Obsolete Paper Money
Issued by Banks in the United States 1782–1866

A Study and Appreciation for the Numismatist and Historian

Q. David Bowers

Foreword by
Eric P. Newman

OBSOLETE PAPER MONEY
ISSUED BY BANKS IN THE UNITED STATES 1782–1866

Whitman Publishing, LLC
PUBLISHING SINCE 1934

3101 Clairmont Road · Suite C · Atlanta, GA 30329

Correspondence concerning this book may be directed to the publisher, at the address above.

ISBN: 0794822037
Printed in China

Disclaimer: Expert opinion should be sought in any significant numismatic purchase. This book is presented as a guide only. No warranty or representation of any kind is made concerning the completeness of the information presented. The author, a professional numismatist, regularly buys, sells, and sometimes holds certain of the items discussed in this book.

Advertisements within this book: Whitman Publishing, LLC does not endorse, warrant, or guarantee any of the products or services of its advertisers. All warranties and guarantees are the sole responsibility of the advertiser.

Illustrations: Most notes in this book are illustrated at or slightly smaller than actual size. However, certain scrip notes (fractional values of less than $1) are shown enlarged, and are so noted.

About the note on the front cover: Illustrated is a $1 note of the Calais (Maine) Bank, dated August 1, 1857, bearing the signature of bank president George Downes. At ten o'clock in the morning of July 18, 1864, four raiders from the Confederate States of America entered the bank with the intention of robbing it. On hand in the vault were many of the bank's bills, similar to this one. Forewarned that a party of Confederates had crossed into Maine by way of Canada, the bank officials and townspeople captured the desperadoes. The exciting story is told in chapter 19. (Collection of C. John Ferreri)

For a complete catalog of numismatic reference books, supplies, and storage products, visit Whitman Publishing online at www.whitmanbooks.com.

CREDITS AND ACKNOWLEDGMENTS

First and foremost, the availability of the American Bank Note Company archives, acquired by John Albanese and his associate Steve Blum in 2005. Both Steve and John worked closely with the author in identifying interesting and obscure bank note plates and related items.

The author expresses appreciation to the many collectors, dealers, and scholars in the field of American paper money who have helped in many ways:

Joseph Adamski corresponded about currency. The **American Bank Note Co.** permitted the author to inspect its archives in 2003. **Irene Axelrod**, librarian at the Phillips Library, Peabody Essex Museum (Salem, MA), assisted greatly with research.

Georgia Barnhill, curator at the American Antiquarian Society (Worcester, MA), facilitated research in that institution's archives. **Jane Beckman** facilitated research by the author at the Sandwich (NH) Historical Society.

Frank Campbell, librarian of the American Numismatic Society, sent extensive information on counterfeit detectors and bank-note reporters. **J. Emily Cowin**, of R.M. Smythe & Co., provided about 10 images from the Schingoethe Collection.

Thomas Denly provided currency for use as illustrations and contributed market information for chapter 21. **Roger H. Durand** made suggestions during the research phase of the book.

Larry Falater provided information on Michigan notes. **C. John Ferreri** provided important notes for photography, including the cover illustration. **Roberta French** assisted the author with the compiling of information from 19th-century periodicals, almanacs, and directories, over a period of years, creating extensive historical files on nearly all of the note-issuing banks in operation from 1782 to 1866.

David Gladfelter corresponded with the author concerning anti-counterfeiting patents and supplied a scrip note for illustration. **Stephen Goldsmith** facilitated the use of R.M. Smythe & Co. images. **Nancy Green**, then American Numismatic Association librarian, filled several requests for information. **Jack Gumbrecht**, of the Historical Society of Pennsylvania, helped with research information and provided images of bank notes from plates with Christian Gobrecht vignettes.

Bruce Hagen reviewed the manuscript, provided selected illustrations, and helped with research aspects of several notes. His commentary about research is in chapter 20. **James A. Haxby** reviewed the text and made valuable suggestions. **Warren S. Henderson** provided notes for photography. **Gene Hessler** furnished a suggestion concerning William Congreve's work. **Peter Huntoon** provided early access to certain archives of the American Bank Note Co.

Katherine Jaeger reviewed the text and made suggestions. She also helped with historical research.

Lawrence T. King provided an item concerning Andrew Dexter Jr. **John Kraljevich** reviewed the early chapters in the text and made suggestions. He also furnished illustrations of items from his reference collection.

George H. LaBarre loaned notes and financial documents for illustration. **Kevin Lafond** provided notes for illustration. **Joseph R. Lasser** read selected parts of the manuscript and provided historical information. **Littleton Coin Co.** (Littleton, NH), provided illustrations and helped in other ways.

Greg Manning discussed aspects of the ABNCo archives. **Robert McCabe** shared extensive information from his files on W.L. Ormsby and helped in other ways. His contributions were essential to the Ormsby information in this book. **Paul McCoy** shared his reminiscences of his employment with the American Bank Note Company. **Hugh McDougall** corresponded concerning Samuel D. Dakin. **Tim Melanson** furnished a historical photograph. **Jenny Moulton** reviewed the manuscript and made many valuable suggestions. **Karl Moulton** reviewed the manuscript and assisted in other ways. **Doug Mudd**, curator, American Numismatic Association Money Museum, furnished an image. **Don Munro** furnished 19th-century newspaper accounts relating to certain banks.

Eric P. Newman reviewed the manuscript and created the foreword. He made suggestions and corresponded during the research phase, including about W.L. Ormsby, William Congreve, and anti-counterfeiting patents. **Douglas A. Nyholm** provided information on Kirtland Safety Society Bank notes.

Donald O'Brien reviewed the manuscript and made suggestions.

Gary Parietti provided currency for photography. **Donn Pearlman** supplied photographs of ABNCo archival items when they were stored in New Jersey.

Fred Reed III, editor of *Paper Money* magazine, reviewed the manuscript and made suggestions, especially regarding the Civil War era. **Gaylen Rust** answered an inquiry on Mormon-related notes.

Harry Salyards provided an 1834 article on paper money and made suggestions. **Amanda Sheheen** furnished a note for illustration. **Hugh Shull** reviewed the manuscript and helped in other ways, including information for inclusion in chapter 20. **R.M. Smythe & Co.**, New York City, made illustrations of Herbert and Martha Schingoethe Collection notes available for use carte blanche, and fine images were selected. **Stack's Rare Coins**, New York City, provided a photograph of an 1840 campaign medal and helped in other ways. **David M. Sundman** engaged in research with the author concerning New Hampshire currency, with one or more books forthcoming on the subject. Certain of that research is used here, including excerpts from a large file of information on the Portsmouth branch of the second Bank of the United States.

Anthony J. Terranova reviewed the text and made suggestions. **Mark Tomasko** reviewed the text and made suggestions.

Steven Whitfield corresponded concerning W.L. Ormsby notes of Kansas and Utah. **Richard Winslow III** provided many historical clippings relating to banking. **Wendell Wolka** reviewed the text, made suggestions and corrections, contributed to research information, and helped in other ways. His far-ranging contributions were very important.

The following institutions were very helpful: The **American Antiquarian Society**, Worcester, MA. The **American Numismatic Association**, Colorado Springs, CO. The **American Numismatic Society**, New York, NY. The **Massachusetts Historical Society**, Boston, MA. The **New Hampshire Historical Society**, Concord, NH. The **New Hampshire State Library**, Concord, NH. The **Ossipee Historical Society**, Ossipee, NH, Arletta Paul, curator. The **Phillips Library** at the Peabody Essex Museum, Salem, MA, Irene Axelrod, librarian. The **Professional Currency Dealers Association** (PCDA). The **Sandwich Historical Society**, Sandwich, NH, under curator Craig Evans, generously allowed the author to examine and photograph the extensive archives the society has for the Carroll County Bank. Jane Beckman facilitated the writer's visits. The **Society of Paper Money Collectors**. The **Wells Fargo History Museum**, San Francisco, CA. Robert Chandler, curator, provided information about 19th-century banking. The **Wolfeboro Historical Society**, Wolfeboro, NH.

The staff of **American Numismatic Rarities** assisted in many ways. John Kraljevich and Frank Van Valen reviewed the text and made suggestions. Susan Novak, assistant to the author, helped with correspondence, research, and coordination of the book. Christine Karstedt assisted with aspects of the ABNCo archives. Douglas Plasencia photographed certain dies and plates from the ABNCo archives.

ABOUT THE AUTHOR

Q. David Bowers became a professional numismatist as a teenager in 1953, later (1960) earning a B.A. in Finance from the Pennsylvania State University, which in 1976 bestowed its Distinguished Alumnus Award on him. He served as president of the Professional Numismatists Guild 1977 to 1979 and president of the American Numismatic Association from 1983 to 1985. He is a recipient of the Founders Award and Farran Zerbe Award, the highest honors of the PNG and the ANA.

He is the author of more than 50 books and has received more honors from the Numismatic Literary Guild than has any other person. He was recently awarded the Society of Paper Money Collectors' First Place Literary Award for 2005, in the obsolete-currency category. His column, "The Joys of Collecting," has been a feature of *Coin World* for more than 40 years and is the longest-running column by any author in the history of numismatics. He is co-author, with Arthur and Ira Friedberg, of *A Guide Book of United States Paper Money,* is also an award-winning columnist for *Paper Money* magazine (certain bank items in this book were featured in his *Paper Money* articles). His *The 100 Greatest American Currency Notes,* co-authored with David M. Sundman, is his most recent study of paper money. As an equity partner in American Numismatic Rarities, LLC, in Wolfeboro, New Hampshire, and as numismatic director for Whitman Publishing, LLC, he is also in the forefront of current events in the hobby.

Eric P. Newman, writer of the foreword, has long been recognized as one of America's most important numismatic scholars and authors, the recipient of nearly every honor in the discipline, including more Heath Literary Awards than any other writer in history. His *Early Paper Money of America* is a classic, as are his other works on coins, tokens, medals, and paper money. Newman has been a friend of the author since the 1950s and was among the founders of the Rittenhouse Society, devoted to numismatic study and scholarship.

CONTENTS

FOREWORD

About 80 years ago, before I was old enough to be eligible to become a member of the American Numismatic Association, I enjoyed reading about the many non-federal American bank notes listed and described each month in *The Numismatist* and written about by David C. Wismer of Hatfield, Pennsylvania. The paper money therein was listed alphabetically by state. It fascinated me because it was of its enormous quantity and complexity. Collectors referred to these as *obsolete bank notes* or *broken bank notes*. I became a customer of Wismer, and was able to buy many bank notes from him for less than $1 each. My numismatic curiosity disregarded whether money was made of metal or paper, or whatever the period in which it circulated. I learned from available publications how many non-federal American bank notes had become irredeemable, and thus, readily collectible. I plunged into that field.

What soon intrigued me further was why the U.S. government under the 1787 Constitution had virtually no paper money until the Civil War period, and why the country was flooded with circulating state-chartered and other private bank and company notes. I sought the reason. Since the capable Founding Fathers of the United States had so diligently worked on the exact wording of the Constitution, I could not understand how they had expected the public to make hand-to-hand money payments when coin was so scarce. I realized that the paper money of the Continental Congress and that of the individual American colonies and states issued before and during the American Revolution and the Confederation period had become virtually worthless, but that the U.S. debt to foreign nations was being repaid for their assistance. I knew that, under the Constitution, the United States reassumed payment of all federal debts, including the Continental Currency, but had failed to pay almost all of the Continental Currency. What was redeemed was at a tiny fraction of face value. The reputation of federal paper money reached low levels.

It was well realized that, when the Constitution was being drafted, the Bank of North America had been incorporated in 1781 by the Continental Congress and was majority-owned by the United States. This institution continued to issue its bank notes; it had been and was handling much banking for the U.S. This situation was not addressed by the language of the Constitution, which gave the federal government the right "to coin money and regulate the value thereof" and denied the states the right to issue "bills of credit." The power of the federal and state governments to issue bonded indebtedness was not affected by the money provisions.

Pennsylvania was opposed to the federal issue of bills of credit or paper money, but no one knows how Benjamin Franklin, a Pennsylvania delegate, voted on the matter. Some feel that Franklin, being a master at compromise and project completion, deliberately left the paper-money issue unclear in order to cut off the wrangling and get the Constitution approved. The meaning of that money wording resulted in off-and-on litigation for more than many decades, and in comments today as to whether the Federal Reserve Bank is a legal, federally incorporated nicety to avoid the language of the Constitution.

The consequence of the early interpretation of the meaning of the Constitutional provisions was the outpouring of American paper money by private banks and companies usually incorporated by individual states. This ended with a 10% tax to destroy that circulation enacted by the United States at the time of the Civil War and made effective in 1866.

Now, focusing on the book at hand:

From the adoption of the U.S. Constitution and through the Civil War, the American monetary scene was unique in world history. Never before had any country had more than 10,000 different combinations of denomination and design for circulating notes at one time. The situation was so confusing it required bank-note reporters of hundreds of pages in length and endless quantities of counterfeit-detecting and valuation publications (in newspapers, almanacs, pamphlets, etc.) to help the public handle the money.

The field is so vast that a number of fine studies have been undertaken simply to cover the currency of almost every state. Further historical detail and data as to bank notes were deemed necessary, and a Wismer Project was organized by the Society of Paper Money Collectors after David Wismer's death. It was realized that many numismatists enjoyed collecting and studying obsolete bank notes from the states in which they resided. Thus further research was undertaken and publications were generated on bank notes of the individual states. Some books include only bank notes, but others add scrip of companies and individuals. Then, in 1988, James A. Haxby, in a four-volume work, undertook a total revision of technical detail and illustration of all American obsolete bank notes.

Even with such studies and other economic and historical writings, there was one thing missing: a comprehensive overview of paper money in one volume—how it was conceived, designed, produced, and spent, and the American economy in which it played such a part, together with specific useful information on how to collect and appreciate obsolete bank notes.

Now comes my long-time friend Dave Bowers (in the 1950s we were both founders of the Rittenhouse Society, and we have been in constant touch since that time) with his study, *Obsolete Paper Money Issued by Banks in the United States 1782–1866,* to fill the gap. With his book in one hand and any specialized book in the other, the big picture can be easily understood. Dave has spent many years in his own research, exploring long-forgotten books, newspapers, and other archives, to draw as much as possible from *original source* material, rather than relying upon modern works.

He quickly discovered that with regard to non-federal American paper money, even the many accomplished writers in economy and finance knew little about how such currency was created or issued, or about how banks were then operated and regulated. For example, it is conventional thinking that for a bank to have been officially in business it should have had a state charter, as each state issued such privileges. However, as the book relates, there are some banking institutions, including some of those that later became very large, which for political or other reasons could not obtain a charter, but bravely went into business nevertheless. It is clear that these banks were accepted as legitimate in their own time.

Still other banks were strictly official, in the sense that they did receive state incorporation—but the arrangement was made by embezzlers who simply used the charters as a basis for distributing large amounts of unreported paper money, bringing great profits to the organizers and operators.

While today we see federal paper money in everyday use, and it is well respected for what it accomplishes, in the era of Dave Bowers' study, 1782 to 1866, this was not generally the case. In some years such obsolete paper money was ubiquitous, with scarcely any coins in sight—such as during the Panic of 1837, when coins were hoarded. In other times, bank notes were scarce, restricting the operations of commerce. As such currency was issued by banks owned by private stockholders, the scenario runs from bank officers whose actions bordered on the improbable or even fantastic, to reliable institutions that year after year earned an honest profit for their stockholders. Dave explores several of these in detail, giving a "you are there" feeling when you read the book.

You will even be able to, in effect, sit at the cashier's desk at a particular bank that opened in 1850 and continued in business to 1865, in the meantime trying to carve a niche in its community and also to distribute as many of its bills as possible, hoping they wouldn't come back to be redeemed in coin. When bank notes were in circulation the bank was in effect borrowing money interest free.

There was no federal bank during this era, but, as the text points out, this did not prevent business people from setting up in Washington, DC, institutions named National Bank, Congressional Bank, Government Bank, etc. Actually there were two institutions named Bank of the United States, and the author covers these in detail.

While currency and banking can be thought of as a technical subject laden with facts and figures, the author shows that it can be exciting and adventurous as well. You may be surprised as you read about the great raid by Confederate troops on a tiny town in Vermont in 1864, when they took over the place, robbed three banks, and escaped to Canada, creating an international incident. Then there is the story of Andrew Dexter Jr., who ran the fraudulent Farmers Bank of Gloucester, Rhode Island, which collapsed in 1808, one of the earliest major bank frauds in America—but certainly not the last, as you will see when you read the narrative.

By the time you finish his book you will know how bank notes were engraved, printed, and distributed. You will also understand the role such paper money played in the American banking and financial system, all important in a numismatic context, as many mysteries are explained. Collecting and enjoying obsolete paper money is discussed in detail, concluding with a state by state view of paper money issued and suggestions on collecting it. Even the most experienced and dedicated numismatist specializing in paper money will find much that is new and interesting to read and contemplate.

This is a book which was waiting to be written, possibly because of the enormous effort involved. Also, few economists and finance scholars have knowledge of numismatics, and apparently few numismatists have knowledge of the other side. Bowers, whose college degree was in finance, has studied economics as a pastime for many years, while at the same time being deeply involved in pure numismatics. Thus, he is perhaps an ideal person to bring all of this together. The effort was too large to do alone, and the roster of contributors reads like a Who's Who in Numismatic and Paper Money Research. In addition, for a number of years he has employed private researchers and helpers to do work for him with archival and other material. He has distilled and edited it well, and I believe you will agree that the result will stand as a classic.

Once this book is distributed it should serve as a catalyst for further research and an essential reference for anyone interested in collecting American obsolete paper money.

Eric P. Newman
St. Louis, Missouri

INTRODUCTION

All roads lead to Rome, it has been said. Similarly, in the study of obsolete bank notes, nearly all activities lead to the American Bank Note Company. In March 1858, seven of the leading private companies in the field met to form ABNCo, as it was abbreviated. The new company was incorporated on April 29 and announced to the public on June 1. All of a sudden, one firm controlled 90% or more of the market.

The ABNCo partners were successors to a long string of individual engravers, partnerships, and companies that had provided currency to state-chartered banks since 1782. The combining of companies was one of necessity. The Panic of 1857, which began with a ripple in early autumn of that year, had by December cast a pall on the American economic scene. Hundreds of banks failed, and many more endured various degrees of distress. Few entrepreneurs thought of forming new banks, and existing institutions pared down their orders for new currency. Times were difficult.

In 2005, John Albanese and Steve Blum acquired the archival currency-printing plates, vignette plates, and other artifacts from the modern American Bank Note Company—more than 200 *tons* of metal plates and cylinder dies in all! While the vast majority of the archives related to stock certificates, foreign paper money, security documents, and the like, a small but wonderful treasure of material relating to the era of obsolete bank notes was acquired. This consisted of nearly 1,000 metal printing plates for paper money (usually four notes to a plate), thousands of small metal vignettes with portraits, scenes, and decorations, and about three dozen plates used to print the advertising broadsides of the firms that combined to create ABNCo in 1858. Marvelously, many of these plates were still wrapped in paper and marked in crayon on the outside.

American Numismatic Rarities was tapped to bring much of the preceding to market. This catalyzed the present book, which I had been writing for several years. Whitman Publishing, LLC, stepped in produce and distribute the book. In a way it can be said that the treasures of the ABNCo archives served to underwrite or at least inspire a book about them!

Today, collectors divide pre–federal era currency into several different specialties. Colonial paper, well chronicled by Eric P. Newman in *The Early Paper Money of America*, covers issues of the various colonies before the Revolutionary War and the later bills of the Continental Congress. Also generally included under this heading are bills produced by the various states after the Revolutionary period, plus the early bills of Vermont (which did not become a state until 1791, mainly due to opposition by New York state, which claimed some of Vermont's real estate). Later specialties include notes circulated by state-chartered and private banks, scrip and fractional bills, and a myriad of issues by railroads, canal companies, and other enterprises, as well as currency of the Confederate States of America and individual states.

Early American bank notes, the subject of this study, are sometimes classified as *obsolete notes,* or in coin-convention slang, simply *obsoletes,* as in, "What do you have in obsoletes?" James A. Haxby, for his magisterial four-volume set published in 1988, used this descriptive title: *Standard Catalog of United States Obsolete Bank Notes, 1782–1866.* This work is absolutely essential to serious collecting of the series.

The Haxby study, along with more than two dozen specialty books on the obsolete paper money of individual states, well serves anyone who wishes to pursue the panorama of different denominations issued by various banks, their designs and their printers, and their estimated rarity as collectibles today. Many of the more useful ones have been published by the Society of Paper Money Collectors. Most are cited in the text to follow.

In addition, specialized monographs, including those by John A. Muscalus years ago and Roger H. Durand in recent times, are assets to any numismatic library. Both of these authors emphasized subjects printed on currency—as Durand did in an excellent book on Santa Claus depictions. Gene Hessler's *The Engraver's Line* is essential to any library, and for good measure, a file of back copies of the remarkable *Essay-Proof Journal* and the ongoing *Paper Money* and *Bank Note Reporter* are foundational.

I learned by reading or skimming all of the preceding, plus several hundred books on bank histories, economics, and finance. All of this has been highly enjoyable. While rare *coins* have been studied in great depth, and it would be difficult to come up with much new information on, say, large copper cents of 1793 to 1857, the field of obsolete bank notes beckons with many mysteries and unanswered questions.

It is my hope that the present book will serve as a useful background for anyone interested in the currency of state-chartered banks and their position in history. I have endeavored to describe the processes of designing, creating, printing, and using these notes. I've also gone into various counterfeits, spurious bills, and the like, in their day called by such nicknames as *wildcat, red dog, blue pup*, and *owl.* Close to 3,000 "real" banks issued these notes, as did many fantasy banks (the latter existing only in the imagination of those who either induced leading bank-note printers to make currency for them or made their own).

I don't recall when I acquired my very first piece of obsolete paper money, but it was probably about 1953 or 1954, soon after I had set myself up in a modest way as a dealer in rare coins and other numismatic items. From that time onward I would occasionally obtain old bills, not by deliberate search, but in the course of acquiring coin collections. Most numismatists, then and now, had a specialty or two, but also acquired odds and ends of interest. Accordingly, when I bought a collection of, say, American cents from 1793 onward, like as not I also got an armful of old books and auction catalogs, a few tokens and medals, and, sometimes, some old currency.

In the 1960s and early 1970s I formed a fairly creditable collection of the bank notes of New England, which was later auctioned by the Numismatic and Antiquarian Service Corporation of America (NASCA). Separately, in the 1970s I donated a fairly impressive display of $3 bills to the American Numismatic Association Museum, where it can be studied today.

Since then I've collected obsolete bills from New Hampshire as a serious specialty, and, apart from that, have selected examples from many other states. For me, a bill with a story is infinitely more interesting than one that simply has rarity as its main claim. Currency from the Owl Creek Bank, the Vermont Glass Factory, the Manual Labor Bank, and the nonexistent Bank of New England (Fairmount, Maine) are in this category. Most pleasing is that often such "story notes" were never redeemed or called in, and today they are neither rare nor expensive.

Other bills can, indeed, be both costly and rare, some so elusive they have achieved the ultimate degree: none are known today. Not far from where I live in Wolfeboro, New Hampshire, the Carroll County Bank of Sandwich was situated from 1850 to 1865. Most of its records survive today and have been a rich archive for research (see chapter 15). However, the bills of this institution are so elusive that scarcely any exist today, and most varieties are completely unknown. The reason is that bills of this bank were redeemed for full face value after it converted to the Carroll County National Bank in 1865.

In contrast, the Wolfborough (as it was spelled) Bank started out with good intentions, but quickly fell into the hands of an adventurer from New York City, Samuel D. Dakin by name, who closed down the legitimate banking operations and proceeded to order a veritable flood of bills from the New England Bank Note Company to put into circulation as a fraudulent scheme. As such bills were not redeemed and became totally worthless in their time, examples are fairly plentiful in numismatic circles today, and I have had the opportunity to examine dozens of them.

Another interesting aspect of obsolete bills is that valuations are often the opposite of what might be found in the *coin* market. Most obsolete notes in Uncirculated grade are "remainders" consisting of bills that may have been signed or partly filled in, or not signed at all, but were stored by banks and never used. Years later large quantities, then of little value, passed into the numismatic market. At one time in the 1950s I had the opportunity to buy 7,000 *sheets* of unused bills from the Canal Bank of New Orleans from Clarence Rareshide. Today, such remainders are fairly widely distributed, and prices have risen. In contrast, a well-worn bill, signed and used in circulation, is usually much more valuable than an unused remainder from the same bank, especially if the used bill is rare.

While one does not normally think of a well-used, perhaps tattered bank note as an *investment,* I dare say that the prices of many if not most bills have kept pace with advances in the closely watched coin market. Obsolete bank notes that used to cost $2 to $5 each in the 1950s sometimes sell for a hundred times as much today.

Recently, Stack's has auctioned many outstanding obsolete notes from the collection of John J. Ford Jr., and R.M. Smythe & Co. has done the same with the vast collection of Herbert and Martha Schingoethe. Each collection was formed by collectors who paid market prices at the time, often setting auction records. However, the sale of these collections has registered a new level, making old records appear quaint in most instances.

The chapters to follow are arranged in approximate chronological order. I have made liberal use of the writings of Waterman L. Ormsby, without question the most fluent and logical author in the bank-note engraving business in the mid-19th century. While Ormsby was a curmudgeon and "character," the contents of his 1852 book, *Bank Note Engraving,* and his 1862 pamphlet, *Cycloidal Configurations,* may well be the best contemporary views of bank notes, how they were engraved, and the politics and subtleties of their distribution. Reading the original texts of these two works greatly contributed to my understanding. In a way, Ormsby can be considered a subsidiary or contributing author to the present book, and my debt to this character of characters is immense. Ormsby formed the Continental Bank Note Company in 1862, which later merged into the American Bank Note Company.

In the course of being interested in obsolete currency I have kept many files and clippings of things that have interested, amused, or informed me. Certain of these are adapted here with the thought that you might enjoy them as well. Many of these things piqued my curiosity years ago, and I could not find ready answers for them. As will be seen, I have preferred contemporaneous sources to modern interpretations. Accordingly, the pages of *Hunt's Merchants' Magazine, Banker's Magazine and Statistical Register, Niles' Weekly Register* (title changed in 1837 to *Niles' National Register*), and state banking-commission and federal Treasury reports have been very valuable.

As a sometime student of American economic history, I have read many if not most of the standard texts prepared by economists and historians—many of which decry banks and their paper money, but not fully understanding how banks operated. To popular writers, for a bank to suspend the redeeming of its notes in specie (silver or gold coins) was an act of fraud. Reality is different, as is demonstrated in the text.

In contrast, the authors of the dozens of bank histories commissioned by the banks themselves often suggest that such institutions were formed, if not *pro bono publico,* then almost to help develop the country, to assist growing businesses, and to promote general welfare. In actuality, nearly every banking report, court document, and business plan I have ever encountered states very clearly that there was one main motive for establishing a bank: *profit* for its owners. This, of course, is the American system—success through entrepreneurship.

Many economists and historians have a difficult time dealing with success—witness the calling of many 19th-century men of wealth *robber barons*. Moreover, nearly all of the modern "economic studies" of banking are based not on original research, but on the reinterpretation of what earlier generations of economists have written, beginning in the 1830s with Condy Raguet's *A Treatise on Currency & Banking* and Albert Gallatin's *Considerations on the Currency and Banking System of the United States* and continuing down to present times. Scarcely anyone seems to have done much present-day study of early newspaper and state legislative reports. This is not particularly unusual, for with the notable exception of Neil Carothers's excellent *Fractional Money* (1930), I am not aware of any economist-writer or general historian of the 20th century who discussed *coins* with significant numismatic knowledge. Accordingly, you can assemble a whole bookshelf dealing with the Civil War, the Jackson administration, or the War of 1812, and find virtually nothing specific about the types of coins and paper money used during these times. This translates into a virtual gold mine of opportunity for numismatic historians. However, the coins themselves (such as the earlier-mentioned copper large cents of 1793–1857) have been studied in great detail.

It is my hope that after reading this book you will be well informed on the entire art and business of designing, printing, and distributing bank notes during the period from 1782 to 1866. You will read of hopes that were dashed and dreams that were realized beyond the projectors' fondest expectations. I believe that after reading this text you can close your eyes and contemplate your knowledge of virtually the entire bank-note scenario.

An attractive aspect of the study of paper money of this era is that there is so much to be discovered. Few obsolete bank notes have been studied for their subtle variations. Styles of lettering, alternations of vignettes, and other details await the curiosity-seeker; moreover, the histories of only a very few individual banks have ever been explored in detail, yielding many opportunities for anyone interested in delving into state and local history in connection with these banks.

As to forming a collection, although prices have risen over the years, today the marketplace is still filled with many rare notes offered for inexpensive prices, usually tiny fractions of what comparably rare coins would bring.

As if the preceding attractions were not enough, perhaps best of all, "paper money people" are among the finest and most helpful in the numismatic hobby.

This is the kind of text that I would have enjoyed reading years ago, as I would have learned much. However, no such study existed. I consider myself fortunate that I have had the *pleasure* of doing all of the reading and research that contributed to the volume you now hold in your hands. My list of contributors includes some of the nicest and most talented people in numismatics. High on this list is Eric P. Newman, who wrote the foreword.

Q. David Bowers
Wolfeboro, NH

Early American Paper Money

Prelude to Bank Bills

Money in Early America

The first paper money in America consisted of notes issued by the Massachusetts Bay Colony under the authorization of December 10, 1690. Before that time and continuing later, there were many other items used in commercial transactions.

Massachusetts 5-shilling note of December 10, 1690, the first government paper money issued in the Western world. This bill, believed unique, is in the Peabody-Essex Museum, Salem, Massachusetts.

Perhaps most familiar in the 17th century were coins of a slightly earlier era. Made in Massachusetts were the New England, Willow Tree, Oak Tree, and Pine Tree coinages struck from 1652 through 1682, most of which bore the date 1652, representing the original authorization. Contemporary accounts often called such pieces *Boston money* from the site of the mint.

However, the circulation of Massachusetts silver was small in comparison to gold and silver coins from other countries, most notably from the possessions of Spain to the south, including Bolivia, Mexico, Peru, and other Latin American countries. Vast quantities of precious metal were converted to Spanish milled silver dollars, gold escudos, and other denominations. Coins from European nations, including Spain, the Netherlands, France, the German states, Portugal, and England (to a very modest amount) also saw wide distribution in colonial America. Availability over the years ranged from plentiful to scarce based on prevailing economic and political conditions.

When a shortage occurred, which happened often in colonial America, coins were not easily replenished given the difficulties of transportation and communication at the time. Because of this and other difficulties, from early times commodities such as food and cattle were used to barter for goods and services. In the colonies such commodities were often assigned specific values for which they could be used in the marketplace.

In Massachusetts, under legislation of March 4, 1634/35 (1634 Julian calendar, 1635 Gregorian calendar), musket balls of full bore were valued at one farthing (a quarter of a penny) each, provided that no one be compelled to take more than a shilling's worth at a time, a shilling being equal to 12 pence (written as 12d.).

Wampum and More

In addition to coins and commodities, wampum, or colored beads made from shells, served as money among both Indians and the white settlers.[1] In early times wampum was made from shells, with white wampum being valued at about half of what the scarcer black, purple, or otherwise

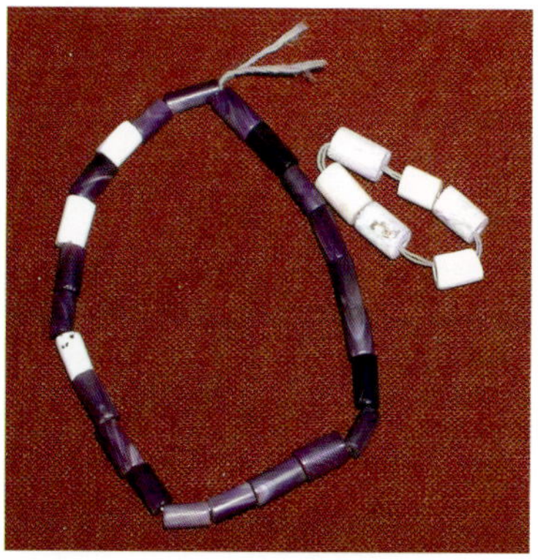

Wampum beads on exhibit at the American Numismatic Association Museum. The string of beads to the right is attributed to the Algonquin Indian tribe, 17th century, and was earlier in the Franklin Institute Collection.

dark-colored beads were valued. Throughout the northern colonies wampum often was used as change in small transactions, paying of taxes, and the like.

On November 15, 1637, Massachusetts valued certain wampum on a string at 6 beads per penny. On September 27, 1642, wheat and barley were valued in commerce at 4 shillings (written as 4s.) per bushel, peas at 3s. 4d. per bushel, and corn at 2s. 6d. for the same quantity. However, by the time that Massachusetts produced its first paper money in 1690, wampum had deteriorated in value due to the availability of manufactured glass beads and other counterfeits. As will be seen throughout this text, virtually from the beginning issuers of money played cat-and-mouse games to track down counterfeiters. Even the penalty of death, exercised on occasion, did not seem to act as a deterrent!

Twilight of the Barter System

By the 18th century, barter had become obsolete in most cities, but in many towns and in the hinterlands it still was used. A list of commodities valued as money by the Massachusetts General Court in 1727 includes pork, beef, wheat, barley, Indian corn, oats, peas, hemp, flax, beeswax, butter, hides, leather, dried codfish, mackerel, oil, bayberry wax, turpentine, bar iron, cast iron pots and kettles, well-cured tobacco, and good tallow.[2] Accordingly, in a broad sense a cow, ear of corn, or peapod could be included in an exhibit of money! In actuality, this idea is not far fetched, for now and again items that are offbeat (by today's standard) are displayed under the heading "odd and curious money."

In the early 19th century, barter was all but obsolete in most developed areas. However, in the American West as well as in rural districts in the East and Midwest, exchanging goods for services remained commonplace. A typical keeper of a country store in that era kept a ledger listing customers by name, debiting them with purchases such as cloth, food, and tools, and crediting them for items brought in for resale, such as livestock, eggs, and produce. Labor was also credited. Several account books kept in New Hampshire in the 1830s and 1840s show that labor in that time and place was valued at about a dollar for a day's work, with a higher value for a man plus a horse.

Cattle and other commodities were used as money in Massachusetts and other colonies, often with values fixed by law. (American Bank Note Co. vignette)

In 1875, S.S. Crosby gave this account of the use of unusual commodities as money long after paper currency and coins achieved wide distribution, such being a curiosity by that time:

> In Marblehead [Massachusetts], some time ago, while Signor Blitz was giving performances, a large number of people who were short of quarters paid for their admission in fish. The receipts in this currency, on one occasion, amounted to 20 dollars.
>
> In some parts of Mexico pieces of soap pass in exchange for merchandise, as a substitute for better currency. In Iowa Territory, in 1840, the marriage fee was 3 goat skins or 4 bushels of sweet potatoes. In the back settlements of Oregon the only money consisted of livestock currency. A hog was $1; a sheep, 50 cents; turkeys 25 cents each; and a pup, 12-1/2 cents; so if A owed B 4 dollars and 9d he sent him 5 hogs and received as change 1 sheep, 1 turkey, and a pup.[3]

Finally, a report from the September 1943 issue of *The Numismatist* shows that some Americans were still using barter generations later, this being in the South Pacific in World War II:

> "Do They Buy Crocodiles For The Sergeant?" Allied Headquarters In Australia.
>
> Here are the exchange rates quoted to Yanks occupying the Trobriand Islands and Woodlark Island, in terms of vile-smelling sticks of twist tobacco used by natives as currency: 20 oranges, 1 stick; 50 pounds sweet potatoes, 1 stick; 40 pounds bananas, 1 stick; 40 pounds pawpaws, 1 stick; Bush pigs, each, 3 sticks; Grass skirts, each, 2 to 3 sticks; Turtles, 2 sticks; Canoes, each, 1 to 4 sticks; Walking sticks, each, 3 to 6 sticks; Crocodiles, 1/2 to 2 sticks.
>
> Lists were distributed to each soldier so he could protect himself against being overcharged.

Commerce in the Cities

In the meantime, in the larger coastal cities paper bills of credit and exchange often served in lieu of coins or paper money, especially for large transactions, for imports, and for the sale of commodities in bulk. Warehouse receipts issued against deposits of tobacco, fish, or hides served as currency and could be exchanged elsewhere by mutual agreement. Merchants in such centers of commerce as New York City, Boston, New Orleans, Baltimore, and Philadelphia conducted their affairs in this manner, never mind that a day's travel away, bartering was still going on in country stores.

International trade in commodities was largely conducted by barter. Lumber, fish, flour, and other products were shipped from New England to the Caribbean and related islands, and there traded for sugar and molasses used in the colonies to make rum. This ardent liquor was "money" in itself, easily transported and used to buy other products, including slaves from African traders. Shipped out of the mid-Atlantic colonies, tobacco was eagerly received in Europe and was exchanged for other goods. Other examples could be given.

The cornerstone of the Philadelphia Mint was laid on July 31, 1792, with Mint Director David Rittenhouse and other officials on hand. By the following March, copper one-cent pieces reached circulation, followed in 1794 with the first federal silver issues and in 1795 by gold coins. But it was many years before the supply of domestically produced coins was sufficient to answer the needs of commerce. In the meantime, many types of foreign silver and gold coins remained in use as official legal tender. Finally, the Act of February 21, 1857, provided for the end of this status two years hence, later extended for a further six months. By the late 1850s, coins as well as paper money were plentiful in commerce, the latter being the emphasis of this book.

THE RISE OF PAPER MONEY

CURRENCY OF THE COLONIES

Beginning with Massachusetts in 1690 and extending into the Revolutionary War era and beyond, the 13 colonies issued their own paper money in many forms. Vermont, admitted as the 14th state in 1791, also issued its own currency.

Most of these notes were *bills of credit* or, in today's parlance, IOUs. Currency was issued and circulated, often in payment for obligations of the state, but it had a redemption date of a later time, such as three years hence. This practice was later used on a few state bank notes (these being called *post notes*) and on all currency issued by the Confederate States of America during the Civil War. Often interest was promised and so stated on the face of the bills.

Certain early bills were *indented,* a practice in which a border of the note was cut in a wavy line to separate it from a stub, the latter being retained by the government so the note could be matched up at a later time; this practice was a way to prove a bill genuine.

Paper money issued by the colonies tended to stay within those particular colonies and was of little value or interest elsewhere. A bill of Massachusetts, if presented in South Carolina, would be accepted only at a discount, if at all. The British Crown controlled the colonies on the coast and did not specifically authorize paper money. However, its use was tolerated as an expedient for commerce or financing projects such as military activities. Generally, bills were receivable for taxes, but they often expired or became invalid after a specific length of time.

In addition to the official issues of the state colonies, many merchants, towns, and other entities issued their own bills, the smaller denominations today referred to as *scrip.* These are delineated in Eric P. Newman's *Early Paper Money of America.*

COUNTERFEITING

Frauds relating to currency were endemic, despite warnings such as "To counterfeit is death" or similar wording on many bills.

A common deception involved altering a low-denomination note to one of a higher value, such as raising 2s. to 20s. by erasing certain lettering and inking new notations.

In other instances a printed note was dampened or soaked in a solvent, then pressed to a blank piece of paper, which in effect became a "printing plate" to create a new note by pressing on still another blank sheet. The result might have been light in impression but good enough to pass. Often these and other types of counterfeits were "aged" and dirtied to give them the appearance of having been used in circulation.

Still other counterfeits were made laboriously by pen, the counterfeiters hand-drawing the various inscriptions and decorations.

What one printer could do under an official contract to a colony, another could do unofficially. Accordingly, in the annals of counterfeiting, more than a few names of well-known printers and engravers appear. Many counterfeits were made abroad in England, the German states, and elsewhere, then imported into America to be distributed. Such foreign sources were difficult if not impossible to prosecute.

In April 1756 in New York City, Owen Sullivan, a notorious counterfeiter of various colonial notes, was tried in court and sentenced to be hanged. An account in the *New-York Gazette, or, the Weekly Post-Boy* of May 17 reads as follows:

> Owen Sullivan, before he was turned off on Monday last, declared that some years ago he struck off near twelve thousand pounds of Rhode Island money, and passed above sixteen hundred of it in one day; that of the New Hampshire currency he made ten or twelve thousands; of Connecticut cash he struck off about three thousand pounds; and of the New York currency he printed large sums of four different emissions. . . .[4]

The *Pennsylvania Gazette* carried this item on October 17, 1751:

> Last week, at a Court of Oyer and Terminer, held in Lancaster, two men (father and son), both named Sigismund Hainly, were tried for counterfeiting the half-crown and ninepenny bills of this province, found guilty, and received sentence of death. . . .[5]

The son was subsequently pardoned, but the father swung from the gallows a few weeks later.

In York, not far from Lancaster, court documents reflected the punishment exacted upon Josiah Pitt in October 1770 for altering a 2s. Pennsylvania bill to 10s. and passing it. He was sentenced to

> stand in the pillory in York Town on the twenty-ninth day of November next, between the hours of ten and twelve in the forenoon for one hour. That then he shall have both his ears cut off and that they be nailed to the said pillory. That the said Josiah Pitt shall then be whipped at the public whipping post in the said town with thirty-nine lashes on his bare back well laid on. . . .[6]

Further Sketches of Counterfeiting

A New Hampshire case set a few months prior to the signing of the Declaration of Independence relates a scenario that in one form or another was repeated throughout the colonies and, later, the states:

> On March 23, 1776, the Committee of Safety for the town of Hanover met in the rooms of John Paine, local innkeeper.[7] To be adjudicated was a matter involving a spurious bill of New Hampshire. In attendance were David Woodman, chairman; Capt. Aaron Storrs; and Bezaleel Woodward, clerk, constituting the Committee of Hanover. In addition the Committee of Lebanon was present, with John Wheatley, Major John Slapp, Major John Griswold, and Azariah Bliss.

The transcript related the course of events:

> Bezaleel Phelps of Norwich, in the colony of New York,[8] yeoman, was brought before this Committee by virtue of a warrant issued by Bezaleel Woodward and Aaron Storrs, two of the Committee, predicated on his having in his custody and detaining a certain note of this colony bearing the face of a six shilling bill which is supposed to have been fraudulently altered and increased as to the value or sum therein expressed by said Phelps, as by said warrant may more fully appear.
>
> Respondent pleads not guilty.
>
> After a full hearing of the evidences in said case said Phelps confessed that he had burnt said bill being conscious that it was altered, and that in case he may be excused from penalty in detaining said bill when he knew that it was counterfeit, he will disclose to this Committee the author of that and sundry other bills, and discover where some of said bills are—whereupon said proposal is agreed to, only that he pay costs hitherto made in the affair, till they can be regularly recovered of some other person. Cost taxed at 40 shillings.
>
> Said Phelps then desired Lemuel Paine of said Hanover to produce a certain 40 shilling bill which he received on the evening of the 15th inst. of Andrew Wheatley of Lebanon, which said Paine on request accordingly did, which bill is adjudged by the Committee to have been altered from a three shilling bill, and which said Lemuel on his oath declared of said Wheatley as aforesaid.
>
> Committee adjourned to tomorrow morning, 9 o'clock, March 24th.
>
> Met according to adjournment. . . .

Charles Hill, a Lebanon innkeeper, was then brought before the Committee and was charged with making and passing counterfeit money, whereupon Solomon Cushman of Norwich "produced a 40 shilling bill of the Colony of New Hampshire, No. 3260, emitted July 25th, 1775, and payable Dec. 20th, 1779," which was judged by the committee to have been altered. Cushman swore that he had received it from Hill in exchange for a silk handkerchief. Hill claimed he was not able to say whence the counterfeit came and was ordered to pay reimbursement of 40 shillings plus costs.

The committee's attention then turned specifically to the 40-shilling altered note shown by Lemuel Paine the day before. Charles Hill swore that he saw Joseph Skinner (a member of Captain Green's company in Colonel Bedel's regiment) "put a bill in the hand of Andrew Wheatley of Lebanon so that he might get it changed." According to Bezaleel Phelps, Wheatley then gave the bill to Lemuel Paine to be changed. Phelps went with Skinner to Dr. George Eager with the bill, during which time Skinner boasted, "And I made it myself, and I have altered a good many bills from three shillings to 40 shillings, and I have known many more altered both here and at Cambridge, and a person may make his fortune by it in a little time."

Although Dr. Eager does not seem to have been involved, he was aware of the crime (as further related).

Skinner also told Phelps that he had spent much spurious money in Cambridge, but "if he told anybody of it he would kill him."

The testimony continued:

> Said Phelps further testifies that he saw said Skinner cut certain pieces from a certain book or pamphlet to use in altering bills, and said Skinner told him he had cut pieces from it before to use for that purpose, and that he would take a thousand pounds for the book.
>
> Phelps described the book and informed particularly where he had left it (which being produced exhibited strong ground to apprehend from its appearance that it had been abundantly used for that purpose).
>
> Said Phelps further testifies when said Skinner had some paste to use in altering bills, Mrs. Winton coming into the room asked what it was for? Dr. Eager replied, "To paste books," when he was sometimes in the room whilst Skinner was altering bills with the paste, both before and after Mrs. Winton asked the question. Said Phelps further testified that he saw said Skinner alter a bill to 40 shillings last Sunday, and this deponent, observing Dr. Eager to be present part of the time, asked Skinner whether the doctor knew of his altering bills, to which Skinner replied, "Damn him, yes." [Remainder of committee account is missing.]
>
> Andrew Wheatley give such an altered bill to Lemuel Paine. . . .

The subject of counterfeiting has commanded the interest of several numismatic writers, most notably Kenneth Scott (the source of the above citations), and excellent studies have been published by the American Numismatic Society and others. These accounts usually draw from a combination of newspaper notices and court documents and provide fascinating reading today.

A pioneer family in 18th-century America. Most of the East was wilderness, roads were often in poor repair, and except for links connecting major coastal cities, travel was difficult. (From a painting by Thomas Gainsborough R.A.)

Features of Colonial Currency

Most colonial bills include at least several of the following features.

- *Denomination*—Usually stated in figures, often in several places on a note. Given in English pounds, shillings, and pence, or in dollars (meaning Spanish milled dollars). Some bills have the value stated both ways.

	Equivalent	Abbreviation/Symbol
1penny (plural: *pence*)		d.
1 shilling	12 pence	s.
1 crown	5 shillings	5s.
1 pound	20 shillings	£

- *Text*—Spelled-out description of the denomination, name of the issuing colony, statement of its use as legal tender, and any other provisions, sometimes including warnings against counterfeiting and the name of the printer (the last only among later issues). The text can be hand engraved on a plate, set in printer's type, or a combination of both. Printing can be on one side, especially for early issues, but it is usually on both.
- *Design*—Usually a border composed of decorative elements is found on notes. Decorative vignettes, sometimes one on each side, include state emblems, motifs from history or mythology, and other objects. Often actual leaves of plants were used to create decorative elements of plates, each leaf having unique details. This practice is called "nature printing."
- *Date*—Usually the date of the authorizing act or legislation, not the day, month, and year that such bills were actually issued.
- *Redemption date*—The time that these bills would be redeemed by the colony, sometimes with interest added.
- *Serial number*—Sequential number added in ink.
- *Signatures*—Prior to release, the typical note was signed in ink by two or three people appointed by the colony.

Other Aspects

The paper used to print notes was usually selected for its quality so as to endure the rigors of circulation.

However, many earlier issues were printed on flimsy stock and deteriorated rapidly. Tiny mica flakes and colored fibers were popular additions to later paper issues as anticounterfeiting measures. Early notes, mostly printed in black, gave way to the use of black plus one or more colors for most issues of the 1770s and 1780s. The term *polychrome,* or multicolored, applies to some.

An overview of these early issues follows in chronological order from the first bills of Massachusetts to the paper money of Vermont.

Paper Money of Massachusetts (1690–1781)

In 1667 the Massachusetts Bay Council reviewed a proposal advanced by the Reverend John W. Woodbridge to create a bank that would issue paper money backed by loans on real estate. A related land bank proposal was made in 1681 and was followed by a proposal in 1686. The last was approved by the council, and a press was obtained "for tryall [trial] of the plates and printing of some bills."[9] Such experimental currency, if produced, is not known to exist today, nor has any information survived concerning the denominations intended. None were placed into circulation.[10]

The Act of December 10, 1690, set in motion the first paper money known to have been issued by any government in the Western world.[11] The order provided for £7,000 in bills to be produced and issued to troops returning from the unsuccessful Phipps military expedition to Quebec. A copper plate was engraved with four denominations: 5s., 10s., 20s., and £5. From the plate, 1,037 impressions were made. The bills were cut apart, given serial numbers in ink, and signed by three of a committee of five persons: Elisha Hutchinson, John Phillips, Timothy Thornton, Penn Townsend, and Adam Winthrop. Each bill had an illustration of an Indian standing, wearing a loin girdle, holding in one hand an arrow and in the other a bow, and with a balloon caption emerging from his mouth, reading COME OVER & HELP US. At first the notes were not accepted in commerce except at a discount of 15% to 20%. But soon the colony agreed to accept them for taxes at a 5% premium, and confidence was restored. The existence of these early notes proved ephemeral, and within a decade nearly all had been redeemed or exchanged for other currency. By the time a numismatic interest arose in them, in the early 19th century, just one example was known to survive. Today that note, of the 5s. denomination, is preserved by the Peabody-Essex Museum, Salem, Massachusetts, descended from the holdings of the former Essex Institute. On February 3, 1690/91, and May 21, 1691, a further £400,000 in bills was author-

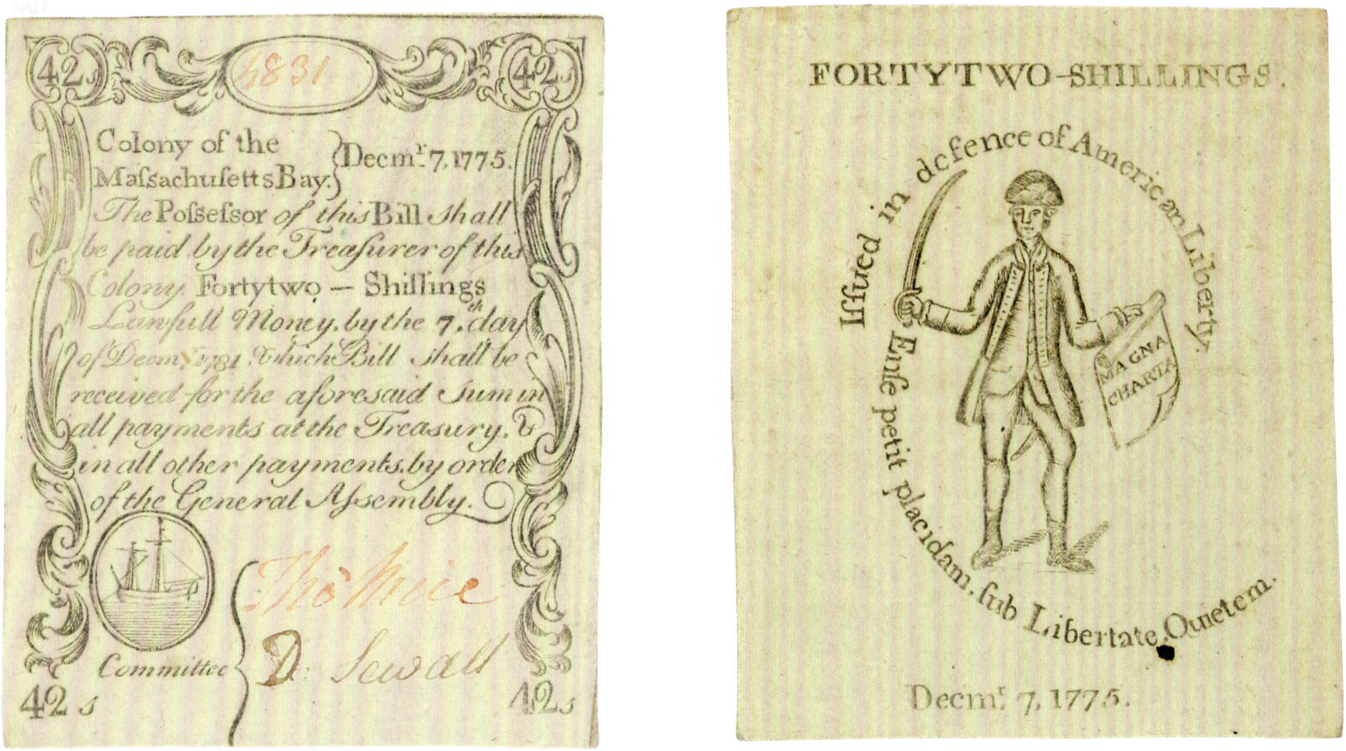

Massachusetts 42s. note of December 7, 1775, from a plate by Paul Revere. The back has the famous Sword in Hand motif.

ized by Massachusetts. Certain of these bear the date as "February the third 1690," but this is the old or Julian calendar, and the actual time of issue was 1691 by today's reckoning.[12] These notes are elusive today, and only about a half dozen are known to exist.

Then followed other issues of the Massachusetts Bay Colony through many authorizations of the 18th century. Certain bills of this colony as well as paper money of some others were from redated plates. As an example, a plate first used in 1714 and with that date was later dated 1718, such later notes bearing both the 1714 and 1718 dates. Continuing the procedure, the plate was eventually dated 1714, 1718, 1719, 1721, 1722, 1723, 1725, 1727, 1731, 1733, 1735, 1736, and 1740. There was an element of practicality of this system, as new plates did not have to be engraved and the design and appearance of each note would remain constant over a period of many years.

As paper money became plentiful in Massachusetts and other colonies, silver and gold coins were prized more than ever, and traded at a premium in comparison to paper. Given a choice, a citizen would rather hold five shillings in silver coins than in currency notes. As certain issues depreciated, there was great public outcry, furnishing fodder for letters and articles in newspapers for many years. In 1751 the British Parliament passed legislation restricting the use of paper money in New England to the payment of taxes and not allowing it as legal tender in commercial transactions or other obligations. The act was loosely enforced, but it did serve to restrict the volume of new issues for a time.

Among Massachusetts bills, perhaps the most famous today, and a type that is readily collectible (although popular and expensive), is the "Sword in Hand" legal tender design from plates engraved and printed by Boston patriot, engraver, and silversmith Paul Revere under acts from August 18, 1775, through November 17, 1776. On these bills a standing patriot is shown brandishing a sword in his right hand and a scroll inscribed "Magna Charta" in his left, with the surrounding inscription "Issued in Defence of American Liberty." Under that is a Latin inscription. Many plate and lettering varieties were made across a wide number of denominations, all denominated in pounds, shillings, and pence. Certain Sword in Hand bills were printed from the back side of a copper plate earlier used for Revere's popular *View of Boston* decorative print.

Massachusetts became part of the United States of America, and as a state it issued its own bills in the late 1770s. One of the most popular from a numismatic viewpoint is the so-called Codfish Note, depicting a fish of that species on the face.[13]

Near the conclusion of the Revolutionary War, the Act of May 5, 1780, provided for Massachusetts currency denominated in dollars at the values of $1, $2, $3, $4, $5, $7, $8, and $20. Several other states issued paper money in the same sequence: denominations from $1 to $8 (except $6) and $20. The "dollars" were Spanish milled dollars, or 8-*real* silver coins, ubiquitous in trade in America.

Paper Money of South Carolina (1703–1788)

The Act of May 8, 1703, launched the paper money of the province of South Carolina. More than 40 series were produced from that time, concluding when South Carolina became a state in 1788.

The first bills under the Act of May 8, 1703, were of two denominations, 50s and £20, and were from plates engraved by Joseph Massey. The intention was to finance the Saint Augustine expedition, which resulted in the burning of that coastal town (now in Florida). It was provided that the bills would be redeemed by March 9, 1703/04.

The Act of November 4, 1704, called in remaining unredeemed notes, but this action was not completed, and the Act of July 5, 1707, made similar provisions. Currency of this and other colonies during the early 18th century tended to be of almost ephemeral existence; it remained in circulation for a few years, then was redeemed by later issues. As might be expected, most of the earlier issues of this and other colonies are essentially noncollectible today, and there are many authorized denominations for which not a single note is known in a numismatic collection.

This constant turnover of authorizing, issuing, and then soon redeeming notes helped reduce the dangers of counterfeiting. At the same time it engendered many complexities for merchants and citizens, who had difficulty in discerning the genuine from the false. Newspaper accounts in this and other colonies warned of counterfeits but could not address the full problem. The penalties—ranging from ear cropping, lashing, and confinement to the pillory to the ultimate punishment proclaimed on the bills as "death to counterfeit"—did not seem to be much of a deterrent in South Carolina or elsewhere.

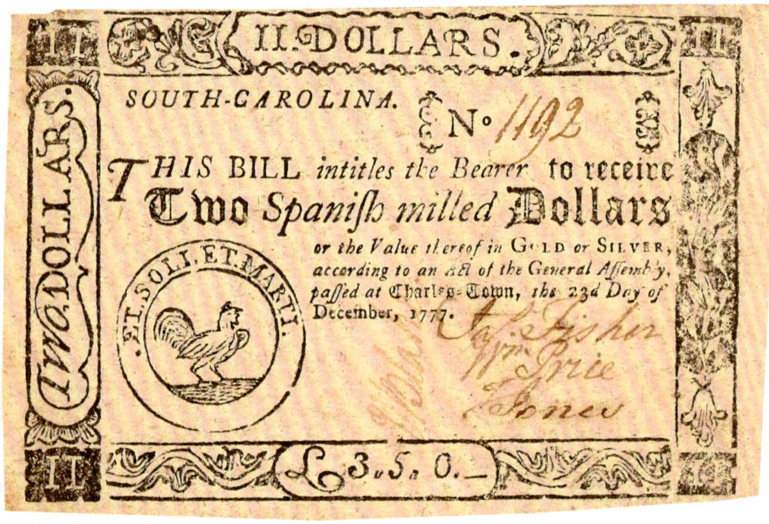

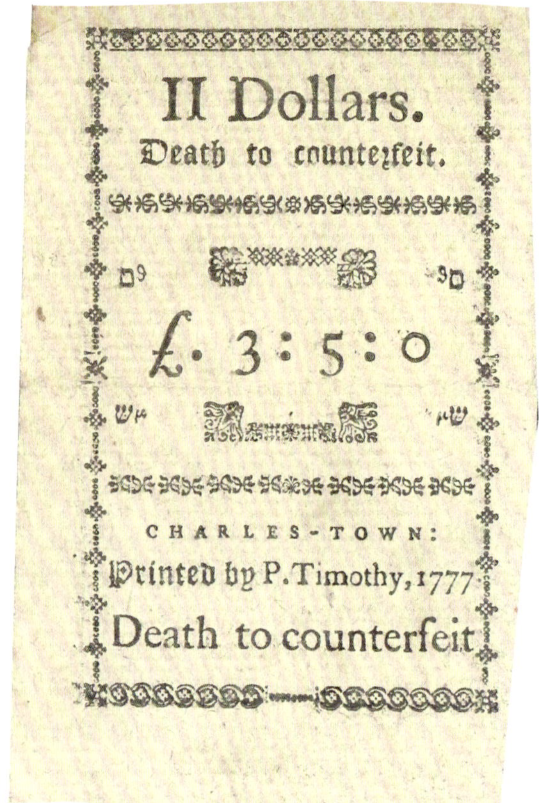

South Carolina note payable in two Spanish milled dollars, equivalent to £3, 5s. in paper, issued under the Act of December 23, 1777. For emphasis, "Death to counterfeit" appears twice. Printed in Charles-Town (Charleston) by P. Timothy.

Among early 18th-century issues were notes referred to as *bank bills,* under a bank authorized by the legislature.[14] The later issues of the colony, then the state, in the 1770s, are remarkable for their interesting vignettes with Latin inscriptions. Certain illustrations on the issue of February 8, 1779, are dramatic, including, as described by the Newman text, "Angel blowing trumpet and holding book entitled ANNALS OF AMERICA; Atlas holding a boulder; Prometheus bound and attacked by a vulture; and Hercules strangling a lion."[15]

Paper Money of Connecticut (1709–1780)

The General Court of the Colony of Connecticut, succeeded by the state of Connecticut, issued many different denominations and styles of paper money. The earliest were made under the Act of May 1709 and are dated July 12, 1709. Denominations were expressed in the British system, including 2s., 2s. 6d., 3s., 5s., 10s., 20s., 40s., and £5. These and bills issued under legislation of October 1709 and October 1710 were intended to finance a military expedition against Canada, but the action did not materialize. Such bills were not intended to be general legal tender but could be used to pay taxes to the colony, valued at a premium of 5%. Jeremiah Dummer of Boston produced two copper plates, one with the four lowest denominations and the other with the four highest. Each bill was serially numbered and signed before issuing.

Each note contained a vine with grapes, the symbol of Connecticut that was later used on certain of its coinage in 1785. The motto, SUSTINET QUI TRANSTULIT (he who transplants sustains himself), appeared on each. Variations of the grape motif appeared on many later notes as well.

Currency authorized in May and June 1711 consisted of essentially the same designs as the preceding, but with a red monogram AR, left and right in mirror image, for Anna Regina, or Queen Anne. The plates were modified later by adding "May 1713" below the first date, this to create a new issue of paper totaling £20,000. By this time the earlier notes had been extensively altered by raising the denominations, and the new issue with the May 1713 date created a fresh series (which in time also attracted those who sought to alter them). These circulated widely. Legislation of the period made them legal tender in payment of transactions that were intended to be paid only in coins, with the notes being valued for a specific amount of silver. In England in July 1740, the Lords Commissioners of Trade and Plantations censured Connecticut for this

Connecticut bill of 10s. issued under the Act of June 1, 1773, and payable two years later. Printed in New London by Timothy Green.

practice. Certain later bills had the wording changed slightly to counter this criticism.

During this era the silver coins struck by the Massachusetts Bay Colony from 1652 through 1682 (but generally dated 1652) were seen regularly in commerce in Connecticut, together with many varieties of foreign gold and silver coins. Bills of New York and the New England colonies were also seen in commerce and were widely accepted by those who were up to date on exchange values. The use of foreign (non-Connecticut) currency varied over a period of time. For example, in May 1752 an act was passed rendering Rhode Island paper money useless within the colony.

Subsequent issues of Connecticut currency included an engraved copper plate to produce the obverse and a typeset reverse. In time, in Connecticut and elsewhere, typesetting became more popular and generally replaced engraved notes, although the borders and certain design elements continued to be engraved.

While most early notes issued by Connecticut range from scarce to rare to unobtainable today, beginning in the 1770s large quantities were issued from typeset plates, and enough have survived today that they are highly collectible. The denominations remained in the British system, such as for the issue of £500,000 in Treasury Notes due on December 31, 1779, produced in the values of 2s, 2s. 6d., 6s., 10s., 20s., and 40s.

Certain of the later issues were denominated both in English and Spanish currency, such as the 5s. bill of March 1, 1780, with the inscription "The possessor of this bill shall be paid by the treasurer of the State of Connecticut 5s. in Spanish milled dollars at 6s each, or other coins equivalent, within interest at 5percent, per annum, by the first day of March, A.D. 1784."

The collecting supply today includes many pieces that were canceled or redeemed by Connecticut but were preserved. After the Declaration of Independence, Connecticut, now a state, continued to issue its own currency in the British system. The last was authorized July 1, 1780, in the amount of £100,000 total.

Paper Money of New Hampshire (1709–1780)

The notes of New Hampshire commence with the date 1709 and conclude with issues under the Act of April 29, 1780. The first issue of 1709 was authorized at £8,000 and was used to pay obligations in force as well as being receivable for taxes at face value plus 5% charge or interest. These were from plates engraved and printed by Jeremiah Dummer of Boston, who also did certain related issues for Massachusetts and Connecticut. The AR monogram on the back was also used on the currency of these other two colonies. These and other bills were from engraved copper plates.

New Hampshire seems to have taken the lead in redating plates (i.e., reusing earlier plates by adding later dates to them sequentially). The first with extensive redating were the issues of May 20, 1717, in denominations from 1s to £4; these were redated in turn as 1717, 1722, 1725, 1726, and 1727, each time with the earlier dates left in their original positions. Motifs on this particular plate included a boar (1s.), bear (1s. 6d.), camel (4s. 6d.), cod (15s.), two-headed eagle (25s.), stag (30s.), pine tree (£3, 10s.), and Indian (£4).

A number of the early plates still exist and are preserved by the New Hampshire Historical Society and the state government. Some of these were used in the 19th century to make reprints to the order of Dr. Joshua I. Cohen of Boston, who began his collection in 1828 and continued it for years thereafter; he was the first person known to have systematically collected paper money of the colonies. Today these are known as *Cohen reprints* and are scarce in proportion to the demand for them. From a numismatic advantage they do offer the opportunity to have impressions from plates for which originals are either exceedingly rare or not available at all.

As was true of most other notes in the American colonies, those of New Hampshire depreciated rapidly

New Hampshire merchants' note, 12d. or 1s., dated December 25, 1734. Bearing interest of 1% annually, the bill was payable in silver or gold *or* in bills of credit of the several New England states. The "or" was an important provision, for gold and silver coins were scarce.

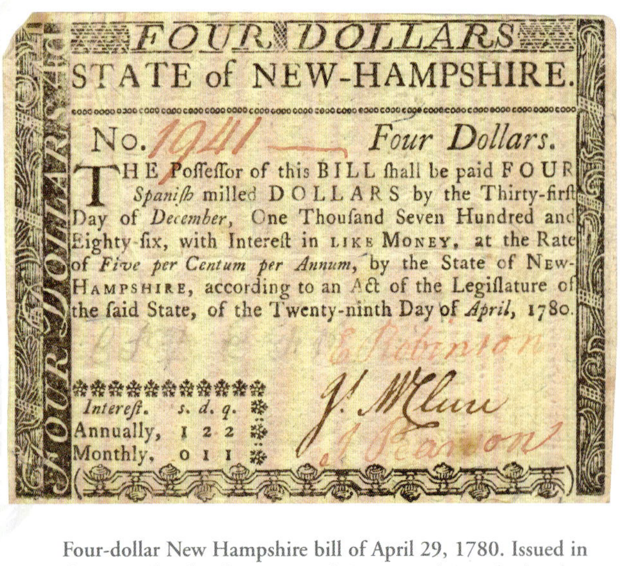

Four-dollar New Hampshire bill of April 29, 1780. Issued in the general style of Continental Currency, this and related notes were printed by Hall and Sellers, Philadelphia.

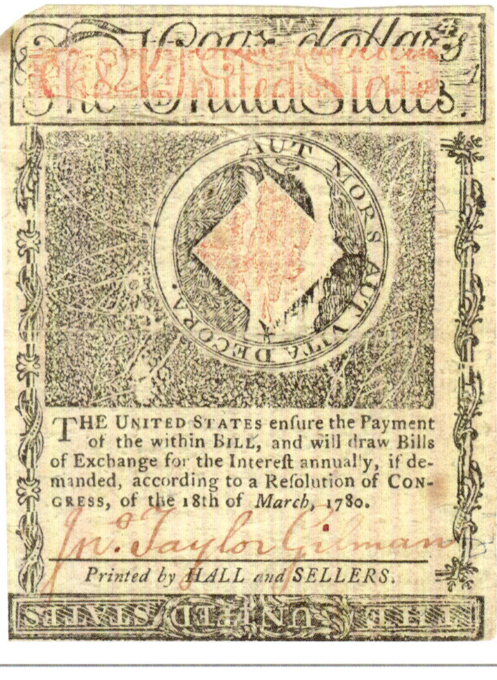

and sold at a deep discount in relation to silver and gold coins. In 1733 it took £3 in paper to exchange for £1 in silver coins.

Bills called *merchants' notes* were issued under the date of December 25, 1734, in five denominations from 12d. to 10s. These were inspired by similar notes issued by private interests in Massachusetts in 1733. Soon after the New Hampshire bills appeared, Massachusetts passed legislation making them illegal for trade in that colony. The use, value, counterfeiting, and circulation of paper money in the colonies provided subjects for many notices in New Hampshire and other newspapers.

Among later notes are a number of varieties from typeset plates by Daniel Fowle of Portsmouth, who had as a partner his nephew, Robert Fowle, a Tory sympathizer. Daniel Fowle was an interesting character, well known in his era, and issued an almanac with sayings somewhat similar to those in Benjamin Franklin's *Poor Richard's Almanack.* Such aphorisms likely were passed around from one printer to another, making their sources difficult to learn today. Robert Fowle was no less interesting. After the partnership dissolved, Robert took some printing plates and ran off some notes for his own account, leading to his arrest on November 3, 1775.

The latest New Hampshire issues, those under the Act of April 29, 1780, were printed by Hall and Sellers, Philadelphia, and were denominated $1, $2, $3, $4, $5, $7, $8, and $20, the same denominations used for certain other state notes. Many of these remained unissued or were redeemed and canceled with a large hole at the center. Later, these notes reached the numismatic market, making them readily collectible today, although hardly common. Early notes of the colony are for the most part very rare.

Paper Money of New Jersey (1709–1786)

Paper money for the province and colony of New Jersey as well as for the later state was issued under dates from July 1, 1709, through 1786. The first emission consisted of five denominations, from 5s. to £5, under the Act of June 30, 1709, dated July 1, 1709, to finance a proposed expedition to Canada. There was an error in the printing design, and problems arose with an unauthorized signer, who sought to take the place of an authorized individual who had died.[16] The currency was not well received because of this confusion, and under the Act of February 10, 1710/11, the bills were revalidated. As is the case with early currency of other colonies, today these and related issues from the early 18th century range from extremely rare to unknown.

From 1755 to 1762, bills known as *war issues* were produced in 13 series, each with a specified period for use, after which they were invalidated.

In time, currency production became more extensive, employed typesetting with woodcut designs, and had the protection of nature printing. The issue under the Act of June 9, 1780, was printed by Hall and Sellers, Philadelphia, and closely resembled currency issued by several other colonies. The denominations were $1, $2, $3, $5, $7, $8, and $20. The final notes were the series of 1786, 1s. to £6, for a total of £100,000.

Today, notes of New Jersey are widely available from the issue of June 22, 1756, onward, although there are exceptions among the varieties.

New Jersey bill for £6, April 16, 1764, payable in 17 ounces, 10 pennyweight of plate (silver). To the left is the British royal crest. On the back is the dire warning "To counterfeit is death." The "nature printing," devised by Benjamin Franklin, is from a mold taken from an actual leaf and was intended to deter counterfeiting. Printed by James Parker in Woodbridge.

PAPER MONEY OF NEW YORK (1709–1788)

Paper money for the colony and, later, the state of New York commenced with issues under the date of May 31, 1709, and continued to include 35 dates, ending with February 8, 1788. The first consisted of £5,000 in bills of credit dated May 31, 1709, under the act of June 8, 1709. These were produced in values of 5s., 10s., 20s., and 40s. as well as £5, from typeset copy plus a decorative woodcut.

Though the English, with a brief pause, had control of New York since 1664, the Dutch economic culture of the colony remained intact at least through 1709. The final of three emissions of New York paper money that year was expressly denominated in "lyon dollars," a reference to the silver crowns of the Netherlands, whose rampant lion insignia gave them a ready nickname. Such coins were found aboard the HMS *Feversham,* which sank after leaving New York in 1711. Archaeological discoveries such as the Castine (Maine) hoard have also offered further evidence of the role of the Dutch trade coins in American circulation.

Under the Act of June 15, 1780, bills printed by Hall and Sellers, Philadelphia, were issued in the values of $1, $2, $3, $4, $5, $7, $8, and $20, conforming more or less to issues that Hall and Sellers created for several other states.

In the 1770s, both New York City and the Committee of Correspondence of the city and county of Albany issued paper money in quantity. The final state series is of February 8, 1788, and is denominated in shillings and pounds.

Similar to scenarios for other colonies, bills of New York can be collected from the second half of the 18th century but are generally very rare before that time.

PAPER MONEY OF RHODE ISLAND (1710–1786)

Currency notes of Rhode Island and the Providence Plantations, later the state of Rhode Island, were issued under dates from August 16, 1710, through May 1786. More than 50 different series were made, a remarkably large quantity for such a small colony. Although Rhode Island did not have a large land area, it was a beehive of commercial activity, including the maritime trade, and was an important factor in commerce in the Northeast.

The issue of August 16, 1710, comprised £13,300 in eight denominations, 2s. to £5, printed from two engraved four-subject copper plates. Counterfeiting

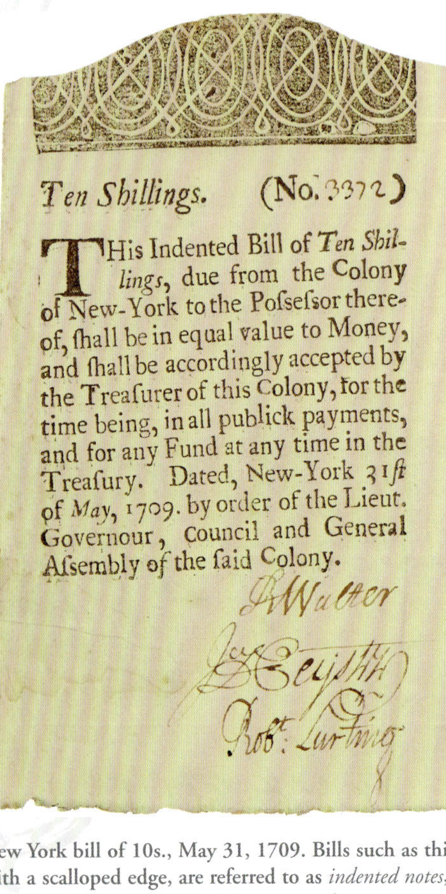

New York bill of 10s., May 31, 1709. Bills such as this, with a scalloped edge, are referred to as *indented notes*, with the matching part of the outline retained in a receipt file.

To the PUBLIC.

THE FLYING MACHINE, kept by John Mercereau, at the New-Blazing-Star-Ferry, near New-York, ſets off from Powles-Hook every Monday, Wedneſday, and Friday Mornings, for Philadelphia, and performs the Journey in a Day and a Half, for the Summer Seaſon, till the 1ſt of November; from that Time to go twice a Week till the firſt of May, when they again perform it three Times a Week. When the Stages go only twice a Week, they ſet off Mondays and Thurſdays. The Waggons in Philadelphia ſet out from the Sign of the George, in Second-ſtreet, the ſame Morning. The Paſſengers are deſired to croſs the Ferry the Evening before, as the Stages muſt ſet off early the next Morning. The Price for each Paſſenger is *Twenty Shillings*, Proc. and Goods as uſual. Paſſengers going Part of the Way to pay in Proportion.

As the Proprietor has made ſuch Improvements upon the Machines, one of which is in Imitation of a Coach, he hopes to merit the Favour of the Publick.

JOHN MERCEREAU.

Advertisement of 1791 for the "Flying Machine," a coach that traveled the popular route from New York City (leaving New Jersey across the Hudson River) to Philadelphia. The fare was 20s.. The trip involved an overnight stay and a ferry trip across the Delaware River at Philadelphia. In this era, financial news of one of these cities was usually published a day or two later in the other.

became endemic for the £3 value, resulting in the Act of June 17, 1718, which invalidated this particular issue.

Early notes were distributed as "loans" or certificates of indebtedness, to be repaid with interest at a later date. Large quantities reached commerce, viewed by some as a boon to business and society but condemned as inflationary by others.

Later series were from engraved plates (some redated for subsequent use), then printed plates, as with the back (not the face) of the issues of February 14, 1743/44.

Some Rhode Island bills of the 1740s and 1750s were so-called New Tenor issues, with different exchange rates. The bills, authorizations, and exchange values were difficult enough to understand within the colony, and nearly impossible to evaluate from a distance; thus, most circulation was regional.

Later issues include bills under the Act of July 2, 1780, printed by Hall and Sellers. The final issue (May 1786) amounted to £100,000 in denominations from 6d. to £3. The fouled anchor (a symbol of the colony) is common on early notes.

Paper Money of North Carolina (1712–1785)

More than two dozen acts and series of notes were issued by the province and, later, state of North Carolina from 1712/13 through December 29, 1785.

The first emission consisted of £4,000 in bills of credit, bearing interest, authorized in 1712, followed by £8,000 in 1713, to finance the war against the Tuscarora Indians. Curiously (at least from a later point of view), these bills are *handwritten,* for the simple reason that there was no printer active in the colony! Denominations consisted of £3, £5, £10, and £20, issued in small quantities of 500, 500, 300, and 250, which certainly must have constituted a formidable writing task. These bills were followed by other handwritten issues under dates of 1715, October 19, 1722, and November 27, 1729.

The next issue, that of 1734 and 1735, consisted of £40,000, was from a copper plate with inscriptions and decorations, and was issued to redeem the most recent handwritten issue. By that time, the colony had issued more than 40,000 handwritten notes! As might be expected, these were not difficult to counterfeit, and, accordingly, there were many problems.

North Carolina bills of the early 18th century continued to be denominated in British currency, evolving by the issue of 1756 and 1757 to typeset style, replacing the engraved plates. Under the Act of May 10, 1780, £1,240,000 in bills of credit was issued, in a series of high denominations of \$25, \$50, \$100, \$250, \$300, \$400, \$500, and \$600. Plate varieties exist. Enough were issued that they are highly collectible today.

Under the Act of May 17, 1783, £100,000 in notes, denominated in the British system from 6d to 40s, were distributed, followed by a like amount under the authorization of December 29, 1785. These bills remained in circulation into the early 19th century.

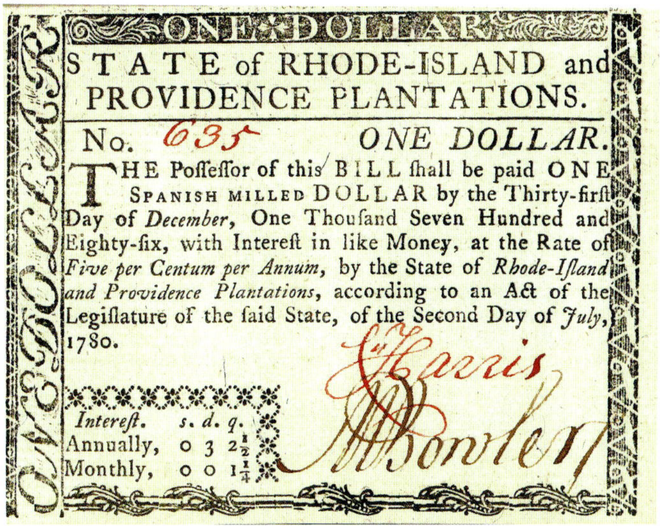

One-dollar note of the state of Rhode Island and the Providence Plantations, July 2, 1780. Printed by Hall and Sellers, Philadelphia.

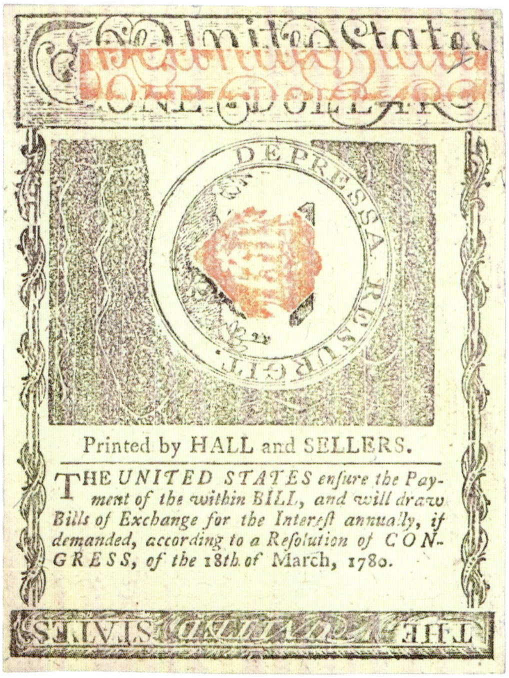

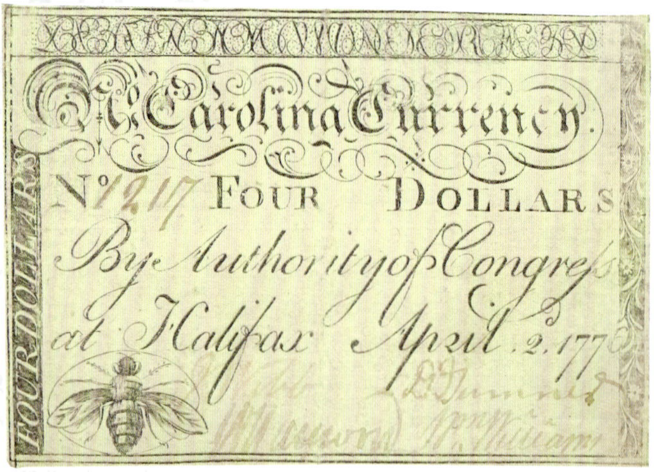

North Carolina note of the $4 denomination, authorized at Halifax, April 2, 1776.

Paper Money of Pennsylvania (1723–1785)

The province of Pennsylvania, later known as the Commonwealth of Pennsylvania, was a relative latecomer in the issuance of paper money, with the first issue dated April 2, 1723. These were called Loan Office Notes; they were to be redeemable by April 2, 1731, at interest, and to be repudiated after August 2, 1731. The printing was from set type plus illustrations, in denominations ranging from 1s. to 20s. By the time of the Act of March 16, 1785, there had been 20 dated issues from the province/ Commonwealth of Pennsylvania.

Many bills of the 1750s and 1760s were printed in Philadelphia by the shop of Benjamin Franklin, who was in England for much of this era. He later proposed Latin mottoes for use on Continental Currency. Hall and Sellers, printer of all Continental Currency Notes, printed many Pennsylvania notes as well toward the end of the series. Certain of these are similar in appearance to the Continental issues.

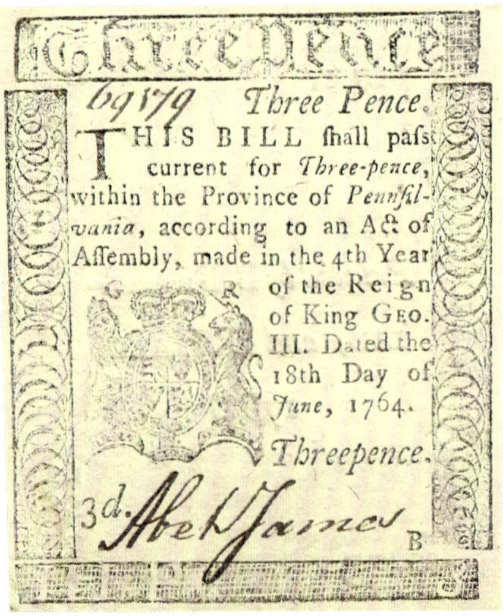

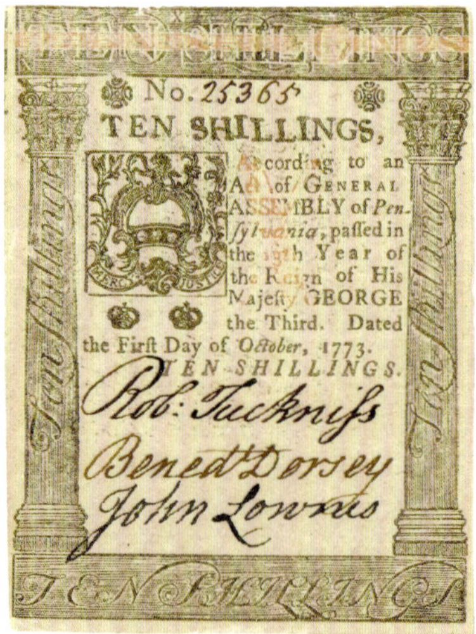

Pennsylvania threepence bill, June 18, 1764. Printed by Franklin and Hall, Philadelphia.

Pennsylvania 10s. bill, October 1, 1773. Printed by Hall and Sellers, Philadelphia.

Delaware threepence note, May 1, 1777. Printed by James Adams. (Shown enlarged)

Six-dollar bill of Maryland, April 10, 1774, payable in bills of exchange receivable in London at the rate of 4s./6d. sterling per dollar. From a plate by T(homas) Sparrow, signed vertically at the left; Sparrow also engraved the dies for the John Chalmers silver coinage of 1783. Printed by A.C. and F. Green.

As Pennsylvania was a well-populated colony, the production quantities of paper money tended to be extensive. Many issues from the mid-18th century onward are highly collectible today, although there are rare varieties.

Paper Money of Delaware (1723–1777)

The colony of Delaware, later the state, including the counties of Kent, New Castle, and Sussex, issued paper money under 14 dates, representing enabling acts, from April 23, 1723, to May 1, 1777.

The notes of this colony are many fewer in number than of certain of the larger provinces. Delaware was closely affiliated with adjacent Pennsylvania, and its currency circulated in the latter place to a limited extent. However, there were always problems when currency of one colony was presented in another, even if the two had a common border. In the early 1720s many people in Pennsylvania refused the notes from Delaware, causing them to depreciate about 25%. However, in October 1726 the Pennsylvania Loan Office and some merchants in Philadelphia agreed to accept them at par, after which they circulated at full value and extensively.[17] Delaware bills are nearly all set in type, plus decorative borders. Some of them have nature printing on the back.

Many of the later notes were printed in Philadelphia, including by Benjamin Franklin. The very latest bills are dated May 1, 1777, in the early period of the Revolutionary War, and are on the same paper (with mica chips and blue fibers) used for Continental Currency bills. Denominations of the last issue ranged from 3d. to 20s. The printer was Hall and Sellers.

Today, Delaware notes dated 1753 and earlier range from very rare to unknown. Most later issues are readily collectible.

Paper Money of Maryland (1733–1781)

The colony of Maryland, later the state, issued paper money under more than a dozen authorizations from 1733 through August 8, 1781. The first consisted of £90,000 in Legal Tender Notes, authorized in the session that commenced March 13, 1732/33, intended to create a Loan Office. Certain of these bills, amounting to as much as 30s. for each taxable person, were paid in 1734 and again in 1735 for the mandated burning of 150 pounds of tobacco, in order to prevent the market from being depressed. Denominations ranged from 1s. to 20s. The printing was done in Maryland from handsomely engraved plates.

Some later issues were denominated in both dollars and shillings, such as a bill worth $6, equal to 27s. For most of the Maryland notes dated 1767, 1770, and 1774, there are secret marks for given denominations, not publicized at the time, but no doubt an aid to determining which notes were genuine (assuming the counterfeiters did not copy the marks). As examples, on the $1 bills each N in INDENTED is rotated 180 degrees, on the $2 bill a period is above the a in "Rate," and on the $6 bill there is a dot after ASSEMBLY.[18]

The Maryland issues of 1767 were expressed in *dollars,* this being the first use of that designation on any paper money issue in the world.

Among the later bills issues, the £100,000 in Maryland currency authorized and bearing the date of July 26, 1775, is of special numismatic interest. The plates were engraved by Thomas Sparrow, who also cut the dies for the 1783 Chalmers silver coinage issued in Annapolis, Maryland. These bills, known as *gunpowder notes,* have unusually elaborate motifs depicting interaction between the colony and Great Britain. They were issued to promote the manufacturing of gunpowder, an industry of rising importance in the colony.

Paper money denominations were expressed in a combination of dollars and British currency. As an example, the $4 note was also valued at 30s. Issues under the Act of June 28, 1780, ranging from $1 to $8, plus $20, were printed by Hall and Sellers, who also printed Continental Currency and notes for other states during this era.

The last Maryland bills are those of May 10, 1781, from 1s. to £3, to be redeemed in specie at the rate of 7s., 6d. per dollar, between December 25, 1784, and June 25, 1785, to be paid for from proceeds received from the sale of property seized from British sympathizers, many of whom had fled the district.

Today most Maryland notes range from scarce to rare in higher grades. Early issues are very rare in any preservation.

Paper Money of Georgia (1735–1786)

The first paper money associated with Georgia consisted of £32,250 in so-called *sola bills,* produced in England and drawn for the "Trustees for Establishing the Colony of Georgia in America." In America these were countersigned by James Oglethorpe, perhaps the most famous individual associated with the colony. These bills circulated in Georgia until they were sent

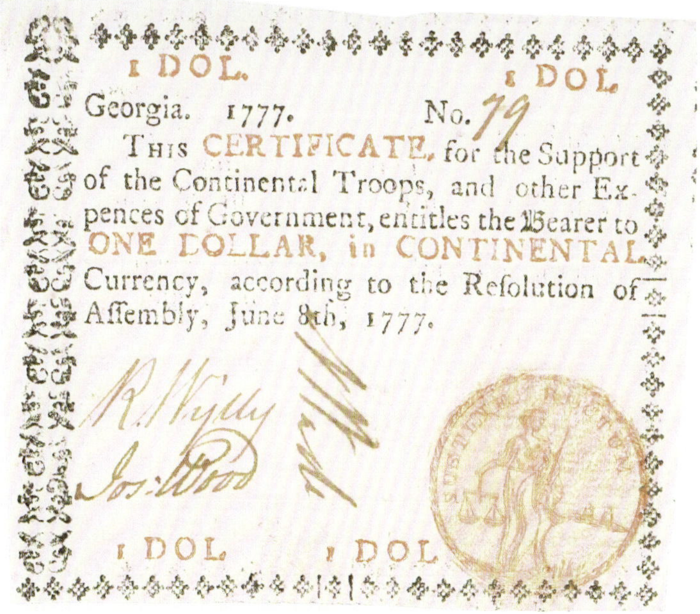

One-dollar note of Georgia, June 8, 1777. Issued for the support of Continental Army troops and exchangeable for Continental Currency.

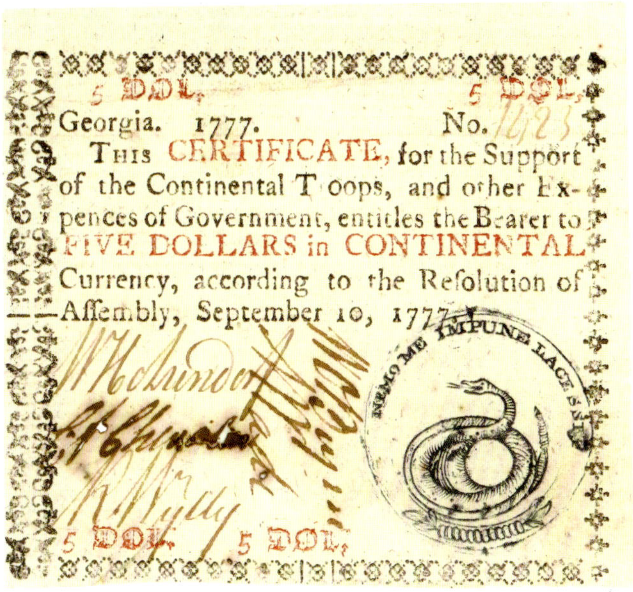

Five-dollar note of Georgia, September 10, 1777, with rattlesnake motif.

back to England for repayment. Denominations included £1, £2, £5, £10, and £20.

Under the Act of February 17, 1755, £7,000 worth of bills of credit were produced, with values ranging from 2d to 20s. Smaller denominations from 2d to 2s were typeset, while higher values were from engraved plates. Other issues followed, from both engraved and typeset plates, mostly the latter, through the Revolutionary War period.

Bills of 1776 and later were denominated in dollars (Spanish milled dollars), some with English equivalents as well. Certain of the later issues have interesting motifs, among the most memorable being a coiled rattlesnake, head raised, with the inscription NEMO ME IMPUNE LACESSET (no one will provoke me with impunity), and another with two jugs floating in the ocean, one representing America and the other England, with the inscription SI COLLIDIMUS FRANGIMUR (if we collide we will break).

Lighthouse certificates, issued to rebuild the structure on Tybee Island, dated May 1769, have scrambled letters in Hebrew, Latin, and English, separately, which if arranged in proper order, designate "To counterfeit is death without benefit of clergy," etc. The £5 note of 1775 depicts an Indian standing, with bow and a quiver filled with arrows, with the inscription AMERICA above. Such inscriptions and designs engender great numismatic interest today. The final early bills bear the date October 16, 1786, and were issued in denominations from 6d to 20s.

As is true of most other colonial notes of the era, Georgia bills of the later authorizations are generally collectible today but are apt to be scarce in higher grades. Early currency ranges from rare to unknown.

Paper Money of Virginia (1755–1781)

It was not until June 1755 that the first authorization for paper money was made by the colony of Virginia, also known as the Dominion of Virginia, the Commonwealth of Virginia, and, later, the state of Virginia. Production continued through the Act of May 7, 1781.

The first emission, that of June 1755, amounted to £20,000 in Treasury Notes issued to finance action in the French and Indian War, these being loan certificates with 5% interest payable on June 30, 1756. These bills are obscure today, and it is not known what denominations were issued.

Other currency issues were produced in the next two decades. The earliest to be generally collectible today are the bills bearing the name of the James River Bank, under April 1, 1773, in five denominations.

The latest authorization was under the Act of May 7, 1781, for £20,000,000 of treasury bills, redeemable by December 30, 1794, at the rate of $1 in silver or gold coins for $40 in these bills—an interesting instance of a piece of currency being devalued at the very time of issue. Actually, this was not the end of the story, for under the Act of November 1781, all were called in, but at an even lower rate, $1 in coins for

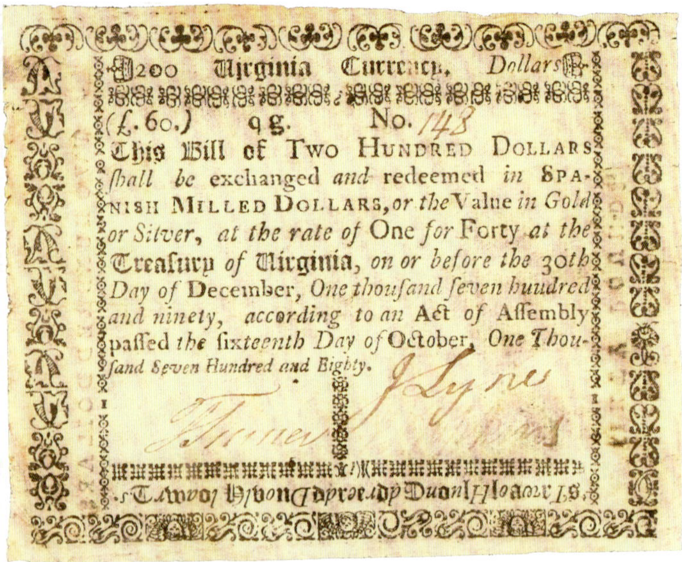

Two-hundred-dollar or £60 bill of Virginia, October 16, 1780, redeemable in gold or silver or in Spanish milled dollars at the rate of $1 paper for $40 in coin.

$1,000 in bills. All became worthless as of October 1, 1782. By this time, Continental Currency issued by the federal government was virtually worthless, and many of the notes of the individual states were likewise. This situation gave rise to the eventual proliferation of bank notes issued under state charters, as citizens would not have accepted any more federal paper money.

Paper Money of Vermont (1781)

Vermont hoped to be one of the original 13 colonies forming the Union under the Declaration of Independence in 1776 and the subsequent Confederation. However, border disputes with New York resulted in the latter state blocking the ambition of Vermont.

Finally, in 1791, Vermont became the 14th state. By that time a short, illustrious, and numismatically rare series of bills had been issued under the date of February 1781. Just 3,600 were issued, from set type, of the denominations of 1s., 1s. 3d., 2s. 6d., 5s., 10s., 20s., 40s., and £3. Each bore "Death to Counterfeit" as part of the inscription, a warning seen on many notes of the colonies. The printing was done by Judah Paddock Spooner and Timothy Green in Westminster, Vermont. Spooner, who saw action in the Battle of Bunker Hill, was later taken prisoner by the British. Green is perhaps best remembered as the printer of certain Connecticut currency. In 1781 the partnership published the *Vermont Gazette, or Green Mountain Post-Boy,* a popular regional newspaper.

Nearly all Vermont bills were subsequently redeemed in good order by the state. By the time a numismatic interest arose in them, hardly any were to be found. Today, notes from Vermont are far rarer than from any of the original 13 colonies.

Other Issues

In addition to the notes of the original 13 colonies plus Vermont (which became the 14th state), paper money, scrip, and related currency were produced for districts that later became part of the Union, such as Louisiana and Florida. Hawaii, which did not become a state until generations later, had its own paper money in the 19th century.

Numismatic Notes

Collecting colonial currency can be a fascinating pursuit. In the absence of any generally agreed upon grading standards and with the added complexity that certain high-quality counterfeits are difficult to differentiate from the genuine, a high degree of expertise is required to maneuver successfully in the marketplace. For many notes, grades such as Fair and Good represent outstanding examples, and none exist in such preservations as Very Fine or Extremely Fine, never mind Uncirculated. Tears, tattering of edges, repairs, and the like are the norm, not the exception, for many bills—the 1781 notes of Vermont being a good case in point.

Although there are exceptions, most colonial notes dated prior to the 1760s range from scarce to rare to utterly unobtainable. Newman's *Early Paper Money of America* often draws from legislative records to delineate what denominations were issued, since actual examples of many no longer survive.

Apart from the Newman text, numismatic information is difficult to find in handy form. For some issues there is little to be found anywhere. The upside of this fact is that, although the pursuit of colonial notes can be daunting, the field of collectors is sparsely populated, and great rarities can be obtained for prices that appear as bargains compared to the values of later (1861 and onward) federal notes. Also, there is a great camaraderie among those who specialize in early paper. Further, it is a fascinating pursuit to correlate the notes, their designs, reason for issue, and even their signers with contemporary history—what was going on in Georgia, or North Carolina, or Massachusetts when such notes were used. Nine signers of colonial notes were also signers of the Declaration of Independence, and one signer of the Declaration of Independence, James Wilson, also autographed Continental Currency Notes (see below).

Colonial currency of the 1770s and the early related state issues of the 1780s are for the most part collectible and in higher grades, with Very Fine and Extremely Fine being realistic expectations for many. Issues that were redeemed bear cancellation marks or punched holes and are accepted as such.

The Continental Army retreating from Long Island in August 1776. As the fortunes of the Continental Army declined, Continental Currency depreciated in value.

Continental Currency

Introduction

On May 10, 1775, the Continental Congress authorized the issuance of paper money. By this time all of the colonies had produced their own bills, making the subject of currency familiar to the delegates. These entities were still under the British Crown, with the Declaration of Independence more than a year away. Under the name of United Colonies, the first issue was followed, through 1777, by others, all denominated in "Spanish milled dollars, or the value thereof in gold or silver," although the well-intentioned colonies had no formal government or any silver coins to fulfill the promise.

Over a period of time, continuing through the early days of the Revolution, through the Declaration of Independence, and then late into the Revolutionary War, bills in values from 1/6 of a Spanish milled dollar to $80 were produced, with higher denominations coming late in the series due to the depreciation of Continental bills.

While early issues bore the imprint of the United Colonies, beginning with the authorization of May 20, 1777, the imprint was changed to the United States. The $20 bill of the first issue was printed on paper ordered in France by Benjamin Franklin and is of unusual dimensions and appearance, the marbled left edge of the face being particularly colorful and distinctive. All others were printed on heavy paper, perhaps more like thin cardboard, made in the United States. Security features included mica chips and threads in the paper, and printing part of the design in orange ink.

During the Revolution the seat of government moved several times. Accordingly, imprints on various series include Philadelphia, Baltimore, and Yorktown (York, Pennsylvania), with the last being the most highly prized today. The Yorktown issue was extensively counterfeited, causing the genuine notes to be questioned in many instances. As a result many of the authentic bills were soon called in, to be replaced by new currency more readily accepted.

All bills were printed by Hall and Sellers, of Philadelphia, well known for producing state currency as well. Certain of the backs featured the already popular "nature printing" devised by Benjamin Franklin.

Continental Currency bills were printed in sheets with multiple bills of different denominations, signed, and then cut apart for distribution. Each bill with a face value of $1 or more bore two authorized signatures, some of whom were also signers of the Articles of Confederation, Declaration of Independence, or other important early documents, thus lending particular interest and value to such bills today. While most numismatists collect Continental Currency by date and denomination, the pursuit of signatures can be an interesting sideline. A roster of signers is given in Eric P. Newman's *Early Paper Money of America.*

In addition to regular issues, impressions of certain issues were printed on blue-tinted paper. Unsigned, these were distributed to aid in the detection of counterfeits. Examples are occasionally seen in the marketplace today, many of which were cut from sheets in recent times.

Counterfeits were endemic and were produced by criminals as well as by the British, the latter using them as economic weapons. Sir Henry Clinton, British commander during the occupation of New York City, encouraged and supervised counterfeiting. A notice in the *New York Mercury*, April 14, 1777, demonstrates how some bills were distributed:

> *Advertisement.* Persons going into other colonies may be supplied with any number of counterfeit Congress notes for the price of the paper per ream. They are so neatly and exactly executed that there is no risk in getting them off, it being almost impossible to discover that they are not genuine. This has been proven by bills to a very large amount which have already been successfully circulated. Inquire of Q.E.D. at the Coffee House from 11 a.m. to 4 p.m. during the present month.

As time went on the financial abilities of the Continental Congress became less and less. The issue of January 14, 1779, was the swan song of the series and included many high-denomination bills not earlier used, reaching as high as $80.

Depreciation

Although early Continental Currency bills traded at or near face value, by early 1777 depreciation had set in, rapidly continuing in a downward spiral. As the Continental Army suffered military setbacks and the government had little in the way of assets, public faith in the bills diminished. This schedule shows the trend—the amount of Continental Currency paper needed to buy $100 in Spanish-American silver dollars:

January 1777—$105 (first listing)

February 1777—$107

January 1778—$325

January 1779—$742

January 1780—$2,934

January 1781—$7,400

February 1781 (last listing)—$7,500[19]

By 1790 the value of Continental bills had diminished to the point at which a $1 coin could buy several hundred dollars or more in such currency. Then came the Act of Congress of August 1, 1790, which provided that old Continental bills would be receivable at the United States Treasury at the rate of $1 in coin for $100 in paper, an action said to have yielded a fortune to certain speculators holding large quantities of such money. This offer expired on September 1, 1791. Then the Act of May 8, 1792, revived the policy, which was extended until March 7, 1793 (the month that the first copper cents of the Chain design reached circulation, an unrelated event). After that time the bills had no official exchange value.

The Continental Issues (1775–1779)

The following is a summary of the various series of these bills, organized by date of congressional session or resolution and denomination (all were authorized in Philadelphia, except as noted). The quantities printed are given after each.[20]

- May 10, 1775 (session)—*Authorized amount:* $3,000,000. *Denominations issued:* $1 (49,000 printed), $2 (49,000), $3 (49,000), $4 (49,000), $5 (49,000), $6 (49,000), $7 (49,000), $8 (49,000), $20 (11,800—French paper issue), $30 (33,333). The border engravings are attributed to David Rittenhouse. The $20 in this series is of a unique nature and is printed on thin paper from France, with colored marbling along one border. This particular issue is considered to be the key variety in the entire Continental Currency series. Thick rag paper with mica flakes and blue fibers was used for other issues and was obtained from Willcox & Co., Ivy Mills, Delaware County, Pennsylvania. Bills from $1 to $8 have nature prints on the back; the higher denominations have emblems.
- November 29, 1775 (resolution, as are the following)—*Authorized amount:* $3,000,000 plus an additional $10,000. *Denominations issued:* $1 (83,611), $2 (83,611), $3 (83,611), $4 (83,611), $5 (83,611), $6 (83,611), $7 (83,611), $8 (83,611). These bills are serially numbered in red ink to differentiate them at a glance from the preceding.
- February 17, 1776—*Authorized amount:* $4,000,000, including $1,000,000 in fractional bills. *Denominations issued:* $1/6 (600,000 printed—Fugio, sundial, and rings design), $1/3 (600,000—design as preceding), $1/2 (600,000), $2/3 (600,000—design as preceding), $1 (130,436), $2 (130,437), $3 (130,436),

$4 (130,435), $5 (65,217), $6 (65,217), $7 (65,217), $8 (65,217). The fractional bills, issued only in this series, each have the sundial/linked rings design similar to that used on the 1776 pewter Continental Currency dollar and later adapted for the 1787 Fugio copper cent. In the $1/6 CURRENCEY is a misspelling. Fractional bills bear one signature instead of the two used on larger denominations.

- May 9, 1776—*Authorized amount:* $5,000,000. *Denominations issued:* $1 (138,889 printed), $2 (138,889), $3 (138,889), $4 (138,889), $5 (138,889), $6 (138,889), $7 (138,889), $8 (138,889). The fractional bills have been dispensed with. The highest denomination is $8. The currency was depreciating, and soon higher value bills would be added to the sequence.
- July 22, 1776—*Authorized amount:* $5,000,000. *Denominations issued:* $2 (76,923 printed), $3 (76,923), $4 (76,923), $5 (76,923), $6 (76,923), $7 (76,923), $8 (76,923), $30 (76,923). The $1 is absent from this issue and the next several, giving rise to the theory that pewter Continental Currency dollars were issued as substitutes. They were authorized on two dates, July 22 and August 13, 1776, but the bills are all imprinted July 22, 1776.
- November 2, 1776—*Authorized amount:* $5,000,000 plus $500,000 for fractional bills (never issued). *Denominations issued:* $2 (76,923 printed), $3 (76,923), $4 (76,923), $5 (76,923), $6 (76,923), $7 (76,923), $8 (76,923), $30 (76,923). Denominations and quantities issued are the same as for the preceding. They were authorized on two dates, November 2 and December 28, 1776, but the bills are all imprinted November 2, 1776.
- February 26, 1777—*Authorized amount:* $5,000,000. *Denominations issued:* $2 (76,923 printed), $3 (76,923), $4 (76,923), $5 (76,923), $6 (76,923), $7 (76,923), $8 (76,923), $30 (76,923). Denominations and quantities issued are the same as for the preceding. This resolution was passed in Baltimore, where the Continental Congress met by necessity, for the British occupied Philadelphia from December 20, 1776, until February 27, 1777.
- May 20, 1777—*Authorized amount:* $16,500,000. *Denominations issued:* $2 (253,850 printed), $3 (253,839), $4 (253,839), $5 (253,840), $6 (253,839), $7 (253,840), $8 (253,851), $30 (253,850). Although the bills are all dated May 20, 1777, the large amount was authorized in 10 separate resolutions extended to April 18, 1778. From this issue onward the bills were imprinted United States instead of United Colonies. This issue was extensively counterfeited. Many bills were called in and exchanged.
- April 11, 1778—*Authorized amount:* $25,000,000. *Denominations issued:* $4 (208,335 printed), $5 (208,330), $6 (208,335), $7 (208,330), $8 (208,330), $20 (208,330), $30 (208,335), $40 (208,335). Authorized by multiple acts at York ("Yorktown" on the bills), Pennsylvania, on April 11 and other times, and in Philadelphia, but all imprinted April 11, 1778. As a class, currency of this series is rarer than any other issue, as many were called back to be replaced with other bills in view of widespread counterfeiting. The $40 denomination was introduced. The depreciation of Continental Currency made it economical to create higher denominations, as was done increasingly from this point to the end of the series.
- September 26, 1778—*Authorized amount:* $75,001,080. *Denominations issued:* $5 (340,914 printed), $7 (340,914), $8 (340,914), $20 (340,914), $30 (340,914), $40 (340,914), $50 (340,914), $60 (340,914). These were issued under nine different resolutions, but all dated September 26, 1778. This authorization was for a greater amount of money than all previous issues combined.
- January 14, 1779—*Authorized amount:* $95,051,695. *Denominations issued:* $1 (139,811 printed), $2 (139,811), $3 (139,811), $4 (139,811), $5 (139,811), $20 (139,811), $30 (182,070), $35 (182,070), $40 (182,070), $45 (182,070), $50 (182,070), $55 (182,070), $60 (182,071), $65 (182,070), $70 (139,811), $80 (139,811). These were authorized by nine different resolutions, but all dated January 14, 1779. This is the final series and also the most extensive in terms of different denominations.

A 1777 Description of the Mottoes

Numismatists and historians have always found the mottoes on Continental Currency as well as on certain notes of the colonies to be fascinating. As most citizens had very little in the way of formal education, the meaning of the mottoes, imprinted in Latin, must have been lost on those who used the bills.

The following account is adapted from an almanac published in 1777, in the era in which such currency was made and used. The bills described are from the first issue of May 10, 1775 (as evidenced by the range of denominations covered), although the same motifs were used on ater issues. The text remains interesting today, although it is likely that, similar to 1777, most current readers cannot translate Latin:

> An explanation of the Devices on the *Continental bills of credit:* with conjectures of their meaning.
>
> An emblematic device, when rightly formed, is said to consist of two parts, a body and a mind, neither of which is complete or intelligible, without the aid of the other. These that I am about to consider, appear formed on that rule, and seem to relate to the present struggle between the colonies and the parent state, for liberty, property, and safety, on the one hand, for absolute power and plunder on the other.
>
> On the $1 bill [see figures 1a and 1b], we have the plant acanthus, sprouting on all sides, under a weight placed upon it, with the motto, DEPRESSA RESURGIT—"though oppressed it rises."—The ancients tell us that the sight of such an accidental circumstance, gave the first hint to an architect in forming the beautiful capital of the Corinthian column. This, perhaps, was intended to encourage us by representing that our present oppressions will not destroy us, but that they may, by increasing our industry, and forcing it into new courses, increase the prosperity on the base of liberty, and the well proportioned pillar of property, elevated for a pleasing spectacle to all connoisseurs, who can taste and delight in the architecture of human happiness.
>
> On the $2 bill [see figures 2a and 2b] is a figure of a hand and flail, over sheaves of wheat, with the motto, TRIBULATIO DITAT—"threshing improves it;" (which we find printed on another of the bills) may perhaps be intended to admonish us, that though at present we are under the flail its blows, how hard so ever, will be rather advantageous than hurtful to us; for they will bring forth every grain of genius and merit in arts, manufactures war and council, that are now concealed in the husk, and then the breath of a breeze will be sufficient to separate from us all the chaff, or toryism.
>
> Tribula, too, in our English sense of the word, improves the mind, it makes us humbler and tends to make us wiser. And threshing, in one of its senses, that of beating, often improves those that are threshed. Many an unwarlike nation have been beaten into heroes, by troublesome warlike neighbors; and the continuance of a war, though it lessen the numbers of a people, often increases its strength by the increased discipline and consequent courage of the number remaining. Thus England, after the civil war, in which her people threshed one another, became more formidable to her neighbors. The public distress, too, that arises from war, by increasing frugality and industry, often gives rise to habits that remain after the war is over, and thereby naturally enriches those on whom it has enforced, those enriching virtues.
>
> On the $3 bill [see figures 3a and 3b] is drawn an eagle on the wing pouncing upon a crane, who turns upon his back and receives the eagle on the point of his long bill, which pierces the eagle's breast; with this motto, EXITUS IN DUBIO EST—"the event is uncertain." The eagle, I suppose, represents Great Britain, the crane America: this device offers an admonition to each of the contending parties. To the crane, not to depend too much upon the success of its endeavors to avoid the contest (by petition, negotiation, &c.) but to prepare for using the means God and nature hath given it; and to the eagle, not to presume on its superiority and strength, since a weaker bird may wound it mortally.
>
> On the $4 bill [see figures 4a and 4b] is impressed, a wild boar of the forest, rushing on the spear of the hunter, with this motto, AUT MORS AUT VITA DECORA; which may be translated—"death or liberty." The wild boar is an animal of great strength and courage, armed with long and sharp tusks, which he well knows how to use in his own defense. His is inoffensive while suffered to enjoy his freedom, but when roused and wounded by the hunter, often turns and makes him pay dearly for his temerity.
>
> On the $5 bill [see figures 5a and 5b], we have a thorny bush, which a hand seems attempting to eradicate; the hand appears to bleed, as pricked by the spines. The motto is SUBSTINE VEL ABSTINE; which may be rendered "bear with me, or let me alone," or thus, "either support or leave me." The bush I suppose to mean America, and the bleeding hand Britain. Would to God that bleeding were stopt; the wounds of that hand healed, and its future operation directed by wisdom and equity; so shall the hawthorn flourish and form an hedge around it, annoying with her thorns only its invading enemies.
>
> The $6 bill [see figures 6a and 6b] has the figure of a beaver, gnawing a large tree, with this motto, PERSEVERANDO—"by perseverance." I apprehend the great tree may be intended to represent the enormous power Britain has assumed over us and endeavors to enforce by arms, of taxing at pleasure, and binding us in all cases whatsoever, or the exorbitant profits she makes by monopolizing our commerce.—Then the beaver, which is know to be able, by assiduous and steady working, to fell large trees, may signify America; which, by perseverance in her present measures, will probably reduce that power within

(continued on p. 26)

The United Colonies
ONE DOLLAR.
No. 26560
THIS Bill entitles the
BEARER to receive
ONE SPANISH MILL-
ED DOLLAR, or the
Value thereof in Gold or
Silver, according to the
Resolutions of the CON
GRESS, held at Phila
delphia, the 10th of May,
1775. ONE DOLLAR.
DEPRESSA RESURGIT.
Continental Currency

1a.

ONE DOLLAR.
PHILADELPHIA:
Printed by HALL and SEL-
LERS. 1775.

1b.

The United Colonies
TWO DOLLARS
TWO DOLLARS.
No. 30606
THIS Bill entitles the
Bearer to receive
TWO SPANISH MILL-
ED DOLLARS, or the
Value thereof in GOLD
or SILVER, according to
the Resolutions of the
CONGRESS, held at
Philadelphia, the 10th of
May, 1775. II DOLL.
TRIBULATIO DITAT.
Continental Currency

2a.

TWO DOLLARS.
PHILADELPHIA:
Printed by HALL and SEL-
LERS. 1775.

2b.

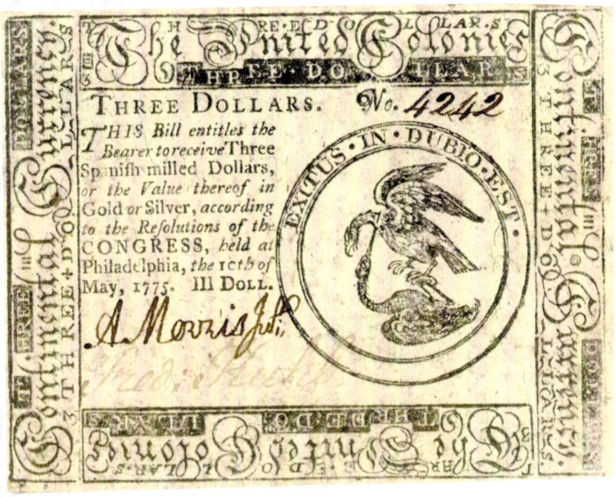

3a.

3b.

4a.

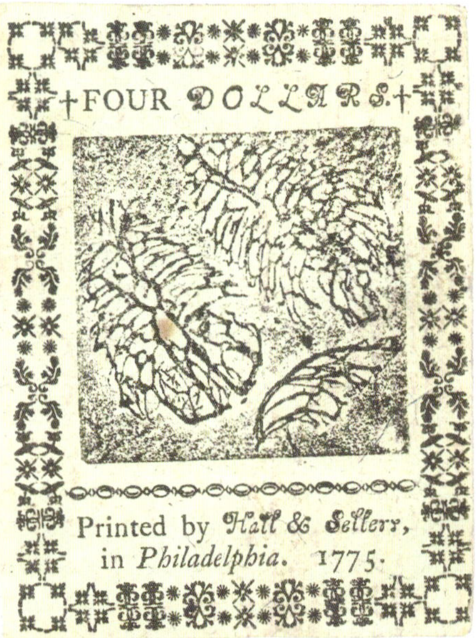

4b.

5a.

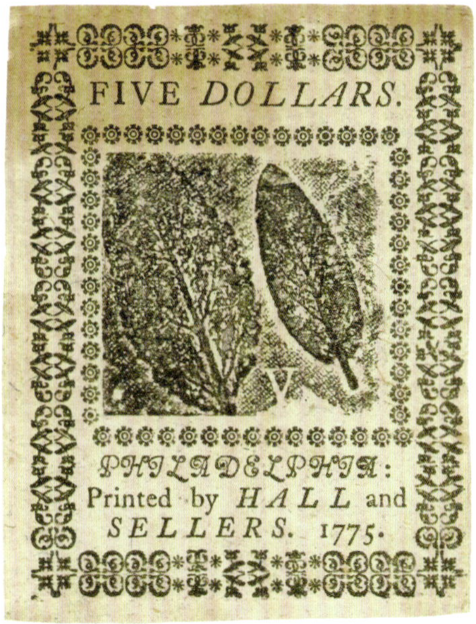

5b.

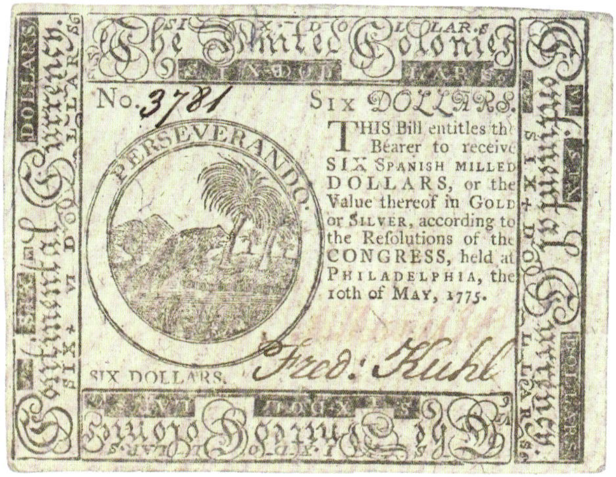

6a.

6b.

7a.

7b.

8a.

8b.

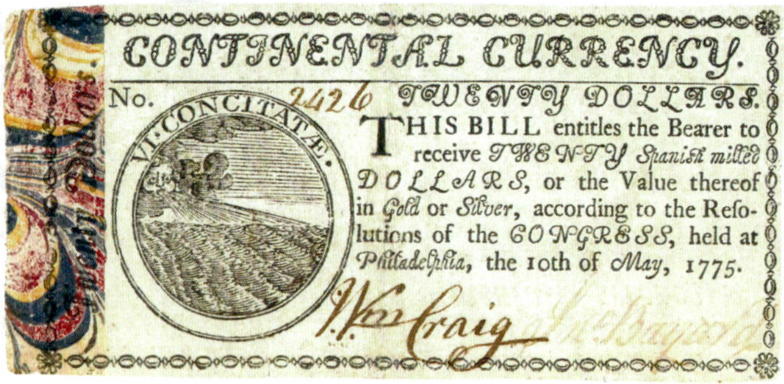

9a.

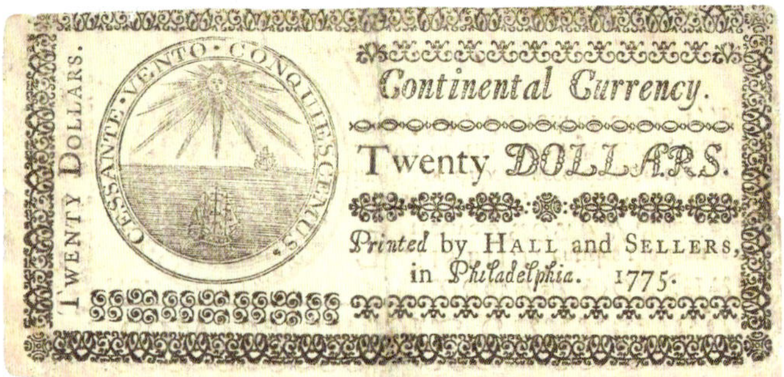

9b.

10a.

10b.

(continued from p. 22)

proper bounds, and, by establishing the most necessary manufactures among ourselves, abolish the British monopoly.

The $7 bill [see figures 7a and 7b] has for its device, a storm descending from a black heavy cloud, with the motto, SERENABIT—"it will clear up." This seems designed to encourage the dejected, who may be too sensible of present inconveniences, and fear their continuance. It reminds them, agreeably to the adage, that after a storm comes a calm. . . .

On the $8 denomination of the bills [see figures 8a and 8b], there is the figure of a harp, with this motto, MAJORA MINORIBUS CONSONANT; literally—"the greater and smaller ones sound together." As the harp is an instrument composed of great and small strings, included in a strong frame, and also so tuned as to agree in concord with each other, I conceive that the frame may be intended to represent our new government by a continental congress, and the strings of different lengths and substance, either the several colonies of different weights and force, or the various ranks of people in all of them, who are now united by that government in the most perfect harmony.

On the $20 bill [see figures 9a and 9b], there is stamped the representation of a tempestuous sea; a face with swollen cheeks, wrapt up in a black cloud, appearing to blow violently on the waters, the waves high, and all rolling one way. The motto, VI CONCITATE; which may be rendered—"raised by force." From the remotest antiquity, in figurative language, great waters have signified the people, and waves an insurrection. The people of themselves are supposed as naturally inclined to be still, the waters to remain level and quiet. Their rising here appears not to be from any internal cause, but from an external power, expressing by the head Eolus, god of the winds, (or Boreas, the North wind, as usually the most violent) acting furiously upon them. The black cloud perhaps, designs the British parliament, and the waves the colonies. Their rolling all in one direction, shows, that the very force used against them, has produced their unanimity.

On the reverse of this bill, we have a smooth sea, the sails of ships on that sea hanging loose, show a perfect calm, the sun shining fully, denotes a clear sky. The motto is CESSANTES VENTO CON QUIECEMUS—"the wind ceasing, we shall be quiet." Supposing my explanation of the preceding device to be right, this will import, that when those violent acts of power which have roused the colonies are repealed, they will return to their former tranquility. Britain seems thus charged with being the sole cause of the present civil war, at the same time that the only mode of putting an end to it, is thus plainly pointed out to her.

The last, the $30 bill [see figures 10a and 10b], has a wreath of laurel on a marble monument or altar: the motto, SI RECTE FACIES—"if you act rightly." This seems intended as an encouragement to a brave and steady conduct in defense of our Liberties, as it promises to crown with honor, by the laurel wreath, those who persevere to the end in well-doing; and with a long duration of that honor, expressed by the monument of marble.

A learned friend of mine thinks this device more particularly addressed to the *Congress.* He says that the ancients composed for their heroes a wreath of laurel, oak and olive twigs interwoven. . . .

Of laurel, as that tree was dedicated to Apollo, and understood to signify knowledge and prudence; of oak, as pertaining to Jupiter, and expressing fortitude; of olive, as the tree of Pallas, and as a symbol of peace. The whole to show, that those who are entrusted to conduct the great affairs of mankind, should act prudently and firmly, retaining, above all, upon an altar, to admonish the hero who is to be crowned with it, that true glory is founded on, and proceeds from piety. My friend, therefore, thinks the present device might intend a wreath of that composite kind, though, from the smallness of the work, the engraver could not mark distinctly the differing leaves. And he is rather confirmed in his opinion that this is designed as an admonition to the Congress, when he considers the passage in Horace, from whence the motto is taken—

Rex eris, aium,
Si recte facies. . . .

Not the king's parliament, who act wrong, but the people's congress, if it acts right, shall govern America.

As to those fascinating mottoes, in the *American Journal of Numismatics,* October 1875, J. Hammond Trumbull discusses the designs, noting that "most of them are taken from the emblem books or from Dutch medals of the preceding century."

NUMISMATIC NOTES

All of the basic dates and denominations of Continental Currency notes are collectible. The rarest of the rare is the May 10, 1775, $20 of long rectangular shape and with the left end of the face in marbled colors. However, examples, though hardly inexpensive, come on the market regularly.

The American Beaver medal, a favorite among collectors of Washingtoniana, depicts the American beaver gnawing at the English oak. Although the medal is dated 1776, it was produced in 1805 (by dies cut by John Reich) using a concept similar to that found on the Continental Currency $6 note, although the latter depicts a palm tree. The obverse has the portraits of Franklin and Washington. (Baker-54A, Betts-549)

The April 11, 1778, issues authorized in Yorktown (York, Pennsylvania) are, as a class, the rarest of all series, as most were called in at an early time.

Generally, earlier issues are found in lower grades than are later emissions. Perhaps the highest average grades are found among the Continental Currency bills of January 14, 1779, the last of the issues and also the one laden with more high denominations than any other.

As signatures were applied separately and with different pens and inks, colors can vary as can their susceptibility to fading. In all instances a given note with clearly recognizable signatures is worth more than one with faded signatures. Sometimes one signature is bright, and the other is so faded as to be illegible.

Centering and trimming can vary. Most desirable are bills that are not trimmed into the border designs, although the borders can be close.

Offerings of Continental Currency bills are more frequent and the prices more standard than for earlier colonial notes.

EARLY BANK NOTES, 1782–1810

THE RISE OF BANKING AND BANK NOTES

With colonial notes and Continental Currency as a prelude, the scene shifts to the subject of this text: bills issued by state-chartered banks and similar entities from 1782 to 1866. The study is divided into sections, somewhat arbitrarily as the evolution of bank notes is a continuum. However, each era had its own innovations.

By 1782, Continental Currency had depreciated to the point of near worthlessness. Although the surrender of Lord Cornwallis and his British troops at Yorktown (Virginia) in 1781 ended the Revolutionary War, the treaty of peace would not be signed until 1783. The inauguration of General George Washington as America's first president would not happen until 1789, which would also see the appointment of Alexander Hamilton as secretary of the Treasury.

During the 1780s the U.S. government was still in the process of being formed. Assets were scarce, but ambitions were high. Despite the optimism for the future engendered by independence, the public would not have been receptive to another federal issue of paper money. Accordingly, the field of opportunity passed to the private sector, primarily to banks that were organized under charters granted by the various states.

THE BANK OF NORTH AMERICA

The first commercial bank established in the United States after the Revolution was the Bank of North America, situated in Philadelphia, authorized by the United States Congress on December 31, 1781. The official name of the institution was The President, Directors, and Company of the Bank of North America, such long titles becoming common with other, later bank charters in various states. In the present text as well as in most contemporary records, the short title was used for this and other banks. The main projector was Robert Morris, superintendent of finance of the United States, a position equivalent to what would later be known as the secretary of the Treasury. Although the federal government would become involved in certain other early banks, including being a prominent shareholder in the first Bank of the United States (1791), soon the states took nearly complete charge.

The Bank of North America in Philadelphia was housed in a Greek Revival building, the architecture of choice for several of the larger early banks. ("Bank Buildings," *Architectural Review,* March 1905)

Capital of the new bank was not to exceed $10,000,000, and there was no time limitation for its charter. In April 1782 the state of Pennsylvania affirmed the charter, after which the bank commenced business with capital of $400,000.

While many modern historians credit the bank with unqualified success, in fact there were challenges and struggles at the outset, as in this 19th century account, although it seems to have an anti-bank bias:

> As the country was deficient in notes of circulation, and its credit stood high, it was enabled to extend its issues vastly beyond its capital. The extensive circulation of the notes of the bank, occasioned by the disbursements of the government, emboldened its directors to overstep the bounds of discretion. The channels of circulation soon became surcharged, and the public, beginning to doubt the ability of the bank to redeem its notes on presentation, they were returned so rapidly for payment that it was compelled to call upon its debtors for payment also. This reduction of loans occasioned a general pressure for money, bankruptcies, usurious extortions, the disappearance of specie, and the impossibility of procuring money at the legal rates of interest.
>
> Petitions were shortly afterwards presented to the Legislature for repeal of the charter, which was granted on 13th September, 1785, but the bank continued its business, claiming the right to do so under the charter granted by Congress; but in March 1787 the Legislature revived its charter, limiting its capital to $2,000,000, of which only $830,000 was paid in, and its duration to 14 years.[1]

Certain early bills of this bank are a combination of an engraved plate and set type. The engraved part was done by Charles Heath and included a small vignette or decoration.

The official history of the bank, published in 1882, includes this commentary regarding the difficulty of gaining acceptance for its paper money:

> It was found that notes of the bank would not readily circulate. Army contractors, when paid in this way, almost invariably carried the bills to collectors and got the amount in specie.
>
> In New England, the people, fresh from the recollection of Continental money, were very loath to receive the bank issues at all, so that they circulated at from 10% to 15% below par. Stories were current, and actually believed, that the bank had a show of far greater wealth than it actually possessed.
>
> [Historian Bolles said] "Gentlemen interested in the institution were in the habit of requesting people from the country and laboring men about town to go to the bank and get silver in exchange for notes. When they went on this errand of neighborly kindness, as they thought it, they found a display of silver on the counter, and men employed in raising boxes containing silver, or supposed to contain silver, from the cellar to the banking-room, or lowering them from the banking room into the cellar."
>
> By these contrivances they were induced to believe that the bank was possessed of extreme wealth.
>
> But all difficulties were soon overcome. A considerable sum in specie arrived from Europe and the West Indies, and little by little the amounts subscribed by individuals for the capital stock were paid into the treasury. The deposits gradually rolled up.
>
> Morris, by skilful management, prevented further issues from floating into that part of the country where they were badly received. The depreciation was quickly checked. Bank bills rose to their par value and were thus sustained without further trouble.[2]

Bank of North America currency of the 1780s is so rare today as to be essentially noncollectible. The same comment can be made for nearly all other bank bills issued in the United States in the 18th century. We know that in 1792, William Harrison Sr. spent six months in Philadelphia engraving plates for notes for the Bank of North America and for the Bank of the United States.

SHOWING STRENGTH

The preceding scenario of displaying silver coins to demonstrate the ability of the bank to redeem its bills has many counterparts in the annals of American finance. In essence, if a bank appeared to be short on coins, then depositors wanted them. However, if it seemed that a bank could redeem bills with silver or gold on request, then the public felt no urgency to do so.

In a related context there were "runs" on several banks in San Francisco in 1855, in the Gold Rush era. Banking historian Benjamin C. Wright describes one incident:[3]

> There was a run upon the bank of Burgoyne & Co. as there was upon other private bankers. There was a sufficient number of idle people in the city to supply a good-sized crowd to look after every person who was compassed with a sea of trouble. It was a very big crowd that filled the small quarters occupied by Burgoyne & Co. Some of these wanted the money due them and they wanted it bad, and the whole amount, and they wanted it right away.
>
> There were probably others in the crowd who did not have a dollar in the embarrassed bank, but they were just there out of sympathy, you know, for the other fellow, and who were insistent that he, at least, should have a square deal. There never was a run on a bank that did not attract some of those disinterested and disgruntled persons, who belong to a class altogether too large that are delighted when trouble comes, provided they are not personally involved.
>
> Well, Burgoyne & Co. had the trouble, all right. They also had more friends on the outside than on the inside of their little enclosure. They were neighbors, too, and near-by. Word was sent to some of them, and soon one of them forced his way to the counter and threw down a bag of gold coins to be deposited. It was like oil on troubled waters. It had a restraining effect on the turbulent crowd.
>
> Soon another man came in with a bag of gold which he wanted to deposit. A little later a third followed. The crowd thinned out, and the run had collapsed.
>
> *One* bag of gold did the business, for as soon as received it was passed to a confederate at the back door and then brought in at the front door to be again deposited.

A somewhat similar caper took place at the bank of Lucas, Turner & Co. during the same excitement, catalyzed by the failure of Adams & Co. and Page, Bacon & Co., two of San Francisco's most important banks. William Tecumseh Sherman (remembered for his later Civil War march through Georgia as Union general) was at the time in charge of Lucas, Turner & Co., an institution with substantial assets. Rumors were spreading quickly, and the public had no way of knowing which banks were solvent and which were on the brink of disaster. There was a rush to withdraw coins.

This is from Sherman's memoirs:

> Meantime, rumors from the street came pouring in that Wright & Co. had failed; then Wells, Fargo & Co.; then Palmer, Cook & Co., and indeed all, or nearly all, the banks of the city; and I was told

> that parties on the street were betting high, first, that we would close our doors at eleven o'clock; then twelve, and so on; but we did not, till the usual hour that night. We had paid every demand, and still had a respectable amount left. . . .
>
> Toward the close of the day, some of our customers deposited, rather ostentatiously, small amounts, not aggregating more than eight or ten thousand dollars. Book-keepers and tellers were kept at work to write up the books; and these showed: Due depositors and certificates, about $120,000, for which remained of coin about $50,000. . . .
>
> I resolved not to sleep until I had collected from those owing the bank a part of their debts; for I was angry with them that they had stood back and allowed the panic to fall on the banks alone. Among these were Captain [Joseph L.] Folsom, who owed us $25,000 secured by a mortgage on the American Theatre and Tehama Hotel; James Smiley, contractor for building the Custom-House, who owed us two notes of $20,000 and $16,000, for which we held, as collateral, two acceptances of the collector of the port, Major R.P. Hammond, for $20,000 each; beside other private parties that I need not name. . . .

By quick thinking, Sherman exchanged some fiscal paper and obtained a check for $40,000 signed by the collector of the port of San Francisco. At eight the next morning this was cashed at the San Francisco Mint in exchange for

> two sealed bags of gold-coin, each marked $20,000, which I had carried to the bank, but never opened them, or even broke the seals.
>
> That morning our bank opened as usual, but there was no appearance of a continuation of the "run;" on the contrary, money began to come back on deposit, so that by night we had a considerable increase, and this went on from day to day, till nearly the old condition of things returned.[4]

In the same account Sherman quoted a panicky Frenchman who had waited in a long line at the bank, seeking to withdraw his funds in the form of gold coins before the institution collapsed—which he hoped it would not do at least until after he reached the cashier's payout window. Upon reaching the head of the line and being pleasantly surprised that, indeed, coins were readily available, the Frenchman remarked, "If you got the money, I no want him; but, if you no got him, I want him like the devil."

Throughout the present text it is demonstrated that time and again, for a bank, appearances were everything, and that confidence of the public was an institution's greatest asset. In the entire era of obsolete currency under discussion, from 1782 to 1866, there was very little in the way of serious oversight for any banks. Certain of the states set up banking commissions, this being especially true after difficulties experienced in the Hard Times era beginning in 1837. However, the commissions usually reviewed the reports submitted by the various banks but did not perform audits. Exceptions included state banks set up by Ohio and Indiana, the latter being especially well managed. Elsewhere, abuses were many.

EARLY BANKS IN NEW YORK

The first bank in the Empire State was the Bank of New York, which commenced business in New York City on June 9, 1784, without a charter.[5] The original business plan was drawn up by Alexander Hamilton. In 1789 it petitioned the legislature for a charter in order to limit the liability of the shareholders, but this was not given until 1791, by which time Hamilton was in office as Washington's first secretary

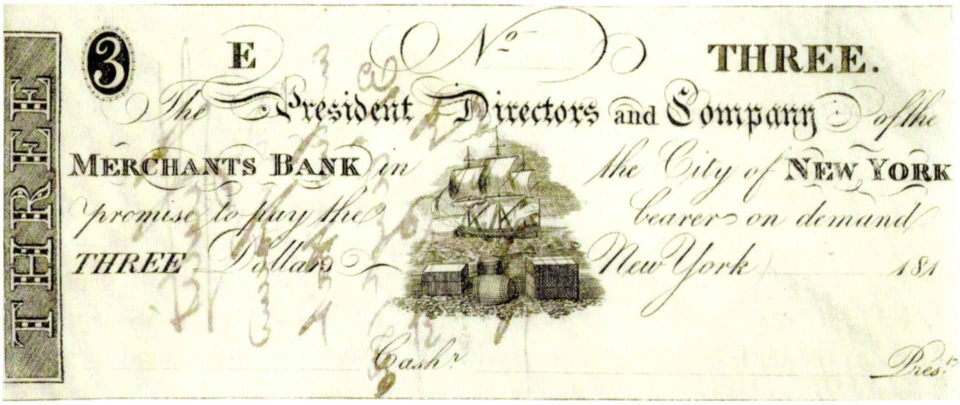

In 1803 the Merchants Bank of New York City was unable to obtain a state charter due to deeply seated political opposition. The bank operated successfully without official sanction until 1805. This unissued note dates from the next decade. On the back is an inked memorandum (traces of which can be seen on the face) noting that A. Curtis had found this bill among his effects on August 21, 1820. It was apparently saved as a souvenir.

Proof impression of a $5 note for the Bank of North America, by Draper, Underwood, Bald & Spencer, a Philadelphia engraving partnership that was prominent in the 1830s. The central vignette depicts the goddess Justice and a portrait of financier Robert Morris.

of the Treasury.[6] By the latter date the bank had capital of $318,250 and bills in circulation to the amount of $181,254.

At the time the procurement of banking privileges was strictly a matter of having the proper political connections. The Federalists, led by Hamilton, controlled the bank's interests and were able to effectively prevent any local competition arising for many years, save for a branch of the first Bank of the United States. Accordingly, the Million Bank, projected with ambitious plans in 1791, went nowhere. In addition to the political milieu, there were many men of prominence who simply were not sure that a commercial bank was a good idea, what with worthless Continental paper money still in the minds of everyone and a general distrust of finance. In commerce, most people wanted "hard money" — gold or silver coins, which continued to be foreign issues, mostly of Spanish America.

In 1799 success at launching a new bank was scored by subterfuge when the Manhattan Company was chartered by the state at $2,000,000 for the purpose of setting up a municipal water supply. The Bank of Albany, with capital of $260,000, was chartered in 1792, and the Bank of Columbia ($130,000) was founded in Hudson in 1792, both along the busy Hudson River watercourse. These and other early banks are discussed below. In 1803 Alexander Hamilton was behind the organization of the Merchants Bank, in New York City, but it could not obtain a charter; yet the ruling politicos had no problem setting up the New York State Bank of Albany (later known as the State Bank of Albany), despite outcry from the opposition.

By 1804, when the Republicans unseated the Federalists in New York City, there were six banks operating in the state. In that year the Merchants Bank of New York City, already in business, applied to the legislature for a charter. This was denied and, further, the legislature enacted a law prohibiting unchartered banking companies from doing business and declaring their contracts and paper money null and void. In 1805 a second application was made, but it was denied. Not to be thwarted, the backers of the Merchants Bank bribed enough members of the legislature that a charter was granted, but not without a notable contretemps.[7] During the next two decades, more banks were established in New York state by those who had the proper political connections.

Roster of Early Banks

By the first decade of the 19th century, the following banks were chartered in the United States, although not all went into successful operation. The figures at the beginning of each study represent the authorized capital, which in many if not most instances was not fully paid in. Historical sketches and casual remarks of possible numismatic interest are included. While space does not permit saying much about the nearly 2,000 other banks that would form later, the sketches of these early banks will give an idea of the situations with which such institutions were faced in the beginning era of the system.

Chartered in 1782

Bank of North America

Philadelphia. $2,000,000 authorized capital. The bank commenced business on January 7, 1782, at which time $200,000 in capital stock was purchased by the United States. Other stock sales lagged, and capital was set at $400,000 in the early years, later increased to $1,000,000. This is the first state-chartered bank and the first issuer of paper money after the Revolution. Its charter specified that its bills were to be exchangeable at par with gold and silver coins.

The Massachusetts Bank as it appeared in the early days. (*Pageant of America,* 1927)

A proof impression of a $2 note of the Bank of Massachusetts by Abner Reed. From the second decade of the 19th century.

During 1782 through 1783 the bank was managed by federal Superintendent of Finance Robert Morris, at which time the bank dealt in depreciated Continental Currency (a great speculation at the time), foreign money, bills of exchange, etc., endeavoring to make a profit in the meantime. Benjamin Franklin Bache produced certain early bills of this bank, including fractional values denominated in pence.

In the 1790s and onward this bank was a favorite depository for coins struck at the Philadelphia Mint. During this era certain bank notes had the printed date 179, with the final digit to be added in ink. Later notes were imprinted 18. Robert Scot, who became the chief engraver at the Mint in 1793, prepared some of the printing plates, although no notes are known today with his imprint.

The years 1806 to 1809 were troubled, an investigation disclosed that most large loans were made under special arrangements with favored individuals, and losses were sustained. After 1808 the bank returned to profitability despite generally unfavorable business conditions resulting from the Embargo Act of 1807 and the subsequent restriction of maritime trade. Although the act was repealed in 1809, the Non Intercourse Act took its place. Commercial travel on the high seas remained perilous in the several years preceding the War of 1812.

From 1837 through 1842, the Hard Times era, the Bank of North America suffered greatly, with more than 80% of its assets tied up in nonperforming loans and illiquid securities. With the resumption of prosperity the bank became profitable again. The bank shared its misery with most other financial institutions at the time.

After the National Banking Act of 1863, this bank reincorporated as a National Bank, an action which stockholders approved on November 14, 1864. This bank alone was allowed by the Treasury Department to retain its original title, without adding "National."

Chartered in 1784

Massachusetts Bank

The Massachusetts Bank, located in Boston, was chartered on February 7, 1784, with capital authorized at $300,000, but $253,500 was the amount paid in when business commenced on July 5. Premises were established in a brick building fronting on Boston Common (now Tremont Street), a structure earlier known as the Manufactory House. In the early days banking was conducted Monday through Saturday from 10 A.M. to 1 P.M., then again from 3 to 5 P.M., except for Sundays, public fast days, Thanksgiving, Commencement Day, election days, Christmas, Good Friday, and the Fourth of July. Early loans were usually short term, for one or two months, by discounting the notes to reflect interest (at the rate of 6% per annum), with the borrower to pay back the face amount in full. The first president was James Bowdoin, who served from 1784 to 1786.

In 1797 there was excitement when it was found that the bank's $5 bills had been counterfeited. The same criminal also faked bills of the Union Bank (chartered in 1792). At the time there were no "counterfeit detector" publications to aid bankers and the public, who had to rely on often incomplete descriptions in newspapers.

In 1811, banking hours were revised, to open at 9 A.M. in the summer and an hour later in the winter, and to close daily at 3 P.M., except Saturday, when the doors were shut at 1 P.M.

Early bills of the bank included such odd denominations as $1.50, $2.50, $3.50, $4.50, $6, $7, $8, $9, $15, $25, $30, $35, and $40, in addition to the usual $1, $2, $3, $5, and other standard values. Authentic 18th-century bills of this bank do not bear the name of an engraver. By the early 19th century, currency was being made for the bank by William Heogland, in the 1810s by Abner Reed, and still later by Jacob Perkins. All 18th-century bills of this bank are rare today. By the conclusion of business in 1865, the amount of currency issued totaled $4,674,177, all of which but $22,111 was redeemed.

On April 4, 1865, the assets of the corporation passed to the newly chartered Massachusetts National Bank of Boston, charter 974.

Bank of New York

The Bank of New York, capitalized at $950,000, went into business in New York City on June 9, 1784, under articles of association drafted by Alexander Hamilton. Alexander McDougall was the first presi-

Detail of a map of New York City as it appeared in 1789. Broadway was the most prominent thoroughfare of the era. Many business and financial interests were on or near Wall Street, where the Bank of New York was situated. (By G. Hayward, 1857, for inclusion in D.T. Valentine's *Manual of the Corporation of the City of New York*)

The Walton house, New York City, where the Bank of New York began business on June 9, 1784. (Harper Brothers)

The northeast corner of William and Wall streets circa 1797. The Bank of New York building is prominent on the corner. (From a painting by A. Robertson in the New-York Historical Society)

Unissued $3 note of the Bank of New York City, by Fairman, Draper, Underwood & Co., Philadelphia. The partnership was active from 1823 to 1827 and included Gideon Fairman, John Draper, and Thomas Underwood. The beehive, a symbol of industry, forms the central vignette.

dent, and William Seton was the founding cashier. At the time there were about 20,000 residents in the city. Premises were maintained at 44 Wall Street in the heart of the financial district. Loans in the form of discounted paper were awarded each Thursday to the highest bids left in sealed envelopes the preceding day. The institution operated without benefit of a charter until 1791, when on March 21 it was granted, the first to be awarded in the state. This was a risky procedure, as stockholders were personally liable in suits arising from the normal course of business. For any bank a state charter offered protection, but in the politically charged climate of the late 18th century, these were not easy to get.

The bank distributed lists of coins, their weights, and the accepted value at which various foreign gold coins would be received in payment. Business in coins and, in time, the bills of other banks was extensive.

In 1794 the Treasury of the United States negotiated a $400,000 loan from the bank at 5% interest, payable in 1796, a large sum in relation to the total domestic debt of the government at the time, which was about $29 million. This action greatly enhanced the reputation of the bank.

On January 3, 1795, the bank issued a warning that $5 and $40 bills of the bank had been counterfeited, the first of many such frauds over a long period of years. The counterfeiting situation was not much different in the 1790s than it had been in pre-Revolutionary times, except that punishments were less severe and did not include death. The typical counterfeiter was apt to make false plates of the notes of several different prominent banks. Some were of such quality that their status can be a point of discussion today in auction and other catalogs.

In 1831 the bank was rechartered for 20 years, with the capital set at $1,000,000. At the time the institution did business at the northeast corner of William and Wall streets. The business proved profitable throughout its existence, except for the economic troubles beginning in 1814 and 1837. Annual dividends ranged from 8% to 10%.

In the 18th century the bank acquired and kept a quantity of several thousand 1787-dated copper Fugio cents. These came to light in 1859. By about 1948 some 1,641 pieces remained in possession of the bank and were numismatically analyzed by Damon G. Douglas. Some are still held by the bank today.

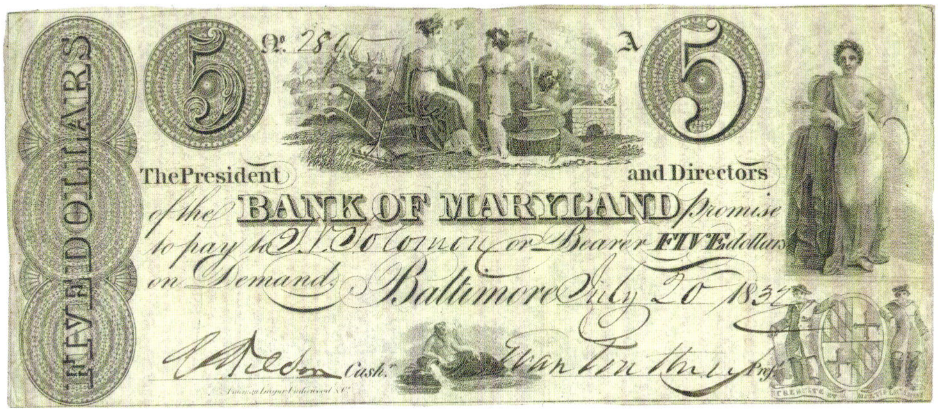

Signed and issued $5 note of the Bank of Maryland, July 20, 1832. At the time the bank was fraudulently operated, a situation that came to a conclusion with its failure in March 1834.

Chartered in 1790

Bank of Maryland

On November 9, 1784, the *Maryland Journal and Baltimore Advertiser* carried this notice: "Such of the inhabitants as are desirous of promoting the establishment of a bank in the town of Baltimore are requested to meet . . . when proposals for carrying into immediate effect an institution so essentially necessary to the commercial interests, not only of the town, but of the state also, will be laid before them." Shares were available for $400 each, payable in specie. Interest was less than anticipated, and only 17 people subscribed for a total of about 300 shares. The plan was laid before the state senate in November 1784, but it failed to pass.

In 1790 the Bank of Maryland gained its charter, capitalized at $300,000. Subscriptions were opened on December 10, and in two weeks some $200,000 worth of shares was sold, this being the minimum amount needed before directors could be elected.[8] Business commenced in 1791. The institution was immediately profitable and soon commenced paying 12% annual dividends. In 1813 the charter was extended after the bank promised to subscribe to help pay for the Cumberland Road extending from Maryland to the West.

On July 18, 1794, the Bank of Maryland made the first deposit of silver at the Philadelphia Mint, thereby making it possible to produce coins in this metal. The shipment consisted of French coins to the value of $80,715.73.

In early 1824 it was disclosed that the Bank of Maryland had been operating at a deficit, and some $100,000 had been lost, equal to a third of its capital at the time. Apparently, little effort was taken to remedy the situation. In 1831 the bank, still in an uncertain position, made significant changes in its personnel, after which time reckless expansion was undertaken. Large numbers of bills were circulated, causing apprehension in local banking circles.

By 1833 the reputation of the bank had gone from questionable to very bad, and its currency was unacceptable to many in the financial community. In March 1834 the bank failed. It was thought that by that time the bank had issued large quantities of worthless paper. The bank officers promised a full explanation, which creditors awaited.

Exasperated after receiving no information for 17 months, creditors and note holders ran riot in August 1835, and mobs raged out of control in the city for five days, destroying houses and personal property of the former bank officers, the most alarming such situation in American banking history. *Niles' Weekly Register,* published in Baltimore, followed the proceedings in detail. In September 1835 a correspondent recommended that a city guard force be established to assist the police should anything like this event ever happen again. It was estimated that worthless bills of this bank were issued in an amount far exceeding its own capital and that of all other Baltimore banks combined, leaving holders with paper with face value totaling about $1,600,000.

The once "worthless paper" of this bank is readily collectible today as the bills were never redeemed. Ironically, nice examples sell on the numismatic market for significantly more than their original face value!

Chartered in 1791

Providence Bank

The bank opened for business in the thriving port of Providence, Rhode Island, on October 10, 1791, following an unsuccessful attempt to establish a bank in the city in 1784. Capital was authorized at $400,000. The office was in a house on a hill on Hopkins Street, soon renamed Bank Lane. Olney Winsor was the first president, and John Brown was the first cashier. The institution had a close relationship with the Providence Insurance Company, which issued coverage for certain borrowers. Loans were made for a stated maximum of 30 days, but as many of the borrowers were in the maritime trade and transactions could take many months to complete, the bank allowed extensions. The charter placed no limit on the amount of paper money the bank could issue.

Over the years there were many notices regarding the bank's paper money. An article in *Bicknell's Counterfeit Detector,* November 22, 1830, reads, "We copy the following from the *Boston Patriot:* There are now in circulation in Boston one dollar bills, purporting to be of the Providence Bank, signed by Wm. C. Billings, president, and James W. Crawford, cashier. These bills have not the least resemblance to the genuine Providence Bank bills. Of the Providence Bank, Thomas P. Ives is president, and Charles L. Bowler, cashier."

A report of January 2, 1860, gave the capital of the bank as $500,000 and the bills in circulation as $112,253. In 1865 it converted to become the Providence National Bank, charter 1302.[9]

Bank of the United States

The Bank of the United States was established in Philadelphia, then the seat of the federal government. Capital was limited to $10,000,000, divided into 2,500 shares of $400 each, payable 25% in gold and silver coins and 75% in public securities. Of this sum, $2,000,000 was subscribed for by the federal government, as allowed by the charter. Branch offices were opened in several cities.

The Bank of the United States, conceived by Secretary of the Treasury Alexander Hamilton, was chartered for 20 years by Congress in 1791, under the precept that it would facilitate the conducting of national finances, would assist the government in quickly securing funds for emergencies, and would facilitate domestic and international trade and commerce. The bank would strengthen the finances and reputation of young America. To the United States it was to be similar in many ways to what the Bank of England was for the British. The charter provided for 24 directors, American citizens elected by stockholders. However, the birth of the bank was controversial, with most opposition, including Thomas Jefferson, stating that it would be unconstitutional.

The bank opened for business in Philadelphia on December 12, 1791. At the time the policy of the bank was to receive bids for loans on Mondays and Thursdays and to evaluate them on Tuesdays and Fridays. Similar to the procedure elsewhere, loans were given by discounting paper from its face value, with the face value of the note to be repaid by the borrower. All throughout the period 1782 to 1866 as studied

Proof impression of a $1 note of the Providence Bank, by Leney & Rollinson. William Rollinson took William Leney as a partner in 1811, at which time he distributed specimen bills that were said to be "impossible to be imitated in the common mode of engraving." In 1812 Rollinson devised a machine to add wavy lines to bank plates, as are featured on the ends of this note.

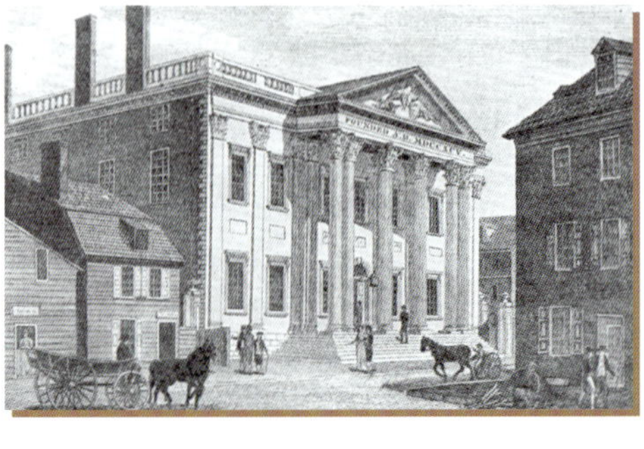

The Bank of the United States. (William Birch, 1799, *Views of Philadelphia*)

here, all banks listed the total receivables from such business on their statements under the title of "discounts," rather than "loans," as might be the practice today.

In the 1790s the bank was a depository for many copper coins struck at the Philadelphia Mint, after which they passed into circulation. Half cents and cents were struck by the Mint for its own account, unlike silver and gold coins, which were made to the order of depositors. The profits on copper accrued to the Mint and helped pay expenses.

Although the Bank of the United States operated successfully from the outset, its affairs caused many political problems and debates. Congress did not renew its charter, mainly on the much-discussed grounds of constitutionality. The charter lapsed on March 4, 1811, at which time the bank ceased business. Beginning with a 70% payment on June 1, 1812, stockholders eventually were given back the par value of the stock they purchased, the final 5% being paid in April 1815.[10] A final dividend of 8-1/2% was also paid. During the years of the bank's operation, dividends averaged about 4% annually. On the market, shares sold as high as 150% of par on occasion.

It was anticipated by some that the expiration of the Bank of the United States would precipitate financial disaster. However, the bank acted slowly in collecting its debts, there were few problems, and other banks, which were numerous by that time, easily took up the business. The handsome bank building and many of its facilities, including more than $5,000,000 in gold and silver coins, were purchased by Stephen Girard of Philadelphia, a prominent figure in the early banking business there.

In 1816 the second Bank of the United States was chartered, operating until 1836. It was based in Philadelphia and operated many branches. Today it is a matter of debate among historians as to whether either bank was a positive or a negative influence on the growth of the American economy. The difference does not deal with constitutionality, but whether each bank was truly objective in the conduct of its business and if the same business could have been handled as well by state-chartered banks.

Chartered in 1792

Bank of Albany

The idea of forming a bank in Albany, New York, arose from a meeting held in New York City on February 2, 1792, in which a need for a bank at the state capital was discussed. It was suggested in a subsequent newspaper account that at least $100,000 in stock would be bought by Albany residents within hours of the time it went on sale, and that in New York City and elsewhere the balance would be taken quickly. The projectors of the bank set up an arrangement for the capital to be a modest but surely successful $75,000, divided into 500 shares at $150 each, to be paid for in specie. A deposit of $15 was required, after which the balance was to be paid in three equal installments. Subscriptions were received for 537 shares, in amounts from one to 50 shares per buyer. There was great excitement, and soon anyone who had paid the $15 deposit could sell that and the right to the share for a $150 profit, even though the share had not been paid for in full.

On April 10, 1792, the legislature granted an act of incorporation to the Bank of Albany, with the capital raised to $240,000, in 600 shares of $400 each. The bank organized in June under its new charter, opened to receive deposits on July 16, and began discounting notes on the 17th. Interest was at the rate of 6% annually.

On July 26, 1792, this resolution was passed by the directors, regarding fractional money denominated in *cents:* "That the cashier cause to be engraved bills of the following denominations: One bill of 25; one bill of 30; one bill of 40; one bill of 50. The said bills to correspond with the paper intended for half-dollar bills."[11]

This anecdote published years later relates to early paper of the bank:

> The old Bank of Albany, since defunct, then presided over by thirteen distinguished representatives of fatherland, issued its first circulating notes. Immediately after their receipt from the printer an application for a loan of a few thousand dollars was made to the bank, by a drover well known in Albany for his ability and financial soundness. The loan was passed by the board, and the cashier ordered to pay the money, who, like a faithful officer, bethought himself as to what *kind* of money he would pay—whether their own new currency or gold. The currency was new; so he reconvened the directors at once, and laid the subject before them. Chairs were drawn to the great fireplace, thirteen clay pipes were lighted, and discussion ensued upon the proposition to pay out the new currency. No satisfactory conclusion was likely to be arrived at until the following speech was made by one of the number: "Gentlemen of the board: These bills of ours, received today, have cost this bank a large sum of money. The engraver, the printer, the papermaker, and incidentals, all have to be paid. The thought of these expenses, so justly incurred, does not stagger me in the least; for the bills are very fine, and an orna-

> ment to the bank. But, gentlemen, when it is proposed to send these new bills into the far West, there to be traded for cattle, torn, soiled, and perhaps utterly destroyed, I, for one, most solemnly protest. I venture this moment, gentlemen, to assert the opinion that should you be so unwise as to allow these new bills to be sent North and West, beyond Lansingburgh, Schenectady, and away the other side of Utica (as I understand this man proposes to take some of them), you will never see them again so long as the Bank of Albany has an existence or a name!" The motion was lost, and the gold was duly paid.[12]

The first office of the Bank of Albany was in an old building of Dutch style on Pearl Street. In 1794 the bank purchased a lot next to the Mansion House to the south and erected its own building. In February 1810 it moved to an elegant new building at the northwest corner of State and Court streets, where it remained until 1832, when it was torn down in order to widen State Street. The next headquarters was at 42 State Street in a new facility under a 21-year lease.

In October 1796 the directors authorized the cashier to send $30,000 in specie to New York City to buy up Bank of Albany bills that had accumulated there at the Bank of New York. At the time there were no clearinghouse facilities, and separate arrangements had to be made for other banks to take its notes, usually on a quid pro quo basis.

In 1797 the New York City newspapers stated that the Bank of Albany had failed, as its paper money had been counterfeited so extensively that the notes were no longer received in commerce. The stories were completely false. Apparently, unknown parties were seeking to damage the bank, perhaps to speculate in its stock, which had been trading about 45% over par, but plummeted on the news.

In the 1803 session of the state legislature, an application was made for the New York State Bank at Albany, under the claim that the existing Bank of Albany was but a political tool of the Federalists and it discriminated against Republicans.

The capital of the Bank of Albany was adjusted several times. In 1832, when the charter was extended to January 1, 1855, the capital was reduced by 25% by returning $100 to each holder of a $400 par value share.

In May 1837 this bank and nearly all others in the United States stopped paying out gold and silver coins in exchange for paper money. In January 1838 the Bank of Albany was early among eastern banks in resuming specie payments. In the same year it reorganized under the Free Banking Law, legislation intended to make bank charters more easily available to entrepreneurs and to add a degree of protection for holders of currency. The bank reorganized (with a new set of books, but containing essentially the same assets and liabilities) two days before its charter expired and began business on December 30, 1854, as an associated free bank with $360,000. In 1861 the Bank of Albany failed, at which time $65,673 circulation was outstanding. The bills were eventually redeemed at par.[13]

Bank of the State of South Carolina

The Bank of South Carolina was set up in Charleston with a capital limit of $1,000,000 (eventually reset at $640,000). This bank was unique to this point in that all shares were owned by the state of South Carolina and none were available to the general public. It was thus the first state-owned bank after the Revolution, although others would follow. At first it operated privately, but in 1801 it was chartered by the state. Loans, given by the usual discount method, were not to extend for more than a year, but could be renewed on good credit. Issuing paper money, including fractional denominations, began at an early date. In 1812, when its charter was revised, the state prohibited all bills for less than $1. In 1813, all *other* banks were forbidden from issuing bills of less than $5, leaving the Bank of South Carolina with a monopoly on the popular lower denominations.[14] Bank loans were nearly all for real estate until 1820, with a maximum of $2,000 per loan, increased to $10,000 in 1825. During the War of 1812 the bank served well the interests of plantation owners who suffered from the inability to export cotton to Europe. In 1820 the institution broadened its loan portfolio and began serving many different classes of customers, becoming a commercial bank. The bank continued in business into the Civil War.

Union Bank

The Union Bank, chartered in 1792 for $1,200,000 and located in Boston, was the first to fall under a new Massachusetts rule whereby the state retained the right to acquire an ownership interest. It did so, signing up for $500,000 in stock. On June 26, 1811, the *Columbian Centinel* reported that the state held $1,000,000 worth of stock in the Union Bank and Boston Bank, and that this investment was worth nearly a 20% premium. Such matters worked against

Ten-dollar proof note of the Union Bank, Boston, by Abner Reed in the second decade of the 19th century. It was customary for bills of this era to have a space, usually left blank, for the payee, normally the first recipient of a bill. In this instance the name of Miles Standish has been engraved in the plate, also a common practice in which names from history were used.

others who desired to form banks, as was being done at the time, for it was feared that new banks would dilute the profits of the Boston and Union institutions. Such were the continuing mix of banking and politics that pervaded this decade.

A Union Bank statement dated January 1, 1838, reveals these figures: Capital actually paid in: $800,000. Bills in circulation $5 and up: $63,595. Bills in circulation less than $5: $5,726. Net profits on hand: $34,485.69. Balances due to other banks: $75,033.14. Cash deposited: $153,081.60. Cash deposited bearing interest: $47,714.03. Total amount due from banks: $1,179,635.46. Gold, silver, and other coined metals in the banking house: $32,222.48.[15] Real estate: $128,178.40. Bills of other banks incorporated in this state: $45,795. Bills of other banks incorporated elsewhere: $27,106.12. Amount of all debts due: $946,333.46. Total amount of resources of the bank: $1,179,635.46.[16]

In April 1865 this became the National Union Bank of Boston, charter 985. Cashier Lemuel Gulliver and bank president George C. Richardson were elected to the same posts in the new bank, this being the usual procedure in such conversions.

New Hampshire Bank

The New Hampshire Bank at Portsmouth, as it was titled, was chartered January 3, 1792, by the state for a period of 50 years, capitalized at an unspecified figure. The amount of paid-in stock was at first $80,000, including $10,400 provided by the state.[17]

Stockholders were allowed to have votes as follows: "For one share and not more than, one vote; for every two shares above two and not more than ten, one vote; for every four shares above ten and not exceeding thirty, one vote; and for every six shares above thirty and not exceeding sixty, one vote." Similar provisions are found in the charters of other banks through the mid-19th century in other states. It was not desirable to have one share equal one vote, but to limit the power of those who held a large amount of stock.

William Plumer, speaker of the New Hampshire House of Representatives (and who in 1812 would be elected governor of the state), in a letter to Congressman Jeremiah Smith, January 2, 1792, commented,[18] "I very much doubt whether the bank will have sufficient applications for loans—or whether the bills will obtain so general circulation as to render the bank profitable to stockholders." The comment about the bank's bills achieving "general circulation" is poignant not only here but also elsewhere in state banking, reflecting an important aspect of an institution's profitability: the longer bills remained in the hands of the public, the longer the bank had free use of the funds. If the bills became lost or otherwise were never redeemed, they became pure permanent profit.

The Bank of New Hampshire at Portsmouth opened for business on June 11, 1792, and began to offer discount loans. John Taylor Gilman served as president, a largely honorary position. John Peirce was cashier and tended to everyday banking affairs. The "discount day" each week was set as Monday, when loan requests were to be presented. On Tuesdays the requested amounts, if approved, were paid out on the discount basis. The bank was open daily except Sunday.

In the meantime, the state decided to go into the banking business for itself, and on January 3, 1792, the same date the New Hampshire Bank at Portsmouth was chartered, it provided for £4,000 sterling lawful money, in the state treasury, to be available for loans.[19] Persons who could collateralize the loan with acceptable state or national securities worth at least 50% more than the amount requested could bor-

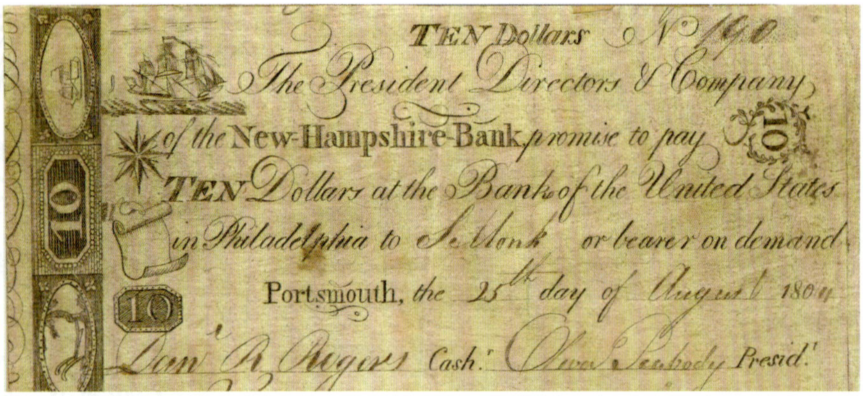

Signed, dated, and used $10 bill of the New Hampshire Bank, Portsmouth, August 25, 1804. The note could be redeemed for coins *in Philadelphia,* a practice that was outlawed in 1803 by the state legislature. However, later-dated bills are known, as here. It is likely that the bank kept using the bills on hand until their supply was exhausted. The note is from a hand-engraved copper plate and bears no imprint of the artist.

Five-dollar note of the New Hampshire Bank from a plate engraved by Christian Gobrecht, circa the 1820s. (Historical Society of Pennsylvania)

row money at 6% interest. In June 1792 an additional £7,000 sterling was made available. Most loans were made to just nine men, five of whom lived in Exeter, New Hampshire. Two were brothers of Governor John Taylor Gilman, first president of the New Hampshire Bank. Politics and banking were strongly interwoven in the state. Although others desired to obtain charters, the New Hampshire Bank fended off all comers, although several entrepreneurs became banks without benefit of charter. Finally in 1802 the second bank in the state was chartered.

Certain notes that were issued by the New Hampshire Bank bore the promise to pay *in Philadelphia,* which of course made them useless for redemption locally—and resulted in the bills being passed around for a long time and not exchanged for coins. Perhaps in response to this situation, a more enlightened legislature passed an act on July 11, 1803, effective September 1, that to give any place of payment other than the town in which the bank was situated would be illegal. However, such bills continued to be issued after that time.

Nathaniel Adams, chronicler of many events in New Hampshire history, included this 1802 account in his *Annals of Portsmouth:*[20]

> Sunday, December 26, about four o'clock in the morning, the town was alarmed by the cry of fire; which was discovered in the building occupied by the New Hampshire Bank. Before many of the inhabitants could assemble, the fire burst out through the sides of the house, which was soon enveloped in flames. The fire was communicated to the adjacent buildings with such rapidity as to render it impossible to arrest its progress, until a large proportion of the town was laid in ashes The bank's records, compiled by former cashier John Peirce, were destroyed, as were other of the bank's possessions.

Fortunately, this proved to be but a temporary setback, and the New Hampshire Bank was soon back in business.

In 1819 the bank was accused of overissuing bills. In July the state legislature resolved to look into the matter, and a committee was appointed for this purpose. In due course the investigators reported that bank affairs were in disarray, and that, among many other problems, the cashier could not account for $72,000 of money his books showed was on hand. The committee could not find it either. The cashier put up $9,000 of his own money and signed notes for a further $20,000. *Niles' Weekly Register* called the situation a "giant peculation and fraud."

The bank was struck a hard blow, and during the next nine years no dividends were paid to stockholders as recovery took place. As late as 1830 there were still negative balances in certain accounts.[21]

The New Hampshire Bank at Portsmouth suffered during the Panic of 1837, as did other institutions in the state. Its business diminished and was finally concluded in 1842 at the expiration of its charter.

Bank of Alexandria

The Bank of Alexandria was chartered in Virginia on November 23, 1792, with a capital of $500,000. The land that later would become Washington, DC, was mainly undeveloped low-lying terrain and swamp. The Federal City, as it was known at first, did not become the seat of government until 1800. Shares were offered at $200 each, limit 50 per buyer, with one vote per share up to 10, and above that amount, one vote for every five additional shares. Early loans were made at the discount rate of 6%. Currency was authorized to be issued, but of no denomination below $5.

In 1793 the Bank of Alexandria opened for business. It seems to have operated successfully in a milieu, soon including the city of Washington, DC, that saw many unofficial banks and frauds. On April 12, 1834, the bank was forced to suspend specie payments for lack of ready funds as part of a panic that swept through the district. Although at first it was expected that it would recover quickly, the doors never reopened.

Bank of Richmond

In Virginia the Bank of Richmond was chartered on December 23, 1792, a month later than the Bank of Alexandria and using essentially the same wording in its charter. It was authorized to open branch offices throughout the state and had impressive plans to become an important factor in the banking business. However, the dreams did not materialize. John Jay Knox later wrote, "Nothing is known of the history of this bank or the measure of success it attained. The names of the men who were authorized to sell its stock were famous in Virginia mercantile history."[22]

Hartford Bank

Formed at a meeting held in David Bull's tavern in Hartford, Connecticut, on the evening of February 27, 1792, the Hartford Bank was dealt with in the May session of the legislature (with the Union Bank receiving its charter at the same time). The capital was set at $100,000, divided into 250 shares of $400 each. The state was allowed to buy 40 shares at $400 each and to name two directors. The bank opened for business on June 16 of the same year. On the first day, deposits totaling $930.69 were received and were secured in a small iron chest. On August 26 the bank announced that it would reckon its accounts in dollars and cents, an unusual step in an era in which many commercial interests reckoned their figures in pounds and shillings. The "dollars" were Spanish milled dollars, as there were no United States dollars struck until November 1794.

Niles' Register, July 19, 1828, carried this account:

> Bank robbery. A clerk of the Hartford Bank, named Hinsdale, has succeeded in defrauding it of upwards of forty thousand dollars. He has been employed in the bank upwards of eighteen or twenty years, and even since his connection with the institution commenced making overdrafts upon his deposits, and contrived to keep the balance by wrong posting, as for instance, adding a cipher to the amount deposited. The large amount of which he robbed the bank was, according to his own account, mostly expended in the purchase of lottery tickets. . . .

In October 1815 the state legislature granted permission for banks to issue fractional currency, this being a time when silver coins were not seen in circulation. Later, June 1, 1816, was set as the latest date such notes could be issued. This bank is among those that circulated such bills.[23]

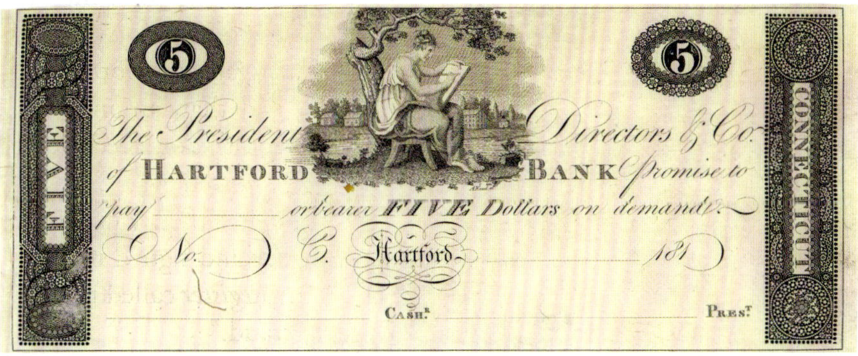

Five-dollar note of the Hartford Bank, signed A. Reed sc, from the second decade of the 19th century. Abner Reed, one of the most prominent bank note engravers and printers during this era, is the subject of chapter 5 of this book.

The stockholders of the Hartford Bank reincorporated to form the Hartford National Bank on July 1, 1865. As is true of most early banks sketched in this chapter, there are still large gaps in knowledge about the paper money it issued, especially in the early years, although an excellent overview is contained in James A. Haxby's *Standard Catalog of United States Obsolete Bank Notes 1782–1866.*

Union Bank

In Connecticut the Union Bank of New London held its first organizational meeting on February 10, 1792. It and the Hartford Bank were both chartered in May. Likely, the Union Bank was in business by early June. As is true of most banks of this state, its affairs were well conducted, although there were enough exceptions to make certain once-worthless notes readily available on the numismatic market (the Eagle Bank comes quickly to mind). During this era, most eastern ports had specialties (whaling for New London, West India trade for Portsmouth, whaling for Nantucket, etc.). Times were good, and New London prospered, although there were setbacks, such as during the Embargo Act of 1807 and the perilous times of the War of 1812.

Following a wave of specie payment suspensions in New York City on May 10, 1837, on May 11 most Connecticut banks suspended payment, the only exceptions being City Bank of New Haven, the Union Bank of New London (studied here), the Mystic Bank, and the Stonington Bank.[24] In later years the bank conducted its business without undue incident, reinforcing its important financial position in the town. On May 20, 1865, the Union Bank of New London became the National Union Bank of New London.

New Haven Bank

The New Haven Bank bid fair to become a very early entry in American banking, following an organizational meeting held February 16, 1792, and the granting of a charter in October of the same year at a capital of $100,000. However, by early 1795 it had not yet gone into business. By December 5, 1795, subscriptions had been received for $80,000 in stock, and some business was conducted, although the official opening date was not until February 12, 1796.

During the coin shortage of late 1815 and early 1816, the New Haven bank issued fractional currency denominated as 5, 6-1/4, 10, 12-1/2, 15, 20, 25, 30, and 50 cents.[25]

The Financial Register, November 8, 1837, reported that the bank had $63,000 worth of bills in circulation. At the time, this and most other banks had suspended specie payments. The New Haven Bank resumed in January 1838, being among the first banks to do so.

In 1847 a contretemps arose when it was learned by the Suffolk Bank, Boston, redemption agency for most notes of New England banks, that original plates had been used to produce unauthorized $2, $5, and $10 bills of the New Haven Bank. The Suffolk Bank ceased trading in the notes for a time, while a Wall Street firm, Carpenter & Vermilye, stepped into the breach and, after careful inspection, redeemed all good notes at standard rates.

However, more information was learned later, and in December 1849 *Banker's Magazine* published a report stating that in actuality *counterfeit* plates had been made, and that similar false notes had been issued, of a quality such as to virtually defy detection. There was great commotion, especially in the summer of 1849, when more fake notes of the New Haven Bank appeared.

The rest of the story, per *Banker's Magazine,* is adapted from coverage in the *New York Journal of Commerce,* November 5, 1849:

> Since the appearance of this third counterfeit, the two banks have been unceasing in their efforts to solve the mystery, and bring the offenders to justice. We rejoice to say that their efforts have at length been crowned with success. Within the last few days, Henry Knickerbacker, William E. Brockway, and a man by the name of Snyder, have been arrested at Hudson, on a charge of being concerned in getting up or passing those counterfeits, or both, and having been subjected to a long and rigid examination, facts were elicited which leave no reasonable doubt that some, if not all of them, were guilty. Brockway was shown to have had an active agency in getting up the counterfeits, and was probably at the bottom of the whole affair.
>
> Besides the above, three persons have been arrested at Brooklyn, one in this city, and one elsewhere, making eight, supposed to have been concerned in the villainy. The officers of justice are in pursuit of still others of the same gang. Altogether, it was one of the most dangerous combinations to defraud the public, that ever existed in this country, and we may well congratulate the community if it is at length broken up. The prominent part taken in the counterfeiting by Brockway, was made known by Knickerbacker, (who was first arrested,) but not till many ineffectual efforts had been made to induce him to confess. Among other things, Knickerbacker states that he received $4000 of the counterfeits from Brockway, for the purpose of getting them

exchanged for other bills, but that finding some difficulty in so doing, he returned $3,500 of them to Brockway. It was conclusively shown that the three counterfeits were perpetrated by the same gang. It is admitted, we understand, by both banks, that the first counterfeits on those institutions must have been printed from the genuine plates.

As to the recent counterfeit on the New Haven Bank, the case is not so clear, but there would seem to be a strong presumption in favor of the supposition, from the fact that Brockway was formerly a journeyman in the office at New Haven, where the genuine bills of both banks were, at that time, printed. It further appeared that the villains had not confined their operations to the New Haven Banks, but had got up and issued counterfeit twos on the North River Bank in this city [New York City], and also counterfeits on one or two other banks. These facts we have obtained from undoubted sources, and they cannot fail to be interesting to the public.

A photographic view of the New Haven Bank in the mid-19th century. (Hasse, *A History of Money and Banking in Connecticut*)

In the 1850s this bank participated in the testing of certain printing techniques said to deter counterfeiting, this in an era in which a half dozen or more "systems" were devised for such. A report of William Grubb of the Suffolk Bank, Boston, was published in the summer of 1856 regarding tests he had made on a $1 bill of the New Haven Bank, under Christopher D. Seropyan's patent said to prevent alteration. The bill *could* be altered, Grubb reported. However, his findings were contested by the inventor and several of his supporters.[26]

It was policy of the New Haven Bank not to accumulate profits as a reserve for contingencies, but to pay out such funds to stockholders. On June 6, 1865, the New Haven Bank converted to become the National New Haven Bank.

CHARTERED IN 1793

Bank of Columbia

In 1792 and early 1793 a group of entrepreneurs from Rhode Island proposed to open a whale fishery business and foreign trade depot at Hudson, New York, on the Hudson River upstream from New York City. The Bank of Columbia was duly chartered at a capital authorized at $160,000. Business commenced on March 6, 1793. The business failed in May 1829, just in time to be included in the inaugural issue of *Bicknell's Counterfeit Detector,* July 31, 1830, on its "List of Broken Banks."

Bank of Columbia

Another Bank of Columbia, this one in Georgetown, in the District of Columbia, was chartered by the Maryland State Legislature for $1,000,000. The bank was to operate in the Federal City (later known as Washington City, then simply Washington), which was in the process of being laid out. It was thought

Five-dollar note on the Bank of Columbia, Hudson, New York, June 1, 1807. Right margin missing. Although bills of broken banks are often common in the market today, those of this bank are fairly scarce.

that the bank would facilitate the city's growth and development. The jurisdiction of the bank immediately passed from Maryland to the federal government.[27] Georgetown became a part of Washington, D.C., in 1801.

The bank was pretentious in its aspect in 1820, per this account:

> The building constructed for, and for several years occupied by the Bank of Columbia, at Georgetown, was considered, at the time of its erection, the most elegant and costly of the finished public buildings of the District of Columbia. Built upon an elevation of at least 100 feet above the river, it commands an extensive view of the Potomac, the City of Washington, a portion of Virginia, (as proposed to be retroceded,) and is now within one hundred yards of the Chesapeake and Ohio Canal.
>
> It was constructed upon a large scale, having a front of 50 feet with a depth of 80 feet, in the centre of a lot 165 feet front and 240 deep: and finished in a costly manner. The entire cost of the property at the time (1811–12) was $109,000. Such were, however, its rapid strides to inflation and insolvency, that although possessing a capital of $940,000, it was compelled during the reverses of 1819–'20, to suspend payment and make an assignment of its property to the Bank of the United States for the benefit of its creditors. These were nearly all paid off, but the stockholders never realized any returns.[28]

Bank of Pennsylvania

In 1793 the Bank of Pennsylvania was chartered with an authorized capital of $2,000,000, with the charter extending to May 1, 1814. Of the capital, $1,800,000 was paid in. Permission was given to open branches, which was done in Harrisburg, Reading, Easton, Lancaster, and Pittsburgh. These branches operated until about 1810 and then were closed. The state subscribed to one-third of the capital, with the expectation that the Bank of Pennsylvania would be to the state what the Bank of the United States was to the entire country. Subscription offices were set up in Philadelphia seeking to sell 2,000 shares, in Lancaster with 300 offered, and in Reading with 200. After 10 days, any unsold stock would be sold to any and all comers in Philadelphia. Later the charter was extended to 1824. Interrupting business in the early days was this incident:

> In the year 1798, the Bank of Pennsylvania, then kept in the Carpenter's Hall, in Philadelphia, was entered, and about $160,000 taken away. As no force appeared to have been committed, the natural conclusion was, that the bank locks had been opened by means of false keys. The directors attached suspicion to Mr. Patrick Lyon, a very ingenious blacksmith, who made the original keys for the iron doors, which he had also manufactured. On inquiry being made for Lyon, it was found that he had, just after the robbery, left the city in a shallop for Cape May, to which place he was pursued, apprehended, and brought back a prisoner to the city, and committed to jail, on suspicion of being concerned in the robbery. The yellow fever was then prevailing in Philadelphia; most of the inhabitants had removed to the country, and the poor honest fellow remained in confinement a considerable time. An upright jury awarded him $12,000 in damages against the directors of the bank.
>
> During the following winter, a journeyman carpenter, I believe his name was Davis, began to move in considerable style, made deposits in different banks, and endeavored to make his way into company other than he had been accustomed to. This excited the suspicion of the mayor, who I believe was Mr. Robert Wharton. He laid his plans, apprehended Davis, and obtained from him within a few thousand dollars of the amount abstracted from the bank. I do not recollect if he was punished, but I believe he was not. It appeared that he had acted in conjunction with the man having charge of the keys to take to the cashier's house. This man died of the yellow fever the same season, being taken ill immediately after the robbery.[29]

Architect Benjamin Latrobe designed a building for the bank, which was completed in 1800 and became a civic landmark. A published statement of February 11, 1812, noted that the face value of the bank's bills in circulation totaled $1,425,203.[30]

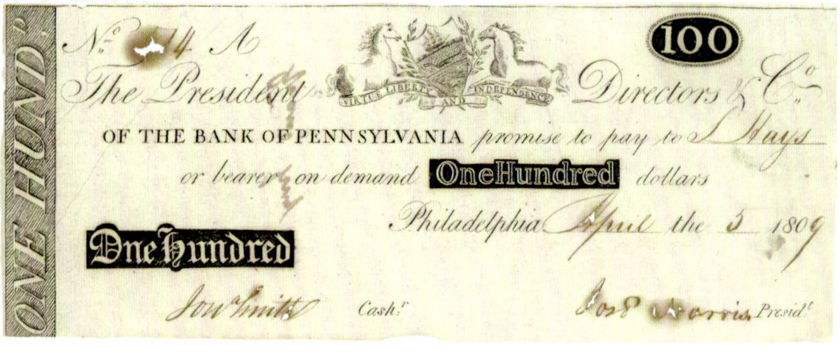

A signed and dated $100 bill of the Bank of Pennsylvania, April 5, 1809.

Dangerous counterfeits of the bank's bills appeared in 1820 and were reported in the issues of *Niles' Weekly Register* of September 23 and October 14, including this note:

> The celebrated plate of Murray, Draper, Fairman and Co. had been successfully imitated. We had seen the fact mentioned in several newspapers, but would not believe it until we saw an imitation of the 100 dollar bills of the Bank of Pennsylvania, which, from his confidence in what may be called the die work, was taken by one of our friends, than whom no man is more generally cautious or a better judge. In this state of the case, it seemed needful to the public security that the fact should be made known.
>
> Last week we received a letter signed "Joshua B. Bacon, attorney for Jacob Perkins," saying that "a plate with work upon it, originally performed by punches, and which was made by Murray, Fairman and Co." had been, within a short period, successfully imitated—but this "was not the plate in which the talents of Jacob Perkins and Murray, &c. were combined."

In 1826 the Bank of Pennsylvania moved to a new building at Fourth and Chestnut streets. In January 1842 the highly regarded Girard Bank failed, causing citizens to worry about the solvency of the Bank of Pennsylvania. A "run" was made on it, compelling the governor to mandate that the doors be closed until matters settled. At the same time the statement was made that the state had just deposited about $800,000 in the bank, as interest to be paid on the state debt.[31] Matters went from bad to worse, and on March 25, *Niles' Weekly Register* stated that the bank had been ruined, along with a handful of other local and regional institutions including the Bank of the United States of Pennsylvania, the successor in interest to the second Bank of the United States. In this time of uncertainty, the currency of the affected banks was discounted up to 60% when received in transactions. The Bank of Pennsylvania recovered and went on to prosperity. In 1856 the impending construction of a new building was announced. However, good times did not last, and it failed in 1857, a year that carried down many banks.

Chartered in 1795

Nantucket Bank

In the 1790s the island of Nantucket, off the coast of Massachusetts, was an active center in the whaling trade. It was logical to establish a financial institution there. In 1795 the Nantucket Bank was formed with an authorized capital of $110,000, of which about $40,000 was paid in. Permission was given for the bank to issue bills in denominations from $2 upward, there being a dislike for fractional or scrip notes that were plentiful in circulation (but which are numismatically rare today).

The bank was not successful, and in 1812 the restrictions on maritime trade precipitated by the Embargo Act of 1807, then the War of 1812, sounded the death knell, and the institution failed.

Bank of Delaware

In Wilmington, the Bank of Delaware, incorporated in 1795 with a capital of $110,000, was for a long time the only bank in the state. Its paper money was highly esteemed and generally traded at par, or very close, in nearby Philadelphia. In the 1830s, after President Andrew Jackson's veto of the charter renewal of the second Bank of the United States, when federal funds were moved to "pet banks," the Bank of Delaware was selected, where funds remained until the Deposite (*sic*) Act of 1836 ended the largesse. However, the institution remained an authorized bank of deposit for funds destined for the Treasury Department.

During the Panic of 1837 the bank stopped specie payments and did not resume them until March 1842. With a few exceptions its affairs were conducted with skill over a long period of years, earning it a reputation for stability even during several eras of financial uncer-

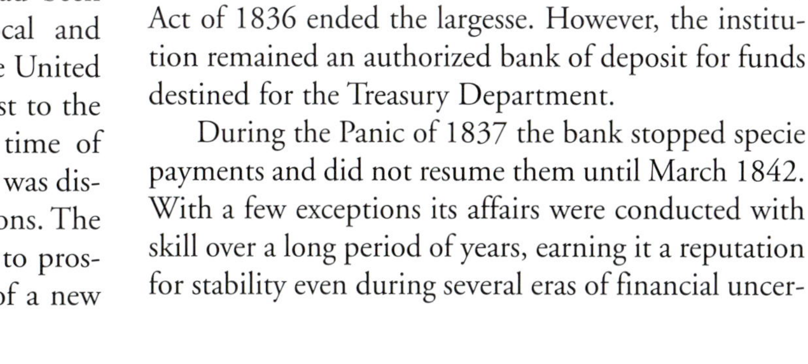

Five-dollar note of the Bank of Baltimore, by Christian Gobrecht for Murray, Draper, Fairman & Co., Philadelphia, which operated from 1811 until 1822. (Historical Society of Pennsylvania)

tainty. In 1865 it evolved into the National Bank of Delaware, charter 1420.

Bank of Baltimore

The Bank of Baltimore was chartered in 1795 for a capital of $1,200,000, or less than the $3,000,000 the organizers had requested. Subscription books were opened in each county within the state, with no person allowed to buy more than 20 shares in a given day. The Bank of Maryland was a heavy purchaser of the stock. In addition, the Bank of the United States had a branch in the city. Baltimore was enjoying an era of glory and was recognized as a center of art and culture in addition to being important for its commerce. The bank opened its doors on January 2, 1797.

Bills were issued in quantity, with denominations commencing at $5. Nearly all bills from the early days have since disappeared, and there are gaps in numismatic knowledge concerning the designs and the values produced. In 1813 this was one of several banks whose charters were extended to January 1, 1835, on condition that the bank subscribe to the road being built to Cumberland in the state.[32] In 1865 the bank reincorporated as the National Bank of Baltimore, charter 1432.

Middletown Bank

The Middletown Bank was chartered in Connecticut in October 1795, with capital authorized at $400,000. Despite the hopes of its projectors, stock purchasers proved to be few and far between. It was not until May 13, 1801, that the bank went into business, and then with a capital of just $75,000.[33]

During the Panic of 1837 this bank and most others in the country suspended specie payments. With some trepidation such exchange of coins for bills resumed in early February 1838. However, a surprise occurred. Very few bills were brought to the bank, but many citizens submitted coins for deposit!

The bank was profitable, and its capital was increased. A report of state bank commissioners, April 1859, gave the capital as $369,300 and the bills in circulation as $120,638. Although circulation fluctuated, the capital was at this level for an extended period. On June 3, 1865, the company was chartered as the Middletown National Bank, charter 1216.

Bank of Rhode Island

The Bank of Rhode Island was incorporated in Newport in October 1795, with a capital of $100,000. It commenced business soon thereafter, in the residence of cashier Moses Seixas, the former Perry mansion on Truro Street.[34] While operating a bank in the cashier's home is unusual in the annals of larger towns and cities, it was commonplace in small towns in the 19th century. The arrangement made a lot of sense. In an era before electronic alarms, the bank was guarded when it was closed. If business was slow at the bank the cashier could do other things around the house. For rural banks the cashier was often the only full-time employee.

The Bank of Rhode Island operated quietly and successfully for a period of many years. Its affairs were not often noted in the larger city papers or in financial journals, save for routine statements and changes of officers. On August 21, 1865, it reincorporated as the National Bank of Rhode Island, charter 1532.

Chartered in 1796

Norwich Bank

The Norwich Bank was chartered in the Connecticut town of the same name in May 1796 and opened its doors later in the same year. Capital was set at $200,000, a figure that was increased only slightly in later years to $220,000.

No news is good news in some instances, and this bank seems to have avoided major scandals, defalcations, and financial troubles. Throughout its existence it circulated currency, usually in modest amounts in comparison to its capital. On June 29, 1865, the Norwich Bank converted to become the Norwich National Bank, charter 1358.

Chartered in 1799

Manhattan Company

The Manhattan Company, often referred to as the Manhattan Bank, was chartered with a capital of $2,000,000 on April 2, 1799, "for supplying the city of New York with pure and wholesome water." It could also engage in financial transactions. At the time the granting of an obvious bank charter was not possible given the political cliques in the state capitol, controlled by the Federalists and inimical to the interests of the opposing party, the Democratic party. Colonel Aaron Burr (who later served as Thomas Jefferson's vice president) was instrumental in arranging a ruse that granted a charter to the Manhattan Company.[35] The projectors of the Manhattan Company did some limited activity in waterworks but devoted most of their energy to banking. Soon, the company were prominent in the field. Daniel Ludlow was the founding president, and the first cashier was Henry Remsen. In 1809, branch offices of discount and deposit were opened in Poughkeepsie and Utica. These branches were closed in 1819, a time of stress in the financial markets.

In September 1835 the second Bank of the United States, then in the process of winding up its affairs, called upon the Manhattan Bank to pay an obligation of $400,000 in coins. In turn the Manhattan Bank made similar requests by submitting obligations held by other banks in the city. There was great alarm, the price of bank stocks fell, and there was worry about the future. However, within a short time business returned to normal.[36] For a time in the 1830s it was a "pet bank" in the Andrew Jackson administration.

After the Panic of 1837 caused specie suspensions by nearly all banks on May 10, the Manhattan Bank and the Bank of America were considered pillars of strength, did much to help city merchants, and inspired confidence. On August 4, this and related reports appeared: "The Manhattan Bank has resumed specie payments in part, or rather gives out specie more freely than before. It pays five dollar notes and half of ten dollar notes in specie, etc."[37] This was a very early resumption scenario on the banking scene. Most banks did not resume until 1838, and some waited until the early 1840s. Meanwhile, many failed.

In March 1841 it was revealed that the head teller at the Manhattan Bank had decamped with at least $49,500, perhaps more, as accounting was in disarray. Confidence in the bank was lessened, and on the first day of the news its stock fell 6%. Later in the month, bank president Maltley Gelston and cashier Robert White each "resigned," as did a director. A special committee was appointed to investigate the affairs of the bank. The bank soon recovered from the temporary difficulty and went on to be one of the most respected institutions in the city. In 1856 its offices at 40 Wall Street were entirely remodeled and substantially enlarged.

Portland Bank

The Portland Bank was chartered by the General Court of Massachusetts on June 15, 1799, to do business in the Maine district of the state of Massachusetts (in 1820 the district became the state of Maine). All bills, etc., of this bank bear the Massachusetts address.

The capital was set at $100,000 with the option of increasing it to $300,000, but cash subscriptions did not meet expectations, and many "bought" stock simply by giving promissory notes (a common practice throughout the country) secured by the stock certificates of the bank, a circular arrangement that produced no real assets, despite the entire $300,000 being taken up.[38]

The bank struggled with a shortage of cash plus problems with loans. It closed its doors in 1808. Affairs were liquidated in 1815.

Essex Bank

The Essex Bank was chartered in Salem, Massachusetts, on June 18, 1799. At the time the city was one of the most active trading ports on the coast, with trade including to the far reaches of the world in the East Indies. In 1819 its charter expired. The liquidation was completed in 1822.

The Essex Bank became prominent in the annals of banking jurisprudence. In the celebrated case of *Foster v. Essex Bank,* depositor Foster left several sealed kegs of gold coins for safekeeping with the bank's cashier and president. The kegs were weighed but not examined, and a receipt was issued for them. In a robbery the kegs were stolen. Foster brought court action to recover the loss and won the suit. In a later action Chief Justice Parker of Massachusetts ruled that the bank was not responsible.[39]

Chartered in 1800

Washington Bank

The Washington Bank was chartered in Westerly, Rhode Island, in 1800, with the modest capital of

Beginning in 1800 the Washington Bank issued bills with the portrait of George Washington, the first bank notes known to bear his image. This $5 note is dated 1803 and is from a plate by Amos Doolittle, New Haven, Connecticut.

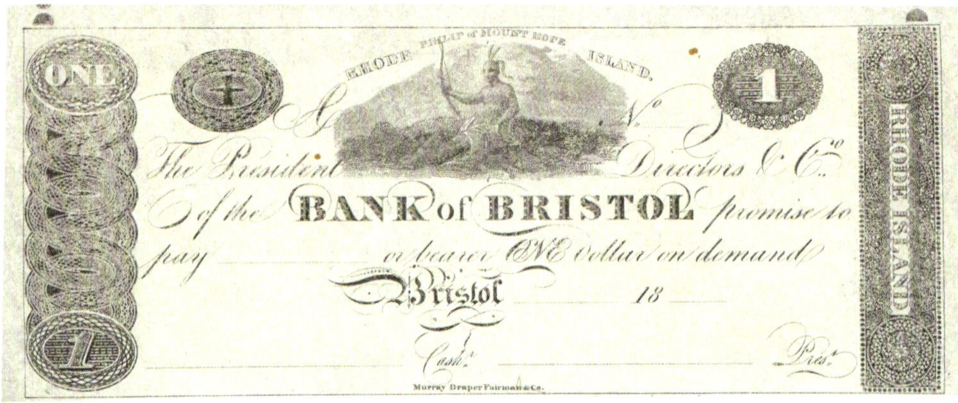

One-dollar note of the Bank of Bristol by Murray, Draper, Fairman & Co., circa 1815.

$50,000. The charter required that two-thirds of the directors and the president should reside in the same county as the bank.

Bills for the bank were made from copper plates engraved by Amos Doolittle, of New Haven, Connecticut. These featured the portrait of the recently deceased George Washington and are considered to be the earliest depiction of Washington on a bank note. At least three types of sheets were made, each with four notes: $1-$1-$1-$1 (dated 1800), $3-$3-$3-$25 (no date), and $10-$5-$5-$5 (dated 1803).[40]

Thomas Noyse was the first president, and Arnold Clark was the first cashier. The bank was run well and proved profitable to the Perry family, its main stockholders, with Perrys holding the position of cashier beginning in the bank's early days. Years later the capital was increased to $150,000. In March 1865 it made the transition to the Washington National Bank of Westerly, charter 953.

Bank of Bristol

The Bank of Bristol was chartered in 1800 and soon opened in the Rhode Island town of the same name. The capital was set at $120,000. The institution began as a holding company for the Bristol Insurance Company, which through political connections held federal deposits in the district.[41] Relatively little information about the affairs of this bank appeared in journals, apart from periodical reports on the officers and capital. In 1865, declining to convert to a National Bank, the directors voluntarily liquidated the bank. By that time its capital stood at $150,000.

Status of Banks

The study of early American currency is spiced with many challenges, not the least of which is determining whether a bank was "real." As can be seen among the scenarios delineated above, a perfectly sound institution could be denied an official charter, or if it had a charter, the renewal of it could be prohibited. In years to come such scenarios would occur many times. Later years in Washington, DC, where banking was regulated by Congress (as with other affairs of the district, for it was not a state), legislators would sometimes overlook bank charter renewals or fail to act on them in a timely basis. In still other instances, entrepreneurs sought to form a bank, raised capital, and were welcomed. Others were denied charters but went into business anyway.

The question then arises: are bank notes legitimate only if the bank issuing them was currently operating under the benefit of a charter? Most numismatic historians would elect to call nonchartered but honestly conducted banks legitimate, with very little question in this regard. Popular historians often disagree, and in absence of facts impute illegal actions to the banks' officers and directors. For this reason, it is difficult to determine the status of certain institutions without delving into *contemporary* records. History books can be misleading.

With this as a background, certain bank notes are easier to understand.

Numismatic Notes

In the late 18th century most bank notes were made locally under contract with printers, who used hand-engraved copper plates. The rise of bank-note engraving and printing firms awaited the next generation. Early bills gave the name and location of the issuing bank, in engraved lettering or script, or a combination, together with the value. Sometimes there would be a small ornament, such as a ship or animal, but nothing in the way of ornate vignettes. Serial numbers and dates were inked in by hand. Notes were signed by the cashier and president of the bank. Throughout the period covered by this book, the cashier was a bank's

Stagecoach and tavern on a road connecting New York City and Philadelphia (a journey that also involved river crossings by boat). Such coaches carried passengers, mail, and money between the two points. (Tinted print circa 1795; this print exists in many variations.)

most important officer. He (no record of a *she* has been found) was responsible for the integrity of the loan portfolio, the management of the bank's assets, and the conducting of everyday business. In contrast, the duty of the president was to preside over meetings of the board of directors and meetings of stockholders. It was not unusual for a bank president to visit an institution only occasionally. Many lived in other cities and towns, and most were involved in other occupations as their main business. Cashiers drew the largest salary at the bank, while presidents received just a token payment each year.

With very few exceptions, the cashier's signature was affixed to the lower part of the face of a note, left of center, and the president's signature to the right.

It was generally considered (and confirmed by legal decisions) that a bank note was not officially monetized until both officers signed. In the absence of one or another, it was permissible for an appointed substitute to sign, such as a vice president, but this had to be noted with "v.p." or a similar inscription.

Filling in dates and serial numbers in advance was common practice. Sometimes the bank president's signature was added in advance as well, if he visited the bank only at intervals. The cashier would sign last, and then pass the bills into circulation.

Serial numbers were often started anew each month or, less often, each day. In this way the numbers were kept in lower ranges, reducing the work needed to add them.

Nearly all early bills were printed on one side only and on flimsy paper. The notes absorbed grease and dirt easily and soon became discolored. Within a few years many were reduced to veritable tatters, but they still kept circulating.

Today, information concerning the currency issued during the early 1782 to 1800 era is very hard to find. James A. Haxby's *Standard Catalog of United States Obsolete Bank Notes 1782–1866* is a good beginning, while Eric P. Newman's *Early Paper Money of America* includes some issues. The bills from this time are generally very scarce, and some denominations reported to have been issued are unknown in collections today. This terra incognita may someday become appealing for specialists to study, similar to what has been done with many once esoteric early series of coinage.

Chapter Three

THE GENIUS OF JACOB PERKINS

Jacob Perkins, from a 19th-century engraving.

INTRODUCTION

This chapter forms a segue to the bank-note *producing* aspect of early state bank paper money.

In the annals of early American bank notes the name of Jacob Perkins looms especially large.[1] Perkins was a true genius, with accomplishments remembered today in several different categories ranging from the engraving of coin dies and medals, to experiments with physics, to proposals for armament, to the subject important here: the engraving and production of bills for state-chartered banks, including his Patent Stereotype Steel Plate (for which no actual patent has been located), and, especially, the siderographic or roll-transfer process that revolutionized the bank-note engraving and printing trade. Three of his better-remembered bank-note clients are also included in this chapter.

BIOGRAPHICAL NOTES

Jacob Perkins was born in Newburyport, Massachusetts, on July 9, 1766, the son of Matthew and Jane (Noyes) Doyle Perkins. Matthew Perkins, a native of nearby Ipswich, had fathered 12 children in an earlier marriage, been widowed, and married again. Jane and Matthew Perkins first had two children, one of whom lived one day and the second just a month. Then came Jacob, the subject of this sketch. The next child was Abraham, who also became important in bank-note engraving (as did Abraham's son Nathaniel). Jacob's second son, Angier Park Perkins, also became a skilled engraver.

When Jacob Perkins was born, Newburyport was one of the most important depots for maritime trade on the East Coast. Vessels continually arrived at and departed from the sheltered port located where the Merrimac River (spelled *Merrimack* in its upper sections in New Hampshire) reached the sea. The same river lent its name to the Confederate ironclad ship that skirmished with the Union *Monitor* in the Civil War. Newburyport attracted citizens of refinement, culture, and even eccentricity, the curious activities of Lord Timothy Dexter being in the latter category. Dexter's home on High Street was a veritable outdoor museum, its lawn decorated with many carved statues of important figures in history. Although facts are scarce, it is said that he made a fortune buying severely depreciated Continental Currency, then redeeming it when the Treasury allowed holders to exchange the bills for coins at the ratio of $100 Continental to one Spanish dollar.

Young Jacob attended public school until he was 12 years old, after which from 1779 to 1781 he was apprenticed to the goldsmith and clockmaker Edward Davis in Ipswich, having signed for a six-year term. There he learned various aspects of the trade, including plating buckles, making beads, and engraving. For use in crafting silver and gold items, Spanish and other current coins were used. In 1781, following the death of Davis and only halfway through his apprenticeship, Perkins assumed the business, continuing there until 1787. The shop's main output was gold-covered beads for necklaces and bracelets. Shoe buckles were another important product, the sales of which were increased after Perkins devised a new way to inexpensively plate them. While there his activities may have included making dies or molds for U.S. Army uniform buttons.[2] He returned to Newburyport in 1787.

On November 11, 1790, Perkins married Hannah Greenleaf, with the Reverend John Murray performing the service. She was from an old family that had settled in Newbury, inland from Newburyport, in 1635. Jacob and Hannah became parents to nine children, two of whom figured importantly in Jacob's businesses.

In Newburyport, Perkins had a small shop in which made belt buckles and other small metal articles. In 1793 he advertised to hire several apprentices to help him in this line. In 1795 he invented a machine for cutting and putting heads on nails in a single operation. He rented premises in the nearby town of Byfield, where he made nails and brads. In spring 1796 he moved the operation a short distance to the town of Amesbury, near the New Hampshire state line.

In 1803 Gideon Fairman, later to become prominent in the bank-note engraving profession in Philadelphia, moved to Newburyport. At the time Charles Toppan, a distant cousin of Jacob Perkins, was seven years old. Toppan would also become well known in the trade. In 1808, *Perkins' and Fairman's Running Hand, Stereographic Copies, Patent Steel Plates,* was published, a guide to penmanship illustrated with engraved steel plates.

During this era Perkins was awarded a long string of patents filed from Newburyport, Boston, and Philadelphia, a list that includes the unimportant bank-note innovation of March 19, 1799 (see Abel Brewster's commentary in chapter 4) and his patent of June 25, 1813. Curiously, no patent has been located for his *Patent* Stereotype Steel Plate system.

- *January 16, 1795*—Machine for cutting nails.
- *February 14, 1799*—Machine for making nails.
- *March 19, 1799*—Bank-Note Check Plate to deter counterfeiting.
- *July 9, 1802*—Innovation in the construction of pumps.
- *June 26, 1809*—Machine for polishing morocco leather.
- *June 16, 1810*—Copperplate printing and mode of preventing counterfeits (an improvement on his 1799 patent).[3]
- *July 17, 1810*—Mechanism for making cut nails, cut points, and brads.
- *August 6, 1812*—Fire engines (Perkins and others).
- *March 22, 1813*—Vault locks for banks and, as part of the same patent, a device for making screw shanks and rivets from lengths of metal rod.
- *March 23, 1813*—Fire engines.
- *March 23, 1813*—Pumps and mechanics of valves, innovations made while working with Commodore William Bainbridge in connection with the outfitting of the SS *Independence* during its construction in Charlestown, Massachusetts.
- *March 23, 1813*—Machine for making screw shanks.
- *War of 1812 era*—Perfected several nautical devices, apparently not patented, but made available to the U.S. Navy and others, for an "orthometer" to ascertain the trim of a ship and a "plenometer" for determining the angle of tilt from upright.
- *June 25, 1813*—Method of impressing all kinds of die work on steel and copper by circular dies; separately, a printing press for copper and steel engravings (both patented with George Murray).
- *June 26, 1813*—Improvements in moving water through a mill, such as a grist mill.
- *June 28, 1813*—Copper and steel plate printing press.
- *June 29, 1813*—Mechanism for making spoons by pressing metal between a steel roll and a table, with designs impressed on two dies. Theophilus Bradbury, Newburyport silversmith, employed the device.

Classical-style portrait of the bust of Jacob Perkins engraved by W.L. Ormsby for the New England Bank Note Co., 1834.

- *November 1, 1815*—Cylindrical nail cutter improvement.
- *December 18, 1816*—Water marks applied to continuous lengths of paper using a machine made by Thomas Gilpin of Philadelphia.
- *February 27, 1819*—Portable progressive lever press on the knuckle joint system.

Among the preceding, the June 25, 1813, patent for "circular dies" (also called *cylinder dies*, but today known as *transfer rolls* or *roller dies*) used by Murray, Draper, Fairman & Co., was described by them as "a roller transfer press or copying machine for more efficiently impressing steel and copper plates by a circular matrix or master die." This is known as the *siderographic process* and is probably the most important patent ever granted in relation to bank notes.

In 1819 Perkins went to London, where he lived for the rest of his life. While in England, Perkins was associated with 20 or more other patents.

Coin Dies and Processes

Perhaps there is no better reflection of Perkins's abilities early in his career than to note that in 1788 he was selected to cut dies for the copper half-cent and one-cent coinage for the state of Massachusetts, his challenge being to make strong dies, and his compensation to be 1% of the value of the coinage from the dies. Today, numismatists recognize his workmanship as among the best in the series of state copper coinages of that era.[4] Earlier the dies had been made by Joseph Callender, also a good artist, but the state considered his charge of £4/4s per die to be excessive. When it was learned that the state-run mint expended twice face value in making each coin, the operation was closed forthwith, by which time about 400,000 copper coins had been produced.

Following the Mint Act of April 2, 1792, Mint Director David Rittenhouse and his associates sought artists to engrave dies. In his fourth annual message to the U.S. House of Representatives, November 6, 1792, President George Washington told of progress made concerning the Mint and coinage, including this improvement: "In execution of the authority given by the Legislature, measures have been taken for engaging some artists from abroad to aid in the establishment of our Mint; others have been employed at home." Although Perkins is not known to have been associated with the early Mint, his talents may have been solicited by that time, this per a newspaper notice of July 10, 1792:

> We hear that the ingenious Mr. Perkins, of Newburyport, has been sent for to Philadelphia, to execute the coinage of the United States.[5]

This related item was published in the *Essex Journal and New Hampshire Packet,* July 18, 1792:

> Several newspapers of the past and present week have prematurely mentioned Mr. Perkins of this town being sent for to Philadelphia, for the purpose of superintending the coinage there. Mr. Perkins' abilities in that line are fully adequate to such an appointment, as the specimens he has exhibited in that line amply testify. Instead of the former method of performing the business, he has invented a new machine, which cuts the metal into such circular pieces as are wanted, and gives the impression at the same time—its motion is accelerated by a balance-wheel, and more than one-third of the time and labor thereby saved.
>
> He has also constructed another machine, of his own invention, for milling or lettering the edge, by which a boy can mill sixty each minute. Were it found necessary, he could apply steam to perform all the most laborious part of the business. . . .[6]

Although Perkins reached Philadelphia in the summer of 1792, it is likely that key positions had already been filled, and there were no openings available. Perkins's interest in the opportunity seems to have been in the line of equipment and production, not in engraving dies. Had he been hired and his knowledge of mechanics employed, the history of early Mint coinage might be much different from what we know today.

Notable Tokens and Medals

Perkins is said by some to have created the dies for the famous SUCCESS TO THE UNITED STATES token, usually seen in brass, in two different sizes, sometimes with light silvering, believed to have been made in connection with Washington's second inauguration in 1793.[7]

Following the death of George Washington at Mount Vernon on December 14, 1799, the nation went into mourning. Many mementoes were made to reflect

Washington funeral medal in silver by Jacob Perkins, 1800. These were made in large quantities and found a wide sale. Today examples are scarce and highly prized.

the life of the "Father of Our Country," including ribbons, badges, medals, and booklets of eulogies. Most famous in this regard is the series of so-called Washington funeral medals, round and of the diameter of a current copper cent, by Perkins, from several different die combinations, most showing a portrait of Washington on one side and a funeral urn on the other. A typical inscription is HE IS IN GLORY, THE WORLD IN TEARS, this being the suggestion of Dudley A. Tyng, collector of the port of Newburyport.[8] Most medals were made in pewter or silver and were holed at the top for suspension on a cord or ribbon. Many of these were worn in parades held in eastern cities on Washington's birthday, February 22. Other varieties included those with a skull-and-crossbones motif and examples of elliptical format. A few were struck in gold.

J. Russell's Gazette, Boston, January 6, 1800, carried this notice:

> Mr. *Jacob Perkins,* of Newburyport, has designed and executed a very beautiful Medal of Gen. WASHINGTON. One side is an excellent likeness of that illustrious personage; and on the reverse, a memoranda of the most remarkable periods of his life. They are struck of gold, silver, or white metal, and may be purchased of Mr. Perkins, or at the Bookstore in Newburyport, and of Mr. *Eben Moulton,* Goldsmith, in this town.[9]

Similarly, the *Essex Journal,* January 10, 1800, printed this item datelined January 7:

> Jacob Perkins takes leave to inform the public that he will now be able to answer orders for the Medals in memory of the late illustrious Gen. WASHINGTON, from any part of the continent, and to any amount, executed on Gold, Silver, or White Metal, with punctuality and dispatch—from 3 to 5 thousand can be made daily.
>
> A liberal discount will be made to those who purchase quantities to sell again. Jan 7.

The preceding report indicates that Perkins was well equipped for quantity production. He operated in a three-story wooden building on Market Square, not far from where the Ocean Bank would later conduct its business.[10] Later in the same town, he produced bank notes in a small three-story building on Fruit Street, which still stands today.

On January 11, 1800, Perkins was in Boston, where he participated in a procession honoring Washington. In the evening he joined others for supper in the home of Paul Revere. Delivering the eulogy for the occasion was the Reverend William Bentley, whose diary noted, "also present was Mr. Perkins so eminent for his mechanic genius and on this occasion so well known by his excellent medals of our General Washington."

Before leaving the subject of Perkins's early medals, it should be noted that the Victor Sine Clade medal honoring Washington is sometimes incorrectly attributed to Perkins but instead seems to have been made in his shop by another artist, Nicholas Pearce.[11]

Bank-Note Improvements of the 1790s

The article about Perkins in the *Essex Journal,* July 18, 1792, earlier quoted in regard to coins, continued with this information:

> What is of more importance, and will be found to be of more public utility . . . is a check which he has invented, for discovering counterfeits [such] that one-eighth of a minute is sufficient to determine, without the possibility of a mistake, whether a piece of money is genuine . . . and any town or merchant can be supplied at a small expense with said checks, and then rest assured that an imposition will be absolutely impossible.[12]

Details of this practice are not known today, but "check" may have referred to a printed section of a genuine note, the edge of which could be matched to a suspected note to see if the two aligned properly—this being the basis of his later check plate system. This could be done quickly and without any expertise needed.

Patent Secured

The forgery-detecting system mentioned may have evolved into the Bank Note Check Plate patented on March 19, 1799. About two months later Perkins ran this notice in the *Newburyport Herald,* complete with several testimonials, one from Robert Scot, engraver at the Philadelphia Mint:

> *JACOB PERKINS.* Having invented an effectual check for detecting counterfeit bank paper, which has received the sanction of several banks, and the approbation of the undersigned eminent artists in Philadelphia, and having obtained a patent securing to him, and his assigns, the exclusive right of the invention, hereby offers to his fellow-citizens the privilege of using it upon terms to be agreed on between him and any person disposed to avail themselves of a guard against counterfeits.
>
> The undersigned having examined Jacob Perkins' new invented method to detect counterfeit bank paper, do approve of the plan; it being impossible to engrave or sink two plates perfectly alike without the original die or hub, the counterfeiter would find it impossible to make an impression which would perfectly gage with the check from the original die.
>
> Robert Scot, Engraver & Die Sinker
James Smither, Engraver
James Akin, Engraver

Description of the Patent Stereotype Steel Plate

By 1803 Perkins devised a method of engraving on soft steel then hardening the steel, a method that permitted plates to produce many more impressions than the copper versions then in wide use. No patent for this invention has been located. He also devised a transfer press whereby engravings could be reproduced in a process known as *siderography.* Later, he made a cylinder die, a die in circular form, patented in 1813, a great improvement in siderography, which was used by the American Bank Note Company and others through the late 20th century. Perkins is believed to have been the first to have used a transfer roll rather than an ink ball to apply ink to a bank-note plate.

In the *Newburyport Herald,* March 8, 1805, an advertisement by Perkins included this information:

> **Stereotype Plates for Banks**
>
> The patentee of the Stereotype Plates for the impression of bank bills informs the public that he has constantly on hand ready made plates (the name of the bank and town excepted), and will be happy to supply banks on the shortest notice. His terms are reasonable and uniform, the plates well executed, and he has the authority of many eminent artists, as well as the sanction of experience, to say that bills impressed from these plates cannot be counterfeited. No attempts of the kind have ever yet been made, tho' it has been adopted and is now used by sixteen banks in New England.
>
> Encouraged by the success of his principle, and the increasing demand for his plates, he has at a great expense improved his former invention by adding beauty to security. He has formed a steel plate of sixty-four dies, impressed by the same dies now used for copperplates, neatly fitted and keyed together in a strong iron frame. The name of the bank and town and the denomination of the bill are removed and substituted at pleasure.
>
> The standing part of the plates are elegantly engraved by Mr. James Akin. When completed there will be from six to seven hundred days' work in the plate, and being well hardened, it will, without injury, print more paper than will be used by the United States. It is now nearly finished, and any orders addressed to him at Newburyport will be punctually honored.
>
> Jacob Perkins

No actual patent for the above device has been located. Perhaps it is an adaptation or derivation of some earlier innovation. Seemingly, by this time Perkins was involved in multiple businesses. James Akin, the engraver of what would be billed as the Perkins Patent Stereotype Steel Plate, had recently moved from Salem to Newburyport, where he would remain until about 1808, when he moved to Philadelphia. In the latter city he was listed over a period of time in directories as a designer, draftsman, druggist, and keeper of an eating house (restaurant)—obviously a jack of many trades.[13]

The basic Perkins bank-note innovation consisted of a plate of rectangular shape on which a design was impressed, the design being more ornate than had been used earlier. Although there were variations, a popular early motif consisted of an approximately elliptical border composed of lettering for the denomination and floral decorations, outside of which the denomination was given as a number in each of the four corners. Within the ellipse was standard lettering, often a plate letter (sometimes designated as Check Plate A, etc.), and a place for the number, payee, date, and signatures of the officers.

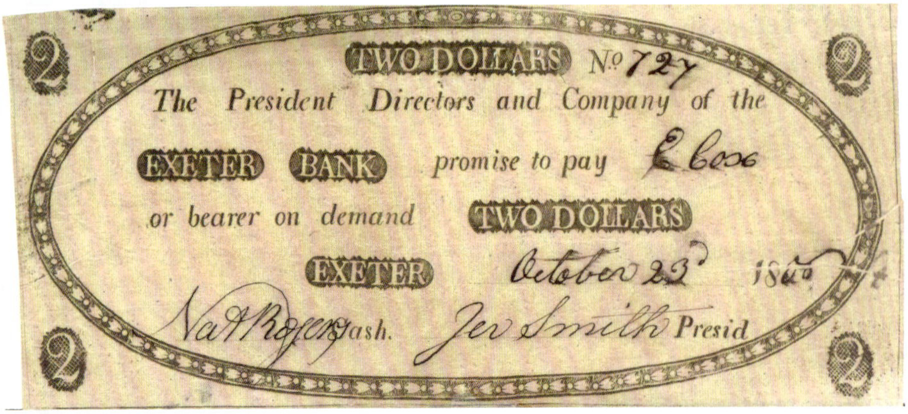

An early Perkins note with "watermelon" border, denomination in each corner, and replaceable elements for the bank name and location—this a $2 bill of the Exeter Bank, Exeter, New Hampshire, ink dated October 23, 1806.

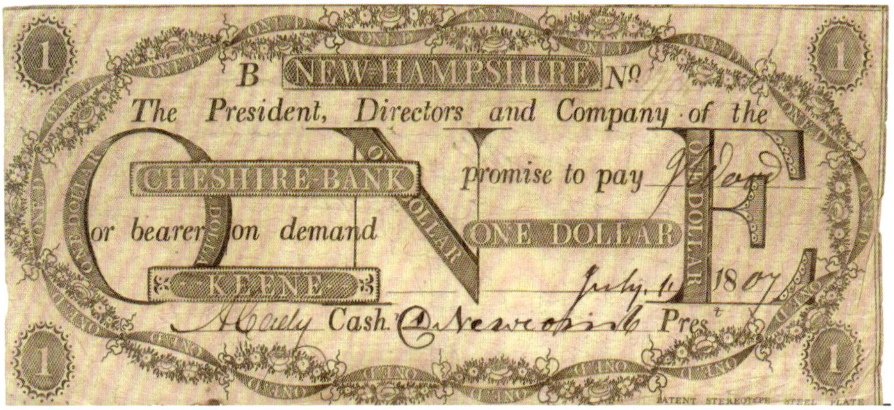

An early version of the Patent Stereotype Steel Plate, a $1 note on the Cheshire Bank of Keene, New Hampshire, ink dated July 1, 1807.

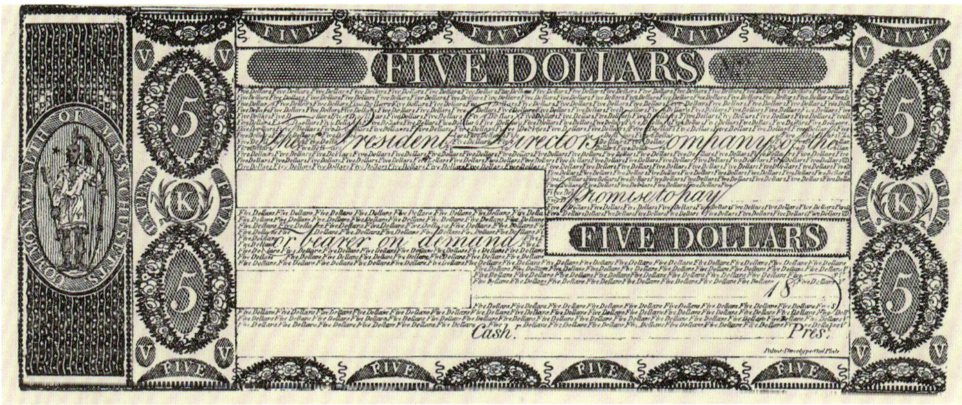

Face impression of a $5 Patent Stereotype Steel Plate note without bank and location added. This note was built up by blocks fitted together, with separate blocks for certain elements such as the Massachusetts emblem on the left edge and the border elements. Plate letters were assigned to the face of these notes, the present example being K.

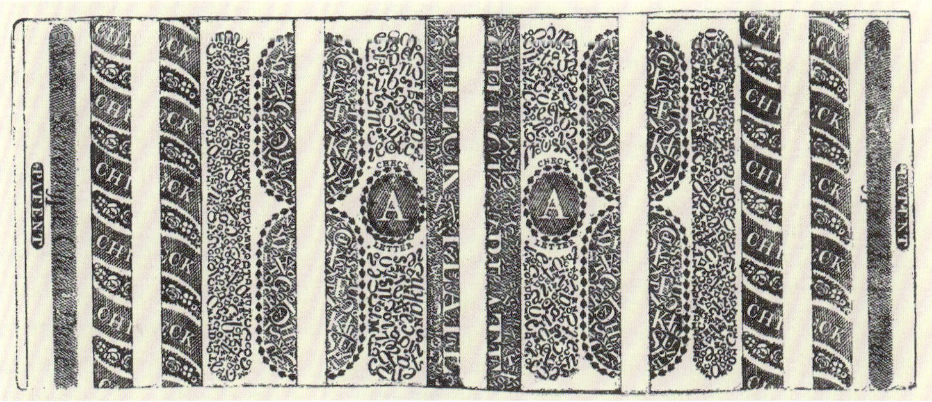

Back impression of a Patent Stereotype Steel Plate note, Check Letter A. To determine the authenticity of a suspected note, it could be folded so that the fold edge would match one of the split vertical elements on the genuine note shown here. If there was a misalignment, the note was apt to be false (although paper could shrink or expand slightly on genuine notes, providing exceptions).

Face of a $5 Perkins Patent Stereotype Steel Plate note signed and issued by the Passamaquoddy Bank of Eastport, Maine, December 1, 1824.

Rectangular openings in the plate provided spaces where steel slugs could be inserted with the bank name, town, and state, such as, in the instance of a particular $1 bill of about 1808, NEW HAMPSHIRE, HILLSBOROUGH BANK, and AMHERST. For another bank the same plate could be used, but with different slugs.

Later versions had large areas of the face of the note filled with tiny repeated italic letters indicating the denomination, such as *Five Dollars Five Dollars Five Dollars,* etc.

Publicizing the Stereotype Steel Plate

In January 1806 Perkins issued a pamphlet titled *The Permanent Stereotype Steel Plate, with Observations on Its Importance, and an Explanation of Its Construction and Uses,* printed in Boston by C. Stebbins. Included was a folded engraving of a four-subject $5-$10-$5-$5 New Hampshire sheet with respective "check letters" (plate letters) C-B-A-D. Instructions were included for comparing questionable bills with those illustrated on the plate. The text, repeating certain information quoted earlier from an 1805 advertisement, included this claim:

> Such is the plan, which the subscriber now offers to the consideration of the public, and which he has, for the last five years, been laboring to accomplish. He flatters himself that, on strict investigation, it will be found in its present improved state to approach nearer to the desired security, than any mode heretofore adopted or proposed. He believes that an exact uniformity in bills, excepting the name of the bank and town, is the only means by which individuals can be enabled to distinguish between spurious and genuine bills.
>
> To effect this uniformity, he has formed a case-hardened steel plate, from which the frontispiece was printed. This he will carefully preserve as, a standard plate for all those banks, which honor him with their attention. It is presumed that all the bills, which the present age would require, might be made from this plate, without defacing it in any perceptible degree.
>
> This plate is made up of fifty seven case-hardened steel dies, an inch thick, and keyed together in a strong iron frame, which is screwed firm to a metal plate of an inch in thickness. It is made of separate parts; in order that it should serve to print bills of any denomination, and for any banks, simply by removing the dies, which contain the name of the bank, town and denomination, and substituting others prepared for the purpose; and also that an exact uniformity might be preserved between banks in general, which could not be effected in the common way of engraving plates. . . .
>
> The standing parts of the plate being always the same, it will exactly gauge or check with any denomination of any bank, while, at the same time, the engraving and etching will compare only with the bill of the same check letter, which may be seen at each end of the bill. . . . This method of checking bills of different banks by one standard has never before been practiced, nor could it be upon the old plan of engraving plates, for such soon wear out; and experience has proved it impracticable to engrave two exactly alike.
>
> In making this plate, together with the machinery and dies necessarily used about it, more than 800 days have been expended. Three years have elapsed since bills from Stereotype plates have been circulating and no attempt has been known to have been made to counterfeit them; twenty six banks have had bills made upon this plan. . . .
>
> Bills of less denomination than five dollars are printed from copper Stereotype plates, of an oval form, which is an infallible check against altering them to any of a higher denomination.

In the same year Perkins addressed a memorandum to the Massachusetts General Court suggesting that the state mandate use of his plates to deter counterfeiting. The idea met with a warm reception, and although it was not enacted into law at the time, much favorable publicity resulted.

In 1808 Jacob Perkins's brother Abraham, a storekeeper in Newburyport, relinquished that trade and joined in the bank-note engraving and printing business. Soon a small three-story brick factory was erected on land behind Jacob Perkins's home.

Success of the Plate

In 1809 the Massachusetts Banking Act was passed, mandating use of the Perkins plate for denominations from $1 to $5. The $5 denomination was to have the Perkins check plate on the back. The use of this extra security was optional for other denominations. In actual practice, some $5 notes were made with this feature but many were not.

In the same year a four-page leaflet was issued under the title *Perkins' Bank Bill Test; consisting of original impressions from the permanent stereotype steel plates of Massachusetts paper currency, executed in conformity of an act of the legislature, passed March 3, 1809; together with the Standard Check Plate, which will apply equally to every bank in the United States which has adopted this principle.* The leaflet was printed by W. and J. Gilman and published in Newburyport by Perkins. Accompanying engravings consisted of two four-subject sheets, with $1-$1-$2-$3 and $10-$5-$5-

$5, and a sheet of four back impressions of his check plate lettered A to D.

Perkins suggested that, to determine the status of a questionable bill, it should be folded so that its lines and features could be aligned with the genuine on the check plate. Alternatively, the suspected bill could be placed over a genuine plate impression and the overlay compared, presumably aided by illuminating the notes from below or holding them up to the light.

In the same era another party issued a listing titled *The Only Sure Guide to Bank Bills; Or Banks of New England, With a Statement of Bills Counterfeited.* This publication seems to have inspired fear in the hearts of its readers, no doubt prompting many banks to investigate Perkins's system. Soon Perkins plates were in general use by many New England banks, predominantly in Massachusetts (which included the district of Maine, which would become a state in 1820).

Characteristics of the Perkins Plate

The Patent Stereotype Steel Plate process offered several advantages. First, the background of the plate was standard. Such plates could be replicated by the siderographic or transfer process. Accordingly, if one plate became too worn to give sharp impressions, another plate could be made—with the same details of design, etc. In contrast, hand-engraved plates, when worn and replaced by new hand-engraved plates, always had some minor differences.

Second, the insertion of slugs could be done quickly. Accordingly, an order could be filled soon after receipt, an improvement over the long time and care needed to make hand-engraved dies.

Third, as little new work had to be done to fill an order for a new bank customer, the bills were less expensive than would have been the case had custom plates been created.

Fourth, as the background details, border, etc., were much more complex than those on a typical hand-engraved copper plate, the Patent Stereotype Steel Plate was difficult to counterfeit—difficult, but not impossible, as will be seen.

Fifth, the printed back plate, used on a minority of such notes (the $5 being a favorite), offered additional lettering and lines and was a further deterrent to counterfeiting.

There were also disadvantages not mentioned in contemporary publicity. In time, certain banks using the Patent Stereotype Steel Plate failed or were determined to be fraudulent, and large amounts of their worthless bills flooded the market. Altering these notes was not difficult, done simply by removing the inscriptions for the bank name, town, and state and printing in new inscriptions. In reality, the Perkins plate was a boon to those who altered notes, an aspect hardly ever mentioned in contemporary reports as well as modern numismatic commentaries. This fatal flaw in the Patent Stereotype Steel Plate process was exposed by Abel Brewster in about 1810 (see chapter 4). It was later treated in detail by Waterman L. Ormsby in his masterful *Bank Note Engraving,* 1852, the details of which are given in chapter 9, "Counterfeits and Counterfeiters." By 1852 the information was largely passé, as relatively few banks were still using the bills made by this process.

Moreover, the Patent Stereotype Steel Plate bills were regarded as unattractive. Some banks simply did not want them, although for a time Massachusetts law provided that banks in the state had no choice in the matter.

Reviews of the Siderographic Process

A British periodical, *Monthly Magazine,* May 1, 1820, included this explanation under the heading, "Varieties, Literary and Philosophical, Including Notices of Works in Hand, Domestic and Foreign." Without question, this was Perkins's most important invention in the field of bank notes:

> Having been permitted to examine the Siderographic process we proceed to lay a concise account of it before our readers. Steel blocks or plates of sufficient size to receive the intended engraving are softened or decarbonated upon their surfaces, and thereby rendered a better material for receiving all kinds of work than even copper itself. After the intended work has been executed upon the block, it is then hardened with great care by a new process which prevents injury to the most delicate work.
>
> A cylinder of steel previously softened is then placed in the transferring press, and repeatedly passed over the engraved block by which the engraving is transferred *in relief* to the periphery of the cylinder, the press having a vibrating motion equaling that of the cylinder upon its axis, by which new surfaces are presented equaling the extent of engraving. This cylinder is then hardened and is ready to indent either copper or steel plates, which is done by placing it in the same press before described, and repeatedly passing it over the copper or steel plates, thereby producing another engraving *identically* like that upon the *original* block; and this may be repeated upon any required number of plates, as the original engraving will remain to produce other cylinders if ever required, and when

> transferred to steel plates and hardened, these will also serve as additional matrices for the production of new cylinders.

This précis of certain of Perkins's innovations was published years later. The first subject is his use of *steel* to make plates, and the second is the transfer press:

> Into an air-tight box, filled with finely powdered animal charcoal, the glittering and beautiful piece of steel is imbedded; the metal box and its precious contents are then submitted to the action of an intense fire for several hours. The steel, previously robbed of its carbon, to render it soft enough for the steel instrument of the engraver, sucks, as it were, from the carbon by which it is surrounded, under the influence of the fiery god, that which it had formerly. Its hardness secured by the workman plunging the reddened plate into water or oil, it now bids defiance to the instrument that previously could plough through its polished surface.
>
> The plate hardened, has become brittle, and, under a severe blow, would almost crumble; still its hardness enables it to despise friction, and the tablet is in a condition which may yield hundreds of thousands of impressions. The artist, pursuing his object, and not content with securing his original engraving, determines that it shall serve as the matrix of copies innumerable.
>
> On the periphery of a cylinder of steel, thoroughly decarbonized, and under the rolling pressure of the transfer press, all the delicate lines in intaglio, every scratch, cut, or even the nervous trace of the carelessly imposed hand, is, however, taken up *en relievo.* This roll, or cylinder, is, then, in turn, submitted to the hardening process, which if successfully prosecuted, gives to the engraver a tool by which his art treasures can be multiplied millions of times.
>
> The transfer press is the triumph of Mr. Perkins' invention; it is the foundation upon which the whole superstructure of the art of bank note engraving rests. It may be likened to the lever of Archimedes, in its power to "move the world." A powerful compound lever over a solid bed of iron, upon which the hardened plate is placed, the soft cylinder or "die" then placed in position, the ponderous lever closes on it, a rolling motion forward and backwards is communicated, and in a few minutes the ductile metal receives the reverse of the engraving with the certainty and accuracy of the electrotype battery. Recent improvements have added greatly to the general utility of this machine. Many of the most beautiful and elaborate ornaments on our notes are produced by transferring process, and though the production of new plates and the "retouching" of those worn by the hand of the printer, brings it into daily and hourly requisition, yet it knows no "idle time" in the various duties it is expected to perform.[14]

The Continuing Story

Bills printed by Perkins remained in wide use until the early 1830s, this being especially true of issues of Massachusetts and Maine banks. The appearance of Patent Stereotype Steel Plates evolved over the years, and by the 1830s most contained at least one large vignette at top center, and, often, vignettes to each

Early-issue $3 bill of the Farmers Bank of Gloucester, with two small vignettes dated January 10, 1806, signed by cashier Henry Smith and president John Harris. This is from a plate engraved by William Hamlin before Perkins began making bills for the bank.

Face of a $5 note of the Farmers Exchange Bank, Perkins Patent Stereotype Steel Plate, inked serial number 507 and dated May 7, 1808. Signed by cashier W. Colwell, who worked day and night to turn out thousands of notes. To aid in the deception, serial numbers were kept low and were started anew each day.

side. Spaces were still reserved for repeating the denomination in tiny letters, sometimes italic, other times in block type.

While most customer banks were managed with all good intentions, there were some conspicuous failures, which captured a lot of newspaper copy while the more honest "good guys" received little publicity.

The following chronicles of three prominent Perkins customers reflect not only the currency issued but also certain intricacies of banking of the first decade of the 19th century.

The Farmers Exchange Bank

The Early Years

The most important customer for Perkins's bank notes in the early days was the Farmers Exchange Bank of Gloucester, Rhode Island. This institution started in a modest way. Incorporated in February 1804, the capital was authorized at $100,000, in 2,000 shares of $50 each, paying in specie in seven installments.

As to whether the Farmers Exchange Bank was a fraud from the very beginning is a matter of question for some historians, but to the present writer it appears to have been a house of cards. This is one of three criminally operated banks of the era, the others being the Detroit Bank (which seems to have been first in the game) and the Hillsborough Bank of Amherst, New Hampshire. History recognizes the Farmers Exchange Bank as an out-and-out fraud, while the other two banks seem to have slipped below the notice of many historians, save perhaps for numismatic scholars. The Vermont State Bank was also a paper mill, but with good intentions and with a satisfactory conclusion to holders of its bills.

Very little of the capital of the Farmers Exchange Bank was ever paid in, and although the directors each remitted the first installment in gold and silver coins, the same amount was quickly borrowed back from the bank by each—without giving any security. Each director eventually held 103 shares, apparently essentially free.

Of the bank's 2,000 shares, only 661 were ever paid for in gold and silver, and deducting the loans taken back by the directors, the capital of $100,000 amounted to only $3,081.11 in actual specie!

Bills were ordered to be printed, and various denominations were soon on hand, made from hand-engraved copper plates with a small vignette, such as of two cows or a farmer hoeing. These notes bore no imprint of an engraver. A statement of March 28, 1805, indicated $288.50 in specie and bills of other banks, backing $22,524 of bills in circulation. On June 3 of the same year, the directors voted to allow each to take $200 from the bank, but no accounting of these funds was ever made, nor were they repaid.

Soon, many more bills were printed through orders placed with Jacob Perkins in Newburyport. Small denominations seem to have been the most popular, not surprising as these were easy to place into circulation. Of the slug-plate type and resembling countless bills issued by other banks, particularly in Massachusetts, such currency was instantly familiar to the public.

Andrew Dexter Jr.

Andrew Dexter Jr., a Boston entrepreneur, became interested in this bank. Born in Brookfield, Massachusetts, on March 28, 1779, Dexter is said to have been a classmate of Daniel Webster at Dartmouth College. With ample financing through his family, he sought to establish a bank in Massachusetts in the early 19th century but could not obtain a charter. By this time he had been involved as a secret backer of the notorious Detroit Bank (of which more will be related later).

In February 1808, eleven of the directors sold their interest in the Farmers Exchange Bank of Gloucester to Dexter for $1,300 in notes payable to each, plus forgiveness of the loans they had taken out to "buy" capital stock. By this time Dexter knew the banking business well, having been involved in the fraudulent Detroit Bank. The notes were signed by Simon Smith and John Harris as principals and Dexter as guarantor. In due course the former directors received their money. It was later learned that Dexter and his associates paid not a cent of this and that the money was taken out of the bank's own funds. Other stockholders were bought out on the same basis. At the time of the management change, $45,821 face value in bills was in circulation from earlier times.

Dexter, who in Massachusetts controlled the Boston Exchange Office, the Berkshire Bank in Pittsfield, and the Northampton Bank—in addition to his involvement with the Detroit Bank in Michigan—realized that he could make money simply by having notes printed by Perkins. With no requirement to make his records available to anyone and with good connections in business, Dexter was able to circulate the remarkable total of $760,265 in bills in the first year the Farmers Exchange Bank was under his control. Through his Boston Exchange Office and deals with other banks, he traded many notes for other bills. Others notes were sold as investment certificates, although not so imprinted. Investors were promised 6% interest if they held them, but if they changed their minds, instant redemption in coin would be made. With such an assurance, the bills seemed to be very sound. Content with their seemingly good investments, most people who had such bills held them tightly.

In the meantime, Dexter was involved in other ventures, including the construction in 1808 of the Boston Coffee House, a place of public accommodation that included dining and drinking facilities and rooms for overnight guests. That business, never a success, allowed Dexter a place to keep his bills secret and to sign them privately and at night, not during times that the bank had customers. As to delaying redemptions, Dexter instructed Colwell on May 21, 1808, that those demanding coins "should be plagued as much as possible, by detaining them as long as it will naturally take to count all kinds of specie change, intermixed, in the most deliberate manner." This tactic later became popular with legitimate banks, and many are the stories of customers holding notes being allowed to redeem only a small number of them on a given day, due to "bank policy."

John Harris, one of Dexter's partners in the scheme, signed as president and was not usually on the premises anyway. More than $500,000 in bills were given to Dexter personally, who gave the bank IOUs in return. Dexter then pocketed the proceeds he received.

In the meantime, although there were no real profits from which dividends could be paid, stockholders were given about 8% dividend on their capital. In addition, the directors received cash payments from time to time. The Farmers Exchange Bank of Gloucester was a true money machine.

THE END

Rumors concerning Dexter and the bank circulated widely, and many suspicions were aroused. In March 1808, cashier Colwell wrote to Dexter,

> Our situation becomes every day more disagreeable. The discontent and irritation among the people is very great. We have been sued to-day, and our bank is the topic of conversation through the country.

Finally, in early 1809 a committee of the Rhode Island State Legislature was appointed to investigate the situation.[15] The report included this finding of the bank:

> The president and cashier were constantly employed in signing bills . . . and Dexter was continually urging them to sign bills as fast as possible, telling them that everything depended on his having them very speedily; that if they were not soon finished, he should not be able to dispose of them, and that at that time he should be able to sell some of them very well.
>
> The bills were made with so much precipitation, and the officers of the bank were so much pressed for time, that said bills were in some instances sent to Boston without being dated or numbered. There is now in said bank $86.46 in specie. . . .

It goes without saying that $86.46 in coins did not do much toward redeeming hundreds of thousands of dollars in bills, and all became worthless. The state closed the operation soon thereafter. Subsequently, an item in the *Providence Gazette* stated that Dexter had "practiced a system of fraud beyond which the ingenuity and dishonesty of man cannot go." The Farmers Exchange Bank became famous as the greatest bank fraud in early 19th-century America and was discussed in banking circles for years afterward, although it is virtually unknown to modern popular historians. (The Detroit Bank fraud was large but was not widely publicized.) In the meantime, Dexter decamped to Windsor, Nova Scotia, to avoid imprisonment for debt. In 1830 some $1,500 in bills on hand from the investigating committee of 1809 was destroyed by the legislators.[16]

In 1816 Dexter was back in business with nothing but profit to show from his Farmers Exchange Bank venture. The next scenario took place in Milledgeville, Georgia, where, using land scrip inherited from his father (so he said), he was the successful bidder for a vast tract for $7 per acre, which was paid for in large part with money claimed to have been supplied by John Falconer (but who knows?), in whose name the title was placed. The town of New Philadelphia was laid out and came into being. Soon, a small community of log structures arose on streets named by Dexter for naval heroes of the War of 1812 and U.S. presidents. Peter A. Remsen, a traveler from New York City, went through the district, and on January 12, 1818, wrote these comments:

> I visited New Philadelphia, one mile back from the river. A high, pleasant place and bids fair to flourish. . . . Lots sell in this place for $50 to $150 per lot. It has 800 laid out and Mr. Dexter is

State capitol building in Montgomery, Alabama, located at the end of Dexter Avenue, after Andrew Dexter Jr. In this chapter of his life, Dexter pursued business interests in the South with few people being aware of his earlier fraud.

> about to have grist and sawmills in operation shortly about five miles distant.

Another entrepreneur, Virginia-born plantation owner General John Scott, acquired extensive acreage and established the town of East Alabama. In 1819 that section of Georgia became part of the new state of Alabama, New Philadelphia and East Alabama merged, and the town of Montgomery was formed.[17] Dexter's partner, John Falconer, became the first postmaster of Montgomery, which later became the state capital. Dexter donated land to Montgomery, and the name of Market Street was changed to Dexter Avenue in his honor, apparently without knowledge of his having committed the largest bank fraud to this point in American history! In fact, on this street you will find today the Supreme Court of Alabama and, at its end, the Alabama Capitol building.

The town prospered greatly, aided beginning in 1821 by steamboat service connecting down the Alabama River to Mobile, on the Gulf of Mexico. In 1861 it was for a brief time the first capital of the newly formed Confederate States of America.

Apparently, Dexter's ambitions exceeded his abilities to turn a profit, and it seems that he drifted from one project to another. In 1833 he visited Texas and became fascinated with its potential. He traded some of his Alabama real estate for dry goods and other merchandise, seeking to sell it in Texas, but the idea did not pan out. Soon he was bankrupt.

Dexter died in debtors' prison in Mobile, Alabama, of yellow fever on November 2, 1837. His burial place is unknown. His wife, born in 1787, the former Charlotte Apthorp Morton, sister of a governor of Massachusetts, died on August 17, 1819, and was buried in Montgomery. Later historians have variously characterized Dexter as a dreamer and a visionary,

Vermont State Bank $10 note issued at the Middlebury branch, location added in ink, issued April 20, 1808.

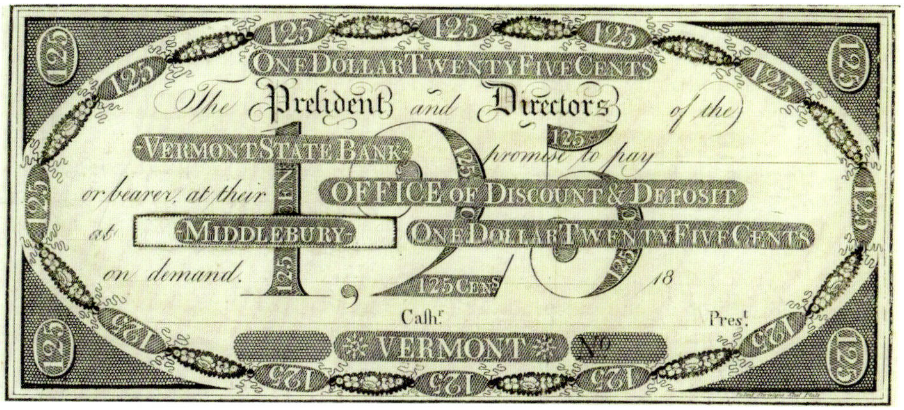

Middlebury branch note with MIDDLEBURY slug identifying the location; $1.25 "remainder" note, never signed or used.

what with helping to found the capital of Alabama, or less charitably and more accurately as a scoundrel. Actually, he seems to have been all of these things.

Today, the Perkins bills of Farmers Exchange Bank of Gloucester are very common, as is often the case with notes from failed banks. With the above narrative in mind, they are certainly among the most interesting currency of the first decade of the 19th century.

The Vermont State Bank

In the Beginning

Another prime user of Perkins's bills in this decade was the Vermont State Bank.[18]

At the turn of the 19th century, paper money in circulation in the Green Mountain State consisted of a ragtag selection of bills issued outside of the state, many of which were counterfeit. Sensing a need and seeing an opportunity, in 1803 projectors of banks in Burlington and Windsor petitioned the Vermont General Assembly for charters. The Windsor applicants stated that they

> were convinced of the importance and usefulness of banks, and that the establishment of a bank at their place would essentially promote the interests of the citizens, by lessening the interest and increasing the quantity of money in circulation, enlarging the sphere of confidence and credit with the contiguous states, removing the loss and inconvenience which flow from the exclusive circulation of notes from other banks at a great distance. . . .

Legislators were divided on the matter, and eventually the proposals were rejected. Nathaniel Niles, reporting for the committee, suggested that paper money would drive other money, presumably meaning coins, out of the state:

> 1. Bank bills being regarded as money, and money, like water, always seeking its level, the bills put into circulation in this State must displace nearly the same sum of money now in circulation among us, and, by driving it into the seaports, facilitate its exportation to foreign countries.
> 2. By introducing a more extensive credit, the tendency of banks would be to palsy the vigor of industry, and stupefy the vigilance of economy—the only two honest, general, and sure sources of wealth. In this view, banks would tend to divert the attention of the speculator, the inexperienced youth, the indolent and incautious, from those honest and sure sources of mediocrity and independence, and to fix it upon imaginary and unjustifiable methods of suddenly accumulating an overgrown property.
> 3. Banks, by facilitating enterprises both hazardous and unjustifiable, are natural sources of all that class of vices which arise from the gambling system, and which cannot fail to act as sure and fatal, though slow, poisons to the republic in which they exist.
> 4. Banks tend strongly to draw off the dependence of debtors from their own exertions as means of payment, and to place it on the facility of increasing new debts to discharge the old.
> 5. Banks have a violent tendency, in their natural operation, to draw into the hands of the few a large proportion of the property at present fortunately diffused among the many. The tendency of banks seems to be to weaken the great pillars of a republican government, and at the same time to increase the forces employed for its overthrow.
> 6. As banks will credit none but persons of affluence, those who are in the greatest need of help cannot expect to be directly accommodated by them.
> 7. Should the bill pass into a law, we apprehend it would be found necessary, at least, to render the bank granted thereby perpetual; a measure too important to be adopted without a more thorough investigation than the novelty of the question and the shortness of the time will allow.
> 8. By the establishment of banks, government would in our opinion go farther than could have been contemplated by its original institution.

This far-reaching and somewhat imaginative condemnation of banks clearly reflected the fear that businesses, if established in Vermont, would become too powerful.

Advantages of a Bank

In 1804 the draft of the charter for a bank at Windsor was printed in a newspaper in that town, as the matter was to come up again before the legislature. Included was this reasoned view of the need for such an institution:

> There is not in the state any bank or public office where the temporary wants of our citizens may be supplied with loans of money at a low rate of interest, and for a term of time convenient to the borrower; in consequence of which usurious loans are more common than in other states, and the rate of interest exorbitant without example; and as illegal interest cannot without some risk to the lender be taken on simple loans, recourse is had to oppressive contracts, whereby the law against usury is evaded. . . .
>
> As there is no bank, or place of deposit, where current coins can be had to make a legal tender, forfeitures are incurred, and much cost and inconvenience arises in cases where notes of foreign banks are refused in payment; and owing to the distance of those banks whose notes are in circulation amongst us, the people suffer a direct tax from defaced, worn out, and counterfeited notes. The circulation of the bills of banks of other states

> in this state is at least $800,000; that money is issued in loans to their citizens, who purchase cattle and other stock from the people of Vermont, by which means an increase of revenue is derived to those states, and speculators take advantage of the scarcity of money amongst our people, and buy their cattle, pork and grain at a reduced price, and make our necessities subserve their interests. Money (coin) disappears in proportion to the increase of the circulation of foreign bills. It is difficult, even at this time, to procure sufficient specie to pay the taxes. Such of our citizens as are stockholders in foreign banks, would be induced to vest their money in banks of our own. . . .
>
> By the state reserving a right to draw considerable sums from the bank at a low rate of interest, and for a certain number of years, she would always be provided for any emergency which might require an *immediate expenditure* of money. The value of such a privilege has been duly appreciated by the sister States, and recognized in all their charters to bank companies.

However, in 1804 the legislature took no action on any bank proposals. In 1805 the matter came up again, and a Committee on Banks was appointed. Proposals were heard for banks at Windsor (with an additional office of deposit in Brattleboro) and Burlington as well as for a state-owned bank. No positive action was taken. In 1805 and 1806 certain of these pleas were renewed and several other banking proposals were brought forth.

Founding of the Vermont State Bank

At long last, on November 10, 1806, there was positive action. Seemingly, the state's citizens were to have their own bank. Legislators incorporated the Vermont State Bank, approving a bill introduced by Titus Hutchinson of Woodstock. After revisions and amendments, the act included the following provisions (summarized):

- *Section 1*—There shall be established a bank, to be called the Vermont State Bank, to consist of two branches (and more if the state from time to time shall direct), one at Woodstock, the other at Middlebury; and all the stock in the bank, and all the profits, shall be the property of the state, and be under the *sole* direction and disposition of the Legislature *forever.*
- *Section 2*—Thirteen directors for the bank shall be chosen annually, by ballot, in joint assembly; they to choose one of their number president. Six of the directors shall reside in the Eastern, and six in the Western District of the state, and the others where prudence shall dictate.
- *Section 3*—Those directors residing in the Eastern District shall be directors of the branch at Woodstock; those in the Western of the branch at Middlebury.
- *Section 4*—Directors have the power to appoint cashiers and clerks, and make necessary rules for conducting business.
- *Section 5*—The directors of each branch shall have discretionary power to borrow money from time to time, to fill the vaults of such branch, on the credit of such branch only; but they shall not give a greater interest than six percent per annum.
- *Section 6*—The bank bills shall be signed by the president, and also by the cashier of the branch at which they are made payable; and the directors of either branch shall not at any time issue or put in circulation bills to a greater amount than the actual deposit of coin in the vault of their branch, until the deposit shall amount to $25,000, after which they may put in circulation bills to three times the amount of such deposit, provided said deposit shall not at any time exceed $300,000.
- *Section 7*—The sum of $500 is appropriated from the state treasury for the purchase of plates and paper necessary in issuing bills, and, after the same are procured, the Legislature may from time to time appropriate any moneys or sums of money, as they shall see fit, to fill the vaults of the branches of the bank and those they may establish hereafter.
- *Section 8*—Each director is required to give bonds to the state treasurer in the sum of $30,000. The cashiers and clerks also to give bonds to the state in such sums as the directors from time to time require, having reference to the amount in the vaults.
- *Section 9*—Each and every officer of the bank shall be sworn to the faithful performance of the duties of his office, and shall receive for his services such sums as the Legislature shall from time to time direct, provided it is not more for them all than the whole profits of the bank for the first year, or more than half of the profits for any succeeding year.
- *Section 10*—Directors have the power to purchase, hold, and dispose of any real or personal property as the banking interest of the state shall dictate, and for the interest of the state only.

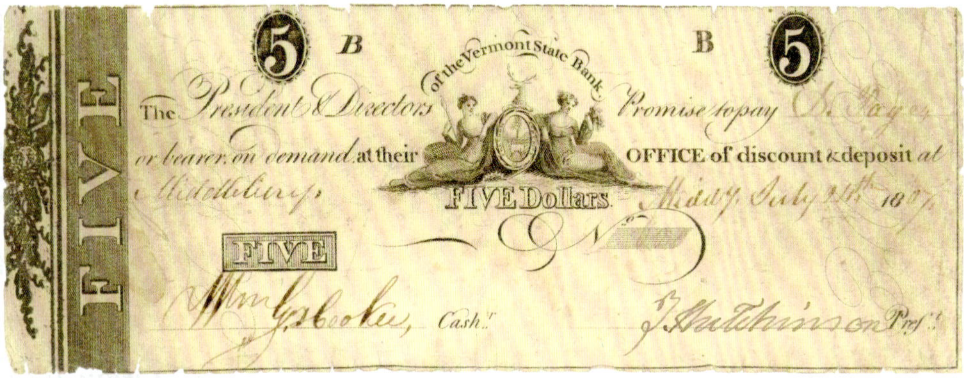

An early-style $5 note from the Middlebury branch of the Vermont State Bank, dated July 11, 1807.

Perkins Patent Stereotype Steel Plate $5 note from the Westminster branch, March 7, 1808.

- *Section 11*—The directors must report annually to the Legislature on the situation of the bank, including the amount of the deposits and bills in circulation; and the Legislature can appoint a committee to inspect and report the situation of each branch.

Thus Vermont became the first New England state to inaugurate its own banking system with offices and branches. The first two offices were to be established at Woodstock and Burlington, per the early proposal, but the last was changed to Middlebury as given above. In the next year branches were established at Burlington and Westminster.

The directors chosen were David Robinson, Apollos Austin, Horatio Seymour, Daniel Chipman, John Willard, William C. Harrington, John Mattocks, James Tarbox, Titus Hutchinson, Benjamin Swan, Elias Lyman, Alexander Campbell, and Mark Richards.

Titus Hutchinson was named president, Job Lyman was selected as cashier of the branch at Woodstock, and William G. Hooker served as cashier of the branch at Middlebury.

Paper Money

The Vermont General Assembly ordered currency with small vignettes. The bills were stock, applicable to all offices, with a space for the location to be filled in with ink. The first bills were released on February 23, 1807.

An example of an early issue is provided by a $5 bill of July 11, 1807, issued in Middlebury. At the top center are two women flanking a shield with a stag's head above, an emblem of the state. Vertically at the left is a decoration of foliage and the inscription FIVE. This note is not signed by its maker, but it seems to be from a copper plate, mostly engraved by hand.

By 1808 an order had been placed for bills with Jacob Perkins in Newburyport, these being of the Patent Stereotype Steel Plate type with slug inserts for the different locations. Denominations known to have been produced include these:

- *Burlington*—50¢, 75¢, $1, $1.25, $1.75, $2, $3, $5, $10, and $20.
- *Middlebury*—50¢, 75¢, $1, $1.25, $1.75, $2, $3, $5, and $10.
- *Westminster*—50¢, 75¢, $1, $1.25, $1.75, $2, $3, $5, and $10.
- *Woodstock*—50¢, 75¢, $1, $1.25, $1.75, $2, $3, and $5.

Ignoring all strictures, the Vermont State Bank issued more than $500,000 in paper money by the time the General Assembly met in its 1808 session. By that time the bills were eagerly accepted in regional

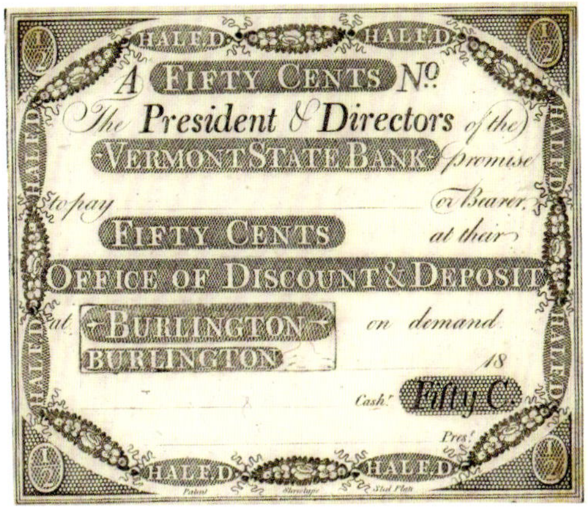

Note for 50¢ of the Vermont State Bank with not one but two slugs identifying the location as Burlington. An unsigned, unissued "remainder."

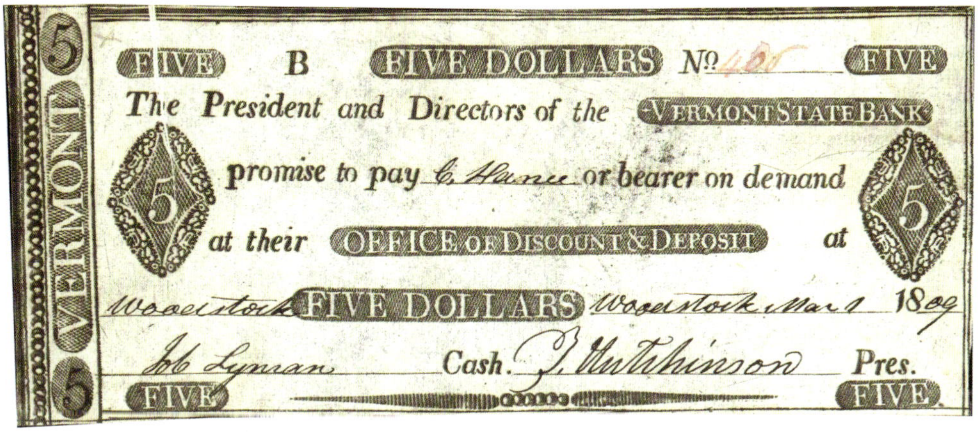

Perkins Patent Stereotype Steel Plate $5 note issued by the Woodstock branch, March 1, 1809, with address added in ink. In the several years that the Vermont State Bank issued paper money, several different styles of notes were used. Job Lyman, who signed as cashier, later corresponded with numismatist George B. Reed concerning the bank.

commerce, and there seemed to be no end of the demand at the outset.

Interestingly, at this same time Perkins was also turning out hundreds of thousands of dollars in bills for the Hillsborough Bank of Amherst, New Hampshire, an amount far in excess of its legislative authorization, not to overlook the infamous Farmers Exchange Bank of Gloucester, Rhode Island, and the Detroit Bank. For these and certain other banks that resulted in great losses to the public, Perkins chose not to ask questions about their remarkably large orders but simply to print currency as requested. As related later in the present text, the general policy of bank-note printers in the early 19th century was to fill orders and ask few questions. However, if asked, such companies would argue that they carefully chose their customers, etc.

Bills of Other States

Prior to the establishment of the Vermont State Bank, the paper money used in the district consisted of issues from New York, Massachusetts, and elsewhere. In the absence of readily available information, citizens could not discern the good from the bad, and counterfeits were widespread. In 1807, with the Vermont State Bank launched, the legislature passed this resolution to address the continuing practice of bringing bills of distant banks into the state:

> *Whereas,* Sundry persons, belonging to this state and elsewhere, have combined together and formed companies for the purpose of bringing bills of banks in other states into this state, and for loaning the same—which bills, considering the great distance of the banks from which they are issued, and the uncertainty of procuring the specie even when the application is made to them, are not equal to the face of them; and whereas, also, such proceedings are not only injurious to the individuals who have received them, but also tending to the injury of the banking institutions of this State: to prevent which combinations and injurious practices,
>
> *It is enacted,* That if any person shall, after the first day of December next, bring into this state any sum or sums in foreign bank bills, or bills issued by the directors of any bank out of this state, with the intent and for the purpose of loaning the same, or assist in so doing, shall forfeit to the state the full value of such bills, to be assessed as a fine. And it is further enacted, if any who have heretofore brought such bills into the state for the purpose of loaning them, or been in any way concerned or interested therein, shall continue after the above date to make any loans thereof; or of any such foreign bills printed or struck off within this state; or of any

> funds thereby created, or in any way aid or assist therein, shall forfeit and pay to the state a fine equal to the amount of such loan, with costs.

Effects of the Embargo Act

The Embargo Act, passed in 1807, was very damaging to American seacoast commerce, as domestic vessels were not permitted to sail to distant ports. The objective was to protect American ships from being seized and their sailors taken captive by the British or French navies, a frequent practice, especially by the British. Although the act was repealed in 1809, the Non Intercourse Act that succeeded it was still restrictive. Continuing attacks on American vessels eventually led to the War of 1812.

Following the Embargo Act, once-busy harbors such as Portsmouth and Salem were largely idled. Stocks of West India goods as well as imports from Europe could not be replaced, and many merchants suffered, including those in interior towns. There was a chill in the economy of Vermont, and loan repayments were often slow. Moreover, "hostile legislation and failure of banks in neighboring states handicapped the institution."[19]

In its 1808 session the Vermont General Assembly was made aware of reports that cashiers of the Vermont State Bank offices were engaging in questionable practices. In Middlebury and Westminster, bills were not being redeemed in coins promptly on request. Instead, the cashiers endeavored to negotiate discounts of 1% to 2% on the notes presented or to redeem them with other paper from distant banks payable in the future. Legislators reported the following:

> The committee find, from the concessions of the directors, and from evidence adduced, that the directors of the bank have directed the cashier that when any person applied to the bank with their bills for payment, whom the cashier or directors thought a *speculator,* or who did not receive the bills in the ordinary course of business, or was unfriendly to the bank, to offer him drafts on Boston, payable in 60 or 90 days; and if he refused such draft, then to proceed to count the money in small change, or weigh small pieces of gold moderately, until he had paid him or he should offer to discount one per cent, and if said discount was made, to pay the bills promptly; which directions the cashier followed, and the cashier certified that all sums so received went to the benefit of the bank.

It is thus seen that there are two sides to every story! Speculators were the bane of banks in all states. These individuals, usually located in the larger cities, often cast aspersions on distant banks and sought to diminish the value of their bills. Strategies included placing fake notices of failure or suspension in newspapers, advertising that bills of a certain bank would not be received in trade, and so on. These bills would then be bought at as deep a discount as might be possible. Afterward, the speculator or an agent would travel to the bank and demand that the bills be exchanged at face value for gold and silver. Often, a given bank did not have enough coins on hand to redeem thousands of dollars' worth of bills at once, and embarrassing situations would result, damaging the bank's reputation.

It was further alleged in 1808 that both the Middlebury and Westminster branches of the Vermont State Bank had currency in circulation far in excess of what state regulations allowed, this, of course, rendering it even more difficult for these offices to have enough coins on hand for redemption. Corrective action was presented to the legislators, but it failed to pass by one vote. For many, the Vermont State Bank still held promise for a beneficial system.

At the Woodstock office Jireh Durkee of Boston sought to redeem $9,000 in bills, but he was accused of being an evil-minded person bent on destroying the very resources of the state of Vermont. The directors sought to get an indictment against Durkee in court, but they were rebuffed. Such scenarios seem improbable today but were repeated in one form or another by many banks of the era and for decades afterward. The objective was to keep bills "out there," and if they were redeemed, to pay them out again as soon as possible. In this instance the otherwise reputable *state* of Vermont was involved in a currency scheme that was bound to fail.

Job Lyman, who served as cashier of the Woodstock office, gave his recollection of the situation in 1808:

> The monstrous disproportion was clearly seen between the capital of the bank and the amount of its notes in circulation. If, for instance, a bank has at one of its branches $151,000 in circulation, and can show only $20,000 and a little moonshine stored away in its vaults to meet so large an obligation, no wonder its bills fall below par.[20]

Events of 1809

In 1809 the situation worsened in step with the spreading effects of the Embargo Act. What did not help was adverse publicity given to several banks, all Perkins customers, that had failed or were about to, due to flagrant over-issue of notes. Prime examples were the notorious Farmers Exchange Bank of Gloucester, Rhode Island, having been conceived in fraud; and the Hillsborough Bank of Amherst, New Hampshire, in hopeless condition. The bad news about the Detroit Bank (discussed later in this chapter) was not well circulated in the East, and although it was a great fraud, few New Englanders knew about it.

At the autumn legislative session of that year, Governor Jonas Galusha endeavored to reassure his listeners that, although the Vermont State Bank might have problems, the situation was far better than if private banks had been established and had collapsed. He argued in part:

> The failure of several private banks in the vicinity of this state, the rejecting of our bills by the law of one state and the policy and caprice of others, has embarrassed our mercantile intercourse with the adjoining states. . . .
>
> The manner to be pursued to meet or remove these impediments, I leave to your consideration. It will be remembered by many that I was not amongst those that favored the institution of country banks; but it is apparent that the establishment of a public bank in this state has saved many of our citizens from great losses, and probably some from total ruin—or it is obvious that but for this establishment, in lieu of our own Vermont Bank bills, our citizens would on the late bankruptcies have been possessed of large sums of the depreciated paper of the failing private banks. . . .
>
> For my own part, I consider the holders of our bills perfectly secure; and, as every person in the state has an interest in the avails of the bank, they will the more cheerfully acquiesce in any prudent measure you may devise to give it support.

The House Committee on Banks furnished this statement of operations to date:

> Since the establishment of the institution, there have been issued and put in circulation, up to September 30th, 1809, bills to the amount of \$760,825.50; of which they have redeemed, and had in the bank September 30th, \$356,225.75; leaving in circulation, \$404,599.75; for the payment and redemption of which they had, in notes, specie and other securities, after paying all expenses attending the establishment, together with a loss of about \$1,100 in bills of some of the private banks which have failed, \$427,012.23; leaving a net gain to the state of \$22,412.48.
>
> Your committee would further observe that the rule with the directors has been, on loaning money, to require a note made joint and several, with three or more signers; and, from the care which has been taken, it is believed that very little, if any, is out on doubtful security. And, although causes unforeseen to the president and directors have produced a temporary suspension of punctual payment at the bank, yet it does not appear that this state of things will long continue. And it is also the opinion of your committee that with some further legislative aid, which is believed to be practicable, the institution will succeed equal to the most flattering expectation of the citizens of this state.

The legislators put several proposals into effect to try to strengthen the tottering bank. One was obvious: that delinquent borrowers should be pursued with vigor and assessed severe penalties if they did not pay within three days. Another mandated that each branch should prepare an annual statement of its limits in borrowing and bill issuing. Yet another provision encouraged citizens to pay real estate taxes with the bills.

Politicians of the state were divided on the issue, with name-calling and charges filling the air. Whigs, seemingly without evidence, stated that Federalist interests had borrowed large sums from the banks, then had tried to discredit the system so that bills could be bought at a discount to repay the loans.

A Curious Incident at Middlebury

In the dark of night in June 1809 the Vermont State Bank branch in Middlebury was broken into, and about \$14,000 in bills was taken.[21] Evidence pointed to Joshua Henshaw, a local merchant and landlord of the bank building, who was in financial distress at the time and later fled to Canada. During construction work he was said to have acquired a duplicate key, which was later found in his home and which today is an exhibit at the Sheldon Museum in Middlebury. Recorded by Samuel Swift in the *History of the Town of Middlebury* (1859), the story became accepted as fact.

Generations later a Vermont historian, Kenneth A. Degree, sought to investigate the matter in depth, revealing the following scenario. The Middlebury branch was controlled by three prominent local men, Daniel Chipman, Horatio Seymour, and John Willard. When state representatives visited the bank they found that accounts were confused and that large sums of money were missing. It was recommended that the bonds of these men be forfeited and suits be brought against them to recover the funds. The three men suggested that the legislature should appoint a committee to review the situation, a procedure simpler than a court action would be, and they would comply with the recommendations. Hearings were to begin in Middlebury on December 16, 1812.

Some highly interesting information came to light. In 1808 the Middlebury men had decided to engage in bill discounting and currency speculation. In Boston they made an arrangement with Deacon Isaac Warren to obtain more than $253,116 in bills at a discount to distribute widely, with the hope that most would never be returned to Vermont for redemption in coin. For these Warren paid the Vermont State Bank $238,959, the difference being his profit, but that was not the full story. Such an arrangement was not at all unusual, and in the same era the Concord Bank in New Hampshire sought to distribute its currency in this manner; in the same state, the Hillsborough Bank sought an arrangement with a bank in distant Marietta, Ohio, to pass its bills there, while Marietta bills would be passed in New Hampshire.[22] The Middlebury directors also made a currency-passing arrangement with an agent in St. Albans, a Vermont town to the north. The Vermont bills were to be exchanged for currency of good banks in the East.

The investigators found the business with Warren lasted from June 1808 to July 1811. The directors maintained that the arrangement was necessary to keep the bills in circulation, to minimize redemptions, and to strengthen the bank. However, when banks began failing, many notes became suspect, and paper money proved to be more difficult to distribute at a distance. It was learned that Warren's remittance of $238,959 to Middlebury included bills of other banks, which the bank received for their full face value, but which Warren had obtained at a 50% discount! Some of Warren's bills proved to be utterly worthless. The loss amounted to more than $15,000, plus the large discount on the true value of the deposited bills. There were further complications when the cashier of the Middlebury bank paid out $1,000 in worthless bills received from Warren, and the directors were sued by the recipient to make good the damages. The whole matter was a free-for-all scam, conducted under the name of the state of Vermont.

Investigators found that, similarly but with less money involved, the Middlebury directors established the St. Albans Exchange Company through which over $75,000 in bills was processed, resulting in a loss of more than $4,000. This operation was short-lived and ended in March 1809. The St. Albans business, not far from the border with Canada, involved transactions in coins from Canada, which was completely illegal under current federal law, as Canada was allied with England during the Embargo period.[23]

Further, the investigators found that the directors made poor and even illegal loans, including $5,000 on February 22, 1811, to John Merriam, who was already in default to the bank for $10,000. Then there was the situation of $13,750 missing from the bank's accounts. The investigators charged that the directors were unwilling and unable to account for the shortfall. In time, the directors offered this explanation.

On a particular Saturday toward the end of June 1809, cashier Adonijah Schuyler was busy at work at the bank, which was housed in a brick building owned by Joshua Henshaw, who operated a dry-goods store adjacent, the two premises being separated by a solid brick wall. Later in the day he left for what he thought would be a short time and secured just the lower of two locks on the single door to the bank. However, he was detained and did not return until Monday morning. At that time he was surprised to find both locks secured, as he had left the key to the upper lock inside the bank.

Unable to gain access he went to director Horatio Seymour, who secured a blacksmith to come and cut away the rivets holding the top lock. Upon entering the bank the cashier found the key to the top lock where he had left it on Saturday. Nothing was discovered missing, but much later it was claimed that more than $13,000 in cash was gone.

The directors viewed landlord Henshaw as a suspect, for he was known to be in serious financial straits due to overextension of his business and unpaid bills for inventory and construction. One of his creditors had obtained a foreclosure judgment. Henshaw soon decamped to Canada. In the words of the historian Degree, Henshaw was thus the ideal scapegoat as the thief of the allegedly stolen funds.

However, there were serious flaws in the directors' story. Recently, the bank had paid Henshaw to construct a vault in the bank, perhaps giving him a set of keys. However, if he had keys, it was a most singular circumstance that he would wait until only one lock on the door was secured, and then after stealing the money, carefully close both locks.

If money were missing, why did the directors wait so long to declare it? The committee considered the various stories, then announced that they would soon be rendering a decision. Tired of hearing the accounts, the judges declined to learn more and rendered a judgment against the directors for $13,869.68. As if this were not enough, the Vermont Supreme Court presented a report to the legislature in autumn 1813 stating that the directors were liable for $22,826.13 for their malfeasances. They were given until April 1, 1814, to pay the debt.

However, there were changes in the political scene at the time. The defendants had strong connections and secured a review by a new group of judges. With a new hearing the story of the theft was accepted. The judgment against them was reduced to just $1,200.

Winding Up Affairs

Matters continued to worsen at the Vermont State Bank, as did the general economy in the East. Remedies for the bank were too little and too late, and distrust in its bills deepened, as did the discount at which they traded. Although many bills were redeemed through various transactions, an 1810 accounting showed $211,831 in currency outstanding with little in the way of coins to back the bills.

In 1811 the balance sheet of the Vermont State Bank included these items:

- *Assets:* Notes discounted (loans due to the bank): $145,313.21; land taken on execution: $9,550.14; specie: $3,046.24; bills of other branches: $8,731.42; total assets: $166,641.01.
- *Liabilities:* Bills in circulation: $94,932.50; checks outstanding: $26,939.40; profit account: $44,769.11.

The caveat was that many loans were of questionable value, thus negating the "profit" on the statement and probably taking the bank into the loss category. Times remained difficult due to the lingering effects of the Embargo Act and a general business slowdown.

The legislature appointed a committee consisting of Samuel C. Crafts, Elihu Luce, and Robert Temple to close the Westminster branch and remove its operations to Woodstock and to prohibit any further distribution of bills unless specie was actually in the vaults of a branch, equal to 50% of the amount of its bills in circulation, a regulation that no bank in New England could have met. Essentially, new business came to a halt. The collection of debts was given a high priority, as loan delinquencies continued to worsen.

In 1812 the state legislature mandated that the Burlington and Middlebury branches be closed and their business transferred to Woodstock. In November of the same year an act was passed to close down the bank and place it in charge of appointees. A report from about that time showed $78,431.75 worth of bills still in circulation, loans due to the bank of $95.418.80 (of which more than half were currently involved in lawsuits!), $6,904.30 in specie, and $3,052 in bills of broken banks, among other entries.

A report of October 11, 1813, stated that outstanding currency of the bank amounted to $66,522.25, of which more than half was in the state treasury, where such were receivable at par in payment of debts. Specie and good bills of other banks on hand amounted to a paltry $2,671.07.

A statement of October 23, 1814, showed $58,680 in currency, with $39,255.25 in the hands of the state treasurer.

The state treasurer, in company with one or more directors, was ordered to burn all of the bills in the treasury except for a small number to be retained for current business. Although the bank was essentially defunct, the legislature continued to choose directors annually until 1822, after which an agent was named to "sell the lands [valued at $21,685, mostly taken in loan foreclosures] and settle up the affairs of the bank." The state continued to receive at face value any and all bills in payment for taxes. It was not until about 1845 that matters were concluded. No one was forced to take a loss on the bills, although in the exchange market they had traded at a discount for a long time.

Postscript

By the early 1860s, George B. Reed became interested in the history of the bank and began gathering data. On January 1, 1863, he received this letter from a former official:

> Burlington, January 1, 1863
>
> Dear Sir,
>
> In reply to yours of the 20th. I have to say I have no papers in relation to the Vermont State Bank. I can give you no light on the subject except reminiscences which at this distance of time would not be very reliable. I was cashier of the Woodstock Branch during its business life, and might give a pretty correct account of its doings those few years. I could say nothing of the doings of the other Branches of consequence. Perhaps the paper you read might bring to my recollection facts which are hidden in obscurity at present.
>
> I conclude there is to be an adjourned meeting of the Society here this month if you attend it. I will endeavor to see you and talk about the old Vermont State Bank.
>
> Respectfully, Dear Sir, Yours, &c.
>
> Job Lyman

In 1879 Reed published a small book about Vermont paper money. In his own copy he appended as a bound-in scrapbook items he had collected, including a selection of bills from the Vermont State Bank branches, the earlier quoted letter from Lyman, and this, a clipping dated September 10, 1870:

> Hon. Job Lyman of Burlington died on Saturday last, aged 89 years. He graduated at Dartmouth College, in the class of 1804. He was cashier of the old Vermont State Bank throughout its existence, and president of the Woodstock Bank for many years. He was court auditor of Windsor County for a long period.

Although many Vermont State Bank bills may have been destroyed, large quantities of "remainder" bills of the Perkins Patent Stereotype Steel Plate type, not filled in with ink, plus many that were signed and used and probably were later disposed of by the state of Vermont, remain today to delight numismatists.

The Detroit Bank

Early Days in Michigan

The following is an account of another highly important customer for Jacob Perkins's bank-note printing business, the third and last sketch of a prolific user of Patent Stereotype Steel Plate currency.

In 1805 the district known as Michigan was on the leading edge of the American West. During this period the rich farming lands and other opportunities in Ohio, Indiana, Illinois, and Michigan attracted many farmers, merchants, and ambitious people from the East. The 1800 federal census placed the number of white inhabitants at just 551. The population grew rapidly, and a decade later it was close to 5,000.[24]

On June 30, 1805, Michigan became an official territory of the United States, a status it maintained until January 26, 1837, when it became the 26th state in the Union.[25] Detroit was the territorial capital and also the center of commerce in the district. William Hull was appointed as the first governor in 1805, and the judicial system of the territory was put into the hands of Augustus B. Woodward, James Griffin, and Francis Bates through their appointment by President Thomas Jefferson. In July of the same year these judges organized a town government for what was left of the settlement of Detroit, all but one residence having been consumed by fire on June 11. An act of Congress provided more than 10,000 acres of land as well as guidance for laying out the new town.

Governor Hull and the three judges collectively represented the law and its enforcement in the territory. Sometimes they relied upon their knowledge of laws in other states, and other times they made up their own rules, some of which defied logic, justice, or both. The men were in the remarkable position of making laws, then convening as judges to determine cases brought under those laws.

Located on the border with the British territory known as Upper Canada, the River Raisin was the site of a fort or blockhouse built in 1806 as a defense against the Indians. On July 2, 1812, General William Hull, in charge of the American Army of the Northwest at that station, received notice that war had been declared between the United States and Great Britain. Hull marched with his troops to Detroit. That town, including Hull's troops, was captured by the British on August 16, 1812, an early success in the War of 1812.

Under British General Isaac Brock the citizens submitted to the rules laid down by the enemy. On August 24, Colonel Henry Proctor announced that earlier regulations for the conduct of civil government would remain in effect, with Proctor now acting as governor and chief justice and Judge Augustus B. Woodward taking the position of secretary, now with

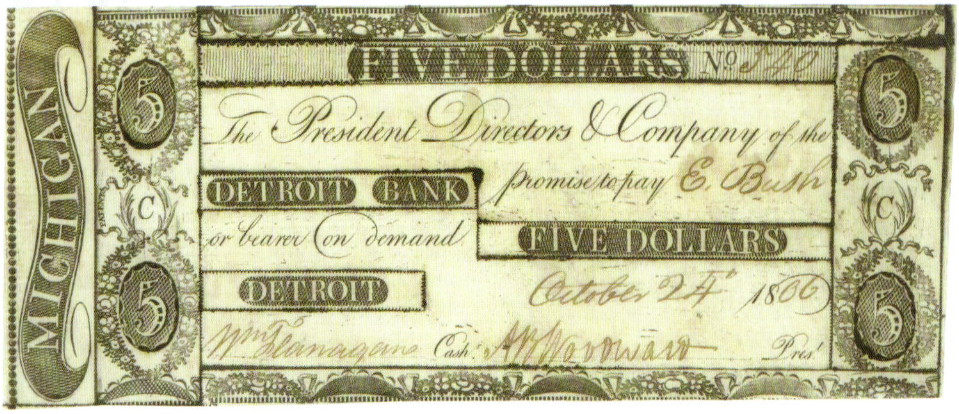

Detroit Bank $5 bill, Perkins Patent Stereotype Plate, signed by A.B. Woodward as president, October 24, 1806. Judge Woodward had a most curious career in the early days of the city.

allegiance to the British Crown instead of the United States. Woodward, the central figure in the present sketch on banking, seemed to have had the mental and ethical elasticity to accommodate himself to various circumstances that he considered either convenient or profitable or both.

On February 4, 1813, Proctor eliminated the civil government in place and set up martial law. In the meantime, American forces were fighting the British on the sea and in several venues on land. During the course of the conflict many towns and cities in the United States were invaded, and some were occupied—a short list of incidents including the burning of government buildings in Washington, the bombardment of Baltimore, and the occupation of the town of Castine in the district of Maine.

Not long thereafter, when the British had been chased out of Detroit, Woodward quickly resumed his loyalty to the American cause, issuing this proclamation:

> Whereas, the encouragement of American manufactures is a duty imposed on the good citizens of the United States, by the dictates of benevolence as well as by the injunctions of patriotism, and whereas the consumption of domestic manufactures is at the same time the most simple and most efficacious encouragement of them, and whereas it is at all times becoming that those who receive both honors and emoluments from the execution of public trusts, should exhibit themselves the foremost in examples of utility, therefore,
>
> Resolved that it be respectfully and earnestly recommended by the legislative authority of the Territory of Michigan, to all officers of this government, to appear clothed in articles the manufacture of the continent of North America at all times when engaged in the execution of any public duty, power or trust from and after the fourth day of July, 1813.

By this time the Detroit Bank was part of the city's history.

EARLY BANKING PLANS

In 1806 Judge Augustus B. Woodward took the lead in establishing the first important financial institution in the territory, the Detroit Bank. The background is revealed by this excerpt from a letter from Governor William Hull, at that time on a visit to Boston, to Woodward, April 1, 1806:

> A very rich and respectable company of merchants, in Boston, have agreed to make an establishment in our Territory to carry on the fur trade. They will place a capital of $100,000 in the business at first instance.
>
> They have petitioned our government for a bank. I have ventured to give them such assurances, that they will immediately make all their arrangements—all the shares are now subscribed for excepting one-quarter part, which is left for the people of the Territory. That quarter they will take, if the people there do not wish for it.
>
> It is impossible that a company of more wealth, intelligence, and spirit could have been formed. A large number of mechanics will go from Boston with me. Between the 15th and 20th of April I shall be at Albany, where I shall expect the pleasure of meeting you.
>
> My family will not go with me, but part of them will come on at their leisure.
>
> I am, Dear Sir, most sincerely your friend,
>
> Wm. Hull[26]

Although per the above the bank seems to have been a fait accompli by April 1806, it was not until later that arrangements were perfected.

This document is dated May 27 of the same year (edited excerpts):

> Know all men by these presents, that William Flanagan of Boston, gentleman; and Russell Sturgis, Samuel Coverly, Nathaniel Parker, Benjamin Wheeler, Samuel Sturgis, Samuel Spear, David S. Eaton, Eliphalet Williams, Dudley S. Bradstreet, George Odiorne, Barzillai Homes, and Henry Bass, Jr., all of Boston, are holden and stand firmly bound and obliged unto the president, directors, and company of the bank which is contemplated to be established at Detroit in the Territory of Michigan, by the name of the Detroit Bank.
>
> It shall be binding on the parties thereto, from the time said bank should make the first discount in the full and just sum of $15,000, to be paid unto the said president, directors, and company, to which payment, well and truly to be made, we bind ourselves. . . .
>
> The condition of this obligation is such that whereas the said William Flanagan has been nominated and has agreed upon condition of his election by the president and directors of said bank to the office of cashier thereof, to accept the same and proceed to Detroit with all convenient dispatch for that purpose.
>
> Now therefore, if said William Flanagan is elected cashier of said bank . . . he will conduct himself with fidelity and faithfully perform all trusts . . . and permit no loss to arise through his inattention or neglect, except that he shall not be answerable for counterfeit bills. . . . [27]

THE BANK IN BUSINESS

The Detroit Bank was chartered on September 19, 1806, by which time the company had erected a banking house, an impressive building at a cost of $8,000 on the northwest corner of Jefferson Avenue and Randolph streets.

Although the remotely located settlement had scarcely 600 residents, the capital of the new bank was set at a remarkable $1,000,000, and it was soon declared that $400,000 had been paid in. Historian Alpheus Felch commented:

> The long distance of the locality of the bank from the great centers of business many have been deemed by the projectors an important advantage. If these eastern capitalists could give the bills of the bank a circulation in the Atlantic states, there would be little fear of their sudden return to the remote banking house for redemption.[28]

Not long afterward the bank placed an order for bills with Jacob Perkins in Newburyport. In time as many as $3,000,000 worth may have been ordered, but the actual figure is unknown. Early commentaries on the matter vary considerably, and Perkins did not disclose the extent of the business he did with his customers. During the same era Perkins obligingly printed a flood tide of paper money for both the Farmers Exchange Bank of Gloucester and the Hillsborough Bank of Amherst, and soon the Vermont State Bank would order prodigious quantities. Seemingly, Perkins and his staff asked no questions but simply tended to their primary business of printing currency. This was also business as usual for others in the bank-note printing business.

In the summer of 1807 none other than the soon-to-be-notorious Andrew Dexter Jr. gained control of the Detroit Bank, installed James Henry as president to replace Woodward, and opened branch offices in Providence, Rhode Island, and several other locations to aid in the passing of the currency to the extent of $1 million in worthless notes. Some notes bore the inked inscription, "Payable at Providence, Rhode Island." When asked to redeem them, Dexter exchanged the bills for worthless bills of other banks. His earlier-studied fraud with the Farmers Exchange Bank of Gloucester, Rhode Island, did not begin until 1808.

Denominations ordered by the Detroit Bank included $1, $2, $3, $5, and $10. All were signed Wm. Flanagan (or W. Flanagan) as cashier. Early notes bore the name of A.W. Woodward then were followed in 1807 by the name James Henry. No doubt it was a godsend to the Boston backers of the project to have one of the most prominent men in Detroit as the nominal head of the bank. At the same time, Judge Woodward could make laws, enforce them, and otherwise conduct his affairs much as he pleased. After Henry became president under the aegis of Dexter, Judge Woodward continued to assist in spreading the circulation of the bank's bills.

Although efforts were made to present the Detroit Bank as a solid institution, it was anything but. The quantity of the bills it circulated, with virtually nothing in assets to back them up, was simply too great. In the eastern cities exchange brokers bought and sold them at a deep discount. In 1807 Conrad Ten Eyck arrived in Detroit from Albany with $500 in currency he had bought at a discount and sought to have the bills redeemed in coins. The bank at first refused, but when it became evident that Ten Eyck would publicize the situation, somehow $500 in coins was located.[29]

Judge Woodward did not operate without drawing attention to himself. He was a controversial figure and had many enemies. The United States Congress, in charge of affairs in the territory, revoked the bank's charter. Undaunted, Woodward and his eastern associates continued in the business anyway. In September 1808, the governor and other judges, *in Woodward's absence,* passed a law making it a crime to conduct an unauthorized banking business. Thus ended the Detroit Bank, which closed its doors on December 10.[30]

The bills of the bank became worthless. In the meantime Woodward had personally converted large numbers of these bills to specie for his personal profit. Most probably, the outlawing of the bank was a blessing to Judge Woodward, who could point to state politicians for the demise of the institution, absolving himself from the brunt of the blame. Just as fraudster Andrew Dexter Jr. was honored by the Alabama capital city of Montgomery, which named a street for him, so Woodward Avenue is today the designation of one of the best-known thoroughfares in Detroit. Because Detroit was remotely located from the centers of financial publishing in the East, the demise of the Detroit Bank received relatively little press, in contrast to the highly publicized demise of Dexter's Farmers Exchange Bank in Rhode Island.

Despite erratic judicial decisions and frauds that were blatant in their own time and seem even more absurd when studied today, Woodward was consistently reappointed as a judge for the territory, apparently through very secure connections in Congress, without regard to his reputation in Detroit. On January 6, 1824, several leading citizens of that city took matters into their own hands and addressed this memorial to the United States Senate (excerpts):

> The undersigned citizens of the Territory of Michigan respectfully remonstrate against the reappointment of Augustus B. Woodward as judge of said Territory, and pray that your Honorable Body will not advise and consent to the same. They remonstrate against his appointment for the following reasons:
>
> 1st: Because the application in the last Congress for a change in the local government of this Territory and in the tenure of the offices of judges was mainly superinduced by the disgraceful conduct of this man. . . .
>
> 2nd: Because he is habitually intemperate and is alike destitute of honor, probity, and respect for established law.
>
> 3rd: . . . We should consider the reappointment of A.B. Woodward as a public calamity, the experience of almost 20 years having rendered him intolerable. . . .
>
> 9th: Because when the British were in possession of Detroit after the capture of Gen. Hull, Judge Woodward accepted a commission under Gen. Proctor to act as secretary under a foreign government, thereby abandoning his allegiances to the United States, while at the same time he held the commission of judge under the United States government and was receiving the emoluments thereof. . . .[31]

Woodward's judgeship was not renewed. Today, his name is well remembered, indeed highly honored, as a founder of Detroit, with few knowing about his never-prosecuted banking peculations for personal profit.

Similar to the Patent Stereotype Steel Plate notes of the earlier-studied Farmers Exchange Bank of Gloucester and the Vermont State Bank, bills of the Detroit Bank are easily enough located today and are interesting to collect. The illegal currency-issuing policies of the Hillsborough Bank in Amherst, New Hampshire, were in many ways similar to those of the Farmers Exchange and Detroit banks and are not treated in detail here. It is indeed curious that each of the fraudsters, Dexter (Detroit and Farmers Exchange banks), Woodward (Detroit bank), and Samuel Bell (Hillsborough Bank), comfortably retained their ill-gotten gains without the slightest legal interference!

JACOB PERKINS IN LATER YEARS

BUSINESS INTERESTS IN PHILADELPHIA

By 1810 the bank-note printing business of Jacob Perkins had hit its stride. Bills with the Patent Stereotype Steel Plate system were widely used, particularly in New England, and likely the firm was dominant in its field. At the time he had a monopoly on the issues of Massachusetts, including banks in the district of Maine. Although he facilitated the above-discussed frauds and a few others, most of Perkins's customers had good intentions and endeavored to conduct their banks honorably. Perkins himself was never charged in any way with aiding and abetting crimes, nor were any other of the many bank-note companies that later furnished currency to fraudulent or even nonexistent banks.

In 1810 Gideon Fairman left Newburyport and went to Philadelphia, a city that was becoming increasingly important in the engraving and printing of bank bills. In 1811 Fairman joined George Murray and John Draper in the formation of Murray, Draper, Fairman & Co. and perfected an arrangement with Jacob Perkins to use his cylinder die and other bank-note processes. The Murray partnership became preeminent in the bank-note trade in this decade. Perkins visited Philadelphia on occasion, sometimes staying there for several months.

In 1813 Perkins was caught up in the excitement of a perpetual motion machine, a seemingly marvelous device that had attracted the attention of Henry Voigt, chief coiner of the Mint, Robert Patterson, director of the Mint, and many others.[32] As this numismatic connection is exceptional and quite remarkable, space here is devoted to some of the details. *Niles' Weekly Register*, March 3, 1813, set the scene:

> **Perpetual Motion**
>
> The following memorial from *Charles Redheffer* was presented to the legislature of Pennsylvania, on the 8th inst. . . .
>
> The memorial of Charles Redheffer, of Chestnut-Hill, in the county of Philadelphia, respectfully sheweth, that your memorialist on the 17th day of December, 1812, received from James Trimble, Esq. deputy secretary of the commonwealth, a certified copy of a resolution passed by both houses of the legislature, reciting that having placed confidence in the integrity and qualification of Henry Voigt, Robert Patterson, Nathan Sellers and Oliver Evans, of the city of Philadelphia, and S.D. Ingham, of the county of Bucks, they had appointed them a committee to make a strict examination of a machine, possessing of self-moving powers, discovered by your memorialist, and to make as specific a representation respecting it as its alleged importance and the public expectation required.
>
> Your memorialist although he felt considerable reluctance at that time to expose the principles of his invention, from consideration of prudence and the necessity that existed of securing his dis-

covery, that he might reap the fruit of many years incessant labor—yet such was the deference and respect he felt for the legislature of his native state, that proud in conscious integrity, he resolved to forego these considerations and submit his machine to the examination of this committee.

In consequence of this resolution your memorialist, on the 12th of January, addressed a letter to Henry Voigt, whom the committee had appointed their chairman, and Robert Patterson, whom, in like manner, they had elected their secretary, acquainting them he would be ready to submit his machine to their inspection on the 21st of that month. This letter was dated from his residence at Chestnut-Hill, and it was there he expected they would proceed to make the examination.

Your memorialist further states that on the 18th of that month, Henry Voigt, the chairman, requested the place of meeting might be changed to his own house in Philadelphia, of which he could notify the committee, and that he might be at liberty to exhibit to the inspection of the committee, a brass machine he had got made on your memorialist's plan and principle, as he could convince them in five minutes by that machine, which he had set in motion and which had gone well, that the machine did possess self-moving powers, and that there was no detection on the discovery.

Your memorialist at this time, possessing the same opinion of the said Henry Voigt's integrity which had influenced the legislature to nominate him to this sacred trust, and not doubting he would discharge his duty with fidelity and impartiality, did consent that the committee should make the examination at the house of said Henry Voigt, without your memorialist being present thereat.

On inquiry of the 21st your memorialist found the committee had met at the house of Henry Voigt, but had made no examination, nor was there any reason assigned to your memorialist for this extraordinary procedure.

At the same time Henry Voigt proposed to your memorialist that he should pay him one thousand dollars each, for two improvements he insisted he had made in the machine, and your memorialist observing if he could convince him he had done so, that he would give him three thousand dollars: the said Henry Voigt then insisted that your memorialist should enter into partnership with him, or that he would patent the improvements and *ruin* him, which your memorialist instantly rejected with strong expressions of indignation.

The foregoing facts will show that your memorialist did submit his machine on the 21st to their inspection, and that they made no report of such examination, but notwithstanding on the 23d he is informed, and believes by a publication which appeared in the public prints, the committee, without examination, without proof, and in the face of the declarations made, both by the president and secretary, announced to your honorable body that the machine was an imposition and your memorialist an imposter, because he would not again submit it to their examination, and because several machines ostensibly made on your memorialist's plan had not been able to be set in motion.

The persons who had made these machines, were, amongst others, Henry Voigt, who had offered your memorialist $2,000 dollars for his discovery; Robert Patterson, or his son, in Bucks County, Lewis Vernwag and Archibald Binny, which they had procured by the honorable mode of sending privately, and surreptitiously taking or causing to be taken, the dimensions of your memorialist's machine, which your memorialist conceived was an absolute forfeiture of their integrity, and therefore for these reasons and from the threats of Henry Voigt, he declined letting them again examine his machine, in which he believes he was perfectly justifiable.

Your memorialist, strong in conscious integrity, repels the foul reproach cast upon him by the committee who have unpardonably descended to deception, but as your memorialist's bare assertion, may be questioned respecting the truth and reality of his statement, he begs herewith to subjoin copies of the affidavits of Woodbridge Grafton, Mathias Smith, Jacob Maylan, Robert Pennick, Martin Ludie, Andrew Arkman, Andrew Bitting, Hirman Plows, Henry Cress and Erasmus Thomas, which your memorialist believes will incontrovertly establish, not only that the committee have most scandalously deceived the legislature, but there is neither fraud nor imposition in your memorialist or his machine, and the original depositions in his hands may be seen and examined at any time.

When your memorialist has taken the proper steps for the security of his discovery, he will then submit his machine to the examination of any number of impartial, disinterested and upright men, and he believes that no sensible man can blame him for wishing to reap the fruits of his labor, and that they may not be pirated and robbed from him, and he further believes that this expectation will be satisfactory to the legislature.

Your memorialist prays, that he may be furnished with an attested copy of the committee's report, and he will ever pray, &c, &c, &c.

Charles Redheffer

Philadelphia, March, 1813.

Niles' Weekly Register printed this notice a few months later:

From the Philadelphia Gazette:

The Perpetual Motion.—I do hereby offer to accept, *on demand,* any bet or bets, from five thousand to one hundred thousand dollars, to the end of proving in a few days, both by mathematical data, and by three separate experiments, to the satisfaction of three enlightened judges, chosen by my very opponents, out of the most respectable gentlemen of this city or of New York City, that Mr. Charles Redheffer's machine is genuine, and that it is incontestably such a *perpetual self moving principle,* as the one alluded to by Sir

Isaac Newton, in his *Principia Mathematica,* book 1st, section 13th, on the laws of motion.

N.B. This to be valid until the 15th inst. at sun setting.

Charles Gobert, Civil Engineer,
No. 157, S. 5th Street,
and at New York City,
No. 78 Pearl Street.
Philadelphia, July 12, 1813.

Niles' Weekly Register, October 2, 1813, concluded the affair, at least for the time being, reprinting this notice from the *Boston Daily Advertiser:*

Perpetual Motion at an End

Mr. Gobert of Philadelphia, who lately advertised that he would take any bet from five to one hundred thousand dollars on the feasibility of Mr. Redheffer's *discovery* of perpetual motion, was taken up for five thousand dollars, by Mr. Jacob Perkins of Newburyport.

After making a series of experiments in vain, to construct a moving machine upon Mr. Redheffer's *self moving* principle, he *discovered* to his infinite chagrin, that Mr. Redheffer had in the meantime moved himself off, with 20,000 dollars in notes of hand given him by Mr. Gobert for his valuable secret.

We understand that Mr. Gobert has acknowledged his bet forfeited, and is now in pursuit of Redheffer, who keeps himself in perpetual motion to elude him.

Redheffer and his machine reappeared in the news in *Niles' Weekly Register,* September 7, 1816, this time with no mention of Gobert or Perkins. A group of prominent men endeavored to examine the machine but could not, and therefore signed a statement that their interest in Redheffer's invention had ended.

The Geometric Lathe

In the second decade of the 18th century the geometric lathe became popular as a device to engrave bank-note plates. Several devices were created to mechanically multiply or reproduce lines, curves, and other elements, including one under an 1812 patent to Asa Spencer.[33] A few years later, Jacob Perkins described the basic process:[34]

> This machine, which is denominated the geometrical lathe, was invented in America by Mr. Asa Spencer. Its powers for producing variety are equaled only by the kaleidoscope; but for beautiful patterns it surpasses everything of the kind. It has one of the peculiarities of the kaleidoscope, viz. that the turning of a screw, like the turning of the kaleidoscope, produces an entire new pattern, which was never seen before, and perhaps would never be seen again. The pattern however may be perpetuated by the transferring process.

Perkins Moves to Philadelphia

In December 1815 Perkins moved to Philadelphia, leaving the Newburyport operation under the direc-

Mechanics Bank of Alexandria proof $20 note by Murray, Draper, Fairman & Co., circa 1815. During this era Alexandria, once located in Virginia, was a part of the District of Columbia. In 1846 it was retroceded to Virginia. This note bears no location other than Alexandria.

Murray, Draper, Fairman & Co. bill of the second decade of the 19th century used decades later in 1861 by the Bank of Westminster in Maryland, at a time when the supply of newly printed bills was exhausted.

tion of his brother Abraham. Apparently, he left a string of debts behind as well. He was no stranger to the City of Brotherly Love, having stayed there from July to October 1792, drawn at first by the possibility of working with the Mint then being established.

By 1815 Murray, Draper, Fairman & Co. had risen to great prominence. Their bills were used by a long list of customers, not only banks but also many companies and other issuers, extending to the lands beyond Pennsylvania, then known as the West. Asa Spencer and Charles Toppan (a Perkins cousin twice removed) were also active in the firm, which was located at 47 Sansom Street, Philadelphia.

Today, many Murray, Draper, Fairman & Co. bills survive from the second decade of the 19th century. Among the more interesting are $1 notes made for the (first) Bank of Westminster, in Maryland, whose charter was effective as of January 10, 1816.[35] This institution evolved into the Farmers & Mechanics Bank of Frederick County. Later, in 1830 the second bank was chartered under the same name and took over some assets of its predecessors. In 1865 the second Westminster Bank became the Union National Bank of Westminster. In the meantime, circa 1861, early in the Civil War, the bank had a shortage of currency. On hand were many of the old $1 bills from the early days, not numbered or signed. These were pressed into service, signed by the cashier and president, dated 1861—and used in circulation, no doubt to the puzzlement of anyone who studied such bills closely![36]

Murray, Draper, Fairman & Co. had a financial arrangement with Perkins for the use of his cylinder die and other innovations in siderography. Prospects were bright, and in 1816 the second Bank of the United States would be formed. The *Aurora,* printed in Philadelphia, June 7, 1816, included this note:

> We learn that the steel dies of Mr. Perkins, are to be put in requisition by the national government, for impressing their new emission of bills. The admirable invention of this great mechanical genius, is the only one we believe, that has triumphed over the arts of a whole host of counterfeiters.

The second Bank of the United States began operations in January 1817. By the end of that year more than $150,000,000 in bills had been printed for the main office as well as its branches. In the meantime, on December 18, 1816, Perkins secured a patent to impress watermarks on a continuous roll of paper. In 1818 the bank-note partnership became known as Murray, Fairman & Co. following Draper's departure that year.

The city also offered promise for the fire-engine business, another major Perkins interest. A factory was set up with Dr. Thomas P. Jones as a partner. In November 1817 Perkins's son-in-law, Joshua Butters Bacon, came to Philadelphia with his wife, Sarah Ann, and family to participate in this enterprise. After Jones left in February 1819, Bacon ran the operation until it was sold in 1821. Perkins continued to be hounded by creditors in Massachusetts, who sought to collect old debts. In 1817 two notes of Perkins for $1,750 each were endorsed by George Murray and Gideon Fairman as sureties. It was not until years later (1834) that the Massachusetts claims against Jacob Perkins were fully resolved.

London

The high quality of Murray, Fairman & Co. currency prompted the British to ask the firm to come to England to do work for the Bank of England. At the time there was a large cash prize in the offing for anyone who could devise a successful method to foil counterfeiting. On May 31, 1819, Perkins, in the company of Asa Spencer, Gideon Fairman, and Charles Toppan, went to London on the packet *Telegraph,* considered to be one of the fastest sailing ships of the day. The men were accompanied by 26 cases of equipment and machinery, a few of which contained various of Perkins's devices for measuring ship speed, tilt, and other aspects, and were unpacked for use during the voyage. The Philadelphia firm of Murray, Fairman & Co. became inoperative.

The arrangement with the Bank of England did not materialize, largely due to interference by Sir William Congreve (1772–1828), present supplier of bills to the bank and an inventor of some repute, one of the commissioners appointed to study Perkins's application. Congreve hired Robert Branston, a well-known engraver, and in just 17 days he was able to copy not only the essentials of Perkins's plates but also medallion head vignettes created by Gideon Fairman and a portrait of Homer engraved by Perkins's son Abraham—engraving art that, per Perkins, took more than 15 years of talent and effort to produce.

Moreover, Branston demonstrated that once a copper plate was made, it could be multiplied easily by a counterfeiter into usable *pewter* plates by simply squeezing the copper plate against a blank of pewter in a common vise.

Congreve's impressive 1820 book, *An Analysis of the True Principles of Security Against Forgery; Exempli-*

fied by an Enquiry into the Sufficiency of the American Plan for a New Bank Note; with Imitations of Four of the Most Difficult Specimens of those Notes, Made by Ordinary Means, laid out all of the details and effectively demolished the case for Perkins's and related Patent Stereotype Steel Plate bills, dismissing their system as "perfectly useless as far as the prevention of forgery is concerned."[37] Fortunately for Perkins, this study was little known in the United States. Blind confidence in the Patent Stereotype Steel Plate continued as more banks in New England adopted the style that, by state law, continued to be the only type of plate permitted for Massachusetts banks.

Despite his failure to do business with the Bank of England, Perkins obtained a contract to produce Bank of Ireland notes, with the work performed by a new partnership, Perkins, Fairman & Heath, which had been established on December 20, 1819, with British engraver Charles Heath as a partner. Business was good, and in 1820 the company moved to larger premises at 69 Fleet Street, London. In addition to other work the firm prepared notes for English provincial banks. This company evolved into Perkins, Bacon & Co., later Perkins, Bacon & Petch.

Joshua Butters Bacon, having sold Perkins's fire-engine business in 1821, went to London, where in 1829 he became a partner in Perkins & Bacon. Jacob Perkins's fifth child and second son, Angier March Perkins, was skilled as an engineer and came to London in 1821 as well.

In the meantime, after the death of George Murray (July 2, 1822), Gideon Fairman returned to Philadelphia, where he continued in the bank-note business under a new partnership, Fairman, Draper, Underwood & Co. Charles Toppan returned to America in 1825.

During the same decade Jacob Perkins engaged in the making of engines and steam machinery and perfected a device for copying bank-note and other engraving plates. He had high hopes for a military cannon that was powered by steam, saving the expense and storage danger of gunpowder. Although tests were performed, the device was not successful. Other Perkins inventions of the era included a device for measuring the speed of ships and one for determining the depth of water. His work was widely cited in philosophical (scientific) journals and notices of the day.

In 1840 the first adhesive postage stamps went on sale, the British "penny blacks," printed by Jacob Perkins on a device styled as the circular matrix transfer press. Accordingly, today philatelists honor Perkins for this accomplishment. Therefore, Perkins's name is probably more familiar to the average philatelist than to the average numismatist.

On July 30, 1849, following an illness of 15 days, Perkins died in London at age 83. He was survived by two sons, Angier M. and Greenleaf, and a daughter. The *United States Patent Office Report* for 1849 devoted three pages to a discussion of his inventions and included this comment:

> A simple and ostentatious notice of the demise of this remarkable man is all the tribute that the public press has yet paid to his memory. The merits of our ingenious countryman deserve more; he passed quietly away from the scene of his labors, but has left his mark upon the age.

NUMISMATIC NOTES

Paper money issued by Jacob Perkins and his successors, ranging from the early "watermelon" or oval style, to the first Patent Stereotype Steel Plate bills, to later ones with vignettes, is widely available on the numismatic market. While bills of failed or fraudulent banks are the most common, examples of many others can be collected as well.

The early bills were mainly used by New England banks. Later examples with large vignettes were employed over a wide territory, including in Michigan and other reaches of what in the 1830s and 1840s was the American West.

Because there is a certain sameness of appearance across the Perkins bills from many different banks, they are not as widely collected as are notes with more distinctive designs. Accordingly, the majority, even rarities, are modestly priced, with just a few exceptions. Although ample remainder notes can be found for a few issuers—unsigned and in Uncirculated preservation—the typical bill shows extensive use, with Fine grade being quite satisfactory for many.

Contemporary alterations of these notes, by erasing the bank name and location and printing other information in the resulting blank spaces, have not been studied extensively. Many are unknowingly offered as genuine today, but are collectible for what they really are. Indeed, James A. Haxby lists and prices many notes of this fabric in his *Standard Catalog of United States Obsolete Bank Notes 1782–1866.*

Chapter Four

THE BANK NOTES OF 1811–1820

COINS AND CURRENCY OF THE DECADE

COINS IN CIRCULATION

During the early years of the second decade of the 19th century, to August 1814, coins in circulation in the United States mostly consisted of foreign silver and gold. American coins comprised a small fraction of those seen in commerce. Most often encountered were half dollars of the Capped Bust type introduced in 1807 and designed by John Reich, assistant engraver at the Mint. Silver dollars, last minted in 1804 (from dies dated 1803 or earlier), were seen on occasion, as were half dimes, dimes, and quarter dollars. Gold quarter eagles, half eagles (especially), and eagles were encountered now and again.

Capped Bust half dollar of 1809, of the design introduced by John Reich in 1807 and used through 1836.

A copper cent of 1813.

In this era the United States $5 half eagle was the largest denomination of federal gold seen frequently in commerce. Last minted in 1804, $10 gold eagles were few and far between. Shown here is an 1809/8 overdate half eagle.

Copper cents, minted at Philadelphia since 1793, were plentiful in circulation, as were coins in the same metal bearing inscriptions relating to several states including Vermont, Connecticut, New Jersey, and Massachusetts. Cent-size copper tokens were also plentiful as were British halfpennies, many of which were counterfeit.

The coins of choice for large transactions continued to be Spanish-American dollars, or 8-*real* silver pieces, and fractional parts, the most plentiful of all being the 2-*real* or two-bit coin commonly traded at 25¢, although its actual value was a bit less. During this era, 50¢ was a common wage for laborers in many areas of thc country, and thus thc 2-*real* coin had significant purchasing power.

In remote towns and rural districts, much if not most business continued to be conducted on the barter system similar to colonial times. At a typical country store a customer desiring flour and cloth yardage might pay in milk or eggs, or offer a credit for a day or two of plowing farmland or building a fence or wall. At such stores ledgers were kept with the name of each customer and the transactions that took place, debiting and crediting accounts accordingly.

Gold coins were used to pay for larger items, especially in the cities. American $5 gold half eagles, obtainable at banks, were a familiar sight in general commerce, but they were not encountered as often as were Spanish-American doubloons or 8-escudo pieces; an escudo was worth $2 and a doubloon about $16. But the average American citizen in the country never handled a gold coin of any kind.

As events would prove, 1813 was the last full year in which United States half eagles would be seen in general commerce until well after the War of 1812, and then only for a short time. Already, $10 gold coins were scarcely in evidence because most had been exported, and quarter eagles, last struck in 1808, were not often encountered.

BILLS IN CIRCULATION

Although the number of currency-issuing banks was modest before 1814, most banks issued bills, usually of lower denominations such as $1, $2, $3, and $5. Only occasionally were higher values of $100, $500, and

$1,000 made, these likely more for interbank transactions than for use by the general public.

The War of 1812, discussed below, brought with it great changes in the economic structure of the country. It was widely thought that, after the war ended with the Battle of New Orleans in 1815 (unknown to the combatants, a treaty of peace had been signed in December 1814), coins would again be seen in quantity in circulation. The opposite happened, and even copper half cents (never plentiful to begin with) and cents disappeared, along with half dimes, dimes, and other silver. Because of this situation, many banks and merchants issued currency of fractional denominations in 1815 and 1816, and some states with laws prohibiting such bills modified their stance, Connecticut being an example.

EFFECTS OF THE WAR OF 1812

A SKETCH OF THE CONFLICT

After the Embargo Act of 1807, businesses in the East suffered greatly. This was especially true of the coastal cities, which were also important banking centers. The export-import trade diminished, causing hardships. The relations between the United States and Great Britain grew increasingly problematic as ships of the Royal Navy controlled the oceans and made their domination clear. French ships made depredations on American shipping as well.

Then came the War of 1812, which forms an important chapter in American history beyond the purview of the present numismatic text. British forces

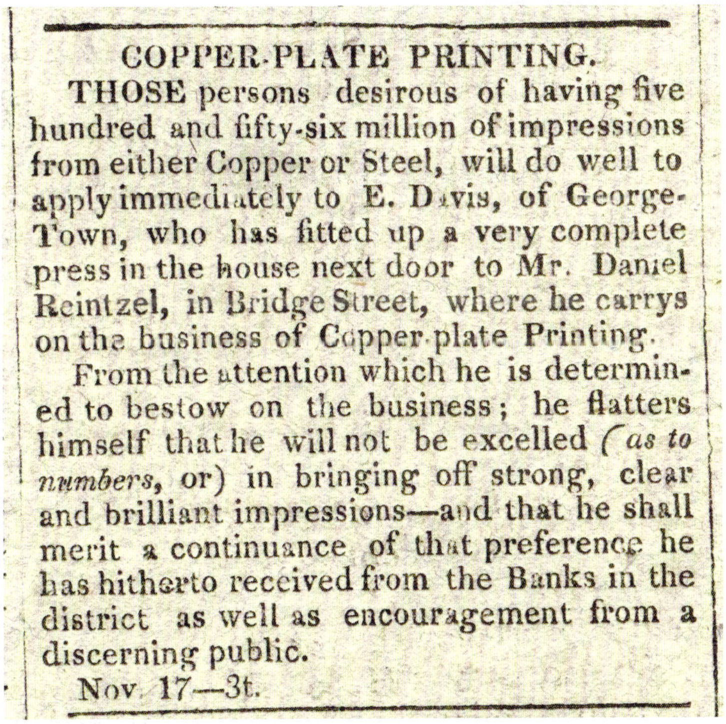

COPPER-PLATE PRINTING.

THOSE persons desirous of having five hundred and fifty-six million of impressions from either Copper or Steel, will do well to apply immediately to E. Davis, of George-Town, who has fitted up a very complete press in the house next door to Mr. Daniel Reintzel, in Bridge Street, where he carrys on the business of Copper-plate Printing.

From the attention which he is determined to bestow on the business; he flatters himself that he will not be excelled (*as to numbers,* or) in bringing off strong, clear and brilliant impressions—and that he shall merit a continuance of that preference he has hitherto received from the Banks in the district as well as encouragement from a discerning public.

Nov. 17—3t.

Advertisement of the Washington Bank, District of Columbia, dated November 17 [1810], as published in the *National Intelligencer.*

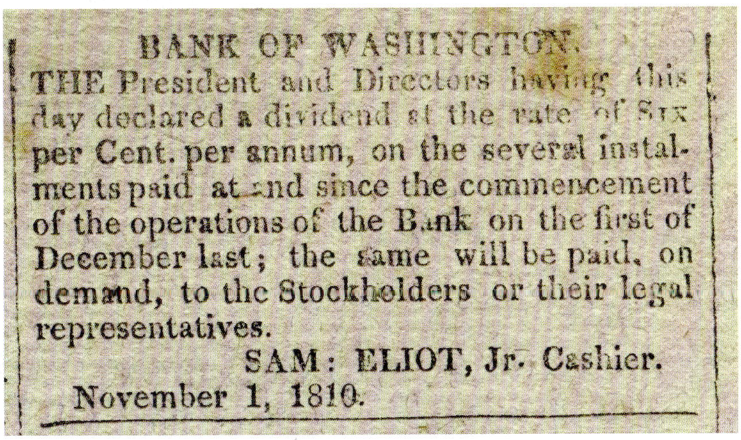

BANK OF WASHINGTON.

THE President and Directors having this day declared a dividend at the rate of Six per Cent. per annum, on the several instalments paid at and since the commencement of the operations of the Bank on the first of December last; the same will be paid, on demand, to the Stockholders or their legal representatives.

SAM: ELIOT, Jr. Cashier.

November 1, 1810.

Advertisement by E. Davis, engraver of copper and steel plates in Washington, D.C., who seems to have done work for banks in the district. Little is known about him today. (*National Intelligencer,* November 17, 1810) engaged American troops on several different fronts, including the border with upper Canada, this including the earlier-mentioned capture of Detroit, plus naval engagements on Lake Erie and Lake Champlain. In 1814 the U.S. Capitol, White House, and other government buildings were burned in Washington, D.C., and British forces advanced toward their greatest prize, the city of Baltimore. However, the bombardment of Fort McHenry, with the Stars and Stripes still waving on the morning after, put an end to that hope. Peace was declared in December 1814, but news traveled slowly, and Andrew Jackson won the Battle of New Orleans in January 1815 when both sides thought the war was still in progress. Jackson, known as the Hero of New Orleans, was elected president in 1828, mainly from the admiration given to this accomplishment. Today, numismatists with an appreciation of history can admire and collect the various medals of great beauty, authorized by Congress and struck at the Philadelphia Mint, honoring various heroes and exploits of the War of 1812. Some events are also featured as vignettes on federal paper money issued beginning in the 1860s.

Coins in Circulation after 1814

On August 27, 1814, the banks in Baltimore suspended specie payments. These were perilous times, and a battle between British and American troops had taken place three days earlier at Bladensburg, Maryland. There was a ripple effect of confidence, and on August 30 the banks in Philadelphia suspended, followed by those in New York City on September 1. This was the first general suspension of specie (gold and silver coins) payments during the state-chartered banking era, except for certain bank failures and regional difficulties.

Writing in 1840, merchant and statesman Condy Raguet commented:

> Specie disappeared in all the states except those of New England, where the banks, coerced by efficient laws and public opinion combined, continued to fulfill their engagements. . . . [1]

However, it should be noted that, in the words of an early writer, in addition to New England, there was "the sole exception of the Bank of Nashville, the steady honesty of whose directors, amid such general knavery, is not less praiseworthy than it is remarkable."[2]

The preceding is quoted simply to reflect that, in most situations involving banking, one rule did not fit all players. In various economic *panics,* as they came to be known (those of 1837 and 1857 being especially memorable in the annals of state-chartered banks studied in the present text), while there were many failures, there were also some banks that experienced profitability.[3]

After late summer 1814, silver and gold coins remained available in the hands of specie brokers, exchange offices, and even banks, but they were not available for face value in exchange for paper bills. Instead, they were traded at a premium, at figures that varied constantly—both by time and by location. Thus, a Spanish-American dollar might trade at one value in New York City on a given day and a few cents higher or lower in Boston or Charleston that day.

An interesting example is provided by the exchange rates in Connecticut. In October 1814, it cost an 11% premium, payable in paper money of sound banks, to acquire specie. In February 1815, when knowledge that the War of 1812 had been peacefully concluded was circulated in the United States, the premium dropped to just 4%. It was thought that normal banking would soon be resumed. However, this did not happen, and in July 1815 the premium rose to 15%.[4] A later writer on the subject noted that during the war the premium on specie varied from 5% to 21-1/2% in Baltimore and from 2% to 16% in New York City.[5]

Copper cents, once ubiquitous, disappeared. During this period not only did the value of gold and silver coins fluctuate, as noted, but also the values of currency issued by a given bank varied. It became the business of exchange brokers to be aware of as many of these situations as possible and to profit in trading. Every large town and city had such brokers, and many bank cashiers engaged in the same activity.

In 1815, although there was peace across the land, the maritime trade had not yet resumed to any extent. Accordingly, as no coins circulated at par (except in New England, and there only in exchange for good New England bills) and as they were not needed for export, mintages dropped to virtually the vanishing point. Mint Director Robert Patterson's report to President James Madison, January 1, 1816, for the year 1815, included this information:

> I have the honor, at this time, of laying before you, a report of the operations of the Mint, during the past year.
>
> From the statement of the treasurer, herewith transmitted, it will appear that during that period there have been struck at the Mint—in gold coins, 635, amounting to 3,175 dollars. . . .

> The high price of gold and silver bullion, for some time past, in the current paper money of the country, has prevented, and as long as this shall continue to be the case, must necessarily prevent deposits of these metals being made for coinage, to any considerable amount. But a fresh supply of copper having lately been received at the Mint, we have again resumed the coinage of cents; and it is believed that we shall, in the course of the year, should no failure in the expected supply of copper take place, be fully able to coin fifty tons weight, amounting to nearly 47,000 dollars; and that with a regular supply of copper, which can readily be procured on terms highly advantageous to the government, we can continue to coin fifty tons per annum, as long as it may be judged expedient.
>
> These copper coins, and of those heretofore issued, from the Mint (amounting to 251,646 dollars), and which be still nearly all in the country, would, it is presumed, soon supply, in a great measure, the place of the small silver coins, which have now almost totally disappeared.[6]

On December 31, 1815, gold bullion on hand at the Mint amounted in value to $721.19. This figure included gold coins valued at $3.87-1/2, apparently representing foreign pieces.[7] Silver coins valued at 6-1/4¢ was on hand, this seemingly representing a *single* Spanish-American half-bit or *medio.*

COINS EXPORTED

During the period of specie suspension but after the War of 1812, although coins were not needed yet for maritime commerce, there were calls for coins from foreign countries due to fluctuations in exchange rates. Banks, exchange brokers, and others who held large amounts of older silver and gold coins continued to profit in a lively trade.

Niles' Weekly Register, July 15, 1815, included this note:

> Specie—Two vessels that lately sailed from Boston for England carried away 500,000 dollars in specie. It is from 28 to 34% advance in that country, compared with Bank of England notes. The people of Boston are getting seriously alarmed about what they so lately prided themselves upon—that, by the "events of the war," they had accumulated much specie, and they have reason to be so.
>
> If the Boston banks were to do business like other banks, they would not have a dollar in 2 or 3 months. With all their pomposity, money is scarcer in Boston than in any part of the United States, and the banks pay specie, because they let few of their notes go into circulation. A history of their *management* is interesting, and we expect to give it at length.

Editor Hezekiah Niles, based in Baltimore, was no fan of the Boston way of banking. In contrast to many other areas, the banks in Boston made a strong effort to maintain the integrity of their paper money. Certain of Niles's thoughts were not clearly expressed, at least in terms of modern understanding. Earlier, during the war, he printed many remarks and accounts concerning New Englanders who privately profited in illegal trading with the enemy, including secretly shipping large amounts of gold and silver coins to Canada under various pretenses. Niles never forgot these doings, and on May 18, 1816, this report was printed in his popular paper:

> *The tide turning.* It is stated that certain persons in New-York have recently demanded and received of the Boston banks, half a million of dollars. . . . It is just as impossible that, in a state of peace and of regular commerce, Boston should be the grand depot for the precious metals in the United States, as that "water should run uphill."
>
> A little while before the war it was as rare to see a specie dollar in the common business of life in Massachusetts, as it was to see an eagle in the middle or southern states—and so it will be again, or like causes will fail to produce like effects, which we do not suppose is very probable. We may forgive, but cannot forget the *enemy* proceedings of the banks and monied men at Boston, and trust they will be taught virtue by suffering that which they themselves inflicted on their country and countrymen.

In the president's annual message to Congress, made this year on December 3, 1816, a report from late Secretary of the Treasury A.J. Dallas was transmitted, noting that due to the absence of coins in circulation, the Treasury had been forced to accept local paper money in various areas, "or abandon the hope of collecting revenue in any convertible medium, for satisfying the public engagements." Only a few such notes were worth par value. Despite the desire of the government to obtain coins in payments due to it,

> There was no magic in a mere Treasury instruction to the collectors of the revenue, which could by its own virtue, charm gold and silver again into circulation. The people, individually, did not possess a metallic medium, and could not be expected to procure it.

Although specie payments were generally resumed by banks in 1817 and 1818, sometimes payment was limited to the exchange of lower-denomination bills only, or there might be a limit on how many bills could be redeemed at a given time. The Spanish-American 8-*real* coin remained the world's standard coin for use in trade, and these continued to sell for a premium in terms of paper money, these items from *Niles' Weekly Register* reflecting the scenario:

October 17, 1818: *Spanish dollars* appear to be in great demand at this moment, and every art is essayed by speculators to drain the vaults of the banks of their contents. The cause of the demand for it will be understood, when it is stated, that specie is, at New York City, and in other commercial cities proportionally, at 7 percent above par.—being bought up at that price for the purpose of exportation, not only in the regular course of the East India trade, but also to Europe. Specie is said to be above par in all the ports of Europe, in some of them even higher than in this country. From the *National Intelligencer.* Spanish dollars at Boston, 6-1/2 to 7 percent premium.

November 7, 1818: *Specie.* So great is the present rage for the East India and China trade, that Spanish dollars are at about 9 percent premium, over the best bank notes—American dollars are not quite so high, though extensively used in this traffic, in which we are altogether willing to wish that many may *"burn their fingers,"* for it certainly is disadvantageous to us. Coin also bears a high premium in every European country much blessed with a paper currency. France is the least plagued with discounts and premiums.

United States silver dollars dated 1794 to 1803 reappeared in circulation, and would be used for the next generation, although they were minted in smaller quantities than Spanish-American dollars and thus were not seen as often.[8]

During this era, privateers sailed on many areas of the sea. Indeed, during the recent War of 1812 many such vessels had been outfitted in American ports and sailed under the Stars and Stripes, carrying letters of marque or permission to engage in such trade. By this arrangement, an armed ship could seize any vessel, government or private, belonging to an enemy nation, in this case Great Britain. The captured ship, called a *prize* in contemporary accounts, would then be manned by Americans who had been hired for that purpose, sailed to a nearby friendly port, and put up for public auction. The amount realized for the ship and contents would be divided in set fractions among the owners, captain, officers, and crew.

After peace was declared, American privateers furled their sails, but those of other countries continued to roam. This account appeared in *Niles' Weekly Register,* December 12, 1818:

The patriot privateer *Constitution,* from Buenos Ayres and a cruise, arrived at Baltimore, a few days since, with nearly 400,000 dollars in specie—probably taken from a Spanish Indiaman, called the *Castilian,* from Lima for Cadiz, which had about $800,000 in specie, and a most valuable cargo. But the rest of the specie could not be got at, and the prize was manned and sent to Buenos Ayres. She was a ship of 20 guns, and of 800 tons burthen. The privateer is owned, as we are told, by several persons at Buenos Ayres.

Lest privateering seem to the present reader to be an unusual way for the American government to have conducted its affairs in the war, it is to be remembered that ships of the U.S. Navy were relatively few in number and were busy on other assignments. Privateers did great service on behalf of the country and interdicted many commercial and military goods that would not have been taken otherwise. Authorized naval raiders and privateers would continue to be used, including in the Civil War. Investors in Portsmouth, New Hampshire; Baltimore; and other ports financed privateer vessels and their crews and generally gained large profits.

After the resumption of specie payments in 1817, the coins in domestic commerce remained essentially the same mix as earlier—mostly foreign coins, dominated by Spanish-American issues, plus a limited quantity of United States silver and gold. By this time, copper cents were plentiful again, as they had been before 1815.

It should also be said that an examination of early bank records reveals that many, if not most, of the established institutions had sufficient specie on hand to have resumed payments significantly before 1817. This fact is reflected in a comment by historian Richard Hildreth, who, like the majority of early writers on finance, was vehemently against the proliferation of paper money:

The suspension it was said, was to continue only during the War. Peace came in five months, but the banks gave not the slightest indication of any desire to return to honest courses. The people, not well acquainted with the subject, purposely puzzled and misled by the specious[9] arguments of the bank directors, and deceived by the apparent prosperity of business, under this new system of banking, did not move in the matter. . . .

A silver dollar of 1802 of the Draped Bust obverse, Heraldic Eagle reverse style. These were common in circulation after the War of 1812 but had not been minted for more than a decade. Half dollars, which were made in large quantities, took the place of dollars in many transactions.

> The banks therefore went on to suit themselves, and the years 1815 and 1816 may be well marked in the calendar as the jubilee of swindlers and the saturnalia of non specie-paying banks. Throughout the whole country, New England excepted, it required no capital to set up a bank. All that was wanted was a charter, and influential politicians easily obtained charters from the blind party confidence, or interest votes of the state legislatures. A whole batch of these banks was created in Kentucky by a single act and other states did the same thing.
>
> These banks, all through the country, immediately commenced lending their paper. . . . This over-issue of notes soon produced a depreciation. Depreciation produced a rise in prices, the apparent value of all kinds of property suddenly went up, and the people imagined they were never growing rich so fast.[10]

While the preceding is overstated, and while one could not start banks with reckless abandon just anywhere (except New England), it is true that specie payments could have been resumed earlier. However, from the bankers' point of view, which has merit, paying out specie would have depleted their stocks quickly, at which time bank balance sheets would have nothing in the way of this highly prized asset to show as evidence of their strength. Moreover, the depletion of specie would have threatened the soundness of the bank itself. The amount of specie listed on a balance sheet was always a mark of a bank's strength, and strong banks were always a boon to commerce.

Economics has been called the *dismal science* by some, and it certainly is highly theoretical. History is subject to very wide interpretations, as various cited commentaries in this book reflect. To reiterate, the writer's view is that in most instances bankers who did not pay out specie were not *bad* or acting with criminal intent, per popular history, but were simply trying to preserve the integrity of their institutions amidst tumultuous national economic conditions beyond their control.

FOCUS ON SCRIP OF 1815 AND 1816

In 1815, when *all* coins disappeared from circulation, many stores, factories, and other entities issued bills of fractional amounts, from a cent up to a half dollar, this in addition to regular values such as $1, $2, $3, and $5. Such denominations as 6-1/4¢, 12-1/2¢, and 37-1/2¢ were popular, among others. These odd values reflected the earlier widespread use of the 2-*real*, or two bits generally reckoned at 25¢, and related coinage, including the 1-*real* at 12-1/2¢ and the quarter real, or *medio*, at 6-1/4¢. Although the United States had its own copper half cent denomination, these were never popular with the public and thus had not been coined since 1811.

As these fractional bills were needed in a hurry, most were made up quickly by local print shops. The typical bill for, say, 25¢ consisted of the name of the issuer (such as a bank or merchant), the geographical location, and often a day, month, and year date. Most were signed by a bank cashier or clerk, and nearly all were serially numbered in ink.

Relatively few fractional bills were printed by bank-note firms, but of those that were, Murray, Draper, Fairman & Co. of Philadelphia seems to have had most of the business, this fact reflected by such bills surviving today. No doubt, the Murray partnership offered quick service, something not always possible for larger bills with vignettes. It is sometimes the case that if a bank paid out fractional and small bills, these were produced locally, while the larger denominations used by the same bank were made by engravers and printers in a distant city, Philadelphia being the center of the bank-note trade at the time.

Most such small bills, called *scrip,* sometimes *shinplasters,* circulated only in the area in which they were issued. A 25¢ bill redeemable in Cincinnati had no value at all in Baltimore or Savannah.

A commentary on bills in circulation, especially of small denominations, was penned by Hezekiah Niles for the October 5, 1816, issue of his newspaper:

> "Yesterday (says a New-York paper of the 27th) all the banks and brokers of this city commenced paying, *in specie,* all sums under a dollar. By this means the small paper trash will gradually disappear."
>
> Yes—and when the good banks re-commence the payment of specie for their notes, a vast quantity of larger "trash in circulation," under the imposing and once respectable character of bank bills, will also "gradually disappear." It is by specie payments, only, that the money can be purged of its "trash."
>
> But the banks, when they re-commence specie payments, will be exceedingly pressed. Everyone that holds a note will be anxious to convert it into specie, and the "run" will be oppressive—much more so, I believe, than it would be if a little *policy* were pursued. The time has been when, except with a few misers and hoarders of money (of no consequence in a general view), bank notes were considered in the same light as specie, under the *idea* that they were always convertible into it, on demands; and this confidence must be restored before the banks can do a business advantageous to their stockholders or the community. . . .

It is not until the 1st of July 1817 that there is a prospect of specie payments becoming general in the middle, southern, and western states. . . . Whether there is or is not as much specie in the United States now as there was before the war is a matter disputed—but it is certain that the people have a much greater desire to possess it now than they did then. Relieve them of this *desire,* and the expected pressure on the banks will also be relieved.

The superior value of specie over a note issued by a good bank is more in idea than in fact—yet the idea operates as a fact, for coin bears a premium. I would therefore attack the *idea* and lessen the weight of the *fact.*

This might be done with considerable effect, if the banks were, occasionally, to throw out a few hard dollars, not of compulsion, any more than they do now, but voluntarily, and I would say, *capriciously*—as if to show that they placed no *particular* value upon them. They would thus, in some degree, bring the public mind back to what it was, and the "run" upon them would be avoided in exact proportion to as this was effected. The distribution of one thousand dollars in this way before the time for specie payments arrives, would save to them ten thousand when it does arrive. For the people, having become *familiar* with specie, would cease their ardent wish to possess it, in preference to approved notes.

The preceding idea can be called wishful thinking. At all times—an apparently inviolable rule—the payment or retention of specie was determined by the *profit* involved and the reputation for soundness that a bank desired to preserve, not by altruistic considerations.

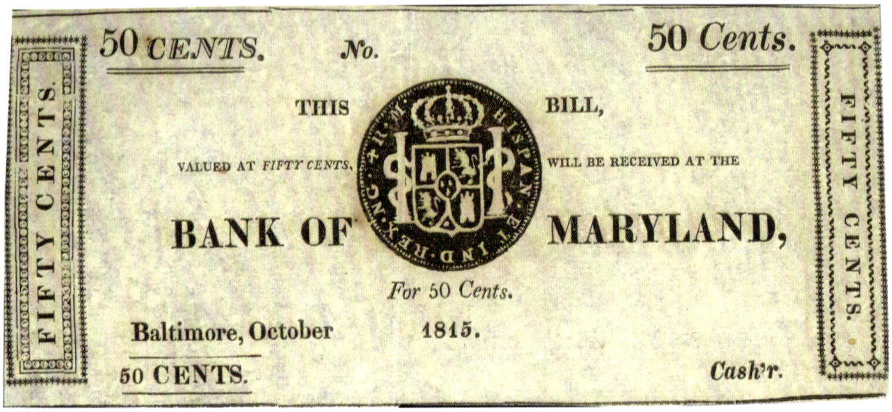

Fractional bill for 50¢ issued by the Bank of Maryland in 1815 (shown enlarged). A Spanish four-bit coin is illustrated on the note. Such scrip, as it was called, was usually turned out by local printers, not bank-note engraving firms.

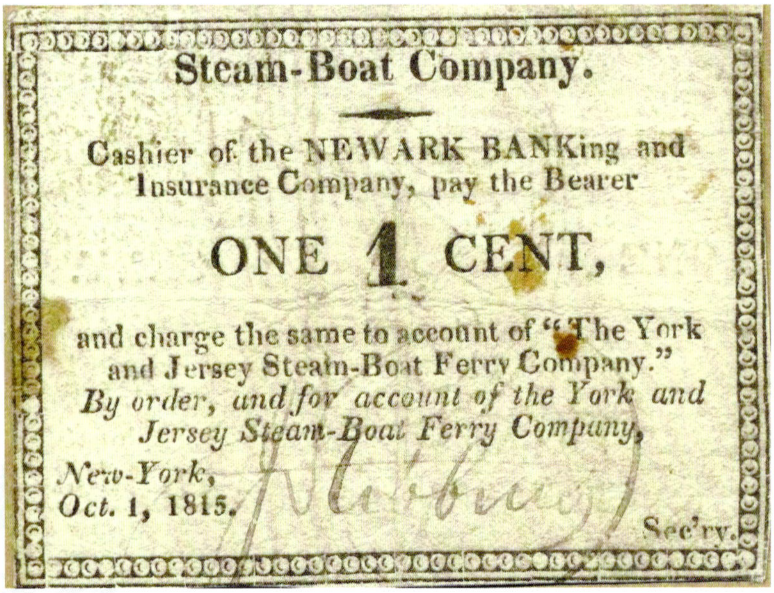

A 1¢ scrip note of 1815 (shown enlarged) that has several numismatic appeals, being connected to New York City, the Newark Bank(ing and Insurance Company), and a steamboat ferry.

Founded in 1804, this bank was one of many that conducted another business in addition to banking, in this instance writing insurance. The response to the organization of the bank was so great that an iron-bound wooden box proved inadequate to hold all of the money deposited, and it was taken to New York City and entrusted with the Manhattan Company. Not long afterward the bank put up its own money and the funds were repatriated. The initial capital was listed as $400,000, then increased in 1836 to $700,000, of which slightly more than $500,000 had been paid in. By that time Newark had become a port for oceangoing vessels, bringing prosperity to the district. The enterprise remained profitable and years later (June 24, 1865) evolved into the National Newark Banking Company, charter 1316.

NILES'S SUMMARY OF THE PAPER MONEY SCENE

Because *Niles' Weekly Register* was the most widely read newspaper on finance and events in America at the time, the editor's comments are particularly interesting to review today, reflecting as they do the scene through his eyes. Most writers of the period were anti–paper money, with a seemingly endless series of news items reflecting bank failures, counterfeiting, reduction in value of bills, and more problems. In fact, one would be hard pressed today to find a single cogent contemporaneous explanation by a national writer to advance the issuance of more paper money.

However, the practical need for a useful medium of exchange took precedence, and state legislators often felt that if a bank was established in a bankless town, and it issued paper money, the general level of prosperity and commerce would be raised considerably. Promoting this concept were the backers of such banks, often very influential in politics.

The years of 1818 and 1819 saw a slump in the American economy, not deep enough to be called a panic but still very stressful—the greatest era of bank problems except for the panics of 1837 and 1857. The 1818-1837-1857 sequence would seem to indicate a 20-year cycle of such slumps.

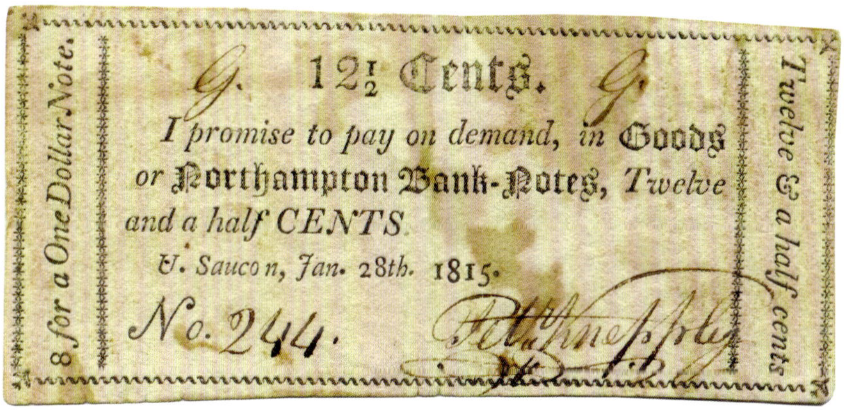

Generic scrip note (shown enlarged) that apparently could be issued by different people, who then signed in ink. Dated January 28, 1815, this 12-1/2¢ bill was issued in Upper Saucon, Pennsylvania. Although scrip notes flooded the country at the time, today as a class they are fairly scarce on the numismatic market.

Scrip note for 10¢ issued by the Phoenix Bank of Hartford, Connecticut (shown enlarged). Interestingly, this bill is payable two years after the end of the war. Unknown to Americans at the time, the war had ended in December 1814. However, the Battle of New Orleans was fought in early 1815, and this scrip note bears testimony to the same lack of information. (See chapter 18 for an illustration of a Phoenix Bank $2 note and a sketch of the bank's history.)

Here is Hezekiah Niles's essay on currency, dated June 12, 1819, in the depth of the current slump:[11]

PAPER MONEY:
The Past, the Present, and the Future

For several years the people of the United States have been rioting on expedients. If a community *wanted* money, it had nothing to do but to *make* a bank. If an individual desired it, he was only required to sign his name to a piece of paper, provided always, the bank-makers thought he was able to meet the obligation.

Millions on millions were daily passed from one hand to another, without much reality in them, save in *anticipated facilities.* Those worth a thousand dollars fearlessly signed for tens of thousands, and others worth ten thousand put down their names for hundreds of thousands. Paper—credit—a directorship or a cashiership in a bank, or a father, brother, cousin or friend, who was a director or a cashier, was the test of respectability!

Sign away, was the word—and it was generally calculated that one debt might be paid by the creation of another! The people were wild—they acted as if a day of reckoning never would come. They bought plantations and country seats; built stately houses and furnished them in the most costly manner; had their coaches and coachmen, feasts and tea-parties—despising industry and economy, and indulging themselves in all sorts of extravagance.

Money, so called, was obtained so easily that few felt the value of it, and we seldom encountered the disagreeable idea that it was not our own!

"Financiering"

Everything was to be done by management—by "financiering" as Jacob Barker says, speaking of the "millions" which he had passed through his hands—or, in plain English, by "causing one rag to do the business of another rag."

Thousands were striving to get to the top of the wheel—to lead the fashion, or rival its prodigality. The country had the appearance of the highest prosperity. The old comfortable farm house was converted into a kitchen for a new mansion, and palaces took the place of cottages. In the cities, every thing was pell mell—reason seemed turned topsy turvy: $15 a yard for cloth for a coat, $9 or $10 for a shawl; $8 or $10 for a gallon of wine, and $50 for a bonnet—town houses—country houses—style—ALL OF PAPER.

The sober and discreet were thrown aside as vulgar folks—creatures without spirit; mere animals—but necessary drudges, producing something to keep the system a-going. Arbitrary distinctions were raised in a society—the borrower of $100,000 was a gentleman of rank; the farmer and mechanic worth $10,000 was nothing; a nobility was fixing itself upon us. The president of a bank, (if bankrupt so much the better!) possessed a mansion more elegant than that of many German princes—and I am told that one merchant who lately failed to the eastward, yet lives in a house for which, and its furniture, he was offered $200,000 in real money, and refused it! Such is a faint picture of the past.

The people thus placed on end, like idle boys put up bricks in a row, looked very promising; but they were out of their natural order, and stood upon a sandy foundation.

Reality

Paper alone could not any longer do the business for them—discounts and interests, with the shaving of bank notes, had eaten up the substance which they possessed before the rage for *signing their names* operated upon them—and one is knocking down another at such a rate as never was heard of before.

Scenes of speculation are revealed, and revealing, that sober people had no idea of. Their effect penetrates through all classes of society—the day-laborer feels it, and suffers, because Mr. Highflyer could sign his name prettily, and thereby cause his paper to pass through *some* of the banks! The farmer who *improved* his plantation by building a costly dwelling, on credit, is compelled to sell both farm and dwelling to pay the debts uncured in erecting the house! A pipe of wine or a cashmere shawl compels some merchants to stop payment.

I have heard of one man who failed for more than $500,000, whose private wine vault, as it stood at the time of his bankruptcy, was estimated to have cost him $7,000. This is said to have happened in the sober city of Philadelphia.

National industry has been paralyzed, and the balance of trade against us makes a mighty amount. It is true, that John Bull will suffer severely by the latter, but in accomplishing the former he will be a gainer in the end.[12] Our manufactories must very generally stop, unless aid is afforded them at the next session of Congress—and tens of thousands of the productive classes will be thrown into the useless and consuming.

Money is scarce, because so much of its representative has been spent on things that cannot now be converted into it—it wants circulation, because confidence is lost and those who have it know not how to part with it safely. The banks, resolved to pay their debts, cannot discount, because few debts are paid to them. If they can stand as they are, they will do very well. No demand for cotton, tobacco or bread stuffs abroad, except at such prices as we cannot afford to raise them at, in the present manners of the times. . . .

Predictions

We have heretofore said that fashion, or pride, wastes more than convenience wants. We are now about to pay for the "whistle." A season of unparalleled distress is arriving; the worst will soon be upon us, and then—things will mend. What ought the people to do for future safety? Speculators have had their day, and the end is exactly what we long ago predicted—such as every reflecting man saw it would be. Now is the time that honest men should combine, to force and sustain a most wholesome purgation.

The war of rags [paper money] against property has had its turn, or is now raging, and will yet rage severely. It must have its course—there is no help for it, any protraction of its consummation will only increase the difficulties heaped upon us, through our own foolish acts or the suffering of folly in others. Any relief afforded by the issue of a new kind of paper money, will only tempt new speculations, and raise up a new race of gamesters, to inflict new calamities, and perish like their predecessors. I am aware that on account of this sentiment, as well as for others which I have lately advanced, there are some who may think me cold to the miseries of my fellow citizens. . . .

It is freely admitted, that the banks, en masse, cannot pay their debts; but there are enough who can pay them, to afford us a criterion of value that will not deceive us. Others, whose discounts have been monopolized by their presidents, directors, and cashiers, and half-dozens of favorites, will go by the board—and they ought to go. The first should be protected and the latter destroyed. . . .

When *two hundred* in the U.S. are dissolved the rest will be able to give us a wholesome currency, in sufficient quantities, and we shall hardly find knots of managers whose discounts and overdrawings amount to more than the capital of their institutions; as now is the case perhaps, in many instances.

We shall have fewer "rag barons"—but ease and comfort will be diffused through society; and economy, superadded to the terror of speculation, secure the future happiness of the people. Let us then resist every succedaneum that may give rise to fresh gamblings in paper. It is the laboring people who at last must pay the losses made by them. They should resolve to bear with, and forbear, for a few months, rather than saddle subsequent productiveness as triumphant seats for new marauders. All that we will have suffered again—if we yield one inch to the monopolizers. The instant that bank notes are no longer the representatives of specie, we shall have a new bank for every day in the year. It is cash payments, only, that can defend the people from swindling banks and bankers.

Bank News

While specie payments had been resumed by many banks by the time Niles wrote this somewhat ranting commentary, it still remained difficult for citizens to exchange bills for coins in some districts.

Occasionally, *Niles' Weekly Register* contained details on the status of specific banks, questionable and otherwise; the item that follows is from the issue of September 11, 1819. However, coverage was erratic, and the editor would often turn his attention to other things and not tell readers what happened later:

> Lexington, Ky. Aug. 25.—Since our last the following have been added to the list of doubtful banks, viz: Georgetown, Shelbyville, Carlisle, Springfield, Burkeville. The list now stands thus: Burlington, Petersburgh, Barboursville, Somerset, Russellville, Hopkinsville, Springfield, Lebanon, Shelbyville, Georgetown, Burksville, Green River, Greenville, Carlisle, Morgantown, Columbia.
>
> The notes of the banks of Springfield, Burkeville, Carlisle, Hopkinsville, Somerset and Greenville, are believed to be good—we have not been able to ascertain that they have forfeited their charters by refusal to pay their notes, and it is said they continue to do business. Nor can we state that all the others on the list are insolvent—on the contrary we are inclined to think, that most of them will be able to wind up by redeeming their notes. But it is sufficient that they are uncurrent to subject the holders to loss.
>
> Public confidence seems to have been almost entirely withdrawn from the independent banks—the notes of the following only are bankable here [in Baltimore, where the *Register* was published], viz. Lancaster Exporting Company, Louisville Commercial Bank, Versailles, Frankfort, Bardstown, and Flemingsburg. The notes of a few others are received at the banks in payment of debts.

The Problem of Small-Denomination Bills

In the second decade of the 19th century and at other times—indeed, almost continuously until the start of the Civil War—small-denomination currency was a subject of great debate. It was universally felt that given a choice, people preferred coins. Indeed, this is a truism not susceptible to serious challenge during any

Note for $5 on the Farmers & Mechanics Bank of Cincinnati, signed and dated July 20, 1816. The copper plate was engraved by William Harrison, a Philadelphia engraver who produced many different bills for various banks in Ohio and surrounding regions.

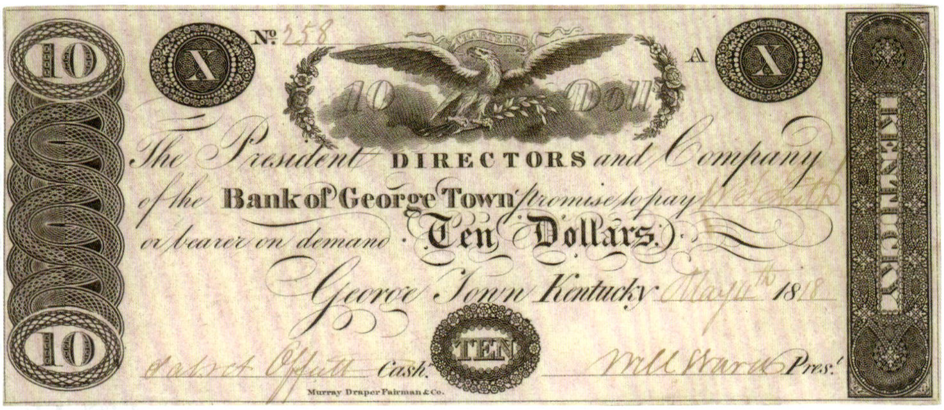

The Bank of George Town, Kentucky, failed in 1819 and was included in an account of Kentucky banks in *Niles' Weekly Register,* September 11, 1819. This $10 note by Murray, Draper, Fairman & Co., Philadelphia, became worthless.

time in the era here studied. If a citizen had a $5 gold piece and a $5 bill of the Farmers Bank and wanted to make a $5 purchase, he would spend the bill and keep the coin.

Similarly, considering paper alone, if he were savvy as to the value among bills, and if the Farmers Bank was solid and exchanged its notes for specie but the Pelican Bank was located in some town he never heard of and was of uncertain stability, a $5 bill of the Pelican Bank would be the first to be spent, and the Farmers Bank bill would be retained.

It was felt by many legislators, newspaper writers, and economic specialists (few and far between at the time) that if laws were passed prohibiting the use of small bills, then coins would automatically appear in circulation and would be used widely. Over a period of time *many* state laws were enacted prohibiting banks from issuing bills of values less than $5, and some proposals called for a ban on values less than $20. However, these laws had little practical effect.

Of this situation, Condy Raguet wrote the following:

> In France, where no bank note is allowed to be issued of a less denomination than 500 francs (equal to about $94 of our money), the whole of the retail transactions of a community of 30,000,000 people, nearly double our population, are carried on by coins of precious metals.
>
> In England no note of a less denomination than five pounds sterling (equal to $24 and upwards) can be issued by the Bank of England, or by any joint-stock or private bank—so that in that country too, the minor channels of circulation are kept well filled with gold. . . .
>
> By the exclusion of all notes of a less denomination than $10 the security of our paper currency would be greatly strengthened in case of an unexpected panic. . . .[13]

Raguet's narrative was ideal in concept but impractical in application in the United States. Indeed, a law such as what he suggested was passed in Pennsylvania during the decade here discussed. As of October 1, 1818, here is what happened:

> The banks of Pennsylvania, having ceased to issue notes of a less denomination than $5, the neighboring states of Delaware, New Jersey, and New York sent an abundant supply, and the chief effect of the law appeared to be, not to give a circulation of specie in the place of small notes, but to fasten upon the citizens a set of notes not known to the public for another set that was known.[14]

The American economy recovered slowly in the early 1820s, then became prosperous. Bank notes were exchangeable at par with silver coins (gold coins remained undervalued and were used only for export; none were in circulation). Then came the Panic of 1837, when specie again disappeared from circulation.

Post Notes, Unofficial Banks, and Other Matters

During the era a type of bill called a *post note* achieved limited popularity. Such bills were similar to regular currency in appearance, but stated that they would be redeemed in specie, or in other bills, only after a certain time, such as a year later than the date the bills were issued. Such bills were often sold at a discount to begin with and thus took the form of a loan to the bank for much of the face value stated. As post notes were apt to be issued by those in uncertain or precarious circumstances, or those engaged in projects yet to materialize (such as building a railroad), most became worthless. The idea was hardly new, and many colonial notes were issued with payment promised later, as were all Continental Currency bills and, later, all Confederate States of America bills.

Throughout this time, and in other decades as well, many manufacturing companies, merchants, and others simply went into the banking business without benefit of a state charter; either because such application had been rejected or, more often, it had never been sought. Because of this situation, it will never be possible to determine with certainty the number of note-issuing *official* banks in the United States. The panorama of obsolete currency includes many bills of attractive appearance issued by companies that operated canals, railroads, and other enterprises, or hoped to. Often, the distribution of such bills was a way to raise needed capital, in essence floating loans by one bill at a time.

Conversely, there were many banks that received charters; ordered currency from the printers in New York City, Philadelphia, and elsewhere; but never went into business. In other instances, entrepreneurs hoped to start a bank, ordered thousands of bills, but never went on to apply for a charter.

The Study of Economic History and Currency

By this point in text, the reader must realize that obsolete currency has a remarkably rich and complex history with much opportunity for further research. Today, bills from real banks, from unchartered banks, and from would-be banks that never materialized are all widely sought by numismatists.

It seems to me, but is generally overlooked in many *modern* American economic texts, that periods of specie-payment suspensions spawned much inflation. The prices of goods and services rose in terms of *paper money,* but when coin payments were resumed, prices did not necessarily return to their former lower levels. In the bank-note issuing era under discussion, widespread specie-payment suspensions took place from 1814 to 1819, from 1821 to 1834 (gold coins only), from 1837 to 1839 (for some banks even later), from 1862 to 1876 (for silver coins), and 1878 (gold).

The late Louis E. Eliasberg Sr., who knew more about American financial history than any other numismatist of my acquaintance, attributed the inflation of American prices of recent generations to the suspension of gold coin payments in exchange for bills in 1933, after which time our paper money has not

State Bank at Newark $3 note of January 2, 1818, bearing the imprint of P. Maverick sc, Newark. The *sc* is for *sculpsit*, or *engraved it*. Such bills became popular in Pennsylvania after that state prohibited new issues denominated less than $5. During this time Peter Maverick was a partner with Asher B. Durand in the firm of P. Maverick, Durand & Co., 2 Pine Street, New York City, but had a Newark office.

Portrait of Peter Maverick, one of the most important bank-note engravers in the early 19th century.

been redeemable in gold coins equal in value to the face value of the bills tendered. By that time silver coins had long been depreciated, and although a Silver Certificate was exchangeable for a silver dollar, that coin, if melted, would not yield a dollar's worth of metal. Today, a $100 note is exchangeable only for other bills or for nickel-clad coins, none of which have any intrinsic value. Come to think of it, the situation was about the same during the specie resumption era of the War of 1812 and later![15]

ABEL BREWSTER, INVENTOR

Abel Brewster was a highly important figure in the bank-note engraving field during the early 19th century, an inventor who claimed that Jacob Perkins pirated certain of his ideas. Although today Brewster is little remembered in numismatic circles, he was well known in his time.

Among his early registered patents was one of July 22, 1808, obtained when he was living in Hartford, Connecticut, for a "vitriolic test for making bank bills." Another was of July 15, 1813, datelined Frankfort, Pennsylvania, for "die work instead of etching." He also obtained two when he was back in Hartford, one on July 15, 1816, "to prevent forgery of bank notes" and one on March 6, 1820, for innovations in "ship building." No other pre-1810 Brewster patents have been found, although he may have submitted applications.

In March 1810, Brewster published a pamphlet, *A Plan for Producing an Uniformity in the Ornamental Part of Bank or Other Bills.* At the time he was in Philadelphia working with Murray & Draper, bank-note engravers.

Brewster's text provides an interesting reflection of his ideas, his resentment of alleged infringer Jacob Perkins, the employment of John Reich (assistant engraver at the Mint), and more. His critique of the Perkins Patent Stereotype Plate cuts to the core of the generally unstated problem of that popular system. Per the narrative, as Perkins had claimed exclusive right to use punches to put small letters in dies, Brewster planned to use engraving tools for "chasing" and/or vitriol (sulfuric acid) for etching, seemingly a more complicated process. As is the case with most early patent applications, dissertations, and commentaries by various engravers, Brewster's thoughts are not always easy to follow.[16]

A post note issued by the Farming & Commercial Bank of Carlisle, Kentucky, with inked inscription noting it was payable 180 days after November 24, 1819. By Murray, Draper, Fairman & Co., Philadelphia.

Proof impression of a $100 post note of the Phenix Bank, New York City, from a plate by Peter Maverick, second decade of the 19th century.

BREWSTER'S PLAN

Objections to the Steel Plate System

Plates made up of various pieces, as the steel plates generally are, afford many and obvious facilities to counterfeiting: the pieces may be made of various kinds of metal, to accommodate different methods of imitating the various kinds of work or parts of the bill; when an error happens in the course of executing, it simply subjects the piece containing of it, to be altered or made over, and not the whole plate: and even after the bills are put in circulation and any conspicuous error detected, by altering or making over the piece containing of it, the public might be deceived again, and again.

Besides, if it should be an object, one such plate would counterfeit bills of all the different banks in a State, by just adding their several names and places, which are contained on pieces. Steel plates tend greatly to increase the temptation to counterfeit. As there is very little difference betwixt making or imitating a bill on steel, than on copper, and when done, one steel plate would produce bills enough, of the common size, to make the fortunes for a great number of undertakers, and in case bills from steel plates were in general use, they would not attract singular attention if they were scattered out for ten, fifteen, or twenty years.

Where the bills have the same general appearance throughout, to an extensive degree, as from steel plates, after being seen a few times, they cease to attract particular attention, and counterfeits, by having the same general appearance, gain currency thereby.

Visiting the Patent Office

As Mr. Perkins, the maker of certain bills used to the eastward [New England], has scrupled my right to use *punches* to produce the standard figures in plates as infringing his patent, I therefore beg leave to trouble the reader with a few particulars relative thereto, which was not in my power to state in former communications—that those who regard justice, may not scruple to patronize this plan, and that they may not encourage the trespass or infringement, which Mr. Perkins is now practicing on my right.

It is necessary to state that before I solicited a patent, I went to Washington City for the purpose of ascertaining the bounds of my right, and on application to Dr. Thornton, secretary of the Patent Department, was informed that my plan did not interfere with anything specified in his office, and that I had an undoubted right to use *punches.* And further, according to recollection, he informed me that everything previously patented for the purpose of preventing counterfeiting had proved worthless and been abandoned.

It now appears from information obtained from said Secretary, that there never has been a patent granted from that Office, to anyone, for "STEREOTYPE." And therefore it appears, as published by Mr. Perkins, a libel.

Alleged Deceptions by Perkins

It further appears that about 11 years since, Mr. Perkins obtained a patent for what he called a "check die," a punch, making the words "public utility" in a circular form, with white lines across the letters. This was soon counterfeited, and abandoned, and a distinct line drawn by Mr. Perkins, between that and what he afterwards pursued.[17]

This distinction was made in a pamphlet, which Mr. Perkins published about the year 1804, wherein he says that "three years have elapsed since bills from 'stereotype plates' have been circulating, and no attempt has been known to have been made to counterfeit them." But he knew that bills bearing the impression of his "check die" had been much longer in circulation and had been counterfeited, and the use of the die had been abandoned. . . .

Mr. Perkins's "check die" is a simple, definite, and limited thing; and which required no great skill to produce; nor had any more to do with the making of bills than the supervisor's stamp that has sometimes been put on. But his "stereotype plates" are complex and extensive, and his method of producing the same, is tedious and critical.

Perkins's Introduction of the Stereotype Plate in 1806

Long after I had devised this plan, commenced the course to secure a patent, and got the plan into use, Mr. Perkins modified his make of bills, from a partial and doubtful uniformity, and took possession of the principal benefits of this plan, as if there had been no laws or sense of justice in the country.

This he did under the frivolous pretext that he had attempted something of the kind, "as early as the year 1805." But, it may be remarked, that however great Mr. Perkins's necessity was for using such an improvement in the making of his bills, he had not—but actually continued to have the mere ornamental part etched directly into the plates as usual, until the latter part of the year 1806, if not longer, and which was long after I had devised this plan.

This infringement on my right, has been peculiarly aggravated by a course of policy which followed it up, on the part of Mr. Perkins, not more cunning than disingenuous.

Brewster's Innovations

It is not for any particular method of perpetuating the ornaments and effecting the uniformity that I claim an exclusive privilege, but for making the mere ornamental part of different bills uniform, by plates, types or vehicles reserved exclusively for communicating the same on to the bills, and a considerable part of chase or vitriolic work (which will distinguish a great variety of objects in form, color, or manner as may please) with the particulars of every different bill incorporated therewith, and furnishing the public with a printed copy thereof, for the mere purpose of TESTING the Bills.

I have shown it to be practicable to produce this uniformity by two different methods, and lodged specifications of the same in the Patent Office, and possibly others might be devised.

Perhaps it would be impossible to please everyone with the same ornaments. I am sensible the present might be greatly improved in beauty and excellence. I have labored under many disadvantages in doing what has already been done. However, if the plan generally merits encouragement, the work may be carried to immense perfection, manifesting as much skill *or* ingenuity as anything that was ever made on a bill and any alterations or regulations made that public good may require.

John Reich Hired to Assist

It is very desirable that all the bank bills in the United States should be made uniform, in a considerable part. If some of the principal banks will agree upon certain ornaments to use as a general standard, and a deposit for the means of communicating the same, the work shall be immediately commenced. Mr. *Reich,* deputy engraver in the Mint, whose taste and abilities as a workman, need no recommendation, has engaged to assist in making ornamental dies, or types, that may be necessary for the promotion of this plan, and with his assistance, I have no doubt of answering every reasonable expectation. . . .

I had it in contemplation to print the ornaments in colors, by a spring type, and have no doubt I might have produced some pretty pictures. However, concluding that ornaments might be counterfeited even if they were printed in colors, and possibly with greater success than usual after the secret was found out, as colors dazzle the sight and are subject to extreme variation from use as a circulating medium, I therefore suspended my operations, and I am fully persuaded that there is nothing superior to good black ink for printing bank bills.

Each bank might have one or more ornamental type or die, made and reserved exclusively to themselves, and use them whether a general standard was adopted or not. Surely it would be important, if only the smallest of the annexed figures were made on the bills.

Used by the Hartford Bank

The Hartford Bank (Conn.) has had bills in very extensive circulation since the year 1807 (the first made according to this plan), and I have never learned that any of them have been counterfeited, although the work was much inferior to the present, and numerous other bills have been counterfeited during the same term of time. I do not mention this as affording conclusive evidence, but as an argument in favor of the plan. . . .

The price of plates impressed with these dies, and finished ready for the engraver, will be ten dollars for every entire impression, and proportionally for plates impressed with any one, or number of them, and anything for the promotion of this plan, will be done reasonable.

By incorporating the denomination of the bills with the standard figures in the plates, within the six circles at each end of the three large figures, in the two blank ovals, and in the ground work of the engraved device, will effectually guard the bills against *alteration*—so that any other precaution may be taken that the banks may deem necessary.

The centre figure is left out to give more latitude and distinction to an engraved device. Every different impression of the dies, will be designated by letters or figures incorporated with them in the plates. . . .

Testimonials to Brewster's Plan

Brewster circulated his plan among engravers and others and was able to procure some compliments regarding it. On March 23, 1810, John Draper (with whom Brewster was associated in business at the time) wrote this comment:

> I am of opinion that Mr. Brewster's Plan for Bank and other Bills, is more difficult to imitate than any thing I have seen, and intermixed with other engravings will be beneficial, as the notes will require more accomplices for counterfeiting, and of course add to the probability of detection.

Brewster prepared a petition with the following text, to which many prominent men affixed their signatures, the listing being a veritable who's who in the Philadelphia engraving world:

> We do hereby certify, that having examined Mr. Brewster's Plan for Bank or other Bills, we are

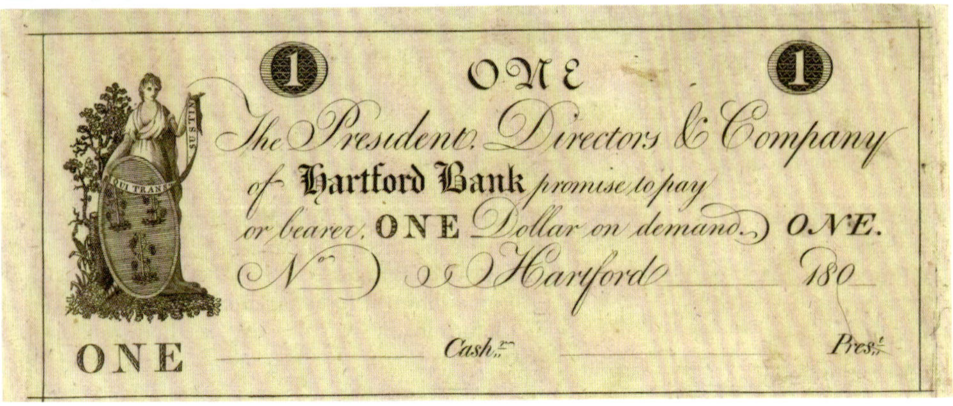

Proof $1 note for the Hartford Bank made toward the end of the first decade of the 19th century, likely by Abel Brewster, as described above. The vignette was from a punch, the details of which had been created in part by acid etching.

Note for $3 of the Huntington Bank, Pennsylvania, engraved and signed by William Kneass, an endorser in 1810 of Abel Brewster's petition and later, from 1824 to 1840, the chief engraver at the Mint.

Detail showing Kneass's name.

> fully of opinion that it is entitled to the merit or advantages which he claims for it.
>
> Robert Scot (engraver, Mint), John Reich, Alexander Lawson, D. Edwin, Samuel Seymour, Cornelius Tiebout, Benjamin Tanner, H.S. Tanner, Josh. H. Seymour, Enoch G. Gridley, William Kneass, William R. Jones.

Interested applicants were invited to contact Abel Brewster at No. 10, Norris's Alley, Philadelphia.

At the time Philadelphia was in the ascendancy as a center for the bank-note engraving business, and the distant Perkins operation in Newburyport, Massachusetts, was a strong competitor, especially for the business generated by banks in New England. Accordingly, certain aspects of the anti-Perkins comments should be viewed in this light.

Numismatic Notes

Bank notes of the second decade of the 19th century are very collectible, especially from banks that failed in 1818 and 1819. There are, to be sure, many rare issues as well, and for some, information is not known today.

Bills that can be specifically ascribed to Abel Brewster's ideas cannot be identified easily today, except that the mentioned issues of the Hartford Bank of 1807 and later are candidates. The etching of vignettes (using acid) was widely practiced. The lines produced were thicker than those created by engraving with a tool on a copper or soft steel plate. Accordingly, acid etching was ideal for depicting ground cover, tree foliage, and the like, but was not well suited for human or allegorical figures, or for any motifs with intricate features. The next chapter continues the discussion of certain currency made in the decade from 1811 to 1820.

Chapter Five

The Work of Abner Reed

Introduction

Among bank-note engravers and printers of the early 19th century, Abner Reed is one of the more prominent figures. Adding to this recognition is the fact that many if not most of his bills bear his name and can be easily identified today. This chapter tells of his life and work and showcases one of his clients, the Vermont Glass Factory.

Early Life

I enjoy studying the life and work of early bank-note and coin-die engravers. Some of these have left long paper (pun) trails, while others are rather obscure. I probably have enough information about Jacob Perkins and W.L. Ormsby to write a *book* on each, and I still keep gathering information.

Among the early engravers for which much information survives is Abner Reed, who often signed his work simply as *Reed* on currency plates.[1] For many years he prepared copper plates and printed bills for banks in the Northeast. Although today his name is well known to collectors of early currency, not much about him has ever appeared in reference books in numismatics. However, there is quite a bit of material out there, especially in archives of early prints and books. The American Antiquarian Society, for one, has a lot of information.

Much of what we know today abut Reed's paper money is from examination of the bills themselves, particularly in connection with material from his scrapbook or specimen book of proof impressions, disassembled and offered by individual notes in the Abner Reed sale of United States paper money, showcased by the Numismatic and Antiquarian Service Corporation of America (NASCA) in 1983 with the descriptions written by Douglas Ball.[2]

Abner Reed was born in East Windsor, Connecticut, on November 11, 1771, the son of Ebenezer and Mary (Fitch) Reed. His education seems to have included elementary and high school, per his recollection of attending a school: "Such was the academical institution in which I received my education, attending three months in the summer until I was eight years old and three months in the winter until I was fifteen years old."[3] Calligraphy was one of Reed's interests if not a pursuit, and there exists a 1786 certificate ornately lettered by his hand.

As a teenager he was apprenticed to a saddler and a supplier of what we know today as tack; his tasks included engraving nameplates on saddles. This work inspired him to learn copperplate engraving, a skill at which he soon achieved success. After his apprenticeship he was offered a local position as a schoolmaster but declined, stating that he wanted to be an engraver. Reed mused that he was planning to take a trip for the summer to New Hampshire, Boston, or New York City, but it is not known whether such a sojourn to these locations took place at the time.

Abner Reed, Engraver

Soon Reed was in Lansingburgh, New York, near Albany. He went to work at his intended profession and soon engraved four plates illustrating scenes of Spanish conquistadors. Later, these illustrated the Reverend W.D. Cooper's book, *The History of South Amer-*

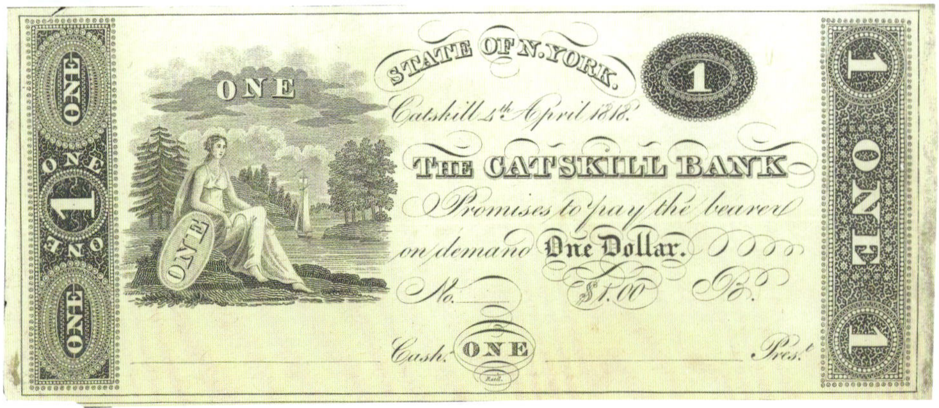

An Abner Reed $1 note for the Catskill Bank, Catskill, New York, dated 4th April 1818 on the plate. (From the Reed scrapbook of proof impressions)

ica. In 1794 he produced two plates depicting the executions of King Louis XVI and Marie Antoinette, timely events in world news. He also created a frontispiece illustrating American and world coins, and he created other scenes, including the allegorical *Navigation, Hope and Fame Inviting Columbus to the Discovery of the New World.*

In 1795 in Lansingburgh he married 14-year-old Elizabeth Loring, this in an era in which it was common for girls to marry in their early teenage years soon after reaching puberty. The union proved to be a happy one. The couple had six children and lived long enough to celebrate their 50th wedding anniversary.

Reed was in New York City for a short time in 1795. During the mid-1790s he is said to have worked, perhaps intermittently, in Albany with silversmiths Isaac and George Hutton. The plates for the first currency issued by the Hartford Bank (chartered in 1792) are said to have been Reed's work.[4] Often, the peregrinations of engravers (both of coin dies and printing plates) are difficult to figure out. Sometimes they lent their names to partnerships in distant cities as a way of receiving orders, but they might never have lived in those places. Town and city directories are of limited help for modern research, as listings are often stale and continue to list people who have moved or died, or overlook existing citizens and businesses. Contemporary documents and newspaper advertisements are better sources, but very little research has been done in these venues.

In late 1797 Abner Reed and his wife moved to East Windsor, Connecticut, re-establishing ties with the scenes of his childhood. In the same year he wrote and published a novel, the first written by a Connecticut author, *Love Triumphant, or Constancy Rewarded.*

In 1798 he was elected a deacon of the Congregational church there, after which he was generally known as Deacon Reed, a designation he enjoyed using among his contemporaries in the engraving profession. During the next several years he worked on bank-note plates, book illustrations, bookplates, and labels, sometimes in connection with Hudson & Goodwin, Hartford printers. Reed also lettered coffins and boxes and applied wood-graining patterns to chairs. As if that were not enough, he was also a farmer.

In 1800 he published *First Step to Learning: or, Little Children's Spelling and Reading Book,* followed in 1801 by a book on penmanship. In 1802 he made many small woodcuts for a new edition of Noah Webster's *American Spelling Book.*

A School for Engravers

In late 1803 in Hartford, Reed set up shop, advertising as an engraver, plate printer, and sign painter. He also continued his work as a book illustrator, completing seven plates for an encyclopedia being prepared by John Low in New York City. During the decade he developed skill in stipple engraving to supplement his standard engraving work. This technique consisted of applying minute dots and curves that, when closely spaced and properly arranged, gave a rich shading to the work. Stipple engraving was considered a special art in itself. A close examination of certain of his engravings seems to reveal that he also employed acid etching.

In 1809 Reed produced two sets of aquatints (a method combining engraving and color) for decorative purposes. In 1810 he turned out a suite of six aquatints depicting Mineral Springs and the Willimantic River, about 15 miles from East Windsor. William Mason, who later achieved recognition as a painter and illustrator, apprenticed with Reed circa 1808 to 1810.[5]

In 1811 Reed moved back to East Windsor. One of the workers in his shop was Edward Bissell, who married a Reed daughter. There was a lot of work to do, and Reed had a group of apprentices and helpers to assist him. One was Samuel Stiles, who later achieved great recognition as an engraver. In 1859, Stiles became treasurer of the American Bank Note Company formed the year before.

John Warner Barber worked in Reed's shop from 1813 to 1819. He went on to success on his own, including creating the "Historical Collection" with various scenes. Oliver Pelton (in the 1830s a principal in Terry, Pelton & Co., Boston and Providence) also studied under Reed. Pelton's future wife, Sarah Wood, may have worked there as well.[6]

Another Reed protégé, Asaph Willard, became a founder of the Graphic Company in Hartford in 1818. Ralph Rawdon, who later became involved in several partnerships culminating with Rawdon, Wright, Hatch & Edson (main component in the formation of the American Bank Note Company in 1858), learned under Reed, as did Lewis Fairchild and William Phelps.

Stonington (Connecticut) Bank $1 note, printed in the 1820s and with the imprint of Reed, Stiles & Co., is ink dated Oct. 20 1831. This bank was a prolific issuer of paper money over a long period, with notes supplied by various firms. Stonington was a whaling port, and many bills feature a nautical vignette, as here.

Continuing Activity

Reed offered a full range of services to his bank-note customers, which by this time were in most states in the Northeast as well as some in what was then known as the American West (beyond Pennsylvania) and to the north in Canada. He and his corps of workers designed and selected the motifs and ornaments, engraved the plates, and printed the bills. When weather permitted, the finished sheets of currency were dried on clotheslines in the back of his shop. What an interesting sight this must have been.

Reed was a man of many business interests in addition to engraving bank-note plates. Certain of his activities included "engraving and printing watch cards and maps, lettering cartridge boxes, graining chairs, making jewels, engraving coffin plates, lettering glass, cutting type and seals, making moulds for beads, making cheese presses, and repairing umbrellas."[7]

A particularly grand project—the largest engraving of his career—was a map of Connecticut dated 1812, commissioned by the state's General Assembly and ordered through Hudson & Goodwin, Hartford printers. The finished work involved the use of several plates to create a map measuring 43-1/4 by 18-3/8 inches. Finished copies were tinted by watercoloring, then framed.

Deacon Abner Reed's trade prospered, and he became a man of means. He took time to follow other pursuits of interest, serving as representative from East Windsor to the General Assembly in Hartford from 1817 to 1828, holding the position of town clerk from 1825 to 1834, and remaining prominent in religious and civic affairs.

Partnerships

Samuel Stiles became Reed's partner in Hartford in 1821, the duo advertising as portrait, historical, landscape, and map engravers upon copper and wood. This relationship lasted for several years. In 1824 Stiles, employing engraver Vistus Balch, opened an office in Utica, New York, to direct work to Reed & Stiles in Connecticut, in addition to the printing they were doing on a press in Utica.

Soon afterward, Balch and Stiles formed their own partnership, a bank-note version of "The Tennessee Waltz." Reed was left out in the cold. It is said that Stiles wanted to include Reed in the business, but Balch did not. Hard feelings erupted. However, in a setting worthy of a soap opera, Stiles married a Reed daughter in June 1825. As to what happened after that, accounts vary. Reed and Stiles became enemies, according to one version. Another holds that Reed was warm to Stiles and corresponded frequently on family matters, but the two had no association in the engraving profession. How this situation worked out with a company said to have been formed circa 1826 under the name of Reed, Stiles, Pelton & Company remains to be learned. Perhaps Stiles was minimally involved, if at all.

About 1828 Abner Reed, always generous and sharing, assisted some others in their business ventures by cosigning their notes. In this era well-run banks often required a guarantor for substantial loans. Because the borrowers themselves were usually not in a position to do this (or they would not have needed to take out loans), they called upon friends. Many financial tragedies ensued when guarantors were called upon to pay. The collapse in Connecticut of P.T. Barnum's financial empire when the Jerome Clock Co. failed is well known. In the 1830s Reed's obligations, made casually and he thought without risk, came due, causing him great distress. He lost most of his assets. Barnum rebuilt his business; Reed did not.

Reed's signature on a Vermont Glass Factory $1.75 note of July 1, 1814.

In ensuing years Reed, then in his fifties, made a modest living by engraving and farming. After 1847, he and his wife moved to New York City to live with a daughter. In 1851 he published *Reed's Guide to the Art of Penmanship,* illustrated with 12 engraved plates. Among his later partnerships was an arrangement in New York with John Scoles, with whom he did stipple portrait engraving work, this being popular in book illustrations of the time and, to a lesser extent, on bank notes.

Mrs. Reed died not long afterward, and Abner Reed moved to Toledo, Ohio, to live with family. There he remained for the rest of his life. He died in Toledo on February 25, 1866, at the home of his daughter, Mrs. Edward Bissell.

THE PAPER MONEY OF ABNER REED

Many of the bank bills made by Abner Reed are recognizable at arm's length for their distinctive style. Most show a goddess or other allegorical figure or scene at the top center, with the denomination of the bill expressed to the left and right. At each end, vertically, are the state of issue and the denomination, often against a dark or shaded background done by acid etching or engraving (or a combination of both techniques) on a copper plate. The signature of *Reed* or *Reed sc.* (*sc* for *sculpsit,* or engraves it) often is found near the bottom of the note, but the location is not standard. On the Vermont Glass Factory bills the signature was below the denomination right of the upper center.

Bills were usually printed on a very thin, sometimes translucent, paper of good strength. Some were printed on opaque paper of a white-yellow hue, the latter not being as durable. Still other bills were made of paper that was delicate and did not hold up well in circulation. The chronicle of activities of Jacob Perkins reveals that it was often the policy for banks to supply their own blank paper to engravers, but in Perkins's instance he and his successors directed most orders through the supplier Crane in Dalton, Massachusetts, achieving a consistency. In contrast Reed's paper is of several different qualities, perhaps indicating multiple suppliers.

The careful examination of a four-subject sheet of sample or proof bills made for the Concord (New Hampshire) Bank yields information as to the engraving techniques practiced by Reed in 1817. The bills are of the $5-$5-$10-$20 denominations. Beyond the left margins are the initials JWB in pencil, perhaps an approval check, for both $5 and the $20 denominations, and J. Barber to the left of the $10, all for John Warner Barber, engraver in the Reed shop. Each note also bears the penciled date "August 14th 1817," and the notation "E. Windsor Con."

Each of the two $5 bills has the same motif (featuring a steamboat on the Merrimack River with the New Hampshire State House in the distance) and layout. However, minute inspection reveals that many different elements of the note were entered separately into the plate, including the main vignette, most of the text as a unit, the denomination in several different units, the vertical border elements as units, and the *Reed* signature. This fact reveals that the siderographic process (transfer of vignettes via a hard steel cylinder die) was not employed by the Reed shop at the time, an observation that can be extended to the slightly earlier Vermont Glass Factory bills discussed below.

The $10 and $20 bills are also composed of different elements, but both have the same motif (a variation on the Merrimack River scene, one showing a steamboat about to enter a canal lock to avoid rapids with the State House in the distance). The use of the same illustration on notes of two different denominations was not good practice, as it facilitated the ease of altering a $10 bill to appear as a $20. For the 1817 era the Concord Bank vignettes are especially attractive, as is the entire ensemble, a pleasing alternative to the Patent Stereotype Steel Plate (Perkins) slug-plate notes that were dominant in use in New England at the time. Unlike the situation in Massachusetts, banks in New Hampshire could order notes from any bank-note printer. As a result, the appearance of bills of this era is quite varied.

Only the $20 on the Reed sheet for the Concord Bank bears a plate letter, an A. Normally, such a sheet would have A and B to distinguish the $5 bills from each other, and A on each of the single denominations. It is generally thought that bills signed *Reed* were engraved by Reed. However, with so much work to do and other talented artists in his shop, it is likely the work was done by someone else, perhaps Warner Barber.

Sheet of Reed notes denominated $5-$5-$10-$20 for the Concord Bank in New Hampshire. (Swasey Collection, ex Boys Town Collection)

Detail of the vignette on the top $5 note on the sheet. The view is of the city of Concord, with the State House to the left, as viewed from the Merrimack River.

Detail of the vignette on the second $5 on the sheet. Although the design is similar to the preceding and the objects have the same spatial relationship to each other, there are many differences in small details. On this note the splash generated by the paddlewheel is larger, the little island in the river at the lower right is slightly smaller, etc. Likely, a damp ink impression from a stock vignette was used to transfer the image to the printing plate, after which the details were engraved by hand. On close inspection, each of the $5 vignettes is as different as two fingerprints.

A comparison of the work in the 1817 bills for the Concord Bank with the 1813 and 1814 bills Reed did for the Vermont Glass Company (discussed below) shows great advances in workmanship. However, the Vermont bills did use a cylinder die or arc-shaped plate with *raised* script engraving, entering the text into the soft copper plate. Perhaps this work was farmed out by Reed to another engraver, even to the Perkins factory in Newburyport.

The local character of both scenic vignettes, which illustrated the New Hampshire State House in the distance, may have precluded these from being used on notes for banks in other cities. But in the world of obsolete currency there are few rules, and who knows what might have been done?

Representative Bank Bills by Reed

The following is a brief listing of some of the banks for which Reed engraved bills, most of these being represented by proofs kept in his personal scrapbook. In addition to work for banks, Reed created many scrip and private bills, the illustrious series of Vermont Glass Factory notes being but one of many examples that could be cited. Beyond that, a listing of Reed book illustrations, prints, and labels would run into hundreds of items.

Connecticut: *Hartford*—Hartford Bank and Phoenix Bank; *Litchfield*—Litchfield branch of the Phoenix Bank; *Middletown*—Middletown Bank and the Middletown Insurance Co.; *New Haven*—Eagle Bank and the New Haven Bank; *New London*—New London Bank and Union Bank.

Maine: *Castine*—Castine Bank; *Hallowell*—Kennebec Bank.

Massachusetts: *Boston*—Massachusetts Bank, Manufacturers & Mechanicks Bank, Suffolk Bank, and Union Bank; *Northampton*—Hampshire Bank; *Pittsfield*—Agricultural Bank; *Springfield*—Springfield Bank.

New Hampshire: *Concord*—Concord Bank; *Exeter*—Exeter Bank; *Haverhill*—Coos Bank.

Abner Reed $5 note, a proof impression, for the Castine Bank, then located in Massachusetts and so noted vertically at the right edge. In 1820, the district of Massachusetts to the east of New Hampshire became the state of Maine. At that time the town became Castine, Maine.

Abner Reed $3 note for the Coos Bank of Haverhill, New Hampshire, with printed partial date 18. (Proof impression from the Reed scrapbook)

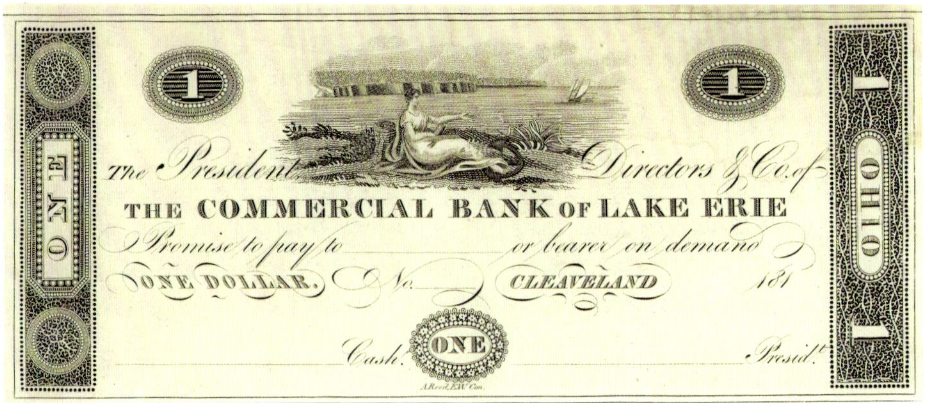

Abner Reed $1 note for the Commercial Bank of Lake Erie, Cleveland, Ohio, with printed partial date 181.

Reed's imprint on the $1 Commercial Bank of Lake Erie note, with the E.W. (East Windsor) address.

New Jersey: *New Brunswick*—Bank of New Brunswick.

New York: *Auburn*—Bank of Auburn; *Catskill*—Catskill Bank; *Geneva*—Bank of Geneva; *Hudson*—Bank of Columbia and Bank of Hudson; *Newburgh*—New Fountain Co.; *New York City*—Mechanics Bank and Phenix Bank; *Watertown*—Jefferson County Bank.[8]

Ohio: *Bloomingville*—Bank of Sandusky Bay; *Delaware*—Bank of Delaware; *Cleveland*—Commercial Bank of Lake Erie; *Mount Vernon*—Bank of Mount Vernon; *Warren*—Western Reserve Bank; *Wooster*—German Bank of Wooster.

Rhode Island: *Bristol*—Freemens Bank; *Cranston*—Cranston Bank; *Kent*—Bank of Kent; *Pawtuxet*—Pawtuxet Bank; *South Kingstown*—Landholders' Bank; *Westerly*—Phenix Bank; *Mount Hope*—Mount Hope Bank.

Concerning certain bills of Newburgh, New York, in the above list, the aforementioned NASCA catalog of Reed's scrapbook included this comment in connection with the same of "three curious proofs, denominations of $1, $5, and $10":

> The New Fountain Company, of Newburgh, with its notes supposed payable at the Bank of America in New York City, has a curious history related by Reed himself in pencil:
>
> "These three bills, with one fifty dollar bill that is missing, were engraved for a counterfeiter (wildcatter) and $5,000 printed. I laid a plan and had an officer ready to take him as soon as the work was delivered; which cost him about $350 besides $250 for the work. The New Fountain soon dried up."

Were it not for these stray remarks by Reed in an obscure book of proofs, we would have virtually no information today on the mysterious New Fountain Company. As it is, the comment invites further research: Who were the principals? In what business was the firm purportedly engaged in? Why did it want bank notes? Had an arrangement been made with the Bank of America? What happened after the officer "took" the counterfeiter? How many such bills exist today?

Among Reed's customers was a private enterprise launched with high hopes, the Vermont Glass Company. Although it is not bank, the workings of the firm is representative of many companies and other entities that issued denominated bills during the era.

CURRENCY OF THE VERMONT GLASS COMPANY

PAPER MONEY

For a brief time from 1812 to 1814, the Vermont Glass Factory was a prolific issuer of paper money, enough that examples of the later varieties are readily available on the numismatic market today. Denominations included $1, $1.25, $1.50, $1.75, $2, $3, and $5. All bills were redeemable at the Farmers Bank of Troy, New York. Among privately distributed paper money of this decade, these bills are among my favorites. Some time ago I wrote an article on this enterprise for *Paper Money,* the journal of the Society of Paper Money Collectors. As is nearly always the case, appreciation of these notes can be enhanced by learning their history—which, as will be seen, even draws Salmon P. Chase (decades later the secretary of the Treasury) for a cameo mention! Similar scenarios for other issuers of paper money in the early 19th century remain largely unexplored and beckon to anyone interested in a combination of numismatics and American history.

In this study, the bills of the Vermont Glass Factory are described by *plate varieties,* with the differences delineated. Presently in the field of obsolete paper money such studies are unusual, as most scholarship deals with major types. However, for rare *coins* the exploration of small differences has been a rewarding pursuit for a long time. As is the case with other focal points and cameo studies in this book, the reader not interested in details is invited to skip ahead to the next chapter.

Early bills issued from at least July 24, 1812 (the earliest date seen), and perhaps before then, were signed on the lower left by Ep. (for Epaphras) Jones, clerk, and at the lower right by Henry Otis, president. Apparently Otis did this for just a short time, as the signature of Samuel Swift, president, (who most often signed as Saml Swift) replaced it by mid-April 1813. Still later issues bore the signatures of Milo Cook, clerk, and continued with Swift as president. The earliest notes, in two different series, were made from woodcut blocks and hand-set type, with no imprint. By summer 1813 bills printed from a copper plate engraved by Abner Reed or another artisan in his shop, and signed Reed or Reed sc., were in use. However, some of the early typeset bills remained on hand and were ink dated into early 1814.

Establishing the Company

In the early years of the state of Vermont, there were four glass houses in operation at various times.[9] Two early businesses were operated by the Vermont Glass Factory, one that issued currency, located on the shore of Lake Dunmore in the town of Salisbury, and the other, not known to have issued bills, situated in East Middlebury. The third glass house was the Champlain Glass Company in Burlington, and the fourth was the Dunmore Glass Works, the successor after a span of years, to the Vermont Glass Factory on the lake of the same name.

The organization of the Vermont Glass Factory, the one of numismatic interest in the present study, took place at the residence of Platt Titus in Troy, New York, in November 1811.[10] Troy, not far from the Vermont state line, was a thriving industrial city, and during the era it furnished many services to the essentially rural areas of Vermont. In attendance at the meeting were Epaphras Jones, a sawmill operator in Salisbury, Vermont, along with John Dickinson, Townsend McCoun, Hugh Peebles, George Tibbits, and Daniel Merritt, all of whom became incorporators or directors of the firm. Dickinson was named chairman of the enterprise and Jones was given the position of clerk, this being the manager of operations. In Salisbury, Jones was well known as a businessman and owned 900 acres of land near the lake. His sawmill was located at the head of the Leicester River, which is the outlet of Lake Dunmore.

The new company was capitalized at $50,000, divided into 1,000 shares of $50 each. The state legislature chartered the business in the same year, granting it through an amendment the exclusive right to make glass in the state for a period of eight years. This action was intended to protect the enterprise from competition during its start-up period.

A few months later the principals of the company and other interested parties met at a tavern in Salisbury. They elected as president Henry Otis, of the nearby village of Leicester. The group determined to set up the Vermont Glass Factory on the west shore of Lake Dunmore immediately east of Epaphras Jones's sawmill.

The lake, a sheet of water extending about four miles in the north-south direction and about a half-mile to three-quarters of a mile wide, is located close to and southeast of Middlebury and north of Brandon. Lake Champlain and the border with New York state are about 15 miles to the west. From the outlet of the lake flows the Leicester River, with several falls that in the 19th century were useful for their water power, including by Jones's sawmill. Later, the lake became acclaimed for the purity of its water and the surrounding scenery, making it an attractive pleasure resort in the warmer months.

The town of Salisbury, on the Leicester River, was chartered on November 3, 1761, by principals from Salisbury, Connecticut, with an arrangement made through Governor Benning Wentworth of New Hampshire. The tract was about six miles square and composed of about 23,040 acres. Of the original 61 grantees, only one person ever settled in the town.

Operations at the Glass Factory

In 1812 a small wooden factory building with a cupola or smoke vent at the center of the peaked roof was erected on the shore of the lake. This structure is depicted on the two earliest types of bills. By August 1813 new bills were made, now showing a large and impressive factory more than 100 feet long with three cupolas, plus the original small building at the right. Equipment was set in place for making cylinder glass, a highly technical procedure.

High-quality sand (silica) was brought to the factory, washed, and ground into tiny particles in a ball mill. The silica and other materials were mixed to create a "batch" for a production run. The batch was put into a special clay pot, taken to the furnace, and brought to a very high temperature, creating in molten form what in the trade was known as "metal."

As the molten mass cooled to a thick consistency, a large blob was gathered at the end of an iron blowpipe by a skilled artisan. The blowpipe was then inserted into the deep end of a hollow metal cylinder about three feet long. As air was blown by mouth into the pipe, it was drawn forward toward the opening of the cylinder, distributing the glass evenly on the inside cylinder wall.

As the glass cooled, it separated from the cylinder wall and was drawn out. With shears it was cut along its length. The glass was then taken to an annealing oven, where it was brought to a high enough heat to render it flexible. It was taken next to a table where workers, using wooden paddles, opened and flattened it into a broad sheet. Afterward it was allowed to cool. Cut into rectangles of various sizes, the product was packaged in wooden crates and shipped to be used as window glass. Certain of the paper-money issues of the factory depict crates of glass as part of the main vignette.

The first factory building, small and with one cupola-chimney on the roof, is the motif of the vignette on a $1.50 Type 1 note dated July 24, 1812. The water of Lake Dunmore is in the foreground.

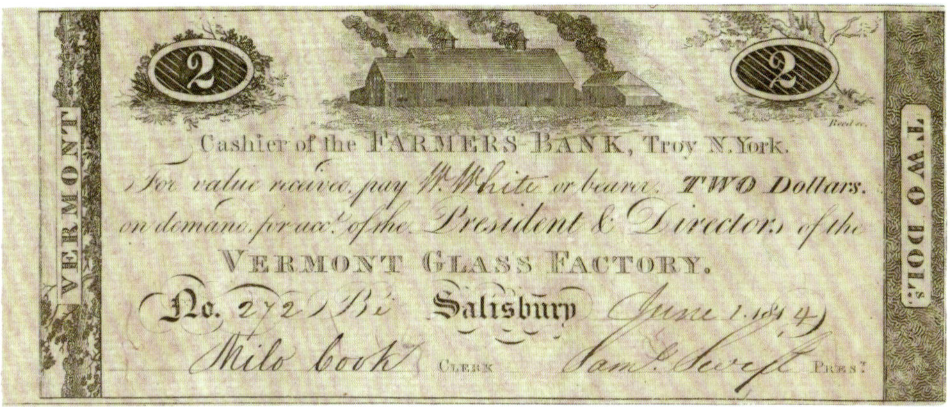

The large factory building with three cupola-chimneys, plus a smaller building to the right (believed to be the first factory), as the vignette on a $2 Type 3 note dated June 1, 1814.

The entire process had to be carefully done at each step, for the product would be ruined by impurities in the sand; the wrong mix of materials in the batch; or the slightest error in melting, blowing, cooling, and cutting. Accordingly, skilled glassblowers were in demand and were often recruited from distant locations.

"Ep." Jones, as he signed currency (or "Eph" as he was known around town), was in charge and hired the factory's personnel, including Peter Schoolcraft. However, Schoolcraft and Jones could not agree, and Schoolcraft left, perhaps soon after April 20, 1813, the date of a bill in which his name is inked as payee, no doubt as the first recipient of the note. Peter Schoolcraft's brother, Henry Rowe Schoolcraft, a precocious young man in charge of a glass factory in New York state, was hired as superintendent for a generous salary of $1,800 per year. In time, Henry Rowe Schoolcraft would rise to become a great name in the annals of exploration of the American West.

It is likely that operations were under way by late spring or early summer 1813, or soon thereafter. By this time paper money had been issued for nearly a year, in denominations of $1, $1.25, $1.50, and $1.75. Later in the year $2, $3, and $5 bills were added.

Henry R. Schoolcraft agreed to work at the Vermont Glass Factory for five years. Samuel Swift, local entrepreneur, was president by late April 1813, as evidenced by his signature on paper money. Bills issued before then were signed by the first president, Henry Otis.

An Early Account of the Business

The *Literary and Philosophical Repertory,* December 1813, published in Middlebury, included this:[11]

> The Glass-Factory is situated in the town of Salisbury on the north shore of Lake Dunmore. This collection of water takes its name from the late Lord Dunmore, who, before the revolutionary conflict, which separated America from England, was governor of Virginia. He owned the land adjoining the lake, made a visit to it, waded into the water, broke a bottle and gave it his own name, by which it is still known. . . .
>
> A large portion of the lake, and the land adjoining it, formerly belonged to Mr. Epaphras Jones. This gentleman was the first who suggested the idea of its being a particularly favorable spot for the manufacture of glass; and who had the honor of being the principal instrument in the formation of a company for that purpose. The Legislature of the state, on petition, cheerfully granted to Mr. Jones and his associates an act of incorporation, to which very liberal privileges

were attached. Mr. Jones now resides in the neighborhood of the factory, and is the company's general agent for the erection of the buildings and the inspection of the works.[12]

The company owns about two thousand acres of land, which lies, chiefly, around a large bay of the lake, and commands its only outlet. On this outlet stands a sawmill, in the vicinity of which exists a sufficient quantity of good timber to keep it in operation for many years to come. Their land also commands the main stream which supplies the lake, and on which a head and fall may easily be made to carry any mechanical works, which this company may hereafter deem it profitable to erect.

It is believed that no establishment of this kind in the northern states enjoys more numerous or greater advantages from its local situation than the Vermont Glass Factory. At least this is the opinion of the ingenious and persevering superintendent of the factory, Mr. Henry R. Schoolcraft. "Sand," says he in a note received from him a few days since, "is found on the shores of the lake. Wood stands in exhaustless abundance in the immediate vicinity of the factory. Firestone, an article hitherto brought at great expense, from Connecticut, has been discovered within ten miles of the works. And the enormous charges heretofore incurred in the transportation of clay from Philadelphia, for the manufacture of pots for melting glass, is about to be avoided by the discovery that the Monkton porcelain earth will answer as good a purpose. From the unusual success," continues Mr. S., "which has attended these works since their commencement, the many advantages which they hold, and the variety of materials with which the place abounds for making all kinds of glass, we are led to believe they will become one of the first establishments in the union."

Respecting the present state of the Vermont Glass Factory, it is necessary to add but few words. It is sufficient to state that the works are now in full and complete operation. The first glass was blown in them about the middle of last September. It is now exhibited for sale in the stores of the village and is beginning to circulate through a large section of the country.

Should the glass produced at this factory prove as good as it now promises to be, the inhabitants of Vermont will derive incalculable benefits from the establishment. To have an article so essential to the convenience and comfort of life, and so difficult of transportation, manufactured within the limits of their own territory is a circumstance of no inconsiderable importance.

The company have it in contemplation to erect before long an additional manufactory for the making of flint glass of various descriptions; and for their encouragement in this enterprise, the Legislature of the State has recently granted them, for twelve years from the time of the last session, the exclusive privilege of manufacturing glass of all kinds.

H.P. Smith's *History of Addison County* includes this information about the business:

About forty operatives were employed in this factory several years. So great was the business done by it that money was made more plenty among us, a good home market was furnished for a part of our agricultural products, and all kinds of business rendered more active.

As the company made its deposits at the Farmers Bank of Troy, N. Y., it issued orders in the form of bank bills, which were stamped and struck off on bank-bill paper, and were in denominations of $1.00, $1.25, $1.50, $1.75, $2.00, and $3.00. These bills, or rather orders, were equally, current with any other bank bills for a number of years.[13]

Products of the Factory

The *Vermont Mirror,* published in Middlebury by the factory's president, Samuel Swift, included this notice in the issue of October 20, 1813:

Vermont Glass Factory

The public are informed that the Vermont Glass Factory is now in complete operation. The glass is warranted equal to any manufactured in the northern states and free from breakage. The following sizes are constantly manufactured and kept for sale at the ware houses in Middlebury, Rutland and Windsor and will be sold at Albany prices:

6 by 8, 7 by 9, 8 by 10, 9 by 11, 10 by 12, 11 by 15, 12 by 16, 12 by 18, 13 by 18, 14 by 20.

Orders for window glass of any other dimensions will be received and punctually attended to by

Ep. Jones, Gen. Ag't

The next issue of the *Vermont Mirror,* October 27, included an advertisement by Henry R. Schoolcraft, superintendent, offering $100 "to any person who shall discover within the state of Vermont . . . a bed of such clay . . . found equal to the manufacture of crucibles for melting pots."[14]

In the same year prospects were sufficiently bright that the state legislature extended the firm's exclusive franchise to 12 years as noted above.

Events of 1814

Apparently, the works operated throughout 1814, and its products enjoyed a good market in the region. However, profits were elusive; by October it could not pay Schoolcraft his salary, and its currency was no longer being redeemed by the Farmers Bank of Troy. Apparently, the company now did business with "a local bank in what later became the Waterhouse Barn."[15] No information has been located concerning *any* bank established in Salisbury, apart from this reference.

By this time the Vermont Glass Factory had set up another facility at East Middlebury for the making of other types of glassware, including bottles of a brown hue.

Soon afterward, Milo Cook, successor in early 1814 to Ep. Jones as clerk of the Vermont Glass Factory, and Artemus Nixon announced that they had leased both the Salisbury and Middlebury factory buildings. However, Jones remained with the firm as general agent.

Not long after the rental agreement had been signed, the Salisbury factory burned, effectively ending the lease. In early 1815 Henry R. Schoolcraft left Salisbury and went to New Hampshire, where he became involved in the new Keene (Marlboro Street) Glass Works. A letter addressed to him in Keene, April 12, 1815, by Peter Starr, his attorney in Middlebury, discussed his efforts to collect salary due Schoolcraft. Apparently, Starr considered claiming certain of the company's property at the Middlebury factory but decided, "I thought not best to attach any little personal property about the Ware Factory." Schoolcraft remained in Keene until the glass works failed in 1817.

More About Henry Rowe Schoolcraft

Henry Rowe Schoolcraft is an important figure in 19th-century American history for his importance later in life in the study of geology and other aspects of natural history, his finding of the head of the Mississippi River, his collecting of folklore and songs, and his connections with Indian tribes and with Salmon P. Chase (later important in the U.S. Treasury and still later chief justice of the Supreme Court).[16] A further numismatic connection beyond the Vermont bills can be made through the bank notes issued by the Farmers Bank of Prairie Ronde in the town of Schoolcraft in the same state. Schoolcraft's ancestors came from England and were known as *Colcroft* or *Colcraft;* the name later was changed to *Schoolcraft.*

Henry Schoolcraft was born on March 28, 1793, in the Manor of Rensselaer, a small village to the west of Albany, New York, son of a glassmaker, Lawrence Schoolcraft. Imbued with a passion for learning, he attended public schools, but supplemented his studies by reading the classics and enlisting a tutor for instruction in French, then teaching himself German and Hebrew. By age 15 he published both a newspaper and a magazine, which printed his own verses and articles. He had hoped to attend Union College in Schenectady, New York, but he was unable to raise the necessary funds. In Geneva, New York, in 1809 he was signed as superintendent of a planned glass factory, continuing the family trade. Meanwhile, he continued private studies with a tutor. On February 4, 1810, before the incorporation date of the Oneida Glass Manufacturing Company of Vernon, New York, Schoolcraft made an agreement with one of the principals, Bryan Johnson, to receive one share of stock for every glass blower he was able to hire for the company.[17] Apparently, the business of the firm did not live up to expectations, and it was soon discontinued.

In late 1812 or early 1813, Schoolcraft moved to Salisbury to become superintendent at the new Vermont Glass Factory in time to celebrate his 20th birthday. He resided on the shore of Lake Dunmore, where he set up a laboratory and a furnace for conducting experiments with glass. While there he studied chemistry and mineralogy under professors F. Hall and Jarius Kennan at Middlebury College a few miles to the north. After his stint with the Vermont Glass Factory and his subsequent work in Keene, Schoolcraft went back to New York, then traveled to Worthington, Ohio. During this journey he supervised the care of young Salmon P. Chase. Salmon's mother lived in Keene and wanted the boy to go west to be under the care of an uncle, Philander Chase, who was the Episcopal bishop of Ohio.

In 1818 Schoolcraft went to the border of what was then the American West, where he pursued mineralogy. In 1819 his carefully crafted study, *A View of the Lead Mines of Missouri,* was published and became recognized as the standard work on the subject. In the following year he was part of a geological expedition under General Lewis Cass, governor of the territory, to the copper regions of Lake Superior. In 1821 he and Governor Cass sought to locate the headwaters of the Mississippi River; they reached as far as Red Cedar Lake (later called Cass Lake) but did not achieve their goal.

Schoolcraft found Indian culture and life to be especially interesting, and in this connection in 1822 he was appointed as Indian agent at Sault Ste. Marie. During the next decade he worked on behalf of the United States in treaty discussions and negotiations with the Indian tribes, some of whom were at war with each other, including the Sioux and Ojibwa involved in a border dispute. He absorbed himself deeply in Indian lore, culture, and traditions, some of which were also used by Henry Wadsworth Longfellow in his 1855 epic poem, "The Song of Hiawatha."

In the meantime, from 1828 to 1832, Schoolcraft was a member of the Michigan Territorial Legislature.

His reports were acclaimed by ethnologists in America and Europe, and he rose to high esteem in the eyes of the academic world. Schoolcraft's interest in finding the source of the Mississippi continued, although his quest was not widely publicized. Cass was among his confidants. Success attended his efforts on July 13, 1832, when Schoolcraft and his companions reached a lake known as Omuskos or, more popularly, Lac La Biche or Elk Lake, now Lake Itasca.

He became important in the early affairs of the University of Michigan, and as a member of the Board of Regents he helped save the institution from financial ruin. He founded the first common-school periodical in America, ***The Journal of Education***, and launched the first literary magazine in Michigan, ***The Souvenir of the Lakes***. He also contributed many articles to scientific journals. Henry Rowe Schoolcraft died in Washington, D.C., on December 10, 1864.

Continuing Vermont Glass Factory Operations

On May 3, 1815, Ep. Jones, as clerk and agent, announced that the Salisbury factory was being rebuilt and would go into operation within a few weeks. It is likely that window glass was again made, but only for a short time. In the meantime the company remained in deep financial difficulties. Its early paper-money issues were worthless.

Strong but unsuccessful efforts were made to raise new capital. The Farmers Bank of Troy continued to refuse to redeem the notes of the Vermont Glass Factory. What remained of the firm's assets, including the Middlebury building, were lost through court attachments. In August 1817 the company completely discontinued operations. By that time other glass factories in America were experiencing great difficulty through competition from inexpensive imports of good quality products.

In 1832 the Lake Dunmore Company was established to continue the glass business. The new firm repaired the buildings of the Vermont Glass Factory and recommenced operations; it lasted about a decade, after which it closed due to foreign competition. The buildings were converted to agricultural use and for the accommodation of tourists during the busy season. In 1849 the property was sold to the Lake Dunmore Hotel Company, which used the existing buildings until a new hotel was built on the site. However, expenses exceeded profits, and the company went bankrupt and was acquired by Florida interests. The hotel burned in July 1877. Another early building, a two-story structure that served as a boarding house for factory employees, was opened in 1818 and was later known as the Waybury Inn.

Currency of the Vermont Glass Factory

Today, little remains except scattered pieces of paper money to remind historians and others of the short-lived Vermont Glass Factory. Printed from type that was set by an unknown shop and later from copper plates by Abner Reed, most of these bills are on durable but thin and flexible paper; imprinted in black ink; and numbered, dated, and signed by hand.

There are four distinct types of notes, each with denominations of \$1, \$1.25, \$1.50, and \$1.75. In addition, Type 3 alone includes the higher values of \$2, \$3, and \$5. The odd values between \$1 and \$2 were useful in an era in which silver coins to make change were scarce.

The early typeset notes employed several different woodblocks, each depicting a small factory with a cupola at the center of the roof, and blocks for the denomination to be printed twice on each note and for inscriptions vertically at each end. The inscriptions at the center were set by hand and varied in their arrangement and style. Apparently, at least two styles of these typeset notes were made, the earliest with a lined panel at top center, above the building, on which the serial number was inked, here called Type 1. These have the inscription,

> The President and Directors of the Vermont Glass Factory promise to pay [payee to be filled in] or Bearer, on demand, at the FARMERS BANK, TROY, N.Y. . . .

Those made slightly later, but seemingly not ink dated until January 1, 1814, here called Type 2, had the small building at the top center, and the serial number at the lower left below the main text. The obligation on this design has the following text, and later issues have slight variations of it:

> Cashier of the Farmers Bank, Troy, N. York. For value received, pay [payee to be filled in] or bearer [face value of bill printed here], on demand, for account of the President and Directors of the Vermont Glass Factory. . . .

The last two issues of bills are from copper plates signed by Abner Reed. The Type 3 depicts the large factory building with the small original structure at the right. Bills of this type were first circulated in the summer of 1813. This type was the only one to include the higher denominations of \$2, \$3, and \$5.

Type 4 bills show a group of wooden boxes containing window glass, with the size of the panes lettered on most of the boxes, a shield, the motto, BY MANUFACTURES WE THRIVE, and branches in the background. The $1.25 bill of Type 4 shows the large factory building in the distance at the upper left, and the $1.50 bill shows the same structure at the upper right. The $1 and $1.75 notes of Type 4 do not show the factory. These vignettes differ in their details, reflecting their production by hand. These seem to have been released in January 1814.

The Reed plates seem to have been made by a process popular at the time. A blank copper plate was coated with a substance (several different substances were used, including wax). With a stylus Reed or an employee drew by hand the various scenic parts of the design. The face was then immersed in vitriol (sulfuric acid). The metal exposed by the stylus was eaten away by the acid, creating rather wide (rather than delicate) lines, curves, etc. The wax was then removed, and a steel cylinder die or arc-shaped plate with raised script-style lettering was impressed into the center part of the plate. Details and finishing touches were added by a hand graving tool. As a result, all of the vignette or design parts of each plate are slightly different from those found on other plates, but the script lettering is essentially identical.

A letter from Henry Schoolcraft's father, Lawrence Schoolcraft, dated March 31, 1813, mentions currency, which by that time had become well known in New York City:

> Yours of the 19 inst duly received, and very pleasant it is to us, that you like your present situation so well. Your bank bills pass as current in this place as Manhattan. You will let me know how you progress, and whether you are likely to remain permanently in Vermont. . . .[18]

The vast majority of bills in collectors' hands today are of the two later types by Abner Reed, the large factory building or the boxes of glass. They are typically dated from December 1813 to June 1814, although earlier dates in the summer of 1813 exist for Type 3. On all bills Epaphras Jones signed as Ep. Jones. On early bills, president Samuel Swift often signed in full, but later abbreviated his first name to Saml.

The Farmers Bank of Troy, New York, acted as redemption agent. Names of inked-in payees on notes vary and may have represented employees or those who did business with the factory. Serial numbers were not continuous for the series, but seem to have been started anew with each inked date for each denomination.

DESIGNS ON THE CURRENCY

As discussed previously, there are four main designs known to have been used on Vermont Glass Factory bills. New VGF (Vermont Glass Factory) reference numbers have been assigned, with cross references to Mayre Burns Coulter, Vermont Obsolete Notes and Scrip, 1972.

Type 1 Notes: Small Factory Building

Serial Number Above (1812 and Early 1813)

Small factory building with one cupola on top. Serial number on lined area above building. "The President and Directors . . . promise." No engraver's imprint.

VGF-1, $1—*Plate letter:* None. Typeset note with hand-set type plus separate vignettes. *Design: Left,* VERMONT vertically • *Top center,* 1 / N followed by two commas, with ruled parallelogram, at top border / 1 • *Below top center,* Small factory building with one chimney-cupola, with lake in foreground • *Right,* 1 / ONE DOLLAR / 1 vertically • Coulter-3

VGF-2, $1.25—*Plate letter:* None. Typeset note with hand-set type plus separate vignettes. *Design: Left,* VERMONT vertically • *Top center,* 1.25 / N followed by two commas, with ruled parallelogram, at top border / 1.25 • *Below top center,* Small factory building with one chimney-cupola, with lake in foreground • *Right,* Vertically, 1 / 1 Dol. 25 Cts. / 25 [line] 100 • Coulter-5?[19]

VGF-3, $1.50—*Plate letter:* None. Typeset note with hand-set type plus separate vignettes. *Design: Left,* VERMONT vertically • *Top center,* 1.50 / N followed by two commas, with ruled parallelogram, at top border / 1.50 • *Below top center,* Small factory building with one chimney-cupola, with lake in foreground • *Right,* Vertically 1 / 1 Dol. 50 Cts. / 50 [line] 100 • Coulter-unlisted

VGF-4, $1.75—*Plate letter:* None. Typeset note with hand-set type plus separate vignettes. *Design: Left,* VERMONT vertically • *Top center,* 1.75 / N followed by two commas, with ruled parallelogram, at top border / 1.75 • *Below top center,* Small factory building with one chimney-cupola, with lake in foreground • *Right,* Vertically 1 / 1 Dol. 75 Cts. / 75 [line] 100 • Coulter-unlisted

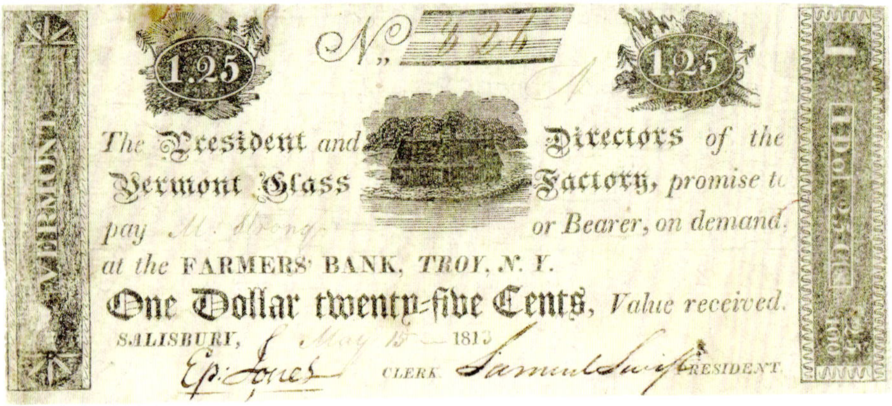

Type 1 note of the $1.25 denomination, dated May 15, 1813, and signed by Ep. Jones as clerk and Samuel Swift as president. Only on Type 1 notes does the obligation read, "The President and Directors." Bills of this type were made by combining hand-set type with individual copperplate vignettes. The same vignettes, with different arrangement of the factory image, were used on Type 2 bills.

Type 2 Notes: Small Factory Building

Serial Number at Lower Left (January 1814)

Small factory building with one cupola on top. Serial number at lower left of note. "Cashier of the Farmers Bank. . . ." No engraver's imprint. Each of the four denominations uses the same end vignettes, denomination vignettes, and building vignette, as employed on Type 1 notes of like denomination.

For Type 1 and Type 2, separate copperplate vignettes were used to depict the factory, the denomination twice, and the inscriptions vertically at each end. Very early bills used additional vignettes for the ruled serial number area at the top border. The arrangement of lettering and capitalization varied from note to note, including within the early and late styles of the same denomination. Apparently, most bills of this style were redeemed and exchanged for later ones, for few exist today. Robert A. Vlack reported that it took him 27 years to gather a complete set of Type I and Type II bills (except for the Type 1 $1.75 and the Type 2 $1.25, which are missing from his collection). C. John Ferreri, a specialist since the 1960s, lacks several varieties.

VGF-5, $1—*Plate letter:* None. Typeset note with hand-set type plus separate vignettes. *Design: Left,* VERMONT vertically • *Top center,* 1 / Small factory building with one chimney-cupola, with lake in foreground / 1 • *Right,* 1 / ONE DOLLAR / 1 vertically • Coulter-4

VGF-6, $1.25—*Plate letter:* None. Typeset note with hand-set type plus separate vignettes. *Design: Left,* VERMONT vertically • *Top center,* 1.25 / Small factory building with one chimney-cupola, with lake in foreground / 1.25 • *Right,* Vertically 1 / 1 Dol. 25 Cts. / 25 [line] 100 • Coulter-5?[20]

VGF-7, $1.50—*Plate letter:* None. Typeset note with hand-set type plus separate vignettes. *Design: Left,* VERMONT vertically • *Top center,* 1.50 / Small factory building with one chimney-cupola, with lake in foreground / 1.50 • *Right,* Vertically 1 / 1 Dol. 50 Cts. / 50 [line] 100 • Coulter-unlisted

VGF-8, $1.75—*Plate letter:* None. Typeset note with hand-set type plus separate vignettes. *Design: Left,* VERMONT vertically • *Top center,* 1.75 / Small factory building with one chimney-cupola, with lake in foreground / 1.75 • *Right,* Vertically 1 / 1 Dol. 75 Cts. / 75 [line] 100 • Coulter-unlisted

Type 3 Notes:

Large Factory Building (Summer 1813 to Early 1814)

View of large lakeside glass factory building at the top, with three cupolas, plus the earlier small factory with one cupola to the right. The cupolas belched smoke and were, in effect, chimneys; the intensity of the smoke varies from light to dark depending on the plate and the amount of ink used. Lettering beginning with "Cashier" and ending with "Prest." is the same in each plate, except that the denomination and plate letter were each added by hand engraving. The left and right borders as well as the glass factory vignette were done by a combination of acid-etching (mostly) and hand engraving. Accordingly, details differ. Type 3 is the only series with the higher $2, $3, and $5 denominations.

VGF-9, $1—Copper plate signed by Reed. ***Plate letter:*** A. *Design:* Left, VERMONT vertically • *Top center,* 1 / Factory buildings with lake in foreground, and with smoke issuing from four chimneys / 1 • *Right,* 1 DOLLAR. vertically • Coulter-1

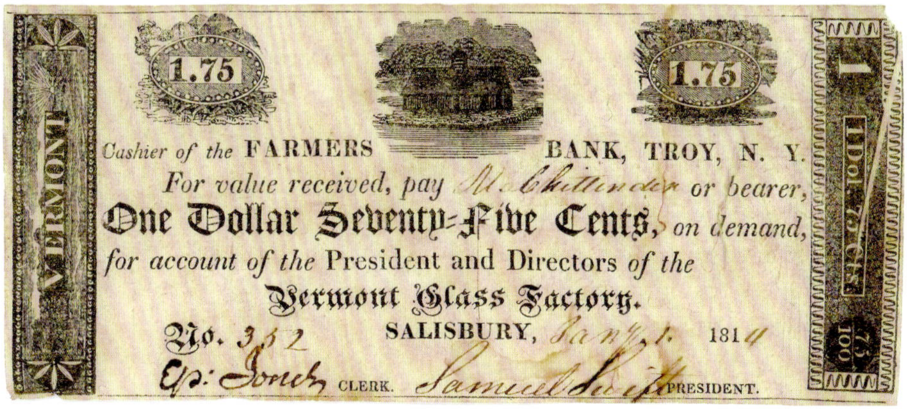

Type 2 note of the $1.75 denomination, dated Jany 1, 1814, and signed by Ep. Jones as clerk and Samuel Swift as president. Bills of this type were made by combining hand-set type with individual copperplate vignettes (the same vignettes, except for the signature grid, as used on Type 1 bills). Most bills of the Type 1 and Type 2 styles were redeemed or replaced with Type 3 or Type 4 bills. Accordingly, the first two types are seldom seen in collections today, and those that do exist are usually in very low grades.

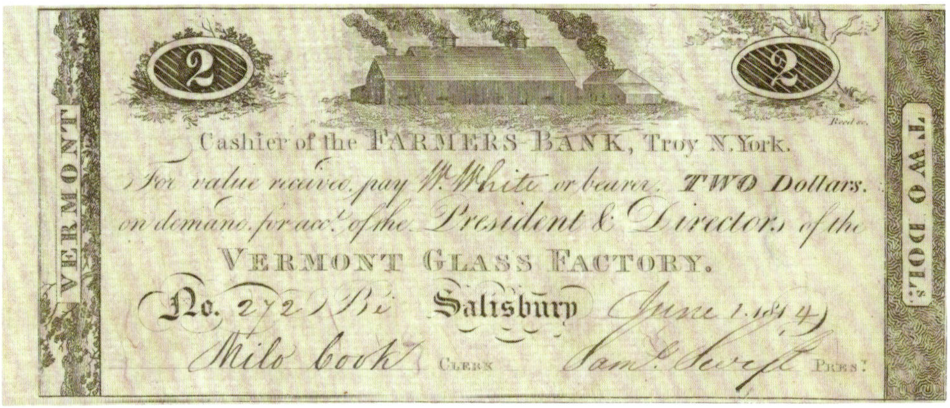

Type 3 note of the $2 denomination, dated June 1, 1814, and signed by Milo Cook as clerk and Samuel Swift as president. Depicted is the large factory with a smaller factory building to the right. Bills of this type combined a standard center imprint (by the siderographic process) with acid-etched vignettes with hand detailing. Such bills bear the imprint of Abner Reed.

VGF-10, $1.25—Copper plate signed by Reed. ***Plate letter:*** B. *Design: Left,* VERMONT vertically • *Top center,* 1. 25 over 100 • / Factory buildings with lake in foreground, and with smoke issuing from four chimneys / 1. 25 over 100 • *Right,* ONE Dol. 25 Cts. vertically • Coulter-7[21]

VGF-11, $1.50—Copper plate signed by Reed. ***Plate letter:*** C. *Design: Left,* VERMONT vertically • *Top center,* 1. 50 over 100 / Factory buildings with lake in foreground, and with smoke issuing from four chimneys / 1. 50 over 100 • *Right,* ONE Dol. 50 Cts. vertically • Coulter-10

VGF-12, $1.75—Copper plate signed by Reed. ***Plate letter:*** D. *Design: Left,* VERMONT vertically • *Top center,* 1. 75 over 100 / Factory buildings with lake in foreground, and with smoke issuing from chimneys, particularly heavy from the rightmost small building / 1. 75 over 100 • *Right,* ONE DOL. 75 Cts vertically • *Notes:* Specimen in author's collection overprinted (not stamped) vertically in three lines: PAYABLE / CURRENT / BANK BILLS • Coulter-11

VGF-13, $2—*Light smoke variety.* Copper plate signed by Reed. ***Plate letter:*** B. *Design: Left,* VERMONT vertically • *Top center,* 2 / Factory buildings with lake in foreground, and with *light* smoke issuing from four chimneys / 2 • *Right,* TWO DOLs. vertically • Coulter-14

VGF-13a, $2—*Heavy smoke variety.* As preceding, but copper plate strengthened and with new details added. Now with heavier details in the VERMONT vertically area to the left and with *heavy* smoke from the buildings. Other areas of the plate were not strengthened, and details are weaker than on VGF-13.

VGF-14, $3—Copper plate signed by Reed. ***Plate letter:*** C. *Design: Left,* VERMONT vertically • *Top center,* 3 / Factory buildings with lake in foreground, and with smoke issuing from chimneys / 3 • *Right,* THREE DOLs. vertically with stippled background surrounding white area • Coulter-15

VGF-15, $5—Copper plate signed by Reed. ***Plate letter:*** D. *Design: Left,* VERMONT vertically

• *Top center,* 5 / Factory buildings with lake in foreground, and with smoke issuing from four chimneys / 5 • *Right,* FIVE DOLs. vertically • Coulter-16

Type 4 Notes:

Boxes, Shield, and Ribbon With Motto (December 1813 to Summer 1814)
Boxes of glass, shield, ribbon with motto BY MANUFACTURES WE THRIVE, etc., at top. Lettering beginning with "Cashier" and ending with "Prest." the same in each plate, but from a different transfer-roll imprint than on the preceding type. The left and right borders as well as the top center vignette were done by a combination of acid-etching (mostly) and hand engraving. The denomination and plate letter were each added by hand. Other details vary from plate to plate. Earliest date seen: January 1, 1814.

VGF-16, $1—Copper plate signed by Reed. ***Plate letter:*** E. *Design: Left,* VERMONT vertically • *Top center,* 1 / Group of boxes for shipping window glass (inscription on one, including 10, 8, and 50) with spade-shaped shield on which are four clusters of wheat or corn; long looping and twisting ribbon inscribed BY MANUFACTURES WE THRIVE. Tree branches and foliage to sides and behind / 1 • *Right,* 1 DOLLAR vertically • Coulter-2

VGF-17, $1.25—Copper plate signed by Reed. ***Plate letter:*** F. *Design: Left,* VERMONT vertically • *Top center,* 1.25 / Group of boxes for shipping window glass (inscriptions on three, including 50 Ft) with spade-shaped shield on which are three visible clusters of wheat or corn with mountains and pine trees above; long looping and twisting ribbon inscribed BY MANUFACTURES WE THRIVE. At upper left, factory building with smoke issuing from three chimneys, smoke drifting up and to the left. Branches at upper right / 1.25 • *Right,* ONE Dol. 25 Cts. vertically • Coulter-8

VGF-18, $1.50—Copper plate signed by Reed. ***Plate letter:*** G. *Design: Left,* VERMONT vertically against stippled background • *Top center,* 1.50 / Group of boxes for shipping window glass (inscriptions on three boxes, in the style of *10 by 8 / 50 Ft,* and related, perhaps indicating window glass dimensions) with spade-shaped shield on which are three visible clusters of wheat or corn with mountains and pine trees above, head of cow partly visible at bottom of shield; long looping and twisting ribbon inscribed BY MANUFACTURES WE THRIVE. At upper center and left, trees in distance. At upper right, factory building with smoke issuing from three chimneys, smoke drifting up and to the right / 1.50 • *Right,* ONE Dol. 50 Cts. vertically on wide ellipse with branches in background • Coulter-9

VGF-19, $1.75—Copper plate signed by Reed. ***Plate letter:*** H. *Design: Left,* VERMONT vertically against tree branches • *Top center,* 1.75 / Group of boxes for shipping window glass (inscriptions on most) with spade-shaped shield on which are three visible clusters of wheat or corn with mountains and pine trees above, cow below; long looping and twisting ribbon inscribed BY MANUFACTURES WE THRIVE. / 1.75 • *Right,* ONE Dol. 75 Cts. vertically on long octagonal panel, with tree branches to left and right • Coulter-12

From a collecting viewpoint, Vermont Glass Company notes are very appealing. Offered are several different odd denominations, two completely different designs, and various subvarieties. There are enough Type 3 and Type 4 bills, nearly all high grade, that a basic set of *denominations* can be assembled without great difficulty, although acquiring each of the varieties, including Type 1 and Type 2, would be daunting.

Numismatic Notes

The notes of Abner Reed form an interesting study. For most of his bank notes and those of the Vermont Glass Factory, examples are seen with some frequency in the marketplace, this being especially true for institutions that failed or otherwise did not redeem their notes. Bills from sound banks can range from scarce to rare. Many Reed bills are on thin paper and are fragile today. Accordingly, chips and minor tears are normal. Generally, market prices are inexpensive.

Proof notes from the Reed scrapbook sold by NASCA on November 2, 1983, are occasionally offered at auction, but as the years go by they are becoming increasingly widely scattered and less available.

Type 4 note of the $1 denomination, dated June 1, 1814, signed by Cook and Swift. Depicted are boxes of window glass, a shield, and a ribbon inscribed, BY MANUFACTURES WE THRIVE, a popular motto during the protectionist era of the War of 1812. Bills of this type combined a standard center imprint (by the siderographic process) with acid-etched vignettes with hand detailing. Such bills bear the imprint of Abner Reed.

Type 4 note of the $1.25 denomination dated June 1, 1814, style similar to the preceding, but with significant differences in the vignette, this with the factory building at the upper left. After the Vermont Glass Factory closed, quantities of used Type 3 and Type 4 bills remained, providing a supply for a later generation of numismatists.

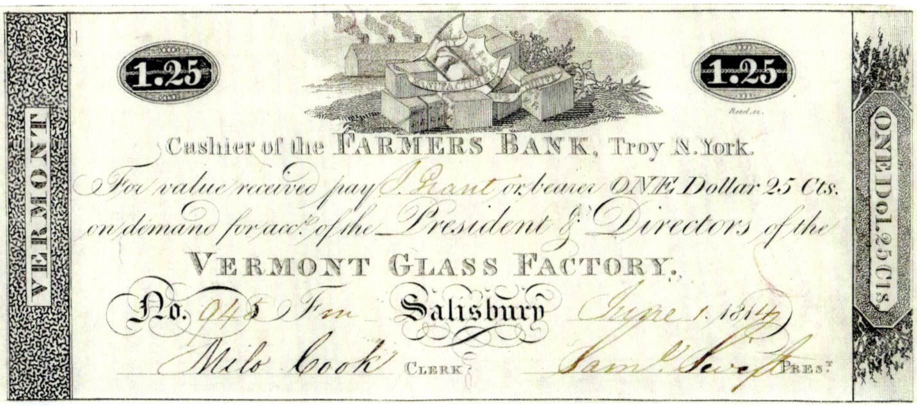

Vignette on the $1.25 Type 4 note.

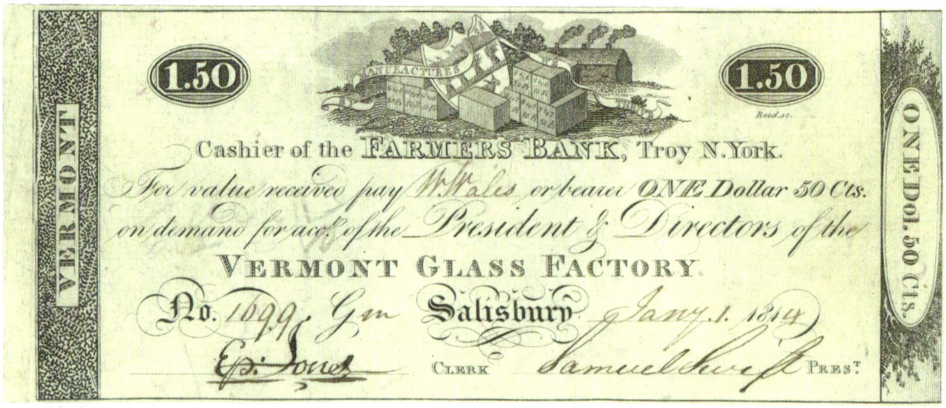

Type 4 note of the $1.50 denomination, dated January 1, 1814, style somewhat similar in concept to the preceding, but with the factory building at the upper right in the vignette.

Vignette on the $1.50 Type 4 note.

Type 4 note of the $1.75 denomination, dated June 1, 1814, style similar to the preceding, but without the factory building. This note is one of several seen with an overprint added later: PAYABLE / IN / CURRENT / BNAK [*sic*] BILLS.

Vignette on the $1.75 Type 4 note.

THE "OWLS" OF THE OWL CREEK BANK

THE NOTORIOUS "OWLS" OF THE OWL CREEK BANK

NILES' WEEKLY REGISTER

The scene now shifts to Ohio, then on the frontier of the American West, where bills by the Harrison brothers carved a niche in the history of paper money. Unlike the situations for Jacob Perkins and Abner Reed, the Harrison name is not well known today. This chapter tells the story of a particular bank, the bills of which are readily collectible. The institution was conceived in good faith by local people who sought a charter but did not receive one, then went on to conduct business—after which it became a victim of circumstances beyond its control. Again, a simple bank note can yield a fascinating story.

I enjoy looking through 18th- and 19th-century magazines and newspapers for interesting tidbits relating to coins, tokens, medals, and paper money. Among the favorite items in my library is a complete run of *Niles' Weekly Register* from its first issue in 1811 to the early 1840s, more than 60 volumes (with a title change to *Niles' National Register* on September 2, 1837). My set used to belong to the Federal Reserve Bank of Philadelphia, but a generation ago, in an efficiency move, someone must have noticed that none of these volumes, each with a slip and card in the back, had ever been checked out. Accordingly, it seemed logical that these volumes were next to useless—and out they went, landing in the hands of a local book dealer, from whom I purchased them. Since that time I have employed these volumes extensively, including citations and quoted articles in this book.

Also tossed out by the Federal Reserve Bank was a full run of the early years of *Bicknell's Counterfeit Detector,* earlier the property of no less an entity than the second Bank of the United States. This reference, too, was deemed useless and discarded. Today, it is another favorite of mine, in fact forming the basis for a discussion later in this book.

Edited by Hezekiah Niles and published in Baltimore, the *Register* was an early version of a national paper—sort of like the *Wall Street Journal* is today—with emphasis on financial and, in the case of *Niles,* also political news. From his writing Niles emerges as a humanitarian, and in an era in which slavery was the standard way of life in the South, including in the shadow of the U.S. Capitol in Washington, D.C., he railed against it—incurring the wrath of many politicians and businesspeople. As related earlier in this book, Niles was an advocate of gold and silver coins and an opponent of paper money. When specie payments were suspended, as happened now and then, the occurrences furnished him an opportunity to fire salvos at the banks that suspended.

I have read and skimmed through the *Register* three times, taking several months for each "tour." Each time I gain a renewed appreciation of American history and life in a you-are-there scenario, as events unfold each week in the newspaper.

In the earliest issues the British capture of American sailors on the high seas commanded much space. England announced that, not only did it rule the waves, but no ship could set sail without its permission. This was overstating the case, but ships of that country were dominant just about everywhere. In the meantime, American ships were prevented from doing much in the way of international trade by the Embargo Act of 1807, a piece of legislation intended to protect ships from capture by the French and the English. This was followed by the Non-Intercourse Act, not as rigorous as the Embargo Act but still destructive to American maritime trade. Much harm was done to businesses on land—especially in coastal towns and cities—by these acts. More than a few citizens cast patriotism aside and smuggled goods in and out of American ports. As noted earlier, the Embargo Act had wide implications on American commerce, the economy, and banking. It is likely that economic conditions resulting from this legislation caused unfavorable conditions in Vermont and were part of the reason the Vermont State Bank was not a success (see chapter 5).

Niles' Weekly Register also covered the War of 1812 as it happened—culminating in the breathtaking scenario of the burning of Washington, D.C., and the bombardment of Fort McHenry in Baltimore Harbor. Earlier, in the British parliament it had been announced that Baltimore was the richest of American prizes, and this city would be captured. As the lyrics of "The Star-Spangled Banner" related, however, it did not work out that way.

Hezekiah Niles wrote much about banking, including many virulent comments relating to the second Bank of the United States, which was chartered in 1816. This institution was cast as a greedy monster, corrupt and insatiable. In the early days there were many malfeasances, but these were mostly straightened out with new management in the mid-1820s. Other causes taken up by Niles were relatively minor, such as repeated comments that a certain river should be spelled as *Susquehannah*, not as *Susquehanna*.

Through the pages of *Niles' Weekly Register* we see battles fought, foreign monarchs deposed, canals prosper and then fade when the railroads took over, the Alamo fall and the Republic of Texas formed, the strongly pro-Jackson faction in Congress struggle with the equally strong anti-Jackson men (there was no middle ground), John C. Calhoun repeatedly threaten to lead South Carolina in leaving the Union, and more—all events fascinating to read. Perhaps in a few years I will start through them all over again.

Hoo-Hoo or Owl Creek

Now and then in *Niles' Weekly Register* a bank whose bills were worthless was sometimes called a "Hoo-Hoo" or "Owl Creek" bank in a generic sense, *hoo-hoo* being the cry of this particular bird.

Some background is provided by this item in the issue of April 17, 1819:

> The Owl Creek Bank has given public notice, that, in order to counteract the injurious tendency of the United States branch banks in that state, it has thought proper to follow the example of the other state banks, and has therefore stopped payment of specie, and will probably [continued to] for some time. So says an Ohio paper.

As a matter of fact, the Owl Creek Bank, located in the small Ohio town of Mount Vernon, did stay stopped. Soon it ceased business entirely.

The fame or, rather infamy, of the Owl Creek Bank spread, and worthless bills of all kinds became known as *owls* or *owl creek bills,* such usage continuing for years thereafter. In a speech in the United States Senate on January 13, 1842, Senator Thomas Hart Benton commented negatively on the chartering of new banks that promised much but would probably deliver little, including this sentence:

> Does he not know that it is the slang upon which every bank charter is obtained—that it is the old worn out, used up, dead and gone slang upon which every red dog, wild cat, owl creek, coon box, and Cairo swindling shop which has disgraced our country, obtained their charter—and that all these paid out specie til they stopped?[1]

As to the origin of *coon box* in relation to paper money, I know nothing. The mention of *Cairo* refers to the Cairo Company and the Bank of Cairo, related phony operations located in Kaskaskia, Illinois, named after the wild and wooly city in Illinois at the intersection of the Mississippi and Ohio rivers, for a long time a hangout for thieves, grifters, gamblers, and others who preyed on the transient population.

The "Owls" of the Owl Creek Bank

Today, bills of the $1, $3, $5, and $10 denominations are known to exist for the Owl Creek Bank. The $3 bill has as its central vignette a snowy owl perched on the ground at the base of a tree. In the distance is a building—not the bank (of which more will be said), but a mill, complete with water wheel, next to a dam. "Richd Harrison fct." is in tiny letters at the upper right, meaning "Richard Harrison *fecit,*" the last for Latin, *made it.* Seemingly, Harrison was the engraver of the plate. Elsewhere on the bills is the tiny inscription, "Prin. by C.P.Hn Pitts'h."

Another of my pet projects, this one a bit more constant than rereading *Niles' Weekly Register,* is keeping a file on people associated with anything numismatic. I was rather surprised to find that I had a fair amount of information on both Richard Harrison, engraver, and C.P. Harrison, the printer, although the Harrisons are footnotes in the annals of numismatics in general and are scarcely more prominent in the specialty of currency.

Richard Granville Harrison, the delineator of the scene and lettering on the bills of the Owl Creek Bank, was born in London in 1793. By this time his father, William Harrison Sr., had spent six months in Philadelphia in 1792, under a contract to engrave notes in Philadelphia for the (first) Bank of the United States and for the Bank of North America. In 1794 William moved with his family to Philadelphia. He taught his sons the art and technique of engraving. On October 18, 1803, he was struck down by yellow fever, which visited the city several times during this era and caused great distress and loss of life. The instruction of Richard in the engraving trade was continued by his three older brothers, including Charles P. Harrison, who was the printer of the Owl Creek Bank notes.

Charles Peter Harrison was born in London in 1783. He learned engraving from his father and was considered to have special talent. In 1806 he is listed in Philadelphia as a copperplate printer. In 1818 he joined with his brother-in-law, James Porter, who learned copperplate engraving and printing from Har-

A $3 note of the Owl Creek Bank, Mount Vernon, Ohio. The plate for the note was engraved by Richard Harrison and was printed in Pittsburgh by C.P. Harrison.

rison. Certain bank bills engraved by his brothers, Richard and William Jr., were printed by C.P. Harrison and bear his imprint. In about 1824, C.P. Harrison moved to New York City, where he engaged in engraving and printing until his death there on November 27, 1854. Some bank bills of the Bank of America, New York City, from plates made by Fairman, Draper, Underwood & Co., Philadelphia, bear the notation, "Printed by C.P. Harrison N.Y.," an interesting confluence of two firms.

This useful information by a descendant of the Harrisons seems to explain the Pittsburgh address on the Owl Creek Bank notes:

> The earliest signed work of Richard Granville Harrison which we have found is the title page of *Works of Robert Burns,* published by F. Lucas and J. Cushing of Baltimore in 1814. Later he did various kinds of engraving . . . but he was principally a bank note engraver.
>
> His business card was engraved in bank note style and printed on bank note paper. Richard G. Harrison must have started his career of bank note engraving about 1815, for a series of Western Pennsylvania and Ohio bank notes dated 1815–16 and 1817 bears his name as engraver along with that of his brother Charles P. Harrison as printer. The signatures of these two Harrisons on some of the notes, such as those of the Westmoreland Bank of Pennsylvania in Greensburg, series of 1815, show them working in Pittsburgh. It seems likely, therefore, that these brothers made a trip through western Pennsylvania and eastern Ohio to engrave for banks springing up in that part of the country, and made their headquarters at that time in Pittsburgh. If this was the case, then Richard Granville Harrison and Charles P. Harrison may well have been . . . the first engravers and certainly the first bank note engravers actually to engrave plates west of the Alleghenies.
>
> During the Panic of 1837, when banks suspended specie payments, a variety of so-called scrip currency was issued. A large volume of such paper money was printed by E. Morris of Philadelphia from plates engraved by R.G. Harrison. These notes were first printed with engraved lathe work at each end and a certain series of vignettes in the top center. Later the denomination and name of the company, town, city, or even person issuing the note, were added by type printing. Very few bank notes dated after 1840 have been found bearing the signature of R.G. Harrison, but portraits and vignettes which he signed were used on notes bearing different engraving

firm names. That he worked for a number of bank note engraving firms is thus indicated, and the fact that during his career he used various forms of signature on his work has led to confusion in regard to his identity.[2]

Redeeming the Bank's Reputation

By 1862 the Owl Creek Bank was a blot on the escutcheon of Mount Vernon and Knox County. However, few knew the story that had played out several decades earlier. Further, I daresay that in later numismatic circles few collectors have known the story either, or at least until I included it as part of an article in *Paper Money* magazine. In bank-note literature it is generally referred to as "broken" or "failed," with little given in the way of details. A. Banning Norton, in *A History of Knox County, Ohio, From 1779 to 1862,* devoted 27 pages to the details in chapter 15 titled "The Owl Creek Bank of Mount Vernon: Its Public and Private History—Let It Be Relieved From Odium!" Following are some excerpts:[3]

> **A True Account**
>
> The history of Knox County would be incomplete without a faithful and true account of an institution with the above euphonious name, located upon the banks of Owl Creek, and within the sacred precincts of Mount Vernon. The engraving above gives a view of one of "the owls" issued by this bank. They were of every denomination from the shinplaster form of 6-1/4 cents up to $10.[4]
>
> The paper, engraving and finish of the notes, although not so perfect in every respect as those issued by banks in the present day, nevertheless is of a higher order than those put forth by the so-called "Confederate States of America," of which cotton is king, and Jeff. Davis vice regent. From the journals and old files of that day, as far accessible, we have compiled the following.
>
> **Currency Needed**
>
> There being great complaint of the scarcity of money after the war [of 1812], large numbers of people in various cities and towns in the United States, and more particularly in the West and Ohio, conceived the idea of multiplying the quantity of paper in lieu of money by manufacturing what is called a "currency." Among other points, those of Mount Vernon determined to engage in the business of making money.
>
> As early as December 1814, a meeting was held, and articles of association for the organizing of a bank, to be called the "Owl Creek Bank of Mount Vernon," were entered into, fixing the capital stock at $150,000, divided into shares of $50 each, payable in installments of not exceeding $5 each, and appointing certain commissioners to open stock books, &c. Petitions were then presented to the Legislature, praying for a charter; and after having petitioned the Legislature for an act authorizing such an association, and been denied the grant, determined to "go it alone," on their own hook.
>
> On the 10th day of April, 1816, the first meeting of record of those who inaugurated the Owl Creek Bank was held at the court-house in Mount Vernon. . . .

At the 1814 meeting resolutions were made to support the bank. It was stated that, although the local citizens had a fair right and privilege to have a bank charter, as the petition had been rejected, plans would go ahead independently, although petitions would continue to be presented. These men were named to draft the articles of association and bylaws: James Smith, Wm. Mitchell, M. Merritt, Abraham Darling, Hosmer Curtis, John Warden, Gilman Bryant, Jonathan Miller, L.S. Silliman, Benjamin Martin, Joseph Brown, John Green, and Jacob Young. From these, L.S. Silliman was later named cashier and James Smith president. Both hand-signed currency.

(Relating to this discussion, modern numismatic historian Wendell Wolka added, "Organizers first tried to obtain a charter for the Bank of Mount Vernon in 1814, but failed. In 1816 and 1817 they petitioned the state four times for a charter, but without success."[5])

On April 17, 1814, the bank's founders, named above, met at the house of Joseph Brown, where articles were drawn up. The official name was to be the Owl Creek Bank of Mount Vernon, and the capital was set as $250,000, current money of the United States, with the privilege of expanding to $500,000 should business warrant this change. Shares were $50 each. As soon as $25,000 worth of stock was subscribed for (but not necessarily paid for), business could commence. Stock sales were to commence on the first Monday of March, "at such places and under such agents as the commissioners may think proper, at the hour of ten o'clock in the morning, and continue until three o'clock in the evening of the same day, and from day to day during said hours, until the whole number of shares are subscribed for." Furthermore:

> At the time of subscribing, there shall be paid to the commissioners or their agents, on each share subscribed for, the sum of $1; the further sum of $2.50 shall be paid on each share, within 90 days thereafter, at such place as the commissioners shall appoint, of which due notice shall be given; the residue in such portions and at such places as the directors hereafter to be chosen shall appoint; they giving at least sixty days notice thereof in the public newspaper of the county. Provided, such installments shall at no time exceed $2.50 neither shall any subsequent installment be called for until a previous one has become payable.

Optimism ran high, and the articles made provisions in case the entire capital was subscribed for on the first day it was offered:

> No person or persons, body politic or corporate, shall be permitted on the first day to take more than one hundred shares, and if the shares are not all taken on that day, the foregoing part of this article is not to operate.
>
> If it shall so happen, that more than the stipulated number of shares may be subscribed for, the commissioners shall apportion them by deducting from the highest subscription; and if more persons subscribe than there are shares, the commissioners shall determine by lot to whom such shares belong; and as soon as may be thereafter, receipts shall be issued to the stockholders, and certificates of the amount of stock held by each.

To manage the bank a board of directors was set up with 13 members, all of whom were to reside within Knox County, a precaution against the practice of outsiders controlling and exploiting banks in distant regions. Other articles dealt with paying dividends, tending to obligations, and normal business.

Banking Operations

It seems that banking activities commenced in 1816. On July 3 of that year, bank commissioners (of the Owl Creek Bank—not state bank commissioners) B. Martin, Joseph Brown, and James Smith published a call for subscribers to pay all installments due by the 20th of the same month.

Per a notice by cashier L.S. Silliman, September 13, 1816, currency was ready at hand. Such bills soon were seen in the channels of commerce. Although the notes had no standing under state laws, they were well received locally, and merchants and others placed trust in them. Elsewhere in America, many other nonchartered banks were experiencing the same scenarios.

Defending the Bank

Although the Owl Creek Bank was successful locally, the idea of its existence raised questions outside Mount Vernon, and some said that its bills would not be redeemed in specie on demand. In August and September of 1816 several letters and comments appeared in newspapers in Lancaster, Mount Vernon, and other Ohio towns. Certain individuals, Dr. Moore B. Bradley and Samuel Williams prominent among them, complained about the bank. President James Smith defended the allegations, and according to historian Norton, "beat them all" in terms of logic.

The bank seems to have stood its course, as per this item in the *Zanesville Express,* December 16, 1816:

> Notwithstanding so much has been said against the Owl Creek Bank of Mount Vernon, we are assured that two gentlemen, a few days since, presented bills at that bank for a large amount, which were redeemed with chartered paper and specie.

Historian A. Banning Norton related this incident:

> About this time an enemy of the bank killed a tremendous big owl, and brought it into the town and rudely threw it down upon the counter, exclaiming, "There, damn you, I've killed your president."
>
> The bank building was located where Adam Weaver's hardware store now is. It was a rough, yet substantial piece of workmanship, a mixture of the Doric and Corinthian styles of architecture, weather-boarded, with four-penny nails thickly driven through its batten-door and window shutters, so thieves should not cut in and steal. On the ground it covered about 14 feet square, and was one low story in height, and painted red!

In late 1816 the bank ordered scrip notes from Murray, Draper, Fairman & Co., bank-note engravers and printers of Philadelphia, a firm enjoying a good trade throughout the East and Midwest. Bills in denominations of 6-1/4¢, 12-1/2¢, 25¢, 37-1/2¢ (possibly), and 50¢ were distributed—small in size and without signatures—no doubt useful locally in lieu of small change.[6] In contrast, most scrip issued by other banks was signed.

Trial by Journalism

Complaints about the Owl Creek Bank and its paper would not stop, and bank president Smith continued to fend off his detractors to the best of his ability. On August 6, 1817, Smith responded in the columns of the *Ohio Spectator* to a meeting of farmers, mechanics, merchants, and innkeepers in the town of Mansfield on July 11. It seems that certain men who had borrowed money from the Owl Creek Bank were now disparaging the institution—not at all unusual in the American banking scene of the time. The annals of finance are strewn with stories of debtors spreading rumors about a lender bank, in the hope of their being able to buy up the bank's currency at a discount to repay their loans or, worse, having the bank fail and become powerless. This was the bank-note equivalent of selling stock short, then spreading false rumors about the stability of the issuing corporation. Smith minces no words in his newspaper comments:

> If, sirs, your sympathy has been awakened for unfortunate persons who have received the paper,

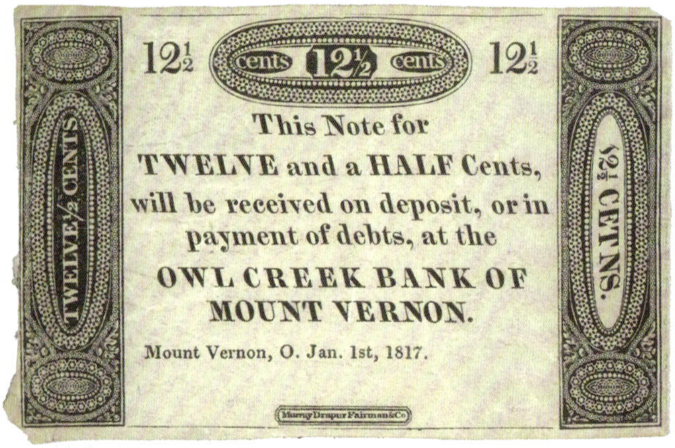

A 12-1/2¢ scrip note of the Owl Creek Bank, by Murray, Draper & Fairman, Philadelphia. The word CENTS is misspelled as CETNS in the right border. (Shown enlarged)

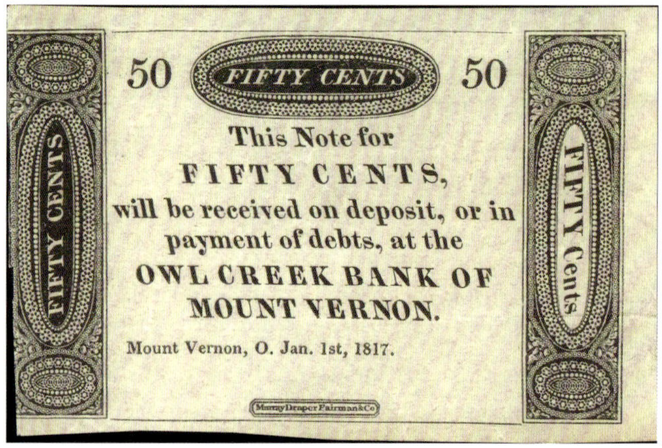

A 50¢ scrip note of the Owl Creek Bank. This and most other fractional scrip bills issued in this era were made by combining vignettes with typesetting. (Shown enlarged)

> I hope you will shortly be prepared to discharge your engagements with the *Owl Creek Bank of Mount Vernon.* It would be an insult upon your good sense for me to tell you, that for you to refuse the paper of this bank, while you are in debt to the bank, is a full sacrifice of every spark of honor.
>
> If you, sirs, and such characters as yourselves, would pay your engagements, or one half thereof, the Owl Creek Bank of Mount Vernon would be completely prepared to pay and give satisfactory exchanges for their notes in circulation. Your honors, sirs, we look after no longer, but your purses and property will have to be tried. Tavern bills and pills ought to be paid for in this paper. . . .
>
> I would advise you to be industrious in collecting the paper, as you know you soon, or at the next court, will have judgment against you. The Owl Creek paper will answer you as well as specie. . . . I censure no person, not in debt to the bank, for rejecting the paper; both the principle of moral justice and honor enjoins on every person indebted, to receive it. The sooner, sirs, you procure this paper, it will be the better for you. This bank will shortly be prepared to make general and satisfactory exchanges.
>
> James Smith
>
> P. S. The editors of the *Ohio Register* and the *Ohio Spectator* will confer a favor on Messrs. Bradley and Williams, as well as myself, by giving the above a place in their respective papers.
>
> J. S.

Tavern-keeper Samuel Williams, a scheming adversary who was in debt to the bank, countered with this item in the *Ohio Register,* August 20, 1817, in an open letter addressed to Smith:

> You, sir, are president of the Owl Creek Bank of Mount Vernon, you are clerk of the Court of Common Pleas, a justice of the peace, and, sometimes, preach the Gospel of Jesus, as I am informed—in politics a professed Republican; all of these callings you profess to fill with fidelity, nay, in some you have sworn to discharge their incumbent duties according to the best of your abilities. . . .
>
> You have prostituted the official duties and obligations as a justice of the peace to subserve its interest by administering unconstitutional oaths. Were you not sworn to support the constitution of this state and of the U. States in the oath of office? Yet swearing individuals not to take advantage of the statute law to prevent the collection of your illegal demands. You loaned us your bills in order to destroy those rights you profess to admire, the rights of managing our pecuniary concerns.
>
> That when we assert our independence, like freemen, you threaten us with destruction and tell us we are in your net, and at your mercy, the mercy of your religion, your integrity, your republicanism—your official virtue, the potent demand of one great Owl debt.

This criticism soon drew a reply from Smith:

> I think it unnecessary to answer your charges against me, when you charge my official, political and religious principles; all you say about it only exposes yourself. Had you kept silent the public had not known your baseness.
>
> Truly, Samuel, you was one of the persons that took a solemn oath to take no advantage of any statute law to prevent or stop the payments of your bank engagements. You brag of your full purse; you are then without excuse if you imagine you took an unconstitutional oath. Will you violate that oath to atone for the crime? You ought to be ashamed to let any person impose on you so far as to publish your black crimes with an idea of injuring me.
>
> If your purse is so full and heavy pay up your bank engagements. Strangers, citizens, and your neighbors too, will have much more confidence in you. FIVE HUNDRED DOLLARS of the trash [Owl Creek Bank bills] you mentioned will be received of you in place of gold and silver.

There are several nuances in this exchange, as it played out in the courts in other states, regarding paper money issued by nonchartered banks. In some venues it was held that if a private or nonchartered bank loaned funds, this action had no basis in state law and thus the debt could not be legally collected. Elsewhere, it was held by courts that as bills of such banks were not legal to begin with, it was no crime to counterfeit them—although this particular aspect did not seem to come up with regard to the "owls."

In the era of obsolete currency, as well as in numismatic circles today, there is no single agreed-upon definition as to what constitutes a legitimate bank.

Depreciation of the "Owls"

The naysayers kept up their attacks, and the bank was not able to maintain adequate specie reserves. The Norton narrative continues:

> The bills rapidly depreciated under the heavy blows given. There seemed to be no stopping the clamor against the bank. The principal circulation in Knox county was Owl Creek, and we find very many advertising for it. Among these were James Miller, and Burr, Green & Co.
>
> "William Stanbery offers to sell the 'Craig Farm,' at present occupied by Major Joseph Brown, to the highest bidder for Owl Creek Bank paper."
>
> "J. Brown offers to sell 156 acres of land near the town of Mt. Vernon, in the Hamtramick section, for such paper.
>
> "OWLs. All persons indebted to the subscriber, are requested to make prompt payment, for I am in want of OWL CREEK PAPER. John Shaw.
>
> "N. B. Those indebted for taxes, for 1817, are also requested to pay with the same."

It seems that such deliberate requests for Owl Creek bills, rather than specie or the currency of a state-chartered bank, reflect local support for the Owl Creek Bank.

Norton continues his discussion:

> The paper when presented was at first redeemed by the bank with chartered paper, and the stockholders and parties interested endeavored to sustain its credit by various devices.
>
> Among other plans adopted to keep up the paper was the following, which we give as showing the disposition of stockholders to pay, and the strenuous efforts resorted to:
>
> "Owls: Owl Creek Bank of Mount Vernon, January 1st, 1818.
>
> "Whereas, several reports have been circulated, some of which are false, and injurious to the credit of the bank, with respect to certain measures adopted by the directors: Therefore, for the purpose of suppressing the further propagating of such false rumors, the directors have thought proper to exhibit to the public, and to the stockholders, a fair and accurate statement of the measures actually determined on by them, and which has been the subject of such reports. The directors have observed with regret the depreciation of the Owl Creek paper of late, and particularly in Knox County. They have been fully convinced that the principal cause of the sudden fall of the Owl Creek paper is owing to the circumstance of the difficulty, or almost the impossibility of obtaining such goods as are wanted by the citizens with this kind of paper.
>
> "With a view, therefore, to obviate these difficulties, and at the same time to draw out of circulation the paper of the bank, we have entered into the following contract with Burr, Green &; Co., viz.: Said company, on their part, have undertaken to bring on a complete assortment of goods, and to retail the same for Owl Creek paper, at prices as low as they can be purchased for in chartered paper [bills of state-chartered banks], and to take assignments on judgments in favor of the Bank, or wait until the Bank can with convenience exchange; and for all paper thus collected, the only privilege granted to said company is a loan of $700 of such money as will pay carriages, to be made use of for that purpose, and to be paid back in good chartered paper, in installments, within one year. Given under our hands,
>
> "James Smith, William Mitchell,
> Jonathan Miller, Benjamin Martin,
> John Warden, John Hawn, Jr., John Shaw,
> Gilman Bryant, Hosmer Curtis,
> Wm. Y. Farquhar."

Further Events of 1818

Not long afterward this notice appeared in the local newspaper:

> Public Notice Is Hereby Given,
>
> That a meeting of the stockholders of the Owl Creek Bank of Mount Vernon will be held at the Banking House in Mount Vernon, on the 12th day of March, 1818, for the purpose of taking into consideration the propriety of closing the business of said company, and to transact any other business relative to said company which may be thought proper when met. Dated at Mount Vernon, this 6th day of January, 1818.
>
> Nathaniel Johnson, Jonathan Miller, Godleib Zimmerman, Benjamin Rush, I. N. Richardson, John Shaw, John Hawn, Jr., William Douglass, Samuel Mott, John Wilson, J. J. Banning, James McGibeny, James McGibeny for Joseph S. Newell, James Miller, Joseph Brown, L.S. Silliman.
>
> N. B. All the stockholders are particularly solicited to attend on said day.

In April 1818 in the *Ohio Register,* Smith ran this notice concerning his own business:

> New Goods for Sale: James Smith has just received and offers for sale a general assortment of mer-

chandise. In the house of Mr. Gilman Bryant, he will sell low for cash in hand, or country produce delivered, but no credit given. Owl Creek paper will be received at par; Granville, Wooster, New Lisbon, and Canton will be received at the present. Clerk's office removed to this stand. . . .

A "PRETTY SLEEK YANKEE"

The Owl Creek Bank figures peripherally in this account of a visitor to Cincinnati, described in *Niles' Weekly Register,* September 11, 1819:

> Cincinnati, Aug. 20.—There came down the river to this place a few days ago, a man from Pittsburgh. He was, what they here call "a pretty sleek Yankee." He brought with him $1,000 in the notes of Piatt's bank. On his arrival he went immediately to the bank, and demanded specie, which was refused.
>
> He expressed much surprise that they should refuse specie, and began to walk backward and forward in the bank. After a short time he asked them to exchange for notes on banks that paid specie. This was also refused. He then told them, that if they had any notes of Owl Creek, Wooster, or Uniontown, he would rather have them, than their notes. This affronted them very much; and they said, they did not suffer strangers to insult them in their bank!
>
> Our Yankee then apologized and declared, he by no means meant any insult, but, if they had any well executed counterfeit notes on any good bank, they would very much oblige him, by exchanging! This affronted them so highly that they ordered him out, which he complied with, after taking a few more turns backward and forward in the bank.

END OF THE LINE

The good intentions of the backers of the Owl Creek Bank and the leading citizens of Mount Vernon are reflected by a document dated February 28, 1822. In this document, these men pledged the amount of $15,000 in cash, services, or goods to settle the affairs of the bank, although they were under no legal pressure to do so:

> Gilman Bryant: $600 • Allen Scott: $200 • Joseph Talmage, in trade at trade prices: $150 • Henry Markley, in trade at trade prices: $700 • Eli Miller, 1/2 in Owl Creek paper and 1/2 in trade: $200 • Jonathan Miller, in good trade or Owl Creek paper: $300 • Wm. Mitchell, in Owl Creek paper or cash: $400
>
> Hosmer Curtis, in something as good as the debts: $400 • Moses Merritt, in Owl Creek paper or trade: $150 • Jacob Young, in Owl Creek paper or trade: $300 • Robert Giffin, in good trade at cash price: $300 • Jas. Shaw, in property: $300 •

A $1 bill of the Owl Creek Bank, October 3, 1816. These bills, similar in production concept to certain of the Vermont Glass Factory issues described earlier, were made by combining acid-etching and engraving techniques for the vignette, engravings for the two ends, and siderographically transferred engraved lettering for the text area. The denomination, in this case ONE, was added separately, as were certain other elements.

Detail of the vignette on the Owl Creek Bank $1 note. A comparison of this with the vignette on the $3 bill illustrated earlier reveals many differences in the details—leaves on the tree, rocks near the mill wheel, etc.

> John Trimble, in good trade at cash price: $250 • Jonathan Hunt, in good trade at cash price: $150 Jos. Brown, in good trade, say whisky: $100 • Samuel Mott, in trade: $100 • Henry Davis, Owl Creek paper or cash: $400 • John Hawn, in property: $70 • John Hawn, Jr., $300 in trade and $500 • John Troutman, in good trade or Owls: $200.

Although these intentions were of a high order, the balances of the bank were never settled, either with regard to the public redeeming the "Owls" at par or, on the other side of the ledger, the bank collecting loans from its debtors.

In the September 1826 term of the Ohio Supreme Court for the County of Knox, one Luke Walpole, a regional entrepreneur and trader and holder of a large amount of "owls," secured a judgment of $8,445.20, plus costs of suit, from the bank and certain related parties, this despite lack of records occasioned by this peculiar circumstance (in the words of historian Norton):

> The stockholders to the bank were never fully known by reason of the mutilation or alteration of the books, which took place pending a suit between Luke Walpole and some of the stockholders. The bank was entered one night, and the large box that contained the papers carried off, and subsequently the box was found in a thicket of hazel, east of town, broken open, and the books and papers scattered about with several of the names of stockholders obliterated.

On August 21, 1829, several individuals, all minor stockholders, brought suit against certain other stockholders of the bank, demanding an accounting of the payments made to Walpole, and other matters. This proceeding, known as "The Owl Creek Bank Case," generated one of the largest files of records in the court. Many records were reconstructed over a period of *years,* including at least a partial list of stockholders. On September 18, 1837, Henry B. Curtis, who had been appointed master commissioner of the case, made his report. He found that $26,796.20 would be needed to "discharge the present unpaid debts of the company, in Owl Creek Bank bills, commonly called." Curtis found that the defendants, being various stockholders, had enough assets to pay this debt.

However, the case dragged on, the complaint was amended, as was the defense, and other stockholders were brought in. In the September 1840 term of the court, special master H.H. Hunter set $17,457.27 as the amount then due. It seems that most of this money was eventually collected after many years, and thus the "Owls" were redeemed.

In the concluding words of historian Norton,

> Finally, after 30 years in the courts, this case . . . was brought to a close, the last dollar of its issue presented was redeemed, and 43 years after its birth, "all that was of earth and earthy" of the Owl Creek Bank of Mount Vernon was consigned to its final resting place—the Great Book of Records.

NUMISMATIC NOTES

As is generally true of bills of the second decade of the 19th century, those of the Owl Creek Bank are inex-

A $2 note of the Banking House of John H. Piatt & Co., Cincinnati, June 1, 1818, from a plate by Murray, Draper, Fairman & Co. This bank, never chartered by the state, was viewed as a sound institution in 1818. Its bills are mentioned in the "Sleek Yankee" article quoted above. The *Liberty Hall and Cincinnati Gazette,* March 2, 1819, stated that the bank had assets of $412,364.15 backing a modest circulation amounting to $242,783 in notes. However, on November 20, 1819, the *Detroit Gazette* stated that Piatt bills were worthless.

Regardless, the bills stayed in the marketplace. In August 1821 the exchange office of V.W. Fish in Cincinnati valued Piatt notes at a 33% discount. As it was not a chartered bank but operated in the shadows, little factual information about it ever reached print. The inaugural issue of *Bicknell's Counterfeit Detector,* July 31, 1830, listed Piatt & Co. as defunct.

A $5 bill of the Owl Creek Bank.

Top central vignette of the $5 note. The details are slightly different from the $1 and $3 vignettes on bills of the same bank.

pensive when found. When a bank failed, as here, the notes are generally more plentiful today than are those of banks that remained solid. For Ohio notes, Wendell A. Wolka's book, *History of Nineteenth Century Ohio Obsolete Bank Notes and Scrip*, is essential. This is one of many volumes published by the Society of Paper Money Collectors on notes of individual states.

Bank Notes of the 1820s

The Banking and Monetary Scene

Banks, Bills, and Business

Following the chaotic monetary conditions during and after the War of 1812, there was little interest or incentive to form new banks in the early years of the 1820s. Many banks and business enterprises had failed recently, and economic times had been particularly onerous in 1818 and 1819. Failures were still occurring.

On January 1, 1820, the Treasury Department estimated that 308 banks were in operation in the country, with bills in circulation amounting to $44,863,344. A decade later the figures of January 1, 1830, showed 330 banks, or an increase of less than 10%, with bills in circulation amounting to $61,323,898.[1]

In earlier times, bank closings were usually precipitated by poor business decisions, unfavorable economic conditions, and lack of capital, these circumstances punctuated with relatively few out-and-out frauds. Those banks that were operated by criminals, such as Andrew Dexter Jr., were exceptions. But the situation changed in the 1820s, when a wave of frauds took place, in which Jacob Barker was especially prominent. As will be seen, Barker's career is not unlike that of Dexter's, in that he was not prosecuted for his crimes and went on to build a new career in the South, with no hindrance from his past.

Such scenarios are puzzling in light of, for example, the fact that ordinary citizens were often sent to prison for not paying their debts, however small. This excerpt from *Niles' Weekly Register,* April 24, 1830, tells of events in New York City:

> The number of persons imprisoned in the debtors' apartment in this city, from June 6, 1829, until February 24, 1830, was 817, of whom there were: 80 whose debts were below $1, 233; above $1 and below $5, 174; above $5 and below $10; 140; above $10 and below $20; 142 above $20 and below $100; 98 above $100. Total 817. Of 252 of these unfortunate people, the debts totaled $663 and the costs $448; of 64, the debts totaled $58 and the costs $120!

Although bank and commercial fraud could be devastating to bill holders and stockholders, in the early 19th century it was not penalized as seriously as was petty thievery or inability to pay minor debts.

Other Changes in Banking

In 1820 the Maine district of Massachusetts became the state of Maine, with the result that banks with Massachusetts addresses in that section now were listed in Maine—without having moved. America continued its westward expansion, and among the new banks chartered were many west of Pennsylvania.

The Suffolk Bank system of exchanging currency of member banks became very popular in New England, and beginning in 1824 it furnished an effective counter to the trading of bills at deep discounts. The system is discussed at the end of this chapter.

New York City, long the premier U.S. business center experienced good times during the decade, providing a setting for several bank frauds. The *Commercial Advertiser* gave this glowing view in August 1824:

The Penobscot Bank of Buckstown, then located in Massachusetts, issued this $3 Patent Stereotype Steel Plate note on July 11, 1809. Later, Buckstown changed its name to Bucksport, and in 1820 the town changed its address to the state of Maine.

A $50 proof note of the Bucksport Bank, dated October 10th 1854 in the plate, with a vignette of Santa Claus. This bank was in the same town and location as the Penobscot Bank of Buckstown, Massachusetts. The plate bears two imprints associated with the same partnership: Bald, Adams & Co., New York City, and Bald, Cousland & Co., Philada.

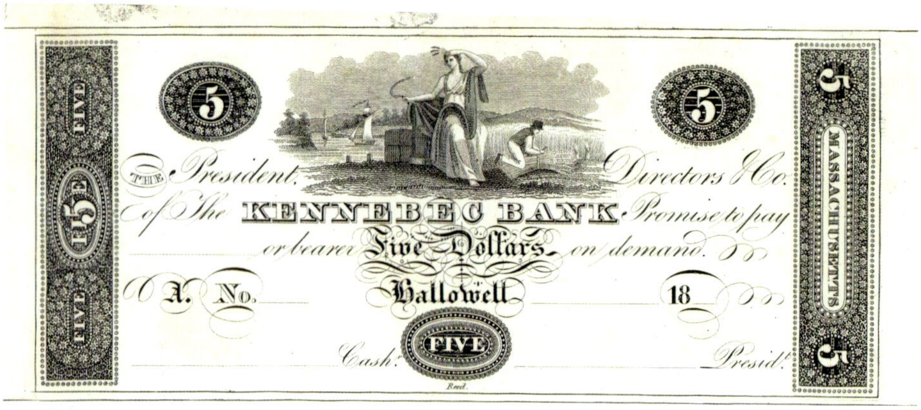

A $5 bill of the Kennebec Bank of Hallowell, with Massachusetts address, circa 1816 to 1820. Proof impression from a plate by Abner Reed. This bank continued business in Hallowell until 1826. Later bills were issued with the Maine imprint.

> We question whether the city of New York ever presented the appearance of greater prosperity, or more rapid growth than it does this season. We are visited by the merchants of every clime, and almost every part of our own country—so that ours may be fairly denominated "the mart of nations." The West Indies and South America pour in upon us their gold and the productions of their soil, and receive in return our own and the fabrics of foreign countries.
>
> We understood early in the spring that as many as 500 or 600 new mercantile establishments were opened in New York this season; and we now learn that more than 3,000 buildings have been commenced and are nearly completed within the city limits. Most of them are of brick and in a style at once rich, simple and substantial. Thirty-five years ago, a prediction of what New York now is, would have been deemed quixotic—equally so would the prediction now be esteemed of what she is yet destined to be.[2]

The Tariff Bill of 1828 placed high tariffs on incoming goods, with the result that domestic manufacturing flourished as never before. In politics and in print this was called the "American system." On the other hand, retaliation in the form of import tariffs levied by foreign countries dampened overseas demand for American goods. South Carolina, in particular, objected to the tariffs, and after they were announced, flags flew at half-mast on ships in Charleston Harbor.[3] Senator John Calhoun espoused the importance of the South, and in coming years he was the chief legislative advocate of the perceived rights of the South, in opposition to the North. This tariff legislation was the catalyst for continuing sectional problems. The bad situation was soon made worse by growing antislavery sentiment in the North, sowing the seeds for the Civil War's start in 1861.

In 1828 Andrew Jackson, the hero of New Orleans, was elected president of the United States, and in March 1829 he was inaugurated. This change initiated the Jacksonian era, in which many changes took place in the monetary system, not the least of which was the closing of the second Bank of the United States in 1836 (discussed in chapter 8). Whether the Jacksonian era was good or bad for America is a matter still not settled by historians.

Bank-Note Engraving

Philadelphia remained the center of the bank-note engraving profession in the 1820s, although New York City and a few other cities and towns were home to scattered businesses. In Newburyport, Massachusetts, the Patent Stereotype Steel Plate notes were turned out in large quantity by Jacob Perkins's business, although

Perkins himself now resided in London, as he would for the rest of his life.

In time, the center of bank-note engraving would move from Philadelphia to New York City. By 1858, when the American Bank Note Company was formed there by consolidation of seven companies, New York City was the focal point of the profession, with Philadelphia being of minor importance.

Siderography became widely used, resulting in more ornate vignettes in the 1820s than were produced at any time before. Now it was a simple matter to transfer the image of a god or goddess surrounded by mythical splendor to any number of bank-note plates. Dramatically diminished was the practice of creating vignettes one at a time for use on bills, such as had been done on the Owl Creek Bank, Concord Bank in New Hampshire, and certain other currency described earlier.

Portrait of Andrew Jackson, engraved by James B. Longacre and published in the *National Portrait Gallery*, 1837.

No Gold Coins

After 1820, federal gold coins were no longer seen in the channels of commerce. Although mintages remained high for half eagles, the highest-valued coin of the realm, nearly all were exported. At the time of their creation it took more than $5 in gold deposited at the Philadelphia Mint to create a half eagle. After mintage, such coins were shipped abroad, where they were valued strictly on their gold content, with the stamped face value being irrelevant. This situation would continue in effect until the summer of 1837, when the authorized weight of gold coins was reduced, after which new lightweight issues circulated freely. Writing in the *National Gazette,* Condy Raguet, a leading economist of the day, stated, "Though the coinage of gold continues to be large, not a gold coin is anywhere to be seen in circulation."[4]

Although gold coins were minted in quantity in the 1820s, nearly all were exported. None circulated in domestic commerce. In the absence of gold coins, paper money was used extensively for large transactions. The illustrated 1827 half eagle is a prime rarity today.

This situation meant that nearly all domestic commerce was conducted in bills of paper money, especially for large transactions. Silver half dollars continued to be minted in large quantities, and dollars of the era from 1794 to 1803 were still seen in circulation but in diminishing numbers.

A reflection on the scene from *Niles' Weekly Register,* March 9, 1822, noted that a British vessel had just arrived at Charleston from the West Indies,

> with 500,000 silver dollars,[5] for that city and New York. A while ago, we never heard of such an occurrence without pleasure, thinking that it furnished conclusive evidence of the prosperous state of the country—believing that specie was chiefly used between the dealing men of different nations to adjust accounts and pay off balances, which could not be settled by a mutual exchange of commodities of their own growth or product. . . . But now we do not feel pleased with such arrivals—we know that the United States was drained of two millions and a half of dollars, in specie, in the course of last year, and we are to understand by such importations that they are made for the purpose of being exchanged for gold, though this may not be the case in the present instance.
>
> The general design cannot be mistaken, when gold is about *eight and one-half percent premium,* and Spanish dollars, until very lately, would not command one percent premium, if any; though at present the brokers sell them at 2-1/2. Our eagles, being worth $10.85 in silver, for the British Mint, have nearly all taken wings and flown away—yet it has been said that "the balance of trade is in our favor"!

In this era and in other times when federal gold coins were not seen in commerce, they could be obtained from bullion and exchange dealers by paying a premium. All large towns and cities had such specialists, most of whom did a lively trade. Specie was always in strong demand by citizens and businesses who did not like paper money. *Niles' Weekly Register* kept up a flow of useful information concerning the availability and movement of gold and silver coins in commerce as well as of the condition of banks.

(continued on p. 128)

The Bank-Note Art of Christian Gobrecht

Relevant to bank-note art of this period, a file of proofs and remainders thought (but not confirmed) to be from plates engraved by Christian Gobrecht circa the 1820s and 1830s is preserved by the Historical Society of Pennsylvania. Examples illustrated here are images that have not been generally known to the numismatic community. If Gobrecht was the artist, he likely engraved the largest vignette illustration on each note, while numerals, smaller vignettes, decorative borders, and the like were simply from the engraving companies' stocks.

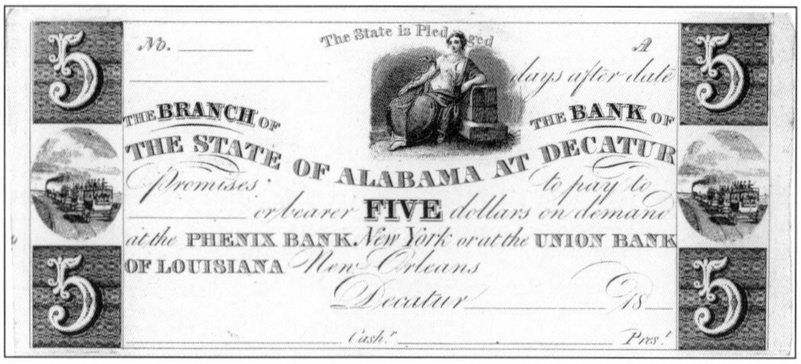

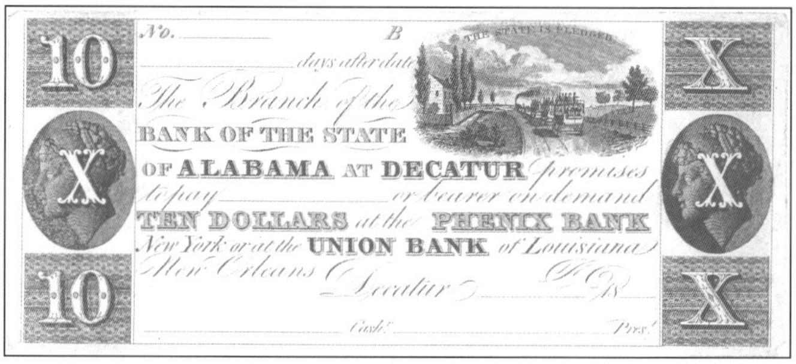

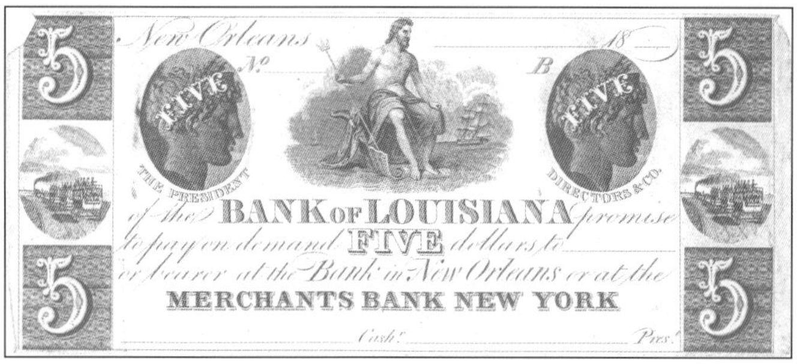

ONE ONE ONE ONE ONE
The President Directors and Company of the
COLUMBIANA BANK
of NEW LISBON promise to pay ONE DOLLAR on
demand to or Bearer
NEW LISBON, OHIO 18
Cash. Pres.

THREE THREE THREE THREE
The President Directors & Co.
OF THE COLUMBIANA BANK OF NEW LISBON
Promise to pay on
Demand to or Bearer
New Lisbon ohio THREE DOLLARS 18
Cash. Pres.
THREE THREE THREE THREE THREE THREE

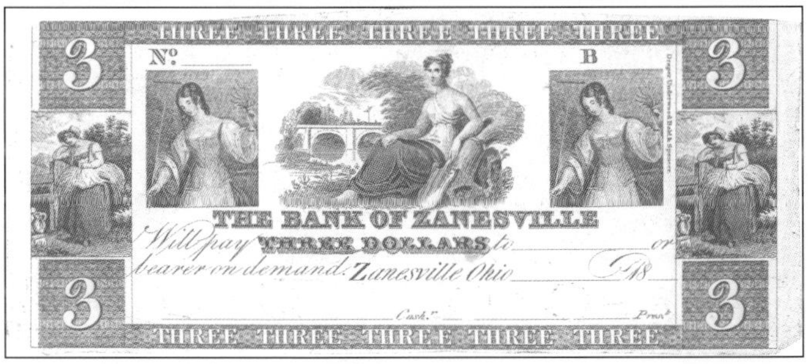
THREE THREE THREE THREE THREE
THE BANK OF ZANESVILLE
Will pay THREE DOLLARS to or
bearer on demand. Zanesville Ohio 18
Cash. Presd.

TWENTY TWENTY TWENTY TWENTY
The HARRISBURG BANK
XX XX
Promises to pay on demand
TWENTY DOLLARS
to or bearer Harrisburg Pa. 18
Cash. Presd.

FIVE FIVE FIVE FIVE FIVE
THE HARRISBURG BANK
V V
Promises to pay FIVE dollars on demand
to or bearer
HARRISBURG Pa. 18
Cash. Presd.
FIVE FIVE FIVE FIVE FIVE

TEN TEN TEN TEN TEN
The UNION BANK of the STATE of TENNESSEE
promises to pay TEN Dollars to or
bearer on demand. Nashville 18
Cash. Pres.

Tales of Two New York City Bankers

Jacob Barker

In the *Merchants and Bankers Almanac,* 1870 edition, space was given for biographical sketches of well-known bankers, including this item:

> JACOB BARKER OF NEW ORLEANS. Jacob Barker is a descendant of the Quakers. He was a resident of New York City forty years ago, and took up his residence at New Orleans, where he now resides. At the age of sixteen years, he came to New York City, a poor boy, and got employment in the counting room of Isaac Hicks, a merchant of this city, He commenced business for himself before his majority, and was soon in possession of four ships and a brig. In the year 1801, Aug. 27, he married Elizabeth Hazard, daughter of Thos. Hazard.
>
> After the war Mr. Barker engaged as a banker, and unfortunately lost his credit, and was prosecuted for his participation in the affairs of certain insurance companies. Many years afterwards he removed to New Orleans, and was elected to Congress after the rebellion, but was declared ineligible.
>
> During the war of 1812, the credit of Mr. Barker was of the highest. In connection with Mr. Girard, Mr. J.J. Astor, Mr. Parish, and others, he bid for the loans of 1813–1815. He is yet a resident of New Orleans, but failed as a broker since the rebellion.

From the above article it would seem that Barker was a banker of outstanding reputation, an associate of Stephen Girard, John Jacob Astor, and others, but somehow lost his credit. No record has been found of Barker doing jail time as the result of any "prosecution." In fact, Barker was a fraud of the same ilk as Andrew Dexter Jr. He controlled several banks, all of which conducted business under false pretenses. Here are a few of many notices published in *Niles' Register* over a period of time concerning his case.

June 26, 1819:

> *Jacob Barker's bank at New York.* Mr. Barker gives notice that he has hypothecated, property in the city to the amount of $100,000, to pay the debts of a bank in the interior of the state, which appears to belong chiefly to him, called the Washington and Warren Bank; and he intimates that he can pay these debts in sixty days. He speaks largely about his resources, and is probably rich.
>
> To effect a liquidation for the Washington and Warren Bank, he is about to repair to Sandy Hill, where it is located, and, while absent, his Exchange Bank in New York will suspend business. He says that the amount of his notes out is not large, and that he is able to pay them all very speedily, though not at present, on account of the great quantities of them which have been pressed upon him, &c. He has made an arrangement however, by which those who had deposits in his bank will receive the balances due them next week.

Barker wrote on his own behalf on July 3, 1819:

> *Exchange Bank, June 29.* Conformable to promise, I have visited Sandy Hill, inspected the concerns of the Washington and Warren Bank, found them in excellent condition, and I do not hesitate to declare, that if there is anything earthly certain it is the solvency of said Bank.
>
> When I have redeemed my pledge as to the paper of the Washington and Warren bank, (which will be within the period mentioned), the public will then know how to estimate what I have said as to the goodness of the notes of the Exchange Bank. JACOB BARKER.

Niles' furnished information on Barker's bank on September 23, 1820:

> *Prices of Bank Notes, at Baltimore: New York:* City banks, par; country notes, generally good, several as par, the rest at 1 to 3 discount. Except the bank of Hudson, the Washington and Warren Bank, Jefferson County Bank, Bank of Niagara, Jacob Barker's Bank [Exchange Bank, New York City], and all the unincorporated banks and other money-manufacturing institutions, few notes of which are afloat, and these very bad.

Legal proceedings made the newspaper on January 1, 1827:

> *The New York Trials.* The case of Jacob Barker, and the company found guilty with him of conspiring to defraud, etc. has been removed to the Supreme Court by a certiorari. Charles Mowatt and Thomas Hyatt, have been sentenced to the penitentiary for two years, and Samuel F. Lambert and Henry B. Lambert sentenced each for one year. Thomas Hyatt not appearing, his recognizance was forfeited.
>
> Certain proceedings in the trial of Barker and the rest, are objected to as having been illegal. The effect of the writ of certiorari may be to grant a new trial.

January 3, 1829:

> *More Disclosures.* Among those charged with some iniquitous doings as to the Tradesmen's Bank, at New York—(a bubble that floated awhile and disappeared)—was Mr. Jacob Barker—who has lately vindicated himself in a pamphlet, and before a public meeting of the people; of which latter we have the following account in the N.Y. *Mercantile Advertiser* of the 24th ult.
>
> The meeting invited by Mr. Barker at the Exchange, on Monday evening, was attended by a large concourse of respectable citizens, exceeding, it was supposed, upwards of 2,000 in number. Mr. Barker exhibited to this meeting, the original papers which he has published in a pamphlet,

proving according to these, that he had no concern in the disposition of the stock of the Tradesmen's Bank, as was alleged against him in the late conspiracy trials; and showing also the real parties engaged in that transaction, one of whom it appears was the Hon. Richard Riker, recorder of the city of New York.

The Capers of Malapar

Then there are the machinations of Malapar, who to the general public seemed to have had just one name. Here are notices from *Niles' Weekly Register.*

April 29, 1826:

> The "Marble Manufacturing Company" of New York City, which lately commenced the manufacture of something which they passed off as bank notes, has already shut up shop. From what is stated, it appears that the managers of this establishment are rightful candidates for the manufacture of marble—in the penitentiary.

July 1, 1826:

> *Speculation!* Malapar, late president of the Marble Manufacturing Company at New York City, who issued a large amount in things like bank notes, has been tried and found guilty of a conspiracy to defraud certain persons named and the public. The development of this affair is said to show as profligate a villainy as ever was exhibited.

July 8, 1826:

> It is thought that Malapar and his associates—a miserable set of irresponsible and obscure individuals, have defrauded the public of about five hundred thousand dollars. The fellow, a short time before he turned money-manufacturer, kept an oyster cellar. He is a Canadian Frenchman, and especially exerted himself to take-in his Canadian brethren, which he did do, to a large amount.

December 2, 1826:

> Malapar, the maker of the Marble (paper-money) Manufacturing Company of New York City, by which many were swindled, is now at Paris—and has proclaimed his intention of "making a book," to give an account of the business of that rag-shop.

July 14, 1827:

> Malapar, the fellow who, in New York City, by speculation, in a few months, elevated himself from a cleaner of boots or vendor of oysters, we forget which, to the highest rank among the nobility and gentry of the city, taking the lead in "good society," has been apprehended at Montreal, and there is some prospect that the honorable gentleman will be associated with the "marble company" at present incorporated within the walls of the state prison; and the charter to carry on his operations, may be granted during life!!

Malapar did have a first name: Antoine.

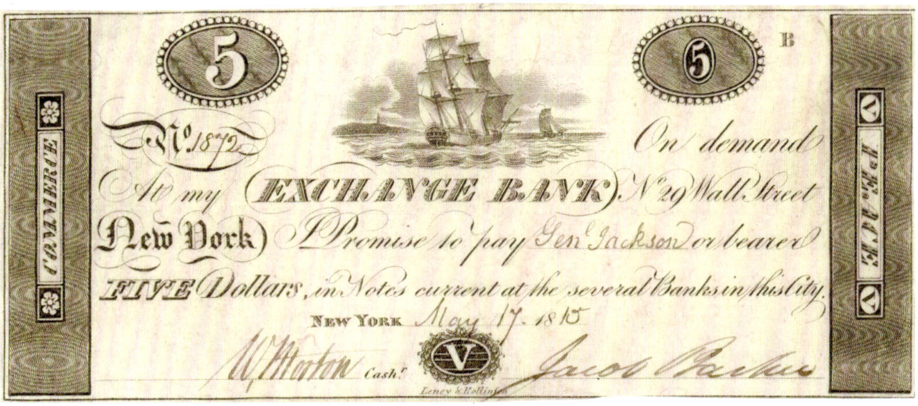

Signed by Jacob Barker, this $5 note of the Exchange Bank, New York City, signed and dated May 17, 1815, was engraved and printed by Leney & Rollinson. *Commerce* and *Peace* at the left and right refer to hopes at the end of the War of 1812. The nominal inked payee is Gen. Jackson, hero of the Battle of New Orleans, whose accomplishment was still echoing when this bill was issued.

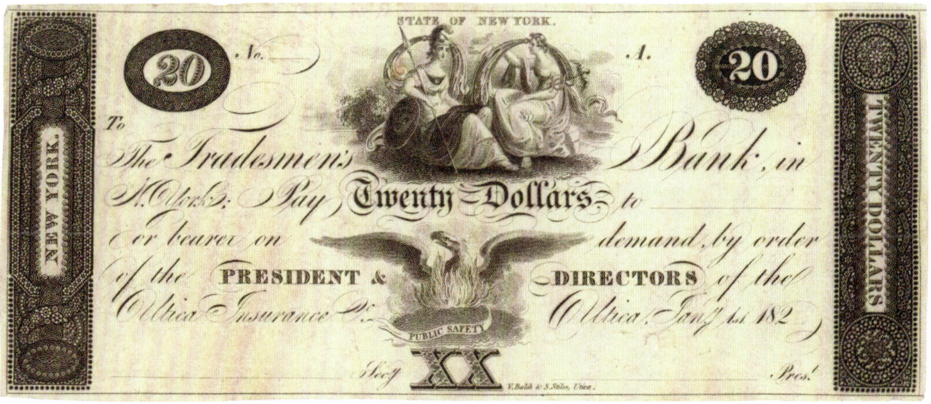

Proof note for another of Barker's peculations, the fraudulent Tradesmens Bank, New York City, from a plate by V. Balch & Stiles, Utica, New York. This bill apparently was issued by the Utica Insurance Company, to be redeemed by the Tradesmens Bank.

Capers in Connecticut

The Eagle Bank

Of the frauds in Connecticut that achieved notoriety in the 1820s, the situation of the Eagle Bank was foremost in the news. Indeed, the echoes of the scenario lasted for a long time as an example of the evils of banking—similar to the lingering poor reputation of the unfortunate Owl Creek Bank discussed earlier.

In May 1811 projectors of the Eagle Bank, to be situated in New Haven, Connecticut, applied for a charter. They were unsuccessful at first, but they persisted, and on October 3 success was theirs. On New Year's Day 1812 the bank opened for business in a building on Chapel Street, west of the New Haven Bank. From the outset the institution was managed for the profits of its directors and officers, not to benefit the general stockholders or the public. Poor loans were made, including substantial amounts to the directors. Through various deceptions the price of the bank stock was manipulated. However, these activities attracted little attention at the time.[6] The president drew an annual salary of $1,500, generous for an era in which most bank presidents served for a few hundred dollars or less (it was the *cashier* who was sometimes paid into four figures).

The Eagle Bank turned out a steady stream of bills, which were used in commerce in the district and received by some banks in New York City. During the coin shortage of late 1815 and early 1816, the institution was one of several in the state that issued fractional bills.

In 1817 the bank president, Simon Baldwin, who had held the post for just a short time, resigned his post, and cashier George Hoadly was elected in his place.[7] In collusion with a new cashier named to the vacancy created by Hoadly's move, Hoadly made secret loans that were not entered on the bank's records, nor were the actions discussed with the board of directors. Large numbers of bills in large numbers were procured and sent to agents

> to give them a forced and distant circulation, and by that means to sustain the operations of the bank. Those operations were not recorded in the regular books of the bank, but vested in loose papers in the custody of the president, and in a book, in which the initial letters of the names of the agents were entered, and the figures containing the amount by them received.[8]

False financial statements were made and distributed to stockholders as well as to the state. In one instance $220,000 in bills was given to president Hoadly of the bank and others in exchange for worthless IOUs, but these notes were not entered on bank records and statements of the currency in circulation. Stripped of its real assets, the bank's flimsy structure was sustained in the early 1820s by issuing large quantities of post notes, sold at a discount to speculators.

In his history of New Haven banking, William F. Hasse Jr. relates this exchange of 1817:

> An interesting incident occurred between the Eagle Bank and the Derby Bank. . . . The Eagle Bank, being jealous of its competitor, at one time started a run on the Derby Bank on a Saturday morning by presenting a large number of Derby Bank bills, $10,000 worth, for payment at the Derby Bank. The Derby Bank stalled around so well that at 12 o'clock Saturday noon, the bank had not finished the transaction and closed its doors to the Eagle Bank until Monday morning.
>
> In the meantime, the president of the Derby Bank, who lived in New Haven, collected $30,000 worth of Eagle Bank bills, which in those days was a fortune. He then presented these bills to the Eagle Bank for payment when it opened for business Monday morning.[9]

Apparently, all bills in this exchange were finally redeemed.

In autumn 1823 this event took place, per a contemporary account:

For the Marble Manufacturing Company the talented partnership of A., B. & C. Durand and Wright produced this beautiful but worthless $100 bill. Fraudsters often called on the leading bank-note companies to create notes that today are high examples of engraving art.

New Haven, November 25. Bank War: The New York banks have engaged with the country banks in "the unprofitable contest of trying which can do the other the most harm." Hostilities, in our quarter, we are informed, commenced by a draft on them, from the Eagle Bank of this city, for 40,000 dollars, which was duly honored, and the specie shipped, transported and safely deposited in the Eagle vaults.

But the money was scarcely stowed away, when the New York agent, a very modest, sleek, grave looking gentleman, appeared with 75,000 dollars in Eagle bills, determined to return the first blow with interest. He was offered the specie or a draft on New York City, at his election. He took the $40,000 back again, and, the expense of freight being considered, he very wisely took a draft for the balance.

Now comes the Eagle's turn again—and they have deposited, in the Bank of New York, one hundred thousand dollars [of New York City bank bills], for which their agent there is instructed to demand the specie. Thus "the combat thickens."

But it is an ill wind that blows nobody good. However, unprofitable the contest may be to the banks, our packet owners[10] are likely to thrive by it: Twenty dollars for bringing the $40,000 up, and twenty dollars for carrying it back again, is forty dollars—so we shall be sure to have some money in circulation as long as they carry on war.

It since appears that 100,000 dollars have arrived from New York City, and we may soon expect to hear of their going back again. A little courtesy among the solvent and honest banks would prevent such things. Paper, passing for money, may thus be transferred, and the money itself be demanded and carried backward and forward almost without end, if the affray be prudently managed, even until nearly the capital of the contending powers is spent in the cost of transportation.[11]

A court case reflects the condition of the Eagle Bank in early 1824:

On the 13th of January, 1824, a citizen of New York offered at the counter of the Eagle Bank in New Haven a certain amount of the bills of that bank and demanded payment thereof in specie. The officers of the bank offered to redeem these bills by giving a draft for the amount on a bank in the city of New York; which was refused. The bills were then left with the officers of the Eagle Bank to be counted and paid.

Two days afterwards the president of the Eagle Bank forwarded a draft to an agent in New York City, with directions to tender the amount of the bills in specie to "A" the next morning. This was accordingly done; and the money was refused, on the ground that two days' interest was then due. Within a day or two afterwards "A" again demanded payment of the bills at the Eagle Bank, which was refused, on the ground of an alleged payment in New York; and then he demanded the bills themselves, which were also refused, and were purposely mingled with the redeemed circulation of the bank.

In March 1824, "A" sued the Eagle Bank in an action for money had and received, and ulti-

Eagle Bank $10 note dated Feby 4th 1815 in the plate, by Leney & Rollinson. George Hoadly signed as cashier, here seen faintly. Later he became president of the bank.

Trimmed proof of a $10 note for the Eagle Bank, possibly engraved byChristian Gobrecht for Murray, Draper, Fairman & Co. (which operated from 1811 to 1822). (Historical Society of Pennsylvania)

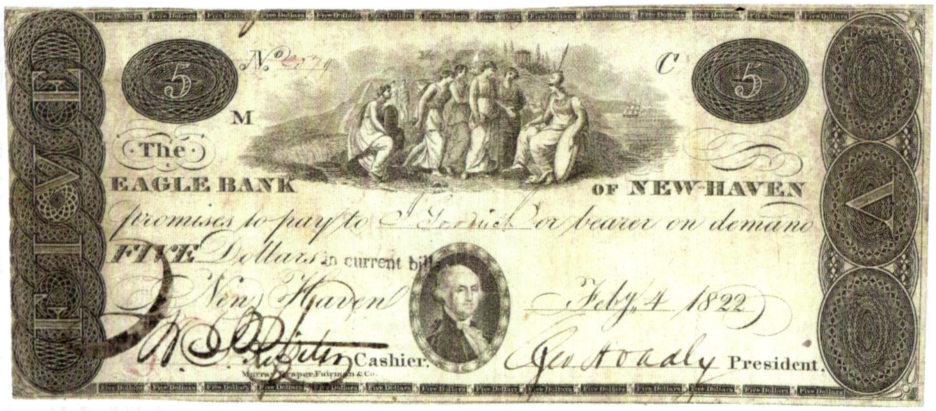

Eagle Bank $5 note made by Murray, Draper, Fairman & Co., Philadelphia, and dated Feby 4th 1822 in the plate.

Eagle Bank $5 note from a plate by N. & S.S. Jocelyn, New Haven, and dated August 4th, 1825. It was issued just before the bank collapsed. The inscription states that it is payable at the Phenix Bank, New York City.

> mately (in 1827) recovered judgment for the amount of the bills and interest.

To help build the illusion of strength even while the rumors swirled, the precariously positioned Eagle Bank commissioned an architect to design an impressive new building in the Greek revival style, to be erected on the corner of Church and Chapel streets in New Haven.

The narrative of the court case continues:

> On the 31st of August, 1825, the affairs of the Eagle Bank being desperate, the funds provided in New York for the payment of the bills were withdrawn, and an entry thereof was made on the books of the bank. On the 19th of September, 1825, the bank failed.
>
> On the 21st, the president assigned a quantity of iron to trustees, first, to secure to a certain amount an endorser of the post-notes of the bank, and then, after paying the Savings Bank the amount of its deposits, "to pay all other persons who had ordinary or special deposits with the Eagle Bank the full amount of such deposit. . . ."
>
> On a bill in chancery, brought by "A" to obtain the benefits of the assignment, as a creditor of the Eagle Bank, by reason of an ordinary or special deposit of money with such bank, it was *held,* that the plaintiff did not sustain that character, and was, therefore, not entitled to the relief sought.[12]

The September 19, 1825, demise of the Eagle Bank marked the first bank failure in the state, but the collapse would soon be joined by another. At the time the Eagle Bank closed its doors, the currency in circulation was stated to be $1,163,237, probably an unreliable figure and perhaps conservative. Against this there were assets estimated to be worth $300,000.[13]

Editor Hezekiah Niles, never one to mince words, printed this report in his *Register* on October 15:

> Banking! It is stated that the Eagle bank, at New Haven, which lately closed its doors, has not met with any material losses; and, it is strongly intimated, that its stoppage of payment may have been brought about that the favored few, largely indebted to this swindling-mill, may pay off their debts, at from 30 to 50 percent discount—that being the present value of its notes in circulation.
>
> When this operation is performed, perhaps, the bank will resume specie payments! If hanging laws are necessary for any other classes of persons than deliberate murderers, pirates and slave traders, fraudulent bankers ought to receive all the benefit of them. It is not easy to comprehend the idea of anything more villainous, than that persons, pretending to respectability, should combine to defraud the public. Common counterfeiters are sinless compared with them. But what else are dishonest bank-managers than counterfeiters? If one of them passes a note for one hundred dol-

> lars, which he knows to be worth only fifty, the injury is the same as though he had uttered falsely made notes to the amount of fifty dollars—and, indeed, the crime is greater, because of the calculating manner in which the fraud is committed.

The same issue included this information in a separate article:

> At auction!—Five thousand dollars, in bills of the Eagle Bank of New Haven, were sold at public auction, in New York City, a few days since, and brought 57-1/2 cents to the dollar. A pretty handsome little job of swindling was this. It is very possible that they will pass into the hands of some director of that respectable institution, and that he will realize the whole amount of them [by using them at face value to pay of debts he owes to the bank].

On October 26th at a special meeting of the stockholders a statement of the bank's affairs was given. According to the officers, $233,681.87 in loans due the bank were considered to be collectible, and $67,000 in good currency of other banks and loans secured by mortgages were of solid value. But these assets were vastly overwhelmed by doubtful loans amounting to $1,604,439.77. Currency in circulation was stated at $430,607 plus $732,630 in post notes. These, too, were "loans" of a kind, the whole placing the bank in an untenable situation. With no alternative in the offing, the shareholders voted to wind down the affairs of the bank. The true condition was not widely appreciated, and local brokers were trading in Eagle Bank currency at 50 to 55 cents on the dollar, hoping for a resuscitation of the institution—as sometimes happened with banks in difficulty, but not often. Within a week the bills dropped to 30 to 40 cents, after which they spiraled further downward to nothing.

Soon afterward, the vaults of the bank were attached by creditors, but upon inspection were found to be empty.[14] This finding set off a financial panic in the city, resulting in losses beyond those taken by shareholders and currency holders of the bank. At this time, local financiers were heavy subscribers to stock for the new Tontine Hotel, then under construction, with the granite basement largely completed. Shares were $100 each, but most buyers had made only small down payments. After the Eagle Bank failure, reeling from losses, most subscribers could pay no more, and the gaping hole of the Tontine cellar remained at the site for years afterward. In a related situation a local entrepreneur envisioned borrowing $500,000 to put up a large group of houses on Church Street. Partially completed, the project was later sold for just $13,900.

Niles' continued the story, this a year and a half later, May 19, 1827:

> The agents of the Eagle Bank of New Haven have made a report of its condition. It appears that almost all the debts which grew out of the ordinary, or honest business of the bank, have been already paid, but that one million and a half of dollars are yet outstanding. The agents further state, that they have "reason to believe that a great amount of property belonging to the debtors, has been secreted or withdrawn from the jurisdiction of the state"; but as some of the principal debtors are now confined to the state, they are not without expectation that further collections, by compromise or otherwise, will be made. Under these circumstances, very little, as yet, has been collected, to constitute a fund for a dividend among the creditors of the bank.
>
> The agents have not deemed it advisable to avail themselves of the provisions of the act of 1826, which authorizes the Superior Court to limit the time of exhibiting claims, and to declare a dividend thereon, believing that the interests of the creditors would be thereby promoted. Really, really, a few did business on a grand scale as the Eagle Bank of New Haven! The sum of all the property appropriated to themselves by the rogues confined in our penitentiaries and jails, is, no doubt, short on these managements!

In 1828 matters were concluded. President Hoadly was committed to prison, and affairs of the bank were wound up with a loss to citizens estimated at $1,500,000.[15]

As a postscript, on November 21, 1829, *Niles'* reported the following legal case, reprinted from the *Democratic Press:*

> A case which may be regarded as of some interest to money brokers, and dealers in bank notes, was recently decided before one of the aldermen of this city. I state the facts exactly as they were admitted by the parties, before the magistrate.
>
> A. keeps a shoe store; a stranger having agreed for the purchase of a pair of shoes handed A., a bank note to take out the purchase money. A. having some doubt as to the goodness of the note, took it to B., a money broker and dealer in bank notes, who said the note is a genuine note. "I will give you the amount in silver if you allow me 12-1/2 cents discount."
>
> A. agreed to this proposition, took the note back to his store, sold the shoes, gave the change and returning to the broker, handed the note to him. B. took the note and paid A. the $4.87-1/2, which he had promised.
>
> Here both the parties expected that the transaction was at an end. B. however, almost immediately on A.'s leaving the office, discovered that the note was not, as he had supposed, a five dollar bank note of the Bank of New Haven, but was in fact a genuine five dollar bank note of the Eagle Bank of New Haven, the word "Eagle" having

been ingeniously obliterated; the Eagle Bank having some time before failed. B. therefore sent for A. who forthwith repaid back the $4.87-1/2 cents, for the recovery of which he now brought suit before the aldermen.

The statement of facts as I have related them, was agreed upon by the parties. The alderman gave judgment for the plaintiff for $4.87-1/2 cents, which was paid by the defendant. The plaintiff entered satisfaction and thus the matter has ended. T.M.

The Derby Bank and Fishing Company

The story of the Derby Bank, located in the town of the same name, is intertwined with the Derby Fishing Company. Under the laws of Connecticut, the Derby Fishing Company was chartered on December 10, 1806, with the intent of engaging in ocean fishing, particularly for cod. Travel on the seas was hazardous, the outward bound did not always return, and both the French and British preyed on American ships in the year before the Embargo Act was passed. The new company did not fare well in its intended objective, and losses to French spoilers amounted to $26,000 or more, per a later claim.[16]

The scenario soon changed, and in May 1807 the firm's charter was amended to allow it to sell marine insurance, perhaps logical enough, as a way to turn a profit for stockholders. Then in 1808 it was authorized to loan money at interest, which seems to have little to do with fishing for cod. The company issued bank notes in profusion. In 1809, following charter changes, it evolved to become the Derby Banking and Fishing Company, later usually referred to as the Derby Bank. The company set about constructing ships for maritime trade, seemingly with good prospects as the Embargo Act was repealed the same year, and it was hoped that the Non-Intercourse Act that replaced it would be less restrictive to maritime commerce.

However, the British retained control of the high seas and interdicted American ships on many occasions, rendering voyages dangerous.[17] Several of the company's ships were lost, and others were captured by the British. In the meantime the Derby Bank issued its own bills. In 1815, Nathaniel Jocelyn, who was to become famous in engraving, is said to have made his first bank-note plate, a $3 note for the Derby Bank. Unfortunately, the Derby Bank failed the same year. End of story. Well, almost.

Derby Fishing Company $5 note, ink dated Sept. 1st 1808, from a plate by Amos Doolittle of New Haven.

Derby Bank $5 note issued on May 2, 1825. The engraving was by Murray, Draper, Fairman & Co. of Philadelphia. The seated goddess in the vignette rests her arm on a shield with grapevine motifs, a symbol of the state. The bill is payable at the Mechanics Bank, New York City.

Surprise! In 1824, with the charter under control of interests from New York City, the Derby Bank reopened for business. In New Haven a Mr. Daggett represented the bank in extensive currency trading and speculation, buying worn and tattered bills of various banks at deep discounts and making a profit by reselling them for higher amounts or, in some instances, redeeming them for face value at banks that were solvent. Without authorization the Derby Bank also made loans to New Haven residents.[18]

In autumn 1825, with untold hundreds of thousands of dollars in new currency in circulation, the Derby Bank closed its doors. This second bank failure in the state of Connecticut quickly followed the Eagle Bank disaster. The greatest victims were holders of paper money, who were mostly citizens of modest means in the area—"widows and orphans," as accounts related.

Sharpers bought up the worthless notes, as such bills of this and other banks always had a market. Exchange brokers would commonly sell quantities at about 2% or 3% of face value and ask no questions of the buyers. *Bicknell's Counterfeit Detector,* January 17, 1831, included this item:

> We have seen advertisements of persons wishing to purchase the notes of broken banks. A gentleman from Liverpool informs us that there are shops in which Derby Bank notes and notes of other broken banks, are sold to emigrants visiting this country. This is so shameful a fraud that every American should unite in ferreting out the perpetrators of so foul an act.

However, because just about every exchange broker did an active business in worthless bank bills, the system did not change.

"New System of Banking"

Under the title, "New System of Banking," *Niles' Weekly Register* ran this item on November 22, 1823. The identities of the two banks involved were not stated:

> The New York *Evening Post* tells us that two banks in the state of Connecticut are engaged in the following new and ingenious mode of banking:
>
> "They place in the hands of many brokers, in New York City, a capital of one or two hundred thousand dollars, for the purpose of purchasing the notes of all the other banks in the state of Connecticut that are below par in New York City, and then employ an agent to go round with these to the different banks and demand either New York City bank paper, drafts on New York City, or specie. The former they prefer, because it immediately, and without much risk or trouble, enables them to keep their funds good in the place of traffic, and turn their capital often, which is a great desideratum in trade, and is supposed to yield a profit of 15 percent, per annum."
>
> The names of these Shylock banks ought to have been given. But the late arrangements of the New York City banks will break up their business—as all the notes of the neighboring banks, deemed good, will be received on deposit as cash.

There was nothing illegal to the above procedure, as currency trading was a business in itself, practiced wherever banks issued bills. Usually, however, it was a central activity for exchange brokers and speculators but merely a peripheral business for banks. New York City in particular was a gathering place for currency from various Eastern banks that found its way there in commercial transactions. Most city banks had supplies of such bills, taken in at a discount from face value if they were from distant banks with which the New York banks had no special relationship. Banks or brokers would hire agents to take the bills to the place of issue and redeem them at face value for coins, the difference representing profit.

The Phoenix Bank in Litchfield

Now and again the actions of a bank officer, acting outside of the policies of the bank itself, would result in the collapse of an institution. In the following instance the officer paid the penalty for his misdeeds, but the bank itself survived. Taken from accounts in *Niles' Weekly Register,* August 11 and September 8, 1821, this story of still another Connecticut bank was used as an example by William M. Gouge in *The Curse of Paper-Money and Banking* (1833). The institution was actually the Litchfield branch of the Phoenix Bank of Hartford:

> Overdrawn! The cashier of a bank at Litchfield, Conn., is tenderly said to have "overdrawn" 30,000 dollars. That is, he appropriated other people's money to that amount, to his own use—a fashionable proceeding, a mere "breach of trust," seemingly not all implicating the character of a gentleman!
>
> We observe by a notice in the *Dutchess Observer* that the farmers in Dutchess County [NY] have been *shorn* of all their wool in a most singular operation—or, in other words, that nearly all the wool in that county has been sold to J. Butler, cashier of the Litchfield Bank, who had recently failed, and assigned his factory, wool, etc., to the bank, as security for his debts, leaving the farmers to suffer.
>
> The story, as told by one of the shorn, is briefly this:
>
> The Wolcotville Factory formerly belonged to Mr. Wolcot, who failed, being largely indebted to the bank. As the bank is prohibited from buy-

ing and selling property, their cashier, Butler, became nominally the proprietor. The belief that James Butler acted on behalf of the bank was so universal that he obtained an unlimited credit. The agents for the factory have recently made large purchases of wool, in the normal manner, upon the notes of James Butler.

A great proportion of the wool raised this year in Dutchess County has thus been purchased and carried over to Litchfield, and as soon as the same is well packed away, James Butler, the cashier, is discovered to be a defaulter to the bank for some $16,000, and he assigns his factory, and the stock thus fairly and recently acquired, to the Litchfield Bank.

The Bank is paid—the farmer has a *Litchfield shearing*—and James Butler, the cashier, is insolvent.

Banking News From Here and There

News from all over, as mainly reflected in *Niles' Weekly Register,* was more likely than not to reflect malfeasances and wrongdoings. Throughout the era if several dozen banks made headlines in newspaper accounts concerning dishonest dealings, at the same time several hundred banks were conducting business in an honest manner, to the satisfaction of stockholders, customers, and the general public.

New Jersey Protection and Lombard Bank

In 1824 the New Jersey Protection and Lombard Bank was chartered in Jersey City.[19] It soon set about having notes printed by Durand & Wright, New York City, a partnership that seems to have had more than its share of fraud-oriented clients. Soon, $170,000 or more face value of bills circulated in New York and New Jersey. Then this information surfaced, per *Niles' Weekly Register,* December 3, 1825:

> The "Lombard and Protection Bank" of New Jersey, which lately failed, is so far exposed as to show us that it was no more than a swindling mill. The commissioners appointed by the state to take possession of its effects, found 4,000 dollars in specie, and a note of the president, a fellow named McLaren, for the sum of one hundred thousand dollars, which note, we suppose, constituted the capital of the bank! Its notes in circulation are ascertained to amount to $170,000—and, from the efforts that had been made to force them into circulation before the bank stopped payment, we must suppose that they are good for nothing—and that the proceeds of them have been pocketed by McLaren and company. Laws must be passed for dungeoning fraudulent bankers. . . .
>
> The legislature of New Jersey deserves much commendation on every account. A law has been passed to compel the banks to receive their own notes in the payment of debts incurred with them, and to revoke the charter of the "Lombard and Protection Bank," and transfer its concerns into the hands of commissioners for settlement—and it seems also, that, though powerfully beset by jobbers, no new banks will be incorporated. Banks are good—so is a glass of generous wine; but too much of either makes a man drunken and dissolute.

Doings in Darien

For a long period of time, including during the 1820s, the Darien Bank in Georgia created more than its share of newspaper accounts through actions that were deemed unusual. Here are some samples from *Niles' Weekly Register.*

April 17, 1819:

> From the first step!—The legislature of Georgia in its last session, but by a small majority and after a warm opposition, wisely resolved to establish a new bank at a flourishing town called Darien. We see in the *Darien Gazette,* a very respectable newspaper, that the subscriptions for this stock were lately made, and that some swindling, "business of sharpers," or as we politely call it, speculation, took place at the beginning.—But, indeed, how can we expect anything else in building up a new bank, in times like these?

A partially filled in $1 bill of the Protection and Lombard Bank, of Jersey City, New Jersey, dated 1 Sept. 1825, from a plate by Durand & Wright, New York.

The actions of August 14, 1819, probably take the prize for making it difficult for holders of currency to redeem the notes:

> Unparalleled impudence! . . . The New York *Evening Post* publishes the following, as an extract of a letter from Darien, Geo.—If the facts stated are true, the directors of this money-making factory must have the credit of having reached "the cap sheaf" of impudence:
>
> "Persons making the demands on the bank of Darien must swear before a justice of the peace in the bank, to each and every bill presented, that it is his own; that he is not agent for any other person; and that oath must be made in the presence of at least five directors and the cashier; it also makes the persons so demanding specie subject to a charge of $1.37-1/2 on each bill, which must be paid on the spot, and unless you find five directors and the cashier together, you cannot make a demand."
>
> Is it possible that this can be true? Can it be that the people will bear with such an arrogant assumption? What manner of a man must he be who would require such an oath, what a mean thing is he that would take it! The bills are payable to bearer without condition, and there is no doubt in my mind but that the directors of either of those banks could be prosecuted and punished for a conspiracy. Would that some honest man within striking distance of them would do his duty to his country by resisting such abominable pretensions! . . .

October 15, 1825:

> A depreciation is said (observes the *National Journal*) to have taken place in the value of Darien notes, to the value of 15 or 20 percent. It is mentioned, in the St. Augustine paper that the notes of that bank, in circulation amount to $1,200,000, and the notes discounted to $1,300,000; and hence arises the present depreciation. No doubt seems to be entertained of the solvency of the bank, as assistance has been tendered to it by other institutions in Savannah. but it is hinted that the bank itself acquiesces in this depreciation, in order to avail itself of the alarm to redeem its paper at an easy rate!!!

July 1, 1826:

> The *Darien Gazette* says that the bank of Darien has recently burnt $930,000 dollars of its bills; $600,000 of which were drawn in while under the management of the old board of directors and the balance under the new direction. The same paper adds—
>
> "We are informed, and we believe correctly, that there are not over $200,000 of its bills now in circulation; thus it is reasonable, to predict a speedy resuscitation of its affairs, and that it will, if allowed to pursue, unmolested by legislative interference, the course it has adopted, soon raise itself into as high repute as ever it was."
>
> There are about 500,000 dollars in Darien notes in the treasury of the state, which are not included, we suppose, in the above amount. If the preceding is correct, though we apprehend some mistake in the figures, it will appear that the bills circulated by this institution must have amounted to the enormous sum of $1,600,000!

FOOLING THE COMMISSIONERS IN MASSACHUSETTS

Now you see it, now you don't. The Sutton Bank of Boston was incorporated on March 11, 1828, with a capital of $100,000. Per the charter the bank could go into operation once $50,000 in specie had been received and was actually in the bank's vault. However, specie proved difficult to obtain. Surprisingly, the bank seemed to have no problem meeting the requirement.

Suspicions were aroused, and on September 26 of the same year the governor of Massachusetts, conforming to a request made by certain subscribers of the bank stock, named "commissioners to examine the money actually existing in said vaults, and to ascertain, by the oaths of the directors of said bank, or a majority of them, that the said capital stock has been *bona fide* paid in by the stockholders of said bank, and towards the payment of their respective shares, and not intended for any other purpose, and that it is intended there to remain as part of said capital."[20]

On the next day the cashier borrowed, by depositing $51,000 in bills of the trusted City Bank in the same city, an equal sum in specie, for one day only, promising to return it quickly. These silver coins were examined by the banking commissioners, who duly completed this certificate:

> We, the subscribers, commissioners appointed for that purpose, have this day been shown, and have examined, $50,000 in specie in the vaults of the Sutton Bank, which was paid in by the stockholders at their first instalment, agreeably to their act of incorporation. . . . Jonathan Leland, Amasa Roberts, Samuel Wood, Commissioners.
>
> Then personally appeared Hezekiah Howe, Jonas L. Sibley, Joshua W. Leland, and Thomas Harback, being a majority of the directors of the Sutton Bank, and made oath that $50,000 in specie by them shown in their vaults was the first instalment paid by the stockholders. . . .
>
> Eliphalet Williams, Justice of the Peace.[21]

It was later determined that stockholders paid for their shares nearly entirely in IOUs with scarcely any specie in sight. "In two instances only, and those for a small amount, it appears any payment was made in money."[22]

A $5 note of the Suffolk Bank, Boston, May 8, 1818. Plate by Abner Reed. The cancellation marks probably indicate this note was redeemed by the bank and retired from circulation.

The sham was exposed but not prosecuted. On February 20, 1829, the Massachusetts legislature granted a request for a delay in raising the additional capital, for $25,000 to be paid on or before June 1, 1829, and the remaining $25,000 on or before October 1, 1829. However, a later report to the state senate shows that little money was ever paid in.[23] In the same year the Sutton Bank failed—essentially before it ever started business.[24]

The Suffolk Bank System

The Beginning

One of the greatest banking innovations of the 1820s was the popularity and growth of the Suffolk Bank system. The plan was centered in Boston and served the New England states, bringing great stability to the value of circulating currency in that district—which included Maine, New Hampshire, Vermont, Massachusetts, Connecticut, and Rhode Island, or all of the states northeast of New York.[25]

The term *country banks* was used during the state-chartered banking era to refer to institutions outside of the large cities. The currency of these banks was generally redeemable at par at the bank itself, with local or regional cooperating merchants, and with other banks. However, at a distance, particularly outside the state, currency would trade at a discount. Paper money from another state was designated as *foreign* in most bank records, statements, and other accounts.

If, for example, a bank in New Hampshire or Vermont was solid, the discount on its bills in Boston, Providence, New York City, or another major city might be nominal, such as half of 1% up to 2%. Often, however, distant banks would not redeem foreign currency at all, especially if the proprietors were not familiar with a note's design, did now know how to determine the genuine from the counterfeit, or had questions about the bank's solvency. Accordingly, a bill issued in Portland, Maine, would likely be viewed with distrust if presented in New Haven, Connecticut, or Montpelier, Vermont.

This chaotic situation was due for a change. In 1814 the New England Bank of Boston commenced competition with exchange offices and money brokers and offered to redeem notes of country banks at a discount, under which arrangement the bills would be remitted in bulk to the issuing bank for specie. This beginning facilitated the exchange, and the discount on such bills narrowed to about 1%. The country banks were required to post a deposit in advance against the notes expected to be redeemed, thus eliminating any risk on the part of the New England Bank.

In 1818 the Suffolk Bank was formed in Boston. Afterward its business plan included the redemption of country bank notes in a fashion similar to that of the New England Bank.

The System Becomes Popular

The foregoing arrangement was not profitable to the Boston banks and was largely discontinued in the early 1820s. Soon, it was decided to return to and improve the deposit system. Six other Boston banks joined the Suffolk Bank, and beginning on May 24, 1824, against deposits from country banks the Suffolk Bank system went into effect. A fee of 1/4 of 1% was charged for exchanging the bills.

Distant banks were required to keep a minimum $5,000 (soon reduced to $2,000) on deposit with the Suffolk Bank, which paid no interest and which constituted an advantage to the Suffolk Bank, plus a generous additional amount deposited by each member bank to be paid out for its bills brought for redemption. The total amount of the deposit funds placed

A $10 note of the Suffolk Bank, proof impression, from a plate by Draper, Toppan & Co., Boston. This engraving partnership, bearing the names of John Draper and Charles Toppan, had offices in Philadelphia, New York City, Cincinnati, and Boston, and operated from 1839 to 1844.

A $1 Perkins plate note of the Kennebec Bank, Hallowell, Maine, April 2, 1824, stamped BROKEN BANK / SUFFOLK BANK / W.G. The Kennebec Bank was chartered in Augusta, in the Massachusetts district of Maine, on or by January 23, 1812. In 1816 it moved to nearby Hallowell. In 1820, when the district became the state of Maine, bills were imprinted with that address. The bank failed on May 1, 1826, after the president made unfortunate investments in western land.

A $10 note purportedly from the Valley Bank of Hillsborough, New Hampshire, but skillfully altered from a $10 note of the Egg Harbor Bank of Egg Harbor City, New Jersey. Dated 1863 and stamped by the Suffolk Bank. By this time the Suffolk Bank was a minority player in bank-note redemption, most of its business having gone to the competing Bank of Mutual Redemption. After the Egg Harbor Bank failed, thousands of its unissued notes were sold to counterfeiters, who used chemicals to remove the original name and location, after which they imprinted the information shown here. An interesting $1 note of this bank is described in chapter 20.

with the Suffolk Bank depended on the volume of the member bank's bills presented for exchange in Boston. Certain strong banks that made regular deposits and did sufficient other business with the Suffolk Bank were exempted from the deposit requirement.[26] Worthless bills from Maine had been flooding commerce in Massachusetts, and the Suffolk Bank system exposed their true nature, preventing further losses.

In June 1824, notes issued by member banks were redeemed to the extent of $330,000, but by 18 months later the volume had increased to more than $2,000,000 monthly. The plan flourished, and by the beginning of the Hard Times era in 1837, more than 300 New England banks were depositors. From 1824 until the mid-1850s, the Suffolk Bank was the dominant redemption depot for bills of New England banks, large and small. This system eliminated the practice, still prevalent in New York City and other banking centers outside of New England, of buying bills at deep discounts and sending agents to redeem them at the issuing banks, taking a generous profit in the trade.

Numismatic Notes

Bills of the notorious banks and paper issuers of this decade are quite collectible—a short list being the Derby Bank and Eagle Bank of Connecticut, several of Jacob Barker's banks in New York, and the Marble Manufacturing Company in the same place.

Currency of this era usually features attractive vignettes, although in Massachusetts and Maine, the Patent Stereotype Steel Plate was standard. Many remainder, worthless, and redeemed notes can be collected from this era. As a class the market for them is rather quiet, although there are exceptions for certain notes and banks.

The Second Bank of the United States

Model Institution—or Monster?

Of all banks of the early 19th century, probably more has been written—and less understood—about the second Bank of the United States than about any other financial institution. For some historians it was at long last the foundation of a national banking system, pioneered by the first Bank of the United States (1791–1811) and now brought to fruition with expanded capital and brilliant planning. To others it was the "monster," a bank with tentacles that reached out across the East to stifle the growth of state-chartered banks and to reduce banking from personal service to a government entity.

Numismatists with an interest in history recognize the importance of the second Bank of the United States, not for its paper money, which is scarce and seldom seen, but for the influence it had on state-chartered banks. In the decade of the 1820s it was a strong competitor to the state banks, especially those in larger cities. During the 1830s, when federal deposits were removed from the second Bank of the United States they went to state banks, which prospered with the influx.

The renewal of the bank's charter, which was intended to take place in 1836, did not happen. After this point there was no strong federal influence on the banking system until the National Banking Act of 1863. The period from 1836 into the 1860s saw the Panic of 1837, wildcat banking in Michigan, the establishment of many rules for safety funds and the like, the Panic of 1857, and more changes—not least of which was the Civil War. Likely, had the charter of the second Bank of the United States been renewed in 1836 the history of both state banking and the currency associated with it would be much different from what we know today.

The second Bank of the United States, Philadelphia. (Bartlett's *American Scenery*)

LAUNCHING THE BANK

The first Bank of the United States, chartered in 1791, operated until its charter expired in 1811. Its franchise was not renewed by Congress, and the bank's assets were distributed. Most historians agree that the bank operated on a sound basis and conducted its business affairs in a reasonable manner.

In 1816, following an extended period of banking difficulty inaugurated by the suspension of specie payments in 1814, Congress felt warmly toward the establishment of the second Bank of the United States, believing it would help curb some of the abuses that had arisen with state-chartered banks, certain of which conducted business with a minimum of assets and were poorly managed.[1]

LEGISLATIVE PROVISIONS

The Act of April 10, 1816, which established the bank, included these provisions, among many others:

> *Sec. 1: Be it enacted by the Senate and House of Representatives of the United States of America, in Congress assembled,* That a bank of the United States of America shall be established, with a capital of $35,000,000, divided into 350,000 shares, of $100 each share. Seventy thousand shares, amounting to the sum of $7,000,000, part of the capital of the said bank, shall be subscribed and paid for by the United States, in the manner hereinafter specified; and 280,000 shares, amounting to the sum of $28,000,000, shall be subscribed and paid for by individuals, companies, or corporations, in the manner hereinafter specified.
>
> *Sec. 2: And be it further enacted,* That subscriptions for the sum of $28,000,000, towards constituting the capital of the said bank, shall be opened on the first Monday in July next, at the following places: that is to say, at Portland, in the district of Maine; at Portsmouth, in the state of New Hampshire; at Boston, in the state of Massachusetts; at Providence, in the state of Rhode Island; at Middletown, in the state of Connecticut; at Burlington, in the state of Vermont; at New York City, in the state of New York; at New Brunswick, in the state of New Jersey; at Philadelphia, in the state of Pennsylvania; at Wilmington, in the state of Delaware; at Baltimore, in the state of Maryland; at Richmond, in the state of Virginia; at Lexington, in the state of Kentucky; at Cincinnati, in the state of Ohio; at Raleigh, in the state of North Carolina; at Nashville, in the state of Tennessee; at Charleston, in the state of South Carolina; at Augusta, in the state of Georgia; at New Orleans, in the state of Louisiana; and at Washington, in the District of Columbia.
>
> And the said subscriptions shall be opened under the superintendence of five commissioners at Philadelphia, and of three commissioners at each of the other places aforesaid . . . and shall continue open every day, from the time of opening the same, between the hours of 10 o'clock in the forenoon and 4 o'clock in the afternoon, for the term of 20 days, exclusive of Sundays, when the same shall be closed. . . .

The charter proposal was passed by Congress, and the capital was set at $35,000,000, with $7,000,000 of this to be stock held by the government, paying for it in obligations (the last one of which was paid years later in 1831). "Of the remaining $28,000,000, one-fourth was to be paid in specie, the balance in specie or government bonds, in three equal half-yearly installments."[2] Shares had a par value of $100 each.

The bank, despite its title, was not a branch of the Treasury Department, nor was it the official bank of the nation; It did, however, hold certain federal deposits, which the secretary of the treasury could add to or remove at his discretion. Rather, it was privately owned, issued its own stock to its own shareholders, and was managed by a board of directors. Federal funds were to be deposited there, but they would bear no interest. The bank was to perform certain services for the Treasury in the care and disbursement of funds.

PAPER MONEY TO BE ISSUED

Because it was anticipated that subscriptions would be paid in specie, surely the bank would exhibit great strength from the outset. Currency was to be issued in an amount not to exceed the total paid-in capital. Denominations were specified to be $5 and higher, with all bills of less than $100 to be payable in specie to the bearer on demand.[3]

At the time, specie was very scarce in circulation. It was widely thought then and for years afterward that if small-denomination notes were prohibited, coins would return to take their place. Regarding paper money, this plan was published in October 1816: "The notes of the *National Bank* are to be engraved by Tanner, Kearny, and Tiebout, in a style that will make imitation of them extremely difficult."[4] In actuality, the engraving on these bills was not much different from that found on other currency of the era.

In the meantime, in the summer of 1816, stock subscriptions were solicited from the public through the various branch offices. This effort was successful, and $24,961,700 was realized.[5] Philadelphia headed the list with $5,833,600. The lowest sales were at the branches, with Nashville, Tennessee, second lowest at $53,600 and Burlington, Vermont, at the bottom of the list with just $6,300. By the end of the sign-up period only $3,083,300 worth of stock remained unsold nationally; on August 26 even this was purchased with due éclat by Stephen Girard, of Philadelphia. Not long thereafter, James Madison rewarded Girard with a directorship in the new bank (along with John Jacob Astor, of New York City, and three others).[6]

In November 1816 *Niles' Weekly Register* reported that offices of discount and deposit "are to be immediately opened at Portsmouth, N.H." and other locations.[7] By this time the annual salaries of the president and cashier of the headquarters of the Bank of the United States, in Philadelphia, had been fixed at $5,000 each. Finally, on January 17, 1817, the home bank in Philadelphia began business, and certain of the branches commenced operations soon thereafter.

In autumn 1816 John Sergeant was commissioned "immediately to embark for Europe, as an agent of the bank, to purchase specie." He was to go to London to buy $5,000,000 worth "on the best terms that may be offered, if he shall deem those terms to be advantageous to the bank."[8] It was apparent that specie expected from stock subscriptions would be slow in arriving.

Growing Pains

For many observers it seemed these were halcyon times for the Bank of the United States and that the shares offered great investment potential. Enthusiasm continued, and by May 1817, "Stock of this bank, for 65 dollars paid, has been selling at $100 a share."[9] Then in July: "The Bank of the United States has declared a dividend of *four per cent* on the stock. . . . and are said to have a *surplus* of profits of about $200,000 more."[10]

Hezekiah Niles, editor of *Niles' Weekly Register*, turned sour on the Bank of the United States, and in 1818 published many condemnatory articles concerning it. Directorships were

> too often bargained for, like *hogs* are bought in the market—*"If you'll give that, I'll give this."* . . . I am convinced, by *casting together* some things that are notorious, that three-fourths of the stock of the Bank of the United States was originally taken by less than 100 persons. . . . [11]

A caper was being practiced, Niles suggested, by certain stockholders pledging their now-appreciated shares against their original stock subscriptions, which still had not been paid for. The balance sheet of the bank of July 1, 1817, showed that of $28,000,000 in assets, not even $2,500,000 was in specie (and, to make matters worse, some of this figure consisted of *notes* of "specie paying banks"—in other words, IOUs) and $11,456,232.87 in notes due for unpaid stock subscriptions.[12] Moreover, according to Niles, many published "prices current" listing values for the bank's stock were grossly inflated, as no quantity of shares could be sold for such prices. Seemingly, the second Bank of the United States was off to a rocky start.

A report issued on November 11, 1818, by Jonathan Smith, cashier (in Philadelphia), stated that as of that time, $34,972,778.63 had been paid in for capital stock of the bank. Of three installments, amounts paid in coin and equivalents had been $14,100,167.97, divided into $1,428,694.45 (entirely in coin, paid by July 23, 1817, one year after the initial subscriptions were taken), plus later installments of $3,534,557.99 (by January 1, 1818), and $9,136,915.53 (by July 1, 1818), the last two in specie *as well as notes and checks* on the Bank of the United States and other specie-issuing banks; thus, much was paid in "paper."[13]

This report by cashier Smith showed that by September 22, 1818, the Portsmouth, New Hampshire, branch had an account totaling $252,264.25 in loans (mostly) and bank bills (of specie-paying banks) on hand. This represented the smallest amount of business, by far, of any of the branches, the next higher figure being $421,470.05 from the branch in Middletown, Connecticut. In terms of money deposited at the branch by citizens and public offices, Portsmouth showed a paltry $19,581.38, again the lowest of any branch and seemingly not worth the bother in terms of overall deposits in the bank, which amounted to $12,128,502.70.

On January 16, 1819, the Honorable J.C. Spencer transmitted a lengthy report of an investigation into the bank's operations to the House of Representatives.[14] Some of the narrative could as well have been written by Hezekiah Niles, as this excerpt:

> Another measurable and probably much more censurable effect of [the various actions of the bank] was to keep the price of the stock constantly advancing, until it reached a point where it exploded and fell. . . .

Later, a historian would write,[15]

> The Bank had suffered not only from bad management, but from downright fraud on the part of its own agents. The branch at Baltimore was managed exclusively by persons who had had a principal hand in bringing the general affairs of the Bank into the condition in which they now stood.
>
> These persons, not content with the enormous loans they obtained under the system of discounting stock notes, had drawn out of

> the branch, without any authority, and without the knowledge of anybody except the president and cashier, upwards of three millions of dollars, the greater part without any security whatever, and more than half of which was ultimately lost to the Bank.

Although a detailed account of the affairs of the Bank of the United States and its more than two dozen far-flung branches is beyond the purview of the present text, suffice it to say that, for several years after the bank opened in 1817, many critics contributed to a seemingly unending stream of negative articles.

A synopsis of what happened regarding bank shares was told by another historian:[16]

> The second installment of subscriptions to shares was then due [in January 1817], but neither this nor the third was paid according to the charter. The bank received less than $2,000,000 (instead of $7,000,000) in specie, having accepted promissory notes and bank notes in lieu of coin. Consequently, the bank was compelled [again] in 1818 to import specie.
>
> The officers permitted the transfer of shares upon the books of the bank before they were fully paid for. A number of the officers and directors speculated in the stock of the bank, discounting their loans for the purpose at the bank or its branches. The first two years' operations showed losses, due largely to these speculations, of more than $3,500,000; nevertheless it paid dividends.

Moreover, in violation of the bank's charter, during several reporting periods there were more notes outstanding than specie on hand for their redemption.[17] Many other actions ranged from questionable to unwise, including William Jones, president of the main branch of the bank, buying and selling stock options on speculation.[18]

SIGNING CURRENCY

In 1818 the president and directors of the Bank of the United States requested for the main bank in Philadelphia, "permission to issue bills and notes signed by other persons than the president and cashier of that bank."[19]

It was recommended that the presidents and the cashiers of the *branches* not be allowed to sign notes, but that there be "the appointment of certain officers whose exclusive business it shall be to sign said bills and notes—thus their uniformity may be preserved, and a part of the evils apprehended will be avoided." Without such a provision, multiple secretaries to the officers might sign notes in multiple styles, confusing anyone who wanted to verify signatures for authenticity. But these suggestions were rejected by the House of Representatives.

Thus, for the ensuing years, one of the primary occupations of these officers was to hand-sign countless thousands of bills, a task that was deeply resented and considered to be a waste of time.

THE BANK OF THE UNITED STATES IN 1819

The second Bank of the United States had issued large amounts of paper money by 1819 and also held as assets many notes of state banks. The main bank facility was in Philadelphia with branches in Portsmouth, Boston, Providence, Middletown (Connecticut), New York City, Baltimore, Washington, D.C., Richmond, Norfolk, Fayetteville (North Carolina), Charleston, Savannah, Lexington, Louisville, Chillicothe (Ohio), Cincinnati, New Orleans, and Pittsburgh—this register of branch offices differing somewhat from the towns and cities listed in the 1816 charter.

In March 1819, Langdon Cheves became president of the Bank of the United States in Philadelphia. Under his administration, which lasted four years, the abuse of overissuing bank bills was ended, and stock shenanigans and speculations subsided. In addition, criticisms in the popular press were fewer.

In September 1819 the bank and its branches held $3,254,479.91 in "specie" (normally silver and gold coins, but in this instance also including some paper money from state banks that redeemed their notes in *specie,* such banks being few in number).[20] The bank held its own paper money to the amount of $10,582,147.09 (from a total of $14,392,258.49 issued), and $1,133,923.86 was held in notes of state banks.

Throughout its existence, the Bank of the United States redeemed its notes in specie, keeping a high reserve for doing so. After 1820, this meant silver coins were used at par rather than gold, as the latter were at a premium in the marketplace. However, the bank also kept reserves of gold. According to rules under its charter, interest to the holder of any unredeemed bill would be paid at the rate of 12% per year.[21] This had the real effect of making the bank's bills worth slightly more than state-chartered bank bills in most areas, and also causing state banks to resent the Bank of the United States's greater strength. In everyday trade, Bank of the United States bills sold at just a tiny dis-

Fifty-dollar note of the second Bank of the United States, Philadelphia, ink-dated 12 of June 1821, bearing the signature of L. (Langdon) Cheves, president, and the imprint of Tanner, Kearny & Tiebout as printers and engravers. Due to a misspelling, some experts have questioned this note, while others believe it to be absolutely genuine.

The national bird as depicted on the vignette of this $50 bill, with PLURIBUS misspelled as PURIBUS.

count on currency exchanges and were generally worth more than the best of state bank bills.

Typically, merchants and politicians would come to the side of home-owned banks and would protest the actions of the Bank of the United States, claiming mismanagement, disruption of the banking system, etc.—this despite the fact that local individuals usually sat on the board of directors of a given branch of that bank.[22] The bank was still referred to as the "monster" in many accounts, a nickname it could never shake.

Biddle at the Helm

The bank went through difficulties for the next several years, but it gained in strength under Langdon Cheves. In 1822 he submitted his resignation, his duty done. In Philadelphia, Nicholas Biddle became president in January 1823, after which time the fortunes of the bank improved. Biddle, the son of a banker, was born on January 8, 1786, into an accomplished family. He demonstrated brilliance at an early age, completing his studies at the University of Pennsylvania at the precocious age of 13 and continuing his education at the College of New Jersey, Princeton, where at age 15 he was valedictorian of the Class of 1801. Not long after, and while still a teenager, he served as secretary to General John Armstrong, the United States minister to France, a position arranged through family connections. Thus situated, he helped finesse the details of the Louisiana Purchase. Afterward he went on a study tour of sites that had been important in ancient Rome and Greece.

In 1807 Biddle came back to the United States and soon became editor of a literary magazine, the *Port Folio.* He also worked with the journals and records of Meriwether Lewis and William Clark, compiled during their journey of exploration in the Louisiana Purchase territory from 1804 through 1806, and created a book from them—a fine and highly acclaimed narrative published in 1814 under the title, *Lewis and Clark Expedition,* with introductory remarks by Thomas Jefferson. His calendar was filled with a swirl of literary, social, and business endeavors. He epitomized the elite set of high society in Philadelphia.

Not long after Biddle's entry, the Bank of the United States achieved a measure of strength, criticism subsided further (but never went away), and it took its place as an important and stabilizing factor in American commerce. Still, the existence of the institution continued to be resented by state-chartered banks, as the Bank of the United States often sought to restrict their enterprise by unfair but legal tactics. Typical capers included sending agents of the Bank of the

Nicholas Biddle in 1826, from a portrait by Thomas Sully.

United States to present a small bank with a large quantity of its notes and demand immediate redemption in specie, and refusing to accept notes of small banks at its own branches, even though the bills of the bank were rated as sound and readily accepted by other banks and merchants. The "monster" deserved its moniker for such activities, although to be fair, many state banks and exchange brokers engaged in similar shenanigans with paper money. The difference was the fact that the Bank of the United States was supposed to represent the epitome of rectitude, standing as a model institution.

On the national scene the Bank of the United States was successful in the 1820s and brought a much-needed stability to certain areas of the country with unsound or speculative banks and their worthless bill issues. However, this advantage was largely redundant in New England, where the Suffolk Bank system became very important beginning in 1824.

Branches and Years of Operation

While most of the "Office of Discount and Deposit" branches opened in 1817, others opened as late as 1830. The branches, locations, and dates of activity are as follows.[23]

Opened in 1817. *Philadelphia* (the "mother" or home bank, center of all activities and administration, eventually situated in a magnificent Greek revival temple-like structure first occupied in 1824, designed by William Strickland, who also designed the branch Mint buildings about two decades later); *Augusta, Georgia* (discontinued in the same year); *Baltimore* (a branch that was very competitive with the home bank in Philadelphia, which clashed with it on numerous occasions, some disputes of which landed in court. In the early days this branch was wracked with scandal. Baltimore was in the ascendancy as a commercial and cultural center, and seemingly the office sought to be more important than just a branch); *Boston* (the prime branch in New England); *Charleston, South Carolina; Chillicothe, Ohio* (closed in 1825);[24] *Cincinnati* (closed in 1820, reopened in 1825; at the time Cincinnati was the prime center for trade in that district of the Ohio River); *Fayetteville, North Carolina; Middletown, Connecticut* (office moved to Hartford in 1824); *Lexington, Kentucky; Louisville, Kentucky; New Orleans; New York City; Norfolk, Virginia; Pittsburgh; Portsmouth, New Hampshire; Providence, Rhode Island; Richmond, Virginia; Savannah, Georgia; Washington, D.C.*

A $10 note of the second Bank of the United States, Philadelphia, ink dated March 1, 1831. The officers were required to hand sign each bill, a boring task. Biddle's cramped signature also appeared on most official documents of the bank. The plate is by Murray, Draper, Fairman & Co.

Opened Later. 1824—*Hartford, Connecticut* (relocation of the Middletown, Connecticut, branch opened in 1817). 1826—*Mobile, Alabama; Nashville, Tennessee; Portland, Maine; Buffalo, New York; Utica, New York.* 1829—*St. Louis, Missouri.* 1829—*Burlington, Vermont.* 1830—*Natchez, Mississippi.*

The main offices and the various branches each issued paper money of common designs—one set of motifs fitting all. Denominations included $5, $10, $20, $50, and $100. The name of the branch location was typically added in ink by hand. After initial production by Tanner, Kearny, and Tiebout, most of the earlier bills were printed by Murray, Draper & Fairman; then Fairman, Draper, Underwood & Co.; then Draper, Underwood, Bald & Spencer, all of Philadelphia.

Counterfeits of these bills were endemic, some so well done that experts do not always agree whether certain bills are false or genuine (a fact that can be observed from reading the fine print in auction catalogs).

Portsmouth Problems of the 1820s

The decade of the 1820s can be described as disastrous for the Portsmouth, New Hampshire, branch of the Bank of the United States, nearly completely from internal influences. Because Portsmouth was just one of many branches, details of its problems would not be given here were it not for the fact that the happenings were pivotal to the future of the entire Bank of the United States and, indeed, the nation, forming the focal point of Andrew Jackson's presidency. Perhaps, just as a butterfly flapping its wings in Hong Kong can catalyze a typhoon (so some say) or a spark can start a forest fire, in the late 1820s a seemingly trivial banking event in New Hampshire altered the course of the government of the United States.

A view of the corner of State and Pleasant streets in Portsmouth. The Portsmouth branch of the Bank of the United States was located on Pleasant Street in the building adjacent to the left of the corner, the third door to the left. After the Bank of the United States ended its operations, the Piscataqua Bank of Portsmouth took over the office. (C.W. Hazlett, *Portsmouth in the Year 1824*)

Edward Cutts, president of the Portsmouth office, was suspected in the disappearance of money from the bank's pension fund and the granting of a large number of bad loans. A clerk at the branch, William R. Parker, blew the whistle on Cutts and was promptly fired.[25] Cutts, who had good political connections and who was a member of one of the state's best-known families, remained in the post until his death in 1824, after which his defalcations were clearly revealed.

Nicholas Biddle, president of the bank system, later gave this statement:

> The office at Portsmouth had originally the misfortune to have at its head a Mr. Cutts, who ended by defrauding the United States of upward of $20,000 of the pension fund, which the bank was obliged to replace.[26]

Cutts was succeeded as president by James Shapley, a well-intentioned man but one who conducted business in a very casual manner, making many unfortunate decisions. By 1828 the branch was in an even worse position, having lost an estimated $112,000 in nonperforming loans, although the full extent of the problems was not realized until 1829.[27] Biddle's retrospective narrative continues:[28]

> At this period the late president [Shapley], a worthy man, had not calculated for such a state of things, resigned his place, and it became necessary at once to adopt the most energetic measures to save the property of the bank.
>
> A confidential officer was dispatched to Portsmouth, who found the affairs of the office in great jeopardy, covered with the wrecks which bad management and the most extensive frauds had occasioned. To retrieve it, it became necessary to select a man of first rate character and abilities. Such a man was Mr. [Jeremiah] Mason. Of his entire competency, especially in detecting the complicated frauds, and managing the numerous lawsuits which seemed inevitable, there could be no doubt. Of his political opinions we neither knew or inquired anything.
>
> In order to induce him to give up so much of his valuable time to the service of the bank, an estimate was made of the probable amount we would have to pay for the professional services of a lawyer, and by engaging Mr. Mason in that character, we were enabled to obtain his consent to accept the appointment.

The Entry of Jeremiah Mason

Mason was a prominent and highly accomplished Portsmouth attorney, whose advice was often sought in complex legal matters. On August 1, 1828, Daniel Webster, senator from Massachusetts, penned this letter to Mason:[29]

> My Dear Sir,
>
> I have seen Mr. Cowperthwaite this morning, and had a full conversation with him, respecting the state of the bank at Portsmouth. At his request I have agreed to write to you, and I come at once to the main matter.
>
> He thinks it important that you should take the presidency of the Branch, if you can be persuaded to do so. He says you manifested no disposition for it, but I did not learn from him that he had suggested a probable increase of the salary, as among the motives. It now stands, I hear, at eight hundred dollars. He desires me to say, confidentially, that if twice that amount would induce you to take the office, it would be given cheerfully. In all probability, the amount of pay would not be a subject of difference between you and the bank, if you were inclined to have the office.
>
> He is to leave Boston on Monday morning, and I am anxious to hear from you before his departure. I suppose you have weighed the *pros* and *cons,* and probably have a feeling one way or the other on the subject. I do not wish to influence your judgment, but should think it a great object with the bank to obtain your services, and am persuaded they would pay as liberally as you should think they ought.
>
> If you have made up your mind fully against it, Mr. Waldron will be appointed. In that case the bank will immediately crave leave to send you a large retainer, at least a proper one, and engage your professional services, with a desire that you should pay particular attention to its affairs and be paid accordingly.
>
> After the receipt of this letter, I will thank you not to enter into any engagement adverse to the bank, until there shall be time to hear from Philadelphia. Contrive to let me have an answer on Sunday. I write this at Beverly [Massachusetts], having come down here to visit Mr. Thorndike's family. I shall return to B. this evening.
>
> Yours truly,
>
> D. Webster

Everything fell neatly into place. On August 14, 1828, upon the recommendation of Webster to Nicholas Biddle,[30] Mason took the presidency of the branch, where he combined his legal and financial skills. As will be seen, Biddle's comment, "of his political opinions we neither knew or inquired anything," was a mea culpa.

Andrew Jackson Goes to the White House

The first term of President Andrew Jackson, elected in 1828, began with his inauguration in March 1829.

Isaac Hill, well-known New Hampshire banker (until recently the president of the Merrimack County Bank in Concord, *the* best politically connected bank in the capital city, and state political figure), was a close friend of Andrew Jackson, who had just taken up residence in the White House.[31] In the presidential election of 1828, Hill had led the Jacksonians to victory in the Granite State. Hill was appointed as second comptroller of the Treasury Department.

Jackson had another strong friend and ally in Senator Levi Woodbury, also from New Hampshire, who would rise in his administration through cabinet positions. In May 1831 Woodbury was appointed by Jackson as secretary of the Navy, a post he held until 1834; on June 27, 1834, he was appointed secretary of the Treasury.

Trying to Oust Mason

Now, with Jackson as president of the United States, Isaac Hill, taking maximum advantage of his new position as second comptroller of the Treasury, sought to cash in some of his political chips. In particular, he coveted the accounts that the United States Pension Agency had with the Portsmouth Branch of the Bank of the United States and desired their transfer to the Merrimack County Bank in Concord, to which he still had close ties. This particular bank was one of the smaller players in the state banking scene. A large infusion of assets from the Pension Agency would certainly be an impressive addition to its deposits and no doubt would help attract other business as well.

To this end, Hill stirred up trouble in Portsmouth and enlisted his fellow New Hampshire-ite, the aforementioned Levi Woodbury, to rally to his cause. Following is a chronology of what happened, the little situation that became of national importance.

June 27, 1829. A petition signed by 56 citizens of Portsmouth, including many of the most influential business and political figures, was sent to Nicholas Biddle and the directors of the Bank of the United States. The document alleged that the Portsmouth branch had been conducted in a manner "partial, harsh, novel, and injurious to the interest of the bank," and that the president of the branch was specifically responsible for the untenable situation.

The petition sought removal of Jeremiah Mason and the board of directors of the Portsmouth Branch and sought their replacement with people who were aware of the business necessities of Portsmouth and were "disposed to dispense the favors of the bank impartially."

June 27, 1829. Senator Levi Woodbury wrote a letter marked "Confidential" to Samuel D. Ingham, Jackson's secretary of the Treasury, endorsing the action of the petitioners. Woodbury added the telling comment that Jeremiah Mason "is a particular friend of Mr. [Daniel] Webster," who was said to have been instrumental in securing the position for him.

Moreover, Woodbury wrote, the appointment of Mason, unpopular from the beginning, "has now become odious through Mr. Mason's ungracious manners and partial, vacillating conduct." Woodbury urged prompt removal of the offensive management personnel of the Portsmouth Branch by not reappointing them, ending with the postscript: "I understand the board is selected for this branch early in July." The directors of the branches were appointed annually.

June 29, 1829. Another petition was sent to Biddle and the directors of the Bank of the United States. This one was impressively signed by 56 members of the New Hampshire State Legislature. The document charged that the Portsmouth branch had refused small, safe loans to established businessmen in Portsmouth, while large and risky loans had been made to distant parties outside the state.

The course being pursued by Jeremiah Mason was "destructive to the business of Portsmouth and offensive to the whole community," it was further alleged. The legislators called for the immediate removal of Mason and his fellow Portsmouth Branch directors and offered a list of suitable men as replacements.

July 11, 1829. Secretary Ingham wrote to Nicholas Biddle, enclosing Woodbury's *confidential* letter, to underscore the importance of the matter. Ingham stated that similar complaints had been received concerning the management of other branches. Most assuredly, Ingham suggested, Biddle would not want to have political relationships influence bank operations.

The secretary closed by complimenting the parent bank on the manner in which it had discharged its trust "in all its immediate relations to the government," seemingly implying that the ousting of Mason and the Portsmouth directors would enable this excellent tradition to continue.

July 17, 1829. Second Comptroller of the Currency Isaac Hill wrote to J.N. Barker and John Pemberton in Philadelphia, enclosing copies of the two New Hampshire petitions and noting that he had encouraged the compilation and signing of such. Poignantly, he observed that "friends of General Jackson have had but too much reason to complain of the branch bank at Portsmouth," and he hoped the men at Portsmouth "may not continue to be an engine of political oppression."

Hill advised that he had reliable information that Jeremiah Mason was "unaccommodating to pensioners" and that he made large loans to his brother-in-law in Boston, "while refusing to accommodate our merchants with two or three thousand dollars, and this, too, on the very best paper."

July 18, 1829. Biddle wrote to Secretary of the Treasury Samuel D. Ingham, acknowledging receipt of his earlier correspondence and stating that if the allegations made by Senator Woodbury were accurate, "an appropriate corrective" action would take place.

Biddle informed Ingham that Webster had nothing to do with Mason's appointment and, moreover, had not known of the appointment until after it had been made. He further noted that the animosity toward Mason was strictly based on politics and had nothing to do with Mason's performance, except that his aggressiveness in trying to collect overdue loans may have offended some people. The bank had never been influenced by politics, Biddle assured Ingham, and it never should be.

However, Biddle was an out and out *liar.* On August 14, 1828, nearly a year earlier, upon the installation of Jeremiah Mason as president of the Portsmouth branch, Nicholas Biddle wrote this to Daniel Webster: "The Portsmouth office which we have this day arranged agreeably to your recommendation."[32]

July 23, 1829. Secretary Ingham replied to Biddle, stating that he was not prepared for such a sweeping statement—that since the founding of the bank it had never been influenced by politics. Ingham found it quite remarkable that 500 men, representing the present and past employees and officers of the central bank and its branches, "had been wholly exempt in all cases from the bias of party feelings." Ingham stated that it was obvious that Biddle's statement represented Biddle's personal feelings, not the true history of the bank.

Ingham stated that he did not assume the accuracy of the charges against Mason unless they were checked, but he objected strongly "to a course of action which either resists inquiry, or, what is of the sane tendency, *enters upon it with a full persuasion that it is not called for.*"

July 31, 1829. Jeremiah Mason, under fire, wrote to Nicholas Biddle to state that the situation was prompted entirely by Isaac Hill seeking to remove the Pension Agency from the Portsmouth branch, "to benefit a small bank at Concord, of which, till his removal to Washington, he was the president."

Although Hill claimed that Concord was a location more central to the addresses of most pensioners in the district, the removal of the agency would be a great loss to the Portsmouth branch. Mason said that he had not seen any correspondence on the matter that might have been sent to the Bank of the United States in Philadelphia, and he expressed a desire to learn its contents. In advance he stated that "absurd untruths were made use of" to induce people to sign the petitions.

August 3, 1829. Secretary of War John H. Eaton wrote to Jeremiah Mason, taking direct action in accordance with the mostly unstated wishes of Isaac Hill, who had precipitated the affair. Eaton advised Mason that "it has been found necessary" to move the Pension Agency from under his control in Portsmouth to a new location in Concord, and that a pension agent had been appointed to reside in Concord.

Mason was requested to deliver to the new agent all the books, papers, and *money* belonging to the Pension Agency.

August 10, 1829. Jeremiah Mason wrote to Nicholas Biddle, enclosing the request from Secretary of War Eaton for the books, papers, and money to be transferred. Mason stated that he thought the request was illegal, and he would not comply unless Biddle authorized him to do so.

August 13, 1829. Mason wrote to Biddle that the newly appointed pension agent from Concord had arrived in Portsmouth and had formally demanded the Pension Agency's records and money. Mason stated that he refused to turn them over, and that due to the present uncertain condition, pension payments now due to deserving recipients would not be paid.

August 17, 1829. Thomas Cadwalader, acting president of the Bank of the United States in Philadelphia (as Biddle was on his way to New Hampshire to personally investigate the situation), wrote to Mason to state that the secretary of war had no authority to demand the delivery of the funds to a new agent, and that Mason was to take no action until instructed from the parent board of directors in Philadelphia. In the meantime, he could continue paying pensions as they were due.

August 20, 1829. Biddle arrived in Portsmouth to interview certain individuals who had complained about Mason. "In two days of interviewing, Biddle accumulated eight serious allegations of harshness, unreasonableness, and personal partiality against Mason," but "not one repeated the charge that loans or renewals had been granted or refused for political reasons."[33]

August 25, 1829. James L. Edwards, pension clerk in the War Department, having been apprised of the situation, wrote to Mason, as Secretary Eaton was not in Washington at the time. Mason was told to continue paying pensions and was advised that when Eaton returned he would learn more.

August 28, 1829. Biddle wrote to Thomas Cadwalader in Philadelphia, advising that "I can now say with the utmost confidence that the whole is a paltry intrigue got up by a combination of small bankrupts and smaller demagogues."[34] One might imagine that while in Portsmouth, Biddle's personal feelings that Isaac Hill and S.D. Ingham and colleagues were "small bankrupts and smaller demagogues" were translated into some of his communications.

September 8, 1829. Biddle wrote to Mason, informing him of a rule change intended to please local Portsmouth merchants. Henceforth, the branch was to accept small notes of the state banks.

A Short-Lived Victory

The correspondence continued, the next letter defying the Jackson administration, thus drawing battle lines that would define the political course of America for the next several years. The following continues the chronology.

September 15, 1829. Nicholas Biddle, now back in Philadelphia, wrote to Secretary of the Treasury Samuel D. Ingham to state that after spending six days in Portsmouth he had concluded that the charges against Mason were "entirely groundless."

In interviews in Portsmouth, Biddle was not able to find anyone who would verify that Mason had been motivated by political sentiments when conducting business. "Mr. Mason, therefore, was immediately re-elected."[35]

Biddle continued: "I deem it my duty to state to you in a manner perfectly respectful to your official and personal character, yet so clear as to leave no possibility of misconception, that the board of directors of the Bank of the United States, and the boards of directors of the branches of the Bank of the United States, acknowledge not the slightest responsibility of any description whatsoever to the Secretary of the Treasury touching the political opinions and conduct of their officers, that being a subject on which they never consult, and never desire to know, the views of any administration. . . ."

October 8, 1829. Secretary of the Treasury Ingham wrote to Biddle to set the matter straight, beginning with the statement that he had been too wordy, and in any event, "Mr. Biddle, you are altogether too touchy; instead of resenting suggestions from the Secretary of the Treasury, you ought to welcome them."

Then came a remark that, ultimately, changed the course of American history:

> The administration is empowered to *act* upon the bank in various ways; in the appointment or removal of five of the directors; *in the withdrawing of the public deposits;* in the exaction of weekly statements, and the inspection of its general accounts. . . .
>
> If it should ever appear to the satisfaction of the Secretary of the Treasury that the bank used its pecuniary power for purposes of injustice and oppression, he would be faithless to his trust if he hesitated to lessen capacity for such injury, by withdrawing from its vaults the public deposits.

October 9, 1829. Biddle wrote to Ingham, concluding their exchange of letters. He explained some passages from his earlier letters and expressed agreement with the secretary's desire that the Bank of the United States be independent of politics.

Jackson Vs. the Bank of the United States

President Andrew Jackson, a military general accustomed to success in *war,* took up the cause, which heretofore seems to have been of little concern to him save for occasional comments. His first inaugural address, delivered on March 4, 1829, did not mention the Bank of the United States.[36] But later in the year, in his first annual message to the House of Representatives and Senate, December 7, 1829, this *manifesto* was included toward the end. The events at the New Hampshire branch had raised his fighting spirit:[37]

> The charter of the Bank of the United States expires in 1836, and its stockholders will most probably apply for a renewal of their privileges.
>
> In order to avoid the evils resulting from the precipitancy in a measure involving such important principles, and such deep pecuniary interests, I feel that I can not, in justice to the parties interested, too soon present it to the deliberate consideration of the legislature and the people.
>
> Both the constitutionality and the expediency of the law are well questioned by a large portion of our fellow citizens;[38] and it must be admitted by all, that it has failed in the great end of establishing a uniform and sound currency.[39]
>
> Under these circumstances, if such an institution is deemed essential to the fiscal operations of the government, I submit to the wisdom of the legislature, whether a national one founded upon the credit of the government and its revenues, might not be devised, which would avoid all constitutional difficulties; and, at the same time, secure all the advantages to the government and country that were expected to result from the present bank.

Jackson's 1830 Message

Jackson's second annual message to Congress, delivered December 6, 1830, reiterated his animus toward the bank:[40]

> The importance of the principles involved in the inquiry whether it will be proper to recharter the Bank of the United States requires that I should again call the attention of Congress to the subject. Nothing has occurred to lessen in any degree the dangers which many of our citizens apprehend from that institution as at present organized.
>
> In the spirit of improvement and compromise which distinguishes our country and its institutions it becomes us to inquire whether it be not possible to secure the advantages afforded by the present bank through an agency of the Bank of the United States so modified in its principles and structure so as to obviate constitutional and other objections.
>
> It is thought practicable to organize such a bank with the necessary officers as a branch of the Treasury Department, based upon the public and individual deposits, without power to make loans or purchase property, which shall remit the funds of the government, and the expense of which may be paid, if thought advisable, by allowing its offi-

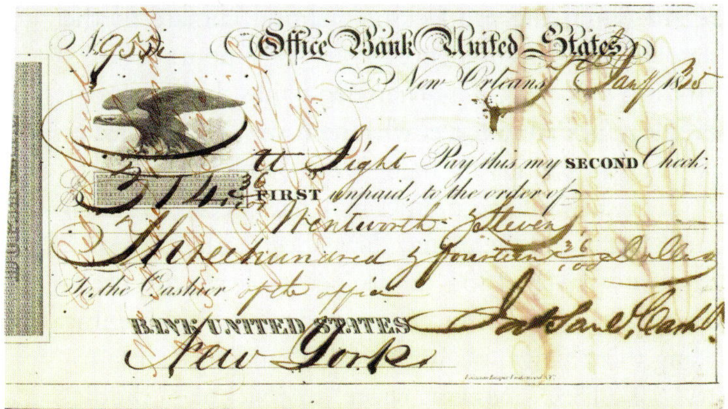

Draft on paper of the New Orleans branch of the Bank of the United States, January 1835.

Across the country a handful of state-chartered banks made their bills payable at the Bank of the United States, Philadelphia, giving such paper the appearance of being especially strong. This remainder $10 note from the St. Joseph branch of the Commercial Bank of Florida is from a plate by Draper, Toppan, Longacre, & Co., which did business in Philadelphia from 1834 to 1839.

Note for $10 of the Susquehanna Bridge and Bank Company, Port Deposit, Maryland, payable at the Bank of the United States in Philadelphia. Ink dated 2 May 1831. From a plate by Fairman, Draper, Underwood & Co., which printed bills for the second Bank of the United States in the same era.

cers to sell bills of exchange to private individuals at a moderate premium.

Not being a corporate body, having no stockholders, debtors, or property, and but few officers, it would not be obnoxious to the constitutional challenges which are urged against the present bank; and having no means to operate on the hopes, fears, or interests of large masses of the community, it would be shorn of the influence which makes that bank formidable.[41]

The states would be strengthened by having in their hands the means of furnishing the local paper currency through their own banks, while the Bank of the United States [the *new* bank proposed by Jackson, not the existing bank], though issuing no paper, would check the issues of the state banks by taking their notes in deposit and for exchange only so long as they continue to be redeemed with specie. In times of public emergency the capacities of such an institution might be enlarged by legislative provisions.

Jackson's political rivals included Daniel Webster and Henry Clay (the latter popularly remembered as a great orator and the man who stated, "I would rather be right than be president," to which a wag responded, "You'll never be either").

EVENTS OF 1831

In 1831 Henry Clay, leader of the Whig Party, championed the renewal of the Bank of the United States charter as fervently as Jackson and the Democrats opposed it. To muster support for the rechartering, Biddle enlisted Mason's help in doing what he could in this regard (amid the pro-Jackson political climate in the state) by using his influence to gain the support of directors and officers of state-chartered banks. In his actions Biddle appeared to forget what he had written to Secretary of War Samuel D. Ingham on October 9, 1829.

The turmoil and politics may have been too much for Mason, or there may have been other reasons, because by May 1831 he decided to leave the presidency of the branch and move to Boston. For the time being this change was not revealed publicly. On January 13, 1832, Mason wrote to Nicholas Biddle, informing him of his decision.

Alexander Ladd, of Portsmouth, who had been a director since the inception of the branch, was named as the new president of that branch, a choice that generated no controversy.

The Vote to Renew the Bank Charter

The renewal of the Bank of the United States charter came up before Congress in the summer of 1832. Battle lines were drawn, with Jackson and his supporters on one side and his opponents, including Webster and Clay, on the other.

The bill was determined in the Senate on June 11, 1832, and was passed by a vote of 28 to 20. It was voted upon in the House of Representatives on July 3 and was passed 109 to 76. It was then sent to President Jackson for his signature, and was returned to Congress on July 4th, marked "Vetoed."

In a message prepared with the assistance of Amos Kendall (in particular), Roger B. Taney, Levi Woodbury, and Andrew J. Donelson, Jackson termed the bank a monopoly against the interests of the common people. The monopoly, he wrote, had these unsatisfactory aspects, among others:[42]

1. Bank stock valued at $8 million was held by foreigners. If the bank were to be rechartered, the stock would increase in value 20% to 30%, thus making this a gift to foreigners, without the slightest advantage accruing to American citizens.

2. If it is granted that the Bank is a monopoly, then a fair price, such as $17,000,000, should be charged for it, instead of the $200,000 annual the government would receive under its current arrangement as an interested party.

3. The Bank of the United States charter excludes any national competition. Other private interests have offered to take a charter on terms more favorable to the United States than offered by the Bank.

4. The Bank of the United States extends more favorable terms to its branches than to general citizens. As an example, the St. Louis Branch can readily have its notes accepted anywhere at par, whereas a merchant in St. Louis has no such possibility, and must offer his paper at a discount outside of the city.

5. Bank stock held by foreigners cannot be taxed, thus depriving the government of revenue and giving foreign-held stock a value 10% to 15% higher than the stock held by American citizens.

6. As states can tax only the amount of stock held by its own citizens in the state, and as most stock is held by out-of-state people, branches can operate within a state on a favorable tax advantage.

7. Of the 25 directors, 5 are appointed by the government and the rest by stockholders who are required to be American citizens. The rechartering of the Bank would accelerate the flow of stock into foreign hands, eventually giving the reduced number of Americans the power to vote 20 directors, even though these Americans might eventually own only a small amount of stock, and would "be able to re-elect themselves from year to year, and who will wield a power dangerous to the institutions of the country."

8. If most of the stock goes to foreign interests in a given country, and we go to war with that country, "all the operations of the Bank within would be in aid of the hostile fleets and enemies without."

Jackson's statement went on to discuss his view of the constitutionality of the Bank of the United States, which had been questioned: "Each public officer who takes an oath to support the Constitution, swears that he will support it *as he understands it,* and not as it is understood by others." The "others" were the justices of the U.S. Supreme Court, thus the Jackson comment: "The opinion of the judges has no more authority over Congress than the opinion of Congress has over the judges, the president is independent of both."

AFTERMATH

Nicholas Biddle, president of the Bank of the United States, professed joy at the veto, a contradiction explained by this letter to Henry Clay, obviously Biddle's choice for president in the contest to be held the coming November:[43]

> You ask what is the effect of the veto? My impression is that it is working as well as the friends of the bank and of the country could desire. I have always deplored making the bank a party question, but since the president will have it so, he must pay the penalty of his own rashness.
>
> As to the veto message, I am delighted with it. It has all the fury of a chained panther biting the bars of his cage. It is really a manifesto of anarchy, such as Marat or Robespierre might have issued to the mob of the Faubourg St. Antoine; and my hope is that it will contribute to relieve the country from the dominion of these miserable people.
>
> You are destined to be the instrument of that deliverance, and at no period of your life has the country ever had a deeper stake in you. I wish you success most cordially, because I believe the institutions of the Union are involved in it.

When in 1829 the Bank of the United States "triumphed over Isaac Hill, Mr. Woodbury, and the administration. It was a dear victory," wrote Jackson's biographer, James Parton.[44] Further:

> I believe myself warranted in the positive assertion that this correspondence relating to the desired removal of Jeremiah Mason was the direct and real cause of the destruction of the bank. If the bank had been complaisant enough to remove a faithful servant [Mason], General Jackson, I am convinced would never have opposed the rechartering of the institution.

Someone challenging the Mason affair while the spark was growing to destroy the bank might point to the fact that, in the course of activities in earlier years, Jackson had made a few anti-bank statements, such as favoring the passing of and later opposing the repeal of legislation in Tennessee taxing the branch in Louisville.[45] At the very least the Mason affair was pivotal, if not the entire cause of the bank's destruction.

LEGALITY QUESTIONED

In an unrelated situation, the legality of the bills, here referred to as "checks," issued by the various branches of the Bank of the United States, and not signed by the president and cashier of the main bank in Philadelphia, was called into serious question, per this report in *Niles' Weekly Register,* October 15, 1831:

> *Checks of the offices of the Bank of the United States.* The greater part of what are called five and ten dollar notes of this bank, are really only checks drawn by the offices of the several branches on the parent bank. The following is from the *Baltimore Republican:*
>
> We mentioned sometime since, that a question had been raised in the state courts of Ohio, as to the legality of the issues of five and ten dollar notes, drawn by the branches of the bank of the United States upon the bank at Philadelphia.
>
> A person named Cunningham was tried "for having in possession certain counterfeit notes, purporting to be notes of the president, directors and company of the United States Bank—knowing the same to be forged and with intent to utter." The counsel for the prisoner contended that the indictment ought to [be] quashed, inasmuch as the document produced in evidence was not a note purporting to be of the United States Bank, but a mere check, drawn by the president of the branch bank at Louisville, countersigned by the cashier—upon the principal cashier of the bank residing in Philadelphia. It was agreed, however, that the case should be referred to the jury, and the man was convicted. His counsel then gave notice that they would move for arrest of judgment—and the case lay over till the 28th ult. when, as we learn, by a letter published in the *Globe,* the motion was made, and the point argued, and it was decided by the court that the indictment had not been sustained, and the prisoner was liberated.
>
> The arguments used were, that the bank had not legal authority for putting into circulation as bank notes, those checks—that no note under one hundred dollars could be legally made payable to order—that the bank had at two different sessions of Congress made application for authority to appoint two additional officers to sign notes, as the president and cashier could not sign a sufficient number of notes for the currency of the country—that the request was refused on the ground, that by multiplying the signers of notes, facilities would be given to forgeries—that notwithstanding Congress had refused to allow two additional signers, yet the bank had increased the number to twenty-five—by the presidents of the twenty-four branches being authorized by the directors to sign notes—that this was an illegal stretch of power, unauthorized by the charter, or any other law—and finally, that there is no law of the state of Ohio for punishing anyone for having forged checks in possession. The decision is of considerable importance to the bank and the public.

THE ELECTION OF 1832

Returning to the political arena in the aftermath of the Mason affair, after Jackson's veto of the bank charter's renewal, sides were polarized for the presidential election of 1832. On one side was Jackson and on the other side was Clay, backed by the Bank of the United

States. Each enlisted friendly legislators to make tedious speeches, complete with personal attacks and accusations of dishonest and dishonorable actions, before the adjournment of Congress, which took place at 6 A.M. on July 16.

The popular press became involved, predicting either the salvation of America or its financial ruin (depending upon the political orientation of the editor) if the charter veto was not challenged. Many if not most readers were thoroughly confused.

About mid-August, President Jackson and a small entourage left Washington, D.C., to visit the Hermitage, Jackson's home in Tennessee. On his trip, Jackson made a point of paying his expenses in gold coins along the way. "No more paper money, you see, fellow citizens, if I can only put down this Nicholas Biddle and his *monster* bank," he was quoted as saying.[46]

A detailed discussion of the campaign of 1832 is beyond the focus of the present text. Suffice it to say that each party was confident of success. In November the results were more one-sided than the most optimistic supporters of Jackson and his vice presidential companion, Martin Van Buren, could have imagined.[47] After the popular vote was tallied (687,502 for Jackson, 530,189 for his opponent), the Electoral College returned 219 of its possible 288 votes for Jackson, leaving Henry Clay a miserable 49 votes, with a few remaining scattered votes going to regional favorites.

Not only had Clay suffered a disastrous defeat, but the Bank of the United States was also dead for all practical purposes. What to do? Perhaps in jest and perhaps not, the *Globe* reported that certain influential members of the defeated party were prompting "the minions of the Bank to save the institution by the only expedient that could save it—the assassination of the president."[48] Rumors abounded to the effect that the bank had $50,000 to give to any man who would render to the future of America such a service.

"Pet Banks"

In an effort to cripple the bank, whose charter was still in effect and would remain so until 1836, Jackson ordered that, instead of future federal deposits being sent to the Bank of the United States, they would be given to various state-chartered institutions, this to take place on October 1, 1833,

> or sooner, provided the necessary arrangements with the state banks can be made. The President thinks that the state banks ought immediately to be employed in the collection and disbursement of public revenue, and the funds now in the Bank of the United States drawn out with all convenient dispatch.[49]

These state institutions were officially called "deposite [*sic*] banks," but popularly referred to as "pet banks." The amount to be deposited in the banks of each state was based upon the number of Electoral College votes of that particular state.[50]

In his fifth annual message to Congress, December 3, 1833, Jackson discussed this shifting of funds, noting that he had instructed the secretary of the Treasury to take appropriate action (through an order by the secretary of the Treasury, September 26, 1833).[51] Further:

> The near approach of the day on which the charter will expire, as well as the conduct of the bank, appeared to me to call for this measure upon the high considerations of public interest and public duty.
>
> The extent of its misconduct, however, although known to be great, was not at that time fully developed by proof. It was not until late in the month of August that I received from the government directors [the government's five directors on the board of 25] an official report establishing beyond question that this great and powerful institution had been actively engaged in attempting to influence the elections of public officers by means of its money, and that, in violation of the express provisions of its charter, it had by formal resolution placed its funds at the disposition of its president [Biddle] to be employed in sustaining the political power of the bank. . . .

On March 28, 1834, the U.S. Senate censured President Jackson for removing the deposits. Jackson protested, and on April 15, 1834, sent a document in reply to the Senate.[52] Years later in 1837, the hotly

Contemporary cartoon showing Andrew Jackson riding a jackass, carrying a bag of money to his "pet banks."

debated "Expunging Resolution" would result in the censure being officially removed from Senate records, this primarily through the efforts of Senator Thomas Hart Benton. A further salvo against the Bank of the United States was included in Jackson's sixth annual message to Congress, December 1, 1834.[53]

History demonstrates that America suffered few if any unfavorable consequences as the power and assets of the Bank of the United States diminished. Indeed, 1834 and 1835 were years of dramatic change for the positive. Today, however, historians are divided on this question.

The Bank Winds Down

There was a general expansion of commerce during the same period.[54] On January 1, 1834, about $200,000,000 was employed in banking capital and about $95,000,000 in bank bills was in circulation. By January 1, 1836, the capital had reached $251,000,000, and the bills in circulation amounted to $141,000,000. Through the actions of Thomas Hart Benton, senator from Missouri and one of Jackson's staunchest supporters, the Act of June 28, 1834, reduced the authorized weight of gold coins, and later in the year $2.50 and $5 coins, absent from circulation for a generation, were available at par.

Times were good, and a surplus accumulated in the United States Treasury. General inflation prevailed, except for the price of federal land in certain districts west of Pennsylvania, which were fixed at $1.25 per acre. Large amounts of paper bills were used to buy such land on speculation, with the result that on July 11, 1836, Jackson issued his "Specie Circular," requiring payments to be in gold or silver coins. The charter for the Bank of the United States was not renewed in 1836. Affairs were wound down, and in time the stockholders and creditors were paid in full.

As the decade progressed, western speculations and unwise expansion came to a head, business was distressed, and the Panic of 1837 ensued. However, by that time the Bank of the United States was history.[55]

The Rest of the Story

Nicholas Biddle determined to carry on the affairs of the Bank of the United States, but in a clever and misleading manner. He formed a new corporation, the Bank of the United States *of Pennsylvania,* a state-chartered bank. Incorrectly at that time, and still by naïve writers today, this institution was popularly called the *third* Bank of the United States.

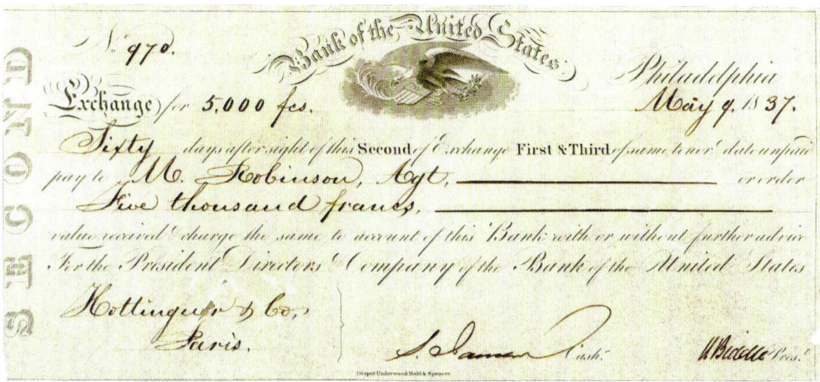

Bill of exchange for 5,000 French francs drawn in Paris on the second Bank of the United States during the process of its dissolution.

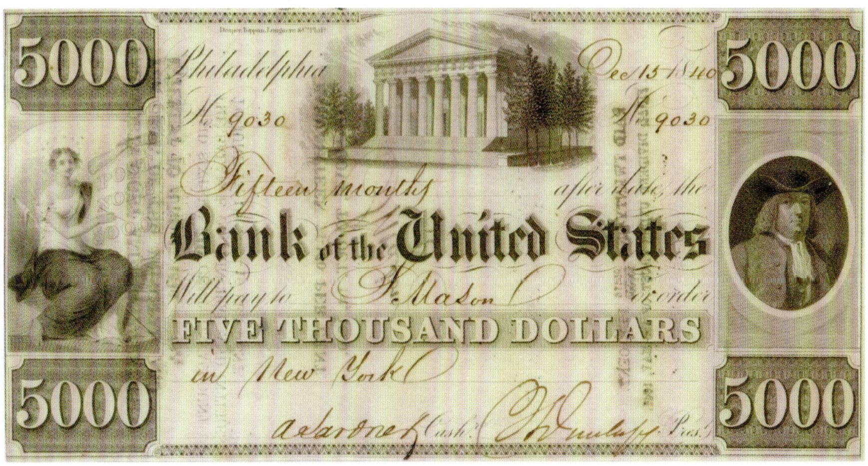

A $5,000 bill of the Bank of the United States of Pennsylvania, although "of Pennsylvania" does not appear on the bill. Such were often mistaken for bills of the second Bank of the United States. All currency of the Bank of the United States of Pennsylvania became utterly worthless.

Perhaps out of desperation spawned by the Hard Times era, Biddle became involved in many questionable activities through 1839. His bank issued large amounts of paper money, including in bills of the high denominations of $1,000, $2,000, $3,000, and $5,000, with "of Pennsylvania" not printed on the notes, leading some to believe that these were from the second Bank of the United States established in 1816 or that, somehow, a third bank had been chartered.

Charles Lyell, a British observer of the American scene who visited Philadelphia in 1842, wrote this, apparently not aware that the third bank was a different institution:[56] "The United States Bank, during its controversy with President Jackson, had accumulated a large amount of specie, and lent it out most lavishly and imprudently, and when it obtained its new charter from Pennsylvania, it again promoted loans of all kinds, which gave an inordinate stimulus to speculation. . . ." This deception, of course, was precisely what Biddle had intended.

The Bank of the United States of Pennsylvania filed for bankruptcy in 1841. Its paper notes became worthless. Perhaps forced by circumstances (although this is never a proper alternative), Biddle immersed himself in lies and deceptions, in the process ruining his reputation—to the dismay of everyone involved, including the minions of Philadelphia society of which Biddle was still very much a part. The reader of the present text knows that lying was nothing new for Biddle and that he had told untruths in 1829 in connection with the Mason affair. After the 1841 collapse, Biddle's friends and associates lost large sums of money. One of Philadelphia's proudest and most important men had fallen. The fall of the bank sent repercussions through the Philadelphia banking community, forcing a run on the banks and prompting suspension of specie payments, which extended to some other banks, including some in neighboring Delaware.

Jackson's *war* against the bank was sufficiently effective, and the results sufficiently long lasting, that it was not until many years later that the Federal Reserve System was established as a federal banking entity in 1913. For the first time, banking was closely regulated nationwide on an effective basis.

Numismatic Notes

Varieties of notes issued by the central office of the second Bank of the United States range from scarce to rare to nonexistent in the marketplace today, as these were redeemable at par when the bank closed. Bills from the branches, with location added in ink, are rarer yet. As the designs were the same for all offices, the most practical approach is to seek an example of each design type, with the realization that your display will never be complete.

Collectors and dealers not aware of the history of the second Bank of the United States are often confused by the large-denomination bills of Nicholas Biddle's Bank of the United States *of Pennsylvania,* and do not realize that they have no connection with the earlier government-sponsored institution. Large numbers of bills of the Bank of the United States of Pennsylvania exist today.

Counterfeits and Counterfeiters

Counterfeits in the News

An ideal introduction to this chapter may be to refer back to the second Bank of the United States, the institution studied in the preceding chapter. Its bills were widely counterfeited, because they were easy to pass into circulation. Their worth was not questioned. No one wondered if the bank was sound. Many notices of such counterfeits appeared in the press. The following have been selected from *Niles' Weekly Register.*

From the issue of April 7, 1827:

> *Alarming Counterfeits.* From the *Baltimore American:* The United States Bank, it is well known, has spared no expense to attain the desirable object of issuing its notes in so superior a style of engraving and finish as to render unavailing any attempts to counterfeit them. It appears, however, that the ingenuity and talent of the gentry who make the business of counterfeiting a regular occupation, have at length succeeded in producing so good an imitation of one of the plates that we are induced to call the attention of the public to the fact, in order that it may guard against imposition from this source.
>
> The counterfeits to which we allude are twenty dollar notes, purporting to be issued by the parent bank, payable at the Charleston office, in favor of Jos. Johnson, president. They bear date 1st February, 1820, and are signed by L. Cheves, president, and Jona. Smith, cashier. The plate is marked with the letter M. The signature of Mr. Cheves, is very well executed—that of Mr. Smith and of Mr. Johnson, but indifferently—but the most perceptible defects consist in the indifferent manner in which the other blanks are filled up when compared with the genuine notes.
>
> Two of these counterfeits were received by our city banks, but were detected at the branch bank, on presentation there. A difference of opinion, however, having been entertained as to their real character, one of them was transmitted to the parent bank, and by it positively ascertained to be counterfeit. We mentioned these particulars to show how well they are calculated to deceive. In this particular state of the case, it will be best to refuse receiving any 20 dollar notes of the issue described, at least for the present, unless of persons well known and responsible.

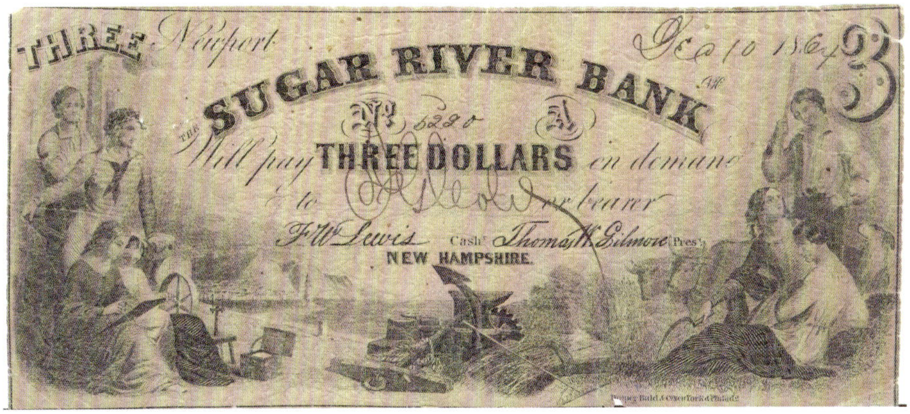

Counterfeit $3 bill of the Sugar River Bank, Newport, New Hampshire, from a false plate. The signatures of the bank officers are *printed.* These were turned out in large quantities.

An authentic $3 bill, signed in ink, of the same bank and design.

Then on October 6, 1827:

> *A batch of counterfeiters.* After the conviction of Newbold the counterfeiter, of whom we have made mention [in an earlier story], he asserted that a trunk containing 100,000 dollars of counterfeit notes, and a number of counterfeit plates had been placed in his hands by a gang of counterfeiters in Philadelphia, with whom he was connected; that on their apprehension he fled, having concealed the trunk in such a manner that it could never be discovered without his agency, he having first helped himself to $8,000 of the notes, in attempting to pass which, he was subsequently convicted at Richmond.
>
> Previous to this disclosure, the police of Philadelphia had received intimation that an extensive fraud was about being practiced upon the United States Bank by a gang of villains in that city, a part of whom after much diligence were arrested at noon day; they were found in a third story back room of a house in Locust ward, busily engaged in signing, trimming, sorting, etc. three men and two women, were found therein, and one man without hat or coat jumped from an upper floor window and escaped, literally cutting his way through a glass window.
>
> So complete was the surprise that the whole were taken, except the man before mentioned—the ink still wet on their pens, and 30,000 dollars of spurious United States notes on the table—and 2,000 of good money found on their persons, together with sundry implements of the trade.
>
> On one of the persons was found two keys, one belonging to a trunk, and the other apparently that of a chamber door, which were found to fit the lock on an upper story room of a tavern in Race Street and a trunk therein—but unfortunately the landlord received an order to deliver the trunk to a man, who packed its contents together with some clothing in his own, and departed—this man proved to be Sutton alias Newbold, and after a very strict enquiry being instituted on or about midnight of the 10th ult. the trunk was found at a tavern on the turnpike road, about half way between the city and Bristol, (Sutton having left the city immediately after making the deposit).
>
> In this famous trunk was found, seven counterfeit plates, principally of banks in the state of New York, and 125,000 dollars of spurious notes belonging to 20 different banks, near 100,000 of which were of the Bank of the United States; 7,000 of Geneva, New York; 6,000 Norristown, Montgomery County; 1,000 Hartford; 7,000 Newbern; 1,600 Merchant's Bank, New York City; 500 Newark Insurance Company; 500 Farmers Bank of Virginia; 900 Orleans Bank; 400 Manhattan Company; 100 Commercial Bank of Philadelphia; 700 Farmers and Mechanics Bank of Philadelphia. In the same trunk was also found about 50 genuine proof impressions of various bank plates, believed to have been cut out of a book that was stolen from the late Gideon Fairman about two years ago.[1]

The remaining members of this villainous band have been arrested in various parts of the United States, and will receive the just desert of their crimes.

From the issue of December 18, 1830:

> *Dangerous counterfeits.* The following circular from the bank of the United States gives notice of some dangerous counterfeits of their notes:
>
> Bank United States, December 8, 1830.
>
> Sir—I lose no time in apprising you of the appearance at our counter, yesterday and today, of three most dangerous imitations of our $100 branch note, Washington and Franklin heads in the margin, two purporting to have been issued by the Washington, and one by the Savannah office. The impressions are fainter, and the notes longer and broader than the original, but the filling and signatures are well executed. I send you annexed our engraver's description of the minuter differences.
>
> I am very respectfully, your obedient servant,
>
> Wm. Ilvaine, cashier.

The scroll at the top of the denomination dies is imperfect, and the white lines of those dies are less distinct than in the original. There is a marked difference between the two fancy heads of the marginal dies and those of the original notes, also in the heads of Washington and Franklin, the former appearing in the counterfeit more like an outline than a finished engraving. There is a want of uniformity in the marginal die work surrounding the heads, etc. The words "Bank of the United States" in the body of the note are much less bold than the original. The same remarks will apply to the general appearance of the counterfeit.

A Long Tradition

In the 19th century, counterfeiting and altering of bills was a widespread crime, beginning long before the era of state-chartered banks commenced. The equipment needed was often minimal, and many types of fake currency could be made at home. In fact, from the very inception of the use of paper money, issuers and counterfeiters played a cat-and-mouse game, each seeking to outwit the other, this being a prime reason why the designs and other features of bills were changed frequently during the colonial era.

As time went on, many innovations and alleged safeguards were developed and used by legitimate engravers to made bills for banks, but their efforts were to little avail as counterfeits became even more numerous. In 1852 and again in 1862, the eloquent writer and engraver Waterman L. Ormsby wrote extensively

Counterfeit $3 bill of the Mechanics and Traders Bank, Portsmouth, New Hampshire. The name of the state is misspelled as "New Hampshier." From a false plate signed Rawdon, Wright, Hatch & Edson, New York City, a well-regarded firm, which by the date printed on the note, January 1st 1859, was a part of the American Bank Note Co.

on counterfeiting, the most erudite chronicler of the era to do so.

While much of what Ormsby and others related—along with various articles that survive from newspapers and periodicals of the day—are of interest to the historian, they also have a practical use for the numismatist. Often, genuine bills were redeemed and destroyed by sound banks, while counterfeits, alterations, and spurious notes remained in quantity and are easily available today.

In the early 21st century many puzzles still remain. Collectors of early notes are blessed with James A. Haxby's four-volume study, *Standard Catalog of United States Obsolete Bank Notes 1782–1866* (1988), plus a library shelf full of specialized works on state bills by various authors, including many texts published under the aegis of the Society of Paper Money Collectors.

In most modern texts, known genuine notes are described along with many bills that were once available, but for which few or none exist today—and descriptions are taken from bank-note reporters (discussed in the next chapter) and other early descriptions. In many instances it is not known today whether certain bills are real or fake, and numerous are the references to banks that *may* be nonexistent or bills that *may* be fake.

Bills that were once despised as fakes are today eagerly collected for what they are—false notes cataloged and described as such, including throughout the Haxby text. This situation is hardly unique to the field of paper money. Numismatists seeking early American and colonial coins often pay great sums for contemporary counterfeits, such as those bearing the imprint of Connecticut or of England, but made in Newburgh, New York, in the late 1780s at Machin's Mills.

To this extent I believe you will find this chapter especially informative and useful. Actually, Ormsby should be listed as coauthor!

Counterfeit Bank Bills

After state-chartered banks began issuing bills in the 1780s—beginning with the Bank of North America, the Bank of New York, and the Bank of Massachusetts—their paper quickly drew the attention of sharpers. Thousands of notes were counterfeited, and others were altered by raising their denominations. There were many criminals active in the field, ranging from those running modest operations conducted at home to proprietors of virtual printing factories with employees in the shop and others on the road passing the forgeries. In news stories the latter groups often were referred to as "nests" of counterfeiters. Over a long period of time, many newspaper accounts stated that counterfeits of various sorts crossed the border in quantity from Canada, where the perpetrators were out of the reach of American authorities.

By the early 19th century there were so many different types of bills in circulation that not even the most experienced bank officer could keep track of them all. Generally, either a bill "looked good" or it did not—a matter of personal judgment. If a bill was obviously false it was handed back to the remitter. If it was taken in and then later found to be a counterfeit, standard practice was to pass it along in circulation to a customer. Few banks were willing to absorb losses.

While the reissuing of counterfeits was nearly always done by those who inadvertently accepted them, little discussion of this ethically questionable practice ever appeared in print. Counterfeit notes in existence today speak for themselves: as a class they show much more evidence of use than do legitimate bills that circulated in the same era. In other instances, bank records, once confidential, reveal cashiers engaging in the practice. Witness the activities of the cashier of the Carroll County Bank, discussed in chapter 17.

"Wildcats" and Other Bills

The American lexicon is strewn with nicknames for paper money, some descriptive, others derogatory. *Owls* have already been discussed, and *red dog, blue pup,* and *coon box* bills have been mentioned in passing.

For counterfeit and worthless bills one of the earliest nicknames was *shinplaster,* referring to a piece of paper money that has little or no value in commerce and might be best used to help bandage a scraped or wounded shin. The term seems to have come into popular use in the 1780s, when Continental Currency bills became next to worthless.[2] The term *shinplaster* remained in use afterward and was applied to bank and private bills that had no value. In the Panic of 1837, when a flood of paper money reached circulation at a time when coins were hoarded, these bills were all tarred with the *shinplaster* designation. In 1838, *Day's New-York Counterfeit Bank Note List and Counterfeit Detecter* (the last word being the spelling used by Day) defined such a bill as one from an "irresponsible or pretended bank."

The term *red dog* may have originated "from bills with red edges, put out by one Jacob Barker, of New York City, who on a certain occasion when asked to redeem his pledges, replied with much indifference that as soon as he could possibly make arrangements to do so, he would publish an advertisement to that effect."[3] As earlier delineated, Barker was a curious figure in the annals of American currency, a charlatan right along with Moses Y. Beach and Samuel D. Dakin, to mention just a couple among currency-issuing scoundrels.[4]

A *wildcat note* was of the same ilk—a piece of paper money issued by a supposed bank, but worth very little, if anything. A *wildcat bank* had little or no financial backing at the outset and was apt to be located in a remote location so as to deter investigation of its circumstances. *Lord's Detector and Bank Note Vignette Describer* (1857), published in Cincinnati, utilized a small engraving of a wildcat for certain bank listings, noting that it "indicates a Wild-Cat concern." *Van Court's Counterfeit Detector and Bank Note List,* Philadelphia, April 1858, included this punning allusion to such currency:

> Minnesota is the paradise of the feline tribe. As in Michigan in earlier days, they flourish with a vigor of growth, and length of claw, and sharpness of voice, that are nowhere else attained.

Harold L. Bowen, whose book on the bank notes of Michigan is a favorite in my reference library, wrote this explanation:

> The term "wild cat" or "wildcat" was first applied to associations organized under the [Michigan] general banking law of 1837, and later to chartered banks, but its origin is obscure. The reader may choose one of the following theories, or formulate his own.
>
> Many of these banks were located in the wilderness, and proved as dangerous as wildcats.
>
> Some early notes had vignettes of lions, tigers, or panthers; hence the name "wildcat."
>
> It is said that Oliver Newberry, a Detroit merchant, refused some new safety fund notes with the remark, "Those banks are springing up as thick as wildcats all over the country."
>
> A diary, written in 1838, states that Michigan notes were classified as "wild cat," "tom cat," "mad cat," and "red dog," according to the fancied solvency of the bank of issue, but few references to "tom cats" or "mad cats" can be found.
>
> Banks having a new location stamped or written (rather than printed) on their notes were called "red dogs." Thus, the Farmers and Merchants Bank, of St. Joseph, was considered a "red dog" because most of its notes were stamped "CENTREVILLE."[5]

Historian Breckinridge Jones described authentic "wildcat" certificates, given that name when they were issued after the governor of Michigan signed legislation "to encourage the killing of wolves, panthers, and wildcats." He ascribed these certificates as the origin of the "wildcat" term:

> The act provided that a premium be paid to any person who shall kill any wolf, panther, or wildcat within ten miles of any settlement in the territory. The rate of such premium in the case of wolves and panthers which shall exceed the age of six months being two dollars, if under that age the sum of one dollar and in the case of wildcats the sum of fifty cents each, regardless of age; to be paid out of the county treasury in which any such animal shall have been killed.
>
> The act provided further, "That any person killing a wolf, panther, or wildcat as aforesaid, shall exhibit the scalp with both ears, . . . to some justice of the peace within said county . . . the justice being directed to execute a certificate in the following form if he was satisfied that the exhibitor was entitled to a premium;

"I, A.B. a justice of the peace, . . . do hereby certify, that the sum of——is due to C.D. as a premium for his killing a wolf, panther or wildcat (as the case may be) and the treasurer of the county is hereby directed to pay the same to C.D. or bearer."

The most interesting part of this early act is the further provision that any such certificate "shall be a legal tender for any county taxes levied within said county, and shall be received by the sheriff or other person collecting any county levy within the same."

These "wildcat certificates" came to be used as currency and led to the name of "wildcat" being given to other kinds of currency that were not redeemable in specie, and being specially applied to the bills of the non-specie paying banks in the adjoining territories.[6]

Confessions of a Banker

Hoyt Sherman, who was a banker in Iowa in the 1850s, told of "wildcat" and other nicknamed bills, with a commentary on what a certain banker did with them:

> To illustrate how the bank note deposits were assorted and treated by the bankers at that interesting period, I copy literally the labels on the several compartments in an old currency tray, in which the notes were assorted as they came in, and from which the checks were paid. These labels were: "Eastern Penn.," "N.Y.," and "New England" in one compartment; "Ohio," "Indiana," and "Missouri" in another; then "Va.," "Md.," and "Ky" in another; then in a further compartment, "Ill." and "Wis,." And, lastly, "Western Mixed."
>
> The first-named notes were choice par funds, rating next to good, and they were shipped to New York for exchange purposes. The next two compartments (with Ohio, Indiana, Missouri, Virginia, Maryland, and Kentucky) were "bankable funds," so called, and graded among the safest of bank notes.
>
> Illinois and Wisconsin took in the few legitimate free banks in those states, located principally in Chicago and Milwaukee, but the last label was more comprehensive than all the others put together. It included "rag tag" and "bob tail," everything not comprehended under the other labels but resembling a bank note—"Western Mixed" was the dignified and formal name for it. Its pet names were "stump-tail," "red horse," "wild-cat," "brindle-pup," and many others of like endearing character.
>
> The vigilant banker watched that pile of currency closer than the others. Its increase in quantity caused much anxious concern—and its decrease corresponding elation. As the close of the business day approached, if the supply was large, he prayed inwardly for checks to come in for payment; and if he could close up the day with that part of his tray empty, his sleep that night would be calm and peaceful. That kind of money reversed the usual order of things in the mind of a banker—a large balance, instead of being a source of satisfaction, was a very disagreeable menace.[7]

"Western Mixed" was no doubt truly a mixed bag containing genuine notes of failed or hopelessly insolvent banks, spurious bills on banks that never existed in the first place, and various types of alterations.

Confessions of a Counterfeiter

Langdon W. Moore, a career criminal who robbed banks, distributed counterfeit bills, and engaged in other sorts of currency misdemeanors and felonies, included in his memoirs this explanation—or perhaps *confessions* would be a better word:

> I went into the business of altering and raising notes. For a sticking substance I used white isinglass that defied detection when the note was held to the light. As my raised notes were, therefore, superior to those put on the market by other men, I realized no difficulty in finding ready sale at fifty dollars per hundred for all I could make, and in a short time I was unable to supply the demand.
>
> I then experimented with acids to see if I could discover some easier way of altering money by extracting the smaller figures and printing in larger ones. I soon learned how to remove the signatures from broken bank bills; but not before I had exhausted the catalogue of powerful acids did I discover that the printing ink in the notes could be extracted with a common fluid found in nearly every New England farmhouse. From that time I did no more pasting.
>
> I visited a number of brokers, purchasing several thousand dollars in broken bank bills on the Metropolitan Bank of Washington, D.C. These bills I altered to a bank with the same title in New York City, by simply changing the location with fancy type, and printing with a typeholder and mallet. I made several hundred dollars by the operation.
>
> I then bought a copying press and made the acquaintance of an engraver, who furnished me with engraved state and location plates, such as I wished to use from time to time, until the following year. As I had never been able to print a perfect impression of a bank title with the press I had been working, I bought a card printing press, and went to work altering notes from failed banks, first extracting the title, state, location, and signatures, then printing in the name of some other bank with the state and location I had selected, taking especial care in selecting inks that would compare with the rest of the notes. I resized the notes, and ran them through the press between cardboards to give them a genuine appearance. I then signed the names of the officers of the solvent banks in their place.

This was a new industry, and as the notes were so much better than a regular counterfeit, I could not keep up with the local demand, to say nothing about the country trade. To supply this, I was compelled to teach a man the business, and as soon as he was able to make a passable alteration, I set him to work on the piece price plan. For every hundred notes, without regard to the denomination, from which he extracted the title, state, location, and signatures, and printed others in his place, resized and milled the notes, I paid him $8, I furnishing the plates and other material. I gave orders to my broker to buy up all or any part of those defunct bank issues not having been put in circulation. Doing this, the broker was brought in direct communication with some of the ex-officers of the banks, and he was able to make large deals with a very little outlay, say one or two percent of the face value of the notes. . . .

This man alone altered many hundreds of thousands of dollars in broken bank bills to other banks, and his weekly earning during the whole time was from $100 to $185. I not only ran this mill, but another, where the real counterfeit [completely printed from false plates] was turned out in large amounts.[8]

In an unrelated situation, in August 1852 the *Philadelphia Bulletin* reported on a raid on a nest of counterfeiters that yielded unexpectedly good results:

Descent Upon Counterfeiters in Montour County

On Monday, August 9, in accordance with admirable previous arrangements, a descent was made upon the principal manufactory of counterfeit paper-money in Pennsylvania. . . . The location of the spurious bank-note factory was in Montour County, about 15 miles from Danville.

The manufactory was in a room on the second floor of the house of Dr. Geitner, a short distance from the tavern of Abraham Hause, the father-in-law of Geitner. The expedition was under the direction of Mayor Gilpin of Philadelphia and Mayor Guthrie of Pittsburg. The police officers selected were High-Constable Hague of Pittsburg, and Captain Jacob Bennett and officers Bunting and Moser of this city. . . .

The police, on approaching the door, were suspected by the wife of Geitner, who gave a signal, when the counterfeiters, who were in the midst of their work, turning out twos on the Harrisburg Bank, instantly leaped through windows and every other avenue of exit, and precipitately fled to the mountains. The officers secured Dr. Geitner, the master-spirit, but the others all escaped. Dr. Geitner had to be shot by officer Moser before he would surrender. He received two or three balls from a revolver, in the region of the shoulder; his wounds, however, are not considered mortal. He was lodged in Danville jail. The escape of his accomplices was a mishap which it was impossible to prevent under the circumstances. There were neither men nor facilities sufficient to give prompt pursuit, and the hills and woods were so close at hand that the fugitives were in their fastnesses ere they could be overtaken.

The whole of the counterfeiting apparatus and implements, consisting of the press, engraving tools, printing materials, chemical preparations; &c., were secured. The press is a complete affair. About $600 in spurious Harrisburg twos were likewise secured, with a number of other spurious bills, purporting to be of different banks. The officers unfortunately did not get the plate of the Harrisburg counterfeit, one of the fugitive counterfeiters who jumped out of a window taking it with him. They had the good luck, though, to recover, in the neighborhood of the scene of operations, two or three other steel and copper plates; one, that of a counterfeit five on the Merchants and Manufacturers Bank at Pittsburg; another, a twenty-dollar copper plate. The latter plate was an alteration from the exploded Millington Bank to the Cape May Bank; and it was being again altered to a Rhode Island Bank. One or more of the recovered plates were originally genuine, and had been stolen.

The prisoner, Dr. Geitner, is a splendid penman, and a most accomplished counterfeiter. He fought bravely before he would give up. His age is about 28. When taken into custody he asked for Police-Marshal Keyser of Philadelphia, saying, that, if he was with the party of officers, all would be right, as they both belonged to the same Masonic Lodge. Officer Hagne told him that he was a member, but could not acknowledge him as a worthy brother of the order. . . .[9]

Counterfeiter Langdon W. Moore found bills of the Metropolitan Bank of Washington, D.C., easy to alter. At the upper right, DISTRICT OF COLUMBIA, and below center, *Washington,* would be erased chemically, after which the address would be changed by imprinting *New York* and *New York City.* Few were the wiser. Depicted is a genuine note.

CREATING FALSE CURRENCY

ORMSBY'S DESCRIPTION OF THE PERKINS NOTES

From the standpoint of the ease of altering a bank's identity, slug-plate bills of the Patent Stereotype Steel Plate format furnished rich opportunities. This type, invented by Jacob Perkins and discussed earlier, consisted of an ornately engraved plate with many flourishes, repeated tiny type, cross-hatching, lines, and more, but not a scenic design or motif. In the steel printing plate there were three rectangular openings into which small slugs could be inserted, to print the name of the bank, its town, and its state.

Waterman L. Ormsby's *Bank Note Engraving* (1852) includes this pointed commentary concerning the Perkins system:

> Perkins' stereotype plate obtained a monopoly of the bank note engraving business, without any opposition, in the New England states.
>
> The plan places more reliance on mechanical, than on artistic skill. One plate is made to print all the bills of one denomination for many banks, by merely changing plugs of steel, on which are engraved the name of the bank, the state, the town, etc. An error in the construction of the note showed itself the moment that one of the banks failed; for the worthless bills are easily altered to represent those of good banks.
>
> So also in the matter of counterfeiting; one good imitation plate can be used for the whole list of those banks that use Perkins' invention. Though the contrivance therefore, may be economical to the banks, because many can use the same general form; it is equally economical to the counterfeiter, who can use his general plate to counterfeit all their bills; and the inducement to make his counterfeit plate equal in workmanship the original, is in exact proportion to the number of banks that employ the original general plate in the manufacture of their bills.

At this point in his text, Ormsby reprinted a letter from Boston that had been published in March 1862 in *Dye's Bank Mirror and Illustrated Counterfeit Detector,* Cincinnati:

> A widely circulated and recently engraved counterfeit of the three dollar general plate of the New England Bank Note Company, on the Tremont Bank, Boston, has lately made its appearance. These bills were sent by parties in Milwaukie, Cincinnati, and St. Louis, to this city for redemption, and your market is, doubtless, ere this, flooded with them.
>
> About thirty New England banks use this plate, and the counterfeiters of it can alter from one bank to another at their convenience. Too much caution cannot be used in taking bills of this plate, and those persons not well acquainted with Eastern money should refuse all those offered by strangers.
>
> The following banks still use the general plate of the denomination of five dollars, so

(continued on p. 166)

A $5 note of the Quinsigamond Bank, Worcester, Massachusetts, from a counterfeit plate. This is a later-generation Patent Stereotype Steel Plate production, issued by the New England Bank Note Company, Boston, successor to the Perkins interests. Counterfeits could be made easily with this false plate and any number of slugs that could be inserted, in this case THE QUINSIGAMOND BANK, WORCESTER, and at the bottom margin, MASSACHUSETTS.

"Phony as a three-dollar bill" is a comment heard today, as most people do not know that $3 notes were once a legitimate part of American commerce. However, here is a phony $3 bill, a note of the Brunswick Bank in Maine, from a false plate with false slugs inserted for the bank name and location. Ormsby mentions this issue in his *Bank Note Engraving* (1852).

The Perkins Stereotype Steel Plate

As W.L. Ormsby explained, Perkins Stereotype Steel Plates furnished a playground for counterfeiters. Here are illustrated $2 notes from the same false plate as used to create fake bills of a string of New England banks, including the Bank of Montpelier (Vermont), Bank of Orange County (Chelsea, Vermont), Bank of Lebanon (New Hampshire), Manufacturers Bank (New Ipswich, New Hampshire), and York Bank (Saco, Maine). All on this list have a prominent break in the plate below the slug with the bank name, creating a black blob on the finished note, as seen, for example, below IER in BANK OF MONTPELIER.

A study of such bills indicates that certain issues for the Eastern Bank (Bangor, Maine) and the Piscataqua Bank (Portsmouth, New Hampshire) were made at an early time from the false plate, as there is no break in the plate at below the lower right inserted plug with the bank name. Alternatively, sheets could be printed with blank spaces for the name and location, and this information could have been added by a separate printing process.

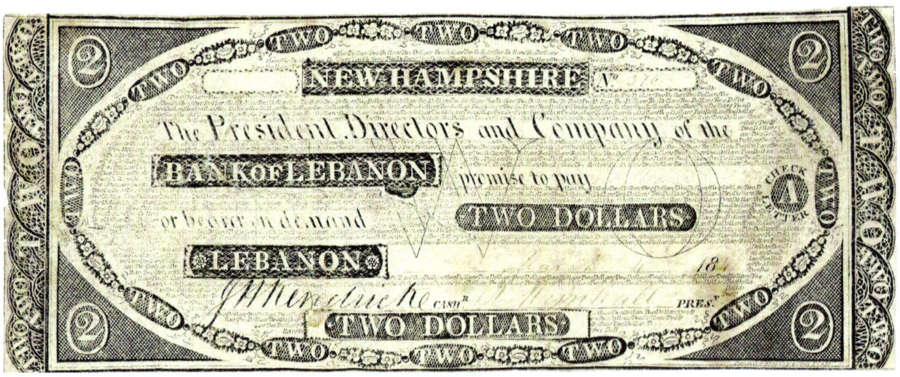

MAINE
The President Directors and Company of the
YORK BANK
promise to pay
or bearer on demand
TWO DOLLARS
SACO
TWO DOLLARS

MAINE
The President Directors and Company of the
EASTERN BANK
promise to pay
or bearer on demand
TWO DOLLARS
BANGOR
SUFFOLK BANK
TWO DOLLARS

PISCATAQUA BANK
NEW HAMPSHIRE
The President Directors and Company of the
PISCATAQUA BANK
promise to pay
or bearer on demand
TWO DOLLARS
PORTSMOUTH
TWO DOLLARS

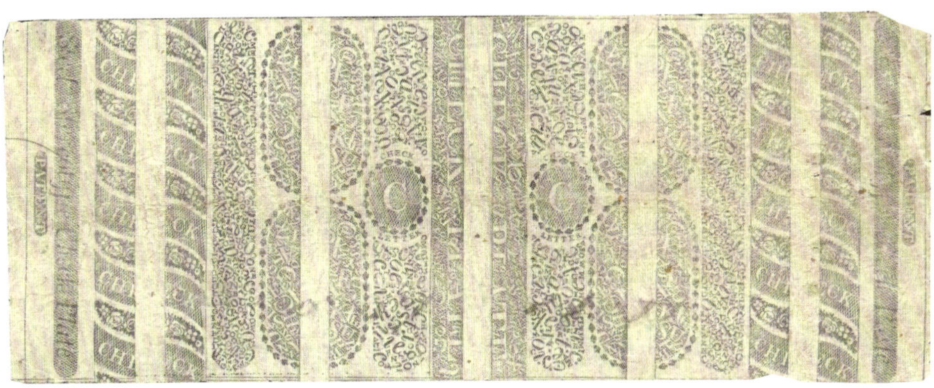

(continued from p. 163)

recently counterfeited:—Bank of Cumberland, Maine; Ashuelot Bank and New Ipswich Bank, New Hampshire; Bank of Montpelier, Vermont; Leicester, Blackstone at Uxbridge, Quinsigamond, Beverly, and Union Bank of Weymouth and Braintree, Massachusetts; Centerville Village, Warwick, Rhode Island; Central, New England Pacific, and Rail Road Bank, Rhode Island.

If there are any of the $5 notes of the above named banks in circulation in your region, I would advise the holder to *send them home for redemption,* and thereby make it for the interest of the banks, who persist in using this plates to adopt a new one.

Ormsby on the Rise of Counterfeiting

In a later publication, Ormsby's 1862 treatise, *Cycloidal Configurations* (of which more will be said in a later chapter), he gave his view of "improvements" vis-à-vis the rise of counterfeiting, from the early dates to the 1820s:

> It is within the memory of living men, that when, in times past, a bank desired to procure plates engraved, and bills printed, an engraver was applied to in person. The distinctive appellation of bank note now attached to his profession, had not then acquired any degree of specialty. If the bank was located in Charleston or Savannah, the engraver would proceed thither with his modest atelier and execute on the spot the work required.
>
> As banks increased, the business of engraving for them increased also; until it was said of a man who practiced in that line, "He is a bank note engraver."
>
> The large profits in the business naturally led to the formation of companies to carry it on—as the Graphic Company and the New England Bank Note Co. [*sic;* actually formed later, in 1833]. These companies introduced mechanical contrivances to embellish their notes, and, at the same time, expedite the work, and make it more profitable.
>
> The application of geometrical lathe work, the invention of engraving on steel, hardening, transferring, etc., forms a remarkable era in the art. At first the engravers honestly thought that they had achieved perfect protection against counterfeiting; but an investigation by the Bank of England proved its fallacy beyond question. Up to this period (1820) there had been few, if any, cases of counterfeiting in this country; nor was such a publication as a "Bank Note List," or "Counterfeit Detector," known in any part of the world.[10]
>
> It is especially remarkable, that, with the advent of this geometrical steel die system, so vauntingly introduced to make counterfeiting impossible, the rapid increase of the crime receives its date; and it was not long ere weekly lists of counterfeits began to appear in the newspapers, and finally to occupy the entire paper itself; the increase in the lists growing more and more disproportioned to the increase of bank note circulation.
>
> From these facts it is self-evident, that the *pretended* improvement in note engraving was, and still is, a *real* auxiliary to note counterfeiting. Still the engravers flourished. New companies were formed, and when a bank complained of counterfeiting, it was urged to greater expenses, and never was urged to anything else.
>
> Rivalry in business was carried to extremes; and special agents, who could not engrave at all, were employed to travel and "drum," like peddlers of pinch-beck jewelry which they sell for gold. Power and wealth accumulated, because the engravers kept every die they were paid for engraving. The circulars read thus: "All plates and dies engraved by us are invariably retained by us."
>
> Another and serious objection to this system of note engraving presented itself. As the original founders of engraving companies passed away, men of capital occupied their places, until at last the latter alone remain, in power supreme, and bank officers are brought face to face with the engraver no more.
>
> When business is dull, the hired engraver is turned away, and still the capitalist lives in affluence on the profits constantly accruing from the use of the artist's previous labor, in the shape of accumulated dies. And still the counterfeiters flourish—still the banks complain—still they are only offered "the protection that vultures give to lambs."

Other Techniques

Ormsby in his *Bank Note Engraving* (1852) sought to demonstrate the ease of making counterfeits:[11]

> **Imitating Lathe-Work by Wood Engraving**
>
> As Congreve showed in 1820, the white line net-work of the geometrical lathe can be imitated on wood.[12] This lathe-work is employed on almost every bank bill in this country. Sometimes it appears in a strip across the end of the note, and more frequently in the shape of an oval, circle, or small end piece in which the denomination of the note appears. In order to illustrate the effect of wood engraving as applied to the imitation of this work, we give the following specimen which was executed by hand, in a few hours, by Mr. J.W. Orr, the well known wood engraver of this city.[13]
>
> One copy only of a denomination figure was engraved by Mr. Orr, from which four electrotype copies were made by Mr. Ward. From these four electrotypes, impressions were printed in an ordinary letter press, by Mr. J.D. Torrey.
>
> The figure was copied from a genuine bank note originally executed by Messrs. Baldwin, Adams & Co. the highly distinguished bank note engravers of this city. We selected their lathe-work, because its openness is favorable to the engraver's process in imitating it. The finest quality of the work, however, can be imitated in the same manner, with a little more care and labor.
>
> The process of producing the facsimile engraving is simply this: the original bill was immersed for a few minutes in a solution of caustic potash which destroyed the oil of the ink. It

was then transferred on a block of wood by offsetting; the design becoming as plain upon the wood as on the original bill. The white line was then cut away with a graver, guided by the hand alone.

This was the manner in which Congreve proved, 32 years ago, that the work of the geometrical lathe possessed no security against forgery. The various parts of any bank note in this country have always been entirely open to the attacks of the counterfeiter, and if any commission of enquiry had been appointed to investigate the subject, the conclusions of Congreve would have been the inevitable result.

The Electrotype Process

This process has been in operation for the last ten years; and it is now generally known and practiced. A full description may be found in the works of Smee and others.

By this process silver, gold, and copper, after being obtained in solution, are deposited again in a solid form upon any metallic surface. Thus a copper medal may be plated with silver or gold to any required thickness. Electroplating is a business now carried on to a very great extent. . . . We will now proceed to show how copper-plates are multiplied.

The copper-plate being immersed in a solution of sulphate of copper, a proper application of a galvanic battery will cause a deposit of pure copper to be made upon the engraved plate. Thus a mould is obtained. This mould is placed in the solution, and a duplicate copper-plate is the result. The thickness of the deposit is determined by the time occupied, and by the intensity of the galvanic battery employed.

The actual cost of the whole apparatus capable of making many duplicates of a copper-plate the size of a bank bill, need not exceed five dollars.

On an accompanying plate is a portrait of Jacob Perkins . . . engraved by the writer for the New-England Bank Note Company in the year 1834. Being desirous of using it to embellish this work, we applied for a copy on copper, or steel, or an impression on a cylinder; but the company declined to furnish a transfer on steel, or to part with a steel cylinder "at any price," and informed us that copper transfers were furnished at $10 each. The effect of the restriction is only to prevent bank note engravers from obtaining duplicates of each others' dies, on steel cylinders; but not to prevent counterfeiting. Where the original artists use a transfer press and dies, to multiply engravings on the plate, the counterfeiter can use one plate, and print it several times on the same plan; thus producing the same effect, by a slower process.

The Ease of Multiplying Copies

Besides, when a counterfeiter obtains an engraved vignette on a copper-plate he can multiply that plate more perfectly by the electrotype process, than can the original bank note engraver by means of his transfer press. A proof of this is seen in the portrait of Mr. Perkins. The copper-plate which was very kindly furnished us is not used at all, to print the impression here shown, but is preserved as perfect as ever. We could produce any number of copper-plates from it for $5 each; though as a matter of courtesy, we would not, unlicensed, take advantage of the means we possess. We will add, however, that this duplicate electrotype plate of the portrait of Mr. Perkins was made by Mr. J.E. Ward of New-York, a practical workman in this branch of business; for which he charged only $1.50.

It must now be obvious that a counterfeiter may collect the copper-plates which the bank note engravers have, from time to time, engraved for checks, drafts, bills of exchange, certificates of stock medicine labels etc. and obtain electrotype copies of the various vignettes upon them; and, after properly filing and fitting the plates thus produced, may compose copper bank plates about as readily as printers can set up a form in type. He can likewise employ good engravers to execute the various parts for cards, labels, etc. and thus procure, piece by piece, a counterfeit plate, which will be equal in workmanship to the original, without being able to engrave a single portion himself.

It must be obvious that a picture or device of any kind ought not to be used more than once on a bank note; because, if it is used twice, the temptation to counterfeit it is exactly doubled. It matters not whether it be the lathe-work oval denomination, the medal head, the vignette, or any other portion of a bank note—thus demonstrating at once the uselessness of the transfer press, the geometrical lathe, and all other machinery, and the employment of dies in any shape or form.

Engravers who already own a large stock of bank note dies, may endeavor to blend them into new forms in the hope of obviating these difficulties; but if they are not permitted to use a design, or vignette, more than once, there will be no economy in using dies, consequently they would soon go out of use in manufacturing bank bills. If we have proved that all contrivances to multiply engravings on bank notes speedily result in their being easily and speedily counterfeited, the private interests of individuals ought not to be consulted, in opposition to the public good.

Ormsby's insights and commentaries, easy enough to understand today, were not widely circulated in the 1850s, and most bank officers, state legislators, financiers, and others involved with paper money and banking were not aware of these basic situations.

TYPES OF FALSE BILLS

COUNTERFEIT BILLS

In 1852 Ormsby related this explanation:

Counterfeiting

Counterfeiting, which is an attempted imitation in every particular of the genuine, can generally be detected by inferiority of engraving. The facilities of the counterfeiter consist in being able to obtain a well executed vignette from one engraver, a denomination die from another, the title of the bank from a third, and so on piece by piece, until he has acquired all the materials, executed in the very best style, which are needed in the execution of his counterfeit plate.

We have seen counterfeit bills so well executed, that we pronounced them genuine, and were only undeceived by a close comparison with proof impressions from the original plates in the hands of the engravers. No artist capable of such workmanship could knowingly lend his talents to such a purpose, and we are firmly convinced that counterfeiters resort to the above trick to obtain their plates. Every patch-work bill in the country is open to this attack; and engravers, though constantly watchful, may still be employed by designing knaves without suspecting their ulterior object.

Thus counterfeiters can obtain the original dies, or, at any rate, the best copies of them, that our best engravers are able to execute.

By this time there were so many dies of denominations, vignettes, etc., left over from past use that any commercial printer could gather a large stock with ease. These could be ordered directly from the engraving companies, bought from old stocks of plates of bankrupt companies, or simply created locally by an engraver who normally did illustrations for letterheads, newspaper advertising, and the like. For the counterfeits as described above by Ormsby, individual elements had to be obtained on a piecemeal basis.

Raised and Altered Bills

Bills with altered *denominations* are occasionally seen in dealers' stocks today, described as "raised notes," and are delineated by Haxby and other authorities. Although raised notes are altered, numismatists group them into separate categories: raised notes, with the denomination made higher, and altered notes, with other features of the bill changed.

Raised notes are less common than are alterations of the *bank name and location,* as described above for the New England Bank Note Company issues and mentioned briefly below, again from Ormsby's *Bank Note Engraving,* 1852:

Alterations can be effected in the titles of banks, by erasing the name of a broken bank, and stamping in the name of a solvent one. The name of the town and state are changed in the same manner.

Thus "The Farmers Bank, Mich." (Michigan) is made to read, "The Farmers Bank, Mass." (Massachusetts) by substituting for ICH the letters ASS!!

[*Raised notes*] The counterfeiter can tear off the corners of $10 notes, paste them over $1 notes—and pass the $1s for $10s, and the mutilated $10s as well as ever. He can procure a copperplate denomination like $10, $20, $50, or $100, and under some ingenious pretence print impressions on thin paper, and procure good $1 by the quantity, and enter into a wholesale business of fraud; after the fashion described in the following extract from the *Boston Atlas,* of June 22, 1847:

"Counterfeits: A remittance was received yesterday at the Suffolk Bank from the Bank of Burlington. Vt. of $900. There were four bills of $100 each, and two of $50 each, of the Shoe and Leather Dealers' Bank, Boston, making $500. Then there were eight bills of $50 each, of the Massachusetts Bank, Boston. All of these bills had been altered from $1 bills of the respective banks. The alterations are so well done, that ninety nine persons out of every hundred would not detect the cheat. The loss to the party who made the remittance, is $886. We hope that the scoundrels who are flooding the country with spurious Notes, may soon be detected."

The following statement in reference to this subject, appears as a standing notice in every number of that excellent periodical, *Thompson's Reporter:*

"Our subscribers cannot too closely scrutinize the larger bills passing through their hands, as every genuine note offers to the adept in this system, a subject for practicing his art, and many of the faculty do it to a nicety scarcely to be detected. It is done by pasting the figures 3, 5, 10, etc., over l's or 2's, and the words expressing the original value of the bill, such as *One, Two,* &c., are defaced (or sometimes erased by the aid of acids) and the fictitious value substituted. These are frauds we do not pretend to keep the run of, as no genuine bill is exempt from its practice."

"Audacious" Spurious Bills

From a numismatic viewpoint, bills called *spurious* are among the most fascinating. These are out-and-out fantasies, audacious (to borrow from Ormsby) capers created with chutzpah and widely passed to the public—who often did not know the difference. Challenging today is sorting out such bills from banks that may not have existed—or perhaps they did. New discoveries are constantly being made, and no doubt researchers will unravel many mysteries as early newspaper and other accounts, town and city histories, and other sources are reviewed.

As one of many examples, in George Wait's 1977 study, *Maine Obsolete Paper Money and Scrip,* a discussion of the bills issued by W.L. Ormsby for the Mousam River Bank of Sanford, Maine, stated that the river should have been spelled *Mousum.* However, I knew that this was incorrect, as the Mousam River, spelled that way, still flows at Sanford. (I have driven through the area many times, for it is just a short distance from my home.) Some numismatic texts say the bank *never existed* based on this spelling discrepancy.

Seeking to learn more about Maine banks, I was able to borrow from Frank Trask a copy of the rare

(continued on p. 171)

ALTERED BILLS

An authentic $10 note of the Commercial Bank, Gratiot, Michigan, from a plate signed by the New England Bank Note Company, which willingly made paper money for a bank that was never fully organized and never went into business. By 1838 this was described as a "wildcat" bank. While numismatists consider this note authentic, a case could be made for it as a spurious issue.

The Commercial Bank of Bath, Maine, was chartered in 1832 and remained in business until about 1856. In the late 1830s and the 1840s, its notes were sound and were well received in commerce. Many Commercial Bank of Gratiot bills were altered by erasing the Michigan information and adding appropriate lettering for Maine, as here, a bill fraudulently signed and dated 1846. For good measure, a red "protector" overprint was added!

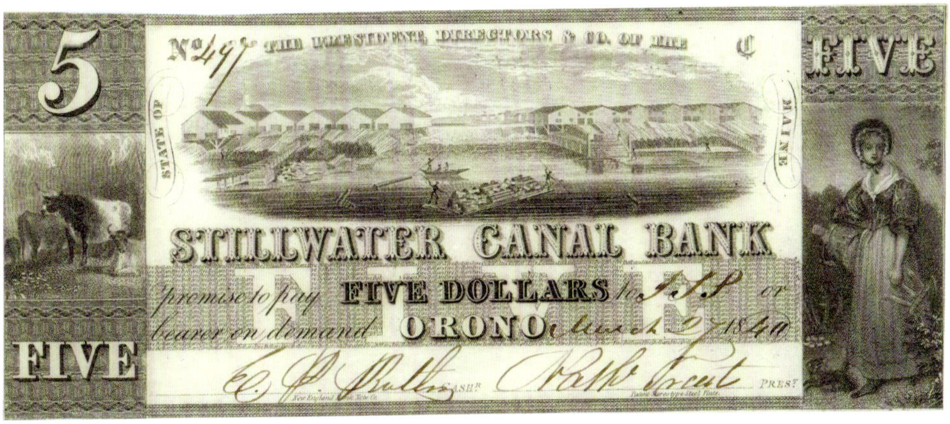

An authentic $5 note of the Stillwater Canal Bank, Orono, Maine, from a late Perkins-style plate by the New England Bank Note Co. Signed and dated March 2, 1840. Chartered on March 1, 1835, the bank operated legitimately for a time. In March 1840 it fell into the hands of "New York speculators," according to a newspaper account. In October 1841, state bank examiners paid a visit and found just $5.41 in copper cents as the bank's liquid assets—not enough to redeem tens of thousands dollars' worth of bills!

What to do with all of those worthless Stillwater Canal Bank bills? The solution was simple: sell them to counterfeiters, who altered them to appear as bills of sound banks, as the Merrimack County Bank of Concord, New Hampshire.

Altered Bills

Do it yourself: This handsomely printed bill, complete with a red "protector" overprint, bears the name of RHODE ISLAND and the fake imprint of Rawdon, Wright, Hatch & Edson, Boston. There is no bank or city printed yet. Such bills were sold "raw" to counterfeiters, who could add whatever information they wished! It is said that some were accordingly printed and distributed with Pawtuxet Bank imprints.

Another do-it-yourself bill, this bearing attractive vignettes, the title UNION BANK, but no city or state. A fake imprint of Toppan, Carpenter & Co. is at the lower right margin. These were sold from one counterfeiter to others in this nefarious trade, who could add information as they pleased.

An imprinted version of this spurious $5 bill with RHODE ISLAND and *Providence*. Inked signatures, date, and serial number have been added.

An *authentic* Union Bank bill printed by Toppan, Carpenter & Co. for the Union Bank of Swanton Falls, Vermont.

(continued from p. 168)

book by Walter W. Chadbourne, *A History of Banking in Maine 1799–1930* (1936). On page 36 this information is given:

> The Sanford Bank was chartered as the Mousam River Bank in 1854, commencing business on August 16 of that year. Only a small part of the capital was subscribed in the vicinity of the bank, nearly all of the stock being owned in Massachusetts. Most of its loan was in that state also. Bank Commissioners felt it their duty to ask for an injunction on these grounds in 1854. The court removed the injunction after a majority of the stock was transferred to responsible parties in Maine. The Bank Commissioners in 1854 stated, after the transfer of stock, that "the bank is in very competent hands." By act of the Legislature, in 1857, the name was changed to the Sanford Bank.

More about the Mousam River Bank will be found in chapter 15, which focuses on the activities of Waterman L. Ormsby, and other information is in chapter 21 under the discussion of Maine.

I have made quite a few minor "discoveries" such as this one by comparing banking and other texts with numismatic references. The state of the art constantly changes, as do opinions of researchers. Most students of paper money are open to new ideas, and often opinions of the past need to be revised. As an example, I recently changed the description of a "counterfeit" Vermont bill in my collection to genuine, and another that I had thought to be genuine I now believe is from a false copper plate.

Accordingly, the area of what have been called *spurious* notes by Ormsby as well as by modern numismatists is especially fertile with research possibilities.

Here is what Ormsby wrote in his 1852 study regarding spurious bills:

A genuine $3 bill printed by W.L. Ormsby, New York City, for the Mousam River Bank, Sanford, Maine. The goddess and eagle vignette is by Asher B. Durand for the ill-starred bank-note partnership of Durand & Co., which failed. Certain remaining vignettes and plates were purchased by Ormsby. Conventional numismatic wisdom has held that this was a fraudulent bank, but records of the state of Maine bank commissioners prove otherwise.

A genuine $100 bill printed by the American Bank Note Co. (with ABNCo monogram at upper left, added to a plate made earlier by the New England Bank Note Co.). This was issued by the Sanford Bank, successor to the Mousam River Bank. Generations later, signed bills of this bank became available to numismatists. Today they are plentiful, but only in the lower denominations. The $100 value is very rare.

Spurious Notes

Another very common and audacious species of counterfeiting consists in the issue of bills, called *spurious notes,* which are not imitations of any genuine bills in particular, but made to bear a general resemblance to all bank notes, and purporting to be the issue of some solvent bank.

The counterfeiter secures his impunity in this case from the perfect confusion of the detached figures and pictures which are used in our notes. The best judges may be thus imposed upon: for no man in the business community presumes to keep constantly at hand a sample of all the bank notes in the country, or to know what particular vignettes are on any one of them.

Judgment is passed upon the general appearance alone. The counterfeiter, therefore, does not find it necessary to imitate the precise vignette of the bill he counterfeits. With the great majority of business men, it will escape detection if it be a Vulcan, a Venus, a ship, a farmer, a steamboat, or a railroad, well engraved.

Ormsby then quoted "a striking instance of this species of fraud," as quoted from a recent issue of the St. Louis *Republican:*

> An extensive system of fraud is at this time carried on in counterfeit notes of the Canal Bank, New Orleans, of the denomination of $100. A few days ago we noticed a counterfeit upon this bank, and we now have information that the rogues have so altered their issues as to vary them from the description we then gave.
>
> The principal in this state, and who has been very successful in giving them circulation, is a fellow who professes to be a southern planter, purchasing Negroes for his plantation. Under this pretence, he has succeeded in passing several hundred dollars on steamboats and hotel-keepers on the Missouri River, and subsequently succeeded in purchasing three or four Negroes with this kind of money. One gentleman was in the city yesterday with $800 which he had received in payment for a Negro. The bank in question has no plate with any such vignette.

Ormsby then suggested that the plate might still be in use, making spurious bills for other banks. Further:

> It may indeed, have been the plate actually used to print $100 notes on the 41 branches of the State Bank of Ohio, which passed over the counters of brokers, bankers, and merchants in Cincinnati to a very large amount, before it was discovered that the bank *had issued no bills of a higher denomination than $50!*

FIVE BILLS FROM FOUR

The fraud of *multiplying notes,* as Ormsby described it, is not reflected in many specimens surviving today. When such bills are encountered in the numismatic market, they are usually of early issues, pre-1820, from copper plates. Ormsby explains the practice in his 1852 *Bank Note Engraving:*

> *Multiplying notes:* Another device of the counterfeiter extensively practiced, is that of multiplying Notes by cutting them into pieces, and patching them together, in such a way that four good bills shall make five shorter ones. In the old system of engraving, almost the only method of fraud known, or practiced, was that of counterfeiting; but at present, frauds in spurious and, altered notes, are far more frequent.

Ormsby went on to quote this item from an issue of the *Mobile Advertiser:*

> A.W. Marsh brought a suit in the circuit court of Alabama, to recover from the Bank of Mobile, the value of one of its $20 mutilated bills, which had come into his possession in the regular course of his business.
>
> The bill was composed of two parts, pasted together, which were less in length by seven eighths, than the original. The name of the cashier was in full on one part of the bill, and the name of the president, with the exception of his initials, on the other part. It was conceded that the owner received it in due course of trade, and when exhibited in court, in the same condition as when it came into his hands. The teller of the bank testifies that at the time the bill was presented to the bank, several bills of a like character had also been offered, and that the bank, in paying them, had been in the habit of deducting from them in proportion as their value was decreased by curtailment.
>
> The witness exhibited six cut notes of the bank, and explained how the seventh was made out of that number, and that it was his belief that the bill in question was cut with a fraudulent design upon the bank. The court in accordance with the above testimony, ruled that the owner was not entitled to anything—in other words, the bill was valueless.

COUNTERFEIT BILLS FROM GENUINE PLATES

If genuine plates were used by criminals to make counterfeits, the deception could be complete—few people, even experts, would have known the difference. In some instances stolen plates were used for this purpose. In other instances, well-known engraving houses were dupes for criminals, as was reported in an item from *Banker's Magazine,* October 1849, in which $500 U.S. Treasury notes were counterfeited, this excerpt being the explanation given by the solicitor of the Treasury:

> A person representing himself to be authorized by a mining company in Illinois, or somewhere West, called at the office of Rawdon, Wright, Hatch, and Co. in New Orleans and requested

> their foreman there to engrave and print a note for the Eagle Mining Company.
>
> He selected the devices which he preferred and the work was done. After a portion of the printing was completed, he called and paid for the engraving and printing, though only a portion of the latter was finished, pretending to some necessity that prevented his waiting for the whole work. The plate was taken to Cincinnati, where an old counterfeiter took out the words Eagle Mining Company," and inserted "The United States," which made the body of it precisely like a Treasury Note.
>
> The words "Secretary" and' "President" were changed to "Register" and "Treasurer of the United States." The words "Receivable in payment of all public dues," were added around the figures "500" at the top. The words "Countersigned" and "Washington" at the bottom and "One year" in: the centre were also added. . . .
>
> I think I ought to state, that no blame can be attached to the person who made the original plate. Nothing appeared calculated to arouse his suspicions. I have seen his original correspondence with his employers which passed at the time, in which he gave a full and satisfactory account of his doing the work, the price etc.

Ormsby commented: "Now, as the original Treasury Notes were executed by the same firm that engraved the principal vignettes on the spurious issues, the best judges of engraving would be the most readily deceived."

Ormsby went on to describe other bills created from genuine plates of various state-chartered banks, but altered in some small way, that had passed as counterfeits.

Then he includes this narrative:

> In August 1851, a stranger of entirely respectable appearance, presented himself at the office of the writer, with an order for a steel bank plate of four notes. He represented himself to be a man of capital residing at Cincinnati, and was about to establish a banking institution in Oregon.
>
> After examining our specimens, enquiring prices, and particularly remarking that it was quite immaterial what designs were used, he selected the vignettes etc., which he desired to have transferred into a plate of four notes, of the denominations $1, $3, $5, and $10 respectively.

Suspicious of the man's intentions, Ormsby contacted John Thompson, editor of a well-known bank-note reporter, who investigated and found him to be a phony. Undaunted, the customer went to another bank-note engraver and had the plates made. He later was arrested for fraud.

Ormsby then told of the career of counterfeiter William E. Brockway, a printer in a bank-note engraving company in New Haven, who was able to use genuine plates to print sheets of bills for himself. The bills were virtually undetectable, "compelling the bank to call in its circulation and to have new plates engraved."

The capers involved $2, $5, and $10 bills on the New Haven Bank and, later, $5 and $10 bills of the New Haven County Bank. Even the banks themselves had difficulty identifying them, and relatively few were ever identified. $2 bills on the North River Bank of New York City were also faked.

Old Plates and Dies Used

It seems to have been the practice of bank-note engraving companies to dispose of for scrap the plates of broken or defunct banks. Ormsby told of this situation:

> A person immediately concerned in a bank note engraving establishment sold from 10 to 15 original plates of broken banks, for a copy of the American edition of Sir Walter Scott's novels. The person who bought, sold the same again to a lithographer in Wall Street for $200. The plates were subsequently used in manufacturing checks, bills of exchange, labels, etc., until we lose all traces of them. . . .
>
> The writer once bought for a few dollars a steel plate containing about 20 vignettes, which an unsuccessful bank note engraving company originally intended for a specimen sheet. At another time he bought for $10 a steel bank plate, nearly new, of the denominations $1, $2, $3, and $5. These plates were cut up, hardened, and cylinder dies, nearly as perfect as the original, were reproduced therefrom. The artists who executed them originally occupy a high position at present in bank note engraving establishments.

In the above statement we see Ormsby admitting that he used original engravings of others for certain of his products. Indeed, his *Bank Note Engraving* book is illustrated with many vignettes made by or copied from others, and attributed as such. One popular and especially beautiful engraving, with a goddess flying through the air toward the right, carrying a shield, and with an eagle to the right, is seen today not only on genuine bills printed by Ormsby, but also on those of other firms. It was created by Asher B. Durand. Another, of a seated goddess and shield, was attributed to the talents of J.W. Casilear.

Ormsby continues his discussion of how such frauds occurred:

> We were recently asked, "How much will you give for *four* steel bank plates, one of which is nearly new?" Though those plates were, not long since, engraved by the firm of Danforth, & Co. we

declined purchasing, unless at a price too trifling to be worthy of notice. The failures of Burton, Edmonds, & Co. and of Durand & Co. at one time flooded the market with the very choicest materials for bank note frauds. The most beautiful lathe-work of Mr. C. Durand's improved machine, consisting of ovals, circles, strips, end-pieces, and borders, all finished with denomination figures, and lettered were sold and exchanged among label engravers, and lithographers from Canada to the city of Mexico and from the Atlantic coast to the Mississippi River.

We have traced one set of dies, most of which were designed and engraved by our highly distinguished artist, J.W. Casilear, Esq., and which formerly belonged to Burton, Edmonds, & Co., to South America; and almost an entire set, together with the transfer press, was lately sold for the small sum of $500; enabling any one therewith to execute facsimiles of many bank bills which are now in circulation!

The splendid vignettes of Durand & Co., some of which were designed and engraved by the renowned A.B. Durand, Esq., which so enriched their specimen sheets of bank note materials, that it is utterly hopeless for any other artists in the country to surpass, if even to equal them, have shared the fate of those of the unfortunate firms of Woodruff & Hammond, of Cincinnati; of Terry, Pelton, & Co., of Boston; of the Boston Bank Note Company; and of Hall, Packard, & Co., of Albany.

A transfer press and genuine dies were recovered from the notorious counterfeiters "Bristol Bill" and Meadows in Vermont, together with bank plates almost ready for use, upon which they had stamped vignettes, originally engraved by our best artists, who are now engaged in the business of manufacturing genuine bank notes. . . .

Transfer presses and duplicate bank note dies are in common use in several places in this country; and impressions of genuine bank note vignettes, lathe-work denominations, etc., are transferred on copper, and steel, for a trifling compensation. . . . Counterfeiters are in possession of these plates, *together with all the machinery of the original bank note engraving establishments,* and are flooding the country with spurious money, changing their attacks from one bank to another, until they wear out their plates in printing, only to supply themselves with those more improved in workmanship. In short, the materials for imitating every patch-work bank bill in the country are innumerable, and easy of access; and the trade is yet in its infancy. . . .

Finally

In the early 1850s, Massachusetts banks united to protest the evils of the Patent Stereotype Steel Plate, the use of which had been mandated in the state in 1809 and which had been generally followed by most banks afterward. On June 15, 1852, regional bankers met in Boston to formulate a strategy to combat counterfeiters. In addition, the overall quality of bills in circulation in America was deemed as being "unfit for circulation," due in part to "a spirit of ill-judged economy that has induced many of our banks to employ second-rate engravers, whose work has been so successfully imitated that neither bank officers nor the community could discriminate between the genuine and the false issues."[14] The state of Massachusetts contributed an annual sum of $2,500 to New England banks that banded together to conduct the Association of Banks for the Suppression of Counterfeiting (the new name as of 1853 for an earlier group), leading to the publication of reports on false bills. This change helped engender a new wave of anticounterfeiting techniques and patents. Then came this twist in the efforts:

> The special agent appointed by the banks to discover the source or sources of counterfeiting, has himself been detected in engraving and printing spurious notes. He has been in the habit of buying the spurious plates from professional counterfeiters, and selling them to the Banking Association, with a view to the plates being destroyed.
>
> Sufficient evidence is brought forward to show that the agent has deceived his employers and has contributed very largely to the numerous counterfeits that have been afloat within a year or two past. The name of this person is William W. Wilson, who is charged with counterfeiting on the Merchants Bank, Boston, and the Tradesmans Bank, Chelsea, and having in his possession dies and bank plates for that purpose.
>
> His case came up in the Police Court on Tuesday, 18th January, per assignment. A fifth complaint was entered against him, charging the same offences of the Housatonic Bank, after which the examination upon the previous complaint proceeded. The government produced about a dozen witnesses. Police officer Galen Holmes and Constable Wm. K. Jones detailed the circumstances of the arrest and what implements, counterfeit bills, &c., were seized, Mr. Pelton, an engraver, testified concerning certain bank plates and dies made by him, which passed into Wilson's possession. and by the use of which, it is alleged by the prosecution, he counterfeited bank bills.[15]

The *Annual Report of the Bank Commissioners of Massachusetts* for 1852 finally acknowledged the ease of counterfeiting Patent Stereotype Steel Plate bills, here called "general plates":

> It is worthy of examination, whether the use of what is called a "general plate," prepared in a manner to be used by any bank, merely by substituting one name for another, does not materially increase the evils of counterfeiting. A successful counterfeit of a general plate may easily be applied to a great number of banks. An

Sheet of sample genuine bank notes issued by V. Balch & Co., Albany, and Durand & Co., New York City. This sheet later descended to the American Bank Note Co. and was sold in 1990 by Christie's, along with other paper items, and still later to the Schingoethe Collection.

The partnership of Durand & Co. was established in 1837 by Cyrus Durand and had its office at 26 Wall Street, New York City. It continued into the early 1840s, by which time Andrew LeMessena was a partner. Afterward, the firm dissolved, and its vignettes became widely scattered. W.L. Ormsby acquired many of them.

> intelligent cashier, in a communication to the Commissioners, remarks that "a large part of the counterfeit bills which have been of late making so much mischief, are of bank notes printed from general plates."
>
> The use of movable vignettes, dies, &c. is regarded as an evil. The haste of banks in procuring new notes, the convenience of artists in manufacturing them, and economical considerations, have much influence in producing a description of notes which are open to the attacks of the skilful counterfeiter in various ways. It has been confidently asserted that, under our present system of engraving, counterfeit bank plates can be manufactured which shall have upon them the genuine work of the best artists without their knowledge or consent. . . .

The December 17, 1853, *Report* from the Association of Banks for the Suppression of Counterfeiting included this information:

> The number of banks belonging to the association is 110; and it is very desirable that every bank in New-England should be a member. . . . [During the past year the] number of "utterers" arrested has been about 38; of this number 14 have been convicted and sentenced to different state prisons. . . . During the present year the business of uttering has been conducted more than usually by females; their operations are conducted with less suspicion, and they more generally elude detection; a few of this class, however, have been arrested.
>
> The banks may do much to remedy the evil of counterfeiting: 1. By withdrawing their worn and defaced bills from circulation; and, 2. By using no plates but those engraved in the highest style of the art.

Andrew T. Hall of the Association of Banks for the Suppression of Counterfeiting made a plea to the Board of Bank Commissioners to outlaw the Patent Stereotype Steel Plate, but in these words:

> Gentlemen: Presuming you will make your usual report to the legislature the coming session, and strongly feeling the necessity of each bank in the Commonwealth being required to use only a special plate, designed and prepared for its own separate use, I venture to ask you once more to call the attention of the legislature to the subject, and to urge upon them some action relative thereto. . . .
>
> Every week, nearly, I see new counterfeits printed from an old plate—or partially old—with the name altered; and which, from the mode adopted by nearly all the banks, is a very easy matter. It will require much time to prepare as many new plates as will be needed, should a law of this kind be passed.
>
> I suggest, therefore, the propriety of an act requiring all banks hereafter chartered, or having their capitals increased, to use a special plate of their own; and that all banks now in existence be subject to the same requirement after the year 1860—thus giving time to procure designs carefully executed by the best talent the country can produce; together with a general design, if a practicable one can be adopted, of having some one general feature, indicating the denomination when under the sum of $10; and that, on the closing up of every bank, all their plates shall be taken possession of by the Bank Commissioners and by them destroyed.

Numismatic Notes

As related in this chapter, various types of counterfeits, alterations, and bills from spurious banks form an interesting aspect of study today. All have significant numismatic value and are eagerly sought. The Haxby text lists and prices many.

The state of the art is that many issues have not been examined carefully, and in the marketplace there are many false notes that are offered as genuine (or offered without comment). Conversely, some notes of "fraudulent" or "nonexistent" banks have been found to be genuine after all.

Bank Note Reporters

Introduction

According to the laws of physics, for every action there is an equal and opposite reaction. The same theory can be applied to the counterfeiting of bank bills. For each method devised to create fake bills of one sort or another, reaction took place in the form of identifying their features and attempting to prevent their passing. However, there were so many counterfeits and counterfeiters that keeping track of them all was a virtual impossibility. As soon as one type of phony bill was described in print, a new plate would be made and a new round of deception would occur. Conversely, whenever a new anticounterfeiting system or technique was devised by the bank-note companies, counterfeiters immediately sought to turn out their own versions of it—sort of a "Spy vs. Spy" scenario, as from an old issue of *Mad* magazine.

The subject of this chapter would fill a *book,* as indeed it did for William H. Dillistin, whose excellent study, *Bank Note Reporters and Counterfeit Detectors 1826–1866,* published by the American Numismatic Society in 1949, remains the authority today.

It seems likely that merchants and bankers found the typical bank-note reporter to be of only limited use, beyond revealing whether a bank was insolvent or that its bills were selling at a deep discount. The descriptions of altered, counterfeit, and otherwise nongenuine notes were often ambiguous. In general, little care was spent to create accurate listings. The aim seems to have been to sell copies of the reporter, a trade in itself. But the business must have had its difficulties achieving profits, for only a few such reporters endured for more than a year or two without change of title or ownership.

Many—if not most—publishers of such periodicals were also exchange brokers and dealt in bills from distant locations or of questioned authenticity. Certain readers of bank-note reporters probably realized the value of an exchange broker in buying or selling worthless bills. The notice that bills had become valueless signaled the call, "Where can I buy some?" No doubt the synergism of publishing and dealing was a major factor in making John Thompson the largest exchange broker in New York City, including in worthless paper, by 1857.

Across the board, virtually all bank-note reporters are rife with errors, with compilations being made from incomplete newspaper reports, hearsay, and scattered sources that were often inconsistent. It is likely that the vast majority of fakes were never seen in person by the publishers of counterfeit detectors but were learned of through correspondence or newspaper reports.

Although documentation is scarce (but see Monroe, Dye, and Taylor below), it is true that, for a wink and the exchange of some hard cash, some publishers would report a bank favorably. That this practice was far from rare is evidenced by use in the trade of the terms *puff a bank* and *blow a bank.* The former referred to listing a weak bank as being strong, and the latter was a way of punishing a bank officer who did not buy an advertisement or who in some other way crossed the publisher.

Today it is possible for numismatic researchers to examine actual specimens of bank notes to learn more than the issuers of such journals ever did. With a library of reference books on paper money, town histories, financial reports, and other data gathering the cumulative knowledge of the past, numismatists who are interested the background of bills and the issuing banks can gain more knowledge today than could any publisher of a bank-note reporter in the 1850s. Today, surviving copies of bank-note reporters and counterfeit detectors (descriptions that are largely interchangeable) have more curiosity value than anything else. However, those that were compiled from information sent by the bank-note companies are quite useful in the descriptions of designs and vignettes, particularly for large-denomination bills, of which examples may not exist today.

While the Dillistin text furnishes a rich source for specific information on many different publishers, descriptions of several bank-note detectors may be of interest, commencing with that produced by Bicknell in 1830, the longest-lasting of the early titles.

Bicknell's Counterfeit Detector

The First Issue

Robert Thaxter Bicknell, a Philadelphia entrepreneur specializing in the sale of lottery tickets and the valuation of bank notes, launched *Bicknell's Counterfeit Detector* as a biweekly commencing with July 31, 1830. His aims were stated thus:

To the Public

The utility of a sheet issued from the press of Philadelphia, embracing a list, corrected semi-monthly, of all broken banks, counterfeit bank notes, a price current, and all such information as is calculated to benefit storekeepers and men of business—the usefulness and want of such a publication will strike every intelligent reader. We have long felt this want ourselves—and under this impression, and at the solicitation of influential friends, we have been induced to commence the present undertaking. . . . The country is already inundated with literary periodicals, from the highest to the lowest grade. [However, a] journal devoted almost exclusively to the more important matter of business, might succeed—indeed, from the liberal encouragement already offered to this publication, we are confident that it will. At all events, the publisher is determined to issue it for a year, so that those who extend to it their patronage may not in any case be disappointed. With these views, therefore, the "Counterfeit Detector" is offered to the public.

The facilities which the publisher of this journal possesses for rendering it serviceable are numerous. He has for many years been engaged in the lottery and exchange business in Philadelphia, is in the habit, daily, of discounting every description of paper money, is familiar with the actual state of the market, and will be indefatigable in an endeavor to render this publication a correct standard, by which his friends and his customers . . . may rely implicitly upon its statements.

Every storekeeper should possess such a publication. Bank notes are being counterfeited in every direction, and with the arrival of every vessel or the creation of every national excitement, the state of the market varies. Some certain guide should . . . be established, by which those at a distance from large cities might receive all such information by the earliest mails, and at such a rate as not to render its possession an exorbitant tax. Such is exactly the description of our design to render this publication—in the effort to accomplish which, neither pains nor expense shall be spared on the part of the publisher.

In addition to what has been stated above, each number of the "Counterfeit Detector" will contain the scheme of the current Union Canal Lottery, with the drawn numbers of that which precede it, so that those who purchase tickets of the publisher may receive the intelligence of the drawing, through the medium of the "Detector," the moment the lottery is decided. By this means our country friends will learn the fate of any tickets purchased, at a cheaper rate than if we informed them by letter—whilst they at the same time learn the state of the markets, and will be enabled to judge of the merits of the ensuing scheme.

INTERNAL IMPROVEMENT.—It may be well enough to mention that the schemes of no lotteries will be inserted in this journal but those of the Union Canal Lottery, authorized by the legislature of Pennsylvania, under the immediate agency of Messrs. Yates & McIntyre, and the proceeds of which, are devoted to internal improvement. The beneficial design of the fund thus created is known to every intelligent reader, and whilst we not pretend to advocate any system of gambling, it is well enough to mention here, that lotteries, like many other means designed for the public welfare, are sometimes perverted to pernicious purposes. Such, however, is not the case with the Union Canal Lotteries.

All information with respect to banking establishments, counterfeit notes, etc., will be gratefully received by the publisher of this journal.

Prospectus of Bicknell's Counterfeit Detector

This publication was commenced inPhiladelphia on the 31st of July. It is handsomely printed on a super-royal sheet, with good type, contains a vast quantity of reading matter as well as a list of prices current, a bank note list, and all such information as is calculated to prove serviceable to the man of business, country merchant and storekeeper. It will be issued every two weeks, is published on Saturday, embraces the latest foreign and other intelligence up to that period, and will be sent away by the mails which leave the city on the day of its publication. The terms of the "Counterfeit Detector" will be TWO DOLLARS per annum, payable in advance. Three copies will be sent for five dollars. Address, Robert T. Bicknell, 119 Chestnut Street, Philadelphia.

Our friends in the country who will give this prospectus one or two insertions, will confer a favor that will at any time be reciprocated, whilst we shall be pleased to interchange with them the courtesies of an exchange. Post masters and editors to whom this publication is sent, are respectfully solicited to act as agents.

List of Broken Banks

An integral feature of Vol. I, No. 1, of *Bicknell's Counterfeit Detector* was the "List of Broken Banks" (below). The compilation, which reflects extensive but not careful study, included state-chartered banks (such as the Hillsborough Bank of Amherst, New Hampshire) as well as unofficial banks (including the Owl Creek Bank of Mount Vernon, Ohio). Some *broken* banks were actually solvent, but perhaps in a period of distress. In 1830 reliable information was very hard to find, and even *Niles' Weekly Review,* the *New York Journal of Commerce,* and the *National Intelligencer* reprinted many allusions and rumors, often in contradiction to fact. Therefore, Bicknell's *Detector* would serve for a long time as a single source for information that in the main was useful.

For present-day numismatists, the following 1830 listing of banks is significant as reflecting the early era of distressed banks, official and unofficial, in the United States. After this point, and continuing to 1866 (the last year of note-issuing by state banks), a veritable deluge of banks failed.

In this early list it will be seen that Ohio, then on the leading edge of what was known as the American West, and Pennsylvania had the most problems, this due to unofficial banking as well as loose state regulations. Certain of the banks listed were able to revive or otherwise continue their business, but most were defunct. This list is by no means complete, but it was based on the best information the publisher had on hand at the time. The histories of several of these banks have been discussed earlier in the present text (illustrations added):[1]

Alabama: Tombeckbe Bank, *St. Stephens*

Connecticut: Derby Bank, *Derby* • Derby Bank, payable at Fulton Bank, New-York • Eagle Bank of *New-Haven* • Eagle Bank of New-Haven, payable at New-York

Delaware: Bank of Laurel, *Laurel*

District of Columbia: Franklin Bank of Alexandria, *Alexandria* • Merchants' Bank of Alexandria, *Alexandria* • Bank of Columbia, *Georgetown*

Georgia: Augusta Bridge Company, *Augusta*

Illinois: Bank of Edwardsville (and its branches), *Edwardsville* • Bank of Illinois (and branches of do.), *Shawneetown* • State Bank of Illinois (and branches of do.), *Vandalia*

Indiana: Farmers' and Mechanics' Bank, and its branches, at sundry places • State Bank of Indiana, and branches of do. at sundry places.[2]

Kentucky: All the banks uncertain

Maine: Castine Bank, *Castine* • Passama quoddy Bank, *Eastport* • Hallowell and Augusta Bank, *Hallowell;* charter revoked • Kennebec Bank, *Kennebec*[3] • Wiscasset Bank, *Wiscasset;* charter revoked [Pre-1820 bills of any of these banks have Massachusetts addresses]

Maryland: Bank of Somerset, branch, *Princess Anne* • Cumberland Bank of Alleghany, *Cumberland* • Elkton Bank of Maryland, *Elkton* • Bank of Somerset, branch, *Snow Hill* • Bank of Somerset, *Somerset* • Planters' Bank of Prince George's County, *Upper Marlborough* • Conococheague Bank, *Williamsport*

Massachusetts: Farmers' Bank of Belchertown, *Belchertown* • Berkshire Bank, *Pittsfield* • Essex Bank of Salem, *Salem*

Michigan: Detroit Bank, *Detroit* • Bank of Monroe, *Monroe*

Missouri: All the banks uncertain

New Hampshire: Hillsboro Bank, broken[4]

New Jersey: Monmouth Bank of New-Jersey, *Freehold* • Hoboken Banking and Grazing Company, *Hoboken* • New-Jersey Manufacturing and Banking Company, *Hoboken* • Franklin Bank of New-Jersey, *Jersey City* • Jersey Bank, *Jersey City* • Jersey Bank, *Jersey City,* same but payable at the Ontario Bank in the state of New-York, dated at Jersey City • New Jersey Protection and Lombard Bank, *Jersey City* • Paterson Bank, Paterson • State Bank, Trenton

New York: Bank of Niagara, *Buffalo* • Aqueduct Association, now the Greene County Bank, *Catskill* • Greene County Bank (formerly the Aqueduct Association), *Catskill* • Bank of Columbia, *Hudson* • Bank of Hudson, once at *Hudson* • Bank of Plattsburgh, *Plattsburgh* • Checks of the *Clinton Manufacturing* Company at *Mechanicville,* on the Jefferson County Bank at Mechanicsville, on the Jefferson County Bank, similar to the notes of said bank, a fraud • Exchange Bank (J. Barker's), *New-York* • Franklin Bank, *New-York* • Franklin Manufacturing Company, *New-York* • Marble Manufacturing Company, *New-York* • Middle District Bank, *Poughkeepsie* • Washington and Warren Bank, *Sandy-Hill*

Ohio: Farmers' Bank of Canton, *Canton* • Farmers' and Mechanics' Bank, *Chillicothe* • Commercial Bank of Lake Erie, *Cleveland* • Bank of Cincinnati, *Cincinnati* • Farmers' and Mechanics' Bank, *Cincinnati* • Miami Exporting Company, *Cincinnati* • Piatt, (J.H.) and Co.'s Bank, *Cincinnati* • Granville Alexandrian Society, *Granville* • Granville Bank, *Granville* • Bank of Hamilton, *Hamilton* • Lebanon and Miami Banking Company, *Lebanon* • Lebanon and Miami Exporting Company, *Lebanon* • Bank of Sandusky Bay, *Lower Sandusky* • Bank of Mansfield, *Mansfield* • Owl Creek Bank, *Mount Vernon* • Columbiana Bank of New-Lisbon, *New-Lisbon* • Farmers' Bank of Salem, *New-Salem* • Jefferson County Bank, *New-Salem* • Hamilton and Rossville Manufacturing Company, *Rossville* • Urbana Banking Company, *Urbana* • Bank of West Union, *West Union* • German Bank of Wooster, *Wooster* • Muskingum Bank of Zanesville, *Zanesville* • Zanesville Canal and Manufacturing Company, *Zanesville*

Pennsylvania: Bank of Beaver, *Beaver* • Allegheny Bank of Pennsylvania, *Bedford* • Centre Bank of Pennsylvania, *Bellefonte* • Pennsylvania Agricultural and Manufacturing Bank, *Carlisle;* charter revoked • Northern Bank of Pennsylvania, *Dundaff* • Farmers' and Mechanics' Bank, *Greencastle* • Westmoreland Bank, *Greensburg* • Harmony Institute, *Harmony* • Bank of Swatara, *Harrisburg* • Huntingdon Bank, *Huntingdon* • Juniata Bank of Pennsylvania, *Lewistown* • Marietta and Susquehanna Trading Company, *Marietta* • Northwestern Bank of Pennsylvania, *Meadville;* charter revoked • Northumberland Union Columbia Bank, *Milton* • New-Hope Delaware Bridge Company, *New-Hope* • Farmers' and Mechanics' Bank of Fayette Co., *New-Salem* • Youghogany Bank, *Perrypolis* • City Bank, *Pittsburgh* • Union Bank of Pennsylvania, *Uniontown* • Bank of Washington, *Wash-ington* • Wilkes-Barre Bridge Company, *Wilkes-Barre*

Rhode Island: Farmers' Exchange Bank, *Gloucester* • Farmers' and Mechanics' Bank, *Pawtucket*

South Carolina: Bank of Cheraw, *Cheraw* • Bank of Hamburgh, *Hamburgh*

Tennessee: Farmers' and Mechanics' Bank of Nashville, *Nashville* • Franklin and Fayettesville Bank, *unknown* • Nashville Bank, *Nashville*

Vermont: Vermont State Bank, *Woodstock* • Vermont Branch of do., *Burlington* • Vermont Branch of do., *Middlebury* • Vermont Branch of do., *Westminster*

Virginia: Virginia Saline Bank, *Clarksburg* • Monongalia Farmers' Company, *Morgantown* • Western Bank of Virginia, *Parkersburg*

Canada: Unchartered Bank of Upper Canada, *Kingston*

Descriptions of Fraudulent Notes

The following is a selection of Bicknell's descriptions of certain bank notes, typical of many different states, this illustration covering Vermont, New Hampshire, and Maine, advising readers what to look for. As proved to be the case for later generations of other counterfeit detectors, in many instances the inscriptions were ambiguous, and the reader would have difficulty distinguishing an authentic note from a false one:

VERMONT

Bank of Brattleborough at Brattleborough. 1's altered to 10's, letter A payable to J. Mann, May 1, 1822.

Bank of Burlington at Burlington. 1's altered to 10's, letter, to whom pay, or date of do. [ditto] unknown.

Bank of Rutland at Rutland. 1's altered to 5's, discernible if held up to the light. The vignette in the true 1's is an ox, and the true 5's a woman.

Bank of Windsor at Windsor. 1's altered to 3's letter, to whom payable or date of do unknown.

Vermont State Bank at Woodstock. 2's let. I payable to bearer at Woodstock, March 1, 1807.

NEW HAMPSHIRE

Cheshire Bank at Keene.

4's old plate letter F payable to F. Alexander, July 9, 1800.

5's letter B payable to J. Welles, dated Nov. 6, 1820.

Concord Bank at Concord.

1's altered to 5's, letter, date &c of do unknown.

1's letter A payable to Roger Vose, dated July 1, 1829.

2's dated July 1, 1820; others dated July 1, 1821, signed W.A. Kent, Cashier; Th. Thompson, President

5's letter A to whom payable unknown, dated Jan. 1, 1822.

10's dated in 1819—letter and other particulars unknown.

Coos Bank, now the Grafton Bank.

3's and 5's letter, date, and to whom payable unknown.

5's letter C payable to J. Gore, dated March 21st, 1818.

Exeter Bank at Exeter.

3's old plate, payable to H. Mann, July 3d, others July 5th, 1805.

5's letter, to whom payable, or date of do. unknown.

Grafton Bank, formerly of Coos Bank at Haverhill. 3's and 10's, letter, to whom payable or date of do. not known.

Hillsborough Bank—Broken. 5's letter A payable to Henry Remsen, dated 10th May 1806.

> *New Hampshire Union Bank at Portsmouth.* 4's and 5's old plate, letter, date, etc. of do. unknown.
>
> *Portsmouth Bank in Portsmouth.* 1's old emission, letter and all other particulars unknown.
>
> **MAINE**
>
> *Bank of the United States, Branch of, in Portland.* 5's letter C payable to S. Greene, dated 4th March 1827, some 1828, and others 1829. The paper is lighter, so also is the vignette.
>
> *Kennebec Bank at Hallowell.* 5's letter C to whom payable unknown, dated May 1, 1818.
>
> *Union Bank.* 4's and 5's letter, date, etc., of do. unknown.

It can be seen from the above excerpt that many descriptions are useless. It would be impossible to determine if a given $4 or $5 bill on the Union Bank in Maine was good or if it was false based on "4's and 5's letter, date, etc., of ditto. unknown." In addition, the Hillsborough Bank of Amherst, New Hampshire, is listed as "broken," so, presumably, the key points for identifying a false note were moot!

Robert T. Bicknell had spent a lot of time gathering this information, useful or not. In ensuing issues of his *Counterfeit Detector* changes were made slowly. Not much new information came to hand from one issue to the next.

Determining Policies

In the second issue of *Bicknell's Counterfeit Detector,* dated August 16, 1830, the publisher had this to say:

> A correspondent asks if the "Counterfeit Detector" will embrace precisely the same matter in each number? Certainly not. The list of bank notes, counterfeit notes, stocks, etc., will, with the utmost care, be corrected every fortnight, and such intelligence will be embraced in every number as will be calculated to interest the general reader, as well as those who take a deep interest in the concerns of business.
>
> As soon as the work becomes more known, it is the design of the publisher to enlarge it to such an extent as will admit the insertion of a larger portion of literary intelligence. . . .
>
> The present number of the "Counterfeit Detector" will be sent to all the banks on which counterfeit notes have been executed and put in circulation. We should be glad to receive the patronage of such institutions. The terms of subscription are not required in advance from post masters and other responsible individuals.

As to "literary intelligence," this referred to news notes, scraps, and fillers garnered from here and there, not necessarily having to do with paper money, but deemed to be of interest to readers. It was widespread practice for newspapers and magazines of nearly all kinds to add items that amused the editors, these being called "exchange" notices and properly credited to the periodical in which they first appeared. Editors maintained exchange lists on a quid pro quo basis, meaning other publications were allowed to copy material with attribution.

Niles' Weekly Register, the leading nationally circulated commercial paper of the day, was laden with such exchange items. In time, *Bicknell's Counterfeit Detector* would treat readers to many notices relating to crimes, politics, and the like. In the meantime, editor Bicknell adhered to business and eagerly reprinted items on counterfeiting as they appeared.

The recruiting of postmasters to help sell the paper was not unusual. At the time most postmasters in small towns and villages also conducted general stores or other businesses on the same premises and often sold whatever could turn a profit. Citizens often called at the post office each day, and it was natural to view them as customers.

More News of Fraudulent Bills

The August 16, 1830, issue included these news items:

> Our correspondent in Harrisburg informs us that a *gentleman* has lately succeeded there in passing several counterfeit ten dollar notes on the Commercial Bank of this city, all of which are made payable to G.W. Ash, letter A, dated June 2d, 1830, Benj. P. Smith, Cash., A. Bayard, President.
>
> Counterfeit five dollar notes, on the Catskill Bank, New York, are yet in circulation in this city. The most of them are payable to C. Hopkins, letter C, dated June 1, 1829.
>
> Counterfeit bills.—Two hoary headed men, named Josiah Hager and N. Pomeroy, the one aged 68 the other 58 years, both of whom served the state many years—*in State Prison*—were arrested on Tuesday night, by Mr. Joseph L. Hays, at Niblo's Garden. It appears they purchased two tickets from the box keeper, and gave him a counterfeit bill for $5, on the Bank of Troy, and received the change. The worthlessness of the bill was discovered almost immediately, and the prisoners were instantly arrested. It appears that both these persons are notorious on the criminal calendar in this city, and were at one time sentenced for life to the prison at Greenwich. They were again let loose on the public by some accident or mistake, and Hager is but just come out of the New Jersey State Prison.

This item from Bicknell's second issue gained attention and was later reprinted in the New York *Journal of Commerce:*

> We saw yesterday a note of the Bank of the State of South Carolina at Charleston, purporting to be of the denomination of one hundred dollars, but

manufactured very ingeniously from a two dollar note. Along the upper and lower margins, the words TWO DOLLARS were repeated in small letters a great number of times. There, and wherever else the denomination was expressed, the original ink had been extracted, and an entirely new impression made. The paper is so little injured by this process, and the new impression is so well put on, that the general complexion of the note is not injured. The vignette is an eagle, holding a shield inscribed with the arms of South Carolina—in the distance a ship. This vignette belongs to the two dollar note, and if remembered, will detect the forgery.

But it will be observed that the same machinery with which this note was altered, is equally applicable to the notes of any other bank, and every other denomination of bills. Villains have become so skilful chemists, for all iniquitous purposes at least, that they find it easier to alter a few words which do not suit them, than to make an imitation of the whole. The great forgeries by Reed and others of checks on the New York banks, were done in this way. If it were possible to bring all the banks of the country into an arrangement, the same vignette might be adopted for all bills of the same denomination, which would at least make rogues a little extra trouble.

The reference to "The great forgeries by Reed and others" is enigmatic today.

The Third Issue

More news of currency capers appeared in *Bicknell's* on August 30, 1830:

> $1 bills of the Merchants' Bank, Newport, R.I. have been altered to 5's. They have the eagle and the paper mill, while the true 5's have the state house.
>
> COUNTERFEITERS.—Two men named Somerset D. Costen and Ed. Sprogle have been apprehended at Port Elizabeth, Cumberland County, N.J. Ten dollar bills on the Commercial Bank of this city, five dollar bills on the Catskill Bank of New York, and on the Eagle Bank, Boston, were found in their possession.

The public's reception to the publication had been favorable, and Bicknell reprinted some testimonials and told of his plans for the future.

> The next number of the "Detector" will give the names of all banks in the United States, and the rates of discount, in Philadelphia, on each.
>
> We have a sufficient number of subscribers to guarantee our publishing the "Detector" for *at least* one year, consequently no more papers will be sent away free of charge.
>
> The following are some opinions that have been expressed, throughout the country, in relation to the merits of this publication:
>
> From the *Centre Democrat.* "This publication will be of incalculable value to every man of business, and should be taken by every merchant and storekeeper."
>
> From the *Lancaster Political Sentinel.* "Such a paper has been long wanted, and will be useful in an eminent degree, to mechanics and traders."
>
> From the *Susquehanna Democrat.* "There is a vast quantity of spurious money now afloat, which makes a paper of this kind particularly desirable. The number before us contains a full list of counterfeit bills, altered notes, and broken banks."
>
> From the *Boston Patriot.* "It is a highly useful work, and appears to be compiled with much industry and skill, and contains a good portion of interesting matter."
>
> From the *Carlisle Herald.* "Every man in the habit of handling bank notes will find it to his advantage to give patronage to this very useful undertaking."
>
> From the *Saturday Evening Post.* "We consider it a work of great public utility."
>
> From the *Pennsylvania Inquirer.* "A journal ably conducted on the plan of the 'Detector' could not fail to merit and receive a liberal share of public patronage."
>
> From the *United States Gazette.* "The publication appears to us calculated to do good and be especially serviceable to traders."
>
> From the *Anti-Masonic Herald.* "It is handsomely printed, and appears to be such a paper as every man of business should have."
>
> From the *Boston Masonic Mirror.* "It contains such information as is calculated to benefit storekeepers and men of business, to whom we have taken the liberty of recommending it."
>
> From the *Saturday Bulletin.* "Those who are fortunately in the way, these hard times, of procuring much money, will, of course, possess themselves of so convenient and valuable a method of shielding themselves from one of the most frequent and vexatious impositions to which the community is liable."
>
> From the *Doylestown Democrat.* "The paper is certainly a valuable one, and ought to be found with every man of business."
>
> From the *Nantucket Inquirer.* "We think every large commercial city needs a paper of this kind; for, as rogues and counterfeiters multiply, the means of detecting them should increase."
>
> From the *Lancaster Gazette.* "To all persons engaged in business it must prove of great utility. It contains a variety of foreign and domestic intelligence, and is altogether an interesting as well as a useful publication."
>
> From the *Western Press.* "It will certainly be a useful paper, and one much required by men of business."
>
> From the *Pittsburgh Mercury.* "As a means of preventing frauds, it is a useful and cheap auxiliary to our commercial men."
>
> From the *Columbia Spy.* "It is a useful publication to those who have much dealing in bank bills, and is printed in a superior style."
>
> From the *Inquirer.* "It is well got up, and promises to be useful."

After the failure of the Farmers Bank of Belchertown, its worthless notes in circulation were eagerly bought up by brokers. Because these notes had been produced as Perkins Patent Stereotype Steel Plate bills, they were among the easiest to alter.

> Terms, $2 per annum. Single copies 12-1/2 cents. All orders must be addressed to Robert Bicknell.

ONGOING ITEMS

On September 13, 1830, Bicknell prefaced a long listing with this information:

> We have been at some labor as well as expense in getting up the copious bank note list, embracing all the banking institutions in the United States, besides that of the counterfeit bank notes, which will be found in our columns of today. It will be seen, on a reference to those lists, that there are *nine hundred and eighty* counterfeit bank notes, of various denominations floating about the country; that there are *three hundred and sixty-nine* solvent banks now in operation—and *one hundred and fourteen* broken banks, many of the notes of which are still in circulation. Perhaps these facts, better than any other representation, show to what an extent the privilege of granting bank charters has been abused in this country.

News of recently encountered counterfeit bills included these reports:

> Counterfeit $5 notes on the United States Branch Bank, New York City, are in circulation, all of those we have seen are dated July 1st, 1829, letter F, payable to M. Robinson, Cashier. Paper flimsy, engraving and endorsement bad; but the signatures are well executed.
>
> Five dollar *spurious bills* of the following description have lately been put in circulation: We promise to pay J. Brady, or bearer, $5 on demand, in specie or paper of the Bank of North America; Philadelphia, July 15th, 1830: signed T. Thomps, Cashier, S. Fry, President. Vignette on the upper part of the bill, head of Washington, No. 47, engraved by S. Hufty, Philadelphia.

FOLLOWING THE ACTION

In reading through *Bicknell's Counterfeit Detector,* one can follow scenarios being revealed as they happened, as in the following series of notices.

On September 13, 1830:

> It is ascertained that the bills, Perkins' stereotype plate, on the Globe Bank, Boston, recently discovered to have been counterfeited, are bills of a broken bank ingeniously altered.

On September 27, 1830:

> Counterfeit five dollar notes purporting to be of the American Bank, Boston, from Perkins' patent steel plate, have just made their appearance, signed I.S. Wright, Cashier, and Geo. Odiorne, president, letter L. payable to B. West, and dated May 1, 1824. The plate is genuine, and probably altered from a bankrupt bank bill. The signatures are well executed, but the filling up bad.

On October 11, 1830:

> COUNTERFEITS.—It is said that the dies were lately discovered in New Hampshire, for altering Belchertown Bank bills to those of the Globe and American Bank, Boston.

The preceding type of caper was common during the era. The Farmers Bank of Belchertown, Massachusetts, capitalized at $100,000, failed in 1829, at which time there was a large quantity of its Perkins Patent Stereotype Plate bills in circulation. These bills soon were recognized as worthless. However, they continued to have some small value at exchange brokers, no doubt about 2% to 3% of face value. Specialists in altering bills bought them in large numbers.

"Dies," per *Bicknell's* terminology, are actually small blocks of wood that had been engraved with details for, in this instance, the Globe and American banks in Boston. They were then inked and pressed into the blank spaces by the counterfeiters. For the Belchertown bills there was no need to change the state name.

BICKNELL'S IN LATER YEARS

When *Bicknell's Counterfeit Detector* was launched in 1830, it was early in the game. The periodical had only two predecessors of significance, both published in New York City, one by Mahlon Day and the other by Sylvester J. Sylvester. Sketches of both are given below.[5]

After about a half year of publication, *Bicknell's Counterfeit Detector* switched to publication on a weekly basis. In June 1831 the title was expanded to more accurately reflect its contents: *Bicknell's Reporter,*

Counterfeit Detector, and Prices Current. In 1835 it became *Bicknell's Reporter, Counterfeit Detector, and Philadelphia Prices Current,* no doubt because "prices current" were often different in Philadelphia, where the sheet was published, than in Charleston, Boston, or elsewhere.

In 1832 a separate pamphlet or booklet listing of bank-note values and counterfeits was published as a handy guide. This publication continued to be issued monthly for more than a decade, then switched to semimonthly. Robert T. Bicknell died on May 7, 1839, at the age of just 33 years. The *Reporter* and certain other business assets were bequeathed to a relative, Robert T. Miller, who had served as cashier in Bicknell's businesses.

Miller continued the periodical until June 30, 1857, when he turned it over to Charles P. Bicknell, the only surviving son of the founder. In time, Charles G. Imlay, a local banking and insurance executive, joined the venture, and it became known as *Imlay's & Bicknell's Bank Note Reporter.* In about 1866 it ceased publication, by which time the bills of state banks had been largely replaced by federal issues.

MAHLON DAY, PIONEER PUBLISHER

THE DETECTER

Mahlon Day, who created the first periodical counterfeit detector of importance, a predecessor to *Bicknell's,* was born in Morristown, New Jersey, on August 27, 1790.[6] On February 21, 1815, in partnership with Charles Turner, he commenced publication of the semiweekly *New-York Shipping and Commercial List.* Some information was carried concerning bank notes, but only incidentally. At the time other newspapers and business periodicals were much the same. Day later claimed to have established a specific counterfeit-detecting publication in 1819, but details are unknown.[7] *Day's New-York Miniature Almanac* was in publication by 1823 (but it may have commenced in 1819, thus supporting the 1819 claim noted), carrying general information plus comments on a few bank notes. This publication lived up to its name and was only about two inches by three inches in size. Although it carried some discussion of bank bills, again this information was incidental to other content.

On December 29, 1826, the *New-York Advertiser* carried this comment:

> Published this day, the *New-York Bank Note List and Counterfeit Detecter,* showing the value of

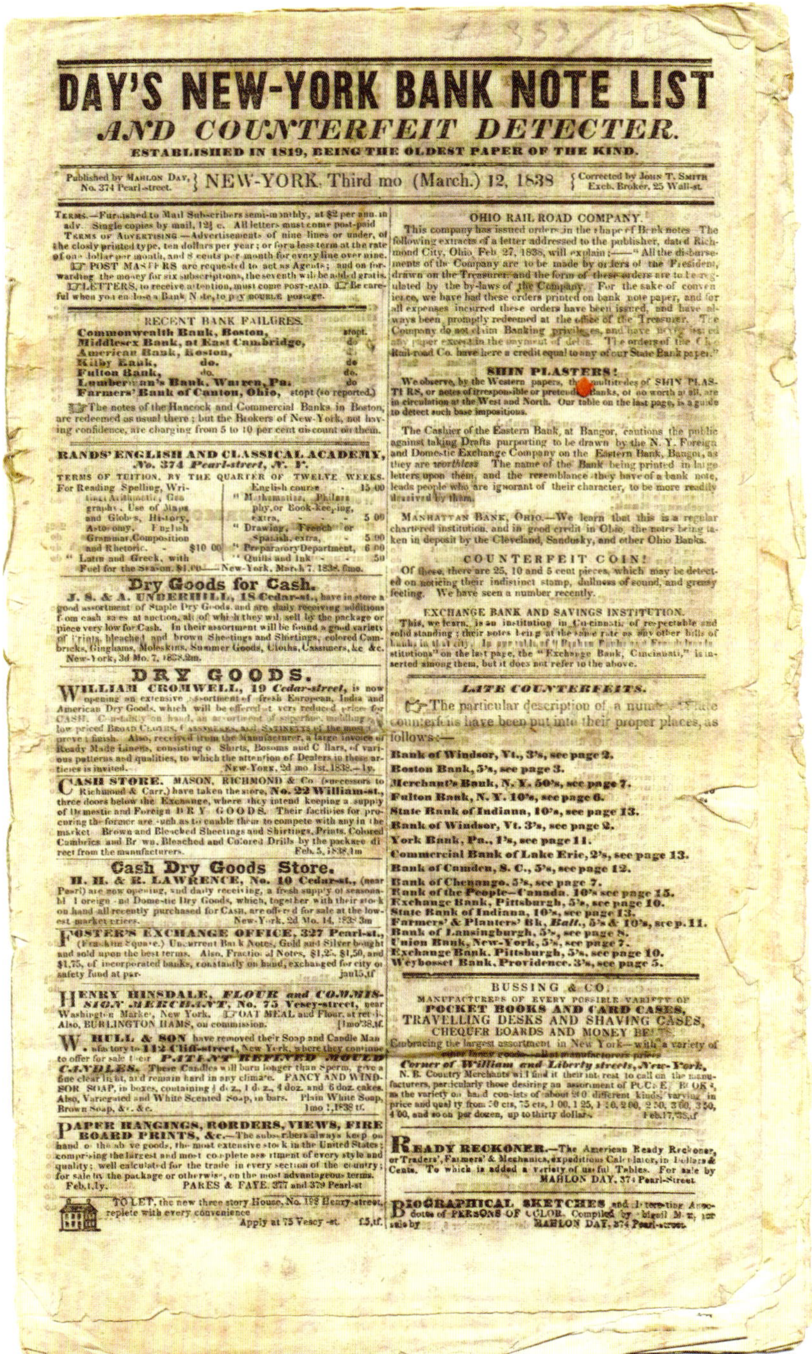

DAY'S NEW-YORK BANK NOTE LIST
AND COUNTERFEIT DETECTER.
ESTABLISHED IN 1819, BEING THE OLDEST PAPER OF THE KIND.

Published by MAHLON DAY, No. 374 Pearl-street. } NEW-YORK, Third mo (March.) 12, 1838 { Corrected by JOHN T. SMITH Exch. Broker, 25 Wall-st.

TERMS.—Furnished to Mail Subscribers semi-monthly, at $2 per ann. in adv. Single copies by mail, 12½ c. All letters must come post-paid
TERMS OF ADVERTISING.—Advertisements of nine lines or under, of the closely printed type, ten dollars per year; or for a less term at the rate of one dollar per month, and 8 cents per month for every line over nine.
POST MASTERS are requested to act as Agents; and on forwarding the money for six subscriptions, the seventh will be added gratis.
LETTERS, to receive attention, must come POST-PAID. Be careful when you enclose a Bank Note, to pay DOUBLE postage.

RECENT BANK FAILURES.

Commonwealth Bank, Boston,	stopt.
Middlesex Bank, at East Cambridge,	do
American Bank, Boston,	do
Kilby Bank, do.	do
Fulton Bank, do.	do.
Lumberman's Bank, Warren, Pa.	do
Farmers' Bank of Canton, Ohio,	stopt (so reported.)

The notes of the Hancock and Commercial Banks in Boston, are redeemed as usual there; but the Brokers of New-York, not having confidence, are charging from 5 to 10 per cent discount on them.

RANDS' ENGLISH AND CLASSICAL ACADEMY, No. 374 Pearl-street, N. Y.
TERMS OF TUITION, BY THE QUARTER OF TWELVE WEEKS.
For Reading Spelling, Writing, Arithmetic, Geography, Use of Maps and Globes, History, Astronomy, English Grammar, Composition and Rhetoric. - $10 00
" Latin and Greek, with English course - 15 00
" Mathematics, Philosophy, or Book-keeping, extra, - 5 00
" Drawing, French or Spanish, extra, - 5 00
" Preparatory Department, 6 00
" Quills and Ink - .50
Fuel for the Season, $1.00—New-York, March 7, 1838. 6mo.

Dry Goods for Cash.
J. S. & A. UNDERHILL, 18 Cedar-st., have in store a good assortment of Staple Dry Goods, and are daily receiving additions from cash sales at auction, all of which they will sell by the package or piece very low for Cash. In their assortment will be found a good variety of Prints, bleached and brown Sheetings and Shirtings, colored Cambricks, Ginghams, Moleskins, Summer Goods, Cloths, Cassimers, &c. &c.
New-York, 3d Mo. 7, 1838.2m.

DRY GOODS.
WILLIAM CROMWELL, 19 Cedar-street, is now opening an extensive assortment of fresh European, India and American Dry Goods, which will be offered at very reduced prices for CASH. Constantly on hand, an assortment of superfine, middling and low priced BROAD CLOTHS, CASSIMERES, AND SATINETTS of the most approved finish. Also, received from the Manufacturer, a large invoice of Ready Made Linens, consisting of Shirts, Bosoms and Collars, of various patterns and qualities, to which the attention of Dealers in these articles is invited. NEW-YORK, 2d mo 1st, 1838.—1y.

CASH STORE. MASON, RICHMOND & Co. (successors to Richmond & Carr,) have taken the store, No. 22 William-st., three doors below the Exchange, where they intend keeping a supply of Domestic and Foreign DRY GOODS. Their facilities for procuring the former are such as to enable them to compete with any in the market. Brown and Bleached Sheetings and Shirtings, Prints, Colored Cambrics and Brown, Bleached and Colored Drills by the package direct from the manufacturers. Feb. 5, 1838.1m

Cash Dry Goods Store.
H. H. & R. LAWRENCE, No. 10 Cedar-st., (near Pearl) are now opening, and daily receiving, a fresh supply of seasonable Foreign and Domestic Dry Goods, which, together with their stock on hand all recently purchased for CASH, are offered for sale at the lowest market prices. New-York, 2d Mo. 14, 1838 3m

FOSTER'S EXCHANGE OFFICE, 327 Pearl-st., (Franklin Square.) Uncurrent Bank Notes, Gold and Silver bought and sold upon the best terms. Also, Fractional Notes, $1,25, $1,50, and $1,75, of incorporated banks, constantly on hand, exchanged for city or safety fund at par. jan15,tf

HENRY HINSDALE, FLOUR and COMMISSION MERCHANT, No. 75 Vesey-street, near Washington Market, New York. OAT MEAL and Flour, at retail. Also, BURLINGTON HAMS, on commission. [1mo'38.tf.

W. HULL & SON have removed their Soap and Candle Manufactory to 112 Cliff-street, New York, where they continue to offer for sale their PATENT REFINED MOULD CANDLES. These Candles will burn longer than Sperm, give a fine clear light, and remain hard in any climate. FANCY AND WINDSOR SOAP, in boxes, containing ½ doz., 1 doz., 4 doz. and 6 doz. cakes. Also, Variegated and White Scented Soap, in bars. Plain White Soap, Brown Soap, &c. &c. 1mo 1,1838 tf.

PAPER HANGINGS, BORDERS, VIEWS, FIRE BOARD PRINTS, &c.—The subscribers always keep on hand of the above goods, the most extensive stock in the United States; comprising the largest and most complete assortment of every style and quality; well calculated for the trade in every section of the country; for sale by the package or otherwise, on the most advantageous terms.
Feb.1,1y. PARES & FAYE. 377 and 379 Pearl-st

TO LET, the new three story House, No. 192 Henry-street, replete with every convenience. Apply at 75 Vesey-st. f5,tf.

OHIO RAIL ROAD COMPANY.
This company has issued orders in the shape of Bank notes. The following extracts of a letter addressed to the publisher, dated Richmond City, Ohio, Feb 27, 1838, will explain:—"All the disbursements of the Company are to be made by orders of the President, drawn on the Treasurer, and the form of these orders are to be regulated by the by-laws of the Company. For the sake of convenience, we have had these orders printed on bank note paper, and for all expenses incurred these orders have been issued, and have always been promptly redeemed at the office of the Treasurer. The Company do not claim Banking privileges, and have never issued any paper except in the payment of debts. The orders of the Ohio Rail-road Co. have here a credit equal to any of our State Bank paper."

SHIN PLASTERS!
We observe, by the Western papers, that multitudes of SHIN PLASTERS, or notes of irresponsible or pretended Banks, of no worth at all, are in circulation at the West and North. Our table on the last page, is a guide to detect such base impositions.

The Cashier of the Eastern Bank, at Bangor, cautions the public against taking Drafts purporting to be drawn by the N. Y. Foreign and Domestic Exchange Company on the Eastern Bank, Bangor, as they are *worthless*. The name of the Bank being printed in large letters upon them, and the resemblance they have of a bank note, leads people who are ignorant of their character, to be more readily deceived by them.

MANHATTAN BANK, OHIO.—We learn that this is a regular chartered institution, and in good credit in Ohio, the notes being taken in deposit by the Cleveland, Sandusky, and other Ohio Banks.

COUNTERFEIT COIN!
Of these, there are 25, 10 and 5 cent pieces, which may be detected on noticing their indistinct stamp, dullness of sound, and greasy feeling. We have seen a number recently.

EXCHANGE BANK AND SAVINGS INSTITUTION.
This, we learn, is an institution in Cincinnati, of respectable and solid standing; their notes being at the same rate as any other bills of banks in that city. In our table of "[illegible]" on the last page, the "Exchange Bank, Cincinnati," is inserted among them, but it does not refer to the above.

LATE COUNTERFEITS.
The particular description of a number of late counterfeits have been put into their proper places, as follows:—
Bank of Windsor, Vt., 3's, see page 2.
Boston Bank, 5's, see page 3.
Merchant's Bank, N. Y. 50's, see page 7.
Fulton Bank, N. Y. 10's, see page 6.
State Bank of Indiana, 10's, see page 13.
Bank of Windsor, Vt. 3's, see page 2.
York Bank, Pa., 1's, see page 11.
Commercial Bank of Lake Erie, 2's, see page 13.
Bank of Camden, S. C., 5's, see page 12.
Bank of Chenango, 5's, see page 7.
Bank of the People—Canada, 10's see page 15.
Exchange Bank, Pittsburgh, 5's, see page 10.
State Bank of Indiana, 10's, see page 13.
Farmers' & Planters' Bk, *Balt.*, 5's & 10's, see p. 11.
Bank of Lansingburgh, 5's, see page 8.
Union Bank, New-York, 5's, see page 7.
Exchange Bank, Pittsburgh, 5's, see page 10.
Weybosset Bank, Providence, 3's, see page 5.

BUSSING & CO.
MANUFACTURERS OF EVERY POSSIBLE VARIETY OF
POCKET BOOKS AND CARD CASES,
TRAVELLING DESKS AND SHAVING CASES,
CHEQUER BOARDS AND MONEY BELTS.
Embracing the largest assortment in New York—with a variety of [illegible]
Corner of William and Liberty streets, New-York.
N. B. Country Merchants will find it their interest to call on the manufacturers, particularly those desiring an assortment of POCKET BOOKS, as the variety on hand consists of about 200 different kinds, varying in price and quality from 50 cts, 75 cts, 1 00, 1 25, 1 50, 2 00, 2 50, 3 00, 3 50, 4 00, and so on per dozen, up to thirty dollars. Feb.17,'38,tf

READY RECKONER.—The American Ready Reckoner, or Traders', Farmers' & Mechanics, expeditious Calculator, in Dollars & Cents. To which is added a variety of useful Tables. For sale by MAHLON DAY, 374 Pearl-Street.

BIOGRAPHICAL SKETCHES and Interesting Anecdotes of PERSONS OF COLOR. Compiled by Abigail Mott, for sale by MAHLON DAY, 374 Pearl-street.

Front page of *Day's New-York Bank Note List and Counterfeit Detecter,* March 12, 1838. The publisher was Mahlon Day. Widely circulated in their era, counterfeit detectors from the 1830s and 1840s are rare today.

> bank notes in New York and a complete list of counterfeit bills in circulation throughout the United States. For sale at the bookstore of Mahlon Day, 376 Pearl Street.
>
> N.B. Persons residing out of the city can have the Detecter furnished them for one year by forwarding two dollars in advance.

Thus, Day was certainly in the *detecter* business as of this time. Spellings of this word varied, not only with Day but also among others, although *detector* was used by most of his later competitors, including Bicknell. At his shop, the New Juvenile Book Store in Pearl Street, where he remained until about 1844, he sold books of general interest with a specialty in titles for children.

Although his *Detecter* was probably well distributed in banking and exchange broker circles at the time, it was ephemeral—and once a new issue arrived there was no reason to keep the old. Such is the dilemma of many historians who today seek to determine the nature of what at one time was common knowledge. In his study on the subject, William H. Dillistin noted that the early issues he was able to locate commenced in 1830.[8] Today, it must be presumed that all *Detecter* copies of 1826 through early 1830 range from exceedingly rare to nonexistent. In addition to his *Detecter,* Day produced a monthly pamphlet on the same subject. The issue of June 15, 1830, bears the masthead designation, *Day's Bank Note Table, and Expose of Counterfeit Notes.* Few examples have survived, and Dillistin located just one copy.

The title of Day's bank-note newspaper changed slightly. On the masthead of the issue of August 16, 1830, just two weeks after the advent of Bicknell's paper, it was called *Day's New-York Bank Note List and Counterfeit Detecter.* In the mid-1840s, Day took in partners, after which the publisher was listed as Baker, Crane, and Day, operators of Day's shop on Pearl Street. The later business course of the *Detecter* is not known in detail. It seems to have wound down in the early 1850s.

DAY'S FINAL VOYAGE

Day met his end in a well-known shipwreck. The large and well-appointed 2,856-ton SS *Arctic* was built by William H. Brown for the New York & Liverpool U.S. Mail Steamship Company, familiarly known as the Collins Line. The ship was launched on January 28, 1850, and was fitted for ocean travel by October 25 of

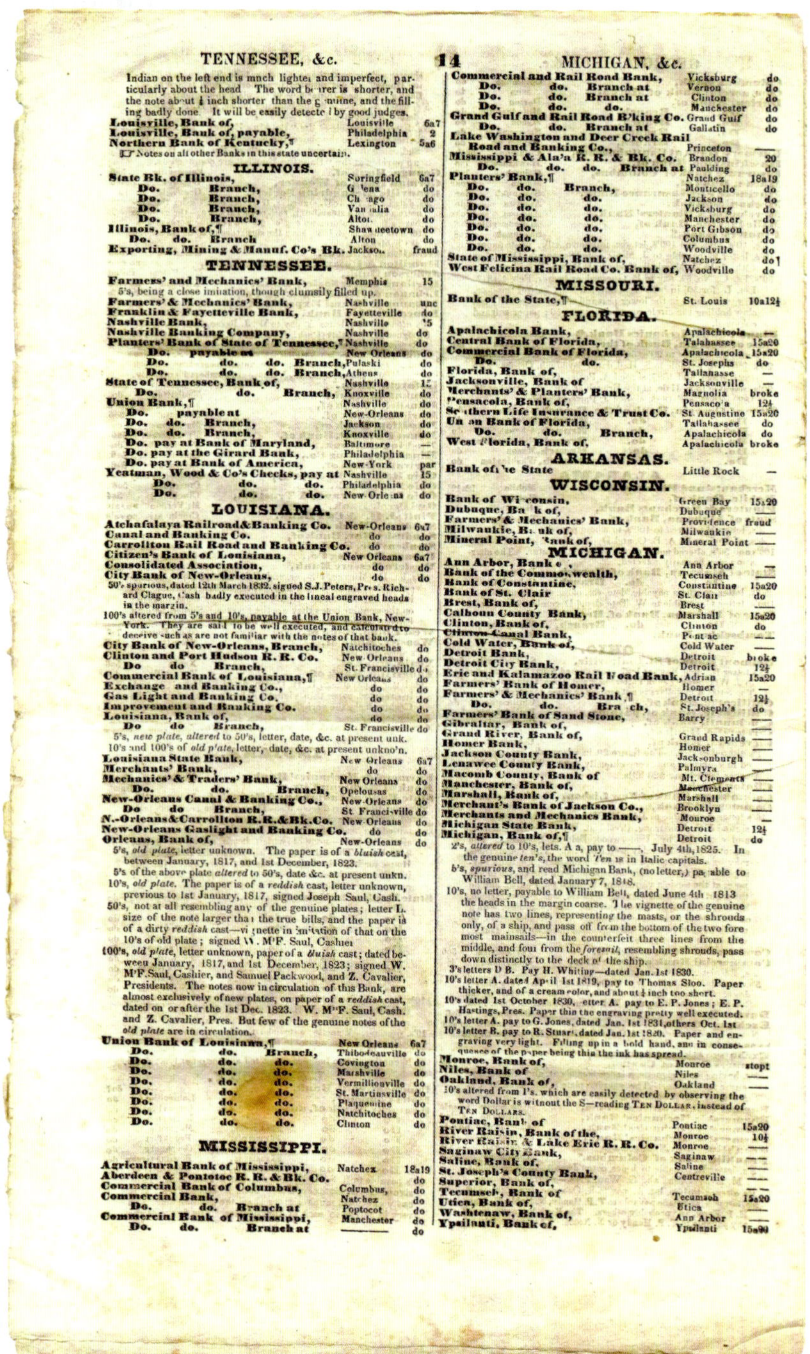

TENNESSEE, &c.

Indian on the left end is much lighter and imperfect, particularly about the head The word bearer is shorter, and the note about ¼ inch shorter than the genuine, and the filling badly done. It will be easily detected by good judges.

Louisville, Bank of,	Louisville	6a7
Louisville, Bank of, payable,	Philadelphia	2
Northern Bank of Kentucky,¶	Lexington	5a6

☞ Notes on all other Banks in this state uncertain.

ILLINOIS.

State Bk. of Illinois,	Springfield	6a7
Do. Branch,	Galena	do
Do. Branch,	Chicago	do
Do. Branch,	Vandalia	do
Do. Branch,	Alton	do
Illinois, Bank of,¶	Shawneetown	do
Do. do. Branch	Alton	do
Exporting, Mining & Manuf. Co's Bk.	Jackson	fraud

TENNESSEE.

Farmers' and Mechanics' Bank,	Memphis	15

5's, being a close imitation, though clumsily filled up.

Farmers' & Mechanics' Bank,	Nashville	unc
Franklin & Fayetteville Bank,	Fayetteville	do
Nashville Bank,	Nashville	'5
Nashville Banking Company,	Nashville	do
Planters' Bank of State of Tennessee,¶	Nashville	do
Do. payable at	New Orleans	do
Do. do. do. Branch,	Pulaski	do
Do. do. do. Branch,	Athens	do
State of Tennessee, Bank of,	Nashville	15
Do. do. Branch,	Knoxville	do
Union Bank,¶	Nashville	do
Do. payable at	New-Orleans	do
Do. do. Branch,	Jackson	do
Do. do. Branch,	Knoxville	do
Do. pay at Bank of Maryland,	Baltimore	—
Do. pay at the Girard Bank,	Philadelphia	—
Do. pay at Bank of America,	New-York	par
Yeatman, Wood & Co's Checks, pay at	Nashville	15
Do. do. do.	Philadelphia	do
Do. do. do.	New-Orleans	do

LOUISIANA.

Atchafalaya Railroad & Banking Co.	New-Orleans	6a7
Canal and Banking Co.	do	do
Carrollton Rail Road and Banking Co.	do	do
Citizen's Bank of Louisiana,	New Orleans	6a7
Consolidated Association,	do	do
City Bank of New-Orleans,	do	do

50's spurious, dated 12th March 1832, signed S.J. Peters, Pres. Richard Clague, Cash badly executed in the lineal engraved heads in the margin.

100's altered from 5's and 10's, payable at the Union Bank, New-York. They are said to be well executed, and calculated to deceive such as are not familiar with the notes of that bank.

City Bank of New-Orleans, Branch,	Natchitoches	do
Clinton and Port Hudson R. R. Co.	New-Orleans	do
Do do Branch,	St. Francisville	do
Commercial Bank of Louisiana,¶	New Orleans	do
Exchange and Banking Co.,	do	do
Gas Light and Banking Co.	do	do
Improvement and Banking Co.	do	do
Louisiana, Bank of,	do	do
Do do Branch,	St. Francisville	do

5's, *new plate, altered* to 50's, letter, date, &c. at present unk.
10's and 100's of *old plate,* letter, date, &c. at present unknown.

Louisiana State Bank,	New Orleans	6a7
Merchants' Bank,	do	do
Mechanics' & Traders' Bank,	New Orleans	do
Do. do. Branch,	Opelousas	do
New-Orleans Canal & Banking Co.,	New-Orleans	do
Do do Branch,	St Francisville	do
N.-Orleans & Carrollton R.R.&Bk.Co.	New Orleans	do
New-Orleans Gaslight and Banking Co.	do	do
Orleans, Bank of,	New-Orleans	do

5's, *old plate,* letter unknown. The paper is of a *bluish* cast, between January, 1817, and 1st December, 1823.
5's of the above plate *altered* to 50's, date &c. at present unkn.
10's, *old plate.* The paper is of a *reddish* cast, letter unknown, previous to 1st January, 1817, signed Joseph Saul, Cash.
50's, not at all resembling any of the genuine plates; letter L. size of the note larger than the true bills, and the paper is of a dirty *reddish* cast—vignette in imitation of that on the 10's of old plate; signed W. M'F. Saul, Cashier
100's, *old plate,* letter unknown, paper of a *bluish* cast; dated between January, 1817, and 1st December, 1823; signed W. M'F. Saul, Cashier, and Samuel Packwood, and Z. Cavalier, Presidents. The notes now in circulation of this Bank, are almost exclusively of new plates, on paper of a *reddish* cast, dated on or after the 1st Dec. 1823. W. M'F. Saul, Cash. and Z. Cavalier, Pres. But few of the genuine notes of the *old plate* are in circulation.

Union Bank of Louisiana,¶	New Orleans	6a7
Do. do. Branch,	Thibodeauville	do
Do. do. do.	Covington	do
Do. do. do.	Marshville	do
Do. do. do.	Vermillionville	do
Do. do. do.	St. Martinsville	do
Do. do. do.	Plaquemine	do
Do. do. do.	Natchitoches	do
Do. do. do.	Clinton	do

MISSISSIPPI.

Agricultural Bank of Mississippi,	Natchez	18a19
Aberdeen & Pontotoc R. R. & Bk. Co.		do
Commercial Bank of Columbus,	Columbus,	do
Commercial Bank,	Natchez	do
Do. do. Branch at	Poptocot	do
Commercial Bank of Mississippi,	Manchester	do
Do. do. Branch at	———	do

14 MICHIGAN, &c.

Commercial and Rail Road Bank,	Vicksburg	do
Do. do. Branch at	Vernon	do
Do. do. Branch at	Clinton	do
Do. do. do.	Manchester	do
Grand Gulf and Rail Road B'king Co.	Grand Gulf	do
Do. do. Branch at	Gallatin	do
Lake Washington and Deer Creek Rail Road and Banking Co.,	Princeton	—
Mississippi & Ala'a R. R. & Bk. Co.	Brandon	20
Do. do. do. Branch at	Paulding	do
Planters' Bank,¶	Natchez	18a19
Do. do. Branch,	Monticello	do
Do. do. do.	Jackson	do
Do. do. do.	Vicksburg	do
Do. do. do.	Manchester	do
Do. do. do.	Port Gibson	do
Do. do. do.	Columbus	do
Do. do. do.	Woodville	do
State of Mississippi, Bank of,	Natchez	do
West Felicina Rail Road Co. Bank of,	Woodville	do

MISSOURI.

Bank of the State,¶	St. Louis	10a12½

FLORIDA.

Apalachicola Bank,	Apalachicola	—
Central Bank of Florida,	Talahassee	15a20
Commercial Bank of Florida,	Apalachicola	15a20
Do. do.	St. Josephs	do
Florida, Bank of,	Tallahasse	—
Jacksonville, Bank of	Jacksonville	—
Merchants' & Planters' Bank,	Magnolia	broke
Pensacola, Bank of,	Pensacola	12½
Southern Life Insurance & Trust Co.	St. Augustine	15a20
Union Bank of Florida,	Tallahassee	do
Do. do. Branch,	Apalachicola	do
West Florida, Bank of,	Apalachicola	broke

ARKANSAS.

Bank of the State	Little Rock	—

WISCONSIN.

Bank of Wisconsin,	Green Bay	15a20
Dubuque, Bank of,	Dubuque	—
Farmers' & Mechanics' Bank,	Providence	fraud
Milwaukie, Bank of,	Milwaukie	—
Mineral Point, Bank of,	Mineral Point	—

MICHIGAN.

Ann Arbor, Bank of,	Ann Arbor	—
Bank of the Commonwealth,	Tecumseh	—
Bank of Constantine,	Constantine	15a20
Bank of St. Clair	St. Clair	do
Brest, Bank of,	Brest	—
Calhoun County Bank,	Marshall	15a20
Clinton, Bank of,	Clinton	do
Clinton Canal Bank,	Pontiac	—
Cold Water, Bank of,	Cold Water	—
Detroit Bank,	Detroit	broke
Detroit City Bank,	Detroit	12½
Erie and Kalamazoo Rail Road Bank,	Adrian	15a20
Farmers' Bank of Homer,	Homer	—
Farmers' & Mechanics' Bank,¶	Detroit	12½
Do. do. Branch,	St. Joseph's	do
Farmers' Bank of Sand Stone,	Barry	—
Gibraltar, Bank of,		—
Grand River, Bank of,	Grand Rapids	—
Homer Bank,	Homer	—
Jackson County Bank,	Jacksonburgh	—
Lenawee County Bank,	Palmyra	—
Macomb County, Bank of	Mt. Clements	—
Manchester, Bank of,	Manchester	—
Marshall, Bank of,	Marshall	—
Merchant's Bank of Jackson Co.,	Brooklyn	—
Merchants and Mechanics Bank,	Monroe	—
Michigan State Bank,	Detroit	12½
Michigan, Bank of,¶	Detroit	do

2's, *altered* to 10's, lets. A a, pay to ——, July 4th, 1825. In the genuine *ten's,* the word *Ten* is in Italic capitals.
5's, *spurious,* and read Michigan Bank, (no letter,) payable to William Bell, dated January 7, 1818.
10's, no letter, payable to William Bell, dated June 4th 1813 the heads in the margin coarse. The vignette of the genuine note has two lines, representing the masts, or the shrouds only, of a ship, and pass off from the bottom of the two fore most mainsails—in the counterfeit three lines from the middle, and four from the *foresail,* resembling shrouds, pass down distinctly to the deck of the ship.
3's letters D B. Pay H. Whiting—dated Jan. 1st 1830.
10's letter A. dated April 1st 1819, pay to Thomas Sloo. Paper thicker, and of a cream color, and about ¼ inch too short.
10's dated 1st October 1830, letter A. pay to E. P. Jones; E. P. Hastings, Pres. Paper thin the engraving pretty well executed.
10's letter A. pay to G. Jones, dated Jan. 1st 1831, others Oct. 1st
10's letter B. pay to R. Stuart, dated Jan. 1st 1820. Paper and engraving very light. Filling up in a bold hand, and in consequence of the paper being thin the ink has spread.

Monroe, Bank of,	Monroe	stopt
Niles, Bank of	Niles	—
Oakland, Bank of,	Oakland	—

10's altered from 1's, which are easily detected by observing the word Dollar is without the S—reading TEN DOLLAR, instead of TEN DOLLARS.

Pontiac, Bank of	Pontiac	15a20
River Raisin, Bank of the,	Monroe	10½
River Raisin & Lake Erie R. R. Co.	Monroe	—
Saginaw City Bank,	Saginaw	—
Saline, Bank of,	Saline	—
St. Joseph's County Bank,	Centreville	—
Superior, Bank of,		—
Tecumseh, Bank of	Tecumseh	15a20
Utica, Bank of,	Utica	—
Washtenaw, Bank of,	Ann Arbor	—
Ypsilanti, Bank of,	Ypsilanti	15a20

An interior page of *Day's New-York Bank Note List and Counterfeit Detecter,* March 12, 1838, with exchange values of notes. The abbreviation "a" means "to"; thus Bank of Louisville bills trade at a 6% to 7% discount from face value. A dash in a listing indicates that, as with many banks in Michigan, the bank is defunct and its bills are worthless. On occasion, however, "broke" is added to mean the same thing.

The SS *Arctic* on the fateful day of September 27, 1854.

the same year. The elegant side-wheel steamer bid well to become a favorite for Atlantic crossings, and for several years it did just that.

On September 27, 1854, in heavy seas about 50 miles off of Cape Race, the *Arctic* was rammed by the *Vesta,* a small French steamer of 250 tons displacement. Among the passengers on the *Arctic* were at least two who figure in the annals of American numismatic history: Mahlon Day, in the company of his wife and daughter, and Jacob J. Morris, prominent Philadelphia collector. Charles I. Bushnell, a New York attorney who was one of the most important numismatists in that city, was also on board.

Those aboard the *Arctic* had little thought they had cause to worry and even launched a lifeboat to assist the *Vesta.* Soon thereafter, despite assurances of the captain and crew that there was no problem, it was learned that the *Arctic* was taking on water and was in serious danger. Nonchalance changed to urgency to escape, then quickly to tragedy as lifeboats became swamped in the high waves and 322 people lost their lives. Meanwhile, the *Vesta* limped into port in Newfoundland under its own power. Echoes of this disaster resounded for many years thereafter, and until the *Titanic* went down more than a half century later, this was the best-known of all passenger shipwrecks.

In his *American Numismatical Manual* (1859), Dr. Montroville W. Dickeson discusses a prime rarity, the 1733 Rosa Americana pattern twopence, noting he knew of the existence of only four, now only three, specimens:

> The fourth was purchased in England for the sum of £7, or $35, for Charles Bushnell, Esq., of New York City, unfortunately placed on board the steamer *Arctic,* to be transmitted to him, on her last and fatal voyage, and its pigmy proportions are now added to the vast accumulations that lie imbedded in the sands of the Atlantic Ocean.[9]

A successor firm, Gwynne & Day, was related to Day's enterprise. In 1860 the company published in bound book form *The Descriptive Register of Genuine Bank Notes,* with text giving printed descriptions of the notes' designs, drawing upon the American Bank Note Co. However, the *Register* would have been of no use in detecting bills from counterfeit plates or bills of the proper design altered from other banks.

SYLVESTER J. SYLVESTER

"THE MINT"

Sylvester J. Sylvester was the other significant early entrant in the counterfeit-detector periodical business prior to Charles T. Bicknell. In about 1825, Sylvester seems to have started in business as an exchange broker and lottery ticket seller, similar to Bicknell. In 1826 his enterprise was designated as The Mint, Sylvester's, with an office at 130 Broadway, advertising as a buyer of obsolete currency among other financial items.

The main reason to buy obsolete currency at the time was to resell it to sharpers, who would either pass it off to unsuspecting victims or alter it to appear to be issued by a solvent bank. Accordingly, it is not difficult to surmise today that Sylvester's ethics were of a rather low order. The same can be said for nearly all other dealers in exchange, except for banks (and banks, too, had some low life on board).

Another and less important element in the trade for worthless bills involved debtors to banks in the process of court actions, who sought to collect money owed. It was a legal and clever practice to buy up bills at a deep discount, then give them at face value to satisfy old debts. However, relatively few "broken banks" had enough potential remaining assets to justify lawyers and courts becoming involved.

Sometime in early 1830, Sylvester commenced publication of *Sylvester's Reporter.* Again, issues are devilishly difficult if not impossible to find today, and the earliest issue seen by William H. Dillistin of this weekly periodical was No. 34, December 2, 1830, from which it can be surmised that it began about April 1830. Not long afterward the title was changed to *Sylvester's Reporter and Counterfeit Detector,* then by June 22, 1831, to *Sylvester's Reporter, Counterfeit Detector and New York Prices Current.* Its content mirrored that of *Bicknell's Counterfeit Detector.*

By 1833, Horace Greeley, the famous newspaperman and, years later, candidate for the presidency of the United States, and his partner, Francis V. Story, trading as Greeley & Story, published Sylvester's sheet, which seems to have found for itself a secure niche in financial reporting.

Unwanted Competition

It has been said that copying is the sincerest form of flattery, but few who are copied are pleased. Such it was in 1838, when E.J. Sylvester & Co., operator of a currency exchange and lottery ticket office at 156 Broadway, with no connection to Sylvester J. Sylvester, began a copycat newspaper. On October 1, Sylvester J. Sylvester published this warning:

> S.J. Sylvester's *Reporter:* A paper having lately appeared in this city under the title of "Sylvester's New Reporter," I deem it advisable in order to prevent my friends and the public from being deceived thereby, to state that the name of my paper remains unchanged, and I am still at 130 Broadway, where I have been for 13 years past, and of course have not removed therefrom.

It is believed that the sham Sylvester publication lasted about three years, then expired.[10]

The original Sylvester newspaper continued to be issued weekly through at least September 24, 1849. By this time it was published by E. Morrison & Co. at 47 Wall Street, premises earlier occupied by Sylvester J. Sylvester for his publishing and exchange business.

John Thompson

The Early Years

John Thompson loomed larger in the field of counterfeit detectors than did the earlier-studied Bicknell, Day, or Sylvester. He was later in the game, but was active in an era in which frauds and failures proliferated to a much greater extent than in the earlier times of the 1830s.

Usually listed in print as J. Thompson, the subject of this sketch was born on November 17, 1802, in the farming town of Peru, about five miles north of Pittsfield in western Massachusetts.[11] He received a good education, remaining in school through age 19, then became a teacher in Poughkeepsie, New York.

By 1828 he was a dealer in lottery tickets in Poughkeepsie, an agent for Yates & McIntyre, of which Charles McIntyre was a partner. (Charles T. Bicknell was also an agent for this partnership.) McIntyre was a member of the old guard in state politics, having served in the state legislature beginning in 1799, then as comptroller of state finances from 1806 to 1821, and later a state senator. In 1840, years after his connection with Thompson, he published *New-York Telegraph, McIntyre's Bank Note List and Prices Current,* also issued under variant titles.

In 1832 John Thompson moved to New York City, the center of American finance, and secured small premises at 12 Wall Street, where he bought and sold uncurrent bank notes.[12] At the time there were 18 active banks in the city, 10 of which were within walking distance of his office. No doubt, bank tellers and officers were ready suppliers of worthless notes as they were acquired, and bill-alterers and other crooks were ready cash buyers. However, probably the main trade was in buying at a discount the currency of perfectly sound banks, but at distant locations. Thompson would then dispatch agents to banks in the hinterlands to redeem the bills for face value in silver and gold coins, taking a profit in the difference.

The Union Bank Incident

Thompson became caught up in a court case involving the Union Bank of New York City in 1835. By this time the Union Bank, incorporated on March 11, 1811, had been well established for many years and was ranked as among the most solid in the city. Occasionally, its name had surfaced in news accounts regarding paper money, such as on April 24, 1819, when *Niles' Weekly Register* advised readers of phony currency in circulation, "on the Silver Lake Bank, payable at the Union Bank, in the city of N. York, subscribed by the fictitious names of Ives Sutton, president, and Daniel Woodbridge, Jun., cashier."

Later, on September 13, 1830, *Bicknell's Counterfeit Detector* warned:

> Counterfeit notes of the Union Bank of the City of New York, of the denomination of five dollars, letter I, No. 1691, drawn in favor of Wm. Browne, dated 1st January, 1829, are in circulation in this city. The paper is good, but the plate is roughly engraved, and particularly the vignette. The signature of Danl. Ebbets, Jr. Cashier, is well imitated, but that of John Low, President, is badly executed.

The matter seemingly ended soon, per this item in the same newspaper two weeks later:

> Two persons were arrested in Pottsville, Pennsylvania, last week for passing counterfeit money in the Broad Mountain, and committed. Counterfeit notes of the New York Union Bank were found in their possession.

However, the foregoing incidents and others of a similar nature had nothing to do with the operation of the Union Bank itself, but simply traded on its good name.

Then came Thompson's involvement with the bank. According to court testimony, at about 10:30 A.M. on October 14, 1835, a young lad employed by Thompson went across the street to Union Bank with a $500 bill in his hand, seeking to redeem it in gold or silver coins.[13] Upon presentation of the $500 bill, the lad was told that the porter of the bank was away, and at the moment the bill could not be exchanged. Typically, the porter had access to the specie stored in the vault of a given bank and was responsible for checking it in and out. This was a highly responsible position, and many mentions of the responsibility of porters (and also of bank messengers) were carried in financial journals of the era.

Thompson himself then crossed the street to the bank and sought to redeem the $500 bill, but with no success. He then enlisted a notary public, Mr. Crooke, to take the note in for official redemption and to record what happened. Crooke asked the teller if he was declining payment, to which this response was given: "I do not decline it, but decline having any further conversation with you."

Angered, Thompson took the bank to court. A representative of the bank stated that what was considered to be an adequate amount of coins had been brought from the vault that morning, but it had been exhausted by the time the $500 bill was presented. It was further related in testimony that Thompson was in the habit of regularly demanding specie for his bills, and that a hostility had arisen between the two parties. Of course, this was Thompson's business—the buying of bank bills and redeeming them for specie.

The court found in favor of Thompson, stating the bank had violated the promise to pay the sum on demand, as printed on its bills. The plaintiff was awarded $500 for the note plus interest on the money and his costs.

Thompson's Bank Note Reporter

On January 4, 1842, John Thompson announced the forthcoming publication of *Thompson's Bank Note Reporter,* a pamphlet of 16 pages. This publication was met with success, and from this time onward his name became one to be reckoned with in this specialty. In time the title was modified, new features were added, and other changes were made.

Later in the decade he issued various editions of *Coin Chart Manual,* usually as a supplement to his *Reporter.* These must have been produced in large quantities, for, unlike certain other periodicals of the era, scattered examples turn up today in the market for out-of-print numismatic periodicals. Another separate pamphlet, launched in 1849 and continued in later editions, was *The Autographical Counterfeit Detector,* listing various banks, printing their names and titles (president or cashier), and reproducing their signatures as they appeared on bills. It can be readily imagined that bank-note alterers and counterfeiters were among the most eager buyers of this useful publication! However, circulation must have been limited, for examples are very rare today.[14]

Thompson's business prospered, and he seems to have enjoyed a fine reputation—a feat not always easy for dealers in obsolete currency to achieve. In 1852 in his book *Bank Note Engraving,* Waterman L. Ormsby presented Thompson's publication as an excellent representative of the genre. Ever alert, after thanking Thompson for loaning plates for illustration, Ormsby used the text as a springboard for pointing out many illogical and contradictory aspects of the business of using periodicals as a guide to detect false notes:

> **Bank Note Lists and Counterfeit Detectors**
> It has doubtless been observed that we have recognized and quoted as a standard work, the *Bank Note and Commercial Reporter,* edited by J. Thompson, banker and broker, corner of Wall Street and Broadway, N.Y., and published by W.

Newspaper postage only is chargeable on this sheet.

Thompson's Bank Note Reporter

NEW-YORK, APRIL 1, 1847.

GOLD AND SILVER COINS.

Thompson's Bank Note Reporter, April 1, 1847. The front page of this particular issue was devoted to coins and exchange rates.

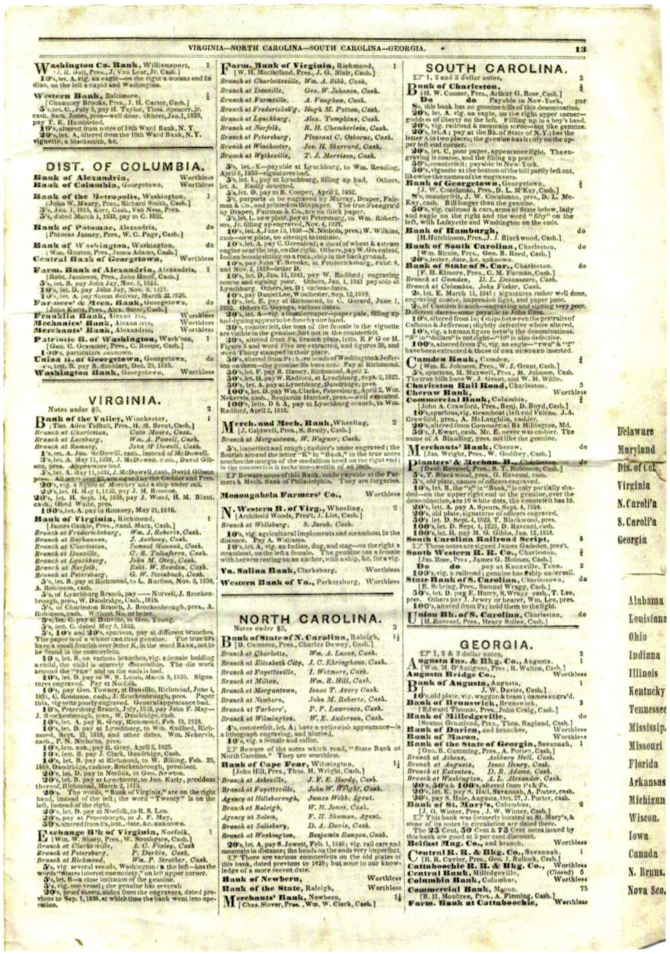
VIRGINIA—NORTH CAROLINA—SOUTH CAROLINA—GEORGIA.

DIST. OF COLUMBIA.

VIRGINIA.

NORTH CAROLINA.

SOUTH CAROLINA.

GEORGIA.

Thompson's Bank Note Reporter, April 1, 1847. This interior page features bank-note listings giving the characteristics of individual counterfeits and alterations.

Lee, No. 12, Spruce Street. These gentlemen evidently take a lively interest in the dissemination of information, in regard to everything connected with a sound and unadulterated currency. The main object of their journal is to describe counterfeit bank bills and to guard the public as far as possible against frauds of every kind in relation thereto.

In the pursuit of this object, they are now presenting their patrons with a series of facsimiles of the most dangerous counterfeit plates, engraved expressly for their work, at great expense. These plates they have generously and freely offered for our use in embellishing this work; thereby evincing a disinterestedness and liberality which calls for this significant acknowledgment on our part.

Bank note lists and counterfeit detectors, though generally useful, sometimes unavoidably aid counterfeiters in their deceptions. The forger will prepare his plate as perfectly as possible in every part but one, which is designedly left imperfect to attract notice. A horse, for instance, will be represented with but three legs. The note will be immediately advertised in the lists as a dangerous counterfeit, with its imperfections specified. The counterfeiter will now correct his plate, and forthwith print and circulate his bills, with less chance

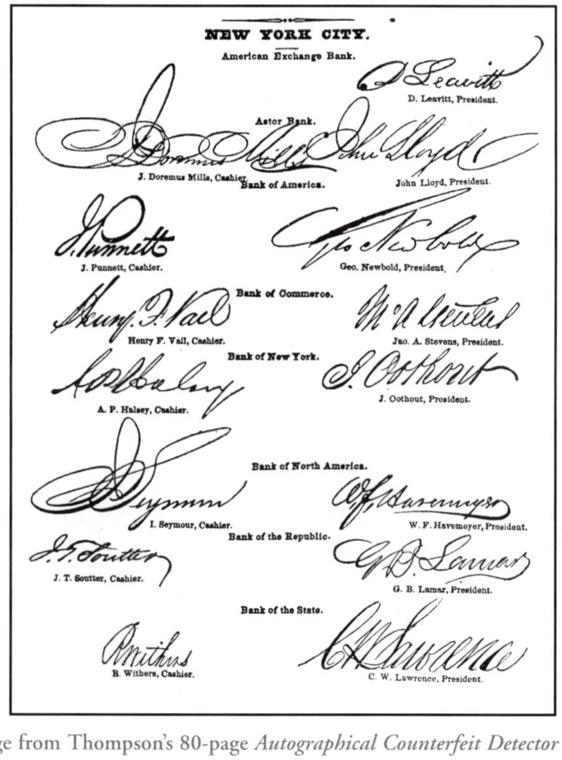
NEW YORK CITY.

American Exchange Bank.

D. Leavitt, President.

Astor Bank.

J. Doremus Mills, Cashier. John Lloyd, President.

Bank of America.

J. Punnett, Cashier. Geo. Newbold, President.

Bank of Commerce.

Henry F. Vail, Cashier. Jno. A. Stevens, President.

Bank of New York.

A. P. Halsey, Cashier. J. Oothout, President.

Bank of North America.

I. Seymour, Cashier. W. F. Havemeyer, President.

Bank of the Republic.

J. T. Soutter, Cashier. G. B. Lamar, President.

Bank of the State.

R. Withers, Cashier. C. W. Lawrence, President.

A page from Thompson's 80-page *Autographical Counterfeit Detector* (1853).

of detection. If the counterfeiter has not the ingenuity to do this by design, he will soon find himself doing it by accident; for it is natural that the first thing he will think of after his fraudulent production has been noticed by the detector, will be to alter his plate so that it will not correspond to the description given.

By referring to Thompson's Reporter, under the head of State Bank of Ohio, the following notice will appear:

"10's, vignette ploughman, etc. The ploughman has no whip, (in genuine he has,) only one of the forefeet of the dog are seen (in genuine both are"

The rogue will now engrave the dog's fore foot, and the ploughman's whip, into the plate, and hasten with all speed to print off a new batch and put them in circulation. Again:

"3's. vig. male and female seated, agricultural implements, etc. Harrison on the left. Justice on the right, 'with sword and scales.'

"10's, vig. six Indians and four whites. Harrison's head on the left. Filling up and signing—bad!

"10's, a figure '10' in the centre. Figure of Justice on the right end—Harrison on the left. Well done, and calculated to deceive."

These figures of Justice and of Harrison remain the same, but a "10" takes the place of a "3," etc., which shows that the counterfeiter makes a few plates, which he can carry in his pocket, answer the purpose of the expensive machinery of the bank note engravers. He may print the vignette on each bill in the exact spot required, and change the relative positions of all the embellishments of his counterfeit note at pleasure. Again:

"20's, excellent imitation of the genuine. Persons not acquainted with the true bill had better refuse all 20's on this Bank. Letter S in the name of the bank not perfect. Female's head in the vignette leans rather too much to the left."

This is a hint to the counterfeiter to improve the letter S and to make the female's head more erect. It is also a hint to the bank that it is necessary to have a new plate or the bills will not circulate; Again:

"10's, letter A, a perfect imitation of genuine. Filling up and red stamp on, the back all well done."

Everything being "perfect" the bank will be relieved from any further expense, in keeping up its circulation! Again:

"100's, on all the branches, none higher than 50 issued."

It is worthy of remark that the number of branches is FORTY ONE!![15] Again:

"10's, excellent imitations of the first plate, having for vignette a male and female figure on either side of a shield, with a large X in centre. Better refuse all 10's of this plate. These are supposed to be from a genuine plate with spurious signatures."

Supposed to be from a genuine plate! Several cases of this kind are recorded, and we can form no idea how a counterfeiter can possess himself of them, except by ordering parts of the engraving done by different persons, at different times and places, and then composing his plates as a printer composes his form, with the genuine work of bank note engravers actually upon them!

Again, the Bank Note List says:

"2's, letter A—The lathe-work on left margin and head of Wm. Penn are poor—the right foot of the Indian in the vig. is poor, and looks more like a stump than a foot, The word 'Cincinnati' after the engravers' names, looks like 'Cincinnali,' The general appearance of the note is good, and very likely to pass unless closely scrutinized."

After this lucky criticism the forger will see that the lathe-work and the head of Wm. Penn ought to change places, or be somewhat improved in their appearance; the Indian's fore-foot will be corrected, or perhaps something will be introduced in the plate to hide it entirely from view; the last T in the word Cincinnati will be rectified, and then the general appearance being good, it will very likely pass, however "closely scrutinized."

It will be found that counterfeiters pay no regard to the vignette in the matter of its resemblance to those on the genuine bill. They do not care whether it is a "Venus," or a "Farmer holding a plough." It is equally immaterial to them, whether the "lathe-work" oval was made in the same net-work style as that of the bill they intend to imitate. They only require a few *vignettes* about the size of those employed on bank bills, a few lathe-work ovals of any pattern, and a few machine copies of plaster medals, all of which can be very easily procured. In fact FIFTY DOLLARS would buy materials enough to make a current imitation of the picture portion of every bank bill in the country; and keep the counterfeit detectors employed in noticing their issues, even if they published an extra every day in the year.

Difficulties

While remaining involved in the bank-note reporting business, Thompson also continued his activity as an exchange broker dealing in coins and paper money. In August 1857, after the failure of the Ohio Life Insurance and Trust Company, there were hard times in New York City. The agent of the company was eventually found to have manipulated funds. Wall Street became distressed, money was scarce, and this precipitated the many bank and other commercial failures that would be remembered as the Panic of 1857.

On the August 25, 1857, Thompson suspended his exchange business, considered to be the largest in the city with regard to dealing in paper money of out-of-town banks, particularly "country banks" distant from large cities. Shortly thereafter he stepped down from the job of compiling data for *Thompson's Bank Note and Commercial Reporter,* turning over that task to Platt Adams, a close business associate for several years previous. Thompson's publication was not helped by the notice published in Cincinnati on September 15 by a rival, *Lord's Detector and Bank Note Vignette Describer,* which described *Thompson's Bank Note and Commercial Reporter* as a fraud filled with false information.

Thompson's difficulties proved to be short in duration, and soon he was back in business, including supplying data on old bills. Later, his bank-note paper evolved into the highly respected *American Banker.* He also was involved in a new company, Thompson Brothers, operated at 2 Wall Street by sons Samuel Clark Thompson and Frederick Ferris Thompson. In 1861, Thompson was an adviser to President Abraham Lincoln on the establishment of a new system of federal currency. His sons were prime factors in 1863 in the establishment of the First National Bank of the City of New York (charter 29). Later, they were investors in the National Currency Bank of New York City. Subsequently they were important in the formation of the Chase National Bank of New York City, named for former Secretary of the Treasury Salmon P. Chase. John Thompson died on April 19, 1891.

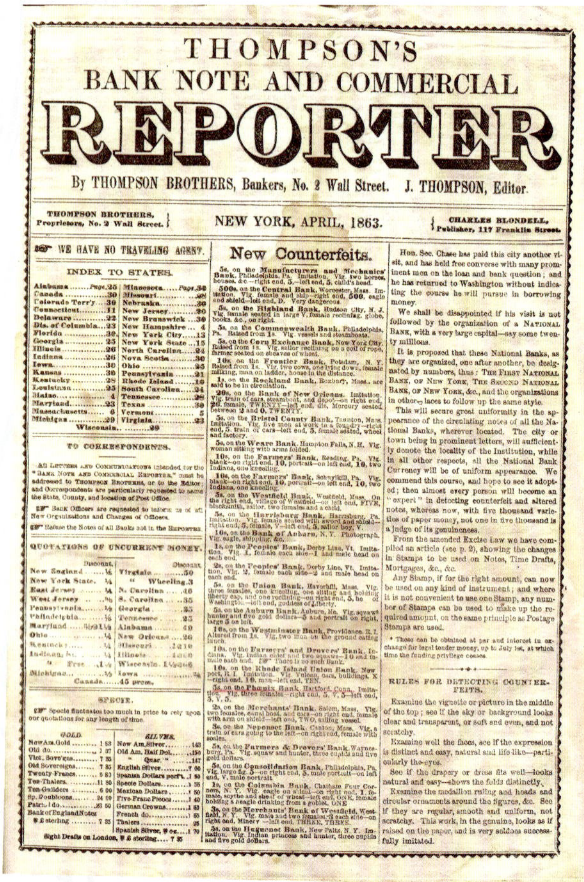
THOMPSON'S
BANK NOTE AND COMMERCIAL
REPORTER
By THOMPSON BROTHERS, Bankers, No. 2 Wall Street. J. THOMPSON, Editor.
THOMPSON BROTHERS, Proprietors, No. 2 Wall Street. | NEW YORK, APRIL, 1863. | CHARLES BLONDELL, Publisher, 117 Franklin Street.
WE HAVE NO TRAVELING AGENT.
INDEX TO STATES.
TO CORRESPONDENTS.
QUOTATIONS OF UNCURRENT MONEY.
SPECIE.
New Counterfeits.
RULES FOR DETECTING COUNTERFEITS.

Front page of *Thompson's Bank Note and Commercial Reporter,* April 1863. The front page, right column, carries news of the new idea of chartered National Banks.

SELECTED OTHER BANK-NOTE REPORTERS

MONROE, DYE, AND TAYLOR

The Litchfield Bank of Connecticut was chartered in 1856. The New York office of the engraving firm, Bald, Cousland & Co., was contacted, sample vignettes were inspected, and attractive bills were ordered. On November 7, 1857, it opened its doors for business. On hand for distribution were bills signed by cashier E.S. Houghton and president Wm. H. Crossman, some ink-dated November 4th. However, all was not well, and when the state bank commissioner filed a report in 1858 he could find no evidence that the capital of $50,000 had been paid in.[16] The bank was insolvent and, apparently, had been conceived and operated in fraud.

Court testimony indicated that the bank had paid nearly $1,000 in various transactions to Monroe, Dye, and Taylor, being three New York City publishers of bank-note detectors; this was done "not to blow the bank."[17]

One person in this allegedly fraudulent threesome was John Monroe, who at the time was associated with John Tyler Hodges at 271 Broadway, New York City, publishers of the weekly *Journal of Finance & Bank*

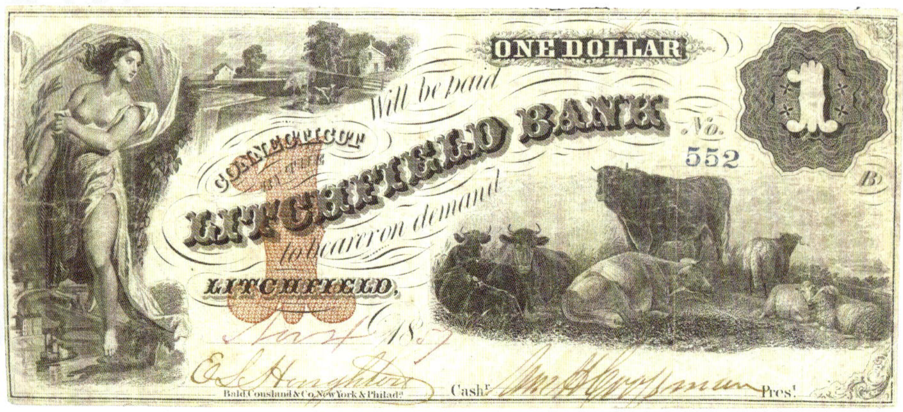

A $1 note of the Litchfield Bank, Connecticut, issued soon after it opened for business. The plate was engraved by Bald, Cousland & Co. of New York and Philadelphia. The bank opened for business on November 7, 1857, a highly unfavorable time since Eastern banks were reeling from the early repercussions of the Panic of 1857. Things did not go well for the fledgling institution, and to bolster its reputation it bribed three well-known New York City publishers of bank-note reporters to give the bank a favorable listing.

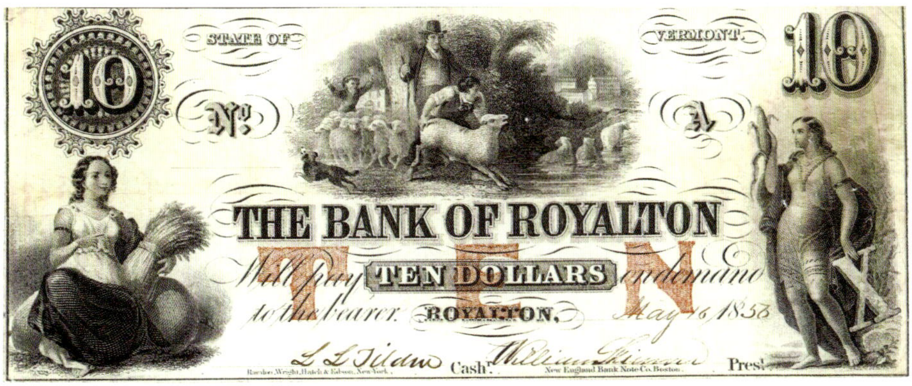

ONE Indian with bow, spear, &c.	Agricultural scene, cattle, &c, Female seated with sickle. BANK of ROYALTON, Royalton, Vt.	The wo.d ONE and figure 1. Man seated with agricultural implements.
Two females embracing each other. 2	Two farmers, one seated; female seated; load of hay in distance. BANK of ROYALTON Royalton, Vt.	2 Head of Jefferson.
Blacksmith and anvil. 3	Three females seated representing Agriculture, Manufactures and Commerce. BANK of ROYALTON Royalton, Vt.	3 Head of Henry Clay.
Large figure 5 and five females. 5	Head of Hon. Jacob Collamer. BANK of ROYALTON Royalton, Vt.	5 Female seated with globe quadrant &c.
10 Female seated with sheaf of wheat.	Men washing sheep; factories in distance BANK of ROYALTON Royalton, Vt.	10 Colossal figure holding corn in right hand and X in left.
Female seated between 2 and 0. XX	Drover and drove of cattle and sheep. BANK of ROYALTON Royalton, Vt.	20 Female churning.
Female feeding a horse. 50	A farmer's family reclining in hay field; load of hay &c. BANK of ROYALTON Royalton, Vt.	50 Head of Webster.
100 Head of Fillmore. 100	BANK of ROYALTON Royalton, Vt. Female seated crowning an eagle with wreath; small head of Washington on left of vig.	100 Load of straw drawn by oxen; man on horseback.

Description of certain bills of the Royalton (Vermont) Bank, from part of a page in the 1858 edition of *Hodges' New Bank Note Safe-Guard.* This volume used typeset rectangular blocks imprinted with text in areas of the block, describing what genuine notes looked like. The system was of little practical use, because it did not aid in the detection of counterfeits or bills of the same designs altered from other locations. Above are shown three actual notes of the Bank of Royalton.

Note Reporter, the book-format *Hodges' New Bank Note Safe-Guard,* and other publications. Monroe is believed to have been the publisher of the earlier *Monroe's Descriptive List of Genuine Bank Notes,* which contained descriptions of 1,323 bills.[18] Although Monroe may have been successful in his time, he has left very little in the way of a paper trail.

On the other hand, Monroe's onetime associate, John Tyler Hodges, was one of the most important names in the business, as was his brother Daniel Milton Hodges. John, who in the mid-1850s was a banker in New York City on Broadway at the corner of Canal Street, became active in publishing, and about the same time issued *Hodges' Gold and Silver Coin Manual.* In 1856, *Hodges' New Bank Note Delineator; A Complete Spurious and Altered Bill Detector, Giving Correct Printed Descriptions of all The Genuine Notes of Every Denomination, of All Banks Doing Business Throughout the United States and Canada* appeared, containing certain information recently used in another publication by John S. Dye, perhaps implying a connection. In the same vein, the 1857 manual, *Hodges' New Bank Note Safe-Guard,* was licensed by or lifted from *Dye's Bank Note Plate Delineator* and contains some of the typographical errors found in the 1855 work.[19] The *Bank Note Safe-Guard* remained in print in various editions through the mid-1860s.

John S. Dye, the second in the threesome of alleged bribe takers, was among the more prolific publishers of his day. His *Wall Street Broker* commenced in 1847, followed in 1850 with a Cincinnati imprint on *Dye's Counterfeit Detector and Universal Bank Note Gazetteer,* also issued by Joseph Arnold of Philadelphia. In Cincinnati in 1852, Dye issued *Dye's Bank Mirror and Illustrated Counterfeit Detector,* which soon was followed by *Dye's Book of Bank Note Plates, an Accompaniment to His Illustrated Bank Mirror for 1853.* In 1854 he moved to New York City, and in the same year he issued *Dye's Gold and Silver Chart Manual* with New York City and Cincinnati imprints.

In November 1853 the *Banker's Magazine* printed this warning:

> **Banks in the District of Columbia**
>
> The Washington *National Intelligencer* thus speaks of *Dye's Bank Note Mirror:* We are in receipt of a semi-monthly publication from Cincinnati, entitled *Dye's Bank Mirror and Counterfeit Detector,* of date September 15th, 1853, which, in all that it says respecting the Banks of the District of Columbia. is so absurdly wrong, that we can account for the fact only by assuming that the editor has been hoaxed by some designing or mischievous correspondent.
>
> For instance, it quotes the rate of Northern discount on the notes of our old established and reliable banks, viz.: the Bank of Metropolis, Bank of Washington, Patriotic Bank, Farmers and Mechanics Bank of Georgetown, and the more recent but respectable institution, the Bank of Commerce, at Georgetown, at *two* per cent, while the *imaginary* establishments of whose successive meteoric passages we have from time to time apprised the public, as the *Bank of America, National Bank, &c.,* stand honored with a mere *one* percent assigned to their fancy names. Other entries and statements are made, of which knowing nothing, we can say nothing more than that we have no confidence in them whatever.

In 1855 the "complete edition" of *Dye's Bank Note Plate Delineator,* a manual of 288 pages, covered about 1,200 banks. Apparently, smaller or regional versions were also published. In 1856, Hodges & Co., New York City, introduced *Hodges' New Bank Note Delineator; A Complete Spurious and Altered Bill Detector, Giving Correct Printed Descriptions of all The Genuine Notes of Every Denomination, of All Banks Doing Business Throughout the United States and Canada.* This contained identical wording and some errors found in an 1855 Dye work and either was pirated from or was a successor to Dye's work. In August 1856, *The Merchants' Magazine* carried a report of a lecture by Dye in which he told of bank-note frauds, the making of fake plates for fake banks, the alternation of plates and notes, and related matters.

Dye, who seems to have been a fraudster or confidence man bearing credentials that many found to be satisfactory, produced many other publications in following years, including some from Philadelphia, where he was located by the late 1870s. In 1883 he was listed as the author of *Dye's Coin Encyclopaedia,* but he was no longer living at the time. This large and impressive-appearing book was not at all encyclopedic; instead, it mainly consisted of miscellaneous essays and articles ranging from the discovery of gold in California to E.L. Mason Jr.'s rediscovery of the 1861 Confederate States of America half dollar die in 1879.

As to the Taylor of the trio, who is said to have pocketed a bribe from the Litchfield Bank, he was H.S. Taylor, a New York printer who published the *Bank & Commercial Reporter* at 208 Broadway, according to a city directory. This seems to have been the final appearance of a series of reporters issued by Edmund Charles and Lewis J. Leonori, later by Leonori alone, which came to be known as *Leonori's New York Bank Note Reporter, Counterfeit Detector & Wholesale Prices Current.* In late 1856 or early 1857,

Taylor took over the publication, after which it seems to have lasted for just a short time.[20]

LABAN HEATH

When publications on counterfeit bills are mentioned in numismatic circles today, the name of Laban Heath is most prominent. He seems to have developed an interest in the subject by 1860 or so, when in Portland, Maine, he was an agent for the sale of a pamphlet titled *The United States Bank Note Detecter at Sight, the Only Infallible System Detecting Counterfeit & Altered Bank Bills as taught by A. S. Gear,* published in 1860 by J.W. Whittemore of Ashland, Massachusetts, himself a "teacher of counterfeit currency detection," according to the text.[21]

During the bank-note issuing era, discussions of counterfeits and forgeries were popular at lyceums and other public venues, and John Thompson and Waterman L. Ormsby are among those who gave such presentations. Often, audience members would be shown examples of currency and challenged to tell the difference between the genuine and the false. Newspaper editors were quick to report on such events, billing them as educational rather than entertainment.

In June 1864, *Heath's Infallible Counterfeit Detector, at Sight. The only infallible method of detecting counterfeit, spurious and altered bank notes, and applicable to all banks in the United States and Canadas, now in circulation or that may be issued, with Genuine Designs, by The American Bank Note Company, New York and Boston,* was published in New York City. The title was more impressive than the contents, which included just 26 pages of text. Inexpensive and small enough to be easily carried, this item became popular as the Pocket Edition and went on to be issued for many years.

In time a larger (quarto) volume was published as a companion, titled *Heath's Greatly Improved and Enlarged Infallible Government Counterfeit Detector, at Sight. The only infallible method of detecting counterfeit, spurious and altered bank notes, government bonds, etc., applicable to all banks in the United States and Canadas, now in circulation or that may be issued, with Genuine Designs from the Original Government Plates. By authority from the United States Treasury Department and the American, National, and Continental Bank Note Cos., New York and Boston, Banking and Counting House Edition.*

Note from a counterfeit plate used as a tip-in illustration in *Heath's Infallible Counterfeit Detector, at Sight* (1864). A $5 note from the Bank of Orleans, Albion, New York. This text accompanied: "For the purpose of more fully illustrating the difference between genuine and counterfeit engraving, we have at great trouble and expense obtained a counterfeit plate engraved by counterfeiters and taken from them at the time of their arrest. This plate is in the hands of the American Bank Note Company, from which these specimens are printed."

Detail of a printed 5 from the false Bank of Albion note. The lines, supposed to be geometric, are seen in close inspection to be irregular.

Detail of a genuine printed 5 vignette of the era, the design being somewhat related. All the arcs and curves are regular. (*Bank Note Engraving,* 1852)

Such publications were launched as the use of state-bank bills was fading, and soon only government currency was included. Accordingly, the story of Heath would be better included in a text on federal bills. Apparently, the government regretted certain aspects of the Heath arrangements, as evidenced by this article published in Washington, February 15, 1892, reprinted from the St. Louis *Globe-Democrat:*

> **Helped the Counterfeiters**
>
> On one occasion the Treasury played into the hands of the counterfeiters by a most astounding act of folly, the ill consequences of which have lasted up to the present day.
>
> In 1866 Secretary McCulloch gave permission to Laban Heath that he might have printed certain designs used on the government currency. The work was done, and the sheets were put in book form and circulated largely in banking and commercial circles. They went through a variety of editions, containing reproductions of the faces and backs of fractional notes, legal tender notes, national bank notes and bonds.
>
> The forgers were quick to take advantage of the material thus provided for them. They flooded the market with false notes and bonds of big denominations by the simple process of reducing the thickness of the paper on which the backs of the designs described were printed, pasting the backs and fronts together. Thus they produced very presentable bonds and notes, actually printed from the government's own plates, and these have been turning up to cause trouble and loss ever since.
>
> During the last year the Secret Service learned where a great quantity of these books were stored in unbound sheets. They seized the whole lot, which represented hundreds of millions of dollars.

Numismatic Notes

Although copies of Laban Heath's counterfeit detector are common today for the pocket-size edition, book-type detectors of other publishers are generally very rare. Seen occasionally are the magazine-style periodicals in this field, although they are sufficiently scarce that forming a run of dates would be difficult.

For research purposes such counterfeit detectors are of limited use. Information concerning bank officers, when such is given, is often woefully out of date. Misspellings are endemic. While in the main *good* banks are described as such, some of the favorable listings are of failed institutions, and, conversely, some banks given negative reportage were actually sound at the time.

The Harry W. Bass Jr. Library of the American Numismatic Society, New York City, has the largest collection of counterfeit detectors. It is open for research by interested numismatists.

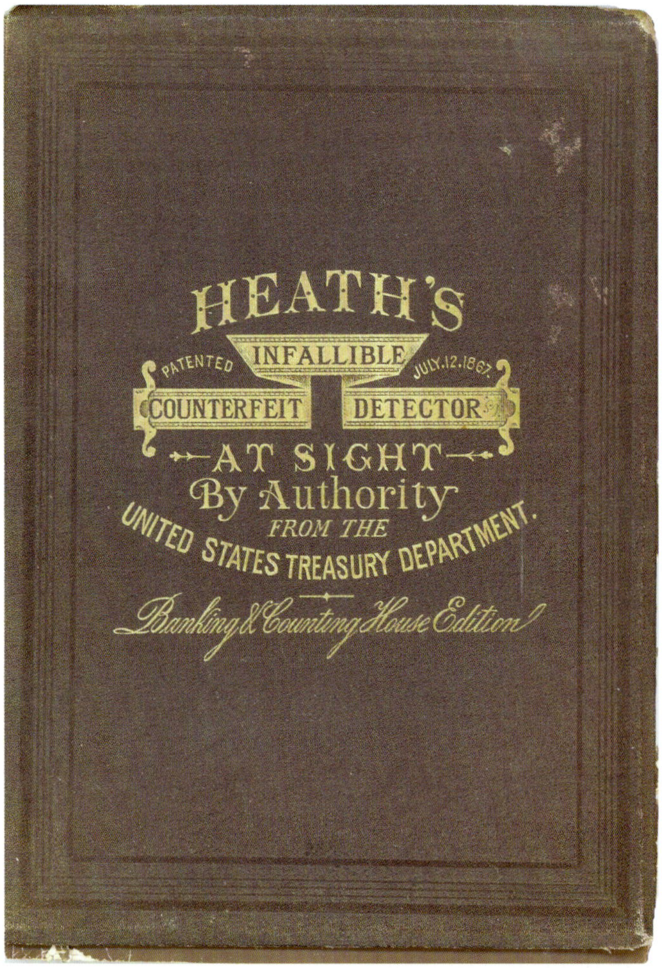

Cover of *Heath's Infallible Counterfeit Detector*, the impressively titled but quite slim Banking and Counting House Edition, 1866.

Into the Age of Elegance

Banking

In 1830 the banking scene was more or less quiet. In the East most banks were sound and well operated under state-granted charters that were often difficult to obtain, except through strong political connections. While there were abuses, as there had been since the early days of the Detroit, Farmers Exchange, and Hillsborough bank scandals, by and large the banks distributing the most paper money were concentrated in major cities and tended to their business of serving commerce.

Currency was obtained from various bank-note companies, mostly located in Philadelphia but increasingly also in New York City.

A review of history demonstrates that partnerships in the bank-note business tended to last for just a short time, and few endured as long as 10 years. Engravers became dissatisfied and left one business to start or become a part of another. When a partner died, his name was dropped from the title, while a new partner signaled a change as well. Successor partnerships usually kept old vignettes and printing plates on hand and used them when required. Numismatically, this system resulted in new issues of bills bearing imprints of firms that no longer existed. Researcher Gene Hessler (in particular in *The Engravers' Line*) and others have spent a lot of time creating time lines of actual operation, and much information on the subject can be found in issues of the *Essay-Proof Journal.*

Philadelphia Engravers of 1830

In Philadelphia at 47 Sansom Street, the partnership of Draper, Underwood & Co., the trade name used following the death of partner Gideon Fairman on March 18, 1827, included John Draper and Thomas Underwood. Draper's experience dated back to the high point of the Jacob Perkins era in America, while Underwood had been in the profession in the city since the early 1820s. Their tradition included the famous partnership of Murray, Draper, Fairman & Co. (1811–1818), which in its day was probably the biggest supplier of bills to the East (except for New England) and Midwest. In 1833 the partnership would be succeeded by Draper, Underwood, Bald & Spencer at the same address. The successive partnerships had been and continued to be printers of currency for the second Bank of the United States.

Asa Spencer, inventor and engraver, an old-timer in the trade, did business at 43 Zane Street. Charles Toppan, also of long standing, conducted a business under his own name, which often was printed on bills as Chas. Toppan & Co. or C. Toppan & Co. For a short time he was also involved in Toppan, Maverick & Co. with Peter Maverick, until the latter's death on June 7, 1831. Maverick, a founder of the National Academy of Design, had maintained offices in several eastern cities. In 1833 Toppan became a partner with John Draper, Marcus Bull, and James B. Longacre in the short-lived Draper, Toppan, Longacre & Bull, bank-note engravers and printers, 60 Walnut Street, Philadelphia, with a branch office at 1 Wall Street, New York City.

George Murray had an engraving business in the city, and James Steel, a talented artist, was among his employees. In the same city the affairs of Tanner, Vallance, Kearny & Co., printers of bank notes, maps, and other items, came to an end in about this year.

New York City Engravers of 1830

In New York City the partnership of Durand, Perkins & Co. at 50 Wall Street included a stellar lineup of talent during this era, including Asher B. Durand, his brother Cyrus Durand, Charles Cushing Wright, Joseph Perkins (no kin to Jacob Perkins), Elias Wade Jr. (brother-in-law of Cyrus Durand), and George W. Hatch (former art student under Asher B. Durand). A quarter century later, W.L. Ormsby's New York Bank Note Company would be operated at the same Wall Street address.

Of all early bank-note artists, Asher B. Durand is probably best remembered today—not for his currency but for his prominence as an American landscape painter and founder of the Hudson River school. Wright, whose 1826 Erie Canal medal had showcased his die-cutting talents a few years earlier, would soon

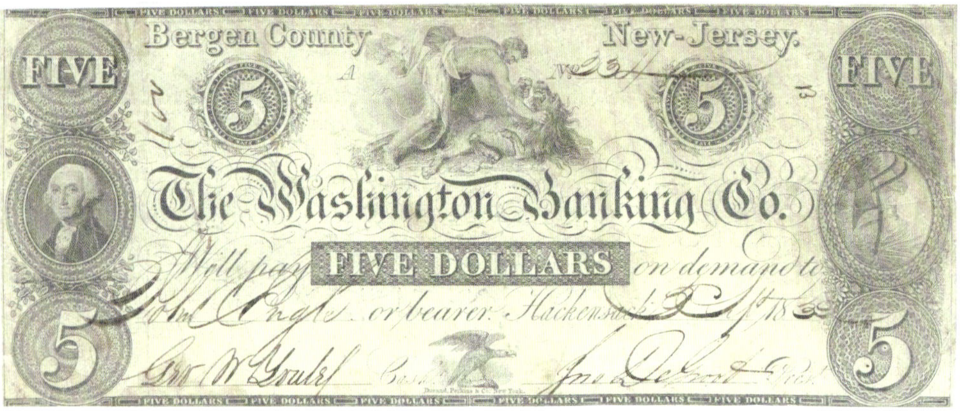

A $5 note of the Washington Banking Co., Hackensack, New Jersey, with a vignette signed by A.B. Durand, depicting Androcles and the lion of mythology. Androcles, a Roman slave, sought refuge from the cruelty of his master and hid in a cave. A lion approached and displayed a swollen paw, which had been infected by a thorn. Androcles extracted the thorn, earning the animal's gratitude. Later, Androcles was thrown to the lions in a circus, and the same lion, a part of the menagerie, rather than attacking Androcles offered him solace and caressed him. Both the lion and the slave were then set free.

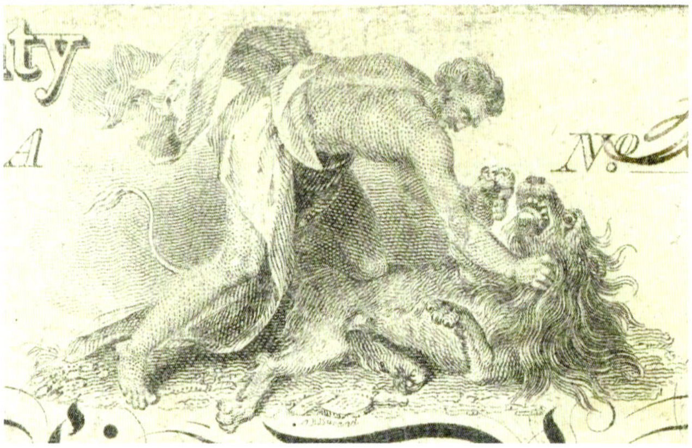

Detail of the vignette. Asher B. Durand was especially well known for his gods, goddesses, and other themes from mythology that decorated bank notes of the era.

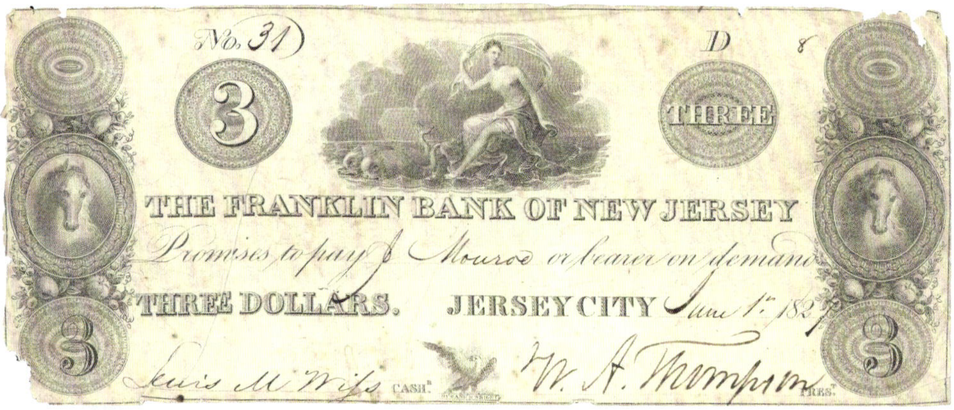

Note for $5 of the Franklin Bank of New Jersey, with a vignette signed by A.B. Durand, featuring a goddess riding a scalloped shell drawn by two dolphins.

Detail of the vignette.

be regarded as the most talented of all medalists in the country. He was less well known for his bank-note engraving. Separately, Wright was a partner in Bale & Wright in 1830, important in the die-cutting and token-issuing field. The Durand, Perkins & Co. firm dissolved in 1832, and some assets were sold to Rawdon, Wright, Hatch & Co.

In New York City in 1830, Vistus Balch and Samuel Stiles operated Balch, Stiles & Co., a small operation that mainly engraved illustrations for books and periodicals but that also issued some bank notes.

Rawdon, Clark & Co., headquartered at 55 State Street, Albany, New York, was the successor in interest to several earlier businesses, including that of the well-known Abner Reed. Ralph Rawdon of the firm lived in New York City in 1830, while Asabel Clark tended to affairs in Albany. The firm was associated from 1828 to 1831 with Rawdon, Wright & Co., 35 Merchants Exchange, New York City, conducted by Ralph Rawdon and Neziah Wright. In the great fire of December 1835, the Merchants Exchange would be destroyed, but the engraving business was soon re-established. Later, this partnership would evolve into Rawdon, Wright, Hatch & Edson, the largest firm in the trade by the late 1850s.

In Newburyport, Massachusetts, the firm founded by Jacob Perkins continued to be the main supplier of currency for the New England banks using the Patent Stereotype Steel Plate, but in 1833 it would transfer its business to the New England Bank Note Company in Boston.

In Boston, William Annin had a small bank-note engraving business as did Oliver Pelton. William D. Terry was active in Providence, Rhode Island, and was a close associate and often worked with Pelton.

Connecticut, which had been home to several important bank-note businesses over the years, in 1830 included the firm of N. & S.S. Jocelyn, conducted by Nathaniel and Simeon Smith Jocelyn, who had been active since the early days of the bank-note business. The Jocelyns, who in the early days spelled their name as Jocelin, had worked in the late 18th century with Amos Doolittle, another pioneer. A related entity in 1830, which lasted for just a short time, was Jocelyn & Munson, New Haven, run by Simeon Smith Jocelyn and Samuel B. Munson.

Most of the preceding engraving firms had stocks of scenic vignettes, which often were rather simple in nature. During the ensuing decade, these illustrations became the focus of the bank-note trade. Year by year bank notes became more artistic and attractive. Siderography was widely used and permitted easy multiplication of favorite designs. Medallion and plaque engravings made by medal-ruling machines achieved great popularity in this era.

THE NEW ENGLAND BANK NOTE COMPANY

FORMATION OF THE FIRM

Among the firms that rose to prominence in the decade of the 1830s, the New England Bank Note Co. was one of the most important.

After Jacob Perkins went to England, his brother Abraham and Abraham's son Nathaniel continued the bank-note engraving and printing business in Newburyport. Their stock-in-trade seems to have been mostly if not exclusively products of the Patent Stereotype Steel Plate style, with complex engraving of repeated tiny letters, small decorations, etc., but with no sweeping scenic vignettes. In the meantime in the 1810s, others such as Abner Reed and Murray, Draper, Fairman & Co. had captured a significant share of the market with their bills depicting goddesses, ships, and other motifs. During the 1820s, Perkins continued to lose market share.

By the 1830s, although the Perkins plate was still difficult to counterfeit, once a false plate was made, it could be used to produce phony bills of dozens of different banks simply by inserting counterfeit slugs with name and address information. Such counterfeits became endemic, as Abel Brewster had warned years earlier in 1810. Seemingly, most bank officers who ordered such bills were not aware of the dangers of counterfeiting. In addition, genuine Perkins bills of failed banks were especially easy to alter to appear as notes of solvent institutions.

Perkins had been the main supplier of currency to the fraudulent Bank of Detroit; Farmers Exchange Bank of Gloucester, Rhode Island; Hillsborough Bank of Amherst, New Hampshire; and the hapless but not criminally operated Vermont State Bank (whose bills were eventually redeemed). These pesky counterfeit bills kept turning up at bank tellers' windows, causing an aggravation for years afterward.

In 1833 the Perkins interests evolved into a new firm, as per this notice in the Boston *Daily Evening Transcript,* March 9, 1833:

> The banking institutions in New England, are respectfully informed that the subscribers have formed a copartnership under the name of the N. ENGLAND BANK NOTE CO. for the purpose of engraving and printing bank notes. Their establishment (now in Newburyport) will be removed to the city of Boston, and located in some building containing secure and fire-proof vaults for the safe deposit of plates and dies, which shall at all times be subject to the inspection of any committee appointed by the banks for the prevention and detection of counterfeits.
>
> The subscribers have spared no expense in procuring machinery of the latest improvements and of the most perfect kind. The assistance of the most skillful artists of this city, of New York City, and Philadelphia, has been secured, and every arrangement made to render their work excellent, and to place every possible obstacle in the way of the counterfeiter.
>
> Abram Perkins, W. S. Pendleton,
> Hazen Morse, Nath'l. Perkins.

NEED FOR CHANGE

Abraham (Abram) Perkins remained in Newburyport, returning to a residence that he had earlier occupied on Fruit Street. Soon, he was finally able to liquidate debts left over from two decades earlier, mostly incurred by Jacob, who was brilliant in science and technology but poor in business. Abraham died in Newburyport on April 2, 1839.

The announcement of the formation of the New England Bank Note Co. included a promise of new, improved machinery and "the assistance of the most skillful artists of this city, of New York City, and Philadelphia." The old Patent Stereotype Steel Plate had become obsolete, and customers throughout the East and Midwest were flocking to secure bills with scenic vignettes offered by other manufacturers, although Perkins plates were still mandated by Massachusetts law. The stereotype plate system was updated artistically by adding small vignettes, but the use of inserted slugs with bank names and locations continued—still making it easy to alter such bills.

THE COMPANY IN 1834

Benjamin Champney, a well-known artist specializing in landscapes including some of the White Mountains of New Hampshire, included this recollection in *Sixty Years' Memories of Art and Artists,* the scene set in the year after the New England Bank Note Co. had moved to Boston from Newburyport:

> When I was sixteen an opportunity occurred for me to enter a store in Boston. Henry L. Daggett, a well-known shoe dealer, wanted a boy, and I left home for a fifty-mile ride in the stage coach for the great city. This was an event of great importance to me. This was in 1834, and Boston was then a large and beautiful town with isolated houses and fine gardens about them. . . .
>
> It happened that the back windows of the shop—204 Washington Street—where I was employed, looked upon a little courtyard, and the place was occupied by the New England Bank Note Co., and by the Pendleton Lithographic Co. I longed to see something of the mysteries of the arts of engraving and printing, but I could find no excuse for trying to do so.
>
> One day I plucked up courage and entered the room where the copper-plate printers were at work, but an old Englishman—the head printer, named Campbell—repulsed me contemptuously. I afterwards knew him well, and found him a jolly, good-natured fellow. I saw the artists going to and fro, and envied them their happy lot. It came about that two of these envied mortals came to my boardinghouse, and I soon became firm friends with them. Robert Cooke, the chief draughtsman, was my room-mate, and we were ever after especial friends. He encouraged me to draw, and gave me good instruction and advice. All of my spare time was given to practice.

COMPETITORS IN THE 1830S

In 1834 Oliver Pelton in Boston wrote to William D. Terry in Providence. (The two in 1836 would form Terry, Pelton & Co., bank-note engravers.) Pelton was probably in the employ of the New England Bank Note Co. at the time:[1]

> If I do any thing more for them I intend to charge them a sound price & the engravers here I believe have made up their minds to that effect. I think in order to continue their business they will be obliged to have a vignette engraver associated with them.

This would seem to reflect the desire to include scenes as part of the firm's designs. Pelton went on:

> The N.E. Bank Note Co. find it difficult and indeed impossible to get the work done that they want. The law I presume will remain as it is another year and as they are dependent upon other engravers for their work I apprehend they will find some difficulty as they already do.

The law in question was the 1809 mandate that Massachusetts bills be of the Perkins format.

The Boston *Daily Evening Transcript,* March 9, 1833, the same issue that had announced the establishment of the New England Bank Note Co., also included this item:

> Annin & Smith, bank note engravers, No. 70 State Street, Boston, inform their friends and the public that, by their arrangements with the well known and long established house of Draper, Underwood, Bald & Spencer (formerly Murray,

Fraudulent note from a plate signed Terry, Pelton & Co., Boston, but not necessarily a plate by that maker. Perhaps the Wolfborough Bank was intended, the real bank having the Wolfeborough name misspelled by dropping the "e."

> Draper, Fairman & Co.), of Philadelphia, they are now in readiness to execute bank notes combining every modern improvement which has been found of real advantage as a security against counterfeits—at the shortest notice.

The bills of Draper, Underwood, Bald & Spencer were of a high order of art and elegance, ornamented with scenic-style vignettes. The addition of an office in Boston aided sales greatly. From the 1830s onward, Philadelphia, New York City, and Boston were the main centers of the bank-note trade in the Northeast. Certain companies based there also had offices in Cincinnati (in particular) and New Orleans.

It seems that the new Boston partnership lasted for just a short time, for on February 18, 1834, Oliver Pelton included this information in a letter to William D. Terry: "Smith the engraver is now at work for the N.E. Bank Note Company in their office. Annin & Smith have dissolved partnership."

After the partnership of Terry, Pelton & Co. was formed in 1836, there were few customers obtained. Even after one year only 11 accounts had been established in Massachusetts, or about a tenth of what the New England Bank Note Co. had in the same state, this in the onset of the Hard Times era. The partnership lasted until autumn 1837, securing a few more accounts including the Wolfborough Bank in New Hampshire. Soon afterward certain assets were sold to the New England Bank Note Co.

Pelton thereafter formed the Boston Bank Note Co., at 39 State Street, Boston, with Joseph Andrews, a company that had modest success at best. This entity terminated its activities in the early 1840s, at which time the New England Bank Note Co. acquired its plates and selected assets. Later, the American Bank Note Company added its ABNCo monogram to certain plates that were reused. In addition, unidentified criminals picked up the Boston Bank Note Co. name to issue spurious bills.

Modification of the Perkins Plate

As discussed earlier, in time the New England Bank Note Co. produced a series of plates combining several scenic vignettes, usually across the top and at each side. At the center of the bill tiny letters such as *Two Dollars* were repeated many times, as on the older Perkins bills but usually in block rather than italic letters. Also similar to the old style, the new bills were of the slug-plate type with rectangular openings for the insertion of the name of the state, town, and bank. These notes, too, were a delight for those who counterfeited or altered notes (see chapter 9).

Later Years

Isaac Cary came to Boston by 1828. In 1845 he joined the New England Bank Note Co., and in 1847 he became its agent (general manager, representing the stockholders). In 1848 he purchased 50% interest in the firm, with the remaining 50% acquired on May 1 of that year by the New York City firm of Rawdon, Wright, Hatch & Edson, probably the most successful partnership in the business at the time.

Cary was the operating officer in Boston for the next decade, and he met with bank officers and others in the course of obtaining business, often assisting with the selection of vignettes. By the late 1850s most bills bearing the New England Bank Note Co. imprint were of the scenic-vignette style, but some paid tribute to the older days by having the denomination printed in repeated tiny letters, such as ONE, at the lower part of the face. By this time, color overprints were in standard use by this firm and many competitors. These overprints consisted of ONE, FIVE, or another denomination printed on the face, often in ink that

A $1.50 note of the New-York Lumber Association payable at the Middling Interest Bank, Boston, from a plate by Terry, Pelton & Co., Boston and Providence. The vignette at lower right is the familiar Androcles and the lion motif by Asher B. Durand, later used by various companies. Many of his vignettes came on the market after the liquidation of Durand & Co.

This bank, chartered in 1836, was investigated by the state in February 1837, but all was found to be in good order. In January 1838, it reported its capital as $1,000,000. Currency in circulation was modest in comparison, with $24,587 in bills of $5 or more and $35,568 of lesser denominations. It became a victim of the Hard Times era and closed down in August 1839.

General-purpose $10 post note with inked name of Bank of Michigan. Dated August 1, 1838, from a plate imprinted Boston Bank Note Co., 39 State Street. The $10 face value was payable 12 months after the date.

was replicated on the back, but with the letters in reverse. Red was the most popular color as it was widely thought to deter the photographic copying of notes, with red appearing as black. Green was the next most popular color.

For years afterward, until the enterprise was merged into the American Bank Note Co. in 1858, many bills carried the double imprint of the New England Bank Note Co. and Rawdon, Wright, Hatch & Edson.

Emphasizing the Ornate

Designs and Illustrations

During the decade of the 1830s, most printers of bank notes built inventories of vignettes, some accumulating hundreds of ornate designs. The intent was to make paper money less susceptible to counterfeiting. Proud of their artistry, they printed posters as well as sample sheets, often illustrating dozens of prominent men in history, mythical gods and goddesses of many styles, women undraped as well as elegantly dressed, Indians, trains, steamships, and more. Indeed, a historian would find it profitable to investigate bank-note illustrations as a mirror of society, art, and technology of the day. Remarkably, many of the printing plates survived, to be included today as part of the American Bank Note Co. archives.

In the 1830s canals were the mainstay of bulk transport in many areas. Most famous was the Erie Canal, connecting the Hudson River with Lake Erie. All around the East and in many areas of the Midwest, dozens of canals were being built or planned in districts in which the topography permitted. Certain of the projectors of these canals also issued bank notes. Reflective of this mode of transportation, many bills showed canals, locks, boats being towed, and related topics.

However, railroads were in the ascendancy and were proliferating just about everywhere. Locomotives and cars were an especially popular subject, and early vignettes depicted trains with passenger cars that often appeared similar to stagecoaches but on iron wheels.

As technology improved, new styles of railroad equipment were illustrated on paper money.

Ships of all types and sizes, from rowboats to seagoing side-wheel steamers, were also widely depicted on bills of the 1830s. Often, those banks that resided in states that bordered the ocean would select illustrations of either ships under full sail or large steamers, while those along the Mississippi River found a wide number of riverboat designs available, including ships whose decks were packed with bales of cotton.

Agriculture was essential to commerce, and bank-note engravers responded with motifs showing horses prancing, drinking from troughs, crossing streams, or just facing forward toward the viewer. Cattle, too, were featured, often with cows or sheep in a field or in a farmyard. Birds on band notes included ducks and ducklings, chickens being fed in a farmyard, and, of course, the American bald eagle. The latter could be found in just about every pose imaginable—perched on a rock in the ocean, on top of a globe, on a shield, or flying through the clouds accompanied by a god-

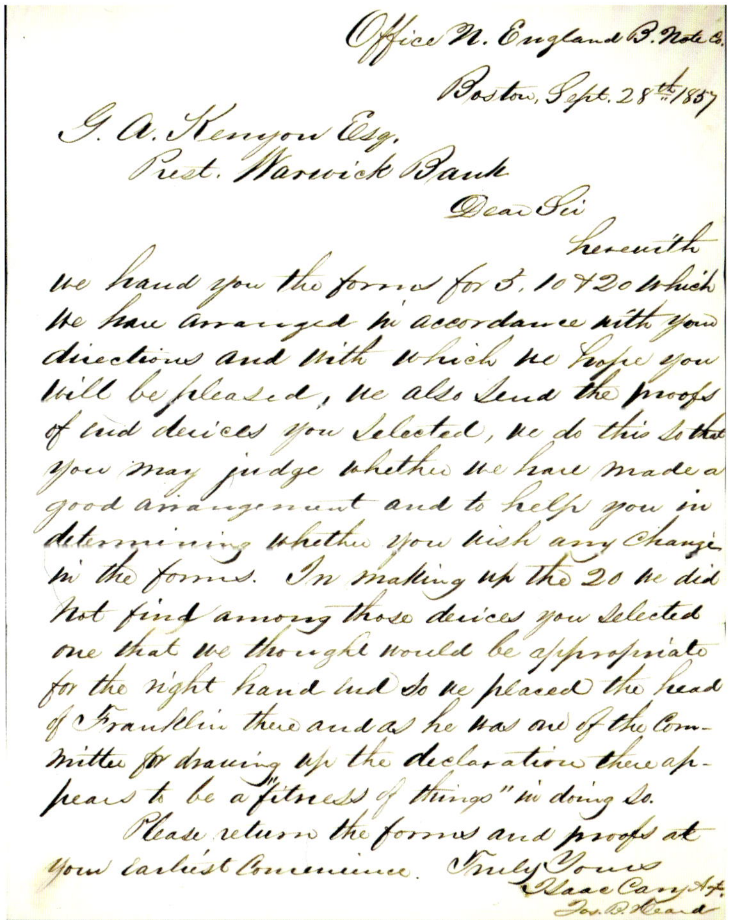

Office N. England B. Note Co.
Boston, Sept. 28th 1857

G. A. Kenyon Esq.
Prest. Warwick Bank

Dear Sir

herewith we hand you the forms for 5, 10 & 20 which we have arranged in accordance with your directions and with which we hope you will be pleased, we also send the proofs of said devices you selected, we do this so that you may judge whether we have made a good arrangement and to help you in determining whether you wish any change in the forms. In making up the 20 we did not find among those devices you selected one that we thought would be appropriate for the right hand end so we placed the head of Franklin there and as he was one of the Committee for drawing up the declaration there appears to be a "fitness of things" in doing so.

Please return the forms and proofs at your earliest convenience. Truly Yours

Isaac Cary Agt.
Jos. B. Heard

Letter from Isaac Cary, New England Bank Note Co., September 28, 1857, to G.A. Kenyon, president of the Warwick Bank in Rhode Island, discussing the bank's new $20 bill design.

An early example of the finished bill, serial number 4, signed and dated, and preserved by president Kenyon.

dess or two. One particularly patriotic bird bore a tiny elliptical portrait of Washington on its neck. Dogs were popular, with the most-often seen pose being of a pooch resting on the floor near a safe or strongbox, securely holding the vital key under a paw.

All U.S. presidents from George Washington onward were used to illustrate bills, often with a portrait within an ellipse, but sometimes with a president on horseback, standing by a table, or in some other pose. Andrew Jackson was perhaps second in popularity, but he nearly always appeared as a portrait rather than posed or in action. Among other historical figures, Benjamin Franklin was the most often used on currency, followed in no particular order of popularity by the Marquis de Lafayette (especially popular from the time of his return visit to America in 1824 until his death in 1834), Alexander Hamilton, Henry Clay, John C. Calhoun, William Penn, and Sir Walter Raleigh, plus dozens of men who were well known at one time but whose identity is not known today. Numismatist Roger H. Durand has published a series of studies of portraits on bank bills, which includes much useful information.[2]

Trades and occupations also were widely depicted. Blacksmiths at the forge, seated with a hammer, standing, or busy at work in a shop illustrated that trade. Sailors standing on deck, holding flags, seated on the shore, and doing other nautical tasks were popular as well. Farmers cutting grain, loading hay, herding cows, sowing seeds, or simply resting in the field with a nearby jug and basket lunch can be seen on bills. Women tending looms; shoemakers plying their trade; and tradespeople making glass, building ships, or plowing and harvesting were all popular motifs, often reflecting a major industry in a particular town.

Buildings were most often seen on notes as part of a town or city scene, such as visible in the distance, or viewed down Main Street, or seen across a river. However, a few banks illustrated their own offices, state capitols and the U.S. Capitol building were popular, and many Greek revival temple-like structures were depicted in detail.

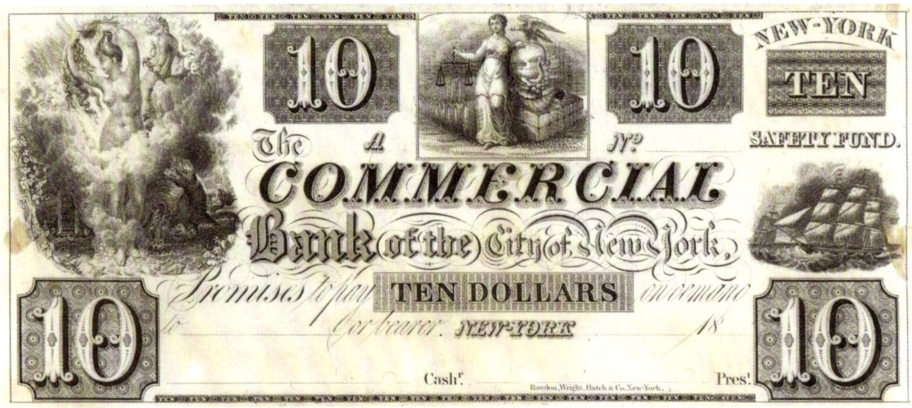

A vignette of Venus adorns this $10 bill by Rawdon, Wright & Hatch, New York City, for the Commercial Bank of the City of New York. The engraver was Freeman Rawdon.

A popular print from a painting by Carl Bodmer, circa 1835, of a steamer on the Ohio River at Cave-in-Rock, a notorious hangout for river pirates and criminals and mentioned widely in the literature of the day. Steamers were in wide use on inland rivers and furnished popular subjects for many bank-note vignettes.

A Gallery of Ornate Art on Bank Notes

Selected bank notes of Michigan in the 1830s reflect the age of ornate art on currency. Nearly all vignettes were stock and also were used for bills of other banks in other states.

Allegorical figures were a prime stock-in-trade, ranging from angels admiring the image of George Washington; to queens in chariots drawn by lions; to all sorts of gods and goddesses, including Archimedes lifting the world with a lever and, especially, Mercury standing, sitting, or flying through the air. There was no substitute for a pretty woman on a paper bill, and many were depicted, from goddesses and angelic creatures to maids holding a bouquet, carrying a milk pail, or feeding chickens in a barnyard.

American Indians were widely depicted, often in bittersweet poses, such as resting with a bow and arrow, or standing near a tent while looking at "progress" in the distance in the form of trains, cities, and the like. Others were on horseback or in canoes. Indian family vignettes depicted a male in feathered attire and sometimes holding a tomahawk, with a woman tending to one or two children.

Objects shown on currency included flags, escutcheons, cannons (not usually in action), poles with liberty caps, coins (often with superb detail appealing to numismatists today), safes, plows, gears, shields, cameos, beehives, trees, monuments, balance scales, and many variations of the caduceus. Sometimes, a woman holding a sickle or standing near a sheaf of grain was referred to as Ceres (goddess of agriculture), and one holding a pair of scales, Justice.

While many activities were depicted on bills, most scenes were of a peaceful nature. Only a few motifs showed conflicts, battle scenes, or disasters. Often a vignette of just about any topic—from goddesses holding shields, to Mercury standing on a dock, to cows grazing—would show in the distance, along with one or more ships at sea, a railroad, or sometimes both. Such arrangements seemingly reflected the combination of art and tradition with the reality of progress.

To see such complex designs was to love them, and, increasingly, bank officers selected designs to produce bills that set a high standard of visual appeal and artistic excellence. At other times, motifs were selected as a veritable hodgepodge, with combinations of irrelevant portraits and designs, creating images that were not at all well balanced.

In combination with scenes, portraits, and other illustrations, ornate geometric designs were used, often surrounding numerals indicating the denomination or employed simply as decorations. These designs were mechanically produced in a dazzling array of loops, curls, and swirls by a geometric lathe.

Archimedes, the early Greek mathematician, lifting the earth with a lever, as depicted on the Tecumseh (Michigan) Bank note, circa 1837. Plate by Rawdon, Wright & Hatch, New York City, using an engraving signed by Freeman Rawdon. "Give me a lever long enough and a place to stand, and I could lift the world," Archimedes stated.

The Medal-Ruling Machine

In 1842 the Assay Office of the Philadelphia Mint published *A Manual of Gold and Silver Coins of All Nations,* by Jacob R. Eckfeldt and William E. DuBois, officers of this institution. On the title page this comment was included: "Illustrated by numerous engravings of coins, executed by the medal-ruling machine, and under the direction of Joseph Saxton of the United States Mint." Saxton used a device that was still considered to be somewhat of an innovation. An overview of it was given in the book:

> There was a process of engraving, yet new to the world, by which coins, medals, and other bas-reliefs could be copied, with comparatively little labor and expense, and so accurately as to present a fac-simile. What is more remarkable, this was a process by *machinery;* and of so great ingenuity

(continued on p. 209)

Three-dollar note of the Tecumseh Bank showing Hebe, cup bearer to the gods, holding a goblet of wine for an eagle. The vignette was engraved by George W. Hatch in 1834. On the right the figure of a standing Indian warrior is labeled "Tecumseh," although this all-purpose vignette was also used for other chiefs.

A $3 note of the Bank of Superior, Michigan, by Underwood, Bald, Spencer & Hufty, Philadelphia. The center vignette shows a Native American contemplating the wilderness, with a canoe on the lake in the distance. Vignettes to each side show frontiersmen, nemeses of the natives.

A $1 note of the Bank of Michigan, by Durand, Perkins & Co., New York. The center vignette shows the Goddess of Liberty and a shield with state symbols. On the right are two steamship vignettes, curiously oriented vertically so they would fit into the allotted spaces.

Note for $2 of the Farmers & Merchants Bank, St. Joseph, Michigan, by Rawdon, Wright & Hatch, New York. The left vignette shows a maiden leaning against a stone post and holding a sheaf of wheat. The center vignette illustrates Benjamin Franklin. Two books are at his feet, one inscribed MIND YOUR BUSINESS, the other the name of A.B. Durand, the famous engraver. On the right is a furiouso depiction, by George W. Hatch, of Mercury approaching Ceres and a seated blacksmith.

A $20 note of the Bank of Saline, Michigan, by Draper, Toppan, Longacre & Co., New York and Philadelphia. The patriotic vignette to the right shows the goddess Liberty with a portrait of George Washington, while an American eagle looks down from a wall, behind which is a shield and E PLURIBUS UNUM.

A $5 note of the Bank of Lapeer, Michigan, from a plate by Rawdon, Wright & Hatch, New York. To the right is an allegorical scene by George W. Hatch, of Mercury bringing a cornucopia filled with coins to the seated Moneta, who is holding a caduceus. The latter emblem, with two entwined snakes on a staff, sometimes with two wings at the top, is a common feature of vignettes with goddesses. Today the caduceus has a different connection, being a symbol used by physicians and related to healing.

An Indian family contemplating a modern plow. (W.L. Ormsby engraving for a book)

(continued from p. 206)

that it is gratifying to affirm that it was invented and perfected by Americans, and (if we may be allowed to show some *esprit de corps*) artists connected with this institution. . . .

It is not difficult to imagine an arrangement of machinery such that while one point is tracing a line across the face of a medal, rising and falling according to the elevations and depressions over which it passes, another point shall draw, on a flat surface, a profile of this line. If now the tracer be made to move successively in a series of parallel and equidistant planes, over the whole surface of the medal, there will be thus drawn a series of profiles corresponding to the sections of these planes with the surface of the medal, and these lines will together form a drawing or engraving of the medal itself.

Such an instrument was invented and executed, in 1817, by Mr. Christian Gobrecht, a native of Pennsylvania, now engraver of the Mint of the United States. In this instrument the "tracing point" moved across the medal in parallel planes perpendicular to the flat surface or "table" of the medal, and the profile lines were drawn on an etching ground laid on copper or steel, by the "etching point."

The first engraving made was of a head of the Emperor Alexander, and the effect was very striking and excited great attention. An instrument constructed chiefly on Mr. Gobrecht's plan by Mr. Asa Spencer of this city was put in operation by him in London in 1819; and thus this art may be justly said to have been first introduced into Europe.

It is true that the general principle of the medal-ruling machine is included in that ancient invention, the rose lathe, and that an imperfect attempt was made by M. Bergeron, in Paris, in 1816, to engrave on copper by this lathe, and by a corresponding instrument which he calls the "machine carré." The whole history of the art of medal-ruling, as now practiced, shows that it had its origin in the invention of Mr. Gobrecht.

The account continued with additional details and information that Joseph Saxton had improved Gobrecht's machine in London in 1829. The improved machine used by the Mint in 1842 was powered by steam. It took about a half hour for it to copy a coin or medal of about an inch in diameter.

The Gobrecht invention and Saxton improvement both created finished engravings that were in mirror image—or backwards. To solve this,

> These copies could not be taken immediately from the coins, because the picture would then be reversed, and the legends would read backwards. It was therefore necessary to obtain impressions of them, and these must be in metal, and that hard enough to bear the tracer. We must then have been at a loss, except for the seasonable invention of the *electrotype,* by M. Jacobi.
>
> By this apparatus a coin suspended in an electro-galvanic battery, with certain adjustments not to be described here, gradually becomes coated with copper, which, when removed in a solid cake, present as complete a counterpart to the coin as if produced from the die, under a coining press. Copies of all the coins were first taken in this way, and from these the rulings were made. It may be added that the finest specimens of coin, belonging to the Cabinet of the Mint, were at our command for this purpose. . . .

It is likely that numismatists can be grateful today that the hard and sharp ruling point was not used on the coins themselves, or otherwise they would have been damaged. Notwithstanding knowledge that must have been common at one time, today information concerning Gobrecht's medal-ruling machine is elusive, as are details relating to his talking doll and improvements in parlor reed organs. A fire in the

U.S. Patent Office, Washington, D.C., on December 15, 1836, destroyed most early records, with the result that certain information once easily obtained does not exist today.

Asa Spencer, an engraver and inventor mentioned in the above 1842 text, was widely credited as the inventor of the medal-ruling machine in the 19th century, and even today not many historians are aware that Gobrecht had prior claim.

While some actual coins and medals were mechanically transferred to bank-note dies by such machines, most often used as models were cheap cameos available in jewelry stores—depicting the heads of gods and goddesses. Unlike coins and medals, these cameos often were elliptical in shape.

Medallion vignettes, as they were called, were widely used by nearly all engraving companies. Their popularity continued for a decade or two but faded by the late 1850s. Additional information concerning medal-ruling machines by W.L. Ormsby is in chapter 15.

Numismatic Notes

Currency of the 1830s with ornate vignettes is easily collected today. Some of the more intricate vignettes were stock-in-trade at the time and were used on many different varieties of bills. While many individual notes from specific banks may be rare, the vignettes themselves usually are not. The availability of bills of this era is due in large part to banks that failed, a topic discussed in the next two chapters.

Medal-ruling machine engraving of the 1804 dollar, and detail, as published on Plate II of *A Manual of Gold and Silver Coins of All Nations* (1842).

Actual medal transferred and reversed in mirror image by a medal-ruling machine. (From a vignette sheet by Draper, Underwood, Bald & Spencer)

Detail of the French artist's name (ANDRIEU) and FECIT in mirror image on the neck truncation.

Note for $5 of the Chesapeake & Ohio Canal Company, by Underwood, Bald, Spencer & Hufty. Two medallion portraits of Athena, mirror images, flank Ceres, the goddess of agriculture. Vignettes were often arranged casually, as here. It would have been better artistry to have had Athena at each side facing toward Ceres, rather than off to the side of the note.

Selection of medallion head vignettes among other vignettes. (From a plate in *Bank Note Engraving,* 1852)

Into the Hard Times Era

Introduction

The decade of the 1820s had been marked by relative stability in American banking. Following the economic problems of 1818 and 1819, many weak banks failed in 1820 and the next year or two after that. Then, economic conditions became stronger as the years went on. The introduction of high protective tariffs in 1828, signaling the advent of the "American System," spurred the growth of domestic industries. The South objected to this new system as it was harmful to the export of cotton. Most banks prospered during the 1820s, punctuated with relatively few exceptions.

In sharp contrast, the 1830s would prove to be a roller coaster of good times and bad in the economy and in banking. In 1830 there were an estimated 330 banks doing business in the United States with a stated capital of about $145,000,000. After Andrew Jackson's veto of the charter renewal for the Bank of the United States in 1832, it was generally realized that the future of banking lay with state-chartered institutions, although proposals for new forms of a national bank were nearly continuous.

Many new banks were formed, with the result that by 1838 there were an estimated 829 banks in operation with stated capital of $317,000,000.[1] In the West, where new towns and cities were being laid out and real estate was booming for much of the decade, banks sprung up like mushrooms after a spring rain (Michigan was especially notorious in this regard); these are the subject of chapter 13.

In the meantime there were significant changes in commerce. This was the decade of the rise of the railroad coupled with the decline of canals, the latter having been the great growth business in recent decades. Commerce was now conducted at a faster pace, with rapid connections laid out between the larger cities. Communications took place at the speed of a train, no longer at the pace of a horse. The telegraph was yet to come. Bank notes reflected the transition, and no doubt an essay on rail commerce of the era could be effectively illustrated with train vignettes on bank notes.

Times were generally good in the early 1830s, and for the bank-note engraving companies the increase in charters was a godsend. Business expanded to a degree not before thought imaginable. It was a wonderland of artistic beauty—with bank notes becoming more ornate than ever before. But the year 1836 was the crest, the top of the roller coaster, after which there came a deep plunge downward into economic and banking problems with no precedent in American history. The date of May 10, 1837, would become etched in history. The last three years of the decade would include the most pivotal, most diverse, and most extensive combination of banking scenarios and currency in the entire era of state bank-note issuing, from 1782 to 1866.

The Asiatic Bank, Salem, Massachusetts, as shown on a $1 note of the 1830s. The bank is on the ground floor at the left side in the India Marine Hall.

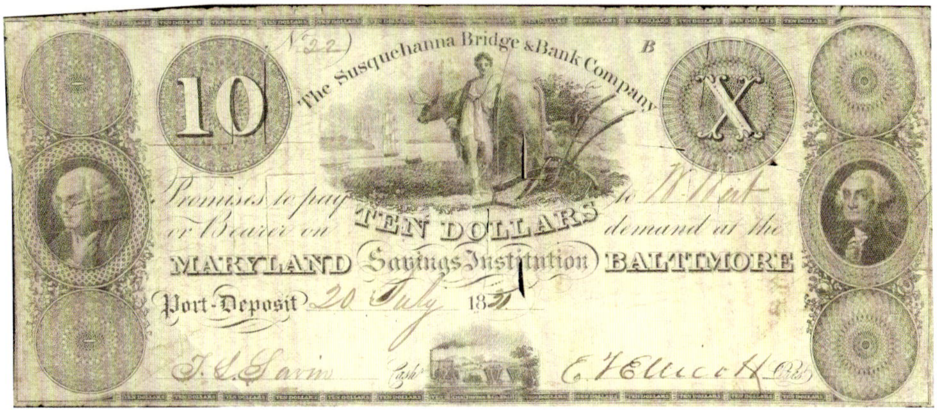

Note for $10 of the Susquehanna Bridge & Bank Company, Port Deposit, Maryland, July 20, 1831. The plate, by Charles Toppan & Co., Philadelphia, has a vignette of a train at the bottom center border. The enlargement gives details. This was in the early days of railroading in America. (For another $10 note of this bank with different motifs, see chapter 8.)

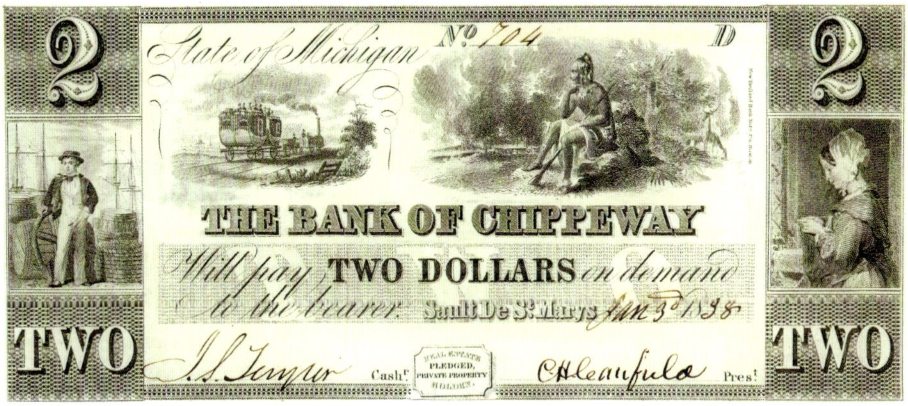

Note for $2 of the Bank of Chippeway, Sault de St. Marys, Michigan, from a plate by the New England Bank Note Co., Boston, and a detail of the passenger train.

PROSPERITY

NO GOLD COINS IN CIRCULATION

In the early 1830s, coins in circulation continued to be dominated by Spanish-American silver issues, mostly from the Mexico City Mint. The most popular domination by far was the two-*real* or two-bit coin, valued at slightly less than the current United States quarter dollar but often interchanged with it in commerce.

Although large quantities of gold $5 coins were minted and a small number of $2.50 coins were also struck, these were not seen in commerce, nor had they been for a decade. It took more than $5 in gold bullion deposited at the Philadelphia Mint to obtain a half eagle. Accordingly, at the outset they were worth more than face value. As in the 1820s, these coins were reckoned on gold value, not bullion value. Most were exported and melted at their destinations. Some were used stateside and were bought and sold by exchange brokers.

On December 15, 1830, Senator Nathan Sanford, of the Select Committee appointed to consider the state of current coins and to make recommendations, issued a report on the subject matter, including this advice:

> We have no gold coins in circulation. . . . The fact that we have no gold coins in use is not the intended effect of our institutions. It has resulted from too low a valuation of gold in respect to silver, when our system was established, and a progressive rise in the value of gold since that time. . . . Our gold coins being much underrated in respect to silver, have never had any general circulation in the country, they have ceased to be used as money; they are merely merchandise, purchased by a considerable premium over silver; and they are used in manufactures or exported to Europe. Our public coinage of gold is now wholly without any public benefit. . . .
>
> We cannot have the use of gold coins while it is more profitable to export them than to export silver; and it is impossible to retain gold coins in the country, unless their legal value in relation to silver, is such that when one metal or the other or both must be exported, there shall be no profit in exporting gold rather than silver. . . .[2]

John White, cashier of the Bank of the United States, Baltimore branch, wrote to Secretary of the Treasury Samuel D. Ingham on May 4, 1830:

> Our gold has disappeared, and possessing silver only, its selection is recommended by the powerful motive of public convenience; besides, generally speaking, dollars [reckoned in silver coins] are our money of account and contract.[3]

On the same day, Secretary of the Treasury Samuel D. Ingham provided a report to the Senate, stating that vast exports of gold coins, and the failure of gold to circulate in the United States in the past decade, was more due to the flood of paper bank notes in commerce than to the values of metals.[4] This situation resulted from an imperfect understanding of the problem, which was not caused by quantities of paper money but by the fact that gold was undervalued in relation to silver.

Gold discoveries in the 1820s had brought many adventurers to North Carolina and Georgia. A report of operations of the Mint, dated January 1, 1831, and covering the previous calendar year, revealed the influx of that precious metal and unprecedented quantities on hand:

> I have the honor to submit a report on the general transactions of the Mint within the last year. The coinage effected within that period amounts to $3,155,620, comprising $643,105 in gold coins, $2,495,400 in silver, $17,115 in copper, and consisting of 8,357,191 pieces of coin. . . .
>
> Of the amount of gold coined within the last year, about $125,000 were derived from Mexico, South America, and the West Indies; $19,000 from Africa, $466,000 from the gold region of the United States, and about $33,000 from sources not ascertained. Of the gold of the United States above mentioned, $24,000 may be sated to have been received from Virginia; $204,000 from North Carolina, $26,000 from South Carolina, and $212,000 from Georgia.
>
> In the last annual report, the progressive development of the gold region of the United States was illustrated by referring to the increase of the annual receipts from North Carolina, which, previous to 1824, had been inconsiderable, but, from that year to 1829, inclusive, had advanced from $5,000 to $128,000, and, also, to the then novel occurrence of gold having been received at the mint from Virginia and South Carolina, about $2,500 having been received from the former, and $3,500 from the latter. The past year exhibits, in relation to all those states, a conspicuous increase in the production of gold, and presents, also, the remarkable fact of $212,000 in gold received from Georgia, from which state no specimen thereof had been presented at the mint in any previous year.
>
> The coinage above exhibited exceeds the amount of any former year. The demand remains, nevertheless, unabated; and the mass of bullion now in the vaults of the Mint is large beyond any previous example.

Gold coins were in abundance, but not in circulation! Relevant to the present text, the absence of gold coins resulted in vastly expanded use of bank notes.

Silver half dollar of the Capped Bust type minted from 1807 to 1836.

Large copper cents continued to be struck in large numbers and were ubiquitous in commerce, while copper half cents were rarely seen. Among United States silver coins, the Capped Bust half dollars, of a design by John Reich introduced in 1807, continued to be made in quantity and were the largest regularly seen native coins of the realm. The silver dollars of yesteryear, dating from 1794 to 1803, were still in the channels of commerce, many of them well worn, but not plentiful.

John Sherman, later the secretary of the Treasury (1877–1881) and a powerful senator, stated this information in a historical review of the state of money in 1830:

> The small and worn Spanish pieces, being legal tender, also drove from circulation our fractional coins coming bright and plump from the Mint. Bank notes and these worn pieces furnished the circulation of our country. The condition of the currency became so objectionable that in 1830 the subject was taken up by a special committee of the House of Representatives, appointed for that purpose. Three reports were submitted, in one of which the committee stated that of $37,000,000 coined at our mints [*sic;* there was just one mint in 1830] only $5,000,000 remained in circulation.[5]

Gold dollar issued by private coiner Christopher Bechtler in the 1830s, the first gold coin of this denomination to be made in the United States. The Bechtler family, located in Rutherfordton, North Carolina, minted gold $1, $2.50, and $5 coins until 1852, without interference from the federal government.

In 1830 in Rutherfordton, North Carolina, German immigrant Christopher Bechtler began producing gold coins, including the first American gold dollars. These coins were used in regional circulation and were valued at a premium in relation to paper money.

This mint would be continued by family members until 1852. In Georgia, Templeton Reid produced a limited number of gold coins for a short period in the summer of 1830.

SECESSION TALK IN THE SOUTH

Trouble between the North and the South, which had been brewing for some time, came to a head when John C. Calhoun of South Carolina declared that state laws nullified federal laws in such matters as trade tariffs. At a banquet held in Washington, D.C., on April 13, 1830, in celebration of Thomas Jefferson's birthday, President Andrew Jackson faced Senator Calhoun and gave this toast (one of 104 toasts at that well-lubricated event), "Our union, it must [and shall] be preserved!"

This saying later would be represented on a wide variety of tokens and medals, among other uses. The Nullification Act would be passed by the state legislature, and several years later, in 1833, President Jackson prepared to use federal troops to enforce the tariffs. Confrontation was avoided when South Carolina revoked its legislative action.[6]

The term *Confederacy* was in use to describe the South, as in this speech given in Charleston, South Carolina, by Langdon Cheves, president a decade earlier of the second Bank of the United States:

> The union—May it be preserved; but, if it be, it will be by a reform which shall make it serve the great purposes for which it was instituted—the equal security and protection of the rights, the interest, the honor and the feelings of all the parts of the Confederacy.[7]

In this period there was much open talk and casual conversation, in South Carolina in particular and the South in general, about seceding from the Union. Slavery was not an issue—it was the tariff. Although abolition was a social cause, it was yet to be a mainstream issue. In the 1830s more attention was paid to temperance, or abstinence from drinking alcohol. Many books and pamphlets were published on the subject, and it became popular for certain public establishments to advertise as "temperance hotels." This trend caused a great rise in the popularity of *medicines* liberally laced with alcohol, which many temperance advocates used in the name of good health.

BANKING AND PAPER MONEY

Hundreds of banks and many factories and other businesses continued to issue paper money, sometimes with the benefit of a state charter, other times not. New York City was the focal point of banking, but Boston, Providence, Philadelphia, Baltimore, Charleston, and other large cities were important. In New England the smoothly functioning Suffolk Bank system brought stability to paper money of that district. There the status of bank notes was well known to merchants and bankers, who suffered from few surprises. Bills of member banks traded nearly at par throughout the several New England states.

Outside of New England, information was less reliable, and the value of paper money varied, often considerably. Bank-note reporters became prominent in this decade, including the earlier discussed *Bicknell's Counterfeit Detector.* Exchange brokers did a lively business buying up bills from distant places as well as depreciated bills, and selling them at a profit.

Although states had chartered banks for a long time, in the 1830s the various legislatures made significant strides in taking interest in the operations of banks that were in business. Safety funds, or deposit accounts set up by the state and contributed to by banks, were intended to repay holders of paper money

Andrew Jackson giving his memorable toast. (From a painting by C.W. Jefferys)

of banks that failed. Most states required at least annual reports. Examiners in certain states visited banks with regularity, but none performed serious audit functions. Cashiers met with state examiners and gave them reports, which were duly filed and printed in annual commission reports.

Today these reports require analysis in order to obtain useful information, and that is not always possible. Capital stock might be "paid in," but the reader of such reports often would have no way of knowing if the payments were simply IOUs of no real value. "Specie" or "specie in the vault" normally meant the number of gold and silver coins on hand, but *paper money* of banks that were "good" and would redeem their bills in specie were sometimes included in the figure. There was little a reader of bank statements could to do determine if the large amount listed under "discounts" (loans due to the bank) represented readily collectible sums or if some debtors were hopelessly insolvent. Often, discounts were worthless IOUs given by bank stockholders and directors.

Because of this situation, the banking scenario was occasionally punctuated by surprises, when an ostensibly sound bank was found to have little in the way of real assets and a lot in the way of liabilities.

The American System

Peace prevailed in Europe, and in the absence of emphasis on war, commerce flourished, including among nations. It was a time of prosperity overseas as well as in the United States.

As bank notes often reflected the times, more than just a few vignettes depicted the sinews of manufacturing and trade—busy city streets, factories, and the earlier-mentioned railroad motifs—the "American System" at work, despite its detractors. In June 1831, the *Portland* (Maine) *Advertiser* printed this description:

> Boston has given us a powerful, and we may say without exaggeration, a splendid illustration of the excellence of the American system. Her trade before the tariff of '28, and for some time after, (till the country was invigorated by new protecting duties), was drooping. Her stores and shops and houses were untenanted. Real estate decreased in value; mechanics were out of employ; and even misery was lifting up its visage. Now the tariff of '28 is under full wing.
>
> An impulse like that of an electric battery is given to trade. Our eastern traders who had purchased goods there this season, tell us, old Babylon was not more noisy. Nothing but bustle;—bustle,—or to use the expressive language of the day (which is always best in matters of this sort) "they are making money hand over fist." All our cities and large towns, certainly, are in a state of wonderful prosperity.[8]

In early April of 1833, the Treasury Building in Washington, D.C., burned, causing a loss that today still affects numismatic research. This description is from a contemporary account:

> In the late conflagration of the Treasury building, nearly all the correspondence of the secretary of the Treasury, from the establishment of the department to the 31st March, 1833, was destroyed, including, as well as the original letters and communications addressed to the secretary of the Treasury, as the records of the letters and communications written by him. . . .[9]

The Treasury Department invited recipients of the correspondence to write out copies of any letters still in their possession, an effort that would be reimbursed at a rate not to exceed 10 cents for every 100 words. However, most information, including much about coins and currency, was lost forever. Spared from the fire were correspondence files to and from the cashiers of banks in the United States, from October 1, 1819, to date.

In October 1833, the Jackson administration moved federal deposits from the second Bank of the United States to "pet banks" scattered through the country. Generally, such banks were sound, and only a few problems resulted. In the meantime, the Bank of the United States set about planning for its demise in 1836. No longer was *Jackson versus the Bank* a leading subject of newspaper accounts.

An 1833 View of Banks

Today, history offers many supposed facts and figures about banks, money in circulation, and the like. In actuality, accurate information is difficult to obtain and in some instances does not exist. The contemporary exchange that follows, published in *Niles' Weekly Register,* September 14, 1833, involving that highly respected publication and also the well-regarded *National Intelligencer,* source of the main commentary, reflects what the experts did not know about banks in that era. The listing endeavors to cover all banks ever formed in the states mentioned and their current status:

> The following addressed to the editors of the *National Intelligencer* presents a fearful prospect before us:
>
> The "rag system" will become as perfect as ever it was, soon after the restraining power of the bank of the United States shall cease—and every nook and corner of our country will again have its own rag-shop, and currency.

To the Editors:

Gentlemen: I have read with very great satisfaction your remarks on the bank question. . . . My purpose is to place in your hands, for use, should you require it, a statement illustrative of a remark in your 5th No. in the following words, viz: "In the year 1816, the number of local banks that generated this 'leprosy,' was 260. How many such banks are there now? We really cannot say; but we have seen a list of 470."

You have not seen the entire list. I have before me an authentic statement of the number and condition of the local banks (with the exception of those of Kentucky, Illinois, Indiana, Missouri, and the Floridas) amounting to 705. The number in the states and territories not enumerated, would probably swell it to 800. [It is proper to observe, that the bank of the United States and branches, are included in this schedule.]

The subjoined table exhibits the localities and condition of these local banks, at the present time. How many more would be invalided, or sent to the tomb of the Capulets, should the madness of the times impel the Bank of the United States to close its concerns suddenly, requires the true spirit of prophecy to foretell. Experience is a severe but most impressive teacher. The annihilation of the Bank of the United States would be, to the stock-jobbers and money-lenders, as an equinoctial gale to the wreckers on our coast. The ship and her cargo would float to the strand; but the "spoil" would be shared by the strongest.[10]

I had no intention to say a word on a subject which you have so ably discussed; and meant simply to put into your hands the annexed table:

Maine, 36 banks, 5 closed, 5 failed.

New Hampshire, 24 banks, 1 failed.

Vermont, 20 banks, 3 failed.

Massachusetts, 118 banks, 4 closed, 1 fraudulent, 12 failed.

Rhode Island, 63 banks, 3 fraudulent, 2 failed.

Connecticut, 31 banks, 1 fraudulent, 4 failed.

New York, 111 banks, 7 fraudulent, 22 failed.

New Jersey, 34 banks, 9 failed.

Pennsylvania, 70 banks, 3 closed, 1 fraudulent, 15 failed.

Delaware, 8 banks.

Maryland, 31 banks, 5 closed, 4 failed.

District of Columbia, 15 banks, 2 closed, 3 failed.

Virginia, 24 banks, 1 closed, 2 failed.

North Carolina, 8 banks, 1 failed.

South Carolina, 12 banks, 2 failed.

Georgia, 19 banks, 1 closed, 10 failed.

Ohio, 42 banks, 2 closed, 19 failed.

Alabama, 7 banks, 2 failed.

Tennessee, 9 banks, 2 failed.

Michigan, 4 banks, 2 failed.

Mississippi, 4 banks.

Louisiana, 15 banks, 3 failed.

705 banks, 23 closed, 13 fraudulent, 123 failed.

Thus, you, see, we have over 700 banking "institutions," with an army of over 8,000 directors, and probably as many clerks and hangers on, to be bought up for the use of the heir-apparent, by the government deposits—if they can! The game is a strong one; but being in the "nine-holes," their "hands" will scarcely avail to secure a triumph.

If the statement I have furnished will afford you any new light in the prosecution of your laborious duty, I shall feel amply rewarded for the little time it has cost me to prepare it.

Your friend, &c.

[Comment by Hezekiah Niles:] The preceding list, though it may be, in the main, pretty nearly correct, has some errors. For instance—the New York *Commercial Advertiser* says the present total of banks in that state does not exceed 80, and that only 8 of those which were incorporated had broken—the names of which are given.]

The public losses, because of the failure of the 123 banks stated—perhaps really 200, if those of Kentucky, &c. were counted, must have amounted to not much less than $20,000,000—out of which, perhaps, the brokers and other dealers in bank notes made more than $5,000,000.

Despite the approximations, the preceding list is valuable from a numismatic viewpoint. It is seen that Ohio and Georgia abounded with failed banks, the track record in Maine, New Jersey, New York, and Pennsylvania was mediocre, while relatively few banks in most other states became insolvent. As a rule, bills from failed banks exist in large numbers in the numismatic marketplace.

By a decade later, the scenario would be much different—with Michigan breaking all records in fraudulent and failed banks.

The good times of the early 1830s were not without financial hiccups. In 1834, banks in some areas experienced problems with failed loans, causing a situation that was widely covered in the press but did not develop into a panic.

As mentioned, federal funds, once stored in the second Bank of the United States, were moved to "pet banks" selected by the Jackson administration. Many new bank charters were granted in view of hoped-for business resulting from the demise of that institution. The tide of sentiment turned toward the Bank of the United States, and its impending charter expiration was widely lamented and regretted. Invectives mounted toward state-chartered banks, but this was a minority point of view. Most citizens enjoyed the prosperity that had settled on all but a few areas of the country.

In 1835 the State Bank of Indiana was founded with a capital of $1,600,000. Ten branches were established across the state, a number later increased to 13. A contemporary report explained the state of affairs: "The directors of the parent bank were to have charge of the plates and bank paper of the branches, and were empowered to deliver to them an amount of such paper not exceeding twice the amount of the stock subscribed for."[11]

Elsewhere in the Union, the good economic times encouraged more banks to open their doors. Among the first actions was the issuing of paper money.

At Last, Gold Coins in Circulation

The Act of June 28, 1834, effective on August 1, reduced the gold content of coins. After August 1, new issues, the $2.50 and $5 denominations of the Classic Head design, entered circulation and remained there. For the first time since 1820, gold coins were exchangeable at par with paper. Gold minted before August 1, 1834, and of heavier weight, continued to sell at a premium through exchange brokers and was referred to as "old tenor" in financial accounts.

Following the 1834 legislation to permit gold coins to circulate, some observers of the social and business scene, such as William Leggett writing in the *Evening Post*, envisioned or at least hoped that the new gold coins would signal the end of widespread use of small-denomination paper money:

> **Small Note Circulation**
>
> Now that *real* money has come into circulation—now that the country is plentifully supplied with gold and silver—we trust the friends of a sound currency will take pains, and adopt all proper measures, to banish small notes from use.[12] We call upon every man who professes to be animated with the principles of the democracy, to assist in accomplishing the great work of redeeming this country from the curse of our bad bank system. . . .
>
> We do not expect and do not desire to overthrow our pernicious banking system suddenly. We would not, if we could, do aught to infringe the chartered privileges of banks already existing. Were they ten times worse in their effects than they are, we would not justify a breach of the public faith to get rid of the evil. But we desire most ardently that it may not be permitted to spread more widely. The legislatures may at least say, 'Thus far shalt thou go and no further; here shall thy proud waves be stayed.' They may refuse to grant any more charters of incorporation, and may take effectual measures to prohibit the small note issues. These measures constitute the proper first step in the great reformation for which we contend, and these measures the democracy of the country—if we do not strangely misinterpret their sentiments—will demand.
>
> But in the meanwhile, the means are within the reach of the people themselves to do much—very much—towards the accomplishment of the desired object. Let employers provide themselves with gold to pay their hands. . . . Let them remember, when paid in small uncurrent notes, that the longer they retain possession of those notes the greater is the profit of the bank that issued them, and therefore let them take the best means within their reach of causing them to be returned to the bank. Every dollar-note in circulation has displaced an equal amount of gold and silver, and, on the other hand, every dollar of gold and silver you keep in circulation, will displace twice or three times its amount in paper money. . . .[13]

Leggett went on to suggest that anyone receiving bills should write on the back, "some short sentence expressive of their sentiments. For example—No Monopolies! No Union of Banks and State! 'Jackson and Hard Money! Gold before Rags!' and the like."

Such actions were thought to end the use of small bills in circulation. It did not happen. Surprisingly, there was not a rush for the new gold coins, and by late autumn of 1834 they were seen only occasionally in the marketplace. The public continued to use paper money for most local and regional transactions.

In 1838, $10 gold eagles of the new lighter-weight standard were made, the first coins of this denomination minted for circulation since 1804. The eagle quickly became the standard coin for export in settlement of international transactions, a status it would maintain until the $20 double eagle was introduced in 1850.

Speculation in Western Lands

In 1834, interest of investors started to focus on real estate in the American West (land west of Pennsylvania), vast tracts of federal acreage were made available to citizens, and in that year $4,800,000 worth was sold. Purchases could be arranged easily enough through federal agents, with payment made in bank bills, promissory notes, and other paper. Prices escalated, and windfall profits were made by some speculators, tripling sales to $14,700,000 in 1834.

The Burrillville Bank was one of the failed banks on the 1833 list. It was incorporated in 1818 but had difficulty in raising capital. In his book, *The Curse of Paper Money and Banking* (1833), William M. Gouge commented, "On an investigation of the affairs of the Burrillville Bank of Rhode Island it was found that only $6,000 of the capital had been paid even in stock notes."

The enterprise was a so-called "paper mill" and ordered hundreds of thousands of dollars' of Perkins' Patent Stereotype Steel Plate bills in various denominations. Shown here are three notes: a $1 note dated September 1, 1831, signed by cashier Samuel Ashley Jr. and president Abraham Baker; a $5 note signed by Ashley and later president John L. Clark; and a $10 note signed by Ashley and, as president, John W. Aborn (a name not located so far in historical sources). The bank, which seems to have been a sham during its existence, failed in 1832.

Representative of the challenges in research on such matters, one of the most highly regarded sources, *The History of Banking* (1900), by John Jay Knox, stated that the bank failed in 1829, but no loss was sustained on its circulating notes, which amounted to $49,000. In fact, all of the notes were utterly worthless to those holding them. For exchange brokers they became a very popular stock-in-trade in the next decade and were bought and sold at pennies on the dollar, the buyers being criminals who used chemicals to remove the bank name and location, printed information pertaining to a sound bank, and then passed the bills into circulation. Most popular were the bills of higher denominations, as it took no more effort to alter a $10, $20, or $50 bill than it did for a $1 bill.

A $2.50 gold quarter eagle of the new Classic Head design, minted beginning August 1, 1834, of lower authorized weight than earlier issues. These and $5 half eagles were made in quantity and in time reached circulation, the first federal gold coins to trade at par with paper money since 1820. Chief Engraver William Kneass prepared the design. Earlier he had been a copper-plate engraver, including those for bank notes.

This design of $10 gold eagles were introduced in 1838 and quickly became the mainstay of international transactions in American gold coins. This denomination was extensively used for this purpose until the $20 double eagle replaced it in 1850.

In the meantime, in eastern cities there were many articles in the press regarding what seemed to be an ever-increasing flood of bank notes. Many of these notices dealt with bills of distant cities being refused, such as New Orleans bills not being accepted in Pennsylvania, except at a deep discount. The second Bank of the United States, still in business, had brought stability to long-distance exchanges involving its own notes, but that bank was rapidly fading in importance.

Exchange values for bank notes given in the May 17, 1834, issue of *Niles' Weekly Register* reflect the fact that the Suffolk Bank system in New England brought great stability to banks in that district, although this network was not specifically mentioned:

> *Currency and the Times, Etc.* The following were the rates at New York on the 10th instant, of the notes of banks regarded solvent.
>
> Bank of the United States and all its branches, par. All of Maine, New Hampshire, Massachusetts, Rhode Island, Connecticut and Vermont, with two or three exceptions only 1/2 percent discount. New York City banks, par, with many of those in the interior—some at 1/2 percent discount but the safety fund banks generally at 1 discount, two or three at 1-1/2. New Jersey, some at par others generally from 1 to 1-1/2 discount. Pennsylvania—Philadelphia 1/2, country banks from 1 to 2, a few at 5 dis. Delaware 2. Maryland—Baltimore 1—country notes 2 to 4 dis. Virginia from 3 to 5. District of Columbia 2-1/2. Ohio, generally, 5. North Carolina, South Carolina and Georgia 5. Tennessee, Louisiana, Alabama and Mississippi 10 dis. Michigan 2-1/2. Canada 3-1/2 to 6.
>
> The uniformly good credit of the numerous banks in New England, is not a little remarkable, in this season of pressure. The credit of the "safety fund" banks has also rallied.

Buildings and commerce on the Ohio River waterfront in Cincinnati in 1838. At the time this was one of the most important trading centers in what was then the American West—the lands beyond the border of Pennsylvania. During the 1830s many towns were laid out and roads built through Ohio, Kentucky, Indiana, Illinois, and other states. Development was especially rapid in the early 1830s, when government land could be bought by paying in bank notes and other paper of depreciated value.

Western speculation continued apace. In 1836, to dampen speculation and end the use of questionable paper money and certificates in such transactions, which eventually totaled $24,800,000 that year, President Andrew Jackson issued his "Specie Circular":

> **Important Treasury Circular**
>
> To receivers of public money, and to the deposit banks.
>
> Treasury Department, July 11, 1836.
>
> In consequence of complaints which have been made of frauds, speculations and monopolies, in the purchase of the public lands, and the aid which is said to be given to effect these objects by excessive bank credits, and dangerous, if not partial, facilities through bank drafts and bank deposits, and the general evil influence likely to result to the public interests, and especially the safety of the great amount of money in the treasury, and the sound condition of the currency of the country, from the further exchange of the national domain in this manner, and chiefly for bank credits and paper money, the president of the United States has given directions, and you are hereby instructed, after the 15th day of August next, to receive in payment of the public lands nothing except what is directed by the existing laws, viz: gold and silver, and in the proper cases, Virginia land scrip, provided, that, till the 15th December next, the same indulgences heretofore extended as to the kind of money received, may be continued for any quantity of land not exceeding three hundred and twenty acres to each purchaser who is an actual settler, or bona fide resident in the state where the sales are made.
>
> In order to insure the faithful execution of these instructions, all receivers are strictly prohibited from accepting for land sold any draft, certificate, or other evidence of money or deposit, though for specie, unless signed by the treasurer of the United States, in conformity to the act of April 24, 1820. And each of those officers is required to annex to his monthly returns to this department the amount of gold and of silver respectively, as well as the bills received under the foregoing exception; and each deposit bank is required to annex to every certificate given upon a deposit of money the proportions of its actually paid in gold, in silver and in bank notes. All former instructions on these subjects, except as now modified, will be considered as remaining in full force.
>
> The principal objects of the president is adopting this measure being to repress alleged frauds, and to withhold any countenance or facilities in the power of the government from the monopoly of the public lands in the hands of speculators and capitalists, to the injury of the actual settlers in the new states, and of emigrants in search of new homes, as well as to discourage the ruinous extension of bank issues and bank credits, by which those results are generally supposed to be promoted, your utmost vigilance is required and relied on, to carry this order into complete execution.
>
> Levi Woodbury, Secretary of the Treasury.

This announcement had the desired chilling effect on wholesale purchases of land by speculators, but at the time the rest of the economy was so robust that little concern was expressed. The Treasury recorded large surplus, and in July, the same month the Specie Circular was issued, Congress declared that the extra millions of dollars would be distributed among the various states, a procedure set for the following January 1st. Even so, there were continuing uncurrent and occasional articles that banks were not as strong in recent times as they had been a few years earlier. Large quantities of bank bills in circulation were blamed for some of this. Many citizens and government officials reminisced about what were now remembered as halcyon days of banking stability under the second Bank of the United States.

Treasury Estimates of December 1836

Although there were no reliable figures, a United States Treasury estimate of December 1836 suggested $80,000,000 in bank bills was in general circulation plus $20,000,000 held in bank vaults.[14] The most popular denomination at the time was probably the $5 bill, as lower values were prohibited by law in some states. Circulation was mostly composed of $1, $3, $5, $10, $20, and $50 notes. Those of $100 were infrequently seen, and $500 and $1,000 bills, although printed for many banks, seem to have been used mostly in bank-to-bank transactions rather than hand to hand in commerce.

The same Treasury report noted that gold and silver coins in circulation rose from $4,000,000, all in silver, to $28,000,000 in 1836, including nearly $10,000,000 in new gold coins (minted after August 1, 1834). The amount of money in circulation (coins and paper) per capita rose from about $6.50 to $10.

The Panic of 1837

Trouble in New York City and Elsewhere

Trouble began early in the year 1837, when the "Flour Riot" erupted in New York City's Chatham Square.[15] A crowd had gathered to protest the high prices of bread, meat, and fuel. They drove off the mayor and the police and stormed a warehouse holding flour.

In March, stock prices on Wall Street fell across a wide front of issues. Anxiety gripped the financial community. New Orleans, the trading center of the Mississippi River valley, was hard hit, and Herman Briggs & Company, a leading cotton brokerage house, failed. Other brokers and factors went bankrupt in that city and elsewhere, and some banks experienced cash shortages.

On March 4, 1837, Martin Van Buren took the oath of office as president, having been elected in November on the coattails of the controversial but popular Andrew Jackson. Van Buren promised to follow "in the footsteps of my illustrious predecessor," while Jackson looked forward to spending time at his home, the Hermitage, in Nashville, Tennessee. By and large his eight-year term had been one of prosperity for America. More than for any other president up to that time, his policies had been divisive. Citizens and politicians either liked him or detested him, it seemed, with few taking a middle ground. The great controversy about the second Bank of the United States was still a topic of casual discussion. Somehow, America had survived, and the vast majority of state-chartered banks had performed well in the 1830s.

The "illustrious predecessor" had left a somewhat confused successor, who would be confronted with what seemed a new wave of economic problems. At a March 1837 meeting in New York City, Daniel Webster told a crowd that the growing financial problems were due to government interference with private bank notes and, in particular, Jackson's Specie Circular of July 11, 1836. An appeal was made to newly inaugurated Van Buren to help strengthen the economy, citing examples of current problems, including the fact that real estate values in the country had dropped by $40 million within the past six months.

At the time there were 788 banks in the United States (as of one reporting period in 1837, but the number was constantly changing), with capital of $291 million. These institutions had $149 million worth of paper money in circulation, backed by $38 million worth of specie. Deposits totaled $127 million. Outstanding loans amounted to $525 million.

The Gathering Storm

On April 3, 1837, the *New York Journal of Commerce* published this disquieting report relating to business in that city:

> The past week will long be remembered by our merchants as a season of trial and difficulty, such as before has not been experienced for many years. It will be remembered also, we trust, as the crisis of the great financial troubles which have been gathering for more than a year past, from the combined influence of speculation, the surplus revenue, bad government, etc.

The first three days of the week were indeed gloomy; a number of failures occurred, chiefly however of houses essentially sound, but which were unable to sustain themselves under the tremendous money pressure which existed; and what was worse than all, in some of its bearings, confidence, that essential element of credit, appeared for panic makers, croakers, and assassins of credit, and well did they improve the opportunity afforded them. We could mention a dozen of our largest and best houses who were reported among the fallen, but who still survive unharmed.

The temporary suspension of payments by Messrs. E.M. Morgan & Co. who were agents for 20 or 30 country banks, gave opportunity by the enemies of such institutions to propagate suspicions concerning them; and all these troubles were aggravated, we will not say wantonly aggravated, by a portion of the press. Thus things were proceeding, when by a concerted movement between the Bank of the United States [of Pennsylvania] and our local institutions, measures were adopted for the relief of the community, and from that moment the state of the money market has been evidently improving.

During the three last days of the week we did not hear of a single failure. Stocks which had been rapidly declining, began to rally—and confidence, though still scarce, was perceptibly gaining ground. We feel assured that these encouraging indications will continue and increase, until the money market shall recover its usual healthy condition. Perfect restoration is not, however, to be expected in a day; the disease was too deeply seated, and some of the exciting causes still remain. . . .

Portrait of Martin Van Buren by E. Wellmore after a painting by Henry Inman. (*National Portrait Gallery,* 1836)

Inviting Disaster

The *New York Mercantile Advertiser* carried this report on April 15:

> *The crisis—the remedy—suspension of specie payments.* An inflammatory handbill under this heading has been posted up in all the principal thoroughfares, and extensively circulated. The intention is to do mischief, and can only aggravate the evils of which we complain.
>
> The example cited of the suspension of specie payments during the war [of 1812] can have no earthly application to the present state of things. Our debts then to Great Britain were necessarily held in abeyance, for they could not be exacted during a state of warfare, and it was imperiously called for by the state of the times. But the adoption of such a measure can only be justified by extreme necessity, which necessity does not at present exist.
>
> A great want of confidence has arisen, and for the banks to adopt the measure recommended would be like pouring oil upon the fire, to make it burn the fiercer. Suppose the measure were to be adopted—what would be the result? Would the merchant or trader be benefited? Not a jot: the banks would hold on upon the specie; but would they extend their line of discount beyond a prudent circumspection? Not a dollar; for if they did, the moment the crisis was past, and specie payments resumed, their vaults would be swept clear of the precious metals.
>
> Would such a measure enable us to create a credit in England, and to make our remittance? Quite the reverse. It would be disgraceful to us in a national point of view, and inexpedient in a financial view. We may be pressed, but we can refrain from compromising our integrity. An individual who cannot obtain facilities equal to his engagements without sacrificing the property of his creditors and the support of his family, may be justified in a temporary suspension; but nations and national institutions have no such plea, and all demands against them should be met to the utmost farthing. We are under the impression that it is a weak invention of the enemy; some Jackson or Van Buren bantling, that should be strangled in the birth. . . .

Satirical cartoon published by M.R. Robinson depicting Van Buren haunted by the ghost of the late Bank of the United States and the fiscal policies of his predecessor, Andrew Jackson.

TROUBLE IN NEW ORLEANS

This account, published in the *Mobile* (Alabama) *Daily Advertiser,* April 18, told of business conditions, including the prices of slaves (considered a commodity, and liens on them were routinely taken as collateral by some banks):

> *New Orleans,* April 18. Our troubles still continue. The failures that have clouded our commercial horizon since the 4th March are now working their way among the middle and poorer classes, cutting off their usual sources of supply, and compelling them in turn to suffer all the evils of deranged credit. The storm is just beginning to reach the West. The heads of several Louisville houses are now here, in the utmost alarm.
>
> *The money market.* Things are in a moody stillness. The disease is working its way into the vitals of the body politic with an awful rapidity. Its progress is silent, but certain. Nothing under heaven can avert the calamity from breaking up the fountains of credit in toto. The failure of Yeatman, Woods & Co. [Nashville bankers] will carry more immediate distress into the West, than any one of the suspensions that has yet taken place. Their house occupied a very high ground in the confidence of millions of people. The result will be ruinous in Tennessee and Kentucky to the poor. Their notes make up almost one-third of the circulation in Tennessee. A constant drain of specie is going on in Mississippi.
>
> Negroes have fallen to $150 to $300, that formerly cost $1,200. Every species of produce is a mere drug among the people of that state. The levee presents a deserted appearance. But few steamboats are lying at our wharves, and every thing wears more the appearance of midsummer than the activity of April.

MAY 10, 1837

Despite the optimism of the *New York Journal of Commerce* and many other newspapers, business conditions and the credit and cash crunch went from bad to worse. On May 10, 1837, New York banks suspended specie payments under a state law that permitted them to do this for a one-year period.[16] By this time there were about 100 bank failures in the city, causing a loss of about $15 million. This occurrence had a domino effect, and within the next few days, most of the larger banks in the East stopped paying out gold and silver coins. In an era before the telegraph, news spread by dispatches sent by rail and, in the interior, by coach or horseback.

In time, virtually every bank in the United States suspended paying out coins. By the end of the year, several hundred banks had closed their doors forever. Many of these had assets of dubious value; some had no assets at all, except a printing press or, more likely, some bank-note ordering forms from one or another of the engraving and printing firms that were all too eager to deliver as many notes as were requested. The country was awash in *broken bank* notes not worth the paper they were printed on.

SHINPLASTERS AND TOKENS

Coins of all kinds disappeared from circulation, eventually and for a short time including copper cents. In order to maintain commerce, paper "shinplasters" were issued by merchants, banks, towns, and others. Denominated in cents, most of these scrip bills were as worthless as the broken bank notes they supplemented. Cent-size copper tokens, known to a later generation of numismatists as Hard Times tokens, were made by the millions and helped fill the need for small change. The pivotal date of May 10, 1837, is included in the reverse inscription on certain of these and is generally cited as the beginning of the Hard Times era.

Scovill's mint and button factory in Waterbury, Connecticut, made many of these copper tokens and sold keg lots at well below face value to merchants who wanted to spend them or give them out in change. Many bore advertisements of merchants; others bore anti-Jackson or anti-Van Buren inscriptions, never mind that Jackson was no longer in office. Still other tokens were neutral in their inscriptions, many simply stating, NOT ONE CENT in order to evade counterfeiting laws. Some depicted Van Buren's "illustrious predecessor," depicted as a jackass. Newspapers ignorantly denounced these tokens as "counterfeits." They were not legal tender, but neither were large cents, to be technical. Customers offered tokens in change could easily enough refuse them, but they risked receiving scrip instead.

ECONOMIC PROBLEMS CONTINUE

Adding to the general misery in 1837 was the failure of much of the nation's wheat crop, leading to expensive importation from the Mediterranean area. By year's end an estimated 39,000 citizens went bankrupt, $741 million was registered in business losses, and all but one textile mill in New England closed

Copper Hard Times token the diameter of a contemporary one-cent piece.

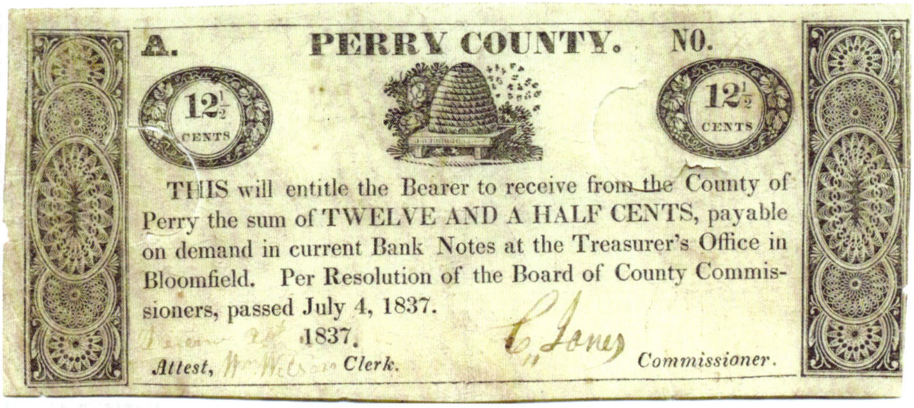

Scrip note of 12-1/2¢ issued by Perry County, Pennsylvania, in July 1837. (Shown enlarged)

down. Bucking the trend, Nathaniel Stevens expanded his textile operation production in North Andover, Massachusetts. His workers were on the job for 76 hours each week and earned an average of $4.50 per week plus $2 for room and board during that time. Relevant to such information, it should be realized that accounts of business and bank openings and closings, failures, and difficulties, varied widely in different published articles, and that today only an approximation can be gathered of what happened. A figure such as $741 million appears to be precise, but in actuality it was simply a published guess. There was no national recording bureau or database, and most companies did not make their figures public.

The year 1838 opened with generally unfavorable business conditions continuing in most sections of the country. A report on Massachusetts banks stated that some of the strongest institutions had just $1 in specie on hand for every $10 to $20 worth of their paper money in circulation. Obviously, redemption of their notes was impossible. Michigan banks broke all rules and are the subject of a separate discussion in the next chapter.

In the meantime, New York banks had been preparing for the resumption of specie payments by reducing their amount of paper money outstanding. In April, 1838, a convention of 143 bankers met in New York City to discuss resumption. Most confreres wanted to delay this event until January 1, 1839, but under state law payments had to resume on May 10, 1838.

Time and again, legislatures in New York and other states attempted to regulate specie payments, but the inviolable laws of economics took precedence. A bank resuming such payments was apt to experience a "run" and have its specie reduced to zero, causing the public to think the bank was on the brink of failure and, in a self-fulfilling prophecy, cause its collapse. It was best for a bank to retain specie and not pay it out until it could do so with confidence. But this concept was virtually impossible for lawmakers and newspaper editors to understand. Instead, an otherwise sound bank was "bad" if it did not redeem its notes in an era of economic stringency.

SPECIE PAYMENTS RESUME

Specie payments did resume on May 10, 1838, in New York City, and many if not most other banks in the United States (except those in Philadelphia) followed suit. The Bank of the United States of Pennsylvania, which continued to mislead many citizens by leaving *of Pennsylvania* off of its paper money, agreed to resume its specie payments on August 13, 1838. Nicholas Biddle was still in charge, but the going was rough.

During 1838, trade and commerce improved, and conditions became somewhat better, although toward the end of the year more financial problems developed. Some banks that had resumed specie payments were forced to suspend again. Some other banks did not pay out gold and silver until early in the next decade. These were among the fortunate ones, for hundreds of banks failed during the Hard Times era. By this time a common sentiment was that the Panic of 1837 was the direct result of Jackson's veto of the charter of the second Bank of the United States and the winding down of that institution in 1836.

In 1838 the bank's successor in name (partial) only, the Bank of the United States of Pennsylvania, engaged in great speculation, which ultimately caused its downfall, and on October 10, 1839, it closed its doors. The entire banking system felt repercussions. By this time, 343 out of an estimated 850 banks in the country were said to have closed entirely and 62 had closed partially. The U.S. government lost $2 million in deposits.

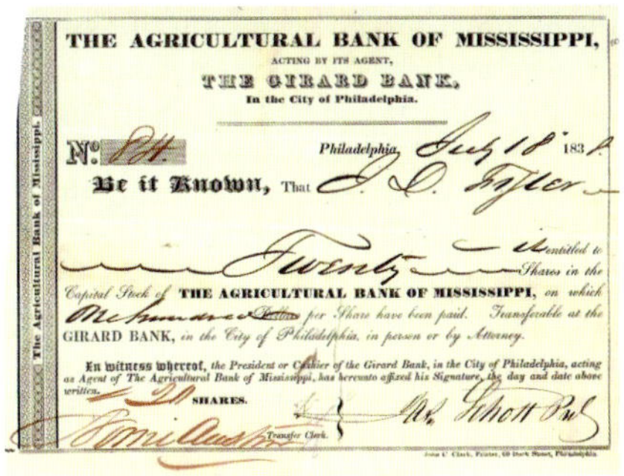

Stock certificate of the Agricultural Bank of Mississippi, located in Natchez, issued in 1838 through its agent, the Girard Bank of Philadelphia.

Railroads continued to be the growth industry of the era. *The American Almanac for 1836* reported that as of January 1, 1835, there were 2,867 miles of completed canals and approximately 1,600 miles of completed railroad track. In 1835, 465 miles of new railroad track were laid, followed by 175 miles in 1836, 224 in 1837, 416 in 1838, and varying amounts from that point onward. Anticipation of land opening up by the laying of track furnished an incentive to buy real estate, although the Hard Times era necessarily inhibited extensive activity in this area. While many canals remained in use, no new large ventures were undertaken.

In 1838, branch Mints were opened at Dahlonega, Georgia; Charlotte, North Carolina; and New Orleans. The Philadelphia Mint continued to be the main facility.

Although no reliable data exist, one historian estimated these figures for currency in circulation during the decade, plus the total of specie held by banks (and not in general circulation) and the ratio to paper notes issued:

1820—Specie: $19,800,000. Paper money: $44,800,000. Ratio specie to paper: 1 to 2.26.

1830—Specie: $22,100,000. Paper money: $61,300,000. Ratio specie to paper: 1 to 2.77.

1834—Specie: No estimate. Paper money: $94,800,000. Ratio specie to paper: 1 to (?).

1835—Specie: $43,000,000. Paper money: $103,600,000. Ratio specie to paper: 1 to 2.4.

1836—Specie: $40,000,000. Paper money: $140,300,000. Ratio specie to paper: 1 to 3.5.

1837—Specie: $37,900,000. Paper money: $149,100,000. Ratio specie to paper: 1 to 3.9.

1838—Specie: $33,100,000. Paper money: $116,100,000. Ratio specie to paper: 1 to 3.5.

1839—Specie: $45,100,000. Paper money: $131,100,000. Ratio specie to paper: 1 to 2.9.

1840—Specie: $33,100,000. Paper money: $106,900,000. Ratio specie to paper: 1 to 3.2.[17]

Hard Times at the Suffolk Bank

The Suffolk Bank system, established in Boston in 1824, worked very well for the New England banks it served, but it was not flawless. Often a member bank would have deposits insufficient to cover an unexpected quantity of its bills presented for exchange. In such instances the Suffolk Bank usually took in the bills, then charged the member bank interest on the transaction and required immediate additional funds to be deposited. In the years from 1831 to 1833, the Suffolk Bank experienced problems when large quantities of bills were in its hands, but member banks were slow in paying into their deposit accounts.

After the general suspension of specie payments in May 1837, the Suffolk Bank was forced to stop redeeming bills in coins. Certain banks in Maine in particular had problems maintaining their deposit accounts during this period, and the Suffolk Bank stopped receiving their bills.

A curious thing happened in certain states, such as Massachusetts, where banks were prohibited from issuing bills of less than a dollar. Large quantities of bills of such odd values as $1.25, $1.50, and $1.75 were ordered and placed into circulation to help with transactions and were enthusiastically received. The New England Bank Note Co. and Terry, Pelton & Co. printed many of them. The practice of issuing such denominations to help take the place of coins was used elsewhere as well, including by the Vermont Glass Factory earlier studied.

As the Hard Times era continued, the Suffolk Bank issued reports advising the public as to which bills it would not receive. The roster of January 1, 1839, included these *broken banks*, as failed or questionable institutions were designated, not including Maine. Certain of these banks later recovered:

> *Massachusetts:* Nahant Bank of Lynn, Chelsea Bank of Chelsea, Franklin Bank of Boston, Commonwealth Bank of Boston, Middlesex Bank of Cambridge, American Bank of Boston, Kilby Bank of Boston, Roxbury Bank of Roxbury, and Farmers and Mechanics Bank at South Adams (new listing)

New Hampshire: Wolfborough Bank

Vermont: St. Albans Bank, Manchester Bank, Essex Bank at Guildhall

Connecticut: Stamford Bank, Citizens Union Bank at Scituate, Fairfield County Bank at both Norwalk and Danbury

Rhode Island: Centreville Bank at Warwick, Citizens Union Bank at Scituate, Pawtuxet Bank, and Village Bank at Smithfield.[18]

Frogtown and Skunktown Capers

As a lagniappe to end this chapter, it may be fitting to include excerpts from a speech given by the Honorable W.D. Kelley in Indianapolis in August 1875, recalling the early days of banking, an ideal introduction to the next chapter:

> Do you know where the phrase "carpet-bagger" came from? The younger men of our day think it was invented to describe a man from the North who went South [after the Civil War] and got an office.
>
> Oh, no; not at all. The older members of my audience will attest the truth of what I say when I state that the phrase "carpet-bagger" arose from the fact that nearly every specie basis bank had its carpet-bagger—a fellow it sent with notes by the carpet-bag full into some distant state to get them into circulation there. If he could not buy cattle, corn, hogs or something else in which there might be a profit, he was to enter into a treaty with the carpet-bagger or other officer of some bank out there for an exchange of notes. For instance:
>
> The Frogtown bank—for I am told there were banks located occasionally in almost impenetrable swamps, and in those days, you must remember, there were no telegraphs and but few railroads—the fellow from Frogtown would get way out into Skunktown, another almost inaccessible place, and he would effect an exchange of ten, twenty, or thirty thousand dollars of Frogtown bank notes for a like amount of Skunktown bank notes, and the Skunktown bankers would put off the Frogtown notes on their customers, and the Frogtown bankers would put off the Skunktown bank notes on their, and thus they would go on with this legitimate business to their common advantage.
>
> I am giving you a historic fact when I tell you that I first became acquainted with that term in designating those fellows who were traveling from one out-of-the-way place to another with a carpet-bag full of notes to exchange, so that the notes put in circulation in Skunktown couldn't find their way back to Frogtown, because the people in Skunktown didn't know where Frogtown was, and the people in Frogtown didn't know where Skunktown was—and if they did they couldn't get there; the people in one place couldn't get to the other to get the specie on which the notes were based.
>
> Then after the bank at Frogtown had paid out the Skunktown notes, the bank at Frogtown would refuse to receive the Skunktown notes, but it would send the holder, who was its debtor, around the corner to a broker, who would buy them at seven or nine per cent discount, and then the broker and the bank would divide the proceeds of this basis transaction. That is what was going on all over the country.[19]

Numismatic Notes

The Hard Times era is especially well documented by a paper and metal trail of items that are highly collectible today. Scrip and bank bills of the late 1830s are plentiful in the marketplace, and a wide assortment can be obtained for modest cost. Copper (mostly) Hard Times tokens are a specialty pursued by many collectors.

Wildcats and Quasi-Banks

Paper Money in Profusion

At the approach of and continuing into the Hard Times era, many areas in the country saw the growth of banks with scarcely any assets other than stacks of freshly printed bank notes turned out by Philadelphia, New York City, or Boston engravers and printers. This newspaper account of August 30, 1837, is typical:

> The *Portland Argus* states that the managers of the Oxford County Bank, Maine, have commenced the issue of notes. This bank was chartered in 1836, but was not organized within the time prescribed by law and consequently has no legal existence. The notes therefore are probably valueless. It is stated in the *Boston Atlas* that they are not intended for circulation in Maine, but are manufactured for New York and the southern market.[1]

The Oxford County Bank, of Fryeburg, Maine, unleashed a flood of Perkins Patent Stereotype Steel Plate bills obligingly furnished by the New England Bank Note Company in Boston and another firm in the same city. As in earlier times, banks that engaged in curious practices or that failed made news accounts, while properly managed institutions generally did not. Accordingly, banks showcased in the popular press tended to be bad examples of the business. It is the notes of such banks that are often the most collectible today, as they were never redeemed. Numismatists are fortunate that many of the most available bills have some of the most interesting stories.

As to whether certain of these institutions were really banks is a matter of question and opinion. Some had state charters, but many did not. Some were con-

These $5 and $10 bills of the Oxford County Bank, Fryeburg, Maine, were issued by speculators who sold them at deep discounts to exchange brokers in New York City and farther south. This bank, granted a charter in 1836, never organized and never went into the banking business. Its owners simply ordered large quantities of bills. The currency was printed by the New England Bank Note Co., Boston, from later-style Perkins Patent Stereotype Steel Plates with inserted slugs for the bank name and address. Nearly all seen in collections today show evidence of extensive use, confirming that the fraud was successful.

A $50 note of the Oxford County Bank, Fryeburg, Maine, from a plate by Terry, Pelton & Co., Boston and Providence. Similar to the Perkins technique, this was also a modular arrangement, with THE OXFORD BANK, FRYEBURG, and MAINE inserted by slugs into a plate that could be used to print bills from anywhere. Probably, by using the services of both the New England Bank Note Co. and Terry, Pelton & Co. at the same time, the operators of the bank could reduce attention being made to the quantities of bills they were ordering. However, it was the practice of bank-note companies at the time to keep filling orders for bills and ask no questions.

ceived with all good intentions, but then their directions changed. There was even an *anti-bank* that issued notes. All of these examples are fascinating to contemplate, and several are discussed in this chapter.

In addition to such issuers as the Oxford County Bank and other paper mills (as they were often called), hundreds of merchants, some banks, and many other entities issued fractional scrip notes. Regarding these, some contemporary accounts of shinplasters and money in general in New York City may be of interest.[2]

New York City in the Summer of 1837

The following are selected items mentioning coins and paper money from the *Evening Chronicle,* New York City, in the several months immediately following the May 10, 1837, suspension of specie payments. They provide a window on how paper money, especially fractional bills, were viewed at the time. The wholesale buying and selling of banknotes is illustrated as well. Modern comments are added in italics after each item, and within the original text some explanations have been added in brackets.

> **June 15, 1837:** Specie and Gold—Benton's mint drops, Mexican dollars, American halves, and sovereigns, bought and sold by THOMAS D. CARPENTER. No. 13 Wall Street. FOR SALE—$5,000 American halves, $1,000 Southern Life and Trust, Lumbermens bank notes bought.

This is a typical advertisement by a specie and exchange dealer. "Benton's mint drops" refers to $2.50 and $5 gold coins minted beginning August 1, 1834, of a lighter standard weight than earlier issues. All gold and silver coins listed were sold at a premium in terms of paper money. Certificates for $1,000 with the imprint of the Southern Life and Trust Company, of Tallahassee, Florida, were essentially worthless (see also Niles' National Register, *December 19, 1840, by which time the matter was in court). The Lumbermens Bank of Warren, Pennsylvania, issued large amounts of worthless paper money. This was bought and sold for cents on the dollar by brokers, who sold the notes to sharpers, who tried to pass such bills to unsuspecting merchants.*

> **June 19, 1837:** Castle Garden—H. MARSH respectfully informs his patrons and the public that the Garden, having been extensively improved and embellished in a novel and attractive style, is now open for the season. His well known and justly celebrated band, under the direction of Mr. Thomas Dilks as leader, is re-engaged, and will perform the most approved overtures, marches, airs, &c., every pleasant evening. N.B.: A piece of fireworks every fair evening at nine o'clock. Admittance one shilling, for which refreshments will be furnished at the bar.

In New York City in 1837, the word shilling *often referred to a Spanish-American two-*real *coin or to a United States quarter dollar (of slightly higher value), not to a British shilling coin.*

> **June 20, 1837:**—Small Notes—Small Notes—Small Notes—For change, engraved expressly for storekeepers, hotels, tradesmen, manufacturers, &c., to supply the present scarcity of specie. The great demand for these notes have made it necessary to engrave an entire new set on Steel Plates, with beautiful vignettes, the high finish of which renders them secure from counterfeit. Notes for $1, 75, 50, 25 and 12-1/2 cents, printed on bank note paper, equal to bank bills in appearance and

The Lumbermens Bank at Warren, Pennsylvania, was a sham operation in which nearly the entire amount of its capital had been paid for by loans to its stockholders. Its bills were essentially worthless in the summer of 1837, as discussed here, but so many were in circulation that they furnished a lively trade for exchange brokers.

Shown here are two proof impressions from plates by Underwood, Bald, Spencer & Hufty, one of the leading engraving firms of the era. Each has handsome medallion vignettes made by a medal-ruling machine. Similar to others in the business, the UBS&H partnership simply printed notes and asked few if any questions. Most of these were passed by agents in western New York state.

On January 31, 1838, the *Financial Register* reported that the bank, which "has been fluttering in the wind for nearly a year past, has finally gone by the board, and its doors are closed." On February 20, 1838, a meeting of interested people was held in Jamestown, New York, across the state border from Warren. It was revealed that up to that point the bank had issued about $345,000 in bills. At the time the bank had $25 in silver and gold coins and eight boxes containing copper cents to the value of about $100. In March, representatives of the bank bravely urged that it would return to soundness, and in the meantime the public should honor its notes!

beauty, payable to bearer at sight in trade or bankable bills. The above notes are now ready for delivery. Orders from any part of the United States promptly attended to, on application to J. NEALE, Engraver and Printer, 6 John St., 5 doors from Broadway, N.B. Tradesmen and country merchants are invited to call and see specimens previous to making their purchases.

Fractional paper notes, often called shinplasters, flooded circulation in 1837 in the absence of silver and gold coins. Most but not all were typeset, not usually made from engraved steel plates, although engraved decorations were often added.

June 26, 1837: MONEY MARKET—Monday, 1 o'clock, P.M. The opinion that the banks in all sections of the Union have been extending their issues [paper money] beyond a wholesome limit since the suspension, is being confirmed every hour. Much has been done *sub rosa.* The position assumed in this morning's *Herald* is a true one. It will be seen that promises to pay will so increase that no power in the country can put a stop to them but a determination on the part of the government and the people to regard them as domestic bills of exchange. We must, in self-defense, cease to regard them as a currency for the value they express on their face. Let every artisan and every *sure* merchant conduct his business with reference to the silver dollar, and all will yet be right.

City notes [currency of New York City banks] are rising, as will be seen by reference to our coin table. This is indicated by the fall in the price of specie. We have every reason to believe that this is the effect of a combination among their lordships, the brokers, in order to buy all they can, to be prepared against the last proximo. A day or two before the sailing of the next packet they will mount it up again, and thus are we to be subject to the variations in the price of bank notes, dependent entirely on the will of a small body of men wielding the great criterion of commerce. There is no other way of accounting for this variation in the price of specie.

The banks are in no better condition for the last two days. They are no nearer resuming specie payments. In shunning the irresponsible body of banks who have preyed so long on the vitals of the country through the special benefit of the *scientific lie,* that they would redeem their notes in specie on demand, we run into the arms of an equally irresponsible body of men, entitled brokers, who to favor their own interests will mount up or knock down the specie value of bank rags at pleasure. There is this difference however. The brokers will pay in specie what they promise to do. The banks have violated that pledge. But the evil of the variations mentioned above is only incident to the present out-of-joint times. The brokers should take care not to lose the public confidence as the banks did.

Stocks are sluggish today. This is pretty much the case every Monday. United States shares;—no sales. The variation since Friday in the price of Mexican dollars is 1-1/2 percent.—We give the following specie rates today—Sovereigns 5.40 to 5.45; Spanish dollars 112-5/8 to 113; Mexicans ditto 111 to 112; Doubloons $18; Patriot ditto 17 to 17.62-1/2; Half dollars 110 to 111.

This report on the money market in New York City includes an observation on the varying premiums of bank bills needed to buy coins. Spanish-American coins were much more plentiful in the hands of the public than were U.S. silver or gold coins, and all traded at a premium. It cost $1.10 to $1.11 in bank notes to buy two silver half dollars.

June 27, 1837:—Specie Paying Banks—The following *small* institutions pay specie for their paper, while the great "Pennsylvania measure" that was to give the people a sound and uniform currency, was forced to close its vaults, to save the Monster [Bank of the United States of Pennsylvania] from destruction, not being able to pay depositors their claims let alone to redeem its paper circulation. The North-Western Bank of Virginia; the Bank of Marietta, Ohio; the Bank of Xenia, Ohio; Bank of Dayton, Ohio; Franklin Bank of Washington, Pa.; and the Paterson Bank of New Jersey. The Brooklyn banks suspended specie payments for a few days, but now redeems all her notes with the constitutional currency, gold and silver.—*Pitt. Bulletin*

A report on certain banks that were currently exchanging their bills at par for United States gold and silver coins, such institutions being only a small fraction of the banks in the country. No reliable listing of specie-paying banks during this period has ever been compiled by historians. The matter is complicated by the lack of nationally published information (most announcements appeared in local papers, rarely in large city papers or financial journals), and banks that paid specie one week might suspend the week after, then resume again—depending on their supply of coins.

July 1, 1837: Small Change—The panic, which induced many persons to secrete and refuse to pay out the small coins in their possession, seems to be removed. Small change circulates about as freely here, for ought we can perceive, as it ever did. This is as it should be. There is enough of it, if it is not hoarded.—*Salem Gazette, June 20th.*

This report from Salem, New Jersey, referred only to that district, and apparently only to small denominations of coins.

July 6, 1837: Banks—Of thirty-five banks chartered in Maryland since its existence as a state, sixteen have failed, and all have stopped payment.

Self-explanatory.

July 8, 1837: Defense of Shin Plasters—Philadelphia, 6th July, 1837. Your great penetration has not taught you that the present condition of what is called the currency of the U. States is more natural and more beneficial to its various classes of trades and occupations, than the monopoly system of banking which had prevailed from the year 1804 up to its last bankruptcy on 10th May, 1837.

Beginning with the first epoch, when the banks began issuing more cash bank notes than they had U.S. coins, we register annually a certain number of citizens buying charters from the state legislatures, ostensibly to loan money to the enterprise of society, but in fact to issue cash bank notes as a standard of value in lieu of the coins of the U.S. Mint. Thus in 40 years we count 800 joint stock companies located in every populous section, exercising the sovereign power of coining the representative of the federal standard of value without comparatively any bullion.

Thus the U.S. Mint, to issue a gold eagle coin, must possess 232 grains fine gold, whereas the banks to issue a rag engraved for $10, which they contract to redeem in specie, only possess about two grains pure gold or silver in their chests. The creation of certificates of stocks by states and improvement companies, promising to pay a higher rate of interest than is paid in Europe, had postponed until 1st Jan., 1836, the foreign demand on these banks to provide hard money for their bank notes; with this request they partially complied up to 10th May, 1837, when as they admit, *i.e.,* necessity or poverty compelled them to confess bankruptcy.

This then, I pronounce, is a grand epoch in the history of the destruction of a mighty order of combination of men uniting the purse and the sword of despotism, even in a republic. They have abandoned the magician's wand by which they governed the spell-bound understanding of the mass of the people, which was the action of paying specie for their bank notes on demand.

However the shin plasters may be denounced, they are the same genus as the bank notes, and probably equally convertible into standard coins. I repeat to you the fact that you have not registered in your *Herald* that the dynasty of chartered monopolies to issue an engraved paper called a bank note, for an exclusive standard of value, has gone by; the liberal party rejoiced in having *de facto* restored to the people their birthright, to exercise in their private station, what any crowd, or next, or bank, may do by the influence of money.

For better for worse we are now rank and file creators of paper money just as sound as that of the illustrious rag barons, holding the patent or sheepskin dooming to eternal disgrace the Tory loafers whose names and signatures are written thereon; but the 10th May came and proved them to be but a nest of impostors and charlatans, who, after 40 years of privilege, had not reserved strength enough to hold but $40,000,000 of specie to pay $230,000,000 millions of their bank notes. Up to this date bank notes were considered by the ignorant as money, as the exact counterpart of the U.S. money or coins; now the banks have proved this but a vision, and an old lie; they admit the said bank notes are but the representative of what they call paper securities, to wit, the promissory notes of citizens, which notes may not represent any tangible substance; hence the bank notes may represent moonshine; certainly they do not represent bullion or coins.

The great effort of the liberal party of the U. States for years has been to open a free trade in banking, by causing charters to be granted by legislatures to every applicant, since such documents are considered by the lawyers requisite to exercise a legal occupation; but the holders of the banking monopoly possessed too many bribed legislators in the halls. I call your attention to the position now occupied on this question by the liberal party; I assert they have triumphed by the suicide committed by the banks, causing their notes to become more collaterals for property, or evidences of transactions, the same as the promissory note of a trader issued on merchandise; in a word, bank notes have ceased to be a standard of value, and have become irredeemable, and are as much merchandise as horses, houses or brick-dust.

The proof then of the triumph of the liberal party, is that every citizen now enjoys the right of issuing bank notes, or any association may issue bank notes and transact any of the business heretofore monopolized by chartered banks, because neither banks, citizens nor combinations of men it is found dare to create coins, and the federal government is too ignorant to provide bullion for this mint.

This lengthy diatribe, partly tongue-in-cheek, against the perceived evils of paper money is representative of countless similar anti-paper commentaries published during this era.

July 14, 1837: Small Notes—Small Notes—Small Notes—Engraved in a superior style, and cheaper than any other in the market. The subscriber has published notes elegantly engraved on steel; of this following denominations, viz.: $1, 75, 50, 37-1/2, 25 and 12-1/2 cents, printed on good bank paper.—The public are solicited to call and examine for themselves, especially country merchants, store keepers, manufacturers, and steamboat proprietors, are solicited to call, as they are cheap and good. C.J. Holyland, Engraver and Printer, 48 Vesey Street, New York. N.B. Orders from all parts of the Union promptly executed. Engraving and printing on reasonable terms.

Advertisement for fractional bills, said to be made from engraved steel plates.

July 14, 1837: Small Notes Plates Engraved—For Twenty Dollars—The first houses in this city and elsewhere having now to issue small notes, frauds are daily committed by the facility of procuring similar blank forms. To remedy this J. Latham being a practical engraver can furnish plates to order for the above sum to suit; for 75, 50, 25, and 12-1/2 cents; thus effectively preventing counterfeits. Those requiring any number, will find the expense less (in addition to the security) than using those in general circulation. J.L.'s superior small notes, the best published, to be had as usual, at 160 Greenwich Street, near Courtlandt Street.

J. Latham promised fractional bills engraved to order, of designs different from those now in the marketplace. In contrast, most bills issued by others were from set type and illustration blocks.

July 20, 1837: Great Shin Plaster Manufactory—These are terrible times in the Jersies, in the shin plaster way.—The authorities of Newark are

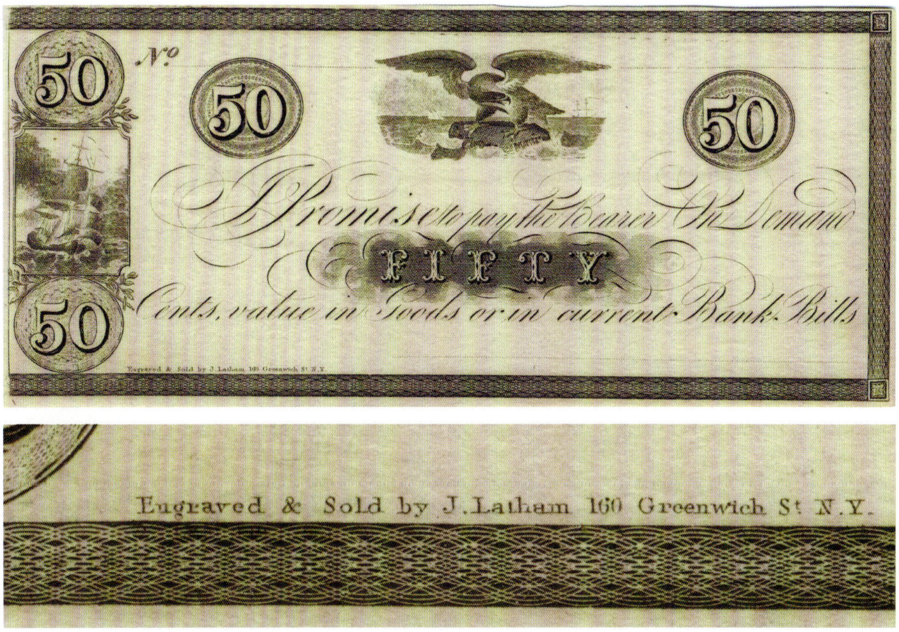

Generic 50¢ scrip note by J. Latham of New York City. Finely engraved and printed, these were available for the imprints of various merchants.

Odd-denomination $1.25 note issued by the Roxbury Bank, from a plate by the New England Bank Note Co. Roxbury, a suburb of Boston, became a part of Boston after the Civil War. Bills of $1.25, $1.50, and $1.75 values were popular in New England in 1837 and 1838, when coins were scarce in circulation.

engaged night and day in signing small bills, which are sold in sheets for current bank notes as fast as signed, and thousands brought to our city. The rule is, not to sell over five dollars worth to the same person, but that is easily evaded, and large quantities are purchased by many of our traders. Look out for counterfeits!

Fractional bills continued to proliferate, and large quantities from Newark, across the Hudson River, were brought to New York City.

July 22, 1837: Shin Plasters. Several Boston banks have issued bills for $1.25, $1.50, and $1.75. This is another expedient to drive all the small change out of the market, and increase the already overgrown circulation of the eastern banks.

In the course of a week, thousands of these notes will be here in circulation. Now is the harvest of dishonest bank directors and scoundrel counterfeiters. Wait till the establishment of the new national bank next fall, and you will see banks, small notes, and shin plasters, melt like dew before the sun, or an ice-cream in the mouth of a pretty woman.

Most Boston banks were solid during the first year of the Hard Times period. The bills of odd denominations were issued to facilitate transactions when coins were not in circulation, not to drive coins from circulation! The "new national bank" is a reference to Nicholas Biddle's Bank of the United States of Pennsylvania, which many people, including more than a few newspaper editors, erroneously thought was simply a new version of the second Bank of the United States.

July 25, 1837: The highest premium given for $10,000 in American halves. Wanted—American gold, sovereigns, and Napoleons—Lumbermens bank notes bought and sold, and also the notes of the State Bank of Alabama, and certificates of deposit payable at Mobile. THOMAS D. CARPENTER, 13 Wall Street. N.B. For sale—A lot of small change, or it will be exchanged for half dollars.

Another advertisement from this exchange broker (also see June 15, 1837). Half dollars were the most plentiful large-denomination silver coins. Many were in the hands of the public and brokers, but all continued to trade at a premium in terms of bank bills or fractional paper.

August 10, 1837: Notice of Partnership.—E.J. Sylvester and Edmund Charles have this day associated themselves as partners under the firm of CHARLES & CO., to carry on the business of exchange and bullion brokers, at No. 7 Courtlandt Street, New York.

Charles & Co., solicit the patronage of their respective friends and the public to the above firm, and assure them that all business confided to their care will be done upon the best terms, and the highest prices will be given for gold, silver, and uncurrent money.

This item reveals a new entry among the dozens of brokers active in the city. In this era numismatists called upon exchange brokers in their quest for interesting coins. In New York City there was just one professional numismatist whose name is known today: John Allan, who had been in the trade since at least 1822.

August 11, 1837: Shin Plasters—Counterfeits upon shin plasters are becoming common in Baltimore and other places. All the better, it will put a stop to the issuing of such trash.

Wishing would not make it so, and fractional bills continued to be plentiful in circulation.

August 14, 1837: Small Notes for Change—Great Reduction in Price.—J. Neale, 6 John Street, 3 doors from Broadway, having engraved three sets of steel plates, is enabled to sell notes for 75 cents per 100, and $1.25 per 100, large size. Having on hand upwards of 30,000 notes, he can furnish them at the above prices, being 25 per cent below the original cost, to storekeepers, manufacturers, and tradesmen generally. Steamboat and railroad companies would do well to give him a call and examine some splendid specimens. The denominations are 12-1/2, 25, 50, 75 cents and

> $1 with beautiful vignettes, and printed on bank paper, superior in execution to any in the city.
>
> Visiting, address and store cards, engraved and printed at prices to suit the times. Small notes for individuals, companies and public institutions, engraved in a superior style, at the shortest notice.

It seems that Neale preprinted currency from his plates, and afterward added the printed names of merchants to order. Also see Neale's advertisement of June 20, 1837.

> **August 15, 1837:** Gold and Bullion Office No. 64 Wall Street, 2 doors from Pearl.—Thomas Barnard, dealer in bullion, &c. continues to give the highest price for sovereigns, doubloons, Bank of England notes, uncurrent notes, &c. Also, on hand and constantly kept for sale fine gold rolled silver and imported plated metal. Gold and silver melted and assays made.

Barnard was one of many exchange brokers in the city. The "assays made" service is typical, as assaying required great skill.

> **August 28, 1837:** Philadelphia shin plasters of every denomination bought at CHARLES & Co.'s Exchange and Bullion Office, No. 7 Courtlandt Street, between the York House and Western Hotel. Also, Lumbermens bank bills, Ohio and Southern money, and American, English and French gold. The highest price given for half and quarter dollars. $5,000 wanted immediately in halves and quarters.

This recently formed partnership bought Philadelphia notes singly or in small groups at a deep discount, bundled them, and then redeemed them in Philadelphia. Deeply discounted bills of the Lumbermens Bank at Warren, Pennsylvania, continued to enjoy a lively trade in New York.

THE MANUAL LABOR BANK

T.W. DYOTT, ENTREPRENEUR

In the annals of the American glassmaking industry the name of Thomas W. Dyott is among the best known.[3] The same can be said for his prominence in the history of patent medicines. In numismatics he is by no means even a supporting actor, so obscure is the memory of him, but the currency produced under his direction forms a very interesting story. Dyott's notes are highly collectible today.

Born in England, Dyott came to Philadelphia in about 1795. Among his first business ventures was a bootblacking shop, for which he made his own blacking by mixing chemicals. By 1806 he was selling patent medicine, a trade for which there were few ethical boundaries. Claims of cures from the marvelous to the absurd could be made without contradiction. Although most patients who were sick eventually got better anyway even without medicine, the taking of medicines produced many "cures." Testimonials from happy customers were easy to get.

In 1807 Dyott was listed as owner of the Patent Medicine Warehouse at 57 Second Street, and in 1809 we find him listed under Robertson's Family Medicine at 116 North Second Street. Among products offered were Robertson's Infallible Worm Destroying Lozenges. In 1811 his Gout and Rheumatic Drops were advertised to "cure all kinds of green wounds, cramps, stones and gravel, and frozen limbs." Pity the poor soul who relied on Dyott's products. By 1812 he

Detail of a scene in a bottle-glass factory such as that operated by T.W. Dyott. (From a Manual Labor Bank note)

was listed as T.W. Dyott, M.D., although whether he ever earned a medical degree is uncertain. There were few rules limiting the titles and degrees one could claim in advertising. In any event, the Philadelphia *General Advertiser,* July 1, 1815, included an item by Dyott, "Long experience and extensive practice in the City of London, the West Indies, and for the last nine years in the City of Philadelphia."

The Philadelphia *Democratic Press,* September 17, 1817, included this item:

> Olive Glass Works. The proprietors of this glass works beg leave to acquaint publishers and the public that as a new blast is commenced they will feel obliged by having early orders for bottles, vials, or any hollow-ware of any form in the mak-

ing of which their attention will be given to please their friends, both in quality and figure, and every exertion made as to punctuality in time for execution.

All orders for this factory are received at the drug store of T.W. Dyott, North-east Corner of Second and Race Street.

The *United States Directory for the Use of Travelers and Merchants* (1822) listed Dyott as "Wholesale druggist and colorman, manufacturer of window glass, bottles, vials, etc. Nos. 137–139 northeast corner Second and Race streets."

Seemingly, by this time Dyott was not only compounding patent medicines, but also making the bottles in which they were sold. In this and other eras, he was sometimes listed as the proprietor and preparer of nostrums bearing the names of others, such as Dr. Thomas Vicker's Embrocation for the Rheum, Robertson's Nervous Cordial, and Tissot's Rheumatic Drops.

During the same decade there was a great demand for glass vials and bottles with patriotic motifs, including images of Washington and Lafayette during 1824 and 1825, the time that Lafayette, French hero of the American Revolution, revisited the United States and was proclaimed by Congress as "the Nation's Guest." A Dyott advertisement in the *United States Gazette,* Philadelphia, October 19, 1824, offered "Washington, LaFayette, Franklin, Ship Franklin, Agricultural and Masonic, Cornucopia, American Eagle, and common ribbed Pocket Flasks." Such products, including some vanity productions with Dyott's own portrait, caused him to be remembered and honored by a later generation of collectors of early American glass.

By 1831 he was sole proprietor of the Philadelphia and Kensington Glass Works, the name of which was soon changed to the Dyottville Glass Works. Certain aspects of production were supervised by Michael Dyott, the owner's brother, who had recently arrived from England.

As profits rolled in, Thomas W. Dyott developed Dyottville, a spread of 300 acres at the mouth of Gunner's Run on the Delaware River. This settlement featured four factories plus facilities offering conditions and amenities said to be ideal for workers, including living quarters, a church, a school, and even a temperance society, the last being one of the most popular social causes of the era. On January 4, 1835, Dyott made his debut as a newspaper publisher with the first issue of the *Democratic Herald and Champion of the People,* indicating that it was pro-Jackson and anti-Whig. In the meantime he enjoyed the trappings of success, including riding through the streets in a fine coach drawn by a span of four horses, flanked by attendants on their own steeds.

Establishing the Bank

In Dyott's position as lord of the manor, so to speak, a bank fit in nicely with his scheme. In 1833 Dyott petitioned the state legislature for a charter, enlisting his influential friend Stephen Simpson in the endeavor. Intended to cast favor on the venture, he published a treatise, *An Exposition of the System of Moral and Mental Labor Established at the Glass Factory of Dyottville,* in which he claimed that workers could achieve unprecedented contentment in ideal surroundings.

However, Dyott's application did not meet with success. Undaunted, on February 2, 1836, he established a Savings Fund into which the public could make deposits. Simpson was named as cashier at a salary of $3,000, Peter Y. Calder took the position of teller, and Dyott assumed the presidency. In May, the Manual Labor Bank, without benefit of a state charter, opened its doors at the northeast corner of Second and Race streets, earlier the location of Dyott's

Note for $50 of the Manual Labor Bank, Philadelphia, Pennsylvania, by Underwood, Bald, Spencer & Hufty, the supplier of currency to the enterprise. Dated February 2, 1836, this is a very early issue. At the center is a glassblowing scene, a common motif used on various denominations. At the left is the portrait of patent medicine king Thomas W. Dyott, while Benjamin Franklin, another famous citizen of Philadelphia, is at the right.

drugstore, which had been relocated next door to 139 Second Street. Among the first deposits was $13,000 from Dyott himself. Capital at the bank was announced as $500,000. The stated goal of the enterprise was to provide a "safe depository for the savings of labor," a lofty objective. The day-to-day operations were conducted by teller Calder, who, it later developed, knew little or perhaps even nothing about bookkeeping or finance.

The engraving firm of Underwood, Bald, Spencer & Hufty was given the contract to print bank notes of several different denominations, illustrated with a scene of the interior of a glass factory with workers engaged in making bottles. A portrait of Benjamin Franklin was on one side of each bill and that of Dr. Dyott on the other, perhaps representing Dyott's opinion of Philadelphia's most prominent citizens past and present.

This bank-note company was new on the Philadelphia scene and had just recently opened its doors in the Exchange Building. The principals and engravers were already well known and included Thomas Underwood, Robert Bald, Asa Spencer, Samuel Hufty, and Samuel Stiles. In New York City an office was maintained at 14 Wall Street under the directorship of Nathaniel and S.S. Jocelyn, well-known engravers who hailed from Connecticut. The firm lasted until 1843, when it was succeeded by the related partnerships of Bald, Spencer, Hufty & Danforth of Philadelphia, and Danforth, Bald, Spencer & Hufty of New York City.

Money rolled in from depositors, and the funds found ready use in financing Dyott's other enterprises. Even President Andrew Jackson seems to have endorsed the bank, per this comment in an advertisement in the Philadelphia *Public Ledger*, January 1, 1837:

> General Jackson says he can see no objection to your plan of business, with reference to your banking, as it is founded on a real security and must depend upon commercial credit for circulation which is all fair; but he is decidedly opposed to chartered monopolies, which sanction a paper credit, without a proper metallic basis.

As bank president, Dyott must have spent a lot of time hand-signing the bank's bills, probably many thousand sheets of them. It is likely that they were the currency of choice in Dyottville and were readily accepted at par elsewhere in the Philadelphia district.

FINANCIAL DIFFICULTIES

Dyott did not foresee the danger of the Panic of 1837—nor did many others. He thought that the unbridled prosperity of the early 1830s would continue forever. On May 11, 1837, in Philadelphia 11 banks suspended the payment of gold and silver coins in exchange for paper. Soon, all paper became dis-

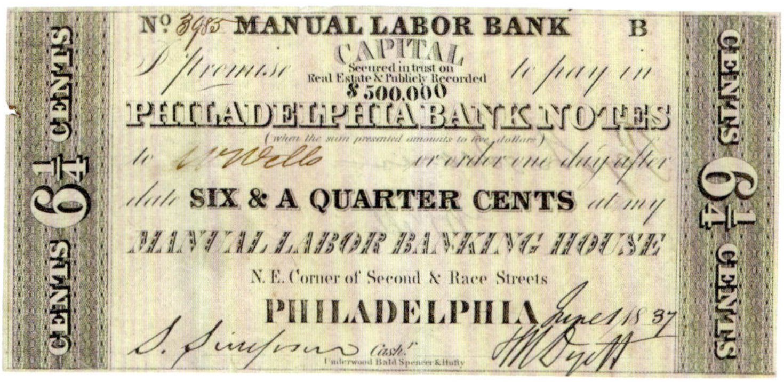

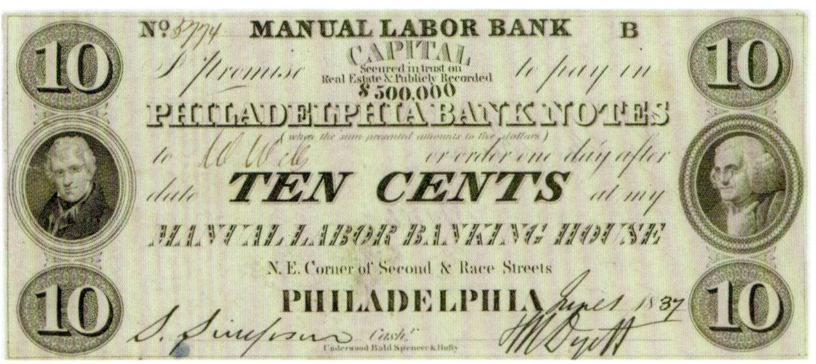

Scrip notes for 6-1/4¢ (equal to a Spanish medio or half-bit, a popular silver coin) and 10¢ issued by the Manual Labor Bank, dated June 1, 1837.

trusted, but there was little alternative to using it. Bills sold at a discount in terms of coins. Large-denomination bills in particular were viewed with suspicion in the marketplace.

On June 30, 1837, the *Saturday Evening Post* printed this item:

> Counterfeit & Loss Prevented: SMALL BANK BILLS
>
> The proprietor of the Manual Labor Saving Fund (at the request of, and to accommodate the public) having caused to be *inimitably* engraved, in first rate style, a series of plates, notes from $3 to 5 cts. printed on bank-note paper, is now prepared to supply a limited amount of same for public convenience.
>
> These bills effectually baffle all attempts to counterfeit them, and being issued on an ample *Security of Real Estate* and redeemed when presented in sums of $5 in the bank bills of this city, no loss can possibly accrue on them. Any amount of the same, not under 50 cents, will always be received on deposit, to the credit of the holder, at 6 percent interest, at the Saving Fund. N.E. corner Second and Race Streets.
>
> T.W. Dyott.
>
> Stephen Simpson, cashier
>
> Manual Labor Bank, June 22, 1837

According to an early account, these small bills were readily accepted by local merchants and tradesmen in return for goods and services, but they were not accepted at the city banks.

Beginning in July, Dyott began the wholesale transfer of his assets and businesses to his close relatives, taking notes in payment and sometimes charging rental, as in the case of the glass factory signed over to brother Michael. His 16-year-old son was set up as Thomas W. Dyott, Jr., & Co., retail grocers. The senior Dyott's stated purpose for making these changes was to permit him to spend more time with the increasingly busy and ostensibly prosperous Manual Labor Bank.[4]

Around November 1, a run on the Manual Labor Bank followed a rash of nasty rumors that the institution was on the brink of failure. Dyott sprang into action and, seemingly lacking silver and gold coins, announced a system whereby the bank's bills would be redeemed at par at local stores—actually a declaration of a system that had been working for a long time. Meanwhile, no other local banks were paying out specie either. On November 6, Dyott published a reward of $500 to be paid for the identification of the person who first circulated the rumor of the bank's instability.

In August 1838, Dyott announced the issuance of a popular type of currency used by many different banks at the time:

> Post Notes: The notes of the Manual Labor Bank dated one year after the date, either with or without interest of the denominations of 1, 2, 3, 5 and 10 dollars, are received at their full par value, the same as those notes payable on demand, at the stores of the subscribers, in payment for groceries, drugs, medicines, paints, glass ware, and every other kind of goods in their line of trade, at the lowest cash prices, either wholesale or retail.
>
> J.B. & C.W. Dyott, 139 and 141 N. Second Street
>
> T.W. Dyott, Jr. & Co., 143 N. Second Street
>
> M.B. Dyott, Dyottville Glass Factories
>
> NB Notes of larger denominations taken by specie contract.
>
> The Messrs Dyotts invite the attention of druggists, merchants, manufacturers, mechanics, store-keepers, farmers and all who are favorably disposed to the Manual Labor System and who may be in possession of any of the Manual Labor bank notes not to part with them below their full par value, but to call at their stores, where every attention will be paid to them.
>
> Fair prices in cash or store goods will be paid for all kinds of country produce and for goods generally of domestic manufacture.

By this time Dyott's debtors operating the businesses he leased and transferred were experiencing losses, as was the bank. However, Dyott endeavored to maintain the appearance of prosperity. He was hardly alone in this situation, for at the time thousands of businesses were failing all across the United States, and the Hard Times era had begun. His *Democratic Herald and Champion of the People* folded, as did a smaller paper he started, the *General Advertiser and Manual Labor Expositor.* Finally, in November 1838, Dyott filed for bankruptcy in the Insolvency Court. Notice of his status was published in December.

Aftermath

As various banks failed around the United States, their presidents, cashiers, and stockholders usually walked away from the enterprise without further obligation. Sometimes legal actions were instituted to recover funds, especially in instances in which shareholders simply gave IOUs rather than paying for capital stock, and owed cash. However, assets were few and far between, and neither stockholders nor the public received much for the shares or bills of failed institutions.

However, with Dyott the situation was different. He had positioned himself as a captain of industry, a man of great wealth living in regal circumstances.

A $100 note dated September 1, 1838, toward the end of the bank's existence.

Creditors of his enterprises denounced him as a fraud and called for his arrest on criminal charges. On February 5, 1839, Dyott's case was scheduled to be reviewed by a jury at the court. Upon arrival, Dyott was met with an angry mob. Hurriedly, he dashed into the nearby store of Jacob Ridgeway and escaped through the back door.

The case was held over, and the judge ordered Dyott bound over for $10,000 on a charge of fraudulent insolvency. On March 30, the grand jury returned a true bill against him. Then followed a long court trial, April 30 to June 1, on 11 indictments, later reduced to seven. Testimony was contradictory, presenting Dyott as everything from a benefactor to mankind who had simply suffered the widespread effects of the panic to a malicious criminal who sought to defraud his associates and creditors. On June 1, the jury returned a verdict against Dyott, guilty as charged on all counts.

The sentence was to be from one to seven years at hard labor, in solitary confinement, the length being at the discretion of the judge. On August 31, however, the judge delivered a sentence of three years of normal imprisonment. The case was appealed, Dyott lost again, and he went to the Eastern Penitentiary. After serving about a year and a half, he was pardoned by Governor David Rittenhouse Porter and became a free man.

Soon, his creditors caused his re-arrest as a debtor, and he was sent to the Debtor's Apartment at the Moyamensing Prison, where he stayed for just a week or two after Daniel Man stood as surety for his future appearances in the Insolvency Court. His assets were liquidated by sheriff's sale and auction in 1841. It was estimated that the approximately $250,000 due to depositors and bill holders of the Manual Labor Bank might yield about 10 cents on the dollar.

In time, although Dyott never became prominent in business, he fit back into the community. Products bearing his name were advertised well into the 1840s, these including Dyott's Toothache Drops, Vegetable Purgative Compound, and Circassian Eye Water, among others.

Dyott lived among his friends in society until he died in 1861.

The Kirtland Safety Society Anti-Banking Co.

Seeking a Charter

The history of the Mormon religion in America has been well detailed in many books and countless studies.[5] Joseph Smith Jr. reported the discovery of ancient engraved plates or tablets on Mount Cumorah, near Palmyra, New York, and founded a religion based on the revelations expressed by the inscriptions. He soon attracted enthusiastic followers. On April 6, 1830, in Fayetteville, New York, the group was organized as the Church of Jesus Christ of Latter-day Saints. Among them was Oliver Cowdery, who had been ordained as an apostle in 1829 and who would later figure in the scenario of Mormon paper money. Members were referred to as "saints," often derisively in the popular press. The Book of Mormon (based upon a translation of the engraved plates), the practice of polygamy, and other aspects of the faith caused much condemnation by some, but others were attracted to it.

In 1836, under Smith's leadership, a large group of Mormons settled in Kirtland, Ohio, about 25 miles from where the city of Cleveland had been incorporated in the same year, following a growth that began with pioneers in 1796. Kirtland grew quickly from about 1,000 residents to more than 2,500. A temple for worship was constructed, and in the district the

Mormons erected houses and attended to everyday activities such as farming. The Western Reserve, as that section of Ohio was known, offered rich lands to those who moved from New York, New England, and other locations where farming was more difficult and land was expensive. Money was scarce in Ohio, and land and buildings were often acquired on credit, with obligations to be repaid from anticipated profits.

On November 2, 1836, a charter was drawn up for the Kirtland Safety Society Bank, with Joseph Smith to be president and Sidney Rigdon cashier. A capital of $4,000,000 was proposed, a very substantial sum for the era. Orson Hyde went to visit state authorities in Columbus with the expectation that a charter would be granted quickly. These were boom times in the Western Reserve, and many new businesses, including banks, were being formed—all necessary to the continuing growth of the region. An atmosphere of optimism prevailed, despite growing evidence of economic problems in coastal cities to the east.

In the meantime, Oliver Cowdery went from Kirtland to Philadelphia, the center of bank-note engraving and printing, and visited the recently formed partnership of Underwood, Bald, Spencer & Hufty, which also had an office in New York City (at 14 Wall Street, staffed by engravers N. and S.S. Jocelyn). The main partners, Thomas Underwood, Robert Bald, Asa Spencer, and Samuel Hufty, were in Philadelphia. Highly regarded as an inventor, Spencer claimed to be the inventor of the medal-ruling machine.

In Philadelphia, Cowdery viewed a selection of stock vignettes on hand and chose a currency series of $1, $2, $3, $5, $10, $20, $50, and $100, this being the same lineup used by many other banks of the era. Topics on the $1 note included farmers shearing sheep and, to the left and right, a passenger train. Medallion engravings completed the suite. Other bills featured more stock engravings, none of which had any particular relationship to either Mormons or Ohio.

Issuing Paper Money

On January 1, 1837, Cowdery returned to Kirtland, taking with him a large supply of freshly printed currency. All was prepared to engage in normal banking practice, except for one thing: the state did not act on the charter proposal, as it could not be demonstrated that even a significant fraction of the proposed capital could be raised.

All set, but with no charter, the Mormons decided to go ahead anyway. As a precaution they changed the name of their proposed business from the Kirtland Safety Society Bank to the Kirtland Safety Society *anti*-Bank-*ing* Society, organizing this on January 2, 1837, with Joseph Smith Jr. as the treasurer and Sidney Rigdon as the secretary. This change was made by printing "anti" and "ing" in small black letters as part of the bank title set in much larger letters on the bills. Shares were sold at varying prices, with 200 buyers participating, yielding a total of $19,644.70 in actual paid-in capital, mostly in specie.

On January 4, bills of the $1, $2, and $3 values were issued—with "president" and "cashier" blanked out, and with "anti" and "ing" stamped in the title. On a note illustrated here, "S. Rigdon Sec" was signed in ink at the left, and "N.K. Whitney Treas P.T." (treasurer pro tem) was inked at the lower right. The *anti-bank* was in business, with a treasurer and secretary. With such care taken, surely banking rules would not be violated.

The above procedure was viewed as clumsy and unnecessary, and later bills were paid out with the full imprints, unaltered, as originally printed. J. Smith Jr. (Joseph Smith) signed as president and S. Rigdon as cashier. Following an estimated $15,000 in *anti* bills issued in January, about $46,000 in unaltered bills of denominations $1 to $20 was circulated in February, and in March perhaps as much as an additional $65,000 was released, now including the higher denominations as well.[6] From the earliest times, it is likely that certain signatures were completed by an amanuensis or scribe, instead of the actual people named. Also, on certain bills the signature positions of Smith and Rigdon are switched, and other names were occasionally used. Beyond the sphere of numismatics, the signature of Joseph Smith is highly prized due to his position as a Mormon leader. However, numismatic historian Douglas Nyholm has written, "It is impossible to authenticate his signature on any single note."

But the operation did not proceed as smoothly as planned. A suit was filed against Smith, Rigdon, and others for operating an unchartered bank. In the meantime, the bank did not have sufficient specie with which to redeem its bills, a situation that created more problems. Soon, the malaise of the Panic of 1837 reached Ohio, and beginning in mid-May, banks suspended specie payments. Mormon residents of Kirtland, in common with many other settlers in the Western Reserve, could not meet obligations they had incurred for land purchases and construction. The situation was grim.

Note for $1 of the Kirtland Safety Society Anti-Banking Co. (top), a detail of that note (middle), and a related $3 bill (bottom), each issued in January 1837. All bills of this era bear the imprint of Underwood, Bald, Spencer & Hufty.

In June, Smith disassociated himself with the bank, and bills fell into the hands of "speculators, renegades, and gamblers who were duping the unsuspecting and unwary by palming off bills. . . ."[7] Smith warned his followers to beware. In November the bank was closed. In the meantime, in October, Smith and Rigdon were convicted in court and were fined $1,000 each for the charges brought earlier in the year. In the annals of banking in America in this era, the case was unusual and probably reflected anti-Mormon discrimination more than problems with an unauthorized bank, although this idea is conjecture. In the summer and autumn of 1837, there were hundreds of unauthorized issuers of bank notes and scrip in the United States, as has been seen in the present narrative, and few charges were ever presented against them.

Smith and Rigdon appealed their conviction, and while the matter was under consideration, they left the state with other Mormons, taking very little in the way of assets and leaving many debts behind. They relocated in Far West, Missouri, then moved to Nauvoo, Illinois. After unfortunate persecution, the saints went to their promised land in Utah and founded the settlement of Salt Lake City, which prospered and in time became a much appreciated stop for forty-niners on their way to seek gold in California.

Quantities of Kirtland Safety Society Bank bills remained and were taken westward to Salt Lake City, where some bills were reissued in 1849, now with the signature of Mormon leader Brigham Young. These were backed to the extent of 80% of face, by gold dust held in the Mormon treasury that had been brought to

A $10 note with unaltered imprint, ink dated March 8, 1837. It is not known today if *any* of the signatures on notes of Joseph Smith Jr., founder of the Mormon Church, are actually by his hand, or if they were done by a scribe.

The Bowery, coinage mint, and Brigham Young's house in Salt Lake City. (Howard Stansbury, *Exploration and Survey of the Great Salt Lake of Utah*, 1852)

Note for $5 of the Kirtland Safety Society Bank signed and issued in Kirtland in 1837, then reissued in Salt Lake City in 1849, now with the signature (by his hand) of Brigham Young, who succeeded Smith as leader of the Mormons.

Utah by Mormon soldiers returning from the war with Mexico. These soldiers had stopped to prospect for gold in and around the American River in California, where their largest encampment was on a sand and gravel area known as Mormon Bar.

The Bank of Monroe

As a postscript in the annals of numismatics, in early 1837 in Kirtland, the Mormons purchased the charter of the Bank of Monroe, located in Michigan, an institution that had been established on March 29, 1827, capitalized at $100,000, with an allowable maximum of $500,000. The institution had its own problems earlier, and in 1830 it landed on the "List of Broken Banks" in the inaugural issue of *Bicknell's Counterfeit Detector*. However, it went on to continue business. In 1835 the capital was stated at $30,000, and the bills in circulation amounted to $31,427. Concerning the Mormon connection, Alvin E. Rust gives this information:

> Notes dated 1 July 1836 were issued by the bank over Cowdery's signature. Cowdery probably served as vice president of the bank before the charter was acquired by the Mormon Church. Cowdery also served as scribe to Joseph Smith, Jr., the Mormon prophet, while the Book of Mormon was being translated.[8]

Notwithstanding the preceding, it was not until February 16, 1837 that Cowdery became an officer of the bank. He did not sign any notes prior to this date, although antedated bills exist. The church sold its interest later in 1837. The bank failed in 1838, with about $80,000 of its notes in circulation.[9] Notes on the Bank of Monroe are seen with some frequency today, but those with Cowdery's signature are rare.

The Free-Banking Era Begins

After the charter of the second Bank of the United States expired in 1836, and the Panic of 1837 became a reality when specie payments were suspended beginning on May 10, 1837, the stage was set to open new banks across the country—to provide more paper money for use in commerce. It was hoped that these new institutions would help business in general, facilitate local and regional trade, and induce prosperity—or at least that was the prevailing philosophy.

Previous to this time, most banks chartered by various states were set up after petitions had been sub-

A $3 note of the Bank of Monroe, Michigan, by Rawdon, Wright, Hatch & Edson, New York. Signed and dated September 21, 1836. Early in the next year the Mormons at Kirtland, Ohio, bought this bank.

mitted, reviews had been made, and political considerations had been weighed. Politics was an important factor—perhaps the *most* important—and those with good connections often could set up a bank, while members of an opposing political party or those who were resisted by individuals in state office met with failure. Because of this fact, existing banks with good connections in the state capital often strengthened themselves by preventing competition from arising. This, of course, had been the scenario from the beginning of the state-chartered bank business in the late 18th century.

Beginning with Michigan in 1837, and soon expanding to include other states, free-banking laws, as they were called, were put in place. Although provisions varied, under a typical law any group of people could apply for a bank charter. This charter would be given provided that securities, or evidence of such securities, could be furnished to the comptroller or treasurer of the state. Acceptable securities varied, but they usually included United States government bonds and state bonds. Sometimes other stocks, mortgages, and other investment paper were allowed. In instances in which bonds were actually deposited with the state, they drew interest, and thus were an investment for the bank at the same time they served as security for bills issued. In actuality, in certain states the *securities* were sometimes little more than IOUs, or mortgages on real estate with inflated appraisals, or worthless or overvalued stocks and bonds. Sometimes institutions with this supposed backing were called "state stock banks" or "government stock banks," titles that sounded impressive.

Free-banking laws were enacted in the following yearly sequence, these being the dates of the initial legislation. Often, the laws were later revised or even canceled. Terms and provisions varied widely:

1837: Michigan

1838: Georgia and New York

1849: Arkansas

1850: New Jersey

1851: Illinois, Maine, and Ohio

1852: Indiana, Rhode Island, Tennessee, and Wisconsin

1853: Florida

1858: Minnesota and Iowa

1860: Pennsylvania

The laws of 1837 and 1838 concern us in this chapter.

ASSORTED RULES AND REGULATIONS

Although policies of Michigan, Georgia, and New York varied and also underwent revision, most banks in these three states were required to redeem their notes in specie (gold and silver coin) on request. However, it soon became evident that with the Panic of 1837 in progress, this could not be done. Accordingly, new as well as old banks were allowed to suspend specie payments. For certain new banks that had little specie to begin with, this change was a godsend. It meant that currency could be issued with no requirement to redeem it except in other paper. Older, established banks enjoyed the situation as well. An examination of bank records during this era shows that most well-managed banks were well stocked with specie, often having about as much on hand as they did before the Panic of 1837 started. As earlier related, for a sound bank to pay out and deplete its stock of coins would reflect poorly on its financial statement and might cast unwarranted suspicion on the strength of the institution. The situation was complex, and no single scenario fit all banks.

In most states, banks were required to keep records and to submit statements on a regular basis, at least annually and sometimes quarterly. During the Hard Times period several states shortened the reporting times. New Hampshire, not a free-banking state, began requiring statements nearly each month. This particular state had relatively close oversight on its banks, and as a result frauds were few and far between. In contrast, in Michigan and certain other western states there was little supervision, and these areas became playgrounds for speculators.

Condy Raguet's Commentary of 1840

In 1840, under a chapter titled, "Of the Creation of Banks Without Capitals, or of Fraudulent Banks," Condy Raguet, well-known Philadelphia student of finance, wrote this definition:

> The term *fraudulent bank* is intended to be applied to a bank commenced without capital, or what is the same thing, a bank the stock of which is held by persons who have not the means of paying for it and who have consequently been obliged to hypothecate it to the bank as collateral security for stock notes discounted to meet the installments as called for.
>
> Books are opened to receive subscriptions to the capital stock, each share of which is to be $100, of which $5 per share is to be paid at the time of subscribing. The capital is to consist of 1,000 shares, equal to $100,000.
>
> The stock is not taken by capitalists, as a mode of investment, but by persons who subscribe as a matter of speculation with the view of selling out at a profit. The first installment, amounting to $5,000 being paid in, the directors are chosen from amongst these very speculators, who are expected to make the payment of the ensuring installments come easy to themselves and their constituents.
>
> A second installment of $10 is called for, but as the holders of the stock have no more money to pay in, they offer notes for discount and pledge their stock to the bank as collateral security. The third, fourth, fifth, and all subsequent installments are paid in a similar manner with stock notes; and, finally, the stockholders obtain an additional loan for the original $5 per share paid in, which may have been originally borrowed, and thus we have a bank with a nominal capital of $100,000, but possessing not one dollar of real capital. . . .
>
> The next step of the directors would of course be to issue bank notes in exchange for the promissory notes of individuals.[10]

The above scenario will be déjà vu to readers of this book, dating back to the era of Andrew Dexter Jr.'s Farmers Exchange Bank fraud. Today, numismatists interested in banking history could argue that not *all* banks organized in this manner were conceived in fraud. Some were simply short of capital and hoped for the best. However, Raguet's example plays well for the majority of such would-be institutions.

Balance Sheets, Good and Bad

At the time, the balance sheet of a typical bank would show assets in the form of bonds or other securities deposited with the state or said to be on hand, plus specie, plus "good" bank bills, plus discounts. Discounts or loans were apt to consist of miscellaneous amounts receivable at the bank and bearing interest—ranging from legitimate loans to individuals and businesses, to IOUs given for the payment of bank stock, the latter generally being of little or no real value.

Liabilities on the balance sheet would include the paid-in capital of the bank (which might include loans to stockholders), bills in circulation, and an account for profit and loss.

Bank statements from this era are difficult to evaluate without seeing original documents and reports of bank commissioners. Over a period of years I have done this for hundreds of banks, including *all* banks in the state of New Hampshire. In contrast to such reports, popularly published data, including annual reports of the condition of banks issued by the United States Treasury Department, do not analyze the numbers. Virtually without exception, books, articles, and dissertations on early 19th-century finance are based on printed reports rather than examination of original bank records or data.

A Tale of Two Banks

As a prelude to the discussion of free-banking and also as possibly useful general information, I insert here two hypothetical balance sheets. One is of a "good" bank, such as a long-established, solid old-line New England institution that has conducted its business profitably and has talented management. The other is of a "wildcat" bank, such as some set up under the 1837 General Banking Law of Michigan.

After each balance entry the *true nature* of the number is given in brackets, such information not being generally available to the casual reader of such statements years ago. As simple as these illustrations may seem when read today, similar information and comparisons are very hard to find in the annals of banking history:

Old-Line New England Bank (December 31, 1837)

Assets

Loans and discounts: $186,000 [Loans to businesses and individuals, not to officers or stockholders; mostly secured by mortgages and cosigners of repute; no single loan more than $10,000. Borrowers must keep interest payments current.]

Banking house: $2,000 [Brick building on Main Street owned by the bank. Offices downstairs. Upstairs rented to a Masonic Lodge.]

Furniture and fixtures: $500

Deposits in city banks for redemption of bills: $5,000 [Deposits at the Suffolk Bank, Boston, and other large city banks for the redemption of bills at par.]

Specie in the vault: $9,000 [Mixture of Spanish-American and United States silver and gold coins; in vault, not being paid out at par, because specie payments of all banks are in suspension.]

Securities: $21,000 [United States Treasury bonds; selected railroad stocks.]

Bills of other banks: $1,500 [Bills of regional banks that are worth par.]

Total: $225,000

Liabilities

Capital stock paid in: $100,000 [All paid in cash long ago; no IOUs to buy stock.]

Bills in circulation: $95,000 [Bills currently in commerce; others are within the bank and have not been issued, and thus are not part of the statement.]

Profit or loss: $18,000 [Accumulated profit on behalf of shareholders.]

Possible losses, reserve: $2,000 [Reserve for loans that may be losses, "slow" paper, etc. Last year only $525 in bad loans were charged off, and the year before that there were none.]

Dividends declared and payable: $10,000 [Declared by the board of directors but not yet paid to stockholders.]

Total: $225,000

Michigan Wildcat Bank (December 31, 1837)

Assets

Loans and discounts: $204,900 [includes $99,000 loaned to directors to buy stock; no director has paid any interest on his loan nor has any loan been reduced; the entire balance of the rest of the loan portfolio is to directors and stockholders and their friends; there are no regular commercial loans.]

Banking house: $0 [Premises are rented for $35 per month.]

Furniture and fixtures: $100

Deposits in city banks for redemption of bills: $0

Specie in the vault: $15,000 [This is for the record; the actual figure is less than $150! In the next month, when the bank commissioners stop by, the cashier will have on hand $15,000 in real coins, borrowed a few hours earlier from the Red Dog Bank of Michigan and returned immediately after the commissioners left.]

Securities on deposit: $0

Bills of other banks: $5,000 [Bills traded for this bank's currency; these are *really* worth very little.]

Total: $225,000

Liabilities

Capital stock paid in: $100,000 [Only $1,000 paid in specie, balance of $99,000 "paid" by loan certificates from the directors, who borrowed from this bank.]

Bills in circulation: $90,000 [This is per the official statement. However, at least $225,000 in bills is actually in circulation and $100,000 more is on hand waiting to be shipped to agents in the East for distribution.]

Profit or loss: $10,000 [Not per any real calculation, but added to the balance sheet for appearance.]

Dividends declared and payable: $25,000 [There is no *real* profit, but if this amount of specie can be obtained in exchange for a much larger face value in the bank's bills, it will be distributed privately to the directors. It is hoped that this number can be increased substantially as more bills are passed out.]

Total: $225,000

To the casual reader of newspapers, Treasury reports, and financial journals, each bank has $225,000 in assets. If anything, the Michigan Wildcat Bank seems to be the more profitable of the two! In actuality, its assets are worth $150 for the specie and perhaps $500 for the bills of other banks—or a total of $650. It is a fraudulent bank, a house of cards. On the other hand the Old-Line New England Bank's assets are worth a solid $225,000.

Actually, the Michigan Wildcat Bank *is* the more profitable, but only in an illegal way. In the past six months the directors have personally benefited themselves by using the bank's bills to buy farms in Indiana and Ohio and to sell tens of thousands of dollars' face value at a deep discount for hard cash to an agent in New York City.

The bills of the Michigan Wildcat Bank are virtually worthless, while those of the Old-Line New England Bank are worth full face value. However, in distant areas the recipients of Wildcat Bank bills might not know that. This is where bank-note reporters are useful—for, unless a deal has been made with a publisher to "puff" the Michigan Wildcat Bank, its bills may be listed at an 80% discount from par or may be listed as worthless. However, the value of bills is *not* a part of bank statements, Treasury reports, and other such data, and perhaps not even the publishers of bank-note reporters could learn the truth.

In 1836 the Michigan Territorial Legislature approved charters for the Calhoun County Bank (in Marshall), the Manhattan Bank (for Manhattan, *Ohio,* but chartered in Michigan), the Bank of Clinton, the Bank of Tecumseh, the Bank of Ypsilanti, the Bank of Constantine, the Bank of St. Clair, and the Bank of Macomb County (in Mount Clemens).

The Manhattan Bank was in an interesting setting, as related by Wendell Wolka:

> The hamlet of Manhattan was located in the so-called "Toledo Strip" in present day Lucas County, Ohio. In 1835 the state of Ohio and the territory of Michigan each sent militia forces to the strip of disputed land to assert their sovereignty over the area. The dispute arose from inaccurate land surveys which resulted in two different locations being reported for the southern tip of Lake Michigan which was used to define the border between Ohio and Michigan.
>
> Somehow the opposing forces missed each other in the swamps, and fortunately not a shot was fired. The United States government finally intervened, giving Ohio the Toledo Strip and Michigan the remainder of the Upper Peninsula not already included in its boundaries. The argument rages to the present day over who got the best of the deal.[11]

The city of Toledo went to Ohio, but some interesting currency from an earlier time issued by the Erie and Kalamazoo Railroad Bank is imprinted Toledo, Michigan.

With the preceding information as background, let us continue the discussion of banking in Michigan.

Wildcats Rampant in Michigan

Before the Free-Banking Era

The curious, indeed unique, financial history of Michigan in the early days drew the attention of a writer whose lengthy article, "Michigan 'Wild-Cats'—Early Banking in the State—Wild Financial Schemes of the Early Days—Banks in the Woods Without Capital," was published in Detroit on August 11, 1892.[12] A few edited excerpts treat the days *before* the "wildcats" roved:

Note for $1 of the Erie and Kalamazoo Rail Road Bank issued in Toledo, *Michigan,* dated December 17, 1840. From a plate by S. Stiles, New York.

A $2 note of the Bank of Gibraltar, Michigan, with the imprint, "Michigan Safety Fund, Secured on Real Estate." The Fund proved meaningless. Depicted as the center vignette is Hebe, cupbearer to the gods, here in the dual role of Miss Liberty, with liberty cap and pole. From a plate by Underwood, Bald, Spencer & Hufty.

> Among the many and varied relics in the possession of the Pioneer Society of Washtenaw County are the financial freaks known as "wild-cat money." . . . The Detroit Bank was the first formed and was set up in 1806. The next bank established in the territory was the Bank of Michigan, incorporated by the governor and judges Dec. 19, 1817, with a capital of $100,000. . . . By the terms of the charter the incorporation was to expire on the first Monday in June, 1839, but the legislative council, Feb. 25, 1831, extended its life 25 years longer, and subsequently it was allowed to increase the capital stock and establish a branch at Bronson, now Kalamazoo. The two banks above named were all the banks which derived their corporate existence from the governor and judges.
>
> The first bank charter granted by the Legislative council was the Merchants and Mechanics Bank of Michigan, approved April 2, 1827. The bank was to be established at Detroit with a capital of $200,000, with liberty to increase it to $500,000. This corporation was also made an insurance company, but there are no records that such a company was ever organized under this charter. March 29, 1827, the Bank of Monroe was incorporated, its capital stock to be $100,000 to $500,000 and to continue in existence 20 years. The Farmers and Mechanics Bank of Michigan was chartered November 5, 1829, and on March 7, 1834, it was allowed to increase its capital stock and establish a branch at St. Joseph.
>
> The Bank of River Raisin was chartered June 29, 1832, and was allowed to have a branch at Pontiac. The Bank of Wisconsin was chartered Jan. 23, 1835, and was to be located in the Green Bay country, but on the organization of the state of Michigan it was thrown outside of its jurisdiction.
>
> March 26, 1835, there were incorporated four banks—namely, Michigan State Bank at Detroit, Bank of Washtenaw at Ann Arbor, Bank of Pontiac, and the Erie and Kalamazoo Railroad Bank at Adrian. The Bank of Pontiac was also a railroad bank, its establishment being an amendment to the charter of the Detroit and Pontiac Railroad Company. The nine banks last named are all that were created by the legislative council.
>
> Next the state legislature in 1836 chartered the Bank of Manhattan, Calhoun County Bank, Bank of St. Clair, Bank of Clinton, Bank of Ypsilanti, Bank of Macomb, Bank of Tecumseh, and Bank of Constantine. The same legislature passed "an act to create a fund for the benefit of the creditors of certain moneyed corporations." Which was in fact the famous safety fund system of the state of New York. It required each bank to deposit with the state treasurer, at the beginning of each year, a sum equal to one-half of 1 percent on the capital stock paid in and the fund so created was to be held and used for the benefit of the creditors whenever any bank subject to its provisions should become insolvent. But this statute was destined to have but little practical effect. The system in New York proved inadequate for the security of the public interests, and it was practically abandoned in Michigan.

The aforementioned provision "to create a fund for the benefit of the creditors of certain moneyed corporations" resulted in the inscription, "Michigan Safety Fund," imprinted on some bank bills to give assurance to those who used them. In practicality, the fund proved useless.

THE 1837 GENERAL BANKING LAW

On January 1, 1837, there were nine banks in operation in Michigan. On March 15 of that year the Act to Organize and Regulate Banking Associations was approved.[13] This is usually referred to as the General Banking Law of 1837 or the Free Banking Law of 1837, the first piece of such legislation in the United States (although numerous historians credit the 1838 New York law as being first). "Free-Banking Law" is the generic term most appropriate to this type of legislation in various states, although actual titles varied.

Under provisions of the Michigan law, any 12 free holders (registered landowners who were also usually voters) who desired to operate a bank could do so by notifying the secretary of state of Michigan, determining a capital amount, and obtaining subscriptions for stock. After 10% of the capital had been paid in specie (gold and/or silver coins) and 20% in notes, securities, or other financial instruments, the bank could begin operations. However, securities and financial instruments often consisted of worthless IOUs, "specie certificates" stating that coins were on hand but were not, and overvalued mortgages, stocks, and bonds.

Starting a bank was so easy that by December of 1837 there were 18 banks in the state, the number having doubled during the year. Two months later, in February 1838, there were 40 banks!

By this time, would-be bankers were filing applications with county clerks, rather than with the state, and payment for stock was being made nearly entirely in IOUs. A common practice was for a director who desired to buy $10,000 worth of stock, to borrow $10,000 from the same bank, then loan the imaginary funds back to the bank, this being illustrated in the hypothetical Michigan Wildcat Bank balance sheet above. Thus, the balance sheet showed $10,000 in stock sold to this person and paid for, and among the bank's assets was a $10,000 loan due from the stockholder. To protect the public, the banks were required to post security assurances with the auditor-general of Michigan attesting to their financial worth. However, these assurances were often worthless. Further, there was no audit system in place, nor did authorities in the state offices even check if certain banks were actually in existence. There was absolutely no oversight.

Somewhat after the fact, in December 1837, the state passed legislation providing for three bank examiners to inspect each institution at least once every three months to verify its soundness and to be sure that the required specie was on hand. At one time these commissioners consisted of Alpheus Felch, Kintzing Pritchette, and Digby V. Bell. Felch, one of only four members of the legislature who had voted against the 1837 banking bill, was especially aware of the problems, and he later wrote of his experiences in the era of wild and wooly banking. Still later he served as governor of the state.

The First Round of Inspections

True to the spirit of the law, the three commissioners set out on their appointed rounds in January 1838 to examine the specie and other assets that banks claimed to have. Felch later wrote:[14]

> In many cases instead of specie a kind of paper denominated as "specie certificates" was used. These were given by bank officers, and sometimes by individuals or firms acknowledging the receipt of specie held on deposit. In some cases specie borrowed for the occasion was used and immediately returned to the owner. Sometimes the notes of the individual subscribers or others, usually denominated "stock notes," were received and counted as *specie.*
>
> How extensive this practice was, and how fraudulent its character, is fully shown by the commissioners' report. We cite a few examples:
>
> The Detroit City Bank had one of these certificates for $9,000, and the Farmers Bank of Oakland, $25,000. The Oakland County Bank was organized on a specie certificate of $10,000, and specie to the amount of $5,000, which was borrowed of another bank and paid in three times and counted for $15,000. The Clinton Canal Bank was started by the means of specie principally borrowed for the purpose in Detroit.
>
> The Farmers Bank of Genesee County was organized by the use of stock notes instead of specie, and in making its reports specie certificates to the amount of $35,000 were used. . . .
>
> The Bank of Kensington used stock notes and specie checks. The Bank of Lapeer used a specie certificate to the amount of $15,000. This certificate was given by an individual interested in getting up the Lapeer Bank without making any deposit or having anything to his credit, and was cancelled by the check of the pretended depositor made simultaneously with the certificate.
>
> The Wayne County Bank had specie certificates to the amount of $30,000, but was originally put in operation on checks of stockholders which were never presented, acknowledged or paid. The Jackson County Bank used a specie certificate of $10,000. The Bank of Saline one of $15,000, which was taken away a few days after the bank went into operation. The Farmers and Mechanics Bank of Pontiac borrowed specie and exhibited it to the bank commissioners as capital stock paid in.
>
> These instances are sufficient to show the gross fraud which tainted the inception of too many of these organizations. The men who got them up had no capital to invest in legitimate banking business, but many of them were unscrupulous and needy adventurers who established banks on fraudulent certificates that they might obtain the notes of the institution for their private benefit.
>
> Some of these fraudulent certificates were issued by chartered banks and some by associations organized under the general banking law. Under such a practice a single bank could, without the expenditure or even the possession of a dollar have supplied the means for the payment of the 30% necessary to put into operation a bank in every hamlet in the state. . . .

In one instance, the books of a bank showed $13,210 worth of currency officially in circulation, but it was learned that a further unreported $18,000 was in the hands of one person and $6,500 was held by another. For another bank, circulation was officially reported at $39,425, ignoring an additional $44,000 paid out without any notation being kept.

Of those running the banks, Felch went on to note, "Many of these individuals were entire irresponsible and their paper worthless," and yet "the same individuals sometimes controlled several banks." Some banks were sold and resold, with the buyers simply paying in worthless or forged obligations. In the meantime, the leading bank-note engravers and printers of New York City and Philadelphia were enjoying the rush of business!

The following notes and caption descriptions of certain of the banks mentioned by Alpheus Felch reveal how fascinating the history of currency can be.

Fast-Moving Money

The situation became increasingly curious as more banks were inspected by the state team. Soon, the commissioners learned that their travel schedule had been made available secretly in advance to certain banks, leaked by politicians who were aware of the investigations. Felch observed:

> In respect to the amount of specie required to be held by the banks the frauds were most glaring. The bank commissioners were carefully watched, with a view to transporting specie from banks already examined to those which it was supposed they were about to visit.
>
> Gold and silver never before circulated so freely or traveled so rapidly, and if the same well-filled boxes or bags were found in several banks in succession, some official at each was ready to swear that the *bona fide* ownership was vested in the present possessor. Sometimes it passed the commissioners by rapid transit on the road, sometimes it was transported by night. Sometimes, arrived too late, it was handed in at the back door of the banking house while an examination was in progress. But the specie held by the banks was largely in foreign coin, and of various mixtures, and little change took place in its identity. A few examinations, with close inspection, would enable anyone to know the character of that held by each bank and to discover ear-marks by which he could afterwards identify it. . . .

However, bank cashiers and directors were always willing to swear that the specie belonged to their bank, and their bank alone!

Few Coins at All

The Exchange Bank of Shiawassee, which employed Penniman & Bemis, a commercial printer in Cleveland, to create a bunch of rather crude-looking bank notes up to the face value of $20 each, was backed by specie certificates for $27,000. Ironically, the bills of this bank are among the great numismatic rarities of the state today, and any one of them, if found, is worth far more than face value! An inspection of this particular so-called institution found no specie (silver and gold) on hand—just "seven coppers." Meanwhile it had $22,261 in bills in circulation.

More from Felch on what the commissioners observed:

> There were found some banks that had no amount of even *borrowed* specie. The Bank of Sandstone, for instance, never had any specie, and although its liabilities exceeded $38,000 it had no assets of any kind at the time when it was examined.

Note for $3 of the Detroit City Bank, one of the banks inspected and found wanting in January 1838, despite the "Safety Fund" and "Real Estate Pledged and Private Property Holden" inscriptions. From a plate by Rawdon, Wright & Hatch, New York. The vignette, by Freeman Rawdon, shows a goddess and an especially patriotic American eagle wearing a brooch with the picture of George Washington.

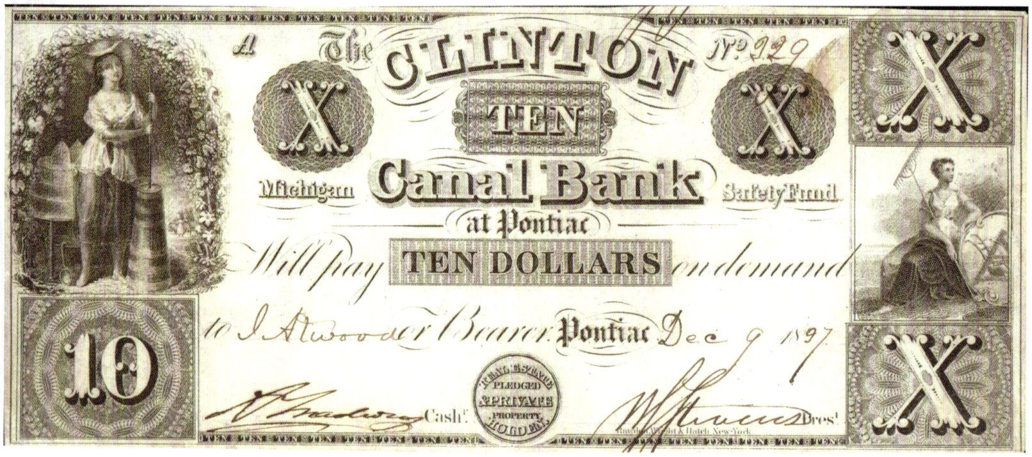

A $10 note of the Clinton Canal Bank, Pontiac, another of the banks that inspector Alpheus Felch found to be dishonest. It was founded on specie borrowed from Detroit, then quickly returned. The capital of $100,000 was never paid, but the bank issued $132,000 in essentially worthless bills, provided by Rawdon, Wright, & Hatch, New York.

The *Detroit Free Press,* October 12, 1838, stated this: "Clinton Canal Bank: Let us see who are the individuals who have been engaged in managing the operations of this institution: First comes William S. Stevens, the notorious Centreville Red Dog speculator. . . . This character was its first president, lately some developments have transpired which cap the climax of all banking operations. From a source of undoubted credit we are informed that a large quantity of notes of this bank are in circulation, signed by him, of the same denomination, letter, and number! Next comes J.S. Davis, cashier, an imported Whig."

A $5 note of the Farmers Bank of Genesee County, located in Pontiac Michigan, still another fraudulent bank. Commissioner Felch found that it was founded on paper, not on specie. The printer was Rawdon, Wright & Hatch, using stock vignettes, the one on the left by George W. Hatch and the center the much-used Androcles and the Lion by Asher B. Durand.

The *Pontiac Courier* reported in March 1838: "The Farmers Bank of Genesee County has gone by the board.… $160,000 of its notes are in circulation. The president left the bank a few weeks since, taking with him $50,000. He has not yet returned. The latest accounts from him state that he was in the western part of Indiana the last of February, purchasing farms with his own bills, taking care to have the deeds made out in the names of some of his particular friends."

Note for $1 of the Bank of Lapeer, Michigan, from a plate by the New England Bank Note Co., Boston. This is a later Patent Stereotype Steel Plate with inset slugs for the bank name and location. Curiously, the bill is stateless—as that space was used for a slug reading "Safety Fund." This bank had no specie backing, and was established with a $15,000 paper certificate of no value.

The *Pontiac Courier* printed this item in March 1838: "A gentleman from Detroit who had been to the Lapeer Bank to exchange the notes of that institution, called on us on his way back and informed us that he could make no arrangement with the president and directors. He had with him $4,000 [in Lapeer Bank bills]. He offered to take wild land, grain, lumber, shingles, or anything else. They refused to do anything. He said there were near 50 men at the bank when he was there, on the same business. Some had $5, some $10, some $20, but they could get nothing for their bills. Fears were entertained that the banking house would be torn down and the officers tarred and feathered."

Numismatic historian Harold L. Bowen wrote this in his *State Bank Notes of Michigan:* "After the bank collapsed its officers were arrested and brought before a justice of the peace, who adjourned the case till next day, placing a witness in his daughter's custody. She felt sorry for the poor man and let him go. Two of the prisoners were removed to an unfurnished room on the second floor of a neighbor's house, where constables guarded the stairs. During the night their host's son brought a ladder, and the prisoners escaped. They were home as usual next day, but the police could not seem to find them, and the suit was finally dropped." Of course, all of this would have made a great scenario for a Keystone Kops movie!

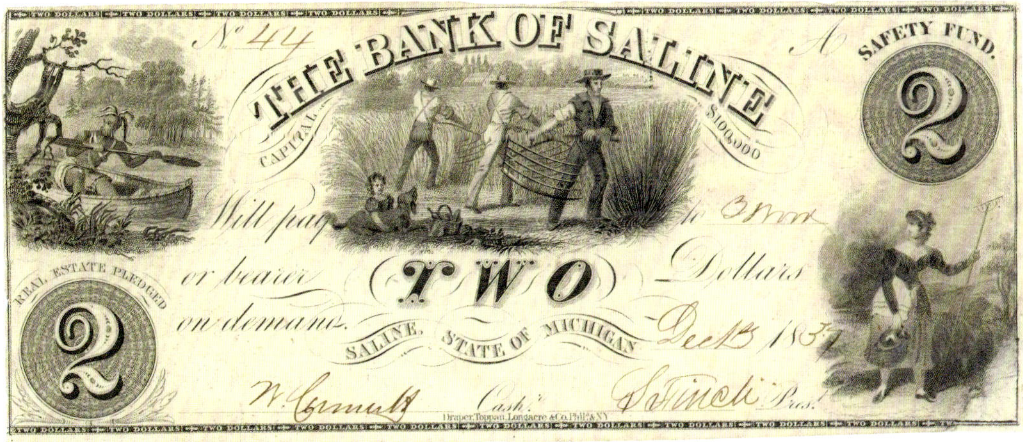

Note for $2 of the Bank of Saline, by Draper, Toppan, Longacre & Co. This bank was organized on September 2, 1837, with a proclaimed capital of $100,000. After issuing $264,000 worth of paper money against virtually no assets, the bank closed in 1838.

The Jackson County Bank placed before the commissioners a goodly number of ponderous and well-filled boxes, but on opening them and examining their contents the top was found covered with silver dollars,[15] but below was nothing but nails and glass. Another box containing silver was then brought from another room and sworn with a director present as being the property of the bank, but he afterwards brought an action against the receiver of the bank claiming it as his personal property. This bank, with an indebtedness of some $70,000, had not more than $5,000 of available assets.

News of the Day

Selected newspaper clippings and articles of the years 1837 to 1839 reflect much the same situation as reported by commissioner Felch.[16]

The *Constantine Republican,* January 18, 1837, reported:

> The River Raisin & Lake Erie Railroad Company, in violation of their charter, have issued notes bearing all the marks and appearing in all respects like bank notes intended to pass as a circulating medium.

A committee of three from the Senate, consisting of Messrs. Manning, Barry, and Moore, and of nine from the House, have been appointed to investigate the matter. The public will do well to refuse these notes as it is not known that there is any security in their redemption.

From the *Detroit Journal and Courier,* August 22, 1837:

> A bold scheme has been exposed at Ann Arbor. Our readers remember that the "Tory" Legislature of last winter passed a General Banking Law. Its first fruits, says the editor of the *State Journal,* are now before us. Under that law diverse office holders, in order to promulgate far and wide their abundant love for the dear people, got up an application for the establishment of an institution which they called the Bank of Ann Arbor.
>
> The *only legal act* in the whole movement was the insertion of a notice of their intention in the village papers. All beyond that was in direct opposition to the law. The specie was not paid in, proper security was not given—nothing was done that the statute required. And yet, extraordinary and barefaced as it may seem, some eight or ten thousand dollars [in bills] were signed by the vice president and the assistant cashier, and entrusted to the hands of J.E. Field, for the purpose of having them pledged to New York for specie upon which to establish the bank!
>
> These bills were signed at the request of Field, but, we understand, without the knowledge of a majority of the directors. Field disappeared clandestinely soon afterward. . . .

Found in the Ann Arbor *State Journal,* April 19, 1838:

> The cashier of the Manchester Bank, we understand, has . . . disposed of some $50,000 in bills without the knowledge of the directors! Hurrah for the General Banking Law! The wildcat Tory currency! Three cheers for Gov. Mason's "principle correct in theory, but mischievous in practice!" One-hundred gun salute for this immortal display of modern democratic, Tory, wildcat, Loco Foco wisdom.

The *Detroit Daily Advertiser,* April 26, 1838, reported:

> The Farmers & Merchants Bank of St. Joseph, located at Centreville, is technically and *par excellence* named the "Red Dog swindling shop." From the last *White Pigeon Gazette* we gather some startling details of this rabid canine monster. That paper states that two of the principal directors are buying up their bills at a discount of 50%. The president, cashier, and directors have all been indicted by the Grand Jury. The conduct of Thomas M. Langley, the president, is represented as having been in a high degree censurable, as he has reiteratingly represented the bank as perfectly sound.

Found in the Detroit Free Press, July 17, 1838:

> It is said that the Grand Jury in and for the County of Wayne has found a true bill against John A. Welles, cashier of the Farmers and Mechanics Bank of this city, for extensive swindling operations. . . . It is said that an individual by the name of Henry H. Brown, generally reputed to be a "stool pigeon" for Welles in a "shaving shop"[17] on Jefferson Avenue, was indicted for similar offenses.
>
> It is said that *specie certificates* were the materials in which these gentlemen dealt. . . . It is said that these *specie certificates* were manufactured for the purpose of establishing "wild cat banks," to which "institutions" they were loaned at very moderate rates, and that the use of them was paid for in the issues of said *wild cats,* to be again reissued at the counters of certain city institutions.

More in the *Detroit Free Press,* August 7, 1838:

> We understand that bills to a large amount are in circulation in the western part of the state, purporting to be of the Bank of Romeo, no such institution having yet gone into operation.
>
> A man recently sold a horse for $40 and received in payment forged bills on the Bank of Romeo. Having occasion to travel near Romeo, he thought he would visit that place and either get the specie for his bills or the notes of some other bank, when to his astonishment he found there

A $20 note of the Exchange Bank of Shiawassee, featuring a rather primitive job of printing by a commercial shop in Cleveland, not a bank-note engraving firm. The printer used type and woodcuts.

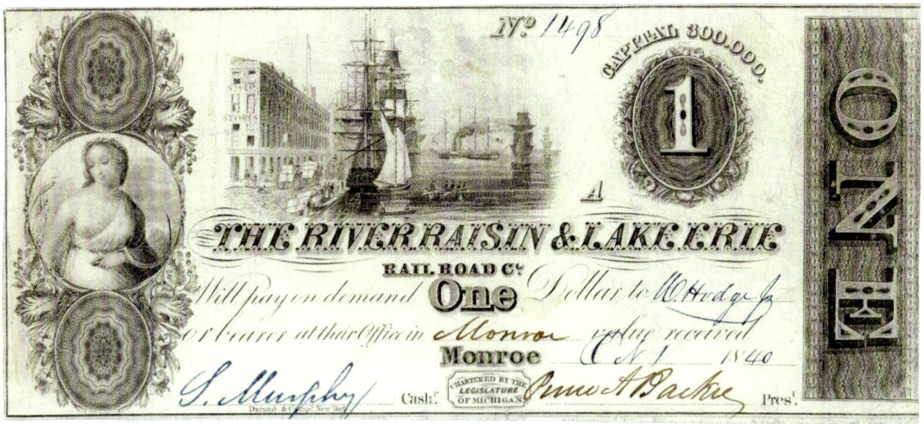

A $1 note of the River Raisin & Lake Erie Railroad Company, by Durand & Co., New York. Railroading, its main business, was more profitable than was banking in Michigan, and this line issued its own paper money into the 1860s.

Note for $10 of the Bank of Ann Arbor, by Rawdon, Wright & Hatch, New York. "Directors and stockholders responsible & security given for double the amount of issues," the bill proclaimed. The vignette depicts the seated goddess Moneta holding a key to an ironbound chest guarded by a griffin, as Mercury approaches with a cornucopia brimming with coins. Although this bank issued an estimated $60,000 in paper money, it never opened for business!

> was no such bank in existence. The bills are of the same plate as those procured for the contemplated Bank of Romeo. —*Macomb Statesman.*

Detroit Journal and Courier, February, 1839, reported the following:

> Bank of Ypsilanti: The institution had not local ties, there being but only one actual stockholder in the place, and he owning but a few shares. Entirely in the hands of strangers, by them was it solely managed, and its proceedings kept as secret from public gazes as the dark mysticisms of Isis from the vulgar herd who worshiped at her shrine.
>
> What the circulation of the bank may be we know not. Rumor places it at over $100,000, one third of which sum, it is said, has been thrown into the western markets within the last 30 days. Some outstanding facts have likewise been detailed, such as *dead men* obtaining facilities from the bank, etc., etc.—*Ypsilanti Republican.*

The End of the Michigan Line

After most damage had been done, on April 16, 1839, an Act to Protect the Public Against Various Frauds provided that no more banks should be established under the General Banking Law. Thus the first law of its kind was an abject failure. Many later financial historians chose to ignore it!

The Michigan bank commissioners reported in December 1839 that only three chartered banks (one with a branch) and four free banks remained in operation in the entire state, a wholesale fall from the recent time when 40 banks had been organized under the free-banking law alone.[18] By that time more than a million dollars' face value in worthless Michigan bills was in state and regional circulation, mostly held by individuals and small businesses who had little real money to begin with and who could ill afford such losses.

On March 25, 1840, the offices held by bank commissioners were abolished, and the state attorney general was placed in charge of overseeing banking. By the time that the Act to Repeal the Charters of Certain Banks was passed on February 16, 1842, the matter was largely moot.[19]

In the meantime, many men had signed as guarantors or sureties for the obligations of banks that had become worthless. Many if not most of these were criminals or adventurers for whom little sympathy was held. However, in instances in which honest banks collapsed in the rubble, there was the possibility that the land, homes, farms, and other assets of upright citizens would be taken away. Not to worry. In 1845 the

Michigan Supreme Court held all such guarantees to be invalid. Everyone was now home free![20]

Over a period of time many engravers and bank-note companies related that *they* were careful with regard to accepting orders, but that *others* would take any business offered. In reality, it seems that any and all bank-note companies were more than eager to print bills for Michigan banks ranging from nonexistent to fraudulent to those of questionable soundness. The firms taking the business ranged from the large and prominent Rawdon, Wright & Hatch of New York City, which got a large share of the orders, to obscure shops such as Penniman & Bemis of Cleveland.

Further Aspects of Michigan Currency

From a numismatic viewpoint the bank bills of Michigan offer a rich playground. Because huge quantities were printed but few redeemed, as a class such currency is plentiful today. However, contrasting the issues that turn up with frequency are certain other bills that are known only from mentions in articles from long ago or in bank-note reporters. We can only contemplate that bank bills produced for a nonexistent Romeo, Michigan, bank were despised in their time, but if found today they would be worth many times face value! Actually, the Romeo bills were worth *something* in their time, to fraudsters who altered them to the Farmers Bank of Rome, New York, by bleaching out certain information and adding false imprints. The once-worthless but now rare and expensive bills of the Exchange Bank of Shiawassee have already been mentioned.

Many bills with Michigan imprints are highly artistic and were deliberately produced to be attractive to the public. A letter from Timothy Tredwell, president of the Bank of Ypsilanti (whose fraudulent operation was not yet known), to John Horton Jr., cashier of the Michigan State Bank, October 27, 1837, discusses the planning for a new bank:[21]

> The name selected for the bank at Lowell is "The Bank of Superior," that being the name of the *town.* The bill is to be dated "Superior."

A $10 note of the Farmers Bank of Romeo, Michigan, altered to the Farmers Bank of Rome, New York. Such worthless notes were purchased in quantity by sharpers, references to Michigan were bleached out, and false information was added by the use of printing blocks.

> I would advise one plate as you suggest of two $1's and $2 and $3. The books will be opened 28th next month, the application having been regularly made.
>
> Get a real furiouso plate—one that will TAKE with all creation—flaming with cupids, locomotives, rural scenery, and Hercules kicking the world over! I will call on you in a few days on my way to Buffalo. . . .

This letter points out another feature common to many Michigan bills: low denominations were preferred, as the citizenry had little money and, in any event, such bills were more readily accepted within the state and at discounts elsewhere than higher values would have been.

The earlier-mentioned August 11, 1892, newspaper article included these further comments, some of which relate to currency:

> Many good specimens of this wild-cat money are in possession of the Pioneer Society of Washtenaw County and are well worth examining. Many of the bills have no date and some even are not signed by either a president or secretary. A collection comprising a $10, $15 and a $20 bill of the Washtenaw County Volunteer Family Relief Fund is especially noticeable, the $10 and $15 bills having written across the face in red ink: "Redeemed, June 28, 1883. Signed Fred. H. Belser, Dept. County Treasurer."
>
> Wild-cat banks originated in this way: In the year 1835 Samuel W. Foster and John Holden of Scio, Washtenaw county, applied to the Bank of Michigan, in Detroit, for a loan of money to buy wheat to stock their mill. The bank could not accommodate them, but referred them to a broker doing business in the basement of the bank building, where they found money, if they would submit to a "shave." On their return home they conceived the plan on which the "wild-cat" banks were gotten up. Foster presented the bill to the legislature and the bill was passed, the four members heretofore mentioned being the only ones brave enough to vote against it. Very soon after the enactment of the law banks sprung up all over the state and their bills were as plenty as raspberries. In Washtenaw County there was one at Ann Arbor, called the Millers Bank of Washtenaw, which was conducted fairly and paid all its indebtedness. Another was started in Lowell, an imaginary place on the Huron River; another at Ypsilanti, one at Saline, one at Manchester and one at the village of Sharon.
>
> In some cases where stockholders had not enough land of their own to give the required security they mortgaged a piece of *government* land to make out enough. Fortunes were made in a few months. New cities and villages sprung up as fast as the surveyor could survey and plat them, and splendid maps, showing contemplated railroads, hotels, mills and large public parks, were shown to the would-be investor. High sounding names were given to the streets and avenues, and the most glowing inducements held out to the stranger, who could not find these mythical places even with a guide and map. In Washtenaw County there were towns called Boston, Saratoga, Windham and Sharon, and the plats of them are on record in the register's office.
>
> The $5 bill of the Exchange Bank of Ann Arbor has a design of a railroad train, the engine of which is of itself a curiosity. This bank presumably won the confidence of its customers by having "safety fund" printed on its bills.

FREE BANKING IN NEW YORK STATE

Starting with the Bank of New York, which began business in New York City in 1784 without a charter, through the next several decades, the granting of bank privileges was a political plum. In ensuing years through the early 1820s, many more banks were chartered, nearly always through corruption.[22] However, the banks that were formed were mostly sound. The first failure in the state did not occur until 1819, at which time there were 33 banks in business. By 1830 there were 43 banks and a record of eight failures, some at the hand of the earlier-mentioned Jacob Barker.

In the meantime, New York City had established itself firmly as the financial center of the United States, with nearly all activity centered in lower Manhattan in and around Wall Street. The city was also becoming a center for bank-note engraving and printing companies, gradually surpassing Philadelphia in this regard. During the late 1830s and early 1840s, several engraving partnerships had offices in both cities.

THE SAFETY FUND SYSTEM

On January 24, 1829, the essentials of what became known as the Safety Fund System were included in proposals sent to the legislature by Judge Joshua Forman, of Syracuse, agreeable to a request to Martin Van Buren, then the governor of New York state.[23] The idea was referred by the governor to Thomas W. Olcott, cashier of the Mechanics and Farmers Bank of Albany. At first Olcott thought it unreasonable to require perfectly sound banks to pay into a fund to support other institutions. However, upon consideration he changed his mind and offered to help discuss the matter with legislators. Soon, the idea became law.

The rule was that each bank gaining a new charter or the renewal of an old one was committed to pay one-half of 1% of its capital into the fund each year, until it had on deposit an amount of 3% of its capital. It developed that, except for the Manhattan Company and the New York Dry Dock Company, each of which conducted banks under unlimited charters not needing renewal, other institutions in the state fell under the law. Capital, which was sometimes not funded in full, must now be fully paid. The levy against capital fell most heavily on the strongest banks, such as those in Albany and New York City, which were also deemed to be the least likely to fail. On the other hand, a rural bank capitalized for a small amount would not have to pay much, but it presented a greater risk.

The system was simple enough: most banks in the state were sound, but if a few should fail, the Safety Fund would provide funds to redeem its bills, and the banks in the state would afterward resume payments into the fund, at the standard rate, until the Safety Fund's assets were restored. The act also included a provision for hiring state bank commissioners, who were to visit each bank at least three times per year. The idea caught on, and in variant forms it was set in place in Vermont in 1831, Indiana in 1834, and Michigan in 1836. The term *Safety Fund* boldly printed on bank notes was intended to give assurance to the holders of such bills.

In 1837 three banks in New York, all in the city of Buffalo, experienced difficulties. The legislature stepped in, and money from the Safety Fund was used to secure the value of outstanding currency. The system was working.

The Free-Banking Law of 1838

All seemed to be going well, creating a fine setting for the enactment of a free-banking law, called the General Banking Law, for the state on April 18, 1838.[24] By this time the nature of the problems experienced in Michigan was not widely known, and as New York's Safety Fund had proved effective, all seemed to be in order to create more banks. The Hard Times era made doing business difficult, and it was felt that banks set up in towns and villages across the state would contribute to the strength of the economy in each place.

The New York law provided that any "person or association of persons" could form a bank and could issue bills. To do this, funds equal to the amount of the bills, in the form of government bonds, approved state bonds, stocks, or mortgages yielding 6% or more in annual interest and for not more than half the appraised price of properties, were to be posted as security, with mixing various combinations as specified in the legislation. The interest received on the

Note for $5 of the Exchange Bank of Ann Arbor, mentioned in the 1892 article quoted in the text. The detail is of the "curious" locomotive also mentioned. From a plate engraved by R. Lowe, Broadway, New York City.

deposited securities would be paid back to the bank.

To regulate the bills and to prevent overissue, Section 1 of the law included this provision:

> The comptroller is hereby authorized and required to cause to be engraved and printed in the best manner, to guard against counterfeiting, such quantity of circulating notes, in the similitude of bank notes in blank, of the different denominations authorized to be issued by the incorporated banks of this state, as he may from time to time deem necessary to carry into effect the provisions of this act, and of such form as he may prescribe.
>
> Such blank circulating notes shall be countersigned, numbered, and registered in proper books to be provided and kept for that purpose by the comptroller, under his direction, by such person or persons as the said comptroller shall appoint for that purpose, so that each denomination of such notes circulating shall all be of the same similitude and bear the uniform signature of such register, or one of such registers.

Among other provisions, each bill was to bear a printed inscription as part of the design, "Secured by the pledge of public stocks."

Further, "the plates, dies, and materials to be procured by the comptroller for the printing and making of the circulating notes provided for hereby, shall remain in his custody and under his direction." This plan would prove unworkable, however, because in order to print the bills, the bank-note companies needed to have the plates on their own premises. No bill of a denomination less than $1,000, intended to be put into circulation, could be made payable at any place except the bank's main registered business office in the state. This provision was made in view of the common practice of certain banks issuing bills payable at remote locations, sometimes in distant states.

After receiving such bills from the comptroller, each bank would cause the cashier and president to affix their signatures, then release the currency into circulation. It was specifically required that any and all such bills be redeemable in specie on demand "during the usual hours of business, between the hours of ten and three o'clock, at the place where such note is payable."

FREE BANKING IN OPERATION

Observers of the economic scene heralded the legislation as the first truly effective law to insure the soundness of banks and the interests of those who held its paper money. A report on the progress of free banking appeared in *Niles' National Register*, February 2, 1839:

> The comptroller of New York reports that up to the 9th instant, the number of banks which have filed certificates under the general banking law, is 54. Capital subscribed is $12,319,175. To what amount the capital may be increased, $487,680,000.
>
> *Duration of charters.* This varies from 25 years, the lowest number (the Farmers Bank of Orleans, in the village of Gaines), to 4,050 years, the duration of the charter of the Bank of Central New York at Utica. The U.S. Bank in Buffalo has a charter for 200 years, and the U.S. Bank in New York City, for 62 years. Two of the banks have a 1,000 years charter, and several 500.
>
> We find in the *New York American* the following statement of the amount and kinds of securities pledged by them.
>
> Bank of Western New York, Rochester, $100,000 state stock Indiana 5%; North American Trust and Banking Company, New York City, $200,000 mortgages, Michigan 6%; Mechanics Banking Association, New York City, $60,000 Maine 5%, and $60,000 bonds and mortgages; Staten Island Bank, Port Richmond, $25,000 Indiana 5%, and $35,000 bonds and mortgages; Lockport Bank and Trust Company, Lockport, $100,000 Alabama 5%, and $29,690 bonds and mortgages.
>
> Bank of Syracuse, Syracuse, $50,000 Michigan 6% stock, and $20,800 bonds and mortgages; Farmers and Mechanics Bank of Genesee, Batavia, $100,000 Arkansas and Michigan 6% stock; Farmers Bank of Orleans, Gaines, $50,000 Indiana 5% stock and $48,300 bonds and mortgages; Merchants and Farmers Bank, Ithaca, $40,000 Michigan 6% stock, and $27,200 bonds and mortgages; Willoughby Bank, Brooklyn, $50,000 Maine 5% stock, and $50,000 bonds and mortgages.
>
> New York State Stock Security Bank, New York City, $25,090, New York 5% stock; Millers' Bank of New York City, Clyde, $100,000 Arkansas 6% stock; the Powell Bank, Newburgh, $50,000 Michigan 6% stock, and $50,000 bonds and mortgages; Bank of Central New York, $10,000 Michigan and Arkansas 6% stock, and $10,000 bonds and mortgages; the Wool Growers Bank of the State of New York, $10,000 Maine 5% stock.
>
> Total $1,170,090 state stocks, and $422,900 bonds and mortgages.

The new law continued to be popular, and before December 1, 1839, a flood of charters had been issued under its provisions, some 133 in all, of which 76 institutions had already commenced business.[25] Many of these were in small villages and towns, including some that had unsuccessfully applied for charters earlier but whose sponsors did not have the proper political connections to succeed at that time.

In addition to the safeguards provided under the free-banking law, the well-endowed Safety Fund

A $10 note of the Wyoming County Bank of Warsaw, New York, showing the special seal mandated by the state. Engraved by Baldwin, Adams & Co., New York.

provided further assurance to the public. Banks that were still in operation from earlier days and had charters still operated under the old system. Accordingly, state bank reports of the era were in two categories—regular banks and "free banks." Each had its own set of regulations.

But what had been envisioned as an ideal Safety Fund scenario soon proved to be otherwise. The Bank of Tonawanda failed in 1840, after which time it was found that its pledged securities were worth just 68% of the amount stated. Things went from bad to worse, and "the mortality of the free banks was so great, by failure or voluntary liquidation, that in 1842 only 46 remained in operation."[26]

Failures continued, and in 1844 the state comptroller reported that of the free banks that had collapsed up to that point, just 76 cents on the dollar had been paid to holders of their currency. Obviously, both the Safety Fund and the free-banking idea had many problems.

The Bank of Central New York

Operations of the Bank of Central New York, located in Utica, are interesting to contemplate. The institution began business on September 8, 1838, and formally filed articles as an associated free bank on September 17. On the same date, director Samuel D. Dakin was authorized to go into the marketplace and locate $100,000 worth of stock that could be used as backing for an equal value of Bank of Central New York stock, this being its stated capital. The *New York Courier* soon printed this notice:

> The Bank of Central New York is the name and style of an institution recently organized at Utica, under the general banking law. About $160,000 is already subscribed to the capital stock, and the books will be opened for 30 days for an increase to $500,000. From the peculiar advantages of location, the stock must give large dividends to the stockholders; and the respectability of the direction warrants the belief that the institution will be conducted on sound business principles. The directors are, Charles Gould, president; Spencer Kellogg, Samuel D. Dakin, Frederick Hollister, Elisha M. Gilbert, Heman Ferry, and George Curtiss.[27]

Banking hours were from 9 a.m. to 12:30 p.m. and from 2 to 4 p.m., except Sunday. Discounts (loans) were to be made at 6% and 7% interest. The entire board of directors was to meet each Tuesday and Friday to review loans and other business. Article V of the bylaws mandated, "The directors shall make no disclosure of the proceedings of the board in the general business of the company. . . ."

The salary of the president was fixed at $2,500 annually, an extraordinarily high sum for this office. The cashier, normally by far the highest paid officer in a bank, was to draw $1,500—about on par with other banks of the time. Each director was appointed for varying terms, with that of Samuel D. Dakin to expire in seven years.

On September 29, 1838, the private minute book of the board of directors recorded this decision:

> Resolved: That we hereby authorize and empower Charles Gould, Samuel D. Dakin, and Spencer Kellogg to make any arrangement they may deem proper with the president and directors of the Belleville Bank in New Jersey and the Wolfborough Bank in New Hampshire, in reference to obtaining their bills for circulation.[28]

By that time the Wolfborough (*sic*) Bank, in Wolfeborough, had been bought by Dakin. That institution, with hardly any assets, operated fraudulently by issuing large amounts of worthless paper money. The Belleville Bank also was controlled by Dakin, who was also involved in the North American Trust & Banking Co. in New York City. The last began business on November 6, 1838, and was forced into receivership in 1841, at which time its $100 par value shares were selling for about $3.[29]

On December 1, 1838, this action was entered in the Central Bank of New York's minutes book, confidentially of course, addressing a proposal from Michigan that had been discussed by the board on October 31:

> Mr. Romeyn presented through the president some modifications of the contract between this institution and himself, the Ypsilanti Bank and the Oakland County Bank. Whereupon resolved that the contracts be modified according to the propositions and that the president and secretary of this board be authorized to complete the contracts with Mr. Romeyn and take Oakland County bills for the $25,000 of stock [capital stock of the Bank of Central New York] instead of Ypsilanti bills. Also to take $350,000 of circulation from the Oakland County Bank instead of $250,000 of that bank and $100,000 of the Ypsilanti Bank.

The Bank of Ypsilanti, discussed earlier in this chapter, was an utter fraud. Its officers were implicated in several other phony institutions in the state. Harold L. Bowen, historian of Michigan currency, wrote that Theodore Romeyn, a "tool or agent," had the principles of a "highway robber or a midnight thief."[30] The Ypsilanti Bank failed quickly.

Chartered on March 28, 1836, the Oakland County Bank issued $143,200 in essentially worthless bills, plus $350,000 face value exchanged with the Bank of Central New York, as above. The Oakland County Bank lasted for a long time, passing out worthless bills, and finally closed in 1846. Its assets were found to consist of $40 in specie in an iron vault, desk, printing press, pair of shears, and other office supplies.

After the paper money deal was consummated, the Oakland County Bank ordered bills from Draper, Toppan, Longacre & Co. The currency was received by that bank and signed by the cashier and president. Each bill had in addition the printed name of T.O. Grannis, cashier of the Central Bank of New York. A board member was sent to Pontiac to bring the bills back to Utica. These were then wholesaled to exchange brokers in distant cities, who offered them for sale at attractive discounts to sharpers, who in turn spent them around the country.

Dakin did the same thing with Wolfborough notes, wholesaling them to money brokers. The bank there kept a double set of records, one for bank examiners and the other for the proprietors' own use.[31]

Somehow the wily and unprincipled Dakin stayed out of the limelight, and except in obscure reports little notice has been found concerning his banking activities.[32] The Bank of Central New York remained in business, without the Oakland County Bank bill fraud ever being prosecuted, to the writer's knowledge. In the Hard Times era hundreds of banks were having deep problems, worthless currency flooded the channels of commerce, and most onlookers gave up and considered the redemption of bills to be hopeless. The bank continued to issue its own paper money. A report filed with the state in 1847, well past the Hard Times era, showed just $3,723 in coins against $76,860 in bills in circulation. The bank survived to 1860, when it was placed in the hands of a receiver. In the meantime, it was involved in several lawsuits, changed officers frequently, and gained control of the Washington Mills factory, which then went bankrupt.

History remembers Dakin as an accomplished individual, with no mention of fraud, as in this account by M.M. Bagg in *Pioneers of Utica,* which does mention without elaboration "a scheming turn of mind":

> Samuel Dana Dakin, born in Jaffrey, N.H., July 16, 1802, came with his parents to New Hartford, in 1815. He entered Hamilton College and was graduated in the class of 1821, after which he spent two years in teaching in the family of Mr. Brent, in Maryland. He next came to Utica and entered the office of Joseph Kirkland.
>
> In the year 1824, while still a student, he bought, in company with William J. Bacon, also a student of law, the Utica *Sentinel and Gazette,* and likewise the *Utica Patriot.* Uniting these papers, they edited them for a few years. After Mr. Bacon had sold his interest to Richard R. Lansing, Mr. Dakin continued to conduct the paper some time longer, until it was disposed of to Rufus Northway.
>
> Mr. Dakin was admitted to the bar in 1826, and opened an office for practice. Literature rather than law was, however, a principal object of pleasure and pursuit. Besides the management of the *Gazette,* he wrote frequently for the *Knickerbocker* and other magazines. Yet he was not solely a *literateur,* but had an inventive and scheming turn of mind, heated many irons, and did not lack of a money-getting ability.
>
> In 1839 he removed to New York. There he became patentee of a floating dry dock, of which he constructed two for the United States govern-

Note for $5 of the Bank of Central New York, by Danforth, Bald & Co., New York and Philadelphia. Proof impression from the American Bank Note Co. archives. Notes of this configuration were designated as spurious by James A. Haxby, who did not see this particular impression, which seems to be genuine. This bank, seemingly conceived in fraud by Samuel Dakin and partners, did issue some legitimate notes.

Evidence of a fraud: $5 note of the Oakland County Bank of Pontiac, Michigan, payable at the Bank of Central New York, Utica, New York. Such bills were brought to Utica and from there they were wholesaled to exchange brokers in distant cities.

> ment, one at Portsmouth, N.H., and one at Philadelphia.[33] Continuing his interests in literary pursuits, he had in progress at the time of his death a *History of Civil Liberty.* This event occurred, suddenly, January 26, 1853. He was the father of five sons, all of whom were graduates of Hamilton College. Attractive in form and feature, and genteel in demeanor, his social rank was with the first.

Trying to Fix Problems

Many of the banks set up in New York state under the Free-Banking Law transacted little or no real banking business, in the sense of making loans to local businesses and individuals who were not shareholders of the bank. Instead, they concentrated on issuing paper money, putting up securities of doubtful value with the state as backing. Few of these corrupt outfits stayed in business as long as did the aforementioned Bank of Central New York.

In 1844 the legislature passed a law requiring that banks could conduct business only in the place specified in their charter. In 1845, banks that only issued bills but performed no other visible services were censured by a committee of the state senate, but nothing further was done about the problem. Matters drifted along, and while the free banks in New York did not draw as many disparaging comments as those in the Michigan debacle, the sight was not a pretty one. An accounting in 1846 revealed that, due to the inflated value of securities deposited, holders of the bills of failed banks had sustained a 39% loss on the average. In the same year the granting of special charters for banking was terminated. So much for free banking in New York state.

The Continuing Story

In July 1846 the first issue of the *Banker's Magazine and State Financial Register* was published by J. Smith Homans of Baltimore. The magazine, with various adjustments to the title, would endure for many years and become the single most valuable record of banking during the era of note-issuing state-chartered banks. In later years, operating in New York City, the publication also issued a yearly almanac. (Over a period of time, a word in the title was variously given as *Bankers'* as well as *Banker's,* with the latter used most often.)

Among the feature articles in the inaugural 1846 issue was "Banks of New York," which reviewed the recent banking history of the state. Several other comments in the same issue dealt with three recent failures: the Farmers and Drovers Bank of Erie County in Buffalo, the Lewis County Bank in Martinsburg, and the White Plains Bank in White Plains.

As of January 1, 1846, there were 72 free banks in operation in the state, with bills in circulation amounting to $6,442,045; and 85 regular or incorporated banks with a circulation of $2,703,451.

By 1850 many free banks had failed. Depending on the value of the securities posted by each bank, bill holders received from 30 cents on the dollar to the full par amount. While there had been a good share of crooks involved in free banks, many other failures were simply the result of ineptness. Often, the fact that well-intentioned citizens in a small upstate New York community desired a bank did not translate into the bank being run on a profitable basis. Then as now, the granting of loans and credit, the investment of bank funds, and other decisions required considerable skill and talent.

BANK-NOTE GAMES IN MISSISSIPPI

INVESTMENT OPPORTUNITIES

During the period of specie suspension, generally from May 10, 1837, through 1838 but also into the early 1840s in some locations, the values of many bank bills remained uncertain, this being particularly true for currency issued by institutions of low capital located in small towns. Accordingly, in Philadelphia, New York City, or Boston, bills of towns in the South and West were available at discounts, often large. At the same time certain of the financiers in those cities were acquainted with the strength of selected distant banks and saw opportunities to acquire bills that were in fact sound. In 1840 Condy Raguet wrote of this scheme:

> Large sums were invested in 1838 by some of the Philadelphia and New York banks, in purchases of the notes of the Mississippi banks from 10% to 25% discount and loaned to the latter at par for their bonds payable at a subsequent period.[34]

Under such an arrangement, a Philadelphia bank would hold a perfectly good $1,000 bond, currently paying attractive interest, which had been purchased for, say, $800 in depreciated bills. As it developed, the bonds were not quite as sound as the smart bankers in Philadelphia believed.

In 1892 in *Cheap Money,* a booklet about various currency schemes published by the Century Company, this scenario appears under the title, "Mississippi's Chief Crop: Moving Currency" (excerpts):[35]

> **Prosperity Everywhere**
>
> Mississippi's experience with cheap money during the period of inflation and speculation which followed the removal by President Jackson of the public deposits from the Bank of the United States, and the refusal to recharge that bank, was more reckless than that of Alabama,[36] and consequently more disastrous. It began in 1833 and ended in 1840. For five or six years the people of Mississippi believed themselves to be the richest and most prosperous on the face of the globe. Everybody had all the money he wanted, and if he needed more the banks would pour it out for him.
>
> Yet when the end came everybody discovered that he was so poor that the state arose as one man and repudiated its most solemn obligations, thus adding breach of faith to its other follies. In this respect its conduct was in most unfavorable contrast with that of Alabama, though the disasters both suffered had been brought on by similar causes.
>
> "Nowhere," says Professor William G. Sumner in his *History of American Currency,* in commenting upon the developments of this period, "had the paper-money mania raged worse than in Mississippi, where the banks operated as cotton factors, manufacturing money to carry cotton as they needed it."
>
> **Banks Formed, Bonds Issued**
>
> The experiment began in 1833 when the state came to the aid of the Planters' Bank of Mississippi, which had been chartered three years before, by issuing $2,000,000 worth of bonds, at 6% interest, to be used as the bank's capital. The avowed object was to enable the bank to "aid in developing the resources of the state." The bonds sold at a premium, and the bank had a remarkable prosperity during the following year. This was so encouraging that nine new banks were chartered in 1834, and many others in following years. In 1838 the state, desiring to get a larger share in the general prosperity brought on by such liberal banking, chartered a bank of its own called the Union Bank of Mississippi, and issued $5,000,000 worth of bonds at 5%, most of which were sold in Holland at their par value, bringing into the state the largest sum of money its people had ever dreamed of possessing. The whole state went wild with a fever of speculation. The smaller banks did their best to rival the Union Bank, and all vied with one another in pouring out currency, making loans and discounts, and publishing fabulous accounts of their great prosperity.
>
> At the close of 1839 the 26 banks in the state professed to have a paid-up capital of over $30,000,000, loans and discounts exceeding $48,000,000, a note circulation exceeding $15,000,000, and deposits aggregating nearly $9,000,000. . . .

A $100 note of the Planters Bank, Natchez, August 3, 1834, two years after its charter. This bank raised a lot of money, passed many bills into circulation, and helped launch a wave of prosperity that eventually was proved illusory. From a plate by Rawdon, Wright & Hatch, New York.

Note for $500 of the Mississippi Union Bank, Jackson, May 1, 1839. Established by the state of Mississippi in 1838, this bank floated $5 million in bonds and large amounts of paper money. The bank seemed prosperous, but it was not. Its failure embroiled the state in bitter disputes that lasted many years when the state repudiated its debts. From a plate by Draper, Toppan, Longacre & Co., Philadelphia and New York.

An Unexpected Turnabout

At the moment of greatest apparent prosperity, when everybody believed himself rich and hourly growing richer, the entire system collapsed. It was then discovered that all of the boasted $30,000,000 of paid-up capital, with the exception of the money that had been borrowed on the bonds of the state, consisted of "stock notes" which had been paid in for capital, the banks discounting them and the proceeds going to pay for stock subscriptions. This was simply an exchange of one form of credit for another. Absolutely no money had gone into the banks except that obtained by the sale of state bonds, and when that was exhausted nothing remained but entries upon the bank records for indebtedness from which nothing was ever to be realized.

In summing up the result, Mr. Henry V. Poor, from whose *Money, Its Laws and History* we have obtained much of our information, says:

"The $48,000,000 of loans were never paid; the $23,000,000 of notes and deposits never redeemed. The whole system fell as a huge and shapeless wreck, leaving the people of the state very much as they came into the world. Their condition at the time beggars description. Society was broken up from its very foundations. Everybody was in debt without any possible means of payment. Lands became worthless for the reason that no one had any money to pay for them. The only personal property left was slaves, to save which such numbers of people fled with them from the state that the common return upon legal processes was in the very abbreviated form of 'G.T.T,' *gone to Texas,* a state which in this way received a mighty accession to her population."

Reneging on State Obligations

The state paid the interest on the bonds issued for the banks for less than a year, when the governor informed the bondholders that the state, "in her sovereign capacity, had refused payment of her bonds." This position the legislature sustained in 1842 by adopting a report of a committee declaring payment of the bonds to be "incompatible with the honor and dignity of the state."

The state's conduct was defended on the floor of Congress by Jacob Thompson, afterward President Buchanan's secretary of the Interior. The bondholders had the question of the constitutionality of the bonds brought before the highest court in the state, and obtained a decision in their favor, the court affirming their constitutionality and declaring them to be binding obligations upon the state, but as no execution could issue against the state, the bondholders could obtain none of their lost money. As late as 1853 some of the bondholders, by persistent efforts, obtained from the legislature an act referring the question of payment to the people. The people voted that the bonds should not be paid, thus adding the final and overwhelming touch to the state's disgrace.

In 1838, early in the paper-money game, the state of Mississippi appointed commissioners to investigate certain banks. However, several of the banks denied access to their records, stating the commissioners had no constitutional authority to meddle in their affairs. Certain of the stronger banks did allow inspection, allowing the commissioners to report that these institutions were strong. However, the strength of banks suspected to be weak remained a mystery.[37]

For the next generation, the credit of the state of Mississippi and the banks in it was at a low level, as was the reputation of the integrity of the state itself. Bills of the Union Bank and others involved became utterly worthless.

Banks and Banking in the 1840s

More Than 900 Banks in 1840

On January 1, 1830, the Treasury Department estimated that 330 banks were doing business in the United States and had $61,323,898 face value of bills in circulation. By January 1, 1840, the number of banks, plus branches, had swelled to an estimated 901, while currency had increased to $106,968,572.[1] To the figures for both of these years can be added many quasi-banks in the form of unofficial institutions as well as merchants and others who issued their own bills.

During this tumultuous Hard Times period most of the big-city banks in the East remained sound, with no losses to currency holders, depositors, or stockholders. New England in particular was a bastion of good banking practice, although there were enough exceptions that hardships were experienced by those holding bills of certain banks. The Suffolk System of bank-note redemption permitted the notes of all good banks to be redeemed at par in Boston, the banking center of that district.

Elsewhere, the situation varied, with the aforementioned troublesome affairs in Michigan being the most improbable. By decade's end the public, state legislators, and others had experienced their fill of banking innovations and consequent problems. Accordingly, the decade to come was relatively quiet.

The Newburyport (Massachusetts) Bank as shown on a $1 note of 1840. The horse's head to the right is opposite the front door of the bank.

Wall Street in the 1840s. (Engraving by J.A. Rolf)

PRICES OF STOCKS.
Exchanges, and Gold and Silver.
Stock and Exchange Board—Feb. 20.

Stocks.	*Off.*	*Ask.*	*Marine Ins. Co's.*	*As.*	*Off*
N.Y. State 5's..1845	95	98	New York..........	—	—
New York, 4½.......	32	—	Ocean	—	—
Ohio Sixes.........	66¾	67½	American	—	—
N. Y. city 5's.......	90	—	Union	—	—
do Bonds, 6's....	—	—	Atlantic....n s......	—	—
Illinois 6's..........	20½	21	Neptune.............	—	—
do Sterling......	—	—	Jackson..............	—	65
Kentucky 6's......	84¼	84½	Washington.........	56	65
do Sterling......	—	—	Merchants	—	—
Indiana 5's.........	23½	23½	State Marine........	—	—
do Sterling......	22½	23			
Arkansas 6's.......	27	35	*Fire Ins. Co's.*		
Banks.			Mutual...............	95	—
Bank of New York.	112½	120	Eagle.................	93	100
Manhattan	67	70	Merchants..........	—	80
Merchants..........	96	100	Manhattan..........	92½	100
Mechanics..........	66	66	North River.........	—	—
Union	109	111	Equitable...........	72	—
Bank of America...	88	92	Jefferson...........	105	—
City	100	103	United States.......	80	—
Phenix.............	73	74¾	Contributionship....	70	—
North River...new	83	84	Ætna.................	95	—
Tradesmen's.......	—	—	Howard	—	—
Chemical...........	—	—	Firemen's...........	90	—
Fulton...............	105	—	Brooklyn............	—	—
D.& Hud.Canal Co.	85	85	New York...........	—	—
Dry Dock	—	30	City..................	—	—
Greenwich	—	—	Bowery..............	125	135
Butch. & Drovers..	87½	—	East River..........	—	—
Mech. & Traders...	90	—	Long Island.........	82	96
National............	94½	—	Greenwich..........	92	95
Merchants Ex......	94	95	North American....	—	—
Leather Manuf....	95	96	Trust Fire..........	—	—
Seventh Ward	70	75	Hudson..............	—	—
Bk of State of N.Y..	8[illegible]	90	Williamsburg.......	—	—
Long Island Bank..	70	—	National	—	—
Atlantic, Brooklyn.	70	—	Guardian...........	—	—
Banking Asso.			*Rail Roads.*		
Bank of Com. full.	91½	95	Mohawk & Hud....	29	29
do do scrip.	96	96	Patterson...........	44½	44½
Mech. Bk's Asso...	70	—	Boston & Prov......	—	—
Am. Exchange Bk..	70	70	N. J. R. R. & T.L...	65¼	65½
Tust Co's.			Camden & Amboy..	—	—½
Life Ins. & T. Co...	51½	60	Prov & Ston.........	18½	19
Farmers Trust Co..	12	13	Boston & Worces...	—	—¼
Ohio Life & T Co..	52½	55	Harlæm	16½	—
Miscellaneous.			Utica & Schenect...	115½	115¼
N Y. Gas Light Co.	97¾	101	Long Island.........	48¾	48
Manhattan Gas Co.	70	75	Utica & Syracuse...	97	91
Merch. Exchange..	—	—	Auburn & Syracuse..	[illegible]5	5
Canton Co. Balt....	19¼	19½	Auburn & Rocherte.r	91¼	91

Active stocks on the New York Exchange on February 20, 1843, were dominated by bank, insurance company, and railroad shares. Many of the larger city banks were publicly traded. (*New York Journal of Commerce,* February 21, 1843)

William Henry Harrison portrait engraved by R.W. Dodson, after a painting by J.R. Lambin. (*National Portrait Gallery,* vol. 3, 1836)

THE ELECTION OF 1840

On the national scene in 1840, the presidential contest between William Henry Harrison, the hero of the Battle of Tippecanoe, and incumbent Martin Van Buren went overwhelmingly to the challenger. Harrison logged 234 electoral votes contrasted with his opponent's 60. This was the first presidential campaign to feature large quantities of tokens, medals, ribbons, flags, and other items to advertise the candidates.

At the nominating convention of the Democrats, Van Buren had been featured as holding true to his illustrious predecessor, Andrew Jackson. These comments in a report of the proceedings relate to paper money and specie, blaming the second Bank of the United States for the Hard Times era, thus seeking to absolve Van Buren of any blame for the inevitable consequences:

> At the commencement of his administration in 1837, Mr. Van Buren found the country excited by the redundancy of paper money, which had produced a mania of speculation and over-trading, and a consequent delusive show of prosperity, which had no other basis than a system of credit without bounds of limitation. The Bank of the United States had, during the years 1834 and '35, thrown wide open the floodgates of expansion, and either allured or coerced the state banks to follow its example.[2] Under pretense of administering to the immediate prosperity of the country, it scattered the seeds of future embarrassment and ruin. The country suddenly became bloated with an unwholesome and sickly expansion, and all men not infected with the madness of the times predicted that this unnatural growth was but the forerunner of incurable weakness and premature decay.
>
> The fulfillment followed close on the heels of the prediction. That invariable and imperative law of nature which decrees that all violent excitements, all over-wrought efforts, whether of body or mind, shall be speedily followed by sudden prostration, produced its inevitable consequences. Within less than three months from the commencement of Mr. Van Buren's administration, and before he had advised or carried into operation a single measure that could, in the slightest degree, operate to produce the catastrophe, more than seven hundred banks, as if by one impulse, violated their charters by suspending specie payments, and by that means locked up in their vaults, and withheld from public uses in a legal currency, more than twenty-seven millions of accumulated revenue, the property of the people. . . .
>
> He remained at the helm, steadily steering his course by the polar star of public faith and national honor. The result was such as ought to fill with honest exultation the bosoms of all who value these as the brightest jewels in the diadem of the sovereign people. The sacred standard of value, which is only of secondary importance to the standard of morality, and constitutes one of the great conservators of human integrity, was preserved inviolate by the government, while everywhere else trodden under foot. The credit of the United States escaped the general wreck of public confidence; and the interest and principal of every debt were paid in the constitutional currency, contemplated by the fathers of the Revolution. . . .

William Henry Harrison campaign medal of 1840. The log cabin on the reverse symbolized Harrison's youth and was a symbol of the election contest. (White metal, 37.1 mm. DeWitt/Sullivan WHH 1840-11)

> The firm adherence of Mr. Van Buren to the obligations of integrity and the behests of the law had forced the great mass of the banks to resume specie payments. But experience had failed to make the most of them wise, nor had corrected their innate, incurable propensity to sacrifice future security to present gain. They played over the same game; the same predictions of its ultimate consequences were renewed, and the same catastrophe followed. Less than two years after the first suspension, a second occurred. In both the Bank of the United States [*sic*] led the way—first by its influence, and secondly by its example. A few honored exceptions mitigated the evil in some degree; but the measure and its consequences were the same in both cases, and the people are now suffering similar evils with those that resulted from the first suspension. . . .[3]

Somehow, this explaining away of the Hard Times during Van Buren's administration did not play upon the heartstrings of voters, with the result that he bid goodbye to the White House.

Unfortunately, his successor, William Henry Harrison, took sick from the cold weather on his inauguration day and a died a month later, on April 4, 1841—the shortest presidency in American history. Vice President John Tyler stepped into the post.

The American Scene in the 1840s

Coming into the social forefront in the middle of this decade was the abolition of slavery, advanced by stories of the mistreatment of black people in the South, attempted escapes to freedom in the North, and popular 1838-dated Hard Times tokens with the inscription AM I NOT A WOMAN & A SISTER, a sentiment borrowed from the antislavery movement in England. Meetings were held, pamphlets published, and newspaper accounts printed. Some abolition societies did not allow women, causing a double prejudice.

In the early 1840s, abolition was still a niche issue, and adherents were often labeled as fanatics, even in the North. The status quo had been in effect for a long time, and not many Northerners were prompted to take action. In 1842, John A. Collins, organizer of the American Anti-Slavery Society, suggested to members that instead of relying on oratory and pamphlets, the movement should adopt *entertainment* and other features that already characterized the temperance movement. By that time, there were temperance hotels and restaurants advertising that no alcohol was served on

John Tyler (Stock vignette from a specimen book presented by the Treasury Department, 1876; Harry W. Bass Jr. Library)

The White House as it appeared during the Tyler administration. (Buckingham's *America,* 1841)

The Erie Canal at Lockport, New York. From the time of its opening in 1825 it ranked as the most important canal in the United States. (Bartlett's *American Scenery,* 1840)

A $5 note of the Canal Bank, one of several financial institutions in Lockport, New York, a busy upstate center of commerce. Rawdon, Wright & Hatch, New York.

Detail of a $20 note of the Columbia Bank, Chatham Four Corners, New York, from a National Bank Note Co. plate of 1860. By this time the railroad had rendered many canals obsolete. This vignette shows the transition.

the premises, and any number of popular poems and songs had captured the public's fancy concerning that cause. Soon the Hutchinson Family singers, a touring group in the Northeast, added abolition to their program topics and drew record crowds.[4]

Temperance remained important, with temperance beverages, medals, hotels, and eating houses (restaurants) catering to those who did not use alcohol. Temperance did not mean tempered judgment, but total abstinence from alcohol. For teetotalers who wanted a secret nip now and then, an entire class of "medicines" called *bitters* prospered during this era. Liberally laced with alcohol and given exotic flavorings, these were available everywhere and were said to cure just about every ailment known to mankind. Women's rights was an increasingly important cause as well, but it was not yet in the forefront.

Religion was one of the most frequently discussed social topics. The Mormon faith was widely condemned, Catholicism, not yet widely practiced in the United States (that would await the mass arrival of immigrants from Ireland and elsewhere in Europe) was criticized, Masons had many detractors, and anything outside of the mainstream Protestant churches was viewed with disfavor. Maria Monk's *Awful Discourses,* published in 1836, gave lurid details of purported orgies and other scandalous activities she witnessed among Catholic nuns and priests when she spent seven years in the Hotel Dieu Nunnery in Montreal. This book continued to be a runaway best seller in the 1840s and onward, with more than 300,000 copies in print by the Civil War.[5] While in this era a patently pornographic book would likely result in legal prosecution for those involved, this so-called biographical and didactic account was found to be acceptable.

William Miller, leader of the Adventist religious movement, attracted many followers with his notion that, per information decoded from the Bible, Christ would return to earth in 1843. The Second Coming failed to happen, and disciples who had sold their worldly goods and neglected their work returned to reality, despite Miller revising the date to October 22, 1844.

In areas where the terrain permitted, canals were still the main method for transporting bulk goods inland in 1840, with about 3,300 miles of waterway in service. However, railroads continued as the growth industry, with trackage at about 2,800 miles in that year under control of about 300 companies, most of which operated for short distances. In the coming decade, rail service would expand greatly, to include most larger towns and cities in the East.

New York City was the main American trade port in 1840, but by 1850 the laurels would go to New Orleans, the service depot for the rapidly expanding economy of the Mississippi River basin. In an era before the use of petroleum, whaling remained a major industry, operating out of New England ports from Connecticut to Maine. Whale oil lamps and wax candles were standard for household lighting. By this time coal gas was used for municipal and other lighting in some areas, New York City having inaugurated such a system in 1827. However, only a few American homes were so equipped.

The Hard Times era wound down in 1843, and by 1844 the country was experiencing a new generation of enthusiasm and prosperity.

Money and Banking in the Early 1840s

The branch mints at Charlotte, Dahlonega, and New Orleans continued their coinage operations, but they were widely viewed as inefficient. A recent scandal had rocked the New Orleans Mint, and the echoes still lingered. In a speech regarding the General Appropriations Bill before the House of Representatives on April 3, 1841, Representative Green of Kentucky stated that these mints had been established as patronage plums of the Jackson administration and were continued by Van Buren. Now they were a wanton waste of public money.[6] However, the mints continued their business. During the era the gold coin denomination of choice for the export trade remained the $10 eagle, made at the Philadelphia and New Orleans mints.

On June 12, 1841, precipitated by a new suspension of specie payments by certain banks earlier in the year, an act calling for creation of the Fiscal Bank of the United States was introduced in the U.S. Senate and was soon passed by both houses, but it was vetoed by President Tyler. Tyler's entire cabinet, with the exception of Secretary of State Daniel Webster, resigned in protest over the president's action. Thus a true third Bank of the United States never came to pass. Scattered problems remained among the state-chartered banks, and as late as March 1842, not a single bank in Philadelphia was redeeming its notes in coins.

"It is death to counterfeit," proclaimed many colonial notes. Now, generations later, death was no longer a penalty under law, but that did not prevent the public from taking matters into their own hands, as per this account published in *Niles' National Register*, September 4, 1841:

Stock certificate of the Mechanics Bank of Burlington, New Jersey, issued on November 22, 1844. Plate by Draper, Toppan, Longacre & Co., Philadelphia.

Arkansas: Terrible Application of the Lynch Law

The *New Orleans Picayune* contains the particulars of a wholesale exercise of lynch law in the state of Arkansas. It seems that Philips County of that state, and the county of Cloohoma on the opposite side of the river, have been the harbor of an extensive band of counterfeiters.

The citizens, enraged at this system of things, resolved to rid themselves of them by any and every means placed within their power. They accordingly proceeded, about 100 in number, in pursuit, headed by a captain Barney Bedford, all well armed. The following stratagem was then resorted to, for their apprehension.

The volunteers engaged a trading boat at Helena, and hid about 50 men in the store room. They then descended the river, landing at every place where they expected to fall in with the counterfeiters. These depraved men came on board to purchase produce, with the intention of paying for it in counterfeit money. They were thus taken and secured in the boat . . . tied hands and feet, and, as the report says, drowned in the Mississippi, near Island No. 69. . . .

The St. Louis papers contain further particulars, giving a still darker hue to this bloody outrage. The number either drowned or shot was from 50 to 75; after which the executioners proceeded up and down the river, burning the houses lately occupied by the victims of their vengeance, and ordering their families to leave their homes forever.

In 1842 an important book appeared, titled *A Manual of Gold and Silver Coins of All Nations, Struck Within the Past Century.* Written by Mint officials Jacob Reese Eckfeldt and William Ewing Dubois, it mainly dealt with the bullion values of world and United States coins, not with numismatics. Various examples, including an 1804-dated silver dollar (without mention of its rarity), were illustrated by means of plates made by a medal-ruling machine constructed by Mint employee Joseph Saxton. Machines of this type made by various inventors were in wide use at the time, creating many illustrations of cameos and other shallow-relief art objects depicted on bank notes.

In 1843, the last year of the Hard Times era, bank bills in circulation in the United States were reduced to about $58,000,000 from about $149,000,000 in 1837, per Treasury reports. Gone were most of the wildcat issues of Michigan and assorted other worthless notes. On August 12 of that year, *Niles'* reported that the Northampton Bank, in the Pennsylvania town of the same name, had $108,217 worth of its bills in circulation, but just *69 cents* in coins in its vault! The trouble was laid at the doorstep of bank president John Rice, formerly the cashier, who had granted unwise loans and allowed his friends to overdraw their accounts.[7] Certain bills of this bank are of special interest today, as their text is given in German, while related issues were in English.

The first demonstration of the telegraph, by Samuel F.B. Morse in 1844, launched a new era of communication. Soon, news from distant places, including financial information and the status of banks, could be learned at the speed of light—not of a railroad train.

On July 23, 1844, Chief Engraver Christian Gobrecht died. He had been employed at the Philadelphia Mint since September 1835 and before that by various Philadelphia firms as a highly accomplished engraver of bank bills and dies. His successor on September 6 was James Barton Longacre, well known for his banknote plates, including those made for partnerships in which he was involved, most notably Draper, Toppan, Longacre & Co., which was in business from 1837 until his resignation in 1839. Similar to certain other Philadelphia-based firms, the partnership also maintained an office in New York City.

A $5 note of the Northampton (Pennsylvania) Bank, January 27, 1836, with inscriptions in German, from a plate by Draper, Underwood, Bald & Spencer. Cashier John Rice, who signed this note, later became bank president, after which time the bank failed.

Laying a telegraph wire across a river. The invention of the telegraph in the 1840s revolutionized communications, including the transfer of banking and financial information. (T.P. Shaffner, *The Telegraph Manual,* 1859)

Telegraph lines appear in a few 19th-century vignettes, usually as part of railroads or commercial scenes, such as this from a $10 note of the Columbia Bank of Washington, D.C. Plate by Danforth, Bald & Co., New York and Philadelphia.

Typical telegraph office in a large city. (T.P. Shaffner, *The Telegraph Manual,* 1859)

Money in the Mid-1840s

In 1845, with James Knox Polk in the White House, Florida and the Republic of Texas both joined the Union as the 27th and 28th states respectively. The era of the *extreme* clipper ship dawned, a high-speed design that found wide use in long-distance maritime trade, including to China. In the meantime, steam-powered ships were being built in large numbers and were omnipresent on navigable rivers such as the Mississippi, with more than just a few in ocean commerce as well. The outlook for canals continued to fade, and that for railroads continued to brighten. Bank bills were the sinews of domestic commerce, with those of sound banks freely interchangeable at par with gold and silver coins.

In 1846 the war with Mexico commenced, with subsequent battles duly reported in the American press. The one-sided conflict, with a string of American victories, had no particular effect on commerce. The economy remained strong.

In August 1846, *Banker's Magazine* suggested that those employed in the banking profession should "diverge occasionally from their legitimate and immediate circle of duties, and devote an hour or two a day, as a relaxation or otherwise, to the more elegant and more refined pursuits of music, painting or literature, of chemistry, botany or mineralogy; of arboriculture, floriculture or horticulture." Popular conception had it that the typical bank cashier, the highest-paid officer of a bank, devoted his life to money and numbers, with little in the way of outside interests. In contrast, bank presidents were usually busy in many other activities, ranging from conducting businesses to running for political office. Over a period of time, many bank presidents also served as governors of their states.

In the same year, *Hunt's Merchants' Magazine and Commercial Review* included these reasons under "Causes of Failure in Business," seemingly still applicable today:

1. The leading cause is an ambition to be rich—by grasping too much it defeats itself.

Portrait of James Knox Polk engraved by H. Velten from a photograph by Mathew Brady.

2. Another cause is aversion to labor.
3. The third cause is an impatient desire to enjoy the luxuries of life before the right to them has been acquired in any way.
4. Another cause arises from the want of some deeper principle for distinguishing between right and wrong, than a reference merely to what is established as honorable in the society in which one happens to live.

Such characteristics also applied to certain bank cashiers and tellers of the era, engendering scattered news accounts of such men disappearing, leaving a *wrecked* (the standard term used) bank behind them.

THE LATER YEARS OF THE DECADE

The war with Mexico ended in 1847, and American troops headed homeward, including many Mormons who passed through California, the territory recently ceded to the United States. On January 14, 1848, gold was discovered by John Marshall in the tailrace of Sutter's mill on the American River, igniting the gold rush. Its effect on paper money, the subject of the present text, was curious. Although the Miners Bank in San Francisco ordered sheets of currency in 1849 and circulated a small amount, in 1850 the state constitution (framed in 1849) forbade the use of bills in commerce. Too many immigrants recalled the Hard Times era and worthless currency, and the new state was determined to operate on specie only.

By the time that this belated report was published in the *Portsmouth* (New Hampshire) *Journal,* May 11, 1850, paper was no longer being used:

> Paper Money.—The new State of California, in the absence of the means of converting the gold dust readily into coin, it seems is favored with the facilities of a paper circulation. The *Albany Atlas* states that it has been shown a $3 bill of the most approved pattern, and in the best style of Danforth & Hufty, of New-York, purporting to be issued by "The Miners Bank of California"—J.E. Fuller, cashier, and William H. Graham, President. The bank is located at San Francisco.

Accordingly, banks in the Golden State did not participate in the use of currency after this time, although scrip bills were issued by some merchants.

NEWS OF BANKS AND PAPER MONEY

A scrapbook of selected news clippings from *Niles' National Register* (with day of publication) and *Banker's Magazine* (with month of publication) mirrors the banking scene of the 1840s. Modern comments are added in brackets. The arrangement is in chronological order:

> **Banks in Florida "extinct" (December 19, 1840):** Grand Jury for the district of East Florida have presented, among other matters, the present condition of the banks in Florida. But three banks are now pretending to be in operation: the Bank of Pensacola, the Southern Life and Trust Co. and the Union Bank; all the others have become extinct. The faith bonds issued to these banks are presented as *null and void,* and the legislature is urged to take immediate measures to cancel them.

> **Commercial Bank of Millington, Maryland (December 26, 1840):** The *New Orleans Picayune* states that F.A. Weed, president of the Bank of Millington, his brother Wm. Weed, and a third person, were arrested in that city on the 2d

instant that F.A. Weed on a charge of fraudulently, obtaining the presidency of the bank, and then passed off and exchanged for a very large amount the bills of the bank which were worthless, for the bills of other banks that were solvent; and further, that a reward has been offered for the apprehension of F.A. Weed—that he is a fugitive from justice, and that William Weed, one of the other parties arrested, has been his aider and abetter in these transactions. The property of the Messrs. Weed, consisting of some $20,000 in current bank notes, has been attached at the suit of Mr. James Jameson. M.M. Cohen, Esq. appeared for the prosecution and Messrs. Elmore, Gaiennie and King were present to defend the prisoners. New Orleans papers of a latter date state that the arrested parties have been discharged for want of sufficient evidence that they had violated either the laws of Maryland or Louisiana.

Jacksonville (Florida) Bank (February 1841): The state of Florida annulled its charter, by which time the officers had engaged in many illegal practices. [In 1842 a fraudulent attempt was made to revive the circulation of its bills in distant towns, including fake advertisements published in New York City to the effect that brokers would redeem the notes at par.[8]]

Stillwater Canal Bank of Orono, Maine (November 6, 1841): We learn from the *Newburyport Herald* that an injunction has been placed on the bank. The report of the bank commissioners of Maine says that this bank has been in the hands of New York speculators, introduced by Mr. Cyrus Moore. The bills are nearly all in circulation in distant states. The amount of the circulation is $25,829. The resources consist—first, of $10,816 past due, and of little value, principally in executions, and $38,354 due from the New York speculators, of which $15,857 was given for stock, and $22,496 bills paid out. There is a deposit of $6,500 in the Washington Bank, New York City, to redeem the circulation, but which is supposed to be exhausted. The bank also owned a dwelling house, but this has been destroyed by fire, and the real estate is now worth little or nothing. The value of its bills, of course, depends upon what may be obtained of the New York speculators.

Bank of Cincinnati, Ohio (January 22, 1842): *Mob in Cincinnati.* A disgraceful and lawless procedure occurred at Cincinnati on the 11th inst. Some of the private banking establishments, not in fair repute perhaps, became the objects of assault, were forcibly taken possession of, and their books, papers, notes and fixtures were destroyed and thrown into the streets. There were some feeble and ineffectual attempts to rally the civil authority in protection of the laws. A few spirited individuals did their duty, but the mass of the community evidently folded their arms and were mere "lookers on." The call made upon the city government to convene and assert their authority was ineffectual. Some of the firemen attempted to arrest the proceeding, but they and the few civil officers that were active were driven off by the mob. The Cincinnati Bank was forcibly entered and the counters, etc., destroyed. The inmates had escaped with the valuables. The Miami Bank was next assailed, its vaults forced and the books, notes, etc., strewed in the streets—$224,000, of which 218,000 were of its own notes!! were in the vaults, and $1,261 in specie. One individual with $24,000 in notes has been arrested. Lougee's office was run upon all day, but paid to the utmost. The Mechanics and Traders Bank was threatened, but escaped.

Bank riots in New Orleans (June 18, 1842): The attempt of the banks of New Orleans to resume specie payments has proved unavailing. They resumed on the 18th and 19th ult.; an immediate depreciation of the Municipality notes ensued, and on the 20th a mob destroyed several brokers' shops, but was soon quelled with the arrest of the ringleaders. In a few days, more than $600,000 was drained from them. Some disagreement amongst themselves led to distrust; a panic and a severe run ensued, which some of them maintained for several days, and finally all had to suspend. The Citizens Bank and Louisiana State Bank on the 31st ult. announced that they suspend until the 5th of December. The Consolidated Bank, the Commercial Bank, and the Canal Bank were overwhelmed on the 1st inst. The crowd was tremendous and some lives were lost. The City Bank held out until the 2d inst. but then gave in. The Mechanics and Traders bank, the Carrollton Bank, Union Bank, and the Bank

of Louisiana continue to pay specie, but except the latter, they are said to have no notes out, and to be doing but little business.

Farmers and Millers Bank of Hagerstown, Maryland (1843): The bank, which failed in 1836, was the report of a committee of the State Legislature in 1843. It was learned that only $100,000 in stock had been subscribed for, of a stated capital of $300,000, and that only $75,000 had been paid, including $60,000 in essentially worthless certificates of deposit from the Commercial Bank of Millington, this being the requirement to begin operations. This amount should have been paid in specie. "At one time there was only $4 in bankable funds in the institution, and the only specie was some boxes of pennies."

Bank of Illinois at Shawneetown (April 29, 1843): An examination of the condition of the Bank of Illinois has been made by a Mr. David Prickett, who was appointed the commissioner to wind up the affairs of the bank. Upon entering the vaults, instead of finding specie to the amount of $307,040 as reported by the cashier, Mr. Prickett found but $138,000, leaving a deficit of $124,000, which the officers of the bank refuse to account for. Of course this development has produced great excitement at Shawneetown. [Conditions went from bad to worse. Finally, in 1853 the bank was liquidated, including sale at auction of the large banking house, which cost more than $60,000 to build.]

Manufacturers and Mechanics Bank of Nantucket, Massachusetts (August 1846): The calamitous fire at Nantucket on the 13th of July, destroyed the Custom House, Post Office, Savings Bank, together with the building occupied by the Manufacturers and Mechanics Bank. The condition of this institution, which failed in February last, is even more deplorable than at first supposed. The defalcation of Mr. Barker Burnell, its recent cashier, is now ascertained to be nearly $150,000, while its entire capital was only $100,000. If the bank hold Mr. Burnell's private property, as it will be enabled to do unless prevented by a legal flaw, the deficit can probably be reduced to $100,000. The directors are the principal sufferers, being large stockholders and depositors. This is one of the most extraordinary and unaccountable instances of bad management that we have ever heard of; a commentary upon the practice of placing *nominal* directors in office, either too ignorant of the routine of business, or too busy with their own affairs, to attend to public duties *for which they receive no compensation.* [Very few bank directors were ever deeply involved in the operating affairs or in auditing the accounts of banks.]

Bank of the State of Alabama (September 1846): *Extensive Fraud.*—A circular, issued by the trustees of the Bank of Alabama, states that some months since, a person by the name of Bryan Hines, of Greene County, Alabama, executed to Mr. Hawn, of Tuscaloosa, a deed of trust, securing to said bank on the payment of over $60,000, a number of slaves, some 60 and upwards, 19 mules, and eight head of horses; that since the date of said deed of trust, Hines has fled, carrying with him all the property pledged. . . . [Slaves were commonly used as collateral for bank loans in the South during this time.]

Plainfield (New Jersey) Bank (February 1847): The legislature of New Jersey adopted a summary process in February, against the Plainfield Bank. An injunction was issued against the bank, and receivers appointed to take charge of the institution forthwith. The accounts as given by the officers to the committee are about as follows [excerpt]: capital stock $100,000, specie $9,000, circulation $115,000. The circulation has been hitherto almost entirely in New York City, having been issued at the office of the *Sun*. . . . Meantime, the redemption of the notes having been suspended by the receivers, the latter are calling in the assets of the bank at Plainfield, and will soon commence taking up the notes in circulation. [Moses Y. Beach, a bank fraudster of the era but best known as the proprietor of the *New York Sun,* was the principal in this bank.

Bank of Milledgeville, Georgia (January 1848): The Bank of Milledgeville (capital formerly $472,270) is now closing its business and will soon be out of existence. A proposition is now before the legislature of Georgia to authorize or compel the several banks of the state to make semi-annual returns to the comptroller general, for publication: showing their capital, circulation, loans, deposits, specie, &c. [Georgia was a laggard among states requiring banks to submit reports.]

Commercial and Agricultural Bank of Galveston, Texas (February 1848): A new bank, and the only one in Texas, went into operation on the 1st January, at Galveston. Col. Williams, (formerly of Baltimore) was elected president and Mr. McMillan, of Akron, Ohio, was elected cashier. The bank goes into operation under good auspices, with a paid up capital of $300,000. the charter was granted to Col. W. many years ago, when Texas was a province of Mexico. When Texas became independent, the constitutional convention adopted a clause prohibiting the establishment of corporations with banking powers in the state. The convention, however, admitted the validity of Col. Williams' charter, and accordingly the Agricultural and Commercial Bank of Galveston will be the only banking institution in that state. Under these circumstances, this bank has one of the best locations in the country.

Bowery Bank of the City of New York (July 1849): The cornerstone of the new building for the Bowery Bank, New York was laid in June last. The lot selected is the corner of Broome Street and the Bowery. The building will be constructed of Connecticut brownstone, a material now much used for public edifices and for costly private dwellings, as a substitute for marble. The dimensions of the new bank building are as follows: The principal front on the Bowery, 30 feet, and on Broome street, 70 feet. The front will have eight windows, three on each of the upper stories, and one on each side of the entrance, all filled with plate glass. The main floor will be occupied for the ordinary business of the bank, and the upper part as a residence for the president, with an entrance on Broome Street. The basement will be occupied by the Citizens Fire Insurance Company. This new structure will be an ornament to that part of the city in which it is located. The cost of the building will be about $22,000. The architect, John W. Rich.

Ontario Bank at Canandaigua, Branch at Utica, NY (September 1849): At a special meeting of the board of directors of this institution, held at the banking-house, on the 16th August, it was resolved, that the decease of Thomas Rockwell, Esq., cashier of this bank, excites our profound regret, and that the directors and other officers of the institution will wear the usual badge of mourning for thirty days; . . . He had been an officer since its first organization in the summer of 1815. During this long connection with the Ontario Bank, his whole energies were devoted to his official duties with a perseverance that admitted of no interruption, and with a vigilance and correctness that were perfect. . . . So closely did he confine himself to his business duties, that he rarely went from home. He never saw the New York City, and only twice was in Albany, and both times on business that could not be avoided. . . . [Truly a cashier who tended to business.]

Rhode Island bank bills stolen (October 31, 1849, from the *Worcester Palladium*): We learn that the Bank at Provincetown was entered on Tuesday night, by boring through an iron door and $20,000 in bills, principally on the Freemens Bank [of Bristol, Rhode Island], were stolen and carried away by the robbers. [The burglary actually took place at the Union Wharf Co., in Provincetown. The criminals were apprehended soon afterward. One of them, Abijah Larned, had been sentenced to 10 years in prison for robbing the Millbury, Massachusetts, Bank, but had been pardoned.]

Bank of Cincinnati, Ohio (December 1849): The last of the Monster [Bank of the United States].—The stone banking house on Main Street, between Third and Fourth, built many years ago by the Bank of Cincinnati, and afterwards owned and occupied by the Bank of the United States, has disappeared—not a single stone is now lying on the top of another! This was a substantial building, and a splendid one in its day, but it occupied too much terra firma for these days of high prices and high buildings. The Bank of the United States sold it to the old Commercial Bank—the trustees settling up the affairs of that bank since its charter expired, sold it to a company for the new Commercial. A part of the house was taken down two or three months since, and a fine new iron and stone building has been since erected, which is occupied as a bank. Now the rest is torn down to make way for two new structures. Thus three buildings take the place of the old one on the Main Street front, and there is a front of equal extent on Hammond Street, formerly Bank Alley.

State Bank at Camden, New Jersey (December 1849): This morning, about 9 o'clock, the office of the Agency of the State Bank at Camden, N.J., No. 12 Church Alley, was entered by means of false keys, and robbed of $6,243. The office is in the second story room of the building, and the robber or robbers opened the front door below, at the foot of the stairway, and also the door entering into the office room. The money consisted principally of the amount three or four of five hundred dollars. It was taken out of an iron chest standing near the desk of the agent. The sum taken had been deposited there but a short time before by the agent, who, as his usual custom is, after bringing the funds from the bank, proceeded to make his exchanges with the banks in the city. He was absent only about thirty minutes, during which time the robbery was perpetrated. A reward of $500 is offered for the detection of the robber.—*Phila. Bulletin, Nov. 24.* [On December 27th the *Philadelphia North American* reported the following: "The Camden Bank, since the late robbery, has been enabled to withdraw from circulation all its notes of $500 except six, which are numbered as follows: 155, 178, 198, 203, 214 and 219; four of which, it is believed, were stolen. And it is also ascertained that about $3000 of the amount stolen was in notes of the denominations of $50 and $100, dated January 1st, 1846, and much defaced by use. After to-day, the bank will be prepared to issue notes on the last named denominations, so altered from the former as to enable the public to be on its guard against the thieves. It is believed that the latter cannot, at the worst, succeed in passing more of the stolen money than about $1,200 in $5 and $10 notes."]

FURTHER DEVELOPMENTS IN THE LATE 1840S

Among the success stories of this decade, the states of Ohio and Indiana each operated banks with many branches. Generally, they served the public well and their currency was sound. Although failures and frauds continued here and there, the state banks in those districts did have a stabilizing influence.

For good measure, an account of the Government Stock Bank, chartered in Michigan in 1849, concludes this chapter. Its office in Ann Arbor operated in a manner reminiscent of the wildcat bank era in the state a decade earlier. The bank sowed the seeds of its own destruction by the reckless overissuing of currency. In essence it was a paper mill, selling its notes at deep discounts to New York City brokers, who were supposed to break them into small parcels and get them into the hands of the public. About $100,000 of these notes, circulated in an era in which the state sought to protect its citizens, had been unwittingly countersigned by the state treasurer. For better or worse, a large number of these bills shipped to New York City were acquired at a deep discount by the Metropolitan Bank there. This sum was large enough for the Metropolitan Bank to take vigorous action to redeem them. The bank was supposed to have been fully backed by securities and was operated under the close watch of the state.

Banker's Magazine covered the Metropolitan's actions in detail, with a large story in June 1852 covering the court case on the matter; two months later, it added this note:

> This institution is chartered by the state of Michigan, and located at Ann Arbor in that state. Its bills are chiefly issued and put in circulation in New York. The charter of the bank, and the laws of the state of Michigan, require the institution, on demand, during the usual and regular banking hours, to pay its notes in specie.
>
> On the 31st of May last, as we learn on good authority, a citizen of the state of Michigan called at the banking-house of the Government Stock Bank, at Ann Arbor, and presented its notes to the amount of $25,000, and demanded payment thereof, in specie, after having made an offer to take a draft upon New York for the amount, which was declined.
>
> The officers of the bank then insisted upon their right to pay *each bill separately.* The first package taken contained $200 in two-dollar bills. The president took one bill at a time from the receiving counter, examined it, and then carried it to a table near by, on which was a box containing coin, and from thence took two one-dollar gold-pieces and returned to the receiving counter, and delivered them to the creditor. The same process was repeated with each bill. This occupied until twelve o'clock noon, when the bank was closed until two P.M. At the opening of the bank, the creditor again presented the bills of the bank for payment. They were taken up in the same manner, and at four o'clock $700 more, had been paid by the bank, in gold dollar-pieces, and the bank then closed for the day.
>
> On the 1st of June the remaining bills were again presented, and the officers of the bank took them up in the same manner, and during the whole of the day paid $3,200 of the bills. Upwards of $20,000 of the bills presented remained unpaid at the close of the second day, and it is probable that the bank will occupy about ten succeeding business days to pay the remainder. The bills redeemed, it is supposed, are sent to New York immediately, to be again put in circulation, and to raise means to continue payments.

In 1855 the bank failed, and a receiver was appointed. Files and records were moved to state gov-

A $1.50 note of the Government Stock Bank of Ann Arbor, Michigan. Established as a "paper mill," not a legitimate bank, it ordered large quantities of currency and shipped them at large discounts to New York brokers. From a plate by Danforth, Bald & Co., New York and Philadelphia. Printed date of March 1, 1853.

ernment offices. Large quantities of old bills that had been redeemed were kept in an unlocked safe in the state treasurer's office. Employees there pilfered many of the notes and quietly put them back into circulation. Truly, this was a caper with many twists and turns![10]

The Suffolk Bank in Later Years

A review of the Suffolk Bank system was given in August 1846 in *Banker's Magazine.* The Hard Times era had been over since late 1843:

> The voluntary system adopted by the banks of New England for the redemption of their circulation at the counter of the Suffolk Bank at Boston, has been for several years in operation, and has been found to work well for all parties—for the country banks, for the people, and for the metropolitan institutions.
>
> There is, we think, no system of redemption in any part of the world more complete or more secure for the bill-holders. A bank there is known to be insolvent, not by the refusal at its own counter to redeem its paper, but by the refusal of the Suffolk Bank to receive it on deposit.
>
> There are now 243 banks in the interior of New England, all of which (with perhaps four or five exceptions) provide a sufficient deposit of specie at Boston for the redemption of their paper. Hence the latter is receivable upon a par with Boston bank bills, and has the same value (or rate of discount) at a distance as that of Boston. The result is, a uniform circulation, known to and by everybody, not subject to those variable and uncertain values which we find attached to country paper in other cities; an instance of which (and one that could be remedied) we may mention, that of New York state country paper in Wall Street.
>
> Such is the variety in the issues of the New York country banks (127 in number) and the different rates of discount even on the paper of one bank, that the community is never posted up as to their value, and daily frauds are committed that might be obviated. The New England system has this decided advantage: the country banks instead of being burdened with, and holding at risk in their own vaults, a large accumulation of coin, place their specie funds at the point where the bills mostly concentrate. These last do not return so much to their own places of emission, but are carried where they are wanted to discharge debts. Beside the saving made from having so little idle capital in the shape of specie, the banks have greater security in having so little cash in their vaults; safe, however, in their holding large balances among the banks of Boston upon which they can draw whenever occasions require.

By 1855, however, many member banks were dissatisfied with the policies of the Suffolk Bank, which had dominated the redemption of bills for a long time and had instituted certain policies that were found to be annoying. The Bank of Mutual Redemption, chartered in Boston that year, but which did not commence business until 1858, offered arrangements that were less cumbersome. After it opened, it took over nearly all of the exchange business in the area. The new system worked equally well and continued through the end of the note-issuing era in 1866.

Numismatic Notes

Many different bank notes can be collected from the 1840s, most of which are from institutions that failed or were fraudulent. Most plentiful are bills from the early years of the decade when the Hard Times era was still affecting commerce.

An Inside View of the Bank-Note Business

Introduction

Today, in the early 21st century, the writings of the most expressive of all bank-note engravers, Waterman L. Ormsby, furnish a clear view of the bank-note business in the 19th century. To his remarkable book, *Bank Note Engraving* (1852), can be added court records, newspaper accounts, and a book published under the name of George Peyton and sponsored by one of Ormsby's nemeses, the bank-note firm of Rawdon, Wright, Hatch & Edson.

Waterman L. Ormsby

One of a Kind

If I were to choose a single subject for a book-length treatment of a bank-note engraver, Waterman Lily Ormsby would be the top candidate. Similar to Jacob Perkins, he was a genius, and the world of bank notes owes much to his innovations. Unlike Perkins, however, Ormsby seemed to be insecure in life, and what might have been the triumph of golden moments dissolved into unfortunate court appearances, continuing complaints about his competitors, and a generally iconoclastic outlook on the entire bank-note engraving field.

In a word, Ormsby was a *character.* The story of his life has attracted several numismatic writers over the years, most prominently Julian Blanchard, Ph.D., in the pages of the *Essay-Proof Journal* in the 1950s and 1960s, and, in a later era, Robert McCabe in *Paper Money.* The information presented here, while featuring Ormsby, in a wider sense reflects the tenor of the bank-note engraving and printing industry, especially the scene in New York City in the early 1850s.

Blacksmithing and Art

W.L. Ormsby, as he signed his works, was born Waterman Lily (or Lilly) Ormsby in Hampton, Connecticut, on September 9, 1809, son of Elizabeth ("Betsey") Ashley Ormsby and Leonard Ormsby, natives of Hampton who had married on May 29, 1806. For all of his life, W.L. Ormsby maintained an affinity with the quiet, rural town and its inhabitants and often visited family and friends there, most particularly his mother in her later years.

W.L. had two siblings: an older brother, Dorman Leonard Ormsby, born in Hampton on January 2, 1807, and a younger sister, Jane Eliza Smith Ormsby, born before June 29, 1817 (the date of her baptism in the Congregational Church, Pawlet, Vermont). Over a period of years, some of his relatives, but not W.L. himself, occasionally spelled their surname as *Ormsbee.*

Ormsby disclosed little of his early life in his abundant writings, but we know that he showed an aptitude for art and mechanics. As a teenager in 1825, he was a "young blacksmith in William Cobb's shop" in Rochester, New York.[1] It would seem that this was his intended career, perhaps logical from his roots, as blacksmithing was an essential trade in his hometown of Hampton. However, he seems to have aspired to higher art than that afforded by the forge and anvil.

He is believed to have married Julia Ann at age 17 or 18, entering a union that was anything but a love match, according to later accounts.[2] In any event, we

Advertising note of the fictitious New York City Bank, circa 1853, from a plate by W.L. Ormsby, illustrating his *Unit System.* (National Archives)

know little about the romantic sorrows or joys of young W.L. By 1827, soon after his marriage, he was absorbed in the study of engraving, apparently under several instructors, including for a time those at the National Academy of Design in New York City. From that year until 1830, one of his fellow students was Tracy R. Edson, later (1860) named as the president of the American Bank Note Co.[3]

Engraver of Illustrations

Ormsby's innate and learned skills became apparent, and soon he produced engraved plates for book illustrations, some in Albany, New York, and others for the firm of Carter, Andrews & Co. of Lancaster, Massachusetts. For Carter, Hendee & Co., Boston publishers, he engraved several plates, including the frontispiece for the first American edition of Thomas Carlyle's *The Life of Friedrich Schiller* (1833).

One of many engravings Ormsby did to illustrate books, this is "The Twins," from the *American Common-Place Book of Prose,* 1833.

W.L. and Julia Ann Ormsby had a son, Waterman Lily Ormsby Jr., sometimes referred to as the 2nd, born on December 8, 1834. The senior Ormsby is said to have had a second spouse later in life. In the next year, on November 27, 1835, W.L. Ormsby Sr.'s mother, Betsey, having been a widow since March 2, 1831, married Zenas Loomis of Coventry, Connecticut, after which she was known as Betsey Loomis.

In 1834, and perhaps earlier, W.L. Ormsby did contract work providing unsigned vignettes for the New England Bank Note Co. of Boston (established in 1833). His products include small rectangular illustrations that could be mixed and matched in the newer-style Patent Stereotype Steel Plates.

The Medal-Ruling Machine

In 1832 Ormsby completed his first invention in the medal-ruling machine line, a device for impressing curved as well as "waved" lines into metal plates. This invention was followed in 1833 by a ruling machine "for medallion, upright," and in 1834 by a similar device, but "for medallion, horizontal." In the latter year he also contrived an "automaton operator" for both of these devices, driven by a weight on a cord that actuated clockwork. At the time, Ormsby was in Lancaster, Massachusetts.

On June 17, 1834, Oliver Pelton wrote to his partner William D. Terry, who during the decade were proprietors of Terry, Pelton & Co., engravers with offices in Boston and Providence:

> The machine for meddle [*sic*] ruling Ormsby is a going to get it pattented [*sic*] and then will sell us one—He is a doing something for me. He can rule with it as perfect as the Phil. Co.[4]

Some years later in 1852, in Ormsby's *Bank Note Engraving,* Plate II illustrated two medal-related devices, described as follows:

> **The Ruling and Medallion Machines.**
>
> *Figure One.* The Friction Ruling Machine, in common use among engravers. It is represented in a position to execute straight lines. By the application of a brass rule, having an indented edge, waved lines can also be executed by the same machine.
>
> Number 1—The sliding carriage, which has a motion backward and forward. The use of this is to mark parallel lines, with the diamond point, through an etching ground, on the plate.
>
> Number 2—represents the plate as placed upon the bed of the machine, which has a lateral motion. The diamond point is represented as resting upon the plate.
>
> Number 3—The index, to regulate the width of the lines.
>
> Number 4—The connecting bar.
>
> *Figure Two.* The Medal Copying Machine, which is made precisely like the plain ruling machine, with the exception of the four upright supporters of the medal, and a very simply tracing apparatus, which is attached to the carriage.
>
> Number 1—The supporters of the medal.
>
> Number 2—The medal in a horizontal position, with the face downwards.
>
> Number 3—The steel point tracer; the uneven motion of which, in passing over the medal, conveys a corresponding lateral motion to the diamond point in passing over the surface of the plate.

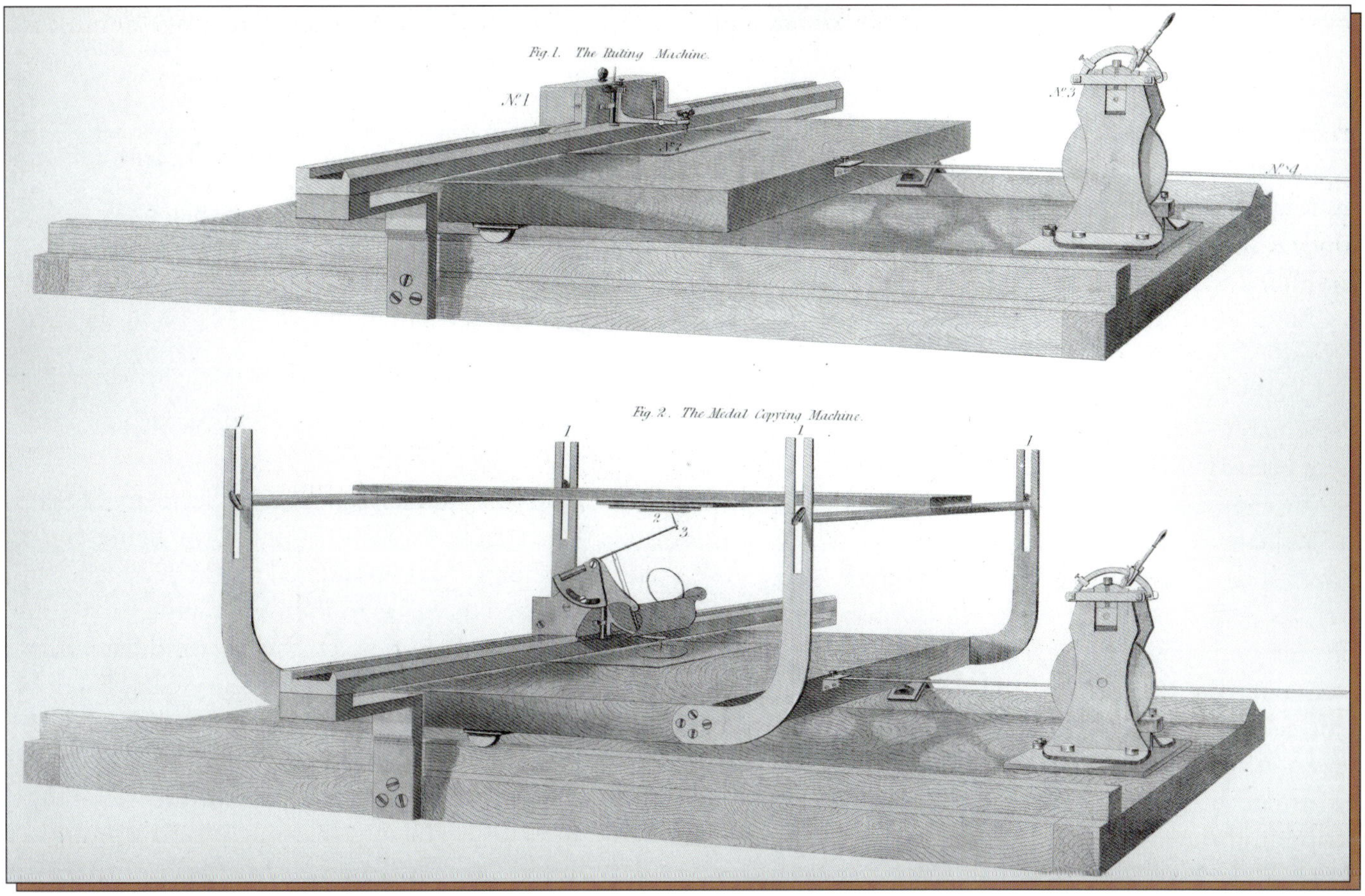

Plate II from Ormsby's *Bank Note Engraving* book showing a medal-ruling machine (top) and a medal-copying machine.

> The medal, which is being copied, and the plate, are moved along together, by means of the index, and connecting bar.
>
> There are many kinds of ruling machines, some of which are very ingenious and complicated. Those represented in the engraving are substantially the invention of the writer. Their simplicity and accuracy are generally commended.
>
> The writer has another machine in actual use, which is wound up like a clock, and is made to propel the ruling machine for several hours without the personal attention of any one. The weight employed is about three hundred pounds, and the fall, sixty feet.

IN NEW YORK CITY

By 1835 he set up in trade in New York City as the proprietor of Ormsby's Pentographic Establishment. *Pentographic* was Ormsby's term for illustrations produced by his medal-ruling machine. His business was at 142 Nassau Street, and he resided at 26 Vandam Street, close to the 32 Vandam Street location of his brother, Dorman, who was a grocer for a long time before going into other lines, including beer and soda.

Ormsby's 1835 publication, which must have achieved only limited success because copies are scarce today, was titled *Ormsby's Pentographic Illustrations of the Holy Scriptures; Being Accurate Copies of Sir Edward Thomason's Celebrated Medals with a Condensed History of the Bible.* A modest volume of octavo size, the work included just four pages of plates, each with two medals illustrated. Descriptions were printed on facing pages. Edward Thomason, an English medalist and engraver, produced many large-diameter medals, including a set showing scientific and philosophical discoveries and curiosities, a beautiful medal for the opening of the Erie Canal in 1825, and a set of biblical scenes. It was an easy matter for Ormsby to make illustrations by mechanically tracing the medals.

In 1835 Ormsby created a quarto-sized engraving of George Washington, the most popular figure in American history at that time. Other engravers well known to numismatists today, including Christian Gobrecht and James B. Longacre, also produced portraits of the Father of Our Country. Other popular historical figures engraved by Ormsby included DeWitt Clinton (1769–1828) and Samuel Finley Breese Morse (1791–1872), the artist and inventor of the telegraph. It is said that Ormsby knew Morse and helped him and his associate, Henry A. Munson, devise the Morse code alphabet. Among lesser figures whose portraits were engraved was Emanuel Swedenborg (1688–1772), Swedish philosopher, scientist, and mystic. A large print of Thomas Jefferson signing the Declaration of Independence achieved wide sales. Examples of this piece are occasionally met with today.

Scrip notes ink dated 1838 were made with W.L. Ormsby's imprint, such as some with $1.50, $3, $5, and $10 values issued by the Manhattan Association. Presumably, Ormsby made the plates, and the bills were printed elsewhere.[5]

In 1841 *Longworth's New-York Directory* listed him as William [*sic*] L. Ormsby, engraver, 142 Nassau Street. The *William* error is found in other listings as well, as is *Walter.* In the same year Ormsby invented the "grammagraph," which he described as a device "for engraving map letters."[6] The next year an important celebration was held in New York City. For the occasion, Ormsby used his grammagraph to prepare an ornate badge that was sold for 12-1/2¢ by subscription through Edward P. Whaites, No. 1 Cortland Street. This description appeared in the *New York Journal of Commerce:*

> *Croton Aqueduct Celebration.* Mr. W.L. Ormsby, 142 Nassau Street, has prepared a beautiful badge to be used at the celebration of the completion of the Croton Aqueduct. It is printed on white satin, from a steel plate, the letters of which, 3,000 in number, were engraved at the rate of seven a minute by a machine just invented by Mr. Ormsby.
>
> At the head of the badge is a vignette exhibiting the city arms, the dome of the City Hall, the fountain in the Park, and the arches of the Aqueduct. Underneath the vignette is a summary history and description of the most important bridges, reservoirs, syphons &c. This badge has been adopted by the Joint Croton Water Committee and is to be worn by the Common Council and the invited guests on the day of the celebration, Oct. 14th.

In October 1844 this notice appeared in the *New York Tribune:*

> CLAY BREAST-PINS. W.L. Ormsby, 116 Fulton Street, has got up a cheap Breast-Pin embellished with a likeness of Mr. Clay. Price 12-1/2 cents.

In the 1844 presidential election, Secretary of State James Knox Polk, a relatively unknown figure and a true "dark horse," was nominated for the presidency by the deadlocked delegates to the Democratic Party convention. Opposing him was the Whig candidate, Kentucky senator and famous orator Henry Clay, billed as "the people's choice." In November, Polk beat Clay handily by 170 to 105 electoral votes. Ormsby's entry into campaign novelties is reflective of his wide-ranging outlook for engravings that might turn a profit.

Ormsby's business seems to have been situated at 116 Fulton Street from June 1, 1844, through the end of the decade. However, the 1843/1844 issue of *Doggett's New York Directory* has him at 12 Beekman Street, corner of Nassau Street, which seems to be about the same as the 1844/1845 issue of the same publication, where his location is stated as 136 Nassau Street, corner of Beekman Street. The 1846/1847 issue

Ormsby's popular print of Thomas Jefferson signing the Declaration of Independence.

of *Doggett's New York Directory* noted that he maintained his residence in Newburgh. If so, then Ormsby must have commuted to his office by either rail or the Hudson River Day Line steamship.

By 1847, per directory listings, he was living in Jersey City, New Jersey, where he remained for years afterward, while maintaining his business in New York City at 116 Fulton Street.

More successful in the medal-ruling line of images was Ormsby's later contribution to Thomas Wyatt's 315-page book published in 1848, *Memoirs of the Generals, Commodores, and Other Commanders, Who Distinguished Themselves in the American Army and Navy During The Wars of The Revolution, and 1812, and Who Were Presented With Medals by Congress, For Their Gallant Services. Illustrated by Eighty-Two Engravings on Steel from the Original Medals,* published by Carey & Hart, Philadelphia. This is the first American book of importance to deal with medals, and, as such, is a prized addition to a numismatic library today.[7]

Patent medicine labels were a rich source of business for engravers, including Ormsby, who in 1851 produced such for Judson's Chemical Extract of Cherry & Lungwort, a nostrum put up and peddled by Comstock & Brothers, New York City. He also did labels for Moffat's Vegetable Life Pills and other cure-alls. Moffat's Vegetable Life Pills was actually a counterfeit for a crook who was peddling cheap imitations of the Moffat product, although Ormsby thought he was filling a legitimate order.

In the early 1850s, Ormsby produced an octavo-size print, *View of Sacramento City as it appeared during the great inundation,* a scene from the memorable flood of 1850.[8] Later, he issued a panorama of San Francisco as it appeared in 1849. Both illustrations were based on paintings by George W. Casilear. Easterners were eager to learn of life and scenes of the gold rush, and there was a lively market for such prints made by several different manufacturers.

In July 1852, Ormsby issued a 20- x 28-inch print of *Gen. Franklin Pierce,* a native son of New Hampshire who was campaigning for the November election. The general is shown in uniform, on horseback, against a background of a battle scene from the war with Mexico, the Chapultepec castle, and, for good measure, the famous Popocatépetl volcano.

Among his later popular engravings was a large print titled *Maj. Gen. Geo. B. M'Clellan, Commanding United States Army,* the general being a well-known figure in the Civil War. However, McClellan seems to have developed a case of the "slows," per the contemporary term, and President Lincoln relieved him from command early in 1862. Afterward, this same print was reissued by Ormsby with the word *Late* added before *Commanding* in the title. In the 1864 election McClellan opposed Lincoln in November, but lost.

Ormsby continued making single vignettes of scenes, numbers, and decorations for various bank-note firms. Some of these were his own art, but many of them were old steel vignettes by Asher B. Durand, G.W. Casilear, and other artists, from which he made many transfer copies. Although siderography was well known by this time, the method required technical skill to execute properly, and it seems that other firms found it convenient to farm out work to Ormsby. Among his clients were Rawdon, Wright & Hatch (and their later partnership with Edson), of New York City, and the New England Bank Note Company (which was 50% owned by Rawdon, Wright, Hatch & Edson).

Decorating Colt Pistols

In 1836 Ormsby patented a device for applying engravings to the pistols made by the Colt Arms company in Hartford, Connecticut.[9] The engravings themselves were made by the standard method, an adaptation of siderography, by cutting the motifs into flat plates of soft steel, hardening them, then transferring the designs to become relief impressions in soft steel cylinder dies. These dies were then hardened and used to apply the designs to the pistols. This program was a great success for both Ormsby and Colt, as decorated pistols had wide appeal to customers (as they do to firearms collectors today). Certain of the cylinder dies were used so extensively that Ormsby's signature was worn away, becoming faint and incomplete on the impressions.

Certain early Dragoon, Navy, and Metropolitan Navy model Colts bear the imprint "W.L. Ormsby Sc. N.Y." Motifs attributed to Ormsby included mounted soldiers vanquishing Indians, a stagecoach holdup, a sea battle between ships of the Republic of Texas and Mexico (May 15, 1843), and Admiral Farragut's ship *Hartford* battling the Confederate *Varina* on the Mississippi River on April 22, 1862, when New Orleans was recaptured by the Union. Ormsby's relationship with Colt lasted for many years and was probably the most enduring of his career.

Engraving Bank-Note Plates

By Ormsby's own account, in 1842 he began the business of bank-note engraving, at which time he would have been located at 142 Nassau Street. Apparently, his earlier work had been limited to making and reproducing vignettes and, to a lesser extent, bank-note plates with imprints of other firms. Likely, in 1842 he began producing bank-note plates as his main, but not exclusive, business. Most of these plates must have been made for others, with no signature or imprint by Ormsby.

By the time of publication of his *Bank Note Engraving* book in 1852, Ormsby was still producing plates for others. The book illustrated hypothetical designs for the Bank of North America and the Bank of the Republic, New York City (both Rawdon, Wright, Hatch & Edson customers). Likely, most of the art on the bank-note plates Ormsby engraved, printed, and sold to banks in the 1850s came from old vignettes and was not his original work. Smaller vignettes, ornate numerals, and the like were stock items from various sources—items that he had supplied other engravers for years.

A Popular Eagle

In 1844 W.L. Ormsby engraved the plate to produce one of two stamps used by the American Letter Mail Co., a private post. He signed the work at the bottom edge, "Engraved by W.L. Ormsby."[10] However, he was not the originator of this motif. He simply adapted and signed an earlier work. In the 1850s, Ormsby used this same eagle elsewhere, including on $1 and $2 bills of the Hartford Exchange Bank, Hartford, Indiana.

This same eagle, with no Ormsby signature, was used in the late 1830s on $1 and $3 bills of the Bank of St. Albans, in Vermont, currency made by S. Stiles, Sherman & Smith. Certain $1, $2, and $3 bills of the Republic of Texas, issued in the late 1830s and printed by Childs, Clark & Co., New Orleans, also have the eagle, as does a $3 bill of the Bank of Louisville (Kentucky), by Underwood, Bald & Spencer, Philadel-phia, with the date 1843. An undated proof $5 note of the Weybosset Bank of Providence, Rhode Island, by Balch, Stiles, Wright & Co., from the early 1830s shows it as well. This stock engraving, an Ormsby favorite, was everybody's eagle.[11]

On or about June 1, 1851 (June 1 being the standard annual moving day in New York City), Ormsby relocated his business to 12 Vesey Street, New York City. By that time his teenaged son, W.L. Ormsby Jr., was assisting him in the business and had achieved a high degree of technical and artistic skill.

A $1 note of the Hartford Exchange Bank, Hartford, Indiana, imprinted W.L. Ormsby, New York. This "double eagle" bill had two eagles on the face. The smaller one was widely used elsewhere. It was probably one of the many vignettes copied and widely sold by Ormsby.

A $2 note of the Hartford Exchange Bank, by Ormsby. This set of bills violated one of Ormsby's prime rules: that different denominations should have different appearances. Here the same large spread eagle used on the $1 note was employed.

A $3 note of the Bank of St. Albans, Vermont, by S. Stiles, Sherman & Smith, employing four stock vignettes, including the small eagle at the bottom.

Bank-Note Engraving (1852)

Description of the Work

In 1852 Ormsby's elegant and impressive book, *Bank Note Engraving,* was published in New York and London. This work is an exposition of the title subject that remains definitive today, a rich source for art and technique. The volume measures about 10-1/2 inches wide, 13-1/2 inches high, and is hardbound with gold imprinting on the front and back covers. The interior is a lavish production on heavy paper, set in type with large margins. There are 13 full-page engraved plates at the back, plus various smaller illustrations elsewhere. No other bank-note engraver or firm ever produced such a large, important work on the subject. Today, copies are highly prized, and the work stands as a classic.[12]

At the time the book was published, Ormsby was at 12 Vesey Street, close to the famous Astor House hotel. During this era he was riding high, enjoying a fine reputation earned from supplying plates, vignettes, and decorations to bank-note printing companies and producing many high-quality illustrations for books as well as engraving plates for labels and other works.

Prospectus for the Book

In August 1852, Ormsby mailed this circular letter or prospectus describing his work, offering copies of the book for $12 each and reprinting the preface to demonstrate the worth of the book (adapted):[13]

> Dear Sir,
>
> Will you allow me to call your attention to a work which has just been published, specially addressed to banking institutions and those connected with monetary affairs. It is entitled "A Description of the Present System of Bank Note Engraving, Shewing [*sic*] Its Tendency to Facilitate Counterfeiting; to Which is Added a New Method of Constructing Bank Notes to Prevent Forgery."
>
> As it is the first work of the kind ever issued in this country, and discloses the principal source of danger to which the issues of our banking institutions are exposed, it has an evident importance to the class for whom it is proposed. It is designed to be a true guide to banks in the construction of their notes, so as most effectually to prevent imitation, alteration, or forgery.
>
> It is well known that banks have often been compelled to call in their issues, and procure new plates, at great expense, because they have been successfully imitated by counterfeiters; and yet their new issues, possessing the same inherent faults, are exactly as liable to imitation as were the old ones. A knowledge of the *causes* of this insecurity, which would enable banks to avoid this expense as well as to guard the purity and safety of their issues, it is the purpose of this book to clearly indicate, and to suggest an effectual remedy.
>
> I beg therefore to solicit your attention to the following preface as giving a concise, though accurate representation of the scope and purpose of the work.
>
> The work is published in royal quarto form, elegantly bound in gilt morocco, and embellished with numerous steel engravings. Price twelve dollars. It may be had of the undersigned.
>
> Very Respectfully,
Your Obedient Servant,
W.L. Ormsby
New York City, 12 Vesey Street,
August, 1852
>
> **Preface**
>
> It is with unaffected diffidence that this work is offered to the public. To expose the defects and dangers of the work of eminent artists, with whom the author has none but the most friendly relations, and for whose genius and character he entertains the highest respect, is a task too unwelcome to have been undertaken but from a deep conviction of its importance and necessity.
>
> For many years a professional bank note engraver himself, the defects and bearings of the system of engraving universally employed in this

country upon bank notes, became, in the course of the author's experience, so painfully evident, and the facilities which it afforded the counterfeiter so obvious, that he was unavoidably constrained to seek some adequate remedy. An investigation of the subject soon disclosed the evil to consist in the use of labor-saving machinery and dies, and in the piecemeal or patch-work system of engraving necessarily resulting from their use. The more the subject was considered, the more apparent its weakness became; until there arose in his mind a moral constraint to make it known, and to awaken the public attention to an evil so alarmingly prevalent, and so unavoidable under the existing state of things. The present work has had its origin in this feeling: and he cannot but persuade himself that the candid reader of his pages will arrive at the same conclusions to which his own sincere research led him, that there is no security against counterfeiting so long as the present system of engraving continues to be practiced. The remedy proposed, is simple and practicable; and it is the writer's firm conviction that if it be universally adopted, counterfeiting as now ordinarily practiced will be impossible.

This is, assuredly, an end in which all banking institutions, as well as the public generally, have a vital interest. The losses occasioned by counterfeiting are already enormous; and, under the present system of engraving, they must inevitably become greater. The multiplication of banks and the increase of dies and machinery are rendering the business of counterfeiting so easy and so safe that its rapid increase will be inevitable. But few persons whose attention has not been directed to the subject are aware of the alarming extent to which this dangerous crime is now carried. Our bank note directories teem with cautionary notices and descriptions of counterfeits, alterations of denominations, and other kinds of forgery, all of which can be distinctly traced to the system of engraving now universally in use. This evil will go on till the paper currency of the country becomes worthless, unless some remedy, covering all the sources of danger, be adopted.

Whether that remedy shall be adopted, it remains with banking institutions mainly to decide. It is for them to determine whether the perilous system now in use shall be prolonged, or whether a new system, avoiding the defects of the old, and affording the greatest possible amount of security, shall take its place. From bank note engravers, whose interest, reputation, and capital are involved in the continuance of the present system, no aid in effecting the needful reform is to be expected.

Without imputing to them any motives other than the natural instincts of interest, to which all men are subject, the author anticipates their opposition in any and every form—by the authority of professional knowledge, by the imputation of unworthy designs, and by means of the pre-secured confidence of banking institutions. It is not natural to expect from parties whose interests are affected by a proposed reform, any thing less than an opposition proportioned to the amount of their anticipated losses. If reform there be, therefore it must spring from the enlightened convictions and wisdom of the banks themselves. They can see the evil, and without any professional assistance they are able to judge of the merits of the remedy proposed.

As they are the only sources from which bank notes emanate, they alone have the power to effect the change proposed. These institutions have suffered more from misinformation on the subject of engraving than from the depredations of counterfeiters; and if they continue to rely upon the suggestions of interested parties, every change will be likely to result, as heretofore, in making the original engraving easy and profitable to the artists, and still more expensive to themselves. And, as an inevitable consequence, rendering counterfeiting easy of accomplishment and difficult of detection.

We enter the field of inquiry untrammeled by interest, seeking for no exclusive privileges, no emolument except the natural support of those for whom we labor, no favor except that of being heard and respected, and without any other aspirations than those of being useful—firstly, to banks, by rendering their circulation secure against forgery; secondly, to artists, by opening a new resource for the exercise of their talents and enterprise; thirdly, to business men, by inspiring them with confidence in our great circulating medium, which now requires their constant watchfulness, and deserves their distrust; and, lastly, to aid the cause of morality by closing a royal road to crime, fraught with excitement, temptation, and ruin. . . .

Though complete in itself, the arguments and demonstrations of the present work would be greatly confirmed by a more minute description of the ways and means by which the genuine work of bank note engravers finds its way into the hands of counterfeiters. If duly encouraged in his undertaking, the author proposes another and more elaborate work, giving a circumstantial history by the best professional engravers, which have passed from the hands of their original owners into other hands. Some of these involve deeply instructive lessons and much romantic interest; and their history will go to confirm the impression of the present work, that so long as dies and machinery are used, there is no security from the counterfeiter.

W.L. Ormsby

New York City, August 13, 1852.

For the Public Good or for Profit?

Ormsby presented the work as *pro bono publico,* to protect citizens and banks from the evils of counterfeits. In the work, in fact, he was critical of himself, as his earlier plate engraving had been accomplished by using the methods he now condemned. As he saw it, the great savior for the bank-note engraving world was his *Unit System,* and the thrust of this work seems to have been directed toward promoting it—never mind that in 1852 it was an untested concept.

A fluent writer, either from training or innate ability, Ormsby in the preface and the main text of the book expressed himself clearly and in a highly readable manner, often interweaving classical references, metaphors, and philosophical tidbits. It is clear that he was a student of human nature. At the same time he was a curmudgeon, never losing an opportunity to criticize the actions of others, particularly his competitors. Ormsby felt that the field belonged to artistic engravers, and he curiously railed against corporate executives who simply purchased groups of dies made by others and used them to produce new notes, scarcely with an eye to quality or tradition—although he had been a prime supplier of such dies. In a self-destructive way, Ormsby reveals in the book that he often used old vignettes acquired from defunct firms and, in fact, used certain of these as book illustrations. Ormsby was a man of contradictions and would probably make a good case study in psychology. As will be seen, his emotions overwhelmed any business sense he might have had, leading him into great controversies.

For numismatists, Ormsby's book is exceedingly valuable for the basic information it gives on engraving and bank-note printing. Most current techniques are explained, some in great detail.

His competitors, some of which were his customers at the time, are described as having poor processes and little ability to create notes that could not be easily counterfeited. In contrast, Ormsby's Unit System was featured as being absolutely foolproof, a counterfeiter's nemesis. As might be expected, this claim put his competitors in a defensive position. In time, it would become Ormsby versus the rest of the bank-note engraving world.

PRESIDENT PIERCE

In 1852 and 1853, the book achieved modest distribution, selling, it is believed, many hundreds of copies if not more. Today, at least a few dozen exist in numismatic libraries, and more are located in public institutions and elsewhere. A copy presented to Franklin Pierce, president-elect of the United States, was accompanied by this letter from Ormsby:

> New York, Jan 31 1853
>
> Dear Sir:
>
> Allow me to present you with a copy of my late work on bank note engraving which will explain the cause of the vast amount of counterfeiting in this country. This is the first publication on this subject, and it is daily growing more and more important to every person in the community.
>
> I beg permission to call on you, at some future time, when my plans for constructing bank notes to prevent forgery are mature, that I may have an opportunity of convincing you of the utter insecurity of our present paper money, and the necessity of legislative action on the subject.
>
> At present I will only ask your attention to the important requisites of a bank note which constitute its value. There are but two—first that the bank be good, second that the note be genuine. The people loose [*sic*] more by counterfeiting money than by broken banks. It is therefore of as much importance to the poor people to have the note genuine as it is to have the bank good.
>
> It is my object and aim to instruct the people in the art of bank note engraving to the end that our General Banking Laws may be amended, so that they should define no less particularly the manner in which a note must be engraved than the manner in which the bank must be organized.
>
> Many of the counterfeit bills in circulation are absolutely the work of the original engravers. Counterfeiters obtained their work in spite of their utmost efforts to prevent it. This is all owing to the patch-work system of constructing the note and the use of dies in the engraving of plates.

President Franklin Pierce in 1853. *(Gleason's Pictorial Drawing Room Companion)*

My plan is to have a bank note one design or picture, with all the lettering interwoven in it. The whole to be engraved on the plate by the hand of the artist without the use of dies. A counterfeiter would be obliged to do the work himself instead of employing others who do not know for what purpose their work is to be used.

On turning to page 52 you will learn how a counterfeit plate of a five hundred dollar Treasury note was engraved for a counterfeiter by the very engraver who executed the original plates! Such things have frequently occurred. The matter is seriously alarming to every business man. Any encouragement which I may receive from you will be gracefully received by

Your most obedient humble Sevt,

W.L. Ormsby

The flyleaf of this copy is inscribed, "Presented to Gen. Frank. Pierce by his humble Sevt. The author W.L. Ormsby."

The Unit System

Ormsby's key thesis, the eureka-moment process that was set to eliminate counterfeiting forever, was the Unit System, described but not named in the letter to Pierce: "My plan is to have a bank note one design or picture, with all the lettering interwoven in it." Under this process, the entire face of a note would be devoted to a specific scene, a *unit*—such as goddesses or a landscape—unique to a specific bank and bill denomination. In that way a bill could not be altered to another denomination, as this would involve re-doing the entire plate. Nor could the bills of one bank be altered to give the name of another, for no other bank would have the same vignette.

In his 1852 book Ormsby gave these details of the plan:

A New System of Bank Note Engraving

In offering a new system of bank note engraving, adapted to avoid the evils and imperfections which have been proved to be inherent in the present system, the writer would pretend to no infallible remedy. Perhaps it is not possible for the highest order of genius to invent that which may not be imitated. There is no such thing as a *perfect* protection against imitation; it would be a proof of charlatanry to claim it. The most that can be exacted of a system is the best possible approximation to a perfect security. And this, it is claimed, that the system developed in the following pages, fairly and undeniably attains.

Bank bills will be most secure against the arts of the forger when they are so constructed as to *compel* him to resort to the same methods in imitating the note as are employed in the original construction; or if not the same, methods equally difficult and costly. And this forms the principal feature and distinction of our plan. It does not propose to baffle the counterfeiter by secrecy, but to set his arts at defiance—to render imitation too difficult to be remunerative, and impossible without the aid of artistic skill nearly equal to that employed upon the original note. It may serve to show in some degree the merits of the system that we are unable to illustrate it by a multitude of engravings, as we have already been able to do in reference to the old system. For, while it is easy to produce bank notes of the present style at trifling expense, the illustrations of the proposed plan cannot be furnished at a less expense than would be required to provide original work for banks.

The New Plan

We recommend the entire disuse of all mechanical contrivances and machinery, and a resort to the simplest means, openly, and in defiance of the forger. The main features of the plan we propose are the following:

First Requisite: One Design

The whole surface of the bill should be covered with one unbroken and inseparable design, with the lettering so interwoven by the hand of the artist, as to form an integral part of the design. If this be done, then the security against imitation or alteration will be exactly in proportion to the ingenuity of the design, the talent of the artist, and the amount of labor bestowed upon it. The forger will be obliged to encounter all the difficulty in imitating, which the artist experienced in constructing.

The obstacles which the adoption of this principle will throw in the way of the counterfeiter are obvious. If the artist designs and engraves the *whole note* at once, on the whole surface of the plate, and never himself engraves another like it, it cannot be copied without the employment of talents, nearly equal to those by which it is first produced.

If the original plate is the workmanship of the best artist in the country, it is plain that the utmost difficulty will lie in the way of its imitation. If the artist bestows upon the original plate a great amount of work, the forger will encounter a corresponding amount of difficulty. If the artist employs no dies in the execution of the original work, no *part* of the genuine plate can get into the hands of the counterfeiter. If there be but *one* picture upon a note, it will be readily remembered, and counterfeits will be readily detected. If the artist employs only *one* design, or vignette, to cover the whole note, the forger cannot get his work done by professional engravers, a little here, and a little there. If the artist will not assist the forger, the forger will be compelled to rely upon his own skill, and, in all probability will not succeed in producing a passable imitation.

The use of a variety of designs and dies, arranged together in the patch-work system, renders it perfectly easy for the forger to obtain the genuine work of honest artists for his fraudulent purpose. But the employment of a single design covering the whole bill would put an end to this. If a counterfeiter wished to imitate a portrait, he could not obtain from one artist an eye, from another a nose, and from a third a forehead; the very nature of the work demands that it should be done by one and the same artist; and no part of it could be engraved without a knowledge of the design for which it was to be used. So would it be if a single design, or vignette, were used upon the bank bill. Being inseparable, no part of it could be engraved without the whole, nor without a knowledge of the purpose to which it was to be applied. Of course, by this, the forger's greatest facility would be removed entirely.

The benefit of weaving the lettering into the design, is, that neither the name of the bank, nor the denomination of the note, can be changed, or altered. This would, at once, prevent that large class of frauds.

Second Requisite: Copyright

The second requisite of our plan is the following: that the bank, which obtains a new design for its bills, shall *copyright* the notes, so that the design upon it shall never be used for any other purpose. Let the bank also retain possession not only of its plates, but of every part of them, in whatever shape or form they may exist.

The benefit of this precaution would be, that if a bank should fail, and the steel-plates of its bills be sold, the counterfeiter could not, by obtaining them, and altering their denomination or name, make them represent the bills of good banks, as he can now easily do. And if the bank note engravers should fail, and their stock be sold, their plates and dies could not be used for counterfeits, as they now can be. Under the present system, the failure of one of the large engraving establishments, might prove fatal to the circulation of every bank that had employed it.

Third Requisite: State Arms

Another safeguard, in the case of all issues of free banks, would be obtained by entirely covering the back of the note with the Arms of the State—splendidly, and, if possible, inimitably engraved, with the denomination of the note inseparably interwoven. This plate should be sedulously kept in the bank department, and in no other place; and the printing upon all bills done by the department; for which, if a small remuneration were charged, the profit might defray, perhaps, the entire expenses of the department.[14]

It being also one design, would not only ornament the bill, but double the difficulty to the counterfeiter, who being unable to procure it piecemeal and by fraud, would be obliged to engrave it himself. It would moreover furnish the people a ready means of comparing one note with any other, and would give an additional means of influence to the bank department.

Fourth Requisite: Open to All Artists

Another source of safety we recommend, is, to throw the business of engraving bank notes open to all artists who are competent. Let any artist design and execute a single note plate, of any denomination, according to the preceding rules: and let a plate of three or four notes be made by multiplying it, by means of the electrotype process, which is the simplest and most accurate of all "transferring" processes. The original plate being thus only used for producing the copies, could never wear out or require repair.

Fifth Requisite: Different Sizes for Different Denominations

It would furnish another great security against that species of counterfeiting which consists in altering the denomination of notes, to enact a law requiring uniformity of sizes in all the bills of a state. The different denominations should be of different size—the ONE DOLLAR notes being a trifle smaller than those of TWO—and increasing in size, with the increase of the denomination. This would enable every observer to detect any alterations of denomination, and to measure the amount of a note by a foot rule. It would put an end also to another frequent and dangerous species of counterfeiting, the cutting of notes into pieces, and making five forged notes out of four genuine ones.

Sixth Requisite: Local or Regional Designs

It would add much to the convenience and security of a system of bank note engraving, to require that the designs for bills should observe some principle of indicating the locality of the bank, or of the town, or state, at least, the section of country, to which they belong.

A view, for example, of the Falls of Niagara, might form a part of a design to designate an institution created in that section of the country. The Bunker Hill Monument for a bank in Charlestown or Boston.[15] By this means the public might become more easily familiar with the designs of the various bank notes of the country, so that a spurious vignette could not be passed off. As it now is, there is perfect confusion of designs. Not even the most scrutinizing broker pretends to keep account of all the vignettes adopted for the various bills of the banks on all their denominations.

It will be observed that, completely to realize the benefit of the proposed plan, legislative enactments will be necessary. But the principle of these benefits can be secured at once, without any such legal interpositions. A form may be commenced by any banking institution, the result of which will surpass any preconceived conceptions.

Objections

It is not to be supposed that every objection which interested and ingenious minds may suggest to the details of our system can be anticipated. No criticism nor reproach will be withheld to dispute its claims. But some of the more obvious of these objections which will be apt to rise in the mind of the candid inquirer, we will consider.

If it be asked, "Will bank notes engraved upon the proposed system *cost* more than those engraved upon the present system?" we answer, unhesitatingly, "No."

The charge now made for engraving a bank note plate, is $125 each note. A plate constructed upon the new system, might cost $200, including the design and engraving for the single note. But this may be multiplied by the electrotype process, so as to make a plate of two or four notes, for $10 each copy. The cost therefore of a plate of four notes, of one denomination, would be $240, while the cost of such a plate of four notes, in the present system is, as bankers well know, $500. The printing a plate of four notes, *ought* not to cost the bank more than $2 per 100 impressions.

Will the proposed system require a longer time to execute the work?

Not in the aggregate; for if speed be required, one artist would be employed on each note separately: and two, three, or more plates would be obtained just as readily as *one,* both in the engraving, and in producing plates of four notes, by the electrotype process; and any number of presses could soon be put in requisition to print a large number. The time lost in the engraving would be more than made up in the printing.

Are there good engravers enough in the country to execute the work required by the banks, on the proposed system?

We answer, unhesitatingly, that there are. And no inconsiderable benefit of the proposed system would be found in the distribution of the business of bank note engraving which it would affect. Instead of being confined to three or four firms, a hundred or more artists would be employed in the business, and the public security would be promoted by it. The safety of the public ought not to be sacrificed to the interest and convenience of a few engravers. It should also be borne in mind, that while the skill and genius of the best engraver may find proper scope in bank note engraving, the highest style of art is not requisite as a means of guarding against counterfeiting. It is well known that the beauty of the engraving upon a bank note is soon effaced by circulation. The counterfeiter, therefore, never imitates a newly issued bill, but reserves his attacks for those which have been worn. There is but little practical utility, therefore, in employing highly finished vignettes, unless the practice of the bank of England be adopted, of destroying the notes which have been once issued and returned. If bank notes are made by means of dies, there is no security against counterfeiting, however elegant they may be.

Is the proposed system as safe in respect to the fraudulent circulation of loose bills from genuine plates?

It cannot be more *unsafe* than the present system. If any practical artists were inclined to dishonesty, the present system enables them to obtain the genuine dies and genuine work in a variety of ways; and the country might be flooded to a still more alarming degree with well engraved counterfeit bank notes without any clue to their source.

But in the new plan, the artist would be strongly interested in guarding the trust reposed in him by the banks, since the appearance of his genuine work on a counterfeit note would be traced directly to him, and could not be obtained from any other source without incurring an amount of labor and expertise which would not remunerate the counterfeiter. He could not obtain a part of the plate of one engraver, on one pretense, and a part of another, on another pretense. Nor could he obtain old broken bank plates and alter the lettering upon them, as he now does. The design being one and indivisible, no part of it could be obtained without the other part, nor without the purpose of it being known. The design also covering the whole surface of the plate, and embracing as an integral part of it, all the necessary lettering and devices, it could not be altered, without so defacing it, as to make the counterfeit at once discernable.

Under the present system, a counterfeiter can collect plates here and there and compose them together into the required form, so as to imitate any or all the bank notes in the country, with the genuine work of the very artists employed by the banks to do their work. As the different parts of the bill can be separated from each other, one portion may be obtained of one and another of another, and the fraudulent intent may not be detected till the last finishing touch of printing be given. Counterfeiters now seldom attempt the superfluous folly of engraving a note anew: their work is done to their hands, and scattered over the country in the form of checks, labels, bills of exchange, etc.

Will the new system prevent the alteration of bank notes?

We confidently assert that it presents the *greatest amount* of difficulties to the counterfeiter.

If artists turn counterfeiters, there is no protection in any work of art. All we pretend to do is to compel the counterfeiter to resort to the same process to produce a copy that is used in producing the original; thus, we *fix* upon the forgery *all* the difficulties of the original. We make it impossible for the counterfeiter to obtain any part of his plate from the honest artist, under any pretense. We make the intent of the forger evident at the very first step in the process of counterfeiting—namely, that of tracing the whole design of the note on the plate, preparatory to engraving. And we render it impossible for him to use the plate for any other purpose than the one first designed. The counterfeiter, being forced to use his own skill in engraving, would be obliged, in order to be at all successful, to possess the combined talent of a landscape, portrait, historical and writing engraver, which is rarely found in any professional artist, in any country. If he should be a good picture engraver, he might not be able to execute letters well; and *vice versa.* But let it be borne in mind, that in the present patchwork system, the counterfeiter is not compelled to execute anything himself, except the mechanical process of filing, fitting, and electrotyping his separate pieces.

Modern Critique of Ormsby's Thesis

In his 1852 book Ormsby had no sample of an actual bank note to illustrate his Unit System, this omission pointing to a fatal flaw in his innovation: few, if any,

These two scenic vignettes were used by Ormsby to illustrate the advantages of his Unit System, as sample currency had not been created. It seems that Ormsby rushed to get the book in print, losing the opportunity to show examples of the main thesis of his book.

engravers, including Ormsby himself, had the time to create a unique panoramic vignette for use on a single note of a given bank. The system was untried. The expense would have been considerable for his clients—in sharp contrast to the Perkins Patent Stereotype Steel Plates still being used, with plugged-in vignettes, names, and addresses, which could be done quickly and inexpensively. As to the plates that cost $125 each to create, per Ormsby's comment above, these, with ornate vignettes and decorations, could be made by the siderographic process much more quickly than creating custom dies for each denomination of each bank. Ormsby's ideal Unit System was completely impractical.

His lack of a sample Unit System bill to exhibit the ideas was remedied in the same year, when he applied for a patent and entered a record in the Clerk's Office of the Southern District of New York. (This note is illustrated at the beginning of this chapter.) His product was a note for the fictitious New York City Bank with an elaborate scene covering all of the face, except for the corners. Depicted from left to right was a forest, tepee, seated Indian, shield displaying a windmill motif and surmounted by an eagle (this being an adaptation of the seal of the city of New York), a soldier, and a distant panorama of the sea. The numeral 1 was placed at each corner, and ONE was lettered three times as part of the design, but the word DOLLAR was not used, perhaps to avoid the charge of creating spurious currency. At the lower right appeared a registry notice of the State Bank Department, a requirement of the time for bills issued in New York.[16]

Still, the production of this sample must have been very time consuming. Otherwise, a selection of different denominations might have been made. The standard denominations used by most banks were the $1, $2, $3, $5, $10, $20, $50, and $100 values, and many banks ordered $500 and $1000 notes as well. To create a full suite of 10 different bank-note designs would have required many weeks of effort, even by the most highly skilled engraver.

Although Ormsby himself was such a highly skilled engraver, combining formal schooling in the art with a lot of practice in commerce, such work could not be done by just anyone. In his presentation Ormsby suggests that large numbers of artists could

By 1854 this sample note of the fictitious Security Bank was included in a broadside advertising Ormsby's services. The three goddesses are the same as those used on his fictitious New York City Bank bill and, later, on the authentic $1 note he did for the Carroll County (New Hampshire) Bank. To bolster one of his key arguments, bills for different banks should have had different designs. The ideal techniques described in *Bank Note Engraving* were often at odds with what Ormsby did in his business.

His technique of printing the denomination on the back, repeated many times in tiny letters (here O, N, and E) was widely used on bills he made for banks in the 1850s, these notes being of regular format (not the Unit System).

The one and only *Unit System* bank note of any denomination ever made by Ormsby for an actual customer, the Carroll County Bank of Sandwich, New Hampshire. Curiously, the Unit System was not used for other denominations made by Ormsby for the same bank at the same time. The face of the $1 note is the same as used on several of his sample notes. *Very curiously,* the plate for this bill later passed to the American Bank Note Co. (see tiny ABNCo monogram added at the upper right above the N in BANK), which printed this bill!

engrave notes—though not artistically—and that artistry did not matter, because subtleties of the design were soon worn away. This was a specious argument at best. By 1852, crude engraving on bank bills was a thing of the past. Moreover, Ormsby seemed to overlook the fact that crude or poor work on bank-note plates was not likely to appeal to bank officers and, further, it would be easier for amateurs to counterfeit—to make their own crude products to be launched in a commercial sea in which other crude bills were being used. Someone in, say, New York City would have no way of knowing if a crude-appearing note bearing the name of an Ohio bank was genuine or false.

Despite Ormsby's highly readable text and, in many instances, logical conclusions, there were enough illogical statements and vituperations against just about the entire bank-note trade (excepting Ormsby himself) that readers could not have been left with a sense of satisfaction.

The proof of the Unit System was in the pudding, and the pudding was never made. The production of such bills was so labor-intensive, expensive, and time-consuming that not even Ormsby himself attempted it during the remainder of the time he was in that business, except for a single known variety (the $1 on the Carroll County Bank of Sandwich, New Hampshire).

It is fair to say that Ormsby's *Bank Note Engraving* was an excellent delineation of many principles of the art, but that his conclusions in many instances were flawed, and what he accused other bank-note companies of doing he did as well and would continue to do.

Among his competitors this impressive, handsome hardbound book, complete with gold stamping on the cover, seems to have created consternation. Although Rawdon, Wright, Hatch & Edson and other firms had a larger business and were better known that was Ormsby, none had a *book* to show their clients. While the reception of Ormsby's book among bankers in 1852 may have been uncertain, today *numismatists* appreciate the text highly. Other citations from this work are included in chapter 9 of the present book.

Making Plates for Bank Notes

Ormsby's views of making plates and engaging in the bank-note business form the most comprehensive view of such known from the era. Described below are the technicalities of making vignette and ornamentation dies:[17]

> **Bank Note Dies**
>
> We will now proceed to describe succinctly the mode of preparing the bank note dies. All the vignettes, portraits, and scroll ornaments that adorn the usual bank note are first engraved on soft pieces of steel, of about the thickness of window glass, which are called in professional parlance, "bed pieces." . . . When finished, this bed-piece undergoes a process called "case-hardening," a process so fully described in mechanical books, as to need no description here. It is then placed in the transfer press.
>
> The die is a steel cylinder, about two inches in diameter, of width varying from half an inch to about three inches, according to the size of the vignette or ornament to be transferred to it.
>
> Now in order to obtain the engraving on the cylinder, or to "take it up," as it is technically called, it is placed upon the bed-piece in the transfer press. A heavy pressure is put upon the cylinder by means of the foot-lever, and the beam moved backward and forward by means of the hand-lever, by which the soft steel of the cylinder is pressed upon the hardened bed-piece, until a complete impression is made upon the cylinder in relief. The cylinder die thus produced, without the slightest possible defacement or injury of the bed-piece, is then case-hardened, and is ready for use in transferring the engraving upon it to any required place, in a steel plate for a bank note, or any other purpose.
>
> **Geometrical Lathe Work**
>
> The figures on the bank note denoting denomination, as 1, 2, 3, 5, etc., are obtained on the die in a finished state, in the following manner:
>
> The lathe-work is taken up on a cylinder in the manner previously described, and the figures, or letters, are scraped off, to produce the white face figures. An impression of the die is made on a steel bed-piece, and the letters are "finished up" by the engraver. The bed-piece is then hardened, and a die is again taken up, to give the finished impression. By this process, the various figures are made ready on the several dies, to be used in transferring these engravings into plates for bank notes.
>
> **Multiplying Geometrical Figures**
>
> A single lathe-work oval can be multiplied into an almost unlimited variety by the following process. The oval is taken up in relief on a cylinder die, and scraped off again, except a section of one-eighth of a circle. Thus prepared, the die will give the impression, which is then transferred to a steel bed-piece eight times. A die is then taken up and scraped off again, leaving another section of one-eighth. The figure will now be larger. [Other figures are then transferred individually to the plate in the same manner. Letters, figures, stars, and numbers can also be transferred.] These figures can be changed, varied, and multiplied by continuing the process, to any length.
>
> **The Medallion**
>
> The medallion is the ornamental portion of the bank note engraved by machinery, resembling *bas relief.* It is made principally by the plain ruling machine, with the medal attachment, which copies, by a succession of lines running entirely across the design, whatever medal, coin, or relief pattern is placed in it. The medals most generally used for bank notes are selected from specimens obtained from plaster image vendors; though original designs are sometimes procured for the purpose.[18]
>
> **The Lettering**
>
> The name of the bank, the state, and the town; the number, check letter, cashier and president; the words "will pay," "to bearer," "on demand," "Ten Dollars," etc., are all transferred to the bank-plate, in a short space of time, by means of dies, which will answer the purpose for any number of plates.
>
> The title of the bank is most usually required to be engraved anew; though in the regular course of business for years, an engraving establishment will be apt to accumulate a number of titles such as Farmers Bank, Merchants Bank, or Mechanics Bank, which will answer for plates of any bank of the same name.
>
> **The Comptroller's Die**
>
> This die is peculiar to the bills issued by the free banks. The vignette design embraces the arms of the state in which the bank is located. The words "Countersigned and Registered in the Bank

A $5 bill of the Lancaster Bank of Lancaster, Massachusetts. The back of the note has reverse red printing for the denomination and also, imprinted at the same time, the MASSACHUSETTS surcharge. This surcharge was an extraordinary procedure and was done to differentiate the bills at quick glance from the similarly named Lancaster Bank in New Hampshire, the state to the north.

A selection of vignettes that were stock-in-trade for Ormsby, this being part of Plate 11 in *Bank Note Engraving.* Ormsby commented, "Nearly all of the vignettes on this plate were originally employed by Casilear & Co. and Burton, Edmonds & Co. in bank note engraving. Exact duplicates of them may be found on genuine bank notes now in circulation."

Department," or others of similar import, usually make the border of the vignette, in an oval form.

The Red Letters

The red letters, ONE, TWO, THREE, etc., seen on the back and face of many notes, as if the ink had penetrated the paper at one impression, are made by the following simple process: wood or metal cuts of the required letters are placed in a common printing-press; the "form" inked with red. The first impression is pulled upon the "tympan sheet," which moves on a hinge. The form is inked again with red; the bill placed upon it, and an impression made upon its face, while at the same time, a corresponding impression is made upon the back, by an offset from the tympan sheet.

Such are the processes by which a bank note is engraved in this country. The simplicity and ease with which they are performed, will thus be seen.

Expenses, Equipment, and Profits

Ormsby gave this information relating to the business end of bank-note engraving. In this illustration he presumes that the actual printing is contracted to others off-premises:[19]

Requirements for Success

The business of bank note engraving is usually conducted by professional artists; though personal ability to engrave is not indispensable to the conductor of it. A capital of about $2,000, an extensive acquaintance and influence with directors of banking institutions, and apt business capacities, are all that are necessary to the prosecution of the art.

The usual components of an establishment of this kind are: an office for the transaction of business; rooms for the engraving, hardening, and transferring of the dies to bank-plates; and a printing department of greater or lesser extent.

No restraints are placed upon the workmen employed in the various departments of the business which are not imposed upon those engaged in any other branch of mechanical labor. Whatever merit, therefore, is due to the establishment for integrity and secrecy, belongs equally to all the members of it, from the humblest errand boy to the principals themselves; for all have it equally in their power to take advantage of the facilities which the establishment affords, for illicit purposes. The various instruments and machines used in the engraving of bank notes we will now severally describe:

Essential Machines

The most important of the bank note engraver's implements is the transfer press. The function of this is to multiply the small engravings of the note, without re-engraving, in perfect facsimile, and to any extent. The facility which this machine affords for multiplying the finest engravings, enables the artist to spend more of his labor and skill in finishing his vignette, since it may be used many times over, in different designs for notes, checks, certificates, labels, etc.

The next in importance is the ruling machine, now universally in use among engravers. It is employed in a variety of forms, as in executing the sky of a vignette, the back ground of a portrait, the shading of letters, etc. which constitute no inconsiderable part of the actual labor to be done in bank note engraving.

The medal copying machine is used for the execution of that portion of bank bills which resembles bas relief, and is generally attached to the ruling machine.

The geometrical lathe is used to produce the white line network seen in ovals, circles, and strips of bank bills, in which the figures denoting the denomination of the bill are placed. It is seldom used after a few specimens are obtained; and many establishments dispense with it altogether, content to purchase the productions of others.

In his book, Plate I showed the transfer press, with this description on the facing page:

The Transfer Press

Figure 1.—The Transfer Press, represented in a position to take up in relief, on a cylinder die, the engraving on the bed-piece.

Number 2—The bed-piece, which is case-hardened.

Number 3—The steel cylinder, which has been made soft by annealing.

Number 4—The foot lever; by means of which the cylinder is pressed upon the bed-piece.

Number 5—The hand lever, which forces the beam (number six) backward and forward.

Number 6—The beam, which has a motion backward and forward.

Number 7—The screw, for elevating and depressing the bed of the machine.

Figure 2.—The engraved bed-piece.—The vignette upon it is produced by concave lines cut into the steel by the hand and implements of the Artist.

Figure 3.—A side and front view of the cylinder die. The vignette upon it is produced by pressure upon the bed-piece. The lines, of course, are convex, and after the dies have been case-hardened, are readily transferred again in any required spot in a bank plate.

It will be seen that only one half of the cylinder can be used to take up the engraving, as here represented; but an arbor, or mandrel, may be employed in a manner which will permit the engravings to be taken up on the entire periphery of the cylinder.

The honor of the invention of this method of transferring engravings from one piece of steel to another, belongs to our distinguished countryman, Jacob Perkins.

Transfer presses have been made in various ways. The one represented in the engraving is, we believe, the best, and is the invention of our ingenious fellow citizen, James Bogardus, Esq. The writer has constructed one of these presses for Mr. Wellstood; one for Messrs. Rawdon, Wright, and Hatch, the well-known bank note engravers, of this city; and is now constructing

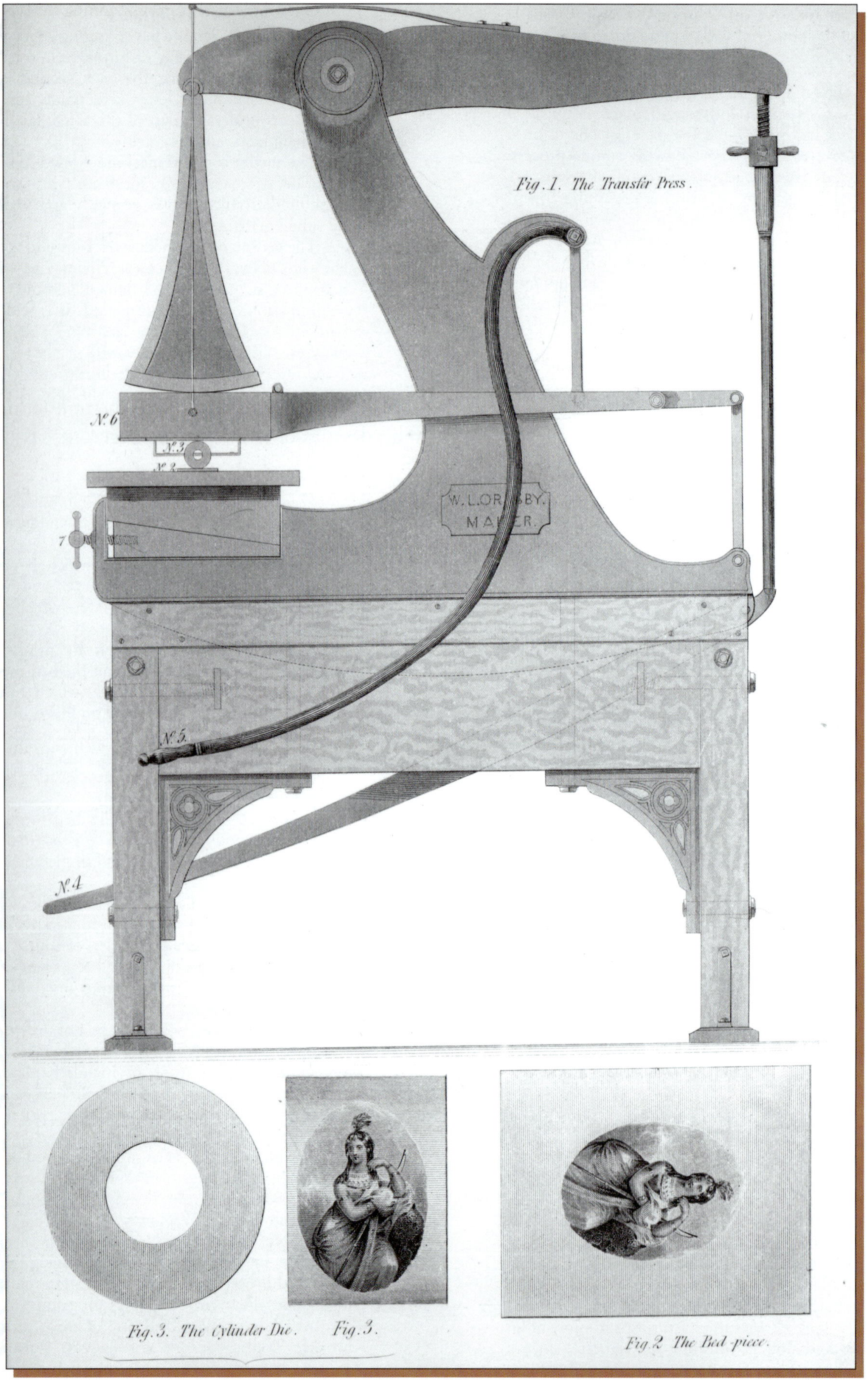

Plate I of Ormsby's 1852 book, the transfer press.

one for his own use. The cost of such a press is about five hundred dollars.

The preceding description seems to indicate that, while Ormsby had made several such transfer presses for others, perhaps including the one he had been using for some time in his own business, the next one constructed was to be kept. Soon, he would be going into the bank-note *printing* business, but in 1852 this plan was not disclosed.

Costs of Equipment

These implements constitute all the machinery necessary to furnish the bank note engraver's atelier on the prevailing plan in this country. They are few and not expensive. Their average cost may be estimated to be as follows:

The Bogardus transfer press: $500.00

The friction ruling machine: $100.00

Above, with the medal attachment, variety of geometrical lathe work: $50.00

Desk tools, together with a stock of blank plates and dies sufficient for the commencement of business: $150.00

Total: $800.00

Capital

To complete our survey of the bank note engraver's business, let us estimate the necessary amount of capital required successfully to carry it on.

The amount of capital required to purchase the machinery and the stock requisite to commence the business we have estimated to be $800. To this must be added the cost of engraving and preparing the first set of dies. If the conductors of the business are themselves professional artists, they will produce by their own labor, in a few weeks, vignettes, denominations, etc., sufficient for the execution of a bank-plate, without any further outlay of capital. But if not professional engravers, which is sometimes actually the case, the sum of $1,000 would be sufficient for this purpose; making the total amount of capital required, $1,800.

Prices

The established prices for engraving and printing bank notes are the following:

Engraving a steel plate of four notes, of any denomination, $500.00; half plate, $250.00

Printing a plate of four notes, per 100 impressions, $2.50; half plate. $1.50

Commencement of Business

At the commencement of business, if an order be received for a full suite of plates for the Rail Road Bank, for example, which has a circulation, we will suppose, of $300,000, the plates may be arranged as follows:

One whole steel plate, containing four Ones.

One whole steel plate, containing three Twos, and one Three.

One whole steel plate, containing two Fives, one Ten, and one Twenty.

One half steel plate, containing Fifty and One Hundred.

The supposed circulation of the Rail Road Bank will require the following amount of printing:

20,000 impressions of the plate of four Ones, giving $80,000

10,000 impressions of the plate of Twos and Threes, $90,000

1,500 impressions of the plate of Fives, Ten, and Twenty, $60,000

500 impressions of the plate of Fifty and One Hundred, $75,000

Making the supposed circulation of $305,000

The printing may be procured, without expense to the engraver, of the best copper-plate printers, for $1.50 for 100 impressions.

32,000 impressions will therefore cost the engraver $480.00. Add the amount invested in dies, machinery and stock, as before estimated, $1,800.00, and we have a total of $2,280.00

This comprises the whole amount of capital requisite to commence the business of bank note engraving and to execute the first order.

The Artist's Charges

For the above work the artist's bill to the bank will be as follows:

Engraving plate of four Ones, $500.00

Engraving plate of Twos and Threes, $500.00

Engraving plate of two Fives, one Ten, and one Twenty, $500.00

Engraving half plate of Fifty and One Hundred, $250.00

Printing 32,000 impressions, full plate, at $2.50 per hundred, $800.00

Printing 500 impressions, half plate, at $1.50 per 100, $7.50

Total: $2,557.50

Estimating Profits

If we now deduct the whole amount of investment as before estimated, $2,280.00, we shall have a remaining balance of profit, on the completion of the first order, of $277.50, without taking into account the small profits on bank-paper, certificates of stock, cashier's checks, drafts, etc.

Extensive influence with the presidents and directors of banking institutions is only necessary to secure a rapid succession of orders, which, after the first outlay for machinery and the accumulation of dies, can be executed with great rapidity and cheapness.

The system of engraving the bank note as we have shown, requires only a few dies in order to effect a great variety of changes. As these dies have never been known to wear out by use, it would be quite possible to make one set answer the engraver's purpose for any length of time. If the use of dies in the engraving of bank notes were, as is

"One" note without "Dollar" mentioned, engraved by W.L. Ormsby, 1853, with the name of the Morrisania Bank, New York. No record of such a bank operating has been found by the author. Likely, this was a speculative issue made as a sample the year after his *Bank Note Engraving* book espoused the Unit System. Ormsby had just announced that he was going into the bank-note printing business. The general design later was used for a $1 note of the Carroll County (New Hampshire) Bank. (Ex Thomas Morris Jr. and Schingoethe collections)

> supposed, really a security against forgery, it would be desirable in a moral point of view, not less than for the pecuniary profit, to make use of but one set for the execution of any number of plates.
>
> But if on the other hand, the temptations to counterfeit any vignette or design upon the bank note be in proportion to the number of times that vignette is repeated on other notes, it must be obvious that the dies ought not to be used more than once.
>
> If every repetition of bank note dies facilitates the imitation and illicit use, no one unconnected with bank note engraving establishments will presume to recommend the employment of them any longer, at least, for the purposes under consideration.

Ormsby, Bank-Note Printer

The *Bank Note Engraving* book was a limited success, and it prompted Ormsby to go into the bank-note printing business. In spring 1853 he announced that he had left 12 Vesey Street and was preparing new premises. Soon, he advertised that as of June 1 he was located at 50 Wall Street and would offer a full service to banks and others desiring currency. Likely, his clients for vignettes and bank-note plates did not like this change, and business in this direction diminished or ended. His former customers were now his competitors.

After this time his currency plates bore the imprint W.L. Ormsby, New York City, and still later, the New York Bank Note Co., both with variations. In numismatic circles, few people are aware that the two are actually the same enterprise. His first bank-notes plates for his own account may have been those bearing the names of the Morrisania Bank of New York and the New York City Bank. Finally, his Unit System saw application on a piece of currency, even if the bills were created as advertising samples, bearing names of banks. However, it was not until well into 1854 that he used the system for bills of an actual bank in operation, this being the $1 note of the Carroll County Bank.

Sensational Allegations in Court

The Slanders of 1854

In his new 50 Wall Street location, W.L. Ormsby found himself in the heart of the financial district and close to nearly all of the other engravers in the city. While there were engravers and bank-note printers in Philadelphia, Cincinnati, and a few other places, by the mid-1850s New York City had become the epicenter of the trade.

While Ormsby had done his share of complaining about others in his *Bank Note Engraving* book, he did not expect others to do the same to him. After all, he was trying to right the many engraving wrongs of the past, including his own methods. In reality, he was tilting at windmills.

Babcock Disparages Ormsby

In June 1854 it seems that Avery C. Babcock, an employee of the Mercantile Agency (a credit-reporting service in New York City owned by Benjamin Douglass), made a point to spread rumors and gossip about Ormsby. The victim took Babcock to court, where this affidavit laid the groundwork for the complaint:[20]

> It is alleged that the defendant, Babcock, on or about the first day of June last, contriving and wickedly and maliciously intending to injure the plaintiff, Ormsby, in his good name, fame and credit, and to bring him into public scandal, infamy and disgrace, with and amongst all his neighbors and other good and worthy citizens caused it to be suspected and believed by those neighbors and citizens that the plaintiff had been and was guilty of these offenses and misconduct hereinafter mentioned to have been charged upon him by the defendant.
>
> The plaintiff has been informed that these offenses took place in the city of New Haven, in the state of Connecticut, and also in the city and county of New York. In the presence and hearing of diverse good and worthy citizens he did falsely

> and maliciously speak, declare and publish of and concerning the plaintiff, and of and concerning the plaintiff in the way of his profession and business of bank note engraving and printing, and of engraving generally, the following false and scandalous, malicious and defamatory words against the plaintiff, that is to say:
>
> "He has left his wife and is living with a prostitute," and, "He had and has been engaged in counterfeiting. He is a licentious man and of bad reputation; a counterfeiter and bad fellow. He has been a counterfeiter and works at counterfeiting."
>
> By reason of the speaking of which said false, scandalous and malicious words the plaintiff is greatly injured in his good name, fame, credit and reputation as an individual and a man of business, to his damage ten thousand dollars, for which amount he prays judgment and costs.

The Mercantile Agency Strikes Again

A month after Babcock defamed Ormsby, Buckley T. Benton, a jeweler residing in Brooklyn, was considering accepting a promissory note signed and endorsed by Ormsby, to be discounted through Mr. Blair (actually E.J. Blake, but "Blair" in court documents), cashier of the Mercantile Bank.[21] He sought to obtain information regarding Ormsby's financial integrity, although he had known Ormsby for 12 years. He applied to the Mercantile Agency, the New York City credit-reporting firm for which aforementioned Babcock worked. Visiting its office in the Trinity Building, 111 Broadway, Benton submitted his request by filling an application stating, in part,

> Give us in confidence, and for our exclusive use and benefit in our business, whatever information you have respecting the standing, responsibility, &c., of Waterman L. Ormsby.

Although Benton had known Benjamin Douglass, the owner of the agency, for about four or five years, this written inquiry was handed to a clerk. In the words of Benton,

> I made an application and presented it at the counter. One of the clerks came and turned to a book. He looked at the book, turned round and beckoned to another clerk, and he came. He looked at the book and then turned to Mr. Douglass himself. [Douglass] said that he could not give me a report of Mr. Ormsby in writing. He said the report was very bad.
>
> I told him that I was somewhat surprised that there should be a bad report of him, as I had known Mr. Ormsby very favorably during the time that I have been acquainted with him. I also told him that I thought he must be mistaken. . . . Mr. Douglass said that Mr. Ormsby was a bad man, a man of no responsibility, and advised me not to have anything to do with him. He said he . . . worked for counterfeiters and was a counterfeiter.[22]

The commentary further given to Benton included information that Ormsby "was in the habit of engraving for any casual applicant for plates without inquiring into his character or the object for which the plates were to be used, and in this way he engraved counterfeit plates on a number of banks in this and other states."[23] Other wording included, "He is a counterfeiter—he is a man of no credit."[24]

Apparently, this information had been given not only to client Benton, but also earlier to "three or four others" who had asked about credit.

In Court in January 1856

In the New York Superior Court, special term of January 1856, Ormsby sought redress and claimed that he had been slandered. He stated that there was "a combination of certain engravers" who desired to crush him "and drive him from his business." Defendant Douglass countered by stating that he had made his report in confidence in the course of his regular business, and he believed that it was truthful. In the meantime, Ormsby's similar case against Douglass's employee, Babcock, was still pending.

The Douglass case was amended and continued. Meanwhile, as part of a formal answer to Ormsby's complaint, Douglass, in an affidavit of March 14, 1856, denied the substance of the action, and then went on to give specific commentary concerning the plaintiff's business.[25] He stated that Ormsby had widely publicized the fact that he "was engaged in the business of bank-note engraver and printer," and that, accordingly, he had the responsibility to conduct this trade with great care. Otherwise, as he pointed out, Ormsby

> was liable to be and to become an instrument of great fraud and injustice, by enabling evil-disposed persons to make counterfeit resemblances of trade-marks and bank notes by which they could deceive purchasers of goods and dealers to whom such evil-disposed persons might tender such counterfeit resemblances of bank bills as payment or in exchange for gold coin or good bank bills.

According to Douglass, engravers "who pursued such business in a lawful and proper manner, and who conducted their said business honestly" would not make bank-note plates "except for persons well known and respectable character." Moreover, "such engravers retained in their own possession the plates so made or engraved by them, and this prevented any use thereof otherwise under their own immediate supervision, whereby they were enabled to confine and did confine the use of such plates within the limits required by fair dealing and the law of the land."

The reader of the present book will realize that this statement is utter nonsense! Just about every other well-known bank-note engraving firm in business at the time, and in earlier times, recklessly accepted orders from just about anyone ordering plates. Witness all of the worthless paper money put out by insolvent or even nonexistent banks in the wildcat era of Michigan, nearly all of which bore the imprints of leading firms. However, those in the court did not have the benefit of this knowledge.

The Mousam River Bank

Further contrary to good business practice, Douglass claimed, W.L. Ormsby "was in the habit of engraving in whole or in part as required by *any* applicant to him, without any knowledge or inquiry of or concerning his intent or object, plates adapted to the purpose of making paper, having the form and simil-

A phony $5 bill of the Mousam River Bank, of *Sanford*, Maine, similar to the one presented as "evidence" in the court case. The town name is misspelled as "Sandford," the vignettes are crudely done, and it in no way resembles Ormsby's authentic work. The back is plain.

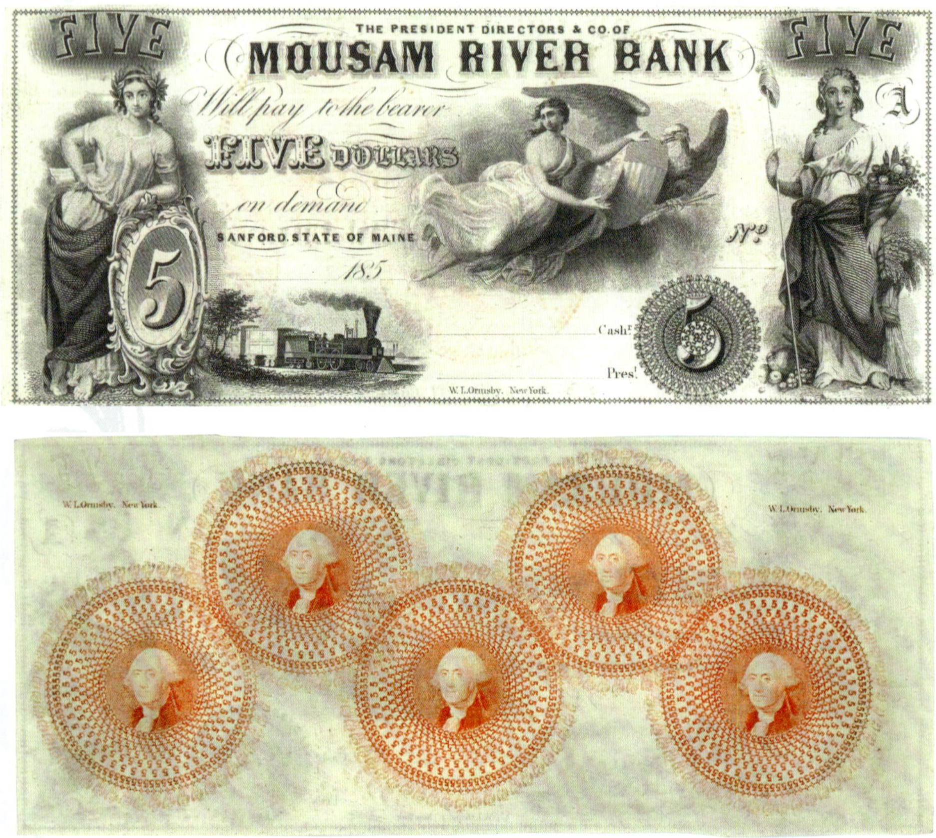

Face and back of an authentic Ormsby $5 note of the Mousam River Bank. Unlike the counterfeit, the genuine has a brightly printed back, with five design areas, each of which has a vignette and repetition of the letters F, I, V, and E.

Face and back of an authentic Ormsby $1 note of the Mousam River Bank, also with a bright orange back. The tiny letters O, N, and E are repeated many times.

itude of bank notes and trade marks." Per the affidavit, Ormsby,

> In disregard of the mischievous consequences to be apprehended as aforesaid, impressions from which were afterwards, by such last mentioned persons or their confederates, used and put into circulation fraudulently, that is to say, plates for printing the similitude of bank bills, each purporting to be issued by a supposed bank called the Mousam River Bank, located at Sandford,[26] in the state of Maine, by which the similitude of bank bills in large numbers, dated August 30, 1854, were made, passed off, and fraudulently put *in* circulation, by persons to the defendant unknown, purporting to be for two dollars, three dollars, five dollars, and ten dollars respectively.

As to what *really* happened with the "supposed bank," in fact it was a real bank, and at the outset appeared legitimate, including to bank commissioners and legislators in the state of Maine.

It is apparent that as part of his defense, Douglass had acquired a counterfeit $5 bill of the Mousam River Bank, on the face of which the artist had misspelled Sanford as "Sandford." A modern examination of such a bill verifies it to be a contemporary counterfeit, including Ormsby's imprint, with workmanship not up to Ormsby's high standards. It was no different than other counterfeits of the era bearing the imprints of Rawdon, Wright, Hatch & Edson and other well-known firms. (A discussion of certain of the Mousam River Bank bills is given in chapter 9, and a history of the bank will be found under the Maine entry in chapter 21.)

The scenario continued. . . .

More Allegations

In his 1856 affidavit, Benjamin Douglass, proprietor of the Mercantile Exchange and, apart from this court case, not known to be an expert on bank notes, went on to list other alleged frauds by Ormsby. Likely, one of Ormsby's competitors had been keeping a file, probably casually (as evidenced by the Mousam Bank information above), of his products:

> [Ormsby also created] plates adapted in whole or in part for making the similitude of bank bills, from which were made and put in circulation fraudulently by some person or persons to the defendant unknown, false and forged bank bills

purporting to be of the denominations and issued by the banks following, that is to say:

Counterfeit $3 bills purporting to be of the City Bank of New Haven, in the state of Connecticut;

Counterfeit $3 bills purporting to be of the Merchants' Bank of Salem, in the state of Massachusetts;

Counterfeit $2 bills purporting to be issued by the Mechanics' Exchange Company, of New York City, in the form of checks of two dollars each on the Bank of St. Albans, in the state of Vermont, payable to bearer on demand;

Counterfeit $10 bills purporting to be of the Farmers' Bank of Schuylkill, located at Schuylkill-Haven, in the state of Pennsylvania;

Counterfeit $1 bills purporting to be of the Delaware City Bank, located at Delaware in the state of Delaware;

Counterfeit $2 bills purporting to be of the North River Bank, located in the city of New York.

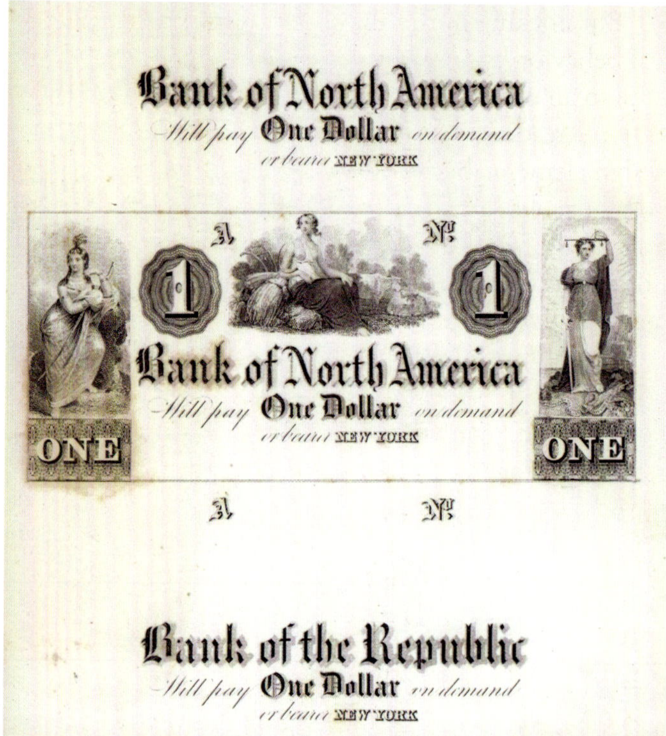

Detail of a plate in *Bank Note Engraving* showing a bill made up as an illustration, the Bank of North America of New York being fictitious. This was part of a narrative on how bank-note plates are made and had nothing to do with fraud.

Ormsby was further charged with engraving a plate for a counterfeit label "by which the venders of spurious and inferior medicines were enabled to place thereon a similitude of the trade mark of Moffat's Vegetable Life Pills, sold by William B. Moffat at the city of New York City, and bearing a *facsimile* of John Moffat's signature." Today the study of patent medicines has been a specialty of collectors of old bottles and old advertising as well as the focus of attention by many historians. In general, most patent medicines of the nature of the "Vegetable Life Pills" were completely worthless, even if "genuine" and "original."

Other of Ormsby's alleged nefarious plates or separate vignettes contained such varied images and inscriptions as: "Boston," "State of New York," "New Jersey," "Fifty Dollars," "Massachusetts," "10," a "medallion enclosing a shield bearing the figures '50,'" "The Manufacturers' and Mechanics' Bank," "Merchants' Bank," "Bank of North America," "Bank of Commerce," a "medallion enclosing the figure '3,'" a "large medallion enclosing a helmeted head," a "larger medallion enclosing a head and a bust of a man believed to be Harrison," "a *female* angelic figure,[27] bearing a shield which is also supported by an eagle with arrows in his claws," and such terms as "Cashr" and "Prest."

Certain of the above images, such as "Bank of North America," had been publicly and obviously used as illustrations in his 1852 *Bank Note Engraving* book!

A $20 note of the Farmers Bank, Orwell, Vermont. This is a spurious note of a fantasy design, signed by the nonexistent Eastern Bank Note Company. The workmanship is poor, and it can in no way be compared to Ormsby's engraving. A related note was mentioned in court testimony as "Orwell Bank."

But nothing in the above statement proved unethical behavior by Ormsby. Of course, any visitor at the time to an ordinary *print shop* might find a plate or set of type reading "Massachusetts," or whatever. Such design elements by accomplished engravers were freely bought, sold, and traded in the marketplace in the normal course of business. Rawdon, Wright, Hatch & Edson, for example, had thousands of such design elements and vignettes in stock.

W.L. Ormsby was further accused of making up a set of six bank-note plates, bank name and location not specified, "for a person to the defendant unknown, who obtained the same from the said plaintiff for the purpose of *making* counterfeit bank bills therefrom for fraudulent purposes, as the said plaintiff well knew when he so engraved the same."

Digging Into the Past

A fairly large file on Ormsby must have been presented to Douglass for his use, for in his 1856 affidavit he went deep into the past concerning his adversary:

> And in 1841, the said defendant engraved and delivered to Edwin Ely a plate containing all the important parts requiring for their formation artistic skill in the engravers, which was shortly thereafter, by said Ely or his associates, used to make counterfeit similitudes of the bank notes of the Bank of Orwell, in the state of Vermont, which were fraudulently put in circulation to a very great extent.
>
> And, long *prior* to the said alleged grievances, and on or about the first of January, in the year 1848, it was stated and represented to the said plaintiff that his said habits and practice of placing in the hands of persons not known him to have lawful and just occasion to use them, engraved plates, or part of plates, capable of being used for the purpose of making counterfeits, was immoral and improper; whereupon he, the said plaintiff, replied that no man had a right to inquire for whom he worked, that it was *not* his place or duty to inquire into the object of his employers, or the uses to which they intended to apply his work after it had passed out of his hands, and that it had been his practice to work, and that he intended for the future to work in his said business for any person who would employ and pay him, without regard to their characters or purposes in possessing themselves of his work.

In the summer 1856, Ormsby's motion against Douglass was denied, but Ormsby elected to continue the matter.

Back in Court

In March 1858 in the New York Superior Court, the case of W.L. Ormsby v. Benjamin Douglass was heard by the Honorable Judge Edwards Pierrepont.[28] He stated that if the case were to go to trial he would charge the jury with determining, first, whether this was a privileged communication, and, second, whether there was any evidence of malice. Robert G. Pike, of Pike & Galpin, was lead attorney for Ormsby, and Fullerton & Dunning served as attorneys for Douglass.

The lineup of witnesses called in by the defense to testify against Ormsby was a veritable who's who in American bank-note engraving, all of whom were on hand for four days during the proceedings. Not long thereafter, on April 29, 1858, the American Bank Note Company was incorporated by combining certain firms in which some of the witnesses against Ormsby were owners or employees. In March, most of the terms among the partners in the new firm had been agreed upon. Unbeknownst to the court, most of those testifying against Ormsby were not independent but were associates with each other in business.

Samuel Stiles, a partner in Danforth, Wright & Co., 1 Wall Street, was there to condemn Ormsby, as was William C. Smillie, talented engraver at Toppan, Carpenter & Co., 111 Broadway. Neziah Wright was present from Rawdon, Wright, Hatch & Edson, the most prominent of all bank-note companies (and whose customer list included a long inventory of questionable and failed banks—one that would far exceed the list attributed to Ormsby—but this fact was not mentioned in court). Nathaniel Jocelyn represented Jocelyn, Draper, Welsh & Co., another leader in the industry. These men all were currently involved in forming the American Bank Note Company.

Marius Schoonmaker, who had been superintendent of the state Banking Department from 1854 to 1856, and whose self-serving practices Ormsby had criticized, was reimbursed at the rate of four cents a mile for his 800-mile trip to and from the trial. As if the preceding and nine other witnesses were not enough, John Thompson, leading publisher of counterfeit detectors and bank-note reporters, 2 Wall Street, was also in the courtroom to testify, never mind that in his 1852 *Bank Note Engraving* book, Ormsby had praised Thompson highly.[29]

Many people whose engraving and printing methods Ormsby had maligned in his 1852 book and elsewhere were ready, willing, and eager to see Ormsby get his comeuppance. Seemingly, Ormsby had sown the seeds of his own impending destruction.

A lovely $5 bill of the fraudulent Ship Builders Bank of Rockland, Maine, produced by Rawdon, Wright, Hatch & Edson, which supplied large quantities of notes—far more than Maine law allowed.

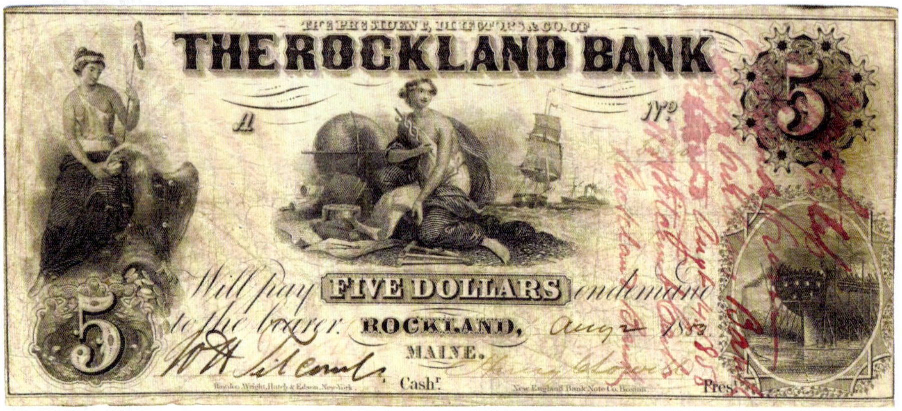

After the Ship Builders Bank failed, many of its notes were fraudulently altered, as in the case of the illustrated bill changed to the Rockland Bank.

Skeletons in Closets

With the advantage of hindsight, it is easy for any historian of banking to recite today a long list of spurious and failed banks for which currency had been provided by Ormsby's "reputable" competitors in New York City during the 1850s—this long past the earlier-mentioned "wildcat" era of Michigan banking.

For example, in his study, *A History of Banking in Maine 1799–1930* (1936), Walter W. Chadbourne related this fact:

> The Ship Builders Bank of Rockland was a most disastrous private speculation. The bank was incorporated in March 1853 and commenced business on June 7th of that year. In less than two years its mission was fulfilled, its credit doubted, and an injunction placed upon its further proceeding with business.
>
> It had finally suspended in October 1854, at which time a committee reported the value of the assets as $82,439 with liabilities of $33,015, leaving a surplus of $49,424. The books, however, did not show the true financial condition, and the surplus was later turned into a heavy loss.
>
> The cashier of the bank, by name W.L. Pitts, was entrusted with the affairs of the bank. With the help of the president, H.C. Lowell, he wrecked the institution. The records showed that the whole amount of bills ordered from the engravers had been $356,000 for a bank with $100,000 nominal capital. $296,596 were actually delivered.
>
> When the receivers took charge of the bank they found that bills outstanding amounted to $149,513 although the books of the bank showed only $97,149. The books also showed that $48,663 had been destroyed, but whether or not this was correct could not be proved.
>
> The assets consisted of notes and drafts for $76,156. There were four notes amounting to $30,700 signed by Jane Pitts, the wife of a brother of the cashier. The brother had also borrowed directly or had endorsed paper from about $32,000 more.
>
> The final amount realized from the assets was $4,068. A criminal indictment was found by the grand jury in Lincoln County, but the creditors of the bank recovered practically nothing.[30]

The willing supplier of paper money to that bank was none other than Rawdon, Wright, Hatch & Edson, of New York City. If that firm did any inquiry into the integrity of the bank's founders, it must have been superficial at best. Even allowing that a good credit report may have been obtained, the engraving firm still provided far more in paper money to the bank than its widely published and easily available capitalization figure of $100,000 would have allowed.

Many of the remaining bills were snapped up by counterfeiters who altered them to resemble issues of other banks, including the Rockland Bank in the same town.

A beautifully engraved $10 note of the Citizens Bank of Gosport, from a plate by Wellstood, Hay & Whiting.

As another example, this commentary appeared in a modern numismatic reference, *Indiana Obsolete Notes and Scrip* (1978), by Wendell A. Wolka, Jack M. Vorhies, and Donald A. Schramm:

> The Citizens Bank of Gosport [Indiana] was one of the more notorious of the many banks which were in operation as private ventures in Indiana during the 19th century. It would seem that this bank put out paper as fast as it could be signed. According to the December 1858 issue of *Banker's Magazine,* one Judge Perkins in that year ruled:
>
> "The Citizens Bank of Gosport is an illegal institution and because of its illegality its issues are void, and being void no action can be brought, founded on such notes of issue, although the consideration given for them may be recovered. There is no statute making it a penal offense to issue such paper."
>
> This bank was, therefore, a glaring example of the conditions which allowed wholesale larceny under the guise of "banking."[31]

An ally in the perpetration of this, the greatest of Indiana frauds, was none other than the New York bank-note printing firm of Wellstood, Hay & Whiting, which in 1858 became a partner in the American Bank Note Company.

As a reader of this book, you could cite dozens of other examples. The record shows clearly that those who testified against Ormsby produced far more plates for fraudulent banks than Ormsby ever did!

The View of the Judge

After hearing testimony and reviewing documents, Judge Pierrepont expressed his opinion that the communications made by the Mercantile Agency were "privileged," and that no express malice was intended. Pierrepont stated that in the course of normal activities or business, such as hiring a servant, it was normal to make inquiries to someone familiar or holding an opinion on the person in question, this being a privileged communication for a specific purpose, not for wide public dissemination. Another illustration was given:

> So a bank is about to be started, and the teller of another bank applies to become the cashier of the new bank. It is proper that the officers should make inquiries of the persons by whom he is employed, and although they may reply that they believe he has secretly taken money from the bank, that they suspect he has made false entries, that they believe he has forged notes—yet if they communicate this in reply to an inquiry made in good faith, and without any malice, it is a privileged communication, and an action of slander does not lie.[32]

Similarly from the justice:

> If four banks in Wall Street should associate themselves together for the purpose of ascertaining the character and standing of their correspondents in Boston, and should select one of their number, and pay his expenses to Boston for that

> purpose, and he should, on his return, state that he ascertained that Mr. Jones, of Boston, was a man of bad character—that he had committed many outrages against society—and he communicated that to his four associates in the confidential relation in which they stood—it would be a privileged communication, and no action could take place, unless express malice were shown.
>
> Now, it is difficult to see how there would be any difference between four men and twenty-four, or any number, associated for the purpose of gaining honest and truthful information of this description, and without malicious motives. I am not able to see why the information given by this commercial agency, so far as it appears before the court, may not come under the class of privileged communications, if made in a proper manner, and without any evil intent or malicious motive, and if made in good faith and honesty.[33]

Judge Pierrepont stated that if the case were to go to a jury, "it is not proper for the jury to speculate about secret motives, of which no evidence has been given." In this case, if the jury were to find for the defendant, "the Court would be obliged to set it aside."

The case did go to trial, and the jury agreed with the judge. Soon this ruling was handed down:

> Motion for non-suit granted. Twenty days' time allowed the plaintiff to make a case—to be heard in the first instance at General Term; all proceeding in the meantime enjoined.

Back in Court Another Time

In 1859, Fullerton and Dunning, attorneys for Douglass, filed a motion to recover costs of $284.50 from Ormsby, for expenses in the 1858 suit. This payment was granted by the court on July 9.[34] Ormsby was not satisfied, and the matter dragged on, eventu-

The W.L. Ormsby imprint appears on this 1854 stock certificate of the American Submarine Tunnel Co. The high-decked steamer in the vignette was added by Ormsby to the sea scene.

All bank-note engraving companies of the era also did security printing, the latter including stock certificates, checks, receipts, and official documents, plus general commercial printing requiring engraving or vignettes, such as letterheads.

The ship alone, with a small amount of sea, was a stock-in-trade vignette for Ormsby. It is an adaptation of a related vignette acquired at the dissolution of another engraving firm years earlier, illustrated as vignette 32 on Plate 11 of *Bank Note Engraving*.

ally being heard years later by the Court of Appeals, January 1868, where the earlier ruling was affirmed.[35]

In essence, except for an airing of accusations, claims, counterclaims, and defenses that are interesting and even amusing to the bank-note historian today, there was little value to anyone from all of the effort Ormsby made in court. Clearly, Ormsby was the loser in these court encounters. He was persona non grata in his own profession, and the otherwise close-knit community of bank-note engravers considered him to be an outcast.

Today, it is not possible to know what might have been, but we do know that Ormsby's commissions by major banks in the 1850s were virtually nonexistent. What little trade he was able to garner was mostly from small-town banks or those situated in remote locations.

In 1855 and 1856, and possibly at other times, Baker & Duyckinck, New York City, published books, leaflets, and other material. It seems that on occasion they partnered with W.L. Ormsby and his New York Bank Note Co. to provide paper money to bank customers and others. Certain 1856 printing work (not bank notes) is signed "Baker & Duyckinck Steam Presses." Other than this, he seems to have had no special business connections with others in the printing or bank-note engraving business in this era. Likely, by 1856 Ormsby's *Bank Note Engraving* book was no longer in active distribution.

The history and operations of these two banks are not known today. Legitimate or fraudulent? Both are by Ormsby and seem closely related.

A $5 note of the State Bank of Lecompton, Kansas Territory, by W.L. Ormsby. A related $3 bill had three cherubs on the face. Notes of this bank seem to have circulated effectively.

Ormsby's Success

By 1856, Ormsby had many currency commissions from small banks to his credit, but orders from important banking districts, including the entire state of New York, seem to have eluded him. His competitors, especially Rawdon, Wright, Hatch & Edson, controlled most of the business and had much more extensive facilities. Ormsby's operation was modest at best, with just a handful of employees.

Ormsby's clients, some of whom had less than honorable intentions, were far ranging in their business locations, real or intended. Ormsby's imprints are found on bills from Maine to Utah. Some are considered legitimate by historians today, while others are viewed as questionable. It is likely that Ormsby readily assented to making plates for most comers, but—as we have seen—his competitors did the same thing. There is no single prominent bank-note firm of this era whose products were exempt from being used by banks that failed or by those with fraud in mind. In fact, among his competitors, the biggest firms were involved with far more worthless banks than was Ormsby, as earlier noted.

Ormsby's Inventions

Perhaps to establish his credentials for those who did not know him, Ormsby published this schedule several years later in 1862:[36]

> The following mechanical inventions adapted to the business of engraving have been designed and perfected by the author of this work during the last thirty years. They are respectfully submitted as a partial testimonial to the writer's familiarity with the subject on which he treats:
>
> 1. Ruling machine for straight and waved lines: 1832
> 2. Ruling machine for medallion, upright: 1833
> 3. Ruling machine for medallion, horizontal: 1834
> 4. Automaton operator of the above: 1834
> 5. Hardened steel dies for Iris Buttons made with the above: 1835
> 6. Machine for engraving on Colt's pistols: 1836
> 7. Machine for registering the movements of bank note printing presses: 1839
> 8. Kaleidoscopic combinations of geometrical lathe work: 1839
> 9. Improvements on the Bogardus transfer press: 1840
> 10. The grammagraph for engraving map letters: 1841

11. Machine for engraving piano and carriage plates: 1842
12. Machine for engraving on metal combs: 1842
13. Engravers' rolettes: 1844
14. The Kaleidograph: 1846
15. Mathematical instrument for turning minute circles and ovals: 1849
16. THE UNIT SYSTEM of engraving bank notes: 37 1851
17. Geometrical lathe combining the Rose engine: 1854
18. Machine for engraving on wood: 1855
19. Machine for engraving on pencil cases: 1857
20. Machine for engraving on locket and watch cases: 1858
21. Ruling machine combining cycloidal, geometrical, straight, and waved lines: 1858
22. Improvement in engraving metal signs: 1859
23. Machine for printing steel plates in two or more colors: 1860
24. Kaleido Mosaic Engraving: 1861

Indeed, this list was impressive and had no equal among his competitors, although a strong challenge can be found in the career of Jacob Perkins, the subject of chapter 3. However, his genius was scarcely ever acknowledged by his peers, and few of the devices yielded a profit. Moreover, it was relatively easy to obtain a patent on any device with new or different features, this having no relationship to its practicality or commercial application.

PEYTON'S BANK-NOTE BOOK OF 1856

DETECTING COUNTERFEITS

By early 1856, Ormsby remained anathema to other bank-note engravers, most of whom had "violated" the various rules for currency security outlined in his 1852 text. The earlier-delineated court case demonstrates the ill will harbored by the various parties. The time had come for someone else to create a book on bank-note engraving, preferably in a small format to permit wide distribution.

In March 1856, such a book appeared, written by George Peyton and published as a small, hardbound book of 45 pages plus plates, under a lengthy name that, in its entirety, essentially comprised a table of contents. Such sesquipedalian titles were hardly uncommon in the era, this per the first page: *How to Detect Counterfeit Bank Notes; or, an Illustrated Treatise on the Detection of Counterfeit, Altered, and Spurious Bank Notes, with Original Bank Note Plates and designs, by Rawdon, Wright, Hatch & Edson, Bank Note Engravers, of New-York, the Whole Forming an Unerring Guide, by which Every Person Can, on Examination, Detect Spurious Bank Notes of Every Description, No Matter How Well Executed They May Appear.*

Likely, most used the short title on the cover, *How to Detect Counterfeit Bank Notes.* Peyton, whose address was 418 Broadway, styled himself as an exchange broker who had been in that line of business for 15 years. Associated in the project, and likely its sponsor, was the well-known and highly regarded New York firm, Rawdon, Wright, Hatch & Edson, bank-note engravers and printers, the largest in the field. Two years later the partnership would become most important of the seven components that formed the American Bank Note Company.

Ormsby's thesis had been that individual vignettes arranged on a plate were an invitation to counterfeiting, and that such bills could be easily reproduced, even by a teenager. Ironically, however, by 1856 Ormsby's Unit System was a failure. Ormsby was using individual vignettes and decorations to create bank notes in exactly the same manner as his competitors.

Such individual vignettes were the mainstay of the Rawdon, Wright, Hatch & Edson business, and, accordingly, the idea of using multiple stock illustrations on a bill was viewed by them as being the best technique. An oblique reference to Ormsby is given by Peyton's mention of a person unnamed:

> Two or three years since, an engraver of this city, supposed he had hit upon a method which was perfect, and wrote a book to prove its value, but, I believe it has been but in one instance adopted. Indeed, it would be a very difficult matter to invent a method, or system of engraving bank notes, that would be superior to the one used at the present time. . . .

Peyton was correct in his statement, as all that Ormsby had to show for the adoption of his system was a particular $1 bill he had created for the Carroll County Bank of Sandwich, New Hampshire, with the date of January 1, 1855.

However, Peyton's credentials in the logic and writing departments fell short of Ormsby's. A comparison of the two texts reveals that Peyton was often contradictory in his own discussions, seemingly more so than Ormsby. However, it was a book and could be given out to bank officials, probably accompanied by sample vignette sheets, examples of notes printed with others, and more—a flood of material known to have been distributed by Rawdon, Wright, Hatch & Edson, for which Ormsby had but a small counterpart. The Peyton volume was probably given out for free to many clients.

Peyton's Commentary

In his introduction to the work, Peyton included this *sentence,* indicating that a picture, in this instance a bank-note engraving, is worth a thousand words (although Peyton was obviously ready to supply the words as well):

> Proficiency in any art or science, must always be the result of practical experience; and although the knowledge by which we perceive the difference between the counterfeit bank note and the genuine one, cannot be strictly called a science, yet it can only be acquired by attentive observation of certain laws; which we always see harmonized in the genuine, and transgressed in the counterfeit; and as no language, no matter how lucid, can convey to the mind an adequate conception of what those laws are, I have had engraved by Messrs. Rawdon, Wright, Hatch & Edson, the accompanying bank note designs, or illustrations, which are of so general a character as to embody all the particulars that make up the genuine bank note.

Then comes the remarkable comment, shrouded by many words, that, in essence, any one of the several bank-note engravers is about as good as any other:

> To fully appreciate the advantage which these plates offer, it will be necessary to know that there is a standard of excellence in bank note engraving, at which all, who claim the title of bank note engravers, must arrive before their ability can be acknowledged.
>
> With the present few established firms, which, I believe, constitute all the bank note engravers in the United States, this ability, both in design and execution, is beyond question; and the degree of excellence to which bank note engraving has been brought, is about equal with each of them; hence, comparatively, no difference can be discovered between any branch of it, engraved by one firm, and a similar one engraved by another: thus establishing a general uniformity by which the characteristics of *all* can be acquired by learning those of *any one.*

The "Formation of a Note"

Perhaps Peyton had not read Ormsby's 1852 book carefully, or if he had, perhaps he forgot that one of Ormsby's theses was that counterfeiters as well as reputable bank-note engravers often possessed precisely the same equipment and dies, and that often genuine dies were used to make counterfeit notes. In the light of Ormsby's philosophy, Peyton's list of essential foundations of a genuine note are meaningless, nor can the modern student of bank notes learn much:

> This will appear evident, by considering the following branches which are used in the formation of a note.
>
> **1st.** The round hand, "will pay on demand to the bearer," is the same in all bank notes—that is to say, the curves and hair lines are drawn with mathematical accuracy, and although there may be occasionally a slight difference in the style of letter, yet a comparison of the curves and hair lines, one with another, will instantly disclose the precision to which I allude.
>
> **2nd.** The shading of letters and all the parallel ruling on the notes, are executed by the parallel ruling machine, used by all bank note engravers, consequently the work is the same.
>
> **3rd.** The geometrical lathe work—that is the ends, borders, counters, &c., though apparently dissimilar—springs from a common origin, and is essentially the same, being like the various patterns in lace, in each of which the same thread, though differently woven, is used.
>
> **4th.** The bas-relief is made by similar machinery, and necessarily presents the same appearance in all genuine work.
>
> **5th.** The human figures which form the principal characteristic in vignettes, are drawn in accordance with a certain ideal standard of perfection; and, as this is one and the same with all artists, no essential difference can possibly exist between their productions in this particular.
>
> It will now be manifest that an intimate acquaintance with the engraved illustrations, aided by the explanatory text connected with them, will insure a skill in judging of bank notes that can only otherwise be acquired by years of practical familiarity with the routine of a broker's business.

In the last statement Peyton certainly was correct—while at the same time he inadvertently suggested that his book was useless to the typical reader apt to lack "intimate acquaintance" with the thousands of engraved illustrations currently employed!

Detecting Counterfeits

Peyton continued his view that the only way to detect counterfeits was to study the quality of the engravings, still overlooking the fact that genuine dies engraved by leading artists were often employed by counterfeiters:

> **How to Detect Counterfeit Bank Notes**
>
> *Counterfeit notes* are those which are fac-similes of the genuine.
>
> *Spurious notes* are those which differ entirely from the genuine.
>
> *Altered notes* are those whose title, locality, or denomination has been extracted and some other one pasted or printed in its place.
>
> Fifteen years' active experience in the exchange business has convinced me, conclusively, that the multiplicity of counterfeit, altered and spurious bank notes, which have, from time to time, been forced into our circulating currency, has been owing more to the very imperfect knowledge we possess of what constitutes good

bank note engraving, than to any ability, in point of workmanship, displayed by the counterfeiter in producing those fraudulent issues.

So diffused, indeed, is this ignorance, that not one percent of the community knows the object or character of those beautiful devices which are to be found on every genuine bank note, and which constitute the only safeguard against fraud it can furnish. With the remaining ninety-nine percent paper money is strictly enigmatical. Some judge from the first impression their minds receive on glancing at a note; others place great faith in pin holes; others, again, consider certain conditions of the ends, whether they be thumbed or not, infallible.[38]

Numerous other methods might be mentioned, if it were at all necessary, which would show the apparently hopeless condition we are in respecting a correct knowledge of our paper currency. The cause of this confusion unquestionably arises from the multitude of banks issuing notes, together with the universal idea that to be a good judge of paper money, it is essential to be acquainted with each individual issue in the country.[39]

I shall endeavor to prove that this idea is as erroneous as it is impracticable, and that a correct and certainly rational method may be determined from investigating and reducing the science of bank note engraving to a few fundamental principles, which must, from the peculiarity of the present style, enter into and form an integral part of each genuine bank note issued.

Peyton went on to suggest that careful examination of a note, including the quality of engraving of the geometrical designs, human figures, animals, and other features, was essential in determining the nature of a note. In genuine notes the fine or delicate lines would all be sharp, whereas "in all counterfeit work the lines are coarse and irregular, and cross each other in a confused manner; consequently producing blurred and imperfect figures."

This may have been the case if counterfeits were amateurishly engraved. However, a number of makers of such notes had authentic vignettes available, purchased from engravers or made to their order by skilled artists.

In due course, the apparent sponsor of the book was highlighted:

The steel plates which illustrate this work were engraved, as the reader will perceive, by the eminent house of Rawdon, Wright, Hatch & Edson, of this city, which has, for the last thirty years, by the beauty and artistic superiority of the bank note engraving executed by it, successfully resisted, strictly speaking, the many attempts, to imitate its work. The plates, it may be proper to state, were engraved on condition that they should remain in their hands, to be destroyed when the impressions were printed.

It appears that every order for engraving is investigated in the most rigorous manner, and no price can purchase an atom of their work, until the party applying is ascertained beyond doubt to be acting in good faith and for a legitimate purpose. Their sources of information, in consequence of the extent of their business, which compels them to have branches in the principal cities, are so reliable, that the character of an individual, or an institution may be obtained a in a few hours' notice.

Again, the reader of the present text will find the preceding to be humorous.

Explaining the Transfer Process

Peyton then gave this useful account of the transfer or siderographic process:

The various parts of the note, whether the engraving be mechanical or artistical, are executed on thin squares of steel, after which they are TRANSFERRED on cylinders, thus becoming the "rolls," or dies of the bank note engraver.

In using the term *transfer,* it may be necessary to state what is understood by the word. If you take a coin and press it on the surface of a piece of wax, or any other equally soft substance, certain indentations corresponding to its letters and characters will be reduced; if these indentations are filled with ink, and paper or cloth pressed over them, an exact printed copy of the original coin is the result.

In bank note engraving, a piece of softened steel, about three inches square and one-eighth of an inch thick, is selected, and upon its surface engraved, either by hand, or machinery the design required. After it is finished in every respect, it undergoes the process of carbonization, or in other words, it is converted into the hardest steel.

It is now ready to be transferred. This is performed by means of a powerful machine termed a transfer press, weighing about a ton, and capable of exerting an immense pressure; the design is brought under a small cylinder of softened steel, which is rolled over it with such force by the machine, as to take up in relief every line in the most perfect manner.

The cylinder is hardened, and is then capable of transferring its design on a bank note plate, by being rolled over it in the same manner. . . .

Engravings in the Hands of Counterfeiters

The preceding led to a refutation of the problem of good engravings falling into the hands of bad people, one of the warnings Ormsby had given in his 1852 text, although, again, Peyton made no mention of Ormsby. To Peyton it was not a problem at all:

The argument put forth was, that in case these dies should get into the hands of the counterfeiter, either by his breaking into the engraver's establishment and stealing them, or by purchas-

> ing them honestly if the engravers should fail, and their dies be sold at public auction, the country would, in a very short time, be flooded with counterfeit notes bearing genuine impressions.
>
> In a strict argument, both conditions would, of course, be untenable; but permitting the broadest license, let us suppose that one of the present houses should fail, and that their immense stock of dies, &c., were sold at public auction; let us suppose also, to shorten the matter, that a counterfeiter has purchased all the dies necessary to make a bank note, what then?
>
> The possession of the dies by no means makes him an artist: the thief who steals the painter's palette and brush, would certainly find some difficulty in making the picture. After buying the dies, he must of necessity, before he can use them, procure the transfer press before mentioned. This would incur a large expenditure of funds, quite sufficient to place the machine beyond the reach of nine-tenths of the fraternity. It must be recollected that the ordinary counterfeiter is not a capitalist, but on the contrary, belongs to a class of vagabonds whose means are always limited. The pecuniary obstacle, however, is very trifling, when compared with the danger of having the transfer press on his premises: its weight, in case of a surprise, is so great that it is impossible to dispose of it with any ordinary dispatch, and it stands an incontrovertible witness, whose silent testimony is fatal.
>
> But waiving these considerations entirely, to put an end to this side-issue, it does not follow that the counterfeiter who possesses the dies, and even has a transfer press at his service, can use them effectually.
>
> Transferring is an art, and like every other art, it has certain elementary rudiments which must be mastered before any satisfactory progress can be made in it: enthusiasm can never take the place of skill, neither can the workman be created without the qualifications which experience can alone impart. And yet it must be admitted that on many of the spurious notes in circulation at the present day, the genuine work of the lathe and designs not originally intended for counterfeiters are to be found.
>
> To account for this, is not difficult, since bank note engraving, like many other arts, has its pretenders, who, after failing to prove their merit before the proper tribunal, like charlatans, dispense their wares to any purchaser, without questioning his object, or character. To say that their professional ability being limited, the injury they can do will be trifling, would be advancing a very weak argument, since it is evident that they are only restricted from doing a great injury by the circumstances of the case.

Peyton went on to say that legislatures should enact laws to prevent established engravers from engaging in illicit activities, a comment which seems to indicate that, indeed, there was a problem in this regard.

A "Genuine Bank Note"

"I shall now carefully analyze a GENUINE BANK NOTE," Peyton continued, "for the purpose of making the reader thoroughly familiar with its principal points."

No fewer than 26 features were discussed, ranging from paper and the signatures of officers to headings such as "hair," "eyes," "nose," and "neck," to the appearance of railroad cars on vignettes. No doubt to check each of these aspects on a particular bill, even an expert would have to spend many minutes with a magnifying glass!

In practice, Peyton's guide, as well as *all* bank-note reporters and counterfeit detectors, were generally useless against well-made forgeries, of which there were many in circulation.

Overlooked was the *main problem* with worthless bank bills conceived in fraud: by the late 1850s most false notes were *alterations* of the real notes of failed banks, with certain original inscriptions removed and new names and addresses added. Ornateness was the prevailing style of bank notes of the era, and relatively few counterfeit printing plates were made.

The Golden Era of the 1850s

A New Era of Prosperity: California Gold

Gold was discovered in quantity in the American River, near Sacramento, California, by James Marshall in the tailrace of Sutter's Mill on January 24, 1848. By year's end many adventurers were headed to the land of opportunity, one of them being Edward E. Dunbar. In the present text Dunbar will be relevant in connection with his importance in the bank-note industry, although most numismatists may remember him for his remarkably rare Dunbar & Co. $5 gold coins struck in San Francisco in 1851.

In 1849 gold bullion began arriving in large quantities in the East. Much was converted to coins at the several mints, most importantly in Philadelphia, but also in Charlotte, Dahlonega, and New Orleans. With this influx came great prosperity. By this time the Hard Times years of 1837 to 1843 were history, and the American economy was prospering.

The Later Era of Free Banking

The Olden Days

It will be recalled that in 1837 the first free-banking law in the United States was passed by the Michigan legislature. Under its provisions any group could form a bank by applying for a charter, giving suitable proof of assets, and agreeing to a few basic rules. The General Banking Law, as it was called in this particular state, proved to be an unmitigated disaster. The term *wildcat bank* was applied to bills issued by banks with little or no real capital, often situated in obscure locations, and sometimes without an office at all.

Then in 1838 Georgia and New York each enacted free-banking laws. These states achieved better results—not hard to do in view of the utter chaos in Michigan. However, these laws had the unintended consequence that many banks were set up by applicants with little experience in the field, or by people

California Gold Diggers—A Scene from Actual Life at the Mines. (*Ballou's Pictorial Drawing-Room Companion*)

A paying teller at a metropolitan bank in the 1850s. (J.S. Gibbons, *The Banks of New York*)

with criminal intent, or by those with other deficiencies. Failures were extensive in New York in particular, but not to the degree that Michigan sustained. In 1838 and 1839, there was so much unfavorable publicity about new banks, including hearings in the U.S. Congress, that few state legislatures thought of enacting free-banking laws.

Although new banks were formed in many states during the 1840s, the number was far fewer than would be seen in the decade of the 1850s. By this time memories of the Hard Times era had faded, and new players were eager to get into the banking game.

New Free Banks

Within a few years the scenario changed dramatically. More banks meant more prosperity, it was thought—a replay of the Michigan philosophy of 1837. In the West small communities were eager for financial institutions to set up, and in the East many smaller towns and villages desired to have their own banks. Times were good, and banks were expected to make them even better.

Arkansas was the first state to loosen up its banking laws in the new wave of activity, followed by other states over the next decade to 1860:

1849—Arkansas

1850—New Jersey

1851—Illinois, Maine, and Ohio

1852—Indiana, Rhode Island, Tennessee, and Wisconsin

1853—Florida

1858—Minnesota and Iowa

1860—Pennsylvania

In the frontier prairie lands known as the American West, hundreds of new banks were formed, including under the free-banking laws by which just about any group of investors could form a bank, subject in some instances to depositing security with the state. Not since the heady times of the late 1830s had there been such activity. There were some restrictions that banks be located in settled areas. In 1857 in Illinois a law provided that a community desiring a bank had to have at least 200 people, and in 1858 a similar law was passed in Wisconsin.

Each of these new banks needed currency, and quickly—preferably to be on hand by start of business (and before its reputation was established). But history repeated itself, and free banks were not the hoped-for catalyst to propel prosperity to new heights.

In Indiana 68 banks were set up during the first three years of free banking, but three years later only 38 remained. Indiana paper became a wide subject of derision, especially as many of the state's bills had very attractive vignettes, making them beautiful to look at but worthless to spend.

In Illinois, nearly 90% of the banks were out of business by the early 1860s. In Wisconsin in 1861, there were 108 banks in business at the beginning of the year, but within the next two years 36 failed and 15 others shut down.

Maine as an Illustration of Eastern Activity

A useful example of new banks in the East is provided by those in the state of Maine. In the years from 1840 to 1849, just two new banks had commenced business in the state. In contrast, in Maine from 1850 to 1859, a long list of new banks went into operation, 55 total, plus some unofficial or fraudulent banks and some few entries caused by name changes. Unless noted otherwise in the following list, each bank was located in the town reflected by its name. Banks that failed or were liquidated during the currency-issuing period are so noted.

A listing of later Maine banks follows, together with what happened to them and the names of the firms that made their currency in later years. Collectively the bills represent a rich panorama of designs in use in this period. Most bills printed in black with bright white backgrounds are proofs from the Norman Pullen and/or Herbert and Martha Schingoethe collections:[1]

1847: Biddeford Bank—Capital $50,000.[2] Became the Biddeford National Bank in 1865. New England Bank Note Co., Boston (50% owned by Rawdon, Wright, Hatch & Edson, New York).

1848: Veazie Bank of Bangor—$200,000. Became the Veazie National Bank of Bangor in 1873. New England Bank Note Co., Boston.

1850: Atlantic Bank of Portland—$100,000. *Liquidated in 1855.* Baldwin, Bald & Cousland and Bald, Cousland & Co. Imprints.

1850: Exchange Bank of Bangor—$50,000. *Failed in 1856.* Toppan, Carpenter, Casilear & Co., New York and Philadelphia.

1850: Merchants Bank of Bangor—$50,000. Became the Merchants National Bank of Bangor in 1865. New England Bank Note Co., Boston / Rawdon, Wright, Hatch & Edson, New York.

1850: Union Bank of Brunswick—$50,000. Became the Union National Bank of Brunswick in 1865. New England Bank Note Co., Boston / Rawdon, Wright, Hatch & Edson, New York.

1850: Waterville Bank—$50,000. This was one of two banks with this name, the first having existed circa 1814 through 1831. The second became the Waterville National Bank in 1865. New England Bank Note Co., Boston. Later issues with the ABNCo monogram of the American Bank Note Co.

1851: Bank of the State of Maine at Bangor—$150,000. Became the Second National Bank of Bangor in 1864. Toppan, Carpenter, Casilear & Co., New York and Philadelphia.

1851: Ellsworth Bank—$50,000. Second bank to use this name. *Liquidated in 1855.* New England Bank Note Co. / Rawdon, Wright, Hatch & Edson, New York.

1851: Lewiston Falls Bank of Lewiston—$50,000. Became the First National Bank of Lewiston in 1865. New England Bank Note Co. / Rawdon, Wright, Hatch & Edson, New York. Later bills have the ABNCo monogram.

1851: Rockland Bank—$50,000. Became the Rockland National Bank n 1865. New England Bank Note Co. / Rawdon, Wright, Hatch & Edson, New York.

1852: Bank of Hallowell—$50,000. *Failed in 1856.* New England Bank Note Co.

1852: City Bank of Bangor—$50,000. Charter expired in 1857. Toppan, Carpenter, Casilear & Co., New York and Philadelphia.

1852: Cobbossee Contee Bank of Gardiner—$50,000. Became the Cobbossee Contee National Bank of Gardiner in 1865. New England Bank Note Co., Boston.

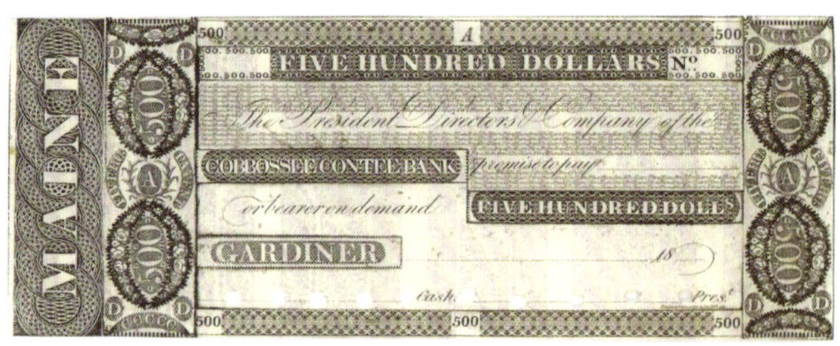

1852: Georges Bank of Thomaston—$50,000. Became the Georges National Bank of Thomaston in 1865. New England Bank Note Co., Boston.

1852: Lumbermans Bank of Old Town—$50,000. *Liquidated in 1865.* New England Bank Note Co., Boston / Rawdon, Wright, Hatch & Edson, New York.

1852: Orono Bank—$50,000. Became the Orono National Bank in 1865. Toppan, Carpenter, Casilear & Co., New York and Philadelphia.

1852: Peoples Bank of Damariscotta—$50,000. Became the Marine Bank of Damariscotta in 1853. Not known to have issued currency under this name.

1852: Richmond Bank—$50,000 Became the Richmond National Bank in 1865. Toppan, Carpenter, Casilear & Co., New York and Philadelphia.

1853: Bank of Winthrop—$50,000. Became the National Bank of Winthrop in 1864. Used old-style Perkins Patent Stereotype Steel Plate format (by New England Bank Note Co.). Later issues with ABNCo imprint.

1853: China Bank—$50,000. *Liquidated in 1855.* New England Bank Note Co. / Rawdon, Wright, Hatch & Edson, New York.

1853: City Bank of Bath—$50,000. Charter expired in 1868. Imprint not recorded by Haxby or Wait.

1853: Farmers Bank of Bangor—$50,000. Charter expired in 1867. New England Bank Note Co.; also Toppan, Carpenter & Co., New York and Philadelphia.

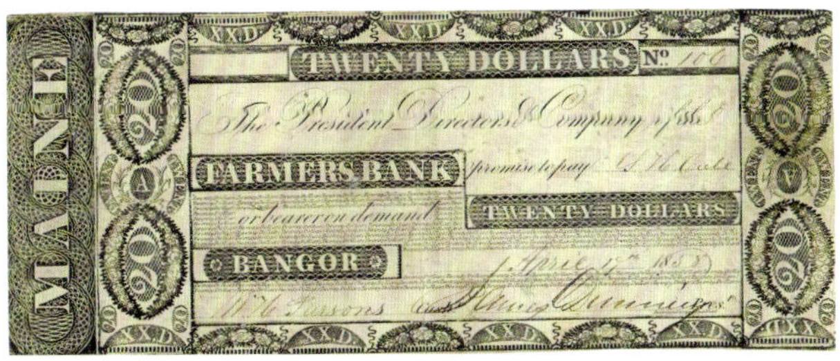

1853: Hancock Bank of Ellsworth—$50,000. *Failed in 1857.* New England Bank Note Co. / Rawdon, Wright, Hatch & Edson, New York.

1853: Marine Bank of Damariscotta (new name for the Peoples Bank of Damariscotta)—$50,000. Became the First National Bank of Damariscotta in 1864. Toppan, Carpenter & Co., New York and Philadelphia.

1853: Maritime Bank of Bangor—$75,000. Charter expired in 1857. Danforth, Wright & Co., New York and Philadelphia.

1853: Sandy River Bank of Farmington—$50,000. Became the Sandy River National Bank of Farmington in 1865. Toppan, Carpenter, Casilear & Co., New York and Philadelphia.

1853: Searsport Bank—$50,000. Charter expired in 1867. Toppan, Carpenter, Casilear & Co., New York and Philadelphia. Later notes with ABNCo monogram.

1853: Ship Builders Bank of Rockland—$100,000. *Failed in 1855.* New England Bank Note Co. / Rawdon, Wright, Hatch & Edson, New York.

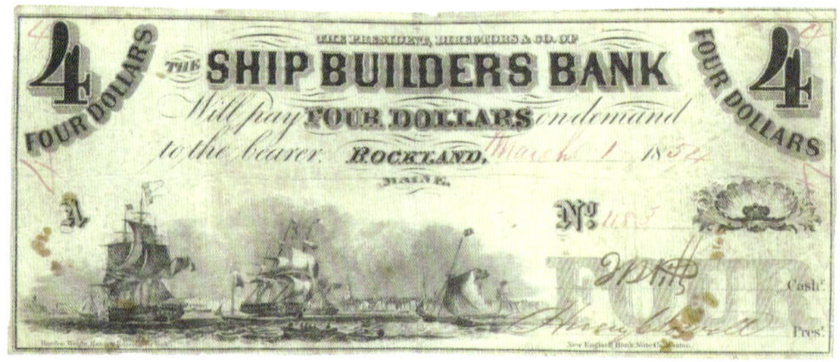

1853: Traders Bank of Bangor—$50,000. Became the Traders National Bank of Bangor in 1865. Danforth, Wright & Co., New York and Philadelphia.

1853: Waldoboro Bank—$50,000. Became the Waldoboro National Bank in 1865. Toppan, Carpenter, Casilear & Co., New York and Philadelphia. Later notes with American Bank Note Co., New York.

1854: American Bank of Hallowell—$75,000. *Failed in 1865.* New England Bank Note Co. / Rawdon, Wright, Hatch & Edson, New York. Later bills have the ABNCo monogram.

1854: Bank of Commerce of Belfast—$75,000. Charter expired in 1867. Baldwin, Adams & Co., New York; also American Bank Note Co., New York.

1854: Bank of Somerset of Skowhegan—$50,000. *Liquidated in 1864.* New England Bank Note Co. / Rawdon, Wright, Hatch & Edson, New York.

1854: Bucksport Bank—$50,000. Became the Bucksport National Bank in 1865. Bald, Adams & Co., New York City, and on the same notes, Bald, Cousland & Co., Philadelphia. The $50 of this bank has the popular Santa Claus vignette.

1854: Grocers Bank of Bangor—$75,000. *Failed in 1857.* New England Bank Note Co. / Rawdon, Wright, Hatch & Edson, New York.

1854: Market Bank of Bangor—$100,000. Became the First National Bank of Bangor in 1864. New England Bank Note Co. / Rawdon, Wright, Hatch & Edson, New York.

1854: Mechanics Bank of Portland—$100,000. Became the Second National Bank of Portland in 1865. Toppan, Carpenter, Casilear & Co., New York and Philadelphia. Later issues with ABNCo monogram.

1854: Mousam River Bank of Sanford—$50,000. Name changed to the Sanford Bank (see listing) in 1857. W.L. Ormsby, New York. Also, per one historian, some by Toppan, Carpenter, Casilear & Co., New York and Philadelphia.[3]

1854: New Castle Bank—$50,000. Became the New Castle National Bank in 1865. Danforth, Wright & Co., New York and Philadelphia.

1854: North Bank of Rockland—$50,000. Became the North National Bank of Rockland in 1875. New England Bank Note Co. / Rawdon, Wright, Hatch & Edson, New York.

1854: Ocean Bank of Kennebunk—$50,000. Became the Ocean National Bank of Kennebunk in 1865. Danforth, Wright & Co., New York and Philadelphia.

1854: State Bank of Augusta—$50,000. Became the First National Bank of Augusta in 1864. New England Bank Note Co. / Rawdon, Wright, Hatch & Edson, New York.

1855: Alfred Bank—$50,000. *Liquidated in 1865.* Danforth, Wright & Co.

1855: Auburn Bank—$50,000. Name changed in 1855 from the Danville Bank of Auburn. Became the First National Bank of Auburn in 1865. New England Bank Note Co.

1855: Bath Bank—$50,000. Became the Bath National Bank in 1864. Baldwin, Bald & Cousland, New York City, and on the same notes, Bald, Cousland & Co., Philadelphia; also American Bank Note Co., New York.

1855: Canton Bank of China—$50,000. *Failed in 1856.* New England Bank Note Co. / Rawdon, Wright, Hatch & Edson, New York.

1855: Danville Bank of Auburn—$50,000. Name change in the same year to the Auburn Bank (see listing). Not known to have issued currency under the Danville Bank name.

1855: Oakland Bank of Gardiner—$50,000. Became the Oakland National Bank of Gardiner in 1864. Danforth, Wright & Co.; also American Bank Note Co., New York and Boston.

1855: Peoples Bank of Waterville—$50,000. Became the Peoples National Bank of Waterville in 1865. Toppan, Carpenter, Casilear & Co., New York and Philadelphia. *1856: Atlantic Bank of Portland*—$100,000. *Liquidated in 1860.* Toppan, Carpenter, Casilear & Co., New York and Philadelphia.

1856: City Bank of Biddeford—$50,000. Became the First National Bank of Biddeford in 1865. New England Bank Note Co. / Rawdon, Wright, Hatch & Edson, New York.

1856: Village Bank of Bowdoinham—$50,000. Became the National Village Bank of Bowdoinham in 1865. Baldwin, Bald & Cousland, New York City, and on the same notes, Bald, Cousland & Co., Philadelphia.

1857: Bank of New England of Fairmount—None. *Nonexistent bank.* Fraudsters ordered about $500,000 face value of these bills from Rawdon, Wright, Hatch & Edson, New York. Apparently, the firm did not make even a basic check on the standing of this bank! According to W.L. Ormsby, these notes were "for the sole purpose of altering them to represent the issues of the New England Bank, Boston. The best are often deceived."

1857: Central Bank of Gray—None. *Fraudulent bank.* Certain bills have inked 1857 date. Wellstood, Hay & Whiting, New York. No background investigation was made of the perpetrators when they ordered the bills.

1857: Long Reach Bank of Bath—$100,000. *Liquidated in 1864.* New England Bank Note Co., Boston; also Bald, Cousland & Co., New York and Philadelphia.

1857: Maine Bank of Brunswick—$75,000. Became the First National Bank of Brunswick in 1864 New England Bank Note Co. / Rawdon, Wright, Hatch & Edson, New York.

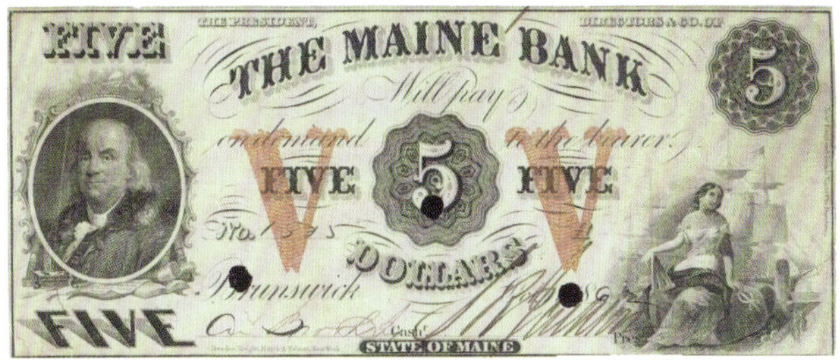

1857: Norombega Bank of Bangor—$100,000. *Liquidated in 1860.* New England Bank Note Co. / Rawdon, Wright, Hatch & Edson, New York.

1857: Pejobscot Bank of Brunswick—$75,000. Became the Pejobscot National Bank of Brunswick in 1865. New England Bank Note Co. / Rawdon, Wright, Hatch & Edson, New York.

1857: Sanford Bank—$50,000. Name change in 1857 from the Mousam River Bank of Sanford. *Failed in 1861.* Toppan, Carpenter, Casilear & Co., New York & Philadelphia. Some bills with the ABNCo monogram.

1859: International Bank of Portland—$250,000. Became the First National Bank of Portland in 1864. American Bank Note Co., Boston.

1859: Mercantile Bank of Bangor—$50,000. Second bank to bear this name. *Liquidated in 1876.* Toppan, Carpenter & Co., New York and Philadelphia, with ABNCo monogram added. This was a reuse of a plate made earlier for the first Mercantile Bank, whose charter expired in 1857.

1860: North Berwick Bank—$50,000. Became the North Berwick National Bank. American Bank Note Co., New York.

1861: Lincoln County Bank of Wiscasset—$50,000. *Fraudulent.* American Bank Note Co., New York.

For most of the failed banks in the above list, their currency proved to be worthless. Most banks failed from mismanagement, but a few were fraudulent. As to how much the bank-note companies promulgated frauds by not investigating applicants, answers will never be known.

The Panic of 1857, the effects of which were felt for the next two years, curtailed the formation of new banks. In Maine, only two more were incorporated during the note-issuing period: the North Berwick Bank in 1860 and the fraudulent Lincoln County Bank of Wiscasset in 1861, the last never having been chartered.

Free Banking in the West

During this era several states either closely regulated the issuing of paper money or went into the banking business. Now, in good economic times, banks were being opened with reckless abandon. In 1852 the *New York Journal of Commerce* published this item:

> The list of new banks is increasing so rapidly, that it is almost impossible to keep a record of them; and unless the public exercise more than their usual caution, there will be some notable swindling carried on under this guise. Foiled at the seat of government, the operators have turned to the West, and, under the free banking laws of Illinois, Indiana, and Wisconsin, are preparing more than one million of dollars in notes with which to flood the channels of circulation at the East.
>
> There can be no mistake on this point. It is not the Western capital thus seeking profitable employment; nor is it Eastern capital invested at the West to afford accommodation to the residents there. Not a dollar of the new currency will be issued where it is likely to be presented: at the bank for redemption. The object of the distant location is to *avoid par redemption,* and to shave those who may be induced to receive the bills, out of such a rate of discount as may best suit the purposes of the Wall-Street owners.[4]

"It is often said that the happiest and most prosperous of nations have no histories. . . . This is apt to be true of banks as well as of nations." Included in the preface of a bank history, this statement reminds us once again that the annals of banking are filled with columns about charlatans and fraudsters, not to overlook decent banks that simply failed, while banks that operated quietly and profitable attracted little notice.[5]

Banking Games in the Prairie States

In Indiana in the 1850s, 94 banks were chartered under the free-banking law of 1852; the state was a latecomer to the scenario. Some of these banks were paper mills ordering large quantities of currency to be distributed at distant points. An 1853 report commented:

The House called on the Auditor of the State for a report of such of the banks in Indiana, organized under the general law, as were doing business in conformity with the provisions of the law. In response to this call, the Auditor sent in the following report:

> "In answer thereto I have the honor to submit the following statement: The following banks are doing a local legitimate business, to wit: The Bank of Connersville, at Connersville; State Stock Bank of Indiana, at Peru; the Indiana Stock Bank, at Laporte; the Wabash Valley Bank, at Logansport; the Gramercy Bank, at Lafayette; and the Prairie City Bank, at Terre Haute. These banks have an aggregate capital of $1,300,000.
>
> "The notes of the following banks are taken principally to New York City and there put in circulation, to wit: The State Stock Bank, at Logansport; the Plymouth Bank, at Plymouth; the Government Stock Bank, at Lafayette; the Public Stock Bank, at Newport; and the Bank of North America, at Newport. The aggregate capital of these banks is $365,000. These also have agencies at the localities named, for the redemption of their notes. No notes have been issued to any other institution."[6]

The American Exchange Bank

In New York City the American Exchange Bank, founded on October 1, 1838, and operated since that time, was knee deep in the paper money-trading business in 1853. It served as an exchange office and bought and sold worthless notes—a great source for those who sought to alter or pass such bills.

In 1853 it instituted what was a phony counterpart to the real and highly effective Suffolk System then operating in New England. Banks of uncertain reputation in Indiana and Illinois made private arrangements to have the American Exchange Bank redeem their notes at a token 3/4 of 1% discount. Although details are not known, this plan could have been arranged by exchanging such services for stock of the banks in question, or having the distant banks put up small cash deposits. The American Exchange Bank then advertised to buy and sell such bills, giving them the aura of being especially sound. Typically, bills of far-away banks sold for deep discounts. The banks serviced included these:

> *Indiana:* Bank of North America (Newport), Public Stock Bank (Newport), State Stock Security Bank (Newport), Government Stock Bank (Lafayette), Gramercy Bank (Lafayette), Merchants' Bank (Lafayette), Southern Bank (Terre Haute), State Stock Bank (Logansport), Plymouth Bank (Plymouth), and Drovers' Bank (Rome).
>
> *Illinois:* Bank of America, Chicago Bank, City Bank, Commercial Bank, Marine Bank, Mechanics and Merchants Bank, and Union Bank, all of Chicago; Clark's Exchange Bank (Springfield), and Stock Security Bank (Danville).

In March 1853, *Banker's Magazine* wryly observed this fact concerning the American Exchange Bank:

Proof impression of a $5 note of the Wabash Valley Bank of Logansport, Indiana, by Danforth, Bald & Co., New York and Philadelphia. Dated January 1, 1853, bills of this bank were issued at a time when the citizens of Indiana were often confused as to which banks were legitimate and which were not.

> We consider this a retrograde movement in banking—one that reflects no credit upon parties who endeavor to bolster up such issues and one that, sooner or later, will bring loss upon our own citizens, if the plan be pursued. It is a somewhat curious coincidence, that on the very day in which this arrangement is announced, our exchange papers inform us that a large portion of the so-called circulation of the above institutions has been rejected by the responsible private bankers of St. Louis, as unfit for use in that city.
>
> And it is further announced, that several of the parties who have recently established banking concerns in Illinois, have been indicted by the public authorities of the state of Illinois for malpractices, swindling, &c. In Indiana, the character of the new banking concerns is not much better, and it is an admitted fact that the new currency of both states is issued by, or in behalf of, parties at remote points, who avail themselves of the law to fasten an illegitimate circulation upon the community. Finding that the new currency of these states is not well received at home, it is now attempted to engraft these issues upon New York and its people, under color of law.

These currency capers resulted in a lot of business. *Banker's Magazine* printed this item in July 1854:

> *Girls as Bank Clerks.*—The American Exchange Bank, of this city, employs upwards of thirty boys and young men, to count country bank bills, at an average salary of about $500 per annum. Now, then, why cannot girls do this work as well as boys? Their nimble fingers can slide off the bill as expeditiously, and more so, than the clumsy thumbs of boys. Then as to the reckoning of counting, they certainly have the capacity to do

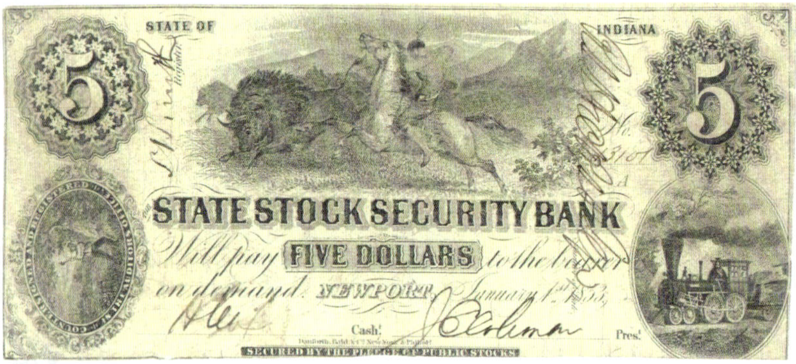

A $5 note of the questionable State Stock Security Bank of Newport, Indiana. From a plate dated January 1, 1853, by Danforth, Bald & Co., New York and Philadelphia.

A $5 note of the Merchants Bank of Lafayette, Indiana, an institution of uncertain reputation. Engraved and printed by Danforth, Bald & Co., this bill is dated December 15, 1852. Phony banks in Indiana and Illinois provided much business to bank-note printers in New York and Philadelphia.

Proof impression of a $10 note of the Southern Bank of Indiana, Terre Haute, by Wellstood, Hay, Hanks & Whiting, New York. Although this bank was viewed as questionable in the early 1850s, it remained in business until the mid-1860s.

> that. It requires the smallest amount of hard work, next to opening oysters, or any business that men ever engage in. We go for introducing girls into banks. Who objects?—*New York Day Book.*

The American Exchange Bank pursued its business unhindered, its deeds unpunished. Prosperity attended its efforts, and in 1857 it erected an impressive banking house at the corner of Broadway and Cedar Street. In the same year the General Assembly of New York questioned certain of its practices, and a report was filed. In 1859 the bank had a capital of \$5,000,000 but just \$177,229 of its own bills in circulation, a figure that dropped to just \$23,000 by January 1863. By that time the bank had changed its direction and had become legitimate in its practices. In 1865 it became the American Exchange National Bank, charter 1394.

EVOLUTION IN INDIANA

In a message in 1853, the governor of Indiana commented on banking in his state:

> The speculator comes to Indianapolis with a bundle of bank notes in one hand and the stock in the other; in twenty-four hours he is on the way to some distant point of the Union to circulate what he denominates a legal currency authorized by the Legislature of Indiana. He has nominally located his bank in some remote part of the state, difficult of access, where he knows no banking facilities are required, and intends that his notes shall go into the hands of persons who will have no means of demanding their redemption.[7]

Here we have a situation of déjà vu—Michigan banking of the 1830s reincarnated as Indiana and Illinois banking of the early 1850s. By autumn 1856, some 51 banks in Indiana had suspended, and their bills on the New York market were discounted up to 75%.[8]

A \$5 American Exchange Bank bill of the 1860s, a colorful proof impression by the American Bank Note Co. "Patented 30 June 1857" appears at the left above the bank's seal and refers to the *Canada Green* printing tint said to deter counterfeiting.

A \$5 note of the Bank of the State of Indiana, Madison branch, with "Madison" inked in, American Bank Note Co. The back is a custom plate with the bank's name printed. The note is signed at the lower left by H. McCulloch as president. The Bank of the State of Indiana circulated large numbers of notes and was a well-run organization. In 1863 Hugh McCulloch left to take a post as the first comptroller of currency in the Treasury Department in Washington, D.C.

In 1855 the General Assembly of Indiana incorporated the Bank of the State of Indiana, which in time was set up with branches in important towns and cities, operated from headquarters in Indianapolis. This institution succeeded the interests of the State Bank of Indiana, whose charter had expired.

In 1835 Hugh McCulloch became associated with the State Bank of Indiana, and in 1857 he became president of the Bank of the State of Indiana, in which position he signed bills for all the branches. The bank under his direction operated virtually problem-free and was a model of what a state could do, with good people and planning. He later went on to serve as the first comptroller of the currency under Abraham Lincoln in the early 1860s, during the launch of the National Banking system and its paper money issues. Later he served as secretary of the Treasury from 1865 to 1869 and again in 1884 and 1885.

Meanwhile in Ohio

On March 21, 1851, Ohio enacted a free-banking law. Capital for new banks had to be at least $25,000 and no more than $500,000. To secure integrity, stocks were to be deposited with the state to the full amount of bank notes in circulation. The state published bank information on November 15, 1851, revealing that 12 free banks had been established, adding to 41 branches of the State Bank of Ohio (formed in 1845), 5 "old banks," and 12 independent banks, with a total capital of $7,949,356. In time 17 free banks were established.[9] In the summer of 1851, a new law ended the formation of new free banks.[10] By 1856 ten such banks remained in business with a total capital of $738,050 and with $769,397 face value of currency in circulation.

The Ohio banking scene was shattered in the summer of 1853, when quantities of notes of five free banks were said to have been stolen from the printer, signed falsely, and put into circulation. The story of the false bills was told by a later historian:

> Great care had been exercised in all recent acts in those provisions regulating the furnishing of circulating notes to prevent fraudulent or unauthorized issues. However, during the summer of 1853 the business community was startled by finding a circulation of quantity of the notes of the free banks of Ohio, printed on genuine plates, with forged signatures of the officers of the banks and of the registrar, who was required to number and countersign them.
>
> As the law made it the business of the auditor of the state to provide the notes, he naturally felt his responsibility for their appearance. For a long time every effort to find the ones who had put them in circulation failed; but finally it was discovered that the engraving establishment had been betrayed by the person entrusted with the printing of them. This individual eventually confessed, and with four accomplices was tried in the criminal court of Hamilton County and sentenced to imprisonment in the penitentiary. The old plates were abandoned, new ones procured, and the old circulation withdrawn.[11]

The miscreants were employees of the Cincinnati branch of Rawdon, Wright, Hatch & Edson, which had made notes for all of the free banks in Ohio. A common design was used, with slugs inserted into the plate for the bank name and location. "The designs were crude and apparently went to the lowest bidder," Wendell Wolka commented in his study of Ohio notes.[12] The contract for new and replacement notes was given to Bald, Cousland & Co. and its partner Bald, Adams & Co. (sometimes Baldwin, Adams & Co.), which turned out bills of exceptionally high quality.

The news of false notes in circulation caused great consternation, and more than $1,000,000 in bills was brought back to the banks, severely decreasing the amount of their authentic currency in circulation. This shortage caused Tennessee banks to distribute large quantities of their notes in Ohio.

In 1852 the General Assembly of Ohio passed the Tax Law, which doubled or tripled the tax on bank property within the state. This became known as the "Crowbar Law," as law officers were authorized to enter banks without notice and use crowbars and other means of force to open money chests to seize assets of any bank that did not pay the tax on a timely basis. Soon, most of the remaining legitimate Ohio bills were withdrawn by the banks, causing Indiana paper, much of it worthless, to flood into the state. In 1856 one of the oldest and wealthiest citizens of Cincinnati reported that in the past six years he had received only four Cincinnati bank notes.[13] The law was eventually taken to the United States Supreme Court and declared unconstitutional.

In the meantime, branches of the State Bank of Ohio provided reliable service to the citizenry. Although a few banks closed their doors, safeguards built into the system assured that all holders of currency could redeem their bills at par. All told there were 41 branches, including these few that had problems or experienced changes, but with no loss to holders of bills:

Akron branch—Failed in 1854.

Franklin branch at Cincinnati—Voluntarily with-

A $1 note of the State Bank of Ohio, Farmers Branch at Mansfield. This branch began operation in 1847. In February 1865 it evolved into the Farmers National Bank of Mansfield, charter 800. American Bank Note Co.

Before 1856 the president of the entire system of branches signed all currency. After that time the vice president of the entire system signed $1, $2, and $3 notes, and the president signed denominations of $5 and upward.

A $3 note of the State Bank of Ohio, Piqua Branch. This branch began operation in 1847 with Joseph G. Young as cashier and William Scott as president. It aggressively issued paper money. In 1862 it had $217,055 in bills in circulation. In April 1865 it evolved into the Piqua National Bank, charter 1006, with the same officers. A $1 bill of the National Bank is illustrated here.

drew from the state system in 1852 and continued as a private bank.

Newark branch—Closed by the state Board of Control in May 1852.

Mechanics and Traders branch at Cincinnati—Suspended on November 20, 1854, and was subsequently placed into receivership by the Board of Control.

Commercial branch at Toledo—Failed on May 23, 1855, and closed by the Board of Control.

Cuyahoga Falls branch—Had difficulties but did not fail. The Board of Control supervised its sale to new owners.

Toledo branch—Had difficulties but did not fail. The Board of Control supervised its sale to new owners.[14]

Anticounterfeiting Plans and Patents

Early Anticounterfeiting Plans

The use of systems to prevent or deter counterfeiting dates back to colonial times, when secret marks and letters, the nature printing process, and other techniques were popular. Early in the era of state bank currency, Jacob Perkins' Patent Check Plate was widely admired.

An innovation of the 1820s was "Mr. Star's [*sic*] typographical colored printing plan," the idea of using different-sized bills for different denominations and having the number of vignettes be the same as the value of the bill in dollars (a $1 bill would have one vignette, a $5 would have five).[15] This colorful technique was ephemeral in its use if the absence of such bills in existence today is an indication.

In 1837, Philadelphia engraver Benjamin Tanner advertised that he could offer:

> STEREOGRAPHIC NOTES . . . which cannot be imitated or altered without immediate detection. The losses which institutions as well as the public sustains, are obviated by procuring notes which cannot be imitated by every apprentice in a printing office, as is the case with most of the small notes now in circulation.[16]

The Congreve Patent Check Plate

The Congreve Patent Check Plate back was originated in England by Sir William Congreve, the same man who challenged Jacob Perkins in the latter's quest for Bank of England business in 1820 (see chapter 3).[17]

Advertising note with multiple denominations, $1 to $50, by E. & C. Starr, imprinted Mechanics Bank in the City of New York, February 10, 1824, demonstrating the Starr anticounterfeit printing method. While the bill is certainly colorful, it does not transmit to the viewer the nature of the Starr system. W.L. Ormsby called it a "typographical colored printing plan."

A 1837 50¢ scrip note with TANNER'S STEREOGRAPH LABEL imprinted on the left border. Payable at the Bank of Granville in the Ohio town of the same name.

Sir William Congreve (1772–1828). (Portrait by James Lonsdale, National Portrait Gallery, London)

Similar to Perkins, Congreve had a particularly inventive turn of mind and developed innovations in many different fields, including some for ships and banknote printing. From 1808 until 1827, the year before his death, he filed 18 British patents, most of which were criticized as trading on the work of others. He was often abrasive to his associates and was viewed by many as a curmudgeon.

About 1824, James Whiting and Robert Branston acquired the rights to the compound printing system from Congreve. The process was later used on labels and other printing in which counterfeiting might be a problem. On some items "Whiting Patentee" was imprinted. After Sir William's death in 1828, his widow married to became Mrs. James Whiting.

Historian Elizabeth M. Harris described the compound printing system procedure:

> Congreve's compound plate was made by first cutting or stamping a design through a plate of fairly strong metal, such as brass or copper, to make a stencil. The stencil was then put on a flat surface and another more fusible metal was melted and poured over it. This formed a second detachable plate covering the back and filling the holes of the first.
>
> Next the face of the entire plate was engraved with lettering and mechanical patterns in a continuous design over both metals. Commonly the stamped holes were in wormlike shapes. . . . or roughly circular. The linear engraving on the surface was not governed by the pattern of the stencil; in both . . . the engraving formed a more or less independent design laid over the two colors.
>
> For printing, the two interlocked plates were separated, inked in different colors, fitted together again and printed at one pull. A special machine was built to ink and print the plates. In his patent specification Congreve claimed that other materials such as wood or ivory could be used as well as metal, and that three, four, or more colors could be combined and printed by the same machine with a slight adjustment.[18]

The Congreve Patent Check Plate back is seen on certain American bills with the Patent Stereotype Steel Plate face, issued by the New England Bank Note Company, which formed in 1833 and combined the Perkins interests. The back is filled with engraving in geometric designs. Eric P. Newman reports:

> In my collection I have in a frame a set of 8 different colored Congreve Patent Check and Plate bank note size backs. They are several FIVEs and other designs. They are identified as SPECIMENS OF CONGREVE ENGRAVING AND PRINTING by Abel Bowen, 1 Washington St., Boston.[19]

A $3 note of the Duxbury (Massachusetts) Bank, with Congreve Patent Check Plate back, circa 1835. This anti-counterfeiting plate was used on notes of only a few banks. Those reported date from the 1830s and are combined, as here, with a face from the Patent Stereotype Steel Plate of the New England Bank Note Co.

The Duxbury Bank was active from October 1, 1833, until September 1, 1846. It was headquartered on Washington Street at the Powder Point junction. Many loans were made to those engaged in the maritime trade.

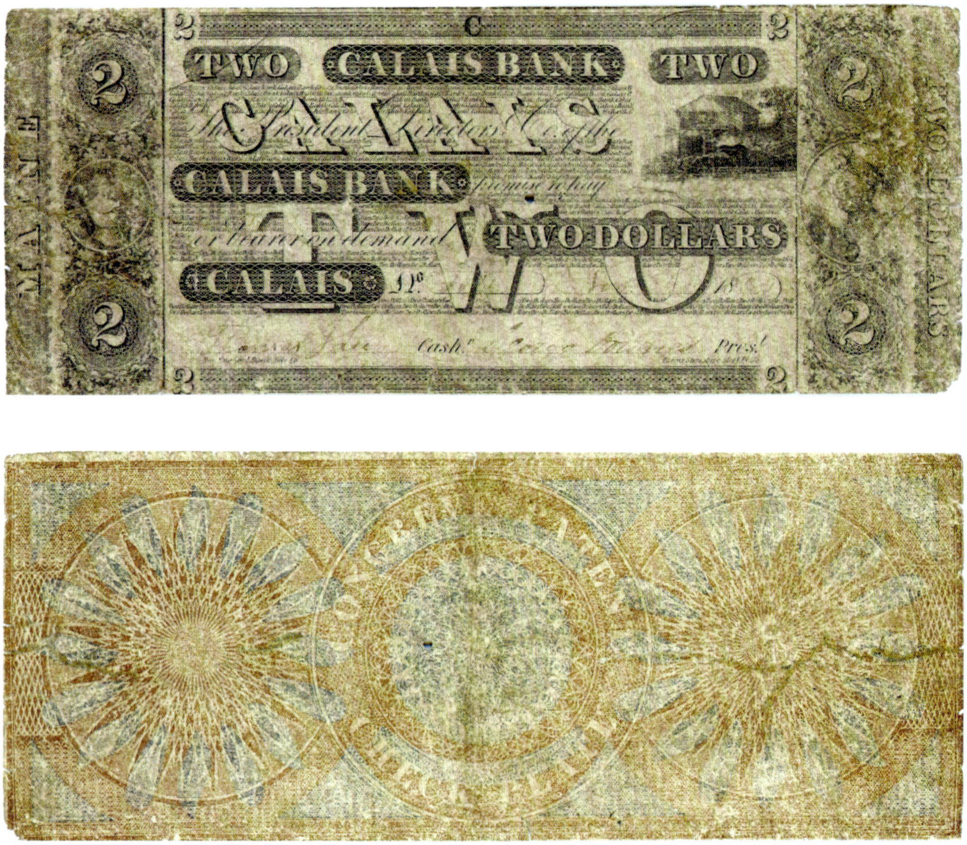

A $2 note of the Calais (Maine) Bank, 1834, with a two-colored Congreve Patent Check Plate back. The Calais Bank was founded in 1831 with a set capital of $50,000. It was located in the town of the same name, a seaport near the border with Canada. By 1848 it was one of only two banks in the state that had not joined the Suffolk Bank system for redeeming its currency. Its bills mostly circulated regionally in Washington County, where they were the main form of paper used in commerce. They were seldom taken out of the district, for they were valued at a deep discount elsewhere. On May 30, 1865, it converted to become the Calais National Bank, charter 1425. (See chapter 19 for an account of the bank in the Civil War.)

A $3 note of the National Bank, Washington, D.C., featuring Danforth, Bald, & Co.'s anticounterfeiting layout. "These are the most unique and pleasing specimens of bank note engraving, we have ever seen," cooed *Thompson's Reporter.*

According to Gene Hessler in *The Engraver's Line,* Abel Bowen, born in Greenbush, New York, in 1790, was engraving on wood as early as 1811. In 1816 he was a printer in Boston and soon took up copperplate engraving. By 1821 he was a partner with copperplate printer Alexander McKensie, publisher of *Shaw's History of Boston,* with engraved illustrations by Bowen. At the time, "Bowen resided at 4 Washington St. in Boston, where, in 1833 he designed and engraved multi-colored, cycloidal backs for bank notes. Some of his designs were used by the New England Bank Note Co Features similar to those of Bowen's designs had been developed in England by William Congreve."[20]

For many years Bowen engraved copper plates for printing and on various metals for plaques, door signs, and labels. Several engravers who later achieved prominence, most notably Joseph Andrews, worked under him at various times.

The Atwater Plan

The patented system of a Mr. Atwater was described by *Banker's Magazine,* December 1852, in connection with its use on bills of the Hartford County Bank of Hartford, Connecticut:

> Mr. Atwater's plan is to manufacture the bank-note paper in such a way that no alteration can be made from a low to a higher denomination. He introduces borders on the end of the notes, in addition to the figures which indicate its value, a single border for a one-dollar bill; two borders for two dollars, and five borders for five dollars. These are inserted at the left hand of the note. For the ten-dollar notes, a single border is introduced on the right end; two borders for a twenty-dollar bill. These various borders change the positions of the names of the president and cashier, and also of other portions of the bank-note, so that the general appearance of each denomination is entirely different from any other.

Atwater's patent may be related to the process called "Atwater's Secret Stripes." In *Bank Note Engraving* (1852), W.L. Ormsby quoted this explanation from a recent issue of *Thompson's Reporter,* seemingly describing a system with at least some of the same features:

> In executing the notes for the National Bank, D.C., the engravers, Messrs. Danforth, Bald, & Co., have adopted a perfect guard against altering notes from a lower to a higher denomination. It is simply this: on the right margin of the ONES is one border, on the TWOS, two borders; and on the THREES, three borders, etc.
>
> The reading of the notes comes plumb up to the borders, rendering it impossible to alter the notes without distorting their proportions. These notes are peculiar, and unlike any other bank notes in another particular—on the left end is a very large vignette or hemisphere, surmounted by an eagle. Altogether these are the most unique and pleasing specimens of bank note engraving, we have ever seen.

But Ormsby did not agree that this design was foolproof. He delineated how such a note could be altered easily by removing printed areas and adding new information. A $3 note could be changed by substituting FIFTY in place of THREE, and the numerals 50 where the 3 was. The average recipient of such an altered bill would not be aware that three segments on the right border had anything to do with the denomination.

Seropyan's Patent Among Others

In 1856 Christopher D. Seropyan published a circular telling of his chemical methods to prevent counterfeiting by "photographic," "anastatic," "photo-lithographic," "transfer," and other nefarious practices, the maker including an endorsement from Professor Emeritus Benjamin Silliman of Yale, one of the most famous scientists and writers of the era. "The protection which I offer against counterfeiting . . . does not depend upon the tint of the paper, but upon the translucent blue ink (which is exclusively prepared by myself) and the solid surface of the paper."[21]

Although currency with the Seropyan's patent *yellow* overprint was used as far west as Wisconsin, most attention regarding this innovation was played out in New Haven, Connecticut, where such bills were issued by at least two banks: the Elm City Bank and New Haven Bank. The latter institution commissioned local printer L.S. Punderson to add a yellow overprint to certain of its own notes, perhaps for comparison or experimental purposes.[22] It is not known what happened to the translucent *blue* ink idea first announced by Seropyan.

In the same year Seropyan's patent was given a big play by Danforth, Wright & Co., with offices in New York City, Philadelphia, and Boston. In 1857 the patentee had a special agent in New York City, Stille Manning, working with local engravers. A great controversy regarding the worth—or lack thereof—of Seropyan's patent was carried in several issues of *Banker's Magazine,* commencing in August 1856 and continuing into the next year, some based on articles in the New York *Journal of Commerce,* July 15, 1856, and the Boston *Evening Transcript,* July 20, 1856, and in *Annual of Scientific Discovery, or Year Book of Facts in Art and Science,*

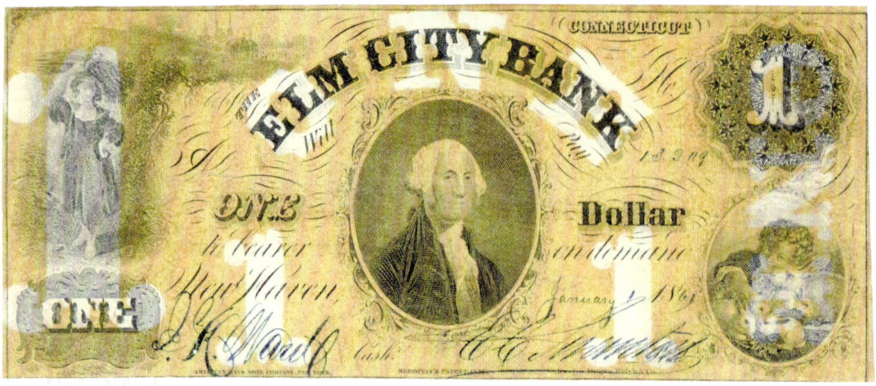

A $1 note of the Elm City Bank, New Haven, Connecticut, imprinted "Seropyan's Patent 1856" at the border below Washington's portrait. Relatively few banks used this anticounterfeiting system. This bank was chartered on July 11, 1854. P.T. Barnum subscribed for $50,000 worth of stock but never made payment, for reasons not known today. On February 1, 1864, the bank converted to become the Second National Bank of New Haven, charter 227.

A $5 note of the New Haven Bank with a yellow overprint imitating Seropyan's patent. This was applied locally by L.S. Punderson Print. Separately, certain currency of this institution utilized Seropyan's innovation. In 1856, New Haven Bank bills were the subject of experimentation in this regard, with the findings duly discussed in the *New York Journal of Commerce* and *Banker's Magazine.* This bank, organized in 1792, is discussed in chapter 2.

for 1856.[23] In brief, a committee representing New England banks found the invention to be utterly useless, while Seropyan and his endorsers claimed the test to be incomplete and the findings to be distorted. No matter, the Seropyan patent method soon disappeared from usage on bank bills, fading into history.

Canada Green

The prevalence and danger of counterfeits was highlighted by an article in the *New York Herald* in 1856, which noted that there were 1,317 banks in operation in the country, and counterfeit bills were known to exist of all but 463 of these! Included in the survey were counterfeit, altered, and spurious notes.[24]

The popular press as well as financial journals told of false notes that virtually defied detection, including many made by the photographic process. Alarm was raised across banking circles in the mid-1850s. To counter this evil, several new anticounterfeiting systems and techniques were proposed, adding to others that dated back to the days of the Perkins Check Plate. Some systems proved useful, but others did not. The record shows clearly that more counterfeits were in circulation in the 1850s than ever before.

In the 1850s, many hocus-pocus claims were made for certain printing techniques, ink colors, design arrangements, etc., that were said to deter or prevent altering or counterfeiting notes. These techniques would be a boon to later numismatists, who appreciated owning currency with all sorts of colored overprints, lacework, and other embellishments. Although color had been added to certain bills for a long time, including in the colonial era, most state bank bills were black and white until the 1850s. Such systems had a long history dating back to the Perkins Check Plate of the turn of the 19th century.

The most popular color addition was the so-called *Canada Green,* an allegedly antiphotographic green overprint said to make the photographic copying of a note impossible, as the green-imprinted section would appear as a black blob on a photographic print. This process was the brainchild of Dr. Sterry Hunt, who registered it in 1857 under Canadian patent number 715 and U.S. patent number 17,688. As was the case with patent medicines and elixirs, a patent for a green tint did not reflect that the Patent Office had approved of any claimed merits of the innovation. However, the fact of a patent looked good in advertising and publicity.

Hunt sold the rights to the Patent Green Tint (as it was officially designated) to George Matthews, Montreal agent of Rawdon, Wright, Hatch & Edson, who quickly sold it to Tracy R. Edson, president of that firm in New York. Edson lost no time in promoting it as the wonder of the age, including on colorful cards mailed to banks. "PATENTED 30 JUNE 1857" was boldly printed on such bills, said to have been made with the ink of sesqui-oxide of chromium, a name at once mystical and marvelous enough to have been used on a patent medicine. In the federal paper money contract awarded to American Bank Note Co. in August 1861, the government agreed to a surcharge of $5 per 1,000 impressions of this tint added to currency sheets. Some researchers have suggested that this tint became the "color of money" and gave rise to greenbacks in the federal paper money system, explaining why green is still used on bills today.

At the Strafford Bank in Dover, New Hampshire, the Canada Green tint impressed the cashier, who on March 2, 1859, recommended that a supplement of $150 be paid to imprint the bank's next order for bills, ordered in sheets of $1-$1-$3-$10 and $5-$10.[25] Many other banks did the same, but the idea soon died out, especially after news spread that the Associated Banks for the Suppression of Counterfeiting, an industry group, had submitted the Canada Green to testing and found it could be removed easily by an amateur.[26]

"Patent Green Tint" Press Agentry

In 1861 a reporter for *Harper's New Monthly Magazine* visited the holder of the Patent Green Tint to gather information for an article, "The American Bank Note Company," and for the February 1862 issue wrote this—after hearing from company president Tracy R. Edson about the advantages but, of course, not of its failure in certain tests:

> At one time it seemed that photography and kindred arts would destroy every guarantee against counterfeit notes. Give the photographer a camera, a few dollars' worth of chemicals, and a quire of paper, and he could produce fac-similes of any note without limit. No matter how perfect the engraving, or how elaborate the machine work, he could in a few minutes make a copy exact to the minutest point. Science was invoked to remedy the evil which it had occasioned. Now photography can not, as far as we know, reproduce colors.
>
> Red, yellow, blue, and green act like black upon the photographic plate. A red-haired man, for example, when photographed, wears a head of unimpeachable raven hue; the yellow of a footman's gorgeous plushes appears black in his photographic picture. So parts of bank notes were printed in red, blue, yellow, or green. These parts when photographed appeared black, as well as the part which were so in the genuine notes. But unfortunately all the colored inks in use were of such a nature that they could be discharged, with more or less facility, without disturbing the black ink.
>
> The counterfeiter would remove those colors, photograph the remainder of the note, and then print in the proper colors an imitation of the colored parts. An additional process was thus rendered necessary for the manufacture of a photographic counterfeit, but this was an easy one, and the labor was more than repaid by the security which was supposed to be given to any note printed in colors.

Patent Green Tint on a $5 note of the Strafford Bank, Dover, New Hampshire. This process was widely used by Rawdon, Wright, Hatch & Edson until that firm became part of the American Bank Note Co. in 1858. Afterward, it was used extensively by ABNCo. This $5 note is from an earlier plate by Toppan, Carpenter & Co., New York and Philadelphia, imprinted with ABNCo (just below the S in STRAFFORD).

Section of an advertising sheet for the Patent Green Tint issued by the American Bank Note Co., but mentioning the Rawdon, Wright, Hatch & Edson name. Tiny vertical lines as well as a heavier latticework are printed in green over black printing in the background.

The production of an indestructible colored ink thus became a desideratum. This has been held impossible. Absolutely it is probably so. We presume no ink can be devised which may not be removed by chemical or mechanical means, or by a combination of both. Thus the coloring matter of the black ink used by printers is carbon finely pulverized. Put this dry upon paper, and it may be brushed off with a feather; mix it with water, and when the liquid evaporates the powder can be rubbed off. In printer's ink the carbon is mixed with oil, which binds it to the surface of the paper. An alkali combined with the oil produces soap which can be washed away. Let a piece of printed matter be saturated with alkali; wash it carefully with water and the oil disappears, leaving the carbon free. The problem, however, was to produce a colored ink, not indeed absolutely indestructible, but one which could not be removed from a part of the note without, at the same time, discharging the black in of the remainder. Even this was pronounced impossible.

The *New American Cyclopaedia* says: "No tint has yet been discovered which may not be chemically removed from the paper." This important desideratum has, we believe, been attained in the "Green Ink," for the use of which the American Bank Note Company holds the exclusive patent. Four years ago it was submitted to the examination of the most eminent chemists. Among these were Messrs. Hunt of Montreal, Gibbs of New York Free Academy, Torrey of the Assay Office, Horsford of Harvard, Silliman of Yale, Henry and Hilgard of the Smithsonian Institution. The composition of the ink was explained to them, and they were requested to apply to it the most searching tests known to chemistry, with such new ones as they could devise. They all replied, in substance, that they knew of no chemical means by which the green ink could be destroyed without, at the same time, destroying the texture of the paper on which it was printed; and it could be removed mechanically only by means which would, at the same time, remove the black carbon ink combined with it on the same note.

Most of these eminent chemists have recently been asked whether in the interim any new discovery has been made which would lead them to change their former opinion. They all reply in the negative. We may therefore assume that the green ink which appears so largely upon the bank notes and United States Treasury Notes prepared by this company, affords a perfect security against photographic counterfeits. The public must learn just what parts should be in green. If they do not in any bill appear of that color, or if they do appear in any other, the note may be assumed to be a photographic counterfeit.

The Lyman Patent

George D. Lyman devised and patented a layout for bank bills, consisting of two panels, one with vignettes, occupying the left side of the note, and the other without vignettes but with spaces for signatures, at the right side, the entire printed with a patterned reddish orange background. The idea was to have the panels of different sizes for different denominations, with, for example, a $1 bill to have a large left-side panel and small right-side one, a $2 bill to have the panels both the same size, and so on. Although the idea may have been a good one, it came late in the game, and today,

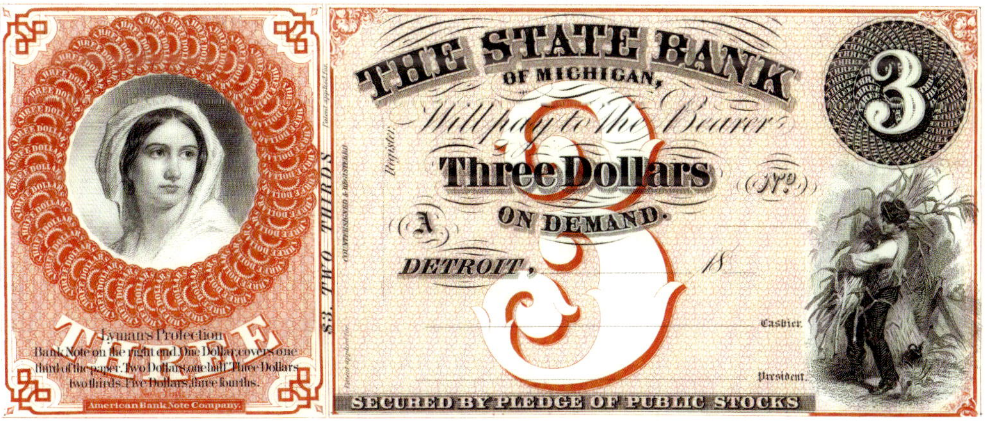

Several notes of the "Lyman's Protection" system printed by the American Bank Note Co. for the State Bank of Michigan in Detroit.

A $2 note of the Merchants Bank, New York City, with the "Lyman's Protection" arrangement. American Bank Note Co.

while American Bank Note Co. $1, $2, and $3 remainder bills from the State Bank of Michigan in Detroit, dated in the 1860s, are sometimes seen, those of other banks range from scarce to rare.

The $5 Lyman bill printed by the American Bank Note Co. for the State Bank of Michigan, Detroit, includes this inscription in multiple lines:

> Lyman's Protection. Bank Note on the right end One Dollar covers one third of the paper. Two Dollars one half. Three Dollars, two thirds. Five dollars, three fourths.

It seems to the modern viewer that Lyman's Protection was resistant to alteration or other abuses, but such bills have a rather mechanical appearance, more like checks or documents than paper currency. In any event, the system was never popular. Time and again, bank officers and the public preferred ornate notes—the more goddesses, landscapes, and ships the better. Security methods that interfered with artistry were doomed to fail.

Geometric Gobbledygook

Among other anticounterfeiting systems were Captain Glynn's Anti-Anastatic Bank Note Paper and "Desopyn's patent red tint," both of which were quickly forgotten.

Certain bills produced by the National Bank Note Co. included the inscription, "Patented April 23, 1860." Ormsby checked into the matter and found the patented claim consisted of:

> 1st. The combination in repetition of the valuation or denomination, and the configuration.
>
> 2d. Combined use in repetition of the valuation or denomination with the title of the institution or corporation, and the configuration of the geometric cycloidal waved-line or rosette.

Ormsby considered the claims to be nonsense, and present-day readers will probably agree.[27]

Commercial Success

Many other anticounterfeiting ideas were tried over the years. Some methods simply evolved without any claims to patent, such as the use by Rawdon, Wright, Hatch & Edson of one central object in a vignette for a $1 bill, three for a $3 bill, and so on. In this context, one, two, three, and five Liberty Seated silver dollars dated 1853 (on some plates altered to 1857) were used on bills of like denominations, and 10 gold dollars were on a $10 note.

The technique of repeating the denomination was of course used by Perkins on his Patent Stereotype Steel Plate notes, with *Three Dollars Three Dollars Three Dollars,* etc., endlessly reiterated. More attractively, small vignettes with goddesses or other figures holding a shield emblazoned 1, 2, 10, or some other number could be scattered on a note, in addition to the denomination spelled out and printed in the corners. W.L. Ormsby devised colored backs with the number of vignettes corresponding to the denomination, each composed of the letters of the denomination (such as F, I, V, E) in concentric circles, sometimes with a portrait at the center.

Both the Canada Green tint patent of 1857 and the National Bank Note patent of 1860 proved especially profitable, because, beginning with large quantities of federal paper money printed by these companies in 1861, a surcharge was added to invoices for these colored overprints.

Many of the notes of various companies printed in the 1850s and early 1860s have colored protectors or surcharges, such as ONE, FIVE, or some other denomination, usually in red or green ink, but sometimes in other colors. These have been called by various names over the years, including *guard, protector,* and others. In other instances printing was accomplished this way:

(continued on p. 334)

Sheet of $1-$2-$3-$5 notes of the Millers River Bank, Athol, Massachusetts, proofs by Danforth, Wright & Co. from the American Bank Note Co. archives, later in the Herbert and Martha Schingoethe Collection. Geometric arrangements are used to identify the four different denominations, a design intended to deter altering the notes.

The Millers River Bank was chartered by the state in 1854. With a stated capital of $100,000, it went into operation the same year. Success attended its efforts, and a few years later the capital was raised to $150,000. On December 15, 1864, the bank converted to become the Millers River National Bank of Athol, charter 708. Alpheus Harding Jr., cashier of the state bank, later become president of the National Bank.

Red overprint as an antiphotographic protector on a note of the Mechanics Bank, New York, November 1, 1861. From an earlier plate by Toppan, Carpenter & Co., now with the ABNCo monogram in the field at the upper left.

(continued from p. 332)

> The die [plate bearing the letters FIVE or another denomination] is covered with ink, and an impression is taken from that on a piece of thick paper. The note is then laid on that paper face up and the die stamped on the face, so that the back of the note takes the impression from the thick paper, and both sides being printed from the same die, one side will correspond with the other.[28]

The sheet was then dried, after which it was imprinted with a regular plate. In a variation of this, the number was simply printed directly on the back of the note, reading properly, not visible on the face side. (W.L. Ormsby's description of this process is given in the preceding chapter.)

While their security features can be debated, the various overprints and arrangements did add to the color and attractiveness of the notes. By the 1860s the majority of bills in circulation had security tints of one type or another.

THE PANIC OF 1857

Clouds gathered in the financial sky in the summer of 1857, perhaps a natural progression in a long-term economic cycle of about 20 years, including problems beginning in 1818 and 1837. In the winter and spring of the year little seemed to go wrong, and bankers, brokers, land buyers, and others made many investments based more upon enthusiasm and optimism than on sound business practice.

By June and July, many uncertainties were expressed concerning unsound loans, but such editorial musings went unheeded for the most part. Then came this event, adapted from the words of J.S. Gibbons, a historian who wrote about it soon thereafter:

> On the 24th of August the suspension of the Ohio Life Insurance & Trust Co. was announced. It struck the public mind like a cannon shot. An intense excitement was manifested in all financial circles, in which bank officers participated with

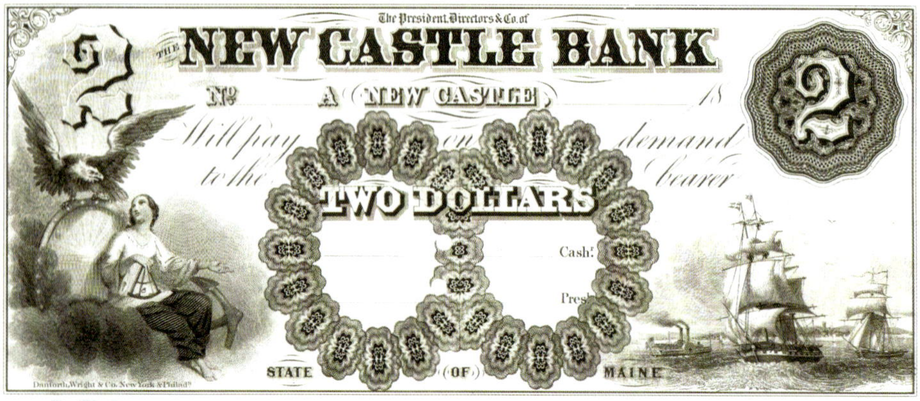

This $2 note of the New Castle Bank, Maine, emphasized the denomination by adding two prominent decorative ellipses on the face. Danforth, Wright & Co., New York and Philadelphia.

There can be little doubt as to the denomination of this note of the South Royalton (Vermont) Bank, from a plate by the American Bank Note Co.

A note by W.L. Ormsby for the State Bank of Lecompton, Kansas Territory. The number of cherubs on notes of this bank reflected the denomination. A $5 bill of this bank is illustrated in chapter 15.

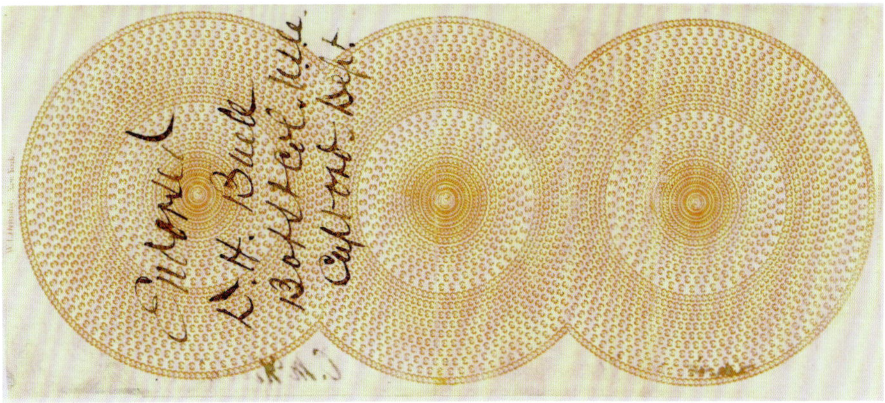

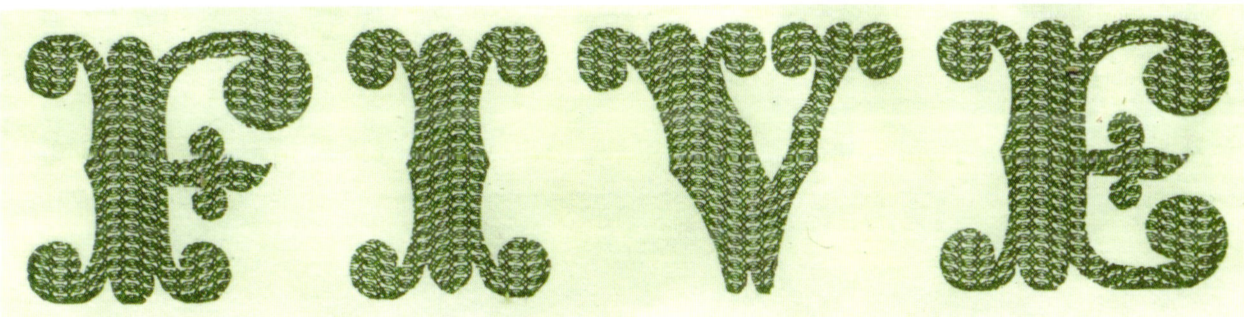

Protector of the $5 denomination (enlarged) as displayed on a plate in *Heath's Infallible Counterfeit Detector,* 1864.

unusual sensitiveness and want of self-possession. Flying rumors were exaggerated at every corner.

The holders of stock and of commercial paper hurried to the broker, and were eager to make what a week before they would have shunned as a ruinous sacrifice. Several stock and money dealers failed, and the daily meetings of the Board of Brokers were characterized by intense excitement. Every individual misfortune was announced on the news bulletins in large letters and attracted a curious crowd which was constantly fed from the passing throng.

The New York City office of the Ohio Life Insurance & Trust Co was not a bank of issue, nor, to any appreciable extent, of deposit. Its principal business was to receive remittances from the home office in Cincinnati and numerous correspondents in the West, and to hold them subject to draft. It was not a discounter of bills receivable, but, on the contrary, a large borrower from other institutions. The consequences of its stoppage, therefore, did not fall directly on New York City merchants, as in the case of a bank on which they are depending for continuous loans. The capital of the company was $2,000,000.

The general circumstances of this failure, so far as they were published, were not in themselves very alarming. The home office was reported, by telegraph, to have its doors open as usual, with its affairs apparently unembarrassed, notwithstanding the stoppage of the New York branch. It was soon known, however, that the entire capital of the institution had been virtually embezzled, and serious alarm was immediately manifested in banking circles.[29]

Panic!

Following the August news, "conditions in the money market rapidly approached a state of panic."[30] More from Gibbons:

A $100 note of the City Bank of New Haven with a surcharge printed on the back. American Bank Note Co., New York.

A $1 note of the Dubuque Central Improvement, not a bank, but one of many nonbank issuers of denominated paper money. This shows the ONE protector applied to both sides. In addition, a list of stockholders is printed on the back, an unusual procedure that may have lent credibility to the notes. Wellstood, Hay & Whiting, New York and Chicago.

A $2 note of the Bullion Bank, Washington, D.C., with green security printing on the back. Printed by the Union Bank Note Co., Newark, New Jersey, a small firm operated by J.W. Hayes & Sons.

A $100 note of the Phoenix Bank, Hartford, Connecticut, circa 1860, when Henry A. Redfield was cashier and John L. Bunce was president. The bill is from a Murray, Draper, Fairman & Co. plate of the 1810s, now with red latticework as an anticounterfeiting measure.

> On the day after the failure of the Ohio Life Insurance & Trust Co. our merchants found that the terms of business between them and the banks were changed. The discounting of commercial paper was stopped. . . . It suddenly dawned on financial managers that the city loans were tens of millions of dollars higher than ever before—a very gratifying fact during their accession, but now inspiring only fear and distrust, which in a few hours, comparatively, ripened into symptoms of alarm.[31]

All of a sudden there were scarcely any new investments in land or in businesses. In ensuing weeks hard money in the form of gold and silver coins was hoarded, as it was far more preferable to have a $5 gold half eagle than a piece of paper imprinted with FIVE DOLLARS and the name of a bank.

Gibbons continued his relation of events:

> The [New York] Clearing House report for the 29th of August—the first report after the suspension of the Ohio Life Insurance & Trust Co.—showed a reduction of four millions of dollars in the bank loans during the previous week. The most substantial securities of the market fell rapidly in price at public sale. The safety of bank notes in circulation was suspected or denied. The publishers of counterfeit detectors spread alarm among the shopkeepers and laborers by selling handbills with lists of broken banks, which were cried about the streets by boys, at "a penny apiece."
>
> One of the Associated Banks [a member of the New York City bankers' alliance] fell into default at the end of August, and a fraud of $70,000 by the paying teller roused suspicion of

> similar misconduct in other institutions. The regular discounting of bills by the banks had mostly been suspended, and the street rates for money, even on unquestionable securities, rose to three, four, and five percent a month. On the ordinary securities of merchants, such as promissory notes and exchange, money was not to be had at any rate. House after house of high commercial repute succumbed to the panic, and several heavy banking firms were added to the list of failures.[32]

By mid-September in the larger cities, there was a general apprehension concerning banks. The momentum to exchange paper bills for coins accelerated. On September 25, the Bank of Philadelphia stopped paying out coins, and the next day the other banks in that city followed suit, three of which subsequently failed. On September 28, the banks in Providence suspended specie payments, as did all but one bank in Pittsburgh. New York remained a bastion of strength, but its defenses were weakened. In that city banks bravely paid out gold and silver on request.

From Uncertain to Bad to Worse

Conditions remained uncertain for the next two weeks as dozens of banks in the East closed their doors forever, including 30 in New York state alone. The news arrived that the SS *Central America,* a steamship carrying more than 500 people and more than $1,600,000 in gold, bound for New York City, had been lost in a hurricane on September 12, far off the coast of North Carolina. Such gold normally infused strength into New York commerce, but not this time. Presciently, *Harper's Weekly,* June 20, 1857, had commented:

> The country is prosperous, no doubt, but we are going ahead so fast, and living so absolutely from hand to mouth, that the first hitch in the machinery may upset the whole concern. The loss of a single specie-steamer from California would break no one can tell how many mercantile houses in New York City, Philadelphia, and Boston.

On Tuesday, October 13, a run was made on New York City banks, and by late that afternoon 19 leading banks stopped paying coins, a policy made official the next day. The Chemical Bank was the only holdout, and it continued to redeem its notes in gold and silver. As "punishment" for this action, when a new association of bankers was formed the Chemical Bank was not allowed to join!

By year's end several thousand companies were bankrupt. A later government report, *Condition of Banks in 1857,* revealed that throughout the year most banks in America issued paper money equal to many multiples of the amount of coins on hand for the purpose of redeeming such notes if they were offered.

During the same year, railroad shares fell precipitously, examples being the January to October crash of Michigan Southern stock from $88 to $15 per share and Illinois Central from $123 to $79. At the time rail stocks dominated Wall Street trading. Concerning New York City banks, the report noted that on January 1, 1857, banks had liabilities of $43,974,000 and held $6,557,000 (in gold and silver coins). By June 6, specie had increased sharply to $14,370,000, but liabilities had increased far more dramatically, to $127,703,000. Thus, although there were more coins in banks' hands, wild speculation in railroads, lands, and other areas put many bank assets in nonliquid form.

The Panic of 1857 changed the bank-note printing business forever. Orders for new bills dropped almost to the vanishing point, and few new banks were chartered. For the printing and engraving companies, the outlook was dismal. In March 1858, seven firms, including the leading ones, merged to form the American Bank Note Company, which was incorporated on April 29.

A $1 proof impression of a Chemical Bank note of the late 1850s, by Danforth, Bald & Co., New York and Philadelphia. During the Panic of 1857 this was the only bank in New York City that did not suspend specie payments.

Commotion on Wall Street on October 14, 1857, the day that all but one bank in New York City stopped redeeming their paper money with coins.

A run on a bank in the Panic of 1857, as customers sought to withdraw their deposits and also to exchange paper money for coins.

An Inside View of a Currency-Issuing Bank

Introduction

In 2003 I spent time at the Sandwich Historical Society in New Hampshire. Curator Craig Evans made available the institution's extensive file on the Carroll County Bank. Eventually, the New Hampshire Currency Project, conducted by David M. Sundman and me, will publish extensive documentation on this and other banks in the state.

This chapter tells the story of the Carroll County Bank using a time line, attempting to create a you-are-there experience. I felt just this involved as I completed my research and wrote up the notes that form the basis of this chapter. Many aspects of paper money circulation, redemption, and valuation mentioned earlier will be found in this study.

The town of Sandwich is located in Carroll County, about 25 miles from my office in Wolfeboro, New Hampshire. It is set in verdant rolling hills, inland a few miles from Lake Winnipesaukee. In the 1850s, most of the local business was related to farming and light manufacturing, such as milling. As was true of most towns in America at this time, Sandwich was essentially a self-sufficient place. The various local industries, stores, farms, and services took care of nearly all of the residents needs. There was no railroad link to distant places, but roads in every direction connected to nearby towns such as Moultonborough on the lake and inland to Ossipee, Ashland, and other communities. Concord, the capital of the state, could be reached in a few hours by coach or wagon—and perhaps faster on horseback.

Today the small business district is referred to as Center Sandwich, as it was years ago (then variously spelled as *Centre* or *Center*).

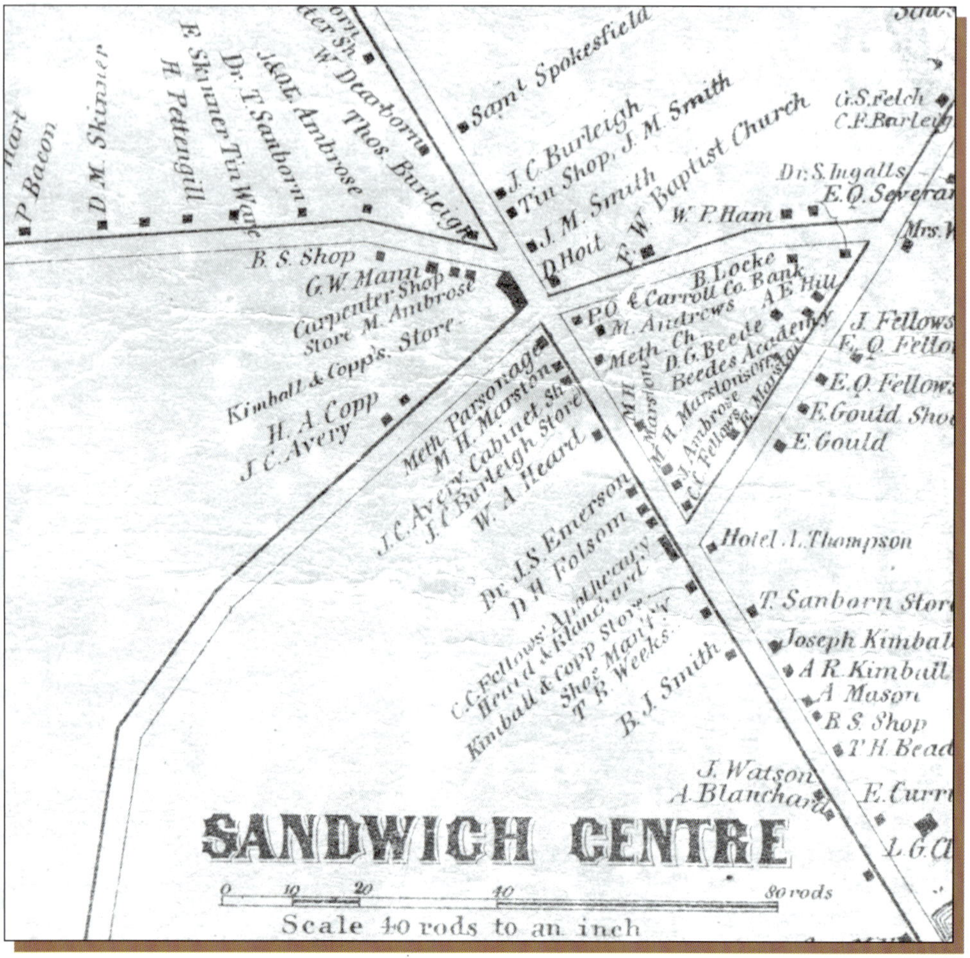

Map of the center district of Sandwich, New Hampshire, in 1860. The Carroll County Bank and the post office are on the southeast corner of the main road intersection. (From a map of Carroll County by C.C. Walling)

ESTABLISHING THE CARROLL COUNTY BANK

On July 12, 1850, the Carroll County Bank was chartered by the New Hampshire State Legislature.[1] The capital was set at $50,000, divided into 500 shares. Incorporators included Daniel Hoit (misspelled *Hoyt* in some records), Josiah Dearborn, Samuel Emerson, Josiah H. Hobbs, Luther D. Sawyer, Moulton H. Marston, Thomas Burleigh, Augustine (listed as *Augustus*) Blanchard, and Jesse Ambrose. These were men of local and regional importance. At the time there were no other state-chartered currency-issuing banks in Carroll County, although the Wolfborough [*sic*] Bank had operated briefly in 1837 and 1838, after which it was taken over by fraudster Samuel D. Dakin and floated large amounts of worthless paper money. A few years later in Carroll County the Pine River Bank of Ossipee would be founded. But in 1850 the new Carroll County Bank was unique.

The charter was to begin on March 1, 1851, and to continue for 20 years, the typical length for a bank in the state. Assuming the bank conducted its affairs in a businesslike manner, it would likely be granted a charter extension or renewal as the expiration date drew near. The bank was mandated to go into effective operation on or before the second Wednesday of June 1851, or the charter would be voided. This schedule gave the founders of the bank about a year to raise the necessary capital.

Currency circulation was permitted up to the actual value of the paid-in stock. Bills were required to be signed by the president and countersigned by the cashier. Other terms were typical for bank charters of the era. Such rules were written into the bank bylaws and were approved by the state legislature. Up to this time in New Hampshire history, there had been just two banking frauds or scandals: the Hillsborough Bank of Amherst and the Wolfborough Bank. A few other banks experienced difficulties or were closed for other reasons. In comparison to the situation in most other states in the early 19th century, New Hampshire's banks were solid, well respected, and their notes generally traded at par minus a fractional handling charge. In 1850 all currency-issuing banks in the state had agents in Boston for the redemption of their bills, mostly but not entirely through the Suffolk Bank system.

The directors of the Carroll County Bank, seven in number, were required to be citizens and residents of the state. No stockholder could have more than 20 votes. The annual meeting date was to be set by the directors. Other meetings could be called by "posting up a notice thereof in two public places in said town of Sandwich." In practice, stockholder meetings were held in August, when the weather was warm and travel was convenient.

PREPARING FOR BUSINESS

After the incorporation was accomplished, this announcement was posted at the store of Joseph Wentworth at Lower Corner in Sandwich, from August 3 to 19, 1850:[2]

> **Notice**
>
> The grantees of the Carroll County Bank, incorporated by the New Hampshire Legislature, June Session 1850, are hereby notified to meet at the Inn of Enock [*sic*] B. Beede in Sandwich on Monday the 19th day of August next at one of the clock in the afternoon for the purpose of organizing agreeably to the provisions of the act of incorporation.
>
> Sandwich July 27, 1850
>
> Daniel Hoit, Josiah Dearborn,
> authorized to call the first meeting

DELAYS

Daniel Hoit was named as the founding president, and Stephen Beede was the first cashier. The board of directors included Daniel Hoit, Samuel Emerson, Moulton H. Marston, Joseph Wentworth, John M. Stevenson, John Bryant, and Jeremiah Furber, some of whom had been incorporators. The prominence of these individuals made it unnecessary to establish confidence in the bank's operation and facilitated the gaining of business.

The Carroll County Bank directors and officers found that progress was slow, and by summer 1851 business had not commenced. By this time the charter technically had expired, obviously an impediment if the bank was ever to operate.

On July 2, 1851, the state legislature granted a reprieve in the form of an amendment to the act of July 12, 1850.[3] "The grantees or stockholders of the Carroll County Bank may at any time after the passage of this act and before the first day of October, A.D. 1851, commence the business of banking agreeably to the provisions of the act to which this is in amendment. . . ."

On September 30, 1851, this document was registered with town clerk N.G. French, for which a fee of 25¢ was paid:[4]

> Whereas Daniel Hoit, Samuel Emerson, Moulton H. Marston, Augustin [*sic*] Blanchard, and certain others were at the June Session of the New Hampshire Legislature A.D. 1850 made a body politic and corporate by the name of the Carroll County Bank with a capital stock of fifty thousand dollars—which act was amended by the Legislature at the June Session A.D. 1851.
>
> Now this is to certify that said capital stock of fifty thousand dollars has this date, the thirtieth day of September A.D. 1851 been all paid in as required by Chapter 321 Section 2 of the law of the state of New Hampshire passed & approved July 8, 1846.
>
> Stephen Beede, Cashier

When a tally was made of the shares sold, the roster showed that all but three buyers lived in the state.

THE FIRST DAY OF BUSINESS

On October 1, 1851, the bank issued its first bills, received from the New England Bank Note Co. of Boston. These were of the late-style Patent Stereotype Steel Plate with small vignettes, and with slugs inserted for the bank name and location. Other banks throughout New England used identical notes, but with their own names and addresses added. Such bills were easy targets for criminals to alter, but it seems that the directors of the Carroll County Bank were not aware of this fact and did not investigate other avenues.

October 1 was also the first day of business, per the institution's records. The beginning page on the ledger indicated the following discounts (loans) had been made by October 1, demonstrating that cashier Beede, the chief operating officer, had been busy, no doubt with the advice and consent of the directors. The loans were carefully made, either with two or more endorsers or with a pledge of stock:[5]

> Stephen M. Alton, Walter Bryant: $10,000. Walter Bryant, Stephen M. Alton: $10,000. Gould & Varney, Timothy Varney, Ezra Gould: $2,000. Elisha Marston, stock pledged: $250. Jeremiah Furber, stock pledged: $250. Jacob Hale, stock pledged: $500. Beede Varney, stock pledged: $100. Noah Varney, stock pledged: $250. I.C. Wiggin, Jos. Wentworth, Esq.: $300. John M. Stevenson, Timo. Varney: $100. Ruel Ladd, Wm. Ladd, H.M. Ladd: $100. Walter Bryant, John Bryant, Sam Emerson: $669.50. Heard & Prescott, Augt. Blanchard, Elisha Marston: $2,500. Jesse Cook, Daniel Hoit, Esq.: $106. John F. Coffin, Geo. Marston note pledged: $1,500. Daniel Hoit, stock pledged: $1,000. M.H. Marston, stock pledged: $2,000. [Total]: $41,625.50.

The loans to the directors for "stock pledged" *actually* represented unpaid amounts on pledges to buy stock, as all of the stock was reported as having been paid for in full. At the time such a procedure was legal and was very common among state-chartered banks, as related many times in the present text. However, the practice made it impossible to decipher bank statements unless extensive details of the discounts were given. Records of the bank show that enough money was on hand to conduct business properly, even though the capital was not fully paid in specie.

On November 24, 1851, a listing of stockholders and their locations was prepared and subsequently filed with the town clerk. Isaac Cary of Boston was the manager of the New England Bank Note Co. in Boston, a firm 50% owned by Rawdon, Wright, Hatch & Edson of New York City. Cary's shares were acquired in payment for paper money printed for the bank, part of a solicitation to secure the contract for printing bills:[6]

> Stephen M. Alton, West Roxbury, Mass. • Walter Bryant, Boston, Mass. • Isaac Cary, Boston, Mass.[7] • Edwards & Holman, Boston, Mass. • Jacob Smith, Holderness • Daniel Hoit, Sandwich • Moulton H. Marston, Sandwich • Joseph Wentworth, Sandwich • Jeremiah Furber, Sandwich • Augustin Blanchard, Sandwich • Gould & Varney, Sandwich • Beede Varney, Sandwich • Noah Varney, Sandwich • Jacob Hale, Sandwich • Samuel Emerson, Moultonborough • Mary Anne Emerson, Moultonborough • John M. Stevenson, Tamworth • Theophilus Gilman, Sandwich • Elisha Marston, Sandwich • Enoch Lewis, Sandwich • John Bryant, Moultonborough

THE FIRST EXAMINATION

Frederick Vose, a state examiner, paid a visit to the Carroll County Bank on May 24, 1852. By that time business was well under way. Outstanding discounts and debts due the bank totaled $83,119.29, deposits in Boston banks amounted to $12,406, and $3,127.81 in specie was on hand. Bills to the extent of $44,365 were in circulation. Already a modest profit had been made, totaling $204.61. On April 1 a dividend of $1,000 had been distributed among the 35 stockholders. The new bank enjoyed a fine reputation.

Later in the summer, cashier Beede issued this notice of the first meeting of shareholders since the bank commenced business:

Carroll County Bank

Notice is hereby given that the annual meeting of the stockholders of the Carroll County Bank will be held at their Banking Room at Centre Sandwich on Wednesday the 26th day of August instant at 12 o'clock noon for the choice of directors and the transaction of such other business as may legally come before them.

August 3d 1852

Stephen Beede, cashier

Currency Capers and Counterfeits

In time, bills of the bank circulated widely in New Hampshire, Massachusetts, and, to a lesser extent, in other places. In Boston the Bank of Commerce acted as a redemption depot in the early days, after which a switch was made to the Suffolk Bank.

In keeping with the prevalent but largely unrecorded practice of many banks in operation in America at the time, the directors did what they could to see that as many bills as possible would stay in circulation and not be redeemed, as such currency represented pure profit. This letter from Albert Little, a principal in Little, Bridgham & Co., a Boston agent for the bank, reflects that he was doing his part in this regard, sending "small bills into the interior."

Boston, Feb'y 7 1853

Carroll Co. Bank

Herewith please find certificate of three shares of your stock as per request of Messrs. Beede & Marston. Edwards Holman & Co. reserve to themselves the dividend due October 1st 1852, which they say has not been claimed till a day or two since. So you will please forward them the amount of their dues and remit to me the amount of three shares and interest from Oct 1/52 according to contract.

Since writing the above, I have obtained of Mr. Clark's broker the four shares standing in his name for which I paid some more than par and interest since the last dividend. But as I did not pay full interest for the first three above named I shall ask of you only the regular interest on the seven shares since Oct. 1, 1852, and I shall make a small commission on that.

I sent $500 of your small bills into the interior of the state.

Yours Truly,

Albert Little

Luther D. Sawyer, an Ossipee lawyer and a director of the bank, sent this letter to cashier Beede, including information on a counterfeiter and also a recommendation for a Mr. Drew of that place, a cattle drover who would be in a position to distribute the bank's bills far and wide, helping with the bank's cash position ("if your exchange is short"):

Ossipee Feb 12, 1853

Friend Stephen,

Mr. Drew, who has exchanged a good deal of money with me, wants to get two shares of stock in your bank. And Mr. Taylor of Effingham wants to get 3 or 4 shares. They have the money ready if the stock can be had. I hope you can get two shares for Drew as he is a drover and is buying cattle more or less all the time. Please write soon. If your exchange is short, Drew and others will help any time when you can send to us.

I see by the papers that they have hauled up [arrested] a fellow by the name of Storer at Portland with some of your counterfeit threes.

When I was at Conway mountain Peirse [?] Fabyan told me he thought he had seen one's and two's counterfeit on C.C. Bank. He thinks all the counterfeits have been brought into that region by a fellow of the name of Dresser. Fabyan (who by the way does not want his name mentioned) says that Dresser is a smart likely looking fellow, 40 or 50 years old, and has been hauled up several times but they never could catch him with any of the stuff about him and he has so far got clear.

Rep'y yours,

L.D. Sawyer

These counterfeits were made from a false plate, with slugs added for the bank name and address. Similar phony $3 bills, representing a counterfeiter's delight, were made for other banks in New England. Apparently, many phony Carroll County Bank $3 notes were circulated, as they are seen with some frequency today. Little is known about the false $1 and $2 issues mentioned in the above letter.

Further from Sawyer, the following note requests a "package of money" for Sanborn B. Carter, an Ossipee lawyer, to take to Concord. Both Sawyer and Carter would become involved in the Pine River Bank of Ossipee when it was formed in 1856:

Ossipee, March 11, 1853

Friend Beede,

Mr. Carter goes to Concord today & returns the first of next week. If you have no earlier opportunity you can send a package of money to Mr. Emerson or some place that Mr. Carter may name for him to take

We are getting short of funds here.

Rep'y yours,

L.D. Sawyer

Bank president Daniel Hoit was spending time in Urbana, Ohio, one of this favorite homes away from

Counterfeiters had a field day with this fake $3 plate used to make bills from several different banks, including this of the Carroll County Bank, stamped COUNTERFEIT by the Suffolk Bank. Separate slugs were added for CARROLL COUNTY BANK and SANDWICH. The state name was added in ink by hand, causing this feature to vary among the several different examples seen.

Bank of Orleans, Irasburgh, Vermont, counterfeit from the same $3 plate but with different slugs inserted. These dangerous counterfeit $3 notes were mentioned by W.L. Ormsby in *Bank Note Engraving,* 1852.

home, and sent a long letter to his friend, cashier Beede (addressing him formally, as was Hoit's custom), including these excerpts:

> Urbana, March 14, 1853
>
> My dear Sir,
>
> Your good long interesting letter of the 28th ult. did not reach me till the 8th inst. I can hardly be thankful enough for our promptness in bank reports and other transactions in and about home.
>
> It seems our loans are below par and our deposits in the Bank of Commerce above. The balance Feb. 28 (exclusive of interest) is $19,652.86. Our loans ought to average 90 thousand dollars. A capitalist in this place informed me a few days ago that he owned stock in the Springfield Bank which netted him 16 percent in the bank in this place.[8]
>
> I have an offer for a loan of our bills of $10,000. Our bills would be thrown into the country circulation, so that we should not be troubled as we are now in the redeeming of them almost weekly. The bills [would be] forwarded from Boston and the principal and interest paid there or at our bank without any expense to us for exchange or any interest. [The bank in this place would make a similar offer to us for their bills.]
>
> Now there can be no question but what we should find it for our interest to effect loans of this kind, if we could do it with safety. I mention these facts that you would bring it before the directors and give me an answer. I have no particular wish to enforce my own opinion on the board of directors nor will I recommend any paper unless Mr. Bean as well as myself shall pronounce it unquestionable.
>
> I however see by Thos. Ambury's paper of Cincinnati that a number, say three or more, banks in Connecticut have failed and the Cincinnati Bank had or was about refusing to receive any eastern or N. England [bank bills] except Boston bills. It is understood these banks were the N. York brokers' begetting—no wonder at their failure. It will however injure the sound banks very much in their circulation in the West, it will drive them [bills of eastern banks] home at a rapid rate. What a pity these brokers should be suffered to impose upon the public in this manner.
>
> You will I suppose take measures to procure a plate for our bank, to prevent any more counterfeits. If so I would suggest it should embrace on it four denominations 2-3-5 & 10d—or two threes and no twos.
>
> If you should take any order on the subject, I would open a correspondence with some company beside N. England [Bank Note Co.]. Perhaps W. Foster, the cashier of the Bank of Commerce, and Albert G. Hoit, or Foster alone, would be a good agent.[9]
>
> March 17. Since the above was written, the same day in the afternoon the news of the failure of three banks in Conn., plus as above stated, was seen, and if their failure has the effect, which is

feared by many, it will injure our N.E. currency very much. Only think $180,000 of bills in circulation of one bank of $50,000 capital & this mostly in the West—rather a heavy tax. You see the necessity of having a daily paper.

Hope our folks will keep a good look out for brokers.

D. Hoit

The newspaper account of Connecticut banks mentioned by Hoit involved a scandal with false records, large amounts of paper money circulated, and other irregularities. In that state the Woodbury Bank and the Eastern Bank of West Killingly collapsed when W.E. Chittenden, a New York City broker who held many of their so-called assets, claimed to have failed. In any event, the assets were of questionable value. W.E. Chittenden aided and abetted president Frederick Chittenden of the Eastern Bank in the distribution of worthless notes and kept two sets of books for that bank: one for public reports and the other giving the actual state of business. Frederick Chittenden resigned from the bank in West Killingly in January 1853 and immediately became president of the Bank of Litchfield County, which also collapsed.

But more problems were brewing outside of Connecticut. This was a tempestuous year in Ohio banking, with many worthless bills from Indiana and other states in circulation, and many Ohio banks experienced difficulties under the new Tax Law (the earlier mentioned "Crowbar Law").

Meanwhile, throughout 1853 Boston agent Bridgham, Little & Co., kept busy trying to wholesale quantities of Carroll County Bank bills, which cashier Beede obligingly shipped in quantity to them. In turn the agent endeavored to place the bills in the hands of others, as per this letter:

Boston, Dec. 8, 1853

S. Beede, Esq.

Dear Sir—

We have tried to find an outlet for your bills to the whole amount of our discount $2,280.65, but have succeeded only to the sum of 800 or 1000 dolls. But we will venture to engage to distribute the balance over your draft on the Bank of Commerce for $1,000, provided you can give us all small bills.

One firm which have engaged to distribute 3 to 5 hundred dolls want all the bills below the denomination of 5's. The balance is wanted in bills below 10's. Perhaps a very few 10's would pass in this crowd, but they are not desirable.

You will please forward the above by express. Perhaps you can afford to pay freight on the bills—if not, we will.

Little, Bridgham & Co.

[Note added by cashier Beede:]

The above insured and sent by Drews & Niles Express Dec. 12, 53.

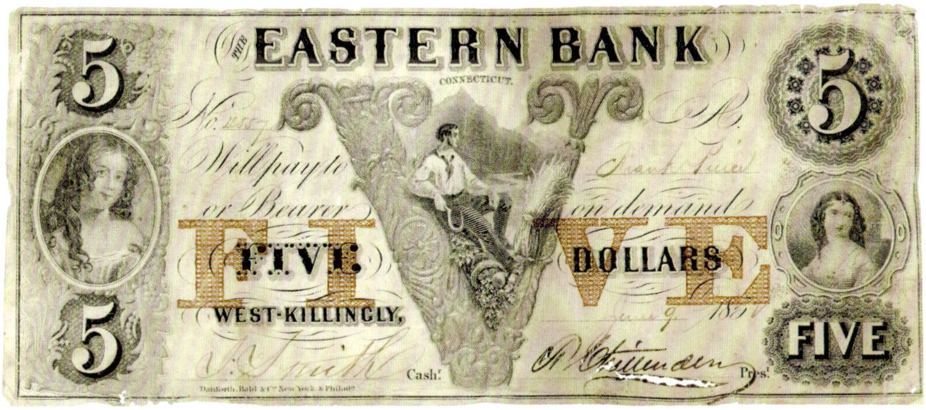

A $5 bill of the Eastern Bank of West Killingly, Connecticut. In the same state, president Frederick Chittenden was also involved in the Bank of Litchfield County in Milford and the Woodbury Bank of Woodbury, all three of which distributed large amounts of worthless paper. Danforth, Bald & Co., New York and Philadelphia, printed this note.

A $2 bill of the Litchfield County Bank, New Milford, Connecticut. Overstamped COUNTERFEIT, the note is from a failed bank.

John (Jonathan) T. Coffin, formerly the cashier of the Winnipissiogee Bank in Meredith Bridge, New Hampshire, and now a director of the Belknap County Bank in the same place, was also involved in the scheme of "scattering" the Carroll County Bank's bills, most probably on a quid pro quo basis in which Beede did the same for Coffin's bank:

> Meredith Bridge, Dec. 16 [1853]
>
> S. Beedee [*sic*] Esq., Cash.
>
> Dear Sir—
>
> We should like the money for the note, making the interest right, from the time sent, with exchange.
>
> I exchanged and scattered 1500 of the other before I sent it to the office.
>
> I will look for it on Tuesday.
>
> Yours Truly,
> John T. Coffin

Bills printed by the New England Bank Note Co. were used for the balance of 1853 and all of 1854. In particular, counterfeits of the $3 denomination continued to be pesky and turned up with some frequency, as, for example, in a bunch of bills accumulated by the North Bank in Boston, a redemption agent, which sent large quantities of Carroll County Bank bills back to Sandwich, averaging more than $1,000 per week for much of 1854. On July 21, 1854, a shipment consisted of $1,500 in good bills plus a note: "Your account is charged with counterfeit of $3 enclosed."

Banking as Usual in 1853

Year in and year out in the 1850s, the Carroll County Bank operated under the aegis of Stephen Beede, cashier, with the advice and consent of Daniel Hoit, president, and the board of directors. The principals were businessmen par excellence, and the bank did well accordingly. The only other currency-issuing bank in the Lake Winnipesaukee region was the Belknap County Bank in Meredith Bridge. Then in 1855 the Lake Bank was established in Wolfeboro, and in 1856 the Pine River Bank would commence in Ossipee, the latter being inland from the lake.

The economic milieu of Sandwich and, in the same town, Center Sandwich and North Sandwich, plus the small settlement at East Sandwich, was not sufficient to sustain a vigorous business. Loans were made to customers in surrounding towns, most notably Tamworth, Ossipee, Conway, and other districts to the east.

The Carroll County Bank preferred to make discounted loans on a short-term basis, for less than a year. Generally, cosigners or sureties were required, or assets such as stock could be pledged. Those with loans of six months or more were encouraged to keep in touch with cashier Beede every three months or so, simply to assure the bank that all was still in good order.

However, most loans were secured through Boston brokers, including Little, Bridgham & Co. and Peirce & Bacon, who regularly wrote to Beede offering him lists of available paper. As an example, following instructions from Beede on March 18, 1853, Peirce & Bacon sent documents on March 21, for short-term (six-month) loans consisting of $2,550.74, dated November 27, 1852, for Rice & Nichols; $2,634.67, December 24, 1852, to the same partnership $907.78; $1,024.36 on February 22, 1853, for Peirce & Jewett; and January 16, 1853, for Flynn & Jewett, for a total of $7,127.55.

The function of Boston brokers was to find good loans, investigate credit, and, as another branch of their business, place the currency with distant banks, collecting a commission in the meantime. Such brokers negotiated the purchase of currency at a discount, often

A $1 note of the Winnipissiogee Bank in Meredith Bridge, New Hampshire, signed by J.T. Coffin.

A $2 note of the Lake Bank of Wolfeboro. In 1865 this would convert to become the Lake National Bank. Rawdon, Wright, Hatch & Edson and New England Bank Note Co. imprints.

A $10 note of the Pine River Bank of Ossipee, a proprietary proof made by the American Bank Note Co. in the late 20th century. No original bills of this bank are known to exist today. The vignette depicts a family gathering hops in a field. This plate was made for the bank by Rawdon, Wright, Hatch & Edson in the 1850s. Bills printed from the plate after April 1858 had the ABNCo monogram added to the plate at upper right.

requesting deep discounts by offering the promise that small-denomination bills would be sent hundreds of miles away and would likely never be seen again.

The Carroll County Bank did no independent investigation of loans received through brokers but relied upon the brokers' due diligence, nor were the borrowers in Boston and other distant places necessarily personally known to Beede or president Daniel Hoit. The brokering of loans was a legitimate practice and was convenient for small banks that did not have enough business in their own towns. The brokering of loans continues in the banking profession today.

Selected bank correspondence of 1853 reflects regional business of the era.

Luther D. Sawyer, attorney in Ossipee and a director of the Carroll County Bank, often brokered loans and met with borrowers. The following letter relates to various activities Sawyer conducted on behalf of the bank:

> Ossipee, March 26/53
>
> Friend Beede,
>
> Enclosed I send the certificate of deposit left by J. Smith. He wants a certificate of two shares [of Carroll County Bank stock] made out in the name of Andrew J. Drew of Wolfboro [*sic*] and sent to me by mail.[10] He has left Mr. [William L.] Wentworth's money with me.
>
> I sent $600 to Smith but he did not get it in season, and I told E. Gould to call for it. Have you received it? Drew would like larger bills when he exchanges money. You may keep out of my dividend interest for 60 days on the note [Asa] Beacham signed for L. Brown.
>
> Yours &c.
>
> L.D. Sawyer

John Peavey wrote concerning transactions:

> Moultonborough, June 14th 1853
>
> Stephen Bedee [*sic*] Esqr.
>
> Dear Sir,
>
> I here send you two hundred and thirty dollars. You will take the check on the note of G.B. Canney which is nearly due and send me the balance in your bills. This check I think is about $54.
>
> Please send it by the stage driver to be left with Andrew L. Hersey, Esqr., Tuftonborough.
>
> Very respectfully,
>
> Your obt. sev't
>
> John Peavey

Following is another letter from Peavey:

Moultonborough, September 19, 1853

Stephen Beedee [*sic*] Esqr.

Dear Sir,

Enclosed I send you one dollar to pay the interest on my last note for thirty days longer. I do this that I may be able to pay out the pension certificate that I have on hand. I have not yet been able to attend to making out the pension papers upon the certificates which I have in my possession, owing to having to attend to our Camp Meeting, and consequently I desire to keep the $200 for 20 days longer, and this with what money I have at my command will be sufficient for the above purpose without asking further accommodation.[11]

I herewith send $200 to be exchanged and returned by stage driver in care of Andrew L. Hersey, Tuftonborough. If you cannot do, please write me.

Yours in haste,
John Peavey

The next letter was written from a town about 20 miles to the northeast, near the Maine border:

Eaton Centre, N.H. June 25th 1853

Gen. Hoit

Dear Sir,

I should like to get a few hundred dollars at the Carroll County Bank if I can take it out for six months without the trouble of checking in, say from the first of July until the first of January. I want it for the purpose of buying cattle through the season and therefore should not want the trouble of paying or checking in at the close of three months.

I will endeavor to secure you with people that will be satisfactory if you would like to let it out upon the time named. Please inform me by mail upon your reception of this.

Yours, &c.,
Benjamin Glines

The proprietor of Gilman Cooper & Co., who did a mercantile business on Main Street in Wolfeboro, sent this request:

Wolfborough [*sic*], Sept. 29/53

Mr. Bedee [*sic*]

Enclosed I send $200 to take up the note signed by myself, Moses Varney & Nath. Morrison. I want to get a note discounted at your bank of one thousand dollars with Hiram & John Barker as sureties. In case you discount this note I want to take up my old note on which there is due (I believe) $400. Please write me by return of stage whether I can be thus accommodated.

Yours respectfully,
Gilman Cooper

On October 10, 1853, George M. Burleigh, of Centre Harbor, sent this letter in regard to money owed to the bank:

Stephen Bedee [*sic*] Esqr.

Dear Sir,

I am going to Concord Monday to get some money and will call and see you immediately on my return. I think some of going to N. York to meet my brother. If I do go I shall not be back till next Saturday.

I am not posted upon in bank rules and regulations as I have never taken money from a bank before. Therefore if I have transgressed you must excuse me. Had I the money on hand I should call before I leave.

Respectfully yours,
Geo. M. Burleigh

The Bank's Condition and Standing in 1854

On May 1, 1854, cashier Beede prepared this "statement of the condition and standing of the Carroll County Bank" for the governor of New Hampshire:[12]

Means

Amount of debts due: $91,068.76
Deposits in Boston banks: $6,222.85
Specie: $2,132.92
Bills of other banks: $359.00
Real estate: $400.00
[Total]: $100,182.53

Liabilities

Capital stock: $50,000
Bills in circulation: $48,226
Dividends unpaid: $188
Due depositors: $650
[Total]: $99,064[13]

The Bank's Offices

In the early years the Carroll County Bank may have been located in the building on Main Street occupied by Moulton H. Marston as an office, to the right of the Marston residence and two buildings to the right of the Methodist church.[14] The post office was there from 1846 to 1849.[15]

Later in the decade bank was located in a two-story (plus attic storage) building across the street on the left from president Daniel Hoit's fine house, which he constructed in 1810, and, on the front, across the street from Hoit's store.[16] To the right of the bank on

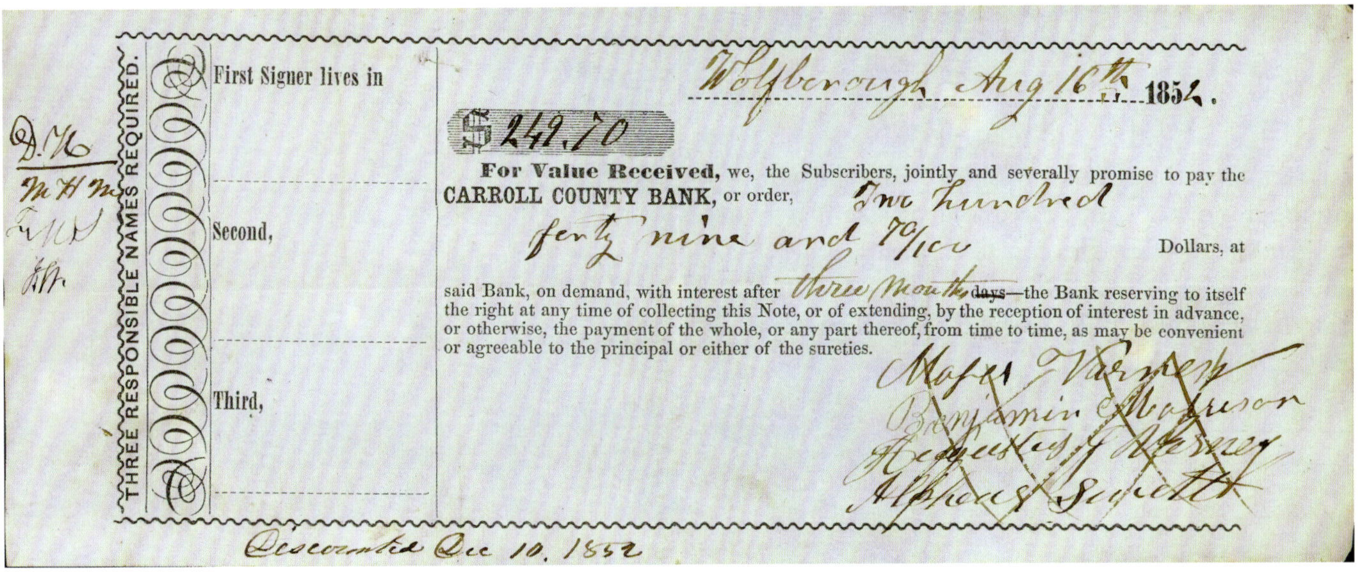

THREE RESPONSIBLE NAMES REQUIRED.

First Signer lives in

Second,

Third,

Wolfborough Aug 16th 1852.

$249.70

For Value Received, we, the Subscribers, jointly and severally promise to pay the **CARROLL COUNTY BANK,** or order, Two hundred forty nine and 70/100 Dollars, at said Bank, on demand, with interest after three months ~~days~~—the Bank reserving to itself the right at any time of collecting this Note, or of extending, by the reception of interest in advance, or otherwise, the payment of the whole, or any part thereof, from time to time, as may be convenient or agreeable to the principal or either of the sureties.

Discounted Dec 10, 1852

A promissory note issued by the bank in 1854.

the same side of the street and just a short distance away, stood the Methodist church (built in 1848). It is likely that the structure was erected to the order of Hoit, as it completed his domain in that section of Center Sandwich. The building was carried on the bank's books at a value of $400.

The lower floor, made of brick, housed the Center Sandwich post office and a drugstore. Christopher C. Fellows was postmaster there in the early 1860s. In 1864 he would become cashier of the bank. The bank's office was upstairs, the top half of the structure being made of wood. Access to the bank was by a walkway nearly at ground level on the left, as the building was built into a slope, with the left side of the first floor into an embankment and the right side exposed. Daniel Hoit could walk across the street from his house and enter the bank without using stairs.

An 1860 map locates the Carroll County Bank on the east corner of an intersection near the center of town, with the Methodist parsonage on the south corner, the store of Kimball & Copp on the west corner, and the home of Daniel Hoit on the north corner.[17] Fellows's house, located across the street from his apothecary shop, was several hundred feet to the southeast of the bank. Hoit's heirs sold the bank building and lot to Moulton H. Marston in 1863. The Carroll County National Bank later occupied the premises in the early part its existence, 1865 to 1867 (after which the office operations were moved to the homes of the cashier and president).

Bills in Circulation

Bills of the Carroll County Bank, printed by the New England Bank Note Co., continued to circulate widely in the early 1850s. The official accounts made public by the bank showed an average amount in the $45,000 range, or close to the legal limit of $50,000. It is very likely that official figures were one thing and private figures another, as indicated years later by the bank's statement, on May 23, 1868, that during the entire operation of the bank, in which over $175,000 in bills had been printed, only $1,055 remained unredeemed. The fact that records could be altered or fudged involving the New England Bank Note Co. quantities of bills is vividly demonstrated by a vast unofficial overage of bills printed during this era for the White Mountain Bank of Lancaster, located in the north part of the state. Original state Banking Commission records, all of which I have examined in detail, reveal no instance in which a commissioner contacted a printer of currency in regard to the quantities delivered to a bank.

Intense efforts were continued by the Carroll County Bank in the 1850s to distribute its small-denomination bills in distant locations, including in Ohio, with the specific desire that most would disappear and never be redeemed. The bank continued its eagerness to sell packages of bills at a discount to parties who traveled to other towns in the state, including stagecoach men and cattle drovers.

NEW BILLS FROM W.L. ORMSBY

In 1854 the time came to order new bills, and no doubt following the direction of Daniel Hoit, cashier Stephen Beede contacted firms other than the New England Bank Note Company. On July 15, this letter was sent to Toppan, Carpenter, Casilear & Co. in Philadelphia:

> Gentlemen—
>
> As we are about to get new special plates for our bills of the denominations of 1-2-3-5-10 & 20 and having seen some of your work, and feeling anxious to have any work done in a workmanlike manner on the very first quality of paper and at as low as possible rate as such work and materials can be furnished, induces me to write to you for your lowest terms for the above described work. The five first [to be on] steel plates and the 20s copper.
>
> We have a capital of only $50,000 and do not want a much larger amt. than the capital struck off at first as it will take some little time before we can get our old bills in.
>
> Please advise me on the subject.
>
> Respectfully,
>
> Stephen Beede, Cashier

Late 19th-century photograph of the building, on the left, that housed the Carroll County Bank from the late 1850s onward. The bank was on the top floor, made of wood and with white columns in the front, and the post office was on the ground floor, made of brick. (Sandwich Historical Society)

The response, if any, has not been seen. That autumn an arrangement was perfected with W.L Ormsby, proprietor of the New York Bank Note Co. of New York City. Bearing the printed date of January 1, 1855, a new series of bills was produced by Ormsby. The $1 note was made of the *Unit System* promoted by

A $1 Carroll County Bank note, December 1, 1853, from a New England Bank Note Co. plate. Stephen Beede signed as cashier and Daniel Hoit as president.

A $500 Carroll County Bank note. New England Bank Note Co., early 1850s. (Unique; ex Leonard Finn and Schingoethe collections)

Ormsby. As related earlier, this Carroll County Bank $1 note seems to be the only actual Unit System bank note Ormsby ever produced!

Other bills were also produced by Ormsby, also dated January 1, 1855, but of a normal configuration, with multiple small vignettes with a motif, denomination, etc. It is likely that some included the portrait of bank president Daniel Hoit.

The Ormsby File

Correspondence from Ormsby to the bank provides a remarkable window on his enthusiasm and business practices.[18] The first item is a letter to the bank on September 30, 1854, apparently in response to a general inquiry as to his services:[19]

> Sept. 30th 1854
>
> $1. $2. $3. $5: $300.
> $10. $20: $150
> $50. $100: $150
> [Total] $600
>
> [The design of each bill to be the same:] Like form, Indian and lake vignette, including an original portrait to belong exclusively to the bank. Denomination figures to be larger and to stand up straight.
>
> Printing 100 impressions, whole plate, face: $2
> Printing 100 impressions, whole plate, back: $1
> Printing 100 impressions, half plate [face:] $1.50
> Printing 100 impressions, half plate, back: $0.75
>
> I will make 10 pr. cent discount on the whole bill if I have the order immediately. I will engage to engrave a new set of plates and furnish a new one for the bank gratis, if the notes I now propose to engrave are counterfeited or altered so as to cause the bank any trouble.
>
> W.L. Ormsby

The preceding shows that Ormsby considered the full plate to have four bills, such as $1-$2-$3-$5, and the half plate to be used for higher denominations, $10-$20 and, separately, $50-$100. His printing charge for four notes, front and back, was $3, and for two notes, $2.25. As to original sheets of blank paper, these were made double-size and cut in half for a four-subject bank-note sheet and in quarters for a two-subject sheet.

On November 28, 1854, Ormsby wrote this letter:

> New Haven, Nov. 28th 1854
>
> To the President, Directors & Co. of the Carroll County Bank
>
> Gent.
>
> I started from New York this morning to visit you, but [since] I could not reach Center Sandwich before Wednesday night and knowing that Thursday would be Thanksgiving, I concluded to stop here and send my message forward by mail.
>
> I have taken more pains to execute this work well, than I anticipated, and as you told me to take what time was necessary, I have not forced anything beyond the proper course.
>
> The portrait of Mr. Hoit is not yet finished enough to submit to his son in Boston, but will be so in two or three days more. I want a better sketch of Center Sandwich village. I intended to take it myself—but perhaps you have a daguerreotypist or someone among your people who can make a sketch—however made—from which I can make a view which will include in it the bank and perhaps the president's house, &c. I want the view for the one dollar note.
>
> Now as to the forms for the notes, you will observe that I have made a one dollar note according to the true method recommended in my work on Bank Note Engraving which, by the way, I take the liberty of presenting for your acceptance.[20] I used this form in my guide, but I see no impropriety in giving the use of it to you, although this plate alone cost me nearly five hundred dollars.
>
> You will perceive that I have used four principal vignettes. With few exceptions every piece of work is entirely new. You recommended me to have the lettering under the vignettes, but I have done so only up to the five denomination. On the 10s and upward the lettering is above. I like this arrangement but can alter it if you require it. In fact I will make any alterations you may suggest.
>
> I propose of course to use back plates for all the notes, which I will submit for your examination before I commence printing.
>
> As to the paper I have done the best I could—have specimens from 6 different houses—have tried them all, and might puzzle you with some dozen or more that you would finally reject. I send two specimens only, and if you do not like either I will still try other kinds until I find what you desire. I recommend the paper of the National Exchange Bank.
>
> As the one dollar note will attract much attention not only in the New England states but in all the other states I recommend that you have a large circulation of this denomination, and to be economical in printing have a steel plate of two ones, a two, and a three, a half plate five and ten, a half plate twenty and fifty, and a single one hundred. If these forms are satisfactory without material alteration I can have all the plates ready to print inside of two weeks.
>
> Your Obt ser't
>
> W.L. Ormsby

On the 29th he wrote two letters, one to president Daniel Hoit, with a sketch of the bank and Hoit's house, the text indicating that Ormsby had visited there, and the other to director Moulton Marston:

> New Haven, Nov. 29th 1854
>
> Mr. Hoit.
>
> Dear Sir.
>
> I have come to a sudden stop on my way to your town. An explanation is in the letter to the directors.
>
> You will find a small proof of the portrait die in the package. I shall improve it much before I submit it to your son, and I am sure we shall have a strong likeness and a good piece of work.
>
> If you have a view of Center Sandwich or if any of your family are able to make a sketch—however rude—so that the buildings are located properly, I should like to have it for the one dollar note.
>
> A sketch with a pen something of this fashion will suit. [Sketch here of Main Street, as viewed across the street from the bank, showing the front of the bank to the right, Hoit's house to its left, and trees and buildings uphill farther to the left.] I have imagined myself in front of the tavern and made a remembering sketch of the right hand or upper end of your street including the bank, the president's house, &c. A daguerreotype view would be preferable.
>
> Your Obt sev't
>
> W.L. Ormsby

> New Haven, Nov. 29th 1854
>
> Mr. Marston.
>
> Dear Sir.
>
> You will see by my letter to the directors why I write from this place. It is now snowing violently and I think myself fortunate in not being caught in a storm among the mountains.
>
> There was, indeed, no occasion for my writing to you in person, but to talk over the matter of paper—any variation in forms—and to take a little sketch of the village for the one denomination. My object in visiting in person was mostly to save time, as a correspondence in case any change was suggested would occupy several days.
>
> It has taken longer than I at first expected to progress so far. This is owning to my dependence on others in the execution of the portrait, but the time has been occupied in beautifying all parts of the notes, engraving totally new designs, &c. Everything will be ready by the time I hear from you, and I can have the plates finished in a very few days ready to print.
>
> I hope you will be pleased with the forms as I have arranged them. And I suggest that you adopt the paper of the Marshall County Bank & Potomac R.R. (both the same) for the denominations of five and under and the other for the tens and over.
>
> Your Obt sev't
>
> W.L. Ormsby

More on the Ornate $1 Bills

Seven years later, on April 9, 1862, this letter was sent to the bank by Ormsby, enclosing a printed commentary about the bank's memorable $1 bills:

> New York City, April 9th 1862
>
> Cash. Carroll County Bank, N.H.
>
> Dear Sir,
>
> Having frequently had occasion to refer in newspaper and book publications to the one dollar note which I engraved for your bank in 1854 as embodying great security against alterations and counterfeiting, I respectfully request that you will favor me with your opinion of the merits as practically obtained from the circulation.
>
> Respectfully
>
> Your Obt Servt
>
> W.L. Ormsby
>
> Proprietor, New York Bank Note Co.

Sent along by Ormsby was a clipped excerpt from his "Rules to Prevent Alterations," in which Ormsby reprinted a "certificate," a testimonial from John S. Dye, publisher of counterfeit detectors, but first telling about Dye himself:

> The following certificate is from a gentleman said to be the best judge of paper money in the United States. He gave a series of public lectures on counterfeiting at the Tabernacle, in this city, and announced to the audience that he could alter the denomination of any circulating note that might be handed to him.
>
> He succeeded in altering a two-dollar note of the Unadilla [New York] Bank into a fifty, and provided by the Hon. M. Schoonmaker that if it was not a fifty, at least it ought to be so, as the state die was placed precisely in the position required.
>
> He failed to alter the one-dollar note of the bank mentioned below, which was engraved by me, and volunteered the following:
>
> *"New York City, Jan'y 14th, 1856*
>
> *"W.L. Ormsby.*
>
> *"Dear Sir:*
>
> *"The most secure notes against alterations and counterfeiting that I have ever seen in circulation are the one-dollar notes of the Carroll County Bank, New Hampshire. Such is my candid opinion.*
>
> *"Respectfully yours,*
>
> *"John S. Dye"*

On April 22, 1862, a reply was sent to Ormsby's request:

(continued on p. 354)

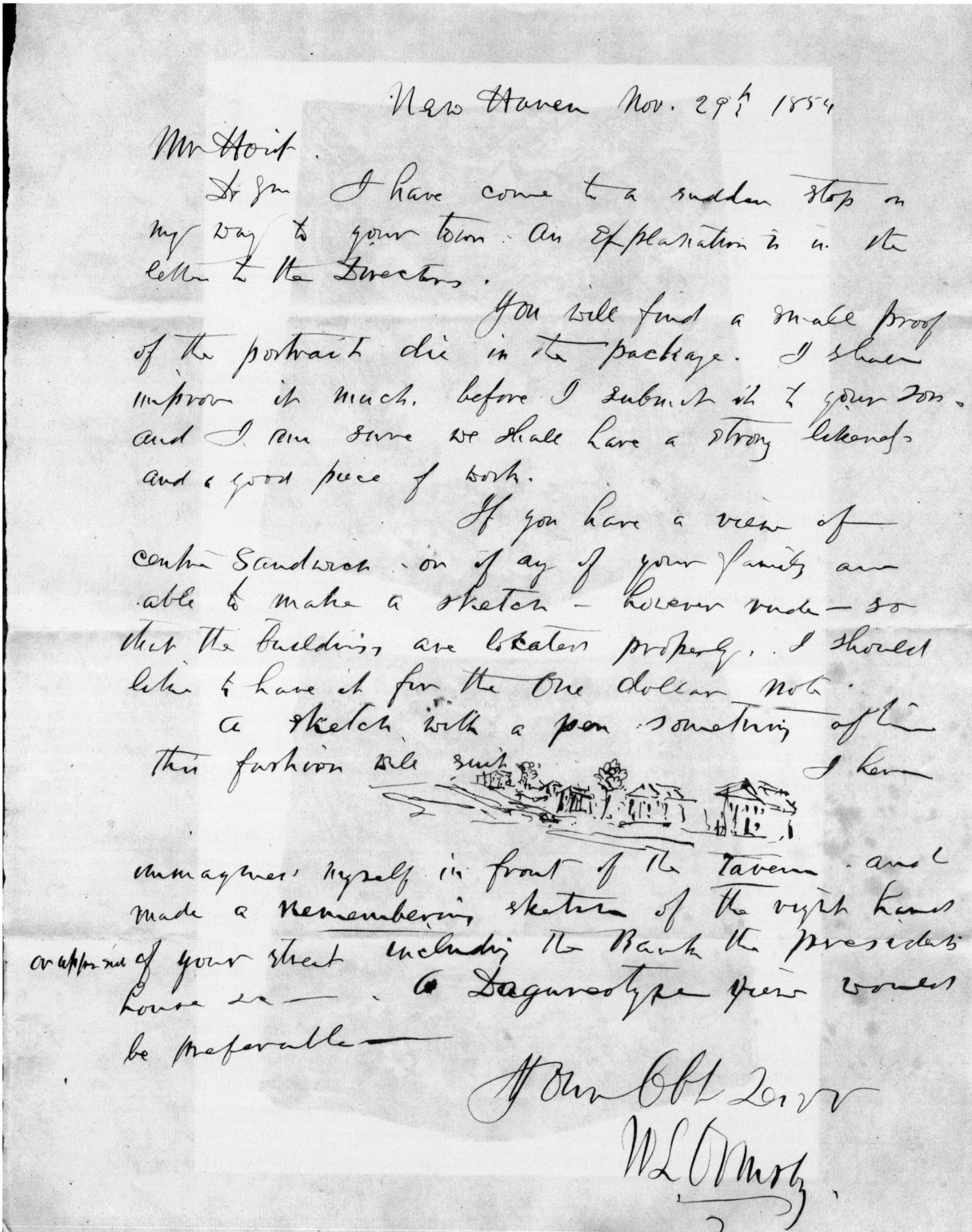

New Haven Nov. 29th 1854

Mr Hoit.

Dr Sir I have come to a sudden stop on my way to your town. An Explanation is in the letter to the Directors.

You will find a small proof of the portrait die in the package. I shall improve it much, before I submit it to your son. and I am sure we shall have a strong likeness and a good piece of work.

If you have a view of centre Sandwich - or if any of your family are able to make a sketch - however rude - so that the buildings are located properly, I should like to have it for the One dollar note.

A sketch with a pen something of this fashion will suit. I have imagined myself in front of the Tavern and made a Remembering sketch of the right hand or upper end of your street including the Bank the presidents house &c — . A Daguerreotype view would be preferable —

Your Obt Servt

W L Ormsby.

Ormsby's letter to Hoit, November 29, 1854, with a sketch from memory. (Sandwich Historical Society)

A $1 note of the Carroll County Bank, of the Unit System design by W.L. Ormsby. Variety without red ONE protector.

(continued from p. 352)

W.L. Ormsby, Esq.

Dear Friend—

In answer to thy request of my opinion of the merits as practically obtained from the circulation of our one dollar notes engraved by thee in 1854—

There has never been an attempt to my knowledge to alter or counterfeit them, and I believe them to be as secure from a successful operation of that kind, more so than any engraving that I have ever seen. But their appearance after having been a little worn is not what I would like, as a handsome bank bill with an attractive picture upon the face will be taken better care of and carried longer in the pocket than one of an opposite character.

Respectfully,
Stephen Beede, Cash'r

Ormsby's comment on the preceding was given in a pamphlet, *Cycloidal Configurations,* published in 1863:

> I am very glad that the gentleman has referred to the beauty of a bank note as one of its requisites. My mind has been so intent on the qualities that our soldiers and their families would value, viz *genuineness* and *redeemability,* that I had quite forgotten this excellence. On this point I am quite sure that if I could make bank notes so perfectly beautiful that people would *keep them in their pockets* as gems of art, all banks of issue would throng my studio. But I know that all banks of issue are not, by design, banks of redemption. I know, also that this class of banks is the first to profit by any prevailing fashion.
>
> The Carroll County Bank note was the very first design on the Unit System. It was engraved with my own hands, simply with a view to protection against counterfeits. Both the designer and engraver can improve upon it. Let us have the true system of security first; and we can embellish and beautify in the highest degree required. It is enough that the foundation of the Unit System has proved sound by actual experiment. The following is additional testimony on this point:

Philadelphia, Feb 1st, 1863

The undersigned has been engaged in teaching the science of detecting counterfeit, altered, and spurious notes, to rail road officers, bankers, and in twenty mercantile colleges during ten years past, and hereby certifies that, in his opinion, the one dollar notes of the Carroll County Bank, N.H., engraved by W.L. Ormsby, combine more security against alterations and counterfeiting than any other notes in circulation in this country.

A. Thompson

It is seen that the Carroll County Bank $1 bill of 1855 is of particular importance in the annals of American paper money. In fact, it is remarkable that no other Unit System bills were ever made.

BANKING ITEMS OF THE LATE 1850S

During the 1850s various banks in New Hampshire collected loans and accounts on behalf of the Carroll County Bank, charging a small fee in each instance. Conversely, other banks would send paper for due loans to Sandwich region citizens and merchants and request that collections be made.

Shares of bank stock were taxable by the state. Each year the cashier was required to send lists of shareholders to the assessors of New Hampshire towns in which they resided. On April 3, 1856, cashier Beede sent letters to the following places: Sandwich, Effingham, Freedom, Tamworth, Wolfeboro, Moultonborough, Somersworth, Holderness, and Ossipee. This situation reflects the fact that there was no equity interest held in any of the larger towns and cities such as Portsmouth, Concord, or Manchester; Somersworth was the only exception.

In 1857 the Suffolk Bank in Boston was the main redemption agent for bills of the Carroll County Bank.

A $100 proof note of the Carroll County Bank, by Ormsby. This denomination was unknown to scholars until this specimen was found in 2005 in a small group of proof bills that had remained hidden since the late 19th century. This was the only note from this bank found in the cache.

Cashier Beede described the design in a memorandum to the publisher of a bank-note reporter: "In lower center figure of an Egyptian with wings seated, a female seated beside him, a globe between them. Right end 100 on a die above & below. Left end same as the right."

However, the relationship between the banks was strained, seemingly for good reason, this per a letter from an assistant cashier of the Suffolk Bank:

> Boston, 11 July 1857
>
> S. Beede, Esq., cashier
>
> Dear Sir,
>
> Your account is overdrawn about $10,000. It has been overdrawn a long time and altogether is not profitable to us, without you can keep us supplied with funds in advance of your redemptions.
>
> Without you can make some change which will be more favorable to us, we would prefer to have you keep your account at some other Boston bank that is able and willing to accommodate you.

Sometimes banks would cooperate on matters of common interest, as indicated by this letter from the Peterborough Bank:

> Peterborough Bank, Sep. 21 [1858]
>
> S. Beede, Esq., Cash.
>
> Dear Sir—
>
> We have received a latter from Mr. J.W. Butler of Boston, asking on behalf of the directors of the Verd Antique Marble Co. for a meeting of their creditors in Boston on Thursday, Sept. 30 at 3 o'clock P.M. at the office of A.G. Peck on Kilby St., to see if it is possible to make any settlement.[21]
>
> Our bank will send a delegate and we think it desirable that all parties should be represented, and trust your bank will take the same view of it.
>
> Yours truly,
>
> C.G. Cheney, Cash.

Shipment of Bank Bills Lost en Route

The *Portsmouth Journal,* February 20, 1858, printed this account:

> **Lost Money Recovered**
>
> Several weeks since, notice was given that a package of money, consisting of $3,200 in bills of the Carroll County Bank, had been lost between Wolfeborough Bridge and Sandwich, and a reward of $100 was offered for its recovery. The money had been brought from the Suffolk Bank, Boston, by Niles's Express, and delivered to David Lawrence, the express man between Dover and Alton. At Alton Mr. Lawrence delivered the package to Joseph W. Wiggin, then driving the stage from that place to Wolfborough Bridge.
>
> At the latter place, according to the explanation given, Wiggin transferred the package to Mr. Rogers, stage-driver on the Sandwich route. On arriving at Sandwich, Mr. R. discovered the loss of the money. His account of it was that Wiggin placed the package in his (Rogers's) breast pocket, and buttoned the inside coat over it. Whether the

The Peterborough Bank was a very active and successful institution in the southern part of New Hampshire. This $1 note is from a plate by Danforth, Wright & Co., Boston, New York City, and Philadelphia.

A $2 note on the Bay State Bank of Lawrence, Massachusetts. Proof impression of a plate by Toppan, Carpenter & Co., New York and Philadelphia.

> package was in reality delivered to Rogers, was doubted by the friends of the latter. Both persons, however, were closely watched.
>
> No clue to the affair was obtained, until a few days since, when Mr. Wiggin paid a bill in Dover amounting to $40. All the notes being on the Bay State Bank, of Lawrence [Massachusetts], an investigation was set on foot, which revealed the fact that Wiggin had exchanged $200 of the Carroll County Bank for an equal amount of Bay State Bank money. It was subsequently ascertained that Carroll County Bank bills to the amount of $300 had been exchanged at another bank in Lawrence, and at Portsmouth.

These circumstances led to the arrest of Wiggin, who, on learning what had been discovered of his movements, confessed the crime and promised to make restitution.

According to his story, two other persons were engaged in the affair, one of whom was to take the money and drop it in the road, another was to find it, and the three were to divide the plunder between them. About $2,300 of the money, we understand, has been recovered, and the balance secured—a fortunate circumstance for Mr. Lawrence, upon whom the loss would have fallen.

The Bank of Mutual Redemption

In 1855 the Bank of Mutual Redemption was set up in Boston with the specific purpose of acting as a redemption agent for currency. Business commenced in 1858. In time this entity largely replaced the Suffolk Bank as exchange agent for many New England banks. James C. Carney was president and Henry P. Shed was cashier. In coming years Shed would correspond almost daily with Stephen Beede, in the course of Beede sending bills of other banks and checks for collection.

This completed form letter was received by the Carroll County Bank:

> **Bank of Mutual Redemption**
>
> Boston, Aug. 20, 1858
>
> To the President and Directors of the Carroll County Bank, Sandwich, N.H.
>
> Gentlemen:
>
> Referring to the circular of this bank sent to you under date of July 9th last, as to its proposed plan of doing business, I am instructed to notify you that the required portion of the capital having been paid in, and examined, according to law, the bank will commence business on Monday next, the 23rd inst.
>
> Respectfully,
>
> Your Most Ob't,
Henry P. Shed.
Bank of Mutual Redemption
>
> [Postscript] Will you please say where you wish your bank notes presented for redemption, as requested in the circular referred to.

In the meantime it seems that the Carroll County Bank's relationship with the Suffolk Bank had deteriorated, per this message:

> Bank of Mutual Redemption
12 Exchange Street
Boston, Massachusetts
>
> Sep. 11, 1858
>
> To the Cashier of the Carroll County Bank
>
> Sir:
>
> In conformity with your request we have presented to the Suffolk Bank your notes for 100 dollars for redemption, and the president thereof refuses to redeem the same. You will please make provision therefor at your earliest convenience.
>
> H.P. Shed, Cashier

On another matter, cashier Beede wrote to cashier Shed on November 22, 1858:

> At a meeting of the board of directors held this day I was instructed by a unanimous vote of said board to subscribe on behalf of this bank for twenty shares of one hundred dollars each of the capital stock in the Bank of Mutual Redemption in Boston—and I herewith enclose the certificate of our deposit of three thousand dollars in the Suffolk Bank, which please collect by giving the proper notice—and forward me a certificate of stock—or advise me what further is necessary to be done to obtain it.

Similar to the cash-flow problems Beede had with the Suffolk Bank, now a similar situation arose with the Bank of Mutual Redemption. On April 19, 1859, cashier Shed wrote to Beede: "Your account stands overdrawn $1,881.74. Please remit funds to make your account good."

General Daniel Hoit

During the 1850s Daniel Hoit was no doubt the leading figure in local commerce in Center Sandwich, conducting his store at the intersection known as Hoit's Corner. A genealogy of his family, published in 1857, noted in part:[22]

> Hon. D. Hoit is still living in Sandwich, N.H., where most of his life has been spent. He has retired from active business, but still retains much of his vigor, and is president of the Carroll County Bank, located within a few rods of his residence.
>
> Though he has been chiefly engaged in mercantile pursuits, yet he has found time to interest himself somewhat in politics, and has been, for many years, a prominent public man in New Hampshire. Of course he has filled town offices of all kinds. He was first chosen representative to the Legislature of New Hampshire in 1807, and has 15 times been elected to represent his native town, but once resigned on account of being chosen senator. He has been senator four years and councilor two years. He early identified himself with the old Liberty or Free Soil Party, and was for several years their candidate for governor.
>
> One or two of his years were spent in Ohio, and it was while returning from a visit to Urbana that his first wife, Sally, died at Jersey City, N.Y., May 31, 1837. [His second] wife, Betsy, died May 13, 1856.

Transition

In 1859 and 1860 there were major changes at the bank. Daniel Hoit died on August 11, 1859, and his place as president was taken by Moulton H. Marston.

The composition of the board of directors was altered, and Ira Bean, William M. Weed, and Ebenezer Wilkinson were new faces, joined by Augustine Blanchard, who had served much earlier.[23] Bean was a local attorney who had done much work for the bank in earlier times. Wilkinson was a physician in Tamworth and an investor in bank stock.

The bank had seen difficult times, as did nearly all banks in America after the Panic of 1857. The dividend of 7% for the earlier 12-month period had been reduced to 4% for the most recent 12 months. After this was paid, the bank had an operating deficit of $258.57. In the loan portfolio, $32,000 of the $76,395.96 total was to out-of-state parties. Bills in circulation amounted to $33,073, according to the ledger.

William M. Weed

New board member William H. Weed, born in North Sandwich on July 29, 1814, was a local character who became active in business in 1836, when he was employed in the store of Jeremiah Furber in Sandwich Lower Corner. Success attended his efforts, and soon he acquired Furber's interest.

In 1839 Weed was a trustee of the Sandwich Academy, one of several trustees who were later associated with the Carroll County Bank. In that particular year Weed and his friend, young Dr. Andrew J. McFarland, engaged in a caper that was illegal, but humorous in its retelling years later. The two men conspired to create documents exempting local men from military service. McFarland had been appointed by the governor to serve as surgeon to a regiment of the state militia. At the time many local and regional men were members of the militia, such service typically consisting of one day a year in which they attended a fun-filled encampment, often being tucked into bed in a tent after a day and evening of heavy drinking. Then came the unexpected prospect of a genuine war: New Brunswick and Maine were in a boundary dispute, and the countries of Great Britain and America might have to settle it by military action against each other. The matter eventually was resolved without war, indeed amicably.

McFarland remembered that time:[24]

> This pacific outcome was not at all anticipated in our town of Sandwich. Nothing was seen but the iron front of grim-visaged war. And, I blush to record it, the prospect was viewed with a most craven spirit. Not a man talked of raising a regiment—not even a company—but all ran helter skelter to the surgeon's office to get certificates of disability.
>
> To such details as the giving of disability certificates I had bestowed but little thought, only knowing that to keep the office pure the law was

strict that no fees were to be charged in any case. But I believe it is human nature everywhere, that where work is done, payment is made for it, some way or other, prohibitions to the contrary notwithstanding. It was not in reason that such a crop of lumbagos, sciaticas, rheumatisms, and invisible sprains would be investigated and passed upon for nothing, for it was a curious fact that in most of the cases the applicant's word was about the only proof. Men limped up before me who I had seen scores of times before walking as stiff and straight as grenadiers. Old ulcers, never before heard of, were brought to light

At length a happy thought enabled me to get a "corner" in the business. I discovered (or pretended to) that these loose and formal applications were all contrary to law, and all proceedings void and had to be done over again. Applications were to be drawn up in precise compliance with the strict forms, oaths upon certain specifications, all to be *secundem artum.*

This branch of business was declared outside of the surgeon's office, Mr. W.M. Weed, whose ready pen had been enlisted by a mutual understanding. His fees were made proportionate to the purse and panic of the applicant, in some cases quite handsome.

The nomination of William Henry Harrison and his running mate, John Tyler, in the "Tippecanoe and Tyler too!" presidential campaign of 1840 ignited public sentiment, coming as it did after the advent of the Hard Times era. Dr. McFarland remembered that time:[25]

Without question the affairs of the country were then at the lowest ebb ever known, and the unparalleled excitement of the campaign of 1840 was a species of reaction from the gloom that for some years had settled over the country.

I think that the "Corner," as [Sandwich Lower Village] was then termed, must have been the focus of prevailing feelings. This was due to the presence there of certain very enthusiastic spirits who went into the strife *con amore.*

Immediately after the nomination, William M. Weed caused to be erected a mast at least a hundred feet high, from which floated a huge banner emblazoned in big capitals, "HARRISON AND TYLER." It was an object conspicuous for miles over the country in every direction. It must have been a tough piece of canvas, for, after standing the battle and breeze for eight months or so, it did good service as the mainsail of a boat navigating the perilous waters of the pond east of the town [Lake Winnipesaukee] for some years afterward.

In 1845 Weed built a handsome two-story red brick store in Sandwich, at the Lower Corner intersection. In 1847 he was one of only three people in town licensed to sell liquor (Daniel Hoit, later associated with the bank, was one of the other two).[26] During this era pro-alcohol and the more prolific anti-alcohol (temperance) feelings ran high and were sometimes topics at annual town meetings. One way or another, over the years the residents managed to have all the liquor they wanted, if not officially, as in Weed's store in 1847, then by prescription as *medicine.* In 1862 Weed issued scrip notes payable at the Carroll County Bank.

Continuing Operations in 1859

In 1859 the Carroll County Bank continued its business satisfactorily, returning to profit after the dip caused by the Panic of 1857.

Demand for local and regional loans remained low, and, as before, the bank did much business with brokers in Boston and elsewhere. This letter, apparently unsolicited, reflects the eagerness of a bank in Wisconsin to distribute the Carroll County Bank's bills as part of a proposed relationship:

Bank of Eau Claire
Eau Claire, Wis.

July 25, 1859

[to] Stephen Beede, Esqr., cashier

This bank would like to obtain a line of discounts of $2,500 per month. We can give your currency a first rate circulation, and will give you thirty day drafts on John Wright & Co., No. 35 Park Row, New York City, accepted.

We have a greater demand for money than we can supply. Our bank capital is $50,000 amply secured by state stocks. One active business account is kept with Messrs. Clark & Williamson, No. 1 Wall Street, N.Y., to whom we respectfully refer. Please answer.

Respt. Yours,
Charles Whipple, Cashier[27]

In the meantime, as the Bank of Mutual Redemption was experiencing sufficient business, a more expedient method was adopted for correspondence, this per a form letter dated August 3, 1859: "All acknowledgments of letters received from you, will, in future, be enclosed with your packages of redeemed bills."

A Run on the Bank Averted

In September 1859, rumors were afloat that the Carroll County Bank was insolvent, although no such problem actually existed. Such false notices were common, indeed endemic, in American banking and were

Weed's store in Sandwich, on the road toward Moultonborough and Lake Winnipesaukee, as photographed in 2003.

Scrip note (shown enlarged) issued by William M. Weed in 1862, payable at the Carroll County Bank.

sometimes started by brokers and currency dealers in an attempt to buy bills at deep discounts from panicked citizens. In other instances, debtors to the bank would be involved, hoping to buy bills at deep discounts to use to repay their loans. As news spread, sometimes there would be a run on the bank, and an otherwise solid institution would be unable to redeem its bills at par, with the rumor becoming a self-fulfilling prophecy. No bank in existence maintained enough gold and silver coins in its vault to exchange for all of its paper money. Instead, it was anticipated that bills would be redeemed only in small amounts, continuously and over a long period of time.

Regarding the bank in Sandwich, as might be expected, facts were scarce as to its true financial condition, and opinions were abundant. No doubt the recent death of longtime president Daniel Hoit and his replacement by a lesser-known (although eminently sound) person, Marston H. Moulton, may have raised doubts to some in distant locations. A careful reading of the results of the annual state examination on May 18, 1859, by George W. Pinkerton, given to members of the state legislature in June, showed surplus or undivided profits of $1,206.41, but with $5,000 in overdue loans and a further $2,000 considered to be bad or doubtful, ill omens to those knowledgeable in banking circles. Of the $77,669.01 in loans, $30,000 had been placed out of state, not considered by analysts to be an indication of local or regional strength. In October 1858 a semiannual dividend of 3% had been paid to stockholders, which was increased to 4% in April 1859, a good sign.

Reflective of the critical situation, on September 16, 1859, this note was appended to a notice of other matters sent to Beede by the Bank of Mutual Redemption, for some time now at a new location, 91 State

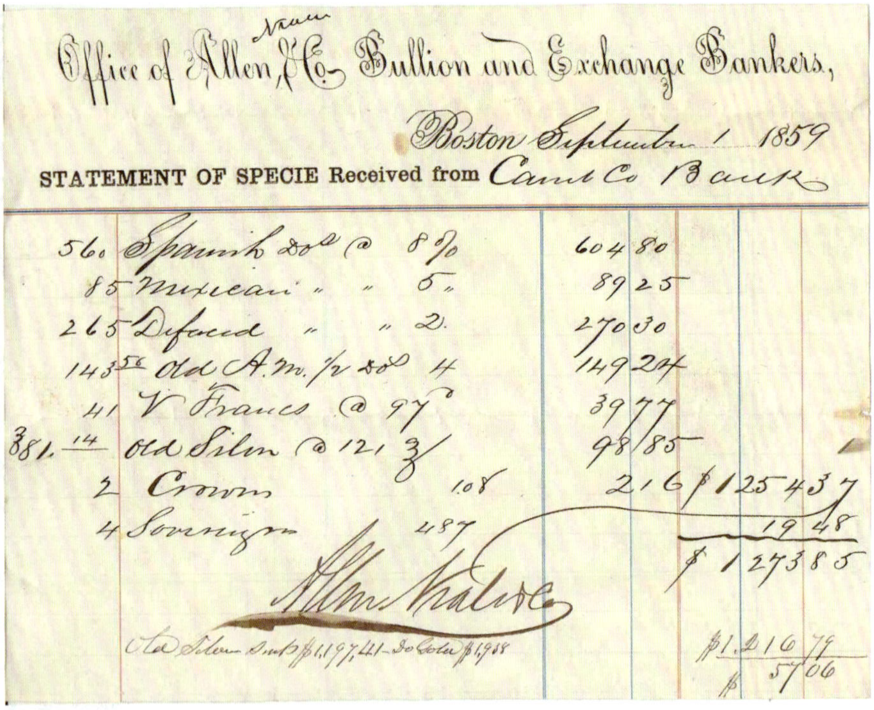

Office of Allen & Co. Bullion and Exchange Bankers,

Boston September 1 1859

STATEMENT OF SPECIE Received from Carroll Co Bank

A shipment of specie received by Allen & Co., bullion and exchange bankers in Boston, September 1, 1859, consisted of worn foreign silver coins and four British sovereigns that the bank or its customers had on hand. Such coins were flowing into exchange brokers, as their legal tender status had been repealed.

Street, Boston: "On your draft on us for $10,000 we have delivered to Mr. Weed same amount in coin, ten thousand dollars."

No doubt, this immense trove of silver coins did duty to demonstrate the fact that the bank could redeem its bills in *hard money.* Likely, the coins were mostly half dollars, for silver dollars did not circulate in America at this time, and had not since 1850. No doubt the conspicuous display at the bank of thousands of dollars in silver coins effectively ended any doubt of the bank's strength.

On September 23, 1859, cashier Henry P. Shed of the Bank of Mutual Redemption wrote to Beede in Sandwich:

> Dear Sir:
>
> Yours of the 22nd inst. is at hand and contents have attention. I am glad to learn that all is quiet at Sandwich, and hope that the temporary inconvenience to which your bank has recently been subjected will not be repeated.
>
> The card of your directors affords a satisfactory explanation to the public, and will effectually silence any rumors which may have arisen from the original paragraph in the Journal, in regard to the "run" upon you.
>
> The reference to us in the card was proper, and we shall not hesitate to clear up the doubts of any over anxious person who may call to inquire in regard to the solvency of the Carroll County Bank.
>
> The amount of your bills on hand is $11,200, having redeemed on the 19th, $1,300; 20th, $1,200; 21st, $3,800 & 22nd, $4,900.

The Bank of Mutual Redemption was having some of its own problems counting currency, as reflected in these items, both circular notices apparently sent to multiple banks:

> December 8, 1859
>
> Sir:
>
> Please examine with care our package of the 23 ult. as we were short on that day $100.

> December 22, 1859
>
> Cashier of the Carroll Co. Bank:
>
> Did the package or packages of your bills put up here on the 17th inst count correctly? If not examined, please do examine such package or packages, AT ONCE, and report to us the result, as there is a package missing, which may have been put in your package.

CURRENCY IN USE IN JANUARY 1860

On January 12, 1860, cashier Stephen Beede wrote to the *Metropolitan Bank Note Reporter,* commencing with descriptions of the bank's current notes, apparently all by the New York Bank Note Co. (W.L. Ormsby), although this was not stated. Leading the list is the ornate $1 note. At the end, Beede included a short message:

1s: In the center, three large female figures floating in the air, and extending nearly across the whole note. Right end, a portrait; 1 on upper corner. Left end ONE above; 1 on lower corner. ONE ONE diagonally in capitals on left end & near right end.

2s: Upper center, an Indian seated and an Indian woman holding a child & kneeling on one knee, plows, sickle, sheaf & landscape. 2 on each side. Right end w female seated; 2 below. Left end a female seated, oval portrait of Gen. Taylor below.

3s: Upper center same as the twos. Right end an oval male portrait. THREE above and below. Left end, front of a train of cars, 3 above & below.

5s: Upper center same as the twos & threes. 5 on a die on each side. Right end oval portrait of a girl. V in upper corner. Left end a dog's head in a circle with key in his mouth. V in upper corner.

10s: Lower center a train of cars; two laborers in the foreground. 10 on a die at each upper corner of the picture. Right end a female seated. X on a shield in upper corner. Left end the same as the right end.

20s: Lower center same as the tens. Right end an oval male portrait. 20 on a die above. Left end, oval portrait of Franklin. 20 on a die above.

50s: In the center, figures of an Egyptian with wings seated, w female seated beside him, a globe between them & a bust at her right hand. Indians in the background. Right end, 50 on a die above & below. Left end the same as the right.

100s: In lower center figure of an Egyptian with wings seated, a female seated beside him, a globe between them. Right end 100 on a die above & below. Left end same as the right.

The above is a description of the genuine bills of the Carroll County Bank at Center Sandwich, N.H.

Stephen Beede, Cashier

Please send me a copy of the descriptive register of genuine bills when issued, together with the bill for the same receipted and I will return one dollar by mail when so received.

The use of the same images on bills of different denominations—as the Indian motif on the $2, $3, and $5 bills; the same train on the $10s and $20s; and the same Egyptian design on the $50 and $100—was a violation of good practice, because it made the alteration of bills simpler.

A "Malicious Enemy" Kept at Bay

President Moulton H. Marston, new in the office in 1859, entered 1860 with the slate of directors elected the previous August, consisting of Marston himself plus Thomas Burleigh, Nathaniel Hubbard, Ira A. Bean, Augustine Blanchard, William M. Weed, and Ebenezer Wilkinson. In earlier times president Daniel Hoit had brought much talent to the bank, including that gained in several decades of operating a store along with knowledge from his regular reading of

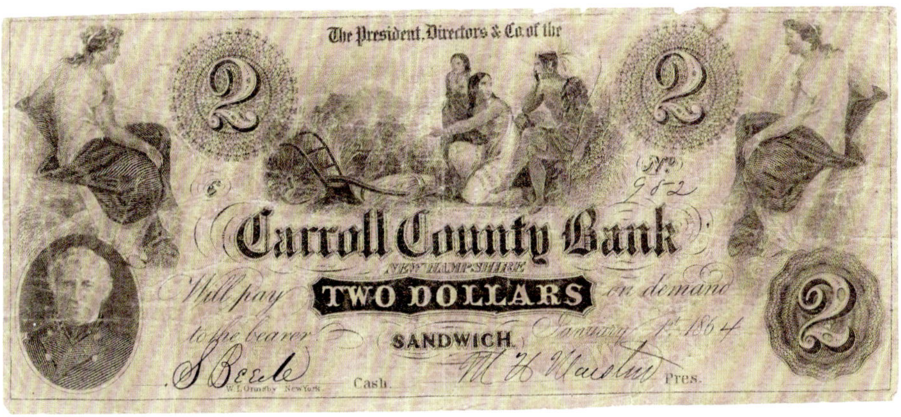

A $2 note by W.L. Ormsby, issued January 1, 1864. This was a leftover note, for by this time the American Bank Note Co. was supplying new bills to the Carroll County Bank.

A $20 note by Ormsby, with printed date of January 1, 1855. This was from the first order done for the Carroll County Bank.

newspapers and financial journals published in distant cities. Stephen Beede, competent as a cashier, mainly followed the directions given by Hoit.

Apparently, the specter of a run on the bank arose again in early 1860, as reflected in these letters, the first from Beede to local merchant Charles Blanchard, with instructions, and the second from Beede to the Bank of Mutual Redemption:

Carroll County Bank
Center Sandwich, N.H.

February 14, 1860

Chas. Blanchard, Esq.

Dear Friend—

Enclosed please find a draft on the Bank of Mutual Redemption for $4,000—for which please obtain one half in small silver coin from 5 cent pieces up to 1/4d and 1/2d, the more small, the better—the other half in gold dollars.

If so much silver cannot be had please get the balance in gold dollars.

When obtained please have it sent from the Bank of M. Redemption by Cheney & Co.'s Express on our contract with them & write me what day it will come, that we may meet it at Meredith.

All trouble & expense in negotiating this business will be paid beside being under much obligation for the favor.

Carroll County Bank
Center Sandwich, N.H.

February 14, 1860

H.P. Shed, Cashr.

Dear friend—

Chas. Blanchard, Esq., will present you our draft for $4,000 which we wish to appropriate for small coin & when made we will return to you the same amount in gold of a larger denomination as we find no law of our state regulating the denomination of coin in payment of our bills.

We think that small coin, a good proportion of which in silver, will not be easily exchanged again (by a Malicious Enemy) for our bills.

We very much regret the necessity of so often calling on you for favors of this kind. We would send the gold in advance but fear an unfriendly call in its absence.

Reference to the bearer for further particulars.

On November 23, 1860, cashier Stephen Beede sent to I.W. Beede, presumably a relative, at an unspecified location, a quantity of Carroll County Bank bills to be exchanged for "foreign money," this being a term for out-of-state bills of other banks. Seemingly, the bank was short of ready funds other than its own bills:

Fifteen hundred dollars in our bills and twenty five dollars in specie, $1,525, for the poultry dealers & enclose a blank note to be executed.

Please forward as much foreign money as may be as our exchanges are growing somewhat harder.

In the same era cashier Beede wrote notes to debtors near and far, attempting to collect loans, some of which were two years in arrears.

On the lighter side, perhaps, or at least with no long-lasting consequences, is this letter to a Boston supplier of safes, Edwards & Kershaw:[28]

Gentlemen—

Your favor of the 9th inst., relative to our safe, is before me. In reply will say that I cannot operate the lock with the right hand door open any better than shut. The bolts are not distinct from the lock but are thrown by operating the lock.

We have taken the inside plate of the door off, thinking it might expose the lock to view, but found that it was bedded in a kind of hardened sand which must be removed to get at the locks, & when taken out we cannot replace it, which perhaps is not essential.

I lock & unlock the safe daily by throwing the bolts very lightly, or if I happen to turn the key quickly, I have sometimes worked an hour before I could open the door again.

Yours respectfully,
Stephen Beede, Cashr.

Various events came together to create a situation in which the bank was operating at a slight deficit—of just $258, but a deficit nonetheless—by the time of the state examiner's visit on May 15, 1860. Matters did not improve for the rest of the year. This negative situation persisted into the next year, with a similar deficit posted in spring 1861.

The Civil War

During the coin shortage of 1862 (see chapter 19), William M. Weed, the *character* who prospered at Lower Corner, issued his own scrip notes, printed by McFarland and Jenks in Concord and redeemable by the cashier of the Carroll County Bank. These were printed in sheets of three notes, well done with a gold-colored overprint on the face. Denominations produced were 5¢, 10¢, and 25¢, but of those that survive today, most are of the 5¢ type.

It is likely that Weed's notes circulated through Sandwich and, perhaps, in surrounding districts as well. This was a time of substitutes for federal coins, and in New Hampshire dozens of banks, merchants, and others issued scrip. In the meantime, larger transactions were conducted with paper money, including the bills of the Carroll County Bank, with values from $1 upward, as well as Federal Legal Tender *greenback* notes.

From time to time the Carroll County Bank acquired silver and gold coins. Because they were worth a premium during the war, they were boxed up in even amounts (values ending in an even hundred dollars) and sent to Boston to be sold to exchange dealers, with the proceeds charged to the bank's account there.

Certain Aspects of Currency

Mysteries surround the paper money issued by the Carroll County Bank, not the least of which is the reuse by the American Bank Note Co. (formed in April 1858) of the Ormsby plate for the Unit System $1 bill (see chapter 15). These bore the original printed date of January 1, 1855.

During the 1860s the bank issued bills printed or at least distributed by the New England Bank Note Co. division of the American Bank Note Co. Whether these were from old plates with the ABNCo monogram entered or whether they were of new designs is not known today.

The report for the Carroll County Bank prepared by state examiner C.H. Powers, May 2, 1862, gave for the first time details on currency, noting that $141,741 worth of notes had been issued during the bank's existence, $92,016 had been destroyed, $23,882 was signed and in the bank, and $25,823 was in circulation.

Whether the recorded amount issued was correct is not known today, for, as noted, cashier Beede, with the blessing of the board of directors, sometimes made deals for the bank's bills to be distributed widely at distant locations. Likely, many tens of thousands of dollars' face value in currency, possibly more, was ordered secretly. Probably, most such bills were shipped to banks and brokers in distant places and were never redeemed. The profit from them was not recorded.

In 1863, this order for currency was sent:

> June 1st 1863
>
> Isaac Cary, Esq. Agt. N.E. Bank Note Co.
>
> Dear Friend—
>
> We are in want of a few more small bills. Please print for us 1000 1/2 sheets of 1-1-2&3, best quality of paper.[29] The denominations printed in red upon the back—similar to those you last printed for us—and advise me when they will be ready for delivery.
>
> Respectfully,
>
> Stephen Beede, Cashier

The above was an official order, which was duly entered on the bank's books.

Prosperity

The examination of March 24, 1864, conducted by C.V. Dearborn, noted that for the first time the bank's assets went into six figures and stood at $100,002.92. Bills in circulation were at an all-time high of $48,287.

In the third week of August 1864, there was dissension among the stockholders, Daniel Beede was ousted as cashier and replaced by Christopher C. Fellows, and the Joseph Wentworth family, always important in the bank, began to dictate policy.

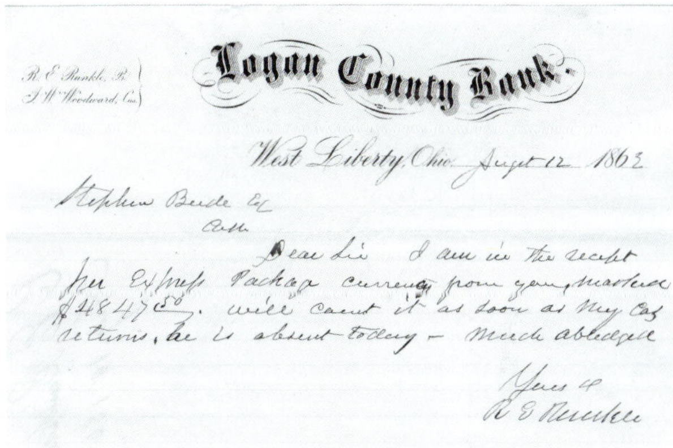

R. E. Runkle, Pr.
J. W. Woodward, Cas.

Logan County Bank.

West Liberty, Ohio, Augst 12 1863

Stephen Beede Esq
Cash

Dear Sir I am in the receipt per Express Package currency from you, marked $4847.50. will count it as soon as my Cas returns, he is absent today — Much obliged

Yours &c
R E Runkle

R.E. Runkle, president of the Logan County Bank of West Liberty, Ohio, writes to the cashier of the Carroll County Bank, September 12, 1863. He had just received a package of paper money amounting to $4,847.50. This probably consisted mostly of Carroll County Bank bills. During the bank's existence it shipped large numbers of bills to distant places, either at a substantial discount for cash payment, or in exchange for another bank's bills. Each bank would then try to pass the bills into circulation, usually small amounts at a time, so as not to attract attention. These unofficial transactions were not reported to state examiners.

Converting to a National Bank

On November 17, 1864, following a resolution of the stockholders, a request was made to the comptroller of the currency to convert the Carroll County Bank to a National Bank.[30] On November 28 another letter was sent from Sandwich, this with more information:

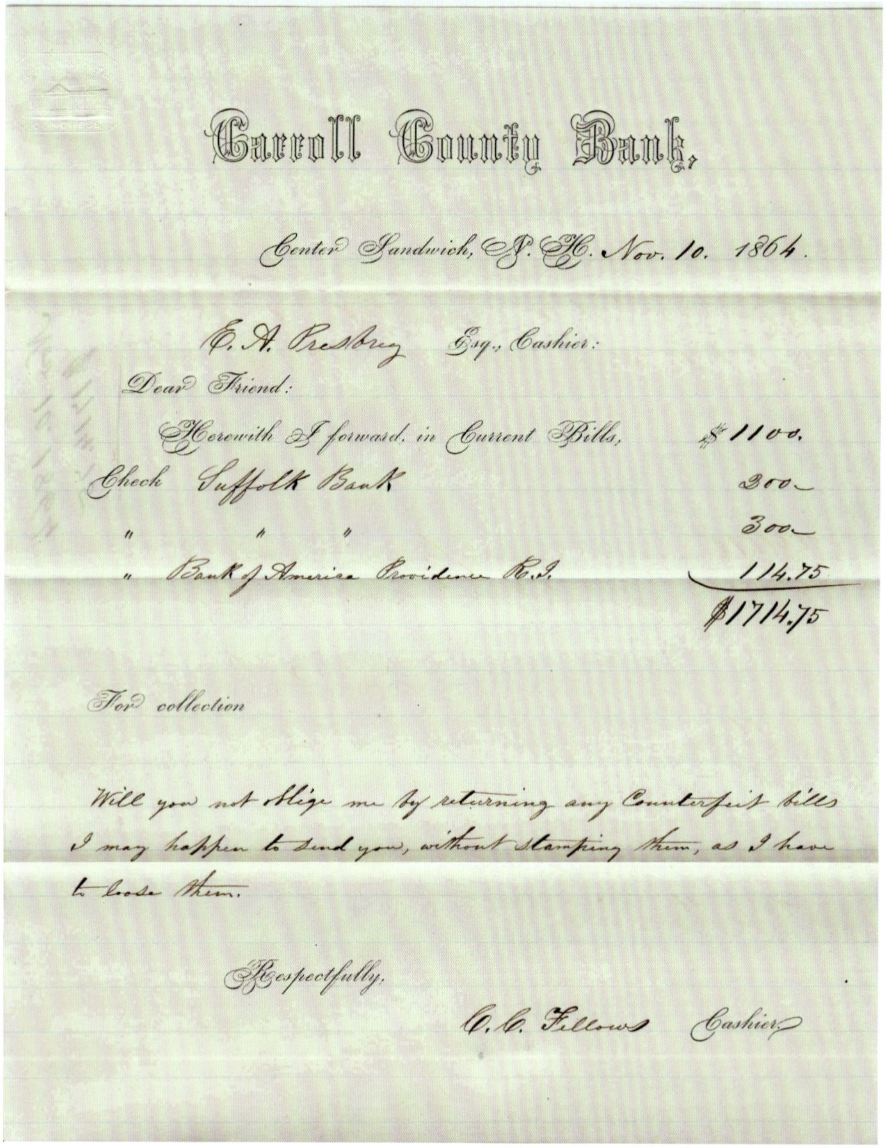

Carroll County Bank,

Center Sandwich, N.H. Nov. 10. 1864.

E. A. Presbrey Esq., Cashier:

Dear Friend:

Herewith I forward in Current Bills, $1100.

Check Suffolk Bank 300

" " " 300

" Bank of America Providence R.I. 114.75

$1714.75

For collection

Will you not oblige me by returning any Counterfeit bills I may happen to send you, without stamping them, as I have to trade them.

Respectfully,

C.C. Fellows Cashier

A very telling letter, November 10, 1864, from cashier C.C. Fellows to E.A. Presbrey, cashier of the National Bank of Mutual Redemption, Boston (successor to the Bank of Redemption), noting at the bottom:
"Will you not oblige me by returning any counterfeit bills I may happen to send you, without stamping them, as I have to trade them."

Fellows did as many other cashiers did: if a counterfeit came to hand, he passed it out again. If he inadvertently sent a counterfeit in to be redeemed, he wanted it back!

To the Hon. Comptroller of the Currency.

The undersigned, citizens of the town of Sandwich in the County of Carroll and State of New Hampshire, respectfully represent that the Carroll County Bank is located in said Sandwich and has been in successful operation for the past thirteen years, and has afforded important facilities to the business of said town and vicinity, which facilities are likely to be as much needed hereafter as heretofore, there being no other bank within a distance of twenty miles from said Carroll County Bank. The facilities are ample for doing banking business with a capital of $50,000.

The average circulation of the bills of said bank for the past year is $44,564 as per Bank Commissioners' Report.

M.H. Marston, president.
Isaac Adams, Joseph Wentworth, John M. Stevenson,
Augustine Blanchard, Enoch Q. Fellows, directors
Gilman Moulton, deputy sheriff
Wm. A. Bean, attorney at law
William A. Heard, merchant
Merritt Ambrose
Albert K. Kimball

On December 1, cashier C.C. Fellows wrote to Larkin D. Mason, a Tamworth, New Hampshire,

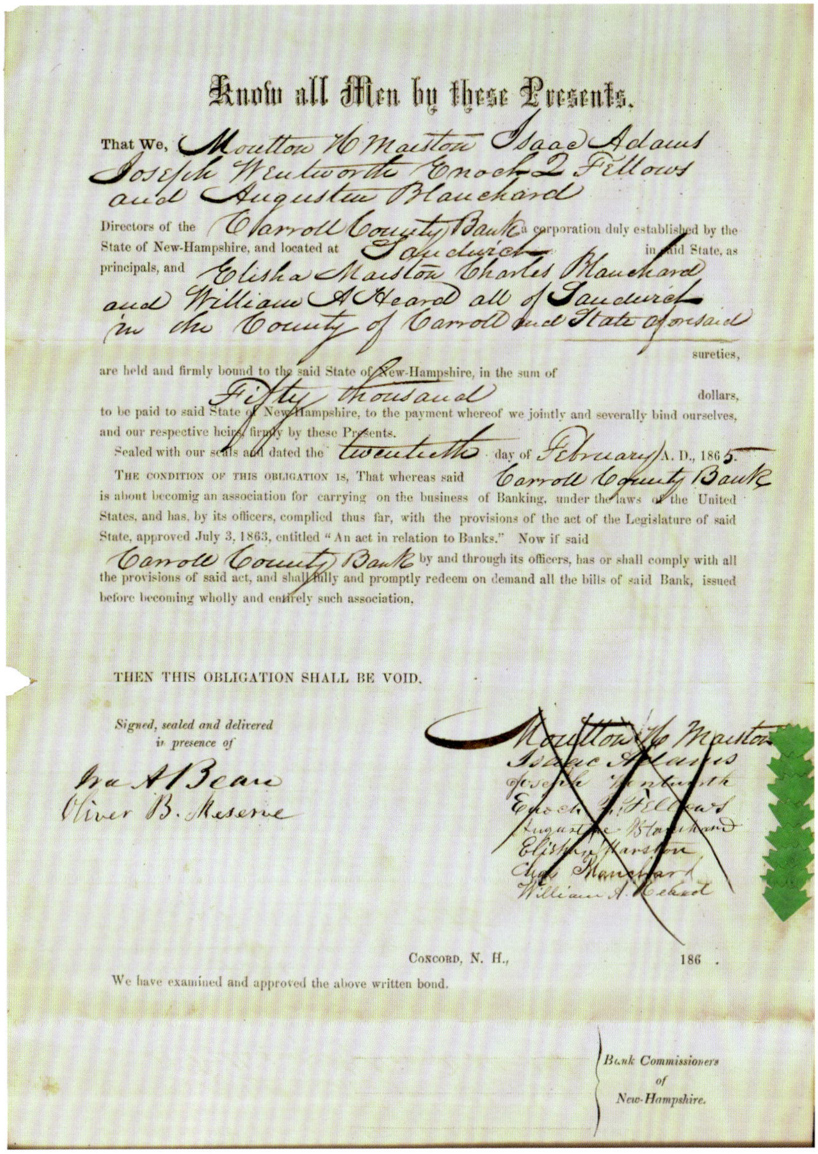

Know all Men by these Presents.

That We, Moulton H Marston Isaac Adams Joseph Wentworth Enoch L Fellows and Augustus Blanchard

Directors of the Carroll County Bank a corporation duly established by the State of New-Hampshire, and located at Sandwich in said State, as principals, and Elisha Marston Charles Blanchard and William A Heard all of Sandwich in the County of Carroll and State aforesaid sureties, are held and firmly bound to the said State of New-Hampshire, in the sum of Fifty thousand dollars, to be paid to said State of New-Hampshire, to the payment whereof we jointly and severally bind ourselves, and our respective heirs, firmly by these Presents.

Sealed with our seals and dated the twentieth day of February A. D., 1865.

THE CONDITION OF THIS OBLIGATION IS, That whereas said Carroll County Bank is about becomig an association for carrying on the business of Banking, under the laws of the United States, and has, by its officers, complied thus far, with the provisions of the act of the Legislature of said State, approved July 3, 1863, entitled "An act in relation to Banks." Now if said Carroll County Bank by and through its officers, has or shall comply with all the provisions of said act, and shall fully and promptly redeem on demand all the bills of said Bank, issued before becoming wholly and entirely such association,

THEN THIS OBLIGATION SHALL BE VOID.

Signed, sealed and delivered in presence of

Ira A Bean
Oliver B. Meserve

Moulton H Marston
Isaac Adams
Joseph Wentworth
Enoch L Fellows
Augustus Blanchard
Elisha Marston
Chas Blanchard
William A Heard

Concord, N. H., 186 .

We have examined and approved the above written bond.

Bank Commissioners of New-Hampshire.

Application of the Carroll County Bank to become a National Bank, February 20, 1865.

politician then residing in Washington, D.C., to encourage the influential Mason to help expedite the process:

> Dear Sir,
>
> We contemplate changing our bank into the Carroll County National Bank. We wrote to the Department and the Comptroller of the Currency required certain statements from us. A copy of said letter I herewith send you.
>
> I send a list of our Stockholders to you and also some statements relative to the wants and facilities of our place for banking business. I wish you to take the papers to the Comptroller and do the best you can for us. If they are not satisfied with you alone, please call on Mr. Craigan, to whom Wentworth has written, and he will assist you. You are acquainted with the most of our stockholders and can vouch for them.
>
> Respectfully yours,
>
> C.C. Fellows, Cashier

Relevant to the application, the latest report, November 1, 1864, listed these stockholders with 10 or more shares:

Moulton N. Marston (20 shares), Joseph Wentworth (20), Isaac Adams (40), Enoch Q. Fellows (20), Mary E. Fellows (10), Susan Jones (10), Samuel S. Weed (10), George W. Lang (10), Mary F. Porter (10), Margarette J. Morrill (10), Timothy Cook (15), Levi F. Smith (29), Elias Towle (16), Ebenezer Wilkinson (15), W.F. Ulman (20), and Alfred Ambrose (15)

On March 8, 1865, the cashier furnished this notarized statement of the condition of the bank:

Carroll County Bank
Center Sandwich, N.H.

March 8, 1865

I do hereby satisfy that the following is a true statement of the condition of the Carroll County Bank at this time.

Capital Stock paid in: $50,000

Present circulation: $48,000

Average circulation for the past year about $48,000

U.S. 5-20 Bonds now deposited at Washington par value $20,000

U.S. 6-81 Bonds now deposited at Washington par value $25,000

The market value of the above bonds is now about 10-1/2% above par

U.S. Compound interest notes on hand $2,590

Stock owned in the National Bank of Redemption, Boston $3,600. Notes on interest due from the state of New Hampshire $10,000. Notes on interest due from the County of Carroll $2,000. Notes on interest due from Town of Sandwich & other towns: $20,350. Notes on interest due from individuals $14,973.95

On the 2 day of January last the directors made a discount of 10 percent upon notes amounting to $36,450, which was carried to profit & loss account. The discount was made upon all notes which had been due more than 6 months, the most of which were town & state notes. That discount of $3,645 should be taken from the above gross amount of notes, although a part of the notes on which that discount was made have since been paid and I consider them all good.

C.C. Fellows, Cashier

In 1865 the bank converted to become the Carroll County National Bank of Sandwich, chartered on February 20. The last day of official banking business under the state charter was May 9, 1865. The cashier and president remained the same at the new bank, and business continued as usual, with Joseph Wentworth being the controlling stockholder.

The American Bank Note Company

Forming the Company

Aftereffects of the Panic of 1857

By early 1858, virtually all banks in America had experienced effects of the Panic of 1857. Many no longer existed, and others had portfolios heavy with loans of failed businesses, or for which payments were not being made on a timely basis. Accounting practices were quite different from what they would be a century later. For most banks, if a loan client was in great difficulty, or even defunct, the full face value of the loan was apt to remain on the books as a receivable. Often, it required the urging or threats of state bank commissioners to have bad debts recognized for their true nature. Because of this widespread practice, the balance sheets of even the stronger banks were apt to be somewhat optimistically crafted, not really indicative of the banks' assets or cash flow.[1]

The influx of currency printing orders from newly formed banks, a flood tide before the panic, slowed to a trickle. It was gloom and doom in and around Wall Street and the New York City financial district, the epicenter of the engraving and printing business.

Misery loves company, it is said, and there were talks of mergers and consolidations among the bank-note printers. In time, these rumors became reality, and plans were laid to create a new company that would virtually monopolize the bank-note business—that is, what was left of it.

Meetings in March 1858

Tracy Edson was the leading light in the formation of the company, assisted in the planning stages by Nathaniel Jocelyn and Moseley Danforth.[2] George D. Lyman, who would later patent a system of variable-size panels for different denominations of bank notes (see chapter 16), was secretary of the New York Clearing House at the time. His office served as a common meeting place for discussions, including in March 1858, when most details were finalized. Later, he received 20 shares of the new company, valued at $50 each, for his services. The American Bank Note Company name, used since 1854 by Jocelyn, Draper, Welsh & Co., was a natural choice for the new firm. April 19, 1858, was the official date of incorporation.

Edson arranged with Isaac Cary to contribute his 50% interest in the New England Bank Note Co. to the new firm in exchange for shares. The former Danforth, Wright & Co., as it had been known, was changed to Danforth, Perkins & Co. just before the merger, as certain of its partners elected not to become part of the American Bank Note Company (ABNCo). The partners of Toppan, Carpenter & Co. were permitted to retain their interest in a contract to print stamps for the United States Post Office. Otherwise, all assets of the seven firms, plus Cary's interest in the New England Bank Note Co., became the property of the new enterprise.

Ownership interest was divided among the seven companies as follows: Rawdon, Wright, Hatch & Edson, 23.9%; Toppan, Carpenter & Co., 22.4%; Danforth, Perkins & Co., 21.8%; Bald, Cousland & Co., 13.3%; Jocelyn, Draper, Welsh & Co., 8.4%; Wellstood, Hay & Whiting, 8.2%; and John E. Gavit, 2%. Some historians state that nine companies were actually involved by considering the New England Bank Note Co. (half owned by Rawdon, Wright, Hatch & Edson) and the two divisions of Jocelyn, Draper, Welsh & Co.

The articles of agreement of the new corporation contained restrictions on the sale or transfer of American Bank Note Company (ABNCo) shares. Any new partners seeking to join had to have the approval of four-fifths of the members. A board of trustees that was set up to supervise included Tracy R. Edson, Freeman Rawdon, Samuel H. Carpenter, Moseley I. Danforth, Edward J. Danforth, J. Dorsey Bald, Nathaniel Jocelyn, and William H. Whiting. Most of these were accomplished engravers.

The founding president was Charles Toppan, born in 1796 in Newburyport and a cousin twice removed of Jacob Perkins. Over the years he had been involved in many engraving partnerships, including Draper, Toppan, Longacre & Co., founded in 1835, with James B. Longacre, who later became chief engraver at the Philadelphia Mint. The creations of Toppan's firms were well known for their dramatic vignettes and crisp engravings. In 1860 he was succeeded in the post by Tracy R. Edson, who since 1858 had supervised much of the business.

Neziah Wright, of Rawdon, Wright, Hatch & Edson, took the office of treasurer in 1858 and remained in the position until he retired in April 1873.

The American Bank Note Company

On May 1, 1858, the American Bank Note Company was officially announced to the public. It was well received by the financial community and promised an end to the various engravers' partnerships, which seemed to evolve constantly. Here at last was a solid and seemingly permanent institution.

For several years after this, there was little competition within the industry. The small partnership of Edmonds, Jones & Smillie was merged into ABNCo in May 1858. Waterman L. Ormsby was not invited to join, and thus his New York Bank Note Co. remained in business on its own account. Certain members of the Danforth, Perkins & Co. partnership, and several others, joined forces in November 1859 to form the National Bank Note Company (an important firm of which more will be said later). However, in practice, the American Bank Note Company owned the lion's share of the business, probably at least 90% by January 1, 1860, although no figures are available to the modern researcher.

The Merchants Exchange, New York City, where the American Bank Note Company had its headquarters in the premises formerly occupied by Rawdon, Wright, Hatch & Edson.

Printing room at the American Bank Note Co. Bills were printed one sheet at a time on hand-operated spider presses. ("American Bank Note Company," *Harper's New Monthly Magazine,* February 1862)

Rawdon, Wright, Hatch & Edson

The lead partner, Rawdon, Wright, Hatch & Edson, owner of 23.9% of the new stock, was America's most successful bank-note engraving firm by the time it merged into the American Bank Note Co. The company had offices in New York City, Cincinnati, New Orleans, and Montreal, and from 1848 onward it had a half interest (with Isaac Cary having the other half) in the New England Bank Note Co. of Boston. The New England firm, founded in 1833, was the successor to the business of Jacob Perkins, which was moved to Boston from Newburyport. George Matthews, the Montreal representative of Rawdon, Wright, Hatch & Edson, also had an ownership interest. The New York office of Rawdon, Wright, Hatch & Edson occupied large premises in the Merchants Exchange. This became the home of ABNCo.

The firm traced its ancestry to Abner Reed (see chapter 5), who began engraving bills in the late 18th century and grew to prominence in the field. The company evolved into Rawdon, Wright & Hatch in 1832, with Freeman Rawdon, Neziah Wright, and George W. Hatch. With the addition of Tracy R. Edson, the name changed in 1835 to Rawdon, Wright, Hatch & Edson, a name it maintained with continuity at the New Orleans branch for more than two decades—remarkable longevity in a field in which some changes were made almost yearly. In December of 1835 it was in the Merchants Exchange when that and dozens of other commercial buildings were laid to waste by one of the largest fires ever to plague New York City. By 1858 the principals included the men in the company name plus James P. Major and Peter Hall.

The following were antecedents of Rawdon, Wright, Hatch & Edson:

1793 to 1798, Abner Reed—Apprentice to Isaac and George Hutton, Albany, New York, silversmiths.

Plate room at ABNCo, where small vignette plates as well as larger plates for full sheets were stored. ("American Bank Note Company," *Harper's New Monthly Magazine,* February 1862)

1798, Abner Reed—Engraver and copperplate printer. East Windsor, Connecticut.

1803 to 1821, Abner Reed—Designer and bank-note engraver. Hartford, Connecticut. These were glory years for Reed, who had a large shop (see chapter 5).

1821 to 1824, Reed & Stiles—Copperplate engravers and printers. Hartford, Connecticut. Abner Reed and Samuel Stiles.

1813 to 1815, Ralph Rawdon—Apprentice to Thomas Kensett, Cheshire, Connecticut.

1816, Ralph Rawdon—Engraver. Albany, New York.

1816, Willard & Rawdon—Bank-note engravers. Albany, New York. Asaph Willard and Ralph Rawdon.

1820, Rawdon & Balch—Engravers. Albany, New York, 55 State Street. Ralph Rawdon and Vistus Balch.

1827 to 1834, Rawdon, Clark & Co.—Albany, New York, 55 State Street. Ralph Rawdon (lived in New York City during 1828–1834) and Asabel Clark. N. & S.S. Jocelyn, New York and New Haven, used certain of this partnership's plates.

1828 to 1831, Rawdon, Wright & Co.—New York City, 35 Merchants Exchange. Ralph Rawdon and Neziah Wright.

(continued on p. 373)

Transfer press room at ABNCo, where copies of vignettes as well as bank-note plates were made by using steel cylinder dies (today known as *roller dies*) mounted in transfer presses. The process, known as *siderography*, required a high degree of skill. ("American Bank Note Company," *Harper's New Monthly Magazine,* February 1862)

Counting and packing room at ABNCo. Sheets of notes were counted and wrapped for shipping. Notes were not cut apart. ("American Bank Note Company," *Harper's New Monthly Magazine,* February 1862)

The old Merchants Exchange during the great fire of December 16, 1836. The equipment and effects of Rawdon, Wright, Hatch & Edson were destroyed in the conflagration.

(continued from p. 370)

1832 to 1834, Rawdon, Wright, Hatch & Co.—New York City, 35 Merchants Exchange. Ralph Rawdon (1832), Freeman Rawdon (1833 and 1834), Neziah Wright, George W. Hatch, Tracy R. Edson (1834), Albert G. Durand (1833 and 1834), Asher B. Durand (1833), and William C. Smillie (1833 and 1834).

1833 to 1858, New England Bank Note Co.—Formed from the Perkins business relocated from Newburyport to Boston. Abraham Perkins, Hazen Morse, and Nathaniel Perkins were partners in 1833. *1837 to 1848,* 204 Washington Street. Nathaniel Perkins (agent), W.S. Pendleton (1837), Isaac Cary (1845–1848), and J.H. Bufford (1847). *1848 to 1858,* Owned 50% by Isaac Cary and 50% by Rawdon, Wright, Hatch & Edson, New York. *1858,* Merged into ABNCo.

1835, Rawdon, Wright, Hatch & Edson—New York City, 35 Merchants Exchange. Freeman Rawdon, Neziah Wright, George W. Hatch, and Tracy R. Edson. Merchants Exchange burned December 1835; thereafter, Albany, New York, 55 State Street.

1836 to 1847, Rawdon, Wright & Hatch—New York City, 30 Wall Street (1836–1840); 48 Merchants Exchange (1840–1846). Ralph Rawdon (1841–1846), Freeman Rawdon (1842–1846), Neziah Wright, George W. Hatch, Tracy R. Edson (1836), John G. Wellstood (1840–1845), William H. Whiting (1839–1846), and James Parsons Major. *1843 to 1847,* Boston, 25 Merchants Exchange (1843–1846); 24 Merchants Exchange (1847). Timothy House (1845–1847), Timothy House Jr. (1847). *1842 to 1846,* Cincinnati, 3rd and Main streets. William F. Harrison, manager (1842–1843), George T. Jones (1843), George T. Jones, agent (1844).

1837 to 1858, Rawdon, Wright, Hatch & Edson—New Orleans beginning in 1837. Royal and Canal streets (1843–1850); 10 Royal Street (1851); 12 Royal Street, upstairs (1851–1858). Tracy R. Edson, partner and manager (1837–1847); Solomon Schmidt, engraver (1843–1850), engraver and agent (1851–1858). *1847 to 1858,* New York City, 48 Merchants Exchange. Freeman Rawdon, Neziah Wright, George W. Hatch, Tracy

(continued on p. 377)

Small sheet of vignettes by Rawdon, Wright, Hatch & Edson, from the 1850s.

Selected Notes From Rawdon, Wright, Hatch & Edson Antecedents

Reed & Styles $5 note for the Cheshire Bank of Keene, New Hampshire. Proof impression.

Chartered in 1803, this bank was among the earliest in the state. The opportunity to issue paper money beckoned, and at one point the ratio of bills in circulation to coins in the vault was an astounding 175 to 1. In the absence of either good banking procedures or legislative oversight, profits flowed in, and the bank declared an incredible 18% yearly dividend during this period. Then came reality, a state investigation, and closing in March 1811. Then, phoenixlike, the bank arose, and after rearranging its policies, reopened in November 1813. The bank wound up its affairs when its charter expired in 1843.

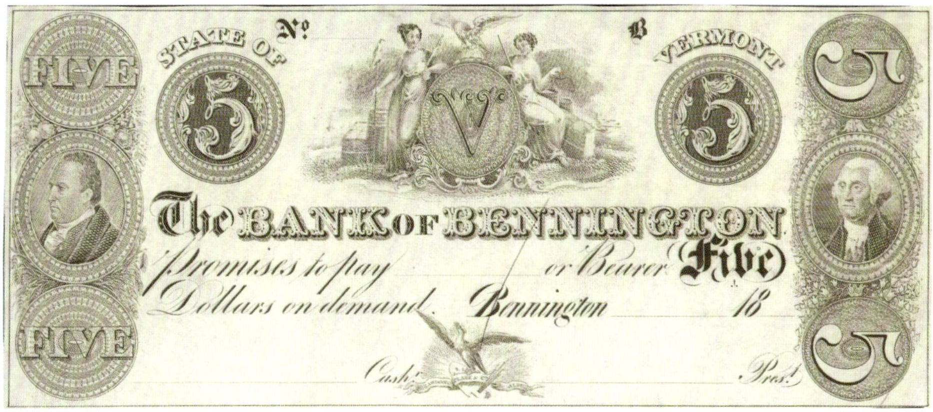

Rawdon, Clark & Co. $5 note for the Bank of Bennington, Vermont. Proof impression.

The Bank of Bennington was chartered in 1827. It failed in 1841, with a loss to note holders as this bank was not covered by the state safety fund. Early bills were by Rawdon, Clark & Co., Albany, New York, as here. Albany is a short distance from Bennington and is the nearest large city. Later bills bear the imprint of Rawdon, Wright, Hatch & Edson, New York.

Selected Notes From Rawdon, Wright, Hatch & Edson Antecedents

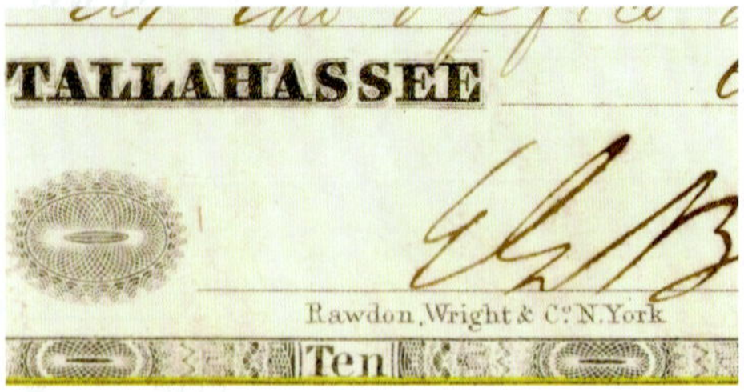

Rawdon, Wright & Co. $10 note for the Bank of Florida, Tallahassee, August 1, 1843, signed and numbered in ink.

This bank was chartered in 1828 and rechartered in 1845. In 1843 the state made shareholders liable for three times the par value of their stock. In case of suspension of specie payments, the directors were liable to indictment, and if convicted, were subject to a $20,000 fine and imprisonment for five years. Two years later another draconian law made stockholders individually liable for *all* debts in case the bank failed to redeem its notes or was dissolved.

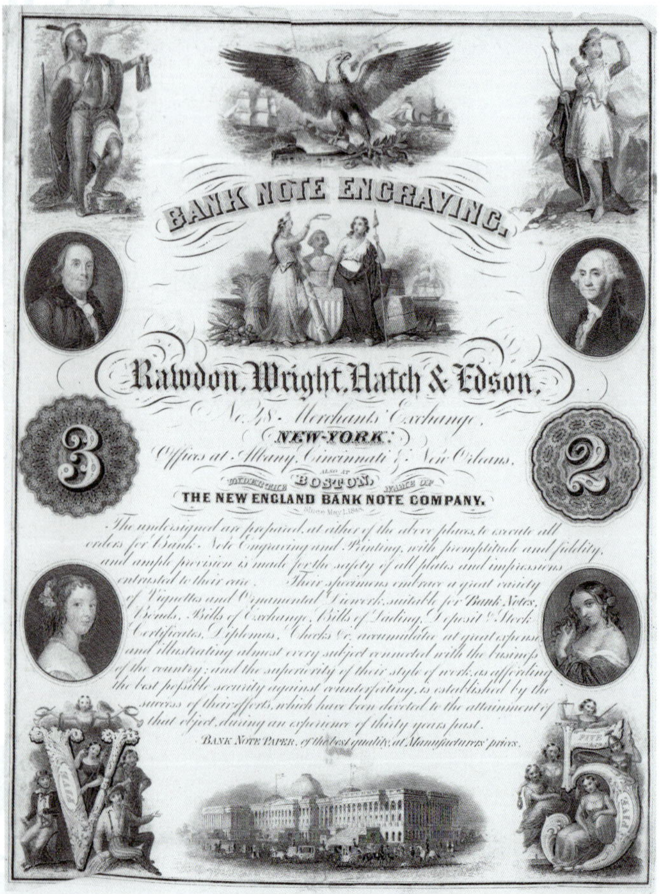

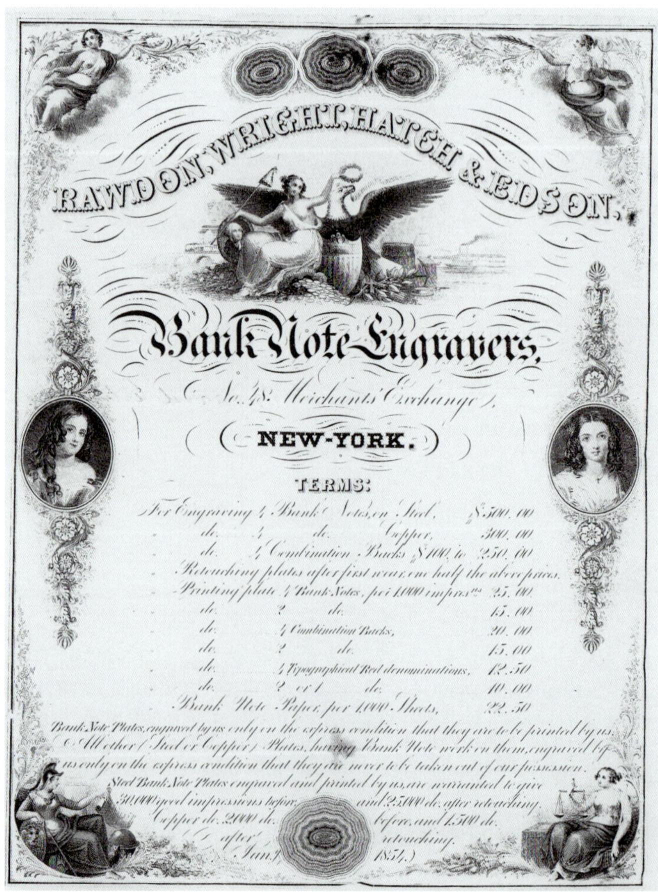

Rawdon, Wright, Hatch & Edson advertising sheet, face and back, of the mid-1850s.

(continued from p. 373)

R. Edson, James P. Major, and Peter Hall. In 1847 Edson, who had proved himself to be a highly efficient businessman, was put in charge of RWH&E. *1853 to 1858,* Cincinnati, 148 Main Street. George T. Jones (agent) and Thomas F. Harrison. *1849 to 1857,* Boston, 24 Merchants Exchange. *To 1858,* Montreal, Canada. George Matthews.

1842, Rawdon, Wright, Hatch & Smillie—Pictorial engravers. New York City, 48 Merchants Exchange. Ralph Rawdon, Freeman Rawdon, Neziah Wright, James Smillie, and others on the staff of Rawdon, Wright & Hatch.

1858, ABNCo.—Merger of Rawdon, Wright, Hatch & Edson with the New England Bank Note Co.

Toppan, Carpenter & Co.

Toppan, Carpenter & Co., with 22.4% of the new stock, was next in importance, with its partners gaining an equity interest nearly that of Rawdon, Wright, Hatch & Edson. It too was widespread in office locations with facilities in New York City, Philadelphia, Boston, and Cincinnati. Charles Toppan became the president of American Bank Note Co. In the meantime, the entity of Toppan, Carpenter & Co. was maintained to fulfill certain contracts in place with the United States Post Office to print stamps.

The tradition of the company was long and illustrious, with most activities centered in Philadelphia until about 1835, when a branch was opened in New York City at the popular address of 1 Wall Street. By the time of the merger in 1858, Toppan, Carpenter & Co. had its New York office at 111 Broadway, where the principals included Charles Toppan, Samuel H. Carpenter, William C. Smillie, James Smillie, Charles T. Carpenter, Samuel H. Carpenter Jr., Henry E. Saulnier, and Paul S. Casilear.

The following lists describe the seven firms that merged in 1858 and their antecedents. This information will bring into focus many of the engravers and illustrations of their bank notes presented in this book. Dates are mostly from directory listings and are not precise.

The following were antecedents of Toppan, Carpenter & Co:

1819 to 1823, Charles Toppan—London, England.

1829, Charles Toppan—Engraver and printer. Philadelphia, 28 Sansom Street.

1830 to 1834, Charles Toppan & Co.—Philadelphia, 28 Sansom Street.

1830 and 1831, Toppan, Maverick & Co.—Charles Toppan and Peter Maverick (died on June 7, 1831).

1833, Draper, Toppan, Longacre & Bull—Philadelphia. John Draper, Charles Toppan, James B. Longacre, and Marcus Bull.

1835 to 1839, Draper, Toppan, Longacre & Co.—John Draper, Charles Toppan, and James B. Longacre. Philadelphia, 60 Walnut Street; New York City, 1 Wall Street.

1839 to 1844, Draper, Toppan & Co.—John Draper (resigned 1844), Charles Toppan, Simeon Smith Jocelyn (1840–1844), Peter H. Draper (1843–1844), William Cumming Smillie (1840–1844), and Charles Harrison (1840–1841). *Philadelphia,* 60 Walnut Street (1839); 103 Locust Street (1840); 5 Bank Place (1840–1842); 76-1/2 Walnut Street (1843 and 1844). *New York City,* 1 Wall Street (1839–1842); 16 Wall Street (1842–1844). *Boston,* 60 State Street (1843). John Draper, Charles Toppan, and Samuel B. Carpenter.

1844 to 1850, Toppan, Carpenter & Co.—Philadelphia, 76-1/2 Walnut Street. Charles Toppan, Samuel H. Carpenter, Simeon Smith Jocelyn, Nathaniel Jocelyn (1849 and 1850), Henry E. Saulnier, and William Cumming Smillie. *New York City,* 16 Wall Street (1844 and 1845); 31 Wall Street (1845–1847); 29 Wall Street (1848–1850). *Boston,* 60 State Street (1844); 24 Merchants Exchange (1845); 66 State Street (1846–1850).

1850 to 1855, Toppan, Carpenter, Casilear & Co.—Philadelphia, 76-1/2 Walnut Street. Charles Toppan, Samuel H. Carpenter, John W. Casilear (1850–July 1855), Simeon Smith Jocelyn (1850–1853), Nathaniel Jocelyn (1850–1854), Simeon Starr Jocelyn (1850–1854), Henry E. Saulnier, William Cumming Smillie, James Smillie, William Main Smillie (1853–1855), and Francis A. Casilear (1853–1854). *New York City,* 29 Wall Street (1850 and 1851); 111 Broadway (1851–1855). *Boston,* 68 State Street (1852–1855). *Cincinnati,* 119 Walnut Street (1853–1855). Charles A. Jewett, agent. *Montreal, Canada,* Great St. James Street.

1855 to 1858, Toppan, Carpenter & Co.—New York City, 111 Broadway. Charles Toppan, Samuel H. Carpenter, William C. Smillie, James Smillie,

Selected Notes From Toppan, Carpenter & Co. Antecedents

Charles Toppan & Co. $5 note for the Bank of Louisville, Kentucky, payable at the Bank of North America in Philadelphia. Proof impression from the American Bank Note Co. archives.

Historian John Jay Knox wrote, "In the session of 1833–34 charters were granted to three banks—a new Bank of Kentucky with a capital of $5,000,000, the Northern Bank of Kentucky with a capital of $3,000,000, and the Bank of Louisville with a capital of $5,000,000—$13,000,000 possible capital in all, although the actual aggregate paid in capital never exceeded $9,030,000."

Toppan, Carpenter & Co., Boston office, $2 note for the New England Bank, Boston.

The New England Bank in 1814 set up a program to redeem bills of various other banks in the New England states, a precursor of the Suffolk Bank system but not ultimately successful. In early 1836 the bank's officers were the subject of an official investigating committee that found that it and certain other banks had "transcended the limits of their charters" in certain activities in the exchange of paper, along with other matters. However, the matter was soon forgotten. The bank, located at 67 State Street, Boston, converted in 1864 to become the New England National Bank of Boston, charter 603.

Toppan, Carpenter & Co., Cincinnati office, $5 note for the Bank of Kentucky in Louisville. Proof impression from the American Bank Note Co. archives. The transfer agent for this bank was the Schuylkill Bank of Philadelphia. It was learned in 1839 that the agent commissioned the printing and then issued $1,250,000 of spurious stock of the Bank of Kentucky. The matter went to court, where it dragged out for a long time. Finally, a judgment of $1,343,000 was obtained.

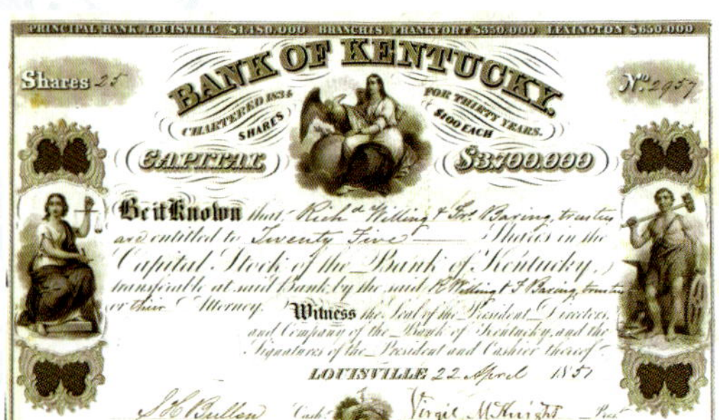

Toppan, Carpenter & Co. stock certificate for the Bank of Kentucky in Louisville. Ink dated April 22, 1851. As a general rule, banks ordered certificates from the various bank-note engraving companies and kept them on hand for years afterward, using them as needed.

Charles T. Carpenter, Samuel H. Carpenter Jr., Henry E. Saulnier, and Paul S. Casilear (1856–1858). Philadelphia, 760 Walnut Street. *Cincinnati,* 119 Walnut Street (1855–1858). Charles A. Jewett, agent (1855–1856), E.C. Middleton, agent (1857), and Charles Toppan (1858, lived in Philadelphia). *Boston,* 20 State Street (1856 and 1857).

DANFORTH, PERKINS & CO.

Some of the principals of Danforth, Perkins & Co. signed on as shareholders, gaining an impressive 21.8% of the stock, while others declined to join. The company was widely spread and had its main office in New York with branches in Philadelphia, Boston, and Cincinnati.

No firm had a finer tradition, this partnership tracing its origin back to Jacob Perkins, the genius inventor and engraver of Newburyport, Massachusetts, sharing with the unrelated New England Bank Note Co. this distinction. By 1858 the principals were Moseley I. Danforth, Edward J. Danforth, and Henry Perkins.

The following were antecedents of Danforth, Perkins & Co.:

1790s to 1819, Jacob Perkins—Engraver, of Newburyport, Massachusetts; later located in Boston, then Philadelphia, after which he spent the rest of his life in England.

1803, Gideon Fairman—Engraver and artist. Newburyport, Massachusetts. In Albany by 1811, then in Philadelphia beginning the same year.

1800 to 1809, William Carr—Engraver. Philadelphia, 118 South Front Street, 87 South 2nd Street.

1801 to 1806, John Draper—Engraver. Philadelphia, 87 South Front Street in 1804; 446 North 2nd Street in 1804.

1809 to 1810, Carr & Draper—Copperplate engravers and printers. Philadelphia, 3 Norris Place. William Carr and John Draper.

1807, George Murray—Engraver. Philadelphia, 398 Race Street.

1810, Murray & Draper—Book-plate and bank-note engravers. Philadelphia. George Murray and John Draper.

1811 to 1818, Murray, Draper, Fairman & Co.—Philadelphia, 47 Sansom Street. George Murray, John Draper, Gideon Fairman, and Jacob Perkins. This was one of the largest and most important bank-note engraving partnerships of its era.

1815 to 1818, Asa Spencer and Charles Toppan.

1819, Asa Spencer—Newburyport, Massachusetts. Spencer improved the medal-ruling machine invented by Christian Gobrecht in 1817. *London, England* (1819–1823).

1818 to 1822, Murray, Fairman & Co.—Philadelphia. 47 Sansom Street. Commenced in July 1818. George Murray died on July 2, 1822. Gideon Fairman was overseas in 1822.

1823, Fairman, Draper & Co.—Engravers. Philadelphia, 45–47 George Street.

1825 to 1833, Asa Spencer—Engraver. Philadelphia, 43 Zane Street (1825–1832); 50 George Street (1833).

1823 to 1827, Fairman, Draper, Underwood & Co.—Philadelphia, 47 Sansom Street. Gideon Fairman, John Draper, and Thomas Underwood. This was one of the most important companies of its time.

1828 to 1833, Draper, Underwood & Co.—Philadelphia, 47 Sansom Street. John Draper and Thomas Underwood.

1833 to 1835, Draper, Underwood, Bald & Spencer—Philadelphia, 47 Sansom Street. John Draper, Thomas Underwood, Robert Bald, and Asa Spencer. This was a very important firm. Christian Gobrecht engraved many vignettes for the company. *New York City,* 14 Wall Street, N. and S.S. Jocelyn, agents.

1835 to 1837, Underwood, Bald & Spencer—Philadelphia, 47 Sansom Street. Thomas Underwood, Robert Bald, and Asa Spencer. *New York City,* 14 Wall Street, N. and S.S. Jocelyn, agents.

1837 to 1843, Underwood, Bald, Spencer & Hufty—Philadelphia, Exchange Building. Established in July 1837. Thomas Underwood, Robert Bald, Asa Spencer, Samuel Hufty, and Samuel Stiles. *New York City,* 14 Wall Street (1837–1849), N. and S.S. Jocelyn, agents.

1839 to 1843, Danforth, Underwood & Co.—New York City, 14 Wall Street. *1839 and 1840,* N. and S.S. Jocelyn were agents. *1840 and 1841,* Moseley I. Danforth, Thomas Underwood, and Charles C.

Selected Notes From Danforth, Perkins & Co. Antecedents

Draper, Underwood, Bald & Spencer $5 note for the New Hampshire Bank at Portsmouth.

The New Hampshire Bank at Portsmouth, as it was titled, was chartered January 3, 1792, by the state. Its projectors had powerful political connections, effectively preventing any other banks from being chartered in New Hampshire until the next decade. In 1819 the cashier could not account for $72,000 in funds and nearly wrecked the bank. The New Hampshire Bank at Portsmouth suffered during the Panic of 1837 as did other institutions in the state. Its business diminished, and it was closed in 1842 at the expiration of its charter.

Underwood, Bald & Spencer $5 note for the Mechanics Bank of Augusta, Georgia, signed in ink and dated October 1, 1856.

This bank, with a capital of $500,000, was profitable and a mainstay to the city. At the time this bill was issued, the cashier was Milo Hatch, who took that post in June 1849, and the president was Thomas S. Metcalf. That duo continued the bank's management into the Civil War era. Metcalf did not sign this note, and in his stead the signature of I.B. Bishop was used "for" the president. This is unusual, as typically other signers were vice presidents and indicated such.

Danforth, Spencer & Hufty $5 note for the State Bank of Ohio, Columbus. There is space for the name of a branch to be added.

The State Bank of Ohio was incorporated in February 1845 with a capital of $6,150,000, plus additional capital of five banks later provided for by legislation. The 80 counties in the state (today there are 88) were divided into 12 districts, with each assigned a specific capital, which ranged from $300,000 to $1,200,000. One district had just three banks and another had 11, with a total of 61 branches provided for.

In the Panic of 1857, ignited by the failure of the Ohio Life Insurance and Trust Co., the State Bank of Ohio had so much money tied up with that company that for a time brokers refused to receive Ohio notes. Fortunately for the branches of the State Bank, two members of the Ohio Board of Control were in New York City at the time of the failure and were able to quickly obtain a contract from the cashier, setting aside assets of the Ohio institution.

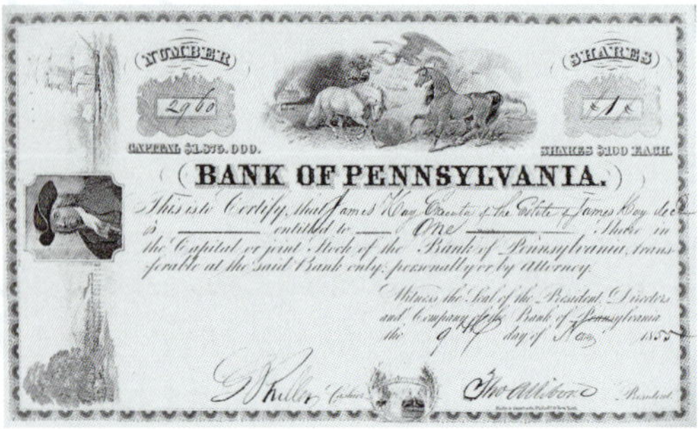

Hufty & Danforth stock certificate for the Bank of Pennsylvania, ink dated November 9, 1855, but printed a few years earlier.

The Bank of Pennsylvania, chartered in 1793 as one of the nation's earliest financial institutions, remained in business until its failure in 1857. Benjamin Latrobe designed its headquarters, which were started in 1798 and completed in 1800. It issued paper money over a long period of time, such bearing the imprints of different engravers.

Wright. *1841 to 1843,* Samuel Stiles. Charles Cushing Wright was an especially talented engraver and today is considered to be the leading medalist of the second decade of the 19th century.

1843 and 1844, Bald, Spencer, Hufty & Danforth—Philadelphia, Exchange Building.

1843 and 1844, Danforth, Spencer & Hufty—New York City, 34 Wall Street (1844 and 1845); 1 Wall Street (1845–1847). Moseley I. Danforth, Robert Bald, Asa Spencer, Samuel Hufty, Samuel Stiles, and Alfred Sealey.

1844 to 1847, Bald, Spencer, Hufty & Danforth—Philadelphia, Exchange Building.

1844 to 1847, Danforth, Spencer & Hufty—New York City, 34 Wall Street. Moseley I. Danforth, Asa Spencer, Samuel Hufty, Samuel Stiles, and Alfred Sealey.

1847 to 1850, Hufty, Danforth & Co.—Philadelphia, 95-1/2 Walnut Street. Some imprints as Hufty & Danforth with both Philadelphia and New York addresses.

1847 to 1850, Danforth, Hufty & Co.—New York City, 1 Wall Street. Moseley I. Danforth, Samuel Hufty, Samuel Stiles, Alfred Sealey, and Fitch Shepard, 1849 and 1850.

1850 to 1852, Danforth, Bald & Co.—Philadelphia, 950 Walnut Street; *New York City,* 1 Wall Street. Moseley I. Danforth, Edward J. Danforth, Nicholas D. Danforth, Samuel Stiles, Robert L. Bald (resigned 1852), Alfred Sealey, Fitch Shepard, James McDonough (1851 and 1852), and Cyrus Durand (1851–1852). *Boston,* 78 State Street (1851 and 1852); 228 Washington Street (1851). David Russell (1851), S.A. Schoff, Henry Kurtz, and Lloyd Glover (1852). *Cincinnati, Ohio,* 38 West 4th Street (1851–1852). Samuel B. Munson and James E. Smith.

1853, Danforth, Wright & Co.—New York City, 1 Wall Street. Moseley I. Danforth, Edward J. Danforth, Nicholas D. Danforth, Henry Perkins, James McDonough, Samuel Stiles, Cyrus Durand, Fitch Shepard, William D. Nichols, James Wright, Frederick Girsch (1855–1856), and Charles Harrison (1855–1858). *Philadelphia,* Exchange Building, 3rd and Walnut streets. *Boston,* 228 Washington Street. Lloyd Glover (1853–1854), D.L. Glover (1853), S.A. Schoff (1853), and A.C. Warren (1854). *Cincinnati,* 25 West 3rd Street (1853); 3rd and Walnut streets (1854–1858). Samuel B. Munson (1853–1855), Samuel B. Munson, agent (1856–1858), and Charles A. Jewett (1853–1857).

1858, Danforth, Perkins & Co.—Formed in March 1858 and merged into ABNCo on April 19, 1858, by March the firm had lost certain of its partners. *New York City,* 1 Wall Street. Moseley I. Danforth, Edward J. Danforth, and Henry Perkins. *Philadelphia,* Exchange Building. *Boston,* 228 Washington Street. *Cincinnati,* 3rd and Walnut streets.

Bald, Cousland & Co.

Bald, Cousland & Co., with 13.3% stock interest, had offices in New York and Philadelphia. Over a period of time both offices, each with a slightly different trade style, double-imprinted many notes, as Bald, Adams & Co., New York City, and on the same notes, Bald, Cousland & Co., Philadelphia. This firm was also laden with tradition, with the past including such luminaries as Peter Maverick, Asher B. Durand, and Charles Cushing Wright.

Today, Durand is remembered as one of America's greatest painters of the early 19th century and less so as a bank-note engraver, although his work in the latter field is unsurpassed. Charles Cushing Wright was the foremost medalist in the country in the second decade of the 19th century. Today, the currency of this firm is admired for its especially high level of artistry.

The following were antecedents of Bald, Cousland & Co.:

1802 to 1817, Peter Maverick—Engraver and copperplate printer. New York City, Nassau Street, Duane Street, Walker and Liberty streets.

1817 to 1820, P. Maverick, Durand & Co.—New York City, 2 Pine Street. Peter Maverick and Asher B. Durand.

1821 to 1822, Asher B. Durand—Engraver. New York City, 27 Provost Street.

1823 to 1824, Durand & Wright—New York City, 8 Varick Street. Cyrus Durand and Charles C. Wright.

1824 to 1828, A.B. & C. Durand, Wright & Co.—New York City, 8 Varick Street (1824–1826); 50 Wall Street (1827). Asher B. Durand, Cyrus Durand, Charles C. Wright, Joseph Perkins, and George W. Hatch (1827 and 1828).

Selected Notes From Bald, Cousland & Co. Antecedents

Durand, Perkins & Co. $10 note for the Bank of Burlington, Vermont.

The charter of this bank became effective on November 1, 1818, one of two new banks that year—the first since the star-crossed Vermont State Bank (discussed in chapter 3). During the Jackson administration this was a *pet bank.* The institution enjoyed a long career, and in 1865 it was succeeded by the First National Bank of Burlington, charter 861.

Casilear, Durand, Burton & Edmonds $50 note for the Bank of Kentucky, Louisville.

This bank operated for many years until 1865. In June 1852, *Banker's Magazine* reported on a theft from the Rawdon, Wright, Hatch & Edson branch office: "The *Louisville Courier* of June 3rd states that the genuine plates of this bank, of the denomination of tens, have recently been stolen, and a large batch of new notes printed. Of course they will be put in circulation. The theft was managed so adroitly that no clue can be obtained to its discovery, or to lead to the detection of the perpetrator. The plates were stolen from the engraver in Cincinnati."

Baldwin, Bald & Cousland $10 for the Bank of Greensborough, Georgia. The vignette depicts Zoe (so identified in microscopic letters) under a palmetto tree.

This bank had its ups and downs. In early 1857, before the Panic, articles in various Georgia newspapers stated that the bank and its bills were of questionable credit. Somehow the bank, with a modest capital of $50,000, survived and continued business into the Civil War era.

1828 to 1832, Durand, Perkins & Co.—New York City, 50 Wall Street. Asher B. Durand, Cyrus Durand, Joseph Perkins, Elias Wade Jr., George W. Hatch (1828–1830). In 1832 this partnership was liquidated. Its plates became widely scattered, accounting for their use in later years by several firms. Certain equipment went to Rawdon, Wright, Hatch & Co.

1833 to 1835, C.C. Wright & Durand—New York City, 45 Maiden Lane. Charles C. Wright and Cyrus Durand.

1834 to 1835, Casilear, Durand & Co.—New York City, 53 William Street. John W. Casilear, Theodore Durand, James R. Burton, and William Edmonds.

1835 to 1837, Casilear, Durand, Burton & Edmonds—New York City, 50 Wall Street. John W. Casilear, Theodore Durand, James R. Burton, William Edmonds, William C. Smillie (1836 and 1837), and Albert G. Durand (1835–1837).

1837 and 1838, Burton, Gurley & Edmonds—New York City, 26 Wall Street. James R. Burton, Royal Gurley, and William Edmonds.

1838 and 1839, Burton & Gurley—New York City, 20 Wall Street. James R. Burton and Royal Gurley.

1839 to 1842, Durand & Co.—New York City, 26 Wall Street (1839–1841); 115 Merchants Exchange (1842). Cyrus Durand and others. The partnership was dissolved and its properties scattered.

1840, Woodruff & Hammond—Cincinnati, corner of 4th and Main streets. William Woodruff (resided in Pennsylvania.) and John T. Hammond (resided in New York).

1842, Durand, Hammond & Mason—Cincinnati, corner of 4th and Main streets. Albert G. Durand, John T. Hammond, and Daniel Mason.

1847 and 1848, George D. Baldwin—Copperplate printer. New York City, 35 Spruce Street.

1848–1850, Durand, Baldwin & Co.—New York City, 40 Wall Street. Cyrus Durand, Albert G. Durand, and George D. Baldwin.

1851 to 1854, Baldwin, Adams & Co.—New York City. George D. Baldwin and William H. Adams.

1853, Robert L. Bald & Co.—Philadelphia, 95 Chestnut Street. Robert L. Bald (died on July 20, 1853) and J. Dorsey Bald.

1854, Bald, Adams & Co.—Philadelphia. J. Dorsey Bald and William H. Adams. Certain of their bills were also imprinted Bald, Cousland & Co., Philadelphia.

1854 to 1857, Baldwin, Bald & Cousland—New York City, 40 Wall Street (1854–1855); 9 Nassau Street (1856 and 1857). George D. Baldwin, J. Dorsey Bald, William Cousland, and David R. Harrison (1855–1857).

1858, Bald, Cousland & Co.—New York City, 9 Nassau Street. J. Dorsey Bald, William Cousland, and David R. Harrison. *Philadelphia,* 74 Walnut Street (1854–1857); 326 Walnut Street (1858). J. Dorsey Bald, William Cousland, Frederick E. Bliss, Edward A. Moss, and Albert G. Goodall.

JOCELYN, DRAPER, WELSH & CO.
AMERICAN BANK NOTE CO.
DRAPER, WELSH & CO.

Jocelyn, Draper, Welsh & Co., of New York City, already trading as the American Bank Note Co., had an 8.4% share in the new partnership with the same name, or about a third as much as the main owners. Draper, Welsh & Co. was located in Philadelphia. Charles Welsh later worked as an engraver at the Philadelphia office of the firm. The Jocelyn family was well known in the profession, tracing its prominence in the profession to the turn of the century. Amos Doolittle, famous engraver of maps, bank notes, and other items, was also important as an antecedent.

In 1858 the firm was at 7 Wall Street. Principals included Nathaniel Jocelyn, Simeon Starr Jocelyn, Robert Draper, Charles Welsh, and Alfred Sealey.

The following were antecedents of Jocelyn, Draper, Welsh & Co.

1775, Amos Doolittle—Copperplate engraver. New Haven, Connecticut.

1782, Jocelin & Doolittle—Copperplate printers. New Haven, Connecticut. Nathaniel Jocelin and Amos Doolittle.

1800, Amos Doolittle—Bank-note engraver. New Haven, Connecticut.

1815, Nathaniel Jocelin—Bank-note engraver. New Haven, Connecticut.

Selected Notes From Jocelyn, Draper, Welsh & Co. Antecedents

Graphic Co. $2 note for the Phoenix Bank of Hartford, Connecticut.

The bank was set up in 1814 by prominent Episcopalians in Hartford, who felt that the Hartford Bank, in operation and quite successful, was controlled by the Congregational Church. In final form the capital was set at $1,000,000. Across the years, many anecdotes and stories were printed about the bank, including one of a cache of $270 in $10 bills hidden in West Springfield, Massachusetts, in 1827 and not found until November 1845. On January 1, 1865, the Phoenix Bank of Hartford became the Phoenix National Bank of Hartford.

N. & S.S. Jocelyn $1 note of the Hamilton and Rossville Manufacturing Co., Hamilton, Ohio, a "pure fraud," according to historian Wendell Wolka.

Many factories, railroads, canals, and other entities that were not banks issued paper money. Generally, such issues had little value outside of the area in which they were issued and were not desired by distant banks or exchange brokers.

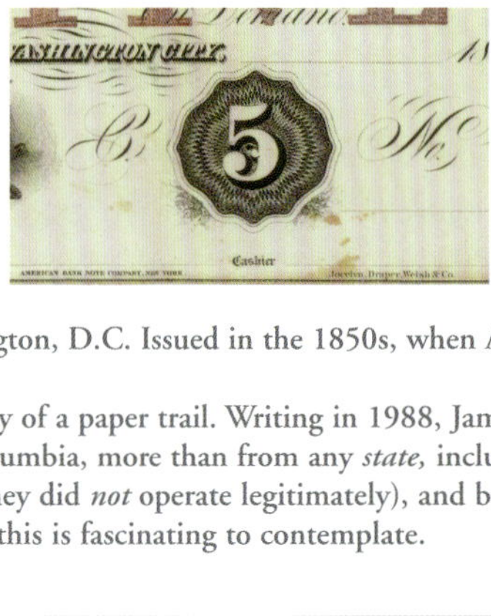

American Bank Note Co. / Jocelyn, Draper, Welsh & Co. $5 note for the Congressional Bank, Washington, D.C. Issued in the 1850s, when American Bank Note Co. was a trade style of this partnership.

Whatever the Congressional Bank of Washington City did do or did not do, it left little in the way of a paper trail. Writing in 1988, James A. Haxby called this bank "fraudulent or non-existent." Whatever the case, paper money from the District of Columbia, more than from any *state,* includes mystery notes—fraudulent issues, banks that operated legitimately but without benefit of charter (or perhaps they did *not* operate legitimately), and banks whose charters were not renewed because of the inattention of Congress, but kept issuing bills anyway. All of this is fascinating to contemplate.

1815, Jocelin & Munger—Engravers and printers. New Haven, Connecticut, Nathaniel Jocelin, George Munger, and Simeon Smith Jocelin. (The Jocelins soon changed the spelling of their surname to *Jocelyn.*)

1817 and 1818, Hartford Graphic & Engraving Co.—Sometimes imprinted as Graphic Co. Hartford. Elkanah Tisdale, Moseley I. Danforth, Asaph Willard, Nathaniel Jocelyn, and Abel Brewster.

1817 to 1841, N. & S.S. Jocelyn—Publishers and engravers. New Haven, Connecticut. Glebe Building (1818); Bradley Building (1819). Nathaniel Jocelyn and Simeon Smith Jocelyn.

1819, Jocelyn & Goldsmith—Engravers and printers. New Haven, Connecticut. Nathaniel Jocelyn, Simeon Smith Jocelyn, and A.B. Goldsmith.

1819, Jocelyn & Doolittle—Engravers and printers. New Haven, Connecticut. Nathaniel Jocelyn, Simeon Smith Jocelyn, and Curtis M. Doolittle.

1819, Nathaniel Jocelyn—Engraver. New Haven, Connecticut. Affiliated with Murray, Fairman & Co., Philadelphia.

1822 to 1823, N. & S.S. Jocelyn—Savannah, Georgia (branch). Nathaniel Jocelyn (artist).

1830, Jocelyn & Munson—Engravers and printers. New Haven, Connecticut. Simeon Smith Jocelyn and Samuel B. Munson.

1831 to 1834, Jocelyn, Darling & Co.—Engravers and printers. New York City, 36 Wall Street (1831); 31 Merchants Exchange (1832–1834). Simeon Smith Jocelyn and Charles Darling.

1833 to 1841, N. & S.S. Jocelyn—New York City, 14 Wall Street (branch). Nathaniel Jocelyn and Simeon Smith Jocelyn. Certain plates of Rawdon, Clark & Co., Albany, New York, were used by the firm. In 1841 they also had a connection with Draper, Underwood, Bald & Spencer, continuing to successive partnerships.

1841 to 1845, Charles Welsh—Engraver. Philadelphia, 191 Christian Street.

1844, Welsh & Walter—Bank-note engravers and printers. Philadelphia, 98 Chestnut Street. Charles Welsh, A.B. Walter, and Joseph Walter.

1845 to 1850, Draper & Co.—Philadelphia, 60 Walnut Street. John Draper, Robert Draper, and William Draper.

1851 to 1854, Draper, Welsh & Co.—Philadelphia, 220 Merchants Exchange. John Draper (resigned in 1853), Robert Draper, and Charles Welsh.

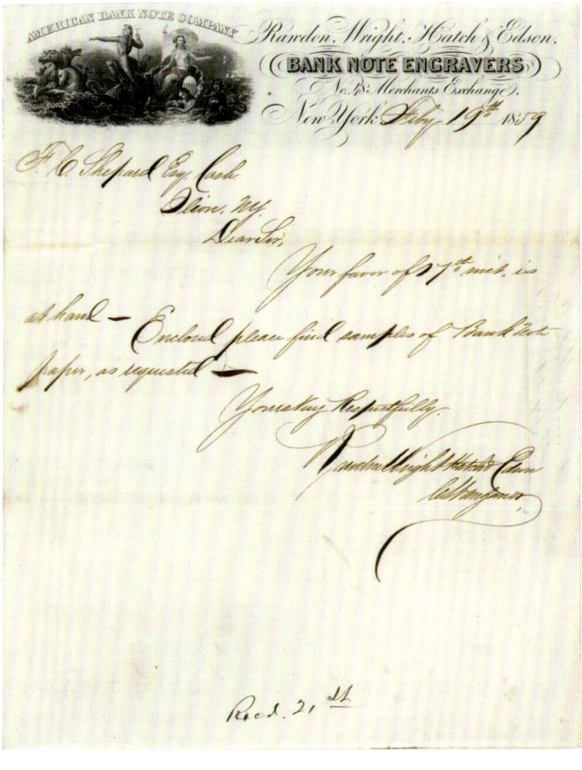

AMERICAN BANK NOTE COMPANY
Rawdon, Wright, Hatch & Edson.
BANK NOTE ENGRAVERS
No. 48 Merchants Exchange
New York Feby 19th 1859

F.C. Shepard Esq. Cash
Ilion, N.Y.
Dear Sir,
Your favor of 17th inst. is at hand — Enclosed please find samples of Bank Note paper, as requested —
Yours truly Respectfully
Rawdon Wright Hatch & Edson

Recd. 21st

Detail of letterhead vignette.

Letter from American Bank Note Co. to F.C. Shepherd, cashier of the Ilion (New York) Bank, February 19, 1859. The letterhead, formerly used by Rawdon, Wright, Hatch & Edson, has been modified by adding American Bank Note Company above the vignette. Otherwise, all features are the same. The note is signed on behalf of Rawdon, Wright, Hatch & Edson. Although seven companies had merged to form ABNCo, they often maintained their old identities when corresponding with customers.

1854 to 1858, Draper, Welsh & Co.—Philadelphia, 220 Merchants Exchange. Robert Draper, Charles Welsh, Nathaniel Jocelyn, and Simeon Starr Jocelyn.

1854 to 1858, American Bank Note Co. / Jocelyn, Draper, Welsh & Co.—New York City, 7 Wall Street. Nathaniel Jocelyn, Simeon Starr Jocelyn, Robert Draper, Charles Welsh, and Alfred Sealey (1856).

Wellstood, Hay & Whiting

Wellstood, Hay & Whiting, with 8.2% ownership interest in ABNCo, was about equal to Jocelyn, Draper, Welsh & Co. in this regard. Offices were maintained in New York City, Boston, and Chicago. John G. Wellstood was well known in the trade, and partners DeWitt Clinton Hay and William H. Whiting were likewise talented. The firm and was admired for its splendid vignettes, some being of nearly panoramic nature.

The following were antecedents of Wellstood, Hay & Whiting:

1836 to 1846, John G. Wellstood—Engraver. New York City, 20 Bedford Street (1836–1840); 48 Merchants Exchange (1840–1846).

1836 to 1846, William H. Whiting—Engraver. New York City, 20 Bedford Street (1836–1840); 48 Merchants Exchange (1840–1846).

1844 to 1849, DeWitt Clinton Hay—Engraver. New York City, 14 Leroy Street (1844–1846); 120 Leroy Street (1847–1849).

1846 to 1848, Benjamin W. Benson—Merchant (1846 and 1847), engraver (1848). New York City, 35 Spruce Street.

1846 to 1848, Owen G. Hanks—Engraver. New York City, 235 West 21st Street.

1848 to 1851, Wellstood, Benson & Hanks—New York City, 52 Merchants Exchange. John G. Wellstood, Benjamin W. Benson, Owen G. Hanks, and William H. Whiting (1850 and 1851).

1852 to 1855, Wellstood, Hanks, Hay & Whiting—New York City, 52 Merchants Exchange. John G. Wellstood, Owen G. Hanks, DeWitt Clinton Hay, and William H. Whiting.

1856 to 1858, Wellstood, Hay & Whiting—New York City, 52 Merchants Exchange. John G. Wellstood, DeWitt Clinton Hay, and William H. Whiting. Boston, 12 School Street. Chicago.

John E. Gavit

John E. Gavit, located for many years in the Exchange Building in Albany, New York, was a minor figure at 2%, but he brought a long tradition in the industry. His business in recent times was more with book illustrations and related engravings than with paper money.

Born in New York City on October 29, 1817, Gavit commenced his career in engraving in 1833, entering the trade with Burton, Durand, & Edmonds. In time he set up his own business, and for a long period he was either a partner or a single owner of shops in Albany. At a later time, from 1866 to 1874, he was president of the American Bank Note Co.

The following were antecedents of John E. Gavit:

1839 and 1840, Hall, Packard & Cushman—Albany, New York, Exchange Building. John W. Hall, Rawson Packard, and Thomas H. Cushman.

1840 and 1841, Packard & Gavit—Albany, New York, Exchange Building. Rawson Packard, John E. Gavit, and John H. Hall.

1841 to 1849, John E. Gavit & Co.—Albany, New York, Exchange Building. John E. Gavit and Daniel E. Gavit.

1849 and 1850, Gavit & Duthie—Albany, New York, Exchange Building. John E. Gavit and James Duthie.

1851 and 1852, Gavit & Co.—Albany, New York, Exchange Building. John E. Gavit.

1852 to 1858, John E. Gavit—Albany, New York, Exchange Building.

The Continuing Growth of ABNCo

In ABNCo the partners referred to each other as "associates." By temperament artists often have their own fixed ideas, and bringing different associates and employees together was no easy task. Each of the founding partnerships had different policies, salary schedules, and other arrangements. There were more workers than needed, and some were laid off. The salaries of others were adjusted. Each of the seven member companies continued to maintain its own accounting department and to communicate with old letterheads, now with *American Bank Note Company* added. It was months before ABNCo had its own central billing department.

(continued on p. 389)

SELECTED NOTES FROM WELLSTOOD, HAY & WHITING ANTECEDENTS

Wellstood, Hay & Hanks $1 note for the Bank of Central New York, Utica.

This bank, in which the notorious Samuel D. Dakin was a director in its founding year of 1838, was involved in paper money fraud (see chapter 13). An interesting collection could be made of notes from Dakin-related banks, none of which were signed by him, as he operated quietly and behind the scenes (except when hauled into court).

Wellstood, Hay, Hanks & Whiting $3 note for the Mechanics Bank of Georgetown, D.C., ink dated November 26, 1852.

The Mechanics Bank of Georgetown is another mysterious institution from today's standpoint, leaving little in the way of records or newspaper accounts. James A. Haxby called it "fraudulent or non-existent." A $1-$1-$2-$3 plate for currency survives today in the ABNCo archives.

Wellstood, Hay & Whiting $1 note for the New Haven (Connecticut) Bank, July 1, 1863. The vignette is captioned with FIRST SABBATH above and QUINNIPIACK 1638 below.

The New Haven Bank, chartered in 1792 and opened for business on February 12, 1796, was one of the nation's first banking institutions. It went on to serve its city for many years. On June 6, 1865, the bank converted to become the National New Haven Bank.

Selected Notes From John E. Gavit Antecedents

Gavit & Co. $2 note for the Presidents Bank, Washington, D.C., 1852.

The Presidents Bank is yet another District of Columbia bank of which little is known today. Perhaps there is little to be known, and it simply represents either a fraud or a banking dream that never saw fruition through a charter.

"Printed by Gavit & Co. Albany," added to a $1 note plate for the Lewis County Bank of Martinsburgh, New York, made by Rawdon, Wright, Hatch & Edson, New York. The nature of this arrangement is not known today.

This bank began business on April 30, 1833, with a capital stated as $100,000, under the Safety Fund. By the next February it had $86,242 face value in bills in circulation. The bank suspended in spring 1846. The state sent an investigation committee, which arrived on May 26. It was learned that the bank had traded, loaned, or otherwise placed $18,000 of its bills in the hands of the Bank of Watertown, New York. At the time the bank had $128,273 of new bills in circulation and $2,548 of older issues. It was found that of the bank's assets, only the amount of $2 (yes, two dollars!) was in gold or silver coins. Years later the state made an arrangement to redeem bills with its Safety Fund, but it seems that most had been discarded as worthless or had otherwise disappeared. By 1866, $105,211 remained unredeemed.

"Printed by Gavit & Co. Albany," added to a $10 note plate for the Chemung Canal Bank of Elmira, New York, made by Rawdon, Wright, Hatch & Edson, New York.

The Chemung Canal Bank was established in 1833, when canals were still a growth industry for inland transportation, and the railroad was just getting started. The bank operated successfully, and in 1865 it evolved into the Chemung Canal National Bank of Elmira, charter 811. In a curious twist of events, in 1870 the National Bank was bought out by private interests, and a new state charter was acquired under the old name of the Chemung Canal Bank.

On March 4, 1860, Charles Toppan retired as president, and Tracy R. Edson took his place. With seemingly untiring energy, Edson had built the fortunes of Rawdon, Wright, Hatch & Edson, and for the new company was the prime negotiator and business-getter.

Branches were maintained in Boston and in New Orleans, with the managers of each receiving $2,000 per year. George Matthews, earlier the Rawdon, Wright, Hatch & Edson representative in Montreal, was encouraged to drum up more business, which apparently slackened in that district. Cyrus Durand had been in the bank-note business for a long time and was skilled in the operation of the geometric lathe used to engrave decorations and borders. He demanded and received a special salary and contract, but he was not satisfied and left a year later. In 1859 a recently formed bank-note engraving partnership, Edmonds, Jones & Smillie, of the same city, joined ABNCo. In the autumn of the same year, certain partners of Danforth, Wright & Co., together with some former employees of ABNCo, formed the National Bank Note Company in the same city. Twenty years later National became a part of ABNCo.

American Bank Note Company operated in the former Rawdon, Wright, Hatch & Edson premises in the Merchants Exchange, but until the owner of the building made expanded space available, the printing presses and additional equipment of the other companies were not brought in. This was accomplished about May 1860. At one time there were as many as 100 spider presses in use there for bank notes and security printing.

In Philadelphia some of the former partners of Charles Toppan who had continued the business of printing postage stamps continued independently as bank-note printers under the old trade style of Toppan, Carpenter & Co.

Aspects of ABNCo Plates and Currency

Paper Money Imprints of ABNCo

The firm's primary trade was the printing of bank notes and financial documents, the last including checks, stock certificates, loan certificates, and letter heads, among other products, generally referred to as security printing. The company was also a leading maker of postage stamps, inheriting the former business of certain firms that formed American Bank Note Co. in 1858. Government bonds and currency were also important lines of business. In time, extensive commissions were received from overseas governments and businesses. ABNCo issued specimen books in foreign languages for these clients.

Today, obsolete bank notes with the company's imprint usually have the monogram ABNCo (with the N being somewhat difficult to discern, sometimes visible only with its upper right tip, appearing overall as ABCo) added to existing plates still bearing the names of Rawdon, Wright, Hatch & Edson; Wellstood, Hay & Whiting; or another firm that had created the plate prior to April 1858. The ABNCo monogram was imprinted in various locations on the face of bills, with no rhyme or reason for the locations, providing a little seek-and-find game for interested collectors today.

Accordingly, if a bank note has ABNCo on it along with the name of an earlier firm, it was made from a plate taken from old stock, to which the monogram was added. On the other hand, if a long-existing bank had plates of a new design created by American Bank Note Co., or if a new bank was formed after April 1858 and ordered currency from ABNCo, then these new plates usually included American Bank Note Co. or a variation thereof. Sometimes a location is given, typically New York City, but often not. Some notes have a Boston address, others are imprinted Philadelphia, and there are several further variations.

As relatively few new plates were made after April 1858, bills with solely American Bank Note Co. identification are few and far between. For example, in the entire state of New Hampshire, only the Valley Bank of Hillsborough (established in 1860) is known to have had such bills.

Although there are exceptions, most bills from earlier plates with the ABNCo monogram added were printed with colored (often red, occasionally green) overprints such as 1 and ONE, even though in their earlier use the bills may have had no color. New plates made after April 1858 tend to be even more colorful, some having a network background in red, pink, green, or some other color covering all or most of the surface.

The tradition was maintained, with few exceptions, of having the imprint only on the face, although sometimes color protectors with denomination imprints were used on both sides (mirror-image letters on the back).

(continued on p. 393)

Selected Notes From New ABNCo Plates

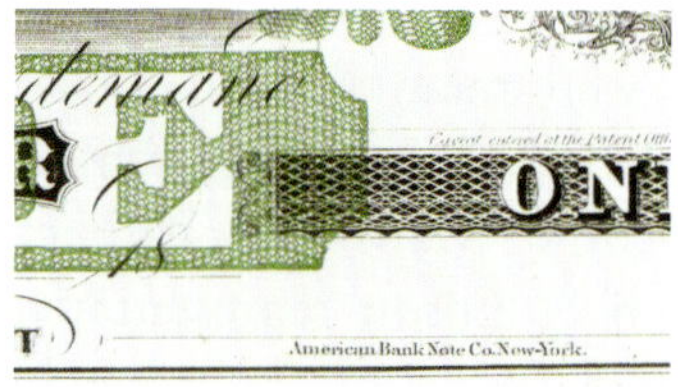

American Bank Note Co. $1 note for the Bank of New England at Goodspeed's Landing, East Haddam, Connecticut. The existence of large quantities of unused remainder notes, as here, make bills of this bank easily collectible today.

This bank was another chartered under the Free Banking Law of 1852. It opened for business on August 1, 1853. Historian William F. Hasse Jr. commented: "East Haddam was a prospering community with two hotels, an opera house, and a successful river business. Steamboats left from its docks for Europe and the West Indies." On July 22, 1865, the bank converted to become the National Bank of New England. Thomas Gross Jr., cashier of the former bank, and president George E. Goodspeed took the same posts with the new bank.

American Bank Note Co. $5 note for the Farmers Bank of Kentucky in Frankfort.

The Farmers Bank of Kentucky was authorized by the state house of representatives and senate in 1850. The arrangements were these: Mother bank (as it was called) at Frankfort, capital $300,000. Branch at Covington, capital $600,000. Branch at Maysville, capital $400,000. Branch at Mount Sterling, capital $200,000. Branch at Henderson, capital $250,000. Branch at Princeton, capital $300,000. Branch at Somerset, capital $100,000. Branch at Bardstown, capital $150,000. Total Capital $2,300,000.

In September 1852, *Banker's Magazine* reported: "The Farmers Bank of Kentucky has now opened, at the Bank of America, New York, books of subscription for an increase of its capital stock. The Farmers Bank has now been in operation about two years, and has made regular semi-annual dividends of five percent. An addition of $200,000 to its capital, which is now desired, will enlarge the business of the bank to a much greater extent, without adding to its contingent expenses."

Wellstood, Hanks, Hay & Whiting $2 note with ABNCo monogram added, for the Elmwood Bank of Cranston, Rhode Island. Ink dated July 7, 1865 (a relatively late date for *any* bank note; very few were issued in late 1865 or early 1866). This plate was used by Wellstood, Hanks, Hay & Whiting prior to 1858, when the Elmwood Bank was a customer. The plate, modified by adding ABNCo, was used by ABNCo after May 1, 1858.

A $1-$2-$5-$10 proof sheet of notes of the Bank of Carmi, Illinois, by Danforth, Perkins & Co., with the ABNCo monogram added to each, after May 1, 1858. The primarily agricultural motifs reflect the economy of the region. The auction of much of the paper section of the ABNCo archives by Christie's in 1990 brought to the market many hitherto uncataloged varieties. Quite a few of these, including this sheet, were bought by Herbert and Martha Schingoethe and were auctioned years later by R.M. Smythe & Co. All but the $2 note on this sheet had been listed by James A. Haxby as "SENC" (surviving example not confirmed) in 1988.

This was a small bank capitalized at $50,000. In 1861 the cashier was G.T. Pomery, and J.H. Cain served as president. A few years earlier the town had been home to the Peoples Bank, a paper mill with a stated capital of $464,000(!), whose notorious actions engendered many warnings and notices in newspapers.

A $1-$2-$3-$5 proof sheet of notes of the Wisconsin Pinery Bank, Stevens Point, Wisconsin, with the imprint of the American Bank Note Company in addition to the earlier imprint of Danforth, Perkins & Co. Usually, when the company reused old plates they entered the ABNCo trademark, not its full name. The vignettes are stock and were used on other bills as well. The $5 note illustrates the apotheosis or glorification of George Washington, a recurrent theme on vignettes of the era.

The Wisconsin Pinery Bank was a small institution capitalized at $50,000. In 1861, L. Scheffer served as cashier and Herman Huyssen was president. Local competition included the Frontier Bank (capital $30,000, later increased to $50,000) and the Northwestern Bank (capitalized at $60,000, later reduced to $50,000, then to $40,000).

(continued on p. 389)

Plate-Letter Technicalities

Generally, on a four-subject plate with an ABNCo imprint, the plate letter A was assigned for the first note of a given denomination. If there is more than one note of a certain value, then sequential letters such as B and C would be used. Accordingly, a sheet with values of $1-$1-$2-$5 would have plate letters A, B, A, A. On a sheet with $5-$5-$5-$5, a popular arrangement, the plate letters A, B, C, and D would be used.

On some early sheets, instead of using other letters, an A would be used for all notes of a given denomination by varying the appearance of the A on the same sheet, with one being as a block letter, the second in flowing script, etc.

While A, B, C, and D were the most popular letters, sometimes a much later letter in the alphabet would be used for high denominations, such as a K for a $500 bill. Certain of the companies that joined ABNCo in 1858 routinely used letters past D, the New England Bank Note Co. being an example. Such letters were carried over on the reuse of earlier plates.

Sometimes after long use, a plate would have its life extended by re-entering certain vignettes or inscriptions that had become weak, sometimes called "retouching" the plate. When this was done, a second or even a third letter sometimes would be added, such as an A plus two small a letters, etc. This practice was particularly extensive on slug-plate style produc-

Among the most curious bank notes ever to bear the ABNCo monogram are those of the Freemen's Bank of Bristol, Rhode Island. The bank was robbed in 1862, and stolen notes were placed into circulation. As a safeguard, new bills were issued from an old Abner Reed plate on hand in the ABNCo archives, given an ABNCo monogram, and rushed into print, complete with green overprints not used on original notes.

tions, in which the same basic plate was used many times for different banks simply by replacing the slugs indicating the state, town, and bank name. Many Rawdon, Wright & Hatch plates—and later Rawdon, Wright, Hatch & Edson plates—have multiple plate letters for the same note position on the plate. Such a plate might have "aA" and then another "a" some distance away, perhaps on the other side of a small vignette or ornament.

The Curious Bills of the Freemen's Bank

Among the most curious of all bank notes by ABNCo are those of the Freemen's Bank of Bristol, Rhode Island.[3] The face of each is signed "Reed," from plates engraved by Abner Reed after the bank's incorporation in January 1817. However, each note also bears the ABNCo monogram of the American Bank Note Company, established in April 1858.

This state of affairs came about after a burglary of the bank in autumn 1862, as described in the *Phenix,* a local newspaper, issue of November 29 of that year:

> The Freemen's Bank on State Street in this town was entered by means of false keys sometime between Saturday evening and Monday morning last. The bank was robbed of some $20,000, about $16,000 of which was in bills of the Freemen's Bank and other banks.
>
> About $3,200 in new bills of the bank signed by the president but not by the cashier were also taken. About $5,000 in government notes belonging to the Bristol Institution for Savings were also stolen. A number of private trunks that were deposited in the bank for safekeeping were broken open and their contents scattered about the floor, the most valuable of which were carried away. Three bags containing several thousand dollars in specie were left behind.

It is likely that the stolen bills were from the extensive series made by the New England Bank Note Co. in the late 1850s—these having ornate vignettes and red overprints. Probably, from the time of the burglary onward, bills of this style were redeemed with caution, with track kept of the serial numbers. To facilitate an issue of new bills without delay, a plate left from the days of Abner Reed decades earlier and held by ABNCo was rushed into service, with the new features of the denomination in green on the face and an ornate design in green on the back, and, for good measure, an ABNCo monogram added to the old plate. This is one more indication that for every rule in bank-note printing and distribution there are exceptions.

In 1861 the American Bank Note Company secured contracts for the printing of federal paper money, of which more will be said in the next chapter. From the outset, the company had been a great success.

Bank Notes and the Civil War

Historical Background

The Civil War, which began in April 1861 and ended four years later, furnished the setting for the most complex of all eras in the American coinage and currency system. The fortunes of the private bank-note companies were profoundly affected. The following is a historical background.

Prelude to the Civil War

Beginning in a significant way in the 1830s, differences in philosophy between the North and the South polarized the sections. The South was loosely defined as the district below the Mason-Dixon Line (the lower boundary of Pennsylvania), although the status of Maryland was uncertain. The states above the Mason-Dixon line comprised the North. In the Midwest the boundaries were less clear, and California (which became a state in 1850) was more or less neutral. Although there were many spokespeople, Senator John C. Calhoun of South Carolina was the best-known representative of the South. His rallying call was for states' rights—which simply meant that state laws that governed the commerce and politics should supersede regulations made by the federal government in Washington, D.C. Many Southerners felt that lawmaking in the U.S. Senate and House of Representatives was dominated by Northern interests.

In the South, slavery was viewed as a right to be granted by the states, not one to be restricted or regulated by the federal government. The "peculiar institution," as many deemed it, was considered to be an economic necessity to the South, as black people in servitude provided cheap labor. Black workers in servitude were found to be effective in farm fields but not in factories. Accordingly, the South evolved with emphasis on agrarian activities, while the North became known for its manufacturing. A famous token made in Cincinnati in 1860 bore the inscription "Wealth of the South" and displayed cotton, corn, tobacco, and rice.

The encounter between the *Monitor* and the *Merrimack* is one of the best-remembered incidents of the Civil War. On March 8, 1862, the ironclads engaged each other off the coast of Virginia. Neither scored a victory, but the days of wooden ships were numbered. As to the winner, the contest was a draw.

Cotton in particular was essential to commerce and was a profitable export to supply the looms of England and elsewhere. At one time the Virginia state legislature suggested that the commercial breeding of slaves would be a profitable endeavor. There was a ready market for these unfortunate humans, and public auctions of them were held within walking distance of the U.S. Capitol building.

In the early 1850s Harriet Beecher Stowe's novel *Uncle Tom's Cabin* was published, creating one of the greatest literary sensations ever. Readers, particularly in the North, could feel the emotional experiences of slaves who were willing to risk their very lives crossing an icy river or facing other dangers. Of course, this knowledge of the hardships of slavery was hardly new, and abolitionists had been active in the North for many years. Stories of captured runaway slaves, the sale at auction of black families in the South, and related matters furnished continuing fodder for newspapers to the north of Maryland. During the Hard Times era, the 1838 token "Am I Not a Woman & a Sister" achieved wide circulation. Beginning in the early 1840s, legislators from the North became increasingly insistent that slavery be abolished. The Free Soil Party (1840s) was based on this platform, and when the Democratic Party would not go against slavery, the Republican Party was formed, entered the presidential election for the first time in 1856, and lost.

While slavery was considered by the South to be a non-negotiable institution, states' rights also involved commerce. In particular, the high protective tariffs of the 1820s encouraged manufacturing in the North but dampened the export of cotton for the South.

Following his win over Republican candidate John Fremont in 1856, Democrat James Buchanan went to the White House in 1857. In office he tried to appease both the North and the South, amidst ever-escalating controversy and more printings of *Uncle Tom's Cabin.* During Buchanan's tenure, John Brown and a small band of followers in the antislavery movement raided

James Buchanan, president of the United States from March 1857 to March 1861, endeavored to please both the North and the South but satisfied neither. (From a Bureau of Engraving and Printing vignette book, 1876)

Secession rally in Charleston, South Carolina, held soon after the 1860 election outcome was announced. (*Frank Leslie's Illustrated Weekly*, November 24, 1860)

the federal arsenal at Harper's Ferry, Virginia (later West Virginia), and seized it, expecting that this action would spark an uprising by slaves to join a movement for freedom. This did not happen. Instead, Brown was viewed as a criminal and was captured and shot. Somewhat similarly, the Dred Scott decision of the U.S. Supreme Court declared that a slave who risked his or her life for freedom and escaped to the North could be captured and returned by force to the South.

In November 1860, Abraham Lincoln was elected president on the Republican ticket with a stance against slavery. He was roundly detested by Southerners of means. Secession rallies were held throughout the South. On December 20, 1860, South Carolina withdrew from the Union by a state legislature vote of 169 yeas and no dissents. Such actions had been threatened for a long time. Soon, other southern states pulled out, and in early 1861 the Confederate States of America was formed, with its capital in Montgomery, Alabama (it later moved to Richmond, Virginia).

Lincoln Becomes President

Lincoln was inaugurated on March 4, 1861, and in his address commented on secession: "This country, with its institutions, belongs to the people who inhabit it. Whenever they shall grow weary of the existing government they can exercise their constitutional right of amending it, or the revolutionary right to dismember it or overthrow it." If anything, the statement was realistic.

After the formation of the Confederacy, military officers, government officials, and others had been

Abraham Lincoln, elected president in November 1860, served from March 4, 1861, until his assassination on April 14, 1865. With the exception of less than two months, his administration was immersed in conducting the Civil War. (From a Bureau of Engraving and Printing vignette book, 1876)

Howell Cobb, who had served two terms as the governor of Georgia, was appointed as secretary of the Treasury on March 6, 1857, and served until his resignation on December 8, 1860. He was commissioned in the Confederate army but saw no important service there. After the war he moved to New York City, where he died on October 9, 1868. (From a Bureau of Engraving and Printing vignette book, 1876)

forced to declare their loyalty to one side or the other. Howell Cobb, secretary of the Treasury, resigned his post on December 8, 1860, and later served the Confederacy. Many others packed their bags and bid the federal government goodbye.

Most merchants and suppliers in the North and the South hoped their differences would be resolved amicably, and in the meantime they endeavored to conduct business as usual. Many members of the government of the Confederacy, in a standoff with the Union, hoped that the new country embracing the South would be recognized, and afterwards that it would be life as usual. Slavery would continue, but it would be irrelevant to the North, or the Union.

The Confederacy envisioned producing its own coins and currency at the captured federal mints in the South, and for a time it did use federal dies to make coins at New Orleans and Dahlonega. Orders for bonds and currency were placed with bank-note engraving companies in the North, this important to the present text. The National Bank Note Co. in New York City used stock vignettes to create a suite of $50, $100, $500, and $1,000 "bonds," as they were called—actually interest-bearing notes from a numismatic viewpoint. This undertaking launched what would become a panorama of nearly 100 different major designs and types of Confederate paper. Bills of the Confederacy were all *post notes,* as each promised payment at a later date.

However, other Southerners were more belligerent and did not want to see harmony between the North and the South. In the weeks after the inauguration of Lincoln, it appeared certain that the two factions were on a collision course. A focal point was Fort Sumter, the federal garrison situated on an island in the harbor of Charleston, South Carolina, the most aggressive state in the Confederacy. The fort was held by Major Robert W. Anderson and about 100 men, mostly soldiers plus some laborers. On April 8, General Pierre G.T. Beauregard, in command of the Confederate forces at Charleston, received notice that a federal squadron was on its way by sea to reprovision and strengthen the garrison. Beauregard communicated to his superiors and was directed to "reduce" the fort. This meant to destroy it by artillery shells.

On April 11, Anderson was ordered by the Confederacy to evacuate the fort, but he refused to comply. On the morning of the next day, batteries at Fort

Moultrie on the nearby shore began shelling the fort, a bombardment that continued for 34 hours, setting the wooden buildings on fire and reducing to rubble certain of the stone fortifications. This was a grand event for the 7,000 Confederate soldiers massed in the area and rich entertainment for the citizens of Charleston, who watched from rooftops and the shore.

Anderson and his men were allowed to surrender, and they went by ship back to the North.

THE CIVIL WAR

On April 15 the United States of America declared war against the Confederate States of America (C.S.A.). By this time, in both the North and the South, many citizens were simply itching for a fight, hoping to settle once and for all disputes that dated back even before the time in 1830 that Andrew Jackson lifted his glass in a toast stating that the Union must be preserved.

In New York City, Philadelphia, and elsewhere, there were much excitement, parades, parties, and other observances, as men signed up under Lincoln's call for a three-month term of service. The war was expected to be swift and decisive, an easy win. It was the North that had manufacturing and commercial abilities, while the South was properly viewed as agricultural—producing the aforementioned cotton, corn, tobacco, and rice. The Southerners were referred to as rebels, and the conflict as the War of the Rebellion. Northerners were called Yankees.

Soon, the Union soldiers, despite their general lack of training, would be returning home as heroes, the Confederacy would be vanquished, and it would be back to life as normal. The states would be re-United, so to speak.

However, by July 1861 the easy win envisioned by the North had not come to pass, and both the Yankees and the Confederates were coming to realize that the war was going to last for more than just a few months. Then, on July 21, the Battle of Bull Run settled the question with an overwhelming victory, albeit a short-lived one, for the South. In the meantime, the Union was in desperate need of funds to finance its side of the war. The United States Treasury had low reserves even before the war began.

A partial solution was provided by a $250,000,000 loan, mostly bonds, but including $50,000,000 in currency to be known as Demand Notes, authorized by the acts of July 17 and August 5, 1861, and supplemented early the next year on February 12 by an additional $10,000,000. The backs of the notes, $5, $10, and $20, were printed in green ink, quickly giving rise to the popular term *greenback,* although this term was more widely applied to the later Legal Tender Notes issued in far greater quantities. The American Bank Note Company was tapped to print the bills.

By the end of the year, the outcome of the war was uncertain. In the money markets of Europe, England in particular, many were rooting for the South, and

An example of a $5 Demand Note dated August 10, 1861. Printed by the American Bank Note Co. and with "Patented 30 June 1857," for the "Canada green" tint, below "New York." Variety designated as Friedberg-1.

arrangements were made whereby Confederate bonds were sold in England. Various British merchants, including shipbuilders, helped the cause of the South. Officially England was neutral, but in practice the South was favored, mainly because it was a prime source of cotton for the mills of Manchester and other textile towns and cities.

During the next four years battlefields and many inland waterways were bloodied in the conflict. The pivotal event was the battle of Gettysburg, which lasted for three days, July 1 through July 3, in 1863. General Robert E. Lee, emboldened by a string of victories in Virginia, led 75,000 men across the Mason-Dixon Line and into the North. He hoped that a decisive victory over Union troops would end the Civil War and that the Union would officially recognize the Confederate States of America as a separate country. In the quiet agricultural town of Gettysburg, Pennsylvania, Lee encountered Union forces under several generals. The battle there was hard fought. On July 4, with about a third of his men wounded or killed, he made a retreat. All told, on both sides about 6,000 to 7,000 were killed. No *major* invasion of the North would take place after that. However, a July 1864 raid earned a footnote in numismatic history and an October 1864 raid proved memorable (both related in this chapter). Sutlers are writ large in numismatic annals, what with tokens and scrip, but other camp followers, such as the much-appreciated vivandières, left hardly a trace in the way of collectibles.

The Civil War ended with a string of Union victories. Northern troops occupied Columbia, South Carolina, on February 17, 1865; Charleston surrendered to the Union fleet on February 18; and Petersburg, Virginia, surrendered on April 3. General U.S. Grant took the Confederate capital of Richmond on April 3. On April 9, General Robert E. Lee surrendered to Grant at Appomattox Court House, Virginia. More than a million men had been killed or injured in the conflict, making it America's bloodiest war before or since. President Abraham Lincoln was assassinated by actor John Wilkes Booth on April 14, 1865, while attending a performance of *Our American Cousin* at Ford's Theatre in Washington, D.C. This is, of course, but a microsketch of the conflict that since that time has engendered thousands of studies and reference books.

Money of the Civil War

In December 1861, with the outcome of the war continuing to be in serious question, people began hoarding gold coins. On the 28th of that month banks in New York City stopped exchanging gold at par for state bank notes, although Demand Notes, specifically redeemable in such, continued to be honored. In the spring of 1862, when a flood of Legal Tender bills was put into circulation by the Treasury Department, the public feared that such paper would lose value, and citizens began hoarding silver coins. By the second week of July, even one-cent pieces had disappeared.

Filling the void as money were ordinary postage stamps, private scrip, tickets, and other substitutes, and, beginning in August 1862, Postage Currency notes of small denominations issued by the Treasury Department, these later called Fractional Currency notes. In the meantime, Legal Tender bills served for large transactions. John Gault patented the encased postage stamp, displaying a stamp behind a pane of clear mica, fitted into a round brass case with an advertisement embossed on the back.

Thousands of merchants, banks, towns, individuals, and other entities continued to order scrip notes from local printers and flooded circulation with bills, tickets, and other printed pieces of paper denominated from one cent upward, with 3¢, 5¢, 10¢, 25¢, and 50¢ being the most popular values. Millions of cent-size copper and brass tokens filled the channels of commerce, especially in 1863. Today, collectors enthusiastically seek these and divide them into two main categories: those with patriotic themes ("patriotics") and those with advertisements ("store cards").

In the meantime, banks continued to issue paper money, mostly in denominations of $1, $2, $3 (which became less popular during this period), $5, $10, and $20. The American Bank Note Co. had most of the business, National Bank Note Co. had a small share, the New York Bank Note Co. (W.L. Ormsby) had even less, and in time the newly formed Continental Bank Note Co. carved out a business niche. A few other engravers and printers, none important, added to the supply. It was not until well into 1863 that federal one-cent pieces were seen in circulation in quantity. Scrip notes continued to be issued in quantity into the year 1864.

Encased Postage stamp issued by George G. Evans, operator of a bookstore, California wine agency, and other businesses in Philadelphia. His emporium at 439 Chestnut Street was very impressive. Evans advertised widely his "gift book" scheme, whereby those who bought books by mail order or in person received trinkets and cheap novelties.

Cartoon showing Secretary of the Treasury Salmon P. Chase pumping out *postage stamps* to use as money in a time when coins were not in circulation due to hoarding. A law hastily passed on July 17, 1862, permitted the use of stamps as money. Soon, private scrip, Encased Postage stamps, Postage Currency notes and other substitutes took the place of coins, and stamps were no longer used. (*Frank Leslie's Illustrated Weekly,* November 15, 1862)

A 3¢ scrip note issued by A.W. Gale, restaurant operator at the railroad depot, Concord, New Hampshire, March 20, 1863. During the Civil War, thousands of merchants and others issued Fractional Currency bills, which enjoyed local circulation at the time.

A 25¢ scrip note issued by Howell & Co.'s Coal Office, Hyde Park, Pennsylvania, December 1, 1862.

Large-Size Federal Paper Money

Although a few scattered issues were circulated during the War of 1812, and although the first and second Bank of the United States, in which the government held stock, issued many bills, no popular federal paper money was issued after the last Continental Currency bills of 1779. These had depreciated to near worthlessness, and it was thought the public would not be receptive to new issues. Thus was set the stage for currency issued by state-chartered banks, the focus of the present text.

The first of the new federal issues of the Civil War era were Interest-Bearing Notes (as they are called today), in effect loan certificates, authorized under the Act of March 2, 1861, a month before the war began. These were to yield 6% annual interest and to be redeemed in 60 days. Under several acts from 1863 to 1865, bills of $10 to $5,000 were authorized for periods of one and two years at 6% interest, and three-year notes at 7.3%, the last issued in denominations from $50 upward. The bills of 7.3% had *daily* interest printed on them, of one cent per day for the $50, and proportionately for higher values. No specimens are known to exist today.

Interest-Bearing Notes, some imprinted as Treasury Notes, were very popular as a way to earn interest and help alleviate the ever-depreciating value of Legal Tender and state bank bills. Banks were large purchasers of these, listing them as "bonds" in their reports to stockholders. Nearly all were redeemed in due course, with the result that any example is a great rarity today. Certain of the large denominations are not known to exist.

The earlier-mentioned Demand Notes, provided for by the acts of July 17 and August 5, 1861, supplemented early the next year, on February 12, 1862, by an additional $10,000,000, added to the paper in circulation. These were redeemable in gold coin. By April 1, 1862, $60,000,000 worth had been printed and issued.

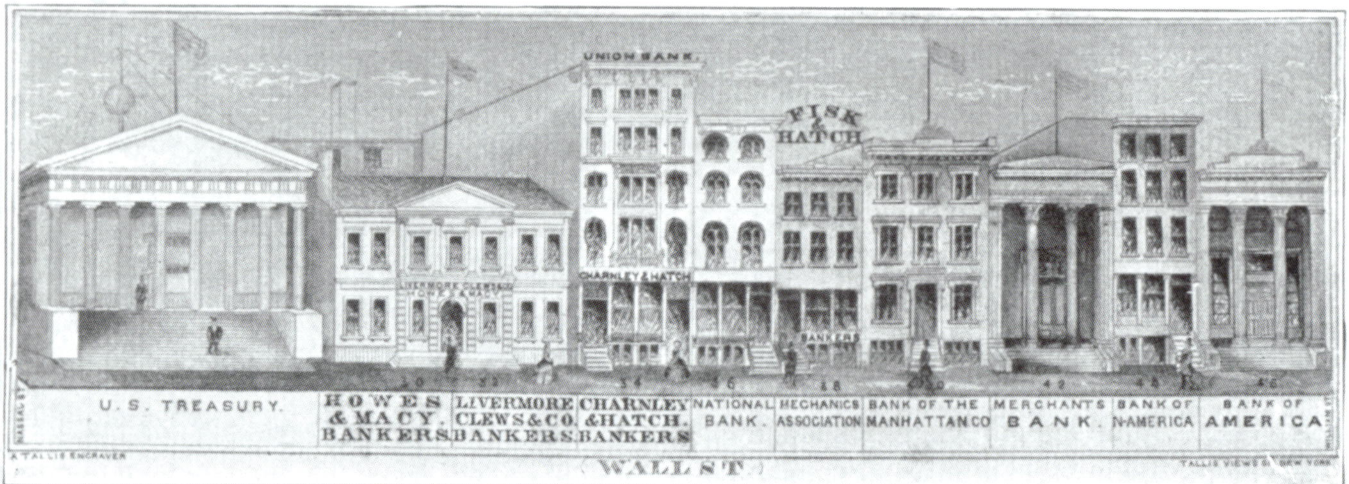

Plan view of a portion of Wall Street, New York City, showing a row of banks, all of which issued their own paper money during the Civil War.

A $20 Legal Tender Note dated March 10, 1862. These and other denominations, $5 upward, reached circulation in the spring of that year. The public was wary of their value as they were not redeemable in coin. At the time of release, and continuing for years afterward, such bills traded at a discount in terms of gold and silver coins at banks and exchange brokers. The face was printed by the American Bank Note Co., the back by the National Bank Note Co. Friedberg-126b.

In 1862, issues of federal paper reached flood tide with the Legal Tender Notes. These had no backing in coin or anything else solid but were issued on the good faith of the government. The first were dated March 10, 1862, and were of denominations from $5 to $1,000, followed by those dated August 1, 1862, of the values of $1 and $2. A $3 value was contemplated, this being a popular denomination with state banks, but was never issued. Eventually, $5,000 bills were made.

Legal Tender bills depreciated from the very beginning, with their value fluctuating in step with the Union's battlefield victories and defeats. Soon, a double system of pricing arose in the marketplace—a larger price if paid in Legal Tender bills, or a lower price if coins were tendered in payment. Indeed, at the outset, there were many merchants who would not accept Legal Tender Notes at all and demanded coins. Not even the Philadelphia Mint would accept Legal Tender Notes in payment at par for the Proof coins it struck for collectors, a situation that endured for many years. To buy such pieces, numismatists had to buy older silver and gold coins from an exchange broker and submit them to the Mint in payment.

Another major class of federal currency was authorized on February 25, 1863, by the Loan Bill, better known as the National Banking Act. Under its provisions, all banks granted charters by the national government were allowed to deposit government bonds with the treasurer of the United States, after which they could issue paper money in an amount limited to 90% of the par value of bonds so given.

Secretary of the Treasury Salmon P. Chase sent a notice soliciting designs for bills for denominations of $5 upward (it was not until later that the $1 and $2 denominations were considered):

> **To Artists, Engravers, and Others**
>
> Designs for National Currency Notes are hereby invited, of the denominations of $5, $10, $20, $50, $100, $500, and $1,000. . . .
>
> The designs must be national in their character: and none will be considered that have been used, in whole or in part, upon any currency, bond, certificate, or other representative of value, and completed bills must all be of the uniform size of seven inches by three inches. Designs must be for both the obverse and reverse of the note. . . .
>
> Proposals and designs must be enclosed in sealed envelopes, and directed to the Secretary of the Treasury, and plainly endorsed, 'Designs and Proposals for National Currency,' and will be opened on the 28th day of March, 1863, at 12 o'clock, M.

Provision was made under the 1863 legislation for issuing denominations of $5, $10, $20, $50, $100, $500, and $1,000. A secondary act, June 3, 1864, included other provisions, including for $1, $2, and $3 denominations, but with no more than one-sixth of a bank's bills being of these low values. The $3 denomination was never employed, but the others were.

Each bank was given a charter number, awarded in sequence. By the end of the National Bank Note issuing era in 1935, the numbers had reached 14,348. Not all of these banks exercised the privilege to issue currency, but the majority did.

From the first bills of 1863 through July 1875, National Bank Notes were printed in New York City by the American Bank Note Co., National Bank Note Co., and Continental Bank Note Co. In these times, the face of each note required one printing while the back, with black and green ink, required two. Certain of the black printing on the back of $5 bills was done in Washington, D.C., by the Columbian Bank Note Co. The bills were then sent to the National Currency Bureau within the Treasury Building in Washington, in sheets of four subjects (two for certain high denominations). There they were imprinted with the Treasury seal in red, the bank serial number in red, and the Treasury serial number in red (or, on some notes, in blue). On $5 bills the Continental Bank Note Co. added the bank serial numbers at the lower left, and at the National Currency Bureau the federal serial numbers were imprinted at the upper right and the Treasury seal was added.

Procedures for printing these notes evolved over a period of years, and beginning in the 1870s the Bureau of Engraving and Printing, Washington, D.C., took over the work. National Bank Notes issued during the Civil War, continuing to 1875, are correctly called Original Series bills by collectors today, although some designate them as *First Charter* notes, a designation with no official basis.

Bills of another class, Gold Certificates, were first printed under the Act of March 3, 1863. Most of these early bills were of higher denominations, $100 to $10,000 (also some of the $20 value). These early

A $10 note of the Citizens National Bank of Sanbornton, New Hampshire. One side was printed by the American Bank Note Co., the other by the National Bank Note Co.

This bank was chartered in 1865 and was located in Sanbornton at the time. In 1875, the name of the town was changed to Tilton, as a wealthy entrepreneur of that name offered to bestow civic improvements and other benefits if the change would be made. Although the idea was opposed locally, it was rushed through the state legislature and became effective. National Bank Notes were issued with both names.

A $1 note, proof impression, made in the early 1830s for the American Bank of Providence, Rhode Island, by Charles Toppan & Co., New York and Philadelphia.

This bank was one of the largest in Providence, capitalized at $1,414,050 by 1864, after a series of increases. It was located in handsome headquarters at 21 Market Square. In 1865 it converted to become the American National Bank of Providence, charter 1472. Cashier William Olney and president Shubael Hutchins made the transition from the old to the new bank.

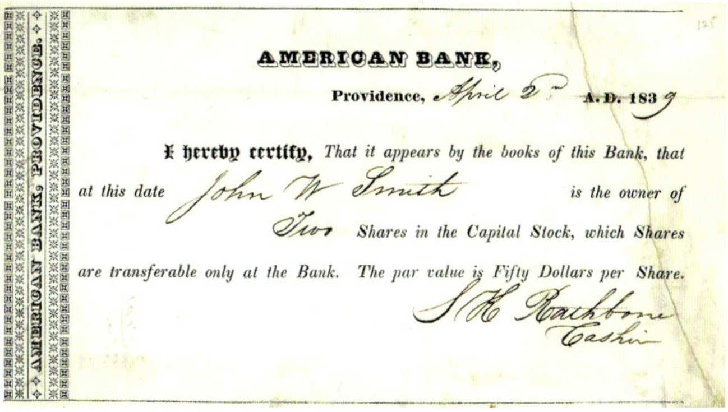

Early stock certificate issued by the American Bank of Providence, Rhode Island.

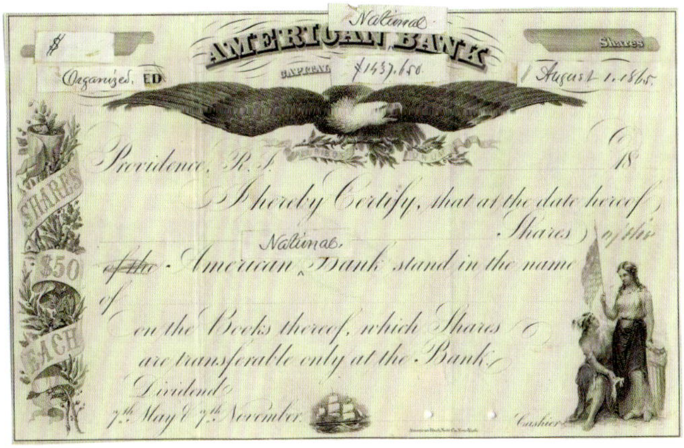

This stock certificate of the American Bank of Providence, Rhode Island, was sent to ABNCo with pasted-on and inked instructions for creating a new certificate for the American *National* Bank.

A $1 note of the American National Bank, Providence, Rhode Island.

During the planning stage for Legal Tender Notes, Spencer M. Clark, head of the National Currency Bureau in Washington, D.C. (predecessor to the Bureau of Engraving and Printing), advocated the use of panoramic scenes extending across the face of notes, paralleling W.L. Ormsby's Unit System.

Such scenes did not come to pass on Legal Tender Notes, but Clark continued to persist, including this item in a lengthy letter to Secretary of the Treasury Salmon P. Chase on March 28, 1863, with regard to National Bank Notes:

"[An] advantage of such a currency would be, that a series properly selected, with their subject titles imprinted on the notes, would tend to teach the masses the prominent periods in our country's history. The laboring man, who should receive every Saturday night a copy of the "Surrender of Burgoyne" for his weekly wages, would soon inquire who General Burgoyne was, and to whom he surrendered. His curiosity would be aroused, and he would learn the facts from a fellow laborer or from his employer. . . ."

Shown here is a Treasury Department proof, unique, mounted on cardboard, of a proposed design for a $1 note, August 4th, 1862. The art work, *Surrender of Gen. Burgoyne at Saratoga, N.Y., Oct., 1777,* by John Murdoch, is from a John Trumbull painting of the same name (now in the Frick Museum). General John Burgoyne is shown surrendering his sword to General Horatio Gates on October 17, 1777.

The first type of Legal Tender Note for $1, dated August 1, 1862, Friedberg-16. The idea of using a scenic or Unit System design was discarded in favor of a standard layout, with a portrait of Salmon P. Chase and a green overprint on the face, among other features. The first Demand Notes of 1861 and Legal Tender Notes of 1862 were similar in concept, but with different portraits for various denominations.

It is likely that the face was printed by the National Bank Note Co. (whose name is printed twice), and the back was done by the American Bank Note Co. National's "Patented April 23rd 1860," the much discussed *cycloidal configuration* scheme, appears at the lower left. Also shown is a detail of the patented feature.

issues did not circulate in general commerce and are seldom seen today.

Authorized by acts of Congress on March 3, 1863, and June 30, 1864, Compound Interest Treasury Notes, yet another category of federal paper, were in essence loans to the federal government. Made in denominations of $10, $20, $50, $100, $500, and $1,000, each featured on the reverse a schedule of the accumulating interest, compounded at 6%. These bills were to be held for three years, at the end of which the principal and interest would be paid. For a $10 note, this amounted to a total of $11.94. Today all are rarities.

THE NATIONAL BANK NOTE COMPANY

ORIGINS

During the Civil War era, the National Bank Note Company rose to importance in the industry, a distant second to ABNCo in the field of currency for state-chartered banks, but also with significant business in the printing of federal paper money, again second to ABNCo.

The company was organized in November 1859 by partners of Danforth, Perkins & Co. who had left the firm when others joined their interest with ABNCo. Founders included George H. Danforth, Fitch Shepard, Samuel Stiles, William D. Nichols, Lloyd Glover, and James MacDonough, a lineup that included well-known longtime engravers Danforth and Stiles. Other engravers with the company included James Smillie, Cyrus Durand (who had joined ABNCo but had become disaffected there and resigned), William Edgar Marshall, Joseph I. Pease, J.P. Ourdan, and George W. Thurber. Danforth was known as an expert siderographer and Durand was known for his skills with the geometric lathe. George E. Perrine was an early engraver with National, but he left a year later to conduct an independent business. Another engraver, Alfred W. Cunningham, was with National in its early days but moved to ABNCo.

GAINING A FOOTHOLD

The new firm took over existing business from Danforth, Perkins & Co. and signed a few new clients as well. Relatively few state-chartered banks were formed after the Panic of 1857, and the field of opportunity was narrow. Still, at least a few dozen banks went with National, including some that had been ordering currency from the former ABNCo partners earlier. It was often the practice of banks to switch from one supplier to another—reaching for perceived improvements, or perhaps yielding to the importunities of bank-note company salesmen, or possibly even gaining a lower price.

The National notes of this era were usually ornate, embellished with "cycloidal configurations," this being the process whereby repeated engraving, often including the denomination of the bill, was arranged in lobes or overlapping petals as well as in latticework overlays containing inscriptions. This technique was patented in 1860 and was trumpeted as highly important in preventing counterfeiting, National's answer to ABNCo's patented green tint of 1857.

In 1860 contracts for security printing were perfected with the Treasury Department and the U.S. Post Office. Postage stamps had always been printed by private firms, who often used bank-note vignettes to illustrate them. On August 15, 1861, National landed a contract to make all stamps for the next six years, a major coup.

Headquarters of the National Bank Note Co. at the corner of Wall Street and Broadway, New York City, in the 1860s. (From a stereograph card)

GAZAWAY BUGG LAMAR

In the spring of 1861, the newly formed Confederate States of America, with its capital in Montgomery, Alabama, sought to have its own paper money. Envisioned by Secretary of the Treasury C.G. Memminger as "bonds," these were to be denominated $50, $100, $500, and $1,000. The Act of March 9, 1861, authorized such bills. Gazaway Bugg Lamar, president of the Bank of the Republic, headquartered in its own impressive building at the corner of Broadway and Wall Street, the same address as the bank-note firm, perfected the arrangements. Lamar was a man of considerable wealth, with investments in several different businesses, mainly in the South. In the 1850s an

A $5 note of the Bullion Bank, Washington, D.C., by the National Bank Note Co. In keeping with location of the bank, the upper left vignette shows George Washington's tomb at Mount Vernon, while on the lower right is a stock vignette of Washington.

Although some signed notes of this bank are known, most are unissued remainders. Two others are shown later in this chapter. Whether the Bullion Bank really existed or was another smoke-and-mirrors fantasy is not known today. The author has located no record of its having engaged in the banking business.

A $10 note of the Wyoming Bank, Wilkes-Barre, Pennsylvania. Proof impression by the National Bank Note Co. Nearly all of the National bills are ornate and colorful.

A $1 note of the Market Bank, Boston. Proof impression by the National Bank Note Co.

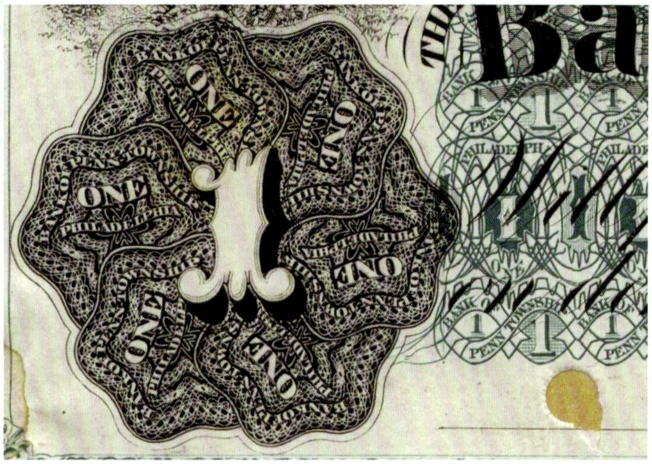

The National Bank Note Company's well-known and attractive *cycloidal configuration* scheme for bank notes featured petals or other ornaments repeating the denomination or the bank's name and colored overprints in the field with similar inscriptions. The illustrations are details from National bills of the 1860s.

oceangoing steamship and a Nashville & Chattanooga Railroad locomotive had each been named after him. He also was involved in the Great Western Marine Insurance Company, based in New York but controlled by Southerners.

In the 1850s, as a supporter of Buchanan during the presidential election of 1856, Lamar established close ties with appointed officials in the federal government, including the head of the Custom House in New York City, who was empowered to examine, or else choose to overlook, certain maritime activities, including those of Lamar's shipping interests. After Lincoln's election in 1860, the rebellious South Carolina needed munitions. Through John B. Floyd, Buchanan's secretary of war, Lamar arranged for South Carolina to purchase 10,000 muskets from the federal arsenal at Watervliet, New York. Georgia seceded from the Union in January 1861. Three days later, on the January 21, Police Superintendent Kennedy of New York City confiscated 38 crates of weapons purchased for Georgia by Lamar and awaiting shipment to the South. In retaliation, the governor of Georgia ordered the seizure of New York ships in the Savannah harbor. Finally, through action of Secretary of War Floyd and New York City Mayor Fernando Wood, Lamar was able to resume filling various orders for arms placed by his friends in the South.

When the National Bank Note Co. was formed, James T. Soutter, then president of the Republic Bank and the Great Western Marine Insurance Company (and married to G.B. Lamar's daughter), was named vice president and trustee of the firm. Soutter's name was also on the side of a Nashville & Chattanooga Railroad engine. Simultaneously, Lamar was president of the Bank of Commerce in Savannah, Georgia. Connections were certainly complex! By arrangement, Bank of Commerce notes could be redeemed at the Republic Bank for a charge of 3/4 of 1%.

In May 1861 Lamar left New York City and took up with the Confederate cause. Later investigations revealed that he had been in the slave trade in the late 1850s; in late 1860 and early 1861, before the onset of hostilities, he had engaged in covert operations in New York City on behalf of the Confederacy. He was the focal point of business, secret transactions, and other matters involving the C.S.A. At the time, the Confederacy viewed the idea of conducting business in New York City as reasonable and even hoped to sell $1 million in Confederate bonds there through Lamar's bank.[1] However, the Confederacy kept most of its activities secret. In the South during the war, he ran a fleet of blockade runners. After Lincoln was assassinated, Lamar was accused of complicity in the plot but was released. He lived to enjoy continued prosperity in later life.

As to New York City Mayor Fernando Wood, he and his brother Benjamin bought the *New York Daily News* before the war started, and they went on to condemn Lincoln and all of his policies. After the fall of Fort Sumter the newspaper's attacks became so extreme that a federal grand jury brought charges that the *News* was printing material that was "calculated to

A $100 note of the Bank of Commerce, Savannah, Georgia, signed by G.B. Lamar as president. From a plate by Danforth, Wright & Co., Philadelphia and New York. Ink dated November 1, 1856. The Bank of Commerce was one of the most important financial institutions in the South. It operated into the Civil War, then closed.

aid and comfort the enemy." The postmaster general of the United States issued an edict forbidding the mails to transport the paper.

The subsequent actions of Secretary of War John B. Floyd were also peculiar, at least in the eyes of Northerners. It seems that the shipping partnership of Russell, Majors & Waddell and several other express companies were in deep financial troubles in the late 1850s. Certain of these virtually bankrupt firms had close connections to Secretary Floyd, who started a letter-writing campaign to persuade bankers and other moneyed interests to loan large amounts of money against expected revenues from freighting contracts to be placed by the War Department. From March 1858 until just before the election of 1860, the incredible sum of $5,036,127 was placed through what became known as *Floyd acceptances,* as Floyd endorsed the loan papers with his own signature. It was a surefire investment.

With fresh money on hand, Russell, Majors, & Waddell set about reorganizing their businesses, renaming one the Central Overland, California & Pike's Peak Express Company, an appealing title as Colorado was in the midst of the *Pikes Peak or Bust* gold rush. The company circulated information that it was going to get a contract for overland mail valued at up to $900,000 per year. However, the contract did not materialize, and other operations experienced great problems as well. When the first Floyd acceptances came due, there was no money to pay. In September 1860 a meeting of acceptance holders was held in St. Louis, where it was stated that an infusion of an additional $200,000 would carry the company through the temporary crisis, which was also alleviated with money embezzled from the federal Indian Trust Fund. The situation came out in the open in December 1860, when it was realized that the Floyd acceptances were completely worthless.

Congress launched an investigation, and on January 29, 1861, three perpetrators, including Secretary Floyd, were indicted for conspiring to "combine, confederate and agree together by wrongful means to cheat, defraud, and impoverish the United States." This included stealing or falsifying records of federal bonds and trust funds, arranging for large shipments of munitions to be sent to the South, and other actions. For Floyd, the Civil War was a special blessing. He resigned as secretary of war and decamped to the South, where he became an important official in the Confederacy. George H. Lovett, a New York diesinker, soon memorialized him on his "Gallery of American Traitors" medal of 1861.

The worthless Floyd acceptances profoundly affected the fortunes of certain banks that held them, some in distant locations. In New Hampshire the *Reports of the Bank Commissioners,* June 1863, gave a status report:

> We found the acceptances of Ex-Secretary of War John B. Floyd in the Dover, Cochecho, Langdon, and Dover Five Cents Savings banks, at Dover, remaining unpaid. There has been no material change in the condition of these claims since our 1st report. . . .

National Prints C.S.A. Notes

In March 1861, after the Confederacy made connections with the National Bank Note Co. through Gazaway Bugg Lamar in New York City, these instructions were given:

> Notes are to be at one year at the rate of one cent per day for every hundred dollars. Put the calculation on the back. None to be below fifty dollars.[2]

The bills, now numismatically considered as *Treasury Notes,* were printed in March in sheets of four notes arranged $50-$100-$500-$1,000. The interest-bearing information was printed on the face of each note in the final version, with the back left blank. By April 2, 1861, a shipment of 607 sheets, having barely escaped capture, was in the hands of Memminger in Montgomery. The ship carrying the C.S.A. notes refused to comply with an order by federal authorities to stop and be boarded in the harbor of New York City. The bills were sent on April 8 to Treasurer E.C. Elmore. Today, these are known as *Montgomery Notes* by numismatists. Later bills by other printers have the Richmond address, where the capital moved.

Leaders of the Confederacy believed that more money could be raised by selling smaller denominations.[3] Accordingly, 999 half sheets were printed with the $50 and $100 values. These denominations did circulate as currency.

After war was declared on April 15, 1861, the National Bank Note Co. surrendered the Confederate plates to agents of the Treasury Department, and the American Bank Note Co. did likewise for plates it had made to produce C.S.A. bonds.

In *Cycloidal Configurations,* published by W.L. Ormsby in 1862 (and discussed below under the heading of New York Bank Note Co.), the author

The famous $1,000 "Montgomery Note," one of four denominations printed for the Confederacy by the National Bank Note Co. in the spring of 1861 before the Civil War commenced. Serial number 15 is the second lowest known today for this issue.

The portrait of Senator John C. Calhoun of South Carolina is at the lower left, and that of Andrew Jackson is at the lower right. Both images were used widely elsewhere, including Jackson on a United States 2¢ "Black Jack" postage stamp. The overlapped petals surrounding the Roman number M in the denomination are of the *cycloidal configurations* patent held by National. Signed by Alex. B. Clitherall, register, and E.C. Elmore, treasurer of the C.S.A.

quoted an article from the *New York World,* April 26, 1861, eleven days after war had been declared against the Confederate States of America. On April 25, United States deputy marshals Bersch and Horton "made an important seizure" at the offices of the American Bank Note Company of 18 printing plates made for the Confederacy.

Ormsby continues his account:

> "The officers of the company state that they ceased printing from them as soon as the President's proclamation was issued. The informer against them asserts that they were being printed as late as four days ago. An hour after the above seizure the United States deputy marshals entered the office of the National Bank Note Company and took into their keeping two plates of cancelled Treasury Notes of the Southern Confederacy, of the denominations of $50, $100, $500, and $1000.
>
> "The engraving of the plates is of the best quality, and not unlike the United States Treasury Notes now in circulation. The presidents of both companies are held to await investigation in the matter."
>
> A few words in the above are italicized, because it looks as if the C.S.A. intended to embark in the counterfeiting business on a large scale. The fact, too, that the American Bank Note Co has a branch in New Orleans, with duplicate dies, transfer presses, &c (which branch, it is rumored, has been taken possession of, and removed to Richmond, by Mr. Jefferson Davis's government), and that an expert in the use of those materials suddenly left the parent company in N.Y., and has been heard from in that locality, together with several accomplished engravers—one of whom was captured at Bull Run, and two of whom subsequently emigrated by the way of Chicago, where they were temporarily detained, on suspicion, for having in their possession an extensive assortment of engraving implements and materials—by no means discourages the entertainment of the idea suggested in the italics referred to. . . .

THE NEW YORK BANK NOTE COMPANY

ORMSBY AND THE CONFEDERACY

Ormsby's narrative in *Cycloidal Configurations* continued with an account of his own firm, standing alone it its absolute loyalty:

> We now come to the third company, viz The New York Bank Note Company, established in 1842. The title has been recently adopted with a view to future incorporation. At present, the writer is sole owner and proprietor. The following is one of its latest recommendations:

United States Marshal's Office

New York 23d, May, 1861

I take pleasure in recommending the New York Bank Note Co., W.L. Ormsby, proprietor, to the patronage of the Bank Department; this being the only engraving company that has voluntarily surrendered to this office the plates and bills of the banks in the seceded states, while other companies were compelled to surrender secession bonds and treasury notes.

Robert Murray,
U S Marshal

ORMSBY CREATES A STIR

As to the background to *Cycloidal Configurations,* in April 1862 Waterman L. Ormsby was still trying to right what he perceived as numerous malfeasances, bad practices, and other undesirable aspects among his competitors in the bank-note engraving and printing profession. No doubt he was smarting from the checkmate, or no-win situation in his lengthy court cases of a few years earlier, and recalled important figures in the business lining up to call him an unethical businessman and counterfeiter.

The straw that broke the camel's back for Ormsby was added the year before, when the Treasury Department in 1861 sought to have private firms print large quantities of new Demand Notes and other securities. The biggest plum went to the American Bank Note Co., and, later with the Legal Tender Notes, some business went to the much smaller National Bank Note Co.

However, John J. Cisco, assistant treasurer of the United States, based in New York City, could not or would not meet with Ormsby to consider involving him in the business. Salmon P. Chase, secretary of the Treasury, with his office in Washington, D.C., considered Ormsby to be a nuisance, an eccentric, and a troublemaker—all this by reputation as the two had never interviewed. No doubt the executives at American Bank Note Co., with close ties to the Treasury Department, passed along many of the rumors and accusations of the 1850s involving Ormsby. Further, ABNCo, in its impressive headquarters with 100 presses and many employees, could not be compared to the small shop maintained by Ormsby.

What to do? In April 1862, Ormsby took his revenge against the American Bank Note Company, the actions of the Treasury Department, and, for good measure, the continuing poor practices of the entire bank-note industry. For the last he reprised much of the philosophy he had used a decade earlier in *Bank Note Engraving.*

This time around his comments were printed in a slim 45-page pamphlet titled *Cycloidal Configurations, or the Harvest of Counterfeiters,* with the continuing

A $2 note of the Mercantile Bank, Washington, D.C., by the New York Bank Note Co. (W.L. Ormsby). Ink dated March 4, 1861. This a late-style note of highly unusual appearance; printed in three colors, changing from orange-brown at left to black at center to green at right, an anticounterfeiting technique. A tiny "Patent Applied For" notice may relate to this coloring.

Little is known about this bank, one of many District of Columbia mysteries. The American Bank Note Co. either issued bills for it or acquired by legacy the plates of others. Today two plates are preserved in the ABNCo archives, a regular plate $1-$2-$3-$5 and a "tint" plate of the same denominations, used to apply color.

subtitle, *Containing Matter of the Highest Importance concerning Paper Money, also Explaining the Unit System of Bank Note Engraving.*

The cover noted it was published by W.L. Ormsby, proprietor of the New York Bank Note Co., 50 Wall Street. The publication was priced at 25 cents and included no illustrations. Later, Ormsby referred to this as a *book* he issued in *1863*. Apparently, relatively few copies were ever sold or distributed, for they are very rare today.[4] The title was taken from wording, considered by Ormsby to be gibberish, in the earlier-mentioned April 23, 1860, patent issued to the National Bank Note Co., for an anticounterfeiting system: "Combined use in repetition of the valuation or denomination with the title of the institution or corporation, and the configuration of the geometric cycloidal waved-line or rosette."

At this point, some information concerning the Treasury Department's man in New York City is relevant.

John J. Cisco. (From a Bureau of Engraving and Printing vignette book, 1876)

THE REMARKABLE RISE OF JOHN J. CISCO

John J. Cisco (1806–1883), a rare Democrat among Lincoln appointees and a holdover from the Buchanan administration, was the assistant treasurer of the United States, with an office in New York City. As noted in Ormsby's narrative above, Secretary of the Treasury Salmon P. Chase instructed Cisco to make satisfactory arrangements to have currency printed on behalf of the government.

Cisco, who had once operated a clothing store in the city at the corner of Market and Cherry streets, had risen somehow to wealth and prominence. His position as assistant treasurer resulted in many connections in banking and industry. For the Lincoln administration, Cisco proved to be of great utility in securing loans for the government and enlisting the aid of New York City bankers in many of the Treasury Department's programs.

It seems that on one particular day in 1861, Cisco received proposals from certain bank-note firms in New York City, while Waterman L. Ormsby was endeavoring to pursue a similar arrangement, but at the wrong location. From *Cycloidal Configurations:*

> Representatives . . . were competing for the largest contracts, in their line of business, that any nation ever offered before.
>
> By one of the most peculiar coincidences, the American and National companies alone presented themselves to Mr. Cisco as the only engraving companies in the country (the New York Bank Note Co. being kept in Washington, waiting on the Treasury Department, in blissful ignorance of what was occurring).

The arrangement with the American Bank Note company was perfected by Cisco. To make matters worse in the eyes of Ormsby, the Treasury Department licensed rights to use an anticounterfeiting patent that he considered worthless. From his 1862 text:

> Notwithstanding public testimonials to the insufficiency of the "Patent Green Tint" for the prevention of counterfeiting, Mr. Cisco contracted for the mere use of it at the moderate rate of $5 per thousand impressions, and the entire contract for engraving and printing fifty millions of Treasury Notes was awarded about the 25th July, 1861, to the American Bank Note Company, the National not caring to accept even a part of it at such low prices!
>
> The New York Bank Note Co at this juncture arrived and was at once informed by Mr. Cisco that the contracts were closed to the entire satisfaction of the government. Consequently this company had no opportunity of submitting to Mr. Cisco any specimens of work whatever.
>
> The writer could not but bring to mind the exciting scene that occurred only a few weeks previously, when an infuriated mob rushed wildly through the streets of New York city, crying "Hang out the American flag"—"Death to all Traitors"—when, as the surging multitude came yelling through Wall Street, the establishment [of the American Bank Note Co.] was closed and barred with trembling hands, and its officers were pale and blanched with fear, lest some one should shout—"In that building they are printing Secession Bonds and Treasury Notes"

The scene was now changed, and those who had been working *"night and day"* for the enemies of government, were rewarded with a princely contract

This mighty contract for engraving, that, under a true system would have called into employment every man who could wield the burin, was patched together in a few days by mere mechanical labor and the use of old dies—while the most talented engravers were enlisting in the army at thirteen dollars a month, leaving for the South for want of employment here, or suffering in idleness in our midst. And here let us repeat the rule, in engraving a note to prevent forgery, that "that which is easy and profitable to the original workman, is easy and profitable to the counterfeiter also."

By casting the influential Cisco as well as the Treasury Department in the category of traitorous, stupid villains, W.L. Ormsby became persona non grata with the Treasury, a situation that would later have wide repercussions.

As to Cisco, similar to the recently discussed Lamar and Floyd, a book could be written about the intrigues in his life. After the Civil War, Cisco, by now a man of impressive wealth, became prominent in railroading and was a prominent stockholder in several lines. The town of Cisco, Texas, bears his name, in connection with his financing of the Texas Central Railroad. He died in 1884, just in time to avoid seeing his private banking firm, John J. Cisco & Son, close its doors (in 1885) when millionairess Hetty Green, "the Witch of Wall Street," withdrew large deposits. She was the mother of Colonel E.H.R. Green, collector of paper money, coins (he had all five of the known 1913 Liberty Head nickels), and other items. In numismatics, all sorts of people, events, and things are interwoven!

Counterfeits Inevitable

Next in his 1862 essay, Ormsby tilted at another windmill:[5]

United States Notes Will Be Counterfeited

In no country in the world has the art of bank note engraving presented such seeming excellence as in the United States, nor has counterfeiting attained elsewhere such perfection and success.

From the fact that an enormous issue of Treasury Notes—made a legal tender—has been engraved in direct opposition to the experience of the past, as to the means of preventing counterfeiting and in direct conformity with the best method of tempting and facilitating it, the writer is willing to hazard an opinion, based on a practical experience of over 30 years in the note engraving profession, that a grand jubilee of counterfeiting is near its advent.

Instead of having the notes made payable in one place entirely unlike those payable in another place, so that a counterfeit on one locality would not affect the others, they are all alike, and one successful counterfeit of each denomination will ruin the whole, and cause their repudiation or withdrawal from circulation.[6]

There is no exception to the rule, that the greater the number of notes of the same similitude, still greater, in proportion, will be the number of people enticed to counterfeit them, and the higher those notes may stand in public favor the more care will be taken to counterfeit them successfully.

In these Treasury Notes there is just enough seeming security to gain public confidence—a confidence which has often been abused, and of which the counterfeiters will again take advantage. Similar experiments have been tried before (See Ormsby's *Bank Note Engraving,* page 47). . . .

Criticizing the Competition

To Salmon P Chase, Secretary of the Treasury, Congress assigned the task of issuing Treasury Notes, in denominations from five dollars upwards, and in amounts sufficient to displace almost the entire paper currency of the country; and to the Honorable John J. Cisco, assistant treasurer in N.Y., he transferred the power to make contracts for furnishing these notes, without any guide or instructions as to the manner of executing them.

However honest in his intentions, Mr. Cisco could not acquire in one day's notice any knowledge of the best method of constructing bank notes to prevent forgeries; therefore he was entirely dependent upon the suggestions of those engravers with whom he consulted.

Who were the applicants for the patronage of Mr. Cisco?

At this period there were only three bank note engraving establishments in actual operation in the country, all of which were located in Wall Street, New York City. Nearly every bank and bond plate was on deposit there, or at least the "dies" or "types" that could have reproduced them, in what is equivalent to absolute identity.

The names of the three companies are as follows:

The National Bank Note Company, incorporated in 1859;

The American Bank Note Company, a consolidation of nine companies into one; incorporated in 1858. (The president [Tracy R. Edson] and the writer were boys and fellow apprentices together in 1827, '28, '29, and '30.)

The New York Bank Note Company, not incorporated.

The business interests of the two first named companies are identically the same. The managers, skilled in diplomacy, have but one object in view, viz. to make money; and in dealing with banks—let whichever obtain advantage—the people, owing to the peculiar system of bank note engraving already noticed, must necessarily suffer in various ways.

In the second place, where the engravers, designedly, induce the bank to have a plate of four 1s, another of four 4s, another of four 3s, and a fourth of four 5s, at a cost of $2,000, when one plate of 1, 2, 3, 5 would suffice at a cost of $500.[7] This certainly quadruples the bank's expenses, without much injury to the people. The case is different, however, when the bank is induced to use "red letters," "patent stripes," or red, yellow, and green "tints," because all such things enable the counterfeiter to serve up his old frauds in new dresses, cheating the people over and over again, in cycloidal progression.[8]

In the third place, where the bank designedly imposes upon the engraver; and in forging his certificate (*vide* the Boone County, Indiana, fraud[9]), and as obtaining plates for apparently a valid purpose, and subsequently using them for an invalid purpose (see Ormsby's *Bank Note Engraving,* page 52); and, as obtaining $500,000 in 10s and 20s for a pretended New England Bank, Maine (having no charter), for the sole purpose of altering them to represent the issues of the New England Bank, Boston,[10] the best are often deceived.

And in the fourth place, when the climax of audacity is reached where both the engravers and the bank, by collusion, flood the country with fraudulent, spurious, and counterfeit issues—as making bills for circulation in Rhode Island with imitation state seals, "payable at Paddy Mills, Va.," making $5 checks on the Government Stock Bank, Ann Arbor, Michigan, in exact *similitude* (state seal or "comptroller's die" included of the bills of the bank)—engraving *absolute frauds* in *similitude* of stock-secured notes,[11] and in making the City Bank and Ocean Bank bills, Washington, a counterfeit resemblance of the bills of the banks of the same name in New Jersey.[12]

ATTACKING ORMSBY

Although Ormsby may have had the best intentions for championing the public good and also advancing the merits of his rather small New York Bank Note Co., his attempts to share information did not have their desired effect. Instead, his longtime repetition of criticism of his competitors, of the Treasury Department, and of certain government officials and practices came back to bite him, as Ormsby himself reiterated in *Cycloidal Configurations:*

> The writer considered it a professional duty not only to criticize the manner of giving out the Treasury Note contracts, but the manner of executing them also; and the consequence was, that when, on the 8th January, 1862, the Secretary of the Treasury asked Congress for an appropriation of $150,000, in addition to $300,000 already appropriated, to pay for the engraving, &c, the money was refused by the House on the ground of fraud in the contract. Not, however, on the part of the Secretary or Mr. Cisco.
>
> A month later, the Hon Mr. Pearce presented to the Senate a statement of the Secretary, together with the agreements, and correspondence with the engravers, giving his reasons for the course pursued. In allusion to the writer, as one of the applicants for the engraving, the Senator said, *"one of them had skill but he had not capital,"*
>
> What higher compliment could be paid to a professional man?
>
> No objection being made, the Senate re-passed the appropriation, and on the 13th February it came before the House again for concurrence. The principal champion for the American Bank Note Co., the Honorable E G Spaulding, of Buffalo, made a personal attack upon the reputation of the writer, of which the following is an extract:
>
> "This witness, who had skill, but who could not give security either for the performance of the contract or for his integrity, is the person to whom nearly all these slanders against the Treasury Department and against the parties who have executed this contract can be traced.
>
> "Who is this witness?
>
> "It turns out here in evidence that he was prowling about Washington *to get an office;* he went to the Treasury with a view to see whether he could not get some contract for engraving, when in New York City, where he is known, no banker would employ him for a moment to execute engraving. Why? Because they would not dare to entrust him with plates for the performance of the work. His character was of such doubtful reliability all over the country with those who knew him, that he could not be entrusted to execute work for any banker in the country, in New York City or elsewhere. . . .
>
> "I know the vigilance of this man, Ormsby, in undermining and traducing respectable houses and respectable officials attached to the government."

To the above, Ormsby mounted a long defense. A logician would question why he brought up the Spaulding matter. However, after his defense, this:

> **Visit Suggested**
>
> If the Hon. Mr. Spaulding will favor the New York Bank Note Co with a visit, he will find that the proprietor, notwithstanding the troubles and depressions of the times, can say, "I am Monarch of all I survey," or, in the language of Senator Pearce, on the floor of Congress, "president, director, and company himself."
>
> He will find him surrounded with the implements of his profession—the works of his own hands—and the inventions of his own brain—transfer presses, dies, machines; geometrical, cycloidal, and rosette. He will be shown entirely new bank note configurations—the only truly original and useful inventions in note engraving of the last 40 years; in short, he will find a "man and not a monster." . . .
>
> After the Hon Mr. Spaulding has visited my humble establishment let him visit the favorite of the government over the way. He also may

be shown a geometrical lathe, and told that *"it is the only one in existence,"* though they know that there are three others as good, if not better, in New York City. . . .

He will, undoubtedly, be shown the wonderful *red letters,* for the use of which banks have paid thousands of dollars during the last ten years, under the impression that "the red ink is of such penetrating quality that it strikes through the paper, and appears on the other side, making alterations and photographic counterfeiting totally impossible"—but which are not worth as much even as the green tint for the purposes indicated *(See* Ormsby's Bank Note Engraving, page 10).

Ormsby continued his text with this, a fine testimonial to himself:

Speech of the Hon Henry L. Dawes

A better and more effective answer to the Hon. Mr. Spaulding was made on the floor of Congress by the Hon Henry L Dawes, of Mass. The following is an extract from his speech:

"Mr. Speaker:

"I am not going to argue the matter which I submitted to the House a moment ago, or to tire the House with a repetition of it. I am content to leave upon the record, just as I put it there, my sentiments.

"I desire, however, to correct my friend from New York [Rep. Spaulding], who is troubled night and day with this witness who appeared before the committee of investigation—sometimes called the Van Wyck Committee—and who says that he traces all I said to him, and all these 'slanders' upon the Secretary of the Treasury and Mr. Cisco, to him.[13]

"Why does my friend persist in saying that I am slandering the Secretary and Mr. Cisco? He says he is going to stand by them. He cannot stand by them any more faithfully than I do. He cannot bear testimony to their integrity any more sincerely than I do; and I am not to be bluffed off from this thing by any such talk as that.

"I will relieve him, however, by telling him that not one particle of what I stated here to the House today came from that awfully wicked witness. I have not seen him, conferred with him, heard from him, or cared for him in this connection. I do not know him from Adam. I do not know him from Eve *(laughter).* I do not care anything about him. I will tell the gentleman who my witness is. I do not know that he is my better; but I tell him that it is myself, my own eyes, and my own ears. I have been to New York City, and personally I have possessed myself of the facts I here state to the House, without any man's help, without any man's knowledge, without any man's attempt either to deter or to buy me.

"Now, he may talk about 'slanders,' and he may heap his anathemas upon this man Ormsby as much as he pleases; but I say to him that it is due to Mr. Ormsby that he should bring some scintilla of evidence here touching Ormsby, before he contents himself with justifying this contract by declaring him to be unworthy of credit.

"I have possessed myself of the facts in that case, not dependent on any officer or on any man engaged in engraving in New York or elsewhere, but on men of my own personal acquaintance in my own state (Mass.)—bank presidents, bank cashiers, and others.

"Mr. Speaker, men from my own state, occupying high public positions, who have had occasion to know, have voluntarily to me borne testimony to the integrity as well as to the skill of this man Ormsby, who is whistled down the wind by this combination of nine corporations in one, incorporated, over and doubled so as to be above suspicion of want of integrity in the eyes of any New York man. . . .

Dawes went on to suggest that while Spaulding of New York was no doubt honest, he had been unknowingly influenced by the American Bank Note Co. He went on to say that in any event, the government should be aware that under current arrangements, if that company ceased to exist, the United States would be without paper money. He respectfully suggested that Spaulding do some investigation on his own to ascertain the facts.

Ormsby noted that the debates in Congress occupied 20 columns in the *Washington Daily Globe* in January and February 1862. He went on to cite specific requirements of the Treasury in awarding currency contracts, some of them so worded that Ormsby could not possibly comply, such as "the names of the president and directors of the New York Bank Note Co., the act under which the charter was granted," etc. However, the company was not incorporated (chartered) and had no board of directors.

A proposal for a *second* contract also favored the American Bank Note Co., inasmuch as applicants were allowed to use plates already engraved for the Treasury Department. Of course, Ormsby had no such plates.

After all of this, American Bank Note Co. remained unscathed. Ormsby's reputation with the paper money decision makers such as Secretary of the Treasury Chase and New York assistant treasurer John J. Cisco fell to zero. No investigation was made of Cisco and his dealings, and he continued to amass a personal fortune. Likely, Secretary Chase had no involvement in Cisco's dealings other than endorsing them from a distance.

All of this leads to the third contender in the bank-note world, one that would join American and National.

THE CONTINENTAL BANK NOTE COMPANY

EARLY OPERATIONS

In January 1863, the Continental Bank Note Company began operations under the direction of W.L. Ormsby, who essentially turned over the business and expertise of his New York Bank Note Company to others. Premises were occupied in the upper four floors at 114 Greenwich Street, New York City, a building owned by none other than Assistant U.S. Treasurer John J. Cisco, a combination of circumstances admitting of no explanation thus far encountered in print. Sometimes things are beyond a person's knowing!

Ormsby was given the position of superintendent, but he was removed from this office almost immediately, as Treasury Secretary Chase believed he had an unsavory reputation. This bias was not supported by any facts but was probably the result of comments made by Cisco and Ormsby's competitors in the bank-note trade who were smarting from the allegations and accusations in *Cycloidal Configurations.* Although Ormsby was no longer an officer, he continued to receive a salary of $5,000, an extremely impressive figure.

THE RECOLLECTIONS OF EDWARD E. DUNBAR

A later account by company president Edward E. Dunbar noted:[14]

> Difficulties arose between Mr. Ormsby and the company, arising in the first instance from a doubt expressed by Secretary Chase as to the character of Mr. Ormsby and as to his being a proper party to be entrusted with so important a work. Under that doubt raised by the secretary, Mr. Ormsby was removed from his position, and Mr. William D. Wilson, then vice president, was put into his place.
>
> Wilson remained as general superintendent for a few months, when for some reasons which I do not precisely remember the tenor of for I was then treasurer or financier, and Mr. A.C. Wilson was president and had the management of that part of the business principally, Mr. W.D. Wilson retired from the general superintendency, and a young man named Truro Robertson was appointed in his place. Thus matters went on until December 1864, when I was elected president of the company.
>
> As soon as I was elected president I made a change in all these departments. I placed Mr. Ormsby back at the head of the practical part of the business, removed Mr. Mainwell, who was then in charge of the transfer department, made a general change in all that respect; and Mr. Ormsby having been reinstated, he having had an examination of the charges against him in Washington, and having been entirely exculpated by Mr. McCulloch, then acting Comptroller of the Currency, he came back with a letter to that effect. It was done at my instigation. . . . I made him general manager of the business, and he went on very successfully to the end of that term.[15]

TOURO ROBERTSON'S DIARY

A rich source of information on the early days at Continental, when W.L. Ormsby was active behind the scenes but was not an officer of the company, is provided by the diary of Touro Robertson, on the Continental staff beginning in January 1863:[16]

> *March 8 1863:* Our business arrangements have all been changed. We had the promise of government work, but Mr. Chase will not allow Mr. Ormsby to have anything to do with it, and therefore we pay Mr. Ormsby $5,000 per year salary and give him $1,000 cash for his transfer press. We have given up all thoughts of the lofts we were trying to get and have taken the four upper lofts of the building, No. 114 Greenwich Street. The building belongs to Mr. Cisco, and it will be another feather in our cap. Everything is going well and we expect to get in operation the first of April. It is a great undertaking.
>
> *March 10th:* Everything going on well at office.
>
> *March 11th:* Everything going on well at counting room. [The counting room was known as that part of the establishment where the sheets of banknote paper were kept. The sheets were "counted" before being turned over to the printer and checked and recounted upon their return.]
>
> *March 12th:* All day at counting room.
>
> *March 14th:* Secretary Chase is at present in the city, but the loan bill is occupying his attention. The question of contract will probably be decided this visit.[17]
>
> *March 20th*: Nothing new in business.
>
> *March 23rd:* Plenty of work at office, and I remained downtown until half-past 8:00, copying a document to lay before Secretary Chase, in order that Uncle Alex [Alexander C. Wilson] may have it this night and start for Washington tomorrow morning.
>
> *March 26:* This morning Uncle Alex returned from Washington unexpectedly, failing to accomplish anything. Secretary Chase says he will not give us one-third of the present hundred millions, but to send in our models for the next issue. I am afraid that everything is lost. How can we survive until then—no work, no money and many inevitable expenses. Can it be that we are to fail?
>
> *March 27th:* Things still look dark in business. We have been very busy today in completing and sending off our models for the new issue. They went this evening and will be opened tomorrow in Washington at noon.
>
> *March 28th:* Things look somewhat brighter today. Mr. Dunbar thinks he can probably procure from a friend of his—Mr. Russell—the amount of money we need to hold over

Vignette sheet issued by the Continental Bank Note Co. in the 1860s.

the storm—$15,000. It will be decided on Monday, probably.

April 1st: Our business is once more beginning to look like a success and I hope our financial measures will not prove abortive.

April 2nd: Everything has transpired today to our advantage. Mr. Russell and Mr. Edwards have each concluded to take 15 shares of stock at $500 (par value) per share, immediately putting the company in command of $15,000. Now we are saved from ruin. We also have received a very gratifying letter from Secretary Chase, and Mr. Cisco received a telegram from Mr. Chase, saying: "Demand of the National Bank Note Company why they do not furnish the 5-20 bonds according to contract, and if they do not give a satisfactory answer, divide the work between the American and Continental." This is even more than we could have hoped for. I hope our presses will not stand idle long.

April 3rd: All going on well in the counting room.

April 4th: This has been a great day for us. Mr. Edwards and Mr. Russell have both come up to the mark and have paid each $2,500 towards their share of the stock. When all the papers are in order, then the remaining $5,000 each will be paid up.

April 6th: Nothing of any importance occurring. Business going on quite well.

April 10th: Nothing of any importance transpiring at office.

April 11th: Very busy at counting room, getting off designs for the new Treasury notes, to be opened at the Treasury Department on Monday at 12 noon. Some of our designs are very pretty, and I am in great hopes the government will adopt some or all of them.

April 15th: I have had much to do today copying the by-laws, but have now finished and I will have time to get accounts straightened out.

April 16th: This morning we received a dispatch from Secretary Chase saying: "Alex C. Wilson please come on immediately and bring your designer." Uncle Alex, Will, and Mr. Fenwick start for Washington this evening. I hope they may bring things to a successful issue.

April 17th: The day has passed in conjecture of the Washington operations.

April 18th: Uncle Will has returned from Washington. Secretary has rejected all the proposals and gives the three companies—American, National and Continental—three weeks longer to send in new designs. We will make a hard struggle for it.

April 28th: Today the Hon. S.P. Chase, Secretary of the U.S. Treasury, visited our buildings and expressed himself very much pleased with the arrangements.

May 6th: Everything going on well. Almost all our designs finished.

May 8th: This morning our designs for the national currency and Treasury notes go to Mr. Cisco to be sent by him to Washington. Some of them are very beautiful and no doubt will bring us some work from the government.

May 11th: This morning a telegram was received from Uncle Will saying that our designs are the only ones yet in Washington. The American and National are the only companies competing, and they, it seems, are taking their time.

May 13th: Another letter from Washington, from Mr. Wilson, but nothing definite in regard to the national currency notes. I hope Secretary Chase will do the fair thing by us and give us a share of the government work; if not, I am afraid we will be ruined. Sometimes I wish I was out of it with all the money and interest I have spent, and yet again I would not sell out if I had the chance.

May 25th: Our business is getting along well and we learn from Washington that eight out of 14 of our designs have been selected. The other companies I am afraid are going to kill themselves.

May 27th: Today Uncle Will and Alex have both returned from Washington. After a hard fight we have won the victory. We have the engraving of the 5s and 10s, and if we do that well we will have the printing.[18] This is all of the work that has been given out. Thanks to a good God who has answered my prayers and to the kindness of Secretary Chase we are now on the high road to success and a good income. The profits are enormous.

Nov. 30th: Today I have been down to the office and seen the first complete proof of the $5 national currency ever printed. It has decided the question of registry, and our faces and backs register perfectly. Clark arranged the borders so as to print dry and though we could not finish wet, we have shown his error and the last great difficulty is done away with. Our future appears certain. On Tuesday I give up the secretary's position and take that of general superintendent. I hope that I may be able to carry the position properly and make all things work together harmoniously and smoothly. Today at the post office I met Febre, and he walked down and surveyed our building and was very much pleased and astonished. He had no idea that we had such a great establishment as was presented to his vision.

Nov. 30th: Mr. Dunbar and Mr. Wilson [W.D.] went to Washington tonight with impressions of the national currency ($5 notes) printed on bank note paper with and without the bronze. They go to procure the abolishment of the detestable bronze and I believe they will accomplish it. All looks well for business, and all that I could have wished for is happening.

Dec. 1st: We have today received the telegram saying that we must go on printing with our own paper (300,000 sheets), that the bronze will not be used and that we also get the printing of the two-year Treasury notes. We can now go on printing with 20 or 30 presses immediately, and begin with the last of this week to deliver the notes of the First National Bank of Washington. We are now fairly launched upon a clear sea and may consider ourselves safe from storm if the vessel is kept under good guidance.

Dec. 2nd: Everything seems to look well and the die of the whole note is progressing toward completion. The notes of the First National Bank of Washington will not be ready before the middle of next week, and they will be the first notes given to the public. This evening I went down to the office and worked on my books until 11:00 and succeeded in getting my trial-balance out correctly. I confess to feeling tired and of course it brings with it a feeling of downheartedness.

Dec. 3rd: Nothing of any importance happened today. Everything seems to be gliding along smoothly; and although the increased delay on the large die makes me somewhat uneasy, I am content with the daily result.

Dec. 5th: All day busy at the counting room getting things so that they will work smoothly. We have found the black plates in such a condition that we will have to wait for the new die, and I fear it will be but little better. I trust that all will be well and that we shall escape from the dilemma as we have from all others. The anxiety about business is almost intolerable and I feel the wear and tear.

Dec. 7: This day the great die went into the fire and came out hardened splendidly and without a blemish. It only remains now to take up a roll and all will be well. In the great glee of a successful hardening the danger of taking up the roll is almost lost. This is a great gain and will yield us the requisite number of plates.

Dec. 8: All day dressing the bed piece preparatory to taking up the roll.

Dec. 9th: All the morning preparing the press and bed piece for the enormous pressure. In the morning our adjourned annual meeting of stockholders took place. The president and treasurer were re-elected. The office of vice-president created and given to Mr. D. Wilson and the post of secretary to Mr. Russell, Jr. I have taken the post of general manager or superintendent and have now the place for which I have long wished. I believe myself better able to hold it than any of the rest. I feel the responsibility of the position and shall hope to be able to go through with it successfully. After the meeting all the officers went upstairs into the transfer room to see the great roll taken up. Upon the face of all was easily marked the intense anxiety for the result. As each foot of the tooth check received the bar, and additional pressure was applied, it seemed as if something must give way. The immense mass of metal composing the standard of the press creaked and sprung perceptibly and I confess to a feeling of fear during the operation and of great relief when Mr. Ormsby announced that the bed piece was unharmed, although the roll was not quite up. Before night it was fully up and the great deed was accomplished.

Dec. 22nd: Everything going well but slowly at counting room. It seems as if the business must drag.

Dec. 23rd: Drag, drag, go things along and it seems impossible to expedite them. I trust all will develop well.

Dec. 26th: I find the letters from the government complaining about the delay in getting out the plates and in printing. We must hurry up and increase our delivery.

Dec. 27th: The morning found me at the office seeing how affairs were getting along. The plates were being turned out rapidly and I have great hopes of our being able to complete our contract in contract time.

At this insertion the diary ended for the time being, and nothing more was added until several years later in 1866. In the meantime Continental kept up its business printing federal currency. Its $5 National Bank Notes were the most popular denomination in that series.

W.L. Ormsby kept busy at Continental, mainly with the transfer or siderography process and the mak-

Serial number 1, plate position A, of the very first National Bank Note sheet, First National Bank, Washington, D.C. (*The 100 Greatest American Currency Notes;* note discovered by Littleton Coin Co.)

ing of plates, most notably for federal currency, but also for other security documents. After about 1866 he left Continental and moved to Hampton, Connecticut.

Ormsby Writes to Chase

After leaving Continental, Ormsby wrote to Salmon P. Chase, former secretary of the Treasury, but since December 6, 1864, the chief justice of the United States Supreme Court:

> Hampton, Conn. March 29th, 1867
>
> You may remember that I called upon you about the time of the Battle of Bull Run in 1861 in relation to the engraving of the first US. greenbacks, at which time you informed me that the matter had been referred to Mr. Cisco of New York City.
>
> The competitors for this work were the American, the National and the New York Bank Note Co., of the latter of which I was sole owner and proprietor. Your letter to me at that time having been delayed four days, gave the other companies opportunity to secure the work, and I was left with nothing to do, under the necessity of discharging my employees and business almost entirely destroyed. You will remember also that you advertised for proposals to engrave the last hundred millions which were to be precisely like those already engraved. No one could compete for the work because the dies were owned by the other companies and it would have been wrong to copy them.
>
> When the last hundred millions was authorized, the Continental Bank Note Company first approached you. This was my company with a new name. I entered into partnership with the two brothers Wilson and their young nephew, Touro Robinson [*sic*], all of whom were totally ignorant of the business. You will doubtless remember that you favored the Continental but objected to me, although I was the only engraver in the company. You gave a promise to give one third of the government work to the Continental and ordered the other companies to give up copies of their dies with which the greenbacks were made. They desired to possess my share of the stock.
>
> "This thing has arrived at a magnitude that none of us ever dreamed of" was their remark when they were conspiring to have me sell out my interest of thirty thousand dollars for fifteen thousand, which, because they were not in funds to make a settlement, they agreed to pay in weekly installments for three years. In their arguments they laid great stress in your objection to me.
>
> Now Sir, let me assure you that during all this I was your truest friend. I saved you from being swindled by the other companies. I sold out knowing that the Continental could not execute their first contract without me and so it proved.
>
> The [illegible] Wilson wrote you about five months afterwards as follows:
>
> "July 3, 1863 The most expert and ingenious living artist in bank note work is confessedly Mr. W.L. Ormsby. We claim that Mr. Ormsby is a man whose integrity is beyond all honest doubt. It is of the highest importance to us and to the rapid execution of government work that Mr. Ormsby should be permitted to enter our service. Many of the bonds now in our hands can only be prepared by Mr. Ormsby under the contract which the Secretary has desired us to inspect &c."
>
> They had previously written to Mr. Cisco, "Our company is based on Mr. W.L. Ormsby's establishment."
>
> Thus I was the sole founder of the Continental, the sole engraver, and the sole means of making yourself and the government independent of the American and National companies. I was the means also of placing in the hands of S.M. Clark a knowledge of the business by my book on bank note engraving—the only written work in the subject in any written language—the means of forcing the other companies to surrender their dies, which enabled Mr. Clark to do what he has done.
>
> I have carried the Continental through their contract for fives, on the Unit System—my invention. The fives have not yet been counterfeited. The Continental having become a losing concern, discharged me, who had [served] them so fully and are now selling out their stock, saving their rich dividends, and not knowing into whose hands the company will pass. I feel that any disaster that may fall upon the Continental Co. will naturally reflect upon me. My desire, therefore, is that if the company is to be wound up, that I may be in some way appointed to do it.
>
> In regard to the above facts, I refer to the late president of the Continental B.N. Co., Edward E. Dunbar, New York City, and the Hon. Eli Thayer, New York. A word from you will I presume help Mr. McCulloch (who I think is my personal friend) to a safe action on the subject. I am now forced into retirement on a farm in the interior of Connecticut where I had provided a home for my mother, now aged 82 years.
>
> Your action against me, honestly on your part, has had the effect of depriving me of many well earned professional laurels and or enriching those who do not deserve it to my entire ruin. I am out of business—all bank note work is now done by government. I have many new inventions which I could introduce in the establishment at Washington and make that establishment the finest in the world.
>
> Yours with respect,
>
> W.L. Ormsby

Epilogue: In 1879 Continental was merged into the American Bank Note Co.

Progress of the American Bank Note Company

Onward and Upward

Despite the slings and arrows wielded by Ormsby, and despite much negative press arising from government investigations in the 1860s concerning federal paper money contracts, bribes, and the like (fascinating to read today, but beyond the purview of the present text), the American Bank Note Company continued to prosper. As much has been said about the antecedents of ABNCo and of the formation of the company, the following accounts emphasize the processes in use by the firm to make currency.

An 1861 Account

On October 5, 1861, this account was picked up and published by the *Portsmouth* (New Hampshire) *Journal:*

> **How Bank Notes Are Made**
>
> *The New York Evening Post* informs us that the American Bank Note Company located in that city, is the most extensive establishment of the kind in the world. It employs some of the best artists in the country in sketching designs.
>
> In some cases the artists send original sketches, but generally embody the ideas suggested to them. Darley's designs are frequent in our bank note circulation, and are at once recognized by those who are familiar with his style.
>
> The vignettes are combined with portraits of individuals, and the letters and lathe work which make up a bank note. The drawings are sent from the design-room to the pictorial engraving department. The best artists are employed in this department, and there are fifteen men, each at his own desk, who work eight hours per day, and earn from $2,000 to $4,000 per year.
>
> Some of them work exclusively upon "heads;" others upon human figures. In some cases a vignette which comprises landscape sky, architecture and figures will pass through as many different hands, and the separate parts of the work, finished by artists who have made that style a specialty, make the whole as perfect as possible; indeed, a first-class vignette, unless a portrait, is hardly ever by one hand, and a portion of it is "bit in" with acids, and afterwards finished with a graver.
>
> The portrait engravers become so skillful, that they produce a perfect likeness from a photograph, painting or engraving, and whatever is in hand is given to the artist who is best qualified to make a finished picture of the kind required. All of the vignettes, and much of the larger letter work, are engraved on separate pieces of steel, from which proofs only are printed. These pieces are taken to the hardening-room, where two men who are experienced in handling steel, harden them, by heating and plunging them into water or oil.
>
> The hardened plates are placed under presses of enormous power, and are "taken up" upon decarbonized dies of a cylindrical form, which are afterwards hardened, and used to transfer the impression to the plate from which the notes are printed [the siderographic process]. Thus the work is doubly transferred before it is printed.
>
> The shading of the letters is done by machinery, and in this way also is executed that curious complicated and beautiful ground work for the figures, and from which the tints on the face and back of a note are printed. Such is the accuracy and uniformity of the geometrical lathe-work and cycloidal ruling that, it is impossible to imitate them by hand.
>
> The production of these lace-like figures is the result of a mathematical problem worked out beforehand; so many turns of certain wheels will produce a certain figure, which can be multiplied by the transferring process indefinitely. The machines are very complicated and expensive, (though to one unacquainted with them, they seem cheap and simple) and require great skill and experience in their management and operation. We were shown in this department a geometrical lathe, not twice as large as an ordinary sewing machine, and less than half as noisy, which was three years in building, and cost about $10,000. These machines are never patented, as the secret of their construction is worth more than a patent, and improvements and alterations are made from time to time, while their great cost prohibits their coming into general or improper use.

Harper's Calls on ABNCo

In 1861 and 1862, *Harper's New Monthly Magazine* featured a series of articles, "Making Money." One installment dealt with the Philadelphia Mint, another with the New York Assay Office and Sub-Treasury, and one with bank-note printing. The last, published in February 1862, included a description of the leading firm in the business.

The unnamed author of the article enlisted ABNCo president Tracy R. Edson as his guide through the company's headquarters in the Merchants Exchange, but had to wait until he concluded a meeting with visiting Secretary of the Treasury Salmon P. Chase and Assistant Treasurer John J. Cisco. The account began with this discussion, which also gives an estimate of the number of banks in operation at the time and of the dangers of counterfeiting:

> The *Bank Note Reporter* is a suggestive if not a very entertaining work, brim-full of facts. The lists of this *Index Expurgatorius* are headed with the significant warning, "Refuse the Notes of all Banks not found here," branding in a phrase a crowd of broken and fraudulent concerns.
>
> There are in the United States and the British Provinces, as we count, about 2,000 banks whose notes are worth something—say from 20 to 100 cents on the dollar. Upon quite four-fifths of these fraudulent notes have been detected, usually several kinds upon each.
>
> Thus, of the 57 banks in the city of New York not one has escaped, the total number of their fraudulent issues being about 350. The same ratio would give 12,000 for the whole country; but this is too large, since banks in the commercial parts of the country offer the greatest temptations to forg-

ers. Still there are noted about 6,000 different issues of spurious notes. Theoretically every man is liable to be defrauded by any one of these.

At first view this would shake our confidence in the genuineness of any bank note. But the fact is that in nineteen cases out of twenty a bad bill is detected almost as soon as its circulation is attempted. The number of "dangerous" counterfeits is very small. Not one person in a hundred has ever lost a dollar in this way.

For this almost complete immunity from loss we are indebted to the artistic and mechanical skill which is lavished upon our bank notes. This perfection has been attained by slow degrees. Nothing can be more rude than the Massachusetts notes issued in 1690, the first American paper money. Hardly better are the Continental bills, first issued in 1775. These were engraved by Paul Revere, the best of the four engravers then in the country [*sic:* in fact, Revere had nothing to do with them]. A comparison of these with a United States Treasury Note of 1861 will show the progress of the art during the interval.

When our financial system began to assume its present form banks were multiplied, each of which demanded distinctive notes. Demand creates supply, and the best artistic talent in the country was attracted in this direction. At first a single artist engraved an entire plate, and not infrequently printed it with his own hands. Afterward several combined to produce a plate, each doing that part of the work in which he excelled. Various machines were also invented, some of which, as Perkins's Transfer Press and Spencer's Geometric Lathe, contain the germs of the complicated instruments which . . . perform such an important part in producing a bank note of the present day.

Subsequently private companies were organized, each containing artists excelling in some particular branch. Each of these companies produced excellent work, but as no one had all of the best talent, and as each had the exclusive control of some valuable mechanical invention which the others could not use, no one note could combine all attainable perfection. Banks meanwhile demanded the most perfect notes that could be produced.

In 1858 the leading bank note firms, nine in number, united themselves into an Association which was incorporated under the title of the "American Bank Note Company." The plates prepared by them are decidedly superior to any ever before executed. More recently another Association for the same purpose has been organized under the name of the "National Bank Note Company." The generous rivalry for artistic perfection between these two companies affords a sure guarantee that bank notes executed in America will continue to be, as they now are, superior to any others in the world. No other country has yet anything to compare with them.

The account in *Harper's* went on to discuss the making of bank-note plates and the printing of currency in its very informative account. Then this on engraving, which was accomplished in the Modeling and Designing Rooms at company headquarters:

[These rooms comprise] a handsome suite of apartments with a lofty groined roof. The walls are covered with original drawings by Darley, Casilear, Edmonds, Herrick, and others. Portfolios filled with such drawings are opened for our inspection. A connoisseur in art could nowhere spend a more pleasant day than here. . . . These drawings have been used as designs for vignettes. They are made much larger than the engravings from them. A favorite size for the drawings for elaborate vignettes is about twice that of a page of this magazine [pages measured about 8 inches wide by 10 inches deep]. When an engraving is to be made after one of these drawings, it is photographed in the exact size desired upon a plate of steel; the outlines are cut faintly upon the plate, which is then given to the engraver to fill up.

It is seen that photography, the tool of counterfeiters beginning in the 1850s, had become essential for making steel-plate vignettes in the 1860s. Then this item relating to making plates and printing from them:

Copper-plate Engraving. In this the lines and dots which make up the picture are cut, one by one, upon a plate of metal. To print from this, the whole plate is covered with ink, which also fills up the engraved lines and dots. This ink is carefully wiped off from the surface of the plate, leaving only that which fills the engraved lines. Then the paper is laid on the plate, which is passed under a heavy roller, which forces the surface of the sheet into the lines, taking up the ink. This process of inking, wiping, and rolling must be repeated for each impression.

Engraving on steel is precisely the same as on copper. Copper, being a soft metal, wears out rapidly in printing, so that but few perfect copies can be obtained from a copper plate; steel, being much harder, furnishes a greater number of copies.

The reporter was razzle-dazzled by accounts of security measures to check the integrity of clients, which, by now, the present reader will know were patently untrue:

When a person wishes a note or series of notes prepared, he must first show that the bank is legally established and that he is authorized to procure its plates. Without this precaution the company will not undertake the work.

Then this more useful information:

In designing a note there are several points to be considered. The various denominations must all be different in appearance, and none of them must resemble any note of any other bank. Each must combine the various kinds of work adopted as securities against frauds, and must, moreover, present a handsome appearance.

Steel cylinder die used to imprint a large horizontal numeral on a plate for the famous "Lazy 2" National Bank notes. This process was in use during the bank-note engraving industry for many years. (*Scientific American,* December 1872)

A hand-operated spider press of the type in use at the American Bank Note Co. and other printers of currency, including the Bureau of Printing and Engraving when it went into operation in the 1870s. At one time ABNCo had 100 such devices. By the early 21st century just three remained.

Geometric lathe on exhibit at the Smithsonian Institution as part of the National Numismatic Collection, 2004.

A transfer press in use in the 19th century. Operating such a device required extraordinary skills. The machine enabled design elements in raised relief on steel cylinder dies (today called *roller dies*) to be transferred to form a part of a bank-note plate or to create a duplicate vignette die (as they were designated). (*Scientific American,* December 1872)

> Then a bank frequently wishes its notes to have some special adaptation to its title or location. A "Farmers Bank" will naturally wish an agricultural scene to appear on its notes; a "Merchants Bank" will wish a commercial scene; an "Artisans Bank" a mechanical scene; and so on. Then there will be prepossessions in respect to portraits. If the directors are Democrats, they will probably wish Jefferson or Jackson, Douglas or Wright; if Republicans, Lincoln or Seward, Scott or Chase. An Eastern bank will likely wish Webster, a Western one Clay, a Southern one Calhoun.
>
> The agent examines the portfolios containing proofs of the dies in the possession of the company. He has ample scope for choice, for there are some 20,000 of them. Of these probably 5,000 are vignettes, 5,000 portraits and emblematical figures, and 10,000 checks and counters.[19] Aided by the officers of the company, who take care that in combination and arrangement the notes of each bank shall be easily distinguishable from those of any other, this part of the plate is agreed upon.
>
> Then the general style and arrangement of the lettering is settled, and a sketch of the note is made. The vignettes, portraits, checks, and counters are now put upon the plate in their proper places by the transferring machine, and the plate is passed to the Letter Engraving Room, where the lettering is performed by hand. Here also is room for the display of artistic talent, for a good and bad lettered line differ almost as much as a good and a bad vignette or portrait.
>
> The Lettering Room employs a much larger number of artists than the Pictorial Room, because the lettering of each note must be to a great extent peculiar to it, while vignettes or portraits may be used in different combinations on any one of a thousand. Here also the principle of division of labor comes in.
>
> One man's forte is German text; that of another is ornamental letters; that of a third is script. Each executes that part in which he excels, and the combined result of their skill appears on every note. Our plate is now finished; the main one, that is, which is to be printed in black; for most bank notes now have the back and a part of the face in colors, for which separate plates are used. This complicates the process and renders the work of the counterfeiter more difficult. But its special object is to afford security against photographic imitations.

After this explanation, a visit was made to the Printing Room:

> This room, or rather series of rooms, present a busy aspect. They occupy three sides of a hollow square, of which the rotunda of the Exchange forms the center. . . . Rows of presses are ranged through each division. On some are being worked the black plates of a note; on others the green backs and checks; on others the red patterns which appear on various parts of the notes.
>
> According to our count there are in this room about 100 presses, giving employment to nearly 200 persons. The necessity for this large force will appear when we remember that each note, as now produced, requires at least three separate printings: First the black, secondly the green upon the face, and third the green check upon the back. A fourth printing, usually red, is frequently added upon some part.
>
> Notes also wear out more rapidly than is generally supposed. A curious table compiled from the records of the New York Banking Department has been prepared by Mr. Gavit, showing that the average "life of a bank note" is about three years. That is, taking one with another, notes in three years become so worn and defaced as not to be fit for circulation. When such a note comes back to the bank it is destroyed and is replaced by a new one. This period might be shortened with advantage to the public. . . .
>
> A portion of the colored work of a note is printed from raised plates, like type, upon the ordinary hand-press. But the greater part of the printing is "copper-plate." The plate is laid on a brazier containing fire, for it must be warm to keep the ink in a sufficiently fluid state. The ink is applied with a roller all over the plate. The workman gives it two or three dexterous wipes with a cloth, and one or two more with his bare hand, removing all the ink except that which fills up the lines of the engraving; then places it on the press, lays the sheet of paper upon it, and by turning a winch passes it under the roller, which gives the impression.
>
> The whole operation is one of great nicety, for if the plate were not wiped perfectly clean the whole note would be blurred over; the paper also must be laid on in exactly the proper place, otherwise, when the colored pattern is added, it will not fall exactly in its right position. The presses must therefore all be of the most accurate description.
>
> Bank notes were formerly numbered with a pen. The numbers are now usually printed in red by means of a very ingenious little press, so arranged that the action by which one number is printed changes the type for the next impression to the number immediately succeeding without any possibility of error. Thus, if 666 has been printed on a note, the figures for 667 are presented for the next. The machines are arranged to present any number up to 7 figures. That is, they will give any number from 1 to 999,999. No two notes of the same "letter" can have the same number; so that a record of the "letter" and "number" is sufficient to identify any note numbered by the machine. . . .
>
> In all the American Bank Note Company employs about 350 persons, of whom more than 100 are females. There are about 60 artists and engravers; 250 are employed in the Printing and Counting Rooms; the remainder being superintendents and clerks in the various departments. The presses and lathes are all worked by human power. Still there is employment for a steam-engine of 20-horse power. It pumps water, moves the elevator, works the hydraulic presses, turns the ink mills, heats the building, and makes itself generally useful in a variety of ways.

A $50 note printed for the Confederate States of America by the Southern Bank Note Co. branch of ABNCo. The design combined stock vignettes widely used earlier on notes of state-chartered banks. All C.S.A. bills were IOUs in that they were redeemable in the future. This one is payable 12 months after the date of September 1, 1861, inked on the note. Made in limited quantities in comparison to many later C.S.A. issues, the Southern Bank Note Co. bills are highly prized by numismatists today.

The New Orleans Branch of ABNCo

On January 26, 1861, the state of Louisiana seceded from the Union. A popular referendum had been held, but no results were announced. Instead, a convention of secessionists met in Baton Rouge and formulated the declaration. On May 1, 1862, New Orleans was taken by General Benjamin Butler, and the city was again part of the Union. The city was inhabited by citizens who had taken vows of allegiance to the Confederacy. Nearly everyone of commercial or political importance who had sympathies with the North, and who had declined to swear loyalty to the Confederacy, had departed. The rule of *Beast* Butler, or *Spoons* Butler, as he was called, remained controversial for decades afterward. Butler's view is that he had to take strong measures with the citizens in order to control them. The view of many of the inhabitants, in contrast, was that Butler and his troops stole and pillaged the towns (taking, among other things, silverware including spoons) and used unnecessary force.

While the city was under the control of the Confederacy, the Southern Bank Note Co., the branch of ABNCo in that city, obligingly printed bills for the Confederate States of America, these being some of the finer issues of that government. Most later bills were made in locations closer to the capital at Richmond and included work by engravers imported from England. Certain of these artists asked for and received payment in gold coins, even in times when the C.S.A. Treasury was nearly empty. Although there are exceptions, most bills are of fairly rustic quality, some made by lithography rather than printing from copper or steel plates.

The New Orleans office was under the direction of Solomon Schmidt, an engraver of long experience who had emigrated from Germany to the United States about 1840 and went to work for Rawdon, Wright & Hatch's branch in New Orleans in 1843. Beginning about 1851 he became agent (business manager) of the branch. In 1858 it came under the supervision of the new ABNCo.

After the Union forces reoccupied New Orleans in April 1862, Schmidt kept the office open. Later in the year he made an accounting, which showed an operating profit of about $17,000 for 1861 and 1862, although some equipment had been lost.

Further Aspects of ABNCo

With hefty federal contracts on hand, in November 1862 ABNCo opened new offices in the former Merchants Exchange in New York, now known as the United States Custom House. The facilities were more impressive than ever.

Tracy R. Edson resigned as president in 1863. Ever the entrepreneur, he became involved in other corporations, eventually including the Celluloid Company, the Metropolitan Telegraph & Telephone Co., and the American Speaking Telephone Company. His successor as president was George W. Hatch, one of the more accomplished engravers of bank notes, whose vivid vignettes of mythological scenes enlivened many bills. Hatch died in 1866, the last year of use of bills by state-chartered banks. In 1867 the company relocated to the corner of Broadway and Liberty Street, where it remained for 17 years.

ABNCo went on to fill federal currency contracts into the 1870s, until the Bureau of Engraving and Printing took over that business. In the meantime, it developed many customers in foreign countries, including exclusive arrangements to print paper money. The printing of stock certificates, bank letterheads, checks, bonds, and other security items continued.

The National Bank Note Co. and the Continental Bank Note Co. were merged into ABNCo in 1879, the same year that a handful of smaller engraving firms were also acquired. During the 20th century, ABNCo remained dominant in the security-printing business, including paper money for so many countries that a world map filled in to show its customers would have very few blank spaces.

THE CALAIS BANK CAPER

THE CIVIL WAR

The Calais (Maine) Bank, established with a capital of $50,000 in 1831, conducted a strictly regional business for a long time. It elected not to have its bills redeemed by the Suffolk Bank in Boston, and therefore its currency sold at a deep discount at places distant from home. Located on the Atlantic seacoast adjacent to the border with New Brunswick in Canada, the bank did an active business financing the maritime trade.

During the Civil War, Canada was a neutral country. A possession of England, if anything Canada was sympathetic to the interests of the Confederate States of America, a trading partner with the home country, furnishing cotton for the inland textile mills. Many Union men who sought to avoid conscription or who agreed with the Confederate cause were living in Canada, as were Confederate soldiers who had escaped from prison camps or who were simply there on undisclosed missions.

In December 1863, rumors spread through Calais and other border towns that Confederate soldiers were about to mount an attack, but such an event never materialized. The danger was real, as evidenced by the capture by 16 men, mostly inhabitants of New Brunswick, under the leadership of a Confederate naval officer, of the 460-ton wooden passenger steamer SS *Chesapeake*. The vessel was intercepted on December 7 in the seas off Cape Cod, Massachusetts, where it was en route from New York City to Portland, Maine. The attackers, claiming to be operating under a letter of marque or authorization for privateering, took their prize to Sambro Harbor in Nova Scotia. In a turnabout, she was captured there by the American warship USS *Ella and Annie* and soon repatriated.

Rumors continued to fly, including warnings of an uprising by the Passamaquoddy Indians who had been enlisted by the Confederacy to massacre residents along the St. Croix River in Maine. In ensuing months the stories subsided, but many citizens kept up an armed guard. On July 16, 1864, Governor Samuel Cony of Maine received information from two sources that an attack was being planned. Consul J.Q. Howard had wired from Canada, "A small raiding party left St. John last night to commit depredations on the Maine frontier."

Printing paper money at the American Bank Note Co. in the 19th century. (Modern watercolor, courtesy of ABNCo)

A $10 proof note of the Calais Bank with the printed date April 1st 1852. Patent Stereotype Steel Plate by the New England Bank Note Co. Certain Maine banks continued using these old-style bills long after most institutions elsewhere had turned to popular designs with large ornate vignettes. This is an archival specimen with notations on the back, dated March 26, 1852, that it is printed on "Crane's old" paper (made in Dalton, Massachusetts, by the Crane Co.).

The governor wired warnings to the mayors and others in towns and cities, alerting them to the possible danger. Along the border, citizens were on high alert. A unit of the state guards, under Captain Benjamin Flint, became overly enthusiastic and crossed into Canada to position themselves in the New Brunswick town of St. Stephen.

Acting on information received from the Reverend John Collins, brother of William Collins, Howard sent another message, including this warning:

> Satisfactory evidence has been furnished me that one William Collins, late of the rebel army, is now organizing in this vicinity a force to commit depredations on the Maine frontier. There is reason to believe that the somewhat notorious James McDonald and a precious scoundrel by the name of Jones, are concerned in this new military movement. . . .
>
> Collins is well known here and although a man of energy, is such an eminent fool as to suppose that he can march a small force through the Northern states to Kentucky. He affirms that he is authorized by the "Confederate authorities" to burn and destroy and to show no quarter.

An Unexpected Incursion

In 1864 the capital of the Calais Bank was $100,000. Signing bills were cashier Joseph A. Lee and president George Downes. At 10 A.M. on July 18, Consul Howard wired cashier Lee in Calais:

> Fourteen men left here in a lead-colored sail and row boat for Calais. Would touch at Robbinston. Intention was to rob your bank in daytime. If they have not been alarmed, you can apprehend them quietly in the bank. William Collins is the leader.

A newspaper account told what happened next:

> CALAIS, Me., July 18. At midday today there was an attempt to rob the Calais Bank by a small party of rebel raiders who came here from St. John. Three men were arrested. The leader of the gang is Collins, a captain in the 15th Mississippi regiment. They say some 30 associates promised to meet them here, but failed. The vigilance of the state guard prevented the consummation of this bold scheme of pillage. The three men have been committed. The citizens are arming in expectation of an attack tonight.[20]

It was learned that four raiders entered the bank and put some gold coins on the counter in front of cashier Lee to exchange for Legal Tender Notes, which would be sold at a deep discount. At the same time another of the intruders reached for a pistol in his pocket, and another shouted a warning to the bank employees.

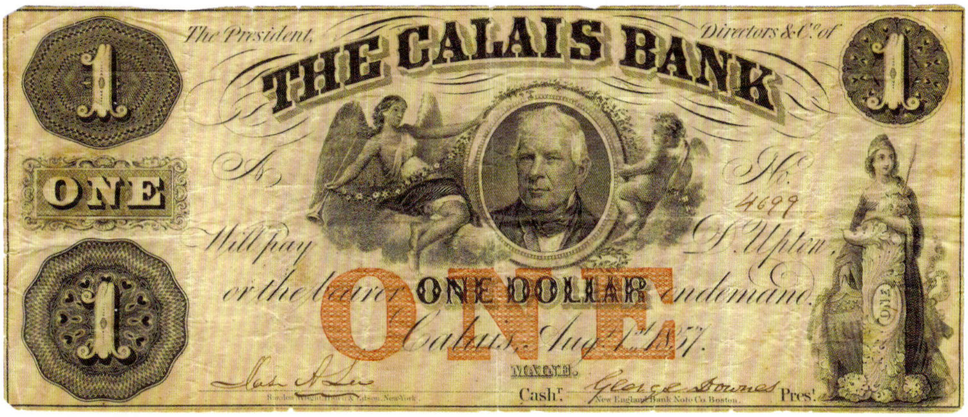

A $1 note of the Calais Bank, August 1, 1857, bearing the signature of president George Downes. The back, with CHECK, illustrates one of the various security imprints of the New England Bank Note Co.

Forewarned, the bank was prepared. Four men behind the bank counter brandished their own pistols, while other armed citizens stormed the building. The raiders had no chance. William Collins was captured with a Confederate flag in his pocket, which he said he had planned to fly over the town. He and the others related that they were going to burn the town, but a reinforcement of 25 men did not arrive to help them.

Although townspeople were set to kill the invaders on the spot, reason prevailed and three of them in handcuffs were hauled off in the night to the Washington County Jail in nearby Machias. The fourth young man was turned free, and he went back to St. John. It was learned that Collins, earlier a captain in the 15th Mississippi Regiment, was now a master in the Confederate navy, although he had stated to his associates that he was a major in the Confederate army. It was also learned that for a moment in Calais he had taken his flag and had shaken in it the breeze.

Although the trio of inmates requested to be treated as prisoners of war, Judge Charles Danforth found them guilty of the crime of bank robbery and sentenced each to three years in the Maine State Prison in Thomaston. On their way to Thomaston, traveling by stage through Ellsworth, they shouted a hurrah for Confederate President Jefferson Davis.

It turned out that Collins was not imprisoned for very long. Thirty-six days into his sentence, on November 26, 1864, he escaped. Traveling in secrecy, he went back to St. John, then to the South. On May 18, 1865, a month after the Civil War ended, he was pardoned by the federal government. Another raider, Francis X. Jones, was pardoned by Governor Coney on January 15, 1866, and the third, William Phillips, was given his freedom on May 7 of the same year. Today, the poignant Confederate flag is on view at the Maine Historical Society in Portland.

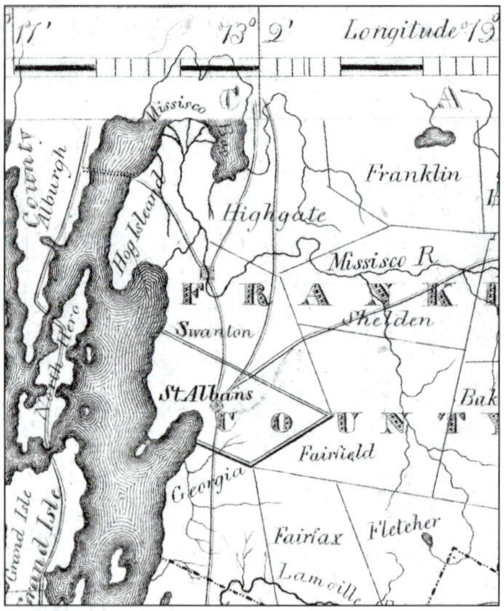

Detail of a Vermont map showing St. Albans. The border with Canada is near the top margin (Thompson, *History of Vermont,* 1842). The town of Sheldon, connected by a road going northeast, also figures in the present story.

A $5 note of the Franklin County Bank, St. Albans, Vermont, signed by cashier Marcus W. Beardsley, who would figure prominently in the historic events that took place in the town on October 19, 1864.

THE GREAT ST. ALBANS RAID

SETTING THE SCENE

If one searches long enough, just about any obsolete bank note can be linked to a story.[21] For some notes, the story is dramatic. Such is the case for certain bills issued in St. Albans, Vermont, a quiet community of about 2,800 citizens on the shore of Lake Champlain at the northwest corner of the state, just below the border of Canada. The time is Wednesday, October 19, 1864. The Civil War continued to be fought far to the south. The story of the incursion into Calais, Maine, had been newsworthy but not sensational, and most citizens of St. Albans were not aware that it had happened—in view of important battles and skirmishes in the war zone in the South.

Vermont was largely unaffected in a direct sense, although more than 34,000 of its young men were in the service, of whom more than 5,000 would never return. The economy of St. Albans, largely agrarian, was enhanced by railroad machine shops and facilities that employed several hundred men. A staffed recruiting station for the Union army was also in the village.

It was an especially quiet day on the main street of St. Albans. Light rain in the morning had kept most people indoors. Main Street was muddy, and few people were to be seen. On this particular Wednesday, about 40 leading citizens were out of town, attending the session of the legislature in Montpelier and the state supreme court in Burlington. Meanwhile, around the town, citizens were involved in everyday affairs, clerking in stores, conversing, catching up with office work—a very ordinary scene, nothing unusual. In contrast, the day before had been crowded with activity, as Tuesday was market day each week. The population about doubled as farmers, merchants, traders, tourists, and others arrived to buy, sell, and exchange information. The village was easily accessible by road and by rail and was a popular regional destination.

Nine days earlier, on October 10, Bennett H. Young, age 21, and two companions had come to town on the Montreal Express train from Canada. They secured accommodations at the Tremont House on Main Street, which took in boarders. Three of their friends arrived the next day and checked in at the American House Hotel. The young men were a friendly bunch, typical tourists, and arrived from several different directions, including some from Chicago. Young read the Bible aloud in room 6, suggesting to guests who could hear him from the narrow hall that he was a theology student. He and his roommate, William Hutchinson, attracted the attention of two other boarders, Margaret Smith and Sarah Clark.

On the third day, Young had breakfast with the two girls. He invited Sarah to be his guest the next day for dinner at the American House, the finest dining spot in town. She was thrilled. During their repast they enjoyed each other's company, talked about the attractiveness of St. Albans, and discussed biblical prophecies. Afterward they walked around town and Sarah pointed out and discussed buildings and other points of interest, including Governor J. Gregory Smith's mansion on Bank Street, a highlight of the village. Sarah knew the governor's family well and soon arranged a tour of the grounds for the next Saturday morning. In the meantime, she was falling in love with Bennett, despite her roommate Margaret's advice that she learn more about him and go slowly. In due course Bennett and Sarah were guests at the mansion, where Bennett paid particular attention to the stable and its fine horses.

Bennett H. Young and his friends were sociable and of an inquiring turn of mind. Around town they asked many questions of local folk in a casual manner, such as which livery stables had good horses for rent. They visited the three local banks and tarried to watch business being transacted, making mental notes of where their safes were located and judging the temperament of the clerks and cashiers. As they hoped to go hunting, so they said, they checked on the possibility of borrowing or renting guns. On October 18, six more travelers from Canada arrived, with four of them checking into the Tremont House. On the morning of the 19th, six more young men came to town and registered at the St. Albans House, while five others took accommodations in the American House Hotel.

As to the sequence of memorable events in St. Albans, newspaper accounts tell the story. These are from the *Daily Spy,* a widely read paper published in Worcester, Massachusetts:

October 20, 1864:

A Tragedy at St. Albans, Vermont
Three Banks Robbed and Citizens Shot

ST. ALBANS, VT., Oct. 19.—An invasion of this town took place today. Some twenty or twenty-five armed desperadoes supposed to be in rebel employ, from Canada, made an assault on the several banks about 4 o'clock this afternoon. The National Bank was robbed of about $50,000, mostly in bills; the St. Albans Bank was robbed of between $70,000 and $80,000, and the Franklin County Bank of a considerable amount.

Some twenty horses were also seized by the desperadoes and carried off. Several citizens who resisted were deliberately shot, two were wounded seriously, and it is feared fatally, E.J. Morrison, a contractor, and C. Huntington, a jeweler. Several others are reported slightly injured. The raiders threatened to burn the town and left in the direction of Canada. A large party of armed citizens have gone in pursuit.

St. Albans is about eight miles from the Canada line, and three from Lake Champlain. It is the residence of Gov. Smith.

The attack began about 4 o'clock P.M. The cashier of one of the banks was locked up in his safe, where he remained a considerable time. The raiders came in the guise of travelers and may have been roving about town sometime before the attack.

The issue of October 21, 1864, included multiple accounts:

WE HAVE GRATIFYING INTELLIGENCE that nine of the robbers who made a successful descent upon the banks of St. Albans, Vt., Wednesday, have been arrested, and that one hundred and fifty thousand dollars, or nearly the whole amount of their booty, has been recovered.

The authorities of Vermont and of Canada are in sharp pursuit of the rest of the gang, with a fair prospect of bringing them to grief. No difficulty is apprehended in bringing the desperadoes before our courts under the extradition treaty, the Canadian authorities seeming to manifest equal interest with our own officers in securing justice for the scoundrels.

ST. ALBANS, Vt., Oct. 20—Later advices from the parties who are pursuing the raiders, under Capt. Newton, Capt. Conger and Lieut. Stranahan, confirm the capture of nine freebooters and $50,000 stolen bank bills. Considerable excitement prevails, though all apprehensions of any further danger at present from the marauders is removed. Capt. Nickerson, of the veteran reserve corps, is garrisoning the border with 115 convalescents from the hospitals at Brattleboro.

Judge Alihe of the supreme court has just returned from Montreal, where he has had a satisfactory interview with the Canadian authorities, and he is now preparing the necessary papers to bring the captured raiders before our courts, under the extradition treaty. Major Austin has dispatched Major Bantow to St. Johns. C.E., in order, if possible, to secure the arrest of a party of the raiders who are approaching that place from St. Ansted.

The banks in this place have suffered severely, but the St. Albans Bank announces that it will redeem its bills. We learn that in the skirmish last night at Freeleighsburgh four raiders were captured. Wm. Hunt, one of the bailiffs of that municipality, left mortally wounded while gallantly endeavoring to capture the raiders. The provincial authorities of the frontier towns did everything in their power to accomplish the arrest of the rascals. Six horses taken by the scoundrels have been re-captured.

The raiders were pursued so close that they had no time to rob the Sheldon Bank, as no doubt they intended, but pushed through the village and thence took the nearest route for the Canada line. Two were arrested at Freeleighsburgh, three miles north of the line, and six more at Stanbridge, five miles further.

> BURLINGTON, Vt. Oct. 20.—The St. Albans Bank and the First National Bank of St. Albans will redeem their bills as usual. The robbery has not affected their solvency.
>
> ST. ALBANS, Vt. Oct. 20.—Six of the bank robbers were arrested in Stanbridge about midnight, and $50,009 of their booty recovered. Three others were arrested at Freeleighsburgh. They will be lodged in jail at St. Johns, to await a requisition from the United States authorities. Major Austin, provost marshal of the state, arrived here this morning, and has assumed direction of all military matters.
>
> LATER—4 P.M.—Capt. Conger's party have returned, and report that they caught the leader of the raiders at Stanbridge, and recovered $100,000 in addition to $50,000 received this morning. The Canadian authorities are still after the villains, and there is a good prospect of the capture of the whole gang. The governor general of Canada has telegraphed that he will respond to a requisition from the United States government for the surrender of the robbers already arrested, and such as may be hereafter arrested.
>
> The St. Albans Bank lost $15,000, Franklin County Bank $85,000, and the First National Bank $50,000.
>
> MONTPELIER, Vt., Oct. 20.—Immediately after the depredations in St. Albans by the raiders, governor Smith telegraphed to the governor general of Canada relative thereto, and messengers were sent to various points to confer with officers of the Canadian government. It is worthy of mention, that all communications, written and oral, upon the subject, have been treated with great interest and kindness by the British authorities, and so far, every facility and assistance possible has been rendered our pursuing party to hunt down and capture the raiders.
>
> The communications of the governor general to governor Smith, are papers worthy of that high official, signifying as they do an interest on his part equal to that of our own people, to have the marauders brought to a speedy retribution. Maj. Austin has ordered the citizens of the frontier towns to organize themselves into home guards, and arms have been distributed to them, and they will shortly be prepared for any emergency.

The story became increasingly complex. In its December 1864 issue, *Banker's Magazine* included this item in its coverage:

> One of the most daring bank robberies of the past fifty years was that of the banks at St. Albans, Vt., on the 19th of October, by a party of freebooters, since representing themselves as officers and men of the Confederate service.
>
> They attacked and robbed the Franklin County Bank, the St. Albans Bank, and the First National Bank, all of that place. About half-past three two or three young men, very well dressed, and evidently men of intelligence, came into the St. Albans Bank. All were fair in appearance save one, who is described by our former townsman, M.A. Seymour, who was in the directors' room of the bank at the time, as of most malicious visage.
>
> These fellows approached Mr. C.N. Bishop, teller of the bank, and, presenting a pair of pistols, proceeded to rob the institution. Mr. Bishop ran into the room where Mr. Seymour was, and attempted to bolt the door, but they were too quick for them, and, forcing the door, Bishop was dragged out by the throat, and Mr. Seymour presented with a rebel argument in the shape of a pistol at his head. They were then obliged to swear an oath of allegiance to the Southern Confederacy, and not to divulge any of these proceedings for two hours.
>
> The leader of the party said: "We are here under the order of General Early. You have been down in the Shenandoah Valley, burned our houses, and wasted our property; and now we propose to pay you back in the same coin." Mr. Seymour, being an extremely good Union man, hesitated about taking the oath prescribed; but a threatened application of "cold lead" soon brought him to the rebel terms.
>
> The First National Bank is comparatively a new institution, having been started last spring. The party who robbed this bank had a scrimmage before they went in with a young man named Blaisdell, clerk in an adjoining clothing store. He saw these armed men coming towards the bank, and started to notify the cashier that there was set of "blacklegs" proposing to visit him. Before he entered the bank, however, he was stopped by the raiders, who, presenting a pistol, after a brief scuffle marched him and other prisoners to the Green, where a guard was set over them.
>
> Upon entering the bank Mr. Sowles, the cashier, was urbanely invited to hand over what money he had and the keys of the safe. The request was complied with, the funds abstracted, and Mr. Sowles marched off to the Green. The losses of this bank amounted to $52,650, as follows: $29,650 in 7 3-10 Treasury bonds, in denominations of 50's, 100's, 500's and 1,000's; $15,000 in five percent legal tender interest bearing notes[22]; $8,000 in currency on New England banks and greenbacks.
>
> A reward of one thousand dollars will be given for the necessary information which will lead to the conviction of any of the robbers, and all persons are cautioned against purchasing any of the above lost bonds, as payment has been stopped. After the raiders had procured their horses they congregated in front of the American, and near the store of George H. Farrar, when they strolled up and down Main Street, firing at random. Nearly all the parties implicated are now under arrest, and undergoing an examination at Montreal.

The Rest of the Story

What was first thought to be a daring daylight robbery of several banks developed into an international incident. The raiders were, indeed, Confederate soldiers. Most were from Kentucky and all but one were from 20 to 26 years of age. Their position after capture was that they were on a wartime exercise, for the glory of the Confederacy, and, seeking refuge in neutral

Canada, they were immune from the laws of the United States. American troops were commanded to charge into Canada and capture the raiders by force. However, President Lincoln revoked the order, realizing that it would violate neutrality and that an invasion of Canada could be construed as a warlike act. Such publicity would benefit only the Confederacy and likely make Canada its ally. For several years that country had been a refuge for northerners who sympathized with the Confederate cause.

The exact amount of money taken was never ascertained precisely, but it seems to have been about $208,000, most of which was never recovered. In time the story of what happened was pieced together.

It was learned that Bennett H. Young, leader of the raid, had been a Confederate soldier with the Lexington (Kentucky) Rifles under General John Hunt Morgan (*Morgan's Raiders,* they had been called). He and many others were captured by the Union and confined at Camp Douglas, near Chicago. Young and some fellow prisoners were able to escape to Canada, remaining for a time in Toronto. Later he made his way to the South, via Halifax, Nova Scotia. He arrived in Richmond, capital of the Confederacy, where he presented his ideas for breaching the security of Camp Douglas, which was lightly guarded, allowing all the prisoners to escape.

In 1862, C.S.A. Secretary of War James A. Seddon had authorized the formation of "partisan rangers," to consist of from three to 50 men who, dressed as civilians, were to live and work in the North to aid the Confederacy by providing intelligence, cutting telegraph lines, starting fires at strategic places (wooden bridges were to be targets), and aiding in the freeing of Confederate prisoners of war.

Then, on June 16, 1864, Young received this commission from Seddon:

> Lt. B.H. Young is hereby authorized to organize for special service a company not to exceed twenty in number from those who belong to the service and are at the time beyond the Confederate States. They will be entitled to their pay, rations, clothing, and transportation but no other compensation for any service which they may be called upon to render. The organization will be under the control of this department and liable to be disbanded at its pleasure and the members returned to their respective companies.

Lieutenant Young left with a group of others and went to St. Catherine's in Canada, where he conferred with Clement C. Clay, the Confederate commissioner in that country. Both Canada and England, of which Canada was a possession, were neutral in the war but had warm relations with the Confederacy. Young then went to Chicago, arriving in early August, where, in the company of other Morgan's Raiders and Southern soldiers who had escaped from prison, he assessed the situation. From there it was back to visit with Commissioner Clay to lay plans to raid Camp Douglas and free all the men held there.

Word of the plan leaked to the commander at the camp, guards were reinforced, and, learning of the change, Young and his men canceled the foray. A new plan was hatched. News was fresh about General Philip Sheridan and his Union army troops tramping through the Shenandoah Valley of Virginia and destroying all the food they could find, under the mantle of keeping it from provisioning the Confederate army. However, most inhabitants of the valley were women, children, and older people, who suffered terribly under the depredations.

Young, Commissioner Clay, and the others devised a plan to attack several towns in northern Vermont to give the Yankees a taste of their own medicine. Citizens were not to be harmed if they offered no resistance, but buildings were to be burned and banks robbed. On October 6, 1864, Clay gave Young official approval.

Carrying out their strategy, 22 young men came into St. Albans casually, as described, and selected Wednesday, October 19, as the time to carry their plan into effect, being as it was the least busy day of the week. Main Street was muddy, the town was chilly and damp, and few people were outdoors. Three o'clock was the appointed hour when each of the three banks would be entered simultaneously. All were on Main Street and within short walking distance of each other. Some men would enter the banks, while others would stand on Main Street, preventing passersby from sounding an alarm. If the men at work in the railroad shops were alerted, they could quickly overwhelm the unwelcome visitors.

At the Banks

At the St. Albans Bank, the raiders consisted of Marcus Spurr, Thomas Bronson Collins, Turner Teavis, and two others, some smelling of alcohol. Upon entering, the five men found teller Cyrus Newton Bishop seated by a window counting paper money. Teavis waited outside. Bishop went to the reception desk to help the men and was greeted by drawn revolvers and threats (as early described in a quoted news account). He ran toward the directors' room, where a clerk, Martin G. Seymour, was working with bank records, and tried to close the door, but the raiders pried it open. Collins, the leader, proclaimed that the strangers in town were all part of Morgan's Raiders, a group from Kentucky that had distinguished itself with derring-do earlier in the Civil War with its incursions into Ohio and Indiana. Three more robbers joined the first two. Teller Bishop was directed to get the bank's gold and silver coins. There was no gold, he said, but several bags of silver coins were in the safe, amounting to about $1,400. This amount of coins proved too heavy to carry, weighing close to 80 pounds, so the robbers took about $400 worth.

A cash drawer under the counter containing about $9,000 was not noticed. All of the currency in the safe was taken, including St. Albans Bank bills and federal Legal Tender Notes. In the meantime, two customers came into the bank and were robbed. The whole affair lasted about 12 minutes and netted $73,522. The bank currency consisted of 400 notes of $50, 1,000 of $20, 1,000 of $10, 2,000 of $5, 10,000 of $2, and 2,000 of $1.

Left behind, oddly enough, was a pile of sheets of St. Albans Bank currency, face value about $50,000, that had been numbered, dated, and signed but not yet cut apart. Also not taken was about $50,000 in bonds and securities left with the bank for safekeeping by customers. Perhaps some of the robbers had imbibed a bit too much earlier in the day.

The Franklin County Bank was quiet at the appointed hour when William H. Hutchinson entered. Cashier Marcus W. Beardsley was on hand, sitting by the stove, talking with James Saxe. The bank, which opened for business on April 20, 1850, with a stated capital of $100,000, had been a successful operation. Beardsley had been cashier for a decade, succeeding founding cashier E.W. Parker. The bank had issued paper money from the earliest days, with the first bearing the printed date of February 1, 1850, and the address of St. Albans Bay. The *Bay* word was soon removed from the printing plate, leaving St. Albans on issues printed later. Today, two canceled plates remain in the ABNCo archives, one for $10-$20 and the other for $1-$1-$2-$5.

Another man, Jackson Clark, a sawyer, was in the room as well when raider Hutchinson came in. Beardsley stood up and went to his place behind the counter to help the visitor. Hutchinson casually asked the price of gold, a popular speculation at the time. Beardsley said that the bank did not deal in such coins. Soon, a local businessman, J.R. Armington, arrived. Beardsley told the stranger that Armington dealt in gold, whereupon the stranger exchanged with him some Legal Tender Notes for two gold coins. Armington and Saxe then left the bank, while Hutchinson remained in his conversation with the cashier.

Four more raiders came in to join Hutchinson. One of them pointed a revolver at Beardsley to make their real business known. The cashier was ordered to first bring out all of the *greenbacks* the bank had, then all other money. He was told that a band of 100 sol-

Main Street, St. Albans, Vermont, as it appeared years later in a postcard mailed in 1909.

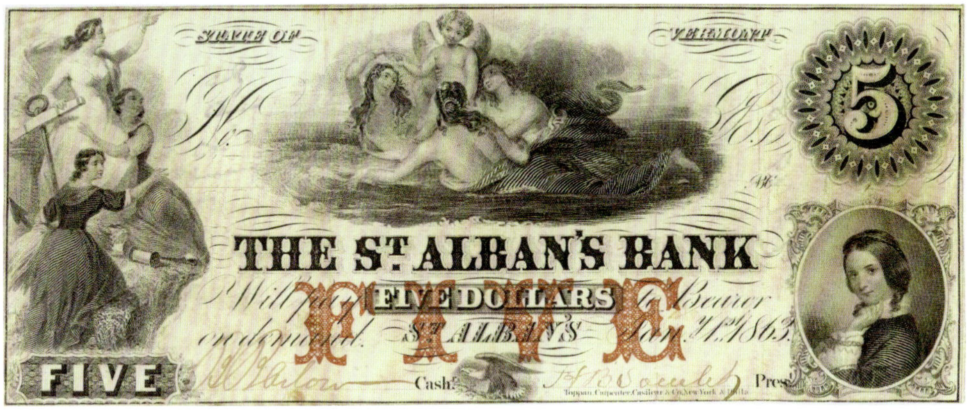

A $5 note of the St. Albans Bank, dated January 1, 1863, in the plate. The apostrophe in Alban's represents erratic usage. Printed by Toppan, Carpenter & Casilear, New York and Philadelphia. Could this note have figured in the October 1864 scenario?

diers was going to burn down the town in retaliation for Union raids in the South. The cashier was then pushed into the bank vault, where Jackson Clark had already been placed. Over Beardsley's protests that he would smother in the airtight space, the door was slammed shut and locked. Both confined men had visions of dying as the bank burned. Armington, the bank customer and gold trader, entered the bank after the robbers left, heard shouts from within the vault, and, following instructions called out by Beardsley, was able to open the safe. The two men had been trapped for about 20 minutes.

At the First National Bank of St. Albans, a similar scenario took place, this time with four raiders. Caleb McDowall Wallace (a nephew of John J. Crittenden, the famous Kentucky statesman) and a companion entered the bank, where they encountered cashier Albert Sowles, who was standing behind his counter. The only person in the bank was John Nason, a retired general who was nearly 90 years old and who had severely impaired hearing. While Sowles was held at gunpoint in front of two pistols held by Wallace and a long revolver held by his accomplice, Joseph McGroarty ransacked the safe and took all the bills and securities he could find, amounting to $58,000 in currency. Five sealed bags of coins were found, and McGroarty asked Sowles what was in them. "Cents," was the reply. To verify this, he undid the cords on one of them and scattered the coins around on the floor. McGroarty was 38 years old, the only one of the St. Albans raiders who was older than 26. The fourth raider, Alamanda Pope Bruce, stood inside the door as a guard, later going over to the park to help with guard duties there.

While all of this was going on, General Nason sat in the room casually reading a newspaper. After the robbers left, he inquired as to what the gentlemen had wanted. Cashier Sowles was taken to Taylor Park in front of the American House Hotel nearby and placed under armed guard with a few other citizens, Main Street being nearly empty.

In the meantime, while 13 of the men were robbing the banks, the other raiders, about nine in number, commanded several citizens to gather in the park. Some ran away, and other citizens took matters into their own hands. However, the workers at the railroad shops did not learn of the incident in time to help. The raiders, mounted on horses stolen from citizens (some detached from their buggies and carts) along with seven taken from Fuller's livery, started on their way out of town. The robbers threw "Greek fire," an inflammable concoction of phosphorus, on several buildings in an attempt to burn the village. At Atwood's and Brainerd's stores the fires were inconsequential. The American House Hotel was set on fire, but just a small part suffered damage. Shots were exchanged during these hectic moments, and Elinus J. Morrison, a contractor from New Hampshire who was doing the bricklaying during the construction of the Welden House, was mortally wounded. Ironically, Morrison was later remembered as a northerner who was sympathetic to the Confederate cause.

On the way north to Canada, the raiders stopped at the Missisquoi Bank in Sheldon but found the door locked. From there it was across the border to safety, setting small fires at two wooden bridges along the way.

Consternation and fear reigned in the towns in the United States that were close to Canada. A rumor arose that Burlington would be attacked next and that smaller towns would fall victim to depredations. Local guards and sentinels assisted by military personnel were on alert in many villages for the rest of the autumn and into the next year.

A $5 note of the Franklin County Bank, St. Albans *Bay,* Vermont. "Bay" was later removed from the plate. Signed by Marcus W. Beardsley and O.A. Burton. Wellstood, Benson & Hanks, New York.

A $5 note from the same plate, but with "Bay" removed, leaving the remaining imprint off center.

BACK IN CANADA

In Washington, D.C., Secretary of War Edwin Stanton received word that St. Albans had been pillaged and set on fire by Southern refugees, after which the telegraph service district failed. The next morning he learned the details of the robberies and escape.

Most of the raiders soon were arrested in Canada and sought protection under international law. Canadian authorities were indecisive, resisting the request to prosecute those in captivity and to issue arrest warrants for others at large. On October 21, 1864, Secretary of State William H. Seward demanded that Canada turn over the men and money to American authorities. However, Lord Monck, the governor general of Canada, directed that they be tried in court there. The prisoners were taken to Montreal, where crowds cheered them as they arrived. Soon the men were taken to prison, but they were assigned to apartments that were nicely furnished in the manner of a fine hotel and given special food service. Bennett H. Young penned a nice letter to Sarah Clark, his former boardinghouse friend in St. Albans, sending her $3 with a request for copies of the *Vermont Daily Messenger* so he could read the accounts.

The hearing of evidence began on November 7. The United States had observers on hand but could not bring any attorneys to the court as none were licensed to practice in Montreal. Young, leader of the raiders, stated that the action was a military attack under the authority of the Confederate States of America, and nothing more. His statement included this claim:

> The course I intended to pursue in Vermont, and which I was able to carry out but partially, was to retaliate in some measure for the barbarous atrocities of Grant, Butler, Sherman, Hunter, Milroy, Sheridan, Grierson and other Yankee officers, except that I would scorn to harm women and children under any provocation, or unarmed, defenseless and unresisting citizens, even Yankees, or to plunder for my own benefit.

After hearing testimony, Judge LeCharles Coursol stated that in actuality he had no jurisdiction in the case as the raiders had not been arrested under legal warrants, and dismissed the prisoners to the cheers of onlookers. A waiting sleigh took Mr. Porterfield, a Confederate agent who had attended the proceedings, to a nearby bank, where what remained of the stolen money had been stored. This money was given to the agent, who distributed it among the

Note for $5 of the Missisquoi Bank of Sheldon, Vermont, named for the Missisquoi River that flows nearby. Plate by Rawdon, Wright, Hatch & Edson / New England Bank Note Co. The eagle vignette is the most wingspread of any in the bank-note series.

prisoners. The value was calculated to be about $88,000 in terms of paper money, equivalent to about $50,000 in gold coins.

The released men then scattered in several directions. The United States raised sharp protests, including through Francis Adams, United States minister to Great Britain, as Canada was a possession of that country. Call was made for a further investigation. Judge Coursol was commanded to appear before the Police Committee of Montreal after inquiries revealed that he had made certain arrangements with Confederate agents before and while the trial was in progress, suggesting what the verdict would be. He admitted that he had associated with Confederates, but he declined to answer further questions. Coursol was suspended from his office, and the statement was made that he was indictable for malfeasance. Later, the attorney general restored him to the bench, and still later he was elected to several terms as mayor of Montreal.

The improprieties were considered, and Justice James Smith of the Superior Court of Canada issued a warrant for the re-arrest of the raiders, but only five could be found, one being Bennett H. Young. In the meantime, the freed men had turned over most of the St. Albans money to Clement C. Clay, the Confederate commissioner in Canada. A new trial was scheduled for December 27, then continued into the next year.

The trial took place, and testimony was again heard, this time including as a main charge the robbery of Samuel Beck, a merchant who had entered the St. Albans Bank while the robbery was taking place. On March 29, 1865, Justice Smith announced that the raid was indeed a military expedition carried out under the auspices of the Confederacy, and that the raiders could not be extradited to the United States to face other charges. Rousing cheers in the courtroom and outside were raised as the prisoners were given their freedom.

Another arrest warrant was soon issued, and the men were taken to Toronto for yet another trial. Throughout these court scenes, United States representatives persisted in their argument that the actions of Bennett H. Young and his raiders were not those of soldiers but of common criminals. To counter this claim, and easily, the prosecution had a field day parading similar and even worse depredations committed by Union soldiers on innocent people in the South, including in the Shenandoah Valley, where houses were pillaged. For good measure the defense attorney brought forth a volume of *The Rebellion Record*, published by Putnam in New York, and read this account of the invasion by Union troops of the quiet town of Darien, Georgia:

> On June 11, 1863, an old ferry boat converted to a gunboat came up the Altahoma River to Darien. On board was a federal officer, Montgomery, commanding a party of Negro soldiers. Their purpose was to "present their compliments to the rebels of Georgia."
>
> As they approached, they threw shells into the village scattering the terror-stricken inhabitants. Not a single armed person appeared at the wharf to dispute their landing or to offer resistance. Pickets were sent to the outskirts of the town; orders were given to take everything of value to the boat and then to burn Darien. Officers with squads started off in every direction. Soon they began to return to the boat loaded with all types of furniture, even pianos. Tools, mirrors, jewelry and money were taken. One private returned with a pair of chickens in one hand and leading a cow by the other. Papers, letters and books weren't neglected.
>
> Darien contained between 70 and 100 houses on a street running along the river shaded on both sides by large oaks and mulberry trees. A town of age and respectability, it never looked so grand and beautiful as it did in its destruction. As soon as a house was ransacked the torch was

> applied, and by 6 o'clock the whole town was in a sheet of flame.
>
> Montgomery's reason for the raid was, "The South must be conquered inch by inch and what we can't put a force in to hold ought to be destroyed." Later he described how the plunder was divided at camp and that "some of the quarters look really princely with their sofas and pianos."

The trial of the St. Albans raiders was still in progress when the war ended in April. The men were set free. Soon afterward the Canadian government made restitution to the Franklin County Bank of $31,000 of the paper money bearing the imprint of that bank, to the First National Bank of $19,000 in paper money, and to the St. Albans Bank of $20,000 in gold coins.

After the war, Bennett H. Young achieved prominence in Louisville, Kentucky, as an attorney, author, and president of the Southern Railroad, one of the nation's largest lines. In 1911 he remarked concerning the raid, "I wonder how I ever undertook it. I am now as loyal to my reunited country as I was then to my cherished Confederacy." He lived to the age of 76, and died as an honored American citizen.

The End of an Era

Few New State Banks Formed

As the Civil War progressed, monetary conditions remained chaotic. While most banks in business remained solvent, there was little interest in forming new institutions. Existing banks reordered currency from American Bank Note Co. primarily, National Bank Note Co., and a small handful of others. By the time the Continental Bank Note Co. entered business in 1863, the opportunity for new business was slim.

Moreover, the flood of federal paper money that entered circulation with the Legal Tender Notes of 1862 served to diminish public interest in state bank bills. Both state and federal bills traded at a discount in terms of gold and silver coins. Given a choice, most people preferred to own a Legal Tender Note or, later, other series such as National Bank Notes. By early 1865, with the Civil War still in progress, the circulation of new notes by state-chartered banks diminished sharply.

After the passage of the National Banking Act in 1863, the directors of most banks considered the option of converting to become a National Bank. This process involved organizing stockholders, securing an affirmative vote, and applying for a charter. If a charter was granted, a new corporation, called a "national banking association," would be formed, and assets would be transferred from the state bank to the new one. In many instances, only some of the stockholders wanted to convert (as the process was called), instead choosing to sell out their interest. In other instances, banks were not sound enough to have their charter accepted, and new National Banks were set up with just some assets purchased from the old. Under other scenarios, entrepreneurs not affiliated with any state bank applied for and received charters to operate a National Bank.

Under federal regulations, a portion of a bank's capital could be pledged to the Treasury Department, earning interest on the investment. Up to 90% of this amount could be taken back in National Bank Notes. An account in the *Portsmouth* (New Hampshire) *Herald,* April 23, 1864, touches upon the process:

> *National Banks:* There are already 25 National Banks in New England alone; *i.e.,* banks which issue United States bills, founded on public credit, the capital for security being in United States bonds, deposited in the public Treasury. The United States new loan, called 10-40—(*i.e.,* the United States having the option to pay the principal in ten years, or to extend the time to forty years, interest semi-annually 5 per cent. payable in specie, principal also payable in gold) is likely to have a complete success.
>
> It is being taken up at the rate of one to two millions a day. The late sudden rise of gold cannot be long maintained. The new tax bill increasing the revenue, or the surety of suppressing the rebellion immediately, will at once *tend* to a nearer equalization of government paper, and gold the standard—both are demanded, and must be realized; or *Southern* misery, to some extent, at least, would be the result. Failure in either is not contemplated.

This was a win-win situation for many parties. The federal government acquired significant new funds to aid in the fighting of the war. In this time of conflict, and with the future economy uncertain, banks were secure in the ownership of interest-bearing federal bonds. For the American, National, and Continental bank-note companies, having huge government contracts to print notes from just a few different plates was far more profitable than filling small orders from many different plates for state-chartered banks.

There was a rush to convert to become a National Bank. By the end of the 19th century, more than 2,000 state banks had taken this step—including nearly all of the sound, profitable institutions—with most conversions taking place in the 1860s.

Certain notes issued by the Bullion Bank of Washington, D.C., were specifically payable in either Demand Notes or Treasury Notes, as stated on the face. These represent an interesting transition between bills of state-chartered banks and federal issues. Printed by the Union Bank Note Co., Newark, New Jersey.

The $1 bill has the inscription, "Will pay on demand one dollar in United States demand notes. . . ." There was a problem with this promise, as the smallest denomination of the federal Demand Note was $5. With the printed date of July 4, 1862, this bill must have traded at a premium in relation to other state-bank paper of the era, as federal Demand Notes were redeemable in gold. The point may be moot, for James A. Haxby suggests that this bank was "fraudulent or non-existent," and little mention has been found of it.

The $3 note reads, "Will pay on demand three dollars in United States Treasury Notes. . . ." Such bills were exchangeable for Treasury or Legal Tender Notes, which traded at a discount in terms of silver and gold coins. Printed date of July 4, 1862, the same as the preceding.

At first the Treasury Department required that National Banks in a given city be assigned names serially, such as the First National Bank, Second National Bank, and upward, in New York City reaching the Tenth National Bank. However, it was often the case that the largest bank in town did not apply in time to become the First National Bank and did not want a title such as Second or Third National, which sounded inferior. Soon, the Treasury permitted banks to choose their own names, with approval, and the rush to convert became more intense than ever.

Accelerating the Demise of State Bank Notes

With the National Bank system a reality, Secretary Chase wanted to hasten the removal of state bank notes from commerce, as did Senator John Sherman, the latter important in the passage of the National Banking Act of 1863. A letter from Chase to Sherman, October 2, 1864, included this information:

> There is now not the slightest uncertainty about the re-election of Mr. Lincoln. . . . You ask about Mr. Fessenden's remaining in the cabinet. He will be a candidate for re-election to the Senate; and if successful will leave his communication with me since he took charge, and in every step, with perhaps one slight exception, his judgment has corresponded with mine. He sees several matters now in quite a different light from that in which they appeared to him when senator.
>
> He would now, for example, *cordially support* your proposition for a heavy discriminating tax upon all unnational [state bank] circulation. . . . How clear it is now that if Congress had come boldly to the act of marked discriminative taxation on all non-national circulation and final prohibition after a few years, say two—or at most three—gold would now have been at not more than fifty percent premium and that resumption of specie payments might have been effected within a year. I trust the next session will witness bolder and better legislation. It will be one of your brightest honors that you so clearly saw and so boldly followed and path of reform; for certainly no greater boon—except liberty itself—can be conferred upon a nation than a truly national and thoroughly sound currency.[23]

An excerpt from another letter from Chase to Sherman, March 1, 1865 is complimentary:

> Your speech on the finances is excellent. There are one or two points on which I shall express myself otherwise; but, in the main, it commands the fullest extent of my judgment. Your appreciation of the currency in question exactly corresponds with my own; only I would not give up the national currency even if we must endure for years depreciation through the issues of state banks before getting rid of them.

> The clause in the bill, as it came from the House, imposing a tax of ten percent on all notes not authorized by Congress which may be paid out after this year by any bank, whether state or national, will do much towards making our currency sound.
>
> I will briefly indicate what I should prefer and what I should most zealously labor to have sanctioned by Congress if I were at the head of the Treasury Department.
>
> 1. Let the monthly tax on state bank circulation be increased to one-half of one percent.
>
> 2. Provide that any bank may pay into the national treasury the amount of its circulation in United States notes or national currency and that on such payment the bank making it shall be exempt from taxation on circulation.
>
> 3. Provide for the application to the redemption of the circulation represented by such payments, of the United States notes or national currency so paid in, and strictly prohibited the paying out of such notes for any other purpose. . . .[24]

Chase went on to envision "an exclusive *national* currency," without state bills. Congress obliged, and a tax of 10% was levied on transactions taking place on July 1, 1866, or later involving currency of state-chartered banks.

All National Banks that converted from state banks were required under various state laws to redeem their notes. The time limit varied. In New Hampshire it was three years, after which such bills became worthless. A review of various state banking–commission records reveals that converted banks often redeemed all but a tiny fraction of the bills they had issued. Unlike gold or silver coins, bills of state banks had little sentimental attraction to the holders, nor were they considered to be a store of value. With the prospect of becoming worthless, all notes that could be found were redeemed—with relatively few remaining outstanding by 1870. Although in many states they were not legally bound to do so, some National Banks considered it a point of honor to redeem stray bills in later years, well into the 20th century.

Scenarios of Two Banks

The following selected excerpts from the *Bank Commissioners' Report* of two New Hampshire banks show the rapidity with which bills were withdrawn from circulation.[25] The first example is the Union Bank of Concord, which did *not* convert to a National Bank. The second is the Cochecho Bank of Dover, which converted to become the Cochecho National Bank of Dover. The progenitor of the latter bank was plagued with worthless Floyd's acceptances, discussed earlier in the text. As these had no value, they could not be transferred to the National Bank.

Some figures not relevant to currency are retained simply to reflect the finances of typical state-chartered banks.

Union Bank of Concord

April 20, 1865: *Bank Commissioners' Report* examination this date • *Capital:* $100,000 • *President:* Nathaniel White • *Cashier:* Augustine C. Pierce (salary $1,400) • *Directors:* Nathaniel White, Onslow Stearns, Woodbridge Odlin, Peter Sanborn, John K. Woodman, Calvin Howe, and N.B. Walker • *Number of stockholders:* 132 (stock owned by directors: 184 shares) • *Bills of other banks and checks:* $35,957.87 • Specie: $7,440 • Stock in National Bank of Redemption: $5,400 [central redemption depot for the bank's notes in Boston] • *Currency:* Total amount of bills printed and received since the inception of the bank: $261,000; bills destroyed: $51,000; bills unsigned in bank: $99,000; bills duly signed in bank: $25,253; bills in circulation: $85,747.

April 10, 1866: *Bank Commissioners' Report* of examination of this date (selected data): • *Capital:* $100,000 • *President:* Nathaniel White • *Cashier:* Augustine C. Pierce • *Directors:* Nathaniel White, Onslow Stearns, Woodbridge Odlin, Peter Sanborn, John K. Woodman, Calvin Howe, and N.B. Walker • *Number of Stockholders:* 131 (stock owned by directors, 197 shares) • Two dividends past year, April and October, 5% each • *Loans and discounts:* $211,587.64, including $112,500 in U.S. securities • Stock in National Bank of Redemption: $5,400 • Cash: $32,125.32 • Specie: $640 • *Currency:* Whole amount bills printed: $261,000; bills destroyed: $58,000; unsigned bills in bank: $73,000; signed bills in bank: $42,810; bills in circulation: $87,190.

April 12, 1867: *Bank Commissioners' Report* of examination of this date (selected data): • *Capital:* $19,300 • *President:* Nathaniel White • *Cashier:* Augustine C. Pierce • *Directors:* Nathaniel White, Onslow Stearns, Woodbridge Odlin, Peter Sanborn, John K. Woodman, Calvin Howe, and N.B. Walker • *Number of Stockholders:* 124 • *Total assets of bank:* $70,183.18, including $51,905.25 bank balance and $5,400 stock in the National Bank of

A $10 note of the Union Bank of Concord, New Hampshire, ink dated April 7, 1857. From a plate by Toppan, Carpenter & Co., Philadelphia, New York, and Boston. This bill was found in an old scrapbook formed generations ago by a New Hampshire banker.

Redemption • *Currency:* Whole amount bills printed: $261,000; bills destroyed: $258,351; bills in circulation: $2,649.

1868: Bank closed this year. Each holder of a $100 share received $132.50.[26]

April 9. 1868: *Bank Commissioners' Report* of examination of this date (selected data): • *President:* Nathaniel White • *Cashier:* Augustine C. Pierce • *Notes:* This bank is winding up its affairs under the statute. The stock has been divided, $132.30 per share. There are no liabilities except $1,234 for the outstanding circulation; and this sum the president, Nathaniel White, has agreed with the corporation to redeem, filing the proper bond with the state. • *Final analysis in a Bank Commission report.*

Cochecho Bank of Dover

March 24, 1865: *Bank Commissioners' Report* of examination this date (selected data): • *Capital:* $88,075 (reduced; see note below) • *President:* Thomas E. Sawyer (salary $75) • *Cashier:* Ezekiel Hurd (salary $1,000) • *Directors:* Thomas E. Sawyer, William B. Wiggin, Oliver E. Wendell, J.E. Lathrop, Harrison Haley, Joseph Morrill, Chas. W. Rollins • *Number of stockholders:* 162 (shares owned by directors: 43) • Real estate owned by bank: $4,244.51 • Specie: $25 • *Total assets of bank:* $247,723.72 • *Currency:* Whole amount of bills printed since the inception of the bank: $326,071; bills destroyed: $145,671; bills unsigned in bank: $65,600; bills duly signed in bank: $21,026; bills in circulation: $93,774 • *Selected liabilities:* Doubtful paper (including $25,000 in Floyd's acceptances): $29,000; amount of paper deemed bad: $5,000 • *Notes:* At a special meeting of the stockholders held February 25, 1865, it was voted to close up the affairs of the bank, leaving the details to the directors, who voted, March 7, to pay to stockholders a dividend of stock at the rate of $25 per share; and on March 21st they voted to pay a further stock dividend of $25 per share, payable March 27. On the 24th day of March, $14,925 of the first stock dividend had been paid out to stockholders, leaving the $85,075 capital, as above stated, though $35,075 *was* to be divided. The stockholders of this bank are in the process of starting a National Banking Association, to take the place of the Cochecho Bank.

March 29, 1866: *Bank Commissioners' Report* of examination of this date (selected data): • *Capital:* $15,000 • *President:* Thomas E. Sawyer • *Cashier:* Ezekiel Hurd • *Directors:* Thomas E. Sawyer, William B. Wiggin, Joseph Morrill, J.E. Lothrop, O.E. Wendell, and Charles W. Rollins (stock owned by directors: 50 shares) • *Number of stockholders:* 185 • *Currency:* Whole amount of bills printed: $326,071; bills destroyed: $310,071; signed bills: $1,575; bills in circulation: $14,425 • Since our report last year the capital has been reduced to $15,000. The Cochecho National Bank is in operation in the rooms heretofore occupied by this bank.

March 18, 1867: *Bank Commissioners' Report* of examination of this date (selected data): • *President:* Thomas E. Sawyer • *Cashier:* Ezekiel Hurd • *Directors:* Thomas E. Sawyer, William B. Wiggin, Joseph Morrill, J.E. Lothrop, H. Haley, and

A $10 note of the Cochecho Bank, Dover, New Hampshire, August 1, 1855, from a plate by Toppan, Carpenter, Casilear & Co., New York. In this era the average lifespan of a bill in circulation was about three years, a contrast from decades earlier, when currency would circulate for much longer and become tattered and ragged. This well-worn bill seems to have used up its three-year allotment.

Charles W. Rollins (stock owned by directors: 50 shares) • *Number of stockholders:* 165 • Whole amount of bills printed: $326,071; bills destroyed: $323,671; signed bills: $134; bills in circulation: $2,266 • Since our report last year the capital has been paid, and the bank is winding up.

May 4, 1868: *Bank Commissioners' Report* of examination of this date (selected data): • *President:* Thomas E. Sawyer • *Cashier:* Ezekiel Hurd (salary $100) • *Directors:* Thomas E. Sawyer, Joseph Morrill, W.B. Wiggin, Charles W. Rollins, H. Haley, and J.E. Lathrop • Bank balance in Cochecho National Bank: $6,735.05 • Entire amount of bills printed: $326,071; amount of bills destroyed: $323,671; bills signed and on hand in the bank: $732; bills still in circulation: $1,668 • *Bad debt:* $25,000 "J.B. Floyd acceptance" • *Final analysis in a Bank Commissioners' Report.*

Banks of the Confederacy

Bank Bills in the South

After the Civil War began on April 15, 1861, banking in the South went on as usual—at least for a time. Most banks had ample supplies of paper money on hand from the leading bank-note engraving companies, mostly in the North, but also including the Southern Bank Note Co. in New Orleans, the branch of ABNCo now under Confederate control. While the Southern Bank Note Co. had the equipment to turn out new steel plates with custom inscriptions, throughout the rest of the South there was little in the way of such expertise.

There were, however, many regular printing companies in the South. Lacking equipment for platemaking and siderography, these firms made do with what techniques and materials they had—including typesetting, printing from stock wood block or steel ornaments set among the type, and lithography. The aesthetic results ranged from acceptable to rustic and crude.

In 1864, Keatinge & Ball, important as a printer of bank notes for the Confederacy, issued a booklet, *Remarks on the Manufacture of Bank Notes and Other Promises to Pay, Addressed to the Bankers of the Southern Confederacy, Columbia, S.C.* The text included this comment, or perhaps lament would be more appropriate, relating to the inadequacy of bank-note printing in the South at the time, beginning with a discussion of lithography:[27]

> **The Lithographic Process**
>
> Lithography, which is nearly dependent on the efforts of the steel engraver, and has been in vogue for many years, has met with very great success. It is simply the transferring of impressions of engraved plates to stone, and printing from the transfer. The enormous multiplying power of this mode will readily be perceived by the reader, on being informed of the fact that an engraved steel plate will print, say twenty-five thousand copies, and each one of these impressions, when transferred to stone, will yield, when printed by a careful hand, six thousand.
>
> This branch of the business is devoted mainly to what is technically called "commercial work," such as bank checks, bills of exchange, promissory notes, and all the blank documents required in commercial transactions. Notwithstanding the cheapness and utility of this method of reproduction, it carries upon its face the inevitable stamp of inferiority, and has never been brought into requisition by banks of issue in this country for their notes of circulation.
>
> **Problems of "Surface Printing"**
>
> An impression from a steel plate, taken on the enameled paper of the lithographer, however beautiful and perfect the engraving may be, when

(continued on p. 447)

The Exchange Bank of Salem, Massachusetts, which converted on February 18, 1865, to become the Exchange National Bank of Salem, charter 817, dutifully redeemed its old bills for years afterward. Cashier Joseph H. Webb and president John Webster took the same offices with the new National Bank. Shown above is a detail of a scrapbook kept by the bank, affixing the redeemed bills, crossing them out, and entering details of redemption to the left.

On the following page are selections from the records kept by the bank of the issuance and redemption of its bills. The bank was chartered on January 1, 1823. (Peabody Essex Museum, Salem)

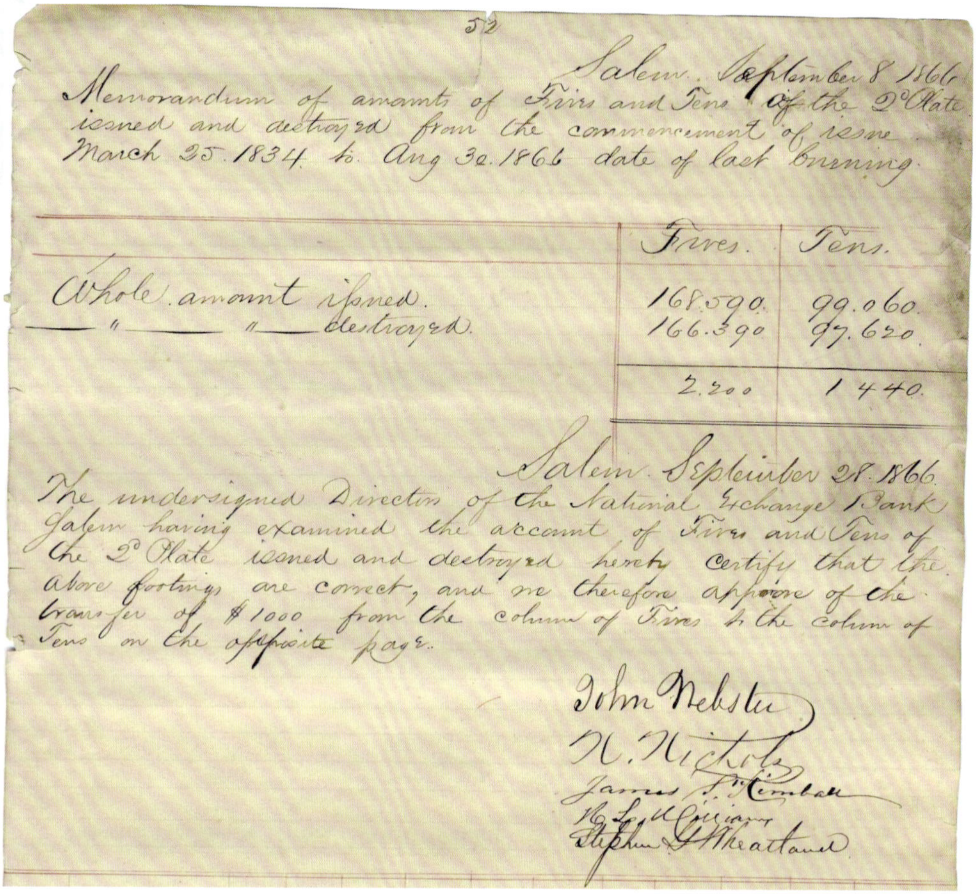

52

Salem. September 8 1866

Memorandum of amounts of Fives and Tens of the 2d Plate issued and destroyed from the commencement of issue March 25. 1834 to Aug 30. 1866 date of last burning

	Fives.	Tens.
Whole amount issued.	168.590.	99.060.
" " destroyed.	166.390	97.620.
	2.200	1.440.

Salem September 28. 1866.

The undersigned Directors of the National Exchange Bank Salem having examined the account of Fives and Tens of the 2d Plate issued and destroyed hereby certify that the above footings are correct, and we therefore approve of the transfer of $1000 from the column of Fives to the column of Tens on the opposite page.

John Webster
N. Nichols
James [illegible]
[illegible]
[illegible]

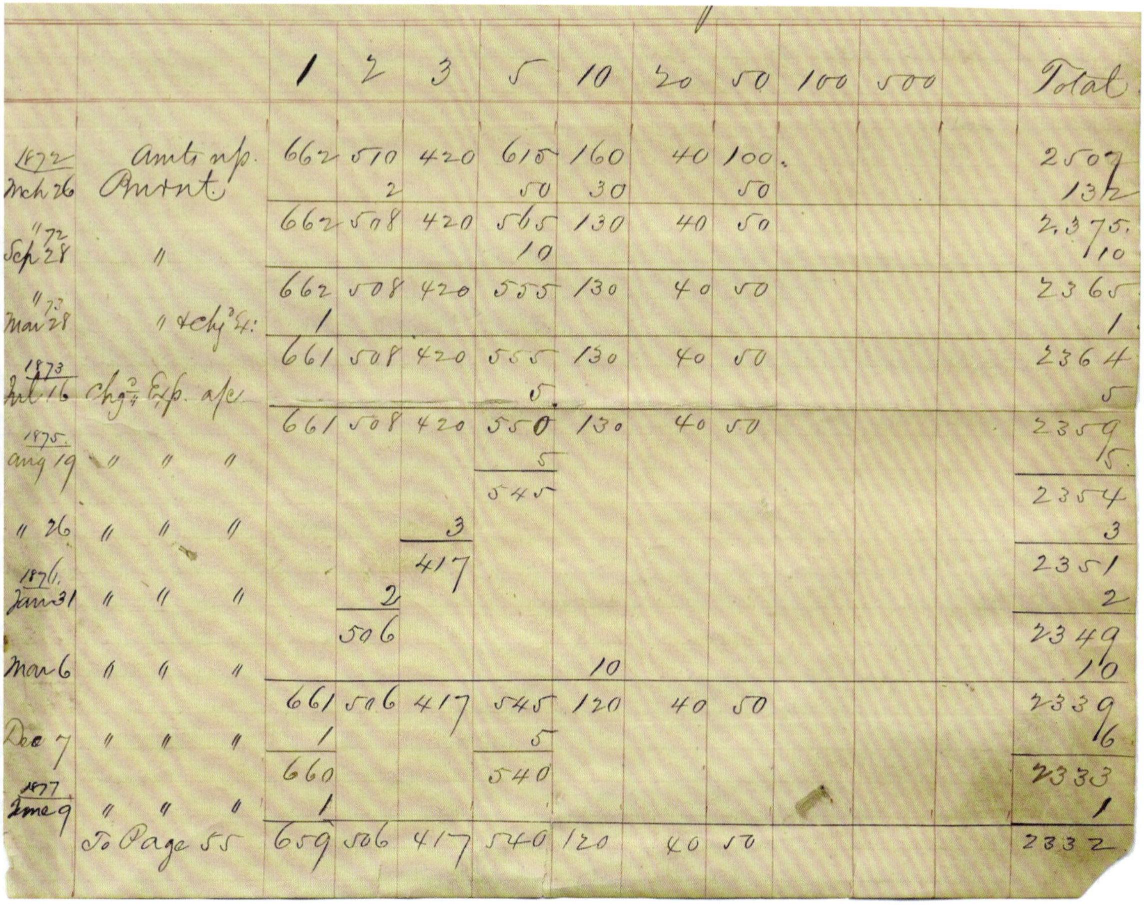

		1	2	3	5	10	20	50	100	500		Total
1872	Amt. n/p.	662	510	420	615	160	40	100				2507
Mch 26	Burnt		2		50	30		50				132
		662	508	420	565	130	40	50				2375
"72 Sep 28	"				10							10
		662	508	420	555	130	40	50				2365
"73 Mar 28	" & chgd Ex.	1										1
		661	508	420	555	130	40	50				2364
1873 Jul 16	Chgd Exp. a/c				5							5
		661	508	420	550	130	40	50				2359
1875 Aug 19	" " "				5							5
					545							2354
" 26	" " "			3								3
				417								2351
1876 Jan 31	" " "		2									2
			506									2349
Mar 6	" " "					10						10
		661	506	417	545	120	40	50				2339
Dec 7	" " "	1			5							6
		660			540							2333
1877 June 9	" " "	1										1
	To Page 55	659	506	417	540	120	40	50				2332

A $5 note of the Bank of the State of South Carolina, by the American Bank Note Co., ink dated November 5, 1861, by which time the Civil War had been in progress for seven months. The "Sweet Potato Dinner" image, from an 1836 painting by John Blake White, was very popular in the South. It was used on various paper money and was the subject of a Currier & Ives print.

Depicted is a famous incident in history. During the Revolution, British General Banastre Tarleton relentlessly pursued Brigadier General Francis Marion, the "Swamp Fox," of South Carolina. Under a flag of truce, Marion invited Tarleton to dine, the meal being simply a repast of sweet potatoes, a staple of the local economy, reflective of the hard times Marion had experienced. It is said that years later, Tarleton commented that men who could flourish without the comforts of life could never be subdued.

A $10 note of the Bank of Selma, Alabama, by ABNCo. Ink dated June 1, 1862, well into the war, this bill was from earlier stock.

The Bank of Selma, with a capital variously stated as $101,000 or $100,000, remained in business into the Civil War. R. Lapsley served as cashier, and W.M. Smith was president. Among the bills printed by ABNCo for this bank were some of the $100 denomination.

(continued from p. 444)

laid on the stone, and passed through the press repeatedly, under a powerful pressure, loses a great portion of the delicate tracing and finish of the lighter parts, as well as the rich velvety tones of the shadows of the original; the sharp, well defined lines of the artist's "burin" [hand engraving tool], the free and flowing expressions of the practiced etcher in landscape, the clear and carefully traced details of the human form, the delicate gradations of light and shadow in a sky or cloud, are partially lost, and what remains, is but a grey, broken mass of lines, offensive to the eye of the true connoisseur.

Again, impressions from stone are liable to the same objections as may be urged against all "surface printing," the paper receiving a mere film of ink from stone, and, consequently, soon obliterated by constant handling; it is a well known fact that the quantity of ink deposited on the paper from an engraved steel or copper plate, would be sufficient to produce ten or more from the transfer on stone; this fact accounts for the great durability, so to speak, of the engraved bank note. The ink used, being a pure carbon, will retain its color and sharpness as long as the paper upon which it has been deposited will hold together.

Notes which were issued by our government at the commencement of the war, engraved by Keatinge & Ball, were in circulation, (having been re-issued many times) up to the time of funding them while stacks upon stacks of the lithographic issue were cancelled or destroyed, never being in a fit condition for re-issue, even after a few months' circulation.

The pressing wants of our government have forced into use this process of lithography, in which, it is easy to perceive, there is little protection, and, unfortunately, offers a premium to crime by simplifying its commission.

A $20 note of the Exchange Office, Holly Springs, Mississippi, printed by Rawdon, Wright & Hatch in the 1830s. Sheets with this and other bills, signed but not issued, were overprinted on the back during the Civil War with a new plate for fractional scrip notes. This note, cut off the sheet after overprinting, shows part of the scrip.

A $1 note of the state of Georgia, Milledgeville, January 1, 1863. Signed "Howell, Engraver," this bill was printed by lithography. The vignette of a train with a steamship in the sky in the distance was popular in prewar times and was widely used by W.L. Ormsby and others.

A $1 note of the state of North Carolina, January 1, 1863, printed by T. Paterson & Co., Augusta. Bills such as this appeared primitive in comparison to earlier steel-plate engravings.

> **Easy to Counterfeit**
>
> In lithography, or where movable types are used, the ease with which fraud can be committed, unfortunately, renders crime too frequent. An impression of the most elaborate plate taken with what is known as "transfer ink," easy of access and not at all difficult to make from the abundant receipts and instructions published, can, if a workman is so disposed, be taken off, concealed, taken elsewhere, transferred to stone, and copies, to any extent, put into circulation, differing from the genuine only in the signatures, which afford no protection to the public, and require the keen-eyed expert for their detection. Knowing that great frauds have been committed, have we not a perfect right to doubt the security of a system that gives to a common workman the opportunity as well as the temptation of enriching himself, with so little risk, and so few chances of detection, and of the punishment due to his crime?
>
> **Difficulty of Finding Material**
>
> It is in the want of material that the prosecution of bank note engraving and printing in the Confederacy has met with the greatest difficulties. Many of the most important articles are not to be obtained in Europe of the quality desired; others have to be improvised, as it were, on the spot. The swamps of South Carolina furnish the vegetable carbon for the inks, and the hills of North Carolina and Virginia, the oils. Plates and dies made from the crude steel. The manufacture of machinery and presses gives employment to mechanism of all entirely novel character in the South; in fact, to establishments of this kind, necessity has added to the machine shop the laboratory of the chemist.
>
> One of the peculiarities of this business is, that time as well as capital, is necessary for its successful prosecution, where large demands are made upon it; the accumulation of the labor of the artist, the immense variety of embellishment required at his hands can be obtained only by patient and persevering labor. The progress made, under these difficulties and peculiarities, in the Confederacy is, therefore, gratifying, and gives assurance that when the clouds of war are dissipated, the commerce of the world admitted again to our silent wharves, and peace, with healing wings, brings health, activity, and her innumerable blessings to the once happy people of the Confederacy, this important branch of industry will take its legitimate rank, bestowing its benefits upon the commonwealth, as well as honor and profit upon those engaged in its prosecution.

The bittersweet comments at the end of the narrative, about the "once happy" people of the Confederacy and that healing wings will bring happiness and blessings, is in contrast with the general sentiment in the North at the time, where "obliterate the Confederacy" was the rallying cry. The burning of Richmond, General Sherman's march of needless destruction through Georgia, and other activities bear testimony to that other side. In the North a traveling tent show, *Retribution,* was very popular into the early 20th century, with narrative and illustrations suggesting that the South still should be punished, even at that late date.

SOUTHERN BANKS IN OPERATION

Banking in the South faced many of the same conditions as in the North. Gold and silver coins were completely absent from circulation after the early months of the war, and reliance was on substitutes. While encased postage stamps and copper tokens were not issued in the South, millions of scrip notes of fractional denominations were used, probably more so than in the North. Larger denomination bills, from $1 up, were issued by states, cities, towns, railroads, and other entities, again to a greater extent than in the Union. Both the Union and the Confederacy were in need of funds to conduct the war, and the floating of loans through bonds and paper money was done by each.

When existing bank-note supplies became exhausted, the services of local and regional printers were enlisted, as described above. In the meantime, the regular business of making loans, receiving deposits, and otherwise engaging in business continued in about the same way on both sides of the conflict.

Scattered and incomplete reports of many Southern banks were printed in *Merchants and Bankers Almanac* and other publications, often giving the names of officers but little in the way of financial data. Thus the Bank of Montgomery, in Alabama, is listed in 1863 as having a capital of $100,000, with E.M. Burton and E.C. Hannon as president.

Historian John Jay Knox told this incident about a certain institution in Alexandria, Virginia, founded on March 29, 1851:

> The Bank of the Old Dominion secured its financial integrity through its discount clerk, Mr. J.W. Lockwood. On the advance of the federal troops to Alexandria the bank's gold was shipped to Lynchburg, and it was afterwards moved to Richmond in Mr. Lockwood's care. The demand for gold by the government was so great that nearly all the banks surrendered their gold and took Confederate securities, and when the end came the banks were swept out of existence with the general destruction.
>
> But not so with the Bank of the Old Dominion, its faithful discount clerk secured its gold and fled with it South at the evacuation of Richmond, and two months later returned it to the board of directors at Alexandria intact along with two thousand dollars in silver, which he buried in a sarcophagus in Charlottesville and dug up after his return. The president of the bank was William

N. McVeigh; P.E. Hoffman was Cashier and G.W.D. Ramsey, a near relative of Gen. Washington, was teller. He was afterwards teller of the First National Bank of Alexandria.[28]

NATIONAL BANKS

In many instances, Southern bankers who had been active in state-chartered institutions signed on as cashier or president of newly formed National Banks, these taking hold beginning in 1865. Thomas W. Dewey, cashier of the Bank of the State of North Carolina, Charlotte branch, became the founding cashier of the First National Bank of Charlotte, charter 1547, founded on August 26, 1865, just a few months after the April conclusion of the conflict. In Salem in the same state, Israel G. Lash, cashier of the local branch of the Bank of Cape Fear, segued into the cashiership of the First National Bank of Salem, charter 1659.

Soon after the end of the war, George W. Williams & Co., leading brokers in Charleston, South Carolina, expanded the business, built 15 large brick warehouses to store cotton and other goods, and established credit connections in New York City and London. The firm, earlier engaged in banking, was the leading light in organizing the First National Bank of Charleston, charter 1622, with a capital of $200,000 and the authorization to expand to $1,000,000 if so desired.

In the same year, the Peoples Bank of South Carolina, in Charleston, reorganized as the Peoples National Bank of Charleston, charter 1621, one of relatively few instances in the South of a state bank directly converting to a National Bank. Many other scenarios could be given.

After the war was over, the American Bank Note Co. jumped back into the business of serving customers in the South, such as with this 1866 $1 note for the state of South Carolina. By this time, orders for bank notes were few and far between, but there was much activity in other areas of security printing.

Collecting and Enjoying Obsolete Bank Notes

Buying, Selling, and Collecting

Bills of state-chartered banks, essential to commerce in their time, form a fascinating numismatic specialty today. No one knows how many banks issued notes from 1782 to 1866—more than 3,000 but probably fewer than 4,000 is a good estimate. The number of different denominations and designs is also unknown, but it certainly runs into the tens of thousands.

While obsolete currency has been collected for a long time, it still remains a largely undiscovered niche in numismatics in relation to activity in United States coins and federal paper money. Still, within this niche there are rich resources for information. The *Essay-Proof Journal,* published in 50 volumes by the Essay-Proof Society from 1944 to 1992, is essential for the study of engravers and their art. The Society of Paper Money Collectors (SPMC) has sponsored what now amounts to a bookshelf of titles relating to the obsolete currency of different states, and its journal, *Paper Money,* has included many fine articles over a long period of time. In the early 20th century, *The Numismatist* ran many features on bank notes, including a lengthy series by D.C. Wismer and many articles by Waldo Moore, among others. A file of these articles is a great resource today.

The *Bank Note Reporter,* a modern newspaper put out by F+W Publications, brings monthly news of the market, auctions, and other events and includes occasional articles on obsolete paper. James A. Haxby's four-volume *A Standard Catalog of United States Obsolete Bank Notes 1782–1866,* published in 1988, is essential to appreciation of the series, but copies are not easy to find. Gene Hessler's *The Engraver's Line* gives much useful information about those who created the artwork and designs for currency. Roger H. Durand has published a series of monographs in the *Interesting Notes* series, such as *Interesting Notes About Denominations* (1988), *Interesting Notes About History* (1990), *Interesting Notes About Territories* (1992), and *Interesting Notes About Indians* (1991), to mention several titles. His studies are indeed interesting and will add to the appreciation of bills in your collection.

Auction sales of obsolete paper money are held frequently, the Internet has many offerings, and within the Professional Currency Dealers Association (PCDA) there are specialists with notes for sale.

At the same time, there are many aspects to obsolete bank notes that remain unexplored. Having read this book, you realize that whether certain banks actually existed and if certain bills are legitimate may not be known. Among remaining currency, not even the most expert of experts can always tell a genuine note from a cleverly altered one. Out-and-out counterfeits from false plates are easier to discern, but the changing of the imprint of a bill from one location or bank to another can be challenging to discover. In the marketplace, including in some great auctions held by the finest firms, there are apt to be counterfeits and alterations among bank notes. General policy within the hobby is that bills are offered *as is,* but returns can be made within a specified period of time. This possibility might seem strange to a collector of United States coins or federal paper money, in which authenticity is usually guaranteed, but to a specialist in obsolete bank notes, it goes with the territory. Besides, the Haxby text lists and prices certain false notes known to him, and they are highly collectible in their own right.

The marketplace for obsolete currency offers many opportunities to you as a buyer. Prices are hardly standard, and for a given note one qualified seller may charge $100, while another seeks $200. Not so long ago I bought a $50 note from the Somersworth (New Hampshire) Bank for $800, while at about the same time a friend paid $1,500 for a virtually identical bill. Both sellers were knowledgeable professionals and members of PCDA. To a buyer of Morgan silver dollars, such variations would be unusual indeed. For obsolete paper money this happens often. Later in this chapter, I will discuss some techniques for buying. However, many notes are so rare that if one is offered, it is best to buy it—never mind that next year one may be offered for less. It could also be that next year one sells for twice the price at auction. If you are a collector of antiques, prints, autographs, or books, you will know that such variations are part of the market. Some might say that freedom from bid and ask prices, extreme focus on high grades, and other trappings of buying, selling, and evaluating federal coins is a blessing for currency collectors. Perhaps a salvation from the grading obsession prevalent elsewhere is the fact that for bank notes, a used Extremely Fine note is *usually* worth more than a superb Uncirculated, flawless, etc., note, the latter being a remainder.

The above said, the field of collecting obsolete bank notes beckons and is filled with many opportunities. This chapter will explore the techniques I have found to be useful. A nod of appreciation goes to dealer Tom Denly for much advice on aspects of buying and selling paper money and other traits of the marketplace discussed in this and the next chapter. To begin with I give some basics.

THE ANATOMY OF A BANK NOTE

At first blush an old note from the Citizens Bank, or the Farmers Bank, or the Canal Bank might seem to have but two aspects: the grade assigned and the price asked. This may seem especially true if you enter currency collecting with experience based on collecting silver dollars or gold coins. However, each bill invites exploration, and close inspection can yield a panorama of interesting features. With tens of thousands of varieties of notes in the offing, and no two the same, this aspect can lead to new discoveries and heightened appreciation.

The following paragraphs give major elements found on many bank notes as well as some characteristics occasionally seen on bills.

BANK NAME

This will be one of the more prominent features on the face of a bill and is apt to be found at the center in large letters. Bank of Michigan, Corn Exchange Bank, Eighth Avenue Bank, and Liberty Bank each identify the issuer. Although there are exceptions, it is a general rule that at a given time no two banks in the same *state* had the same name. There are many instances, however, in which a name used and abandoned years earlier was resurrected by a new banking corporation. Punctuation in a bank title can be erratic, such as *Farmers, Farmers,'* and *Farmer's,* even for bills from the same bank. Numismatic protocol is to drop punctuation in titles when describing notes.

The name of the bank is usually located in the middle of the face, either centered or high. An inscription such as CENTRAL BANK, FARMERS AND MECHANICS BANK, or some other name identified the issuer and is usually large and prominent.

Some titles are descriptive of local or regional commerce, trade, or activity that is serviced by the bank.

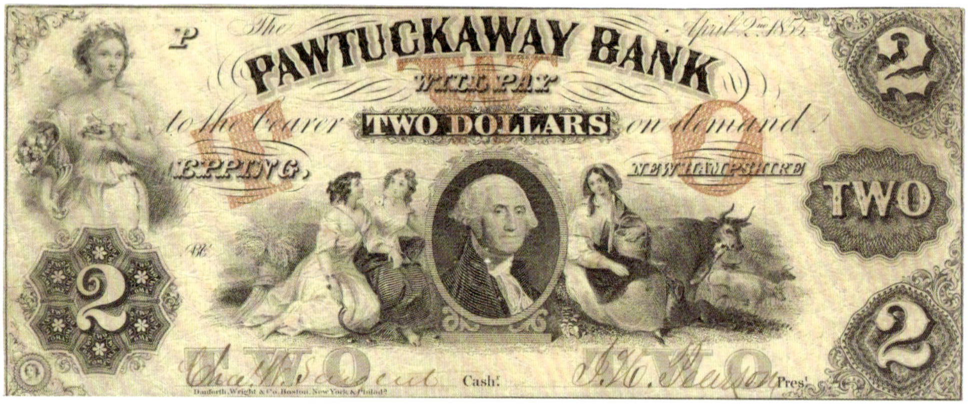

A bank note can be fascinating to contemplate. Upon close examination of this typical bill from the Pawtuckaway Bank a numismatist will see how many of these features he/she can find: bank name (Pawtuckaway Bank; the history of this or any other bank can be fascinating to explore); town or city (Epping); state (New Hampshire); denomination (expressed both as 2 and TWO, multiple times); payee (to bearer); obligation (two dollars will be paid to the holder of the note); ornaments and vignettes (one large and one small vignette, embellishments around the denomination imprints to each sides, decorations in the corners; study of the vignettes can be an interesting pursuit); (8) Imprint of the bank note maker (Danforth, Wright & Co. Boston, New York and Philadelphia, also ABNCo monogram; each engraver has a story to be learned); plate letter (P); other imprints on the face (red protector TWO overprint); back imprint (none on this note); imprinted date or date of issue (April 2nd 1855 printed); serial number (none on this issued note, and thus highly unusual); inked signature of the cashier (Chas W. Sargent; details of his life and career might be interesting to learn); inked signature of the president (J.H. Pearson; similarly, his biography might be worth investigating).

The typical bank note has most or all of the above. In addition, the numismatist contemplating the purchase of this note will want to know its rarity (not known, but perhaps up to a dozen or so), its approximate grade (Very Fine); what to expect in a grade for this note (most are Fine to VF); and its market value ($365 was paid for this note in 2003).

As will be seen from the accompanying text, some bills have even more features. Upon study an "ordinary" bank note can reveal many fascinating aspects.

Examples include Hatters Bank (Bethel, Connecticut), Merchants Bank (Portland, Maine), Agricultural Bank (Troy, New York), and Ship Builders Bank (Rockland, Maine). Some title elements, such as Merchants, Manufacturers, Mechanics, and Farmers, were widely used. A whole display could be made of different Farmers Bank bills from different locations.

Other bank names seem mysterious to those not familiar with local history and events. Some research may be needed to learn about such choices as Pahquioque Bank (Danbury, Connecticut), Bank of Shiawassee (Owasso, Michigan), Cobbossee Contee Bank (Gardiner, Maine), Middling Interest Bank (Boston), and Mahaiwe Bank (Great Barrington, Massachusetts).

Many titles simply reflected a bank's location, such as Calais Bank (Calais, Maine), Goodrich Bank (Goodrich, Michigan), Bank of West Union (West Union, Ohio), and Bank of Montpelier (Montpelier, Vermont).

Some bank titles seem to reflect different locations than the town or city imprinted, such as Oakland Bank (Gardiner, Maine) and Bank of Oakland (Pontiac, Michigan), as well as Farmers Bank of Sandstone (Barry, Michigan), Hillsborough Bank (Amherst, New Hampshire), Farmers Bank of Jessamine (Nicholasville, Kentucky), Bank of Cairo (Kaskaskia, Illinois), and Bank of Newbury (Wells River, Vermont), among many others.

Still other titles seek to reflect strength or official status, never mind that they were usually private operations, often of uncertain stability, as these in Washington, D.C., none of which had anything to do with the federal government: Government Bank, Bank of the United States (of the 1850s, not related to *the* Bank of the United States of earlier renown), Congressional Bank, and National Bank. One might imagine that if someone in a foreign country had been offered a $10 note on the Bank of the United States, Washington, D.C., it might be taken as a government issue, much like a Bank of England note would be in the country of its origin.

In the strength-projecting title categories there are many banks named for famous figures, including Franklin Bank (Boston), Washington Banking Co. (Hackensack, New Jersey), Jefferson Bank (New Salem, Ohio), and John Hancock Bank (Springfield, Massachusetts). Probably the gold crown goes to the Atlas Bank (Boston).

A quick glance at a bank title can sometimes give a different impression than a detailed examination of the bill. What is ostensibly a certain bill of the Canal Bank, of Middleton, Ohio, is found upon close inspection to be a private issue, by "the undersigned, who has an office on the CANAL BANK." This soggy (perhaps) office, nothing to do with an official bank, seems to have been located on the Miami Erie Canal in the same town! Certain bills of the State Stock Bank of Indiana, which failed in 1855, have the word *Stock* in small letters so as to give the impression that the bills are from the highly regarded State Bank of Indiana, an unrelated institution.[1]

Fraudsters who altered bank bills from one address to another had a field day with common bank names. Farmers Banks were located in Connecticut, Michigan, District of Columbia, Delaware, and other places. The bills of a defunct Farmers Bank could be bought up and altered to another town and state.

Location

Each bank note is imprinted with the town or city of its origin and usually its state. In many cases these words are not near each other. An imprint such as Vermont or Michigan may appear on one part of a note, and the town name on another. Often the town name will be directly below the bank name, but there are many exceptions.

For a given town there can be variations in spelling. District of Columbia bills exist with Anacostia as a town and also Anacastia, along with other variations including Washington and Washington City. Some notes of Elizabeth, New Jersey, are imprinted as such, while others have Elizabethtown. Sometimes "borough" is shortened to "boro" in bank titles and locations. A certain city in Vermont can be spelled as Brattleborough or Brattleboro. Similarly we have Marlborough as well as Marlboro spellings in Massachusetts.

As noted earlier in the text, some banks and towns can change state locations without actually moving. All towns now in Maine were in Massachusetts prior to 1820; Alexandria was in Virginia, then for a while in the District of Columbia, then back in Virginia; and today's Toledo, Ohio, was once claimed to be within the boundaries of the territory of Michigan. Certain bills of the Pocasset Bank of Fall River have no state name imprinted. This bank was in a section of Fall River that was once in Rhode Island but then was assigned to be part of Massachusetts. Perhaps it was safer just to say "Fall River" and nothing more.

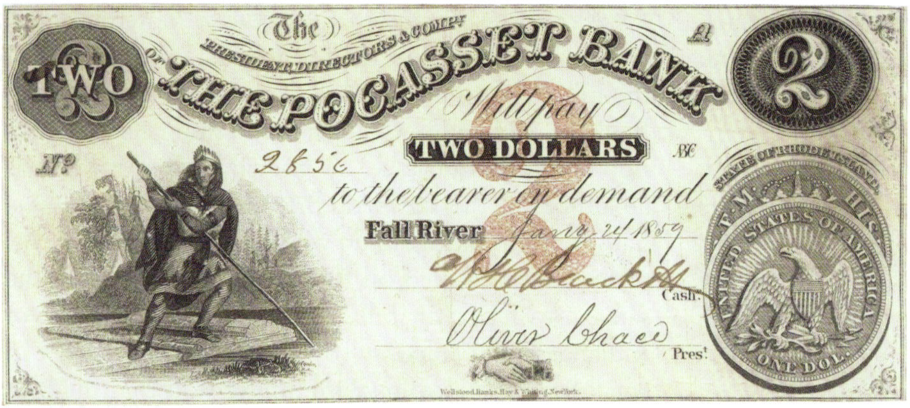

Where is this $2 bill from? The Pocasset Bank was on land that at one time was in Rhode Island and another time in Massachusetts after a border alteration in 1860. Perhaps to avoid confusion, this bill gives no state! From a plate by Wellstood, Hanks, Hay & Whiting, New York.

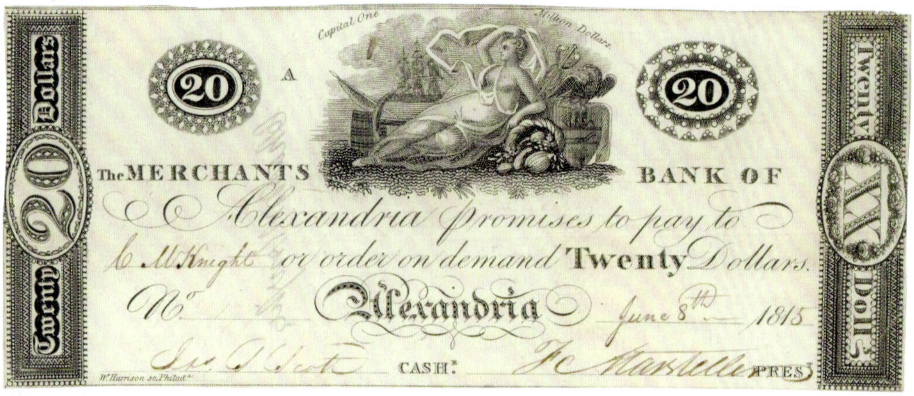

A $20 note from the Merchants Bank of Alexandria, June 8, 1815, with no further location given, to avoid confusing the public. At one time Alexandria was in Virginia. Then it was ceded to the District of Columbia, later to be retroceded to Virginia. From a plate engraved by William Harrison, Philadelphia.

Various territories in the Midwest later became states. A location abbreviation such as K.T. translates to Kansas Territory.

The Farmers Bank of Saratoga County was established in Half Moon Village, New York, in 1851, then became located in Crescent, New York, when the name of the place was changed. Great Falls and Somersworth, New Hampshire, are the same city, Great Falls being a district of Somersworth. Certain bills of the State Bank of Camden (New Jersey) have "near Philadelphia" as part of the address. Certain banks in New Jersey and Michigan were deliberately located in remote villages or even uninhabited tracts so their notes could not be redeemed easily. In Washtenaw County, Michigan, in the 1830s surveys were laid out on charts and filed for towns named Boston, Saratoga, Windham, and Sharon, but they existed only on paper. Bank examiner Alpheus Felch stated that the town of Lowell was completely imaginary in the 1830s (although such a place was later created). Collecting fictional or fraudulent banks with remote or nonexistent addresses could be a specialty in itself.

Denomination

The denomination or face value of a note is one of the more prominent elements, usually appearing multiple times and as a numeral as well as spelled out. In the trade in the bank-note issuing era, these elements were called *counters.* A $5 bill is apt to have "5" (without a dollar sign) several places on the face, often with an ornament made by a geometric lathe. FIVE is likely to appear one or several times in green, red, or other color overprints on notes of the 1850s and 1860s. Patent Stereotype Steel Plate bills and certain Ormsby back designs repeat the denomination dozens of times. On some notes by various engravers the denomination is carried out further, such as by having a goddess holding a shield emblazoned with a 5, or cupids or pretty girls sitting on or holding a large ornate 5 numeral.

Standard denominations for bank bills included $1, $2, $3, $5, $10, and $20, these being the most popular. Now and again a state or even a city would enact a rule that no notes of less than a certain amount, say $5, could be used. The intent was to promote the circulation of coins, which usually did not happen. Higher denominations printed for many banks included $50, $100, $500, and $1,000. The $500 and $1,000 values in particular did not circulate extensively but were used in bank-to-bank transfers. Accordingly, when such bills are seen today, which is not often, they are apt to be in higher circulated grades. Most in collectors' hands are proof impressions, most

The casual viewer might think this note was issued in Philadelphia, Pennsylvania, but in actuality it was paid out from Salem, New Jersey. In distant places, Philadelphia bills were apt to be highly valued, while few people would have heard of Salem. Only with a magnifying glass is Salem visible in the title!

Regarding such notes, *Bicknell's Counterfeit Detector* printed this item on December 6, 1830 (original emphasis maintained):

> We copy the following from a late New Orleans paper: Of importance to the public.—Our readers will remember, that some time in August last, information was received in this city, of the wreck of the ship, *Superb,* bound for this port, from Philadelphia. One half of the cargo paid a salvage of fifty percent, and was purchased by the underwriters, and forwarded to Philadelphia. Among other articles sent on to this city was a bundle about a foot square, which, on examination, was found to contain *bank notes on the Salem and Philadelphia Manufacturing Company,* to the amount of about 10,000, in notes of one, two and three dollars value, and executed in such a manner, as manifestly shows, they were intended to defraud the public.
>
> The word *Salem* is in small letters, scarcely visible, while that of *Philadelphia,* is in a large bold letters, and the word *Manufacturers* is in letters nearly the size of that of Philadelphia, but very indistinct, and requires a close examination to distinguish it correctly. These notes were intended to be forwarded to the state of Illinois, and there, in all probability, the fraud was to have been practiced. We have seen these notes; they are beautifully executed, and would deceive any person who was not habitually a narrow observer of paper currency. We trust this publication will hinder any person being deceived by this party, and hope it will deter all persons, of felonious intentions, from attempting soon to put similar cheats on the public.

notably from the dispersal of the American Bank Note Company's printed archives a generation ago.

There were many other values used as well, including cent-denominated scrip as well has higher denominations such as $1.25, $1.50, $1.75, $4, $6, $7, $8, $9, and onward, to the thousands of dollars. The Bank of the United States of Pennsylvania (sometimes incorrectly called the third Bank of the United States), issued bills up to $5,000, examples of which are met with frequently today.

Obligation and Payee Information

The inscription on each bill typically includes a "promise to pay," "redeemable in," or some other inscription. Some bills are payable at a later date than the date of issue and are called post notes. An inscription may read: "Will pay One Dollar on demand." As noted and illustrated earlier, certain bills of the Bullion Bank, Washington, D.C., issued in 1862, are payable in Demand Notes, with later versions of the bill payable in Treasury Notes.

While most bills were payable and receivable at the issuing bank, many bore addresses of distant places where they could be exchanged. Michigan notes that were payable at the Bank of Central New York in Utica, New York, have been described. In the same vein, certain bills of the Bank of Macomb County (Mount Clemens, Michigan) are payable at, of all places, the Bank of Tonawanda, New York. Many bills have imprints noting they are payable at the bank of issue and also in a large city such as New York.

On many early bills there was a blank space for the name of the payee to be inserted, after "pay to" or a related inscription. Originally this seems to have been for the first recipient of the bill, perhaps someone who took out a discount (loan) from the bank. Likely, the payees on notes of the Vermont Glass Factory (Salisbury, Vermont) were employees or suppliers. Later, many issuers either left that space blank or else filled it in quickly with an initial and fictitious three- or four-letter surname. Actual examples include E. Eon, W. Weir, S. Wot, and J. Hill seen on Hillsborough Bank (Amherst, New Hampshire) bills. Names of prominent people were often used, such as H. Clay, A. Jackson, and B. Franklin. Some banks had such payee names engraved on the bills, possibly for whimsy, but real enough in their use. Bills of the Piscataqua Exchange Bank (Portsmouth, New Hampshire) of the 1850s include those with printed payees James Monroe, B. Franklin, William Penn, and W. Raleigh.

ORNAMENTS AND VIGNETTES

While some early bills feature just inscriptions and numbers, most have some form of artistic embellishment. Many bills from the 1790s up to about 1806 include one or more small decorations, such as a ship, cow, or plow. By 1810, goddesses, scenes, and other artistic motifs were used on many notes, and during the next decade these became standard. As the years progressed, vignettes became more elaborate, with the 1830s and 1840s seeing wonderfully ornate illustrations, often allegorical or from mythology. Engravers tried to outdo each other, sometimes signing their work.

The standard arrangement for most notes of the 1820s onward includes a large vignette at the center, usually at the top of the bill, above the bank name. At the left and right margins are other vignettes, often unrelated in theme to the central one—with political portraits, ships, medallion heads, trains, or

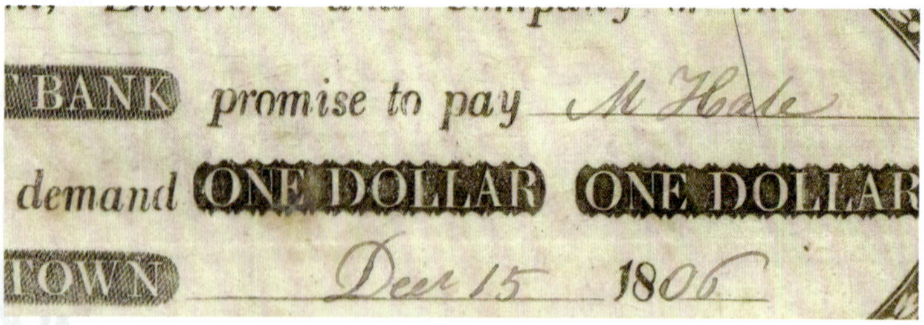

A selection of manuscript and printed payees from a wide range of years (enlargements not to scale).

other topics—compactly arranged. Sometimes just above the bottom center margin is a very small vignette, such as a dog guarding a safe, a woman's head, or a group of birds.

Gods, goddesses, and allegorical scenes were especially popular in the 1830s, continuing into the 1840s. Hebe, cupbearer to the gods, is seen in many poses, including with the American eagle. Mercury, with wings on his cap, is another popular figure, in one vignette bringing a cornucopia overflowing with coins to the seated goddess Moneta. Names have been assigned to certain figures. A goddess holding a sheaf of wheat is often referred to as Ceres, an ancient blacksmith as Vulcan, a figure holding balance scales as Justice, and a woman with a liberty cap on a pole as Liberty. Some engravers' proofs have titles for vignettes, but the names of most are not known today.

By examining small sheets of sample vignettes, bank officers could select the themes they desired. Often the large central vignette reflected local or regional commerce or industry. Iron forges, weaving looms, whaling scenes, shoe manufacturing, and shipbuilding motifs are among the dozens that were used. Bills of banks in coastal towns might show sailing ships, harbors, or shorelines. A bank on a large inland river might use a steamship or river scene. In the Midwest, farming and prairie scenes often were selected.

In the 1820s and 1830s, vignettes of canals and canal boats reflected the times. Progress from the late 1820s onward could be epitomized on a bank note by showing a steam locomotive racing down the tracks, at a station, or hauling a long string of cars. Cityscapes as well as street scenes were popular with metropolitan banks. Some institutions commissioned pictures of their own buildings, but for the most part illustrations were taken from an engraver's stock. Similarly, a few bills depict bank presidents, although such are not only few and far between today, but also hard to identify if they are not captioned.

A portrait of George Washington or Benjamin Franklin represented tradition and stability. Political leanings of the time were reflected by images of John C. Calhoun, Andrew Jackson, Henry Clay, Daniel Webster, and others. A silver dollar, half dollar, or Spanish milled dollar illustrated on a note implied that it was as good as a coin. Battle scenes from the Revolution or the War of 1812 might seem like obvious choices, but few were ever used on paper money. However, portraits of military heroes were widely employed. The United States Capitol was the most popular building depicted on currency.

It was not until the 1850s that weekly pictorial magazines made their appearance with the *Illustrated News, Frank Leslie's Illustrated Weekly, Ballou's Pictorial Drawing-Room Companion, Harper's Weekly,* and others. Prior to that time, most scenic illustrations were found in books, not in newspapers. In their era bank notes thus served as pictures for the people, with illustrations reflecting mythology, history, and the current American scene.

Occasionally, new bills with attractive motifs would make the news, such as in this account in the *Portsmouth* (NH) *Journal,* April 22, 1854:

> **Rockingham Bank Bills**
>
> A complete set of bills from new plates have just been issued by this bank. We have feasted our eyes with the sight of eight denominations ranging from $1 to $100.
>
> The *One* is ornamented by the head of John Jay—the *Twos* by the heads of presidents Taylor and Fillmore—the *Threes* by the heads of Clay, Webster and Calhoun: thus showing the denomination by the number of portraits on each.
>
> The *Five* exhibits an original sketch of Portsmouth Navy Yard, taken from Peirce's Island, and the head of Mrs. Crittenden, the belle of Kentucky.
>
> The *Ten* exhibits the blacksmith with his sledge—and the head of a lady.
>
> The *Twenty* shows the Capitol with the emblem of Young America in front, and eagle and the head of Webster.
>
> The *Fifty* has a view of the steamer *Pacific* on the ocean.
>
> The *Hundred* presents the head of Washington and the National Eagle, the proper emblem of the most valuable bills the bank issues.
>
> These are the leading characteristics of the bills, although there are many elegant decorations on each, such as Amphitrite on the *Ones,* the ships on the *Twos,* &c. The whole design is neat and elegant, the engraving is beautiful, and the checks such as will render futile all attempts to alter or counterfeit.[2]

The bills were the work of Toppan, Carpenter, Casilear & Co. of New York City and Philadelphia. The designs remained in use for years, and after May 1, 1858, new printings from the old plates had the ABNCo monogram added.

IMPRINT OF THE BANK-NOTE MAKER

Although most early bills are unsigned, nearly all later ones bear the imprint of the person or partnership who printed the notes.

Maria Knox Innes Todd Crittenden (Mrs. John J. Crittenden), the "Belle of Kentucky," as illustrated on currency. In lieu of locating a Rockingham Bank $5 note, this portrait is from a bill of the same denomination issued by the Farmers Bank of Kentucky, Frankfort. John Crittenden was important in Kentucky politics, including serving as governor with Maria as his first lady. John Crittenden resigned in 1850 to become attorney general under President Millard Fillmore. Maria, who as a widow married John in 1826, died in 1851.

Printers signed their bills in different ways. Abner Reed imprinted notes with Reed, A. Reed, A. Reed sc, A. Reed E.W. Con. (for East Windsor, Connecticut), and other variations. Rarely, a vignette will have two signatures, one for the artist who created the scene and the other for the engraver who rendered it on a copper or steel plate. An example is the $1 bill issued in 1837 by United States Exchange Company, of New York City, which issued bills payable in Portland, Maine. A vignette depicts a ship under full sail to the left, and to the right, Mercury seated on box, holding a caduceus in his left hand. Below is "A.B. Durand Del / C.C. Wright Sc." This indicates the artwork was by Asher B. Durand and the engraving by Charles Cushing Wright.

Companies gave their names in different ways, such as American Bank Note Company spelled out on one plate, American Bank Note Co. on another, and the monogram ABNCo imprinted on another (the latter usually a reused old plate). American also used different addresses including New York, Boston, and Philadelphia. Except under very close examination, the ABNCo monogram seems to appear as "ABCo," as only a tiny part of the letter N is visible. Rawdon, Wright & Hatch gave its location as New-York, hyphenated, while some others used N. York, N.Y., and other variations. The New York Bank Note Co. usually included "50 Wall St." as part of its address.

Among early bills, imprints can be almost anywhere on the face, arranged horizontally or vertically. Most later issues have it horizontally on or above the bottom border. Perkins bills are often imprinted with "Patent Stereotype Steel Plate," but no mention of Perkins. Others have the same, but with the addition of New England Bank Note Co.

The Engraver's Line, by Gene Hessler, gives the operating dates of many bank-note engravers and partnerships. However, neither these dates nor those in any other reference are reliable guides as to when bills were issued. While most notes were printed while the businesses were in operation, old plates were kept on hand through evolutions of partnerships and were often used later without changing the imprint. Another element was introduced by banks keeping stocks of unissued bills on hand. Because of this habit, bills printed by a partnership that expired in 1839 might be issued with inked dates into the 1840s.

Some vignettes made in the 1850s have very long copyright or registration notices printed in microscopic letters along the border. When copies were made of certain vignettes by siderography, or when the vignettes were trimmed, sometimes part of the lettering was removed, leaving only a few traces.

Plate Letter

Most but not all bank notes have one or more plate letters, most often from early in the alphabet. These identify the position that a note had on a sheet of multiple subjects. A discussion of these will be found under "Plate Letter Technicalities" in chapter 18.

A selection of engravers' and printers' imprints from a wide range of years (enlargements not to scale).

In many instances, four steel plates for single notes would be clamped together in a frame to create four subjects. Sometimes plates with odd letters would be used, such as K for a $100 note in the frame, while other bills had letters such as A, B, or C. Among Patent Stereotype Steel Plate letters, called check letters, letters such as I, L, and M are seen more frequently than are such earlier letters as F and J.

In nearly all instances there are minute plate varieties among notes of the same design and denomination. Close comparison of a $1 note from plate A with a B note from the next plate position will reveal tiny differences in the placement of the vignettes, ornaments, and lettering in relation to each other, as these elements were entered separately by the transfer press during the plate-making process. Such differences have not been studied in the literature and are not of interest to currency collectors at present. It may be poignant to remark that *coin* collectors often seek and pay high prices for coins with minute differences in the arrangement of letters and other features—some of which require high magnification to discern. Large copper cents of the 1850s provide an example of such a specialty.

Other Design Elements

Several state banking departments—New York and Michigan are examples—required certain banks to have the seal of the state treasurer or other office imprinted on the face. Other terms such as "Safety Fund," "Real Estate Pledged," etc., were often used, sometimes with real meaning in terms of security, but often not.

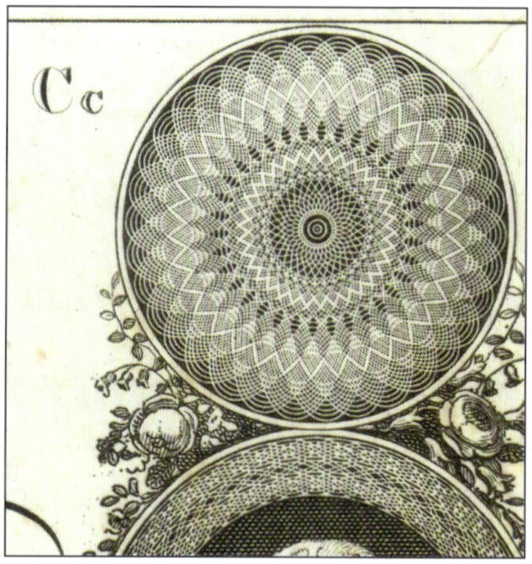

A selection of plate letters from a wide range of years (enlargements not to scale).

Beginning in a large way in the 1850s, many bills had security or anticounterfeiting imprints, including the earlier-mentioned patented Canada Green tint, Lyman's Patent, and more. Overprints in color on one or both sides, such as THREE or FIVE, were common. These are sometimes referred to as *protectors* or *guards.*

Back Plate Designs

Most notes were printed only on the face. However, from the days of Jacob Perkins' Patented Check Plate in the first decade of the 19th century, some bills were also printed on the back. In the 1850s and 1860s, back printing was common, although except for red, green, or other color protectors with the denomination in large letters, such notes remained in the minority. Later issues of the state banks of Ohio and Indiana had colorful backs with the name of the branch imprinted. W.L. Ormsby used colored ink with the denomination repeated many times in tiny letters, and still others used geometric lathe designs. Most later bills have the back printing in color, rarely in only black.

About Bank-Note Paper

In the early days of bank notes, paper was obtained from local sources and varied widely in quality and durability. Bills of the period up to about 1810 are often on thin paper that is susceptible to tearing. Abner Reed stated that banks often supplied their own paper to him, after which he printed the notes. Some such bills are fragile today.

By the 1820s most printers of bank notes used special paper, and this continued through the end of the note-issuing period in the 1860s. The Crane Paper Company of Dalton, Massachusetts, was a leading

A selection of state seals, pledges, etc., on bank notes of the 1830s onward (enlargements not to scale).

supplier of bank-note stock and offered it in many different grades. A few years ago an archive album of Patent Stereotype Steel Plate notes came to light, with many bills being test impressions, with the stock numbers of Crane paper inked on the back.

Willcox & Co., located in Ivy Mills, Delaware County, Pennsylvania, was founded in 1729. The company furnished paper for printing certain colonial bills as well as Continental Currency notes. James M. Willcox, a later-generation member of the founding family, issued this circular in 1850:

> Dear Sir:
>
> Enclosed are three samples of bank-note paper, each a quarter of a sheet, of different thicknesses, but made in the manner (handmade) and of the same material. The subscriber has been a manufacturer of bank-note paper for nearly a half century, and for the last twenty years has made it almost an exclusive business.
>
> After various experiments, he thinks he has succeeded in making a paper peculiarly adapted to that purpose. It is made of a material different from any heretofore used, being tough and flexible, having a surface not liable to crack or wear rough, and susceptible of receiving the finest steel or copper plate impressions, of which the samples are specimens.
>
> He has also in store a large quantity of bank-note paper that is well seasoned, being from eight to ten years old, of which samples will be forwarded without delay when required. Every sheet is warranted perfect, and equal to sample.
>
> The price of this paper is $22.50 per 1,000 sheets, and is for sale by Jas. M. Willcox & Co., No. 7 Minor Street, Philadelphia, and at manufacturer's prices by
>
> Messrs. Rawdon, Wright, Hatch & Edson, engravers and copper plate printers, New York, New Orleans, and Cincinnati.
>
> New England Bank Note Co., Boston.
>
> Messrs. Toppan, Carpenter, Casilear & Co., engravers and copper plate printers, New York, Philadelphia, and Cincinnati.
>
> Messrs. Danforth, Bald & Co., engravers and copper plate printers, New York and Philadelphia.
>
> Messrs. Wellstood, Benson & Hanks, engravers and copper plate printers, New York.
>
> Messrs. Draper, Welsh & Co., engravers and copper plate printers, Philadelphia.
>
> Very respectfully yours, &c.,
>
> James M. Willcox[3]

Generally, bank-note paper was tough. Some higher grades had embedded fibers to add strength and to act as a deterrent to counterfeiting.

Information Added by Banks to Notes

The preceding features were all part of the bank-note engraver's plate. Sometimes late in the state-banking era the printer would add serial numbers by means of a machine, but otherwise the following features were all added by the bank once the bills were received. Ser-

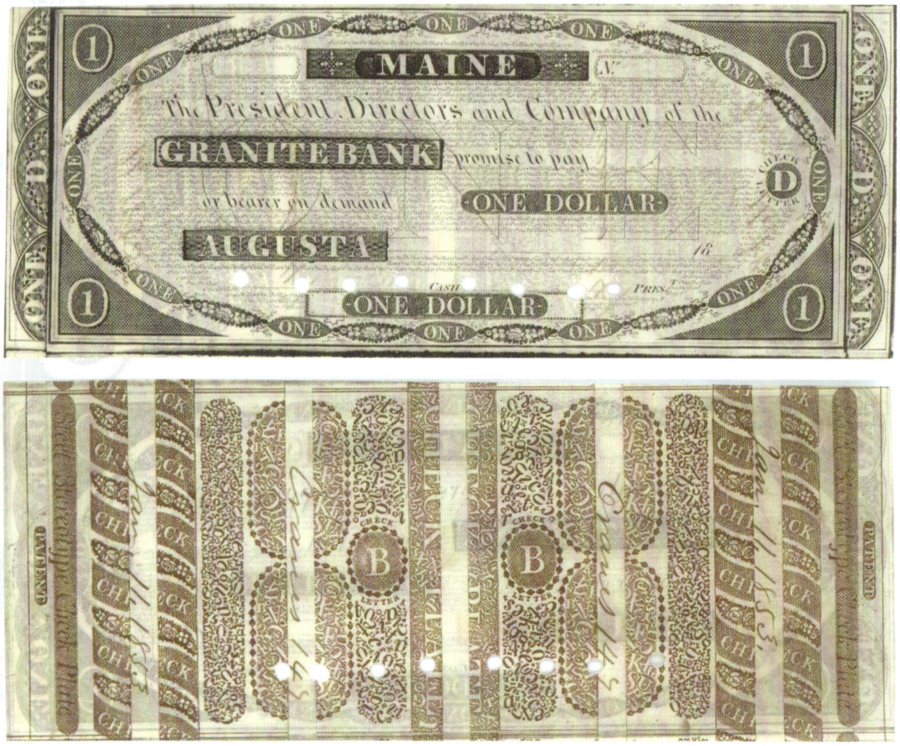

A $1 note of the Granite Bank of Augusta, Maine. Proof impression by the New England Bank Note Co., and from a scrapbook kept by that firm. The back bears notations as to the stock number (145) of the Crane paper used. Dated January 11, 1853.

ial numbers, dates, and signatures were added at different times by different people. Accordingly, a given bill can show several shades or colors of ink.

Imprinted Date or Date of Issue

Each bank note bears a calendar date, sometimes printed in full as part of the printing plate, but usually filled in by a bank clerk or officer. The most popular partially printed date is 18, allowing it to be used in more than one decade. In ink the month, day, and two final year digits would be added. Other partial dates included three numerals such as 185. Still others had a printed month and day date, but an incomplete year, such as January 1, 185. Bills with the full date printed, such as Oct. 10th 1854 on the Bucksport Bank in Maine, or May 1st 1850 on bills of the Mechanicks Bank of Concord, New Hampshire, might be used for years afterward. Hence, such printed dates are of little use.

Bills with the day, month, and year filled in with ink were generally issued about the time of that date, although it was common for cashiers and clerks to fill out bills in advance. It seems to have been the practice of many banks to pick one or two days per month, often the 1st, and use that date for all bills issued in that month. Other banks used the correct day date.

Serial Numbers

Although some banks in the 1850s and 1860s had serial numbers imprinted on their notes by num-

A selection of serial numbers from a wide range of years (enlargements not to scale).

bering machines at the bank-note companies, the usual practice was to add them in ink at the bank. Some bills had the same serial number written twice on a note, a seemingly redundant imprint. Rarely, banks issued bills without serial numbers, certain issues of the Pawtuckaway Bank of Epping, New Hampshire, being an example.

To keep the numbers smaller and make them easier to write, many banks started new sequences with each new day date on a note. Because it may have been felt that low numbers would raise questions, likely many banks started with 100 or another three-digit number. It was usual practice to number the notes when they were still in uncut sheet form. The same serial would be used on all of the notes on a given sheet, the different plate letters and denominations making the distinction necessary for accounting purposes.

Some banks numbered sheets far in advance, as this was a task that could be done anytime. Later, the dates and signatures could be added. Bank cashiers were supposed to keep a record of denominations, plate letters, and serial numbers of notes paid out, but in practice few did. During the course of state bank examinations it was common for agents to learn that the bank had only a vague idea of the number of its bills in circulation, and that precise-appearing numbers were really only guesses. In such instances the examiners sought to see delivery receipts from bank-note companies, but sometimes these were nowhere to be found. This cozy arrangement worked well for the many banks that recklessly and illegally ordered paper money far in excess of authorized limits. The bank-note companies were willing accomplices. Such companies did not give information to inspectors or inquirers except in a few instances of tight state regulation, such as New York.

Signatures of the Cashier and President

Each bill provided spaces for the cashier and president to sign in ink, often with "Cashier," "Cash'r," to the left, and on the right "President," "Pres.," "Pres't," or a related imprint. While the cashier nearly always signed on the left, a few bills provided for the signatures to be one above the other. In instances of factories, railroads, towns, and other non-banks issuing denominated bills, other offices such as "Clerk," "Agent," or "Treasurer" were used.

For nearly all small and medium-size banks, the office of president was held by a man (no woman has been found) who did not spend much time at the bank, except to chair board meetings and, sometimes, to approve discounts (loans) and other policies. Because of this fact, presidents often would sign many notes in advance. According to much of the law in force, a bill was not monetized or legal until it was signed by both parties. Thus the cashier usually only signed bills that were ready to be paid out.

Sometimes a vice president would sign, by inking "v" or "vice" in front of the "President" imprint. Less often, in fact very rarely, would an assistant cashier sign. It is generally thought that bills bear authentic signatures of the officers, not the work of clerks or secretaries. However, counter to this belief, the Mormon Church historians state that Joseph Smith's signature on Kirtland Safety Society (Kirtland, Ohio) bills cannot be authenticated with certainty. Nicholas Biddle's tiny cramped signature was applied to thousands of bills of the second Bank of the United States, and other officers did likewise, despite pleas to the government to allow secretarial signatures.

The State Bank of Indiana, the Bank of the State of Indiana, and the State Bank of Ohio issued notes that were signed by the *branch* cashier and the *system* president. For the State Bank of Ohio, after 1856, denominations of $1, $2, and $3 were signed by the *system* vice president.

Determining the identity of bank cashiers, presidents, or other officers at a given time can be an arduous task, and this has been done only for a few states, such as Rhode Island (Roger H. Durand) and New Hampshire (the yet-unpublished New Hampshire Currency Project files). Information in bank-note reporters and counterfeit detectors can be inaccurate or stale, and these sources cannot be relied upon. Often a person such as "Samuel Smith" would sign variously as Samuel Smith, Sam'l Smith, or S. Smith over a period of time.

In many instances, bills examined by editors and writers for the *New York Journal of Commerce, Niles' Weekly Register,* and other periodicals had hastily scrawled signatures that could not be deciphered. Because of this fact, financial journals are filled with misspellings and wrong names. The best sources are printed reports issued by the banks themselves and state bank commissioners.

Because fraudsters who obtained quantities of unsigned notes of failed banks sometimes did not know the identities of the officers, it was common practice for them to use fictitious names.

Bank Overprints and Surcharges

For control, redemption, or other purposes, some banks stamped or inked letters on the face of a note, often in a color such as red and often at the upper right.

Overprints or surcharges were added by some banks, such as CENTREVILLE in bright red on certain bills of the Merchants Bank of St. Joseph, Michigan, that were sent to its Centreville, Michigan, branch. Other overprints, sometimes on the back, give places of redemption, such as the Bank of Commerce, of Savannah, Georgia, with a red overprint on the back stating that its bills would be received by the Bank of the Republic in New York City. Bills of the Commercial Exchange Bank of Terre Haute, Indiana, are often seen with a vertical overprint at left of center: "GUARANTEED AND REDEEMED AT / KEOKUK, IOWA / BY THE / Keokuk Exchange Bank." Certain New Orleans bank bills issued after the retaking of New Orleans by Union troops in 1862 are imprinted, such as "FORCED ISSUE / REGISTERED / P.H. MORGAN / Commissioner," seen on certain Bank of Louisiana bills.

In Boston the Suffolk Bank and the Bank of Mutual Redemption each stamped worthless bills with bold letters reading COUNTERFEIT, BROKEN BANK, or similar wording.

Countersignatures and Marks

The unofficial way to mark a counterfeit was to draw a large X in ink across the face. However, the stand ard practice was to pass such notes along, not to withdraw them from circulation. Many bills have inked notations on the back relating to when they were redeemed by a bank or when interest was paid on interest-bearing notes. Still other marks were added by users of the bills, giving the name of the person from whom it was received.

Collecting Obsolete Bank Notes

Gathering Information

The logical first step to being a smart buyer of obsolete currency is to obtain as much information as you can. If you've read this book and retained a good measure of it, you probably have as much technical and historical knowledge as most dealers and advanced collectors.

To this it would be worthwhile to add selected books on areas you find interesting. A good way to do this is to borrow copies from the American Numismatic Association Library in Colorado Springs or to view copies owned by a collecting friend. Unless you want a comprehensive library on the subject, you may not want to acquire a specialized text on Maryland or Pennsylvania bills if your main interest is the state of Ohio. In that instance, Wendell Wolka's 2004 book, still in print, *A History of Nineteenth Century Ohio Obsolete Bank Notes and Scrip,* is essential. The four-volume *A Standard Catalog of United States Obsolete Bank Notes 1782–1866* (1988) by James A. Haxby is a must-have for its comprehensive nature. Beyond that, pick and choose titles that appeal to you. Joining the Society of Paper Money Collectors is worthwhile and will gain you a subscription to *Paper Money.* Also subscribe to the *Bank Note Reporter.*

Watch advertisements and notices, and when auctions of bank notes take place, get a printed catalog. The second-best method is looking at lot descriptions on the Internet, but the catalog is handier.

Open the Professional Currency Dealers Association (PCDA) Web site and browse the fixed-price offerings for sale. The reliability of PCDA listings is far finer than offerings on Internet auction sites unless the sellers are PCDA members. There are many phony things on the Internet, including obsolete currency. It will pay to deal with an established professional.

Attend a few coin shows and examine dealers' stocks of obsolete bills. These are usually arranged by states, such as in a pile of New York bills, each in a Mylar holder, or a selection of Florida notes. Most dealers don't mind if you browse, but is it good form to make a purchase after spending extensive time looking and perhaps asking questions.

Categories of Currency

The James A. Haxby text groups obsolete bills into the following categories, which I list here, followed by my own expanded comments. In the Haxby numbering system, for example, a genuine note has a G before the final number, such as Georgia 310-G4a. In this instance, 310 is the number Haxby assigned to the Mechanics Savings Bank of Savannah, Georgia, and this is number 4 in the listing, with the suffix "a" representing a red overprint. Maine 85-C28 refers to a bill issued by the Kenduskeag Bank (assigned number 85 among Maine banks), variety 28, but a counterfeit. It is popular among sellers to blithely list a note with a C,

R, A, or S and assume the buyer knows that it is counterfeit, raised, altered, or spurious. In practice, some buyers are not aware of this custom, although the notes are described properly.

The state of the art is that for some bills it is not known whether a given example is genuine. A degree of opinion intervenes. Various counterfeits and alterations are enthusiastically collected for what they are, and some sell for strong prices. Recently I paid $200 for a bill of the "Farmers Bank of Rome," New York, offered correctly as being altered from the Farmers Bank of Romeo, Michigan. As I had no genuine Romeo note, this was a fine purchase (it is illustrated in chapter 13).

Categories of Collectible Bank Notes

***G** (Genuine)*—Such bills are those ordered by an operating bank and intended to be legitimately used as currency. These comprise most offerings. Usually included as well are bills that were distributed by fraudulently operated banks, such as the *wildcats* of Michigan in the late 1830s. Bills of completely fictitious banks, such as the New England Bank of Fairmount, Maine, are listed under the *Spurious* category below. There are many instances in which banks operated successfully without benefit of state charter. Notes of these are usually considered to be genuine.

***C** (Counterfeit)*—This type of bill is made from a false printing plate, or in the instance of some early issues, laboriously created by hand, to circulate in the era in which related genuine bills were used. These may appear similar to originals, or they may have phony signatures and incorrect features.

***R** (Raised)*—from one denomination to a higher value. A $1 bill of a good bank could be raised to a $10 by pasting "10" ornaments (counters) from a worthless bill of another bank on the good $1, making it appear as a $10 note. These bills are fairly scarce in the numismatic marketplace.

***A** (Altered)*—On these notes, the bank name and/or location has been changed. A worthless note of a Farmers Bank or a Merchants Bank in one town or state could be altered to resemble a good bank of the same name in another state. As explained earlier in the text, altering was a fairly easy process and could be done on a production line basis with many notes. Information on the worthless note was dissolved chemically, leaving blank areas that were then imprinted with different information. There are many such bills in the marketplace today, most identified if offered by established professionals, but others whose true nature is not known.

***S** (Spurious)*—These represent fantasy banks or designs used on bills of the note-issuing era. These include bills of nonexistent banks as well as bills of real banks, but made with the wrong designs. The last could be passed easily at distant locations, for most recipients would not know what real bills looked like. Spurious notes are highly interesting and very collectible.

***N** (Unattributed)*—This is a nongenuine note. This designation was used by James A. Haxby for bills of which he had no complete description or had not seen an example.

***SENC** (Surviving Example Not Confirmed)*—This Haxby notation is not a category but is an indication of rarity. An SENC note might be described from an old listing such as in a bank-note reporter, but no examples have been seen in modern collections. Since the publication of the Haxby text in 1988, *many* bills once listed as SENC are now known to exist, especially among those that came to light in the vast treasure trove of nearly 15,000 proof and sample impressions (in total, counting as four impressions a single four-subject sheet) released from the ABNCo archives through Christie's in 1990 and 1991.

While all of the preceding have numismatic values, there are other bills that are worthless. These include modern reproductions made on copy machines, photographic copies, reprints in imitation of the original, and so on. These are endemic in Internet auction offerings and are sometimes accompanied by naïve but seemingly appealing descriptions, such as this: "I know nothing about old bills. This $1,000 note of the Bank of the United States came in with a bunch of antiques from an estate." Or "This old Continental Currency bill certainly looks interesting. Wish I knew more about it."

And so on. While it may be possible to get your money back after buying a phony bill, it is far easier to buy only from established professionals. That is what I would do.

The Grading of Obsolete Currency

There are no hard and fast rules for grading obsolete currency. Interpretations vary widely.[4] A note that is Fine to one dealer may be another's Extremely Fine. Similar to the situation for coins, grading has become looser over the years. A bill I bought from Richard T. Hoober in the 1960s as Fine will easily be Very Fine today. Years ago a bill with even a slight trace of a fold or crease was automatically excluded from the Uncirculated category. Today, bills described as such can have such traces, and, perhaps, one without such traces would be given a loftier designation such as Choice Uncirculated or Gem Uncirculated. And so it goes.

These categories reflect my observation of current grading by many dealers and collectors. Beginning in the early 21st century, numbers have been attached to grades by some sellers, based on the *ANA Grading Standards for United States Coins.* However, as bills were printed, not minted, the term *Mint State* is not used for paper money.

Grade Categories

Choice or Gem Uncirculated—Unc.-63 and 64 (Choice), Unc.-65 (Gem). A crisp, bright bill with no evidence of creases, folds, or stains. Tom Denly comments, "I consider centering to be a most important part of grade. For instance a poorly centered note possibly cut into the design can never be called Gem or even choice no matter how nice it otherwise is."[5]

Uncirculated—Unc.-60. A new, never-circulated bill, but perhaps with slight evidences of a fold, crease, or smudges from handling (presumably by bank officers). If part of the margin is trimmed away, this fact should be mentioned, but often it is not.

About Uncirculated—AU-53, 55, and 58. A bright, attractive note, with some creases, folds, or light discoloration, but with only slight evidences of use in commerce.

Extremely Fine—EF-40 and 45. Bright and attractive, but with some slight stains or discoloration, perhaps with a pinhole or two or some small defect, but with overall excellent appearance. This is a bill that saw limited service in circulation.

Very Fine—VF-20 and 30. This is a widely used grade for a "nice" note, worn but with nice features. Such a bill may be somewhat faded, but the printing and vignettes will be clear and the note will have an attractive overall appearance. There may be an edge chip or two, or perhaps a tiny piece off of a corner (but not into the printed part of the note). Much inventiveness is displayed in the description of missing pieces in the margins of notes, with such terms as *chip, pull,* and *nick* employed, among others. As most bank tellers and users were right-handed, the right side of a note usually has some discoloration from everyday handling.

Fine—Fine-12. A note with even more wear, often limp or flimsy from extended use in commerce, but with all printed areas intact and most of them sharply defined. May be stained or discolored in areas.

Very Good—VG-8. Well circulated, usually with some problems, tears, or perhaps a small piece missing from the border, etc. Flimsy and often faded or discolored.

Good—G-4. Extensively circulated and with evidence of such, including small tears, perhaps edge pieces missing, areas of the printing and vignettes indistinct, and, often, old writing on the face of the note.

Poor, Fair, and About Good—Poor-1, Fair-2, AG-3. Notes that have been in circulation for a very long time, now with ragged edges or pieces missing, and often with significant areas of the note faded or otherwise not discernible. A filler. There are quite a few very early bills from the late 18th and early 19th century for which these grades may represent the finest known.

Grade as a Determinant of Value

Surprise! In the field of bank notes, a well-worn example often is worth more than an Uncirculated bill of the same variety! Up is down, black is white, things are topsy-turvy, you might say. However, the explanation is simple: Most Uncirculated bills are "remainders" that were never distributed. Most have no officers' signatures. Years after certain banks closed, large quantities of their unissued notes became available. In most instances, a nice Very Fine bill of the same denomination and design, signed and serially numbered, is worth more.

Among signed and numbered notes, higher-grade examples are more desirable than ones in lower levels of preservation. In all instances, an About Uncirculated bill is worth more than an Extremely Fine one, an EF is worth more than a Very Fine, and on down the line.

Commercial Grading Services

In 2005 the Professional Coin Grading Service (PCGS) began grading federal paper money, as did Paper Money Grading (PMG, a division of the Numismatic Guaranty Service Corporation of America). By that time several others firms were grading federal notes. By late 2005, obsolete bank bills offered in commercial holders appeared in the marketplace, joining the federal issues. If this movement expands, and many obsolete bank notes are graded, the change will have several implications.

First, it will bring many new buyers into the market, as they will believe that such aspects as authenticity (presumably guaranteed, but best check) and grade, formerly requiring knowledge to determine, have been settled for them. It will be interesting to read what guarantees such services offer if a note is found to have been cleverly altered.

Second, it will probably lift the prices of common remainder notes, for these are the bills that can be found in very high grades such as Uncirculated-65 and upward. Naïve investors will consider these to be the crème de la crème of the field. Of course, they are eminently desirable now, but they are hardly the focal point of any specialist with whom I am acquainted.

Third, the seeming assurance of third-party grading will be used as a selling tool, perhaps rightly so, by vendors who are otherwise clueless about paper money. This will be a good thing for Internet sellers, for an imprint such as PCGS or PMG carries with it a numismatic tradition. However, if currency grading follows what has happened with coin grading, there may be exploitative or phony services established, with impressive-sounding names and attractive holders.

Fourth, the holders, if made of Mylar or some other inert substance, will have the benefit of preserving the notes against the elements and mishandling.

Fifth and perhaps most important, it will require that absolute faith be placed on the employees of the grading services, for expert collectors, dealers, and others would no longer be able to examine bills for hidden creases and folds, starching or strengthening, and other traps.

Recently, Lyn F. Knight, well-known paper money auctioneer who has been active for many years (my company was his best client in the early 1970s), stated this under his terms of sale (here excerpted):[6]

> We currently offer notes for sale that have been graded and encapsulated by various third-party grading services. Because we are unable to grade the notes outside of any holder we make no representation whatsoever to the quality or grade of that item. We sell all third-party graded items AS-IS and there are no returns accepted for any reason. All guarantees or warranties in force are those offered by the grading service, and it is the responsibility of the buyer to understand each grading service's guarantees. If a lot has been graded by a third party, and you buy it—you own it. . . . I suggest buying elsewhere if we are not on the same page as far as grading is concerned.

As these words are being written, it is too early to see what the general reaction will be across the community of currency collectors. However, as Knight says, there is no way that he or anyone else can lend expertise to grading when the notes cannot be examined!

Unlike the situation for coins, in which the surface quality and many other aspects can be determined by viewing through a holder, every currency expert with whom I am acquainted grades notes by examining them by touching, seeking traces of starching or the pressing out of folds, etc. Dealers will be placed in the position of implying, "I cannot state how I would grade this bill if I could examine it. All I can say is that Grading Service XXX calls it Uncirculated-65," or whatever.

I have always cautioned numismatists to "buy the coin, not the holder." However, for paper money it seems that "buying the holder" precludes examining the note carefully.

Perhaps the Professional Currency Dealers Association (PCDA) can monitor a forum on the Internet or in print, in which the guarantees of each third-party grading service are specified. What protection do buyers have?

Aspects of Availability of Collectible Notes

Among the 3,000 or so note-issuing banks, why are the bills of some easy to find while others are rare? Pondering this question, I compiled the following factors.

Sound Banks

Notes from well-managed banks can be rare. Banks that were on sound financial footing eventually redeemed their notes. Most notes were burned, torn apart, or otherwise destroyed, although in some instances these redeemed bills were saved (see hoards below).

A bill from a sound bank: $10 note of the Amoskeag Bank, Manchester, New Hampshire, August 3, 1863, from a plate by Rawdon, Wright, Hatch & Edson, New York. Although this bank had $680,000 of currency in circulation over a span of years, with less than $200,000 at any given time, all but a few were redeemed when the institution converted to a National Bank in 1864. Such notes are rare today.

Because of this fact, for the vast majority of banks that were still in business in 1865 and 1866 and redeemed their bills, such notes are rare today. Within the field of sound banks, bills of those that issued large amounts of currency and were capitalized at $1,000,000 or more are generally more available than bills from small banks with a modest capital such as $25,000.

Note from a failed bank: $1 note of the Hallowell and Augusta Bank, June 4, 1816. This bill has a Massachusetts address, as that district of Maine was part of Massachusetts at the time. Incorporated on March 6, 1804, the bank was capitalized at $200,000 but later reduced to $150,000, mostly "paid for" by giving IOUs back to the bank, which then treated them as assets. Paper money was then issued in large quantities, and reckless loans were given in exchange for it. The bank failed, and at one term of the court more than 100 actions were brought against the directors. However, the cashier in charge of financial matters claimed that the books and papers of the bank had been lost, and he could not recall certain questioned transactions. The worthless currency is still common today.

FAILED BANKS

Bills from failed banks constitute the vast majority of collectible issues today. Many of these exist in large quantities. Unredeemable in their own time and worthless in commerce, these were kept by unfortunate citizens who received them, or were confiscated and held by state authorities, who later disposed of them to numismatic interests. Notes from these banks tend to be in higher grades such as EF to Uncirculated, as they were used only for a limited time, if at all.

Because of this fact, it is much easier to assemble a large collection of different bills from Michigan banks, where the failure rate was more than 90% by the early 1840s, than from New Hampshire, where only a handful of banks became insolvent.

Bills from a fraudulent or nonexistent bank: sheet of $1-$3-$5 notes, no imprint of an engraving firm, bearing the name of the Cass County Bank, LaGrange, Michigan, style of the 1830s during the "wildcat" bank era. LaGrange consisted of a few buildings on a small lake. No record has been located that any such bank ever was chartered or conducted business. Until about 300 sheets of notes were found in the late 20th century, such currency was unknown, and neither Harold L. Bowen nor James A. Haxby listed such issues.

FRAUDULENT AND NONEXISTENT BANKS

Among bills available in the market today are many from banks that are known to have been fraudulent, such as many in the state of Michigan in the 1830s, or completely fictitious (the New England Bank of Fairmount, Maine, is an example).

Somewhere in between are bills from quite a few banks whose true status is unknown. Are some of the bills from unchartered, undocumented banks in Washington, D.C., from fictitious banks? Most such bills survive today in high grades, usually unsigned and unissued. Most of these banks did not make the news as being fraudulently operated.

Every once in a while information is located that repositions a bank as being legitimate or a fraud. In the meantime, bills that are available play to a wide numismatic audience.

Remainder: $5 note from the Salmon Falls Bank, Rollinsford, New Hampshire. Although this bank remained perfectly sound, large quantities of unissued notes were saved by the bank and later came on the numismatic market. Lower-denomination remainders of this bank are very common today.

Remainders

For several hundred state-chartered banks and some spurious ones, large quantities of unused sheets remained on hand in later years. Usually, these were arranged four notes to a sheet. Sometimes the bills were partially filled in with ink, such as with a serial number and the signature of one or both of the officers, but they were never cut apart and issued.

After the notes became worthless, they remained stored in vaults of banks that were successors to the state banks or that had acquired assets and interests of other banks. In still other instances they remained in the families of bank officers or in storage elsewhere.

Beginning in a significant way in the 1920s and 1930s, when D.C. Wismer produced an extensive serial feature on obsolete currency for *The Numismatist,* which ran from 1922 to 1936(!), a great interest developed among collectors. Dealers sent mailings to banks and other institutions offering to buy stocks of

Redeemed used bill: $10 note of the Merrimack County Bank, Concord, New Hampshire, June 20, 1856, by Rawdon, Wright & Hatch. This bank operated profitably. In 1865 the stockholders and directors voted *not* to convert to a National Bank. The institution wound up its affairs. By 1869, every stockholder received $146.50 per $100 par value of stock owned. Although over $220,000 in face value in bills had been issued, by this time only $1,210 remained outstanding. Years later many of the bank's redeemed bills, punch canceled (as here) or with blocks cut out of the signature area, came on the numismatic market.

old sheets, often enclosing a sample bill, such as one of a high denomination from the Canal Bank of New Orleans, to emphasize the fact that these notes were no longer worth face value. Today, many of these remainder notes are on the market, usually cut into separate notes but less often sold in sheets. Nearly all are in crisp Uncirculated condition.

Redeemed and Used Bills

In other instances, banks would keep bundles of redeemed notes on hand, sometimes canceling them with punch holes, cuts, or inked marks. Similarly, bundles of bills from failed banks would be kept by state authorities or by successor banks, later to be distributed into numismatic channels. There is no information in print as to which bank bills fit into this category, but often, if a common and inexpensive bill is dated from the 1840s to the mid-1860s and shows extensive circulation, it is one of these. Common bills of the Cochituate Bank of Boston (which failed in 1854) are good examples.

A $10 note of the Thompson Bank located in the Connecticut town of the same name. Overprinted by the Bank of Mutual Redemption, the acidic ink has eroded the paper.

For many New England banks, bills exist today with various overprints by the Suffolk Bank and the Bank of Mutual Redemption, usually with COUNTERFEIT, BROKEN BANK, or some other lettering added to signify the status of the bank or the bill. Sometimes bills from failed banks were incorrectly stamped COUNTERFEIT, probably by a lazy clerk, for in any event the currency had no value. These are interesting to collect today, but the overprints can be so bold they blank out sections of the design. In some instances, ink erosion has eaten into the paper. Such stamping detracts from a note's value, but these bills are still eagerly collected.

Gold and Silver Vs. Paper

Over the course of American history, *coins* have been saved as souvenirs, gifts, and stores of value. A gold dollar given as a gift in 1851 may survive today as a memento. In great contrast, in their era the bills of state-chartered banks were not considered to be of permanent value, and there was always the specter that a note would become worthless.

In 1857, Aaron White, a Connecticut attorney, observed the panic of that year and the difficulties with paper money, later issuing a token inscribed "Never Keep a Paper Dollar in Your Pocket Till Tomorrow." For this reason, many bank bills that were common in their era are exceedingly rare now. There are some banks that issued thousands of notes of certain varieties in the 19th century, of which not a single example is known in a collection today.

PROOF AND SPECIMEN NOTES

SPECIAL IMPRESSIONS

From the first decade of the 19th century through the mid-1860s, engravers and bank-note printers often made sample impressions from printing plates. In many instances these were sent to bank officers to suggest designs or to seek approval for motifs already selected. At other times, proofs (usually not capitalized in numismatic use for paper money, unlike for Proof coins) were made to be kept in company files.

Typically, such proofs were made on very thin paper, sometimes called *India paper,* not as durable as that used to print circulating bills. Many such India paper proofs were lightly glued to card stock. Proofs, if printed singly (rather than as part of a sheet), nearly always had wide margins, again unlike those made for use in commerce. To prevent these proofs from being signed and passed, they were often canceled, sometimes by putting a row of punch holes in the signature area of the bill, making ink marks, or cutting out portions of the note.

Proofs can be brittle, and it is not at all unusual for a bright, crisp proof bill to have a piece or two missing from an edge or corner or to have a slight tear. While it would be nice not to have these imperfections, often there is not much of a choice. Besides, such defects are usually minor and do not noticeably impair the beauty of the note.

Today, the buying of proofs can be a dangerous game, as many ordinary remainder bills—regular notes that were never signed or issued—are offered as *proofs,* sometimes even with rows of punch cancels emulating a proof. This problem has been around for a long time, and years ago it was an occasional topic for discussion in the *Essay-Proof Journal.*

DETERMINING WHETHER A NOTE IS A PROOF IMPRESSION

Here are some guidelines, signs to help determine if a note you are offered truly is a "proof" note.

Good sign: *Wide margins*—If the margins are wide *all around,* this is a good sign. An ordinary note cut from a remainder sheet may have a wide top margin if it was the highest note on the sheet, or a wide bottom margin if it was the lowest note, but both margins will not be wide.

Good sign: *Card stock*—If the proof is on card stock this is a good sign. Most card-stock proofs also have wide margins.

Good sign: *Thin paper, crisp details*—If the paper is very thin, almost diaphanous, and the printed impression shows exquisite details, this is a good sign.

Good sign: *Usual color overprint absent*—If circulated examples of the type were made with red or other color overprints, while this bill has no overprint, this is a good sign.

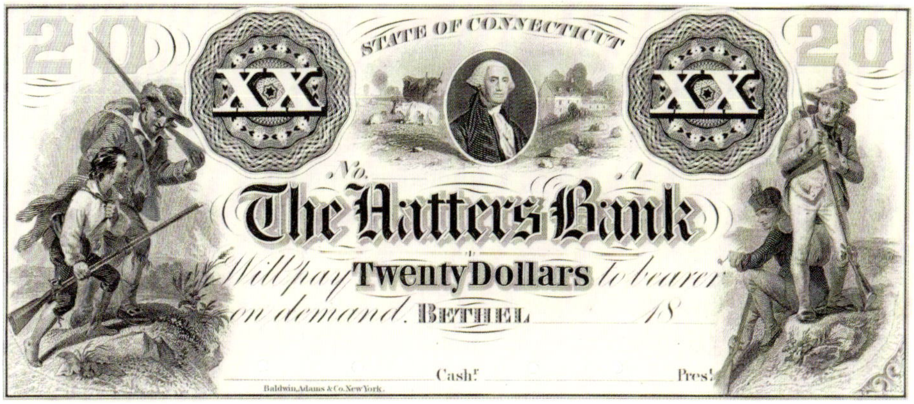

A $20 note of the Hatters Bank, Bethel, Connecticut. India paper proof on card stock, from the American Bank Note Co. archives. Plate by Baldwin, Adams & Co.

Paste-up model or concept on card stock, wide margins, made by the American Bank Note Co. Different elements were pasted in place. This is a fantasy issue intended to show what a design might look like. Lifton, Massachusetts, does not exist. The tiny print refers to an institution other than the large Thames Bank imprint!

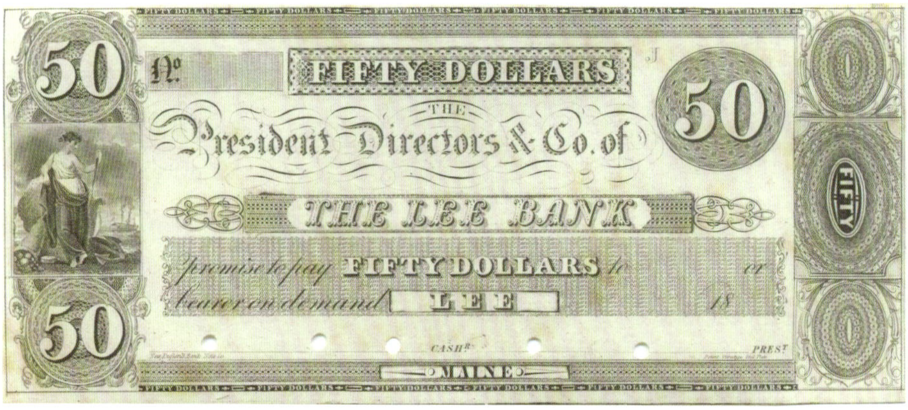

A $50 proof of the Lee Bank, Lee, Maine, Patent Stereotype Steel Plate by the New England Bank Note Co. There is no record of any bank being founded in Lee. Perhaps this proof was made as a sample to send to other banks, or perhaps a Lee Bank was planned, but no charter application was ever made.

Good sign: *Bill is a great rarity*—If it is listed as SENC (Surviving Example Not Confirmed) by Haxby or is of a high denomination, such as $50 upwards, this is usually a positive sign.

Good sign: *Seller is an expert*—Many dealers in paper money have a problem with distinguishing proofs, and even the most expert of experts sometimes disagree. However, it is always best to buy from an expert. Auction catalog listings by leading firms are usually—but not always—reliable.

Here are some guidelines to use when offered a proof note, the "red flags" that nearly always indicate that a note is not a proof at all.

Bad sign (beware!): *Note is common as a remainder*—If large quantities of Uncirculated examples of ordinary bills (made for use in commerce) exist, be ultra-aware if such a note is offered as a proof! Check Haxby or consult a trustworthy dealer if you are not sure.

Bad sign (beware!): *Tight margins*—If margins are close to the printed border, be careful.

Bad sign (beware!): *Seller is not a recognized expert*—Do *not* buy, or even think of buying a proof note offered casually, such as on the Internet, by someone who does not have expertise. Chances of buying a real proof are close to zero.

Bad sign (beware!): *Signatures on the note*—Although real proofs are sometimes (rarely) seen with inked-in serial numbers in low digits, or an inked date, they *do not* have signatures of bank officers.

Bad sign (beware!): *Indistinct printing*—If under a strong magnifying glass the details of the vignettes are not crisp and distinct, beware. This will also help detect modern copies made on computers or copying machines (quite a few such notes are around).

Bad sign (beware!): *Ordinary paper*—If the paper of an offered proof matches that used for circulating notes, beware. This is a difficult concept, however, because so many different styles of paper were used.

Venture carefully before buying any proofs. This is a very technical area.

The Blanchard Commentary

The late Julian Blanchard was one of the great numismatic scholars in the field of bank notes and vignettes. His published research and commentaries, mostly in the *Essay-Proof Journal,* have stood the test of time and are still highly useful today. The following item, from the issue of October 1945, addresses proofs and bank-note paper (slightly edited):

Bank Note Proofs as Distinguished From Bank Note Remainders

by Julian Blanchard, Ph.D.

It has been noticed that collectors, dealers, and auction catalogers occasionally fall into error in their use of the term "proof" in relation to bank notes. Unfamiliarity with this field, and in addition the real scarcity of such proofs, no doubt account for the wrong use of this term.

The mistake that we refer to consists in applying the term proof to unissued remainders of bank notes. These remainders are frequently to be seen in sheets of four notes (sometimes only two), just as received from the printers, but perhaps more often as singles cut from such sheets. They are nearly always unsigned and undated, though some may be partially completed in this respect, and some may have spurious signatures and dates that were applied at a later time. They were never issued as currency, but were left on hand after a change of issue, or because of the dissolution or failure of the bank. We call them, for short, bank note "remainders." They are clean, crisp, and unblemished in appearance. The difference between such a specimen and the average worn and soiled bank note is even more striking than that between a stamp proof and a used postage stamp, and affords some additional excuse, perhaps, for putting it in the wrong category.

But the test for distinguishing remainder notes from proof notes lies in the difference between the kinds of paper upon which they were printed. And furthermore, with regard to appearance, one has but to compare these unissued notes, as beautiful as they are, with genuine proofs to realize the great superiority of the latter in the perfection of printing and the bringing out of detail.

India Paper Used for Proofs

As in the case of stamps, proof impressions of bank notes were nearly always made upon India paper, backed by cardboard. Proofs of this kind were made of the individual vignettes and other portions of the design, for certain purposes, as well as of the completed plate of notes. We find the India paper sometimes still adhering to the card, but perhaps more often removed therefrom. Generally, but not always, we find the proof notes with small holes (2.5 to 3.5 mm. in diameter) punched along the lines for the signatures, a special indication that they were not to be used as actual notes. Of course, the presence or absence of the punchings does not prove anything, for they could be added if originally absent, and remainder notes have been seen with such holes.

The India paper thus employed is quite different from bank note paper. It is in reality a Chinese paper and is made of bamboo fiber. It is rather thin, soft, and absorbent. Being handmade, it may vary considerably in thickness even within a small area; individual fibers, or clusters of fibers, are here and there distinguishable with the unaided eye, and there may be thin spots, and other irregularities and small defects. It is fairly opaque, and very absorbent; a slight wetting on one side will show through almost instantly. Its thinness and its soft and absorbent qualities enable the finest lines of the engraving to be clearly impressed in the printing. But these characteristics also require that it be backed with cardboard to prevent destruction by the pressure of the printing press.

Another kind of paper used for proofs, and called proof paper, is a white handmade rice paper. This is somewhat thicker and more opaque than India, and more uniform, and it does not require the use of cardboard backing in the printing process. Most of the bank note proofs that have been seen are on India paper.

All handmade papers, India, rice and bond, are made on laid moulds, but since no pressure is used the laid lines may or may not be apparent. Modern laid paper is a machine made wove paper with a "laid" watermark impressed upon it.

Bank Note Paper

The paper upon which the actual notes were printed is bond paper, made of linen rags. Being handmade also, it likewise varies considerably in thickness and uniformity. It is somewhat thicker and much tougher and stronger than India, and is less absorbent, affording a less perfect impression. It has a hardness and stiffness not possessed by the soft and yielding India paper, so that when "snapped" it has much more of a crispy and crackling sound (that is, when unworn). As thin and fragile as it is in comparison with that used for our paper money today, it nevertheless has immeasurably greater lasting qualities than India paper would have for this purpose; wherefore an India proof note is not likely to be mistaken for an unissued remainder. The mistake that is made is in thinking a remainder to be a proof.

It has been found that a little experience is generally quite sufficient to enable one to make the distinction. In the absence of any such experience, and without examples of each for comparison, attention must be paid to the different paper characteristics that have been pointed out above, to avoid error.

In the examination and study of a large number of bank notes, both issued and in sheets of remainders, a considerable variation in paper has been observed, in thickness and in other characteristics.

Modern *Proprietary Proofs* and Related

In the late 20th century, many printing plates held by the American Bank Note Co. were dusted off and new impressions taken from them, after which a high-resolution photographic process was used to make new bills and sheets (this per a gentleman earlier associated with the project). These do not have the "embossing," or deep-printing, characteristics of notes made directly from metal printing plates. Many of these were stamped SPECIMEN or had American Bank Note Co. wording on the back, in bright red, but others were unmarked. Complicating matters, many *old* proofs (printed from plates) remaining in ABNCo archives from the early 19th century and sold by Christie's at auction in 1990 and 1991 were also stamped this way. At the sale, the modern proofs were grouped in large lots, neither described nor counted, and designated as "reprints." They did not attract much attention at the time. Other notes filtered out of ABNCo one way or another and came on the market privately. Generally, modern bills are designated *proprietary proofs* or *modern proprietary proofs.* No accounting has been seen of the total number made, but the quantity may have been in the low thousands. Many are very rare today.

Some of these ABNCo proprietary proofs are quite curious in that they were also produced with colored overprints, such as the large inscription ONE, or with green, orange, or other latticework, heavily applied or of different tints from those on original notes. Nearly all of the plates used to make master prints for the modern proprietary proofs were later melted down as scrap steel. More than just a few are impressions from plates of which no original proofs or circulating notes are known.

In addition to modern ABNCo productions, certain collectors, museums, and others possess original plates for the printing of notes and have used them. I have some in my own holdings. In New Hampshire, the Bank of America, successor to certain interests of the Indian Head Bank of Nashua, has a fine set of plates left over from the 1850s.

Plates in private hands have been used, and will continue to be used, to make modern proofs. Although these could be called *proprietary proofs,* as the current owner of the plates sponsored their making, it would seem that *modern proofs* would be a better notation.

The advantage of modern proofs, proprietary or otherwise, is that impressions of bills not otherwise available are now collectible. I have quite a few such proofs from Vermont, New Hampshire, and Maine in my reference collection, nearly all of which represent bills for which originals are either great rarities or completely nonexistent.

There is no catalog or source to find out what exists and what does not among modern proofs, although auction appearances can be a guide. Perhaps it would be of benefit to all if the Professional Currency Dealers Association could devise an accepted procedure, perhaps a light (ink not to soak through) back stamp, indicating a modern proof. Even better would be to include the number printed, as limited edition art prints have. However, there is no guarantee, in numismatics or in art, that other impressions will not be made later.

To me, this is a dynamic niche of collecting that merits some study as to ethics and descriptions.

Ways to Collect Obsolete Bank Notes

There is no right or wrong way to select notes for your collection. A wide world beckons, and there are many choices. Below are some favorite or interesting ways to determine what you want to collect. You may think of others.

Collecting by Bank Location

This is probably the single most popular way to form a large collection of obsolete paper money. Typically, the state of one's residence is a logical choice. Such a

A specialist in the bills of New Jersey would find this Cataract City Bank, of Paterson, $2 note to be a colorful addition to an album or display. Bearing the printed date of November 18, 1856, it also has the ABNCo monogram entered into the plate, revealing that it was actually printed after May 1, 1858, the launching time of American Bank Note Co.

collection of notes will include issues from towns and cities not far from where you live. In many instances the old bank buildings still stand, providing the opportunity to locate and photograph them.

States vary in the number of banks that issued notes, a discussion of which is given state by state in chapter 21. To form a representative collection of different banks, a collector specializing in Delaware, which had relatively few banks, has an easier time of it than the numismatist who seeks New York state bills, of which there are thousands of different possibilities. Within any state there are apt to be common notes as well as great rarities. My own specialties include Maine, New Hampshire, Vermont, Michigan, and the District of Columbia. While the first three comprise upper New England, where I live, I picked Michigan for its fascinating *wildcats* and Washington, D.C., for its generous share of banks with mysterious histories.

Finding just one note from each of the different states in which banks issued currency may be a good way to become acquainted with the field. When bills with a *Bank* title imprint are considered (as opposed to scrip or government issues), the three most difficult states seem to be Texas, Utah, and Arkansas. At present this situation is not widely known, but I confirmed it through checking with other dealers including Tom Denly, Bruce Hagen, and Hugh Shull.

Within the specialty of collecting bills of a given state, one method is to try to obtain a note from each of as many different banks as possible. For New York state, with more than 600 banks, building a specialized collection by bank, denomination, and design would be a lifetime pursuit, and even then there would be many pieces not obtainable. Collecting one of each bank imprint is more feasible, and over a period of time the majority of banks will be represented. For many if not most other states in which certain bills are rare, particularly from institutions that redeemed their notes in the 1860s and burned them, collecting a single example from a bank is feasible.

If there exists a specialized book on the notes of a state you find interesting, this will be helpful. Otherwise, as in the case of New Hampshire, Connecticut, the District of Columbia, and a few other places, the path is unmarked except for the listings by Haxby. To me the unknown is more interesting than mysteries that have been solved, but not many people share this preference. No matter what state you choose, there will be new things to discover. In contrast, if you are a collector of large copper cents dated from 1793 to 1814, you know that if not researched in extremis, at least this series has been extensively documented, with possibilities of significant new discoveries being few and far between.

Towns and cities can form a specialty as well, except that most small towns offer little challenge or scope due to the limited number of banks or notes. On the other hand, bills of Philadelphia, New York City, Cincinnati, or Buffalo, along with many others, comprise many different banks and varieties. Bills from a certain district within a state, such as the greater Boston area of Massachusetts, offer another opportunity.

For many, bank notes of the Southern states form a focal point. Such a collection will include many issues from Georgia, South Carolina, and other areas south of the Mason-Dixon Line, with not a Connecticut, New York, or Maine note in sight.

Generally, if you become involved in collecting obsolete notes, you will be happiest if you are able to add items to your collection on a regular basis. Accordingly, it is best to choose a large arena rather than a small one, perhaps by selecting several different states or cities. Another path often taken is to work on one specialty until new purchases are infrequent, at which time you can add another specialty.

Collecting by Type

Similar to the situation with rare coins, bank notes can be collected by general types. There are no definitions to this method, but such a display could consist of at least one bill from every state that issued such, and one of each different denomination that you can find.

For extra sport, see how many different engraving imprints you can find—a field relatively unexplored, in which a "rare" engraver is apt to cost no more than a common one.

Collecting by Vignette Topic

Vignettes offer a wonderful glimpse of the American scene from about 1810 to the 1860s. A beautiful book could be created, "America as Illustrated on Bank-Note Vignettes." Scarcely any aspect of life would be overlooked.

Topics on vignettes can form an interesting specialty. Collecting vignettes depicting Santa Claus, for example, can be both interesting and expensive. A bill in Very Fine grade of a particular bank, with a miscellaneous vignette, might be worth $100, while another variety from the same bank, this one illustrating Santa

Claus, might sell for several thousand dollars. John and Nancy Wilson, frequent contributors of articles to numismatic papers, have Jolly Old Saint Nick as among their specialties.

Dozens of vignettes depict Native Americans, ranging from chiefs to family and pastoral scenes. Especially popular are depictions of Indians contemplating the trappings of civilization in the distance—railroads, factories, and the like.

Nautical and whaling scenes are popular, the more action the better. A ship under full sail is more interesting than one resting in a harbor with sails furled. Whaling motifs can be dramatic, depicting life-threatening situations.

Railroad vignettes are plentiful and varied. A "History of Railroading on Bank-Note Vignettes" would be another book possibility. All sorts of equipment from locomotives of the late 1820s and early 1830s to high-speed express trains of the 1850s and 1860s can be seen. Canals could also form a specialty, although I have never encountered anyone with this focus of interest. Certainly there is no lack of collecting opportunity in this category.

Portraits on bills range from the well-known to the obscure. George Washington is a favorite, of course, and many notes of the 1820s and 1830s feature either a portrait or standing figure of General Lafayette. It is ironic that Washington tokens and medals are collected intensely—the more varieties the better—but such enthusiasm has not extended to his portrait on paper money. Scenes from mythology comprise some of the most wonderfully ornate vignettes, a specialty worth exploring. Battle scenes from American history are scarce, but enough exist that a collection could be made of them. Often they are unattributed, offering the opportunity for research.

Animals abound on obsolete bank notes. Many different depictions of horses can be found, including grazing, drinking in a stream, or running wild across the plains. Dogs, cats, chickens, sheep, and cows are common. Fish are not seen often, and frogs, turtles, and goats are rare. With some patience, however, you can create a bank-note zoo! The national bird crops up frequently, sometimes in fierce or defensive poses, while at other times in the company of goddesses or perhaps contemplating the bust of George Washington.

You could make a coin collection via illustrations on notes. Spanish-American silver coins abound, early Draped Bust and Liberty Seated dollars are familiar, and others can be found with some

A dramatic Revolutionary War battle scene is the motif on this Central Bank of Tennessee note, July 10, 1855, from a plate by Danforth, Wright & Co., who registered the design in 1854 (according to tiny lettering at the bottom of the vignette).

A $5 proof note of the Nassau Bank, New York City, from a plate by Baldwin, Adams & Co. Depicted is the magnificent glass and steel Crystal Palace opened to the public in 1853. Sponsored in part by P.T. Barnum, the structure remained an attraction but never returned a profit to its owners. It burned in 1858, inspiring the "All Is Vanity" medalet issued by Augustus B. Sage.

A $1 note of the Egg Harbor Bank, Egg Harbor City, New Jersey. The portrait of the youth at the upper left is that of Philip M. Wolseiffer, who became a numismatist and a prominent stamp dealer.

persistence. The late George Hatie had a collection of such paper money.

Buildings suggest another specialty. The U.S. Capitol building can be found in several stages of construction, the New York Crystal Palace of 1853 is wonderfully depicted on notes, and P.T. Barnum's palatial Iranistan home depicts the elegance of a bygone era. Bank buildings, state capitols, and business blocks offer other possibilities. More than just a few banks commissioned vignettes showing their own building standing alone or as part of a street scene.

Vignettes and Their Stories

Exploring the art and significance of vignettes can be a fascinating pursuit. Roger H. Durand's series of *Interesting Notes About . . .* books is based on art found on paper money. Each is well worth having.

Julian Blanchard, who studied notes in detail and was one of the most important contributors to the late *Essay-Proof Journal,* contributed this essay to the Fall 1959 issue (excerpted). This piece also illustrates how one researcher (Blanchard) can build upon the work of another (Frank Duffield, editor of *The Numismatist* in 1928):

> **A Stamp Dealer Pictured on a Bank Note**
>
> Once in a while we run across a real "human interest" story in our bank note collecting and here is one that concerns a stamp dealer. He is the only such dealer whose picture ever appeared on a piece of paper money, so far as we know. This man was Philip M. Wolsieffer, of Chicago and Philadelphia, about whom we have gleaned some interesting facts.
>
> We had heard vaguely of the story some years ago, but it was while clipping some old back numbers of *The Numismatist* recently that it was more fully unfolded. In the issue of that magazine for September, 1928, on page 518, there was found a little piece with the heading, "The Egg Harbor Bank Note and Mr. Wolsieffer's Portrait," which reads as follows:
>
> "Among the obsolete bank notes of New Jersey in Mr. Wismer's list this month is one for $1 of the Egg Harbor Bank, of Egg Harbor City. To the average person this note would attract no more attention than any other one of the many thousand similar notes, unless it was because of the rather unusual name given to the town of issue.
>
> "But most collectors of paper money know, or at least have heard, that the portrait of the child at the upper left of the note is of P.M. Wolsieffer, of Philadelphia, formerly of Chicago. Mr. Wolsieffer has been a member of the A.N.A. for many years and has long been one of the prominent stamp dealers in this country. Although his collecting interest is centered largely in stamps, he has an extensive acquaintance among coin collectors. For several years he was associated with the late Capt. John W. Haseltine in the stamp business in Philadelphia. Captain Haseltine was for a long time a collector of and dealer in coins in that city.
>
> "To set at rest any doubt that may exist about the child's portrait on the note of the Egg Harbor Bank, a letter was sent recently to Mr. Wolsieffer, asking him to verify the story. His letter follows:
>
> "'Egg Harbor City, N.J., was incorporated as a city in 1857, when there were but few residents there. My father was the secretary of the Gloucester Farm and Town Association and laid out the city in even blocks with wide streets and avenues. The avenues running north and south were named after great cities and the streets running east and west after great men. Although my father lived and conducted his regular music profession in Philadelphia, he also lived part of the time in Egg Harbor and at the time I was born, on May 28, 1857.
>
> "'I am the last living member of a family of ten, a sister having just passed away a few months ago. The records of Egg Harbor City show I was the first baby born there after it was incorporated as a city, and when a bank was established there they had my father supply one of my photographs as a small child for the purpose of putting it on one of the notes. I was in Chicago from 1882 to 1914 and lost track of family affairs, but was always told the facts were as stated. Only a short time ago an old resident of Egg Harbor City sent

me one of those bills, because, as she said, I might like it as a souvenir on account of my picture being on it.'"

The same portrait of Mr. Wolsieffer also appears on a $1 note of the Bank of Ocean County, Tom's River. Egg Harbor City is in Atlantic County, about 15 miles north of Atlantic City, while Toms River is in Ocean County, about 45 miles from Atlantic City.

The $1 note of the Egg Harbor Bank is seen to have the imprint of the American Bank Note Co. As often happened, this special portrait engraving became a "stock die" and was afterwards used on other notes. In Dr. John A. Muscalus' pamphlet, "A List of State Bank Notes that Illustrate Characters and Events" (1938), there are found the following notes under P.M. Wolsieffer: $1 Egg Harbor Bank and $1 Bank of Ocean County, as mentioned above; $1 New York County Bank, New York City; $1 Bank of Germantown, Pa.; $1 Farmers and Mechanics Bank, Shippensburg, Pa.; and $100 Union Bank of Tennessee, Nashville. Possibly there are others. . . .

COLLECTING PROOF NOTES

Until the early 1980s, proofs of obsolete bank notes were considered to range from scarce to rare. The *Essay-Proof Journal* discussed varieties and their characteristics, and dealer Christian Blom, for one, made them a specialty. Relatively few came up for sale, and it was impossible to form a meaningful collection of them. Likely, no more than a few thousand were in the hands of collectors.

Then came a vast quantity into the marketplace, mainly through Christie's auction house. These included the Alexander Vattemare albums sold in the early 1980s and, a much more extensive group, the American Bank Note Co. archives auctioned in the early 1990s. In addition to original impressions from the 19th century, the earlier-mentioned modern proprietary proofs, mostly from plates held by the American Bank Note Co., became available. Old proofs as well as modern imprints sometimes have red stamping on the back to indicate they were the property of the American Bank Note Co. As this stamping has been forged, it is essential that you buy modern proprietary proofs from a reliable source.

While collecting only proof notes might be limited as to scope and also rather colorless (few have tinted overprints), adding proofs to a collection of notes by states or design topics is worthwhile. My collection of Maine currency has been greatly enhanced by proofs of notes that do not exist in any other form.

COLLECTING BANK EPHEMERA AND INFORMATION

Ephemera: things that are here today and gone tomorrow. Collecting items relating to note-issuing banks can be fascinating. I have pursued this interest for a long time. Checks, announcements, letters from bank officers (nearly always written by the cashier), printed announcements, and related items make a nice addition to a collection of currency. Now and again bank records, such as minute books and ledgers, become available. Some of these can yield interesting information about paper money.

Tracking down buildings that were once related to obsolete bank notes often yields surprises. Here in Wolfeboro, New Hampshire, the structures that once housed the Wolfborough (*sic*) Bank and the Lake Bank are still standing. In Newburyport, Massachusetts, the brick building erected on Fruit Street in about 1808 and used by Jacob Perkins and his associates to print paper money is still there. Old maps and directories

Photograph circa 1855 of the Lake Bank of Wolfeboro, New Hampshire (entrance in building at far right), and nearby buildings, and a view of the same on May 28, 2006. Tracking down buildings that were once used as banks can be an interesting pursuit.

can yield information about where banks were once located. Photographs are especially helpful, but relatively few exist for the era before 1866.

Learning as much as you can about a favorite bank can be an exciting pursuit. To me it is just as interesting to collect information as it is to collect bank bills themselves. Town histories, old newspapers, maps, and, now, the Internet offer vast resources. In nearly all instances you will be in uncharted waters, for there are many banks to study, and only a tiny fraction have ever been the subject of specialized articles or books.

"I Like It"

Back to the marketplace and collecting currency: the "because I like it" reason may be best of all for buying a note. I like notes with stories, as you can tell!

If you envision that you will enjoy owning a bill you've seen illustrated or have read about, by all means put it at the top of your "want list." I didn't know that I wanted a Kirtland Safety Society Anti-Banking Co. note until I read about them in books by Alvin Rust and Douglas Nyholm, after which I sought to learn even more. A natural conclusion was to acquire one of these notes (from the John Ford Collection) and, later, a Brigham Young later-signed bill from Gaylen Rust (son of Alvin Rust) and Tom Denly. As to the price of the Brigham Young note—ouch! I am still trying to figure out the full story of why the Mormons bought the Bank of Monroe (Michigan) in 1837, along with information about the involvement of Oliver Cowdery, a Mormon who earlier was an officer of that bank.

To me a bill issued by the notorious Farmers Exchange Bank of Gloucester, Rhode Island, is fascinating to contemplate. If asked I could probably stand on a soapbox and talk for 15 minutes on this particular bank. Make that a half hour.

I collect bills made by W.L. Ormsby, simply because he was probably the most interesting and complex figure in the bank-note engraving business in the 1850s and early 1860s. Dealer and collector friends are aware of my interest, and scarcely a month goes by without my being offered a new (to me) variety of Ormsby note. However, collecting bills by engravers is not particularly popular, although you might think that notes bearing the imprint of Longacre, famous Mint engraver, would be. Mint engravers Robert Scot, John Reich, William Kneass, Christian Gobrecht, and James B. Longacre each engraved bank-note plates, but most of their work was not signed.

I have Owl Creek Bank and Manual Labor Bank bills, as illustrated and described in this book. These were and still are very inexpensive. To me, a bill with an interesting story trumps one that is simply rare but otherwise undistinguished. The beauty is that bills with stories—involvement in frauds, capers, and other roundabout activities—mostly became worthless in their own time and are easily collected today.

Other "story" notes are ones that are mentioned in old banking journals and accounts, such as those in connection with anticounterfeiting systems. I would be a buyer for a bill imprinted with some patent in this area if I do not already have an example, such as a Seropyan imprint in *blue* instead of the usual yellow.

Every collector has a preference. Jim Ruddy liked $3 bills and formed a collection of hundreds of different examples of this once common but later curious denomination. An Ohio client once chased bills depicting George Washington and found many. New York City specialist Bruce Hagen likes whaling scenes. If a bill from Milford, Massachusetts, comes up for sale, you'd better have a well-filled wallet to outbid dealer Tom Denly.

Aspects of the Marketplace

The following section reiterates some early commentary and also gives suggestions for being a smart buyer of obsolete currency.

Where to Buy

There are many sources for buying obsolete notes. Among the best are the Internet sites of established dealers who have knowledge of such bills. Such sellers are nearly always members of the Professional Currency Dealers Association (PCDA). While dealers who are not experienced with paper money might have some worthwhile items for sale, until you gain enough knowledge to determine authenticity and grade, it is best to buy from a professional.

As prices are apt to vary, and as some dealers take a larger profit margin than do others, it is worthwhile to do some comparison shopping in this regard. This can be accomplished by selecting common notes and the prices asked. Even if you do not want to buy the bills in question, you will gain an idea of pricing policies.

Terms of sale can vary, and before ordering you should ask about them. Most professionals who sell notes allow a return period if an item is not satisfactory. This will give you time to inspect your purchase and, if need be, consult others about it. Read terms of sale carefully.

Auctions conducted by PCDA members on the Internet as well as with public attendance can be a fine source for bills. However, such sales are usually final, not only with certified bills but with all others as well, unless the auctioneer has made a grave error. Before bidding, examine the illustrations carefully. Most auction houses post color images on the Internet, and this method of viewing is better than a catalog page. Determine the maximum price you want to pay, and bid up to that amount. Many professionals offer their services to represent you at the sale, examine the notes personally, and bid on your behalf. I often take advantage of this service, with the usual representation fee being 5%.

A trustworthy dealer can be one of your finest assets in building a collection. Pick one who will guide you along, answer questions (even basic ones), and be helpful. If a dealer is too busy to do this or is more interested in "big business," find someone else. You'll find that most professionals who handle obsolete currency are very friendly.

Collectors who have been acquiring notes for a long time often have duplicates for sale, and this can be another source.

Realistic Expectations

When you are offered a note, contemplate its appearance, rarity, and price. The availability of a given note is very important. Deciding whether to buy a common bill can be a different process of decision-making from deciding about a great rarity. In the first instance, you can take your time and be choosy. In the second, it may be now or never, or now or not for a long time.

This is vastly different from what you might have experienced while buying *rare coins*. Even for classic rarities and *trophy coins,* if you miss a gem 1879 Flowing Hair $4 Stella today, by a year from now you can find perhaps a dozen more purchase opportunities. However, if you are offered a certain bank bill from Alfred, Maine, whether you own it in your lifetime may depend on today's purchase decision. Making things easier is the little secret that perhaps 100 or more gem Stellas exist, at $200,000 each, while that Maine note at $2,500 may be absolutely unique.

Here are some of my thoughts on how to consider a potential purchase.

Remainder Notes: Availability, Quality, and Price

Many bills are remainders that have survived in four-subject sheets, or have been cut from those sheets by modern owners. If a bill is frequently offered, such as a remainder bill of the Canal Bank (New Orleans), Bank of New England at Goodspeed's Landing (East Haddam, Connecticut), or the West River Bank (Jamaica, Vermont), insist on one that is crisp Uncirculated, bright, and with good margins. You can also take your time. If you determine through the viewing of catalogs and Internet offerings that a certain remainder note generally sells for about $100, and now you would like to buy one, you can seek one at a price of, say, $90 to $110. If one is offered for $175, wait for another opportunity.

Other remainder notes can range from scarce to very rare. In such instances allow yourself some leeway as to both grade and price, although in every instance the bill should have an attractive appearance. The 1988 Haxby text prices nearly all remainder notes. Although the values today are apt to be multiples of what they were back then, you can get a relative idea of scarcity and availability. Auction sales, priced catalogs, and Internet offerings can be a good market guide.

Because remainders exist in high grades, are usually colorful, and are often inexpensive, they furnish an ideal way to start a collection.

Notes of 1782–1805: Availability, Quality, and Price

Currency from the cradle days of bank notes in America present a challenge—more so than for later eras, as counterfeits and alterations abound among the earlier notes. Often there is little factual information in reference books or elsewhere to aid in determining the genuine from the false. An experienced dealer can be helpful, but he or she may not know either.

With few exceptions, grades of early bills are apt to be low. Poor, Fair, and About Good are par for many bills dated before 1800, and even these notes are not offered very often. Genuine bills usually range from scarce to very rare. The territory is so uncharted that for some banks it is not known what denominations were issued in the early years, who engraved the plates and printed them, and what the notes looked like.

Perhaps these notes are the currency-collecting equivalent of what Pine Tree shillings are to the coin collector: rustic, irregular, and often in low grades, but

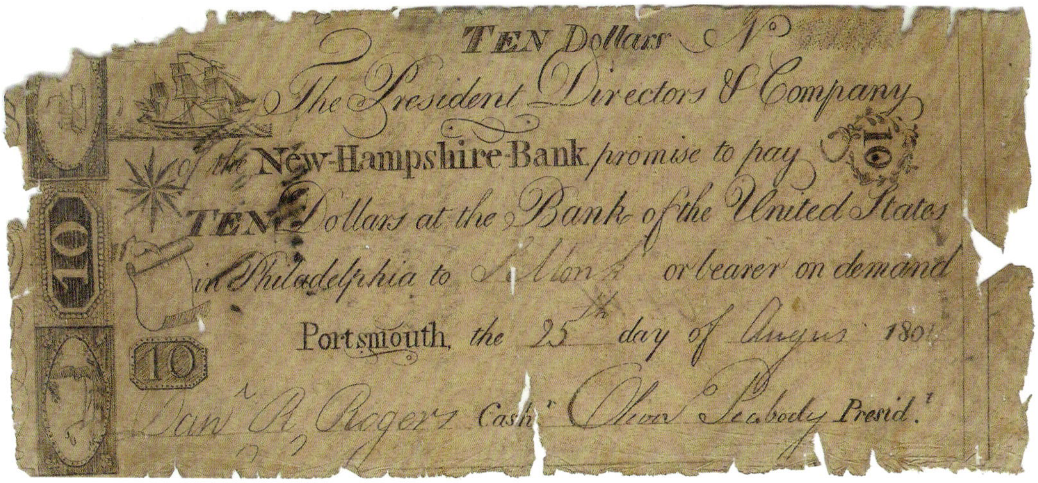

A $10 note of the New Hampshire Bank of Portsmouth. Although the grade of the note is perhaps just Fair or About Good, such preservation is acceptable for many very early issues.

very desirable to own. Proceed slowly, ask advice, and make purchases only from trusted sources.

NOTES OF 1805–1820: AVAILABILITY, QUALITY, AND PRICE

This era saw the rise in the use of illustrations on bills, with nearly all issued in 1810 and later having attractive vignettes. The Patent Stereotype Steel Plate notes by Perkins are exceptions, and they continued to be out of step with artistic progress in later years.

Abner Reed and Murray, Draper, Fairman & Co. were among the most prolific printers of notes. Bills can be collected from the Eastern states as well as from the Midwest, even to Detroit, Michigan. Bills of failed enterprises such as the Farmers Exchange Bank (Gloucester, Rhode Island), the Hillsborough Bank (Amherst, New Hampshire), and the Vermont State Bank exist in quantity and are inexpensive. Other bills can range from common to rare.

Although there are exceptions, grades for *nice* notes of this era are Very Good and Fine—better if you can find them, but VG and Fine are very acceptable. Exceptions include some hoard notes and remainders in higher grades.

As currency from this era is not as ornate as that from later times, notes are apt to be very reasonably priced in relation to their rarity. Patent Stereotype Steel Plate bills have never been particularly popular, except for adding to collections by city or state, and these can be quite inexpensive. Although the subject has hardly been explored, notes of this period can be found with many interesting plate variations. The earlier discussed Vermont Glass Factory (Salisbury, Vermont) and Owl Creek Bank (Mount Vernon, Ohio) bills are from this era.

NOTES OF 1820–1850: AVAILABILITY, QUALITY, AND PRICE

These three decades saw many evolutions in bank-note printing. By the late 1830s, ornate vignettes with gods and goddesses were very much in vogue, as were scenes with ships or trains. Color overprints were not yet popular, and most bills were simply black on white. Medallion vignettes were in common use.

There were many failed banks in this era, most famously in Michigan but also in many other states. Bills from these institutions are often easy to find, although most show evidence of circulation. Some unissued remainders exist from certain banks. These decades are also rich in history.

For notes of this period, Very Fine is a popular grade. Unless it is a great rarity, a bill in Poor to Good or even Very Good preservation should be ignored until a better one can be found. Quite a few issues can be located in grades from Extremely Fine to Uncirculated, but the last are mostly unsigned remainders. Prices vary according to popularity and rarity. The market is very strong for this area.

NOTES OF 1850–1866: AVAILABILITY, QUALITY, AND PRICE

Many collectors consider this era to be the golden age of bank notes. Canada Green, overprinted protectors, anticounterfeiting systems, and other colorful supplements add much to the beauty of bills of this era.

Because many redeemed bills were saved by banks and later made available to numismatists, and as many unissued remainders survived as well, there are ample opportunities to collect whatever you like—notes from a favorite state, or with interesting motifs, or whatever. Offerings of the more common issues are frequent in catalogs and on the Internet, allowing price comparison and evaluation. The era is punctuated with rarities, these often being the bills of banks that redeemed their issues and then destroyed them. Such currency can be difficult to obtain.

Grades of bills tend to be higher for this period, with Very Fine and Extremely Fine examples available for many signed and circulated issues. There are exceptions, and for great rarities you cannot be choosy.

PROOF NOTES: AVAILABILITY, QUALITY, AND PRICE

Proof notes are interesting to collect. Now that the ABNCo printed archives have been distributed, thousands of bills are in the marketplace. However, even though up to several dozen may exist of certain issues, no single type is common. Others range from scarce to unique.

These early proofs are found in several different formats. Scarce are proof impressions printed directly on card stock with wide margins. Most proofs have regular margins, or slightly wider than normal margins, are on white paper, and have punch cancellations or cutout cancels on the signature lines. Some are pasted to heavier paper or card stock. While some proofs have colored protectors or overprints, most are black and white. Some *progress proofs* may be from an unfinished plate, with an inscription or vignette yet to be added.

In the marketplace today, as in 1945 (see the Julian Blanchard article on proofs quoted above), there are many remainder notes offered as proofs, even by well-known dealers. Be careful when buying, and observe the guidelines given earlier.

Early proofs from the 19th century are apt to be brittle, sometimes with tears or splits. It is perfectly fine to buy bills that have been professionally strengthened or restored. Certain proofs in the remarkable John J. Ford Jr. and Herbert and Martha Schingoethe collections, marketed in 2005 and later, were professionally conserved and described in the catalogs as such.

As to modern proprietary proofs, most on the market are acceptable. However, some sharpers have made their own "proofs" by using laser printers, some even embellished by fake American Bank Note Co. backstamps! Buying from a reputable dealer is your best protection.

Prices of proofs are apt to vary widely, even among the more available issues, of which a couple dozen are known. However, by reading auction prices as well as fixed price offerings you will soon get an idea of the ranges involved. In all cases, proofs with special vignettes, such as Santa Claus, bring more.

My recommendation is to go very slowly when buying proofs. Start your collection with remainder notes, common circulated bills, and other more available currency. After you have gained experience and are well on your way to assembling a fine holding, then by all means investigate the fascinating field of proofs.

COMMENTS FROM TWO DEALERS

In the following commentaries prepared for this book, Hugh Shull, who has been dealing in obsolete paper money since 1976, looks back on 30 years in the hobby; and Bruce Hagen, a well-known professional, discusses how he has enjoyed paper money and gives advice for beginning collectors, in most instances paralleling my own thoughts.

In addition, Tom Denly's comments about the current market, grading, and other matters have been incorporated into many sections of chapters 20 and 21.

Thirty Years As a Dealer

by Hugh Shull

When I entered the hobby of obsolete paper money as a dealer in 1976, the market was very active. Several dealers were prominent, and many others engaged in the field in a small way. Thousands of notes were available for very modest prices. I recall Grover C. Criswell Jr. as being the leading figure through publicity and the publishing of reference books. Although Grover's main emphasis was on Confederate bills, he was very active in bank notes as well. Other leaders included Don Fisher (Currency Unlimited), Paul Garland, Claud Murphy, and Douglas B. Ball (who worked with NASCA).

For RARCOA (Rare Coin Company of America) in Chicago, Dennis Forgue prepared numerous advertisements featuring bank notes, many for less than $10 each. The famous DIX note from New Orleans cost all of $19.95 in one of my early offerings, and was a favorite then, as it is now. It is likely that the word *Dixie* was derived from similar notes, as David Bowers mentions in this book. Proof notes were not very popular in the 1970s, except with a few of the most advanced collectors. Today, the situation is much different, now that quantities of specimens from the American Bank Note Company archives have been marketed.

Grover Criswell started the *Bank Note Reporter*, filling it with stories and advertisements. Many of the early issues had so few advertisers that he ran ads for friends and acquaintances to whom he had supplied currency from his inventory. Later, the paper was sold to Austin M. Sheheen Jr. of Camden, South Carolina, and still later to Chet Krause. Under the auspices of Krause Publications it became widely distributed and read.

The first all-paper money show was set up by Mike Crabb and the Memphis Coin Club. In the 30 years since its founding, the Memphis show has become the yearly focal point of the hobby. I recall my first setup there, as a new face in the business, but placed next to Mr. Paper Money—the late, great Amon Carter Jr. of Dallas. The notes he had in his display were simply mind boggling, especially in comparison to my fledgling inventory and display. His willingness to show me notes and answer the questions of a new dealer will always be a great memory.

I have enjoyed being part of the rise and development of the Society of Paper Money Collectors (SPMC), which helps sponsor the Memphis show each year and provides many services to collectors. The Professional Currency Dealers Association (PCDA) has been dynamic, and puts on an annual show in St. Louis each autumn.

Today my greatest challenge is to find good notes and maintain my inventory. This is in contrast to the situation when I started, when several of the larger dealers had extensive quantities of currency to offer, including on a wholesale basis. Now that the Internet has opened the hobby to many newcomers, and the PCDA has offered guidelines on collecting and dealing, there are more collectors than ever. As the supply of notes has not changed, this has meant increases in market prices as well as more competition to find desirable examples.

Thirty years ago, reference books were few and far between. Determining the rarity and value of a piece of paper money was often a trial-and-error procedure. Today, a couple of shelves could be filled with good books on obsolete paper money, and each year sees new titles published. Modern collectors have wonderful resources and advantages that were not available years ago.

In case you are wondering, it is still a wonderful hobby with lots of potential. It is just a bit more challenging than in the past, but the rewards are equally gratifying. That little $19.95 DIX note of 30 years ago now is worth about $700, with demand outstripping supply. They sell every bit as well today as they did 20 years ago.

Have fun with paper money, and enjoy collecting!

Paper Money Research and Collecting

by Bruce Roland Hagen

Now that you have read this far into David Bowers's epic endeavor into the field of obsolete currency enclosed within these covers, I hope you will enjoy some comments from me. Such terms as *research* and *study* could bring back memories of term papers or cramming for tests, perhaps enjoyable at the time, but likely not. However, in more than 30 years of collecting and nearly 20 years as a professional numismatist, research has been very enjoyable, satisfying, and profitable to me in the pursuit and enjoyment of U.S. obsolete currency. Bowers, of course, has covered both the broad view of the subject and many of the details that make obsolete currency such an interesting subject. His list of acknowledgments is amazing and reflects the depth of the content in this book. I would like to delve into the subject of obsolete currency research and the benefits attached to that endeavor, certainly closely related to collecting paper money.

Some people think of research as finding obscure information contained within voluminous tomes held hostage amid the dust and allergens of libraries, archives, and basements. That may be the case for some avenues of investigation, but it is only part of a much wider picture. One of the greatest research resources any collector can have is relationships with other collectors and the sharing of knowledge with them. When I first started collecting as a child, I was always hungry for knowledge simply for the sake of learning about interesting things in the world around me. I couldn't get my hands on enough numismatic books (including several by Dave Bowers) and auction catalogs. Auction catalogs were fascinating since they described things that you could buy if you had enough money (unfortunately, when I was 16 I was basically an observer). I never realized that 20 or so years later, the auction catalogs written by Doug Ball for the NASCA firm in 1970s and 1980s would be an inspiration for me to write auction-catalog descriptions myself. Doug was an amazing colleague to work with when I began my professional career in 1988. Today, his friends and colleagues remember him as one of a kind.

As a collector of obsolete currency I was fortunate to be an early client of Hugh Shull, Barry Wexler, and Douglas Ball. I was often more aggressive in chasing notes than I should have been based on my knowledge at the time. Fortunately, I soon gained patience, after which my purchases were made more carefully. The market for paper money in the 1980s and early 1990s was not as well honed as it is now, and many sellers knew little about the notes they offered.

Although there is more information available today, much is unknown about even the most plentiful notes on the market. A basic research library would be of great help in this regard, starting with the specialized texts that Dave Bowers mentions in chapter 21. Equally important is developing good relationships with other collectors and with dealers. In this way you can share your research findings, ask questions, and discuss the notes you are seeking or ones you have acquired. In the course of writing descriptions for more than 150 auction catalogs since 1988, I have come to depend on others in the hobby for information to supplement that which I already have.

If you enjoy research you will enhance your enjoyment. However, if that is not an area of interest, you can enjoy your collection simply by reading articles and books written by others and contemplating the descriptions in auction catalogs.

I share some recommendations about buying and collecting notes to anyone who is about to emerge as a collector of paper money. Some of these comments, which follow, are standard, but essential.

First of all, know your dealer. Seek someone who can not only help you acquire notes, but who has the knowledge and interest to share information. I was lucky to work with several dealers who were from the "old school." All of them encouraged building a proper library of books and auction catalogs, which brings me to the second point: build a useful research library.

In the past several years, the sale catalogs for the collections of John J. Ford Jr. (by Stack's) and Herb and Martha Schingoethe (by Smythe & Co.) have added much information never available before on obsolete notes in specialized subject areas. Even if information is not of use to you initially from those sources, don't be surprised if, 10 years from now, you look at a lot description and say, "I wish I had bought that note." Never feel any regret in that situation. On many occasions I sat in the same auction room as Herb and Martha Schingoethe and watched them buy notes on which I'd passed because I didn't understand them at the time. Now they are selling for factors of 5, 10, and sometimes 20 times as much as the record prices the Schingoethes paid to acquire them. Possibly, a future generation of collectors will find today's record prices to be similar bargains.

Build a basic library, as Bowers has suggested. In addition to books, a copy of the first 1990 Christie's ABNCo Archive Sale is a must. Over time, other auction catalogs should be added, with emphasis on those that contain the most information (in addition to descriptions of condition and value). Each note has a story to tell, and clues to those stories are often contained in the previously mentioned sources.

While the printed page offers much, there are other avenues for appreciating and learning about bank notes. Recently, I took a road trip to the Midwest, mixing business with numismatic pleasure. I visited with two of my favorite researchers and authors at their homes for the first time. Not all research is reading, and sometimes the best work is done strictly by talking with others and observing the notes themselves.

While riding along the banks of the Ohio River where it separates the states of Ohio and Kentucky, I was able to picture the early banking in that region of our emerging nation. I guarantee that any note you own, from any state, might inspire an interesting day trip or perhaps an extra stay-over on a longer business or vacation trip. Place names that were just listings in Haxby, Wolka, Wait, or other books you use will take on new significance for you.

The longer you collect these special pieces of American history we call United States obsolete currency, the more they will reach out and invite you to search into their fascinating stories. I can't promise financial profits to you as a motivating force, but I can promise tremendous enjoyment if you learn as much as you can about your notes while you are collecting them.

Obsolete Bank Notes: A State-by-State Analysis

Review of States and Their Bank Notes

The following listing covers each of the states with banks that issued paper money during the period from 1782 to 1866. Numismatic comments are given for each state, with the author's text augmented from suggestions by Thomas Denly and Hugh Shull. This chapter is a handy guide to the depth and breadth of the notes available and ways of collecting them.

At the beginning of each state is listed the number of different banks described by James A. Haxby in his essential study, *Standard Catalog of United States Obsolete Bank Notes 1782–1866* (1988), part of approximately 3,091 banks listed there. This number does not include branches (if a given bank operated in more than one place), nor does it include the first or second Bank of the United States.

The general guideline used by Haxby was that to be listed an issuer had to have the word *bank* or *banking* in the title. Accordingly, for most states there are many other issuers, often dozens, that were not titled as banks—including railroads, canals, manufacturing companies, and the like. Information concerning these issuers can be found in other specialized texts, including those published by the Society of Paper Money Collectors, the titles of which are given below, in addition to privately published titles.

A sketch is given of banking during the state-chartered era, primarily from 19th-century sources (rather than modern numismatic texts), after which there are numismatic comments.[1]

Currency of Alabama

Number of banks in the Haxby *Standard Catalog:* 23.
Specialized text: Walter Rosene Jr., *Alabama Obsolete Notes and Scrip,* 1984.

Historical Notes

Although Alabama did not achieve statehood until December 14, 1819, limited banking took place in the district earlier when it was part of the Mississippi Territory, achieving territorial status of its own in 1817. Alabama has had five state capitals, the first being St. Stephens, seat of government for the territory. In 1820 the legislature first met in Cahawba, chosen as capital of the state. The legislative session of 1825 to 1826 voted to leave Cahawba, which was considered to be an unhealthy place subject to flooding, and relocate the capital to Tuscaloosa, where it remained until the General Assembly in 1846 moved it to Montgomery. Andrew Dexter Jr., erstwhile head of the Farmers Exchange Bank of Gloucester, Rhode Island, held a large tract of land there.

The Planters and Mechanics (later known as the Planters and Merchants) Bank at Huntsville was chartered in 1816, followed in 1818 by the Bank of Mobile and the Tombeckbe Bank at St. Stephens, the last earning many mentions in eastern newspapers and financial journals of the era, including when it sustained a $35,000 robbery in 1819. The Huntsville Bank opened soon afterward. By 1823 both banks in Huntsville closed, causing a loss to the Treasury Department, which had deposited special funds in each. In its issue of July 7, 1827, *Niles' Weekly Register* printed this information:

A $2 note of the West River Bank, Jamaica, Vermont—one of several varieties of bills from this bank showing cupids sporting with Liberty Seated silver dollars. Rawdon, Wright, Hatch & Edson.

> We learn from the *Alabama Sentinel,* that the Tombeckbe Bank has stopped payment. It seems to have had a large amount of paper in circulation. A good deal of excitement prevailed among the people. The paper had fallen from 2% to 25%, and even to 50% below par. A letter from the president of the bank gives but little encouragement as to a recovery from its present embarrassments.

The Tombeckbe Bank did not recover, and in 1830 it earned the doubtful distinction of being the only failed bank in Alabama listed in the inaugural issue of *Bicknell's Counterfeit Detector,* the two defunct banks at Huntsville having been overlooked by the compiler.

On December 21, 1820, the Bank of the State of Alabama was approved, to be located in Catawba, for an amount of $2,000,000 ($800,000 in stock to be subscribed for by the state, the balance by citizens). It was anticipated that this would be a very profitable venture for the state. However, the project failed when investors did not materialize. On December 20, 1823, another act provided for a bank under the same title, "to provide for the safe and profitable investment of the funds of the state, and to secure an extended and undepreciating currency." As the prospect of selling stock subscriptions was uncertain, the bank was given no specific capital amount. Instead, the state was to provide the necessary funding from rents on lands, sale of real estate, and the issuance of bonds bearing not more than 6% interest. This money was mostly theoretical, not in hand, based on the expectation that all would work out well, citizens would enjoy a sound currency, and the state would profit.

The Bank of the State of Alabama commenced business in 1825, first in Cahawba, then in Tuscaloosa in 1826, when the capital relocated there. Branches were operated in Decatur, Huntsville, Mobile, and Montgomery. All seemed to develop as hoped for, and $15,859,420 was raised, a generous sum seemingly sufficient to operate a substantial central bank and various branches. During the next decade, cotton crops were excellent and the economy of the state flourished. Real estate prices rose dramatically, adding to the feeling of prosperity.

However, the bank was poorly managed. A statement of June 1, 1837, showed its capital to be $7,889,886, bills in circulation totaling $4,600,000, and deposits of $6,700,000 from citizens and others. To service these liabilities it had a respectable $492,000 in specie, discounted notes (loans receivable) of $17,694,000, and $1,200,000 due from branches. The Hard Times era, not anticipated, soon caused problems, and it was found that there was $6,300,000 in bad debts in the discount portfolio. There was a shortage of cash, and in December 1837 the state issued $7,500,000 in bonds to make up the deficiency. The directors of the bank had been appointed politically, despite woeful lack of banking experience. These officials granted large loans at favored rates to legislators who made the selection. Members of the Alabama General Assembly continued to use the bank as an electioneering tool, offering favorable discounts to those who could help secure their reelection. The directors tapped the bank for personal loans, which amounted in 1839 to nearly $780,000.

The bank was mentioned often in newspaper accounts in connection with such activities as nonredemption of bills, allowing only a small amount of currency to be exchanged each day, issuing post notes, and refusing perfectly good bills of other banks (stating that to do so in each instance required the approval of three directors). In 1841, the house and senate branches of the state legislature each passed resolutions to investigate the bank, which had become the subject of many rumors. A subsequent report of the committee of inquiry included this information:

> They have discovered the existence of a disgraceful league to plunder the banks and swindle the people of the state. Men high in office, members of the Legislature, and bank directors are supposed to be implicated. . . . With all these facts before them the Senate has seen fit to dissolve their portion of the committee. This renders it impossible for us to act efficiently and we therefore tender our resignation.[2]

In 1842 and 1843 the state closed the four branches, and after the bank's charter expired, on January 1, 1845, it was liquidated. The papers and the journal of the joint committee were given to the governor. In 1849 the Capitol building in Montgomery was destroyed by fire, and the journals were allegedly consumed, apparently to the great relief of the many politicians mentioned in them. When matters were settled, the state recorded a debt of $14,000,000 to the state of Alabama's creditors. Including interest, the amount eventually totaled about $35,000,000, an unmitigated financial disaster.

The second Bank of the United States had a branch in the coastal city of Mobile. After its closing, the Planters and Merchants Bank of Mobile was chartered in 1836, with $500,000 capitalization. Launched into the Hard Times era it failed in 1842. In

A $500 note, proof impression, of the Central Bank of Alabama, Montgomery, from a plate by Bald, Cousland & Co. Circulating examples had an orange tint across the face.

Chartered on February 5, 1854, with a capital of $500,000 (later increased to $900,000), this bank remained in business through the end of the Civil War.

1850 an unsuccessful effort was mounted to establish a State Bank in Mobile, with branches in Montgomery, Tuscaloosa, Huntsville, and Tuscumbia. The Bank of Montgomery was also proposed, and it later went into operation.

In the 1850s and early 1860s new banks were chartered and operated with varying degrees of success, most into at least the early years of the Civil War.

NUMISMATIC COMMENTS

Bills of state-chartered banks in Alabama comprise an interesting specialty, but a rather short one in the context of Obsolete Currency. Tantalizing are bills of the Bank of the State of Alabama, so common in their day but elusive now, with many being listed as Surviving Example Not Confirmed (SENC) in the Haxby text. Helping fill the need are some, but not many, proof examples released from the paper archives of the American Bank Note Co.

Beyond the rarities there are many available issues, including from the Hard Times era of banking difficulty as well as those dated from the 1850s onward, the last being colorful and frequently overprinted. Among later bills are many that were redeemed but not destroyed. For other banks that burned their notes there are some incredible rarities—having just two or three examples of their bills known today.

Some Alabama banks continued operation into the Civil War, a collecting specialty in itself. A latecomer was the Farmers Bank of Alabama in Montgomery, established during the war by James Farley, a Confederate official. This particular institution did not last very long, and today its notes are readily available as a result.

Scrip or fractional denomination notes are enthusiastically collected as well, but they are beyond the purview of this text. Dealers report that obsolete Alabama notes of all kinds enjoy a very active market.

CURRENCY OF ARKANSAS

Number of banks in the Haxby *Standard Catalog:* 2.
Specialized text: Matt Rothert Sr., *Arkansas Obsolete Notes and Scrip,* 1985.

HISTORICAL NOTES

The first recorded action involving a bank in the state took place in 1836 at the inaugural session of the state legislature. Proposed was the Real Estate Bank of the State of Arkansas, to be capitalized at $2,000,000, financed by bonds guaranteed by the state. With headquarters in Little Rock, there were to be branches in Columbia, Helena, and Washington. The bank went into operation and added a branch in Van Buren.

Next, the Bank of the State of Arkansas was incorporated, capitalized at $1,000,000, with headquarters in Little Rock and branches in Batesville and Fayetteville. The authorization permitted the bank to do a general banking business, which included dealing in bullion and silver and gold coins.

Niles' National Register included this item on March 2, 1842:

> The *Little Rock Gazette* of the 16th March says, "Few persons now receive Arkansas bank paper except at a discount of one-half."
>
> A review of the condition of the banks of that state which appears in the same paper, over the signature of *R. C. Byrd,* strongly urges the whole of the banks of the state to go into a state of liquidation. He says, "It is not right to disguise the true condition of our banks; and I assert, without fear of successful contradiction, that not a suspended bank in the state is able to pay her interest and resume the payment of specie on her notes, or will be in the next five years to come, if ever."
>
> Count all their specie, their bills receivable, bad and doubtful debts, banking houses, &c., and you will find, (taking all to be money) that the state has made nothing, or but a very small amount, by her banking operations. But deduct the bad, and half the doubtful debts, and she will

> be $150,000 minus. To arrive at this delectable state of bank prosperity, has required four years only, with a specie capital to begin on of $1,500,000. What are our prospects for the next four years, with neither specie, nor credit at home nor abroad, if we must still bank?

Matters quickly went from bad to worse, and both of the state banks and all their branches were defunct by 1843. A cause celèbre arose and lingered for a long time, after $1,000,000 in Arkansas state bonds issued to fund the State Bank of Arkansas were used as security for a loan of $250,000 with the Ohio Valley Trust Co. in Cincinnati. The bonds changed hands at a deep discount and eventually were acquired by Holford's, an English firm, which demanded the full face value from the state. After the Civil War the state legislature repudiated any amount of the bonds beyond the actual cash benefit derived from them when they were pledged.

In 1846 an amendment to the state Constitution outlawed banks in the state. Years later in 1874, after the note-issuing era had ended, this provision was nullified by the new state Constitution.

Numismatic Comments

Collecting bank notes of Arkansas is a quick study, at least so far as what was made at one time. However, acquiring actual currency can be a challenge. Bills of the Real Estate Bank of the State of Arkansas and Bank of the State of Arkansas and their branches, once common, range from rare to SENC.

Although there were a few private banks and other businesses that engaged in finance, these two were the only issuers of bank notes. From the mid-1840s through the Civil War, no Arkansas state-chartered bank bills were current in the state, a remarkable situation. Scrip issues, not studied here, were abundant and are popular to collect today.

Currency of California

Number of banks in the Haxby *Standard Catalog:* 0.

Historical Notes

The Constitution of the state of California, adopted on November 13, 1850, forbade the use of paper money in circulation in that state. However, before that time at least two San Francisco bankers and gold dust traders had bills prepared by Eastern firms.

Although various merchants traded in gold dust beginning in the spring of 1848, following the discovery of gold in the tailrace of Sutter's sawmill on the American River on January 24 of that year, it was not until the next year that the first banking office opened. On January 9, 1849, the Exchange and Deposit Office of Henry M. Naglee and Richard H. Sinton began business in the Parker House on Kearny Street facing Portsmouth Square.[3] Sinton retired in July, after which the remaining partner traded as Naglee & Co., until a run took place in September,

Note for $5 of the Exchange Bank, Helena, Arkansas, ink dated June 1, 1862, from a plate by Rawdon, Wright, Hatch & Edson. A $5-$5-$10-$20 plate of this bank is preserved in the ABNCo archives. Matt Rothert Sr. commented in his book: "Some are printed on the backs of other notes or bonds." The illustrated note has on its back a portion of a sheet of scrip notes. The signatures are probably false (various other names appear on notes of the same era illustrated in the Rothert text). The bank had no legal status under Arkansas law. The bill, which does not have an ABNCo monogram on it, may have been printed before May 1, 1858. However, RWH&E would not have used the scrip sheets for bank-note paper. Seemingly, its authenticity is in question, even though it and its kin have been accepted by many as legitimate issues. Here is a bill that invites investigation!

and the bank closed its doors. Burgoyne & Co. began in the banking business on June 5, 1849, at their office at 165 Montgomery Street.

Wright & Co., which traded as the Miners Bank (the name of which was variously given as *Miners, Miners,'* and *Miner's*), was active by early 1849 and seems to have been organized in the East by entrepreneurs who headed westward, taking with them a supply of currency. It conducted business in rented premises on the Plaza, an early center of commerce. The history of this firm is for the most part an enigma. On August 27, Thomas G. Wells started business in a room in a canvas and wood structure on Montgomery Street. B. Davidson & Co. entered banking in September 1849 with an office at 135 Montgomery Street, as an agent for Rothschild in London. Two months later the Exchange and Deposit Office of James King of Wm. was established at 131 Montgomery Street. In early 1850, Felix Argenti, Tallant & Wilde, and Page, Bacon & Co. joined the lineup of bankers. Except as noted, the early banks did not issue paper money, although it would have been legal to have done so. Doubtless the travel time of about a month to the East Coast (via Panama; the route around Cape Horn took more than three months) and the back-and-forth communications needed to select, approve, and receive printed bank notes precluded interest.

Most banking business in San Francisco and other towns consisted of buying and selling gold dust and exchanging it for coins.

Numismatic Comments

By early 1849, the Miners Bank had arranged for Danforth & Hufty to print paper money for the firm in anticipation of issuing it in San Francisco. A four-subject \$1-\$3-\$5-\$10 plate was made, with each bill having the printed date March 1, 1849. The \$1 notes, some of which are known to have circulated in California, bore as their central motif an eagle on a shield. The other Miners Bank denominations known to exist in unissued proof sheet form include the \$3 note, illustrating various ships, including a steamer with stacks issuing smoke; the \$5 note, showing a ship under full sail on the high seas; and the \$10 note, with a depiction of the signing of the Declaration of Independence. The unrelated Miners Bank of Savings issued scrip notes payable in gold dust.

Felix Argenti, a Swiss trading as F. Argenti & Co., contemplated issuing currency "payable in specie," and four-subject sheets of \$50, \$100, \$500, and \$1,000 notes were made by Rawdon, Wright, Hatch & Edson. The denominations suggest that their intended use may have been as deposit certificates in bulk transactions, not in general commerce.

The above-described bills are so rare as to be essentially noncollectible today.

Currency of Colorado

Number of banks in the Haxby *Standard Catalog:* 0.
Specialized text: Nolie Mumey, *Colorado Territorial Scrip,* 1966.

Historical Notes

Although Clark, Gruber & Co. of Denver did not have the word *bank* in its name and therefore did not qualify for a listing in the Haxby text, on the top front of its building was the sign BANK AND MINT.

In his *History of Banking* (1900), John Jay Knox took notice of the firm, but he seems to have been unaware that it issued paper money:

> Legitimate banking in Colorado began after the adoption by Congress of the Legal Tender Act of February 25, 1862. In the meantime, the principal circulating medium was gold dust, carried in

A \$5 note bearing the imprint of the Miners Bank, San Francisco, March 1, 1849, from a plate by Danforth & Hufty. This bank seems to have flourished in 1849, in which year it issued \$10 gold coins. Later, its fortunes declined when assays indicated the coins were short in gold content. Likely, the bank's paper money circulated on a limited basis in 1849.

small buckskin sacks, and as the smallest price of anything was twenty-five cents, a good deal of waste occurred in making change. . . .

Clark, Gruber & Co. organized the first, most extensive and useful of all the institutions classed as banks in the period 1859–1865. Their establishment sprang from a house instituted in Leavenworth, Kansas in 1858 by Milton E. and Austin M. Clark and E.H. Gruber. In 1859 they purchased considerable quantities of gold from the Rocky Mountains. They were paying five per cent. expressage on the dust brought in, and equal cost on the coin and currency returned, in addition to the expense of armed messengers or guards each way. To avoid this burdensome expense, they finally conceived the idea of planting coining machinery in Denver and making their own coin. . . .

In September 1859 Chas. A. Cook and Jasper P. Sears established a wholesale provision house in Denver . . . and later opened a banking house in connection with their mercantile trade. A few months later they issued from steel plates a fractional paper currency in denominations of ten, twenty-five and fifty cents, with one dollar notes, all redeemable at their counters in lawful currency. This paper entered into general use and in the absence of anything better, served the purpose of its creation. During 1863 the issues ceased and the outstanding notes were duly redeemed.

Numismatic Comments

Notes of the $5 denomination were issued by Clark, Gruber & Co. in the early 1860s and, indeed, were in circulation in and around Denver before Legal Tender (National Treasury) bills arrived. These are great rarities today, with fewer than a half dozen believed to exist.

Currency of Connecticut

Number of banks in the Haxby *Standard Catalog:* 103.

Historical Notes

Although the New London Society United for Trade and Commerce, chartered by the colony in 1732, issued paper money, it was not a bank. The first in the state was the Hartford Bank, chartered on February 27, 1792, and opening its doors a half year later on August 8. The New Haven Bank and the Union Bank of New London were established in the same year, followed in 1795 by the Middletown Bank and in 1796 by the Norwich Bank. By this time, Connecticut was among the leading states with banking facilities.

In 1805, James Hillhouse (earlier a contractor for Connecticut copper coins) and others petitioned to establish the Bank of the State of Connecticut. After discussion, the proposal was turned down in 1806. In 1812, with the threat of war and coastal invasion, the New London Bank packed up and moved inland to Norwich, where it conducted business for a short time before returning home. Now and again, paper money was issued by nonchartered enterprises, such as the Manufacturers Exchange Bank, incorporated in Bristol in 1814. Its bills were payable at an "office of deposit" in New York City.[4]

By 1828 there were 15 state-chartered banks in operation. Most were permitted to issue paper money to the extent of 50% more than their capital, but this limit was seldom challenged. Banks in the state operated conservatively, and save for the spectacular failures of the Eagle Bank of New Haven and the Derby Banking and Fishing Co., they were regarded as being quite sound.

In 1835 banks were prohibited from issuing $1 and $2 bills, but many continued to circulate from banks in neighboring Massachusetts and Rhode Island. In May 1836 the Connecticut General Assembly set up a committee to evaluate the banks. After that time, reports were published on a regular basis. Within the year, examiners had visited 30 of the 31 banks in the state and three branch offices and found that all was in order. Beginning in 1838 examinations were made on an annual basis. By that time there had been complaints of

Note for $5 issued by Clark, Gruber & Co., Denver, Colorado Territory, by the American Bank Note Co. Issued in about 1861, such bills, known only in the $5 denomination, were payable in "Denver coin" at the company's combined bank and mint. This is from the Herbert and Martha Schingoethe Collection of Obsolete Currency sold by R.M. Smythe & Co., where this specific bill was highlighted as the centerpiece of that remarkable offering.

a scarcity of loanable funds to citizens. State regulations capped interest on discounts to 6%, and money was being loaned outside the state at interest rates of up to 18% under the guise of "bills of exchange."

With the onset of the Hard Times era, banks in the state suspended specie payments. Nearly all continued business on a sound basis, the Jewett City Bank being an exception. However, after some illegal loans and other matters were corrected, it continued in operation. By 1839 specie payments were again widespread in the state. Many banks in New York, Rhode Island, and other states suspended in that year. The public rushed to exchange Connecticut bank notes for coins, sharply depleting reserves in the process. However, gold and silver continued to be paid out, and not a single Connecticut bank failed. The Suffolk Bank in Boston was the redemption center for Connecticut bills. Currency was so actively and intensely in use that, on the average, about an eighth of a bank's circulation flowed through the Suffolk Bank *each week.* The notes were then sent back to Connecticut, where they were paid out again.

By 1841 no more bank failures had taken place since the Eagle and Derby closings. In that year there was a scare: post notes and demand notes issued by the Housatonic Railroad Bank became depreciated when the railroad lacked money to redeem them. Unfairly, this sent a shiver through holders of the bills of *real banks,* causing many redemptions. This was the last year of the Hard Times era, after which prosperity reigned. Banks expanded their business and the issuance of paper money.

In 1852 the Free-Banking Act provided that newly organized banks had to post securities with the state, after which they could issue a like amount of bills. Five banks organized in 1853 under this law. In the same year, the Eastern Bank of Killingly and the Woodbury Bank collapsed under a cloud of fraud. By 1855 there were 67 banks in the sate, including 13 organized since 1852. On October 14, 1857, the Panic of 1857 forced most banks in New York City and Boston to suspend specie payments, creating a ripple effect that spread to Connecticut the next day. All banks in the state, by that time 73 in number, experienced problems, and seven were placed into receivership, but some of those reopened.

In 1858 a new law limited circulation of paper money to 75% of a bank's capital. In 1856 the Merchants Exchange Bank of Bridgeport was chartered by the state, but it never conducted a legitimate banking business. However, it did float a lot of paper money with no backing, placing it into the category of a fraudulently operated bank. In 1856 the Colchester Bank opened for business, but its charter was revoked the following year "for unwarranted issuance of bills." Depositors received their money back, but citizens who unwittingly bought bank stock lost nearly all as the out-of-state promoters ran off with their ill-gotten gains.[5] This was a time for blots on the state banking escutcheon, and the Litchfield Bank chartered in 1856 was a phony operation involving forged notes and documents.

One of the most curious operations was that of the Granite Bank of Voluntown, which incorporated in 1857 but never opened for business. "From an office in a saloon in New York City, the Granite Bank's currency was put into circulation. The Bank Commissioner found no place of business, vault, safe or books in Voluntown. It was a fraud and collapsed quickly as such," a historian related.[6]

After the National Banking Act of 1863, most sound Connecticut banks converted to become National Banks. Thus ended the issuance of notes by state-chartered institutions.

Numismatic Comments

The state of Connecticut is a fine example of bank-note collecting opportunity. Activities by state-chartered institutions, including issuing currency, began in the 1790s and continued through early 1866. Along the way there are enough available notes and variations among these notes that a collection of Connecticut bills is particularly interesting. There are some home-grown aspects as well, as such well-known engravers and partnerships as Abner Reed, the Jocelyn family, Amos Doolittle, and the Graphic Company produced issues widely used in the eastern states. In 1856, New Haven was the focal point of certain investigations involving alleged anticounterfeiting methods, including the Seropyan patent.

While many notes from the 1790s and the first few years of the next century range from scarce to rare to unknown today, we have currency of the Derby Fishing Company and its related bank, Derby Banking and Fishing Company, the Eagle Bank, and other institutions, of which large numbers of bills survive.

In time, more banks were chartered while, simultaneously, designs became more ornate and complex. Along the way there were several fraudulent or rogue institutions that have interesting histories, adding to the appeal of their currency. Generally, in Connecticut and elsewhere, bills of such banks are among the more available in the marketplace, as they were never redeemed, and the public was left holding worthless paper. In contrast, many bills of well-managed banks were redeemed at par and later destroyed. Although such notes may have been issued in large quantities, they can be rare today. Notes of certain other perfectly good banks are common today, because many unissued remainders exist. Examples include the Bank of New England at Goodspeed's Landing in East Haddam and the Stonington Bank, sometimes found in four-subject sheets. However, many sheets, inconvenient to store, have been cut apart to fill the demand for single notes.

Vignettes on Connecticut currency include quite a few interesting topics, among which can be found scenes of whaling on the high seas and other nautical adventures, the palatial Iranistan mansion built for P.T. Barnum, a large frog pinning down a small frog (Windham Bank), and, for good measure, the iconic Charter Oak. There is no standard reference on collecting bills from this state, which adds to the challenge.

Currency of Delaware

Number of banks in the Haxby *Standard Catalog:* 18.

Historical Notes

The Bank of Delaware, chartered in 1795 and located in Wilmington, was the first such institution in the state. It acquitted itself well and in 1865 evolved into the National Bank of Delaware. On February 3, 1807, the Farmers Bank of Delaware was chartered. Capitalized at $500,000, the bank's shares were allotted 20% to the state and the rest to citizens in the several counties. The bank was headquartered in Dover and had branches in New Castle and Georgetown. Later, the authorized capital was raised to $1,000,000 and a branch was opened in Wilmington. The bank had 27 directors, nine of whom were appointed by the state. The institution was well managed and earned profits for its shareholders. In the 1860s it elected not to become a National Bank but continued business as a state-chartered institution.

On November 6, 1819, *Niles' Weekly Register* reported that banks in the state were "All good except the Commercial Bank and Bank at Laurel—the former at 7% discount [on its paper money] the latter at from 50% to 60%." A list of currency-issuing banks in 1820 included the Bank of Delaware, the Farmers Bank of Delaware, and the Bank of Wilmington and Brandywine. In 1837 there were eight banks operating in the state, with a capital totaling $818,020. The number fell to just two by 1849, with a capital totaling only $210,000.[7]

The proximity of the state to Philadelphia resulted in that city strongly influencing the market value of Delaware paper money and other matters. When in early 1841 the banks of Philadelphia suspended specie payments, most Delaware banks followed. There were a few scattered failures in the annals of Delaware banking, the first being the Bank of Laurel, which earned a spot on the list of broken banks in the first issue of *Bicknell's Counterfeit Detector.* The Bank of Milford closed its doors in 1854.

A $10 note of the Stonington (Connecticut) Bank, serially numbered, payee named, and dated February 1862 in ink, but with the day date never completed and without signatures affixed. From a plate by Rawdon, Wright, Hatch & Edson. Many colorful bills of this bank exist as remainders today.

Chartered in June 1822, the Stonington Bank opened its doors later the same year. At the time the town was a seaport active in the whaling trade. Its importance had been recognized during the War of 1812, when the British Navy bombarded the village from offshore. However, no troops landed, and little damage was done. Reflective of the whaling industry, certain bills of this bank show related motifs. The bank ceased business in the mid-1860s, while in the same era the Mystic Bank and the Ocean Bank of the same town each converted to a National Bank.

Numismatic Comments

As might be expected, the small state of Delaware did not have many currency-issuing banks, actually fewer than 20. Wilmington was the financial headquarters of the state and in 1795 was home to the Bank of Delaware founded that year, an early entry in American finance. This particular bank is known to have issued many different notes in the early years, but most range from very rare to unknown today, and little is known about certain designs. Some $30 bills were issued in addition to standard denominations.

Fortunately, enough notes were issued over a sufficiently long period of time, and by enough banks, that a nice collection of Delaware currency can be obtained today, including many inexpensive pieces. The sale of the American Bank Note Co. archives in 1980 brought to market some, but not many hitherto unavailable or even unknown proofs, adding to the supply of Delaware notes for the advanced specialist.

Currency of District of Columbia

Number of banks in the Haxby *Standard Catalog:* 80.

Historical Notes

In tracking down the facts and lore relating to various state-chartered banks, I have often encountered situations in which institutions seem to have been functioning well, including issuing currency produced by the better-known engraving firms, but for which no official state-generated information can be found. In some such instances, including in Washington, DC, when charters expired and were not renewed, or when charters were not granted to begin with, banks went into operation anyway, publicly and successfully, being known generally under as *private banks.* The *Banker's Magazine,* the trade journal from the late 1840s onward, recognized this fact and also called them private banks. In looking through the Haxby text for Washington, D.C., there are any number of banks listed as being fraudulent, questionable, or whatever. While some of these may have been such, others seem to have been private banks, conducted fairly and responsibly.

An account in *Niles' Weekly Register,* March 9, 1816, seems to indicate that banking was confused even at that early date:

> Banks in D.C. and nearby: Bank of Washington, Bank of Columbia, Union Bank of Georgetown, Bank of Alexandria, Bank of Potomac, Farmers Bank of Alexandria, and Mechanics Bank of Alexandria. There are also *nine* other banks in the district, unincorporated, viz., the Bank of the Metropolis and the Patriotic Bank, in Washington City: the Farmers and Mechanics Bank and the Central Bank, with an "Importing Company," issuing notes as a bank, in Georgetown, and the Merchants' and the Union Bank, with a bank said to be bottomed out on "real estate," and, we believe, yet another, in Alexandria.

The Columbia Bank was the first to be authorized to operate in the District of Columbia. The charter was given by the General Assembly of the State of Maryland, December 23, 1793, as Washington was still in its planning stage. In early times it was referred to as the Federal City; later, after the death of our first president, Washington City, usually shortened to Washington. In 1800 government offices began operation there. Control of the affairs of the District of Columbia was vested in Congress, this including the chartering and regulation of banks. During the early 19th century, the District included Washington, Georgetown, Anacostia, and Alexandria.

On February 15, 1811, the Bank of Washington was chartered. On March 3, 1817, the Franklin Bank of Alexandria, the Union Bank of Alexandria, the Central Bank of Georgetown and Washington, Farmers and

Note for $1 of the Farmers and Mechanics Bank of Milford, Delaware, October 20, 1862, from a plate by the American Bank Note Co.

Little is known about this bank, and it seems to have slipped beneath the notice of contemporary financial journals reviewed by the writer. James A. Haxby states that it opened in 1861 and remained in business until about 1867.

Mechanics Bank of Georgetown, the Bank of the Metropolis, and the Patriotic Bank of Washington were all incorporated. At the same time, Congress prohibited any individuals or companies from engaging in banking unless they were chartered. Despite this ban, over a period of years quite a few banking houses sprang up and issued paper money without official sanction.

On February 1, 1834, *Niles' Weekly Register* commented: "There are large sending out of notes of the banks of the District of Columbia to the West and to the South—where they are promptly sold, as other merchandise." For much of the note-issuing era, banks of the District were regarded as paper mills. Seemingly, Congress was too busy with other matters to pay much attention to local banking.

A listing of banks and their conditions published in the *National Intelligencer,* January 16, 1836, showed these seven conducting authorized business: Bank of Washington, Patriotic Bank of Washington, Bank of the Metropolis, Union Bank of Georgetown, Farmers and Mechanics Bank of Georgetown, Farmers Bank of Alexandria, and the Bank of Potomac. These had \$964,799.90 worth of paper money in circulation, backed by the remarkable amount of \$643,585.52 in gold and silver coin.

The inattention of Congress to such urgent matters as bank charter extensions is exemplified by a report by the Select Committee on June 20, 1836, which included extensive testimony from bank officials and then issued this statement:

> It is respectively proposed to postpone the final action of Congress on the application of the banks until the next session, that ample opportunity may be afforded to all the members to examine and scrutinize the documents now presented. . . .

Similarly, four years later this comment on deliberations was published in *Niles' National Register,* July 25, 1840:

> Mr. Merrick presented the memorial of Messrs. Kurtz, Van Ness and Bradley, president of the Metropolis and Patriotic banks, and of the Farmers and Mechanics Bank of Georgetown, praying the continuance of their banking powers, and that of other banks, on the condition of their resuming and continuing specie payments, and concluding with the form of a joint resolution, which, if passed by Congress, would be acceptable to them. . . .

The same issue reprinted this item from the *National Intelligencer:*

> No act has passed for continuing banking powers to the banks of the District of Columbia.—The resolution for extending banking powers till the 4th day of March next to such banks as should resume and continue specie payments (a small boon, indeed, but still a symptom of relenting tyranny) which passed the Senate on Monday, was not taken up at all in the house of representatives. Strenuous efforts were made by those sterling friends of this District, Mr. Wm. Cost Johnson and Mr. Jenifer to get the resolution of the Senate taken up, and a majority of the members of the house were willing to take it up. But the consent of two-thirds of the members present was necessary to get at it, and the obduracy of the friends of the hard money anti-bank policy could not be subdued even by the prayers of a suffering people. The banks are left to wind up their affairs, and get their money in, as best they can.

Comments such as the preceding contribute to the numismatic understanding of why so many banks in the District of Columbia have been regarded as unofficial or fraudulent. Faced with lack of cooperation by Congress, they continued in business after their charters expired or simply entered banking without a charter. This act entailed some risk, as in an interesting case involving Peter B. Hogge, a clerk in the Scottsville, Virginia, Post Office who was caught stealing currency from the mail. The issuer was the Exchange Bank of Selden, Withers & Co., Washington, which had no charter but was considered to be of excellent reputation. The defendant was dismissed, as it was found "that the notes stolen had not such value as the law will recognize and protect."[8]

In addition to the bills of banks that operated with or without benefit of charter, some fantasy issues were circulated, as in this 1857 account from the *Boston Traveler:*

> *Destruction of Counterfeit Money at Boston:* Sheriff Clark, of Suffolk, received from Charles B. Hall, Esq., Secretary of the Society for the Suppression of Counterfeit Money, and commenced the destruction thereof, in conformity with the law, a large amount of counterfeit bills, coin, plates and moulds. The whole amount was nearly \$50,000. About \$18,000 consisted of bills on the Potomac Bank of Georgetown, which institution never existed. The rest of the bills were mostly counterfeits of various New England banks. There were also thirty-one steel and copper plates engrossed for bank notes, and some \$200 in counterfeit coin, consisting of quarter, half and whole dollars, Spanish milled dollars, gold dollars, and half and quarter eagles; also, three plaster moulds for the casting of coin.[9]

Also see "Banks in the District of Columbia" in chapter 10. Suffice it to say, if anyone ever writes a history of bank notes of the District, they will have to do diligent research in local newspapers and nationwide financial journals in addition to official records kept by Congress in order to create a useful text.

Numismatic Comments

Paper money from the District of Columbia is among the most fascinating in the American series. Scratch the surface of this specialty and interesting twists and complications arise as suggested by the historical comments above. Bills bear the imprint of Washington City, Washington, Anacostia (*Anacastia* in one instance), Georgetown, and Alexandria. Currency of the last city can bear the address of Virginia, District of Columbia, or no address at all other than Alexandria. The latter town was part of Virginia until 1792, when it was ceded to the District of Columbia, where the Federal City (later Washington) was being laid out. In 1846 Alexandria was retroceded to Virginia. All during the time it was part of the District of Columbia, most residents considered themselves to be Virginians in spirit and tradition.

Attractive vignettes abound among District of Columbia bills, as do interesting inscriptions, such as "payable in Virginia notes," "payable in Demand Notes," etc. Names of banks are likewise diverse, often with lofty-sounding titles relating to commerce, politics, and the government.

The supply of proof notes turned loose from the American Bank Note Co. archives a generation ago has made it possible to collect many issues that were not known to James A. Haxby in 1988 and which, in any event, are still rare.

Currency of Florida

Number of banks in the Haxby *Standard Catalog*: 17.
Specialized texts: Daniel G. Cassidy, *The Illustrated History of Florida Paper Money*, 1980; Ronald J. Benice, *Florida Paper Money*, 2006.

Historical Notes

In its early years of banking, Florida was a territory. Statehood was achieved in 1845. Under the territorial government these banks were in operation by 1833: Bank of Pensacola, Bank of West Florida, Central Bank (successor in 1833 to the Bank of Florida), Commercial Bank, Merchants and Planters Bank of Magnolia, and Union Bank of Florida, the last being the most important.

In 1838 there were five banks doing business, with a total capital of $2,113,302 and bills in circulation amounting to $774,040. Located in Apalachicola, Magnolia, Pensacola, and Tallahassee, each of these failed later, and their currency became worthless. In the meantime, out-of-state banks and companies did banking in Florida through offices in the territory. The situation caused great turmoil. On December 30, 1839, after learning details of fraud within the Union Bank, the United States Senate called for an investigation of bank incorporations and issues.

Niles' National Register printed this item on December 19, 1840:

> *Banks in Florida.* The grand jury for the district of East Florida have presented, among other matters, the present condition of the banks in Florida. But three banks are now pretending to be in operation: the Bank of Pensacola, the Southern Life and Trust Co. and the Union Bank; all the others have become extinct. The faith bonds issued to these banks are presented as *null and void,* and the legislature is urged to take immediate measures to cancel them.

The state annulled the charter of the Jacksonville Bank in February 1841, following the exposure of fraudulent activities by its officers. However, this act did not deter the miscreants involved, for in 1842 many of its worthless bills were sent to distant locations, and false advertisements were published in New York City newspapers to the effect that brokers would redeem the notes at par.[10]

A $1 note purporting to be of the Farmers and Merchants Bank, Washington City, DC, February 15, 1862. From a plate by the American Bank Note Co. This note appears to be spurious.

The Farmers and Merchants Bank is one of quite a few Washington, D.C., banks for which information is scant or altogether absent. The writer has found a listing indicating that the bank began business on April 1, 1852, and ceased business on or by January 1, 1861. The Haxby text suggests that is was "fraudulent or possibly non existent," and that certain plates were later modified to make bills for the Metropolitan Bank of the same city. Haxby gives the time of operation as about 1852.

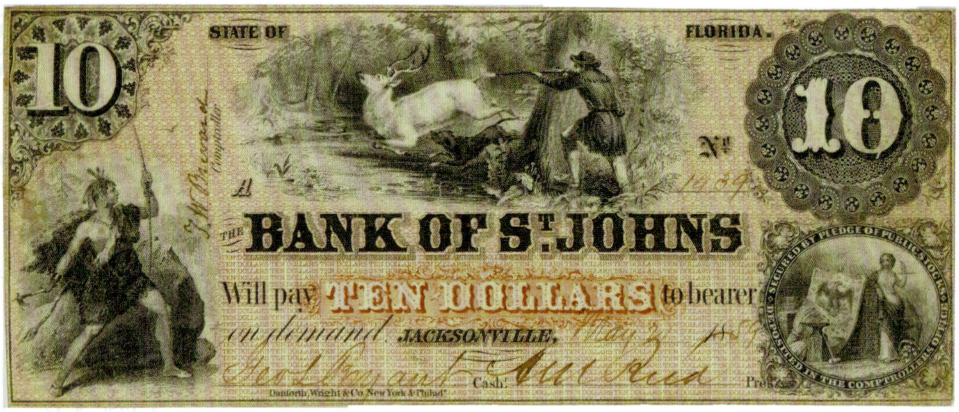

A $10 note of the Bank of St. Johns, Jacksonville, Florida, May 21, 1859, from a plate by the American Bank Note Co. This bank was capitalized at $100,000 and commenced business on May 2, 1859. It ceased business during the Civil War.

In 1853 the state passed a General Banking Law. In December 1855 the Bank of the State of Florida was chartered, but in 1856 *Banker's Magazine* informed readers "we know of no regular bank in the state." From then until the Civil War, many banks were incorporated. However, the state did not set up any system of regulation, nor did it require regular reports. Not surprisingly, there were many abuses.

Numismatic Comments

The obsolete paper money issued by banks in Florida offers a rich and interesting field for numismatic study and acquisition. Many different varieties of notes are available from the 1830s through the 1860s. Many if not most of these survive as remainders, others from banks that failed—the latter always a good numismatic source. The history of the banks is interesting as well, such as the Bank of Fernandina, founded in 1859 in the town with the same name, but which moved to Starke in 1862 when Union troops took over Fernandina. Bills of this particular bank are known for their bright red left and right margins, an anticounterfeiting measure.

Florida is a popular retirement destination, and more than a few longtime numismatists from other areas of the United States have collected Florida notes upon their arrival in this sunny land of the South. The market today is very active for such bills and has been for a long time. The general level of prices is higher than for nearly all other eastern states. "Deep pockets" are a necessity in this field, a leading dealer remarked.

Florida had enough failed banks, banks with interesting history, and unusual locations that a display of bills from this state has many facets.

Currency of Georgia

Number of banks in the Haxby *Standard Catalog:* 69.
Specialized text (related, but not about bank notes): W. Mack Martin and Kenneth S. Latimer, *State of Georgia: Treasury Notes, Treasury Certificates & Bonds,* 2006.

Historical Notes

The earliest effort at establishing a bank under state charter was in 1807, when the Planters Bank, of Savannah, was authorized. However, capital was not raised, and nothing came of the venture at the time. In 1810 the Planters Bank received a new charter. With an authorized capital of $1,000,000, it soon went into operation. In December 1810 the Bank of Augusta was chartered with a capital of $300,000, later raised to $1,200,000.

By 1815 these two remained the only chartered banks in the state, but a host of private companies issued currency, causing great confusion in commerce and tending to impair the reputation of bills of the Planters Bank and the Bank of Augusta. Seeking to end these unofficial issues, in that year the state passed a law levying an 8% tax on all non-bank currency. On December 16, 1815, the Bank of the State of Georgia was chartered. For the next two decades, many more banks were chartered throughout the state. These had the privilege of issuing paper money up to three times the amount of their capital. Most were small institutions, but there were exceptions. The Bank of Darien, capitalized at $1,000,000, attracted much attention in its day (see "Doings in Darien" in chapter 7). During the Hard Times era, nearly all of these banks closed their doors, including the one in Darien.

The Central Bank of Georgia was formed in 1828 under state auspices and control in Milledgeville, then the capital of the state. According to accounts, this bank prospered greatly, to the extent that taxes on citizens and commerce within the state were nominal, as revenue from the institution was sufficient. However, in 1842 it was revealed to be a house of cards in that many assets that looked good on paper could not be turned into cash. The bank closed but was not fully liquidated until well into the 1850s.

In the early 1850s, the Chicago firm of George B. Smith & Co. controlled the Atlanta Bank and the International Bank, the latter in Griffin, Georgia. The company also controlled the Bank of America, chartered in Illinois, and the Wisconsin Marine and Fire Insurance Company Bank. Bills were shipped around the country by these banks, and markets in them were made by exchange brokers in New York City and elsewhere. Many suspicions were aroused, and warning notices were given, but, somehow, proof of illegal activities remained elusive. The Bank of St. Mary's, headquartered in Columbus, Georgia, circulated a large quantity of bills through agents and offices in the state as well as in Alabama and Florida. The bank collapsed in 1854.

Certain bridge, railroad, and insurance companies in the state obtained banking privileges and issued paper money, the Georgia Railroad and Banking Company, of Augusta, the Augusta Bridge Bank Company, and the Central Railroad and Banking Company, of Savannah, being examples. An insurance company in the banking business was the subject of this account in *Niles' National Register,* April 29, 1843:

> The Western Insurance and Trust Company at Columbia, Georgia, had their bank robbed on the 14th instant, of $75,000 in gold and notes, by persons in disguise who entered and secured the officers of the bank whilst they escaped with the booty. A reward of $5,000 was offered, and four persons have been arrested, and have heretofore been considered of the first respectability. Thomas C. McKean, and John Lane Lewis, former mayor of the city, and now solicitor of the Circuit Court. The former is in jail—the latter gave bail; J.B. Jackson and Allen Bass the bookkeeper of the institution, who it is said let in his accomplices, and then suffered himself to be seized by them and locked up with the other officers in the vault. The money except about $5,000 has been recovered.

Most banks in Georgia did well in the 1850s and into the 1860s. Then came the Civil War, which only a few survived. During the war many banks, the state, and others issued a flood of scrip notes, which soon became worthless. The state repudiated its own notes, raising legal questions, but not to any useful effect for its creditors.

Numismatic Comments

The evergreen popularity of bills from this state is exemplified by this comment from dealer Tom Denly: "Georgia has so many notes it isn't funny, and everybody loves them. In Georgia there are banks for which there may be a thousand examples of a given variety in the marketplace, and they still get bought."

Obsolete bank notes of Georgia comprise issues from 69 banks listed by Haxby, plus many other commercial issuers. Imprints range from early, such as the Bank of Augusta, organized in 1811, down through institutions that continued in business during the Civil War. While scrip notes are often, but not always, collected with Obsolete Currency, the field of scrip is particularly rich during the Civil War era, when these were made up by local and regional printers and bore bank names (in addition to many more with private imprints). The November 10, 1861, Bank of Whitfield denominations bear the name of prominent Civil War currency printer Jules Manouvrier. In the absence of skilled engravers and spider presses for turning out

Note for $2 of the Augusta Insurance and Banking Company, Georgia, December 20, 1861, from a prewar stock of currency obtained from the American Bank Note Co.

Capitalized at $375,000, this combined business was active and profitable from the late 1820s until the middle of the Civil War. Headquartered in Augusta, it maintained a branch in Savannah.

notes in the traditional method, these and certain others are lithographed or typeset.

The Bank of the State of Georgia, incorporated in 1815 with headquarters in Savannah, issued bills through its branches. The historical record for these notes is extensive, but in many instances surviving examples are not known today. In Savannah the Bank of Commerce, operated by Gazaway Bugg Lamar, who also had ties to the Republic Bank in New York City prior to the Civil War, continued to do a flourishing business during the conflict. Old bills continued to be in use, but the overprint on the back, stating that the bills were redeemed by the Bank of the Republic in New York, was crossed out. Enough varieties were issued that a specialized collection of Savannah notes would be very extensive.

Generous supplies of remainders and redeemed bills that surfaced after the Civil War are responsible for the availability of Georgia notes today. Most of these date from the 1840s and the colorful decade of the 1850s and can be interesting to collect.

Currency of Illinois

Number of banks in the Haxby *Standard Catalog:* 175. **Specialized text (about banks rather than currency, but useful):** Francis M. Huston, *Financing an Empire: The History of Banking in Illinois,* 1926.

Historical Notes

The first bank in what became the state of Illinois in December 1818 began business under the territorial government at Shawneetown (*Shawanoe-town* to many) in 1813, at which time there were only about 1,500 people in the district. Known as the Bank of Illinois, it was chartered under state rules in 1816. Success attended its efforts, the federal government kept funds there, and its currency stood in high regard. As coins were very scarce in the district, the legislature did not require that the bank redeem its bills in them. In August 1821, following widespread suspension of payments by banks in Kentucky and elsewhere, the Bank of Illinois was forced to stop redeeming paper, and in 1823 it closed. Settlements were made with creditors, so it did not lose its charter. It remained moribund until February 1835, when the state extended its charter to January 1, 1857. Now capitalized at $300,000, within a month the figure was increased to $1,400,000 through the sale of bonds payable in 1861.

In 1814, under territorial laws, the Bank of Kaskaskia, the Bank of Cairo, and the Bank of Edwardsville were formed. In 1819 the Bank of Edwardsville failed, costing the federal government the $54,000 in land sales funds on deposit there. The Bank of Cairo was part of a grand project that included building a city at the confluence of the Mississippi and Ohio rivers. The bank was to be financed by the sale of building lots. This did not happen. In 1836 some men with criminal intent acquired the wreckage of the bank, moved it to Kaskaskia, but kept the Bank of Cairo name. Paper money was issued for a time, but it had no real backing.

The state Constitution of 1818 forbade the incorporation of any *new* banks other than those operated by the state itself. In March 1819, the State Bank of Illinois was incorporated at $4,000,000, with a charter of 25 years, with half to be owned by the state and the remainder by public stockholders. The bank was not formed, because the nation was in an economic slump, and in 1821 its charter was revoked. Another bank, with a capital of $500,000, was formed, to be owned by the state. The bank was headquartered at Vandalia, then the state capital, with branches at Brownsville, Edwardsville, Palmyra, and Shawneetown. "The capital consisted of its office furniture and bank note plates only," commented *Banker's Magazine,* continuing,

> It had hardly commenced operations before its bills fell to 75 per cent.; shortly after to 50 per cent., and finally to 25 per cent, when they ceased to circulate at all. The members of the legislature received their pay in the depreciated currency at the market value, and on one occasion received $9 per day for their services, which the State was compelled to redeem at par; and a loan of $100,000 received in these notes at par was paid out at fifty cents on the dollar.[11]

On February 12, 1835, a new State Bank of Illinois was formed, capitalized for $1,500,000 with authorization to increase that amount to $2,500,000. The state subscribed to $100,000 worth of stock. Headquartered in Springfield, the State Bank set up branches in Alton, Belleville, Chicago, Danville, Galena, Jacksonville, Mt. Carmel, Quincy, and Vandalia. Under the charter provision the bank was allowed 50 days to redeem its bills. At the time the Mississippi River town of Alton was mounting a campaign to challenge and hoped to surpass St. Louis as a trading port. The State Bank of Illinois made substantial loans to Alton merchants, based on rosy expectations but little in the way of assets. These were optimistic times, and this bank was viewed as the gate to increased prosperity, a fount from which all blessings (easy money) flowed. Seemingly, nothing could go wrong with the State Bank, not even with its seemingly wise investments in lead and other commodities. Surprise! The Alton loans proved disastrous, ultimately resulting in a loss estimated at $1,000,000. Speculations, loans to insiders, and other irregularities worsened the bank's finances. The institution was further crippled by the Panic of 1837 and went into receivership in 1842.

In the meantime, the capital of the Bank of Illinois at Shawneetown was increased by $1,400,000, with the state subscribing for $1,000,000 of this. To encourage rapid growth, branches were authorized at Alton, Jacksonville, Lawrenceville, and Pekin. The Panic of 1837 carried this bank down in the early 1840s. Liquidation took a long time. Citizens were reeling from heavy losses, and *bank* was a bad word. After this there were no authorized banks in operation until 1851, when the Free-Banking Law was passed in February.

Illinois became a target for the distribution of out-of-state currency, with paper money bearing the names of banks of Georgetown and Washington in the District of Columbia being particularly prevalent (perhaps explaining the reason for the existence of some of those mysterious institutions). Today, a reader might wonder why District of Columbia bills had any value in distant Illinois. The answer here, and for many other situations, is simply that as long as merchants received them and passed them along, they served in commerce. There was no particular reason for anyone in the chain to consider shipping them off to Washington, D.C., to be exchanged for coin.

One suspected but never convicted sharper, George Smith, with offices in Chicago, controlled more than a half dozen unofficial banks, an insurance company, and other enterprises that issued paper money in quantity, the confidence for which was bolstered by his advertisements to redeem bills in gold (notice of him is given in the Georgia commentary above). Private banks sprang up like mushrooms. In 1852, after the state tried to shut down the quasi-banks operating and issuing paper, Smith obtained a charter from neighboring Wisconsin for the Wisconsin Marine and Fire Insurance Company Bank, an outgrowth of his former insurance company. He also controlled the Atlanta Bank and the International Bank of Griffin, Georgia. Active trading in Illinois bank notes was done in Chicago and St. Louis.

By December 1854 under the Free-Banking Law, 36 banks had incorporated, of which the bills of 10 of them were trading at discounts of 25% or more, and several others were closed or in liquidation. Illinois was a haven for crooks, and nearly a dozen paper mills were opened (banks that did no real business but ordered large quantities of paper money to be shipped off to brokers in distant cities and sold at large discounts, with the expectation that few bills would ever find their way back home).

In 1857 an investigator sought to find out more about the Bentonville Bank and found that

> [It was in] a small hamlet, consisting of three houses and a grocery store, situated on a prairie, about 10 miles from the railroad. The back part of the grocery was occupied by the bank, but as this institution has now suspended operations, the president and cashier have gone to Chicago. I saw no safe or other evidences of cash, and so conclude the assets are now in the breeches pocket of the president and cashier.[12]

Speculation in bank bills was rife, aided by tricks and espionage, such as publishing false reports that a truly sound bank had failed, and buying up its notes in distant places for deep discounts. Another ruse was for a bank or broker to advertise that it would not accept the bills of certain other banks, which it had a right to do. The game was to try to damage the reputation of the concerns. By this time, you will recognize this as being a very familiar scenario in state banking throughout the country. In Illinois the pace of bank incorporations continued, and by the end of 1860 there were 110 banks operating in the state. By that time the business was largely legitimate, with just a few scattered reports of tricks and capers appearing in the newspapers.

Numismatic Comments

With 175 banks listed in the Haxby text and a sufficient number of *wildcats* among them, plus some banks not listed by Haxby (for example, the Bank of Golconda, which in 1863 had $6,000 in bills in circulation, and the early Bank of Cairo located in the town of the same name), the state of Illinois offers a rich panorama of numismatic exploration. There is no modern reference on currency from this state today, but word has it that Smythe and Company, picking up the traces of Herbert and Martha Schingoethe's interest in this state, plans to fill the void.

Murray, Draper, Fairman & Co. of Philadelphia furnished bills to the Bank of Illinois in Shawneetown, but few have survived. Notes of the State Bank of Illinois, issued at Springfield and branches, range from

A $1 proof note of the Grand Prairie Bank of Urbana, Illinois. Unsigned, unissued remainder. Plate by Baldwin, Bald & Cousland, New York, in combination with Bald, Cousland & Co., Philadelphia. A bill of this denomination was unknown to Haxby in 1988.

The Grand Prairie Bank, whose capital varied but was typically in the low $70,000s, operated from October 1, 1856, to January 1, 1861. Currency issues seem to have been small and were composed of the denominations of $1, $2, $5, and $10.

scarce to SENC today, the last being particularly true of the branch bills.

As is true with all states, the American Bank Note Co. proofs sold in 1990 and 1991 dramatically increased the supply of rarities from this state, including many that were either reported as SENC by Haxby in 1988 or were completely unrecorded.

Most Illinois bills on the market today date from after the passage of the Free-Banking Act in 1851—the era with ornate vignettes and color overprints, making an album filled with bills of this state a display of artistic beauty. Pursuing these in combination with the often fascinating history of the banks that issued them can be a very rewarding pursuit.

Currency of Indiana

Number of banks in the Haxby *Standard Catalog:* 140.
Specialized text: Wendell Wolka, Jack M. Vorhies, and Donald Schramm, *Indiana Obsolete Notes and Scrip,* 1978.

Historical Notes

In his *History of Banking,* John Jay Knox included this explanation, the best and worst of situations:

> Indiana presents the anomaly of having been the state organizing the most admirable system of banking of any state in the Union, and also of having a banking system at one time so vicious that under it the banks bankrupted nearly the whole people.

The first authorized banks in the area were chartered by the Legislature of Indiana Territory in 1814: the Bank of Vincennes with $500,000 capital allowed, and the Farmers and Mechanics Bank of Madison with $750,000.

In 1817 the Bank of Vincennes under state law became the Bank of Vincennes, The State Bank of Indiana. Branches were set up in Brookville, Corydon, and Vevay. The capital was augmented by $1,000,000. On September 11, 1819, *Niles' Weekly Register* printed this item:

> The *Western Sun,* printed at Vincennes, Ind. states, that the Vincennes bank has emitted a new batch of paper, payable nine months after date at their branch in Vevay. It is said that the "nine months after date" is printed on a dark ground in a small letter at the top of the bill, and so contrived as to require careful scrutiny to distinguish them from those payable on demand.

This institution issued bills recklessly and fraudulently, refused to redeem them in specie, and was closed down by the state supreme court in 1821. On July 29, 1825, per a contemporary account, "a fool broke into a house in Vevay and stole $16,000 or $17,000 in bills" of this bank. "It is said that a corn-basket full of them would not purchase a dinner for him."[13]

The Farmers and Mechanics Bank, headquartered in Madison, opened branches in Lawrenceburg and Lexington and had a good reputation. In time its charter was extended to 1834. However, it wound down its operations in the mid-1820s with years left to go. A void in official banking for the next decade furnished opportunity for private concerns, such as insurance companies, merchants, plank-road companies, and others to issue a spate of bills. The state of Indiana issued its own currency, interest bearing and receivable for taxes, in denominations of $5, $10, and $20. Most but not all of the bills issued during this era became worthless. Historian Knox relates that the state of Indiana bills were known as *red dogs,* while worthless issues of plank-road companies and other firms were referred to as *blue pups.*

Chapter 16 gives an overview of the State Bank of Indiana, whose branches operated from 1834 to 1857, and which effectively ended the *doggy* notes mentioned above, and the Bank of the State of Indiana, which operated from 1857 to 1865. In 1852 the General Banking Law, also discussed in chapter 16, set the scene for many abuses among newly formed institutions. Again from Knox:

Halcyon Days of Wildcat Banking:

The organizers of a bank were required to deposit with the auditor of the state the bonds of the United States or of some state. At that time the bonds of several of the states, especially those in the South, were at a discount. A few men would get together, purchase the bonds of some state at a discount, file them with the auditor, and receive authority to establish a bank. With that authority they could enter upon the manufacture of paper money wholesale. They were permitted to have the custody of the plates and dies from which their bills were printed, and notwithstanding the law required that the bills should be countersigned by the auditor, there were practically no guards to prevent them from issuing bills *ad libitum,* and in many cases bills were issued to an amount two or three times greater than the value of the bonds deposited.[14]

Then the bank, officers and directors would disappear, leaving the bill holders to mourn. A thousand or two dollars in cash was all that was required to start a bank. This was needed to pay for engraving the plates and printing the bills. An embryo banker would go to New York with a thousand dollars, order an engraver to make the plates and print $50,000 in bills. He would next visit a broker and negotiate for $50,000 of the bonds of some state, get them at a discount, and instruct the broker to send them to Indianapolis in care of the auditor of the state, the price to be paid on their delivery at Indianapolis. He would then go to Indianapolis with his $50,000 of new bills, get the auditor to countersign them, and pay for the bonds with the bills and have a surplus left. Thus a new bank would be established, without banking-house, furniture, or anything else. . . .

Within two years nearly 100 banks were started with a total circulation of more than $9,500,000. Fifty-six of them collapsed before the end of the first year of their existence, representing a circulation of nearly $3,000,000.

In 1855 the Legislature undertook to remedy the matter by amending the law limiting the circulation to $6,000,000, and requiring that all stockholders should be bona fide residents of the State, and also that the deposit of securities should be ten per cent. in market value in excess of the issue. All banks failing to meet the requirements of the new law were required to go out of business. This cut off a number more of them, and the number grew less each year.

The financial panic of 1857 drove more of the banks to the wall, and those remaining finally redeemed all their notes. The securities of the broken banks were disposed of and their bills redeemed by the auditor, most of them at a discount.

Notwithstanding the precautions in effect in the late 1850s, there were still opportunities for fraud. The Citizens Bank of Gosport is mentioned in chapter 15. The passing of bills of the nonexistent Manufacturers Bank of Hartford was another such caper.

Numismatic Comments

The state of Indiana, with 140 banks listed in the Haxby text, plus dozens of branch banks, plus a host of non-bank businesses that issued paper money, is a playground and challenge for the numismatist. The collectible notes are mostly from the 1830s to the early 1850s and are not as bright and colorful as later issues, but there are enough of those to add visual spice to any display.

Bills of the State Bank of Indiana and its successor, the Bank of the State of Indiana, are collectible as to general types, but many issues of the branches range from rare to unknown. In connection with this, the memoirs of Hugh McCulloch, *Men and Measures of Half a Century* (1889), is worthwhile reading. McCulloch left the Bank of the State of Indiana in 1863 to become the first comptroller of the currency in the Treasury Department in Washington, D.C.

Note for $5 of the Manufacturers Bank, Hartford, Indiana, December 27, 1857, with space for the signature of just one officer, given as *banker*. Rare imprint of J. Sage & Sons, Litho-Bank-Note Engravers, Buffalo, New York, who welcomed business from con artists.

This bank was an out-and-out fraud perpetrated by a Mr. Williams, who later claimed that he had paid $1,900 to the publisher of a "certain New York counterfeit detector" to "quote the money right!"

Beyond the two state banks, the many other note-issuing banks were dispersed across the state in large cities as well as small villages. Most ordered bills from companies in New York and Philadelphia, or from a branch in Cincinnati. Designs varied but are similar to those used elsewhere. Many Indiana bills from the 1840s onward are in numismatic channels and furnish a rich collecting opportunity.

As always, fascinating stories beckon, such as that of the Boone County Bank of Lebanon, chartered in 1860, genuine bills for which were furnished by W.L. Ormsby to the extent of $289,000 face value. Although $54,000 value of the bills was given to the state auditor and countersigned, at least $10,000 worth, perhaps more, was fraudulently signed and passed into circulation. The state closed down the bank and redeemed genuine bills at par from its reserve fund. All but $1,552 was taken in. Today, bills of this bank are easily obtained in the marketplace.

The Bank of North America, Newport, was the subject of an investigation in 1853 by the Select Committee of the Indiana House of Representatives, which found it was a "movable" bank set up to issue bills. When a holder of $1,500 in currency sought to redeem them, he was told the bank was only open on Tuesdays and Fridays. He returned on the next open day, at which time payment was refused. The bank later moved to Clinton and closed in 1856. Today, $5 notes from both locations are collectible but scarce. How curious it is that such bills, worthless in their day, are so treasured now! In fact, it would be difficult to name *any* bill from a fraudulent bank that today is not worth more than its face value.

As always, owning a note from a bank might be worth one point in interest value, and for the historian, knowing the background of the bank might be worth a point. The numismatist who combines collecting with history will find that 1 + 1 = 3.

Currency of Iowa

Number of banks in the Haxby *Standard Catalog:* 2.
Specialized text: Dean Oakes, *Iowa Obsolete Notes and Scrip,* 1982.

Historical Notes

The political boundaries of what is now the state of Iowa were adjusted often. In June 1834, this area and other lands north of the state of Missouri and west of the Mississippi River were made part of the Territory of Michigan. This arrangement was superseded on July 4, 1836, when the Territory of Wisconsin was defined, including within its boundaries the present states of Iowa, Minnesota, and Wisconsin.

The Miners Bank of Dubuque was incorporated on November 30, 1836, with a Wisconsin address. On July 12, 1838, the Territory of Iowa was formed, with land comprising the present state plus much of Minnesota northward. The Miners Bank of Dubuque now had an Iowa address. The capital was set at $200,000, with the provision that currency could be issued as soon as $40,000 was paid in, and no loan (discount) business could be conducted until $100,000 was paid in. No bills were to be less than $5. Unfortunately, much of the paid-in capital was in the form of IOUs. Rumors swirled around the district, and in March 1841 the bank was no longer able to redeem its bills in gold and silver coins. On July 1, 1842, the bank started redemption with high hopes, but after being presented with $25,000 of its bills in a few days, it ran out of coins and had to suspend. In April 1844, it resumed payments for a short time. An investigation revealed that the so-called capitalization was fraudulent, and the bank's charter was revoked in 1845.

Iowa became a state in 1846 but remained without a state-chartered bank until 1858. During this time the prairie lands were desolate. Grain farmers and stock raisers and herders were widely scattered amidst activity from incoming settlers. Improvements such as the telegraph and railroad did not yet connect the towns. Business was mostly conducted in towns along the Mississippi River, where private bankers maintained offices, gaining much business by loaning money to immigrants to buy government land for $1.25 per acre, and demanding repayment of $1.75 per acre one year later. This was a usurious interest rate, but it was taken up eagerly by buyers who had no other choice. These bankers also traded in exchange, selling gold and silver coins that were needed to pay the government, as paper was not allowed. Land speculation was another avenue of profit. Historian John Jay Knox gave this wild and wooly scenario in his *History of Banking:*

> Because of the fact that Iowa had made no provision for the banking needs of her people, and because of the demand for money, the state was made the dumping ground for much fluctuating currency from Indiana, Illinois, and Wisconsin. The value of these bank notes was constantly changing, and they were the source of great trouble and loss to the people at large and to

A $5 note of the Miners Bank of Dubuque, Iowa, which closed in 1845. Leftover bills fell into the hands of sharpers, who issued them years later with illogical dates and false signatures. This one is ink dated July 17, 1860. From a plate from the Cincinnati office of Rawdon, Wright & Hatch.

> the banker, who could not tell their value from day to day. . . .
>
> Some of Iowa's business men determined to start banks of issue in the Territory of Nebraska; there were no restrictions on its Legislature chartering all the banks called for. . . . In less than two years eight banks were organized. The first of these was The Western Fire and Marine Insurance Company, organized in March 1855 by Thomas H. Benton, Jr. Until January 1856 when five more of these banks were organized, there were more of the issues of this bank in circulation in Iowa than any other; but after that time they with the notes of the Bank of Florence (controlled by Cook & Sargeant, of Davenport, and Cook, Sargeant & Downey, of Iowa City), the issues of the Bank of Nebraska (by B.F. Allen, of Des Moines), and those of the Bank of Fontenelle (by Green & Weare, of Cedar Rapids), were a large part of the circulating medium [in Iowa].
>
> When the panic of 1857 was precipitated, the Western Fire and Marine Insurance company was one of the first banks in the West to go. In closing up the concern only $191.30 in specie and $121 in bills of solvent banks were found, and its notes became worthless. The Bank of Florence was kept up as long as the credit of its backers held out, its issues being quoted at discount. They were all finally redeemed. The Bank of Fontenelle followed with the others. Cedar Rapids, Marion, Vinton, Osage, Des Moines, Council Bluffs, Fort Dodge, and Sioux City each had a banking house from which the notes of this bank were floated. The Bank of Nebraska, with a smaller circulation, was the last of these Iowa-Nebraska banks to succumb, for the credit of the founder was still good, and the bills were so promptly redeemed that it was the last to go. . . .

Iowa legislators framed a new constitution in 1857. Provisions were included for individuals to form banks as well as for the possible establishment of a state bank. On July 29, 1858, the State Bank of Iowa was incorporated. At first, branches were set up in Davenport, Des Moines, Dubuque, Iowa City, Keokuk, Mt. Pleasant, Muscatine, and Oskaloosa, later followed by offices in Burlington, Council Bluffs, Fort Madison, Lyons, Maquoketa, McGregor, and Washington. Each of the 15 branches was separately capitalized. Bills were furnished by the central office of the State Bank, against which each branch had to deposit federal or state interest-bearing securities into a safety fund. Bills could be issued up to twice the value of paid-in capital. Should a branch fail to redeem its bills in coins, it would be declared insolvent and closed. With the advent of National Banks, the State Bank decreed that as of March 15, 1865, no more bills could be paid out, and all notes in circulation must be redeemed and sent to the central office to be burned. Most of the branches became National Banks.

Numismatic Comments

Although the Haxby text lists just two banks for Iowa, this claim belies the fact that large quantities of notes were issued to the State Bank of Iowa to supply its 15 branches scattered across the district. The vast majority of such issues, which typically ranged in denomination from $1 to $10 for each branch, are very rare today, although there are a few exceptions. All bear the imprint of the American Bank Note Co. (mostly) or the National Bank Note Co. and are very colorful. Competition for scarce varieties is fierce among specialists.

Bills of the Miners Bank of Dubuque exist with Wisconsin and, later, Iowa imprints and come on the market occasionally. These are appreciated for the interesting story they have attached to them and are considered to be key issues, expensive when offered. Various private bankers and other companies issued paper money, but these are beyond the purview of the present text.

Currency of Kansas

Number of banks in the Haxby *Standard Catalog:* 11.
Specialized text: Steven Whitfield, *Kansas Obsolete Notes and Scrip,* 1980.

HISTORICAL NOTES

The Steven Whitfield text lists currency from just a handful of banks associated with Kansas Territory and Kansas, several of which are fraudulent or nonexistent. These date from the late 1850s into the 1860s, a time of great turmoil in *Bleeding* (or *Bloody*) *Kansas,* a term said to have been coined by Horace Greeley of the *New York Tribune.* Whether the territory would be admitted to the Union as a slaveholding state or whether slavery would be prohibited was not decided yet. Gangs and ruffians from both sides of the dispute raided and looted towns and private houses, murdered citizens, and engaged in other depredations. Hostilities were not fully resolved until Kansas became a free state in January 1861.

This was hardly an atmosphere conducive to establishing banks. Those listed as legitimate by Whitfield include the Exchange and Kansas Valley banks of Atchison and the Bank of the State of Kansas of the same place; the Delaware City Bank; the Easton Bank; the Lawrence Bank in the town of that name; and the Redwing Bank, also in Lawrence.

Among the questionable banks are the Drovers Bank of Fort Leavenworth, the Merchants Bank of Leavenworth City, and the State Bank at Lecompton, all of which had bills printed by W.L. Ormsby. Whether certain of these notes were ordered by speculators who intended to start banks in the conflict-torn area, or whether the banks were conceived in fraud is not known today. Another issuer of Ormsby notes, the City Bank of Leavenworth City, operated briefly but failed.

Certain Drovers Bank bills are identical in design to those of the Drovers Bank of Salt Lake City, Utah. Regarding this fact, in a letter to the author, July 9, 2004, Steve Whitfield commented:

> One of Ormsby's notes, the Drovers Bank of Salt Lake City, was in effect an open invitation to fraud. These notes were originally prepared for the Drovers Bank of Kansas, located at Fort Leavenworth. This bank never existed although Ormsby prepared a book of stock certificates, a book of CDs and a book of promissory notes (all surviving), in addition to a large quantity of notes.
>
> It was easy to modify the location of the bank from Ft Leavenworth, Kansas to Salt Lake City, Utah by simply replacing the location slugs. Another change was made from Ft Leavenworth to Leavenworth City about the same time. One problem was that the locations were not part of the overall vignette. Most of these notes, the Kansas editions and the Utah editions, wound up as scrap paper utilized for printed advertising. I believe the two "bank" locations, at opposite ends of the Leavenworth/Salt Lake City Army trade route, were intended to pass the notes of the other state. The notes were all dated about the time of the Mormon War.

NUMISMATIC COMMENTS

Kansas, a territory for part of the note-issuing time, then a state, offers interesting collecting possibilities, although it was too far west and developed too late to participate in the early decades of the bank-note issuing era. Circulated notes as well as proofs are available from the legitimate banks, but all range from scarce to rare and are expensive. W.L. Ormsby's bills are fairly ornate and have mysterious histories and very interesting characteristics.

CURRENCY OF KENTUCKY

Number of banks in the Haxby *Standard Catalog:* 64.
Specialized text: Earl Hughes, *Kentucky Obsolete Notes and Scrip,* 1998.

HISTORICAL NOTES

Dominating the field of note-issuing banks in Kentucky are institutions that operated various branches, commencing alphabetically with the Bank of Ashland, which operated from the late 1850s through the

Note for $5 of the Drovers Bank, Leavenworth City, Kansas, with printed date of November 1st 1857. From a plate by W.L. Ormsby. This features perhaps the most "horsy" of all vignettes. This bank is considered to be fraudulent. Other banks for which Ormsby printed bills in Kansas Territory, and for the Drovers Bank in Salt Lake City, seem to have been either fraudulent or speculative ventures that never opened for business, or banks that opened but quickly failed.

1860s, from the city of that name but also had branches in Mayfield and Shelbyville. The Peoples Bank of Kentucky, which was in business during the same period, commenced in Bowling Green, later moved the head bank to Louisville, and had branches in Hartford and Paducah.

The Bank of the Commonwealth of Kentucky, early in the game and active in the 1820s, was headquartered in Frankfort and had branches in Bowling Green, Falmouth, Flemingsburg, Greensburg, Harrodsburg, Hartford, Lexington, Louisville, Mount Sterling, Princeton, Somerset, and Winchester. The Farmers Bank of Kentucky, operating in the 1850s and 1860s, had its head office in Frankfort but also did business in Covington, Georgetown, Henderson, Maysville, Mount Sterling, Princeton, and Somerset.

Chartered in 1806, the Bank of Kentucky, also headquartered in Frankfort, operated in Bardstown, Danville, Glasgow, Hopkinsville, Lexington, Louisville, Paris, Richmond, Russellville, Shelbyville, Springfield, Washington, and Winchester. This bank was especially prominent in its time and was central to commerce in the early years of the state. In early 1816, a report stated that it had $1,308,129.47 worth of bills in circulation.[15]

The Northern Bank of Kentucky, headquartered in Lexington, also did business in Barboursville, Covington, Glasgow, Louisville, Paris, and Richmond. The Bank of Louisville, operated from the 1830s to the 1860s, had branches in Burksville, Flemingsburg, and Paducah. The Bank of Kentucky, centered in Louisville, had branches in Bowling Green, Burksville, Columbus, Danville, Flemingsburg, Frankfort, Glasgow, Greensburg, Hopkinsville, Lexington, Maysville, Mount Sterling, and Paducah. The Commercial Bank of Kentucky, operated in Paducah in the 1850s and 1860s, had branches in Cynthiana, Harrodsburg, Lebanon, Louisville, Monticello, Newport, and Versailles. The Southern Bank of Kentucky, in Russellville, branched out to Carrolton, Hickman, Lebanon, Louisville, Owenboro, and Smithland.

The above said, the first bank in the state was established on December 6, 1802, under the name of the Kentucky Insurance Company, capitalized at $150,000, with authorization to issue paper money, through a clause not studied carefully by the legislators. On December 7, 1806, the Bank of Kentucky was chartered, the first institution with *Bank* as part of its name. This institution went into branch banking as noted above. In 1817 there were 40 new banks incorporated in the state. This was at the onset of difficult economic times, 1818 and 1819, during which there were many failures.

In 1819, a man giving his name as Hunter, but really a Mr. Morse, a graduate of Rhode Island College, was arrested in Savannah, Georgia, with hundreds of thousands of dollars' face value in $50 and $100 bills and post notes of the Newport Bank. By some devious method he had obtained these bills from Murray, Draper, Fairman & Co. in Philadelphia. Authorities dubbed him the "classical scoundrel" in view of his education.[16]

Over a period of time, many other banks and branches were established, with mixed results. Commerce was flooded with paper money. In a May 25, 1828, article, *Niles' Weekly Register* remarked on the progress in eliminating at least some worthless currency from commerce:

> In Kentucky the people of that state, relieved of the leeches, are returning to the good old fashion of paying their debts as fast as they can and, rapidly recovering from the demoralizing and ruinous effects of the miserable expedients resorted to obstruct the ordinary course of the laws—which lost to the state 100,000 inhabitants

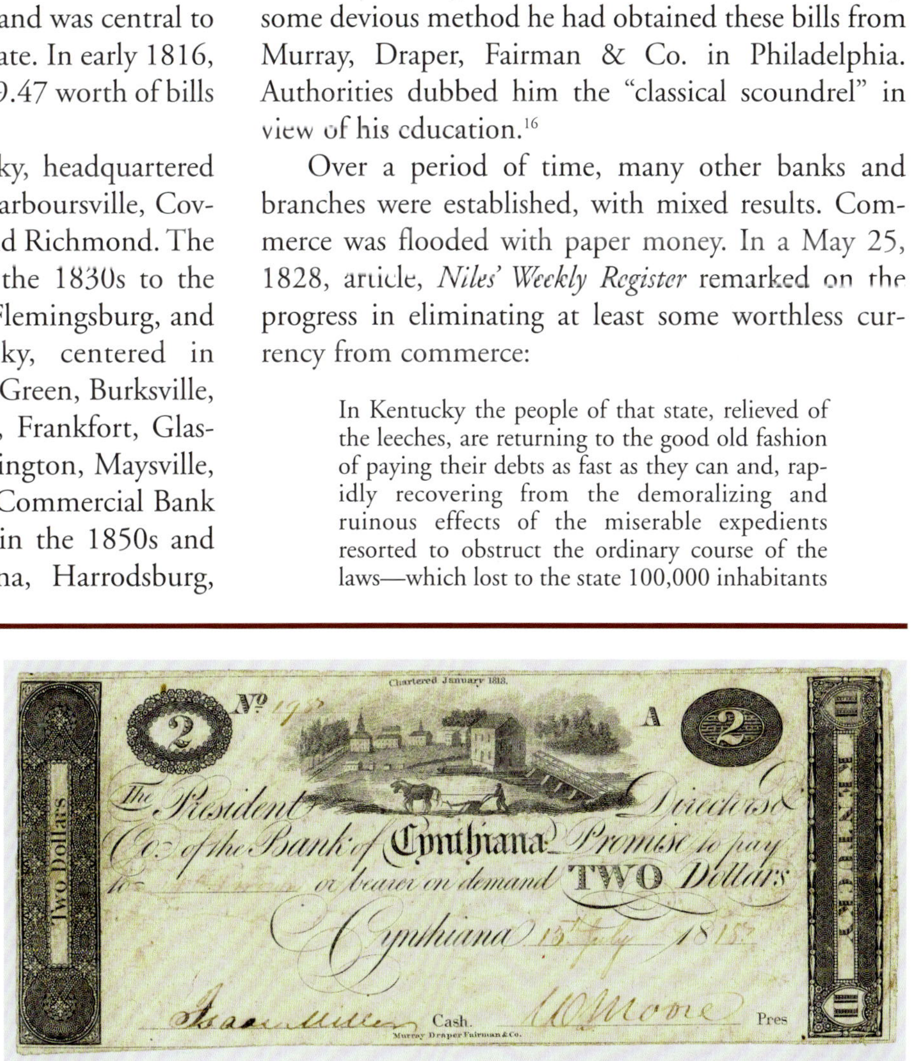

A $2 note of the Bank of Cynthiana, Kentucky, July 13, 1818, from a plate by Murray, Draper, Fairman & Co. During this decade this firm was the main supplier of bank notes to states west of Pennsylvania.

This bank seems to have operated briefly in 1818 and 1819, a time of difficult economic conditions in America. Bills were printed of the denominations of $1, $2, $3, $5, and $10.

> and many millions of wealth. Bills of the banks of Kentucky are now simple articles of trade, among men of business, like hemp or hogs—so much for so much; and every now and then large quantities are burned. There is nothing like fire to purify a currency.

Notwithstanding such commentary, the amount of paper money in commerce continued to grow. In 1830 the banks in the state had $61,000,000 in bills, a figure which soared to $149,000,000 by 1837.

For a long time the Bank of Kentucky had as its stock transfer agent in Philadelphia the Schuylkill Bank. On July 30, 1839, the agent was changed to Nicholas Biddle's Bank of the United States of Pennsylvania, later to be recognized as a star-crossed venture. After the switch it was learned that the Schuylkill bank had passed off $1,250,000 in phony stock certificates of the Bank of Kentucky. The matter was thrashed out in the courts for a long time, after which the Bank of Kentucky was awarded $1,343,000, but the victory was Pyrrhic as the defendant had assets of only $430,000 at the time.

In November 1856, *Banker's Magazine* told of the earlier days, down to 1852, then brought readers up to date:

> Since then, charters have been granted to the Farmers Bank, with $2,300,000 capital; the Commercial Bank, with $400,000; the Kentucky Trust Company, with an *unlimited* capital; and the Newport Safety Fund Bank, with $300,000 capital. Both of these institutions failed in 1854, and their notes are now selling at 50 per cent. discount; and the small notes of the latter bank at 90 per cent.
>
> With the exception of the charters of these two last banks, the legislation of Kentucky has been of a fixed character, and her circulation has ever been esteemed in the Western states as of the highest character. There are now 34 banks and branches in the state, but aggregate of whose capital is $11,730,000, and circulation about $13,300,000. In the session of 1854, it was proposed to charter six new banks, with capitals amounting to $6,100,000; but the governor having vetoed one of the bills of incorporation, the bills all failed to pass, and there for the present the matter rests.

Numismatic Comments

All of the bank branches in the Bluegrass State do not translate into a great opportunity to buy hundreds of varieties of notes in the marketplace, for as a general rule bills are quite scarce, and for many there are no surviving examples. Beyond the dizzying array of branch banks, throughout different towns and cities there were many single-office locations, many of which were active during the earlier years of the 19th century, typically using bills printed by Murray, Draper, Fairman & Co. in Philadelphia. Because many early institutions failed and their bills became worthless, they can be found without difficulty today, although the condition of these is apt to be poor, mostly from Fair to Very Good, reflecting their intense use in circulation. There were only a few stand-alone banks (those not affiliated with branches) in business in the later years.

The release of long-hidden proofs from the American Bank Note Co. paper archives in 1990 and 1991 was a boon to specialists, and many rarities and SENC bills became available. As time goes on these proofs are becoming widely dispersed, and in some future day the opportunities of the present market will be but wistful memories.

Currency of Louisiana

Number of banks in the Haxby *Standard Catalog:* 28.

Historical Notes

The first bank in Louisiana Territory, in the part of that vast expanse that was to become a state in 1812, was established in 1805 with a capital of $500,000. The Louisiana Bank, as it was called, was based in New Orleans and did business until the early 1820s. By 1815 there were three banks operating in Louisiana. The Commercial Bank, an outfit of which little is known today (and which is different from the Commercial Bank established in 1833), was set up to supply water to New Orleans, but it pursued banking and issued paper money. The Planters Bank is numismatically remembered for counterstamping cut sections of Spanish dollars in the 1810s. In 1819 the cashier of the bank, B. Blanchard, disappeared, and it was rumored that he had decamped with a large sum of money. Hurried examination of the bank's assets revealed that all was in good order. Blanchard's body later was found in the Mississippi River; he had fallen prey to thugs.

On March 14, 1818, the state proposed to enter the banking business for its own account by subscribing for $500,000 of the proposed $2,000,000 capital of the Louisiana State Bank. However, only $100,000 was eventually paid in. Headquartered in New Orleans with a branch in Baton Rouge, the bank remained in business through the Civil War and later became the State National Bank of New Orleans. However, it cannot be considered a "state bank."

On April 7, 1824, the Bank of Louisiana was capitalized at $4,000,000, with the state having half interest. The head office was in New Orleans, and five branches were required to be established. This bank also operated for a long time, later evolving into the National Bank of New Orleans. The Union Bank of Louisiana, incorporated in New Orleans for $7,000,000 in 1832, failed in 1842. The bank was financed by state bonds. Subscribers to the stock pledged mortgages as surety. A decade later another bank opened with this name and eventually became the Union National Bank.

Over a period of time, many other banks were set up in Louisiana, with New Orleans being their location. The New Orleans Canal and Banking Co., known as the Canal Bank, went into operation in 1831 and soon did an extensive business. By January 1, 1837, there were 16 banks in Louisiana doing business through 31 offices, these in addition to brokers and other businesses trading as banks and often issuing bills. The New Orleans Gas Light and Banking Co., called the "Gas Bank" in popular accounts, purchased the branch of the second Bank of the United States in 1835.

In the twilight of the Hard Times period, banking conditions precipitated anarchy in New Orleans. *Niles' National Register*, June 18, 1842, reported:

> The attempt of the banks of New Orleans to resume specie payments has proved unavailing. They resumed on the 18th and 19th of May, but an immediate depreciation of the municipality notes ensued, and on the 20th a mob destroyed several brokers' shops, but was soon quelled with the arrest of the ringleaders. In a few days, more than $600,000 was drained from them.
>
> Some disagreement amongst themselves led to distrust; a panic and a severe run ensued, which some of them maintained for several days, and finally all had to suspend. The Citizens Bank and Louisiana State Bank on the 31st ult. announced that they suspend until the 5th of December. The Consolidated Bank, the Commercial Bank, and the Canal Bank were overwhelmed on the 1st inst. The crowd was tremendous and some lives were lost. The City Bank held out until the 2d inst. but then gave in. The Mechanics and Traders bank, the Carrollton Bank, and Union Bank and the Bank of Louisiana continue to pay specie, but except the latter, they are said to have no notes out, and to be doing but little business.

In July conditions improved, and four banks in New Orleans were able to resume specie payments: the Gas Bank, the Bank of Louisiana, the Union Bank, and the Mechanics and Traders Bank. However, these banks had very few bills in circulation. Those that did saw their currency trade at deep discounts—as much as 30% to 35% for the Canal, Commercial, and Consolidated banks and up to 40% for the Citizens Bank. This change wreaked havoc on the holders of such bills who sought to use them in everyday transactions and commerce.

In the pivotal year of 1842, following difficult times and bank failures, the state enacted a law requiring banks to maintain a reserve in specie equal to one-third of its public debts, to place restrictions on its loans, and to submit to quarterly examinations, among other features. This legislation was widely regarded as a model of excellence. However, it was not foolproof. In July 1851, this advertisement appeared in various New Orleans newspapers:

> *Free Banking.* The subscriber will commence banking on his individual account at No. 107 Gravier Street, on the 26th instant, under the name and title of the "Bank of Commerce," associating others with him as soon as the existing tax laws shall be modified as to render an association of individuals for banking practicable; for which purpose arrangements have been made. No revi-

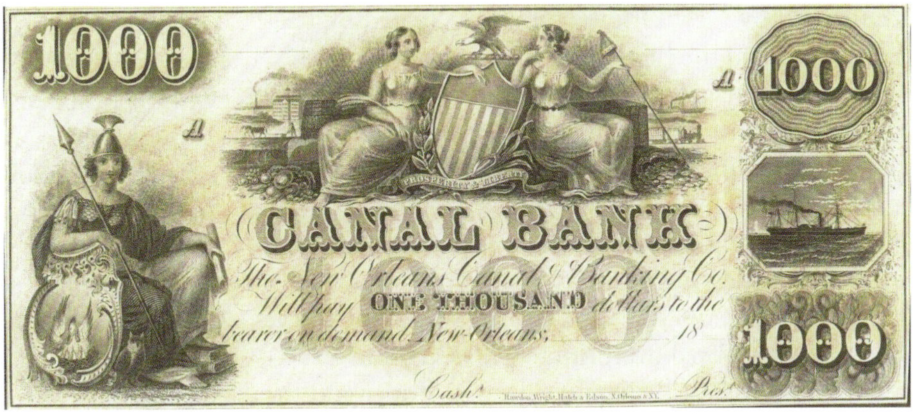

Note for $1000 of the Canal Bank, New Orleans, Louisiana, from a plate by Rawdon, Wright, Hatch & Edson. Vast quantities of unissued bills of this bank came on the numismatic market. Most were of lower denominations. The $1000 denomination is somewhat scarce for the Canal Bank, and for most banks around the country it is very rare. Nearly all known examples from various banks are either proofs (most often) or unissued remainders, as here.

The Canal Bank, also called the Canal and Banking Company, was the largest bank in New Orleans before the Civil War. In 1848 its capital was more than $3,000,000, and in 1849 it had $1,714,835 face value of bills in circulation.

> sion or enactment of other laws is necessary to give full scope to free banking. The funds of the savings bank department will be kept separate from the other concerns of the bank. Manager and trustees to be elected by the stockholders as soon as the association shall be formed.
>
> Jacob Barker. New Orleans, July 24th, 1851.

Readers of this account had no way of knowing that this was the notorious Barker who was implicated in bank frauds in New York in the 1820s. In April 1853, Louisiana enacted the Free-Banking Law, also with strict requirements. The first to organize under this law was the Bank of New Orleans. In due course Jacob Barker's Bank of Commerce opened and issued a flood of bills.

Due in large part to these well-crafted laws, during the Panic of 1857 not a single bank in Louisiana—not even the Bank of Commerce—suspended specie payments, a remarkable record. However, Barker's bank failed several years later. The Canal Bank, the largest issuer of paper money in the state, closed in the early 1860s.

During the secession and subsequent Confederate occupation of New Orleans, a period from January 26, 1861, to May 1, 1862, banks continued to operate, as they did afterward. Certain currency under the repatriation of the city bore special overprints.

Numismatic Comments

The Haxby text lists 28 different banks in the state of Louisiana, to which number many branches can be added. New Orleans was the focal point of banking, and nearly all institutions were headquartered there. Contemporary newspaper and financial accounts reveal that private banks and many other entities issued bills in New Orleans, but their nature and extent is not known today, except for those recorded by Haxby.

Louisiana notes in the numismatic marketplace are dominated by New Orleans bills, punctuated by relatively few from the branches. Large quantities of unissued bills remained from the Canal Bank of New Orleans, in particular, and were extremely plentiful on the market (including sheets) until recent times, although they remain easy enough to find. Certain bills used during the Confederate occupation form an interesting study in themselves, as do bills issued after the repatriation of New Orleans in 1862, some of the latter having special overprints such as "Forced Issue," relating to General Benjamin ("Beast") Butler and the demands he made on banks.

Certain bills of the Citizens Bank of Louisiana, in New Orleans, are bilingual and have the French word DIX in addition to the English TEN. It is said that early DIX bills, and perhaps similar bills of other institutions, were a familiar sight to river men who came down the Mississippi to the *land of the dix notes,* evolving into *land of Dixie* or *Dixieland.* This is the generally accepted origin of *Dixieland* and remains unchallenged, unless someone can come up with a use prior to the 1830s, when the banks started issuing these notes.

Many surviving Louisiana bills are from the 1850s and 1860s and have bright colors and ornate vignettes. These are relatively inexpensive to collect and yield what is perhaps an ideal numismatic situation. If you are contemplating starting a general collection of obsolete bills, it might be well to buy a dozen or so common Louisiana notes, study their characteristics and enjoy their features, then go on to other states.

Currency of Maine

Number of banks in the Haxby *Standard Catalog:* 132.
Specialized text: George W. Wait, *Maine Obsolete Paper Money and Scrip,* 1977.

Historical Notes

The first bank authorized in the Maine district of Massachusetts, in the years before that area became a separate state in 1820, was the Portland Bank, organized on June 15, 1799, and capitalized at $100,000. Its life was brief, and it closed its doors in 1808. On June 23, 1802, the Maine Bank was incorporated in the same city at $300,000, later lowered to $200,000. When its charter expired in 1813, it ceased business. The Lincoln and Kennebec Bank was chartered in the whaling port of Wiscasset in 1802, and in 1803 the Saco Bank at Pepperellboro (a town later known as Saco) was set up.

The Penobscot Bank was incorporated in 1806 and did business in Buckstown (today's Bucksport), with its office in the home of Joseph R. Folsom. Capitalized at $150,000, the bank began issuing bills printed by Jacob Perkins in Newburyport. Cashier John Shaw took care of everyday business. President John Crosby, a man of wealth, lived in Hampden, a town 15 miles to the north. Money was aplenty in Buckstown when the new bills were readily given out to applicants for discounts (loans). The local economy was stimulated, and all went well. Then the discounts became due, borrowers had difficulty repaying, and in

1810 the bank collapsed. A later investigation revealed that the bank's officers and directors had little knowledge or experience in banking.

The Embargo Act of 1807 and the Non-Intercourse Act of 1809 hit the economy of Maine hard, as ships were prohibited from trading with foreign countries. This legislation was widely perceived as unfair by coastal New Englanders, who often took steps to evade it. Many were the accounts of heavily laden ships sailing out of Maine, New Hampshire, or Massachusetts, ostensibly bound for other legal coastal ports such as Baltimore or Charleston, that were "blown off course" and were forced to land in the trading centers of the distant Caribbean!

On January 23, 1812, the General Court of Massachusetts chartered six new banks in the Maine district, these being the Bath Bank, the Cumberland Bank of Portland, the Hallowell and Augusta Bank (in Hallowell, a town adjacent to Augusta), the Kennebec Bank of Augusta (which in 1816 relocated to Hallowell), and the Saco Bank, the last a recharter. In 1813 another six banks were chartered in the state.

In 1814 the Manufacturers and Mechanics Bank of Boston crafted a scheme to send runners to the Kennebec Bank in Augusta with quantities of Kennebec Bank bills and demand instant payment in the form of coins or in bills negotiable at par in Boston. The hope was that the bank would not have sufficient funds on hand for such a large amount and would be embarrassed, after which the market value of its bills would drop for a time. The Boston bankers could then buy the depreciated currency, and, after it rebounded, could profit by turning it in. After several visits by Boston agents carrying thousands of dollars in Kennebec Bank bills, this and other regional banks published notices in newspapers giving new rules on dealing with such incidents, particularly with agents from the Manufacturers and Mechanics Bank. Boston entrepreneurs considered banks in the Maine district to be fair game for paper money manipulation. In the process of this battle, many Maine cashiers came to dislike and distrust Boston bankers, and justifiably so. Such maneuvers continued for a long time, as noted below. A similar attempt to foil Maine banks was tried in 1824.

Banking in the Maine district continued to be a challenge, for the War of 1812 took its toll on the economy, and in any event much of Maine was a desolate rural area inland from the seacoast. Money was scarce at nearly all times. On December 17, 1817, a report of banks in the district reflected information received from 12 institutions, with a total capital of \$1,846,000 (nearly half in promissory notes) and \$581,466 of currency in circulation. Nearly all of the bills were of Patent Stereotype Steel Plate type, the use of this system having been mandated by Massachusetts in 1809. Each note bore the Massachusetts address. Banks receiving them usually shipped the notes off to Boston, where through correspondent banks they were sorted and sent back to the issuers. John J. Knox in his *History of Banking* described the process:

> Prior to 1819 the redemption of bills in Boston had rested with agents of the individual banks, who both interested themselves in putting the bills in circulation and sometimes in their redemption. It was a constant source of trouble, and the utmost skill had to be used to keep these bills from being returned to the banks. Maine was so far removed from Massachusetts that it finally became necessary to collect all the Maine bank bills held by the Boston banks and send a man with a team down the shore to exchange these bills for specie. It was no uncommon sight to see the team in the inn yards with kegs filled with specie and two dogs guarding the treasure. There is no account of any attempt being made to rob this specie collector—a striking instance of the honesty of the inhabitants of Maine in the early part of this century.
>
> So great was the loss of interest in the collection of these bank bills from the remote districts, that in 1809 the leading merchants of Boston signed a paper agreeing to take no country bank bills after that date. This circular set forth in considerable detail the wrongs which they suffered in consequence of receiving these bills, and their determination to take them no longer.

Bills of the Maine district continued to be received at nominal discounts for sound institutions at various banks in Boston. Bankers and exchange brokers in Boston had to be constantly aware of the status of Maine bank notes, because the fortunes of banks there were constantly changing, no public records were available for study, and communications each way involved travel by horse-drawn coach, entailing delays.

In 1820, Maine became an independent state. At the time about 152,000 people lived there. The coastal towns included many citizens of wealth, while those who resided inland typically were poor, often living a hardscrabble existence. In its first report on banking, the new Maine Legislature reported that the capital of the Hallowell and Augusta Bank was to a large extent fictitious and composed of loans to stockholders. Despite this fact, dividends were declared in the form of more IOUs. Soon, other banks were investigated, and many irregularities were found, including false names and amounts on loan documents.

In 1831 a new law was enacted to regulate banks. This did not prevent further improprieties, but it probably diminished them somewhat. In 1833 a law provided:

> That besides the Perkins stereotype bills, it shall be lawful for any bank to issue bills of such other plates of finer engravings, superior workmanship, and greater security against counterfeiting, as may from time to time be allowed and approved by the Bank Commissioners of the State, by their certificate in writing.[17]

In 1834 some 30 banks were doing business in Maine. By that time, nearly all of the larger ones depended on the Suffolk Bank system in Boston for the exchange and redemption of their bills against deposits placed with this bank. The arrangements were clumsy, and the Maine banks filed protests urging legislative action to smooth the system. In 1835, when $2,380,000 worth of bills were suddenly in circulation (an increase of close to $1,700,000 from the 1834 figure), the system became particularly onerous. A report made to the governor of Maine on January 25, 1837, showed that by that time only 14 of the 55 reporting banks did business with Suffolk. This had the result of keeping most banks' bills in circulation in and around the towns where they were issued, but seldom beyond that, where they were apt to trade at deep discounts. This system worked well in remote areas, as bills of local banks were trusted, exchanged at par, and everyone was satisfied.

An act passed in 1835 prohibited the issuance of bank bills less than $5. This change resulted in notes flooding into the state from elsewhere to fill the gap. The next year the legislature sought to ban odd denominations and made illegal any bills from $6 to $9 and from $11 to $19, not that such were ever popular in states where they were legal.

At the onset of the Panic of 1837 in May of that year, all 55 Maine banks suspended specie payments. In the last six months of the year, the average circulation of banks in the state was $1,414,564, with an average of $559,433 passing through the Suffolk Bank system *each month,* even though most smaller banks were not members. These figures are dramatic and indicate that on an annualized basis, the circulation of Maine banks turned over about four times. No wonder bills became so worn and ragged. At that time most continued to be of the Patent Stereotype Steel Plate type, now usually of the improved style with small vignettes. The depression took its toll, and in 1841 only 42 banks were active, some of them just marginally so.

The *Report of the Bank Commissioners* for 1837 described many illegalities, including giving loans to stockholders before 50% of the capital stock was raised, with the Damariscotta Bank, Frontier Bank, Lime Rock Bank, Neguemkeag Bank, St. Croix Bank, and the Bank of Westbrook being cited in this regard. In other instances, banks kept no records of meetings held by the directors or with the stockholders. In some banks the cashier conducted business as he pleased, without consulting the directors or anyone else.[18] As is seen from studying banks in other states, such practices were hardly unique to Maine.

On August 30, 1837, this note appeared in a New York financial journal:

> The *Portland Argus* states that the managers of the Oxford County Bank, Maine, have commenced the issue of notes. This bank was chartered in 1836, but was not organized within the time prescribed by law and consequently has no legal existence. The notes therefore are probably valueless. It is stated in the *Boston Atlas* that they are not intended for circulation in Maine, but are manufactured for New York and the southern market.[19]

Among the smaller frauds in Maine banking is a scheme that took place in 1841. Founded in 1833, the Citizens Bank of Augusta was well regarded. By 1840, business was very slow, loans were small, little currency was in circulation, and the directors considered liquidating it. Then on November 25 of that year, the directors received a letter from S.G. Langdon, a Hartford, Connecticut, entrepreneur, offering to buy the bank outright. The terms were attractive, and the transfer was made on January 23, 1841. The former cashier was given about $15,000 to redeem the outstanding bills and pay depositors.

Immediately, Langdon set himself up as cashier and began issuing paper money. The Suffolk Bank declined to receive it, and general suspicion was aroused. The governor looked into the matter, and on March 29 the bank's charter was revoked. By that time about $6,850 in bills had been paid out. Afterward, Langdon departed for an unknown place, taking with him $28,500 in new bills, many if not most of which he put into circulation.[20] Such currency, in denominations up to $100 and signed by Langdon, is readily collectible today.

In 1840 and 1841, the Globe Bank of Bangor became involved in a paper money scheme through the machinations of one of its directors, Benjamin Wiggin. An alliance was made with J.M. and H.M. True and their associates, currency traders and speculators in New York, who in essence took over the bank's ownership. Large quantities of bills were sold at discounts and sent to the West, where they were used to buy goods from unsuspecting persons. Learning of the arrangement, the state legislature revoked the bank's charter. The Trues, in cahoots with confederates in western New York state, also gained control of the Frankfort Bank, which issued large amounts of worthless bills and failed in 1841. New York speculators also wrecked the Stillwater Canal Bank of Orono.

The *Annual Report of the Bank Commissioners of the State of Maine* for 1841 showed 42 banks active, reflective of the toll taken by the panic. The charters of the Citizens, Frankfort, and Globe banks had been revoked, and the charters of two more, the Lafayette and Washington County banks, had been surrendered. A wide trail of worthless bills was left behind, mostly the work of crooks and currency speculators, not from unwise legal practices or economic conditions.

In 1846 a banking law for the first time regulated the paper money that could be paid out, limiting it in essence to 50% of capital stock paid in. The same law extended the charters of present banks as well as those yet to be formed, to October 1, 1857, provided that a given bank accept this rule in writing.

Maine banks continued to offer opportunities for scheming individuals in Boston, New York, and elsewhere. Over a period of time, more than a half dozen institutions were owned or controlled by out-of-staters, although state residents were nominally listed as directors. Most such banks collapsed, leaving quantities of worthless paper in circulation. There was not much Maine authorities could do to either prevent such frauds or prosecute those involved if they lived in distant states.

Economic necessity to maintain the value of their bills drew all but two banks in the state to sign up with the Suffolk system by 1848, although the arrangement was still widely disliked. The 1852 *Annual Report of the Bank Commissioners of the State of Maine* included this information:

> Since our last annual report, five new banks, with an aggregate capital of $300,000, have gone into operation; and the sixth, the City Bank at Bangor, with a capital of $50,000, was to commence discounting in a few days, when we made our examination at that place. The old banks have added to their capital, in the same period, $219,350, making the increase for the year, $569,350, and the sum total of the banking capital of the State, (including a small amount not yet paid in by the new banks, which have commenced business) $4,470,000. The circulation has increased within the year $1,078,488, and is now $1,772,431 larger than at the time of its highest inflation in 1835, and $2,656,005 larger than at its lowest depression in 1843.
>
> There has been an increase of $270,147.63 in the specie, which now, exclusive of permanent deposits in the Suffolk Bank, amounts to $836,504 89, a sum greater by $650,455 20 than in the Maine banks in 1835. The Commissioners would be recreant to their trust should they withhold their deep conviction that no more banks are at present required. Including the Peoples Bank at Damariscotta, 13 new banks have gone into operation within the last two years. In the same time the capital stock has been increased $1,222,000; the circulation in the same time has been increased $1,507,473, or nearly sixty percent of the whole circulation of 1850; and the present loans exceed $8,000,000.
>
> If anything can be learned from the experience of the past, the time is not far distant when a heavy percent of this circulation must be sent home to the banks from which it issued, and the present large loans diminished at the very moment when the customers of the banks stand most in need of their accommodation. To multiply bank charters, thereby increasing to a greater extent the indebtedness of the business community, can only tend to increase the embarrassments and disasters in business, which no contingency can prevent when the bubble is fully blown. It may be found that at some very few points in the state the people are so remote from all bank facilities that an additional bank or two may add to their business and convenience; but they will be required, so few in number, and small in capital, as not materially to vary the total amount of bank capital in the state.

The commissioners were a conservative lot, and their policies shepherded state banks through the rest of the decade with only a handful of problems. Their *Report* for 1856 included these remarks pertaining to paper money:

> Every bank which is obliged, in order to retain a fair circulation, to resort to undue means, by way of exchanging its own for other bills, inflicts a serious injury upon general credit, and if it cannot acquire sufficient circulation and standing by its regular discounts and a fair business, it may well be doubted whether its continued existence is having a salutary effect on either the currency or the community.
>
> Banks of this character are eventually but too apt to seek a wider field through the agency of brokers in the far West, or else are induced by

tempting promises to transfer to individuals residing beyond the jurisdiction of our state, and of whose responsibility they cannot be certainly assured, the control of a majority of their stock, and that upon conditions wholly unauthorized by their charters.

We made inquiry of each bank as to the custody of the plates and dies from which its notes are engraved, and found that 15 only had them in their own possession. The remaining 62 permit theirs to be in the keeping of the respective engravers, whose places of business are in Boston, New York, and Philadelphia. We required each bank to furnish us with the number of bills received by them, and where a *bill register* was kept; this was easily ascertained; but all do not keep this important record.

In the matter of the bill-plates, the number printed, signed and issued, the people have a direct interest, as well as the banks, and we know of no better guardian than the state or one of its departments, to have the custody of the several plates, and that suitable legislation should regulate the issue of every bill. . . . [21]

It will be seen that the Ship Builders Bank ordered $356,000. If a bank finds itself in trouble, or if its officers are disposed to do wrong, it has the power, or may be tempted to pledge its own bills, or put them afloat in the community, in order to raise funds to meet its circulation. No well-conducted bank would be guilty of this, of course, but every bank should be deprived of the temptation as far as possible.

If a package of unsigned bills should be abstracted from the vault, skillful penmanship would soon make them current until information of the fact was known. If all the bills of each bank should hereafter be registered, countersigned and delivered at the office of the State Treasury Department, by some officer of state, we fully believe that it would afford the best protection which can be devised, and in a great degree remedy the evils to which we have alluded. . . .

Regarding the aforementioned Ship Builders Bank, this was established in Rockland in March 1853 with a capital of $100,000. Its doors opened on June 7th, at which time it began distributing paper money ordered from the New England Bank Note Co. (50% owned by Rawdon, Wright, Hatch & Edson). Problems arose, and the bank stopped redeeming its bills. All seemed fine, however, as the state bank commissioners found assets of $82,439 on hand, with liabilities of $33,015, leaving a surplus of $49,424.

It soon developed that the cashier, W.L. Pitts, in collusion with president H.C. Lowell, had falsified the records, and instead of issuing paper money for slightly less than its capital, per sound banking practices, it had illegally ordered $356,000 in bills. The New England Bank Note Co., which had easy access to public records showing the $100,000 capitalization, filled the request, normal practice notwithstanding various proclamations that the customers were carefully checked, etc. Assets of the Ship Builders Bank were found to be just $4,068. Criminal indictments were brought against the officers.

In 1856 the number of state banks peaked at 77, the number given in the *Annual Report of the Bank Commissioners*. In that year the Exchange and Grocers banks of Bangor and the Hancock Bank of Ellsworth were closed by court injunctions and went into liquidation. The Canton Bank of China was placed into the hands of receivers, who found it to be a phony venture set up to issue paper money. In 1857 the New England Bank of Fairmount issued paper money, or at least those who received the bills, beautifully printed by Rawdon, Wright, Hatch & Edson, thought it did. There was no such bank.

Maine passed through the Panic of 1857 without much difficulty, with just three banks unable to maintain their solvency. In that year the charters of solvent banks were appropriately extended. In 1858 the Sanford Bank (a new name in 1857 for the Mousam River Bank), capitalized at $50,000, ran short of capital funds by $37,000, a remarkable sum. The stockholders made up the deficiency in good funds (the details of which are given in a later paragraph), and it was allowed to reopen. Bank commissioners found that:

> All the bills issued by the Mousam River Bank and the Sanford Bank appeared by the records to have been destroyed, except the amount of $8,972, of which sum $7,214 were in the bank, leaving bills in circulation to the amount of $1,758, with a sufficient amount in specie on hand to redeem them on presentation. All the blank bills having been destroyed, new bills have been ordered. In the resumption of its business this bank will, for a time, have to struggle against prejudices growing out of its former mismanagement, which will only be overcome by placing it under the control of an honest, wise, and safe directory, and a full statement of its condition in the outset; all of which the commissioners were assured would be done.[22]

The bank reopened in 1860 with a generous supply of currency printed by the American Bank Note Co. from old Toppan, Carpenter, Casilear & Co. plates. Soon, these bills, with colorful overprints, were common in circulation in the southeastern part of Maine. However, suspicions were aroused, the bank was investigated, and on May 17, 1861, it was closed under an injunction. Later court documents revealed this information:

> All the defendants who have answered allege that the Mousam River Bank (the name of which was

> afterward changed to the Sanford Bank) had lost 75% of its capital; in other words, that its stock had been reduced in value from $50 to $12.50 per share. It was on account of such loss that an injunction was issued against the bank Nov. 13, 1857 and continued in force until Aug. 29, 1859.
>
> It however appears that about August 29, 1859, some of the defendants, being possessed of a speculative turn of mind and disposed to better their fortunes by a new system of banking, conceived a plan by which to resuscitate the bank and carry their purposes into effect. Accordingly they undertook to make new stock, or to "make the stock good" as it is expressed; or more accurately speaking, make it appear to be so. This had to be done to remove the injunction resting upon the bank.
>
> [Directors] Thompson, Emery, Mills, Vose, and Hill put their heads together in council to do this. Thompson undertook to carry $7,500, Emery $4,000, Mills $7,000 to $10,000, Vose $8,500, and Hill nearly $9,000. They proposed to pay in on the "old stock," so called, *i.e.,* their own shares and of such other stockholders as would surrender them, 75% and thus make the original capital whole. . . .
>
> The parties contemplating the resuscitation of the bank provided themselves with funds, carried the money before Judge Goodnow on August 29, 1859, and made it appear to him that they had paid in on the "old stock" $37,500, being the amount necessary to make up the 75% loss. Having thus obtained a dissolution of the injunction, on their return they took the money immediately from the bank, leaving in place of it their own checks, and then let the bank sleep until May, 1860, because, as Emery expresses it, "they were not ready to run the notes through the bank until then."

The receivers found hardly any assets, the bank capital was mostly worthless IOUs, and the public was left with a large supply of bills having no value. The saga of this bank is interesting in that over a period of years from the mid-1850s until 1861, it was variously described as solvent and fraudulent, with no particular conclusion as to its real situation. Early notes were printed by W.L. Ormsby when the institution was known as the Mousam River Bank.

The Lincoln County Bank of Wiscasset was chartered on March 8, 1861, with $50,000 authorized capital. Its organizers promptly ordered a large quantity of paper money from the American Bank Note Company and put it into circulation. However, when a holder of $3,000 in bills presented them for redemption at the bank's office, he was told that the only exchange would be for a draft of uncertain value on a Boston Bank. The whole operation was fraudulent, as the capital stock was never paid in.[23]

By the time the National Banking Act was passed in 1863, there were 69 banks in business in Maine with a total of $6,019,156 in circulation. Most of the stronger ones evolved into National Banks. After July 1, 1866, when it became illegal to keep using state bank notes without paying a transaction tax of 10%, at least one institution, the Veazie Bank in Bangor, blissfully ignored the regulation but was not prosecuted.

For some years the state law had mandated that all redeemed bills be burned in the presence of a justice of the peace, with the directors in attendance. Each director violating this order was subject to a $500 fine. The law had unfortunate *numismatic* consequences, as redeemed bills of sound Maine banks are for the most part very rare today.

NUMISMATIC COMMENTS

Collecting the currency of banks in Maine forms an interesting challenge. As Maine was a district of Mass-

A $3 note of the Richmond (Maine) Bank, May 1, 1854, by Toppan, Carpenter, Casilear & Co., New York and Philadelphia. While this bill is in low grade, it is an ultra-rarity, and many specialists have never *seen* one, let alone owned an example!

The Richmond Bank was one of eight banks chartered in Maine in 1852, each with a capital of $50,000. The Richmond Bank soon raised it to $75,000. On December 31, 1864, the stockholders voted to close the bank and to reorganize as the First National Bank of Richmond, charter 662. This was done, but with a new cashier and president, unusual in such transitions. Bills of the old Richmond Bank, which by then had totaled $155,000 over a period of years (with circulation below the capital of the bank at any given time), were called in. By 1867 only $650 remained unaccounted for.

achusetts prior to achieving statehood in 1820, early bills from that area are imprinted with the Massachusetts name. Interestingly, nearly all banks that were active before 1820 and used Massachusetts imprints failed by 1820, so the prospect of collecting the exact same bank with both Massachusetts and Maine imprints is small. Early Massachusetts-Maine bills are typically of the Patent Stereotype Steel Plate format. Bills of 1809 and earlier from hand-engraved copper plates exist, but these are especially rare.

Into the 1820s and beyond, Patent Stereotype Steel Plate (PSSP) bills remained popular, modified in due course by adding vignettes. Because these slug-plate notes were used by multiple banks in Maine and also by other institutions around the country as far west as Michigan, when some banks failed, the notes of the distressed institutions became counterfeiters' delights. The identifying bank name and location slugs were bleached out, and names of other banks were inserted. Some of these are so well done that even experts have difficulty in telling them apart. Genuine notes of the PSSP format can be rather boring, a situation also confronting specialists in New Hampshire and, in particular, Massachusetts bills. However, they are what they are, and if a measure of history is added, many PSSP bills can be downright exciting to own.

Maine bills of the 1850s and early 1860s were made by the leading manufacturers in Boston, New York, and Philadelphia and display the usual attractive vignettes, with colored overprints on many. Thanks to the disposal of the American Bank Note Company printed archives through Christie's in 1990 and 1991 along with assorted distributions elsewhere, plus the making of modern proprietary proofs, proof impressions of certain banks are fairly available today. The Santa Claus bills of the Bucksport Bank are a prime illustration. As a specialist in Maine notes myself, I have been thrilled with the purchase opportunities offered for these single proofs and sheets. However, as time passes these become ever more widely distributed, and they are not as often seen now as they were in the 1990s, save when specialized collections come on the market. Especially remarkable are the Herbert and Martha Schingoethe offerings (R.M. Smythe & Co.) and the Maine collection formed by Norm Pullen and offered by Currency Auctions of America in January 2003.

As a general rule, Maine currency from all eras falls into two distinct categories: *quite common,* these being notes that are from failed banks (of which Maine had a particularly large number) or remainders, and *quite rare,* this being true of issues of the 1850s and 1860s in particular, from sound banks that redeemed them for face value. As is true for the bills of any state, the enjoyment and interest of owning them can be enhanced by learning the history of the issuing banks.

Currency of Maryland

Number of banks in the Haxby *Standard Catalog:* 82.
Specialized text: Denwood Kelly, Armand Shank Jr., and Thomas Gordon, *Banking in Maryland: A Catalogue of Maryland Paper Money 1790–1865,* 1998.

Historical Notes

The Bank of Maryland, capitalized at $300,000, was the first such institution in the state. At the time the economy was strong, and the port of Baltimore had excellent demand for food and other exports. In 1792 a branch of the Bank of the United States was opened, and in 1793 the state legislature chartered the Bank of Columbia, intended to operate in the District of Columbia when it was ready. During the next decade the demand for export goods remained strong, but the two Baltimore banks could not meet the demand for discounted paper (providing loans to merchants). Accordingly, much trade went to other ports, particularly Philadelphia.

The Union Bank of Maryland, which had filed its articles of association on February 24, 1804, opened for business the following June, although as yet it was unchartered. The founders declared they would continue in banking until 1825 unless a charter was secured to permit longer operation. In Annapolis the Farmers Bank of Maryland was organized in August 1804, with a branch in Easton. Another branch was set up in Frederick in 1807. With an address in Charlestown, a community planned but not yet built, the Fishermans Bank of Charlestown was formed in 1804, capitalized at $1,000,000, with a branch at Turkey Point. A charter was sought but never granted. The Haxby text lists currency from both offices of this bank, observing that "the denominations and designs are unknown."

The Mechanics Bank was chartered in Baltimore in 1806, and others soon followed, mostly located outside Baltimore. Some of these were chartered, and others simply did business by what they considered to be a common-law right. The last option was restricted slightly in 1817 by action of the legislature. Individuals and other entities were allowed to issue paper money, so long as they followed the rules required of chartered banks, a policy that remained in effect until 1842. In the absence of official charters, the stories of some of the early banks of this state will probably remain largely unknown.

Meanwhile, the legislature mandated that all official banks in the state be rechartered in 1815. In 1813 this law was amended by an act "to incorporate a company to make a turnpike road leading to Cumberland, and for the extension of the charters of the several banks in this state, and for other purposes." Through this move, banks agreeing to be rechartered had to subscribe for stock to build the Cumberland Road to the west and fund schools, at which time their charters would be extended to November 1, 1835. Such unrelated add-ons to bank charters were used in a few other states, Connecticut being an example.

The War of 1812 brought action to Maryland. British troops landed in 1814 and roved through the countryside, burning federal buildings in adjacent Washington, D.C. The enemy fleet approached Baltimore but did not secure a foothold. Banks in the state continued operation during the conflict, but in 1814 they had to suspend specie payments, as did many in other states. In Baltimore specie payments were resumed on February 20, 1817.

The Susquehanna Bridge and Bank Company of Port Deposit was chartered in 1814 with a capital authorized at $250,000.[24] In 1817 it had difficulty redeeming is paper money, of which situation Hezekiah Niles took proper notice in his *Register.* This fact prompted the president of the company to write to Niles in January 1818 to suggest that he be more gentle in his remarks, to "spare an institution which has effect such a splendid improvement as the bridge of the Susquehanna River." Niles stood by his earlier comments.[25] This was not the last word on the subject, for the following item was printed on July 11, 1818:

> *Bank-note Manufacturers.* Letter to the editor of the *Weekly Register,* dated "now in Gettysburg," July 2, 1818, from a former subscriber to the paper:
>
> Dear Sir: I took the within yesterday at par, which I hope will be good in Baltimore, let me hear from you upon receiving it. I received it for a debt of one dollar, and gave Baltimore paper in change. The balance due, I will send to you, if not shortly in Baltimore. Yours—G.N.
>
> Reply: Baltimore, July 6, 1818. Sir: I received your favor of the 2d inst. inclosing a piece of paper curiously marked with various letters and figures, purporting to be issued by the "Susquehanna Bridge and Bank Company of Maryland," for five dollars, and said to be redeemable at Baltimore. The amount of the debt that was due to you, is exactly equal to the discount payable on this bill to reduce it to "Baltimore paper," and I sincerely congratulate you that no more is lost than the whole sum for which you changed it!!—this is lucky, as counterfeited notes and notes-counterfeit go at this time! . . .
>
> I sincerely regret that justice compels me to speak thus of the institution as a "bridge" company, for it has effected a splendid national improvement, to which, however, it unnaturally associated a bank; and, by putting upon the notes "redeemable at Baltimore," has deceived many. Yours respectfully, H. Niles

The bridge company and bank combination suspended the same year. However, in 1824 it revived, changed its name to the Susquehanna Bank, and issued more currency. This lasted until 1834, when it failed to the extent that it had $328,359 in bills in circulation, but only 97¢ in specie![26]

Economic times were difficult in 1818 and 1819, not only for the Susquehanna outfit, but also for just about every other financial enterprise in the state. The situation was made even worse by the reckless actions of the Baltimore branch of the second Bank of the United States. Operations of that office were of concern, and national newspapers carried many accounts. The office was reorganized, and in the early summer of 1819 new officers were installed, including Robert Gilmor, father of Robert Gilmor Jr. (perhaps America's most ardent numismatist of the era).

By 1820, one Baltimore bank and nine at other locations were insolvent, and in that year eight other banks notified the legislature that they intended to close. All banks experienced hardships, and those that remained open suffered from losses on credit unwisely granted in happier times and from inability to collect on the promissory notes given back to the bank in exchange for capital stock. The era was perhaps epitomized by Baltimore's City Bank, in the words of historian John Jay Knox, drawn from extensive accounts in *Niles' Weekly Register:*

> The only failure which occurred in Baltimore at this time was that of the City Bank, which failed in 1819. Some account of its affairs will illustrate the extreme form of reckless banking.
>
> The cashier had entire control of the concern, and ran it according to his own ideas. The causes of loss were mainly negligence and embezzlement. Many accounts, especially the largest ones, were not posted up; nearly every one was incorrectly kept; in some cases no account at all was on the books. Individual accounts amounting to hundreds of thousands of dollars were not set-

> tled for three or more years in some cases. Under such careless supervision embezzlement was easy.
>
> All the officers and clerks (except one) had received large discounts; the directors also received discounts without proper security. The overdrafts amounted to $426,000. The immediate occasion of the failure was a call upon it by the branch of the Bank of the United States at Baltimore, which it could not meet. A run upon it was the result.

In the wreckage, among the assets of the City Bank were IOUs from the cashier for $166,546 and those to a friend of his for $185,382. The liquidation of the bank extended for two decades, until 1840. Although certain officers were found to have embezzled funds, they were never brought to justice.

Of necessity, because coins were often scarce, scrip and small-denomination bills were widely used in commerce. By fiat the Maryland Legislature decreed the elimination of small bills in the hope that coins would magically reappear. This item is from *Niles' Weekly Register* (published in Baltimore by anti-paper money editor Hezekiah Niles), February 24, 1821:

> *Small Notes.* The legislature of Maryland, at the late session, passed a very severe law against the circulation of bank notes of a less denomination than of five dollars, or of any denomination between five and ten, by the banks within the state; and imposed a penalty of five dollars on any person who shall pass such notes of banks not chartered by this state, after the first day of June next. So, we shall get rid of an amazing quantity of filthy rags.

Silver coins became available in quantity in the 1820s in Maryland and elsewhere, but gold coins were not seen again until the late summer of 1834. Banks in Maryland, loosely regulated, were generally profitable during this period, in step with the American economy. A few problems occurred here and there, capped by three failures in the state in 1834. The Bank of Maryland was the most sensational and is discussed in chapter 2. In the same era, the Commercial Bank of Millington, chartered in 1832, went down in 1836, but not before its wily president moved certain assets to a new bank he formed in Hagerstown (an account of this bank is given in chapter 14). These and other incidents precipitated new banking laws in 1835, 1836, and 1842 that strengthened the system.

On March 12, 1837, banks of Baltimore suspended payments during the first concussion of the Panic of 1837. However, most banks maintained their assets and awaited better times. Then came a crisis in 1839, when public works and other projects slowed, and the state treasury bordered on insolvency. During the panic several more banks closed, including the Citizens Bank and Franklin Bank in Baltimore.

Finally, in 1844 general prosperity returned to most of America. In that year the legislature officially permitted *savings* banks to issue notes, a unique privilege among the states, although various private institutions in the savings and loan business had issued bills for a long time. In the ensuing years of growth, many banks in the state were short of the capital needed to service good loans. Many expanded their capitalization with permission of the legislature. By this time a number of non-bank companies, including the Chesapeake and Ohio Canal and Baltimore and Ohio Railroad, had issued large quantities of paper money.

The currency-issuing banking house of J.I. Cohen, Jr., & Brothers was conducted in a two-story Greek revival–style building at the northeast corner of Baltimore and Calvert streets, in premises later occupied by Josiah Lee & Co., also a banking house. Among the principals was none other than Colonel Mendes I. Cohen, collector and antiquarian extraordinaire, who had interests in art, rare coins, Egyptian relics, ancient artifacts, armor, and more. As a teenager he aided in the defense of Baltimore during the bombardment of Fort McHenry (of "rockets' red glare" fame) in the War of 1812. Numismatically, Cohen is remembered as the owner of several thousand bright Uncirculated 1773 Virginia half pennies (the "Cohen hoard") and the owner of a rare 1804 silver dollar, among other things. From October 25 to October 29, 1875, his memorable coin collection was sold in, shall we say, an *unmemorable* catalog prepared by Edward D. Cogan. The event seems to have been a financial disappointment to all concerned.

In the spring of 1834, the Bank of Salisbury failed. Its charter remained in effect and was purchased by speculators in New York City, who in 1848 commenced issuing a flood of paper money eagerly supplied by the partners of the engraving firm of Danforth & Hufty. The revived bank had not a penny of financial backing. The fraud collapsed in the last week of September 1851.[27]

Up to the early 1850s, the state had discouraged the issuance of bills of less than $5. Now, with silver coins absent from circulation due to the rising price of that metal on international markets, Maryland banks issued many smaller notes. In May 1852, the legislature officially forbade the issuance of such bills after

March 1853 and also decreed that no bills of banks located outside of the state could be received or paid out, under penalty of $5 per offense. This was an echo of a law passed three decades earlier. By summer the Coinage Act of February 21, 1853, which lowered the authorized weight in silver coins excepting the dollar, resulted in half dimes, dimes, quarters, and half dollars being seen in quantity once again.

In 1853 the General Banking Law contained few new concepts but was mainly a condensing and modification of existing regulations. The Panic of 1857 and its lingering effects resulted in the failure of the Mineral Bank of Cumberland on October 5, 1857, and the Cumberland City Bank on November 26, 1858. The latter had been chartered for just a few months, only since May, but had managed to distribute a lot of paper money. Remarkably, the bank was revived in 1862, but it sputtered out again a short time later. On balance the banks of Maryland conducted their affairs well from the 1840s through the Civil War, in which latter time many converted to become National Banks.

Numismatic Comments

With more than 80 banks issuing paper money from the 1790s to the 1860s, the bills of Maryland offer an interesting prospect. This state is one of just a few that allowed *savings* banks to issue currency. There were enough insolvent, irregular, and otherwise unfortunate banks that issued notes that bills of these institutions are quite plentiful today. Examples include the star-crossed Bank of Maryland, which failed and in 1835 precipitated a public riot, the Susquehanna Bridge and Bank Co. of Port Deposit, and others. In addition, certain banks that received bills but did not issue them, or redeemed but did not destroy them, provided supplies for a later generation of collectors.

The notes of Maryland are nicely described in the text by Kelly, Shank, and Gordon, which incorporates much in the way of bank history as well as descriptions of individual notes. Although it does not treat the identities of specific bank officers, otherwise it is quite thorough and includes circulation impressions as well as proofs, each attributed by a unique numbering system.

With relatively little effort, a nice representation of dozens of different bills can be acquired across quite a few different Maryland banks. However, as might be expected, there are some issues that are rare and seldom seen, this being particularly true of early varieties. Designs vary from rather simple lettering and rudimentary vignettes—for early issues—through the evolution of the use of larger vignettes and printing techniques, to the 1850s and 1860s, the last often having colorful overprints. Notes were supplied by the usual engravers and printers, mostly in Philadelphia and New York. Proof notes of this state remain scarce as the state of Maryland was underrepresented in the 1990 and 1991 ABNCo archives offerings.

Currency of Massachusetts

Number of banks in the Haxby *Standard Catalog:* 286.

Historical Notes

This state was an early entry in American banking, with the Massachusetts Bank chartered on February 7, 1784, followed in 1792 by the Union Bank, and in time by others. By the early 19th century, the banking profession was thriving, with Boston maintaining its position as the center of commerce in New England. In June 1805, there were 16 authorized banks in business in the state, with a capital of $5,760,000 (of which $5,460,000 had been paid in).

In Newburyport, Jacob Perkins perfected his innovations in bank-note plates and printing. After July 1809, all chartered banks in the state were required to

Note for $3 of the Somerset and Worcester Savings Bank, Salisbury, Maryland, November 1, 1861, from a plate by the American Bank Note Co. The vignettes include a blacksmith adjusting a wheel on an upside-down wheelbarrow and a girl blowing on a dandelion gone to seed. This bank was chartered on February 27, 1857, and continued in operation to the early 1860s. Later, large quantities of remainder notes were sold into the collectors' market.

use his Patent Stereotype Steel Plate (PSSP), as the legislators were convinced this would put an end to counterfeiting. It did not, but use of the PSSP continued for years afterward. The Berkshire Bank of Pittsfield and the Northampton Bank, both controlled by the scheming Andrew Dexter Jr. (of Farmers Exchange Bank of Gloucester, Rhode Island, infamy), were both good customers of Perkins. These two banks failed. Upon examination, one bank was found to have $30 to $40 in its vaults, and the other absolutely nothing.

Before and during the War of 1812, the despised Embargo Act, the Non-Intercourse Act, and the conflict itself caused hardships for all New England ports and, consequently, the banks in port towns. This difficulty was strongly felt in Boston, the most important commercial center of the region. To raise specie to provide for note redemption, bills circulating from Vermont, New York, and other states were shipped to New York City or other clearing centers to be redeemed. By 1814 hardly any other than New England bills were in circulation in Massachusetts.[28]

In August 1816, the Dedham Bank issued a quantity of bills payable at the Middletown Bank, a venerable (established in 1795) institution in the Connecticut town of the same name. This action prompted the Massachusetts Legislature to pass a law prohibiting currency from being payable at any other place, unless the bills were also redeemable at the office of the issuing bank.

Banking regulations in the state were lax. By January 1, 1825, six chartered banks had failed (Nantucket, Merrimack, Essex, Northampton, Bedford, and Berkshire), and three others never opened, out of 49 chartered. In 1819 the Farmers Bank of Belchertown exploded (the term generally used). Its notes, of the PSSP type, became worthless. Quantities were bought up at pennies on the dollar by speculators, who dissolved the ink in certain portions and overprinted the names and addresses of other banks, including the Globe Bank and the American Bank in Boston.[29] In November 1832, a Mr. George Vezey was arrested and charged with passing PSSP-style counterfeit bills of the Franklin Bank of Boston. Bills of this type were very easy to alter or counterfeit, but in Massachusetts the banks kept up a code of silence about this deficiency lest the public distrust their genuine notes.

By early 1837, long-simmering problems among state banks caused special concern. The usury laws of Massachusetts (which were to remain in effect for decades afterward) prompted a flight of bank capital to New York (in particular) and other states, where loans could be made much more profitably, similar to the situation in Connecticut. Separately, the legislature set about investigating several new banks that had been chartered in 1836, but whose operations seemed questionable: the Chelsea, Kilby, Middling Interest, and Lafayette banks. The bank cashiers must have presented documents that satisfied the examiners, for all were allowed to continue business. However, each of these banks closed its doors in the next few years, with losses to the holders of their currency. The Chelsea Bank folded on April 12, 1837, with just $36.71 in cash available to redeem more than $110,000 of its bills![30]

Officially inaugurating the Hard Times era, New York City banks suspended specie payments on May 10, 1837. The next day, Boston bankers met in Faneuil Hall and reluctantly agreed to do the same thing. On May 12, the suspension took effect. Almost immediately, gold and silver coins became worth a premium of 10% to 13%. In July the Franklin and Lafayette banks in Boston, both large issuers of bills, collapsed.

Many solvent banks took the opportunity to vastly increase their currency, because in the absence of gold and silver coins at par in circulation such bills were likely to stay in the channels of commerce and not be redeemed. In any event, they could only be redeemed for other bank bills. As Massachusetts banks were forbidden to issue bills for less than $1, such odd denominations as $1.25, $1.50, and $1.75 immediately became popular and served well in commerce. These were generally of the PSSP style with several small inserted vignettes. Terry, Pelton & Co., of Boston and Providence, issued bills closely resembling the PSSP format.

On September 1, 1837, the *New York Journal of Commerce* ran this piece:

> Banks have been more freely incorporated in Massachusetts than in any other state, if we except Rhode Island. Charters have been given so freely that the necessity of getting them was but a form, for they have been granted whenever asked under circumstances which gave any tolerable warrant for the grant. Charters have been granted until chartered monopolies have been brought upon the ground of free trade; for the charters are so numerous that anybody can have one.
>
> The business has in fact been overdone, and free trade will probably cause a considerable number of the charters to be given up, and the capitals divided. So there will be charters to be had gratis. We know that a considerable number of the Massachusetts banks are seriously considering the question of winding up their affairs. . . .

The large and important Lafayette Bank folded in 1837. The legislature appointed a special committee to investigate the affairs of this bank. A report issued on January 6, 1838, related that very little of the stated $150,000 in capital was ever paid in, $124,558.50 of bills were reported to have been circulated plus unstated amounts not recorded, false reports had been filed, the books of the bank "had been in disarray since the beginning of business," and at the time of collapse, the officers of the bank were trying to work out a currency-distribution scheme with a New York City bank.[31]

On January 11, 1838, the Commonwealth Bank of Boston failed. With outstanding paper money and other liabilities of $915,946, this was the greatest loss to the public up to this point in the state's history. Contemporary accounts laid part of the problem to the recent death of bank president John K. Simpson, who was heavily indebted to the institution. Simpson in collusion with the cashier had issued $120,000 in bills for which no record had been kept, and had secretly reissued $40,000 in notes that were stated to have been burned.[32] On January 16, the Middlesex Bank of Cambridge closed up. Many others experienced difficulties.

In spring 1838, many Massachusetts banks began to redeem their smaller bills (up to $3) in coin. The City Bank of Lowell was chartered at $75,000 and immediately set about ordering quantities of bills from the New England Bank Note Co. Soon, banking authorities learned that it had borrowed on short term some specie from Boston and had IOUs for the rest of its capital, and there were no assets at all. In July 1838, an injunction was issued forbidding it to open. Also in July, the Roxbury Bank, a phony operation run by swindlers in New York City, was enjoined from continuing. However, this did not deter its owners from passing out a further $50,000 or so of bills, including some of the popular $1.25, $1.50, and $1.75 denominations.

In 1837 the legislature revoked the charters of three banks, followed by 10 more in 1838, but this did not stop the flood of worthless notes. The prime supplier was the New England Bank Note Co., which accepted orders for bills and never asked questions.

Economic conditions worsened, and in the next several years quite a few banks closed their doors. The value of their bills ranged from slight discounts, to deep discounts, to utter worthlessness. Historian Dudley P. Bailey viewed the scene:

> Out of 138 banks, with an authorized capital of $40,830,000, on the 1st of January, 1837, the North American, in Salem, India and Blackstone, in Boston, and the Woburn, with capitals of $1,900,000, never went into operation. The only two banks chartered from 1837 to 1844—the Cabot, in Springfield (1837), and the Fishermens, in Provincetown (1839)—both failed of getting into operation. Of the remaining 134 banks, 17 had their charters repealed, in most cases for insolvency, and 15 surrendered or forfeited their charters, making in all 32 banks which failed or discontinued in consequence of the crisis. . . . The magnitude of the calamity is without a parallel in the previous or subsequent history of banking in Massachusetts.[33]

From 1837 to 1844, the last year seeing the resumption of strong economic conditions in America, 32 Massachusetts banks failed, a sorry showing among New England states. After the Hard Times era there was not much interest in forming new banks. Per historian Bailey:

> For the five years 1845–49, little new capital was asked for or authorized for banking purposes. Twenty-five new banks were incorporated with $3,300,000 of capital. Of these 25 banks, three, the Hampshire and Franklin, of Amherst, the Bank of Barre, and the Cape Cod Bank, of Provincetown, with $300,000 of capital, never went into operation.[34]

The legislature mandated that all banks chartered before 1849 had to apply for new charters in 1851, at which time their affairs could be studied. At that time, of the 115 banks involved, all but the Manufacturers Bank of Georgetown (which was first located in Rowley, then in 1838 moved to nearby Georgetown) continued in business. This bank was solvent, liquidated its affairs, and returned a profit to its shareholders.

In 1851 the Free-Banking Law was passed, permitting any group of 50 or more stockholders to set up a bank, with capital to be at least $100,000 and no more than $1,000,000. Half the capital had to be paid in before the bank could commence business. Bills could be issued, backed in part with securities posted with the state, no less than $50,000, or no more than 25% of the face value, whichever amount was larger. In 1852 the number of people needed to form a bank was reduced to just 10.

Unlike the situation in many other states, in Massachusetts the new law elicited no interest from investors. It was not until the Bank of the Metropolis opened in Boston in November 1858 that an institution was organized under its provisions. It folded in November 1863. No more than a half dozen other banks were founded under the law.[35]

By the early 1850s the state of Massachusetts had on its books a long list of banking rules and regulations dating back many years, including these:

> No bill or note can be issued by or on account of any bank, at any other place than its banking-house.
>
> No bank is allowed to pay out from its own counter any other bills than its own.
>
> All bills are to be issued in the name of the president, directors, and company of the bank issuing them, and to be signed by the president and cashier of the bank; but all bills signed by either the president or cashier, in circulation through the agency or neglect of any officer of the bank, must be redeemed by the corporation.
>
> Banks are liable to pay to any *bona fide* holder the original amount of any of their bills which may have been altered to a larger amount in the course of circulation, notwithstanding the alteration.
>
> Banks may issue bills under five dollars to the amount of one quarter part of their capital actually paid in; but no bank can issue bills of a less denomination than one dollar, under a penalty of one hundred dollars for each offense.
>
> The amount of bills issued by a bank must not at any time exceed its capital actually paid in more than twenty-five per cent.
>
> If the officers of any bank refuse or delay payment in gold or silver money of any note or bill of the bank, presented for payment in their usual hours of business, the bank will be liable to pay to the holder, as damages, at the rate of 24% a year during such delay or refusal.

As might be imagined, many rules were overlooked in practice or were not enforced. By this time the state had racked up the worst banking record by far in the Northeast.

At the same time, 110 banks in New England conducted the Association of Banks for the Suppression of Counterfeiting (see chapter 9) to track down the passers of false bills and, among other challenges, persuade the Massachusetts Legislature to outlaw use of the easily counterfeited Patent Stereotype Steel Plate.

In the meantime, in the 1850s there were scattered failures, the most prominent of which was the Cochituate Bank of Boston in 1854, for which its president had made poor investments in the South and West. Several subsequent failures prompted the legislature to revise banking laws that permitted secrecy, to require banks to publish figures of their condition—every week if located in Boston and every month if elsewhere.

In April 1855, a few banks in the state omitted their quarterly dividends, as they were short of funds. The culprit proved to be unwise or slow-paying investments in the distant West (today's Midwest), where there was great speculation in lands and businesses. Such banks did little in the way of loans locally and were viewed by some as in violation of their chartered purpose.[36] Loaning funds outside of the state, in order to gain high rates of interest, had been practiced by other banks for a long time.

The Panic of 1857 caught the banks unprepared, and the Boston institutions suspended specie payments on October 14, one day after all but one bank in New York City did the same. Only a single Massachusetts bank failed, the Western Bank of Springfield, which was closed by injunction on October 6 with long-standing problems. At this time there were 173 banks operating in the state.

In 1858 there was a fight between proponents of the Suffolk Bank system (see chapter 7) and the perceived upstart Bank of Mutual Redemption, which had been chartered in 1855 but did not begin business until three years later. The last drew much business from banks outside of Boston. In the city of Boston the leading banks banded together to deny the Bank of Mutual Redemption membership in the Clearing House Association. Not long afterward, the Suffolk Bank stated that as of November 30 it would no longer do business with "country banks," these being small institutions. By April 1859, the Bank of Mutual Redemption had 143 banks as members, or about half of the institutions in New England.

After the Panic of 1857, only a few new banks were formed in Massachusetts. By 1862 there were 183 of them in operation, or just 10 more than at the onset of that financial crisis.

Numismatic Comments

The state of Massachusetts offers a vast panorama of obsolete bank bills ranging from prior to 1800 up to 1866. The island of Nantucket, a whaling port, was home to one of the earlier banks. The district that in 1820 became the state of Maine was part of Massachusetts until that time, and banks there issued notes with the Massachusetts imprint. As such, these appeal to Massachusetts specialists as well as those who concentrate on notes from Maine.

The state mandated the use of the Patent Stereotype Steel Plate beginning in 1809, with the thought, actually a delusion, that the Perkins system would put an end to counterfeiting and altering notes. It did not, and many are the false bills that can be found today in

A $3 note of the Continental Bank, Boston, from an ABNCo plate. This is the famous "Polar Bear Note," more formally called the *White Bear* motif, showing a tense moment at sea in the Artic. The artist was F.O.C. Darley, and the engraver was DeWitt Clinton Hay. A display of Darley's artwork greeted visitors to the ABNCo offices in New York City.

The Continental Bank, located at 238 Washington Street, was active in the 1860s. Oliver Ditson, one of America's best-known publishers of sheet music, was president, and continued in the post when the transition was made to the Continental National Bank, charter 524, in 1864.

collecting circles, some of them identified as such and others not. For a long time afterward the bills of this state used these plates, creating a rather colorless numismatic landscape today, although stories of the individual institutions can be interesting.

In the 1850s through 1860s, bills became much more varied in appearance, with different firms supplying currency, including ornate vignettes not different in concept from those used in other eastern states at the time. By that time, the PSSP was discredited, although for years banks were aware of its failings, but dared not tell—for their notes were of that type—a scenario reminiscent of the emperor going without clothes.

The banking history of Massachusetts is particularly rich and diverse, and perhaps someday it will be included as a part of a specialized text on Obsolete Currency. In the meantime the Haxby text lists and describes many varieties. To these can be added hitherto unknown motifs that came to light with the dispersal of the paper archives of the American Bank Note Company by Christie's in 1990 and 1991, plus other ABNCo distributions here and there.

Currency of Michigan

Number of banks in the Haxby *Standard Catalog:* 96.
Specialized text: Harold L. Bowen, *Michigan Obsolete Bank Notes and Early Scrip,* 1956.

Historical Notes

Extensive commentary about the history of *wildcat* banks in Michigan is given in chapter 13, and as the Detroit Bank is studied in chapter 3, there is no need to repeat the details here. Instead, an brief overview and summary is appropriate.

The Detroit Bank, the first bank in the Territory of Michigan, was set up by capitalists in Boston. Capitalized at $400,000, it was to engage in the fur trade and do other business in a sparsely populated district. Judge Augustus Woodward, in charge of the area, became the bank's president. Control of the bank passed to the soon-to-become notorious (with the Farmers Exchange Bank of Gloucester, Rhode Island, fraud) Andrew Dexter Jr., who installed a new president and commenced issuing a flood of paper money. The house of cards collapsed in 1808, by which time its notes were worthless.

The Bank of Michigan was incorporated in 1817 with a modest capital of $10,000 (increased to $60,000 in 1824) and set up in Detroit, which had been bankless for nearly a decade. A branch was set up in Bronson (today's Kalamazoo). The bank seems to have done a good legitimate business, until it was brought down in the aftermath of the Panic of 1837, when bank examiners refused to recognize its well-secured discounts (loans) as assets due to their inexperience. The bank was placed into liquidation in 1842.

On March 29, 1827, the Bank of Monroe was chartered. The capital was set as $100,000, with the possibility of expanding to $500,000. In 1837 control of the bank passed to the Mormons in Kirtland, Ohio, after which little was heard of it. Oliver Cowdery, prominent in the Mormon Church, seems to have been the prime factor in negotiations.

The Farmers and Mechanics Bank of Michigan was chartered in 1829, the Bank of River Raisin in 1832, and the Bank of Wisconsin in 1835. With the establishment of the territory of Wisconsin in 1836, the last-named bank suddenly found itself outside the redefined boundaries of Michigan.

The Michigan State Bank was chartered by the territorial council on March 26, 1835, with the view of it being a state institution when Michigan joined the Union (which happened in 1837). Bonds to the extent of $5,000,000 were floated by the bank to further the development of resources in the district, which was undergoing a rapid expansion. To aid in the sale of bonds, unfortunate arrangements were made with the Morris Canal and Banking Company of New Jersey (which defaulted in 1840) and with Nicholas Biddle's Bank of the United States of Pennsylvania.

The wildcat era, elaborated upon in chapter 13, was described by Knox in his *History of Banking* (excerpts):

> Forty banks were fully organized within a year of passage [of the Free-Banking Act], and others were under way. . . . While in some of the older towns these institutions were carried on prudently and honestly, the general tendency of most of the smaller and some of the larger banks was towards reckless discounting and wild speculation. Competent officers and cashiers were rare. Men assumed to be bankers who had no business knowledge and who could hardly cast accounts, and many went into the business as an easy way of swindling.
>
> The examinations of the bank commissioners were of course the only difficulty that those who started banks for swindling purposes had to encounter. They had to see that the specie required by law was in the bank before they would permit it to commence or continue business. All sorts of tricks and combinations were resorted to deceive them. The specie found by them in one bank was sent by hurried journey ahead of them to be counted at the next. . . . Base metals were packed in coin bags and covered over with thin spreadings of coin. . . . There were banks and individuals in Detroit who made a business of loaning certificates and starting banks.
>
> The bank *starter,* provided with a specie certificate and engraved bills, would proceed to a distant and often inaccessible county and there select such prominent citizens as suited his purpose, who, ignorant of banking, he would beguile by fascinating representations of the profits to accrue to themselves and the community at large. They were to become stockholders and furnish the necessary personal bonds or mortgages upon their lands, which with the accommodating assistance of the county officers were perfected and sent with the necessary certificate to the auditor of the state.
>
> The bank starter was sometimes, though not always, elected president—the cashier was chosen in the neighborhood. The specie certificate was made ready, awaiting the approach of the examiners. When they came and set the seal of their approval on the bank the bills were immediately signed and prepared for circulation. As very often there was small need of the money in the vicinity of the bank, owing to the lack of inhabitants, the bills and the specie circular went with the bank starter, who returned with them to his native place.
>
> Ostensibly he was to put the bills in circulation by exchanging them for bills of other banks, but as often as not he neglected to render any account. . . . Perjury and direct robbery seem to have been frequent, and no legal penalties appear to have been inflicted.

By early 1840, Michigan was a banking disaster. Only six banks remained in operation, and 42 were in receivership. The State Bank of Michigan, chartered in 1839 with a capital of $2,000,000, failed to raise the funds needed to open. Banking limped along during the next 15 years, conducted by a handful of institutions as well as by money brokers and exchange offices. In 1849 the Peninsular Bank was organized in Detroit.

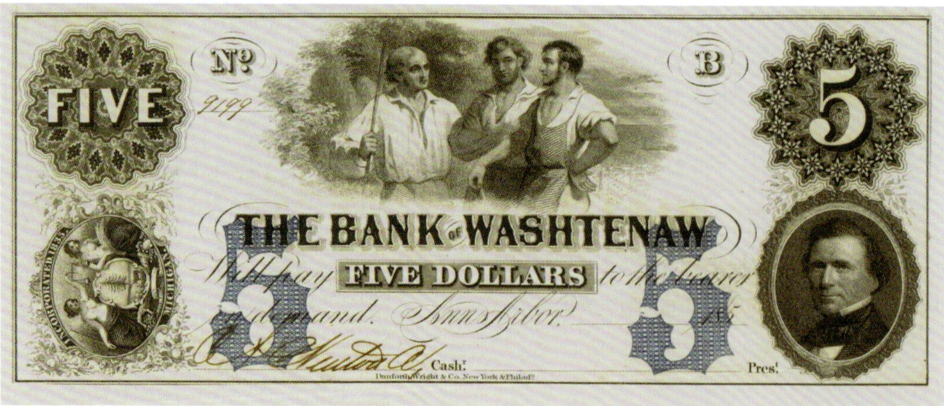

Note for $5 of the Bank of Washtenaw, Ann Arbor, Michigan, from a plate by Danforth, Wright & Co., New York and Philadelphia. This is an unissued remainder note, partially signed by the assistant cashier—a highly unusual situation, for it was the general rule of all banks for cashiers to be the last to sign. Signatures by assistants are rare as well. Bills of this particular bank exist in large quantities and are easily collected today.

The Bank of Washtenaw was chartered on March 26, 1835, prior to the wildcat era in that territory. Its offices were in two small rooms in the Chapin house at the corner of Fourth and Ann streets. The bank succumbed to the effects of the Panic of 1837 and the collapse of most of the Michigan banking system.

This proved to be a sound institution and lasted through the end of the Civil War. In the same year the Government Stock Bank was launched in Ann Arbor, but it collapsed in fraud in 1852.

In 1858 a General Banking Law was approved by state voters, after which a few new banks were organized.

NUMISMATIC COMMENTS

The paper money of Michigan is a veritable numismatic playground, perhaps more so than in any other state, although the District of Columbia (not a state) mounts strong competition. An early specialist in this series was described by Harold L. Bowen:

> The first collector of Michigan paper money was Ford H. Rogers, of Detroit, who started in 1853. Some notes were scarce, even in those days, according to an article in the *Evening News* (October 9, 1883):
>
> "The banks whose notes he has not been able to get are the Commercial bank of Michigan, St. Joe; Commonwealth Bank, Tecumseh; Citizens Bank of Michigan, Ann Arbor; Bank of Marshall; Michigan Centre Bank; Bank of Niles; Bank of Superior; Bank of Shiawassee; and Exchange Bank of Danl. Ball, of Grand Rapids."
>
> No bills of the Commonwealth Bank, or Citizens Bank of Michigan have ever been found, and perhaps none were printed. Rogers compiled an excellent list of Michigan banks, but realized the difficulty of further research. Gaps occurred in many series, official records were far from specific, and several associations had vanished without a trace. A catalogue of Michigan notes seemed quite hopeless.[37]

Bills of the fraudulent Detroit Bank, the first in the territory, while not common, come on the market with some frequency today. Michigan became a state on January 26, 1837. Accordingly, notes dated before that time are territorial issues, although no numismatic attention has been paid to the distinction.

Currency from the wildcat era of 1837 to 1839 exists in large quantities today, although the issues of certain banks and denominations can be hard to find. These were made in the era before color overprints were popular. By the 1850s and 1860s, relatively few banks were in operation. Accordingly, the later and more colorful bills are in the minority in any collection formed of this state.

In addition to banks, several railroads and insurance companies issued denominated notes, highly collectible today. Forming a representative collection from most of the several dozen different wildcat banks is a pleasant pursuit as each one has a story to reveal.

CURRENCY OF MINNESOTA

Number of banks in the Haxby *Standard Catalog:* 52.
Specialized text: R.H. Rockholt, *Minnesota Obsolete Notes and Scrip,* 1973.

HISTORICAL NOTES

The state known as Minnesota as of May 11, 1858, was earlier in Wisconsin Territory. The first session of the new state legislature enacted laws, including chapter 32, "An Act to authorize and regulate the business of banking," amended in the same session. By that time the area had been home to at least 10 banks in the Wisconsin Territory, some of which were located in remote or inaccessible areas reminiscent of the wildcat days of Michigan. None remained in existence. Accordingly, most numismatists group the notes of these banks under the Wisconsin classification, not Minnesota.

The first to be organized under state laws was the Bank of Minnesota, chartered to do business in St. Paul, October 1, 1858. The capital stock of just $25,000 was mainly owned by Sewell, Ferris & Co. in New York, who had hoped to deposit interest-bearing bonds with the state auditor, collect interest, and issue paper money. Cashier H. Thompson and president J.E. Thompson were both experienced bankers. Minnesota 8% bonds to the extent of $25,000 were soon deposited, and paper money was issued. Later, $10,000 in Minnesota bonds was removed and replaced by 10% bonds recently issued by the Minnesota State University.

In 1858 and 1859, the state authorized many other banks, all but a handful being paper mills, according to historian John Jay Knox. Most were located in small out-of-the-way places. The founders of the Bank of Fox Lake, Wisconsin, in 1856, set up the Farmers Bank of Garden City, Minnesota in 1858. The Bank of Rochester, founded in 1859, declared its bills were redeemable in specie at the bank of Galena, Illinois. By 1860, most of the banks organized in 1858 and 1859 were either defunct or teetering on the brink of becoming so.

Sewell, Ferris & Co. collapsed in October 1859 in an unrelated stock speculation, after which the firm's two Minnesota banks, the aforementioned Bank of Minnesota and the Nicollet County Bank of St. Peter, stayed open for a time, then failed. As of January 1, 1863, bills of the Bank of Minnesota were trading at 70¢ on the dollar, while those of the Nicollet County Bank were said to be worth just 35% of face value, as

A $2 note of the Dayton Bank, St. Paul, Minnesota, from a plate by Danforth, Wright & Co., New York and Philadelphia. Instead of "president" at the lower right, there is a space for "banker." An unissued remainder.

The Dayton Bank seems to have operated for a time in the 1850s without benefit of a charter. Because of this fact, it escaped notice in official records. Today we can only speculate on its business activities.

traders hoped they would be redeemed by the state. When the bonds were ultimately sold, their value was found to be just 22% of par.

The bills of other banks in the state offering speculative opportunities at the time were the Bank of Rochester (16% of face), Central Bank of New Ulm (30%), Chisago County Bank (19%), Fillmore County Bank (20%), Exchange Bank of Glencoe (21%), Bank of Owatonna (21%), and the Bank of Saint Paul (98%). The Bank of Red Wing, organized in 1859, sold its assets to a similarly named bank in 1863. Its bills traded at par, a rare situation at the time.

To aid with the circulation of the bills of the Bank of Chatfield, publicity included prominent notice that its owner was Selah Chamberlain, wealthy Wisconsin financier and railroad magnate. Unlike most of its contemporaries, this bank remained in business until 1865, by which time the field of banks in the state was sparsely populated.

Numismatic Comments

Currency of Minnesota comprises issues of quite a few different banks and many different denominations and designs from the later era of bank-note issuing in America, as the starting date is 1858. Thus, Minnesota bills are remarkable for their ornate designs and colored overprints. While many are rarities, and others are described by James A. Haxby as unconfirmed, selected issues are available from a handful of banks.

Quantities of bills issued in this state were modest compared to many other places, and what was issued was often subjected to extensive use. Likely, anyone specializing in Minnesota notes alone would run out of stimulation soon (it is always exciting to be able to regularly add bills to your collection). Accordingly, such currency is most often collected in conjunction with other states.

Currency of Mississippi

Number of banks in the Haxby *Standard Catalog:* 45.
Specialized text: L. Candler Leggett, *Mississippi Obsolete Notes and Scrip,* 1975; Guy Kraus, *Mississippi Obsolete Notes & Scrip,* 2003.

Historical Notes

Prior to statehood in December 1817, the Bank of *the* Mississippi, chartered by the territorial government in 1809, did an excellent business in Natchez under private ownership. The capital stock was $100,000, against which three times the amount could be issued in paper money. For any violation the directors were individually liable. The currency served well and was redeemed upon presentation. In 1818 under the state government it was reorganized as the Bank of the State of Mississippi with a capital limited to $3,000,000, and the state was to take a quarter interest. Headquartered in Natchez, the bank set up branches in Port Gibson, Vicksburg, and Woodville. As part of the arrangement the state legislature stated that no other bank would be authorized by the state until its charter expired in 1840.

Notwithstanding this agreement, the state allowed the incorporation of the Planters Bank of the State of Mississippi in 1830, capital of $3,000,000, to be set up in the same city, with the state holding a two-thirds ownership interest. After this fact became known, the directors of the long-established Bank of the State of Mississippi contemplated the current rampant speculation in trading slaves and dealing in undeveloped land and decided to discontinue business. The new Planters Bank started operation and became the depository for state funds. Branches were operated in Columbus, Jackson, Manchester, Monticello, Port Gibson, Vicksburg, Woodville, and Yazoo City. After September 1839 the state transferred its deposits to the Mississippi Railroad Company. The Planters Bank closed down soon thereafter. The Railroad Company operated branches in Canton, Gallatin, and Raymond and issued many bills, many of which were post notes bearing interest. It went out of business in the early 1840s.

By 1837 there were 18 banks in the state, with a capital of about $13,000,000 and a conservative bank-note circulation of about $5,000,000. On February 5, 1838, the state passed a special act to charter the gigantic Mississippi Union Bank, headquartered in Jackson and capitalized at $15,500,000. To finance the operation the act authorized $15,000,000 worth of bonds to be loaned to the bank, the security for which was backed by the state's good faith and credit. Nicholas Biddle, president of the Bank of the United States of Pennsylvania, was given the agency for selling the bonds. These were difficult times, and holders of the bonds or the bank currency frequently made inquiry to the state offices to be sure all was well. In all instances the state replied that it stood fully behind these obligations.

But all was not well, and the Mississippi Union Bank collapsed in 1840, carrying down with it a number of other banks in the state. Governor Alexander G. McNutt contemplated the damages, the difficulty of raising money at current high interest rates, and other options. He sent a form letter to creditors on July 14, 1841, saying that the state "denies all obligation to pay the bonds" on the grounds of a clause in the state's Constitution providing that no loan of money should be made on the credit of the state for the payment or redemption of any loan or debt unless "such law be proposed in the Senate or House of Representatives and be agreed on by the majority of the members of each house and entered on their journals with the yeas and nays taken thereon, and be referred to the next succeeding Legislature, and published three months previous to the next regular election in three newspapers of the state, and unless the next Legislature duly passes the said law."

The state further claimed that the arrangement with Biddle was invalid, as no bonds were to be sold below par, making his commission an "intentional and willful fraud." The very institution of the Mississippi Union Bank was deemed to be illegal. Citing the record of Washington, Franklin, Madison, Jefferson, and other national leaders who repudiated amounts owed to mercenary foreigners, the citizens of Mississippi had no intention of paying the out-of-state money-grubbing people who held these illegal bonds.

> Higher and holier motives than mere pecuniary considerations actuate [citizens of Mississippi]. They have determined that they will never submit to an invasion of their constitution by either a foreign or domestic foe. The rights secured to them under that sacred instrument they will maintain at all hazards; and relying on the correctness of their principles and the justice of their cause they will, with confidence and cheerfulness, submit to the verdict of posterity.

So the argument went, repeated endlessly, while creditors and newspaper editors reacted with shock and disbelief. State courts found the 1838 act was indeed legal. To have the last word, the state legislature passed a law forbidding the state to ever settle the debt, thereby canceling state court decisions.

In his message of January 1, 1844, Governor Tilghman Tucker, ignoring the nationwide revival of business resulting from the end of the Hard Times period, attributed new prosperity in Mississippi as "the natural result of industry, economy and time which have (aided by the bankrupt law), swept off a large portion of the debts and embarrassments of the people created by the disasters of past idleness, prodigality, gambling, and banking operations." Financial journals and newspapers across the United States continued to react in horror, but Mississippi ignored the outcry. For years, up to the Civil War, the financial reputation of the state was in shambles, and frequent mention of this was made in *Banker's Magazine* and elsewhere.

During the 1830s and 1840s, many other banks were formed in Mississippi, nearly all with little oversight. Results were mixed but generally unfavorable, and most eventually failed. Banking in the state was sharply diminished in the 1850s, leading into the Civil War in 1861. Few new banks were chartered. In 1856 the Commercial Bank at Yazoo City opened its doors. Capitalized at $200,000, it operated profitably into the early 1860s.

The Northern Bank of Mississippi, located in Holly Springs, was established in the unpropitious year of 1837, and went on to operate into the Civil War. It was far from being a local bank, and issued paper payable in New Orleans. In the 1850s there were strict rules in Texas concerning the issuance of paper money, and partly for this reason scarcely any native banks issued bills. The banking house of R. & D.G. Mills in Houston, Texas, made an arrangement with the Northern Bank of Mississippi to acquire large quantities of its paper money. It circulated the bills with good effect in Texas, backed by the excellent reputation of the Mills enterprise. In early 1862, Mills

A $10 interest-bearing post note of the Mississippi Rail Road Company, Natchez, payable 12 months after the date of June 15, 1839. From a plate by Draper, Toppan, Longacre & Co., Philadelphia. While post notes were used in many states, they were especially popular in the South.

As a railroad company, not a bank, the Mississippi Rail Road Company could do business much as it pleased, without interference, in a time when the growth of railroads was encouraged as a harbinger of great prosperity. The line featured its banking division, which in the usual manner sought to distribute as many bills as possible, hoping that many would never be redeemed. With offices in Natchez and Jackson, the railroad part of the enterprise laid only about 24 miles of iron rails. The business collapsed, and the bills became utterly worthless. In 1840 a tornado destroyed some of its remaining buildings.

could not redeem the notes, and a panic swept through the financial community. The scare was short-lived, and soon the strength of Mills was regained.

During this era, scrip and other bills were issued by various merchants, railroads, and other commercial interests in Mississippi. In addition, large quantities of New Orleans bills were seen in commerce.

Numismatic Comments

Currency of Mississippi includes bank issues and, also in the Haxby text (and a departure from the listings of some other states), certain bills issued by other entities, such as the Mississippi & Alabama Railroad Company and the Real Estate Banking Company of Clinton, Mississippi. A particularly elaborate title is the Lake Washington & Deer Creek Railroad & Banking Company, located in Princeton, active in the 1830s, which evolved in the same decade to become the Bank of Mississippi, not related to the other institution with a somewhat similar name.

With so many issuers and so many denominations and vignettes, bills of Mississippi are widely collected today and are very interesting to view, although most date from before the colorful era of the 1850s. There are, to be sure, rarities, particularly among those of earlier dates. Currency of the Bank of the Mississippi, headquartered in Natchez and active in the second decade of the 19th century, is uncollectible today. Certain other issues across the banking spectrum are known through proofs.

Rich vignettes, interesting bank titles, and a lot of stories for those who enjoy history come together in the currency of this state. Perhaps similar to specialists in Florida bills, those who focus on Mississippi bills are often imbued with particular enthusiasm that leads to spirited competition in the auction room. When two or more people each say, "I gotta have it!" watch out!

Currency of Missouri

Number of banks in the Haxby *Standard Catalog:* 14.

Historical Notes

Missouri became a state in 1821. From its acquisition as part of the Louisiana Territory in 1803, the district was under territorial supervision. The Bank of St. Louis, chartered in 1813, did not commence business until September 2, 1816, as it took three years to raise the $300,000 capital. The officers engaged in unwise speculations, causing dissent within the board of directors and confiscation of certain bank property. The doors were closed in July 1819.

The Bank of Missouri opened in St. Louis on February 1, 1817, capitalized at $250,000. Its president, Auguste Choteau, was a founder of St. Louis and the wealthiest man in the district, who reluctantly resigned in 1821 due to age and infirmity. At the time, land speculation was in the forefront of commerce, with government land available for $2 per acre for a quarter section, payable at $80 down and the balance in five years. Trading was extensive in such land contracts, but when the time came to pay the balance after five years, few had the ability to do so. The Bank of Missouri did not collapse, but in 1822 it ceased operations and went into liquidation.

In 1829 the second Bank of the United States somewhat belatedly opened a branch in St. Louis. It lasted only four years, after which time a branch of the Cincinnati Commercial Agency, which had banking privileges, was dominant in local finance.

The Bank of the State of Missouri was chartered in 1837 and issued its first paper money on July 31 of that year. Branches were maintained in Cape Girardeau, Fayette, Lexington, Palmyra, and Springfield in the early years. The capital was set at $3,450,000, with the state owning half. In ensuing years it did business very conservatively, redeeming its notes in coin and refusing to take most of the bank notes from distant places that were swirling around in the channels of commerce of the busiest Mississippi River port north of New Orleans. This caused many problems with local merchants and others who felt their business was being unfairly restricted. By 1856 it was the only bank in Missouri and had many branches to service towns and cities across the state. Its bills were as solid as gold, literally, and were often exchanged in California, not as bank notes in general circulation, for such were not permitted under the California Constitution, but as drafts or evidence of value. Soon, enterprising counterfeiters in the Golden State counterfeited the Bank of the State of Missouri bills. The San Francisco branch of Page, Bacon & Co., bankers, took in $15,000 of the phony Missouri bills in exchange for gold.

In St. Louis the banking houses of Lucas & Simonds, Page & Bacon, and E.W. Clarke & Bros. issued their own paper money without benefit of state authorization. An accommodation was reached in early 1853, when the banks agreed to redeem in gold all such bills presented, after which no more would be paid out.[38]

The Bank of the State of Missouri was rechartered in 1857, and branches were operated at Arrow Rock, Canton, Cape Girardeau, Chillicothe, Fayette, Lexington, Louisiana, Palmyra, St. Joseph, and Springfield. It later converted to become a National Bank.

In 1857 the General Banking Law mandated that all bank-note plates and dies were to be under the custody and direction of the bank commissioner, which translated to say he alone could order bills from the various engraving and printing companies. The commissioner or an authorized representative was to countersign and register all currency. This applied to bills of the Bank of the State of Missouri as well as to new banks.

Under the new law the legislature chartered seven banks in 1857, six in St Louis (the Exchange, Mechanics, Merchants, St. Louis, Southern, and Union) and the other in Lexington (the Farmers Bank of Missouri). Branches were set up, and soon banking became convenient across the state.

During the Panic of 1857 in the autumn of that year, all banks suspended specie payments except for the Exchange and Mechanics banks in St. Louis. Eventually, redemption was restored across the state. Bills of the Missouri banks were readily accepted at or very close to par by merchants and other banks, although the policy of redeeming them only at the issuing branches was clumsy as some were in towns without railroad service. Notes from other states, always depreciated and sometimes worthless, were seen less often, but some remained in regional use throughout the Civil War.

Numismatic Comments

Bills of the several banks headquartered in St. Louis form the prime focus of collecting activity. Notes from the many branches of these banks present a greater challenge, for most of them are described only from historical records, with no examples being in collections today.

Designs of Missouri notes vary from early issues, such as by the Bank of Missouri, with simple designs by Murray, Draper, Fairman & Co., to a rich panoply of issues of the 1850s and 1860s with ornate vignettes and colored overprints. The finest collection ever formed, the property of Eric P. Newman (who wrote the foreword for this book), is displayed in museum surroundings at Washington University in St. Louis.

Currency of Nebraska

Number of banks in the Haxby *Standard Catalog:* 17.
Specialized text: Gerome Walton, *A History of Nebraska Banking and Paper Money,* 1978.

Historical Notes

Nebraska, admitted to the Union in 1867, was under territorial law during the bank-note issuing period. The first session of the legislature in January 1855 provided under its criminal code that,

> If any person shall subscribe to or become a member of, or be in any way interested in any association or company formed for the purpose of issuing or putting into circulation any bill, check, ticket, certificate, promissory note, or other paper of any bank to circulate as money in this Territory, he shall be punished by imprisonment in the county jail not exceeding one year, or by a fine of not more than one thousand dollars.

Proof note for $10 of the Farmers Bank of Missouri, Lexington branch, from a plate by Bald, Cousland & Co., Philadelphia and New York. At the lower right of the face is the patent date of June 2, 1857, for the green tint. Seemingly, this proof was made many years later at ABNCo by someone who did not realize the overprint should have been green!

This particular branch, capitalized at $600,000, did a lively business in its day. Although the Panic of 1857 struck in the same year the bank was founded, it steadfastly maintained specie payments.

However, in the same session several banking privileges were bestowed! The Western Exchange Fire and Marine Insurance Company, of Omaha issued many bills and served as the depository of territorial funds. This business proved ephemeral, and in autumn 1857 it failed, with just $191.03 in specie on hand, a total loss to its creditors. A.U. Wyman, the assistant cashier, later served as treasurer of the United States.

At the 1856 session of the legislature, several new banks were chartered, including the Bank of Nebraska at Omaha, the Bank of Florence, the Platte Valley Bank at Nebraska City, the Nemaha Valley Bank at Brownsville, the Bank of Tekamah, the Bank of DeSoto, and the Fontenelle Bank at Bellevue. The teller of the Bank of Nebraska, David H. Moffat, left Nebraska after the bank failed and went to Colorado to make a fortune in mining. He later served as president of the First National Bank of Denver.

In 1857 the criminal code provision prohibiting the banking business, which had not been enforced, was repealed. New banks were authorized, including the Corn Exchange Bank and the Waubeek Bank, both of De Soto; the Omaha City Bank and Land Company, the Chicago Bank, and the Brownville Bank and Land Co., all in Omaha; and the Bank of Dakota in Dakota City. The last bank was owned by the Kountze brothers, who did business in Omaha, not Dakota City, and organized the First National Bank of Omaha in August 1863. They were also involved in banking in the Denver area after the "Pikes Peak or Bust" gold rush of 1859. Certain of Corn Exchange Bank's bills were payable elsewhere, including at the office of W.H. Rice & Company and, separately, the office of Solon, McElroy and Company, both in Chicago.

Although Omaha experienced boom times during the westward expansion, including the rush to find gold in Colorado, most of the banks organized in Nebraska in the 1850s were fraudulently conceived or poorly operated, leaving behind a trail of failures.

On March 10, 1860, this letter was sent to Secretary of the Treasury Howell Cobb in Washington, D.C., who was preparing a banking report to submit to Congress:

> Secretary's Office, Nebraska Territory, Omaha.
>
> Sir:
>
> Yours inquiring relative to banks in Nebraska, and bearing date February 29, came to hand this day. All the banks, except the "Platte Valley Bank" at Nebraska City, have either suspended or broken. The system of chartering banks in this Territory has proved most disastrous to our people and to the good reputation of Nebraska among the financial men of the eastern states.
>
> The names of the suspended and broken banks are as follows: Nemaha Valley Bank, at Brownville; Bank of Nebraska, at Omaha; Western Exchange, Fire and Marine Insurance Company, at Omaha; Bank of De Soto, at De Soto; Bank of Fontenelle, at Belleview. . . .
>
> I am, sir, your very obedient servant,
>
> J. Sterling Morton,
>
> Secretary and Acting Governor of Nebraska.

Numismatic Comments

Although relatively few banks issued notes in Nebraska, the bills of those that did are widely collectible, including unissued remainders. Dating from the 1850s and 1860s, these typically have ornate vignettes across many different designs, and, often, colored overprints. Certain of the institutions have other activities reflected in their titles, such as the Nebraska Land and Banking Company, of Omaha, and the Western Exchange & Land Company of the same place. The last evolved into the Corn Exchange Bank, located in De Soto, which issued colorful bills created by the National Bank Note Company (established in 1859).

A $2 note of the Bank of De Soto, Nebraska, October 1, 1863, by the American Bank Note Co. The center vignette depicts the sidewheel steamer *De Soto*.

The Bank of De Soto was chartered in 1857, not a favorable time in view of the panic that would ripple through the American economy in October of that year. By early 1860, every bank in the territory had suspended, except the Platte Valley Bank in Nebraska City.

Perhaps the first serious collector of such bills was Byron Reed, who moved to Omaha in 1856, made a fortune in real estate and other activities, and died there in 1891. His immense collection of coins, tokens, medals, and paper money was willed to the Omaha City Library, which soon placed the currency and other items on view.

Today, Nebraska notes are among the most widely collected of the state bills. Dealer consultants advise that in a price list, notes of this state are always among the first to sell, and auction offerings typically attract many bids.

Currency of New Hampshire

Number of banks in the Haxby *Standard Catalog:* 78.

Historical Notes

The banking history of New Hampshire begins in 1792 with the establishment of the New Hampshire Bank at Portsmouth. This seaport on the Atlantic, adjacent to Maine, was one of the busiest harbors in the East in the early days, with emphasis on the West India trade. It was also the banking center and most populous city in the state at the time. Concord, which would become the state capital, was a tiny village then, and Nashua and Manchester did not exist. Nearby Exeter was a center for the law and court.

With powerful political connections—and in this state as well as others, banking privileges were mainly political—the New Hampshire Bank at Portsmouth was able to fend off all comers. It was not until a decade later in 1802 that other banks were formed in the state. In that year the New Hampshire Union Bank and the Portsmouth Bank were chartered in the same city. In 1813 the Rockingham Bank set up in Portsmouth, and in time the Piscataqua Bank and its successor, the Piscataqua Exchange Bank; the Commercial Bank; the Mechanics and Traders Bank of Portsmouth; and the Bank of New Hampshire were established there. With Concord's rise in importance in the early 19th century and, especially, the growth of the manufacturing businesses in Manchester from the 1840s onward, Portsmouth diminished in commercial importance. By the end of the currency-issuing period (1865), Manchester was the leading city in the state.

In 1803 four new financial institutions were chartered: the New Hampshire Strafford Bank in Dover, the Exeter Bank, the Cheshire Bank in Keene, and the Coos Bank in Haverhill.

In Haverhill, a village in the upper part of the state on the Connecticut River bordering Vermont, the district court was established, although the settlement was not of commercial importance. The Coos Bank was set up there in 1803 and afterward led a precarious existence. On occasion, newspaper and other accounts stated the bank failed, information that can easily be found today in popular histories. In fact it did not fail, despite suspensions, closing for a time, and other travails, which included the illegal overissue of currency. Its numerous notes became despised after it stopped redemptions on August 15, 1809. With a gentle hand, it seems, on June 21, 1811, the legislature warned the bank that if affairs were not straightened out in a satisfactory manner within nine months it would forfeit its charter. This precipitated an order from the board of directors that all loans on stock issues had to be paid up at least to the extent of 25%. Over a period of time the bank was resuscitated, and by August 1812 it was again redeeming its notes. Trouble loomed again in the economic depression of 1818. With an unredeemable quantity of notes in circulation, including illegal excess, the Coos Bank failed, perhaps fulfilling the statements made nationwide in premature stories of 1809.

The list of irregular, fraudulent, and poorly managed banks in New Hampshire is not a long one, but it includes some interesting accounts. Far and away the greatest fraud was the Hillsborough Bank of Amherst, founded in 1808 with lawyer Samuel Bell as its president. Amherst was another district court town and a center of society. The bank made deals to ship its currency to the West and to otherwise pass out as much as possible, against very little in the way of assets. Violating all banking rules, this activity continued unimpeded until the bank collapsed in 1808. No convictions were ever made, and Bell went on to become the governor of New Hampshire!

Another caper involved the Wolfborough (*sic*) Bank set up in Wolfeboro, which with all good intentions began business in 1837, the worst of all economic times. The Suffolk Bank would not allow it to join for the redemption of its notes. Along came Samuel D. Dakin, fraudster from Utica, New York, and other addresses, who bought out the stockholders, set up a phony bookkeeping system, and flooded the East with worthless notes. The state Banking Commission investigated, and the charter was revoked. This deterred Dakin not a bit, and more bills were printed. Later, it seems that the privilege of fraud was turned over to other criminals in New York City, who in the 1850s had still more currency printed. In reality, the bank operated legitimately for about a year after its formation.

The Exeter Bank failed in the early 1840s and left a large paper trail. In 1864, Jared Williams, former governor and now president of the White Mountain Bank of Lancaster, died, leaving his son George in charge. The latter, the bank's longtime cashier, was found to have stolen from the bank for years, falsified books, and issued large amounts of unrecorded bills (including \$2 bills with a Santa Claus motif). Although his guilt was ascertained, he was never prosecuted. In New Hampshire, as in nearly all other states, an officer stealing vast sums of money from a bank, or hundreds of thousands of dollars from the public by overissuing notes, was apt to go scot-free. Meanwhile, a hungry person stealing a loaf of bread was likely to be locked up in jail.

In the state capital, the Concord Bank was formed in 1806. The incorporators soon were fighting with each other, and two factions emerged, each claiming rights to the bank. In an unusual scenario, after a time they made peace with each other—sort of—with each conducting a separate and unrelated Concord Bank, both on Main Street. To distinguish them, in the state they were referred to as the Lower Concord Bank and the Upper Concord Bank, but their printed material and currency simply said *Concord Bank.*

By the 1850s Manchester was the leading city in the state, coincident with the rise of the Amoskeag mills and other factories that extended for about a mile along the Merrimack River, the source of power. The Manchester Bank was the first on the scene in 1844, followed by the Amoskeag Bank in 1848, the City Bank in 1853, and the Merrimack River Bank in 1855. At a time when Portsmouth banks were experiencing reduced trade, the Manchester banks flourished.

The first bank in another important city to the south of Manchester on the same river was the Nashua Bank, formed in 1835. This was followed by the Indian Head Bank of *Nashville,* formed in 1851 in a district that had seceded from Nashua because of differences with the city government (it later rejoined). The Pennichuck Bank was chartered in Nashua in 1855.

Other banks were active in Dover, Rochester, New Ipswich, Keene, and other towns and cities. Generally, most banks in the state prospered during the early 19th century. During that time New Hampshire changed its emphasis from agriculture to manufacturing, while on the seacoast the maritime trade remained important.

Most state banks signed with the Suffolk Bank system of note redemption after it was established in 1824. When the Bank of Mutual Redemption took over the business in 1858, the New Hampshire banks went there. Throughout the early 19th century there was always a good market in New England and New York City for the notes of sound banks of the state. After the Panic of 1857, only one bank came into being—the Valley Bank of Hillsborough. This institution alone issued bills created by the American Bank Note Co. (not from reused earlier plates by companies that made up ABNCo). In the 1860s, most of the strong institutions converted to become National Banks.

Numismatic Comments

Bills of the first bank in the state, the New Hampshire Bank at Portsmouth, are collectible today but scarce, with very early issues being rare and usually seen in lower grades. From then until the Panic of 1857, several dozen banks were chartered throughout the state.

Note for $1 of the Strafford Bank, Dover, New Hampshire, January 1, 1862, with the patent Canada Green or green tint background. From a plate by Toppan, Carpenter & Co., pre-1858, later stamped with the ABNCo logotype (at upper right) and printed by the American Bank Note Co.

This bank was founded in the early 19th century, prospered, and evolved into the Strafford National Bank. Its success story is well told by Joanne Griffith Domingue in *A History of the Strafford National Bank* (1978), one of the best American banking histories. In the late 20th century, the bank was absorbed in the era of "bancorp" activity, and today in Dover only its impressive granite building reminds knowledgeable passersby of its grand heritage.

Certain banks that failed or were discontinued in New Hampshire left behind trails of paper money, plentiful today. In particular these include the Hillsborough Bank of Amherst, both of the similarly named Concord Banks, the Cheshire Bank of Keene, the Coos Bank of Haverhill, the Exeter Bank, the Wolfborough Bank, and the White Mountain Bank of Lancaster.

Challenging are many bills that were once plentiful, even common in circulation, issued by leading banks, but which were redeemed in the 1860s when the institutions converted to National Banks, and their notes were destroyed. Designs of New Hampshire banks include the Patent Stereotype Steel Plate for many early issues, changing to ornate vignettes in the 1830s and 1840s, then evolving to notes with colored overprints in the 1850s and 1860s.

As a general rule, New Hampshire banks can be divided into two categories: plentiful bills due to failed banks or remainders (in the latter category the Salmon Falls Bank of Rollinsford is particularly plentiful), and those that range from very scarce to rare. It is quite unfortunate that in the latter category are the majority of colorful bills issued in the last decade of the state-chartered bank era.

The story of New Hampshire banks is rich and interesting. The present writer and David Sundman are conducting the New Hampshire Currency Research Project, which so far has accumulated several thousand (!) pages of data, including biographies on more than 4,000 bank officers and directors. This information will be made available, probably in a book of several hundred pages, incorporating scrip notes described by Kevin Lafond, plus a CD or DVD with all of the other information, trivia, and images.

Currency of New Jersey

Number of banks in the Haxby *Standard Catalog:* 122.
Specialized text: George W. Wait, *New Jersey's Money,* 1976.

Historical Notes

In 1804 the New Jersey Legislature chartered two banks, the Newark Banking and Insurance Company and the Trenton Banking Company, in towns of these names. Elisha Boudinot, late director of the Philadelphia Mint, served as the founding president of the Newark institution, which was situated in the parlor of the Smith Burnett residence on Broad Street. Deposits flowed in rapidly and were kept in an ironbound wooden chest. Soon, part of the money was moved to the Manhattan Company (bank) in New York City for safekeeping. In 1805 the bank erected an impressive building in Newark. Capitalized at $800,000, the company had $350,000 of its stock subscribed for. The bank flourished, its 20-year charter was extended several times, and it later became known as the Newark Banking Company.

The Trenton Banking Company, capitalized at $600,000, drew $214,740 in stock payments. Its founding president was Isaac Smith, who later served on the United States Supreme Court. In the *History of Banking,* Knox related this story:

> Early in the history of the bank two or three runs for the redemption of its notes were made by its

> depositors. In 1837 a run on the bank began and there were not enough funds in the vaults to meet the demand. There was no railroad at that time between Trenton and Philadelphia; but something had to be done to save the bank, and Benjamin Fish, one of the directors, drove to the City of Brotherly Love, loaded a wagon with silver, returned to Trenton and unloaded the coin in front of the bank. The sight of the money inspired the excited depositors with confidence and they quickly withdrew, satisfied that the bank had the ability to redeem its notes in coin on demand.

In 1812 New Jersey passed a general banking law outlining rules for loans, liability, the issuance of paper money, furnishing annual reports, and other matters. No bills were to be issued of a denomination below $3, following the common view that low-value notes drove coins from circulation as people would keep silver coins and spend the paper. There was a demand for smaller bills, and in 1813 the rules were amended to allow values down to $1. These laws remained in force, with occasional amendments, until 1850.

By 1820 there were 14 banks in the state, with a total capital of $2,130,949.[39] In time, various manufacturers, canal operators, insurance companies, and even a "grazing company" issued paper money. Reflective of this fact, *Niles' Weekly Register* on October 1, 1836, commented:

> *Beets and banking in New Jersey.* Notice is given to the Paterson *Intelligencer* that "an application will be made to the legislature of this state, at their next session, to incorporate a company for the purpose of manufacturing sugar from beets, to be located in the counties of Bergen, and Essex, with a capital of $500,000, to be styled the Beet Sugar Manufacturing Company, with banking and trust powers."
>
> We eschew this alliance of the root of evil with the beet root. The cultivation of the last, either by private enterprise, or by incorporated companies, will no doubt, prove profitable and advantageous. But if they are to be raised by the aid of a *beet bank,* we fear more attention will be paid to it than to the beet-beds.

Enforcement of banking rules in New Jersey ranged from lax to nonexistent. As a result, many banks violated the laws, others did business without charters, and still others were not much different from the wildcats of Michigan. Of course it was these wayward banks that furnished fodder for newspaper and financial journal accounts, while properly conducted institutions attracted little notice. This was (and is) the American preference. Similarly, in the Wild West outlaws got all the press while ministers and teachers were seldom mentioned.

The Panic of 1837 brought paper money abuses to a head, the legislature appointed a committee to investigate the banks, and many paper mills and phony operations were closed. Meanwhile, all banks in the state suspended specie payments, with the single exception of the Paterson Bank. In time, various banks began paying out coins again, generally excepting those with strong links to Philadelphia banks, for in that city there were many problems (including the Bank of the United States of Pennsylvania). Those New Jersey banks that did not resume were given a deadline of March 5, 1842, the penalty being the forfeiture of their charters. By 1850 the Paterson Bank had regained strength. Along the way, large amounts of the company's bank bills were circulated.

The Morris Canal and Banking Company, chartered in Jersey City in 1824, proposed to build a large canal linking cities in the state. While engaging in this endeavor it also became involved in issuing large amounts of paper money and working with others, including in Michigan during the wildcat era and in Holland, in floating loans and distributing bills. Its activities were viewed with doubt by *Niles' Weekly Register* and many other newspapers, but the company went on and on, strengthening its image by hiring public figures such as erstwhile Secretary of the Treasury Louis McLane and E.R. Biddle, of the Biddle family in Philadelphia. An impressive canal was indeed built, with inclined planes, stations, and more. By 1842 the company owed but could not pay $4,000,000, including $800,000 to the state of Michigan, $2,000,000 to the state of Indiana, and $1,300,000 to British investors.[40]

Replacing the rules of 1812, the General Banking Law was enacted in 1850, under which the state treasurer could commission the printing of paper money in denominations of $1 upward and issue these bills to banks that furnished appropriate surety in the form of interest-bearing securities. The maximum circulation of such paper was to be $3,000,000. New banks were required to be capitalized for at least $50,000 but no more than $500,000. When this law went into effect, already operating were 24 banks with $2,548,352 of currency, according to their reports.

The 1851 report of the New Jersey state treasurer stated that 15 new banks had been formed, issuing $767,602 worth of bills, a figure that increased to 19 banks in 1852 with circulation decreasing slightly to $766,742. In August 1851, *Banker's Magazine* printed this item, adapted from the *New York Evening Post:*

> There is a small locality in New Jersey, under the name of Tom's River, within about a day's journey from New York, which has been selected as the nominal place of issue of two Wall Street banks, in addition to one in the immediate neighborhood at the Bergen Iron Works. From this circumstance, the place derives some interest to us of New York, and it seems desirable to make known that the town or village contains four stores, one public house, and *two banks,* besides the one in the neighborhood.
>
> The landlord of the public house is the president of one of the banks, the Union Bank of Ocean County. The keeper of the dry-goods store, which, like all small country stores, is an *omnium gatherum,* having for sale almost every description of articles, is the president of the other, the Delaware and Hudson Bank of Ocean County.
>
> This out-of-the-way place presents several difficulties in the way of the redemption of the bills. The bills are mostly issued in Wall Street and sold largely to brokers at a discount to put them in circulation. Leaving the city at an early hour in the morning and taking the train by the Amboy Railroad, the locality cannot be reached before six o'clock in the evening—after banking hours. To present them for payment it is necessary to remain a day there, as the train passes before banking business commences, and a third day must pass before New York can be again reached.
>
> By the banking law of New Jersey, banks are entitled to three days' grace in redeeming their notes, after presentation; which enables the officers to send to New York for specie if any large amount of bills is presented for payment. In this manner is working the trade in a depreciated currency, which is on the increase, and which it behooves the state of New Jersey to remedy.
>
> The bank neighboring those at Tom's River is the Ocean Bank at Bergen Iron Works. The bills issued are a *fac-simile* of the issues of the bank of the same name in this city, the names of the officers excepted. This bank has been generally supposed to be located at Bergen in that part of New Jersey neighboring New York, but this is not so. . . .

On the same subject the *Newark Daily Advertiser* commented:

> The new banks established, or at least most of them, instead of being legitimate banks of discount as well as of issue, are simply *manufactories of paper money* for the benefit of their owners residing in other states, having no affinities here and of no advantage to New Jersey. . . .
>
> The more distant and out of the way, the greater the discount they will bear, and the greater the accruing profit. And to extend their circulation, nothing is easier than to adopt the name and general appearance of some well-known bank, in good credit, keeping the place of issue as much in the background as possible. For example, locating a "Delaware and Hudson Bank" amid the sands and pines of Ocean County, making the *title* very prominent, but having the *place* quite the reverse, so that the inexperienced are readily induced to receive the notes.[41]

In his annual message of 1853, Governor George F. Fort recognized the problems but placed much of the blame on out-of-staters:

> In many cases our banks, although ostensibly located in New Jersey, have their whole business operations conducted by brokers in other states. The facility with which they may be organized and located, without reference to the wants of the community or the business of the place, is destructive to all the legitimate ends of banking.

The situation prompted several revisions to the General Banking Law. Still, supervision was lax. When the Bank Commission was asked about the character of the Public Stock Bank in Belvidere, the Passaic County Bank in Paterson, the Wheat Growers Bank in Newton, the Bank of North America in Flemington, and the American Bank in Trenton, the reply was that the commissioners had no information. Seemingly, this situation was perfectly fine, as "no legal complaint has been made concerning them."[42]

Gradually, certain wildcat banks were rooted out and enjoined. *Banker's Magazine* gave this report of three such paper mills in June 1855:

> The American Exchange Bank at Cape May County Court House, the Wheat Growers Bank at Newton, and the Merchants Bank at Bridgeton have been closed by injunction issued from the Court of Chancery, and are now being wound up by order of said court. . . .

Problems continued, as shown in this 1857 account from the State Banking Committee regarding the Commercial Bank of Perth Amboy:

> Only 15 shares of stock are held by the three Jerseymen who are in the board of direction. The company is doing a large business by sending their notes into distant parts of the Union, and yet have not a single officer that is properly qualified for his duty; and there being no directors, duly elected and sworn, the bill-holders are deprived of even the scanty security contemplated by the renewal of the charter. In short, so far as your committee can learn, every act on the part of the bank, since the removal of the injunction, with the exception of the rendering of two quarterly statements to the State Treasurer, has been a willful violation of the law under which they have an existence. . . .
>
> As the present stockholders have shown that they are unworthy of this high trust, your committee cannot hesitate in recommending that it be taken from them. It is a matter for regret that loss will result to the bill-holders from the adoption of the proposed course; but "the public good" demands that the evil should be checked now,

A $2 note of the Morris County Bank, Morristown, New Jersey, with the green tint background. The red letter A was probably a control notation of some kind for the bank, not the plate letter (which coincidentally is also A). Originally the imprint of Rawdon, Wright, Hatch & Edson appeared at the lower right, above "Individually Responsible," but it was removed from the plate before this bill was printed. There are at least three plate varieties of this note, the first with the RWH&E imprint alone, then shared with ABNCo, then, as here, with ABNCo alone.

Chartered in 1836, the Morris County Bank operated until 1861, then closed—a rather unusual time, as this was an era of banking prosperity, and the Panic of 1857 had been relegated to history. At that time its capital was $90,500, William N. Wood was cashier, and Jesse Smith was president. Today, bills of this bank range from SENC to easily available as remainders, as here.

> rather than after its full development, when the same remedy would produce far more serious consequences. In accordance with these views, your committee have attached to their report an act for the repeal of the charter, and the appointment of receivers to wind up the company's affairs.[43]

The state authorities did not seem to get it right, and a few years later the era of note-issuing ended, leaving New Jersey citizens with memories of many frauds, probably outdone only by Michigan in this regard. However, it is only proper to note that, unlike Michigan, the state of New Jersey also had dozens of properly conducted banks.

Numismatic Comments

Carefully studied by George Wait in his 1976 text, augmented by information in the James A. Haxby text (1988), and extended by a flood of hitherto unknown proofs in the Christie's sales of 1990 and 1991 (which included many wildcat issues of the 1850s), collectible bills of New Jersey form a particularly extensive listing today. While there are rarities, enough notes exist that a representative collection can be gathered within the space of a few years. Generally, any auction or fixed-price list of Obsolete Currency has a generous number of New Jersey issues in it. The later notes are especially colorful.

The bank frauds of the 19th century, costly to citizens holding millions of dollars in face value of worthless bills, translate into large quantities of unredeemed and remainder bills being on the market today.

Currency of New York

Number of banks in the Haxby *Standard Catalog:* 654.

Historical Notes

The first entry in commercial banking in the state was the Bank of New York, which commenced business in New York City on June 9, 1784. A review of this and other early banks is given in chapter 2. Suffice it to say that by the first decade of the 19th century, New York City was firmly established as the banking center of the United States, with Philadelphia (headquarters of the Bank of the United States) solidly in second place, followed by Boston. New York City was the *money center* of America as well, the place where exchange rates were often established. It was also the epicenter of the publishing of financial journals, bank-note reporters, and financial data.

In his *History of Banking,* Knox suggests that banks of the state could be "naturally divided" into three groups:

> 1. From the adoption of the Constitution of the United States in 1789 to 1829. This may properly be called the period of chartered banks.
> 2. The next period extends from 1829 until 1838, and is that of the institutions known as the safety-fund banks. These banks were chartered banks, but they were, in a manner not previously known, bound together into a banking system by the provisions of the Safety Fund Law of 1829. Although the period from 1829 to 1838 has been characterized as that of the safety-fund system, because during that

time this system held the prominent place, yet it will be seen that for many years after 1837 the safety-fund system continued to exist alongside of the free banking system.

3. The free banking system went into operation in 1838, and continued [to the end of the era studied here].

For me and other numismatist-historians, these divisions are not as important as is the time line of economics (good times, wars, panics, etc.) in combination with various bank rules. The superb research of John Jay Knox was based mainly on state bank commission reports and reading through much of *Niles' Weekly* (later *National*) *Register*. Banks that operated without benefit of charter were often ignored, as were the important accounts in independent financial journals. Similarly, while state safety funds, free-banking laws, and so on, are useful to contemplate, actual banking often operated outside these restrictions—witness, for example, chaotic banking in the state of New Jersey. Because of this reality, Knox's book serves as a matrix for studying state banks (but not their currency), to which must be added outside information and abundant tweaking of figures and dates.

As related in chapter 2, chartered banking in the state of New York was primarily a matter of having the right political connections in Albany, the state capital. Accordingly, favored banks operated under charters, but some did not. Still others, and the Bank of New York is an example, conducted business for a long time without a charter (1784 to 1791), then became official when a charter was granted.

This account of the Farmers and Mechanics Bank of Albany, chartered in 1811, reflects politics at the time:

> Mr. Solomon Southwick was the first president. This gentleman was at that period in the zenith of his power and prosperity. He controlled the *Albany Register,* which at that time possessed a most commanding influence on the Democratic public of the state of New York.
>
> He was prepossessing in his appearance and generous in his nature. and was almost worshipped by the Republican members of the Legislature. He was printer to the state, and its patronage that year, by means of the insolvent notices growing out of a law passed during the session of 1811, threw into his coffers gold in unmeasured quantities, and now the influence and power of a popular bank were placed in his hands.[44]

From the early days to the onset of the War of 1812 in June of that year, 19 banks were officially chartered in the state by those who had connections in Albany. Because of the difficulty of obtaining official sanction, in the early 19th century unchartered banks and other issuers of paper money sprang up in the state. Bank-note engravers such as Abner Reed supplied them with the notes they needed, and many of these businesses carved a niche in commerce. The Catskill Aqueduct Association, the Utica Insurance Company, the Little Falls Aqueduct Association, and dozens of merchants, turnpikes, and other entities issued currency.

Among the various banks, chartered and otherwise, some were operated in violation of certain banking rules, such as those concerning keeping records and issuing paper money. To prevent violations, in 1818 the legislature enacted a law stating that only corporations expressly authorized by the state could issue currency; this law was widely ignored. For example, the infamous Marble Manufacturing Company (see the Malapar scheme discussed in chapter 7) operated openly in New York City and duped the public with hundreds of thousands of dollars in worthless bills.

Many of the early charters were crafted with special provisions. However, the first charter that mandated bills be redeemed in specie was that for the Bank of Niagara, in Buffalo, incorporated in 1816. Later this rule became standard. However, rules were overwhelmed by reality numerous times when shortages of coins or runs on banks forced specie payment suspensions.

From the beginning of the War of 1812 until 1829, when the Safety Fund Act was passed (effective on April 2, 1829), 24 banks were officially chartered. Safety Fund banks, in operation from 1829 until 1838, were supposed to guarantee safety of currency to the public, backed by deposits in a state fund paid in installments, eventually to reach 3% of a bank's capital. If a bank or two failed, this fund would provide for redemption of the paper money at par. Banks began their contributions in 1831. In 1832 there were 52 banks that were members of the Safety Fund plan and 12 mostly older banks that were not. The idea was fine in concept, but in execution there were so many failures (beginning in 1841 with the Wayne County Bank of Palmyra) that the fund ran out of money in 1842, this being in the Hard Times era. Again, this is why a *numismatic* historian, bringing the history of paper money into the narrative, is apt to get a better picture than is someone who relies on digests of state legislation. Under the 1829 law, three bank commissioners were appointed to visit the various banks at least quarterly and submit an annual report to the legislature.

In 1834 there was a chill in the economy in and around New York, which some blamed on the machinations of New York City bankers. Others stated that the withdrawal of funds from the second Bank of the United States was the cause. Business soon revived, but in the meantime some banks violated the law out of necessity as they were unable to redeem their bills in specie.

In the same year the Coinage Act of June 28 provided for a reduction in the authorized weight of gold coins, which had not been seen in circulation since 1821. This act had the immediate effect of making silver coins scarce in contrast, as silver was considered to be worth full face value, while gold coins were slightly depreciated. Silver half dollars, the most plentiful denomination, disappeared from circulation and commanded a 1% premium at exchange offices. To bring them back into general use, in New York an act of March 31, 1835, forbade the circulation of any bills below the denomination of $2 (effective in September of that year), with reduction below $3 and $5 scheduled later, the last by September 1836. Draconian penalties included $5 for passing a $1 note and forfeiture of the charter for any bank paying out small-denomination bills.

Politicking continued in the granting of bank charters. In 1834 one observer commented:

> The profits of the place of commissioner to make a bank is estimated in the New York papers, at from 500 to 1,000 dollars! We know not how they are realized. The *New York American* states certain things in relation to the legislative operations concerning banks at the last session, which are well calculated to surprise us—yet being local in their character we shall not particularly notice them. But the facts . . . are matters of general interest, as showing the arrangement of public officers, as a privileged class, separated from the people, and entitled to the "spoils."[45]

On September 19, 1835, the *Schenectady Cabinet* quoted Amos Kendall, postmaster of the United States in the Jackson administration, as perhaps being applicable to the new paper money rules: "We owe an obligation to the laws, but a higher one to the communities in which we live, and if the former be perverted to destroy the latter, it is patriotism to disregard them." At great risk the editor of the *Cabinet* went on:

> Believing that the act passed at the last session of the legislature of this state, restricting the circulation of bank notes under the denomination of $5, to be contrary to the spirit of the various laws incorporating the several banks of this state—they being established for the ostensible object of aiding the business operations of the several communities in which they are located, and believing our "obligation to the community in which we live" to be "higher" or greater than our "obligation to the law" or act above referred to, we hereby give notice, that from and after the 1st day of September, proximo, we shall continue to receive bills of the denomination of one dollar, contrary to, and as though said act had never been passed.

The *Oneida Whig* stated this: "We shall take one dollar notes at our office—law to the contrary notwithstanding. We understand this is the determination of the merchants in town generally."

Again, as was often the case in bank rules made by state legislatures in New York and elsewhere, what seemed like a good idea in theory proved to be completely impractical and unenforceable in practice. A new political administration passed a law on May 16, 1837, slightly less than a week into the Panic of 1837, allowing small bills once again.

In 1838 there were about 100 active banks in the state.[46] In that year the Free-Banking Law was enacted, cited by some historians as the first in the nation, and was widely heralded as the answer to all past problems. However, Michigan was actually the first with such a law, and it was a disaster. In New York the Free-Banking Act permitted groups of citizens to form banks, provided they deposited securities with the state. The state had charge of currency, with officials delegated to countersign bills.

This related state report covers most of 1848:

> *Destruction of currency:* There have been received, counted, and burnt, in this department during the year ending 15th December instant, 753,312 mutilated bank notes, amounting to $4,036,833; and during the same period there have been countersigned, numbered, and registered, 683,934 new notes, amounting to $4,530,754, and delivered to the banks entitled to the same.
>
> This vast amount of labor has been performed by the principal register, aided by but one clerk during the larger part of the year, with the occasional assistance of the book-keeper, and of one other person employed in numbering. The large increase of business made it necessary to employ an additional clerk, whose term of service commenced in August last. The expenses of the department during the year were $4,700.35, which amount was refunded to the treasury at the close of the fiscal year, by drawing on each bank for its ratable proportion according to law.[47]

Besides creating a lot of accounting paperwork for the state government, the Free-Banking Law had other problems, such as state inattention to the real value of the stocks and bonds provided for surety, and actions of banks failing to redeem their bills on a timely basis or making them payable at distant locations. Capers such as this one were many under the new law:

> In November 1841 the Commercial Bank of Buffalo was examined and an overissue of $180,000 was found. The cashier swore that these notes were in the possession of agents at New York and Albany and had been redeemed. It was discovered, on inquiry at Albany, that the president of the bank had received notes to a large amount from the redemption agents, but had again put them in circulation. An injunction was at once secured. The overissue amounted to about $190,000, but about $60,000 of this amount the bank claimed as its property, not in circulation.[48]

It is probably fair to say the Free-Banking Law prevented some frauds—certainly more effectively than was done in New Jersey under a related law—but did not prevent criminal abuses by those who had a mindset to deceive the public. During the entire period under discussion, the banks of New York City were more closely watched and received more press notices than did those in other locations in the state. Accordingly, frauds in the city were relatively few.

By 1843 there had been many problems with banks in the state, as elsewhere, long lingering, but brought to a head with the Hard Times era. The Act of 1843 sought to end the paper money problem by requiring all chartered banks to take stock of their outstanding bills, report the amount to the comptroller of the state, and submit redeemed old bills to the comptroller in order to secure new ones. This ruling later was extended to cover free banks as well. The comptroller was to select the bank-note companies to print the bills, thus placing the comptroller or staffers in a position of great power. Favored companies received contracts, while others who applied (W.L. Ormsby is an example) were not considered. Marius Schoonmaker, superintendent of the Bank Department, appointed in 1854 over the objections of bankers in the state, was implicated for taking bribes in 1856, but the matter was hushed up. He went on to hold important positions with the city of Kingston, New York.

By 1851 there were 95 traditional incorporated banks active in New York City, plus many free banks, about 200 in all. Throughout the 1850s more free banks were chartered, some good, some bad. In New York City the manipulations of currency dealers, the paying of bank-note reporter publishers to puff a worthless bank, the dissemination of false information about the soundness of certain banks to depreciate their notes, the buying and selling of large quantities of bills of worthless and even nonexistent banks, and other abuses continued, as they had for a long time.

It was also true, however, that city banks made a market in bills from distant places, often at just a nominal discount, providing a solidity for currency for banks outside the successful Suffolk Bank system in effect in New England. New York City was also a ready market for funding banks and dealing in their shares. The Clearing House, inaugurated on October 11, 1854, facilitated the settlement of accounts, including paper money, among the banks in the city. By this decade New York City was the center of the bank-note printing industry.

The city was often the starting point for pivotal events in the American economy. On May 10, 1837, New York City banks, while not the very first to suspend specie payments, did so across the banking system, and were thus blamed by some for causing the Panic of 1837 and the Hard Times era that followed.

Two decades later the Panic of 1857 began in August 1857 in the city, and in October all but one bank there suspended, catalyzing a wave that caught up most other banks around the United States. At the time there were about 300 banks active in the state. After the Panic of 1857, only a few new banks were chartered in the state of New York. Most were conducted properly. An 1862 report stated that only three insolvent banks were currently in the hands of receivers. No doubt this situation was due as much to the strong wartime economy as to improved honesty on the part of certain financial officers.

Among bankers of the state there were certainly some saints. Perhaps one candidate was a man who for 36 years was the cashier of and signed bank notes for the Ontario Bank of Canandaigua. The beginning of his obituary reads as follows:

> Henry B. Gibson, of Canandaigua, who died in that village the 20th of November, 1863, exemplified the beneficent effects of habitual temperance and undeviating honesty. By abstinence from intoxicating drinks, from tobacco in all its forms, and by simplicity of diet and regularity of conduct, he attained an age verging towards fourscore years of uninterrupted vigor of body and mind; while, by integrity in all his dealings, he amassed, in an uncommercial locality, a fortune which is probably not less than a million of dollars, and may be more; acquired, too, in advancing the welfare of the public, and of all persons connected with him in business. . . .[49]

Beginning in 1863, most of the stronger institutions in the state converted to become National Banks.

Numismatic Comments

New York joins Massachusetts as a large well-populated state with many banks, for which no specific numismatic reference has ever been written. Accordingly, information about the currency of New York can be found in the Haxby text for starters, but after that, you will have to find listings here and there in auction catalogues, articles in *Paper Money* and the *Bank Note Reporter,* and elsewhere.

The state records of bank-note issuance commencing with the Safety Fund era into the Free-Banking Act years are particularly extensive and yield a rich historical archive today. Troubled banks in particular are discussed in detail. Moreover, as New York City was the focal point of American finance and banking, the *Banker's Magazine, New York Journal of Commerce,* and other periodicals gave the state more attention than any other. As to the potential of a specialized text on this state, if banks alone (not scrip issuers and other entities) were treated, the volume would be of immense size.

Bills issued in New York commence in the late 18th century and continue through early 1866, with more than 650 banks involved—more than double the number of any other state. The designs are wonderfully diverse, for the Patent Stereotype Steel Plate was not a factor there, despite its omnipresent use in neighboring Massachusetts in the early 19th century. Imprints of engravers and printers are many, and a collection of different varieties of logotypes of these talented artists and partnerships on bills from this state alone would be extensive. Motifs are diverse. Beginning in a significant way in the 1830s, ornate designs were used, followed in due course with color overprints and other features.

Among early banks there were many operated fraudulently or incompetently, leaving behind them interesting stories, including the Columbia Bank in Hudson, various of Jacob Barker's enterprises, Malapar's Marble Manufacturing Company, Samuel D. Dakins's Bank of Central New York, and others, a number of which are discussed in the present text.

When large numbers of long-hidden proof notes came to market from the ABNCo paper archives through Christie's in 1990 and 1991, and through other distributions here and there, many hitherto unknown designs became available, with the bills of New York being particularly rich in this regard. The collection of John Jay Ford Jr., auctioned by Stack's, brought to light many more rarities in the New York series. Today, these notes are widely dispersed on the collector's market, eagerly sought, and add much to the dimension of a specialized collection, creating possibilities that were not dreamed of a generation ago.

Currency of North Carolina

Number of banks in the Haxby *Standard Catalog:* 23.
Specialized text: J. Roy Pennell, *Obsolete Bank Notes of North Carolina,* 1965.

Historical Notes

The first banks were chartered by the North Carolina State Assembly in 1804. The Bank of Cape Fear, located in Wilmington, had a capital set at a minimum of $50,000, not to exceed $250,000. The bank could go into operation when half the stock, or a minimum of $25,000, was subscribed. A branch was allowed to be opened in Fayetteville. The Bank of Newbern was chartered for a maximum of $200,000.

In 1810 the State Bank of North Carolina was authorized, located in Raleigh and with branches in Edenton, Fayetteville, Newbern, Salisbury, Tarborough, and Wilmington, with capital to be a maximum of

A $1 proof note of the Niagara County Bank, Lockport, New York, from a plate by Danforth, Wright & Co., New York and Philadelphia.

The Niagara County Bank was founded in Lockport in 1856, succeeding certain residual interests of the collapsed Canal Bank. The capital of $200,000 was not raised, and was reduced to a manageable $100,000. Later, the original figure was achieved. In 1864 it became the Niagara County National Bank, charter 639.

$1,600,000. In 1814 the Cape Fear and Newbern bank charters were extended to 1835, and the capital was increased by $525,000 and $575,000 respectively with $100,000 of each amount to be reserved for the state.

In 1816, alarmed at the notes being issued by the Bernie Manufacturing Co. and the Fayetteville School Association, the state assembly forbade any but chartered banks to issue bills.

On June 12, 1819, *Niles' Weekly Register* told of problems and double standards in the practice of banking in a time of nationwide economic difficulties:

> A meeting of delegates from the State Bank of North Carolina, the Cape Fear Bank, and the bank of Newbern, was lately held at Fayetteville "to take into consideration the present state of the country as it affects the business of the banks, and to report whether any measures are proper on the part of the banks."
>
> The report speaks about brokers and runs upon the banks—the difficulty of collecting their debts, &c. and recommends that the banks shall "refuse to pay specie to brokers and others who they believe have obtained their notes by purchase, at a discount, for the purpose of obtaining specie." It appears however, that these banks in some cases, have given draughts on New York, &c. for large amounts of their notes, even to "brokers." And that they pay off, or satisfy, all their notes received in what they consider a *regular* trade.

At the same meeting, the State Bank of North Carolina and the Bank of Newbern resolved to stop paying specie at par for their bills, but to take them only at a discount. The Bank of Cape Fear refused to join the plan. This prompted William M. Gouge, writing in 1833, to observe: "Then commenced the system of usury and extortion, which has since been carried on with such unparalleled audacity, under the name of *exchange.*"[50]

Banking practices continued to be in disarray, with many complaints voiced in the press. The state assembly of 1828 to 1829 studied a report on banks, which related that contrary to charter provisions, the banks' capital had not been paid fully in gold and silver, and that bankers had tried every mode possible to avoid redeeming bills for coins. It was also revealed that it was common practice to give discounts (loans) in paper money, but to require repayment in specie. Further, the banks speculated in their own bills by buying them in New York City and other places at discounted prices.

In the same session the assembly sought to end commercial banks and passed an act for the State Bank to wind up its affairs. No banks were to issue bills under $5 after 1832 and were to make no loans after 1834, at which time existing loans were to be called. This change caused great consternation, and bills of the State Bank, already at a discount of up to 8% because they were difficult to redeem in specie, dropped to discounts of as much as 14%.

At a meeting held in Oxford in 1828, it was stated that the cashiers of the main office of the State Bank and the branch at Fayetteville had resigned, the countryside was burdened with depreciated paper money, and

> People ought to treat the banks, just as the banks treat them; and all rotten banks should be destroyed. The parts of our country that were most cursed with such operations and "rag-barons" have now a wholesome currency.[51]

In ensuing years, the paper money situation continued to deteriorate as citizens continued to have trouble redeeming them, banks were not giving loans to aid business, and the future financial situation appeared bleak.

On November 18, 1833, there was a change. The Bank of Cape Fear had its charter renewed until 1855, with a capital of $800,000, and was allowed to issue bills up to twice that amount, but with no denominations below $3. The Merchants Bank of Newbern was established with a capital of $250,000, and the Albemarle Bank in Edenton was authorized at $200,000. It was expected that a new era of banking would truly benefit the people.

At the same time the State Bank of North Carolina name was revived, and a new corporation received a charter for $1,500,000, with the state reserving 40% of that. Branches were to be opened quickly in Newbern and Tarborough. The directors requested permission to open offices in Charlotte, Leadsville, Milton, and Morganton. By 1856 it had nine branches in operation.

At its session of 1836 to 1837, the assembly further extended the charter of the Bank of Cape Fear to 1860 and granted banking privileges to the Louisville, Cincinnati & Charleston Railroad, under certain requirements. Other sessions provided for adjustments in the rules, capital, and other aspects of banks.

The Panic of 1837 brought problems, and banks suspended specie payments. They continued to deceive the public by trading in their own discounted bills. In 1841 they refused to redeem their paper money, while at the same time they paid heavy dividends to their stockholders.[52] By this time many observers of the banking scene in North Carolina had long since concluded that financial institutions did not

A $5 Bank of Lexington note payable at Graham, North Carolina, signed and dated April 6, 1861, less than 10 days before the onset of the Civil War (on April 15). From a plate by the American Bank Note Co. The vignette at the left shows a slave picking cotton. The double plate letter Aa, in script at the upper right, reflects the fact that plate A was strengthened or re-entered (the term used), or changed in some other way, to permit continued use. The plate survives today in the archives of ABNCo.

operate in a way to truly benefit the population, and that banking in most other states was conducted on a higher plane.

In the early 1850s several savings banks were chartered, but they were not allowed to issue paper money. During the decade other commercial note-issuing banks were set up. In 1856 there were 29 banks and branches active in North Carolina. The thought of having a Free-Banking Law had been discussed by the state assembly, but it did not materialize. Otherwise the number of commercial banks in the state would have been much greater. Writers in financial journals such as *Banker's Magazine* suggested that as a result, the banks in the state were especially solid, a dramatic change from the early 1840s. By this time many of the problems of Hard Times years and earlier had been forgotten.

Numismatic Comments

From an artistic viewpoint collecting bills of North Carolina may be ideal. The early notes of the State Bank, Bank of Cape Fear, Bank of Newbern, and other issues, simple in design, are for the most part scarce to rare today, with many marked SENC in the Haxby text. Accordingly, specialists will not lack challenges. Among Cape Fear Bank bills there are many interesting odd denominations, a numismatic delight. The second State Bank of North Carolina bills may be collectible by general types, but those of the branches are generally unavailable, save for a scattered few varieties, again a challenge.

Many colorful bills from the 1850s survive in the form of unissued remainders as well as redeemed bills that were punch canceled or marked, but not destroyed. These can be collected easily enough today. To the above mix may be added many previously rare and even unobtainable proofs now collectible, but scarce, as a result of the ABNCo archives sales of 1990 and 1991.

Currency of Ohio

Number of banks in the Haxby *Standard Catalog:* 96.
Specialized text: Wendell Wolka, *A History of Nineteenth Century Ohio Obsolete Bank Notes and Scrip,* 2004.

Historical Notes

The state's first official banking company was formed by the initial legislature session of Ohio on April 15, 1803, incorporating the Miami Exporting Co., of Cincinnati, a trader in goods that in 1807 went exclusively into banking. The Bank of Marietta, on the Ohio River, was incorporated on February 10, 1808, and immediately began to distribute its currency far and wide. The fraudulent Bank of Hillsborough, Amherst, New Hampshire, dispatched a representative to make the arduous journey over the wilderness to Marietta to conspire in paper money trading. Later accounts of this bank often told of its problems, and it seemed sure to fail. Somehow it endured, avoided prosecution, and within a decade became respectable, a depository for federal funds, and often maintained specie payments when other banks could not. It went into liquidation when its charter expired in 1843, a matter of law, not fraud. But then, during the process of winding up, the State Bank of Ohio system was instituted in 1845, and a segue was made whereby certain assets of the old bank became the Marietta branch of the State Bank.

Other banks were chartered across the state and issued paper money, to which were added many bills and scrip notes from unauthorized institutions (the Owl Creek Bank of Mount Vernon, studied earlier in the text, was one of many). On February 8, 1815, the legislature passed a law to prohibit the unauthorized issuance of paper money. This law had little effect, as printers and bank-note companies (Murray, Fairman, Draper & Co. was the most prominent) filled any orders that they received. This was a period of great growth, with farmers who had toiled in the rock-littered hillsides of New England eagerly arranging to buy fertile prairie land in Ohio, never mind the effort needed to clear the forests. Towns sprang up everywhere, and the inhabitants of each of them appreciated having bank notes, unofficial or otherwise, as an aid to commerce. If such bills were paid out and received by local merchants, that was all that mattered. The War of 1812 period was particularly chaotic in the state—with rampant inflation, disregard for authority, and instability in the marketplace.

On January 27, 1816, the state legislated another act to prevent unauthorized bills, launching what historian Knox in his *History of Banking* viewed as "beginning a war against unauthorized banks and bank currency that was waged by the state during the continuance of state banks issuing currency." This act had no great practical effect, because mills, societies, and others continued issuing bills, and many banks that were chartered paid out quantities of unreported currency.

Perhaps in anticipation of things to come—what with the impending establishment of the second Bank of the United States—in 1816 the Ohio State Legislature chartered six more banks and extended the charters of seven banks currently doing business. The newcomers included the Commercial Bank of Lake Erie in rapidly growing Cleveland, the Belmont Bank in St. Clairsville, the Franklin Bank in Columbus, the Lancaster Bank, the Bank of Mount Pleasant, and the Bank of West Union.

When branches of the second Bank of the United States opened in Cincinnati in 1817 and Chillicothe in 1818, currency of legal banks in the state depreciated, causing much ill will. The Monster, as the many-tentacled second Bank was called, did not cooperate with regional institutions and had no intention of doing so. With its great financial strength, that bank could buy up bills of competing institutions, then make surprise demands for payment in specie. Few state banks had sufficient coins on hand to ward off such attacks.

The state levied a tax of $50,000 on these branches of the Bank of the United States, to take place if the offices did not stop business by September 15, 1819. The matter was hotly contested, and in 1824 the United States Supreme Court ruled against the state of Ohio. In the meantime, the Cincinnati branch closed in 1820. The Chillicothe branch shut its doors in 1825, after which the Cincinnati branch was reactivated.[53]

The second Bank of the United States, still widely detested in Ohio, expired in 1836, having been in the winding-up process for several years, following Jackson's 1832 veto of its charter renewal. The swan song of the Cincinnati office, or at least its facilities, was given in *Niles' Weekly Register,* November 14, 1835:

> The United States branch bank at Cincinnati has made disposition of all its concerns to the banks of that city, in the following manner: The Commercial Bank takes the banking house on Main between 3d and 4th streets, and the debts due the branch at St. Louis. The Lafayette Bank takes the current debt owing to the branch in the city, amounting to $880,000. The Ohio Life Insurance and Trust Company purchase the suspended debt due the branch, and has the option to take $400,000 of the debt due the agency on bond and mortgage; is to redeem the notes of the branch, receive and collect all collection paper, pay the deposits due to individuals, and generally to become the depository of the Bank of the United States and its agents. The Bank of the United States deposits with the Trust Company $400,000 for 20 years, taking therefore, certificates of deposit at 5 percent.

Years later it was the failure of the New York City branch of the Ohio Life Insurance and Trust Co. that catalyzed the Panic of 1857.

To avert Nicholas Biddle's so called successor Bank of the United States of Pennsylvania from getting ideas about moving into Ohio, on March 16, 1836, there was passed "An act to prohibit, within this state, any branch, office or agency of the Bank of the United States, as recently chartered by the Legislature of Pennsylvania." In 1838 this was backed up by another law prohibiting the issuance of bills in the state by any other than a state-chartered bank. Certain laws were redundant with earlier legislation, and in any event, merchants and others continued to pay out bills. In addition to bills from Ohio banks, currency of Kentucky and elsewhere was common in circulation.

In its issue of August 14, 1819, *Niles' Weekly Register* printed this item:

> *Ohio banks.* The Farmers and Mechanics Bank of Cincinnati, bank of Chillicothe, Bank of Marietta, Bank of Steubenville, Bank of Mount Pleasant, the Lancaster Bank, Belmont Bank, Western Reserve Bank, and Farmers and Mechanics Bank of Steubenville, are "specie paying banks"—the rest redeem their own notes with the notes of other banks, or do not trouble themselves about redeeming them at all.

Similar to actions taken by other states, on February 9, 1839, well into the Panic of 1837, when most banks were not redeeming their bills in silver or gold coins, the state legislated that no bills less than $3 were to be paid out after July 4 of that year, and none of less than $5, or of any denomination between $6 and $9, after October 1. The intent was that silver coins would automatically reappear in circulation. Instead, scrip and other low-denomination bills proliferated as merchants and others paid them out.

Abuses continued to be widespread due to the lack of practical oversight by state authorities. Historian Knox related:

> Numerous banks had been incorporated [since 1816] within that period, some of which had been successful, but many failed. The banks gave no security for their circulation beyond their general assets, and when a bank failed the notes were in many cases found to be worthless. This frequently occurred even when ordinary prudence had been exercised in the management of the bank, because of the inability of borrowers to meet their obligations as well as the inability of the officers to realize on property, the assets of the bank of necessity undergoing shrinkage. Another aggravating source of distrust was the failure of banks which from results appear to have been organized purely for speculation.
>
> One of the most flagrant examples is the Bank of Gallipolis. In 1839 a gentleman claiming to be a capitalist from Buffalo, with two others, arrived in Gallipolis and proceeded to organize the Bank of Gallipolis. These gentlemen were very plausible in their appearance and representations and soon succeeded in starting the bank with a capital of $200,000. The directors authorized an issue of $175,000 of circulation, and it is said that so far as the books of the bank show, that was all that was ever issued. When the bank failed, perhaps two years later, it was discovered that the gentlemanly managers had had printed and issued $1,200,000 without the knowledge of the directors. This currency was scattered all over the South and West. . . .

On February 25, 1839, the state provided for a Board of Bank Commissioners. In this time frame many other states did the same thing. Earlier, rules were aplenty but enforcement of them was erratic and sometimes nonexistent. On March 7, 1842, the General Banking Law sought to codify the operation of such institutions, adapting worthwhile measures from the past and dropping those that were not feasible, taking some provisions from similar legislation that had been enacted in other states. However, the state remained poor in its supervision, and during the decade of the 1840s, worthless bills continued to be issued in large quantities.

The erratic nature of banking in the state is revealed by the numbers: In 1840 there were 37 active banks, with a capital totaling $10,507,521. At the end of 1843 there were but eight, although the capital had increased to $21,171,807.[54] A flap arose when the highly respected *Hunt's Merchants Magazine* ran an article, "Banks of Ohio," which discussed the failure of banks during this era, but got many of its facts wrong, stating, for example, that the long-dead Bank of Gallipolis was among those that survived after 1844 and continued to do good business.[55]

A banking law passed in 1845 provided for new banks as well as the transition of some older institutions to follow the latest laws. A Safety Fund was set up to help protect the public, in connection with the newly formed State Bank of Ohio. This change engendered a period of growth, helped along by the onset of good times in 1844, the first full year of economic well-being after the Panic of 1837.

As of November 15, 1846, there were 17 branches of the Ohio State Bank in operation (mostly with success)—nine new or "independent" banks, and eight that had been established earlier. In ensuing years more banks were chartered, and the State Bank opened additional branches. The Free-Banking Law of November 15, 1851, spurred more growth, and within a year there were 12 free banks joining 12 independent banks, five old-line banks, and 41 branches of the Ohio State Bank. The later banking scene is discussed at some length in chapter 16, including the notorious "crowbar law" and other events.

After the mid-1850s and continuing into the 1860s, bills of most banks in the state remained good. However, many of the privately owned banks suffered greatly with changing rules, taxes, and other matters. Paper money distribution was reduced in the 1850s, but the deficiency was easily filled by a flood of bills of uncertain value from Indiana and Illinois in particular, but also from Kentucky, Michigan, Louisiana—including the distant New Orleans, the last being closely connected with Ohio in the river trade.[56]

When the curtain came down on the note-issuing era, Ohio may have garnered the prize for the most erratic banking laws. At one point in the 1850s, there were four different acts, each with its own rules and regulations, under which banks operated, depending on when and how they were chartered!

Note for $1 of the Miami Exporting Co., payable at their BANK in CINCINNATI, printed in such a way that at casual glance this seems to be a note of the latter bank, although there was no such institution as the "Bank in Cincinnati." Dated March 4, 1844. From a plate from the Cincinnati office of Rawdon, Wright & Hatch.

The Miami Exporting Co., chartered for a maximum of $500,000 (but set at $200,000) in 1803 and with banking privileges, was the first bank in Ohio. The main purpose of the company was to engage in trade on the Ohio River, connecting to the Mississippi River, in the exporting of agricultural products to New Orleans. The charter provided that the company could exchange its paper money for goods or for notes of other banks, but there was no requirement to redeem them in coins. In 1807 the firm discontinued its exporting trade and engaged exclusively in the banking business.

Although the Miami Exporting Co. was well known to those in the banking trade, to citizens and law-enforcement officials at a distance, its bills were questioned. In 1816 in Harrisburg, Pennsylvania, four men with $300,000 in counterfeit bills of the Miami Exporting Co. were apprehended but soon released when the lawmen determined that no crime had been committed, as there was no such bank in existence! (Related court decisions relating to bills of nonchartered banks were handed down in other states.) The bank failed in 1822, but quantities of its notes remained and were passed into circulation later, with current dates, as the example shown here.

Numismatic Comments

Perhaps no better evidence can be given concerning the variety of notes produced in Ohio than to point out that Wendell Wolka's book on the subject is the only specialized text to cross the 1,000-page mark! However, it includes scrip in addition to the bills of state-chartered banks. This volume is a rich combination of banking and town history along with information about the bills themselves.

Quite a few institutions within the state have fascinating stories, some of which evolved into banking through other activities, such as the Granville Alexandrian Society and the Washington Social Library Company. The State Bank of Ohio with its many branches offers collecting opportunities, many of the bills being rather plain on the face or, sometimes, with the branch name inked in, but with ornate colorful imprints including the bank's name on the back. The Mormon notes of the Kirtland Safety Society Bank and, especially, the short-lived Anti-Bank, cause buyers to scramble when they are offered.

A large collection of Ohio bills can furnish an interesting pursuit over a period of time. Despite the excellence of the Wolka book, dealers report that demand for bills of this state is rather subdued, perhaps yielding opportunities. Most currency dates from the era of reckless banking prior to the 1850s and thus is not colorful visually, but it can be extremely colorful romantically and historically. Later currency with ornate vignettes is much scarcer as a class, as many such bills were redeemed.

Currency of Pennsylvania

Number of banks in the Haxby *Standard Catalog:* 166.
Specialized text: Richard T. Hoober, *Pennsylvania Obsolete Notes and Scrip,* 1985.

Historical Notes

A study of Pennsylvania banks and their paper money can serve as a microcosm of currency in America. Just about everything happened here—the good, the bad, the logical, and the illogical. In addition the two Bank of the United States corporations were headquartered there, established in 1791 and 1816 respectively, plus Nicholas Biddle's so-called but unrelated "successor," the Bank of the United States of Pennsylvania. If a quick phrase were to summarize banking in Pennsylvania, it would be that the government over-regulated banking in an effort to gain control of the system and levy taxes, but the results were poor in terms of service to the public, especially with regard to redemption of bank bills. In the meantime, currency was issued in great profusion, by many different engraving partnerships and firms.

The Bank of North America, the first in the country, was chartered in 1782. The Bank of Pennsylvania, incorporated in 1793, was the first other than the Bank of the United States to set up branches. These and other early banks are discussed in chapter 2.

The Philadelphia Bank was incorporated on March 5, 1804, in what was probably America's most important banking city at the time, if the presence of the Bank of the United States is included. The Mint was there, and until 1800, when offices were removed to Washington City, it was the seat of the federal government. The Farmers and Mechanics Bank in the same city was set up in 1809.

The Banking Act of 1808, with a supplement in 1810, forbade banks outside Pennsylvania from doing business in the state and restricted the issuance of paper money to chartered banks. Rules in the state were destined to be ignored. In 1810 the Farmers Bank of Lancaster opened for business, with a capital set at $300,000, and issued bills, but did not have a state charter. This bank turned loose a flood of paper money and generated so much profit for its stockholders that annual dividends of 12% were paid, and loans were provided to insiders for up to double the amount of stock they owned.[57]

In 1811 three chartered banks were doing business in the state, with a slightly larger number of unofficial banks sharing the business and issuing paper. The Farmers and Mechanics Bank had $804,730 of bills in circulation, the Bank of Pennsylvania $1,425,203, and the Bank of Philadelphia $713,309. In this year the first Bank of the United States closed upon the expiration of its charter. "A number of businesses engaged in other operations, such as building bridges, styled themselves as banks and had bills of various denominations printed," wrote historian H.F. Baker. "No record exists today of the extent of such unofficial issues, but they were considerable in their time."[58]

The Act of March 21, 1814 (see below), loosened the currency-issuing rule, but it was reinstated on March 22, 1817. Throughout this era, individuals and others who desired to issue paper money or scrip did so more or less as they pleased. In Pennsylvania, as in other states, oversight was lax and prosecutions for the unauthorized issuing of currency (other than counterfeits) were almost nonexistent.

Concerning the 1814 legislation, Knox in his *History of Banking* noted this suggestion:

> It is hard to account for the demand that led to the passage of the Act of March 21, 1814, providing for the incorporation of 41 banks with an aggregate capitalization of some seventeen million dollars. Nothing appears to show that there was any lack of banking facilities, and it is to be assumed that the existing banks issued sufficient notes for purposes of circulation. It therefore seems probable that the opponents of this measure were in the right when they claimed that there was no popular demand for its passage, and that it was a piece of jobbery, engineered by speculators. . . .

These new banks were given the usual privilege of issuing paper money, but no denominations below $5. Under this bill, 37 banks actually set up in business. Many were small institutions conducted carelessly, with stockholders submitting IOUs to pay the capital. Within the next few years, the reputation of such banks and their bills was very low, worsened by the economy for the rest of the decade. By 1820 the sorry record showed that 15 of the 37 new banks had collapsed.

On August 31, 1814, the Bank of Pennsylvania, Bank of North America, Philadelphia Bank, and Farmers and Mechanics Bank announced that due to a shortage of coin, redemption of bills would be suspended temporarily. The War of 1812, still in progress, had resulted in a call for specie in all aspects of international trade, as the use of bills and credits was not acceptable to foreigners. No one knew the outcome of the war at that time. On August 24, British troops had engaged American soldiers on land in Maryland at the Battle of Bladensburg. The suspension spread. On September 14, 1814, *Niles' Weekly Register* noted:

> The banks of New-York, Philadelphia, and Baltimore have stopped their payments in specie. The great quantity of the precious metals drawn off by the enemy, through his friends amongst us, by the sale of bills of exchange, &c., has rendered this procedure necessary to secure the safety of our moneyed institutions. It is a very proper and prudent measure; unpleasant and inconvenient, indeed, but the preventive of absolute loss, and a guarantee of their future credit and usefulness. . . .

In October 1814, the Mint ran advertisements in *Poulson's American Daily Advertiser* offering to pay a premium for gold and silver coins.[59] Specie payments were resumed in 1817, but only intermittently. General economic conditions in Pennsylvania and elsewhere remained unsettled. Paper money was issued in large amounts by the many banks then in business, plus a host of other entities, the last leading to the Act of March 22, 1817, which reiterated that only chartered banks could do this. The Act of March 28, 1819, provided that banks *must* pay specie. Some did not have the wherewithal to do so, and in September the

Democratic Press, published in Philadelphia, reported that 11 banks had suspended their business and six were being liquidated. On October 9, 1819, *Niles' Weekly Register* commented on the quality of banks in the state:

> A few, prudently conducted, have maintained an honorable reputation. But the majority appear to have striven only to excel in acts of speculation—by which we mean *fraud.* Take the following as a sample: The directors of one of these broken banks privately agreed that after a certain day, known only to themselves, they would refuse to receive the notes of the bank in payment of debts due to it—which latter were to be transferred for the benefit of the concerned! What remedy is there to the people in a case like this? It is possible that the directors have provided for it, by dividing the capital, if any there was, among themselves—as we are told happened in another state, previous to resigning their office.

In 1820 there were 36 legitimate banks operating in Pennsylvania and so many *freebooters,* as phony banks were called, that they could not be easily evaluated, noted a historical account.[60] More phony banks were set up, while others folded. Concerning the last, *Niles' Weekly Register,* February 2, 1822, reported:

> *Pennsylvania.* The Northwestern Bank, at Meadville; the Allegheny Bank, at Bedford; the Centre Bank at Bellefonte; the Huntingdon Bank; the Northumberland Bank; Union and Columbia Bank, at Milton; the Marietta and Susquehannah Trading Company; the Agricultural and Manufacturing Bank, at Carlisle; the Farmers and Mechanics Bank of Greencastle, the Juniata Bank, at Lewistown; the bank of Washington, at Washington; and the Farmers and Mechanics Bank, at Pittsburg—are all officially declared to be "dissolved, unlawful and unincorporated."

By 1823 there were 17 chartered banks operating in Philadelphia and 32 at other places in the state. In addition, many renegade operations continued to turn out paper money in large quantities, mainly from the engraving companies in Philadelphia, who were eager for the business.

In the 1830s more bank regulations were passed, mainly regarding increasing state revenues through taxation. Oversight of bank operations remained lax, and during the decade there were many problems. In May 1837 banks suspended specie payments. On July 10, 1838, the governor directed that banks resume payments on August 13. After conferring among themselves, the banks went along with the proposal and did so. However, problems of the Hard Times era had not gone away, and in October 1839 payments were again suspended. In the meantime, anticipated revenue from taxes fell far short of expectations, and the state government was deep in debt. On January 15, 1841, again by legislative decree, the banks resumed payments under penalty of having their charters revoked. The problems in the state were too overwhelming, the banks had insufficient funds, and the closure of the fraud-shrouded Bank of the United States of Pennsylvania on February 4 was the final straw. A ripple effect spread throughout the state and to Delaware, always close in financial matters to Philadelphia, and banks were forced to stop paying coin. The Act of May 4, 1841, born of necessity, cast aside the charter revocation penalty. Specie payments remained in suspension. The Act of March 12, 1842, again mandated resumption, and most banks complied. By that time most banks elsewhere in the United States had been redeeming their bills for some time, many since 1838.

More rules and regulations were passed in the ensuing years. By that time the economic health of Pennsylvania had improved, and bank failures became less frequent. Studying banking history can be a fascinating pursuit, but even the best of sources are often inconsistent or flawed, this account in *Banker's Magazine,* April 1855, being a prime example. The writer praised the banks of the state dating back to the early part of the century, and seems to have been blissfully unaware of the real situation:

> This state has had well-managed banking institutions under special charters for the last 50 or 60 years. The only failure among them during the past 15 years, was that of the *Lehigh County Bank,* Allentown. This concern, it was well known, was owned and managed by Wall Street, and other New York speculators. It was purchased by these parties for the purpose of making it a mere bank of circulation, and that circulation to be used in and near New York City, where it was issued at par and redeemed soon after at a discount, until the eventual failure of the bank

The same writer overlooked multiple bankruptcies of "the past 15 years," the failure of the Susquehanna Bank reported at length in his own magazine in January 1850, and the explosion of the Northampton Bank in 1843 (with 69¢ in cash available to redeem $108,217 in currency), among many other problems. The great crash of the Bank of the United States of Pennsylvania was also among the failures in that 15-year period, along with the failure of the Girard Bank and other large institutions!

A $5 note of the Western Bank of Philadelphia, an unissued remainder. Plate by Charles Toppan & Co. This interesting bill has the inscriptions in German and depicts the famous scene from the legend of William Tell, with his archer father at the left and young William against a tree to the right.

This bank commenced on November 1, 1832, a time of prosperity in the economy. A minor setback was sustained in 1834, when the bank's porter (in charge of moving money in and out of the vaults and making local transfers), an Irishman named James Fulham, stole $3,000 to $4,000 in specie and departed for parts unknown. With a capital of $500,000, the institution prospered, although it suffered along with other banks in the Panic of 1837. In late December 1840 through early February 1841, some banks in the city suspended specie payments. The Western Bank was able to redeem in coins the approximately $30,000 worth of bills presented during that time, earning the confidence of the public. On December 29, 1864, it converted to become the Western National Bank, charter 656.

In 1856 there were 57 chartered banks in operation in Pennsylvania. The Free-Banking Act of March 31, 1860, a latecomer among legislation in this regard, came after the Panic of 1857, in the era during which there was little spirit for establishing new banks. Afterward only nine new banks were chartered.

Numismatic Comments

With more than 150 different chartered banks as well as many unofficial banks turning out paper money, plus many factories, railroads, turnpikes, and other entities, Pennsylvania offers a particularly wide selection of paper money varieties. Notes date from before 1800, all of which are rare, down to the 1860s. Along the way just about every evolution in bank-note engraving can be observed.

Naturally, the well-known engraving and printing firms of Philadelphia were the main source for bills for the different banks, although there were exceptions. Richard T. Hoober, author of the standard text on banks of Pennsylvania, was a dedicated collector and dealer for many years, a fine fellow who is kindly remembered by all who knew him. Hoober had banking history memorized and could declaim on just about any note that he had for sale.

Similar to those of Ohio, the obsolete bank notes of Pennsylvania offer extensive purchase opportunities. In the marketplace this state is rather quiet, which would seem to be an advantage to any numismatist with long-range thinking. Most bills date from before the colorful era of the 1850s, although there are enough of the last around to add spice to a display.

Currency of Rhode Island

Number of banks in the Haxby *Standard Catalog:* 127.
Specialized text: Roger H. Durand, *Obsolete Notes and Scrip of Rhode Island and the Providence Plantations,* 1981.

Historical Notes

Similar to the coastal states adjacent to it, Rhode Island was early in the banking business. In 1791 the Providence Bank was incorporated in the most important city, followed by the Bank of Rhode Island in 1795. By 1805 there were 13 banks operating in the state. The Farmers Exchange Bank of Gloucester, scene of the Andrew V. Dexter Jr., fraud, began about this time. At the time there was no state regulation regarding currency, and the flood of bills turned out by this bank was certainly unusual, but not illegal. After the bank's collapse in 1809, the state would be free of bank failures for two decades.

In 1820 a law limited currency issuance to the amount of paid-in capital stock. By 1826 there were 44 banks in business, the same number as nearly a decade later in 1835. The Burrillville Bank failed in 1829 with about $49,000 in bills in circulation per official figures (which were often false). Its affairs were wound up in the early 1830s. The Farmers and Mechanics Bank of Pawtuxet closed its doors the same year. Its currency remained good, although the stockholders' equity was lost. The Phenix Bank of Providence was formed under the same charter.

Beginning in 1833, charters specified that stockholders would be liable for debts after the bank's assets were exhausted. An 1836 law provided for a minimum bank capital of $50,000, with half to be paid in before business could commence. The Board of Bank Commissioners was also set up, a fairly early entry, as it was the Panic of 1837 that prompted such groups in many other states. The board was later eliminated, after which time banks sent reports to other officials in the state. In 1857 the board was reconstituted.

Banks in the state operated fairly and profitably for the most part, with only scattered failures after the early years. No banks went under because of the Panic of 1837, but most experienced difficulties and suspended specie payments. In Rhode Island, as elsewhere, the vaults of many suspending banks were well stocked with silver and gold coins. It was the realization that if exchange were permitted the stocks would soon be depleted that prompted most banks to take this action. The Rhode Island Agricultural Bank, located in Johnston, ceased business in 1843, but currency holders were able to redeem part of the bills' value. The Pascoag Bank in the district of that name, within Burrillville, stopped issuing bills about this time. Its books remained in a muddled state of affairs for the rest of the decade, and by 1850 it was still not able to make a proper financial report.[61] It survived, however, and in June 1851, perhaps to start afresh with a better reputation, it changed its name to the Granite Bank, which continued into the 1860s.

The Scituate Bank had a particularly convoluted career. Incorporated in 1818, it seems to have operated normally for many years. In 1836 an investigation revealed that out-of-state parties had secured control of the bank, stripped it of assets, and released large quantities of essentially worthless bills. The bank went into liquidation. In 1841 it reopened with a new name, the Hamilton Bank of Scituate. In the same year a large quantity of new bills was stolen, given forged signatures, and placed into circulation. The bank refused to redeem them, stirring up a big controversy. In the following years the bank teetered on insolvency, and in 1849 an act of the state legislature forced its closing and liquidation.[62]

The *Illustrated News,* April 23, 1853, printed this item, reflective of an action taken when silver coins were absent from circulation, as they had been since 1850:

> Three banks in Rhode Island have issued fractional bills in large quantities. In the present dearth of change, they are found to be a great convenience, and are very generally welcomed wherever they can be obtained. About four weeks since, one bank issued $30,000 in fractional bills, not a dollar of which has yet been presented at the bank for redemption. They are not received at the Suffolk Bank.

Curiously, after most of these bills found their way back to the banks in early summer 1853, when new silver coins of lower authorized weight again reached circulation, the notes had another use, as reported by the *Boston Traveller:*

> *Fractional paper of Providence, R.I.* The circulation of fractional bills is rapidly diminished in this vicinity, and hundreds of dollars of these bills are being returned through the brokers to those banks that issued them. We understand that the Providence banks are very happy to have these bills returned, as there is a large demand for them at the West, where they are used in paying the laborers on the railroads now being built. One bank has an order for $10,000 worth of these bills, and has employed a number of extra hands to prepare them for circulation. The issue, so far, has proved highly successful and profitable.[63]

Why a railroad worker in the American West would accept worn fractional bills of distant Rhode Island banks seems curious.

The Peacedale Bank, incorporated in 1853, never opened. Similarly, in 1854 the Island Bank was chartered, to be located in the village of East Shoreham on Block Island, but it never went into operation. Other banks arose, such as this group of seven chartered by the legislature in early 1856: the Marine, Northern, and Moshassuck banks in Providence; Greenwich Bank; the Pokanoket Bank in Bristol; and the Washington County Bank in Richmond. Again, gaining a charter did not always mean that a bank ever operated.

In 1856 the Bank of the Republic, located in Providence, suspended operation. Cashier Charles M. Howlett, with the advice and consent of the directors, had speculated heavily in the West and sent large quantities of paper money there to be sold at a discount. A large amount of its assets were in drafts on a New York City concern that failed. The state banking commissioners investigated and found that the institution had been incompetently, but not necessarily fraudulently managed.[64]

Note for $2 of the Phenix Village Bank, Phenix, Rhode Island, March 4, 1861 (President Lincoln's inauguration date). From a plate by Danforth, Wright & Co., New York and Philadelphia. Depicted is a townscape of Phenix. This bill was redeemed and canceled by having the signature of the president cut out. Later, certain of these notes reached the numismatic market.

This bank, incorporated in 1856, was first located in Warwick, Rhode Island, according to historian Roger H. Durand. It relocated to Phenix Village, a settlement earlier called Roger Williams Village. This was a mill town, with the Phenix Manufacturing Co. being the mainstay of the local economy and the lifeblood of the bank. On July 17, 1865, it evolved to become the Phenix National Bank, charter 1460.

From 1857, the panic year, to 1859, the number of banks in Rhode Island dropped from 98 to 90. The Tiverton Bank fell victim to the hard economic times, but it was a fraud owned by speculators who used it to circulate worthless bills. The Farmers Bank of Wickford was a similar phony operation that also failed in 1857. Most surviving banks remained strong after 1859, and in the mid-1860s converted to become National Banks.

Numismatic Comments

Paper money of Rhode Island is quite varied in appearance, as the use of the historical but numismatically monotonous Patent Stereotype Steel Plate was not as prevalent here as in states farther north. Many different institutions issued a wide variety of designs over a long period of years. Today, availability ranges from plentiful for failed institutions, as well as those that redeemed their notes but later made them available to collectors, to very rare. The last category primarily covers issues of the 1850s and early 1860s by banks that redeemed their currency at face value, then destroyed it.

There are many Rhode Island notes with interesting stories, as a perusal of the Durand book will quickly reveal. Bills of the fraudulent Farmers Exchange Bank of Gloucester are easily available today. A few other phony institutions sprang up from time to time, and their currency can be found easily on the market today. Notes of the Freemens Bank of Bristol, featuring an Abner Reed imprint from the 1810s but issued in the 1860s, can be found easily enough and are interesting to those who know the story (see chapter 18).

Proofs and remainders exist for the bills of some institutions, these mainly for later issues. Nearly all proofs are from the American Bank Note Co. paper archives and include varieties for which circulating examples are either very rare or altogether unknown. Similar to other New England states, Rhode Island notes are perhaps most often collected by gathering available types, ignoring the expensive rarities, and in the process forming a very nice display.

Currency of South Carolina

Number of banks in the Haxby *Standard Catalog:* 21.
Specialized texts: Austin Sheheen Jr., South Carolina Obsolete Notes & Scrip, 2004; W.A. Clark, The History of the Banking Institutions Organized in South Carolina Prior to 1860, 1922.

Historical Notes

The Land and Loan Bank of the Carolinas, established in the colonial era in 1712, did business until 1775.[65] In an era in which silver and gold coins were hardly ever seen in commerce, the bills of this bank were very convenient and, as paper issues, were part of the reason why coins were not seen. After the Revolution the first bank in the state was the Bank of South Carolina, formed in 1792 and operated afterward, but not chartered until 1801. This bank continued in business for decades afterward, into the Civil War.

In the early 19th century, the following banks were chartered on these dates, this being a list of those through 1836 that had the word *Bank* in their titles:[66]

> Bank of South Carolina, December 19, 1801; State Bank of South Carolina, December 19, 1801; Union Bank of South Carolina, December 20, 1810; Planters and Mechanics Bank of South Carolina, December 20, 1810; Bank of the State of South Carolina, December 19, 1812; Bank of Cheraw, December 18, 1822; Bank of Hamburg, December 21, 1822; Commercial Bank of Columbia, December 17, 1831; Merchants Bank of South Carolina, at Cheraw, December 19, 1833; Bank of Charleston, December 17, 1834; Bank of Camden, December 19, 1835; Bank of Hamburg [second], December 19, 1835; Bank of Georgetown, December 21, 1836; South-Western Railroad Bank, December 21, 1836.

A branch of the first Bank of the United States operated in Charleston in the late 18th and early 19th centuries and did a large business. Not long after its 1801 charter, the Bank of South Carolina was almost victim to the so-called *ground-mole plot,* which caused a sensation at the time. A man of some means, Withers by name, lost his possessions in gambling. In October 1802, he removed an iron grate on top of an opening leading to the drain at the northwest corner of Broad and Church streets. For the next three months, aided by an accomplice, Withers remained underground, tunneling his way toward the bank cellar. Some incaution by his helper led to the unmasking of the plot just before the bank wall was reached.[67]

The Bank of the State of South Carolina (1812) in effect became a state-run institution. Now and again the constitutionality was questioned of this and other state-owned banks issuing their own money (paper bills). This was a right supposed to be reserved for the federal government, the key phrase in the U.S. Constitution being "that no State shall coin money, emit bills of credit, or make any thing but gold and silver a tender in payment of debts." In 1834, in prosperous times augmented by strong prices for agricultural products and the building of railroads, the Charleston, Louisville and Cincinnati Railroad Company was authorized and given banking privileges, but *Bank* was not part of its name. In 1838 much of the downtown district of Charleston was destroyed by fire. The Bank of the State of South Carolina assisted in the rebuilding by loaning $2,500,000 in funds, largely obtained from Dabney, Morgan & Co., London bankers. After the death of famous U.S. Senator John Calhoun in 1850, bank president Franklin H. Elmore was named to fill the remainder of his term. The Bank of the State of South Carolina was in business through the Civil War, but in 1868 it was closed down by an act of the reconstruction legislature.

The Bank of Charleston (1834) was formed by leading merchants of the city. The idea was protested strongly by the Bank of the State of South Carolina, then a tool of entrenched political interests, which claimed that the new bank would destroy the banking system in the state and wreak hardship on citizens, among other specious arguments. The bank acquired the former premises of the branch of the second Bank of the United States. The Bank of Charleston began selling stock in the first week of June 1835 and opened soon thereafter. Over time the bank placed a large amount of paper in circulation, but the total varied widely. With a capital of $3,160,000, the circulation was $1,945,064 in June 1850, and a much lower $873,364 six years later in June 1856. In 1852 the bank issued bills of $5, $10, $20, and $50 payable in New York City (as well as at the home office in Charleston), causing some controversy. This item about its bills appeared in the *Charleston Courier* in 1854:

> A mercantile firm in Selma writes to us to know whether the Bank of Charleston issues bills of the value of $8, as according to *Thompson's Bank Note Reporter,* there are no genuine bills of that denomination. Mr. Thompson, however, is in error, inasmuch as the Bank of Charleston does issue bills of eight dollars, which, as we stated in the *Courier* of the 15th of April last, in correcting a similar mistake into which the *Mobile Tribune* had fallen, are circulated largely in Alabama, in consequence of the scarcity in that state of small change, and the $5 bill law.
>
> There are, however, we understand, spurious bills of that denomination in circulation, and for the information of our Selma correspondents and the public generally, we would again mention that they have a vignette of a stage coach and horses, while the *genuine* have an engraving of a railroad passenger car; the borders have a representation of a head with a helmet on it, but the *genuine* have a figure of Liberty on one side, and of Agriculture on the other. The counterfeits, moreover, are all signed H.W. Conner, President, while the *genuine* are signed Ker Boyce, President.[68]

The Bank of Charleston continued through the Civil War and in 1872 evolved into the Bank of Charleston National Banking Association, charter 2044, one of only a few banks in the South that made such a transition.

The Bank of Georgetown, located in a seaport town and backed to an extent by wealthy rice planters, had the singular distinction of being the only bank in the state not to suspend specie payments during the Panic of 1837 and the consequent Hard Times era. Others suspended on May 18, 1837, and did not resume until September 1, 1838. For some the resumption was premature. Five banks in Charleston suspended again in October 1839 and did not pay out coin again until July 1840.[69] The state omitted passing a law excusing the banks from paying specie during this trying time, and as a result a lawsuit was filed by the state attorney general to revoke the charter of all suspending banks, with the Bank of Charleston singled out as a test case. The affair dragged out in court, until the bank was held harmless in 1842.

The Act of 1840 provided for the extension of the charters of certain existing banks and the creation of eight new ones, not all of which went into business. The Western Bank of South Carolina, in Anderson, never got under way, nor did the Bank of Sumterville.[70]

The state of South Carolina was an exemplar of banking virtue. As an illustration of solid banking, this item is from a report of the Bank of Camden, July 1, 1853, as given in *Banker's Magazine* the following September:

> The profits of the last six months were at the rate of about 13% per annum: From these profits a dividend at the rate of 12% per annum was made this day; leaving, with former profits, a reserve of $40,000, in round numbers. The assets are all *good;* there is not the least apprehension in relation to any portion of them. . . .
>
> The holders of the stock of this bank number about 200; of these, about 100 hold for widows and orphans, and married and single women, ministers of the gospel, and for various religious and charitable societies and institutions; and these 100 holders represent nearly five eighths of all the capital of $400,000. No part of the stock is held, as we believe, for speculation; for the larger portion of the stock held by the others than the class above named, is held by elderly men, and persons not in business. It seldom changes hands; the actual sales have hardly averaged $5,000 a year for years past.
>
> The members of the Board now are W.E. Johnson, Thomas Lang, J.M. DeSaussure, Benjamin Perkins, John Workman, W.D. McDowall, and Edward Haile. All the 200 stockholders, including the seven directors, two of whom are business men, hardly owe the Bank $20,000. At the annual meeting of the stockholders in May last, the Board was directed to apply for a renewal of the charter, which expires on the first of January, 1856. It is proper to remark, that, notwithstanding the exaggerated impression as to the decline of Camden, we are well assured that under a new charter we can continue to make satisfactory dividends. First, or last, we have excited no false hopes, but have fully come up to our promises, By order of the Board. W. E. Johnson, President.

There was, however, some occasional trouble in paradise, but nothing in comparison to what occurred in most other states. The Bank of Cheraw operated briefly and failed in about 1826, as did the (first) Bank of Hamburg. Interestingly, the Hamburg bank is known only by surviving bills, according to a 20th-century historian, for no contemporary records or newspaper accounts have been found concerning it. Henry Shultz, the cashier, was an eccentric individual who set about laying out Hamburg in a "hideous swamp" adjacent to the thriving town of Augusta, which Shultz envisioned that his town would soon rival.[71]

Bills of the Merchants Bank of Cheraw circulated in the 1850s, but there was no such bank—the scheme was a fraud trading on the good name of the Merchants Bank of South Carolina of the same town (which issued odd-denomination bills such as $6, $7, $8, and $9).

In the 1850s up to the time South Carolina seceded from the Union on December 20, 1860, banking was prosperous, and more than a dozen different banks served the state, although most business was conducted by the Bank of the State of South Carolina and its branches. The Panic of 1857, which began in New York City in September, reached South Carolina in October. On October 10, the Bank of the State of South Carolina was the first in the state to suspend specie payments, followed quickly by others. By October 15 these other banks had suspended in Charleston: South Western Rail Road Bank, Bank of South Carolina, Peoples Bank, Planters and Mechanics Bank, and the Farmers and Exchange Bank.[72] As was usually the case with suspension in this and other panics, in all states this provoked a large outcry. Few understood the workings of banks, and many were the allegations of fraud being committed upon the public.

Knox in *History of Banking* gives this related sketch concerning the Civil War and its effect:

> At the beginning of the War of 1861 there were 22 state banks in South Carolina, with an aggregate capital of $18,000,000; circulation, $10,000,000; deposits, $12,000,000. The banks were so carefully and successfully managed that there had not been a failure of a bank in South Carolina since the close of the Revolutionary War in 1783. Early in the War of 1861 C.G. Memminger, secretary of the Confederate Treasury, a Charleston banker, called upon the banks for $10,000,000 of their bills, which were to be returned as soon as the Confederate notes could be printed. . . .

A $5 note of the State Bank, South Carolina (actually, the Bank of the State of South Carolina), Charleston, May 4, 1857, from a plate by Bald, Adams & Co., New York. The main vignette illustrates the bank's headquarters.

Chartered in 1812, this bank operated for many years despite many vicissitudes and much political interference.

> A director in the Bank of South Carolina told Mr. [William] Birnie, the president, that if the request was granted it would break all the banks, as the bills of the banks, which were considered better than Confederate notes, would be hoarded. A majority of the directors, however, voted for the issue, which resulted in the destruction of the banks.

Numismatic Comments

The number of banks in South Carolina was very small, due to the dominance of the Bank of the State of Carolina and its branches, and the strict attention paid by legislators to the banking business, the last preventing large numbers of fraudulent banks from being established. By the time of the Civil War, most banks that had been formed in the state were still in operation. Hard times fell on the banks in the next several years. After the war, large quantities of bank bills became available on the numismatic market, nearly all being from the era of colorful printing of the 1850s and early 1860s. Today, these are highly collectible.

South Carolina Obsolete Notes & Scrip, by Austin Sheheen Jr., is remarkable in that bills of the various banks are all illustrated in full color. Studying these images can help you decide whether to add the bills to your collection.

Currency of Tennessee

Number of banks in the Haxby *Standard Catalog:* 47.
Specialized text: Paul E. Garland, *The History of Early Tennessee Banks and Their Issues,* 1983.

Historical Notes

Tennessee joined the Union as a state in 1796. The first bank chartered was the Nashville Bank in November 1807, capitalized at $200,000. In 1817 the legislature provided for banks to be established in Gallatin, Murfreesboro, Rogersville, Shelbyville, and Winchester. Before they were fully organized, they became branches of the Nashville Bank, now with a capital of $2,400,000. It is recorded that on March 31, 1823, more than $250,000 in older bills was burned. The bank continued in business until it was liquidated in 1827. Stockholders sustained a small loss on their shares.

The Bank of the State of Tennessee was chartered on November 20, 1811, with headquarters in Knoxville. Branches were set up at Clarksville, Columbia, and Jonesboro, followed by offices in Carthage, Franklin, Kingston, Marysville, and Nashville. The state was a shareholder. The bank wound down its operations in the early 1830s, by which time the second bank of the same name had conducted business for about a decade.

The second Bank of the United States proposed to open a branch in Nashville. Upon learning of this fact, the legislature levied a yearly tax of $50,000 per office on any out-of-state bank proposing to do business in Tennessee, an action similar to that taken in Ohio. As was the case with the Ohio tax, this act was later ruled unconstitutional by the U.S. Supreme Court. Afterward, in August 1827, the branch began business.

In 1817 the Farmers and Mechanics Bank of Nashville was chartered. On June 18, 1819, in an era of difficult economic times nationwide, this bank was the first in the state to suspend specie payments, after having paid out more than $30,000 in coin in the preceding two months to redeem bills as presented. Continuing well into the 1820s, this action and the depreciated value of notes of other banks cast a pall on bills of Tennessee. They were viewed with particular disfavor and traded at deep discounts in relation to silver coins, had even deeper discounts in gold, and in some quarters were refused at any price.

On July 26, 1820, the second Bank of the State of Tennessee was chartered with the thought that it would do what other banks had not or could not:

promptly pay specie and issue bills that were worth par in commerce. This was the brainchild of Governor Joseph McMinn, who had convened a special session of the legislature to consider and enact the law of authorization. Headquartered in Nashville, the bank had branches in Columbia, Franklin, and Knoxville. Reality proved to be different from theory. The bank did not operate ideally, but it did play a part in business and trade. Its bills flooded commerce and became so depreciated that two other large banks in the state resolved not to accept them at any price. In 1830 the cashier was found to have secretly run $100,000 in overdrafts through the bank. The system shut down in 1832 by order of Governor William Carroll. The next year in his message to the state legislature, he gave this poignant comment, "The establishment of banks for the purpose of relieving the people from pecuniary distress is, in most cases, ruinous to those who avail themselves of such relief."

State deposits and much other business was transferred to the new Union Bank of Tennessee, chartered on October 18, 1832, with a capital authorized up to $3,000,000. The bank operated successfully with several branches, with most business done in Memphis.[73] The bank closed in 1865. The Planters Bank, chartered on November 11, 1833, began business the following February, became important in the state, and operated until 1865.

The Bank of Tennessee, the third effort at a state-run bank, was chartered on January 19, 1839, capitalized at $5,000,000, financed by the state. Economic times were sluggish, and the sale of bonds did not meet expectations. After many difficulties it went into operation in Nashville, and branches were opened in Athens, Clarksville, Columbia, Knoxville, Memphis, Murfreesboro, Rogersville, Shelbyville, Somerville, and Trenton, followed later by one in Sparta. This bank lasted through the Civil War, but barely. During the conflict, certain officers took assets of the bank and spirited them off to Atlanta, where they were only partially recovered after the war.

The Panic of 1837, which carried through to 1843, was difficult for all banks, and specie payments were suspended, then resumed, then by some banks suspended again. Currency was plentiful in circulation, but gold and silver coins were scarce. In 1843 the Bank of East Tennessee, with private stockholders, was set up in Knoxville and issued much paper money.

The legislative session of 1851 to 1852 passed the Free-Banking Law essentially patterned on the New York legislation. "Quite a number of banks were organized under this law on fictitious capital, and 'wildcat' banks were as plentiful as grasshoppers," historian Knox commented. He continues:

> The issuance of bank notes of a high order of engraving seemed to be the order of the day. The rule of $3 in capital to $1 in specie seemed to be obsolete, and the redundancy of currency was enormous. In 1853 Governor Andrew Johnson, in his message to the General Assembly, did not hesitate to condemn the wretched system of banking the state had gradually fallen into, and he suggested the liquidation of the State Bank, and again in 1855 and in 1857. This ridiculous system of banking which pervaded every state in the Union, had its weight in producing the Panic of 1857.

A writer in *Banker's Magazine,* August 1856, stated this opinion concerning free banks:

> They are decidedly injurious to the trading interests of the community. They discount very little business paper, if any; they gather up all the circulation of the stock banks, which have hitherto been doing a regular banking business, by exchanging their . . . notes therefore, then run upon those banks for specie or eastern exchange, and thereby cramp them so that they ware unable to discount scarcely anything for their customers. These free banks are in fact nothing but broker concerns—they add nothing. . . .

By the end of 1856, there were 46 banks operating in the state, the quality of which varied from poor to solid. After the Panic of 1857, banking was quiet. Then came the Civil War, bringing less harmful effects on state banking than in other states in the South.

Numismatic Comments

As might be expected from the checkered reputation of many banks in Tennessee, ranging from failed early institutions to rampant wildcats of the 1850s, a trail of paper was left behind. As a result, bills of this state are easily collected today as to a general representation. Those of the 1850s and early 1860s are ornate and colorful. The numismatic landscape is also sprinkled with rarities and SENC notes, especially among early issues and those bearing the imprints of branch offices.

Due to the enthusiasm and effort of Paul Garland, notes of this state were very popular decades ago, before the currency of certain other states moved into the mainstream. For many, this enthusiasm continues.

Note for $5 of the Bank of East Tennessee, Knoxville, payable in Chattanooga, January 1, 1855. Plate by Danforth, Wright & Co., New York and Philadelphia. This ornate vignette was used on bills of various other banks as well.

The Bank of East Tennessee was established in Knoxville in 1843, with a capital of $800,000. Branches were set up in Chattanooga and Jonesville. In March 1853 the bank was unable to redeem its bills and suspended payments, although it honored other liabilities. Despite a switch of presidents from J.W.J. Niles to W.M. Churchwell in autumn 1854, fortunes continued to decline, and a few years later the bank wound up its affairs.

CURRENCY OF TEXAS

Number of banks in the Haxby *Standard Catalog:* 3.
Specialized text: Robert Medlar, *Texas Obsolete Notes and Scrip,* 1968.

HISTORICAL NOTES

The history of paper money issued by state-chartered banks is necessarily brief, as just three banks were involved. In December 1856, *Banker's Magazine* stated that "there is one bank in the state, at Galveston, having a capital of $322,000." This bank had a branch in Brownsville.

By that time two others had closed up. The Commercial & Agricultural Bank of Texas was authorized in April 1835 and was headquartered in the town of Columbia, before Texas joined the Union in 1845. The capital was set at a maximum of $1,000,000, and the bank was allowed to establish branches wherever it wanted to. Although on December 14, 1837, the Texas Congress had passed an act prohibiting any person or entity to issue paper money, on February 3, 1841, the congress authorized McKinney & Williams, proprietors of the Commercial and Agricultural Bank, to issue $30,000 worth of bills, as the partnership had provided financial aid to the Texas government earlier. The third entry in the bank lineup was the Bank of Vernon, which may have operated in the 1840s, but facts concerning it are scarce.[74]

Bills of the Northern Bank of Mississippi (see under Mississippi entry) circulated extensively in Texas. In the absence of currency from Texas banks, these were well received.

NUMISMATIC COMMENTS

Collectors of Obsolete Currency can revel in the issues of Texas, but not in those paid out by state-chartered banks. Instead, it is the Republic of Texas notes, an entity not studied here, that provide much of the action, plus bills of more than 200 issuers of scrip.

Within the purview of the present text, bills of Commercial & Agricultural Bank of Texas are rare today except for some remainders of the $1 denomination. Those of the Commercial & Agricultural Bank of Galveston are generally uncollectible, although the Haxby text notes that certain $10 counterfeits dated January 1, 1848, are seen now and then. Rounding out the trio, the Bank of Vernon issued bills, again essentially uncollectible, although some exist in the form of alterations to represent *Ohio* banks. Remainders provide most of the supply of bills of these banks. Dated, signed, and issued notes are very rare.

CURRENCY OF UTAH

Number of banks in the Haxby *Standard Catalog:* 1.
Specialized texts: Alvin E. Rust, *Mormon & Utah Coin & Currency,* 1984; Douglas A. Nyholm, *The History of Mormon Currency,* 2004.

HISTORICAL NOTES

The only entry in the Haxby text under Utah is the Drovers Bank of Salt Lake City, an imprint found on currency issued by W.L. Ormsby in the 1850s. These bills are quite unusual inasmuch as scenic designs are used on each, but all are the same—a violation of

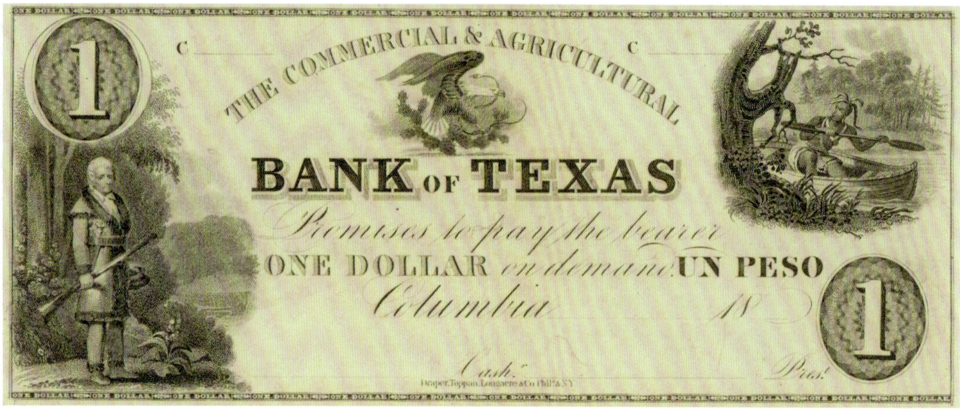

A $1 note of the Commercial & Agricultural Bank of Texas at Columbia. Unissued remainder. Plate by Draper, Toppan, Longacre & Co., Philadelphia and New York.

This bank was set to conduct business in Columbia, Texas, in about 1837, but it never opened its doors. A supply of bills ordered from Philadelphia was thus useless at the time, but generations later proved to be a boon to collectors, especially the four-subject $1-$1-$1-$1 sheets, many of which were cut apart, yielding the available supply of numismatic mementoes of this bank that might have been, but was not.

Ormsby's own rules. Virtually nothing is known about the operation of this bank, which seems to have been active around 1856. Bills are seen with some frequency on the market today, numbered and signed, and are interesting to collect. (Also see comments under Kansas.)

Certain bills of the Kirtland Safety Society Bank, issued in Ohio in 1837, were brought to Salt Lake City in the late 1840s, given additional signatures there, and reissued.

Numismatic Comments

The bank bills of the Utah territory related to the present text are those discussed above, issued by Drovers Bank of Salt Lake City, printed by W.L. Ormsby, and with a background that has not been documented. While not common, such bills are collectible over a period of time.

The reissued Kirtland Safety Society Bank bills with other signatures added to those of 1837, including of Mormon leader Brigham Young, are in strong demand. Certain bills are illustrated in chapter 13. These notes are somewhat scarce today, but they are priced much higher than typical obsolete bills due to the Mormon connection.

Currency of Vermont

Number of banks in the Haxby *Standard Catalog:* 64.
Specialized text: Mayre Coulter, *Vermont Obsolete Notes and Scrip,* 1972. (Created under the direction of George W. Wait.)

Historical Notes

The Vermont State Bank, discussed at length in chapter 3, was the first such institution in the state. Incorporated in 1806, it did business through several offices. The operation was shut down in 1812. Although it had a large overissue of bills, the state eventually redeemed all that were presented. The Burlington and Windsor banks were chartered in

A $3 note of the Drovers Bank, Salt Lake City, Utah, July 1, 1856, by W.L. Ormsby. Little is known of the history of this bank. A similarly named bank with notes of the same designs has a Kansas address.

1818, followed by the Brattleboro Bank in 1821. State regulations permitted banks to issue paper up to three times the amount of their capital and required them to redeem them in specie on demand.

During the next two decades, many other banks were chartered throughout the state. A legislative report giving the condition of banks as of April 1, 1828, showed 10 banks in operation, with paid-in capital of $321,216, specie and good (specie convertible) bills owned of $674,904, and currency in circulation of $949,844. Most banks had deposits for the redemption of their bills in Boston or in Troy, New York (close to Bennington, Vermont, across the state line), and one cleared its currency in New York City.

Some banks changed their names or evolved to become other banks. In Chelsea the Bank of Orange County was established in 1827. Its charter expired in 1843, at which time its business was transferred to the newly chartered Orange County Bank, which operated until 1855, when it was succeeded by the second Orange County Bank. The Bank of Orange County at Irasburgh, as it was titled, not to confuse it with the one in Chelsea, was formed in 1832. Its interests were succeeded by the Bank of Orleans, which on its currency variously spelled the town name as *Irasburg* and *Irasburgh*.

From a title the location of a Vermont bank could not always be determined. The Bank of Caledonia was in Danville, the Bank of Newbury was in Wells River, the Ascutney Bank did business in Windsor, and the Bank of Poultney was in West Poultney. The Bank of Bellows Falls was located in Rockingham, near Bellows Falls, and its bills were so imprinted. Later currency was changed to use the Bellows Falls address, although the bank did not move.

In 1831 a Safety Fund was set up, and banks were made to contribute an amount equal to 4-1/2% of their capital, payable in installments over a period of six years. Should the fund be depleted by paying debts of failed banks, an additional tax would be levied, not to exceed three-quarters of 1% per year.

Without naming the bank, *Niles' Weekly Register*, November 14, 1835, carried this information:

> *"A little monster."* One of the state banks, in Vermont, having been suspected of a violation of its charter, a committee was appointed, by the legislature, to overhaul its affairs and report thereon to that body. In their report, the committee, among other developments of the mysteries of banking, state that "the banking room of this institution is in a wooden building occupied as a store—that the place of deposit for the notes, bills, papers and specie of the bank, is a wooden desk—and that the books of the bank consisted of one or two sheets of paper pinned or stitched together!

The Essex Bank, located in Guildhall, had a poor reputation, and in 1837 the Suffolk Bank in Boston stopped exchanging its bills. The situation became worse, and with $66,262 of bills in circulation, the bank failed in 1839, causing a loss to all involved. The assets of the Safety Fund were inadequate. An investigation revealed that the officers had committed fraud. On these grounds the state refused to redeem the bills, as the Safety Fund was intended to absorb normal business losses and failures due to unfortunate circumstances, not to compensate for criminal actions. Holders of Essex Bank bills were told to look to the bondsmen who had furnished security for the bank.

The subsequent Banking Act of 1840 required that, before a new bank could begin business, half its capital had to be paid in specie. Modifications to the Safety Fund regulations were made in 1842. If a Vermont bank kept deposits in Boston for the prompt redemption of its bills at par, certain rules would be eased. This rule was a reference to the Suffolk Bank system, which had been in effect since 1824. By 1848 all but three Vermont banks had signed up, and by 1850 membership was unanimous.

In 1841 there were 17 chartered banks operating in the state. New banks were chartered over the years. In 1849, for example, the Merchants Bank in Burlington, the Passumpsic Bank in St. Johnsbury, the Missisquoi Bank in Sheldon, and the Franklin County Bank at St. Albans Bay were incorporated. Most banks were small and located in villages scattered throughout the state.

Bills bearing the imprint of the Commercial Bank, in Poultney, were circulated, but were listed as fraudulent in *Thompson's Bank Note & Commercial Reporter* in 1850. There was no such bank. Ditto for the Green Mountain Bank of Rutland, also listed. The Jefferson Banking Company of Vermont was also fictitious. Its nicely engraved bills, by Edward Hulseman of New York City (perhaps best known as an engraver of dies for Hard Times tokens), bore no town name.

The Farmers Bank of Orwell, which operated legitimately from 1833 until it became a National Bank in 1864, was plagued by large quantities of counterfeits of its bills. The Farmers and Mechanics Bank of Burlington was another target for counterfeiters, who issued a wide range of denominations up to $100. All of the phony and spurious bills with Vermont imprints were made out of state and mostly circulated in distant places. These were not Vermont-based frauds.

In 1851 the Free-Banking Act provided that banks could be incorporated by 10 or more persons, with a minimum of $50,000 in capital, not to exceed $200,000, and could issue bills against securities deposited with the state treasurer. Afterward, 13 banks were formed, but all elected to comply with the stricter provisions of the Act of 1840, believing that it would be easier to attract capital if a bank appeared to have a stronger footing. By that time *free bank* was a term that often implied a weak or fraudulent structure.

There were many unsuccessful applications for bank charters in the early 1850s, including the Waloomsic Bank (Bennington), Peoples Bank (Brandon), Bank of Cabot, Eagle Bank (Castleton), Western Vermont Bank (Fair Haven), Fairfax Bank, Hinesburg Bank, Bank of Lamoille (Johnson), Bank at Newfane, Bank of Richmond, Northern Bank of Vermont (St. Albans), Bank of South Hardwick, Bank of Waterville, West Randolph Bank, Bank of Wilmington, and Winooski Bank. Charter petitions seem to have been reviewed with care, no doubt preventing the establishment of paper mills.

The Panic of 1857 had very little effect on banks in the state, and only one suspended specie payments. After the National Banking Act of 1863, many banks converted to become National Banks. By that time, state authorities could look back on the note-issuing era and reflect that there had been very few problems.

Numismatic Comments

Notes of Vermont are especially appealing to collect, as the designs are quite varied. There are, to be sure, many of the Patent Stereotype Steel Plate issues in early years, but they quickly give way to a multiplicity of fascinating vignettes by Boston, Philadelphia, and New York engravers. Although several towns had multiple banks, most bills were issued by banks with small capital located in villages scattered throughout the state.

The earliest issues are those of the Vermont State Bank. Large quantities of redeemed as well as undistributed notes remained in the hands of the state and later found their way into numismatic circles. Today, collecting a representative set of different denominations is easy enough to do, but the challenge can be heightened if early issues are wanted from the different branches. Currency of the Vermont Glass Factory, not a bank, is popular. Except for the early styles, most varieties from this factory are easily acquired with patience.

For bank notes of the 1840s and 1850s, proofs from the American Bank Note Co. archives, plus some modern proprietary proofs, come on the market with some frequency, a remarkable contrast to the times before 1990, when such were great rarities. The Rawdon, Wright, Hatch & Edson $1, $2, $3, and $5 issues of the West River Bank of Jamaica, each with a vignette featuring Liberty Seated silver dollars, have been popular for a long time. As these notes existed in large quantities of remainder sheets, they are much less expensive than might be thought. Bills of St. Albans,

Note for $1 of the Windham County Bank, Brattleboro, Vermont, March 10, 1857, from a plate by Danforth, Wright & Co., New York and Philadelphia. The rosettes around the denominations or counters are not much different from the *cycloidal configuration* patented in 1860 by the National Bank Note Co. The layout of this bill is unusual in that the officers' signatures are near the top.

The Windham County Bank sought a charter in 1854, but the politicians in the state legislature were not ready to say yes. In 1857 the time was ripe, the bank was authorized, and business commenced. The capital of $100,000 was soon increased to $150,000. On June 30, 1864, it was succeeded in interests by the First National Bank of Brattleboro, charter 470 (which in 1880 collapsed in a scandal).

usually seen in circulated grades, are varied. Some have an interesting link with the famous Confederate raid of 1864 described in chapter 19.

Currency of Virginia

Number of banks in the Haxby *Standard Catalog:* 56.
Specialized texts: Charles J. Affleck, *The Obsolete Paper Money of Virginia,* second edition, 1968; Richard Jones and Keith Littlefield, *Virginia Obsolete Paper Money,* 1992.

Historical Notes

The earliest recorded bank in Virginia set up after the Revolution is the Bank of Alexandria (studied in chapter 2), authorized by the Virginia General Assembly on November 23, 1792. Other banks and banking businesses existed in colonial days, likely including a bank said to have been operating in Richmond in 1730. Alexandria was ceded to the new District of Columbia, of which it would remain a part until it was ceded back to Virginia in 1846. During the time it was with the District, most residents considered themselves to be Virginians, at least in spirit and tradition. Certain Alexandria bills of that era bear neither a District of Columbia nor a Virginia imprint.

The Bank of Richmond was chartered on December 23, 1792, but today nothing is known of its history, and no currency has been found with its imprint. A branch of the first Bank of the United States opened in Norfolk in 1800 and closed when the charter of the parent bank expired in 1811. It was not well received in the state. In January 1811, on the eve of that bank's charter expiration, the state assembly passed a resolution urging its senators and representatives to vote against the renewal. Later, some said the vote was selfish, as the state government wanted to control banks within its borders, and the Farmers Bank became the perfect solution.

The Farmers Bank was chartered for $2,000,000 on February 13, 1812, to be located in Richmond. Branches were established in Alexandria, Blacksburg, Charlottesville, Danville, Farmville, Fredericksburg, Lewisburg, Lynchburg, Norfolk, Petersburg, Winchester, and Wytheville. The Alexandria branch was opened in 1847, when the city was back within the boundaries of Virginia, and succeeded the Bank of Potomac. Each branch was originally set up to have 13 directors.

The Bank of Virginia, headquartered in Richmond, was chartered on January 13, 1804, with a capital of $1,500,000. The institution was profitable in its early years, and its currency traded at par, less a tiny discount for handling at exchange brokers. The bank was troubled in the Hard Times era, including by a loss of $540,000 in uncollectible loans made by the paying teller. Branches were operated in Buchanan, Charleston, Danville, Fredericksburg, Jeffersonville, Lynchburg, Norfolk, Petersburg, Portsmouth, and Union.

Each of the preceding two banks was prohibited from issuing any bills under the $5 denomination. To provide a convenience in transactions, they issued odd denominations such as $6, $7, $8, and $9 in addition to such values as $10, $20, $50, and $100.

By the time the sprawling Bank of Virginia and Farmers Bank were organized, many unofficial banks and other companies were issuing currency. The Act of February 24, 1816, mandated that such bills were illegal and must be redeemed. This act caused great problems, as citizens had taken the currency in good faith, and the redemptions could not be made quickly. Among the unchartered issuers were the Leesburg Union Company, Western Bank, Farmers Company, Warrenton Company, Monongahela Bank, Bank of Martinsburg, Salem Company, Charleston Manufacturing and Exporting Company, Bank of Winchester, and the Loudoun Company. Accordingly, the limit for redemption was twice extended.

In the early 19th century, more banks were authorized and allowed to have branches under rules that would extend to 1837. In 1831, veteran financier Albert Gallatin (secretary of the Treasury from May 14, 1801, to March 3, 1809), in *Considerations on the Currency and Banking Systems of the United States,* included these comments in reference to the rise of banking in the state:

> The desk of every agriculturist in Virginia had some gold or silver to spare, if he was a prudent, industrious man; or he had something like money to spare in the hands of his merchant, who, in the days of which I am speaking, acted as a banker to his prospering customers. The currency being specie, was widely scattered through the land, and in diversified hands, so that its concentration at any particular point was impossible and consequently its removal from the country could not happen to any great extent. . . .
>
> No people had more cause to rejoice than the people of Virginia, but alas! the banks came and all things became changed. Like the upas tree they have withered and destroyed the healthful condition of the country, and inflicted on the people political and pecuniary disease of the most deadly character.[75]

The Bank of the Valley, headquartered in Winchester, was established on February 5, 1817, and conducted branches in Charlestown, Christiansburg, Leesburg, Moorefield, Romney, and Staunton. The North Western Bank was chartered in Wheeling on the same date and operated branches at Jeffersonville, Parkersburg, and Wellsburg. The bank continued issuing currency through the early 1860s. In 1863 the western district of Virginia, with Wheeling as its most important city, separated as the new state of West Virginia. However, the former Virginia banks now in West Virginia did not issue any bills with a West Virginia imprint.

The Virginia Saline Bank, which started business in Clarksburg about 1815, was run by a disreputable bunch and ceased business not long after this item appeared in *Niles' Weekly Register,* April 17, 1819, as did the similarly bad Western Bank of Virginia in Parkersburg:

> Of the Merchants Bank of Alexandria—of the German bank of Wooster, and two or three others in Ohio: of the Parkersburg and Saline banks, of Virginia; of several in Pennsylvania; of the Bank of Somerset, or the Elkton Bank, of Maryland [there is a] large heap of trash which we unfortunately have on hand. . . .

In 1834 the Merchants and Mechanics Bank, in Wheeling, was established, and branches were opened in Clarksburg, Morgantown, and Point Pleasant.

The Exchange Bank, located in Norfolk, the last to be chartered under the old rules, was set up by the Act of March 25, 1837, also called the Free-Banking Act, which also created new provisions for banks to be established after that date. The Exchange Bank had branches in Abingdon, Alexandria (opened in 1847, succeeding the Farmers Bank of Alexandria), Clarksville, Lynchburg, Petersburg, Richmond, Salem, and Weston. It is interesting that branch banks were popular in the South and Midwest, but were used only to a limited extent in the Northeast. The law provided that currency could be issued up to five times the amount of specie actually owned by the bank and in its possession, but some banks violated this limit and issued more. Some cheated by calling bank drafts "specie" (a widespread practice in other states as well).

After the Panic of 1837, banks suspended specie payments. The legislature passed a rule that, contrary to earlier law, banks could issue bills less than $5 denomination up to a total value of 6% of their capital. Most banks resumed in due course. Then in 1841 the collapse of the Bank of the United States of Pennsylvania sent shock waves through other states, and many banks again suspended, including those in Virginia. On April 2, 1842, a law was enacted to mandate resumption of specie payments on November 1 and to continue the issuance of small-denomination currency until January 1, 1843.

After the Hard Times era ended, and 1844 became the first full year of prosperity since 1836, the banks in Virginia generally prospered greatly. Currency was issued in large quantities. Bills of banks established under the Free-Banking Law traded at up to 10% discount in New York City in 1855, while those of banks with earlier charters were discounted only up to 2%.[76]

The Panic of 1857 forced the suspension of specie payments. By legislative act, redemption of notes in coin recommenced on May 1, 1858. Conditions continued to be excellent from that time through 1860. The years of the Civil War were a different story. The Confederacy relocated its capital from Montgomery to Richmond in 1861, and that city became the center of financial and military planning. Banks suffered from the depreciation of money and the war itself, and most were ruined.

There were *so many* banking offices in Virginia that it was hardly possible to keep track of them all (the Haxby text lists 56 basic banks, plus branches). Knox in *History of Banking* commented:

> The period from 1834 to 1860 is referred to by the older bankers as "The halcyon days when there was a bank at every cross roads." It is claimed that at one time fully three hundred banks existed in Virginia. The records indicate that there were at least two-thirds that number in the Commonwealth, which at that time also comprised the state of West Virginia.

Knox also told of the Bank of the Old Dominion, a free bank set up in Alexandria in 1851, which operated profitably through the Civil War through the efforts of its honest clerk (see more about this bank in chapter 19).

Numismatic Comments

Virginia notes present a wide panorama of possibilities, due in no little part to a multitude of bills from all the bank branches. However, many of these notes are scarce, and more than just a few are listed as SENC. Much more available are general types, without regard to location.

Most collectible Virginia bills date prior to the colorful era of the 1850s, but those that are exceptions are

A $5 note of the Bank of Pittsylvania, Chatham, Virginia, May 15, 1861, from a plate by the American Bank Note Co. Not much is known about this bank, other than paper money was issued with its name.

attractive. Dating from the enthusiasm spread by Charles Affleck several decades ago, notes of this state have been high on the popularity list, a momentum sustained by the Jones and Littlefield revision with much new information.

Whenever Virginia bills are featured in fixed-price offerings or at auction, any worthwhile old-time group or collection will draw a flock of buyers.

CURRENCY OF WISCONSIN

Number of banks in the Haxby *Standard Catalog*: 177.
Specialized text: Chester L. Krause, *Wisconsin Obsolete Bank Notes and Scrip,* 1994.

HISTORICAL NOTES

Wisconsin was carved out of the vast acreage of Michigan and became a separate territory, made official on July 4, 1836. A century later, a commemorative half dollar was issued to celebrate the centennial.

The Bank of Wisconsin, then in Green Bay, Michigan Territory, was chartered by the latter on January 23, 1835, and organized the following November 12. The bank issued many bills before it closed in 1839, by then located in Wisconsin.

On November 30, 1836, the Bank of Milwaukee and the Miners Bank of Dubuque were chartered. The former never opened for business. The latter did, and later was situated in Iowa when the borders of that territory were laid out. The Bank of Mineral Point received its charter on December 2, 1836. Capitalized at $200,000, the bank was allowed to issue bills of $5 and higher once $40,000 had been paid in. The U.S. Congress reviewed the matter, and on March 2, 1837, made adjustments to the provisions. An investigation the same year disclosed that only $2,000 of the first installment of the capital had been paid in specie, with the rest in bills of the Bank of Detroit and "specie certificates," a class of paper that soon gained infamy in Michigan. The deficiency was made up, and the bank went into operation. Suspicions were aroused, and another examination was made on September 18, 1840, revealing that there had been an overissue of currency and certain assets were worthless. The situation went from bad to worse, and another investigation in March 1841 resulted in the bank being closed down that summer. A further investigation held in January 1847 disclosed that during the liquidation process certain of the officers had fled with a large quantity of paper money and other assets.

In 1838, George Smith, a Scottish immigrant, influenced the territorial legislature to charter the Wisconsin Marine and Fire Insurance Company. While this company had no legal right to issue paper money, it created certificates of deposit that appeared similar to currency and put them into circulation. In the Hard Times era, these were widely used in Wisconsin and nearby states, for the issuing firm appeared to be substantial. By 1843 the circulation reached $100,000, after which, with intermittent dips, it peaked at $1,470,235 in 1851. Smith had wide connections and ownership interests in banks as distant as Georgia. Despite much criticism by skeptics, all presented bills were redeemed in full. In 1853 it acquired banking privileges, after which time its paper money became official. (Notices of Smith are also given under Georgia and Illinois above.)

The Bank of the Fox River Hydraulic Company, chartered in Depere in 1838, the bank of Washburn & Woodman in Mineral Point, J. Hodges's Bank in Plattville, and other individuals and partnerships issued paper money in the territorial era prior to statehood in 1848.

In 1852 a Free-Banking Law was enacted. The number of banks increased rapidly—from January

1854, when there were 10 banks in the state with $519,814 in circulation, to July of the same year, with 19 banks and $768,218 in currency. By July 1856 there were 38 banks in operation with a claimed $1,443,215 in circulation. Seeking new opportunities, A.A. Bliss, formerly the state treasurer of Ohio, and C.T. Flowers from the same state, came to Madison and organized the Merchants Bank in 1856. This was a decade of wildcat banks that saw the reckless issuance of much paper money, no doubt including quantities that were never recorded.

In September 1856, *Banker's Magazine* published this item:

> Such is the active demand for circulation in the Northwest that there are now eight banks in process of formation in Wisconsin alone: Madison, Bank of the Capitol, capitalized at $50,000; Prairie du Chien, Bank of Prairie du Chien, $50,000; Stevens Point, Northwestern Bank, $60,000; Waupun, Waupun Bank, $25,000; Fond du Lac, Exchange Bank of Darling & Co., $50,000; Hudson, Hudson City Bank, $25,000; De Pere, Brown County Bank, $25,000; and Elkhorn, Elkhorn Bank, $25,000.

Numismatic Comments

Today, Wisconsin bank notes make a particularly colorful display, for most banks in the state were formed in the 1850s, when ornateness was the rule. Topping the list of must-have bills is the $2 note of the Waupun Bank with a Santa Claus vignette.

The authoritative book on bills of the state was written by Chester L. Krause, famed founder of *Numismatic News* and the Krause Publishing empire. At the Christie's offerings of ABNCo proofs in 1990 and 1991, Krause competed tooth and nail with Herbert and Martha Schingoethe to acquire prize items, particularly numerous for this state, including many bills that had not been known to exist.

The loose requirements under the Free-Banking Act and the subsequent rise in the population of wildcat banks translated into large numbers of sheets and remainder notes surviving from some banks of the 1850s. Once plentiful, today they are fairly widely scattered, and in some future generation they may be viewed as scarce.

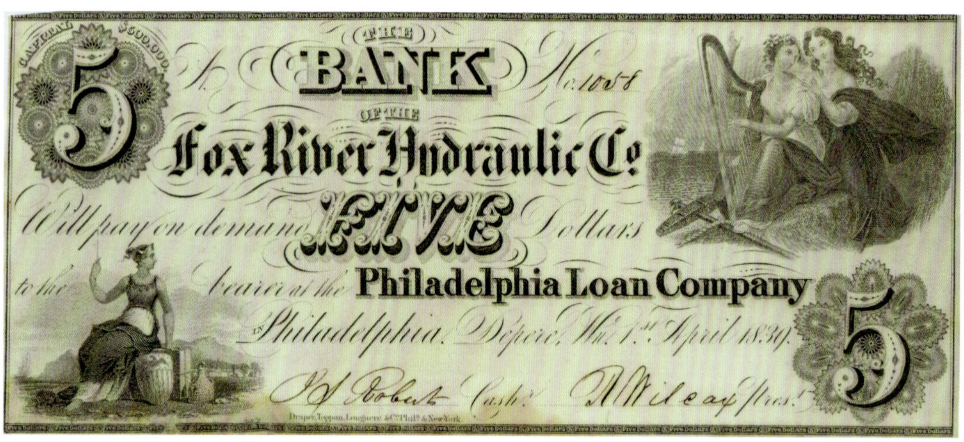

A $5 note of the Bank of the Fox River Hydraulic Co., Depere, Wisconsin, April 1, 1839, payable at the distant Philadelphia Loan Company. Plate by Draper, Toppan, Longacre & Co., Philadelphia and New York.

Treasures of the ABNCo Archives

Plates in the ABNCo Archives

When the plates from the various companies arrived at the American Bank Note Company's building on Wall Street after the 1858 merger, they were either already wrapped, or given a new wrapping of thick paper. In crayon or other marker, the name of the originating firm was noted, often by its initials, plus the name of the bank and its location, sometimes abbreviated and not easily understood today.

The number of bank-note plates on hand in 1858 is not known, but by the late 20th century more than 1,000 still survived, mostly of four-subject sheets. In addition, the company had tens of thousands of small vignette dies, steel cylinder dies (transfer dies or roller dies), and other items bearing paper-money designs of the bank-note-issuing era, this in addition to vast quantities of materials used to print stamps, coupons, stock certificates, bank documents, and various world currency.

In folders, arranged in order by location and bank, were thousands of impressions, mostly proofs, of bills made for banks prior to 1866, including many proof sheets intact from the days when the predecessor firms were in operation. Some of these proofs were in the form of single notes or groups, many were in sheets of two or four subjects, and others were fragments. Although quite a few of these proofs left the firm one way or another over the years, enough remained on hand that the stock was valued at millions of dollars when auctioned by Christie's in 1990.

As the nature of these items had not been disclosed previously, there were many rarities and other surprises for numismatists in this collection—including hitherto unknown designs and issues. In recent years many of these items have reappeared on the aftermarket, a rich source for specialists. Prior to the dispersal of the American Bank Note Co. archives, proofs of such notes were few and far between and could not be easily collected.

In addition to old-time proofs, some plates were dusted off and new impressions were taken from them, from which high-resolution photographic negatives were made to create "modern proprietary proofs." I am not aware that any accounting was kept of the number of such modern bills made, but quantities seem to have been small. In addition to the foregoing, some modern impressions were taken of notes sold as souvenirs to collectors, these usually being on different paper from old-time proofs and with colors different (usually brighter) than on originals.

Now comes the intriguing fact: the selling of modern imprints from old plates, which was anticipated to be quite profitable, did not pay its way. Thus, the idea was abandoned. With the intention of simplifying accounting and storage problems, nearly all the plates used to make master prints for modern proprietary proofs were taken under guard to a steel factory, where, under the watchful eye of a company representative, they were tossed into a melting pot. At the time, batches of steel were being made for railroad rails. Seeing some locomotives depicted on the plates about to be destroyed, an executive commented, in effect, "This is most fitting—from one railroad to another!"

Although many plates were retained by the American Bank Note Co. after their use had ended on or before 1865, many others had been given out by that time. It was often the custom to send plates to the banks that had paid for them, a common practice by Rawdon, Wright, Hatch & Edson. In later years some of these plates, as well as plates from other sources, have come back on the market. They are seen occasionally today.

Sometimes old plates are available as single-note subjects, slightly larger than the note itself, originally intended to be locked together in a frame for printing. In a 2003 visit to the American Bank Note Co., I saw very few of these subjects. Most inventory consisted of plates with multiple notes, typically four. I saw nothing that resembled a multipart Patent Stereotype Steel Plate, nor have I ever encountered these elsewhere on the market.

Examining certain of the old four-subject plates has yielded much information concerning how such plates were made and used. As an example, an old plate for a sheet of $1-$2-$5-$5 bills for the Agricultural Bank of Tennessee was intended to be altered for use by another bank, and was imprinted "Wisconsin," after which no more work was done. Although there were different ways to alter plates, one method was to efface the unwanted name of a bank, state, or other notation by the use of a burin or other small tool, or to carefully grind it off. The plate would then be heated, placed face down on a hard flat surface, and the reverse tapped repeatedly with a peen hammer to flatten the depression caused by the removal. The plate then was polished and taken to a transfer press, where steel cylinder dies would imprint new lettering, in effect creating a plate of a new character.

In another instance, a plate of $5-$5-$10-$20 notes for the Bank of North America in Seymour, Connecticut, was altered by the American Bank Note Co. in 1861 to receive the imprint of the Ansonia Bank of Ansonia, Connecticut.[1] W.L. Ormsby, the exemplar of siderographic expertise, altered several of his plates to print bills of other banks in other states.

Plates Destroyed in Chicago

Paul McCoy, who worked with ABNCo in Chicago, provided these comments for use in this book:

> While growing up, I had the opportunity to work my way through school at the Chicago plant of American Bank Note Company. I started off with summer employment in 1966 while still in high school, and worked there through May of 1972 (at which time I graduated with a degree in electrical engineering from college). In my college years, the employment allowed me to pay my way through school. In my final three years of college, I was going to school during the day and working the evening shift at a nearly full-time number of hours.
>
> My assignment was in the packing and shipping-receiving area (common for part time work), and I like to believe that since I was perceived as a hard worker the company gave me some of the more interesting tasks to do.
>
> In 1970 ABNCo decided that it was time to move from their old facility at 118 East 20th Street on the South Side of Chicago to a brand new printing plant located in an industrial suburb of Chicago named Bedford Park. The 20th Street facility was an early 1900s multi-story printing plant, a picture of which is in the book *The Story of the American Bank Note Company.* At the time of the move, the Chicago plant produced security products printed with the "offset" method, and also served to "finish" stock certificates and bonds which had been produced by the "steel plate method" in the Bronx plant. However, at one time the Chicago plant also did its own steel plate printing, and stored a large quantity of steel plates (thousands) in two vaults on the Chicago plant property.
>
> Now the story gets interesting.
>
> When the move to Bedford Park was imminent, I was tasked with what I viewed, even then, as a sad assignment. Management had decided that the steel plates in storage at the old Chicago plant would *not* be moved to Bedford Park, and decided to *destroy them by melting.* The plates were stored in a vertical position in the vaults in floor-to-ceiling wooden racks. Each rectangular "hole" in the rack was about six inches wide and about eighteen inches high (as I remember). Within each "hole" were stored up to about 10 plates. Each plate's printing surface was coated with a wax to protect it, and all had an actual copy of what had been printed by that plate taped to the plate (with the tape wrapped around the back).
>
> My assignment was to remove the plates in bulk (no one recorded what was being melted), tear off the surface sheet for shredding, and stack the plates on pallets. After that, each pallet (which weighed about 3,000 pounds, and contained about 150 or so plates) was steel strapped for shipment. After all this was done, arrangements were made with the Wisconsin Steel Company to melt the plates in their electric furnace shop on the far South Side of Chicago. On two fateful days, one truck per day was loaded with about 40,000 pounds of plates and driven to the mill. Since these were security items an American Bank Note employee had to accompany the driver to the mill to actually witness the plate melting. I did that on one of the two days.
>
> At the mill, the truck eventually pulled into the "scrap" area adjacent to the furnace. A forklift truck removed the pallets from the semi-trailer, and then an electromagnet-equipped crane picked up each pallet and loaded it into the electric furnace. When the pallets were in the furnace (yes, wood and all), the massive lid was swung into position, the electrodes lowered, and the melting process ensued. Sad.
>
> What was printed at one time by these plates? Well, since I had to tear off the proof sheet from the face of every plate, I had a chance to look at what the plate was engraved with. There were college diplomas by the hundreds, stocks and bonds, postage stamps, professional licenses, legal notices by the states and federal government, commemorative items for both Chicago World Fairs, just to name some.
>
> What I don't know is whether the decision to destroy the plates was made unilaterally at Chicago (I was at the bottom of the totem pole) or had been sanctioned by the corporate offices at 70 Broad Street in New York.

Events of 1990

In July 1990, the American Bank Note Co. was acquired by the United States Banknote Corporation. The buyer announced that the paper archives of the firm, dating back to the mid 19th century, were redundant to current business and consigned them to Christie's, the New York auction house. An article on August 24, 1990, in the *New York Times* included this information:

> "We had been getting tons of letters from collectors who knew we had them, asking if we would sell them privately," said Morris Weissman, board chairman of United States Banknote. Besides, he said, the proofs "were not serving any purpose for us except taking up space in the vault."[2]

The sale date for the American obsolete bank notes and related items was set for September 14 and 15, 1990. A fine catalog, 310 pages describing 2102 lots, was prepared by James Lamb (in charge of Christie's numismatic department) and Gene Hessler. More than 4,000 sheets and individual notes were offered. James Lamb stated that, if the notes on the sheets were added up, plus the single items, the total number of proofs amounted to nearly 15,000; he also observed that prior to the sale, only about 4,000 to 5,000 such proofs were in collectors' hands.

Later in 1990 and in 1991, Christie's sold other ABNCo archives material relating to stocks and bonds, foreign stamps and paper money, and other specialties.

In the *Bank Note Reporter,* February 2006, Mark D. Tomasko discussed the sale of the ABNCo archives of metal plates and dies, concluding with this poignant comment:

> In a larger sense, part of the story of American Bank Note in the last half century and of the industry at large, is the purported technological progress which is moving away from any craft as security to strictly "high-tech" methods. While intaglio continues to survive on currency, picture engraving for bank notes is now increasingly done using computer design programs. Hand done bank note engraving, largely gone from stock certificates ten years ago, is consequently in the process of disappearing from currency too. It's not clear how long the art will survive.

Echoing these comments, it is likely that bank note and other security engraving will fade into history, perhaps completely, leaving ABNCo artifacts as reminders of what once was, but is no longer.

A Gallery of ABNCo Archives Photographs

In 2005, the American Banknote (*sic*) Company, which had gone through several corporate ownership changes and evolutions, operating under Chapter 11 bankruptcy proceedings, became a private company. Today it operates as such in Englewood Cliffs, New Jersey. The demand for security printing diminishes, and in 2001 the New York Stock Exchange waived the requirement that certificates for listed stocks were to be printed by the engraving process. Bank-note plates, vignettes, presses, and other items from the archives were sold to John Albanese and partners, as noted in the introduction to this text.

The photographs on the following pages were taken on several occasions. The earliest are by the author and David M. Sundman, taken in November 2003, when the archives were in Philadelphia, during a visit hosted by Peter Huntoon. In our party were also Don Sundman and Jeff Marsh. Then follow pictures taken by Donn Pearlman (tapped to take charge of publicity) on October 19, 2005, after the archives had been moved to New Jersey, under the care of John Albanese and Steve Blum. The other pictures are of individual plates, cylinder dies, and vignettes on the Wolfeboro, New Hampshire, premises of American Numismatic Rarities, photographed by Douglas Plasencia in 2006.

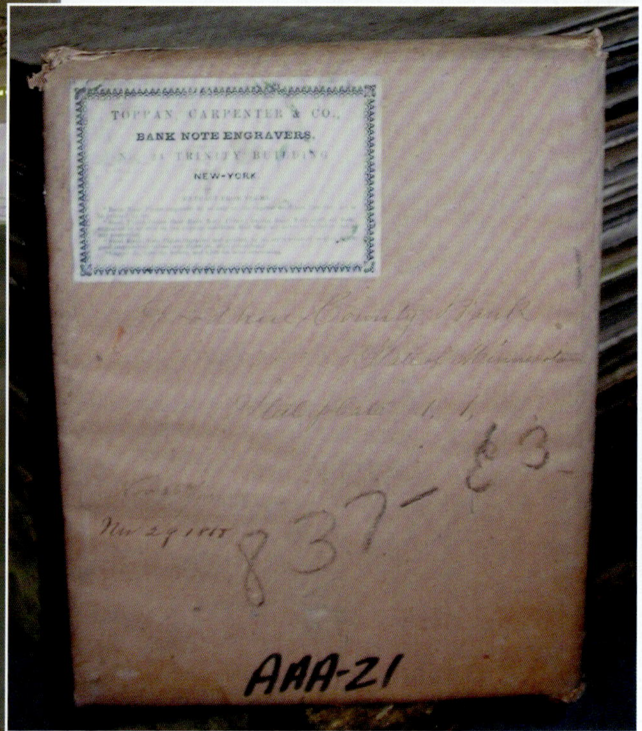

Pink paper wrapping with notations and crayon markings, covering a steel plate used to print Goodhue County Bank (Cannon Falls, Minnesota) bills. The label was affixed by Toppan, Carpenter & Co., located at No. 24 Trinity Building, New York City, in the time before the merger that formed ABNCo in 1858.

The author with about 1,000 bank note plates, arranged in piles on the floor, at the American Bank Note Co., November 2003. Nearly all of the plates were in their original paper wrappers, labeled, as stored in the 1850s and early 1860s.

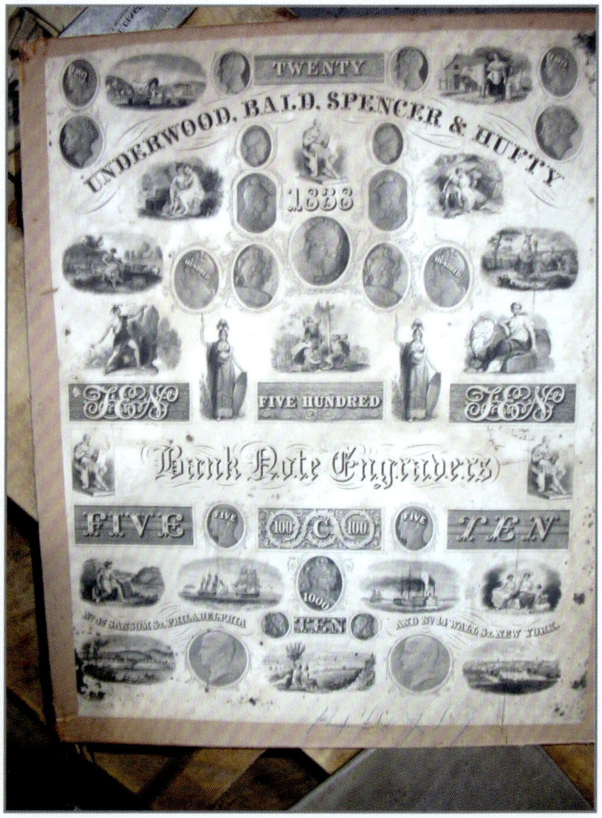

Broadside affixed to the pink paper wrapper enclosing the original printed plate for an advertising broadside issued and dated 1838, by Underwood, Bald, Spencer & Hufty.

A page from a tattered old scrapbook of printed impressions from vignette dies.

A page from another scrapbook shows impression from plates used to print stock certificates and security documents for banks.

Detail from a scrapbook page of bank-note plate impressions from the National Bank Note Co., which was merged into the American Bank Note Co. At the top is an essay or experimental $10 note design proposed but never used. The second is the impression of the back of a DIX ($10) note of the Citizens Bank of Louisiana.

David M. Sundman and Q. David Bowers during their November 2003 visit to the ABNCo archives, shown holding a vignette for the center part of a LaFayette Bank $2 note. The visit was arranged by bank-note historian Peter Huntoon. In the party were also Jeff Marsh and Don Sundman.

Jeff Marsh and David M. Sundman in front of a *small section* of the storage shelves for small vignettes and dies for bank notes, part of an estimated total of 20,000 or more.

One of many small scattered groups of vignettes, each wrapped in paper to which an impression is affixed.

Antique spider press preserved in the ABNCo archives, used in the 19th century to print sheets of paper money.

This old transfer press, with a later coat of paint, was key to the transferring of images from vignette dies to document plates using cylinder dies (transfer rolls).

A small part of the storage facilities for cylinder dies.

Dozens of cylinder dies packed in trays.

John Albanese at the New Jersey warehouse, October 19, 2005, holding a steel printing plate for Miners Bank of Savings scrip notes, San Francisco, Alta California, payable in *gold dust.*

Steel vignette plate with multiple elements for Republic of Texas paper money.

Another antique spider press used years ago by ABNCo to print paper money and other security items.

Steve Blum holding a cylinder die.

An old cabinet filled with cylinder dies, part of thousands of such dies, mostly from the 19th century.

More cylinder dies, close view.

Steel vignette dies with cherubs and girls with Liberty Seated silver dollars as the focal point. These images were popular on bank notes of the 1850s. The top and bottom vignettes have proof impressions taped to the front of the dies.

Boxes filled with steel vignette dies.

More steel vignette dies.

And still more—these being but a small portion of the thousands in the ABNCo archives, as photographed in storage in New Jersey in 2005.

Two vignette dies for counters, photographed with their paper covers bearing a printed impression (images on this page are not reversed).

Cylinder die for an American Bank Note Co. "Specimen Bank Note" with a portrait, possibly of Thomas Edison.

Cylinder die for a stock certificate or other document.

Steel printing plate for a sheet of $10-$10-$10-$20 notes for the Union Bank of the State of Tennessee, Nashville branch (image reversed for easy readability).

A selection of steel vignette dies for counters—indicating the face value of notes (images reversed for easy readability).

ONE
V-39684

3
V-39695

TWO
V 39670

3
V-39699

1
ONE
DOLLAR
V 39652

Copper printing plate for a $100 note of the Ocean Bank, Kennebunk, Maine (most images on this page reversed for easy readability).

Steel vignette die, counter for a $5 United States Treasury Note, using the "cycloidal configuration" patent of the National Bank Note Co.

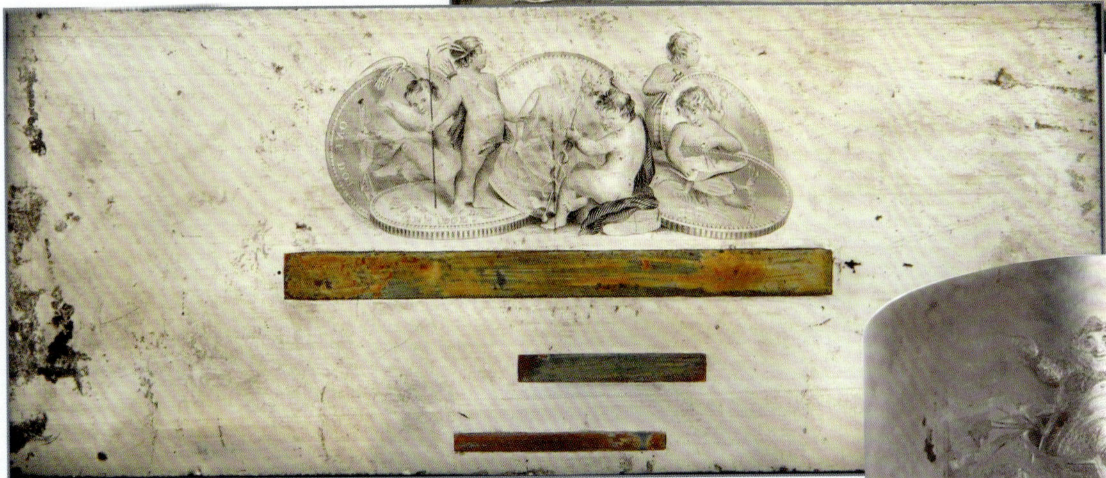

Vignette die for a $5 note with cherubs and silver dollars, with cutout spaces for the insertion of a bank name, city, and state.

Cylinder die for making a bank-note plate depicting Santa Claus (image not reversed).

Vignette die with three elements, not necessarily related in the creation of a specific bank note.

Steel printing plate for a book illustration (images on this page reversed for easy readability).

Copper printing plate with TEN multiple times, used to print a colored tint across the face of a note.

Vignette die with title of the Amoskeag Bank, Manchester, New Hampshire.

A selection of vignette dies (images reversed for easy readability).

Copper printing plate used for a broadside by Rawdon, Wright & Hatch, New York, in the 1830s. Below the title and several counters are standing figures of Washington, Lafayette, and a goddess (image reversed for easy readability).

Ornate vignette die for the Coca Cola Co., early 20th century, one of many commercial dies in the ABNCo archives (images on this page reversed for easy readability).

Vignette die for the Victor Phonograph Co. with Nipper the dog, the famous mascot.

Steel printing plate for the 1907 season's pass issued by the Boston National League Base Ball Co.

Vignette die for postage stamps of Salvador.

Vignette die for the Indian Motorcycle made by the Hendee Manufacturing Co.

Vignette die for the Campbell Soup Co., for use on a stock certificate.

NOTES

Chapter 1

1. S.S. Crosby, *The Early Coins of America,* p. 26, expands on this idea.
2. Joseph B. Felt, *An Historical Account of Massachusetts Currency,* 1839, pp. 82, 83.
3. Crosby, *Early Coins of America,* 1875, p. 25.
4. Adapted from a longer citation in Kenneth Scott, *Counterfeiting in Colonial New York City,* 1953, pp. 92–93.
5. Adapted from a longer citation in Kenneth Scott, *Counterfeiting in Colonial Pennsylvania,* 1955, p. 82.
6. From the manuscript "General Quarter Sessions Docket No. 10, 1769–1775," York County, pp. 78–79, as cited by Kenneth Scott, *Counterfeiting in Colonial Pennsylvania,* 1955, pp. 134–35.
7. Charles A. Downs, *History of Lebanon, N.H. 1761–1887,* 1908, pp. 101–103, from Provincial Papers, Vol. VIII, pp. 115, 116.
8. Today's Norwich, Vermont.
9. Eric P. Newman, *Early Paper Money of America,* 1990, p. 180.
10. Although no "land banks" ever rose to prominence, the idea persisted, and into the 19th century several institutions used titles including Real Estate Bank or, less often, Land Bank. Examples include the Allegheny Real Estate Bank, the Real Estate Bank of Virginia, and the Chicasaw Land Bank.
11. Andrew McFarland Davis, *Currency and Banking in the Province of the Massachusetts Bay,* 1901, gives extensive details of this issue.
12. Borrowing from the English system, the calendar to the year 1752 commenced annually on March 25 and concluded 365 days later on March 24. Historians call this the Julian calendar. After 1752 the year was set in the colonies to commence with January 1 and end with December 31, the system in place ever since, called the Gregorian calendar. According to the Julian calendar, a certain date given as February 4, 1690, would be translated to February 4, 1691, in the Gregorian calendar, as noted in the text.
13. For details of the Massachusetts and other colonial and related issues, Newman's *Early Paper Money of America* is essential.
14. *Niles' Weekly Register,* August 26, 1843, reads *"The first bank in America.* It has been the general opinion that the first bank in America was the Bank of North America, established in Philadelphia. The *Cincinnati Chronicle,* whose editor has been dipping into the antiquities of the country, says that seventy years before the Bank of North America, the legislature of South Carolina established a public bank, and issued forty-eight thousand pounds in bills of trust. These bills were called bank bills, and the establishment was called a public bank. These were lent out at interest, or loaned on personal security."
15. Newman, *Early Paper Money of America,* 4th edition, p. 422.
16. Ibid., p. 244.
17. Ibid., p. 116.
18. Ibid., pp. 167–69.
19. As published in *Niles' Weekly Register,* November 23, 1833.
20. Much information is from Newman, *Early Paper Money of America.*

Chapter 2

1. H.F. Baker, "Outline History of Banking in the United States," *Banker's Magazine*, November 1856, p. 326, largely drawn verbatim from Condy Raguet, *A Treatise on Currency & Banking,* 2nd edition, 1840, pp. 223, 223.
2. Lawrence Lewis Jr., *A History of the Bank of North America, the First Bank Chartered in the United States,* 1882, pp. 41–42; quotation from Bolles, *Financial History of the United States,* p. 273. In actuality, neither Robert Morris nor anyone else could prevent currency from going where people wanted to take it. The statement about "gentlemen interested in the institution" (whatever that means) sending runners to exchange bills at the bank does not make much sense. It indicates that the bank was in difficulty but, by capers involving displaying silver, sought to allay suspicion, which may have been done. However, it does not say that the people were not able to redeem their notes. In instances in which speculators made "runs" on banks, such displays made no difference, for customers would have wanted silver anyway, as would have the runners sent by these supposed gentlemen of interest.
3. *Banking In California 1849–1910,* pp. 103–105.
4. *Personal Memoirs of Gen'l. W.T. Sherman,* pp. 142–45.
5. Horace White, *Money and Banking,* 1896, pp. 334–37.
6. At some point in the early era the bank acquired thousands of newly minted 1787 Fugio copper cents, which in numismatic circles became known as the Bank of New York Hoard. Although many of these coins have been distributed over the years, the bank still retains a large holding.
7. Horace White, *Money and Banking,* 1896, p. 337.
8. Alfred Cookman Bryan, *History of State Banking in Maryland,* 1899, p. 20.
9. For more information see Roger H. Durand, *Obsolete Notes and Scrip of Rhode Island,* 1981.
10. William M. Gouge, *The Curse of Paper-Money and Banking,* 1833, p. 4.
11. As given in an article in the *Albany Evening Journal,* reprinted in Banker's Magazine, March 1855.
12. "Banking in the Olden Time," *Banker's Magazine,* July 1872. This scenario seems unlikely, as sending bills to the "far West" was a common ambition of the era, developing into a wholesale business later in the 19th century when more banks had been chartered. The idea was a simple one: print bills in quantity, spend them in distant locations (even taking the reduction that some notes were subjected to in far away places), and hope that they would never be redeemed. In that instance each bill would represent pure profit, less the cost of printing.
13. John Jay Knox, *The History of Banking,* 1900, p. 323.
14. Dewey, *State Banking Before the Civil War,* p. 68
15. The author's examination of many such statements from banks that suspended specie payments beginning in May 1837, many on May 10 and 11, but which remained in business, revealed that most of these solid banks had ample coins on hand but did not pay them out.
16. *Financial Register,* February 14, 1838.
17. *Laws of New Hampshire,* vol. 5, 1916, pp. 883, 884; Original Acts, vol. 13, p. 74; Recorded Acts, vol. 6, p. 509. Nathaniel Adams, *Annals of Portsmouth,* 1825, p. 25. John N. McClintock, *History of New Hampshire,* 1888, p. 445. *New-Hampshire Annual Register and United States Calendar,* 1858, p. 151, brief history of the bank (with some errors). Joseph B. Walker, "Banking and Currency in New Hampshire," *The New England States, Their Constitutional, Judicial, Educational, Commercial, Professional, and Industrial History,* vol. 3, pp. 1640, 1641. Other sources.
18. Plumer letter book, Library of Congress, cited by Lynn W. Turner, *William Plumer of New Hampshire 1759–1850,* 1962, p. 42.
19. Norman Walker Smith, *A History of Commercial Banking in New Hampshire 1792–1843,* 1967, p. 41, citing state records.
20. Published in 1825, pp. 324, 325.
21. Norman Walker Smith, *A History of Commercial Banking in New Hampshire 1792–1843,* 1967, p. 130.
22. *History of Banking,* 1900.
23. William F. Hasse Jr., *A History of Money and Banking in Connecticut,* 1957, p. 15.
24. Francis Parsons, *A History of Banking in Connecticut,* 1935, p. 15.
25. William F. Hasse Jr., *A History of Money and Banking in Connecticut,* 1957, p. 15.
26. *Banker's Magazine,* August 1856, pp. 132, 133.
27. Alfred Cookman Bryan, *History of State Banking in Maryland,* 1899, pp. 20, 21.
28. Retrospective published in *Banker's Magazine,* August 1846.
29. From a retrospective account in the *New York Courier,* April 6, 1831.
30. *The Weekly Register* (Niles'), February 1, 1812, p. 399.
31. *Niles' National Register,* February 5, 1842.
32. Alfred Cookman Bryan, *History of State Banking in Maryland,* 1899, p. 45.
33. William F. Hasse Jr., *A History of Money and Banking in Connecticut,* 1957, p. 10.
34. Roger H. Durand, *Obsolete Notes and Scrip of Rhode Island,* 1981.
35. Details of this caper can be found in many publications, including the September 1848 issue of *Banker's Magazine.*
36. *Niles' Register,* September 12, 1835. Other sources.
37. *The Financial Register,* vol. 1, p. 74, quoting New York City newspapers (not named) of this date.
38. William Gold, "Portland Banks," *Collections of the Maine Historical Society,* Series II, vol. 4, p. 89.
39. In *Bouvier's Law Dictionary* as 17 Mass. 497.
40. Glenn E. Jackson, "Earliest Use of Washington's Portrait on U.S. Bank Notes," *The Essay Proof Journal,* Spring 1976.
41. Roger H. Durand, *Obsolete Notes and Scrip of Rhode Island,* 1981.

Chapter 3

1. Among many sources: "Jacob Perkins, Die Cutter, Engraver," *The Numismatist,* May 1920, reprinted information from several sources. Grenville and Dorothy Bathe, *Jacob Perkins, His Inventions, His Times, His Contemporaries,* published in 1943 in an edition of 200 copies, is the most important source for biographical information. Various articles in the *Essay-Proof Journal* are also valuable, especially Clarence W. Brazer, "The Fine Art of Line Engraving," October 1945; and Ralph R. Weaver, "Jacob Perkins 1766–1849: Precious Metalsmith, Pioneer Inventor, Engraver and Die-Maker," Spring 1962. See also Samuel L. Knapp, "Memoir of Jacob Perkins," 1835 and 1836, reprinted with expanded notes in *Colonial Newsletter,* vol. 27, no. 3, November 1987, serial no. 77.
2. These buttons are backmarked "PARKI," an apparent attempt to show Perkins's name, according to historians Bruce S. Bazelon and William F. McGuinn, *A Directory of American Military Goods Dealers and Makers 1785–1885,* p. 64. The present author finds the "Parki" signature to be unlikely.
3. In this year he also invented a heating system consisting of a stove in the basement of a building connected to rooms by tubes or passageways. The Massachusetts Medical College, Mason Street, Boston, was so equipped.
4. In this series the copper coins of Vermont (1785–1788), Connecticut (1785–1788), New Jersey (1786–1788), and Massachusetts (1787–1788) were the most prominent.
5. *American Journal of Numismatics,* October 1875; 1792 date of an unattributed newspaper clipping from the scrapbook of J.J. Mickley.
6. Newspaper on file in the library of the American Antiquarian Society, Worcester, Massachusetts. More information from this notice but relating to bank notes is quoted later in the present text.
7. See notations in W. Elliot Woodward's Sixty-Ninth Sale, October 13–18, 1884, Lot 429: "Medal designed and struck by Jacob Perkins for the second presidency of Washington; Bust; rev., a blazing sun, between the rays of which appear fifteen stars represent the Union and the thirteen original states with Vermont and Kentucky, which had been added. Size 16." The next three lots offered other varieties including "another from a different and much larger die." Also, W. Elliot Woodward's Eightieth Sale, Coins and Medals, The Matthews Collection, December 16–19, 1885, Lot 1894: "Success to the United States. Bust; rev. sun and stars; said to have been designed and struck by Jacob Perkins for the citizens of Boston, and worn on the occasion of the second inauguration of Washington as president; brass, very fine, size 12." Notwithstanding this information, modern scholarship suggests that these tokens may date from a later period and have no connection with Perkins.
8. *American Journal of Numismatics,* October 1892.
9. Ibid., April 1896.
10. Ibid., October 1892.
11. W. Elliot Woodward, in a chapter in Franklin B. Hough's masterful study, *Washingtoniana,* 1865, vol. II, p. 281, notes this concerning the "Victor Sine Clade" medal: "Dudley A. Tyng was the designer of this medal and the credit of execution has usually been accorded to Jacob Perkins. The dies were made in the shop of Jacob Perkins, but the work was by Nicholas Pearce, who died within a few years at an advanced age in Newburyport. Mr. Pearce retained in his possession till his death, one of the earliest and finest impressions, always refusing for it the most tempting offers. After his death it was purchased of Mrs. Pearce, and having passed through various hands has found a permanent resting place in a celebrated collection." The *Massachusetts Mercury,* February 11, 1800, included this notice: "A National and Masonic Medal, on one side of which is a bust of Washington, pronounced by judges an excellent likeness; and on the reverse an Urn, on the Pedestal of which is this motto, *'Victor sine Clade'* with Emblems Masonic, national and fanciful, has been received from *Newburyport,* and is for Sale, by E. Moulton, No. 11, and D. Tyler, No. 15, *Cornhill;* T. Pons, opposite Faust's Statue, *Newbury-Street;* S. Sumner, No. 1, S. Turell, and at the Bunch of Grapes, *State-Street;* R. Evans, *Hanover-Street;* and P. Revere, Jun., *Fore-Street."* See also *American Journal of Numismatics,* July 1889.
12. Newspaper on file in the library of the American Antiquarian Society, Worcester, Massachusetts.
13. James Akin was born in South Carolina in 1773. He died on July 18, 1846.
14. *Remarks on the Manufacture of Bank Notes and Other Promises to Pay, Addressed to the Bankers of the Southern Confederacy, Columbia, S.C.,* published by Keatinge & Ball, 1864. Copy digitized by the University of North Carolina—Confederate History Project, "Documenting the American South." Earlier reprinted in the *Essay-Proof Journal,* vol. 19, no. 3, 1962.
15. William M. Gouge, *The Curse of Paper-Money and Banking,* 1833, pp. 6–11, history of the bank and its failure.
16. *Bicknell's Counterfeit Detector,* November 22, 1830.
17. Named for General Richard Montgomery, a hero of the American Revolution, who was killed in 1775 in the Battle of Quebec.
18. Sources for this study include Zadock Thompson, *History of Vermont,* 1832, vol. II, p. 136; George B. Reed, *Sketch of the Early History of Banking in Vermont,* Boston, published by the author, 1879 (Reed's copy, with extra illustrations of authentic bills, etc., ex John Jay Ford Jr., is in the author's library); Walter Hill Crockett, *Vermont: The Green Mountain State,* vol. II, New York: The Century History Company, 1921; Mayre Burns Coulter, *Vermont Obsolete Notes and Scrip,* 1972; Kenneth A. Degree, "Malfeasance or Theft? What Really Happened at the Middlebury Branch of the Vermont State Bank," *Vermont History* 68 (Winter/Spring 2000), pp. 5–34; other sources.
19. Crockett, vol. II, p. 609.
20. Cited by Kenneth A. Degree from Henry Swan Dana, *The History of Woodstock, Vermont* (Cambridge: Houghton, Mifflin and Co., 1889), pp. 328, 329.
21. Information on the Middlebury theft based on Kenneth A. Degree, "Malfeasance or Theft? What Really Happened at the Middlebury Branch of the Vermont State Bank," *Vermont History* 68 (Winter/Spring 2000), pp. 5–34.
22. Details of these and related currency capers will be related in a forthcoming study of New Hampshire currency by the author and David M. Sundman.
23. It should be noted that many large coin transactions with Canada were illegally conducted by Boston financiers and others during this era, many details of which can be found in *Niles' Weekly Register* and other contemporary periodicals.
24. Alpheus Felch, "Early Banks and Banking in Michigan," *Pioneer Collections: Report of the Pioneer Society of the State of Michigan* 2 (1880), pp. 111–24, the source of much other information in this study.
25. Numismatically remembered by the anticipatory use of 26 stars on the reverse of the 1836 Gobrecht silver dollar, expected to go into circulation as a regular design in 1837, but this did not happen.
26. Harold L. Bowen, *State Bank Notes of Michigan,* 1956, p. 164.
27. Ibid., pp. 169, 170.
28. Felch, "Early Banks and Banking in Michigan," 1880, p. 111.
29. Harold L. Bowen, *State Bank Notes of Michigan,* 1956, p. 4.
30. Felch, "Early Banks and Banking in Michigan," 1880, pp. 111, 112.
31. Harold L. Bowen, *State Bank Notes of Michigan,* 1956, pp. 189, 190, reprints a larger excerpt of the text.
32. Henry's surname is spelled "Voight" in the original, standardized to Voigt here.
33. Asa Spencer, then of New London, Connecticut, patented a ruling machine on February 7, 1812, the main purpose of which seems to have been the engraving of watch cases. Others invented related devices that were used on various surfaces including bank-note plates. Today it is difficult to assign specific credit to any individual for being the first.
34. Part of a lengthy 1819 memorial, "Prevention of the Forgery of Bank Notes," from Perkins's London firm, Perkins, Fairman & Heath, to the Society for the Encouragement of Arts, Manufactures and Commerce. The same memorial contained a detailed description of decarbonizing the surface of cast-steel plates, cylinders, etc., to soften the metal to make it easier to receive impressions, after which it could be hardened for use.
35. Denwood N. Kelly, Armand Shank Jr., and Thomas S. Gordon, *Money & Banking in Maryland,* 1996, pp. 510, 512.
36. Variety known today as Shank-150.5.1, Shank, p. 512.
37. Congreve earlier had written a small book, *Protection of the Metallic Currency,* with regard to coins.

Chapter 4

1. Condy Raguet, *A Treatise on Currency & Banking,* 2nd edition, 1840, p. 129.
2. Richard Hildreth, *The History of Banks,* 1837, p. 59. However, "knavery" was often hard to define. Many writers on the subject, including Hildreth, have failed to recognize that most banks stopped specie payments in order to preserve their assets. Suspension was usually a necessity, not a plan to increase bank profits.
3. Although Condy Raguet's text is an example of a useful early work for pres-

ent-day numismatic research and the same can be said for contemporary government and bank reports and, to a lesser extent, newspaper accounts, most modern economic studies are seriously flawed. Typical modern writers in the field of economics know very little about coins and paper money or, indeed, the general working of banks, engraving companies, etc. In their writing a handful of popular sources are quoted, reprinted, and re-analyzed, with the conclusions being quite amusing to serious numismatic students of currency. There are a few good early studies cited now and then, and Raguet's is among them, as are several histories relating specifically to the banking of several states.
4. Francis Parsons, *A History of Banking in Connecticut,* 1935, pp. 11, 12.
5. *International Monetary Conference Held . . . in Paris, in August 1878.* Senate Executive Document No. 48, Forty-fifth Congress, Third Session, study by John White, cashier of the Bank of the United States, Baltimore branch; "Statement of the Price of Specie During the Suspension of Specie Payments," p. 646.
6. The Mint showed a profit on the coinage of cents; when silver and gold coins were minted, no profit was registered on this coinage of precious metals. Thus, extensive minting of cents was highly advantageous. Cents had been coined last in 1814, although the report, dated January 1, suggests that some cents may have been already struck (such as in December 1815 from 1816-dated dies, or from old dies). The new cent coinage of 1816 marked the inauguration of a new motif called the Matron Head by numismatists today. By year's end the mintage total for 1816 cents was 2,820,982, equal to slightly more than $28,000—this being far less than the "nearly 47,000 dollars" projected.
7. Review statement included in the *Mint Report* of two years later, February 28, 1817, covering 1816 and earlier times.
8. Although many United States silver dollars were exported, particularly to the Caribbean, in the early 19th century, large quantities remained stateside. They were familiar enough to citizens that some bank-note vignettes of the 1830s illustrated such coins. The silver dollars used in the China and East India trade were not likely to ever return to America.
9. A subtle pun, perhaps?
10. Richard Hildreth, *The History of Banks,* 1837, pp. 59, 60.
11. This excerpt has been edited and had subtitles added.
12. John Bull was a nickname for England. By this time commerce with England had been restored and, among many other things, copper planchets for making American cents were being imported from Birmingham.
13. Condy Raguet, *A Treatise on Currency & Banking,* 2nd edition, 1840, pp. 128, 129, here excerpted and edited.
14. Ibid., p. 130, edited.
15. America was hardly alone in having specie suspensions, and many countries had them more frequently and for longer periods. As an example, in England specie payments were suspended for a generation, from 1797 to 1821.
16. Excerpted and lightly edited with subtitles added. The text, adapted from an original copy owned by Eric P. Newman, is given in full in the *Essay-Proof Journal* no. 88, 1965, and no. 89, 1966.
17. Little is known today about such bills, seemingly issued beginning circa 1799, the date of Perkins's patent.

Chapter 5

1. Certain biographical information is from Donald C. O'Brien, "Abner Reed: A Connecticut Engraver," *The Connecticut Historical Society Bulletin,* January 1979.
2. The concept of NASCA was conceived by John J. Ford Jr.; George and Douglas Ball were the main backers of the firm, while Herbert I. Melnick was the primary spokesperson. The firm was located in Ford's hometown of Rockville Centre, New York.
3. O'Brien, "Abner Reed: A Connecticut Engraver," p. 121.
4. Foster Wild Rice, "Antecedents of the American Bank Note Company of 1858," *Essay-Proof Journal,* vol. 18, nos. 71 and 72, 1961.
5. Sinclair Hamilton, Introduction, *Early American Book Illustrators and Wood Engravers 1670–1870,* p. 177: "Mason was an apprentice of Abner Reed of Hartford, and admiring the work done by Alexander Anderson on wood, he began in 1808 to experiment himself in this field. When his apprenticeship expired in 1810, he moved to Philadelphia and is supposed to have been the first wood engraver to work in that city."
6. Donald C. O'Brien, "The Early Nineteenth Century Boston Engraving Trade and the Engravers Who Developed It," *Printing History,* vol. XXIII, no. 1, pp. 3–17, American Printing History Association.
7. Rice, "Antecedents of the American Bank Note Company of 1858," *Essay-Proof Journal,* vol. 18, nos. 71 and 72, 1961.
8. Bray Hammond, *Banks and Politics in America from the Revolution to the Civil War,* 1957, p. 178: "In April 1816 New York began, with the Bank of Niagara and the Bank of Jefferson County, to include in all charters a stipulation that the charters would be forfeited upon failure of the banks to redeem their notes."
9. Historical information from George S. and Helen McKearin, *American Glass,* 1941, pp. 195 ff.; Max P. Petersen, *Salisbury: From Birth to Bicentennial,* 1976, pp. 19–21, 93, 94, 106.
10. Minutes of the Vermont Glass Company, preserved by the Sheldon Museum, Middlebury, cited by Max P. Petersen, *Salisbury: From Birth to Bicentennial,* 1976, p. 19.
11. As quoted in McKearin and McKearin, *American Glass,* pp. 196, 197.
12. At the time the term *general agent* referred to the manager and business director of this (or any other) factory, the person in charge who represented the interests of the stockholders.
13. H.P. Smith, *History of Addison County,* p. 606.
14. Per a notice in the *Columbia Patriot,* October 1814, cited by McKearin and McKearin, *American Glass,* p. 199.
15. Petersen, *Salisbury,* p. 20.
16. Abundant information on Schoolcraft can be found on the Internet, in his papers in the Manuscript Division of the Library of Congress (included among other material available on 69 microfilm reels), in the Burton Collection at the Detroit Public Library, and at the University of Michigan, among other locations.
17. McKearin and McKearin, *American Glass,* pp. 190, 191.
18. Quoted by Harry Hall White, "Henry Rowe Schoolcraft, Glassmaker," Part II, *Antiques,* February 1939. A $1.50 bill in the C. John Ferreri collection is ink dated March 5, 1813.
19. Coulter lists only one variety of the small-factory bill, with an ambiguous inscription. It is either VGF-2 or VGF-6 in the present study.
20. Coulter lists only one variety of the small-factory bill, with an ambiguous inscription. It is either VGF-2 or VGF-6 in the present study.
21. Coulter also lists a $1.25 of the VGF-10 style as Coulter-6, with SALISBURY at left end. She lists it as R-6 (5 to 10 known) and stated that she had personally seen one. The present writer has never seen one. If such is located, it can be designated as VGF-10a.

Chapter 6

1. Quoted by William H. Dillistin, *Bank Note Reporters and Counterfeit Detectors 1826–1866,* 1949, pp. 71–72. Cairo referred to the fraudulent Bank of Cairo, also known as the Cairo Company, operated at Kaskaskia, Illinois.
2. "Some Notes on *the* Harrison Family of Engravers," by William J. Harrison (a great-great-grandson of William Harrison Sr.), the *Essay-Proof Journal,* October 1946.
3. The excerpts have been lightly edited with ubtitles added.
4. The scrip notes were printed by Murray, Draper, Fairman & Co., Philadelphia, and bear no relationship to the style of the $1-denominated bills by Harrison.
5. Communication to the author, April 5, 2006.
6. Information about these bills and their current use in Ohio can be found in Joab Squire, "Memoirs of Townships—Florence," *Firelands Pioneer,* September 1861, p. 23. Squire arrived in the district on July 15, 1815. "The first specie currency that we had was cut money. They would take a silver dollar and cut it into ten or twelve pieces, (instead of eight,) and pass them for shillings. The first paper currency was Owl Creek Bank notes, of the denominations of six and one-fourth, twelve and one-half, thirty-seven and one-half, and fifty cents." The 25¢ denomination was overlooked by Squire.

Chapter 7

1. Reports by the secretary of the Treasury as cited by Condy Raguet, *A Treatise on Currency & Banking,* 2nd edition, 1840, p. 242.
2. As quoted in *Niles' Weekly Register,* September 4, 1824.

3. Ibid., June 14, 1828.
4. Horace White, *Money and Banking Illustrated by American History,* 1896, p. 50.
5. Mexican-American silver 8 *reales*, not U.S. silver dollars.
6. William F. Hasse Jr., *A History of Money and Banking in Connecticut,* 1957, p. 13.
7. As his signature on notes was not clear, he is sometimes named as "Bradly" or similar in literature.
8. William M. Gouge, *The Curse of Paper-Money and Banking,* 1833, pp. 119–21, from a report to the state legislature.
9. William F. Hasse Jr., *History of Banking in New Haven, Connecticut,* 1946, pp. 10–14.
10. Owners of coastwise ships connecting from New Haven to New York City and widely used by the public, in an era before the railroads.
11. *Niles' Weekly Register,* December 6, 1823.
12. From a historical account in *Banker's Magazine,* September 1852, pp. 203–204.
13. John Jay Knox, *A History of Banking in the United States,* 1900, p. 320.
14. *Niles' Weekly Register,* November 5 and 11, 1825.
15. *Niles' Weekly Register*, June 28, 1828.
16. As filed in spoliation claims with the Department of State in 1831 as part of a long list presented to the French in the quest for reparations.
17. Hasse, *A History of Money and Banking in Connecticut,* 1957, p. 13.
18. Ibid.; other sources.
19. Bruce H. French, *Banking and Insurance in New Jersey: A History,* 1965, p. 19.
20. Gouge, *The Curse of Paper-Money and Banking,* 1833, pp. 117–19, from report made to the state senate, January 25, 1830.
21. Ibid.
22. Ibid.
23. Ibid.
24. Knox, *A History of Banking in the United States,* 1900, p. 319.
25. Many financial writers for newspapers in New York, Washington, and elsewhere outside of New England had little knowledge of the Suffolk Bank system and its benefits and rarely mentioned it in news coverage.
26. Davis R. Dewey, *State Banking Before the Civil War,* 1910, p. 82.

Chapter 8

1. *American State Papers*, Class III, Finance, vol. III, 1834, pp. 57 ff. M. St. Clair Clarke and D.A. Hall, *Legislative and Documentary History of the Bank of the United States Including the Original Bank of North America*, 1832, passim.
2. A. Barton Hepburn, *History of Coinage and Currency in the United States*, 1903, pp. 82, 83.
3. Ibid., p. 83; other sources.
4. *Niles' Weekly Register*, October 5, 1816.
5. *Niles' Weekly Register*, August 31, 1816, citing a Philadelphia report of August 27; September 7, 1816 (numbers of shareholders in each state). Such numbers were often misleading, for in Baltimore a director of the bank, George Williams, "owned 1,172 shares but registered them under 1,172 different names with himself as attorney for all." So he had 39 times the maximum number of votes the charter allowed any one stockholder. See also *American State Papers*—Finance. vol. III, p. 349; Bray Hammond, *Banks and Politics in America from the Revolution to the Civil War*, 1957, p. 257. The complex involvement of the Baltimore branch is beyond the scope of this study, basically involving a competition between this city and Philadelphia, with Baltimore seeking to assert its financial importance beyond that of a simple branch office.
6. *Niles' Weekly Register*, November 2, 1816.
7. Ibid., November 16, 1816.
8. Ibid., November 30, 1816; December 7, 1816.
9. Ibid., May 14, 1817.
10. Ibid., July 18, 1817.
11. Ibid., March 7, 1818; many other notices.
12. Ibid., June 20, 1818.
13. *American State Papers*, Class III, Finance, vol. III, 1834, pp. 291 ff.
14. Ibid., pp. 306 ff.
15. R. Hildreth, *Banks, Banking, and Paper Currencies*, 1840, p. 73.
16. Hepburn, *History of Coinage and Currency in the United States*, 1903, p. 84, drawing upon House Reports, 15th Congress, 2nd Session, and other sources.
17. Hepburn, *History of Coinage and Currency in the United States*, 1903, p. 84. After 1819, this overissue of notes was checked.
18. *American State Papers*—Finance, vol. III, pp. 306 ff. includes extensive details of the bank operations during the early years, results of congressional inquiries, details on specie importations and use, etc., generally relating to the main office and larger branches (with relatively little about Portsmouth). In general, the Portsmouth branch did not submit reports and was not involved in the investigations.
19. *Niles' Weekly Register*, April 18, 1818, p. 121.
20. Similarly, statements of state-chartered banks during the early 19th century often included under specie certain paper that the bank believed could easily be redeemed in coins, not stating this fact clearly in reports.
21. Various sources including Ralph C.H. Catterall, *The Second Bank of the United States*, 1902, pp. 434, 435.
22. Horace White, *Money and Banking Illustrated by American History*, 1896, pp. 283 ff., gives many details of the problems of the bank.
23. Hammond, *Banks and Politics in America from the Revolution to the Civil War*, 1957, p. 256; American State Papers—Finance; other sources. Throughout this era, "deposite" was used, in this book changed to "deposit."
24. The history of this controversial branch can be found in Wendell Wolka, *A History of Nineteenth Century Ohio Obsolete Bank Notes and Scrip*, 2004, p. 95.
25. "A.B." to William Plumer, April 28, 1827, cited by Norman Walker Smith, *A History of Commercial Banking in New Hampshire 1792–1843*, 1967, p. 181. Identified as surnamed Parker by Nicholas Biddle, letter to James Lloyd, Boston, October 4, 1824; see also Catterall, *The Second Bank of the United States*, 1902, p. 388. Contemporary Portsmouth directories show William R. Parker as the only person of that surname employed by the branch of the Bank of the United States.
26. Quoted by James Parton, *Life of Andrew Jackson*, vol. III, 1861, pp. 262, 263. Biddle's statement was dated July 18, 1829. Thomas Payne Govan, *Nicholas Biddle: Nationalist and Public Banker 1786–1844*, 1959, p. 115, summarized, notes that by this time "the Portsmouth Branch had been badly managed for years."
27. On July 18, 1829, Biddle wrote to Treasury Secretary Ingham, stating that of $460,000 in discounted loans, $148,000 had become delinquent, and of the latter sum $122,000 was likely to be lost. (See also Catterall, *The Second Bank of the United States*, 1902, p. 394.)
28. Quoted by Parton, *Life of Andrew James R. Jackson*, vol. III, 1861, pp. 262, 263.
29. *Memoir and Correspondence of Jeremiah Mason*, 1873, pp. 321, 322.
30. Letter from Nicholas Biddle to Daniel Webster, August 14, 1825, noting that Mason had been named president of "the Portsmouth office which we have arranged agreeably to your recommendation." Mason is believed to have begun his duties on August 25, 1828.
31. Catterall, *The Second Bank of the United States*, 1902, p. 171, dismisses Hill as "a pettifogging politician and newspaper editor," apparently with little information as to the importance and achievements of Hill in the state (at least, these are not discussed by Catterall).
32. Nicholas Biddle, "President's Letter Books," vol. II, p. 410, cited by Catterall, *The Second Bank of the United States*, 1902, p. 174. Moreover, even if Biddle's telling letter of August 14, 1828, had not surfaced to prove his deception, the record is clear that Mason and Webster were very close friends. Irving H. Bartlett's study, *Daniel Webster*, 1978, "drawing heavily on the recently collected Webster papers," furnishes glimpses of Mason vis-à-vis Webster. In view of their longtime personal friendship, which continued for years after the appointment, it is virtually certain that Webster knew just about everything important in which Mason was engaged. Samples from the Bartlett study: Jeremiah Mason soon became a "close friend" after Webster moved to Portsmouth in September 1807 (p. 43). Circa 1807–1810 and later, his wife, Grace Fletcher Webster, was a good companion to her husband when attending formal gatherings in local mansions, "but she was happier in her own parlor in the company of close friends like the Jeremiah Masons and Eliza Buckminster" (p. 47). In summer of 1809, Mr. and Mrs. Mason and Mr. and Mrs. Webster traveled across the state of New Hampshire for Daniel Webster to give the Phi Beta Kappa address at Dartmouth College (p. 50). "Jeremiah Mason was the most important influence on Webster during these years." (p. 48) In 1813 Jeremiah Mason and Daniel Webster both lived in the home of Christopher Gore in Georgetown, near

Washington, D.C. "Once Jeremiah Mason joined the group as a newly elected senator from New Hampshire, Webster felt secure. His domicile, at least would be an island of congeniality and sound New England principle." (pp. 57, 87) In 1816 in Washington, D.C., the Mason and Webster couples enjoyed each other's company (p. 87, with no other friends mentioned in this context). In 1817 Daniel Webster and Jeremiah Mason were two of three attorneys representing Dartmouth College in a famous case involving the U.S. Constitution (p. 77). In 1824 Webster shared with Mason his personal views on the presidential candidacy of John Quincy Adams (p. 105).

33. Govan, *Nicholas Biddle: Nationalist and Public Banker 1786–1844*, 1959, p. 117.
34. Ibid., p. 117, quoting a letter in the Biddle manuscripts in the Library of Congress.
35. In this election, two "Jackson men" had been added to the directors as a concession: Abner Greenleaf and John Harvey.
36. Ronald E. Shaw, *Andrew Jackson 1767–1845*, 1969, pp. 22, 23, text of address. Catterall, *The Second Bank of the United States*, 1902, pp. 183, 184, suggests that Jackson wanted to include anti-bank comments in his inaugural address but was dissuaded from doing so. Marquis James, *The Life of Andrew Jackson*, 1938, p. 866. Among the extant Jackson papers are four drafts of the address, none of which mention the bank. However, in 1833 Jackson recalled that there were two paragraphs on the subject, but they had been stricken before the address was given.
37. Shaw, *Andrew Jackson 1767–1845*, 1969, pp. 23-28, text of message.
38. Earlier the Supreme Court in the case of McCulloch v. Maryland had held that the charter of the Bank of the United States was indeed acceptable under the Constitution.
39. Some of Jackson's detractors disagreed with this statement, and certain popular biographers of recent generations have not examined the situation before completing their manuscripts. However, even the most casual study of American economics and finance during this period will reveal that gold coins, long the pillar of economic stability in civilized modern nations, were completely absent from circulation during virtually the entire existence of the second Bank of the United States, that silver coins were scarce, and that paper currency was subjected to wide variations in value and integrity. In its own dealings the Bank of the United States was stable, and its notes were honored at the time but would become worthless in the 1840s. There was much monetary turmoil during the second Bank of the United States's existence, and one needs but to read a file of *Niles' Weekly Register* to learn about many problems within the bank itself and its branches.
40. Shaw, *Andrew Jackson 1767–1845*, 1969, pp. 33–40, text of message. This would seem to be an excellent synopsis of Jackson's feelings at the time: He favored a government bank as an agency of the Treasury Department, not as a private institution with directors, etc. It would not issue paper money in competition with the state banks, but would relinquish this as the sole province of the state institutions. It would not give private loans in competition with state banks, but would work with them in certain mutually beneficial matters. The majority of popular historians of the 20th century who have written about the Jacksonian era seem to have had very little understanding of Jackson's sentiments and the workings of state banks vis-à-vis his proposed government bank. For this reason, such popular texts have been of relatively little use here, and 19th-century sources, including contemporary documents, have been consulted, as have transcripts of Jackson's speeches and letters.
41. It is seen that Jackson continued to adhere to the alleged unconstitutionality of the Bank of the United States.
42. Shaw, *Andrew Jackson 1767–1845*, 1969, pp. 45–53, for text of message. Parton, *Life of Andrew Jackson*, vol. III, 1861, pp. 407, 408, for analysis by the numbers.
43. Parton, *Life of Andrew Jackson*, vol. III, 1861, p. 411.
44. Parton, *Life of Andrew Jackson*, vol. III, 1861, p. 268.
45. Catterall, *The Second Bank of the United States*, 1902, p. 183. One can review statements of political figures during the period of the existence of the second Bank of the United States to find comments from the same person writing both pro and con on various aspects of the bank, as it was such a highly publicized and discussed issue. Thus, it is almost impossible to say what Jackson might have said in his inaugural address in the absence of the mention of the bank in any contemporary (1829) draft or written memo by Jackson himself. The topic came up soon after his death in a eulogy that Secretary of the Navy George Bancroft delivered in Washington City, June 27, 1845: "He [Jackson] came to the presidency of the United States resolved to deliver the government from the Bank of the United States, and to restore the regulation of exchanges to the rightful depository of that power—the commerce of the country. He had designed to declare his views on this subject in his inaugural address, but was persuaded to relinquish that purpose, on the ground that it belonged rather to a legislative message." (See B.M. Dusenbery, comp., *Monument to the Memory of General Andrew Jackson*, 1846, pp. 33–51.
46. Ibid., p. 421.
47. Ibid., p. 430.
48. Ibid., p. 431.
49. Shaw, *Andrew Jackson 1767–1845*, 1969, pp. 74–79, text of message read to the cabinet, September 18, 1833, outlining the procedure. Parton, Life of *Andrew Jackson*, vol. III, 1861, p. 528.
50. *Niles' Weekly Register*, January 7, 1833, p. 297, showed a report from Secretary of the Treasury Levi Woodbury, January 1, indicating the amounts to be transferred to each of the states during the coming year. John M. McFaul, *The Politics of Jacksonian Finance*, 1972, devotes a chapter to "Domesticated Pets." A sample entry reads: "The Treasury had carried a nominal deposit with the Albany [New York] Regency Bank of $25 through 1833 and 1834, but in 1835 it was appointed a full-time pet, and the government balance swelled to over $100,000 by the end of the year. At the same time, however, $5,500,000 in federal funds were on deposit in the three Wall Street pets" (p. 146).
51. Shaw, *Andrew Jackson 1767–1845*, 1969, pp. 80–83, text of message. John Jay Knox, United States Notes, 1885, p. 172.
52. Shaw, *Andrew Jackson 1767–1845*, 1969, pp. 84–90, text of protest, including additional comment sent by Jackson to the Senate on April 21, 1834.
53. Shaw, *Andrew Jackson 1767–1845*, 1969, pp. 84–97, text of message.
54. Parton, *Life of Andrew Jackson*, vol. III, 1861, p. 590.
55. For information on the Panic of 1837, see the *Chronology*.
56. Charles Lyell, *Travels in North America, in the Years 1841–2*. Vol. I, 1845, pp. 176, 177.

Chapter 9

1. This *Niles'* account reflects the fact that *proof* as a term for specimen or test impressions of bank-note plates was in general use at that time. *Proof* as a description for coins seems to have originated in the 1850s, or at least no earlier official use of this term has been found.
2. William H. Dillistin; *Bank Note Reporters and Counterfeit Detectors 1826–1866,* 1949, pp. 65–66.
3. Lyman H. Low, "Hard Times Tokens," *American Journal of Numismatics,* July 1898.
4. Moses Yale Beach was the primary owner of the *New York Sun.* In 1845 the *Sun* published the 6th edition of *Wealth and Biography of the Wealthy Citizens of New York City.* Beach received the expected hagiographic biography, noting that he was the major stockholder in four banks and was worth $250,000.
5. Harold L. Bowen, *State Bank Notes of Michigan,* 1956, p. 1.
6. Breckinridge Jones, "One Hundred Years of Banking in Missouri, 1820–1920," *The Missouri Historical Review,* vol. XV, no. 2, January 1921, p. 359, as quoted by Dillistin, *Bank Note Reporters and Counterfeit Detectors 1826–1866,* 1949.
7. Hoyt Sherman, "Early Banking in Iowa," *Annals of Iowa,* 3rd series, Des Moines, IA, April 1901, vol. V, no. 1, p. 7, as quoted by Dillistin, *Bank Note Reporters and Counterfeit Detectors,* 1949, p. 75.
8. Langdon W. Moore, *His Own Story of His Eventful Life,* 1893, pp. 47, 48, here adapted.
9. As quoted in *Banker's Magazine,* September 1852.
10. There had been many lists of bank notes published in papers as well as many instances of counterfeiting prior to 1820, although widely circulated bank-note reporters were not yet a reality.
11. Here edited.
12. As delineated by Sir William Congreve in *An Analysis of the True Principles of Security Against Forgery; Exemplified by an Enquiry into the Sufficiency of the American Plan for a New Bank Note; with Imitations of Four of the Most Difficult Specimens of those Notes, Made by Ordinary Means.* This "test" is discussed in chapter 3 of the present work in connection with Jacob Perkins.

13. Orr's illustrations were widely used in books and magazines of the day.
14. *Banker's Magazine,* July 1852.
15. *Banker's Magazine,* March 1853.

Chapter 10

1. List has been adapted for ease of use. Obvious errors in spelling in the original list have been corrected, and states are listed in alphabetical order (in the original they were in random order).
2. This was the Bank of Vincennes, Indiana, and its branches, not to be confused with the later State Bank of Indiana.
3. Augusta, Maine, is the correct location for the Kennebec Bank.
4. This bank, long defunct, had been in Amherst, New Hampshire, but Bicknell did not know this.
5. William H. Dillistin, *Bank Note Reporters and Counterfeit Detectors 1826–1866,* 1949, pp. 96–101 (Day), 109–111 (Sylvester), 125.
6. Dillistin, *Bank Note Reporters,* 1949, pp. 96–101.
7. This claim was in *Day's New York Bank Note List,* September 6, 1837, p. 1, which noted, "Established in 1819, being the oldest paper of the kind."
8. Eight issues of 1830 are preserved by the Henry E. Huntington Library and Art Gallery, San Marino, CA; Dillistin, *Bank Note Reporters,* 1949, pp. 99, 154.
9. Montroville W. Dickeson, *American Numismatical Manual,* 1859, pp. 76–78. For additional information on the numismatic scene of the 1850s, see Q. David Bowers, *American Numismatics Before the Civil War, 1760–1860,* 1992.
10. Dillistin, *Bank Note Reporters,* 1949, p. 111.
11. Ibid., pp. 78 ff.; other sources.
12. Street numbers were changed in about 1845, and the address is where 23 Wall Street (J.P. Morgan) later would be located. Thompson shared some reminiscences in *The Banker's Magazine,* June 1891, p. 989.
13. *Niles' Weekly Register,* April 16, 1836; Dillistin, *Bank Note Reporters,* 1949, pp. 81–82.
14. The American Numismatic Society, New York City, has the largest collection of counterfeit detectors in any library. Francis Campbell, librarian, has generously shared information from this collection with the writer over a long period of years.
15. If anything, Ormsby was *aware.* Probably few others in the bank-note trade at the time had any idea of the precise number of branches of the State Bank of Ohio.
16. William F. Hasse Jr., *A History of Money and Banking in Connecticut,* 1957, p. 42.
17. *Litchfield Enquirer,* November 25, 1858.
18. Dillistin, *Bank Note Reporters,* 1949, p. 144.
19. Dillistin, *Bank Note Reporters,* 1949, pp. 147–48, discusses identity of typographical errors; for example, Ithaca, New York, was misspelled as Ithica; Central Bank was spelled Central Bakk, etc.
20. Dillistin, *Bank Note Reporters,* 1949, p. 96.
21. Eric P. Newman, "Heath's Counterfeit Detectors: An Extraordinarily Successful Comedy of Errors," *American Numismatic Association Centennial Anthology,* 1991. Newman estimated that over a period of years approximately 100,000 copies of Heath's various editions were sold.

Chapter 11

1. This and other correspondence is from Julian Blanchard, "Letters from a Bank Note Engraver to his Partner: Oliver Pelton to William D. Terry, 1834," *The Essay-Proof Journal,* no. 67 (Summer 1960), pp. 107–11, and no. 68 (Fall 1960), pp. 155–62.
2. Roger H. Durand, *Interesting Notes* series, including *About Portraits,* 1996; *About Portraits II,* 1997; and *About Portraits III,* 2004.

Chapter 12

1. *Banker's Magazine,* October 1856, p. 250.
2. "Gold Coins of the United States," a report from Representative White, of New York City, of the Select Committee on Coins, February 22, 1821.
3. *International Monetary Conference Held . . . in Paris, in August 1878,* Senate Executive Document No. 48, Forty-fifth Congress, Third Session, p. 661.
4. A. Barton Hepburn, *A History of Currency in the United States and the Perennial Contest for Sound Money,* 1903, p. 35.
5. John Sherman, *John Sherman's Recollections of Forty Years in the House, Senate, and Cabinet: An Autobiography,* 1895, pp. 458, 459.
6. *Niles' Weekly Register,* April 24, 1830, covered the event in detail.
7. *Niles' Weekly Register,* July 3, 1830. In this context, *Confederacy* refers to the entire United States, not to the entity later known as the Confederate States of America.
8. As quoted in *Niles' Weekly Register,* June 18, 1831.
9. *Niles' Weekly Register,* May 4, 1833.
10. *Equinoctial gale* was the term for what we now call the late summer and autumn hurricane season on the Atlantic coast, earlier so called as they centered about the autumnal equinox in September. Along the southern reaches of the coast, particularly in Florida, *wreckers* (entrepreneurs with salvage equipment) hastened to take what they could from ships cast up on the shore. The wreckers often fought with each other in the division of the spoils.
11. *Banker's Magazine,* November 1856, p. 336.
12. This statement is not true. The new gold coins had not been released as of the time this appeared in print.
13. Commentary in the *Evening Post,* August 6, 1834, later reprinted in *A Collection of the Political Writings of William Leggett* (New York: Taylor & Dodd, 1840). Citation suggested by Harry Salyards, M.D.
14. Report of Secretary of the Treasury Levi Woodbury to Congress, December 6, 1836, with a review of the monetary situation in recent years.
15. Certain commentary is adapted from the writer's text, *Silver Dollars and Trade Dollars of the United States: A Complete Encyclopedia,* 1993, which contains much year-by-year economic news.
16. By this time in scattered other locations, several important banks had suspended, including the Planters and Agricultural banks in Natchez, Mississippi, on May 4 and the State Bank at Montgomery, Alabama, a few days later.
17. William G. Sumner, *A History of American Currency,* 2005, pp. 122–23; adapted from Condy Raguet, *A Treatise on Currency and Banking,* 2nd edition, 1840, plus annual reports of the secretary of the treasury.
18. The *Financial Register,* vol. I, p. 286.
19. As quoted in William A. Berkey, *Money Question. The Legal Tender Paper Monetary System of the United States,* 1876, pp. 151–52.

Chapter 13

1. *The Financial Register*, vol. I, p. 74.
2. Gordon L. Harris, *New York State Scrip and Private Issues*, 2001, gives additional information on certain New York City scrip of 1837.
3. Sources include Thomas W. Dyott, *An Exposition of the System of Moral and Mental Labor Established at the Glass Factory of Dyottville*, in the County of Philadelphia (Philadelphia: T.W. Dyott, 1833); John Thom Holdsworth, *Financing an Empire: The Story of Banking in Pennsylvania*, vol. II, 1928, pp. 547, 548; George S. McKearin and Helen McKearin, *American Glass*, 1941, pp. 95, 431, 457, 468, 469, 470; James Harvey Young, *The Toadstool Millionaires*, 1961, pp. 34–36.
4. "The Case of Thomas W. Dyott," *Saturday Evening Post*, March 16, 1839.
5. Sources for information about the coins and currency issued by the Mormons are many and include Waldo C. Moore, "The Kirtland Bank Bills," *The Numismatist*, May 1914; Alvin E. Rust, *Mormon and Utah Coin and Currency* (Salt Lake City, UT: Rust Rare Coin Co., 1984); Douglas A. Nyholm, *The History of Mormon Currency*, manuscript sent to QDB in 2003; and Wendell Wolka, *A History of Nineteenth Century Ohio Obsolete Bank Notes and Scrip*, Society of Paper Money Collectors, 2004.
6. Estimates from Wolka, *A History of Nineteenth Century Ohio Obsolete Bank Notes and Scrip*, 2004, p. 457, drawing upon Marvin S. Hill, C. Keith Rooker, and Larry T. Wimmer, *The Kirtland Economy Revisited: A Market Critique of Sectarian Economics* (Provo, UT: Brigham Young University Press, 1977).
7. Rust, *Mormon and Utah Coin and Currency*, 1984, p. 14, citing the *Messenger and Almanac*, August 3, 1837, p. 560.
8. Rust, *Mormon and Utah Coin and Currency*, 1984, p. 15.
9. Harold L. Bowen, *State Bank Notes of Michigan*, 1956, from early records.
10. Condy Raguet, *A Treatise on Currency & Banking*, 2nd edition (Philadelphia: Grigg & Elliot, 1840) pp. 110, 111, here edited.
11. Wolka, *A History of Nineteenth Century Ohio Obsolete Bank Notes and Scrip*, 2004, p. 492.
12. Copy in a scrapbook of numismatically related clippings assembled in the

1880s and 1890s in possession of the author. In this instance the publication is not identified.

13. Prime sources for this section on Michigan notes include Harold L. Bowen, *State Bank Notes of Michigan*, 1956; Alpheus Felch, "Early Banks and Banking in Michigan," 1878, reprinted in Senate Ex. Doc. 38, 52nd Congress, 2nd Session; and Horace White, *Money and Banking* (Boston and London: Ginn & Company, 1896).
14. Citations from Felch, "Early Banks and Banking in Michigan," 1878, pp. 111 ff.
15. No doubt these were Mexican dollars, for United States dollars had not been coined since 1804 and were not in general circulation at the time.
16. Selected and edited from Harold L. Bowen, *State Bank Notes of Michigan*, 1956, pp. 176–80.
17. Slang for exchange broker or dealer in bank bills.
18. Felch, "Early Banks and Banking in Michigan," 1878, pp. 122, 123.
19. For a comprehensive list of the banking laws of this era, see Harold L. Bowen, *State Bank Notes of Michigan*, 1956, pp. 173–75.
20. Felch, "Early Banks and Banking in Michigan," 1878, p. 123.
21. See also Harold L. Bowen, *State Bank Notes of Michigan*, 1956, p. 14.
22. White, *Money and Banking*, 1896, p. 338. Also see chapter 2 of the present text.
23. In the 1830s, Forman moved to Rutherfordton, North Carolina, where he founded a newspaper, operated a stagecoach line, and engaged in other activities. At the time the private mint of Augustus Bechtler was in operation in the same town.
24. Wording of the act and other details can be found in Raguet, *A Treatise on Currency & Banking*, 2nd edition, 1840, pp. 243 ff.
25. White, *Money and Banking*, 1896, p. 350.
26. Ibid.
27. As reprinted in *Niles' National Register*, September 22, 1838.
28. The minutes book of the board of directors of the Central Bank of New York is in the possession of the writer and is the source of certain information given here.
29. The March 16, 1843, issue of the *New York Journal of Commerce* listed assets of this bank to be sold at auction on March 21. Included was a listing of various promissory notes given to the bank by Dakin.
30. Harold L. Bowen, *State Bank Notes of Michigan*, 1956, p. 2.
31. These are in the writer's possession.
32. The New York State Historical Association (NYSHA), Cooperstown, includes in its special collections a file of Samuel Dana Dakin's letters, mostly to and from family members, but with little on finances or banking. There is a nearly total gap in the correspondence from about 1829 to 1838. Some materials, believed to have been edited by family members, were given to the NYSHA in 1963 and are under seal until the year 2026. In 1965, Jane Speakes Shadel, a graduate student in the Museum Studies program at NYSHA, wrote her master's thesis, "Samuel Dana Dakin, Esq. 1802–1853," based on certain holdings of the institution but with no information concerning the Wolfborough Bank. In death Dakin deceived historians, as he did with citizens when he was alive. (Information provided to the author by Hugh C. MacDougall.)
33. Actually, the Portsmouth contract, competed for by Dakin & Moody and by Gilbert & Secor (John S. Gilbert and Leno Secor), was awarded to the latter, after much political maneuvering that the Bureau of the Navy found to be very uncomfortable: "The Bureau was much embarrassed by these conflicting claims, pushed as they were by the patentees with the greatest amount of political influence." (George Henry Preble, *History of the United States Navy-Yard*, Portsmouth, N.H., 1892). The Philadelphia dry dock has not been investigated by the writer.
34. Raguet, *A Treatise on Currency & Banking*, 2nd edition, 1840, p. 109.
35. Subtitles added.
36. A description of Alabama's experience was also given in *Cheap Money*.
37. *Niles' National Register*, February 24, 1838.

Chapter 14

1. Raguet, *A Treatise on Currency & Banking*, 2nd edition, 1840, p. 242, quoting reports of the secretary of the Treasury. As precise as these figures seem to be, the Treasury could offer only an approximate idea of banking capital, paper money in circulation, or even the number of chartered banks actually in operation.
2. Actually, in 1834 and 1835 the second Bank of the United States was in a period of contraction, winding down some of its branch offices.
3. *Niles' National Register*, May 23, 1840. The *other* Bank of the United States was the Bank of the United States *of Pennsylvania*, whose misleading name confused just about everyone.
4. For a discussion of this issue, see Brian Roberts, "Slavery Would Have Died of That Music: The Hutchinson Family and the Rise of Popular-Culture Abolitionism in Early Antebellum-Era America, 1842–1850," *Proceedings of the American Antiquarian Society*, vol. 114, part 2, 2004.
5. This figure is, perhaps, the early 19th-century equivalent of having three or four million copies of a book in print today.
6. As reported in the *Log Cabin*, published by Horace Greeley, New York City, April 3, 1841.
7. *Niles' National Register*, August 12, 1843. "The directors have unanimously expelled the president, John Rich, former cashier, who seems to have been the factotum of the institution, and is now charged with 'allowing particular favorites largely to overdraw their accounts,' etc."
8. William H. Dillistin, *Bank Note Reporters and Counterfeit Detectors 1826–1866* (New York: American Numismatic Society, 1949) pp. 49–50.
9. Alfred Cookman Bryan, *History of State Banking in Maryland* (Baltimore, MD: The Johns Hopkins Press, 1899) p. 106.
10. Harold L. Bowen, introductory material, *State Bank Notes of Michigan*, 1956, pp. 1–16.

Chapter 15

1. From an article in the *Rochester Evening Express*, December 10, 1861, quoted in W.L. Ormsby's *Cycloidal Configurations*, 1862, an extract from D.M. Dewey's presentation, "History of the Art of Engraving."
2. Per report by R.G. Dun & Co., circa 1960s, ex Baker Library, furnished by Robert McCabe. "His marriage when but 17 or 18 years of age has been the cause of all his misfortune and led him into errors." The cumulative file on Ormsby, compiled by Dun, is laden with rumors and allegations and cannot be relied upon.
3. Ormsby in *Cycloidal Configurations*, 1862.
4. Part of extensive correspondence reprinted by Julian Blanchard, Ph.D., in "Letters from a Bank Note Engraver to his Partner: Oliver Pelton to William D. Terry, 1834," Essay-Proof Journal (Summer 1960), pp. 107–11, and (Fall 1960), pp. 155–62.
5. Gordon L. Harris, *New York State Scrip and Private Issues*, 2001, p. 115.
6. Some later historians have confused the grammagraph with Ormsby's medal-ruling machine.
7. Much could be related about Thomas Wyatt, a numismatist of repute, but in a checkered way. In about 1856 he created copies and fantasy issues of early Massachusetts silver coins and claimed they had been unearthed as an old-time hoard. W. Elliot Woodward's Sixty-Ninth Sale, October 13–18, 1884, included this description under Lot 343: "New England shilling. . . . These celebrated counterfeits were probably made in New York City. They were offered for sale some 25 years ago by one Thomas Wyatt, who announced that they were found in Chelsea, in a bottle mostly filled with a bituminous substance resembling tar. The alleged find comprised full sets of the Pine Tree money, including the penny, together with N.E. sixpence and shilling and Good Samaritan shilling. The dies were destroyed many years ago, and all these pieces are now rare."
8. An example is preserved in the Sacramento Room of the Sacramento Public Library, Sacramento, California.
9. Information on this connection was mostly furnished by Robert McCabe, including E. Dixon Larson, "The Art of Cylinder Engraving," *American Rifleman*, March 1969.
10. Today this is known by collectors as Scott No. L13.
11. More information may be found in Gordon W. Colket, "Origin of the Eagle Vignette on American Letter Mail Co. Type L13," *Essay-Proof Journal*, October 1952.
12. The text of this book was reprinted serially in the *Essay-Proof Journal*, commencing with Julian Blanchard, Ph.D., "Waterman Lily Ormsby, 1809–1883, Bank Note Engraver," January 1957.
13. Courtesy of George F. Kolbe, copy from the John J. Ford Jr. Library Sale, June 2004. Erratic capitalization and punctuation have been corrected.
14. The reference is to the very active banking department operated by the state of New York—a complicated system whereby notes were registered and dis-

tributed by the state. Elsewhere, most states had departments or commissions that mainly reviewed statements sent by banks and visited the banks on occasion, typically once each year.

15. In this decade the Monument Bank of Charlestown, Massachusetts, featured the Bunker Hill Monument on certain of its notes, from plates made the ordinary (not *Unit System*) way by Toppan, Carpenter & Co.
16. The first numismatic notice of this was by Julian Blanchard, Ph.D., "A Specimen of Ormsby's Proposed Design for Bank Notes," *Essay-Proof Journal* no. 60 (Fall 1958).
17. This passage has been edited, with subtitles added.
18. In the early 1850s, plaster plaques of Greek art and the like were widely sold in art and novelty shops. Most were elliptical or rectangular, rarely perfectly round. Relatively few actual coins or medals were ever used on bank notes.
19. This passage has been edited, with subtitles added.
20. Affidavit sworn by W.L. Ormsby, November 24, 1854, to C.C. Pinckney, commissioner of deeds (from New York Superior Court records). Excerpts have been edited.
21. From information file furnished by Robert McCabe. Sources as cited, particularly *The Superior Court of the City of New York City, Waterman L. Ormsby against Benjamin Douglass, Case* (New York: William C. Bryant & Co., 1858, cited here as *Ormsby against Douglass,* 1858). Buckley's place of business was in New York City at 169 Broadway, where he made gold pens and sold gold pens and jewelry. In the previous year his trade had been conducted at 33 Maiden Lane.
22. *Ormsby against Douglass,* 1858, pp. 11, 12.
23. *New York Times,* March 23, 1858, p. 2, col. 4, this being from the transcript of a later hearing of the same case.
24. *Reports of Practice Cases Determined in the Courts of the State of New York City,* vol. II, New York: Abbott Brothers, 1856, pp. 407–409. The plaintiff was identified carelessly as "Valentine L. Ormsby"!
25. Exhibit reproduced in *Ormsby against Douglass,* 1858. Here excerpted and edited.
26. *Sic.* Should be *Sanford*, but on some counterfeit bills from false plates (not made by Ormsby) it was misspelled it as *Sandford*; an example is illustrated here. Apparently, his adversaries had such a bill on hand.
27. The italics apparently being the technical point that in the Bible angels are *male,* but on bank notes (of just about all engravers, not only those by Ormsby) they are given female characteristics.
28. *New York Times,* March 26, 1858, p. 2, cols. 4 and 5; *Ormsby against Douglass,* 1858.
29. From New York Superior Court records, memorandum of expenses incurred by Fullerton & Dunning, attorneys for the defense.
30. Walter W. Chadbourne, *A History of Banking in Maine 1799–1930,* 1936, pp. 80, 81.
31. Wendell A. Wolka, Jack M. Vorhies, and Donald Schramm, *Indiana Obsolete Notes and Scrip,* 1978, p. 82.
32. *New York Times,* March 26, 1858, p. 2, cols. 4 and 5.
33. Ibid.
34. Superior Court records filed July 30, 1859.
35. Joel Tiffany, *Reports of Cases Argued and Determined in the Court of Appeals of the State of New York City,* Albany, 1868, pp. 477–86.
36. Included in Ormsby, Cycloidal Configurations, 1862.
37. This is the only invention listed in capital letters, emphasizing its importance to Ormsby.
38. In an era before paper clips and rubber bands, bills were often fastened together by steel pins or pinned to the inside of a garment for safe travel. Notes with discoloration at the ends bore evidence of having been counted many times. Most worn bills seen today are darker on the right end, from the thumbs of right-handed users. A recently passed counterfeit note was not likely to have these characteristics of wear.
39. Counterfeit-detecting periodicals based their business on the perceived need to have individual descriptions of various banks and bills across the country.

Chapter 16

1. Adapted from Walter W. Chadbourne, *A History of Banking in Maine 1799–1930*, 1936, passim; George W. Wait, *Maine Obsolete Paper Money and Scrip*, 1977, pp. 13, 14; James A. Haxby, *Standard Catalog of United States Obsolete Bank Notes 1782–1866*, vol. 1, 1988, section on Maine; and other sources.
2. Capital figures represent the amounts authorized by the state legislature. In many instances the amount actually paid in was less—sometimes much less. In Maine as in most other states, payments for stock were often made by exchanging IOUs, creating no real assets for anyone.
3. Wait, *Maine Obsolete Paper Money and Scrip*, 1977, p. 231, for a $1 note.
4. Reprinted in *Banker's Magazine*, January 1853.
5. Comment by Philip G. Hubert Jr. in the preface to *The Merchants' National Bank of the City of New York: A History of Its First Century*, 1903.
6. Quoted in *Banker's Magazine*, February 1853.
7. John Jay Knox, *A History of Banking in the United States* (New York: Bradford Rhodes & Company, 1900).
8. *Banker's Magazine*, November 1856, p. 337.
9. A history of these banks is given in Wendell Wolka, *A History of Nineteenth Century Ohio Obsolete Bank Notes and Scrip* (Society of Paper Money Collectors, 2004), appendix D.
10. *Banker's Magazine*, September 1856, p. 168. The state attorney ruled that the free-banking law was no longer operative under the new state constitution. (Wendell Wolka, comment to the author, April 5, 2006.)
11. Knox, *A History of Banking.*
12. Wolka, *A History of Nineteenth Century Ohio Obsolete Bank Notes and Scrip*, p. 989.
13. *Banker's Magazine*, September 1856, pp. 171–74.
14. Information provided by Wendell Wolka, April 5, 2006.
15. W.L. Ormsby, *Cycloidal Configurations* (New York: Published by the author, 1862).
16. Gene Hessler, *The Engraver's Line*, 1992.
17. Information under this heading is largely derived from Elizabeth M. Harris, "Sir William Congreve and His Compound-Plate Printing," United States National Museum Bulletin 252, Paper 71 in Contributions from the Museum of History and Technology (Washington, D.C.: Smithsonian Institution Press, 1967).
18. Ibid., p. 74.
19. Eric P. Newman, communication to the author, April 4, 2006.
20. Hessler, *The Engraver's Line*, 1992, p. 53.
21. Wording of the patent was printed in *Banker's Magazine*, August 1856, pp. 134–36.
22. See also Schingoethe Collection Part 2, R.M. Smythe & Co., March 2005, Lot 4036.
23. Edited by David A. Wells, pp. 176, 177.
24. Quoted by W.L. Ormsby Jr., "Gold Versus Paper," *Gazlay's Pacific Monthly*, February 1865. The junior Ormsby was an accomplished siderographer and, at one time, a newspaper writer.
25. Cited by Joanne Griffith Domingue, *A History of the Strafford National Bank*, 1978, p. 34.
26. Wendell Wolka has pointed out that "Another downside of the green tint was that it destroyed pen nibs in short order." (Comment to the author, April 5, 2006.)
27. Ormsby, *Cycloidal Configurations*, 1862.
28. Heath's *Infallible Counterfeit Detector*, 1864 edition, p. 13.
29. J.S. Gibbons, *The Banks of New-York*, 1858, excerpts from pp. 344–50. The cashier of the New York office was found to have falsified his accounts and to have assigned certain funds to be in two different places at the same time.
30. Margaret G. Myers, *The New York Money Market*, vol. I., 1931, p. 142. This work also gives many details about the worsening conditions of banks during the year and the high ratio of paper money and credit in relation to coin reserves (specie).
31. Gibbons, *The Banks of New-York*, 1858, p. 350.
32. Ibid., pp. 345, 346.

Chapter 17

1. Laws of the State of New Hampshire, Passed June Session, 1850, pp. 984–87.
2. Posting was a legal requirement and was so docketed and notarized on the back of the statement (Sandwich Historical Society). At the time Sandwich had no local newspaper.
3. Laws of the State of New Hampshire, Passed June Session, 1851, pp. 1112–15.
4. Notarized copy, October 1, 1851 (Sandwich Historical Society).
5. Sandwich Historical Society.

6. On May 3, 1852, Cary wrote to cashier Beede: "You would very much oblige me by informing me what you can get for the stock, with or without the dividend. Of course you must be aware that I do not take stock as an investment, as I am obliged to take a great deal in the way of business."
7. Cary was the agent and 50% owner of the New England Bank Note Co.
8. The Springfield (Ohio) Bank was organized on July 2, 1851, under the Free Banking Law of March 31 of the same year. In 1854 a special bank examiner cited the bank as being "guilty of an improper practice," which was fixed soon afterward. The bank remained profitable through the mid-1860s.
9. The Bank of Commerce, Boston, was organized in 1849. By the time of the correspondence quoted here, it had ordered new bills from plates by Toppan, Carpenter, & Co. William H. Foster was the founding cashier. He resigned in 1854 to take another opportunity in private banking. The board wished him well and gave him a gift of $4,000 in gratitude for his service.
10. Andrew J. Drew was a cattle drover who lived in North Wolfeboro, not far from the Ossipee town line, and who traveled widely in his business.
11. Throughout the district many people received pension payments for past military service, especially for service in the War of 1812. These payments often were deposited with the Carroll County Bank, which forwarded them to Boston to be credited to the bank's account.
12. Pursuant to the act of July 8, 1846, such statements were sent at regular intervals by all banks in the state. It was the practice at this time for a bank examiner to call upon each bank once a year, meet with the cashier, and review operations. However, the statements furnished by the cashier were not audited. Original reports from this era are preserved by the New Hampshire State Library, Concord.
13. The difference between this total and the total of "means" was not stated but represented the profit of the bank. In later statements it was the practice to have the means (assets) and liabilities balance.
14. Nineteenth Annual Excursion of the Sandwich Historical Society (Nineteenth AESHS), 1938, p. 30. The Marston house still stands today, to the right of the Methodist church.
15. In later years the building was removed to a location on the other side of the road that runs to Moultonborough, past the Sandwich Fairgrounds. See also Nineteenth AESHS, 1938, p. 36. Later the building was moved again. Today it serves at another location as the center part of the Sandwich Post Office.
16. Eighth AESHS, 1927, p. 6, with a number of inaccuracies. "Site of the Bank Building," Nineteenth AESHS, 1938, p. 24. After the National Bank moved to Concord (see history of the Carroll County National Bank), the premises were occupied by the Sandwich Savings Bank, incorporated in 1872. The lower part of the building was used for stores and shops, including C.C. Fellows's drugstore, for a long time. In 1871 Robert Russell opened his harness shop there, conducting it for 54 years. For some of that time Daniel Folsom occupied the building's "back shop," where he did carpentry and built coffins. After the Savings Bank moved to other local quarters, William Andrew Heard had a store in the same premises. In later times occupants included Oliver Watson and Denis F. Carter. In the late 19th century the upper or wooden part of the building was moved to Diamond Ledge Road, where it serves as a residence today, and the brick first story was demolished.
17. H.F. Walling, *Topographical Map of Carroll County, New Hampshire*, 1860.
18. Sandwich Historical Society.
19. The original letter is scrawled and has notations in the margins, etc. Here the descriptions of the denominations have been adapted to reflect a logical order. Ormsby's appended message is preserved intact. The letter began with price quotations, with the text following, as given here.
20. No copy of this note remains today with the Carroll County Bank records.
21. The American Verd Antique Marble Co. was located in Roxbury, Vermont (see also New England Business Directory, 1856, p. 464).
22. David W. Hoyt, Hoyt Family: A Genealogical History of John Hoyt of Salisbury, and David Hoyt of Deerfield, (Massachusetts), and Their Descendants, 1857, p. 64. Most of Daniel Hoit's forebears spelled their name as Hoyt.
23. Listed as Augustin on many bank records; his proper name was Augustine; his late father's name was Augustin.
24. In McFarland's words in the Sandwich Reporter (quoted in the Fifty-Second AESHS, p. 9). McFarland lived at Sandwich Lower Corner roughly from 1838 to 1844.
25. Twenty-Eighth AESHS, 1947, pp. 20, 21; letter from Dr. Andrew J. McFarland written in 1883 to the Sandwich Reporter; also quoted in Thirty-Second AESHS, 1951, p. 14.
26. Jane Beckman et al., Sandwich, New Hampshire 1673–1990, 1995, p. 124.
27. In early 1860, the Bank of Eau Claire, capitalized at $200,000, claimed to have $196,165 in bills in circulation. The bank failed in 1863.
28. Full name: Edwards, Fernald & Kershaw. Located on Green Street, Boston, corner of Pitt Street. It is likely that the safe of the Pine River Bank of Ossipee, in existence today, was of similar style to the one described in this letter. On a winter day early in 2003 the writer and Arletta Paul, curator of the Sandwich Historical Society, spent a half hour or more in an unsuccessful effort to open the safe—with the combination and key at hand.
29. The "1/2 sheets" comment indicates that the bank's bills may have been printed in earlier times in eight-subject sheets, four and four, and then cut apart vertically to create sheets of four notes. In numismatic circles intact sheets of eight full-size (not scrip) notes are so rare as to be uncollectible.
30. Letter not seen; mentioned in Treasury files on the bank.

Chapter 18

1. This observation is based on the examination of many state bank commission records and comparisons of them with later data relating to the failure and liquidation of banks.
2. William H. Griffiths, *The Story of the American Bank Note Company* (New York: American Bank Note Company, 1959), and Foster Wild Rice, "Antecedents of the American Bank Note Company of 1858," *Essay-Proof Journal,* vol. 18, nos. 71 and 72, 1961, were important sources for information in this chapter. The antecedents of each of the component firms of ABNCo have been adapted from the Rice study, here with amplifications and some corrections.
3. Certain information is adapted from and the newspaper article is quoted from Roger H. Durand, *Obsolete Notes and Scrip of Rhode Island and the Providence Plantations* (Society of Paper Money Collectors, 1981), p. 26.

Chapter 19

1. Letter from Memminger to Lamar, March 23, 1861, citation from Thian's *Register,* 1880 (as are the other letters quoted here).
2. Letter from Memminger to Lamar, March 13, 1861.
3. On April 2, Elmore wrote to Lamar about the new currency: "There will arise one difficulty about the Treasury notes. There are too many of the $1,000 and too few of the $50 and $100. Our calls will be for the smaller issues. Is there any way by which impressions could be taken of part of the plate?"
4. When the *Essay-Proof Journal* commenced reprinting the text of the pamphlet in 1966, only two copies could be located by Julian Blanchard, who was in charge of the project—one in the Library of Congress and the other in the New York Public Library. The John J. Ford Jr. Library Sale, Part 1, by George F. Kolbe, June 1, 2004, also included a copy, and Kolbe knew of two others that had been sold.
5. Excerpted, with subtitles added.
6. It would not have been practical for the Treasury Department to issue notes with many different places of redemption. The intent was to provide a uniformly accepted currency.
7. This is an invalid illustration. Banks determined the arrangement of notes on a sheet, usually in view of the anticipated use or popularity of each denomination. While many $5-$5-$5-$5 sheets were made, this being the most popular value for state-chartered banks (and, coincidentally, for the federal government as well when it began to issue its own bills), most numismatists specializing in currency today have never heard of a sheet of four $2s, or four $3s, or four $4s. Many banks did, indeed, order sheets with multiple denominations, such as $1-$1-$2-$3.
8. Obviously, "cycloidal" is a favorite word with Ormsby, who used it for multiple meanings.
9. In this incident criminals under false pretenses obtained plates for the Boone County Bank of Lebanon, Indiana, bearing the name of Ormsby's firm, the New York Bank Note Co., per one account. Per another, the criminals obtained a large quantity of genuine bills but forged the signature of the state auditor and, unauthorized, placed them into circulation. Also see comments under Indiana in chapter 21.
10. Notes for the fraudulent New England Bank of Fairmount, Maine, in the denominations of $10 and $20, bearing the engraved date of October 1st 1857, were printed by Rawdon, Wright, Hatch & Edson, Ormsby's most formidable competitor. See George W. Wait, *Maine Obsolete Paper Money and Scrip,* 1977, p. 128.

11. The Government Stock Bank, Ann Arbor, Michigan, had its notes made by Danforth, Bald & Co. and Danforth, Wright & Co., each of New York and Philadelphia. The $5 counterfeits lack the check letter and are dated June 1, 1852. See also Harold L. Bowen, *State Bank Notes of Michigan,* 1956, p. 100. Apparently, this note is the same as Haxby-MI-40-G12, listed as an authentic note (see James A. Haxby, *Standard Catalog of United States Obsolete Bank Notes 1782–1866,* vol. 2, 1988, p. 1041). Complicating matters, the Government Stock Bank of Ann Arbor had notes of the exact same designs printed for its namesake in Lafayette, Indiana.
12. Fraudulent City Bank bills as well as Ocean Bank bills of Washington, D.C., were made by Danforth, Bald & Co. (see also James A. Haxby, *Standard Catalog of United States Obsolete Bank Notes 1782–1866,* vol. 1, 1988, pp. 191, 204, 205). In this text Ormsby accuses that firm of criminal collusion with counterfeiters.
13. C.H. Van Wyck chaired the House Committee on Government Contracts, which published its report in 1862.
14. Edward Ely Dunbar (1818–1871) is an impressive but somewhat obscure figure in the annals of numismatics. Catching the gold fever in December 1848, he went to California, where he became a banker and business broker. In 1852 he commissioned Albert Küner to cut dies for a $5 piece marked Dunbar & Co., a numismatic rarity today. In 1867 Dunbar's book, *The Romance of the Age; or, the Discovery of Gold in California,* was published in New York by D. Appleton and Company.
15. Testimony in "United States Securities," U.S. Senate Committee Report No. 273, March 3, 1869, p. 198.
16. As given by Thomas F. Morris in "Our First National Bank Notes," *The Numismatist,* January 1938. Modern comments in brackets and footnotes are by Morris and the present author.
17. The "loan bill" refers to the Act of February 25, 1863, best known as the National Banking Act.
18. Continental received the contract for the $5 National Bank Notes but not the $10 notes, as this was awarded to American. Continental's submitted design of the back of the $10 note was similar in appearance, except for the counters in all four corners and the borders. The engraved vignette panel of *De Soto Discovering the Mississippi* carried the same picture, except that all the figures contained in the engraving were of larger dimensions. The latter engraving must have taken several months to complete and cost Continental a great deal of money, apparently without any benefit. Similarly, a like amount of labor and money was expended by American in producing an entirely new plate after receiving the award of contract for the $10 National Bank Notes. (Note by Thomas F. Morris, "Our First National Bank Notes," *The Numismatist,* January 1938.)
19. Most of these dies are still preserved in the ABNCo archives.
20. From the *Daily Spy,* Worcester, MA, July 19, 1864. Other sources include Mason Philip Smith, *Confederate Downeast: Confederate Operations In and Around Maine* (Portland, ME: The Provincial Press, 1985), pp. 4–17.
21. Sources, in addition to considerable numismatic research, include, most importantly, L.N. Benjamin, *The St. Albans Raid* (Montreal, Canada: Printed by John Lovell, 1865), being a compilation of warrants, court documents, depositions, and other data; contemporary newspaper accounts; L.L. Dutcher, *The History of St. Albans, Vermont,* 1872; Walter Hill Crockett, *Vermont, the Green Mountain State* (New York: The Century History Company, 1921); John Branch, *St. Albans Raid, St. Albans, Vermont, October 19, 1864,* published in 1935; Edmund H. Royce (comp.), *St. Albans Raid, October 19, 1964,* 4th edition, 1958; National Library of Canada web site; www.vermontcivilwar.org; *Vermont History,* January 1958, including Robin W. Winks, "The St. Albans Raid—A Bibliography," which lists 93 sources.
22. No notes of this specific type were ever issued; there were Legal Tender Notes and, separately, Interest Bearing Notes. Accounts in *Banker's Magazine* and other publications often contained numismatic inaccuracies.
23. John Sherman, *John Sherman's Recollections of Forty Years in the House, Senate, and Cabinet: An Autobiography,* 1895, pp. 341, 342.
24. Ibid., pp. 344, 345.
25. Extract from the New Hampshire Currency Project research files (Q. David Bowers and David M. Sundman).
26. Research by Wayne Rich.
27. Excerpted and edited from a copy digitized by the University of North Carolina–Confederate History Project, "Documenting the American South." Subtitles added.
28. John Jay Knox, *A History of Banking in the United States,* 1900.

Chapter 20

1. Examples suggested by Wendell Wolka, May 10, 2006.
2. Citation provided by Richard Winslow III.
3. As cited by Winthrop S. Boggs, *Ten Decades Ago 1840–1850: A Study of the Work of Rawdon, Wright, Hatch & Edson of New York City* (American Philatelic Society, 1949), pp. 23, 25; the circular has been lightly edited.
4. Certain information is from my *Expert's Guide to Collecting and Investing in Rare Coins* (Atlanta, GA: Whitman Publishing, 2005).
5. Communication to the author, October 19, 2004.
6. Memphis 2006 Sale. Similar statements have been printed in other of his catalogs.

Chapter 21

1. The starting and/or closing dates and certain information given for banks may differ from the Haxby text and is drawn from historical accounts in *Niles' Weekly Register,* the *New York Journal of Commerce, Banker's Magazine* (various issues of the 1850s), and John Jay Knox, *A History of Banking in the United States* (New York: Bradford Rhodes & Company, 1900), among other sources cited.
2. Knox, *History of Banking,* 1900.
3. Ira B. Cross, *Financing an Empire,* 1927, vol. I, pp. 40–53. A numismatic account of Naglee is found in *Walter Breen's Complete Encyclopedia of U.S. and Colonial Coins* (New York: Doubleday, 1988), p. 640; also inter alia, p. 653 (at a later time Wass, Molitor secured space in a large commercial building owned by Naglee).
4. William F. Hasse Jr., *A History of Money and Banking in Connecticut* (New Haven, CT: privately printed, 1957), p. 13.
5. Ibid., pp. 42, 43.
6. Ibid., p. 41.
7. *Banker's Magazine,* November 1856, p. 333.
8. Case cited in *Banker's Magazine,* August 1852. In November 1853, the same magazine stated that this bank had a good reputation. However, *Banker's Magazine* reported in January 1855 that the bank had failed.
9. Reprinted in *Banker's Magazine,* April 1857.
10. Dillistin, *Bank Note Reporters and Counterfeit Detectors 1826–1866* (New York: American Numismatic Society, 1949), pp. 49–50.
11. In a November 1856 retrospective.
12. Dillistin, *Bank Note Reporters,* 1949, pp. 55–56
13. *Niles' Weekly Register,* September 17, 1825.
14. In actuality, few if any banks ever printed their own notes. The plates were kept by the printing companies, which gladly filled additional orders as they were received.
15. *Niles' Weekly Register,* March 9, 1816. The Haxby text does not list bills of the $50 and $100 denominations.
16. *Niles' Weekly Register,* April 24, 1819.
17. Walter W. Chadbourne, *A History of Banking in Maine, 1799–1930,* 1936.
18. Ibid.
19. *Financial Register,* vol. I, p. 74.
20. Chadbourne, *A History of Banking in Maine, 1799–1930,* 1936.
21. For a bank to retain custody of plates currently in use would have been a clumsy procedure involving sending the plates back to the bank-note printer each time more currency was needed. No record has been found of *any* bank or state authority having the proper equipment to print bank notes.
22. *Annual Report of the Bank Commissioners of the State of Maine to the Governor and Council,* 1858.
23. *Annual Report of the Secretary of the Treasury on the Condition of the Banks in the United States at the Commencement of the Year 1863,* p. 2.
24. Alfred Cookman Bryan, *History of State Banking in Maryland* (Baltimore, MD: Johns Hopkins Press, 1899), p. 43.
25. *Niles' Weekly Register,* January 24, 1818.
26. Bryan, *History of State Banking in Maryland,* 1899, p. 104.
27. *Banker's Magazine,* November 1851.
28. Dudley P. Bailey Jr., "The History of Banking in Massachusetts," *Banker's Magazine,* September and October 1876.
29. *Bicknell's Counterfeit Detector,* October 11, 1830.
30. *Niles' Weekly Register,* April 22, 1837.
31. *Financial Register,* vol. I, pp. 304–309.
32. *Niles' National Register,* January 20 and March 11, 1838.
33. Bailey, "The History of Banking in Massachusetts," 1876.

34. Ibid.
35. Ibid.
36. *Banker's Magazine,* May 1855.
37. *State Bank Notes of Michigan,* p. 12.
38. *Banker's Magazine,* March 1853.
39. *Banker's Magazine,* November 1856, p. 331.
40. *Niles' National Register,* August 13, 1842.
41. *Banker's Magazine,* November 1856, p. 332.
42. *Banker's Magazine,* February 1854.
43. *Banker's Magazine,* May 1857.
44. *Banker's Magazine,* April 1853.
45. *Niles' Weekly Register,* May 17, 1834.
46. *Banker's Magazine,* November 1856.
47. Extract from the report of the Honorable Millard Fillmore, comptroller of the state of New York, December 30, 1848.
48. From 136 Assembly Doc. 29, 1842, vol. II, pp. 14–16. The president and cashier of this failed institution formed the Union Bank at Buffalo, which also failed.
49. *Banker's Magazine,* February 1862.
50. William M. Gouge, *The Curse of Paper-Money and Banking; or, a Short History of Banking in the United States of America, with an Account of its Ruinous Effects on Landowners, Farmers, Trades, and on All the Illustrious Classes of the Community* (Philadelphia, PA: 1833), p. 107. This subject is also treated elsewhere, including in the history of an adjacent state, W.A. Clark, *The History of the Banking Institutions Organized in South Carolina Prior to 1860* (Columbia, SC: Historical Commission of South Carolina, 1922), p. 103.
51. *Niles' Weekly Register,* May 5, 1828.
52. *Niles' National Register,* January 1, 1842
53. Wendell Wolka, *History of Nineteenth Century Ohio Obsolete Bank Notes and Scrip,* 2004, gives gripping details of the battle between Ohio and the Bank of the United States.
54. *Banker's Magazine,* September 1856.
55. Details in *Banker's Magazine,* October 1849.
56. *Banker's Magazine,* September 1856.
57. *Banker's Magazine,* November 1856.
58. H.F. Baker, "Outline History of Banking in the United States," *Banker's Magazine,* November 1856, pp. 326, 327.
59. Frank H. Stewart, *History of the First United States Mint,* 1974, p. 54
60. *Banker's Magazine,* November 1856.
61. Letter from the secretary of the Treasury relative to the condition of the banks in the United States, May 16, 1850, House of Representatives, Executive Document No. 68.
62. Letter from the secretary of the Treasury relative to the condition of the banks in the United States, May 16, 1850, House of Representatives, Executive Document No. 68; Roger H. Durand, *Obsolete Notes and Scrip of Rhode Island and the Providence Plantations* (Society of Paper Money Collectors, 1981).
63. Quoted in *Banker's Magazine,* July 1853.
64. Multiple stories in *Banker's Magazine,* December 1856 through May 1857.
65. *Niles' National Register,* August 26, 1843, included this item: *"The first bank in America.* It has been the general opinion that the first bank in America was the Bank of North America, established in Philadelphia. The *Cincinnati Chronicle,* whose editor has been dipping into the antiquities of the country, says that seventy years before the Bank of North America, the legislature of South Carolina established a public bank, and issued forty-eight thousand pounds in bills of trust. These bills were called bank bills, and the establishment was called a public bank. These were lent out at interest, or loaned on personal security."
66. Clark, *The History of the Banking Institutions Organized in South Carolina Prior to 1860,* 1922, p. 45.
67. William L. King, *The Newspaper Press of Charleston, S.C.,* 1872, pp. 94–95, as cited by Clark, p. 54.
68. Reprinted in *Banker's Magazine,* March 1854.
69. Clark, *The History of the Banking Institutions Organized in South Carolina Prior to 1860,* 1922, pp. 129, 149, 152.
70. Ibid., p. 168.
71. Ibid., pp. 111–13.
72. Ibid., p. 230.
73. *Banker's Magazine,* August 1856, p. 84.
74. It is not certain that the town of Vernon was established early enough to have been the location of this bank, a situation inviting research. Some information is from Wendell Wolka, communication, May 24, 2006.
75. The upas tree, indigenous to Southeast Asia, is a species of evergreen growing to heights of more than 100 feet but with a slim trunk. A latex created by the tree, known as antiarin, is highly poisonous. The reputation of this tree, and no doubt it or a derivative was Gallatin's source, can be traced to an account in *London Magazine,* December 1783, later expanded upon by Erasmus Darwin in "Loves of the Plants" in *Botanic Garden.* This lethal tree was said to kill all living creatures within a radius of about 50 feet, or even more, which account was untrue.
76. *Banker's Magazine,* April 1855.

Appendix

1. Foster Wild Rice, "The Altered Bank Note Plates of the Bank of North America of Seymour, Connecticut," *Essay Proof Journal,* Fall 1968.
2. From a column by Eleanor Blau, "Auctions."

INDEX

Page numbers in italics refer to illustrations.

The American Bank Note Co. Archives

One of the most important milestones in my numismatic career was the 2005 purchase of the American Bank Note Company archives.

Since that time I have enjoyed working with my associate Steve Blum, classifying vignette dies, printing plates, cylinder dies (transfer rolls), and other unique items, and sending them to American Numismatic Rarities to be presented at auction. In this way everyone has an equal chance to collect these historical treasures. They have never been offered before and, once sold, in many instances will not come on the market again.

Dave Bowers's new book, *Obsolete Paper Money*, gives you the background and knowledge to appreciate your ABNCo archives purchases. I recommended the American Numismatic Rarities series of sales for your consideration.

JOHN ALBANESE

professional numismatist